The ORIGIN *of the* SECOND AMENDMENT

A DOCUMENTARY HISTORY *in Commentaries*

on LIBERTY, FREE GOVERNMENT

and an ARMED POPULACE

during the formation of the

BILL OF RIGHTS

Edited by
David E. Young

GOLDEN OAK BOOKS
1991

Published 1991

Golden Oak Books
605 Michigan Street
Ontonagon, Michigan 49953

Library of Congress Catalog Card Number 89-85138

ISBN 0-9623664-1-2

Printed in the United States of America

TABLE OF CONTENTS

Preface	xiv
Editorial Method	xvi
Sources and Short Title List	xvii
Chronology	xx
Introduction	xxiii
Documents Section	1
Federal Convention Summer, 1787	2
Federal Convention August 18, 1787	2
Federal Convention August 20, 1787	6
Federal Convention August 21, 1787	7
Federal Convention August 23, 1787	7
Foreign Spectator September 11, 1787	11
Federal Convention September 12, 1787	11
Federal Convention September 14, 1787	12
Federal Convention September 15, 1787	13
Federal Convention (proposed U. S. Constitution) September 17, 1787	15
Foreign Spectator September 21, 1787	26
Confederation Congress September 27, 1787	27
William Pierce (New York) September 28, 1787	28
James Madison (New York) September 30, 1787	29
Seceding Pennsylvania Assemblymen October 2, 1787	30
Richard Henry Lee (New York) October 2, 1787	31
Richard Henry Lee (New York) October 5, 1787	31
Centinel I October 5, 1787	33
Philadelphia *Independent Gazetteer* October 6, 1787	34
George Mason October 7, 1787	34
Governor Edmund Randolph (Richmond) October 10, 1787	35
Foederal Constitution October 10, 1787	37
A Citizen of America {Noah Webster} October 10, 1787	38
A Citizen of Pennsylvania October 12, 1787	41
An Old Whig I October 12, 1787	43
Richard Henry Lee October 16, 1787	44
Impartial October 16, 1787	45
One of the People October 17, 1787	45
A Democratic Federalist October 17, 1787	45
An Old Whig II October 17, 1787	48
Elbridge Gerry (New York) October 18, 1787	51
An Old Whig III October 20, 1787	51
Louis Guillaume Otto (New York) October 20, 1787	54
An American Citizen IV {Tench Coxe} October 21, 1787	54
Louis Guillaume Otto October 23, 1787	56

Essay on Federal Sentiments October 23, 1787 **57**
A Citizen October 24, 1787 57
Centinel II October 24, 1787 **58**
New Haven *Connecticut Journal* October 24, 1787 61
Virginia House of Delegates October 25, 1787 62
An Old Constitutionalist October 26, 1787 64
A Confederationalist October 27, 1787 **64**
An Old Whig IV October 27, 1787 **66**
M.C. October 27, 1787 68
John De Witt II October 27, 1787 **69**
George Lee Turberville (Charleston) October 28, 1787 71
Arthur Lee (New York) October 29, 1787 71
Richmond *Virginia Independent Chronicle* October 31, 1787 72
Philadelphia *Freeman's Journal* October 31, 1787 73
New Haven *Connecticut Journal* October 31, 1787 **74**
Agricola November 1, 1787 75
An Old Whig V November 1, 1787 75
Cincinnatus I November 1, 1787 77
Brutus II November 1, 1787 **77**
Timoleon November 1, 1787 83
George Turner (Philadelphia) November 6, 1787 83
Argus November 8, 1787 84
A Citizen of Philadelphia {Pelatiah Webster} November 8, 1787 85
Centinel III November 8, 1787 85
Hugh Williamson November 8, 1787 **86**
Cincinnatus II November 8, 1787 **87**
Federal Farmer November [8], 1787 **89**
The Monitor November 9, 1787 97
Uncus November 9, 1787 97
Vox Populi November 9, 1787 **98**
Plain Truth November 10, 1787 99
R.S. November 10, 1787 101
William Grayson (New York) November 10, 1787 101
John Adams (London) November 10, 1787 101
James White (New York) November 13, 1787 102
Thomas Jefferson (Paris) November 13, 1787 **102**
One of the Late Army November 14, 1787 103
A Georgian November 15, 1787 103
Brutus III November 15, 1787 104
Cincinnatus III November 15, 1787 104
Publius {Alexander Hamilton} November 20, 1787 **105**
Philadelphia *Freeman's Journal* November 21, 1787 107
Cincinnatus IV November 22, 1787 **107**
A Citizen November 24, 1787 108
Preston, Connecticut November 26, 1787 **109**
Pennsylvania Convention November 26, 1787 110
Pennsylvania Convention November 28, 1787 112
An Old Whig VII November 28, 1787 118

A Federal Republican November 28, 1787 119
Brutus IV November 29, 1787 122
Agrippa III November 30, 1787 123
Pennsylvania Convention November 30, 1787 123
One of the Common People December 3, 1787 127
John De Witt V December 3, 1787 129
Pennsylvania Convention December 4, 1787 135
Publius {Alexander Hamilton} December 4, 1787 136
Cumberland County Petition December 5, 1787 137
Philadelphiensis III December 5, 1787 138
A True Friend December 6, 1787 139
Brutus December 6, 1787 144
Philanthropos December 6, 1787 145
Pennsylvania Convention December 6, 1787 145
"Z" December 6, 1787 146
James Madison (New York) December 9, 1787 147
A Landholder VI {Oliver Ellsworth} December 10, 1787 147
George Lee Turberville (Richmond) December 11, 1787 148
Thomas Johnson (Annapolis) December 11, 1787 149
One of the People December 11, 1787 149
Uriah Forrest (London) December 11, 1787 149
Pennsylvania Convention December 12, 1787 150
A Countryman December 15, 1787 153
Thomas Jefferson (Paris) December 15, 1787 154
Pennsylvania Minority December 18, 1787 154
Philadelphiensis V December 19, 1787 176
Jacob Trusty December 19, 1787 176
Thomas Jefferson (Paris) December 20, 1787 177
Robert Yates and John Lansing, Jr. December 21, 1787 177
Charles Nisbet (Carlisle) December 25, 1787 178
Cassius XI December 25, 1787 178
Philadelphiensis VI December 26, 1787 179
Publius {Alexander Hamilton} December 26, 1787 182
An American {Tench Coxe} December 28, 1787 185
America {Noah Webster} December 31, 1787 186
Thomas Jefferson (Paris) December 31, 1787 186
George Washington January 1, 1788 187
Marquis de Lafayette (Paris) January 1, 1788 187
An Old Soldier January 4, 1788 188
Samuel Osgood (New York) January 5, 1788 188
The Republican January 7, 1788 188
Centinel IX January 8, 1788 191
Indignatus January 8, 1788 192
Thomas B. Wait (Portland, Maine) January 8, 1788 193
Pennsylvania *Carlisle Gazette* January 9, 1788 194
Philadelphia *Freeman's Journal* January 9, 1788 195
Publius {Alexander Hamilton} January 9, 1788 195
Trusty January 10, 1788 200

Supreme Executive Council January 10, 1788 **201**
Samuel January 10, 1788 202
An Impartial Citizen January 10, 1788 203
A Farmer January 11, 1788 **204**
Charles Johnson (Strawberry Hill, North Carolina) January 14, 1788 207
Agrippa XIII January 14, 1788 207
Nathaniel Barrell (Boston) January 15, 1788 208
The State Soldier I January 16, 1788 209
Philanthropos {Tench Coxe} January 16, 1788 **210**
Philadelphia *Freeman's Journal* January 16, 1788 210
Philadelphia *Freeman's Journal* January 16, 1788 **211**
South Carolina Legislature January 18, 1788 215
An Independent Freeholder January 18, 1788 217
Luther Martin January 18, 1788 **219**
An Old Militia Officer of 1776 January 18, 1788 **221**
Agrippa XVII January 21, 1788 222
Massachusetts Convention January 21, 1788 224
A Countryman January 22, 1788 **224**
Helvidius Priscus January 22, 1788 225
Philadelphia *Freeman's Journal* January 23, 1788 **226**
Philadelphiensis VIII January 23, 1788 227
Massachusetts Convention January 23, 1788 228
Massachusetts Convention January 24, 1788 **230**
William Russell (Aspenville) January 25, 1788 231
Publius {James Madison} January 25, 1788 231
The Yeomanry of Massachusetts January 25, 1788 **232**
John Wilkes I January 26, 1788 233
Observator January 26, 1788 233
Publius {James Madison} January 29, 1788 **234**
Civis Rusticus January 30, 1788 235
Philadelphia *Pennsylvania Gazette* January 30, 1788 237
Franklin County Petition January 30, 1788 **238**
Aristides {Alexander Contee Hanson} January 31, 1788 **239**
A Watchman February, 1788 242
Columbian Patriot {Mercy Warren} February, 1788 243
Luther Martin February 1, 1788 **246**
Massachusetts Convention February 1, 1788 246
The Almanac-Maker February 2, 1788 248
Thomas Jefferson (Paris) February 2, 1788 249
Massachusetts Convention February 4, 1788 249
Marquis de Lafayette (Paris) February 4, 1788 250
William Russell February 5, 1788 250
Philadelphia *Pennsylvania Herald* February 5, 1788 **251**
Massachusetts Convention February 5, 1788 251
Agrippa XVIII February 5, 1788 252
The State Soldier II February 6, 1788 253
An Old Whig VIII February 6, 1788 254
Philadelphiensis IX February 6, 1788 258

Massachusetts Convention February 6, 1788 **260**
Thomas Jefferson (Paris) February 6, 1788 264
Thomas Jefferson (Paris) February 7, 1788 264
Anti-Foederalist Nos. I & II February 8, 1788 264
Candour February 12, 1788 265
Thomas Jefferson (Paris) February 12, 1788 265
A Farmer I February 15, 1788 266
George Nicholas (Charlottesville) February 16, 1788 270
William Fleming (Botetourt Co., Virginia) February 19, 1788 270
The Impartial Examiner February 20, 1788 271
A Pennsylvanian III {Tench Coxe} February 20, 1788 **275**
Deliberator February 20, 1788 **277**
Philadelphiensis X February 20, 1788 277
Alexander White February 22, 1788 **280**
Publius {Alexander Hamilton} February 23, 1788 **281**
Richard Henry Lee (Chantilly) February 26, 1788 283
The Impartial Examiner February 27, 1788 **285**
Philadelphia *Independent Gazetteer* February 27, 1788 **286**
Reverend John Leeland February 28, 1788 286
Philadelphia *Independent Gazetteer* February 28, 1788 287
Alexander White February 29, 1788 288
The Landholder X February 29, 1788 289
A Farmer II February 29, 1788 **289**
Hugh Henry Brackenridge March 1, 1788 291
The Impartial Examiner March 5, 1788 292
Philadelphia *Freeman's Journal* March 5, 1788 294
Winchester *Virginia Gazette* March 7, 1788 295
Philadelphiensis XI March 8, 1788 296
Philodemos March 8, 1788 **296**
One of the People March 10, 1788 297
Marcus March 12, 1788 297
James de Caledonia IV March 12, 1788 **298**
An Impartial Citizen March 13, 1788 299
Philadelphia *Independent Gazetteer* March 14, 1788 301
Sommers March 15, 1788 301
Luther Martin March 18, 1788 **301**
A Ploughman March 19, 1788 303
Connecticut *Norwich Packet* March 20, 1788 305
A Farmer IV March 21, 1788 305
Luther Martin March 21, 1788 305
The Political Club (Danville, Kentucky) March 22, 1788 307
A Farmer V March 25, 1788 308
Tullius March 26, 1788 309
Luther Martin March 28, 1788 310
J. T. Chase & J. F. Mercer April, 1788 312
A Plebian April, 1788 312
A Farmer VI April 1, 1788 328
Massachusetts Delegates April 9, 1788 **328**

Aristocrotis April [15], 1788 **329**
George Lee Turberville (Epping, Richmond County) April 16, 1788 335
A Farmer April 23, 1788 **336**
Philadelphia *Pennsylvania Gazette* April 23, 1788 336
Albany Antifederal Committee April 26, 1788 337
Philadelphia *Independent Gazetteer* April 30, 1788 **339**
John Francis Mercer [May], 1788 340
Federal Farmer May, 1788 **342**
Thomas Jefferson (Paris) May 2, 1788 356
Maryland Minority May 6, 1788 **356**
Richard Henry Lee (Westmoreland County) May 7, 1788 361
South Carolina Convention May 20, 1788 **363**
George Mason May 26, 1788 **365**
Thomas Jefferson (Paris) May 27, 1788 366
Thomas Jefferson (Paris) June 3, 1788 367
Virginia Convention June 5, 1788 **367**
Virginia Convention June 6, 1788 374
Virginia Convention June 7, 1788 **375**
A Militiaman June 7, 1788 **379**
George Mason (Richmond) June 9, 1788 380
Virginia Convention June 9, 1788 **380**
Virginia Convention June 10, 1788 384
Virginia Convention June 11, 1788 385
Denatus June 11, 1788 387
George Mason [June 11, 1788] **388**
Virginia Convention June 12, 1788 390
Sydney June 13, 1788 396
Cassandra June 14, 1788 397
A Freeman June 14, 1788 398
Virginia Convention June 14, 1788 **399**
Virginia Convention June 16, 1788 **417**
Virginia Convention June 17, 1788 441
Many June 18, 1788 443
Virginia Convention June 19, 1788 443
Robert Yates (Poughkeepsie) June 21, 1788 444
New Hampshire Convention June 21, 1788 **445**
James Madison (Richmond) June 22, 1788 447
Virginia Convention June 24, 1788 **448**
Virginia Convention June 25, 1788 **451**
A Delegate Who Has Catched Cold June 25, 1788 455
New York Journal June 26, 1788 456
Virginia Convention June 27, 1788 **456**
Philadelphia *Independent Gazetteer* June 27, 1788 463
New York Convention June 27, 1788 463
New York Convention July 2, 1788 **464**
Philadelphia *Pennsylvania Gazette* July 2, 1788 470
Cumberland County (Pennsylvania) Meeting July 3, 1788 471
New York Convention July 7, 1788 **473**
Pennsylvania *Carlisle Gazette* July 9, 1788 475

New York Convention July 10, 1788 476
New York Convention July 19, 1788 **476**
Abraham Clark (New York) July 23, 1788 479
New York Convention July 26, 1788 **480**
New York Convention July 28, 1788 488
North Carolina Convention July 28, 1788 490
North Carolina Convention July 29, 1788 493
North Carolina Convention July 30, 1788 **496**
North Carolina Convention July 31, 1788 501
Thomas Jefferson (Paris) July 31, 1788 502
North Carolina Convention August 1, 1788 **503**
Abraham G. Lansing (Albany) August 3, 1788 509
Tench Coxe (Philadelphia) August 5, 1788 510
Thomas Jefferson (Paris) August 12, 1788 510
James Hanna (Newtown) August 15, 1788 511
Fayette County (Pennsylvania) Delegates August 18, 1788 512
Solon, jun. August 23, 1788 512
James Tilghman (Chestertown) August 24, 1788 514
Bucks County (Pennsylvania) Meeting August 25, 1788 514
Solon August 28, 1788 516
A Friend to Amendments August 28, 1788 517
A Republican September 1, 1788 517
William Shippen, Jr. (Philadelphia) September 2, 1788 518
Harrisburg Convention September 6, 1788 **519**
Boston *Massachusetts Centinel* September 6, 1788 524
A Federal Correspondent September 11, 1788 524
A Marylander September 12, 1788 525
Providence Gazette September 13, 1788 526
A Republican September 17, 1788 527
Civis September 19, 1788 527
DeWitt Clinton (New York) September 19, 1788 529
Pittsburgh Gazette September 20, 1788 530
Thomas Jefferson (Paris) September 20, 1788 532
James Madison (New York) September 21, 1788 532
Abraham Yates, Jr. (New York) September 22, 1788 533
Governor Samuel Huntington (Connecticut) September 23, 1788 533
Federalism September 26, 1788 534
Richard Henry Lee (Chantilly) October 15, 1788 538
James Madison (New York) October 17, 1788 538
Charles Smith (Sudbury) October 18, 1788 542
James Madison (New York) October 20, 1788 542
Real Farmer October 22, 1788 543
Christian Farmer October 23, 1788 543
Theodorick Bland (Richmond) October 23, 1788 545
John Harris (Harrisburg) October 28, 1788 546
Virginia House of Delegates October 29, 1788 546
Charles Lee (Richmond) October 29, 1788 547
Honestus October 30, 1788 548

Virginia House of Delegates October 31, 1788 550
A Friend to the People November 1, 1788 550
James Madison (New York) November 2, 1788 551
Father Abraham November 3, 1788 553
Federal Republican Committee (New York) November 4, 1788 554
Foreign Spectator November 7, 1788 556
A Friend to Liberty and Union November 7, 1788 556
Annapolis *Maryland Gazette* November 13, 1788 559
Federal Republican Committee (New York) November 13, 1788 560
Virginia House of Delegates November 14, 1788 561
Centinel XXII November 14, 1788 566
Foreign Spectator November 14, 1788 567
Patrick Henry (Richmond) November 15, 1788 571
Thomas Jefferson (Paris) November 18, 1788 572
Alfred November 19, 1788 572
Philadelphia *Independent Gazetteer* November 22, 1788 573
James Wilson November 23, 1788 574
William R. Davie November 25, 1788 575
David Humphreys (Mount Vernon) November 29, 1788 575
Jonathan Jackson (Newburyport) December, 1788 575
Thomas Jefferson (Paris) December 4, 1788 579
James Madison (Philadelphia) December 8, 1788 579
Governor George Clinton December 11, 1788 580
A Federal Republican December 11, 1788 581
Belasarius December 15, 1788 583
George Mason (Gunston Hall) December 18, 1788 583
John Francis Mercer December 20, 1788 584
Thomas Jefferson (Paris) December 25, 1788 585
Election Appeal for James Monroe January, 1789 586
Arthur Lee January, 1789 587
Aristides January 1, 1789 588
Adolphus January 1, 1789 591
James Madison (Orange) January 2, 1789 594
Samuel Sterett January 2, 1789 595
A Native of Baltimore January 6, 1789 596
Civis January 6, 1789 597
A True Federalist January 7, 1789 598
Thomas Rodney (Poplar Grove, Delaware) January 10, 1789 601
Elbridge Gerry (Cambridge) January 12, 1789 601
James Madison (Louisa) January 13, 1789 602
New York Assembly January 20, 1789 604
An Observer January 22, 1789 606
Elbridge Gerry January 22, 1789 607
Philadelphia *Independent Gazetteer* January 23, 1789 608
James Madison January 27, 1789 609
New York Election Law January 27, 1789 610
Spectator January 27, 1789 610
Abraham Clark February 4, 1789 611

New York Assembly February 4, 1789 612
New York Assembly February 5, 1789 624
Thomas Jefferson (Paris) February 9, 1789 626
A. B. February 13, 1789 626
Baltimore *Maryland Gazette* February 17, 1789 627
A Republican February 23, 1789 627
Joshua Atherton (Amherst) February 23, 1789 629
Cassius March 3, 1789 630
Thomas Jefferson (Paris) March 4, 1789 634
Thomas Jefferson (Paris) March 13, 1789 634
Thomas Jefferson (Paris) March 15, 1789 635
Thomas Jefferson (Paris) March 18, 1789 637
Thomas Jefferson (Paris) March 23, 1789 638
Paine Wingate (New York) March 25, 1789 639
H.G. April 7, 1789 639
James Madison (New York) April 8, 1789 640
James Madison (New York) April 12, 1789 640
Republican Committee April 21, 1789 641
President George Washington April 30, 1789 642
House of Representatives May 4, 1789 642
House of Representatives May 5, 1789 643
House of Representatives May 6, 1789 643
James Madison (New York) May 27, 1789 643
Richard Henry Lee (New York) May 28, 1789 644
President George Washington [May 31, 1789] 644
James Madison June 8, 1789 645
House of Representatives June 8, 1789 647
William R. Davie June 10, 1789 666
Fisher Ames (New York) June 11, 1789 667
Fisher Ames (New York) June 12, 1789 668
William Grayson (New York) June 12, 1789 668
James Madison (New York) June 13, 1789 669
James Madison (New York) June 15, 1789 669
A Pennsylvanian {Tench Coxe} June 18, 1789 670
Tench Coxe (Philadelphia) June 18, 1789 672
James Madison (New York) June 21, 1789 673
Joseph Jones (Richmond) June 24, 1789 673
James Madison (New York) June 24, 1789 673
A Pennsylvanian {Tench Coxe} June 30, 1789 674
Hugh Williamson (Baltimore) July 2, 1789 676
One of the People July 2, 1789 676
Governor and Council of North Carolina July 9, 1789 678
House of Representatives July 21, 1789 679
Fisher Ames (New York) July 23, 1789 679
House of Representatives July 28, 1789 680
George Mason (Gunston Hall) July 31, 1789 682
James Madison (New York) August 2, 1789 682
Pierce Butler (New York) August 11, 1789 683

Fisher Ames (New York) August 12, 1789 683
House of Representatives August 13, 1789 684
House of Representatives August 14, 1789 687
House of Representatives August 15, 1789 **688**
House of Representatives August 17, 1789 **695**
House of Representatives August 18, 1789 699
House of Representatives August 19, 1789 700
James Madison (New York) August 19, 1789 700
Philadelphia *Independent Gazetteer* August 20, 1789 **701**
House of Representatives August 20, 1789 702
James Madison (New York) August 21, 1789 704
James Madison (New York) August 21, 1789 704
Samuel Adams August 22, 1789 704
James Madison (New York) August 24, 1789 705
House of Representatives August 24, 1789 **706**
Samuel Adams August 24, 1789 708
Thomas Jefferson (Paris) August 28, 1789 709
United States Senate September 4, 1789 **710**
George Mason (Gunston Hall) September 8, 1789 710
Centinel, Revived, No. XXIX September 9, 1789 **711**
United States Senate September 9, 1789 **712**
James Madison (New York) September 14, 1789 712
Richard Henry Lee (New York) September 14, 1789 713
Archibald Maclaine (Wilmington, North Carolina) September 17, 1789 714
State Gazette of North Carolina September 24, 1789 714
United States Congress September 26, 1789 **715**
Richard Henry Lee (New York) September 27, 1789 717
William Grayson (New York) September 29, 1789 717
President George Washington (New York) October 2, 1789 **718**
New York *Gazette of the United States* October 14, 1789 **719**
James Madison (Orange) November 20, 1789 719
New Jersey Council November 20, 1789 **720**
Hardin Burnley (Richmond) November 28, 1789 720
Hardin Burnley (Richmond) [December] 5, 1789 721
James Madison (Orange) December 5, 1789 722
Virginia Senate December 12, 1789 **722**
John Dawson (Richmond) December 17, 1789 725
Maryland Senate December 19, 1789 **726**
Edward Carrington (Richmond) December 20, 1789 726
Governor Alexander Martin December 22, 1789 727
North Carolina General Assembly December 22, 1789 **728**
Philadelphia *Independent Gazetteer* December 28, 1789 728
Philadelphia *Pennsylvania Packet* December 29, 1789 728
Philadelphia *Federal Gazette* January 5, 1790 729
President George Washington January 8, 1790 **729**
South Carolina Senate January 19, 1790 **730**
New Hampshire Legislature January 25, 1790 **730**

Delaware Legislature January 28, 1790 730
Governor John Hancock January 28, 1790 731
New York Senate February 24, 1790 732
Pennsylvania General Assembly March 10, 1790 732
Governor Arthur Fenner (Rhode Island) May 20, 1790 732
Rhode Island Convention May 29, 1790 733
Richard Henry Lee (New York) June 10, 1790 739
Rhode Island General Assembly June [15], 1790 739
Thomas Jefferson (Philadelphia) December 4, 1790 740
A Farmer January 29, 1791 741
Vermont General Assembly November 3, 1791 742
Virginia Senate December 15, 1791 742
Thomas Jefferson March 1, 1792 742
Philadelphia *Freeman's Journal* March 14, 1792 743

Appendix A: The State Bills of Rights and Related Constitutional Provisions 747
Virginia Bill of Rights June 12, 1776 747
New Jersey Constitution July 3, 1776 749
Delaware Declaration of Rights September 11, 1776 750
Pennsylvania Constitution September 28, 1776 752
Maryland Declaration of Rights November 11, 1776 755
North Carolina Constitution December 18, 1776 761
Georgia Constitution February 5, 1777 763
New York Constitution April 20, 1777 764
Vermont Constitution July 8, 1777 765
South Carolina Constitution March 19, 1778 768
Massachusetts Constitution October 25, 1780 769
New Hampshire Bill of Rights June 2, 1784 775

Appendix B: Bills of Rights Provisions Comparison Chart 781

Appendix C: Popular Support for the Constitution and a Bill of Rights 784

Index 787

PREFACE

John Adams wrote Thomas Jefferson in August of 1815 that the American Revolution was not the war for independence, but instead, a revolution in the minds and opinions of the people, which was effected prior to any hostilities of the war for independence. The War of the Revolution was merely a consequence of this change in public opinion. He also wrote that the records of public bodies, newspapers, pamphlets, etc. of the period should be consulted to determine the steps by which the public opinion became enlightened concerning the authority of government. Similarly, it can be said of the struggle for a federal bill of rights that it was completed long before any bill of rights provisons were ever discussed in the new U. S. Congress or offered to the states for adoption. A bill of rights became very important in the hearts and minds of the American people during the ratification struggle over the Constitution. The federal Bill of Rights added to the Constitution as the first ten amendments was simply a consequence of this previous political struggle. The newspapers, pamphlets, records of public bodies, etc., of the ratification period, if consulted, will show the steps by which public opinion in America came to recognize the need for a federal bill of rights, and to expect and insist that one be added to the Constitution by amendment.

The editor has collected a large number of documents relating to the necessity of a bill of rights for the United States Constitution. These originated in the period during which the Constitution was formed, ratified, and carried into effect. This is the period during which the Bill of Rights and the Second Amendment, which is part and parcel of it, were formed. To help understand the Second Amendment, one should understand how it came into existence as part of the Bill of Rights, how the Bill of Rights was derived from the state bills of rights, how the struggle for a Bill of Rights related to the adoption of the Constitution, and how the pressures for previous or subsequent amendment of the Constitution related to all of these things. The documents in this collection have been selected for these purposes. Appendix A of this volume includes the original state bills of rights, the clear predecessors of the federal Bill of Rights.

It is not true that our ancestors joyously accepted the U. S. Constitution. Some of them did. However, the Constitution was perceived by many as establishing a most oppressive form of government since it did not protect the important rights of the citizens contained in the state bills of rights. There was an extensive, enlightened, and often bitter debate over its adoption, and it was ratified with the addition of subsequent amendments intended to protect individual rights virtually assured. Without that assurance, the United States Constitution would not have been ratified. This collection of documents presents the flow of thought of those who participated during the political struggle which produced the Bill of Rights.

The Second Amendment has actually received little historical study until relatively recently. It contains outdated terminology, and therefore, it is open to misinterpretation. There is very clear evidence that this is the case in the entirely contradictory interpretations of the Second Amendment by various political pressure groups supporting and opposing "gun control."

The provisions of the Bill of Rights were certainly not worded to be misleading or unclear. They were worded in such a way that everyone would know his rights and the intended limits upon the government. The problem with the Second Amendment is that one of its phrases is not in common use today. When the editor first became interested in this subject, the need and significance of the reference to a well regulated militia in the Second Amendment was a mystery to him. Why were our ancestors so vague, and what exactly did they mean? The search for answers to such questions has resulted in the volume you are reading. It should be noted here that the terminology was not at all vague during the period the Constitution was ratified. One has "simply" (and this is not simple!) to become familiar with the period and the political thought thereof to answer these questions. In other words, one must read a lot!

December 15, 1991, is the Bicentennial of ratification of the Bill of Rights. The editor is pleased that this in context documentary history of the Second Amendment is being published just in time for the Bill of Rights Bicentennial.

The editor wishes to thank the staff of the Ontonagon Township Library for their assistance in locating various collections of documents. The editor also wishes to thank his wife, Arlene, for proofreading the draft document manuscripts for this volume. More importantly, since this volume has been researched, edited, and typeset in the editor's 'spare time,' he wishes to acknowledge the thousands of hours of time with their husband and father which the editor's family has been deprived of.

This volume is dedicated to my wife, Arlene, and my children, Jonathan, Amy, David, and Thomas Young.

David E. Young

EDITORIAL METHOD

With the exception of a few newspaper articles from microfilmed copies, this documentary history was prepared entirely from published collections of documents. The editorial procedures followed by the editors of those published collections of source documents were not necessarily consistent. The documents in the present collection are literal transcriptions of the cited sources. For this reason, the various documents contained in this collection have been subjected to a variety of editorial methods. Those who require detailed information regarding editorial methods applied to any particular document should consult the cited source for the editorial methods utilized by its editor. The vast majority of documents in this collection are excerpts from longer items with only relevant portions reprinted.

The documents composing this collection consist of newspaper articles, pamphlets, letters, debates in various assemblies, notes of participants in assemblies, and official documents such as ratifications, resolutions, laws, etc. The editor has provided a heading for each document consisting of a title and date, followed by explanatory material. Excerpts are indicated in the heading. This heading material is separated from the text of the document by one blank line. Any original footnotes directly follow the document text in the same type size. Notes relating to the document prepared by the editor follow each document separated by one blank line, and are set in smaller type. Except for some newspaper items where the source is included within the heading material, sources are given in the editor's following notes. Source references consist of a short title or abbreviation assinged by the editor. The full titles of sources corresponding to these short references may be found in the source and short title list which begins on the next page.

The first line of heading material for each document is set in bold type and generally consists of the name of the author (or assembly) followed by the date it was written (or debate occurred). For pseudonymous newspaper articles and pamphlets, the pseudonym is given followed by the true name of the author within left and right braces, if known. For letters, the author is followed by the location the letter was written in parentheses. The second line of the heading material for letters indicates who the recipient was. For published items, "Newspaper Article:" "Pamphlet:", "Broadside:" or "Handbill:" are indicated. These designations are usually followed by a title and/or by the name of the newspaper, where appropriate. All Newspaper and Pamphlet designations include the town of publication. For letters which were subsequently published, appropriate information is on an additional heading line. All documents are arranged chronologically. Where only the month of origin is known for a document, it is included at the beginning of that month.

The documents in this collection which contain references to the right of the people to keep or bear arms, the necessity or desireability of the people being armed, disarming of the people or militia, a well regulated militia, who the militia were, the ability of the people to forcibly resist governmental oppression, usurpation or tyranny, or other subjects directly related to the Second Amendment or its interpretation are indicated by bold page numbers in the Table of Contents.

SOURCES
ABBREVIATIONS AND SHORT TITLE LIST

Ames

Seth Ames, ed., *Works of Fisher Ames* (Boston, Little, Brown and Co., 1854).

Bergh

Albert Ellery Bergh and Andrew A. Lipscomb, eds., *The Writings of Thomas Jefferson* (19 vols., Washington, D.C., 1900-1907).

Borden

Morton Borden, ed., *The Antifederalist Papers* (East Lansing, Michigan State University Press, 1965).

Boyd

Julian P. Boyd, Charles T. Cullen et al., eds., *The Papers of Thomas Jefferson* (20 vols., Princeton, N. J., 1950-1982).

BRDH

Bernard Schwartz, ed., *The Bill of Rights: A Documentary History* (2 vols., New York, Chelsea House, 1971).

Cushing

Harry Alonzo Cushing, ed., *The Writings of Samuel Adams* (New York, Putnam's, 1908).

Debates

Jonathan Elliot, ed., *The Debates in the Several State Conventions, on the Adoption of the Federal Constitution, as recommended by the General Convention at Philadelphia in 1787* (Reprint of 1836 edition vols. I- IV/1845 edition vol. V, Philadelphia, Lippincott, 1941).

DePauw
Linda Grant DePauw, ed., *Documetary History of the First Federal Congress of the United States of America, March 4, 1789—March 3, 1791* (Baltimore, Johns Hopkins University Press, 1972).

DHC
U. S. Department of State, *Documentary History of the Constitution of the United States of America* (Washington, D. C., 1894).

DHFFE
Merrill Jensen, Robert A. Becker, and Gordon DenBoer et al., eds., *The Documentary History of the First Federal Elections, 1788-1790* (4 volumes, Madison, U. of Wisconsin Press, 1976-1989).

DHRC
Merrill Jensen, John P. Kaminski, and Gaspare J. Saldino et al., eds., *The Documentary History of the Ratification of the Constitution* (9 volumes to date, Madison, Wisconsin State Historical Society, 1976——).

Essays
Paul L. Ford, ed., *Essays on the Constitution of the United States Published during its Discussion by the People, 1787-1788.* (Reprint of 1892 ed., New York, Burt Franklin, 1970).

Ford
Paul Leicester Ford, ed., *The Writings of Thomas Jefferson* (10 vols., New York, Putnam's Sons, 1892-1899).

Formation of the Union
Charles C. Tansill, ed., *Documents Illustrative of the Formation of the Union of the American States* (Washington, D. C., U. S. Government, 1927).

Foster
Robert C. Cotner, tr., *Theodore Foster's Minutes of the Convention Held at South Kingstown, Rhode Island, in March, 1790, Which Failed to Adopt the Constitution of the United States* (Freeport, N.Y., Books for Libraries Press, 1929).

Henry
William Wirt Henry, *Patrick Henry: Life, Correspondence and Speeches* (New York, Scribner's, 1891).

Kenyon
Cecelia M. Kenyon, ed., *The Antifederalists* (Indianapolis, Bobbs-Merrill, 1966).

Massachusetts

Bradford K. Peirce, Charles Hale et al., eds., *Debates and Proceedings in the Convention of the Commonwealth of Massachusetts, held in the year 1788* . . . (Boston, 1856).

Pamphlets

Paul Leicester Ford, ed., *Pamphlets on the Constitution of the United States, Published during its Discussion by the People, 1787-1788* (reprint of 1888 ed., New York, Da Capo, 1968).

Papers

Robert A. Rutland and Charles F. Hobson, eds., *The Papers of James Madison* (Volume XI, 1977; Volume XII, 1979; Charlottesville, University Press of Virginia).

Perry

Richard L. Perry, ed., *Sources of Our Liberties* (Chicago, American Bar Foundation, 1959).

Rowland

Kate Mason Rowland, *The Life of George Mason* (reprint of 1892 ed., 2 vols., New York, Russell and Russell, 1964).

Rutland

Robert A. Rutland, ed., *The Papers of George Mason* (3 vols., Chapel Hill, University of North Carolina Press, 1970).

Storing

Herbert J. Storing, ed., *The Complete Anti-Federalist* (5 vols., Chicago, University of Chicago Press, 1981).

Thorpe

Francis N. Thorpe, ed., *The Federal and State Constitutions, Colonial Charters, and Other Organic Laws of the States, Territories, and Colonies, Now or Heretofore Forming the United States of America* (7 vols., Washington, D.C., 1909).

CHRONOLOGY OF SIGNIFICANT EVENTS

	1775
April 19	Americans begin armed resistance to government troops at Lexington and Concord Massachusetts. Hostilities of the Revolutionary War commence.
	1776
June 12-29	Virginia adopts a state Constitution and Bill of Rights.
July 3	New Jersey adopts a state Constitution.
July 4	The Declaration of Independence is adopted.
September 20	Delaware adopts a state Constitution and Declaration of Rights.
September 28	Pennsylvania adopts a state Constitution and Declaration of Rights.
November 11	Maryland adopts a state Constitution and Declaration of Rights.
December 18	North Carolina adopts a state Constitution and Declaration of Rights.
	1777
February 5	Georgia adopts a state Constitution.
April 20	New York adopts a state Constitution.
July 8	Vermont adopts a state Constitution and Declaration of Rights.
November 15	The Articles of Confederation are proposed.
	1778
March 19	South Carolina adopts a state Constitution.
	1780
October 25	Massachusetts adopts a state Constitution and Declaration of Rights.
	1781
February 12	The Articles of Confederation are ratified by all 13 states.
	1783
January 20	The Treaty of Paris brings a formal end to the Revolutionary War.
	1784
June 2	New Hampshire adopts a state Constitution and Bill of Rights.
	1787
May 25	The Federal Convention begins its deliberations in Philadelphia to amend the Articles of Confederation.
September 17	The Federal Convention concludes, proposes the United States Constitution, and sends it to Congress.
September 28	Congress transmits the Constitution to the states where special conventions of the people are to be called to ratify it.
December 7	The Delaware convention ratifies the United States Constitution unanimously.

December 12	The Pennsylvania convention ratifies the United States Constitution by a vote of 46 to 23.
December 18	The New Jersey convention ratifies the United States Constitution unanimously.

1788

January 2	The Georgia convention ratifes the United States Constitution unanimously.
January 9	The Connecticut convention ratifes the United States Constitution by a vote of 128 to 40.
February 7	The Massachusetts convention ratifies the United States Constitution by a vote of 187 to 168, and proposes nine amendments to the Constitution.
February 22	The New Hampshire convention adjourns to avoid outright rejection of the Constitution.
April 28	The Maryland convention ratifies the United States Constitution by a vote of 63 to 11.
May 23	The South Carolina convention ratifies the United States Constitution by a vote of 149 to 73, and states two understandings and two proposed amendments.
June 21	The second session of the New Hampshire convention ratifies the United States Constitution by a vote of 57 to 47, and proposes twelve amendments to the Constitution (the first nine are identical to those of Massachusetts).
June 21	The United States Constitution is put into effect among the adopting states by the ninth ratification of New Hampshire.
June 25	The Virginia convention ratifies the Constitution by a vote of 89 to 79, and proposes an extensive Declaration of Rights and twenty other amendments to the Constitution.
July 26	The New York convention ratifies the Constitution by a vote of 30 to 27, and incorporates a bill of rights into its ratification as well as proposing 33 amendments to the Constitution.
July 28	The New York convention unanimously adopts a Circular Letter to all of the other states inviting them to request that Congress call a convention to amend the Constitution.
August 1	The North Carolina convention refuses to ratify the Constitution until after a declaration of rights and other amendments are proposed by Congress or a Convention, and it adopts the Declaration of Rights and amendments proposed by Virginia.
November 14	Virginia votes to request the calling of a convention by Congress to amend the Constitution, and adopts a Circular Letter to the other states urging similar action on their part.

1789

February 4	The New York Assembly adopts a request for Congress to call a convention to amend the Constitution.
March 4	Congress first meets under the new U.S. Constitution.
May 5	The Virginia application for a convention to amend the Constitution is presented to Congress.
May 6	The New York application for a convention to amend the Constitution is presented to Congress.
June 8	James Madison introduces his bill of rights proposals for amendment of the Constitution. These are widely publicized.
July 28	The select committee to which Madison's amendments and those proposed by the state conventions were referred makes its report.

August 24	The proposed amendments of the House of Representatives are approved.
September 26	The twelve amendments proposed by Congress are approved and sent to the states.
November 21	The second North Carolina convention ratifies the Constitution by a vote of 194 to 77.
December 19	Maryland ratifies all 12 amendments proposed by Congress.
December 22	North Carolina ratifies all 12 amendments proposed by Congress.

1790

January 19	South Carolina ratifies all 12 amendments proposed by Congress.
January 25	New Hampshire ratifies all of the amendments except number two relating to the pay of legislators.
January 28	Delaware ratifies all of the amendments except number one relating to the ratio of representatives.
March 10	Pennsylvania ratifies all of the amendments except number two relating to the pay of legislators.
March 27	New York ratifies all of the amendments except number two relating to the pay of legislators.
May 29	The Rhode Island convention ratifies the Constitution by a vote of 34 to 32, and incorporates a bill of rights into its ratification as well as proposing 21 amendments to the Constitution.
June	Rhode Island ratifies all of the amendments except number 2 relating to the pay of legislators.
August 3	New Jersey ratifies all of the amendments except number 2 relating to the pay of legislators.

1791

November 3	Vermont ratifies all 12 of the proposed amendments.
December 15	Virginia ratifies all 12 of the proposed amendments.
December 15	Amendments three through twelve of those proposed by Congress are adopted and go into effect as the first ten amendments to the Constitution. Article four of the amendments proposed by Congress relating to the right of the people to keep and bear arms becomes the Second Amendment to the Constitution.

1792

March 1	Secretary of State Thomas Jefferson informs the governors of the states that amendments three through twelve of those proposed by Congress have been ratified and adopted as the first ten amendments to the Constitution of the United States.

INTRODUCTION

The Origin of the Second Amendment

The United States Constitution was formed by the Federal Convention, which consisted of deputies appointed by the state governments to meet in Philadelphia during the summer of 1787. The Second Amendment is part and parcel of the Bill of Rights, which consists of the first ten amendments to the United States Constitution. These provisions protecting individual rights and establishing the proper method of construing the powers of the United States government resulted from a great struggle over implementation of the new Constitution between 1787 and 1789.

At that time, most Americans were accustomed to having their individual rights protected from violation by the government because approximately two thirds of the population of the United States lived in states with constitutional bills of rights. In most of the other states some individual rights were protected in the state constitutions. Opposition to the new United States Constitution quickly arose when it was proposed without a bill of rights, and with protection for only a few individual rights within it. Most opponents of ratification of the Constitution, referred to as Antifederalists, bitterly complained about the Federal Convention's omission of a bill of rights in the new plan of government, and they stressed the absolute necessity of amending the new Constitution by adding a bill of rights like those of the states. Since the mode of adopting the new Constitution did not allow for any amendments prior to ratification, proponents of the Constitution, referred to as Federalists, were forced to answer these complaints by arguing against a bill of rights.

Although specific wordings vary, the basic individual rights protected in the federal Bill of Rights are exactly the same rights as those protected in the original state bills of rights.[1] Most of those state bills of rights were adopted in 1776 early in the American Revolution. The provisions they contain relate to conflicts which occurred between the Americans and their former governments, and they were intended to prevent future violations of their rights by the newly formed state governments. For purposes of introduction to this documentary history of the Second Amendment, the general occurrences which led to the adoption of the directly related provisions in the state bills of rights should be reviewed.

Prior to the Declaration of Independence in 1776, the American colonies were a constituent part of the British Empire. Though the colonists controlled the lower houses of the legislative branch in each colony, the executive branch of government in most colonies was under the direct control of the British, who had been attempting for some time to extend their control over the colonies by disallowing colonial legislation and attempting to tax in the colonies. Great Britain claimed a power to "bind the people of America by statutes in all cases whatsoever."[2] Colonial Americans claimed many rights which they believed should not be violated by the government, and which could not be violated by any just government. It became evident to the colonists that the rights which they held dear and their governmental connection with Britain were contradictory and were becoming mutually exclusive—they could either retain the connection and lose their rights and liberty, or sever the connection and preserve their rights. The Americans decided that their liberty was more important than the absolute authority of government. After more than a decade of strife concerning the proper extent of the powers of the administration, their resistance to British policies as supported by colonial governors became armed resistance to the government when the administration resorted to a standing army to enforce British aims. Since practically the entire colonial populace was armed, and the men were trained in the use of their arms due to their past militia establishments, they could not be easily overawed by the simple presence of an army nearby, nor were they at any serious military disadvantage to the government's troops.

Most of the colonies had had a long succession of militia laws to make sure that their adult male populations were armed and trained for military defense. The militia laws provided for military organization and militia officers. The officers were required to list all men in their jurisdictions between the ages of 16 and 60 (ages varied from colony to colony). Generally, the militia laws required every man to obtain their own firearm, ammunition, and other personal essentials which were to be kept in readiness for emergencies. All men with a few exceptions, such as government officials and clergymen, were required to appear for training a certain number of days per year with their firearms and accoutrements. The number of days of training required varied considerably and was directly related to whether or not there was any apprehension of danger which the militia would have to defend against. There were fines imposed for those who did not appear for training, or who did not possess a serviceable firearm.

The colonial governors were in command of their colony's militia, and many of these governors were directly appointed by the British.

Thus, the militia, or adult male population of the colonies, who were generally opposed to British policies as the mid 1770's approached, were led in their military capacity by leaders who were implementing those policies. Clearly, the militia were not going to enforce governmental oppression upon themselves. Instead, they resisted the government.

Prior to the commencement of hostilities in the American Revolution, the people took the militia into their own hands. It had become apparent that armed resistance would become necessary eventually. The people organized, embodied, and trained themselves as a well regulated militia without the sanction of government, and they selected their own officers. Most people strongly supported the resistance against the administration, so they armed themselves and trained assiduously throughout the colonies as the certainty of hostilities with the government became more evident. Even large numbers of Quakers, especially in Philadelphia, took up arms and regularly trained along with their neighbors. There were numerous volunteer companies of foot and troops of horse formed. In Massachusetts and elsewhere the reformation of the militia resulted in select militia as well as regular militia. The minute men, who volunteered to be ready on a minute's warning to march wherever they might be needed, were select militia who comprized from one third to one fourth of the entire militia.

British troops had been stationed in Boston to coerce the people of Massachusetts into compliance with the government's plans. The Americans constantly harped against standing armies in time of peace and pointed out that the proper defense of a country was its militia. In fact, there was a longstanding English Whig tradition of opposition to standing armies which resurfaced in the colonies at this period. As conflict approached, the opinions of the Americans jelled—standing armies were destructive of liberty and of use only to enforce tyranny. Only a well regulated militia of freemen was proper or necessary for the defense of a free country.

The armed populace of Massachusetts mobilized on April 19, 1775, to oppose the British troops sent from Boston to Lexington and Concord. This force of militia skirmished with the government troops all the way back to Boston and continually increased in size as men from distant towns arrived at the scene of action. The militia eventually completely surrounded all land approaches to Boston and kept the governor and his army confined there until the Continental Army was formed. A well regulated militia, composed of the people themselves, had been instrumental in preventing the governor and his appointees, backed by a standing army, from forcing the people to the administration's will.

Such a militia, based upon the experience of the Revolution, was essential to the liberty of men who intended to live in freedom. It made defense of the country possible without endangering liberty. It also made it possible for the people to defend their liberty against the governmental administration itself if necessary. During the formation of the state bills of rights, the beneficial consequences of an armed populace able to protect its own liberty against the government were not forgotten. An armed populace was guaranteed in one way or another in *every* bill of rights of the original states. These provisions were the early progenitors of the Second Amendment since it was the state bills of rights which were cited when the necessity of adding a bill of rights limiting the federal government was discussed later during the controversy over ratification of the United States Constitution.

Prior to the formal end of the Revolution in 1783, the people in most of the former colonies of America had established new state governments to replace the old colonial forms. To avoid any possibility of future dispute, such as their current one with Great Britain about the extent of its powers, *written* constitutions were utilized which clearly stated the powers of the new governments. Most of these constitutions also contained bills or declarations of rights. These were intended to protect specific rights of the citizens against violation by those governments, and proclaim the fundamental principles of free government upon which those governments were being founded.

Seven of the original thirteen states plus Vermont, which was not recognized as a state separate from New York until 1791, formed bills or declarations of rights along with their constitutions.[3] These bills of rights were viewed as limiting all branches and officers of the new governments being formed. In every one of the new state bills of rights, the concept of an armed populace was protected, either by stating the fundamental principle that a well regulated militia is the proper defence of a free state, or by protecting the right of the people to bear arms. In effect, these two ideas are equivalent—they both protect the concept of an armed populace, which is exactly what existed at the time. It was the people themselves, by means of their fundamental laws establishing the governments, who also fundamentally established themselves as a well regulated militia or armed populace in the state bills of rights.

In June of 1776, Virginia became the first state to form a constitution and bill of rights. Its Bill of Rights section 13 stated, "That a well-regulated militia, composed of the body of the people, trained to arms, is the proper, natural, and safe defence of a free state; that standing armies, in time of peace, should be avoided, as dangerous to liberty; and that in all cases the military should be under strict subordination to, and governed by, the civil power." Here the concept of a well regulated militia is defined as "composed of the body of the people." This well regulated militia was clearly the very same armed populace in existence in 1776 which was in the process of resisting the encroachments of the government backed by a standing army. This provision was a statement of a fundamental principle necessary to assure the continued existence of a *free* state, as opposed to the tyrannical state which the government was attempting to impose upon the people by means of a standing armed force.

The reference to a free state in the Virginia provision is of great significance. The Americans believed that, in a free state, the government does what the people want it to do. In an oppressive state, the government does whatever it wants and forces the people to comply by utilizing a standing armed force. A standing army is dangerous to liberty. If the militia is a safe defense for the people who control a free state; the army is a safe defense only for the despot or oppressors who control a tyrannical state. Clearly a well regulated militia, or armed populace, would be detrimental to the continued rule of oppressors, just as a standing army would be detrimental to the liberty of the people. A well regulated militia makes it possible for the people to have ultimate control of the government. If the government becomes oppressive, a corrective revolution, such as the American Revolution, is possible. Section 13 of the Virginia Bill of Rights became the basis for all of the subsequently formed bill of rights provisions on this subject in the original states as well as for the Second Amendment. It was written by George Mason.

Both Maryland in August, and Delaware in September, 1776, as well as New Hampshire in June, 1784, followed Virginia's lead very closely in this respect. Maryland's Declaration of Rights article XXV stated, "That a well-regulated militia is the proper and natural defence of a free government." Delaware's Declaration of Rights section 18 stated, "That a well regulated militia is the proper, natural and safe defence of a free government." New Hampshire's Bill of Rights section XXIV stated "A well regulated militia is the proper, natural, and safe defence of a state." All three also included a statement that standing armies are dangerous to liberty, and that the military should be under civil control, but these were put into separate sections instead of being combined as in the Virginia Bill of Rights. Unlike Virginia, neither the Maryland, Delaware, nor New Hampshire bill of rights provisions specified who that well regulated militia consisted of.

However, it is clear that they were the militia then in existence, the armed populace or entire adult male population, who had resisted their former government just as the Virginians had.

The Pennsylvania Declaration of Rights of September, 1776, was the first to protect the existence of an armed populace by guaranteeing an individual right rather than stating the fundamental maxim that an armed populace or well regulated militia is requisite for free government. Pennsylvania's Declaration of Rights stated "That the people have a right to bear arms for the defence of themselves and the state; and as standing armies in the time of peace are dangerous to liberty, they ought not to be kept up; and that the military should be kept under strict subordination to, and governed by, the civil power." This provision, coincidentally numbered 13, was based directly on the Virginia Bill of Rights also. It simply substituted the right of the people to bear arms statement for Virginia's well regulated militia reference.

The North Carolina (December, 1776), Vermont (July, 1777), and Massachusetts (October, 1780) Declarations of Rights followed the Pennsylvania form. North Carolina's Section XVII stated "That the people have a right to bear arms, for the defence of the State; . . ." Vermont's Section XV was taken vebatim from Pennsylvania's—"That the people have a right to bear arms for the defence of themselves and the State; . . ." Massachusetts' Section XVII stated that "The people have a right to keep and to bear arms for the common defence." All of these state bills of rights provisions should be considered in the context of their formation during the American Revolution—of an armed populace being able to defend their rights, liberty, and free state against any attempts of the government to establish tyranny and an oppresive (not free) state.

During the Revolution, the state governments themselves formed a federal government for the United States under the Articles of Confederation (proposed in November, 1777, and finally adopted by the thirteenth state in 1781). The Articles of Confederation provided that each state was to keep up a well regulated militia. This concept was exactly that militia establishment then in existence—an armed populace, which just happened to be in the process of resisting encroachments upon their liberty. Thus the status quo of the well regulated militia concept at the time the Constitution came into existence was that of an armed populace which would be able to resist the government if it attempted to violate the constitution. This armed populace was fundamentally established by the people themselves in the state bills of rights, either by stating that they were the proper defence for a free state, or by statedly guaranteeing their right to bear (or keep and bear) arms. In this way the people established themselves as the ultimate check upon the governments they had formed.

Governmental powers under the Articles of Confederation were concentrated in a single legislative body, Congress. It had to rely upon requisitions upon the state governments for any actions it took such as collecting taxes or raising troops. No decisions of Congress under the Confederation could go into effect without action by the state governments. Also, the Confederation was specifically limited to the powers "expressly" delegated to it in the Articles of Confederation by Article II thereof.[4] Thus, while the Congress under the Confederation had extensive powers, they were at the mercy of cooperation on the part of 13 separate state governments.

By 1786 it was very clear that the Confederation was not properly organized and Congress was too weak to perform the governmental functions assigned to and expected of it. Thus, the states selected delegates to attend a meeting of such delegates from all the states to gather in Philadelphia in May of 1787. The purpose of this Federal Convention was to propose alterations in the Confederation to remove its defects. It was this Convention which formed the United States Constitution.

The Constitution which the Federal Convention proposed would establish a government fundamentally different than that under the Articles of Confederation. Not a federation of independent and sovereign state governments, the new United States government would be a complete government to be established by the people just as the state governments had been. In addition to expanded powers, the major change was that the new federal government would not rely upon the state governments to implement its actions. Instead, it would be able to pass laws directly affecting the citizens, and would be able to enforce them through its own executive and judicial powers. In addition to this, the powers of the new government would be paramount to state laws, constitutions, and thus, the state bills of rights. Many people immediately perceived a major problem with this arrangement.

Under the Confederation, Congress could not violate the individual rights of citizens because it had to rely upon the state governments to implement its actions. The state constitutions and bills of rights protected the rights of the people from infringement by the state governments. However, under the newly proposed United States government, Congress could pass laws which directly violated any of the provisions in the state bills of rights, and such laws would be supreme, constitutional, and binding. To say that the people would not be likely to accept such a change would certainly have been an understatement. The lack of a bill of rights was a nearly fatal defect which almost resulted in the rejection of the proposed Constitution. This documentary history substantiates the view that the United States Constitution would undoubtedly not have been ratified if amendments protecting essential individual rights had not been virtually guaranteed by the occurrences during ratification.

George Mason, who had been largely responsible for Virginia's state bill of rights in 1776, was a member of the Federal Convention and was very quick to perceive the lack of a bill of rights as a major problem with the newly formed Constitution. Mason brought this up during the last days of the Federal Convention and seconded a motion to form a bill of rights as part of the Constitution. He insisted it would not take much time to form one since the bills of rights of the states could be used as a guide. He also pointed out that even though the state bills of rights were not repealed, they would not protect the rights of the citizens from violation by the federal government because the Constitution specifically stated that it was superior to the state constitutions. The motion to form a bill of rights in the Federal Convention lost on a tie vote of 5 states for, 5 states against, and one state absent.[5] The lack of support in the Convention for a bill of rights may have been due more to the delegates' desires to be finished with the work in Philadelphia, where they had been cooped up all summer, than to any inherent dislike for such a provision. However, once the decision was made to send the Constitution forth without a bill of rights, the lack of one became the major single argument against ratification of the Constitution, and was a main cause of the resulting hotly contested ratification struggle.

A second problem which came up at the end of the Federal Convention was the method proposed for adoption—complete acceptance or total rejection. No means was provided in the Convention proposal for making any amendments to the Constitution prior to its adoption. The Constitution was to be transmitted to Congress and sent on to the states by them. In each state a special convention representing the people thereof was to be called to assent to and ratify the Constitution. Governor Edmund Randolph, one of Mason's fellow delegates from Virginia, was especially unhappy about the lack of ability to amend the Constitution prior to ratification. Mason, Randolph, and Elbridge Gerry, a Massachusetts delegate, refused to sign the new proposed Constitution, partly for the above reasons. Their widely publicized refusal to sign or support the new Constitution was the tip of an iceberg of opposition, most of which was based upon the lack of a bill of rights and a method of adding one prior to adoption.

The dissent of Mason, Randolph and Gerry within the Federal Convention was soon followed by the criticism of others once the Constitution became public. Meetings of the Convention had been held in secret. When it adjourned on September 17, 1787, the proposed Constitution was published and officially sent to the Confederation Congress for transmittal to the states. In Congress, Richard Henry Lee, who had proposed Independence back in 1776, brought up the same complaints against the Constitution which Mason, Randoph and Gerry expressed within the Federal Convention. He insisted the Constitution was defective and needed amendments, especially a bill of rights similar to those which most of the states were founded upon. Congress managed to avoid a prolonged debate over the necessity of amendments and sent the Constitution on to the states without proposing any. The Constitution provided that as soon as nine of the state conventions ratified the Constitution, the new government would go into effect among the ratifying states. This was another major change from the Articles of Confederation which required the unanimous consent of all thirteen member state governments for any alterations.

The Federalist proponents and Antifederalist opponents of the Constitution started publishing their viewpoints concerning it shortly after its publication. Generally, the Federalists wanted the Constitution ratified and the government set in motion prior to any attempts to make amendments to it. Extreme Federalists considered the Constitution as perfect and believed it to be divinely inspired. They were therefore not in favor of any amendment of it, even after ratification. Many Federalists, however, were desirous of having a bill of rights, but they were forced by the mode established for ratifiction to argue against the need of one until after it was ratified. The Antifederalists generally wanted the Constitution amended prior to ratification. Extreme Antifederalists wanted a bill of rights added to the Constitution, as well as amendments which would make major structural changes in the new government. However, most Antifederalists believed that it was a bill of rights which was absolutely essential, that it would solve any problems which the Constitution created, and that it must be added by amendment prior to ratification in order to preserve liberty. Subsequent events proved that a large part of the population merely wished to have a bill of rights added to the Constitution, and were satisfied once it had been so added.[6]

In Pennsylvania, the first state to call a ratifying convention, there were already two parties in existence prior to the ratification debate, the Constitutionalists and Republicans. The former supported the

Pennsylvania constitution of 1776 with its very difficult manner of changing the state constitution, council type executive, one house legislature, and extensive bill of rights. The Republicans wanted a two branch legislature, single executive and easier method of making changes in the state constitution. The Constitutionalists naturally became Antifederalists concerning the ratification of the U. S. Constitution since it would result in changes to the state constitution which would endanger their rights and liberty. The Republicans already were Federalists because the leaders of their party had been instrumental in bringing about the new U. S. Constitution. Virtually all of Pennsylvania's delegates to the Federal Convention had been Republicans in state politics.

The ratification struggle was extremely bitter in Pennsylvania. On September 28, 1787, the Pennsylvania legislature, under the control of Republicans, attempted to vote for calling a ratifying convention prior to official receipt of the proposed United States Constitution from the Confederation Congress. This measure was apparently pushed with great haste and intemperance, and would provide such short notice to the people that ample time would not be allowed for those living far from Philadelphia to be properly informed of what was going on. This resulted in the secession of the minority (Constitutionalist—later Antifederalist) members of the Legislature in order to prevent a quorum and vote on what they considered as a precipitate measure. Several of the minority were physically dragged back to the legislative chambers the following day by a mob and held there while a ratifying convention bill was passed. These overzealous actions of the Pennsylvania Federalists resulted in continual distrust of Federalist intentions by Antifederalists during the remainder of the ratification struggle, not only in Pennsylvania, but throughout the other states as well.

The Pennsylvania ratifying convention met on November 20, 1787. It was the first state convention to meet. In it the Federalists predominated about two to one over the Antifederalists. The opponents of the Constitution were apparently constantly ridiculed, not only by the opposition, but also by people in the gallery of the statehouse. They, however, carefully presented their viewpoints and proposed amendments to the Constitution including a bill of rights. The Antifederalists' amendments were rejected and not allowed to be entered upon the journals of the convention. The convention ratified the Constitution by a vote of 46 to 23 on December 12, 1787.

On December 18, 1787, the Antifederlist minority delegates of the Pennsylvania convention published their viewpoint and proposed amendments to the Constitution.[7] The Pennsylvania Antifederalists did not give up the fight against the Constitution and for a bill of rights just because they lost in the convention. They continued to attack the Constitution and threaten the use of force to resist its implementation. Their viewpoint was that its establishment was a violation of the present Confederation, which required all thirteen states to approve any changes, as well as a violation of their state constitution. The dissent of the Pennsylvania minority was republished at least twenty times including reprints in five other states. This early opposition to ratification was a signal of problems ahead for the Constitution in the larger states.[8]

The other states to take relatively quick action to ratify were smaller ones which stood to gain a lot from the proposed new political arrangement. Delaware, New Jersey, and Georgia ratified by unanimous votes on December 7 and 18, 1787, and January 2, 1788, respectively. Connecticut ratified by a split vote of 128 to 40 on January 9, 1788. Massachusetts, a larger state, followed with a much closer vote of 187 to 168 on February 6, 1788. What had been mostly a tremendous initial surge for ratification was beginning to slow down somewhat. Ratification in Massachusetts could only be achieved by the Federalists offering to support subsequent amendments to the Constitution. This was the first state in which amendments were adopted by a state convention. All of the remaining state conventions except Maryland followed the example of Massachusets in ratifying and proposing specific amendments to be added later.

At the time of the Massachusetts ratification, the protest of the Pennsylvania minority had not yet reached Boston where the Massachusetts convention was meeting. This, along with other similar incidents of delayed intelligence concerning criticism of the Constitution, led to charges that information critical of the new Constitution was intentionally being detained in the mails. It had always been the practice previously for newspapers to be sent gratis through the mails between the newspaper printers throughout America. The new postmaster general had instituted new procedures which interfered with this ancient custom. The Antifederalists interpreted this, along with the precipitancy shown by the Federalists in Pennsylvania, as proof of a conspiracy to foist the Constitution upon the people by keeping them uninformed concerning its defects. The charge that criticism of the Constitution was being suppressed was repeated throughout the ratification struggle, and continued to reinforce the predisposition of Antifederalists to a distrust of the Federalists and the governmental power they seemed to be so much in favor of.

The New Hampshire convention met February 13, 1788, and adjourned within two weeks without taking action on ratification. This, like the proposed amendments and very close vote in Massachusetts, was a setback to the Federalists. It was clear to everyone that the Constitution would have been rejected outright in New Hampshire if the adjournment had not been sought by the Federalist minority.

The Maryland convention ratified by a vote of 63 to 11 on April 28th, 1788. A number of amendments were considered and adopted by a committee of the convention, however, they were not adopted by the convention. Maryland Antifederalists, including some who voted for ratification, felt betrayed by the failure of the Convention to propose amendments to the Constitution. The action of the Maryland convention in considering subsequent amendments but then failing to adopt any were utilized by Antifederalists as a warning to the other states that subsequent amendments could not be relied upon to protect the liberties of the people.

South Carolina ratified on May 23rd, 1788, by a vote of 149 to 73. It ratified with two proposed amendments and with the understanding that the new government was limited to the specific powers given, which was equivalent to the first Massachusetts proposed amendment. So far eight states had ratified, of which two had proposed amendments. The next ratification would carry the new government into effect.

Virginia's convention was scheduled to meet June 2nd and New Hampshire's adjourned convention to meet on June 18th. New Hampshire completed its labors first and ratified by a vote of 57 to 47 on June 21, 1788, while proposing the largest list yet of amendments to the Constitution. Its ratification was copied almost verbatim from that of Massachusetts. New Hampshire proposed basically the same nine amendments as Massachusetts plus three others: protection from standing armies and quartering of troops; freedom of religion; and protection against disarming the populace.[9] Thus, with New Hampshire's ratification, the new Constitution was established among the nine ratifying states, but there was clear evidence that many people did not like the lack of a bill of rights. The state conventions yet to ratify all demanded even more amendments, and very extensive and explicit bills of rights.

The balance between Federalists and Antifederalists in the Virginia convention was very close. However, a large part of those who would have described themselves as Federalists were in favor of a bill of rights. Many of those who were against the Constitution would have been for it if only it contained a bill of rights. Generally, all agreed that amendments were desireable, and many thought they were essentially necessary. The question was not whether there should or should not be amendments, but rather, whether the amendments should take place prior to or subsequent to ratification. With this situation, the Federalists were able to win ratification by agreeing to support subsequent amendments, and Virginia ratified on June 25th, 1788, by a vote of 89 to 79.

The Virginia convention's proposed amendments included a twenty article Declaration of Rights, which was taken largely from the Virginia state bill of rights. Virginia was the first state convention to group proposed amendments relating to indivudual rights and maxims of free government into a declaration or bill of rights, and to follow this with a list of other proposed amendments relating to changes in the structure or powers of the new government.[10] The conventions yet to meet basically followed this lead of the Virginia convention. The sole exception to this was the second convention of North Carolina which did not propose a bill of rights due to the fact that Congress had already proposed amendments to the Constitution, which included what later became the federal Bill of Rights.

The New York convention first assembled on June 17, 1788. It was overwhelmingly Antifederalist, but there were new political pressures and realities now that nine state conventions had already ratified the new Constitution, thus puting it into effect. Congress met in New York City, but it was not likely to continue there under the new Constitution if New York did not ratify the Constitution. After a month of debate and extensive discussion of a bill of rights, New York ratified the Constitution on July 26, 1788, by a vote of 30 to 27. The convention delegates came up with an improvement upon the Virginia ratification plan by actually incorporating a bill of rights into the ratification. New York ratified with the understanding that these provisions were consistent with the Constitution and that the rights listed there could not be abridged or violated. It also proposed 33 other amendments to the Constitution to be added subsequently.[11]

Partially overlapping the New York convention, the North Carolina convention was also overwhelmingly Antifederalist. By a vote of 184 to 84, it decided not to ratify the Constitution until *previous* amendments were added to it.[12] The North Carolina convention adopted the Virginia convention's proposed bill of rights and other amendments verbatim and added six new proposals of its own. The idea of some of the last state conventions refusing to ratify until after a bill of rights was added to the Constitution had been industriously promoted by Thomas Jefferson, minister to France, in many of his letters to friends in the United States. His proposal was debated by the delegates in both the Virginia and North Carolina conventions and was implemented by the latter.

The state conventions which had ratified by close votes should be examined relative to pressures they created for the adoption of a bill of rights. In Massachusetts, New Hampshire, Virginia, and New York, all of which had close contests, the votes indicate almost universal support for amendments. This is evident since the large minority of votes cast against ratification in each of those conventions clearly indicated support for a bill of rights and other amendments *prior to* ratification. The majority votes cast in support of ratification with proposed amendments once again indicated support for amendments. As the latter ratification conventions were meeting, the entire subject was better understood, the people were better informed, and the delegates were insisting that a bill of rights and other amendments be added to the Constitution. The difference of opinion at this period was not whether there should be amendments, but how extensive they should be and whether they should be added before or after ratification of the Constitution.

At this point in time, after the North Carolina refusal to ratify, a bill of rights was virtually assured to be added to the Constitution subsequently. The political pressures created by all of the proposals from the state conventions for amendments, by the continuing refusal of Rhode Island to call a ratifying convention, by the narrow votes for ratification in the large states of Massachusetts, Virginia, and New York, and finally by refusal to ratify by North Carolina prior to the addition of amendments, had their intended effect. The people were demanding that those rights, which they had resisted the British to preserve and which they previously expressed in the state bills of rights against violation by the state governments, must be added to the Constitution. They were intent upon preserving liberty, not establishing tyranny, and would not part with those rights upon which liberty was clearly dependent. Their demands for Constitutional protection for those rights had to be heeded. Americans had recently protected their liberty and gained independence by armed resistance. Because they were armed, they were perfectly capable of such armed resistance again if necessary to protect their rights. This point was made many times during the ratification struggle. The concept of an armed populace was an inherent part of American life which had made not only the American Revolution possible, but also the preservation of liberty, and the ability of the people to be in the position to establish and limit governments rather than have governments imposed upon them.

The mode of obtaining what everyone basically wanted became a major difference between Federalists and Antifederalists not only during the latter conventions, but also during the elections for

Congress. Practically everyone by then wanted at least some amendments. Most Federalists and Antifederalists alike wanted a bill of rights. Many Federalists wanted some minor changes in the Constitution such as increased representation and limits on Congress setting their own pay. The Antifederalists wanted all of this plus many other more drastic changes in the Constitution. Antifederalists did not trust the Federalists to live up to their promises to support amendments, which were made in the state conventions, and therefore, they supported calling a convention to amend the Constitution. This was one of two methods provided in Article 5 of the Constitution for amending it. This method opened up the entire Constitution for changes and did not allow the new Congress any imput concerning them. While a bill of rights was of overriding importance to Antifederalists, they beleived that cutting down the power of the federal government was also important since it was an excess of that power which threatened those rights.

Federalists supported the other method of amendment which provided for Congress to propose constitutional amendments to the state legislatures for ratification. They preferred this method because the entire Constitution was not opened up for changes, and because Congress would not be likely to divest themselves of necessary power. Also, the Federalists hoped Congress would be composed mainly of Federalists, and would willingly provide the needed bill of rights and a few other minor changes. However, a Federalist controlled Congress would clearly not propose such major changes as to destroy the very Constitution they had mainly been responsible for forming.

March 4, 1789, was established by the old Congress as the date of meeting for the new Congress under the Constitution by an ordinance passed September 13, 1788. After this was in effect, the ratifying states began passing election ordinances, the state legislatures began selecting United States Senators, and the people began voting for Congressional representatives. Ratification brought about a new political struggle for the Federalists and Antifederalists. The Federalists wanted to engross as many congressional and senate seats as possible in order to assure that destructive amendments were not tacked on to the Constitution. Antifederalists wanted to gain as many seats as possible so they could take action in favor of a bill of rights and other important amendments. Also, both parties had to seek seats in the state assemblies and senates. If Antifederalists were able to win control in the state legislatures, they could call for a convention to amend the Constitution and open the door to major changes in it.

In order to be elected into the Congress under the new Constitution, candidates had to say whether they would support or oppose the amendments proposed by their state conventions. Federalists increasingly supported some amendments which only had for their object the greater security for individual liberty. They still refused to support any amendments which would change or reduce the powers given to the new government. The Federalists were elected to most positions in Congress, so their plan for amending the Constitution was feasible. However, the Antifederalists controlled several states, noteably New York and Virginia, and these states pursued the Antifederalist plan for pressure to call a convention to amend the Constitution.

The New York ratifying convention had sent a circular letter to the other states on July 28th, 1788, inviting them to support a convention to implement the proposed amendments.[13] Virginia responded favorably, and both states did in fact request the new Congress to call a convention to amend the Constitution. These applications for a convention to amend the Constitution were presented in the first Congress early in its session and helped put more pressure on the Federalists, who predominated in Congress, to come up with a satisfactory bill of rights. Such a bill of rights would quiet the apprehensions of the people regarding the extensive powers of the new government, and dampen the push for other amendments.

When the new Congress met on March 4, 1789, one of its leading Federalist members, James Madison, was under major political obligations to push for a bill of rights. Madison had agreed to support amendments to the Constitution which were intended to protect individual rights during the Virginia ratifying convention in order to gain ratification. He also made many campaign pledges to the same effect in order to win election from Virginia into the first House of Representatives. Obligations aside, he had become convinced that a bill of rights was necessary and proper for the new Constitution. One major influence upon him was Thomas Jefferson, with whom Madison corresponded regularly. In fact, Madison was instrumental in bringing about action on a bill of rights in Congress, even though during the ratification controversy he had always opposed previous amendments.

It was Madison who introduced the subject of amendments in the first Congress on June 8, 1789. He did this to beat the Antifederalists to the punch since he believed they were about to bring up the subject. His initial proposal for amendments contained protection for all of the individual rights finally included in the Bill of Rights. Madison proposed that his amendments be inserted in the Constitution along with related subjects rather than being added at the end of the Constitution. Thus, Madison grouped the rights of individuals which were later protected in the first, second, third, fourth, fifth, sixth, eighth and ninth amendments to the Constitution and proposed that they be inserted in Article I, section 9, between clauses 3 and 4. Interestingly, all of the rights protected in the first, second and third amendments to the Constitution are in exactly the same order that Madison originally proposed them.[14]

Madison had to prod the overwhelmingly Federalist House of Representatives to begin work on amendments since it was so busy setting up the new government that many members felt they did not have time for the subject. His proposals were eventually turned over to a committee of one representative from each state, which reported on July 28, 1789.[15] The committee of eleven report was basically the same as Madison's original proposal. This report was then considered in committee of the whole house which made a report, and that was taken up in the House, which proposed seventeen articles of amendment on August 24, 1789.[16] The proposed amendments were now to be added at the end of the Constitution, and consisted of basically the same provisions as the present Bill of Rights along with two provisions which were never ratified. The seventeed provisions of the House were further condensed into twelve articles after consideration by the Senate.

During the consideration of amendments in the House and Senate, the Federalists tried to quickly push through the bill of rights and a few other provisions and avoid any other amendments changing the new government's powers. Some Federalists did not want to consider any amendments at all. The Antifederalists tried to introduce all of the numerous amendments which the various state ratifying conventions had proposed, but everything other than what Madison had proposed was rejected. Of the twelve amendments which Congress proposed, the first related to the proportion of representatives to population, and the second to the pay of members of Congress. Numbers three through eleven related to individual rights, of which number four protected the right of the people to keep and bear arms and stated the well regulated militia or armed populace concept. Number twelve was similar to Massachusetts' proposed first amendment limiting the powers of the new government to those given to it, and stating all others remained with the states, or the people. Congress approved these on September 26, 1789.[17] In order for them to become part of the Constitution, they had to be ratified by three fourths of the state legislatures.

Madison had pushed to get the amendments passed by Congress prior to the meeting of the second North Carolina convention, which was scheduled for mid November of 1789. The North Carolina convention was the only convention following Virginia's which ratified without proposing or including a bill of rights with its ratification. This was a direct result of the fact that Congress had already proposed the Bill of Rights. On November 21, 1789, the convention ratified the Constitution on behalf of the people of North Carolina by a vote of 194 to 77. The North Carolina legislature swiflty followed up and ratified all twelve of the proposed amendments to the Constitution on December 22, 1789.

In March of 1790, Rhode Island held a ratifying convention, which adjourned somewhat like that of New Hampshire. It proposed a bill of rights and other amendments to the Constitution for the consideration of the people and recommended that the amendments proposed by Congress should be adopted (except for the second one relating to the pay of legislators). On May 29, 1790 the reassembled Rhode Island convention ratified the Constitution by a vote of 34 to 32. It emulated the New York convention's idea of ratifying with certain understandings. The ratification contained eighteen bill of rights provisions which were stated to be consistent with the Constitution and which cannot be abridged or violated, and the convention proposed 21 other amendments to the Constitution.[18] These were nearly the same as those proposed by the March meeting of the convention. The Rhode Island legislature quickly adopted all of Congress' proposed amendments in mid June except for the second proposal relating to the pay of legislators.

Generally, the state legislatures acted fairly quickly on the proposed amendments. The exception to this was Virginia where the Antifederalists were very powerful. Many of the Virginia state senators were quite unhappy that none of the Virginia amendments other than the bill of rights provisons and the two relating to representation and pay had been proposed by Congress. They were wary that if they accepted what had been proposed by Congress, they could not get any other amendments. They took exception to several of the bill of rights proposals and stated their objections at length.[19] It is evident from their objections that they thoroughly considered each amendment proposed and that the right to keep and bear arms provision met with their approval as at least meeting what the Virginia convention desired in that respect. The disagreement between the assembly and senate of Virginia resulted in a delay in consideration of the amendments by Virginia again until December of 1791, when it ratified all twelve proposals.

Vermont became a member of the union in January, 1791. This made it necessary that eleven states ratify amendments before they would become part of the Constitution. Vermont ratified all twelve amendments in November of 1791. Thus, when Virginia subsequently ratified on December 15, 1791, those amendments which had received eleven ratifictions formally became part of the Constitution. Three states, Massachusetts, Georgia and Connecticut, failed to take the necessary actions to ratify any of the amendments at the time.[20] The first two proposed amendments did not receive the necessary number of ratifications. Therefore, the third through the twelfth proposed amendments became the first ten amendments to the Constitution, and the right to keep and bear arms provision became the Second Amendment.

Amendments and a Bill of Rights

The controversy over ratification of the Constitution was basically one over amending the new Constitution since it was proposed as a package to be taken as a whole or rejected. Because no provision was made to add amendments prior to adoption, a bill of rights could not be added even though a large part of the population considered such a provision as essential. The addition of the Bill of Rights by the margins of approval necessary for adoption of constitutional amendments shortly after the Constitution was adopted clearly indicates that it was in fact considered essential by a very large part of the people.[21] Thus the people faced a major dilemma during the ratification period—adopt the Constitution without a bill of rights or reject it. The other possibility was to accept the Constitution as it was and insist that amendments protecting individual rights be added afterward. But if a bill of rights was absolutely essential, as the Antifederalists believed, would it be safe or prudent to adopt without adding one first?

Federalists generally held the view that any changes which were necessary in the Constitution could be made after ratification. This could be done by Congress proposing the amendments as Article 5 of the Constitution provided for. The more extreme Federalists felt that no amendments whatever should be added until experience had shown the necessity of them. The Antifederalists believed there were certain amendments, especially a bill of rights protecting the various individual rights of the citizens, as contained in the state bills of rights, that it was absolutely essential be added to the Constitution prior to establishment of the new government. The idea of waiting until the necessity of a bill of rights was evident was considered preposterous by them. The experiences which would prove the necessity of a bill of rights were tyranny, oppression and the destruction of liberty by the government. When such necessity became evident, it would be too late to restrict the government's powers except by revolution, which might or might not be successful.

With this set of circumstances, a great debate was instituted over the necessity of a bill of rights. This was not a debate over the importance, necessity, or existence of the rights involved, which were protected in the state bills of rights. The existence, importance and necessity of these rights were conceded by both sides in the ratification controversy. The Federalists, however, said that a bill of rights was unnecessary and even dangerous in a Constitution like that proposed. The Antifederalists said it was essential, and must be added before the Constitution was ratified. This was a basic disagreement over how the powers of the new government should be properly construed.

The Federalists' views concerning a bill of rights were inconsistent, and they were never able to convince the Antifederalists otherwise. In fact, the Federalists' arguments may well have convinced more people that a bill of rights was essential, because they were supporting what most people considered then, and would certainly consider now, as a bad cause. Once the Constitution appeared without a bill of rights, Federalists were forced into opposing a bill of rights for purely political reasons unrelated to the merits of the individual rights protected in one. They had to get the Constitution ratified; it contained no bill of rights (or only a few of the many necessary rights contained in the state bills of rights); the ratification system provided no means to add a bill of rights to the Constitution prior to ratification; the majority of people considered a bill of rights essential to their political safety; therefore, the Federalists had to argue against the necessity of a bill of rights in the Constitution to get it ratified. They failed in these arguments. It was very clear that the Constitution was going to be defeated without a bill of rights. As this became evident in the latter Conventions, the Federalists of necessity became supporters of subsequent amendments, especially a bill of rights. They pledging to work for adoption of a bill of rights after ratification in order to secure ratification.

The Federalist position on the necessity of a bill of rights in the Consitution was as follows: Under the Constitution the people give Congress only certain defined powers. It has no other powers. The powers given by the people were not intended for the purpose of violating any of the individual rights protected by the states' bills of rights. In fact, the powers being given to the federal government were being taken from the state governments where their rights are already protected. The total sum of the powers of the new federal government and the state government would be exactly the same as the sum of the powers of the old government and the state government. Therefore a bill of rights in the federal Constitution would serve no useful purpose as Congress was given no powers to violate the individual rights of the citizens.

James Wilson, a leading Pennsylvania Federalist who helped write the Constitution, advanced the premier Federalist doctrine relating to a bill of rights—in the state constitutions, all powers were given to the government unless they were reserved to the people, but in the federal Constitution, all powers were reserved to the people except those given to the government. While Wilson's doctrine is still cited as valid even today, there are problems with it. It implied that states without any bill of rights had absolute control over the rights which the people always considered as too important to trust their governments meddling with. Antifederalists pointed out the fact that Congress could still pass any laws relating to the subjects it had been given authority over, and could conceivably violate any right protected by provisions of the state bills of rights by means of those powers, which were basically unlimited. For example, Congress could constitutionaly tax newspapers. It could pass regulations which would require bonds, licenses, and other regulations which could limit freedom of the press. The power to tax can be used as a power to destroy.

Some Federalists attacked the concept of a bill of rights as useless. They compared it to the English Bill of Rights of 1689, which had been a limitation upon the King or executive branch of government only. The Antifederalists basically ignored Federalist arguments mentioning the English Bill of Rights. Few of the rights considered essential by the people and protected in the state bills of rights were even mentioned in the English Bill of Rights.[22] The Antifederalists argued that the Federal Constitution required a bill of rights which would limit all branches of government, just as the state bills of rights did. They preferred to have written limits to the powers of government rather than to leave so much to construction.[23]

Federalists stated that nothing on paper could stop the government from violating rights. They argued that it was the people's representation in Congress which would check any tendency of the government to infringe individual rights; that if Congress infringed any rights, they were also infringing their own. Antifederalists considered the representation in Congress as a mighty small check upon the tremendous powers vested in the new government. They consistently argued that the representation in Congress was much too small to guarantee that it would not violate their rights.

Other Federalists asked why it was necessary for the people to state that they retained rights which they had never parted with. Still others ridiculed the need for protection of individual rights by mentioning such things as the right to lay on one's side on a cold winter's eve, or to hunt and fish on one's own land.[24] Antifederalists cited historical evidence that those in government are always attempting to incease their power at the expense of the people's liberty. They answered Federalist riducule with riducule. Antifederalists were struck by the appalling naivete of the Federalists, who, in order to explain away the necessity of a bill of rights, were very fond of using a simple land transaction as an analogy for the not so simple transfer of power by the people from the states to the new federal government.

Federalists asked how it was possible to list and protect all of the rights of the people. Antifederalists were not interested in protecting every possible thing which could remotely be considered as a right. Instead, they were interested in protecting those essential and unalienable rights, which governments had often tended to invade, and which no *just* government should have control over. The important rights which they were concerned about were exemplified in the provisions of the state bills of rights. Antifederalists asked pointed questions: Are the people to have no rights? Would a bill of rights consume too much paper? If the new government has only the specific powers given, then why not so state in explicit terms?

Federalists noted that in the Constitution, which specifically lists the powers given to the government, if any particular rights of the people were protected from governmental violation, it would be essential to protect all rights of the people. A clear implication of a few protected rights in a government where no power was given to violate them would be that the government has other powers not specifically given to it in the Constitution. Another implication is that those rights specified were the only ones intended to be protected and that all others were intended to be given up to the control of the government. Thus, to Federalists, a bill of rights was not only unnecessary in their view, it was dangerous in a government like that established by the proposed Constitution.

The Antifederalists were continually pointing out that the Constitution indeed protected several individual rights in Article I, section 9. Therefore, based upon the Federalists' own arguments, it was absolutely essential to protect the rest of those rights the people were accustomed to hold out of control of their governments in the state bills of rights by adding a federal bill of rights. If this were not done, all other rights could be assumed to have been given up to the new government. Also, these reservations of rights which there was no power given to violate implied that the new government did have other unspecified powers. This situation was clearly dangerous and was a major focal point of attack by the Antifederalists.

The Constitution was vague in this and many other respects. Antifederalists, being very distrustfull of the Federalist formed Constitution, believed that this vagueness was no accident. The Constitution allowed those in power to make the decision as to what laws would be "necessary and proper" for them to enact. Not only would Congress be its own arbiter as far as the extent of its powers, but the Constitution specifically made the laws of Congress superior to the state constitutions and bills of rights. If there was a bill of rights in the Constitution, the limits of the government would be written down for all to see, Congress would know its bounds, and the people would know their rights. All would know if the bounds had been passed, and the people would be able to resist the government on universally understood and sound constitutional principles.

There was relative unanimity among the Antifederalists that a bill of rights should be added to the Consitution. Freedom of the press, religious liberty, and jury trials in civil cases were topics relating to amendments and a bill of rights which were often discussed during the ratification controversy. The necessity of an armed populace, protection against disarming of the citizenry, and the need to guard against a select militia and assure a real militia which could defend liberty against any standing forces the government might raise were topics interspersed throughout the ratification period. The Federalists, however, blindly insisted that there were no amendments upon which the Antifederalists could possibly agree. Some Federalists were willing to let the new government pass a bill of rights as a law if it would not actually be part of the Constitution. The Antifederalists sarcastically suggested that perhaps this was the answer to all their problems—as long as Congress would not later rescind such a bill of rights. What was clearly needed, however, and what the Antifederalists insisted upon, was constitutional protection for all of the fundamental and essential rights of the people as contained in the state bills of rights. If these rights were added to the Constitution by amendment, Congress would never be able to rescind or infringe them.

Protection Against Disarming the People

The Antifederalists were fearful of the great powers of the new government—of the few and weak checks upon it. They considered that many of the powers given to the new Congress were vague and open to considerable construction, or were simply too extensive and needed proper checks. The powers over the militia were viewed in the latter light. The militia powers over every man in the country above 16 years old were given to provide for organizing them, for arming them, and for training them so they would be an effective military force which could defend the country. Such powers were very extensive and could be easily abused and perverted to exactly the opposite purposes for which the powers were being given. These unchecked powers could be used to destroy what was considered as the bulwark of liberty—the well regulated militia, or armed populace, as then constitutionally established and protected in the state bills of rights.

From the Antifederalist viewpoint, the state constitutions and bills of rights established free republican governments, which were the basic protection of the individual rights of the citizens. The new arrangement under the federal Constitution would weaken the states to the point of their near destruction, supercede the state constitutions and bills of rights, and thus jeopardize the liberty secured to the people under them. The new Constitution would provide no means of its own for the protection of liberty such as a federal bill of rights. Additionaly, it would take the militia from local state control and put them under federal control, thus increasing federal power and placing the last defence of the people against unconstitutional acts into federal hands without constitutional protection. There would be no assurance that a well regulated militia would be kept up, nor that the concept of an armed populace would be protected in any way. At the same time, the federal government could keep up a standing army as numerous as it would like, pass any laws and collect whatever taxes it wished for whatever purposes it chose to call "necessary and proper," and utilize the army to enforce all of this.

The Antifederalists believed that the government would not obey the Constitution. They believed that the government would use force to violate it, and that the people would not be able to make such a powerful government obey the supreme law of the land. Whenever Antifederalists brought up the spectres of usurpation, tyranny, or other oppressive and unconstitutional actions by the new government, they were *always* given the *same* answer by the Federalists: The people possess the strong arm—they can rely upon the sword—they are armed and can resist the government just as they resisted the British; Congress would be mad to even contemplate projects of ambition against an armed populace. The Antifederalists wanted to insure that the strong situation of the people described by the Federalists would always be a reality, and that the people would be armed and able to defend their liberty in the future just as they were then. But the

Antifederalists pointed out that the government was given such extensive powers over the militia as to allow the new government the ability to destroy the militia if it so desired, and to do it constitutionally.

Outside of directly disarming the people, which was one of the Antifederalists stated fears, there were a couple of ways they envisioned destruction of the militia might be accomplished by the government in the future. One way was to harrass the citizens with militia duty in order to make the people themselves wish to see the militia abandoned and a standing army set up in their place. By having draconian regulations and penalties it might be possible to keep the people under martial law. The government might continually send them to the extreme ends of the union and thus destroy the militia's own desire for a militia system. When the militia was abused and eventually weakened in this manner, the people would not oppose the establishment of a standing army—they would desire one, and there would be no complaints about disuse of the militia.

Another and much more plausible method to destroy the militia as they knew it was to "model" the militia, or form a select militia. The militia consisted of the body of the people. A "select militia" consisted of a small part of the whole militia. For example, if all men from 18 to 21 were made a select corps by the government and trained more often than the rest of the militia, this small part would constitute a select militia. The Revolutionary era minute men were select militia. After the hostilities of the Revolution and previous to the ratification period, there had been proposals for this type of system for the Union. General Washington in 1783 and Baron Von Steuben in 1784 had made proposals concerning a "peace establishment," or peacetime arrangements for military defence. Both had suggested what would have been described at that time as a select militia. The proposal of the latter was in fact decried by some as a standing army.[25] As the Constitution was debated, Federalists (and even some Antifederalists) supported proposals for a select militia establishment. *The Federalist* Number 35, by Alexander Hamilton, contained a specific suggestion for this type of arrangement. It should be noted that Hamilton's proposal assumed that all of the people would be armed.[26]

Most Antifederalists considered that any militia arrangement which did not include the entire body of the people was the equivalent of a standing army, and could be utilized by the government for any and all of the bad purposes which a standing army could be utilized for. If the government could pick who composed the militia, it could in effect disarm everyone else. Antifederalists believed that the government would train and arm the select militia at public expense and disuse the general militia. Thus, over time, the general militia would end up untrained, unarmed, or actually disarmed, and unable to defend their liberty, while the select, or orgainized, part of the militia would be used just like a standing army to enforce oppressive measures of the government.[27]

The Federalist view was that a standing army would not be a threat to liberty because the people were armed and easily an overmatch for any possible army which the government could raise. They did not view any of the powers given to the government in the Constitution as authorizing it to disarm the people just as they did not view those powers as authorizing the government to infringe any of the other rights of the people protected in the state bills of rights.

Power over the militia is power over the entire adult male population. The power given to provide for arming the militia, or adult male population, could be misconstrued as intending a power to disarm the militia. Clearly, disarming the militia was equivalent to disarming the entire population. Some Antifederalists feared that the government would actually attempt to do just that. Antifederalist claims that the militia, or populace, would be disarmed were interspersed throughout the ratification debate.

An early Antifederalist discussion of this topic was contained in a December 3, 1787, Boston *American Herald* article under the pseudonym John De Witt. This piece was reprinted in Philadelphia where it was made even more pointed in its description of how Congress at their pleasure may "arm or disarm all or any part of the freemen of the United States," so as to put it out of the power of the freemen militia of America to defend their liberties against the government's army.[28]

On December 12, 1787, the minority of the Pennsylvania convention introduced their proposed bill of rights.[29] It included the first specific proposal for constitutional protection of the right of the people to bear arms during the ratification debate. It stated "That the people have a right to bear arms for the defense of themselves and their own state, or the United States, or for the purpose of killing game; and no law shall be passed for disarming the people or any of them, unless for crimes committed, or real danger of public injury from individuals; and as standing armies in the time of peace are dangerous to liberty, they ought not to be kept up; and that the military shall be kept under strict subordination to and be governed by the civil power." This is taken directly from the Pennsylvania Declaration of Rights with specific protection added to prevent disarming of the people. The failure to provide for adding this bill of rights to the Constitution was very disappointing to the Pennsylvania minority and their constitutents.

A previous order by the Pennsylvania Supreme Executive Council on December 4, 1787, to collect all publicly owned arms for repairs became a focal point of complaint for the bitterly unsuccessful Pennsylvania Antifederalists after the convention ratified the Constitution and ajourned without adopting or proposing amendments to the Constitution. There were at least twelve different references to this occurrence, mostly in Antifederalist sources, during the ratification period.[30] The Antifederalist references to the Council's action suggested that it was intended to temporarily disarm the militia so that they could not resist while an oppressive government—the Constitution—was to be forced upon them. One Antifederalist suggested that everyone should obtain their own arms and not rely on any supplied by the government. Another stated that no one was planning to obey this order during the Constitutional crisis. In any event, the Antifederalists definitely got everyone thinking about the subject of the militia, their arms, and to what extent it was desireable to have the availability of arms be dependent upon the government.

On February 6, 1788, there was a discussion in the Massachusetts convention over the amendments which the Federalists in the convention had proposed. John Hancock, Governor of Massachusetts, was persuaded to introduced the nine amendments, which were later adopted by the convention. The first article of these amendments was similar to the second article of the Confederation and was described as a "summary" of a bill of rights. Samuel Adams attempted to add a more specific bill of rights as an amendment to this particular article. His amendment specified that the Constitution should not be construed as authorizing Congress to "prevent the people of the United States, who are peaceable citizens, from keeping their own arms," nor to violate freedom of the press, freedom of religion, the right of petition, or freedom from unreasonable searches and seizures. Adams also included a statement against standing armies.[31]

Adams' proposal caused considerable confusion in the Convention. The Antifederalists who actually had a clear majority were upset that Samuel Adams, an old patriot from the American Revolution, would think the Constitution unsafe in that it would allow governmental interference with the rights he had attempted to protect. Some of the Antifederalist delegates who had been convinced to vote for ratification by the original Federalist proposal of amendments changed their minds due to Adams' proposal. This commotion over Adam's proposal, and change of heart by Antifederalists who had decided to vote for ratification, put the adoption of the Constitution by the Massachusetts convention in jeapardy. Adams withdrew his motion as he was under instructions from his constituents to ratify without delay.

His motion was renewed by another delegate. There was apparently extensive debate upon the issues his bill of rights raised. However, no record of the actual debate is known to exist. Samuel Adams was forced to vote against his own proposed bill of rights, and it was defeated. This was not because anyone disagreed about the necessity of the individual rights it protected, all of which were already protected in the Massachusetts Declaration of Rights. The disagreement resulted from the political necessity of the Federalists getting the Constitution ratified without amendments.

The New Hampshire convention ratified the Constitution on June 21, 1788, with twelve amendments, the same nine proposed by Massachusetts, plus several bill of rights type proposals. These included protection for freedom of religion and against quartering of soldiers, and the provision that "Congress shall never disarm any citizen, unless such as are or have been in actual rebellion."[32] It should be noted that the New Hampshire delegates had adjourned for the purpose of going home to sound out their constituents regarding the Constitution. This had been suggested by the Federalists to prevent outright rejection of the Constitution at the first meeting of the convention in February, 1788. On the return of the delegates in June, ratification was possible because the Federalists offered to support the proposed amendments.

In the Virginia state ratifying convention, Patrick Henry stressed the lack of protection for an armed populace as a major defect of the proposed Constitution. He requested that six sections of the Virginia Bill of Rights be read including section 13 protecting a well regulated militia of the people. He then proceeded to point out what to him was so obvious—that the people of Virginia have a bill of rights directed against the abuse of power by their state government, which will be stripped of power under the Constitution, but they will have no bill of rights to protect against the abuse of power by the federal government, which will be in exclusive possession of ***all*** power.[33]

There were extensive debates in the Virginia convention over the militia powers transferred to the Federal government. The fears of the Antifederalists were evident. George Mason asked, "Who are the militia?" He then answered, "They consist now of the whole people, except a few public officers." He could not say who would be the militia in the future because the Constitution gave the new government power which could be interpreted as allowing it to change who composed the militia.[34] In a letter to Jefferson just a couple weeks earlier, Mason had expressed the fear that the government "may disarm, or render useless the militia."[35]

The Virginia convention ratified the Constitution because a majority was obtained by promises to propose and support amendments after ratification. As previously noted, these were divided into a Declaration of Rights and other amendments. Section 17 of the Declaration of Rights stated "That the people have a right to keep and bear arms; that a well-regulated militia, composed of the body of the people trained to arms, is the proper, natural, and safe defence of a free state; that standing armies, in time of peace, are dangerous to liberty, and therefore ought to be avoided, as far as the circumstances and protection of the community will admit; and that, in all cases, the military should be under strict subordination to, and governed by, the civil power." This provision was formed by adding the right of the people to keep and bear arms provision to the existing provision in the Virginia state bill of rights.

The overlapping conventions in New York and North Carolina both proposed amendments relating to the right of the people to keep and bear arms. North Carolina refused to ratify until after amendments were added to the Constitution. Its proposal was exactly the same as that of the Virginia convention. New York's right to keep and bear arms provision was based upon the Virginia proposal, but was more guarded since it clearly defined who the well regulated militia were so as to avoid future governmental manipulation. New York's proposal was "That the people have a right to keep and bear arms; that a well-regulated militia, including the body of the people *capable of bearing arms,* is the proper, natural, and safe defence of a free state." (Emphasis in original.)[36] The "capable of bearing arms," provision was developed from a proposal by a popular pseudonymous Antifederalist pamphleteer, the Federal Farmer, who had suggested the need to insure that the militia of the future would be the same armed populace then in existence.[37]

The state bills of rights provisions constitutionally establishing a well regulated militia, or armed populace, had not been added to the state constitutions to protect the people from foreign invaders, but instead to protect themselves and their liberty from their own state governments. Antifederalists wanted exactly the same type of provision added to the federal Constitution to assure the ability of the people to protect their liberty against the federal government. It was evident that the new government was going to have an army at its disposal and was going to have extensive control over the militia. It was also evident that the Federalists were generally in favor of a select militia system rather than depending upon the general militia.

The Antifederalists wanted the militia in the future to be the same as it was in the past. They wanted a real militia consisting of an armed populace, which would not only be able to help protect the country from foreign invaders, but would *more importantly* make it possible for the people to be able to protect their liberty and free government from destruction by a corrupt or tyrannical governmental administration. Since it would not be possible to assure that the government would always provide for a true militia system, the only alternative for providing a means to the people to protect liberty and prevent gross abuses by the government was to constitutionally assure an armed populace. This was accomplished by guaranteeing the right of individuals to possess weapons free of government infringement.

INTRODUCTION NOTES

1 See Appendix B, p. 781, for a comparison chart of bills of rights provisions. See Appendix A, p. 747, for the provisions of the state bills of rights.

2 From the "Declaration and Resolves of the First Continental Congress," in S. E. Morrison, *Sources and Documents Illustrating the American Revolution . . .* (Oxford, Clarendon Press, 1961) p. 118.

3 See Appendix A, p. 747, for the state declarations and bills of rights.

4 Article II of the Confederation stated: "Each state retains its sovereignty, freedom and independence, and every Power, Jurisdiction and right, which is not by this confederation expressly delegated to the United States, in Congress assembled." See DHRC, I, p. 86.

5 See "Federal Convention," September 12, 1787, pp. 11-12.

6 See Appendix C, p. 784, for an estimate of support for a bill of rights.

7 For the protest of the Pennsylvania Minority see p. 154.

8 For information on reprints of the Pennsylvania Minority protest, see DHRC, XV, p. 575, #353.

9 See p. 445 for the New Hampshire ratification and proposed amendments.

10 See p. 456 for the Virginia convention proposed Declaration of Rights and other amendments.

11 See p. 480 for the New York ratification with bill of rights and proposed amendments.

12 See p. 503 for the North Carolina convention's refusal to ratify.

13 See p. 488 for the New York convention's circular letter.

14 See pp. 654-656 for Madison's proposals in the House of Representatives.

15 See p. 680 for the amendments passed by the committee of eleven.

16 See p. 706 for the amendments proposed by the House of Representatives.

17 See p. 715 for the amendments as proposed by Congress.

18 See p. 733 for the Rhode Island convention ratification with bill of rights and proposed amendments.

19 See p. 722 for the objections of the Virginia Senate to amendments numbers 3, 8, 11, and 12 proposed by Congress.

20 Massachusetts, Georgia and Connecticut all belatedly ratified the Bill of Rights in 1939 as part of their Sesquicentennial of the Constitution celebrations.

21 See Appendix C, p. 784, for an estimate of support for a bill of rights.

22 See Appendix B, p. 781, for a comparison of English Bill of Rights provisions with those of the various American Bills of Rights.

23 See the form of ratification of the Virginia convention on p. 454 for a reference to limits upon all authority of the new government.

24 See "America {Noah Webster}," p. 186, and "Hugh Henry Brackenridge," p. 291, for examples of Federalist ridicule of Antifederalist views on a bill of rights.

25 For Washington's ideas on a proper militia establishment, see *The Writings of George Washington* (Westport, Greenwoood Press, 1970 reprint of 1931-1944 edition), Vol. 26, pp. 387-394. For reference to Baron von Steuben's plan see, note 2, p. 61, in the Documents section.

26 See p. 198 for Hamilton's ideas.

27 See letter number 18 of the Federal Farmer, pp. 353-355, for this Antifederalist view.

28 See "John De Witt V," p. 129, for the original article, and see "Philadelphia *Freeman's Journal*,' p. 211, for a shortened and altered reprint.

29 See p. 150 for the Pennsylvania Minority's proposed bill of rights.

30 See "Jacob Trusty," and note 2 on p. 176 for twelve references to the Executive Council's action.

31 See p. 260 at note 3 for Samuel Adams' proposed bill of rights amendment.

32 See p. 445 for New Hampshire proposed amendments.

33 See comments of Patrick Henry in the Virginia convention on pp. 434 and 437.

34 See comments of George Mason in the Virginia convention on p. 430.

35 See "George Mason," top of p. 366.

36 See p. 480 for the New York ratification. The convention's bill of rights provisions were actually included as part of New York's ratification.

37 See p. 354 for the Federal Farmer's militia comments.

DOCUMENTS

August, 1787 to March, 1792

Federal Convention Summer, 1787
Debates: Speech of Rufus King (excerpt)

We have power to propose anything, but to conclude nothing.

We may expect the approbation of Congress and hope for that of the Legislatures of the States. It is not so sure as some Gentlemen believe it to be, that the Power of the States is the idol of the People, and that they are unwilling to see established a general or national Govt. A citizen of N. Jersey who may be gratified by being called so, will not feel himself degraded by being called a Citizen of the U. S. The object of our Convention is to increase the power of the general Govt. and that too at the expense of the State Govts.

It is not requisite, nor expedient, that the Rights or power of the People should be diminished—they have already given powers sufficient both for the State & general Govt. and all that we are called upon for, is to make a right Division of these Powers between the General and the State Governments. Whether we regard the Power, which makes the Laws, or that which interprets them, or that by which they are carried into execution, nothing further is necessary then a proper division of each Department between the Genl. and the State Govts.

The organization of the State Govts. will remain, or may be altered by the States respectively. Our business is to organize the General Govt., to divide it into Legislative, executive, & judicial bodies; and to do this on safe Principles, neither giving to either too much power, nor too little, beginning with the Legislative and causing the judicial & executive power to be co-extensive. To constitute the Legislature of a free Govt. it must rest upon the Power of the People, and be created by them—not like the Power of Congress, which rests upon the States & is unsound because it rests upon a single unbalanced body.

Formation of the Union, pp. 877-878. From the notes of Rufus King.

Federal Convention August 18, 1787
Debates (excerpts)

Mr. MASON introduced the subject of regulating the militia. He thought such a power necessary to be given to the general government. He hoped there would be no standing army in time of peace, unless it might be for a few garrisons. The militia ought, therefore, to be the more effectually prepared for the public defence. Thirteen states will never concur in any one system, if the disciplining of the militia be left in their hands. If they will not give up the power over the whole, they probably will over a part, as a select militia. He moved, as an addition to the propositions just referred to the committee of detail, and to be referred in like manner, "a power to regulate the militia."[1]

[T]he House proceded to the clause, "to raise armies."

Mr. GORHAM moved to add, "and support," after "raise." Agreed to, *nem. con.*; and then the clause was agreed to, *nem. con.*, as amended.

Mr. GERRY took notice that there was no check here against standing armies in time of peace. The existing Congress is so constructed, that it cannot of itself maintain an army. This would not be the case under the new system. The people were jealous on this head, and great opposition to the plan would spring from such an omission. He suspected that preparations of force were now making against it. [He seemed to allude to the activity of the governor of New York, at this crisis, in disciplining the militia of that state.] He thought an army dangerous in time of peace, and could never consent to a power to keep up an indefinite number. He proposed that there should not be kept up in time of peace more than ______ thousand troops. His idea was, that the blank should be filled with two or three thousand.

Instead of "to build and equip fleets," "to provide and maintain a navy," was agreed to, *nem. con.*, as a more convenient definition of the power.

A clause, "to make rules for the government and regulation of the land and naval forces," was added from the existing Articles of Confederation.

Mr. L. MARTIN and Mr. GERRY now regularly moved,—

"Provided, that, in time of peace, the army shall not consist of more than ______ thousand men."

Gen. PINCKNEY asked, whether no troops were ever to be raised until an attack should be made on us.

Mr. GERRY. If there be no restriction, a few states may establish a military goverment.

Mr. WILLIAMSON reminded him of Mr. Mason's motion for limiting the appropriation of revenue as the best guard in this case.

Mr. Langdon saw no room for Mr. Gerry's distrust of the representatives of the people.

Mr. DAYTON. Preparations for war are generally made in time of peace; and a standing force of some sort may, for aught we know, become unavoidable. He should object to no restictions consistent with these ideas.

The motion of Mr. Martin and Mr. Gerry was disagreed to, *nem. con.*

Mr. MASON moved, as an additional power,—
"to make laws for the regulation and discipline of the militia of the several states, reserving to the states the appointment of the officers." He considered uniformity as necessary in the regulation of the militia, throughout the Union.

Gen. PINCKNEY mentioned a case, during the war, in which a dissimilarity in the militia of different states had produced the most serious mischiefs. Uniformity was essential. The states would never keep up a proper discipline of the militia.

Mr. ELLSWORTH was for going as far, in submitting the militia to the general government, as might be necessary; but thought the motion of Mr. Mason went too far. He moved,—
"that the militia should have the same arms and exercise, and be under rules established by the general government when in actual service of the United States; and when states neglect to provide regulations for militia, it should be regulated and established by the legislature of the United States."
The whole authority over the militia ought by no means to be taken away from the states, whose consequence would pine away to nothing after such a sacrifice of power. He thought the general authority could not sufficiently pervade the Union for such a purpose nor could it accommodate itself to the local genius of the people. It must be vain to ask the states to give the militia out of their hands.

Mr. SHERMAN seconds the motion.

Mr. DICKINSON. We are come now to a most important matter—that of the sword. His opinion was, that the states never would, nor ought to, give up all authority over the militia. He proposed to restrain the general power to one fourth part at a time, which, by rotation, would discipline the whole militia.

Mr. BUTLER urged the necessity of submitting the whole militia to the general authority, which had the care of the general defence.

Mr. MASON had suggested the idea of a select militia. He was led to think that would be, in fact, as much as the general government could advantageously be charged with. He was afraid of creating insuperable objections to the plan. He withdrew his original motion, and moved a power—
"to make laws for regulating and disciplining the militia, not exceeding one tenth part in any one year, and reserving the appointment of officers to the states."

Gen. PINCKNEY renewed Mr. Mason's original motion. For a part to be under the general and a part under the state governments, would be an incurable evil. He saw no room for such distrust of the general government.

Mr. LANGDON seconds Gen. Pinkney's renewal. He saw no more reason to be afraid of the general government than of the state government. He was more apprehensive of the confusion of the different authorities on this subject, than of either.

Mr. MADISON thought the regulation of the militia naturally appertaining to the authority charged with the public defence. It did not seem, in its nature, to be divisible between two distinct authorities. If the states would trust the general government with a power over the public treasure, they would, from the same consideration of necessity, grant it the direction of the public force. Those who had a full view of the public situation would, from a sense of danger, guard against it. The states would not be separately impressed with the general situation, nor have the due confidence in the concurrent exertions of each other.

Mr. ELLSWORTH considered the idea of a select militia as impracticable; and if it were not, it would be followed by a ruinous declension of the great body of the militia. The states would never submit to the same militia laws. Three or four shillings, as a penalty, will enforce obedience better in New England, than forty lashes in some other places.

Mr. PINCKNEY thought the power such a one as could not be abused, and that the states would see the necessity of surrendering it. He had, however, but a scanty faith in militia. There must be also a real military force. This alone can effectually answer the purpose. The United States had been making an experiment without it, and we see the consequence in their rapid approaches toward anarchy [This had reference to the disorders, particularly, that had occurred in Massachusetts, which had called for the interposition of the federal troops.][2]

Mr. SHERMAN took notice that the states might want their militia for defence against invasions and insurrections, and for enforcing obedience to their laws. They will not give up this point. In giving up that of taxation, they retain a concurrent power of raising money for their own use.

Mr. GERRY thought this the last point remaining to be surrendered. If it be agreed to by the Convention, the plan will have as black a mark as was set on Cain. He had no such confidence in the general government as some gentlemen possessed, and believed it would be found that the states have not.

Col. MASON thought there was great weight in the remarks of Mr. Sherman, and moved an exception to his motion, "of such part of the militia as might be required by the states for their own use."

Mr. READ doubted the propriety of leaving the appointment of the militia officers to the states. In some states they are elected by the legislatures; in others, by the people themselves. He thought at least an appointment by the state executives ought to be insisted on.

On the question for committing to the grand committee, last appointed, the latter motion of Col. Mason, and the original one revived by Gen. Pinckney,—

New Hampshire, Massachusetts, Pennsylvania, Delaware, Virginia, North Carolina, South Carolina, Georgia, ay, 8; Connecticut, New Jersey, no, 2; Maryland, divided.

Adjourned.[3]

1 *Debates*, V, p. 440.
2 A reference to Shays' Rebellion.
3 *Debates*, V, pp. 442-445.

Federal Convention August 20, 1787
Proceedings (excerpt)

In Convention.—Mr. PINCKNEY submitted to the House, in order to be referred to the committee of detail, the following propositions:— . . .

"The privileges and benefit of the writ of *habeas corpus* shall be enjoyed in this government in the most expeditious and ample manner, and shall not be suspended by the legislature, except upon the most urgent and pressing occasions, and for a limited time, not exceeding ___ months.

"The liberty of the press shall be inviolably preserved.

"No troops shall be kept up in time of peace, but by consent of the legislature.

"The military shall always be subordinate to the civil power; and no grants of money shall be made by the legislature, for supporting military land forces, for more than one year at a time.

"No soldier shall be quartered in any house, in time of peace, without consent of the owner.

"No person holding the Office of President of the United States, a judge of their Supreme Court, secretary for the department of foreign affairs, of finance, of marine, of war, or of ——, shall be capable of holding, at the same time, any other office of trust or emolument, under the United States, or an idividual state.

"No religious test or qualification shall ever be annexed to any oath of office, under the authority of the United States.["] . . .

These propositions were referred to the committee of detail, without debate or consideration of them by the House.

Debates, V, pp. 445-446.

Federal Convention August 21, 1787
Proceedings (excerpt)

In Convention.—Gov. Livingston, from the committee of eleven, to whom were referred the propositions respecting the debts of the several states, and also the militia, entered on the eighteenth instant, delivered the following report;—

"The legislature of the United States shall have power to fulfil the engagements which have been entered into by Congress, and to discharge, as well the debts of the United States, as the debts incurred by the several states, during the late war, for the common defence and general welfare.

"To make laws for organizing, arming, and disciplining the militia, and for governing such part of them as may be employed in the service of the United States; reserving to the states, respectively, the appointment of the officers, and the authority of training the militia, according to the discipline prescribed by the United States."

Debates, V, p. 451.

Federal Convention August 23, 1787
Debates (excerpt)

In Convention.—The report of the committee of eleven, made the 21st of August, being taken up, and the following clause being under consideration, to wit:—

"To make laws for organizing, arming, and disciplining the militia, and for governing such parts of them as may be employed in the service of the United States, reserving to the states, respectively, the appointment of the officers, and authority of training the militia according to the discipline prescribed,"—

Mr. SHERMAN moved to strike out the last member, "and authority of training," &c. He thought it unnecessary. The states will have this authority, of course, if not given up.

Mr. ELLSWORTH doubted the propriety of striking out the sentence. The reason assigned applies as well to the other reservations, of the appointment to offices. He remarked, at the same time, that the term "discipline," was of vast extent, and might be so expounded as to include all power on the subject.

Mr. KING, by way of explanation, said, that by *organizing*, the committee meant, proportioning the officers and men—by *arming*, specifying the kind, size, and calibre of arms—and by *disciplining*, prescribing the manual exercise, evolutions, &c.

Mr. SHERMAN withdrew his motion.

Mr. GERRY. This power in the United States, as explained, is making the states drill-sergeants. He had as lief let the citizens of Massachusetts be disarmed, as to take the command from the states, and subject them to the general legislature. It would be regarded as a system of despotism.

Mr. MADISON observed, that *"arming,"* as explained, did not extend to furnishing arms; nor the term *"disciplining,"* to penalties, and courts martial for enforcing them.

Mr. KING added to his former explanation, that *arming* meant not only to provide for uniformity of arms, but included the authority to regulate the modes of furnishing, either by the militia themselves, the state governments, or the national treasury; that *laws* for disciplining must involve penalties, and every thing necessary for enforcing penalties.

Mr. DAYTON moved to postpone the paragraph, in order to take up the following proposition:—

"To establish a uniform and general system of discipline for the militia of these states, and to make laws for organizing, arming, disciplining, and governing *such part of them as may be employed in the service of the United States;* reserving to the states, respectively, the appointment of the officers, and all authority over the militia not herein given to the general government."

On the question to postpone, in favor of this proposition, it passed in the negative.

New Jersey, Maryland, Georgia, ay, 3; New Hampshire, Massachusetts, Connecticut, Pennsylvania, Delaware, Virginia, North Carolina, South Carolina, no, 8.

Mr. ELLSWORTH and Mr. SHERMAN moved to postpone the second clause, in favor of the following:—

"To establish a uniformity of arms, exercise, and organization for the militia and to provide for the government of them when called into the service of the United States."

The object of this proposition was, to refer the plan for the militia to the general government, but to leave the execution of it to the state governments.

Mr. LANGDON said he could not understand the jealousy expressed by some gentlemen. The general and state governments were not enemies to each other, but different institutions for the good of the people of America. As one of the people, he could say, "The national government is mine, the state government is mine. In transferring power from one to the other, I only take out of my left hand what it cannot so well use, and put it into my right hand, where it can be better used."

Mr. GERRY thought it was rather taking out of the right hand and putting it into the left. Will any man say that liberty will be as safe in the hands of eighty or a hundred men, taken from the whole continent, as in the hands of two or three hundred, taken from a single state?

Mr. DAYTON was against so absolute a uniformity. In some states there ought to be a greater proportion of cavalry than in others. In some places, rifles would be most proper; in others, muskets, &c.

Gen PINCKNEY preferred the clause reported by the committee, extending the meaning of it to the cases of fines, &c.

Mr. MADISON. The primary object is to secure an effectual discipline of the militia. This will no more be done, if left to the states separately, than the requisitions have been hitherto paid by them. The states neglect their militia now, and, the more they are consolidated into one nation, the less each will rely on its own interior provisions for its safety, and the less prepare its militia for that purpose; in like manner, as the militia of a state would have been still more neglected than it has been, if each county had been independently charged with the care of its militia. The discipline of the militia is evidently a *national* concern, and ought to be provided for in the *national* Constitution.

Mr. L. MARTIN was confident that the states would never give up the power over the militia; and that, if they were to do so, the militia would be less attended to by the general than by the state governments.

Mr. RANDOLPH asked what danger there could be, that the militia could be brought into the field, and made to commit suicide on themselves. This is a power that cannot, from its nature, be abused, unless, indeed, the whole mass should be corrupted. He was for trammelling the general government whenever there was danger, but here there could be none. He urged this as an essential point, observing, that the militia were every where neglected by the state legislatures, the members of which courted popularity too much to enforce a proper discipline. Leaving the appointment of officers to the states protects the people against every apprehension that could produce murmur.

On the question on Mr. Ellsworth's motion,—

Connecticut, ay; the other ten states, no.

A motion was then made to recommit the second clause, which was negatived.

On the question to agree to the first part of the clause, namely:

"To make laws for organizing, arming, and disciplining, the militia, and for governing such part of them as may be employed in the service of the United States,"—

New Hampshire, Massachusetts, New Jersey, Pennsylvania, Delaware, Virginia, North Carolina, South Carolina, Georgia, ay, 9; Connecticut, Maryland, no, 2.

Mr. MADISON moved to amend the next part of the clause, so as to read,—
"reserving to the states, respectivley, the appointment of the officers, *under the rank of general officers.*"

Mr. SHERMAN considered this as absolutely inadmissible. He said that, if the people should be so far asleep as to allow the most influential officers of the militia to be appointed by the general government, every man of discernment would rouse them by sounding the alarm to them.

Mr. GERRY. Let us at once destroy the state governments, have an executive for life, or hereditary, and a proper Senate, and then there would be some consistency in giving full powers to the general government: but as the states are not to be abolished, he wondered at the attempts that were made to give powers inconsistent with their existence. He warned the Convention against pushing the experiment too far. Some people will support a plan of vigorous government at every risk; others, of a more democratic cast, will oppose it with equal determination, and a civil war may be produced by the conflict.

Mr. MADISON. As the greatest danger is that of disunion of the states, it is necessary to guard against it by sufficient powers to the common government; and as the greatest danager to liberty is from large standing armies, it is best to prevent them by an effectual provision for a good militia.

On the question to agree to Mr. Madison's motion,—

New Hampshire, South Carolina, Georgia, (in the printed Journal, Georgia, no) ay, 3; Massachusetts, Connecticut, New Jersey, Pennsylvania, Delaware, Maryland, Virginia, North Carolina, no, 8.

On the question to agree to the "reserving to the states the appointment of the officers," it was agreed to, *nem. con.*

On the question on the clause,—
"and the authority of training the militia according to the discipline prescribed by the United States,"—

New Hampshire, Massachusetts, Connecticut, New Jersey, Pennsylvania, Maryland, North Carolina, ay, 7; Delaware, Virginia, South Carolina, Georgia, no, 4.

On the question to agree to article 7, sect.7, as reported, it passed, *nem. con.*

Debates, V, pp. 464-467.

Foreign Spectator September 11, 1787
Newspaper Article: Philadelphia *Independent Gazetteer* (excerpt)

The present state of human existence is so blended with sin and woe, that the sword must be the last resort against external enemies and internal traitors—let it then be held in the brave hands of a whole federal people; and it will defy any attack from open force or secret malice. When America has better resources, a few thousand standing troops may perhaps be at all times useful. Such a handful could never be dangerous. But great armies, however necessary in Europe, crowded with nations of jarring interests, are with the best regulation great evils; and could, in America, arise from nothing but a fatal corruption. Why should a great standing army be wanted? Because 200,000 militia have not the heart to look an enemy in the face? or because, when their distressed country cries, they only mind their cattle and corn, or how to turn a penny in their shops? or because they cannot refrain from embruing their hands in each others blood? For God's sake let it never be said, Ye true sons of America! Ye noble sons of freedom! *Whether in a palace or in a cottage well-born soldiers and defenders of your country*, protectors of your parents, wives and children!—Think how great you will be by a *valiant federal liberty! You bear on the points of your bayonets the fate of this federal empire*—Let every gun, every ball, every grain of powder be federal—*Let every drop of blood in your veins be federal and heroic.*

DHRC, II Mfm. Pa., pp. 318-319.

Federal Convention September 12, 1787
Debates (excerpt)

Mr. WILLIAMSON observed to the House, that no provision was yet made for juries in civil cases, and suggested the necessity of it.

Mr. GORHAM. It is not possible to discriminate equity cases from those in which juries are proper. The representatives of the people may be safely trusted in this matter.

Mr. GERRY urged the necessity of juries to guard against corrupt judges. He proposed that the committee last appointed should be directed to provide a clause for securing the trial by juries.

Col. MASON perceived the difficulty mentioned by Mr. Gorham. The jury cases cannot be specified. A general principle laid down, on this and some other points, would be sufficient. He wished the plan had been prefaced with a bill of rights, and would second a motion, if made for the purpose. It would give great quiet to the people, and, with the aid of the state declarations, a bill might be prepared in a few hours.

Mr. GERRY concurred in the idea, and moved for a committee to prepare a bill of rights.

Col. MASON seconded the motion.

Mr. SHERMAN was for securing the rights of the people, where requisite. The state declarations of rights are not repealed by this Constitution, and, being in force, are sufficient. There are many cases, where juries are proper, which cannot be discriminated. The legislature may be safely trusted.

Col. MASON. The laws of the United States are to be paramount to the state bills of rights.

On the question for a committee to prepare a bill of rights,—

New Hampshire, Connecticut, New Jersey, Pennsylvania, Delaware, ay, 5; Maryland, Virginia, North Carolina, South Carolina, Georgia, no, 5; Massachusetts absent.

Debates, V, p. 538.

Federal Convention September 14, 1787
Debates (excerpt)

Col. MASON, being sensible that an absolute prohibition of standing armies in time of peace might be unsafe, and wishing, at the same time, to insert something pointing out and guarding against the danger of them, moved to preface the clause, (article 1, sect.8,) "to provide for organizing, arming, and disciplining the militia," &c., with the words,

"and that the liberties of the people may be better secured against the danger of standing armies in time of peace."

Mr. RANDOLPH seconded the motion.

Mr. MADISON was in favor of it. It did not restrain congress from establishing a military force in time of peace, if found necessary; and as armies in time of peace are allowed, on all hands, to be an evil, it is well to discountenance them by the Constitution, as far as will consist with the essential power of the government on that head.

Mr. GOUVERNEUR MORRIS opposed the motion, as setting a dishonorable mark of distinction on the military class of citizens.

Mr. PINCKNEY and Mr. BEDFORD concurred in the opposition.

On the question,—

Virginia, Georgia, ay, 2; New Hampshire, Massachusetts, Connecticut, New Jersey, Pennsylvania, Delaware, Maryland, North Carolina, South Carolina, no, 9.

Col. MASON moved to strike out from the clause, (article 1. sect. 9,) "no bill of attainder, nor any *ex post facto* law, shall be passed," the words "nor any *ex post facto* law." He thought it not sufficiently clear that the prohibition meant by this phrase was limited to cases of a criminal nature; and no legislature ever did or can altogether avoid them in civil cases.

Mr. GERRY seconded the motion; but with a view to extend the prohibition to "civil cases," which he thought ought to be done.

On the question, all the states were, no.

Mr. PINCKNEY and Mr. GERRY moved to insert a declaration, "that the liberty of the press should be inviolably observed."

Mr. SHERMAN. It is unnecessary. The power of Congress does not extend to the press.

On the question, it passed in the negative.

Massachusetts, Maryland, Virginia, South Carolina, ay, 4; New Hampshire, (In the printed Journal, New Hampshire, ay,) Connecticut, New Jersey, Pennsylvania, Delaware, North Carolina, Georgia, no, 7.

Debates, V, pp. 544-545.

Federal Convention September 15, 1787
Debates (excerpt)

Mr. RANDOLPH, animadverting on the indefinite and dangerous power given by the Constitution to Congress, expressing the pain he felt at differing from the body of the Convention on the close of the great and awful subject of their labors, and anxiously wishing for some accommodating expedient which would relieve him from his embarrassments, made a motion importing, "that amendments to the plan might be offered by the state conventions, which should be submitted to, and finally decided on by, another General Convention."

Should this proposition be disregarded, it would, he said, be impossible for him to put his name to the instrument. Whether he should oppose it afterwards, he would not then decide; but he would not deprive himself of the freedom to do so in his own state, if that course should be prescribed by his final judgment.

Col. MASON seconded and followed Mr. RANDOLPH in animadversions on the dangerous power and structure of the government, concluding that it would end either in monarchy or a tyrannical aristocracy—which, he was in doubt,—but one or other, he was sure. This Constitution had been formed without the knowledge or idea of the people. A second Convention will know more of the sense of the people, and be able to provide a system more consonant to it. It was improper to say to the people, take this or nothing. As the Constitution now stands, he could neither give it his support or vote in Virginia; and he could not sign here what he could not support there. With the expedient of another Convention, as proposed, he could sign.

Mr. PINCKNEY. These declarations, from members so respectable, at the close of this important scene, give a peculiar solemnity to the present moment. He descanted on the consequences of calling forth the deliberations and amendments of the different states, on the subject of government at large. Nothing but confusion and contrariety will spring from the experiment. The states will never agree in their plans, and the deputies to a second convention, coming together under the discordant impressions of their constitutents, will never agree. Conventions are serious things, and ought not to be repeated. He was not without objections, as well as others, to the plan. He objected to the contemptible weakness and dependence of the executive. He objected to the power of a majority, only, of Congress, over commerce. But, apprehending the danger of a general confusion, and an ultimate decision by the sword, he should give the plan his support.

Mr. GERRY stated the objections which determined him to withhold his name from the Constitution: 1, the duration and reeligibility of the Senate; 2, the power of the House of Representatives to conceal their Journals; 3, the power of Congress over the places of election; 4, the unlimited power of Congress over their own compensation; 5, that Massachusetts has not a due share of representatives allotted to her; 6, that three fifths of the blacks are to be represented, as if they were freemen; 7, that under the power over commerce, monopolies may be established; 8, the Vice-President being made head of the Senate. He could, however, he said, get over all these, if the rights of the citizens were not rendered insecure—first, by the general power of the legislature to make what laws they may please to call "necessary and proper;" secondly, to raise armies and money without limit; thirdly, to establish a tribunal without juries, which will be a Star Chamber as to civil cases. Under such a view of the Constitution, the best that could be done, he conceived, was to provide for a second General Convention.

On the question, on the proposition of Mr. Randolph, all the states answered, no.

On the question to agree to the Constitution, as amended, all the states, ay.

The Constitution was then ordered to be engrossed, and the House adjourned.

Debates, V, pp. 552-553.

Federal Convention September 17, 1787
Proposed United States Constitution

The Constitution of the United States

We the People of the United States, in Order to form a more perfect Union, establish Justice, insure domestic Tranquility, provide for the common defence, promote the general Welfare, and secure the Blessings of Liberty to ourselves and our Posterity, do ordain and establish this Constitution for the United States of America.

Article. I.

Section. 1. All legislative Powers herein granted shall be vested in a Congress of the United States, which shall consist of a Senate and House of Representatives.

Section. 2. The House of Representatives shall be composed of Members chosen every second Year by the People of the several States, and the Electors in each State shall have the Qualifications requisite for Electors of the most numerous Branch of the State Legislature.

No Person shall be a Representative who shall not have attained to the Age of twenty five Years, and been seven Years a Citizen of the United States, and who shall not, when elected, be an Inhabitant of the State in which he shall be chosen.

Representatives and direct Taxes shall be apportioned among the several States which may be included within this Union, according to their respective Numbers, which shall be determined by adding to the whole Number of free Persons, including those bound to Service for a Term of Years, and excluding Indians not taxed, three fifths of all other Persons. The actual Enumeration shall be made within three Years after the first Meeting of the Congress of the United States, and within every subsequent Term of ten Years, in such Manner as they shall by Law direct. The Number of Representatives shall not exceed one for every thirty Thousand, but each State shall have at Least one Representative; and until such enumeration shall be made, the State of New Hampshire shall be entitled to chuse three, Massachusetts eight, Rhode-Island and Providence Plantations one, Connecticut five, New-York six, New Jersey four, Pennsylvania eight, Delaware one, Maryland six, Virginia ten, North Carolina five, South Carolina five, and Georgia three.

When vacancies happen in the Representation from any State, the Executive Authority thereof shall issue Writs of Election to fill such Vacancies.

The House of Representatives shall chuse their Speaker and other Officers; and shall have the sole Power of Impeachment.

Section. 3. The Senate of the United States shall be composed of two Senators from each State, chosen by the Legislature thereof, for six Years; and each Senator shall have one Vote.

Immediately after they shall be assembled in Consequence of the first Election, they shall be divided as equally as may be into three Classes. The Seats of the Senators of the first Class shall be vacated at the Expiration of the second Year, of the second Class at the Expiration of the fourth Year, and of the third Class at the Expiration of the sixth Year, so that one third may be chosen every second Year; and if Vacancies happen by Resignation, or otherwise, during the Recess of the Legislature of any State, the Executive thereof may make temporary Appointments until the next Meeting of the Legislature, which shall fill such Vacancies.

No Person shall be a Senator who shall not have attained to the Age of thirty Years, and been nine Years a Citizen of the United States, and who shall not, when elected, be an Inhabitant of that State for which he shall be chosen.

The Vice President of the United States shall be President of the Senate, but shall have no vote, unless they be equally divided.

The Senate shall chuse their other Officers, and also a President pro tempore, in the Absence of the Vice President, or when he shall exercise the Office of President of the United States.

The Senate shall have the sole Power to try all Impeachments. When sitting for that Purpose, they shall be on Oath or Affirmation. When the President of the United States is tried, the Chief Justice shall preside: And no Person shall be convicted without the Concurrence of two thirds of the Members present.

Judgment in Cases of Impeachment shall not extend further than to removal from Office, and disqualification to hold and enjoy any Office of honor, Trust or Profit under the United States; but the Party convicted shall nevertheless be liable and subject to Indictment, Trial, Judgment and Punishment, according to Law.

Section. 4. The Times, Places and Manner of holding Elections for Senators and Representatives, shall be prescribed in each State by the Legislature thereof; but the Congress may at any time by Law make or alter such Regulations, except as to the Places of chusing Senators.

The Congress shall assemble at least once in every Year, and such Meeting shall be on the first Monday in December, unless they shall by Law appoint a different Day.

Section. 5. Each House shall be the Judge of the Elections, Returns and Qualifications of its own Members, and a Majority of each shall constitute a Quorum to do Business; but a smaller Number may adjourn from day to day, and may be authorized to compel the Attendance of absent Members, in such Manner, and under such Penalties as each House may provide.

Each House may determine the Rules of its Proceedings, punish its members for disorderly Behaviour, and, with the Concurrence of two thirds, expel a Member.

Each House shall keep a Journal of its Proceedings, and from time to time publish the same, excepting such Parts as may in their Judgment require Secrecy; and the Yeas and Nays of the Members of either House on any question shall, at the Desire of one fifth of those Present, be entered on the Journal.

Neither House, during the Session of Congress, shall, without the Consent of the other, adjourn for more than three days, nor to any other Place than that in which the two Houses shall be sitting.

Section. 6. The Senators and Representatives shall receive a Compensation for their Services, to be ascertained by Law, and paid out of the Treasury of the United States. They shall in all Cases, except Treason, Felony and Breach of the Peace, be privileged from Arrest during their Attendance at the Session of their respective Houses, and in going to and returning from the same; and for any

Speech or Debate in either House, they shall not be questioned in any other Place.

No Senator or Representative shall, during the Time for which he was elected, be appointed to any civil Office under the Authority of the United States which shall have been created, or the Emoluments whereof shall have been encreased during such time; and no Person holding any Office under the United States, shall be a Member of either House during his Continuance in Office.

Section. 7. All Bills for raising Revenue shall originate in the House of Representatives; but the Senate may propose or concur with Amendments as on other Bills.

Every Bill which shall have passed the House of Representatives and the Senate shall, before it become a Law, be presented to the President of the United States; If he approve he shall sign it, but if not he shall return it, with has Objections to that House in which it shall have originated, who shall enter the Objections at large on their Journal, and proceed to reconsider it. If after such Reconsideration two thirds of that House shall agree to pass the Bill, it shall be sent, together with the Objections, to the other House, by which it shall likewise be reconsidered, and if approved by two thirds of that House, it shall become a Law. But in all such Cases the Votes of both Houses shall be determined by yeas and Nays, and the Names of the Persons voting for and against the Bill shall be entered on the Journal of each House respectively. If any Bill shall not be returned by the President within ten Days (Sundays excepted) after it shall have been presented to him, the Same shall be a Law, in like Manner as if he had signed it, unless the Congress by their Adjournment prevent its Return, in which Case it shall not be a Law.

Every Order, Resolution, or Vote to which the Concurrence of the Senate and House of Representatives may be necessary (except on a question of Adjournment) shall be presented to the President of the United States; and before the Same shall take Effect, shall be approved by him, or being disapproved by him, shall be repassed by two thirds of the Senate and House of Representatives, according to the Rules and Limitations prescribed in the Case of a Bill.

Section. 8. The Congress shall have Power To lay and collect Taxes, Duties, Imposts and Excises, to pay the Debts and provide for the common Defence and general Welfare of the United States; but all Duties, Imposts and Excises shall be uniform throughout the United States;

To borrow Money on the credit of the United States;

To regulate Commerce with foreign Nations, and among the several States, and with the Indian Tribes;

To establish an uniform Rule of Naturalization, and uniform Laws on the subject of Bankruptcies throughout the United States;

To coin Money, regulate the Value thereof, and of foreign Coin, and fix the Standard of Weights and Measures;

To provide for the Punishment of counterfeiting the Securites and current Coin of the United States;

To establish Post Offices and post Roads;

To promote the Progress of Science and useful Arts, by securing for limited Times to Authors and Inventors the exclusive Right to their respective Writings and Discoveries;

To constitute Tribunals inferior to the supreme Court;

To define and punish Piracies and Felonies committed on the high Seas, and Offences against the Law of Nations;

To declare War, grant Letters of Marque and Reprisal, and make Rules concerning Captures on Land and Water;

To raise and support Armies, but no Appropriation of Money to that Use shall be for a longer Term than two Years;

To provide and maintain a Navy;

To make rules for calling forth the Militia to execute the Laws of the Union, suppress Insurrections and repel Invasions;

To provide for organizing, arming, and disciplining, the Militia, and for governing such Part of them as may be employed in the Service of the United States, reserving to the States respectively, the Appointment of the Officers, and the Authority of training the Militia according to the discipline prescribed by Congress.

To exercise exclusive Legislation in all Cases whatsoever, over such District (not exceeding ten Miles square) as may, by Cession of particular States, and the Acceptance of Congress, become the Seat of the Government of the United States, and to exercise like Authority over all Places purchased by the Consent of the Legislature of the State in which the same shall be, for the Erection of Forts, Magazines, Arsenals, dock-Yards, and other needful Buildings;—And

To make all Laws which shall be necessary and proper for carrying into Execution the foregoing Powers, and all other Powers vested by this Constitution in the Government of the United States, or in any Department or Officer thereof.

Section. 9. The Migration or Importation of such Persons as any of the States now existing shall think proper to admit, shall not be prohibited by the Congress prior to the Year one thousand eight hundred and eight, but a Tax or duty may be imposed on such Importation, not exceeding ten dollars for each Person.

The Privilege of the Writ of Habeas Corpus shall not be suspended, unless when in Cases of Rebellion or Invasion the public Safety may require it.

No Bill of Attainder or ex post facto Law shall be passed.

No Capitation, or other direct, Tax shall be laid, unless in Proportion to the Census or Enumeration herein before directed to be taken.

No Tax or Duty shall be laid on Articles exported from any State.

No Preference shall be given by any Regulation of Commerce or Revenue to the Ports of one State over those of another: nor shall Vessels bound to, or from, one State, be obliged to enter, clear, or pay Duties in another.

No Money shall be drawn from the Treasury, but in Consequence of Appropriations made by Law; and a regular Statement and Account of the Receipts and Expenditures of all public Money shall be published from time to time.

No Title of Nobility shall be granted by the United States: And no Person holding any Office of Profit or Trust under them, shall, without the Consent of the Congress, accept of any present, Emolument, Office, or Title, of any kind whatever, from any King, Prince, or foreign State.

Section. 10. No State shall enter into any Treaty, Alliance, or Confederation; grant Letters of Marque and Reprisal; coin Money; emit Bills of Credit; make any Thing but gold and silver Coin a Tender in Payment of Debts; pass any Bill of Attainder, ex post facto Law, or Law impairing the Obligation of Contracts, or grant any Title of Nobility.

No State shall, without the Consent of the Congress, lay any Imposts or Duties on Imports or Exports, except what may be absolutely necessary for executing it's inspection Laws: and the net Produce of all Duties and Imposts, laid by any State on Imports or Exports, shall be for the Use of the Treasury of the United States; and all such Laws shall be subject to the Revision and Controul of the Congress.

No State shall, without the Consent of Congress, lay any Duty of Tonnage, keep Troops, or Ships of War in time of Peace, enter into any Agreement or Compact with another State, or with a foreign Power, or engage in War, unless actually invaded, or in such imminent Danger as will not admit of delay.

Article. II.

Section. 1. The executive Power shall be vested in a President of the United States of America. He shall hold his Office during the Term of four Years, and, together with the Vice President, chosen for the same Term, be elected, as follows

Each State shall appoint, in such Manner as the Legislature thereof may direct, a Number of Electors, equal to the whole Number of Senators and Representatives to which the State may be entitled in the Congress: but no Senator or Representative, or Person holding an Office of Trust or Profit under the United States, shall be appointed an Elector.

The Electors shall meet in their respective States and vote by Ballot for two Persons, of whom one at least shall not be an Inhabitant of the same State with themselves. And they shall make a List of all the Persons voted for, and of the Number of Votes for each; which List they shall sign and certify, and transmit sealed to the Seat of the Government of the United States, directed to the President of the Senate. The President of the Senate shall, in the Presence of the Senate and House of Representatives, open all the Certificates, and the Votes shall then be counted. The Person having the greatest Number of Votes shall be the President, if such Number be a Majority of the whole Number of Electors appointed; and if there be more than one who have such Majority, and have an equal Number of Votes, then the House of Representatives shall immediately chuse by Ballot one of them for President; and if no Person have a Majority, then from the five highest on the List the said House shall in like Manner chuse the President. But in chusing the President, the Votes shall be taken by States, and a Majority of all the States shall be necessary to a Choice. In every Case, after the Choice of the President, the Person having the greatest Number of Votes of the Electors shall be the Vice President. But if there should remain two or more who have equal Votes, the Senate shall chuse from them by Ballot the Vice President.

The Congress may determine the Time of chusing the Electors, and the Day on which they shall give their Votes; which Day shall be the same throughout the United States.

No Persons except a natural born Citizen, or a Citizen of the United States, at the time of the Adoption of this Constitution, shall be eligible to the Office of President; neither shall any Person be eligible to that Office who shall not have attained to the Age of thirty five Years, and been fourteen Years a Resident within the United States.

In Case of the Removal of the President from Office, or of his Death, Resignation, or Inability to discharge the Powers and Duties of the said Office, the Same shall devolve on the Vice President, and the Congress may by Law provide for the Case of Removal, Death, Resignation or Inability, both of the President and Vice President, declaring what Officer shall then act as President, and such Officer shall act accordingly, until the Disability be removed, or a President shall be elected.

The President shall, at stated Times, receive for his Services, a Compensation, which shall neither be encreased nor diminished during the Period for which he shall have been elected, and he shall not receive within that Period any other Emolument from the United States, or any of them.

Before he enter on the Execution of his Office, he shall take the following Oath or Affirmation:—"I do solemnly swear (or affirm) that I will faithfully execute the Office of President of the United States, and will to the best of my Ability, preserve, protect and defend the Constitution of the United States."

Section. 2. The President shall be Commander in Chief of the Army and Navy of the United States, and of the Militia of the several States, when called into the actual Service of the United States; he may require the Opinion, in writing, of the principal Officer in each of the executive Departments, upon any Subject relating to the Duties of their respective Offices, and he shall have Power to grant Reprieves and Pardons for Offences against the United States, except in Cases of Impeachment.

He shall have Power, by and with the Advice and Consent of the Senate, to make Treaties, provided two thirds of the Senators present concur; and he shall nominate, and by and with the Advice and Consent of the Senate, shall appoint Ambassadors, other public Ministers and Consuls, Judges of the supreme Court, and all other Officers of the United States, whose Appointments are not herein otherwise provided for, and which shall be established by Law: but the Congress may by Law vest the Appointment of such inferior Officers, as they think proper, in the President alone, in the Courts of Law, or in the Heads of Departments.

The President shall have Power to fill up all Vacancies that may happen during the Recess of the Senate, by granting Commissions which shall expire at the End of their next Session.

Section. 3. He shall from time to time give to the Congress Information of the State of the Union, and recommend to their Consideration such Measures as he shall judge necessary and expedient; he may, on extraordinary Occasions, convene both Houses, or either of them, and in Case of Disagreement between them, with Respect to the Time of Adjournment, he may adjourn them to such Time as he shall think proper; he shall receive Ambassadors and other public Ministers; he shall take Care that the Laws be faithfully executed, and shall Commission all the Officers of the United States.

Section. 4. The President, Vice President and all civil Officers of the United States, shall be removed from Office on Impeachment for, and Conviction of Treason, Bribery, or other high Crimes and Misdemeanors.

Article III.

Section. 1. The judicial Power of the United States, shall be vested in one supreme Court, and in such inferior Courts as the Congress may from time to time ordain and establish. The Judges, both of the supreme and inferior Courts, shall hold their Offices during good Behaviour, and shall, at stated Times, receive for their Services, a Compensation, which shall not be diminished during their Continuance in Office.

Section. 2. The judicial Power shall extend to all Cases, in Law and Equity, arising under this Constitution, the Laws of the United States, and Treaties made, or which shall be made, under their Authority;—to all Cases affecting Ambassadors, other public Ministers and Consuls;—to all Cases of admiralty and maritime Jurisdiction;—to Controversies to which the United States shall be a Party;—to Controversies between two or more States;—between a State and Citizens of another State;—between Citizens of different States,—between Citizens of the same State claiming Lands under Grants of different States, and between a State, or the Citizens thereof, and foreign States, Citizens or Subjects.

In all Cases affecting Ambassadors, other public Ministers and Consuls, and those in which a State shall be Party, the supreme Court shall have original Jurisdiction. In all other Cases before mentioned, the supreme Court shall have appellate Jurisdiction, both as to Law and Fact, with such Exceptions, and under such Regulations as the Congress shall make.

The Trial of all Crimes, except in Cases of Impeachment, shall be by Jury; and such Trial shall be held in the State where the said Crimes shall have been committed; but when not committed within any State, the Trial shall be at such Place or Places as the Congress may by Law have directed.

Section. 3. Treason against the United States, shall consist only in levying War against them, or in adhering to their Enemies, giving them Aid and Comfort. No Person shall be convicted of Treason unless on the Testimony of two Witnesses to the same overt Act, or on Confession in open Court.

The Congress shall have Power to declare the Punishment of Treason, but no Attainder of Treason shall work Corruption of Blood, or Forfeiture except during the Life of the Person attainted.

Article. IV.

Section. 1. Full Faith and Credit shall be given in each State to the public Acts, Records, and judicial Proceedings of every other State. And the Congress may by general Laws prescribe the Manner in which such Acts, Records and Proceedings shall be proved, and the Effect thereof.

Section. 2. The Citizens of each State shall be entitled to all privileges and Immunities of Citizens in the several States.

A Person charged in any State with Treason, Felony, or other Crime, who shall flee from Justice, and be found in another State, shall on Demand of the executive Authority of the State from which he fled, be delivered up, to be removed to the State having Jurisdiction of the Crime.

No Person held to Service or Labour in one State, under the Laws thereof, escaping into another, shall, in Consequence of any Law or Regulation therein, be discharged from such Service or Labour, but shall be delivered up on Claim of the Party to whom such Service or Labour may be due.

Section. 3. New States may be admitted by the Congress into this Union; but no new State shall be formed or erected within the Jurisdiction of any other State; nor any State be formed by the Junction of two or more States, or Parts of States, without the Consent of the Legislatures of the States concerned as well as of the Congress.

The Congress shall have Power to dispose of and make all needful rules and Regulations respecting the Territory or other Property belonging to the United States; and nothing in this Constitution shall be so construed as to Prejudice any Claims of the United States, or of any particular State.

Section. 4. The United States shall guarantee to every State in this Union a Republican Form of Government, and shall protect each of them against Invasion; and on Application of the Legislature, or of the Executive (when the Legislature cannot be convened) against domestic Violence.

Article. V.

The Congress, whenever two thirds of both Houses shall deem it necessary, shall propose Amendments to this Constitution, or, on the Application of the Legislatures of two thirds of the several States, shall call a Convention for proposing Amendments, which, in either Case, shall be valid to all Intents and Purposes, as Part of this Constitution, when ratified by the Legislatures of three fourths of the several States, or by Conventions in three fourths thereof, as the one or the other Mode of Ratification may be proposed by the Congress; Provided that no Amendment which may be made prior to the Year One thousand eight hundred and eight shall in any Manner affect the first and fourth Clauses in the Ninth Section of the first Article; and that no State, without its consent, shall be deprived of it's equal Suffrage in the Senate.

Article. VI.

All Debts contracted and Engagements entered into, before the Adoption of this Constitution, shall be as valid against the United States under this Constitution, as under the Confederation.

This Constitution, and the Laws of the United States which shall be made in Pursuance thereof; and all Treaties made, or which shall be made, under the Authority of the United States, shall be the supreme Law of the Land; and the Judges in every State shall be bound thereby, any Thing in the Constitution or Laws of any State to the Contrary notwithstanding.

The Senators and Representatives before mentioned, and the Members of the several State Legislatures, and all executive and judicial Officers; both of the United States and of the several States, shall be bound by Oath or Affirmation, to support this Constitution; but no religious Test shall ever be required as a Qualification to any Office or public Trust under the United States.

Article. VII.

The Ratification of the Conventions of nine States, shall be sufficient for the Establishment of this Constitution between the States so ratifying the Same.

done in Convention by the Unanimous Consent of the States present the Seventeenth Day of September in the Year of our Lord one thousand seven hundred and Eighty seven and of the Independance of the United States of America the Twelfth In Witness whereof We have hereunto subscribed our Names, [names and correction list deleted.]

DHRC, VIII, pp. 543-553.

Foreign Spectator September 21, 1787
Newspaper Article: Philadelphia *Independent Gazetteer* (excerpt)

They [Congress and the President] could not raise an army without a pretence of war, nor impose on the nation by a false alarm; and though they have a right "to call forth the militia to execute the laws of the union, and to suppress insurrections," sect. 8. art. 1; it is evident, that a people of tolerable virtue would never become tools for enslaving themselves: would any man be ordered to kill himself by his own sword? who but an ideot or a most dastardly wretch would not plunge it in the heart of the tyrant. For the raising and supporting armies no appropriation of money is allowed for more than two years by the 8th sect. 1st art. This term must be prolonged when necessary; but while an enemy is in the country, the army cannot be employed against its liberties; and after the war it is disbanded, or must be for the want of pay. The happy situation of America will generally guard her against long and severe wars—but should any such happen; even the power of a veteran army could not subdue a patriotic militia ten times its number, and rendered perfectly military in the course of such war. Besides, regular troops, who are natives of a country, allied by friendship and blood to the other citizens, bred in the principles of republican liberty, and who have for years defended this country with their blood against a powerful invader, cannot be so generally corrupted, as to turn their arms against those with whom they have so long shared danger and glory; to enslave and murder their friends, and relations, brothers, sons and fathers—in all probability a great part of this army would take part with the nation.

DHRC, II Mfm. Pa., pp. 384-385.

Confederation Congress September 27, 1787
Debates on the proposed United States Constitution (excerpts)

Richard Henry Lee: . . . If I understand, gentlemen, this [Constitution] is to be adopted and no other, with[out] alterations. Why so? [There are] good things in it, but many bad. So much so that, he says here as he will say everywhere, that if adopted, civil liberty will be in eminent danger. . . . he sees not the necessity of pressing this [Constitution] without any amendments. Thinks the [state] conventions had best have had the liberty to alter [the Constitution]. . . .

It is admitted and [a] fact that this [Constitution] was to be sent to Congress, but surely it was to be considered and altered, and not to be sent forward without. The bill of rights will be brought forward. [A bill of rights] not necessary in [the] Confederation because it is expressly declared [that] no power should be exercised, but such as is expressly given, and therefore no constructive power can be exercised. To prevent this [is] the great use of a bill of rights.[1]

[Richard Henry Lee's Proposed Bill of Rights]

It having been found from universal experience, that the most express declarations and reservations are necessary to protect the just rights and liberty of mankind from the silent, powerful and ever active conspiracy of those who govern; and it appearing to be the sense of the good people of America, by the various bills or declarations of rights whereon the government of the greater number of the states are founded, that such precautions are necessary to restrain and regulate the exercise of the great powers given to rulers. In conformity with these principles, and from respect for the public sentiment on this subject, it is submitted,—

That the new constitution proposed for the government of the United States be bottomed upon a declaration or bill of rights, clearly and precisely stating the principles upon which this social compact is founded, to wit:

That the rights of conscience in matters of religion ought not to be violated—

That the freedom of the press shall be secured—

That the trial by jury in criminal and civil cases, and the modes prescribed by the common law for safety of life in criminal prosecutions, shall be held sacred—

That standing armies in times of peace are dangerous to liberty, and ought not to be permitted, unless assented to by two thirds of the members composing each house of the legislature under the new constitution—

That the elections should be free and frequent;

That the right administration of justice should be secured by the freedom and independency of the judges;

That excessive bail, excessive fines, or cruel and unusual punishments, should not be demanded or inflicted;

That the right of the people to assemble peaceably, for the purpose of petitioning the legislature, shall not be prevented;

That the citizens shall not be exposed to unreasonable searches, seizure of their persons, houses, papers, or property. . . .

That such parts of the new constitution be amended as provide imperfectly for the trial of criminals by a jury of the vicinage, and to supply the omission of a jury trial in civil causes or disputes about property between individuals, whereby the common law is directed, and as generally it is secured by the several state constitutions.

That such parts of the new constitution be amended, as permit the vexatious and oppressive callings of citizens from their own country, and all controversies between citizens of different states and between citizens and foreigners, to be tried in a far distant court, and as it may be without a jury, whereby in a multitude of cases, the circumstances of distance and expence may compel numbers to submit to the most unjust and ill-founded demand—[2]

1 DHRC, I, pp. 333-335.
2 DHRC, VIII, pp. 65-66. Provisions have been placed in separate paragraphs.

William Pierce (New York) September 28, 1787
Letter: To St. George Tucker (excerpt)
Published: Savannah *Gazette of the State of Georgia,* March 20, 1788

"Many objections have been already started to the Constitution because it was not founded on a Bill of Rights; but I ask how such a thing could have been effected; I believe it would have been difficult in the extreme to have brought the different states to agree in what probably would have been proposed as the very first principle, and that is, 'that all men are born equally free and independent.' Would a Virginian have accepted it in this form? Would he not have modified some of the expressions in such a manner as to have injured *the strong sense of them,* if not to have buried them altogether in *ambiguity and uncertainty?*

"In my judgment, when there are restraints on power to prevent its invading the positive rights of a people, there is no necessity for any such thing as a Bill of Rights. I conceive civil liberty is sufficienty guarded when personal security, personal liberty, and private property, are made the peculiar care of government. Now the defined powers of each department of the government, and the restraints that naturally follow, will be sufficient to prevent the invasion of either of those rights. Where then can be the necessity for a Bill of Rights? It is with diffidence I start this question; I confess I cannot help doubting the negative quality which it conveys, as some of the greatest men I ever knew have objected to the government for no other reason but because it was not *bottomed with a Bill of Rights;* men whose experience and wisdom are sufficient to give authority and support to almost any opinion they may choose to advance.

"I set this down as a truth founded in nature, that a nation habituated to freedom will never remain quiet under an invasion of its liberties. The English history presents us with a proof of this. At the Conquest that nation lost their freedom, but they never were easy or quiet until the true balance between liberty and prerogative was established in the reign of Charles the second. The absolute rights of Englishmen are founded in nature and reason, and are coeval with the English Constitution itself. They were always understood and insisted on by them as well without as with a Bill of Rights. This same spirit was breathed into the Americans, and they still retain it, nor will they, I flatter myself, ever resign it to any power, however plausible it may seem. The Bill of Rights was not introduced into England until the Revolution of 1688, (upwards of 600 years after the Conquest) when the Lords and Commons presented it to the Prince and Princess of Orange. And afterwards the same rights were asserted in the Act of Settlement at the commencement of the present century, when the Crown was limited to the House of Hanover. It was deemed necessary to introduce such an instrument to satisfy the public mind in England, not as a bottom to the Constitution, but as a prop to it; and hereafter, if the same necessity should exist in America, it may be done by an act of the Legislature here, so that the Constitution not being founded on a Bill of Rights I conceive will not deprive it at any future time of being propt by one, should it become necessary.["]

DHRC, XVI, pp. 443-444.

James Madison (New York) September 30, 1787
Letter: To George Washington (excerpt)

I found on my arrival here that certain ideas unfavorable to the Act of the Convention which had created difficulties in that body, had made their way into Congress. . . . An attempt was made in the next place by R[ichard] H[enry] L[ee]. to amend the Act of the Convention before it should go forth from Congress. He proposed a bill of Rights—provision for juries in civil cases & several other things corresponding with the ideas of Col. M[ason]—He was supported by Mr. Me[lancton]–Smith of this State. It was contended that Congress had an undoubted right to insert amendments, and that it was their duty to make use of it in a case where the essential guards of liberty had been omitted.

DHRC, VIII, pp. 26-27. Also reprinted in *Papers*, X, p. 180.

Seceding Pennsylvania Assemblymen October 2, 1787
Broadside: An Address of the Subscribers Members of the late House of Representatives of the Commonwealth of Pennsylvania to their Constituents. (excerpt)
Philadelphia

If however, after mature deliberation you are of opinion that the plan of government which they have offered for your consideration is best calculated to promote your political happiness and preserve those invaluable priviledges you at present enjoy, you will no doubt choose men to represent you in Convention who will adopt it; if you think otherwise you will, with your usual firmness, determine accordingly. . . . You will also in your deliberations on this important business judge, whether the liberty of the press may be considered as a blessing or a curse in a free government, and whether a declaration for the preservation of it is necessary? or whether in a plan of government any declaration of rights should be prefixed or inserted? You will be able likewise to determine, whether in a free government there ought or ought not to be any provision against a standing army in time of peace? or whether the trial by jury in civil causes is become dangerous and ought to be abolished? and whether the judiciary of the United States is not so constructed as to absorb and destroy the judiciaries of the several states? you will also be able to judge whether such inconveniences have been experienced by the present mode of trial between citizens and citizens, of different states as to render a continental court necessary for that purpose? or whether there can be any real use in the appellate jurisdiction with respect to fact as well as Law?

DHRC, II, pp. 115-116. Also reprinted in DHRC, XIII, pp. 295-296. Nineteen Pennsylvania Assemblymen failed to return to the Assembly chambers on September 28, at 4 PM. This was an intentional maneuver to prevent a quorum, and what they considered as a precipitate vote for calling a convention to ratify the proposed Constitution. Sixteen of these seceding members signed the Address. See "A Federal Republican," November 28, 1787, p. 119, for an Antifederalist answer to Federalist comments on this part of the Address.

Richard Henry Lee (New York) October 2, 1787
Letter: To William Shippen, Jr. (excerpt)[1]

I have considered the new Constitution with all the attention and candor that the thing and the times render necessary, & I find it impossible for me to doubt, that in its present State, unamended, the adoption of it will put Civil Liberty and the happiness of the people at the mercy of Rulers who may possess the great unguarded powers given—And I assure you that confidence in the moderation or benignity of power is not a plant of quick growth in a reflecting bosom—The necessary alterations will by no means interfere with the general nature of the plan, or limit the power of doing good; but they will restrain from oppression the wicked & Tyrannic—If all men were wise & good there would be no necessity for government or law—But the folly & the vice of human nature renders government & laws necessary for the Many, and restraints indespensable to prevent oppression from those who are entrusted with the administration of one & the dispensation of the other—You will see herewith the amendments that appeared to me necessary[.][2]

1 DHRC, VIII, pp. 32-33.
2 See "Confederation Congress," September 27, 1787, pp. 27-28, for Lee's proposed amendments.

Richard Henry Lee (New York) October 5, 1787
Letter: To Samuel Adams (excerpts)[1]

Having long toiled with you my dear friend in the Vineyard of liberty, I do with great pleasure submit to your wisdom and patriotism, the objections that prevail in my mind against the new Constitution proposed for federal government—Which objections I did propose to Congress in form of amendments to be discussed, and that such as were approved might be forwarded to the States with the Convention system.[2] You will have been informed by other hands why these amendments were not considered and do not appear on the Journal, and the reasons that influenced a bare *transmission* of the Convention plan, without a syllable of approbation or disapprobation on the part of Congress. I suppose my dear Sir, that the good people of the U. States in their late generous contest, contended for free government in the fullest, clearest, and strongest sense. That they had no idea of being brought under despotic rule under the notion of "Strong government," or in form of *elective despotism:* Chains being still Chains, whether made of gold or of iron.

The corrupting nature of power, and its insatiable appetite for increase, hath proved the necessity, and procured the adoption of the strongest and most express declarations of that *Residuum* of natural rights, which is not intended to be given up to Society; and which indeed is not necessary to be given for any good social purpose. In a government therefore, where the power of judging what shall be for the *general wellfare,* which goes to every object of human legislation; and where the laws of such Judges shall be the *supreme Law of the Land:* it seems to be of the last consequence to declare in most explicit terms the reservations above alluded to. So much for the propriety of a Bill of Rights as a necessary bottom to this new system—It is in vain to say that the defects in this new Constitution may be remedied by the Legislature created by it. The remedy, as it may, as it may not be applied—And if it should, a subsequent Assembly may repeal the Acts of its predecessor for the parliamentary doctrine is 'quod legis posteriores priores contrarias abrogant' 4 Inst. 43. Surely this is not a ground upon which a wise and good man would choose to rest the dearest rights of human nature— . . .

But I think the new Constitution (properly amended) as it contains many good regulations, may be admitted—And why may not such indispensable amendments be proposed by the Conventions and returned with the new plan to Congress that a new general Convention may so weave them into the proffer'd system as that a Web may be produced fit for freemen to wear? If such amendments were proposed by a Capital state or two, & a willingness expressed to agree with the plan so amended; I cannot see why it may not be effected. It is a mere begging the question to suppose, as some do, that only this Moment and this Measure will do—But why so, there being no war external or internal to prevent due deliberation on this most momentous business—the public papers will inform you what violence has been practised by the Agitators of this new System in Philadelphia to drive on its immediate adoption[3]—As if the subject of Government were a business of passion, instead of cool, sober, and intense consideration.

1 DHRC, XIII, pp. 323-325.

2 See "Confederation Congress," September 27, 1787, pp. 27-28, for Lee's Amendments proposed in Congress.

3 A reference to the forceful return of the Seceding Pennsylvania Assemblymen. See DHRC, II, pp. 95-126 for details on this incident. See "Pennsylvania Minority," December 18, 1787, p. 157, where mention is made of the incident.

Centinel I October 5, 1787

Newspaper Article: Philadelphia *Independent Gazetteer* (excerpts)

TO THE FREEMEN OF PENNSYLVANIA.

Friends, Countrymen and *Fellow Citizens,* Permit one of yourselves to put you in mind of certain *liberties* and *privileges* secured to you by the constitution of this commonwealth, and to beg your serious attention to his uninterested opinion upon the plan of federal government submitted to your consideration, before you surrender these great and valuable privileges up forever. Your present frame of government secures to you a right to hold yourselves, houses, papers and possessions free from search and seizure, and therefore warrants granted without oaths or affirmations first made, affording sufficient foundation for them, whereby any officer or messenger may be commanded or required to search your houses or seize your persons or property, not paricularly described in such warrant, shall not be granted. Your constitution further provides "that in controversies repecting property, and in suits between man and man, the parties have a right *to trial by jury, which ought to be held sacred.*" It also provides and declares, "*that the people have a right of* FREEDOM OF SPEECH, *and of* WRITING *and* PUBLISHING *their sentiments, therefore* THE FREEDOM OF THE PRESS OUGHT NOT TO BE RESTRAINED." The constitution of Pennsylvania is *yet* in existence, *as yet* you have the right to *freedom of speech,* and of *publishing your sentiments.* How long those rights will appertain to you, you yourselves are called upon to say, whether your *houses* shall continue to be your *castles;* whether your *papers,* your *persons* and your *property* are to be held sacred and free from *general warrants,* you are now to determine. Whether the *trial by jury* is to continue as your birthright, the freemen of Pennsylvania, nay, of all America, are now called upon to declare.

Without presuming upon my own judgement, I cannot think it an unwarrantable presumption to offer my private opinion, and call upon others for their's; and if I use my pen with the boldness of a freeman, it is because I know that *the liberty of the press yet remains unviolated,* and *juries yet are judges. . . .*

The framers of it; actuated by the true spirit of such a government, which ever abominates and suppresses all free enquiry and discussion, have made no provision for the *liberty of the press*, that grand *palladium of freedom* and *scourge of tyrants*, but observed a total silence on that head. It is the opinion of some great writers, that if the liberty of the press, by an institution of religion, or otherwise, could be rendered *sacred*, even in *Turkey*, that despotism would fly before it. And it is worthy of remark, that there is no declaration of personal rights, premised in most free constitutions; and that trial by *jury* in *civil* cases is taken away[.]

DHRC, XIII, pp. 328-329, 336.

Philadelphia *Independent Gazetteer* October 6, 1787

Another correspondent observes, that although the tide seems to run so high at present in favor of the new Constitution, there is no doubt but the people will soon change their minds when they have had time to examine it with coolness and impartiality.

Among the *blessings* of the new-proposed government our correspondent enumerates the following: 1. The *liberty of the press* abolished. 2. A standing army. 3. A Prussian militia. 4. No annual elections. 5. Fivefold taxes. 6. Excise laws, customhouse officers, tide and land waiters, cellar rats, etc. 9. A free importation of Negroes for one and twenty years. 10. Appeals to the supreme continental court, where the rich may drag the poor from the furthermost parts of the continent. 11. Elections for Pennsylvania held at Pittsburgh or perhaps Wyoming. 12. Poll taxes for our heads, if we choose to wear them. 13. And *death* if we dare to complain.

DHRC, II, p. 172. Also reprinted in DHRC, XIII, pp. 345-346.

George Mason October 7, 1787

Letter Enclosure: To George Washington (excerpts)
Published: Alexandria *Virginia Journal*, November 22, 1787

Objections to the Constitution of Government formed by the Convention.

There is no Declaration of Rights, and the Laws of the general Government being paramount to the Laws & Constitutions of the several States, the Declarations of Rights in the separate States are no

Security. Nor are the People secured even in the Enjoyment of the Benefits of the common-Law, which stands here upon no other Foundation than it's having been adopted by the respective Acts forming the Constitutions of the several States— . . .

Under their own Construction of the general Clause at the End of the enumerated Powers, the Congress may grant Monopolies in Trade & Commerce, constitute new Crimes, inflict unusual & severe Punishments, and extend their Power as far as they shall think proper; so that the State Legislatures have no Security for the Powers now presumed to remain to them; or the People for their Rights.—

There is no declaration of any kind for preserving the Liberty of the Press, the Tryal by jury in civil Causes, nor against the Danger of standing Armys in time of Peace.

DHRC, XIII, pp. 43, 45.

Governor Edmund Randolph (Richmond) October 10, 1787
Letter: To the Speaker of the Virginia House of Delegates (excerpt)
Pamphlet: Richmond, December [27], 1788.

But when the plan which is now before the General Assembly, was on its passage through the [federal] convention, I moved, that the state-conventions should be at liberty to amend, and that a second general Convention should be holden to discuss the amendments, which should be suggested by them. This motion was in some measure justified by the manner, in which the confederation was forwarded originally, by Congress to the state-legislatures, in many of which amendments were proposed, and those amendments were afterwards examined in Congress. Such a motion was doubly expedient here, as the delegation of so much more power was sought for. But it was negatived. I then expressed my unwillingness to sign. My reasons were the following.

1. It is said in the resolutions, which accompany the constitution, that it is to be submitted to a convention of Delegates, chosen in each state by the people thereof, for their assent and ratification. The meaning of these terms is allowed universally to be, that the Convention must either adopt the constitution in the whole, or reject it in the whole, and is positively forbidden to amend. If therefore I had signed, I should have felt myself bound to be silent as to amendments, and to endeavor to support the constitution without the correction of a letter. With this consequence before my eyes and with a determination to attempt an amendment, I was taught by a regard for consistency not to sign.

2. My opinion always was, and still is, that every citizen of America, let the crisis be what it may, ought to have a full opportunity to propose through his representatives any amendment, which in his apprehension tends to the public welfare—By signing I should have contradicted this sentiment.

3. A constitution ought to have the hearts of the people on its side. But if at a future day it should be burthensome, after having been adopted in the whole, and they should insinuate, that it was in some measure forced upon them, by being confined to the single alternative of taking or rejecting it altogether, under my impressions and with my opinions I should not be able to justify myself had I signed.

4. I was always satisfied, as I have now experienced, that this great subject, would be placed in new lights and attitudes by the criticism of the world, and that no man can assure himself, how a constitution will work for a course of years, until at least he shall have heard the observations of the people at large. I also fear more from inaccuracies in a constitution, than from gross errors in any other composition; because our dearest interests are to be regulated by it, and power, if loosely given, especially where it will be interpreted with great latitude, may bring sorrow in its execution. Had I signed with these ideas, I should have virtually shut my ears against the information, which I ardently desired.

5. I was afraid, that if the Constitution was to be submitted to the people, to be wholly adopted or wholly rejected by them, they would not only reject it, but bid a lasting farewell to the union. This formidable event I wished to avert, by keeping myself free to propose amendments, and thus, if possible, to remove the obstacles to an effectual government. But it will be asked, whether all these arguments were not well weighed in Convention. They were, sir, and with great candor. Nay, when I called to mind the respectability of those, with whom I was associated, I almost lost confidence in these principles. On other occasions I should chearfully have yielded to a majority; on this the fate of thousands, yet unborn, enjoined me not to yield, until I was convinced—

Again may I be asked, why the mode pointed out in the Constitution for its amendment, may not be sufficient security against its imperfections, without now arresting it in its progress?—My answers are, 1. that it is better to amend, while we have the Constitution in our power, while the passions of designing men are not yet enlisted and while a bare majority of the states may amend, than to wait for the uncertain assent of three fourths of the states. 2. That a bad feature in government becomes more and more fixed every day. 3. That frequent changes of a Constitution even if practicable ought not to be wished, but avoided as much as possible: and 4. That in the present case it may be questionable, whether, after the particular advantages of its operation shall be discerned, three fourths of the states can be induced to amend.

I confess, that it is no easy task, to devise a scheme which shall be suitable to the views of all. Many expedients have occurred to me, but none of them appear less exceptionable than this: that if our Convention should choose to amend, another federal Convention be recommended: that in that federal Convention the amendments proposed by this or any other state, be discussed; and if incorporated in the constitution or rejected, or if a proper number of the other states should be unwilling to accede to a second Convention, the constitution be again laid before the same state-conventions, which shall again assemble on the summons of the Executives, and it shall be either wholly adopted, or wholly rejected, without a further power of amendment. I count such a delay, as nothing in comparison with so grand an object; especially too as the privilege of amending must terminate after the use of it once.

DHRC, VIII, pp. 271-273. Also reprinted in DHRC, XV, pp. 131-133.

Foederal Constitution October 10, 1787

Newpaper Article: Philadelphia *Pennsylvania Gazette* (excerpt)[1]

To the FREEMEN *of* PENNSYLVANIA. . . .

The objections to the foederal government are weak, false and absurd. The neglect of the Convention to mention the *Liberty of the Press* arose from a respect to the state constitutions, in each of which this palladium of liberty is secured, and which is guaranteed to them as an essential part of their republican forms of government. But supposing this had not been done, the *Liberty of the Press* would have been an inherent and political right, as long as nothing was said *against* it. The Convention have said nothing to secure the privilege of eating and drinking, and yet no man supposes that right of nature to be endangered by their silence about it.[2]

1 DHRC, XIII, pp. 363-364.

2 See "A Confederationalist," October 27, 1787, pp. 65-66, for a reply from an Antifederalist.

A Citizen of America {Noah Webster} October 10, 1787
Pamphlet: An Examination into the leading principles of the Federal Constitution. (excerpts)
Philadelphia

4. It is alledged that the liberty of the press is not guaranteed by the new constitution. But this objection is wholly unfounded. The liberty of the press does not come within the jurisdiction of [the] federal government. It is firmly established in all the states either by law, or positive declarations in *bills of right;* and not being mentioned in the federal constitution, is not—and cannot be abridged by Congress. It stands on the basis of the respective state-constitutions. Should any state resign to Congress the exclusive jurisdiction of a certain district, which should include any town where presses are already established, it is in the power of the state to reserve the liberty of the press, or any other fundamental privilege, and make it an immutable condition of the grant, that such rights shall never be violated. All objections therefore on this score are *"baseless visions."* . . .

The states in their separate capacity, cannot provide for the *common* defence; nay in case of civil war, a state cannot secure its own existence. The only question therefore is, whether it is necessary to unite, and provide for our *common defence and general welfare.* For this question being once decided in the affirmative, leaves no room to controvert the propriety of constituting a power over the whole United States, adequate to these general purposes.

The states, by granting such power, do not throw it out of their own hands—they only throw, each its proportion, into a common stock—they merely combine the powers of the several states into one point, where they *must* be collected, before they *can* be exerted. But the powers are still in their own hands; and cannot be alienated, till they create a body independent of themselves, with a force at their command, superior to the whole yeomanry of the country.

6. It is said there is no provision made in the new constitution against a standing army in time of peace. Why do not people object that no provision is made against the introduction of a body of Turkish Janizaries; or against making the Alcoran the rule of faith and practice, instead of the Bible? The answer to such objections is simply this—*no such provision is necessary*. The people in this country cannot forget their apprehensions from a British standing army, quartered in America; and they turn their fears and jealousies against themselves. Why do not the people of most of the states apprehend danger from standing armies from their own legislatures? Pennsylvania and North

Carolina, I believe, are the only states that have provided against this danger at all events. Other states have declared that "no standing armies shall be kept up without the consent of the legislature." But this leaves the power entirely in the hands of the legislature. Many of the states however have made *no provision* against this evil. What hazards these states suffer! Why does not a man pass a law in his family, that no armed soldier shall be quartered in his house by his consent? The reason is very plain: no man will suffer his liberty to be abridged, or endangered—his disposition and his power are uniformly opposed to any infringement of his rights. In the same manner, the principles and habits, as well as the power of the Americans are directly opposed to standing armies; and there is as little necessity to guard against them by positive constitutions, as to prohibit the establishment of the Mahometan religion.

Congress likewise are to have power to provide for organizing, arming and disciplining the militia, but have no other command of them, except when in actual service. Nor are they at liberty to call out the militia at pleasure—but only, to execute the laws of the union, suppress insurrections, and repel invasions. For these purposes, government must always be armed with a military force, if the occasion should require it; otherwise laws are nugatory, and life and property insecure. . . .

But I cannot quit this subject without attempting to correct some of the erroneous opinions respecting *freedom* and *tyranny*, and the principles by which they are supported. Many people seem to entertain an idea, that liberty consists in *a power to act without any control*. This is more liberty than even the savages enjoy. But in civil society, political liberty consists in *acting conformably to a sense of a majority of the society*. In a free government every man binds himself to obey the *public voice*, or the opinions of a majority; and the *whole society* engages to *protect each individual*. In such a government a man is *free* and safe. But reverse the case; suppose every man to act without control or fear of punishment—every man would be free, but no man would be sure of his freedom one moment. Each would have the power of taking his neighbor's life, liberty, or property; and no man would command more than his own strength to repel the invasion. The case is the same with states. If the states should not unite into one compact society, every state may trespass upon its neighbor, and the injured state has no means of redress but its own military force.

The present situation of our American states is very little better than a state of nature—Our boasted state sovereignties are so far from securing our liberty and property, that they, every moment, expose us to the loss of both. That state which commands the heaviest purse and longest sword, may at any moment, lay its weaker neighbor under tribute; and there is no superior power now existing, that can regularly oppose the invasion or redress the injury. From such liberty, O Lord, deliver us!

But what is tyranny? Or how can a free people be deprived of their liberties? Tyranny is the exercise of some power over a man, which is not warranted by law, or necessary for the public safety. A people can never be deprived of their liberties, while they retain in their own hands, a power sufficient to any other power in the state. This position leads me directly to enquire, in what consits the power of a nation or of an order of men?

In some nations, legislators have derived much of their power from the influence of religion, or from that implicit belief which an ignorant and superstitious people entertain of the gods, and their interposition in every transaction of life. . . .

Another source of power in government is a military force. But this, to be efficient, must be superior to any force that exists among the people, or which they can command: for otherwise this force would be annihilated, on the first exercise of acts of oppression. Before a standing army can rule, the people must be disarmed; as they are in almost every kingdom in Europe. The supreme power in America cannot enforce unjust laws by the sword; because the whole body of the people are armed, and constitute a force superior to any band of regular troops that can be, on any pretence, raised in the United States. A military force, at the command of congress, can execute no laws, but such as the people perceive to be just and constitutional; for they will possess the *power*, and jealousy will instantly inspire the *inclination*, to resist the execution of a law which appears to them unjust and oppressive. In spite of all the nominal powers, vested in Congress by the constitution, were the system once adopted in its fullest latitude, still the actual exercise of them would be frequently interrupted by popular jealousy. I am bold to say, that *ten* just and constitutional measures would be resisted, where *one* unjust or oppressive law would be enforced. The powers vested in Congress are little more than *nominal;* nay *real* power cannot be vested in them, nor in any body, but in the *people*. The source of power is in the *people* of this country, and cannot for ages, and probably never will, be removed. . . .

Let the people have [real] property, and they *will* have power—a power that will for ever be exerted to prevent a restriction of the press, and abolition of trial by jury, or the abridgement of any other privilege. The liberties of America, therefore, and her forms of government, stand on the broadest basis. Removed from the fears of a foreign invasion and conquest, they are not exposed to the convulsions that shake other governments; and the principles of freedom are so general and energetic, as to exclude the possibility of a change in our republican constitutions.

But while *property* is considered as the *basis* of the freedom of the American yeomanry, there are other auxiliary supports; among which is the *information of the people.* In no country, is education so general—in no country, have the body of the people such a knowledge of the rights of men and the principles of government. This knowledge, joined with a keen sense of liberty and a watchful jealousy, will guard our constitutions, and awaken the people to an instantaneous resistance of encroachments.

Pamphlets, pp. 48-61.

A Citizen of Pennsylvania October 12, 1787

Newspaper Article: Philadelphia *Pennsylvania Packet* (excerpt)

Much observation has been made in regard to the omission of a bill of rights in the new frame of government. Such remarks, I humbly conceive, arise from a great inadvertency in taking up the subject. When the people of these states dissolved their connection with the crown of Great Britain, by the declaration of independence, they found themselves, as to government, *in a state of nature:* yet they were very sensible of the blessings of civil society. On *a recommendation* of Congress, who were then possessed of no authority, the inhabitants of each colony respectively, formed a compact for themselves, which compacts are our state constitutions. These were original agreements among *individuals,* before actually in a state of nature. In these constitutions a bill of rights (that is a declaration of the unalienable rights of each individual) was proper, and indispensibly necessary. When the several states were thus formed into thirteen separate and independent sovereignties, Congress, who managed their general affairs, and their respective legislatures thought it proper (and it was surely absolutely necessary) that a confederation should be prepared and executed. The measure was accordingly adopted; and here let us observe this was *a compact among thirteen independent states* of the nature of a perpetual treaty. It was acceded to by the several states as sovereign. *No individuals* were parties to it. *No rights of individuals* could therefore be declared in it. The rights of *contracting parties* (the thirteen *states*) were declared. Those rights remain inviolate. No bill of the rights of *the freemen* of the union was thought of, nor could be introduced. No complaint was made of the want [of] it, for it was a matter foreign from the nature of the compact. In articles of agreement *among a number of people forming a civil society,* a bill of the rights of individuals comes in of course, and is *indispensibly* necessary. In articles of agreement *among a number of independent states,* entering into an union, a bill of the rights of individuals is *excluded* of course. As in the old confederation or compact among the thirteen independent sovereignties of America, no bill of rights of individuals could be or was introduced: so in the proposed compact among the same thirteen independent sovereignties, no bill of the rights of individuals has been or could be introduced. This would be to annihilate our states constitutions, by rendering them unnecessary. The liberty of the press, from an honest republican jealousy, which I highly applaud, has also been a subject of observation; but the right of writing for publication, and of printing, publishing and selling, what may be written are *personal* rights, *are part of the rights of individuals.* Thus we see when attempts have been made to restrain them in any country, *the individuals concerned* have only been, or indeed could be the objects of attention. They are the rights of *the people in the states,* and can only be exercised by them. They are not the rights of the thirteen independent sovereignties, therefore could not enter into either the old or new compact among them. Every constitution in the union guards the liberty of the press. It has also become a part of the common law of the land. But who is to destroy it? Not the people at large, for it is their most invaluable privilege—the palladium of their happiness—Not the state legislatures, for their respective constitutions forbid them to infringe it. Not the foederal government, *for they have never had it transferred into their hands.* It remains amongst those rights *not conveyed to them.* But who are the foederal government, that they should take away the freedom of the press, was it not out of their reach? *Are they not the temporary responsible servants of the people?* How then, my countrymen, is this favorite inestimable privilege in danger? It cannot be affected. It is understood by all men that it is never to be touched. It is guarded by insurmountable barriers, as you have already seen: and woe betide—the heaviest woe will betide the sacrilegious hand that shall attempt to remove them.

DHRC, II Mfm. Pa., pp. 619-622.

An Old Whig I October 12, 1787
Newspaper Article: Philadelphia *Independent Gazetteer* (excerpt)

The great, and the wise, and the mighty will be in possession of places and offices; they will oppose all changes in favor of liberty; they will steadily pursue the acquisition of more and more power to themselves and their adherents. The cause of liberty, if it be now forgotten, will be forgotten forever.—Even the press which has so long been employed in the cause of liberty, and to which perhaps the greatest part of the liberty which exists in the world is owing at this moment; the press may possibly be restrained of its freedom, and our children may possibly not be suffered to enjoy this most invaluable blessing of a free communication of each others sentiments on political subjects—Such at least appear to be some men's fears, and I cannot find in the proposed constitution any thing expressly calculated to obviate these fears; so that they may or may not be realized according to the principles and dispositions of the men who may happen to govern us hereafter. One thing however is calculated to alarm our fears on this head;—I mean the fashionable language which now prevails so much and is so frequent in the mouths of some who formerly held very different opinions;—THAT COMMON PEOPLE HAVE NO BUSINESS TO TROUBLE THEMSELVES ABOUT GOVERNMENT. If this principle is just the consequence is plain that the common people need no information on the subject of politics. Newspapers, pamphlets and essays are calculated only to mislead and inflame by holding forth to them doctrines which they have no business or right to meddle with, which they ought to leave to their superiors. Should the freedom of the press be restrained on the subject of politics, there is no doubt it will soon after be restrained on all other subjects, religious as well as civil. And if the freedom of the press shall be restrained, it will be another reason to despair of any amendments being made in favor of liberty, after the proposed constitution shall be once established. Add to this, that under the proposed constitution, it will be in the power of the Congress to raise and maintain a standing army for their support, and when they are supported by an army, it will depend on themselves to say whether any amendments shall be made in favor of liberty.

If these reflections are just it becomes us to pause, and reflect previously before we establish a system of government which cannot be amended; which will entail happiness or misery on ourselves and our children. We ought I say to reflect carefully, we ought not by any means to be in haste; but rather to suffer a little temporary inconvenience, than by any precipitation to establish a constitution without knowing whether it is right or wrong, and which if wrong, no length of time will ever mend. Scarce any people ever deliberately gave up their liberties; but many instances occur in history of their losing them forever by a rash and sudden act, to avoid a pressing inconvenience or gratify some violent passion of revenge or fear. It was a celebrated observation of one of our Assemblies before the revolution, during their struggles with the proprietaries, that "those who would give up essential liberty to purchase a little temporary safety deserve neither liberty nor safety."

DHRC, XIII, pp. 378-379. The series "An Old Whig" is reprinted in Storing, III, starting at p. 17.

Richard Henry Lee October 16, 1787
Letter: To Edmund Randolph (excerpts)[1]
Published: Petersburg *Virginia Gazette,* December 6, 1787.

The only check to be found in favor of the democratic principle in this system is, the house of representatives; which I believe may justly be called a mere shread or rag of representation: It being obvious to the least examination, that smallness of number and great comparative disparity of power, renders that house of little effect to promote good, or restrain bad government. But what is the power given to this ill constructed body? To judge of what may be for the general welfare, and such judgments when made, the acts of Congress become the supreme laws of the land. This seems a power co-extensive with every possible object of human legislation.—Yet there is no restraint in form of a bill of rights, to secure (what Doctor Blackstone calls) that residuum of human rights, which is not intended to be given up to society, and which indeed is not necessary to be given for any good social purpose. . . . Upon the whole, Sir, my opinion is, that as this constitution abounds with useful regulations, at the same time that it is liable to strong and fundamental objections, the plan for us to pursue, will be to propose the necessary amendments, and express our willingness to adopt it with the amendments, and to suggest the calling of a new convention for the purpose of considering them. To this I see no well founded objection, but great safety and much good to be the probable result.[2]

1 DHRC, VIII, pp. 62-64. Reprinted in DHRC, XIV, p. 366, and in Storing, V, p. 111.

2 Lee sent Randolph a copy of his proposed amendments to the Constitution. These are the same proposals which Lee introduced in Congress on September 27, 1787. See "Confederation Congress," September 27, 1787, pp. 27-28.

Impartial October 16, 1787
Newspaper Article: Philadelphia *Independent Gazetteer* (excerpt)

But if any illegal and unconstitutional methods should be employed [by Congress], they cannot subsist long in a country where the rights of men are so well ascertained and so generally known. If remonstrances should not be sufficient to procure redress, the militia will always have it in their power to command it.

DHRC, II Mfm. Pa., p. 648.

One of the People October 17, 1787
Newspaper Article: Philadelphia *Pennsylvania Gazette* (excerpt)

To the Freemen of Pennsylvania. . . .
The freedom of the press and trials by jury are not infringed on. The Constitution is silent, and with propriety too, on these and every other subject relative to the internal government of the states. These are secured by the different state constitutions. I repeat again, that the Federal Constitution does not interfere with these matters. Their power is defined and limited by the 8th section of the first Article of the Constitution, and they have not power to take away the freedom of the press, nor can they interfere in the smallest degree with the judiciary of any one of the states. It is essentially necessary that the judiciary of the United States should have an appellate jurisdiction both in law and fact, in cases of disputes between a state and citizens of another state, and between citizens of different states.

DHRC, II, pp. 190-191.

A Democratic Federalist October 17, 1787
Newspaper Article: Philadelphia *Pennsylvania Herald* (excerpts)

The arguments of the Honorable Mr. [James] Wilson, expressed in the speech he made at the State House on the Saturday preceding the general election (as stated in the *Pennsylvania Herald*), although extremely *ingenious* and the best that could be adduced in support of so bad a cause, are yet extremely *futile* and will not stand the test of investigation.

In the first place, Mr. Wilson pretends to point out a leading discrimination between the state constitutions and the Constitution of the United States. In the former, he says, every power which is not *reserved* is *given,* and in the latter, every power which is not *given* is *reserved.* And this may furnish an answer, he adds, to those who object that a bill of rights has not been introduced in the proposed Federal Constitution. If this doctrine is true, and since it is the only security that we are to have for our natural rights, it ought at least to have been clearly expressed in the plan of government. The 2d section of the present Articles of Confederation says: "*Each State retains its sovereignty, freedom and independence, and* EVERY POWER, JURISDICTION AND RIGHT WHICH IS NOT BY THIS CONFEDERATION EXPRESSLY, DELEGATED TO THE UNITED STATES IN CONGRESS ASSEMBLED." This declaration (for what purpose I know not) is entirely omitted in the proposed Constitution. And yet there is a material difference between this Constitution and the present Confederation, for Congress in the latter are merely an executive body; it has no power to raise money, it has no *judicial jurisdiction.* In the other, on the contrary, the federal rulers are vested with each of the three essential powers of government—their laws are to be *paramount* to the laws of the different states. What then will there be to oppose to their encroachments? Should they ever pretend to tyrannize over the people, their *standing army* will silence every popular effort; it will be theirs to explain the powers which have been granted to them. Mr. Wilson's distinction will be forgot, denied or explained away, and the liberty of the people will be no more.

It is said in the 2d section of the 3d Article of the federal plan: "The judicial power shall extend to ALL CASES, in *law* and *equity,* arising under this constitution." It is very clear that under this clause the tribunal of the United States may claim a right to the cognizance of all offenses against the *general government,* and *libels* will not probably be excluded. Nay, those offenses may be by them construed, or by law declared *misprision of treason,* an offense which comes literally under their express jurisdiction. Where is then the safety of our boasted liberty of the press? And in case of a *conflict of jurisdiction* between the courts of the United States and those of the several commonwealths is it not easy to foresee which of the two will obtain the advantage?

Under the enormous power of the new confederation, which extends to the *individuals* as well as to the *states* of America, a thousand means may be devised to destroy effectually the liberty of the press. There is no knowing what corrupt and wicked judges may do in process of time when they are not restrained by express laws. The case of *John Peter Zenger* of New York ought still to be present to our minds to convince us how displeasing the liberty of the press is to men in high power. At any rate, I lay it down as a general rule that wherever the powers of a government extend to the lives, the persons, and properties of the subject, all their rights ought to be clearly and expressly defined, otherwise they have but a poor security for their liberties.

The second and most important objection to the federal plan, which Mr. Wilson pretends to be made *in disingenuous form*, is the entire *abolition of the trial by jury in civil cases*. It seems to me that Mr. Wilson's pretended answer is much more *disingenuous* than the objection itself, which I maintain to be strictly founded in fact. . . .

But Mr. Wilson has not stopped here. He has told us that a STANDING ARMY, that *great support of tyrants*, not only was not dangerous, but that it was *absolutely necessary*. O! my much respected fellow citizens! and are you then reduced to such a degree of insensibility, that assertions like these will not rouse your warmest resentment and indignation? Are we then, after the experience of past ages, and the result of the inquiries of the best and most celebrated patriots have taught us to dread a standing army above all earthly evils, are we then to go over all the treadbare commonplace arguments that have been used without success by the advocates of tyranny, and which have been for a long time past so gloriously refuted! Read the excellent Burgh in his political disquisitions on this hackneyed subject, and then say, whether you think that a standing army is necessary in a free country? Even Mr. Hume, an *aristocratical* writer, has candidly confessed that *an army is a mortal distemper in a government, of which it must at last inevitably perish* (2d Burgh, 349); and the Earl of Oxford (Oxford, the friend of France and the *pretender*, the attainted Oxford) said in the British Parliament, in a speech on the mutiny bill, that "while he had breath, he would speak for the liberties of his country, and against courts martial and a standing army in peace as dangerous to the constitution" (ibid., page 455). Such were the speeches even of the enemies to liberty, when Britain had yet a right to be called free. But, says Mr. Wilson, "It is necessary to maintain the appearance of strength even in times of the most profound tranquility." And what is this more than a threadbare hackneyed argument, which has been answered over and over in different ages and does not deserve even the smallest consideration? Had we a standing army when the British invaded our peaceful shores? Was it a standing army that gained the battle of Lexington and Bunkers's Hill, and took the ill-fated Burgoyne? Is not a well-regulated militia sufficient for every purpose of internal defense? And which of you, my fellow citizens, is afraid of any invasion from foreign powers, that our brave militia would not be able immediately to repel?

Mr. Wilson says that *he does not know of any nation in the world which has not found it necessary to maintain the appearance of strength in a season of the most profound tranquility*. If by this *equivocal* assertion, he has meant to say that there is no nation in the world without a *standing army in time of peace,* he has been mistaken. I need only adduce the example of Switzerland, which, like us, is a *republic* whose *thirteen* cantons, like our thirteen states, are under a *federal government,* and which besides is surrounded by the most powerful nations in Europe, all jealous of its liberty and prosperity. And yet that nation has preserved its freedom for many ages, with the sole help of a militia, and has never been known to have a standing army except when in actual war. Why should we not follow so glorious an example, and are we less able to defend our liberty without an army than that brave but small nation, which with its militia alone has hitherto defied all Europe?

It is said likewise, that *a standing army is not a new thing in America. Congress even at this moment have a standing army on foot.* I answer, that *precedent* is not *principle.* Congress have no right to keep up a standing army in time of peace. If they do, it is an infringement of the liberties of the people—*wrong* can never be justified by *wrong*—but it is well-known that the assertion is groundless. The few troops that are on the banks of the Ohio were sent for the express purpose of repelling the invasion of the savages and protecting the inhabitants of the frontiers. It is our misfortune that we are never at peace with those inhuman butchers of their species, and while they remain in our neighborhood, we are always, with respect to them, in a state of war. As soon as the danger is over, there is no doubt but Congress will disband their handful of soldiers. It is therefore not true that Congress keep up a standing army in a time of peace and profound security.

DHRC, II, pp. 193-197. Also reprinted in DHRC, XIII, pp. 387-392, and in Storing, III, starting on p. 58.

An Old Whig II October 17, 1787

Newspaper Article: Philadelphia *Independent Gazetteer* (excerpts)

MR. PRINTER, Since writing my last, in which I stated some doubts respecting the new federal constitution and expressed a wish that those doubts might be removed, I have met with the printed speech of *James Wilson,* Esquire.—This speech I find was made for the express purpose of removing objections from the minds of those who doubted, like myself, and wished to be satisfied; and except one or two hard names that have escaped the speaker, it bears the marks of more candor than is to be found in most of the productions, which have been ushered into the world in support of the same measure. This speech also deserves the more attention as coming from a man of abilities fresh from "*the impressions of four months constant attention to the subject.*" The subject however is one of those which it imports us all very carefully to examine. I have therefore paid very considerable attention to his arguments, at the same time that I have examined with some care the foundation upon which they are built. Still I remain unsatisfied; and the more unsatisfied, as I have been disappointed in my hope of conviction, from a quarter, from which so much was to be expected—You will give me leave therefore to state shortly in your paper, some of those difficulties which still remain with me.

The first principle which the gentleman endeavours to establish in his speech is a very important one, if true; and lays a sure foundation to reason upon, in answer to the objection which is made to the new constitution, from the want of a bill of rights. The principle is this: that "in *delegating federal powers,* the congressional authority is to be collected, *not from tacit implication,* but from *the positive grant* expressed in the instrument of union," "*that every thing which is not given is reserved.*" *If this* be a just representation of the matter, the authority of the several states will be sufficient to protect our liberties from the encroachments of Congress, without any continental bill of rights, *unless* the powers which are *expressly given* to Congress are *too large.* . . .

There is nothing in the new constitution which either in form or substance bears the least resemblance to the second article of the confederation. It might nevertheless be a fair argument to insist upon from the nature of delegated powers, that no more power is given in such cases than is expressly given. Whether or not this ground of argument would be such as we might safely rest our liberties upon; or whether it would be more prudent to stipulate expressly as is done in the present confederation for the reservation of all such powers as are not expressly given, it is hardly necessary to determine at present. It strikes me that by the proposed constitution, so far from the reservation of all powers that are not expressly given, *the future Congress will be fully authorised to assume all such powers as they in their wisdom or wickedness, according as the one or the other may happen to prevail, shall from time to time think proper to assume.* . . . But to the question;—without force what can restrain the Congress from making such laws as they please? What limits are there to their authority?—I fear none at all; for surely it cannot justly be said that they have no power but what is expressly given to them, whereby the very terms of their creation they are vested with the powers of making laws in all cases necessary and proper; when from the nature of their power they must necessarily be the judges, what laws are necessary and proper. The British act of Parliament, declaring the power of Parliament to make laws to bind America in all cases whatsoever, was not more extensive; for it is as true as a maxim, that even the British Parliament neither could nor would pass any law in any case in which they did not either deem it necessary and proper to make such law or pretend to deem it so. And in such cases it is not of a farthing consequence whether they really are of opinion that the law is necessary and proper, or only *pretend to think so;* for who can overrule their pretensions?—No one, unless we had a bill of rights to which we might appeal, and under which we might contend against any assumption of undue power and appeal to the judicial branch of the government to protect us by their judgements. This reasoning I fear Mr. Printer is but too just; and yet, if any man should doubt the truth of it; let me ask him one other question, what is the meaning of the latter part of the clause which vests the Congress with the authority of making all laws which shall be necessary and proper for carrying into execution ALL OTHER POWERS;–besides the foregoing powers vested, &c. &c. Was it thought that the foregoing powers might perhaps admit of some restraint in *their* construction as to what was necessary and proper to carry them into execution? Or was it deemed right to add still further that they should not be restrained to the powers already named?—besides the powers already mentioned, other powers may be assumed hereafter as contained by implication in this constitution. The Congress shall judge of what is necessary and proper in all these cases and in all other cases;—in short in all cases whatsoever.

Where then is the restraint? How are Congress bound down to the powers expressly given? what is reserved or can be reserved?

Yet even this is not all—as if it were determined that no doubt should remain, by the sixth article of the constitution it is declared that, "this constitution, and the laws of the United States which shall be made in pursuance thereof; and all treaties made, or which shall be made, under the authority of the United States, shall be the supreme law of the land, and the judges in every state shll be bound thereby, *any thing in the constitutions or laws of any state to the contrary notwithstanding.*" The congress are therefore vested with the supreme legislative power, without controul. In giving such immense, such unlimited powers, was there no necessity of a bill of rights to secure to the people their liberties? Is it not evident that we are left wholly dependent on the wisdom and virtue of the men who shall from time to time be the members of Congress? and who shall be able to say seven years hence, the members of Congress will be wise and good men, or of the contrary character.

DHRC, XIII, pp. 399-403. The series "An Old Whig" is reprinted in Storing, III, starting on p. 17.

Elbridge Gerry (New York) October 18, 1787
Letter: To the Massachusetts General Court (excerpt)
Published: Boston *Massachusetts Centinel,* November 3, 1787.

GENTLEMEN, I have the honour to inclose, pursuant to my commission, the constitution proposed by the federal Convention.

To this system I gave my dissent, and shall submit my objections to the honourable Legislature.

It was painful for me, on a subject of such national importance, to differ from the respectable members who signed the constitution: But conceiving as I did, that the liberties of America were not secured by the system, it was my duty to oppose it.—

My principal objections to the plan, are, that there is no adequate provision for a representation of the people—that they have no security for the right of election—that some of the powers of the Legislature are ambiguous, and others indefinite and dangerous—that the Executive is blended with and will have an undue influence over the Legislature—that the judicial department will be oppressive—that treaties of the highest importance may be formed by the President with the advice of two thirds of a *quorum* of the Senate—and that the system is without the security of a bill of rights. These are objections which are not local, but apply equally to all the States.

DHRC, XIII, p. 548.

An Old Whig III October 20, 1787
Newspaper Article: Philadelphia *Independent Gazetteer* (excerpt)

But no treaty ought to be suffered to alter the law of the land, without the consent of the continental legislatures; the powers of the continental legislatures ought to be exactly defined; and there ought to be a bill of rights firmly established, which neither treaties nor acts of the legislature can alter.

Let us however give fair play to the answer which has been attempted to be given to this Objection. The author [James Wilson] of the speech tells us, that a bill of rights would have been superfluous and absurd; because "no powers are given to Congress but what are expressly given;" and "that we shall still enjoy those privileges of which we are not divested either by the intention or the act that brought that body into existence.—For instance, the liberty of the press.—What controul can proceed from the federal government to shackle or destroy that sacred palladium of national freedom?"—What controul!—Suppose that an act of the continental legislature should be passed to restrain the liberty of the press;—to appoint licensers of the press in every town in America;—to limit the number of printers;—and to compel them to give security for their good behaviour, from year to year, as the licenses are renewed; If such a law should be once passed, what is there to prevent the execution of it?—By the sixth article of the proposed constitution, this act of the continental legislature is "the supreme law of the land; and the judges in every state shall be bound thereby, ANY THING IN THE CONSTITUTION OR LAWS OF ANY STATE TO THE CONTRARY NOTWITHSTANDING."—Suppose a printer should be found hardy enough to contravene such a law when made, and to contest the validity of it.—He is prosecuted we will suppose, in this state—he pleads in his defence, that by the constitution of Pennsylvania, it is declared "that the freedom of the press ought not to be restrained."—What will this avail him? The judge will be obliged to declare that "*notwithstanding the constitution of any state,*" this act of the continental legislature which restrains the freedom of the press, is "the supreme law; and we must punish you—The bill of rights of Pennsylvania is nothing here. That bill of rights indeed is binding upon the legislature of Pennsylvania, but it is not binding upon the legislature of the continent." Such must be the language and conduct of courts, as soon as the proposed continental constitution shall be adopted.

As to the trial by jury, the question may be decided in a few words. Any future Congress sitting under the authority of the proposed new constitution, may, if they chuse, enact that there shall be no more trial by jury, in any of the United States; except in the trial of crimes; and this "SUPREME LAW" will at once annul the trial by jury, in all other cases. The author of the speech supposes that no danger "can possibly ensue, since the proceedings of the supreme court are to be regulated by the Congress, which is a faithful representation of the people; and the oppression of government is effectually barred; by declaring that in all criminal cases the trial by jury shall be preserved." Let us examine the last clause of this sentence first.—I know that an affected indifference to the trial by jury has been expressed, by some persons high in the confidence of the present ruling party in some of the states;—and yet for my own part I cannot change the opinion I had early formed of the excellence of this mode of trial even in civil causes. On the other hand I have no doubt that whenever a settled plan shall be formed for the extirpation of liberty, the banishment of jury trials will be one of the means adopted for the purpose.—But how is it that "the oppression of government is effectually barred by declaring that in all criminal cases the trial by jury shall be preserved?"—Are there not a thousand civil cases in which the government is a party?—In all actions for penalties, forfeitures and public debts, as well as many others, the government is a party and the whole weight of government is thrown into the scale of the prosecution yet these are all of them civil causes.—These penalties, forfeitures and demands of public debts may be multiplied at the will and pleasure of government.—These modes of harrasing the subject have perhaps been more effectual than direct criminal prosecutions.—In the reign of Henry the Seventh of England, Empson and Dudley acquired an infamous immortality by these prosecutions for penalties and forfeitures:—Yet all these prosecutions were in the form of civil actions; they are undoubtedly objects highly alluring to a government.—They fill the public coffers and enable govenment to reward its minions at a cheap rate.—They are a profitable kind of revenge and gratify the officers about a court, who study their own interests more than corporal punishment.—Perhaps they have at all times been more eagerly pursued than mere criminal prosecutions.—Shall trial by jury be taken away in all these cases and shall we still be told that "we are effectually secured against the oppressions of government?" At this rate Judges may sit in the United States, as they did in some instances before the war, without a jury to condemn people's property and extract money from their pockets, to be put into the pockets of the judges themselves who condemn them; and we shall be told that we are safe from the oppression of government.—No, Mr. Printer, we ought not to part with the trial by jury; we ought to guard this and many other privileges by a bill of rights, which cannot be invaded.

DHRC, XIII, pp. 426-428. The series "An Old Whig" is reprinted in Storing, III, starting on p. 17.

Louis Guillaume Otto (New York) October 20, 1787
Letter: To Comte de Montmorin (excerpts)

In admiring the wisdom, foresight and talents of those who have designed this new plan, and even agreeing with them that nothing could at this moment be more glorious for the united States, I cannot refrain, My Lord, from submitting to You the reflections of those who consider this plan only from the point of view of *public liberty*. . . . ["]The Congress will be able to raise Armies and fit out fleets; will it not be as concerned as the Roman Senate was with instigating wars in order to maintain many troops and afterwards to employ them in the destruction of liberty?—The Congress will impose whatever taxes it judges appropriate, it will levy imposts, borrow money; will not the Sums raised be used to corrupt the elections? to whom will it be accountable for the Sums raised?—to the people? they will not know how to judge; to the President? he will have a good share of the spoils.—The Congress will suspend the writ *of habeas corpus* in case of rebellion; but if this rebellion was only a resistance to usurpation, who will be the Judge? the usurper.—The Constitution is not even accompanied by a *Declaration of rights*, so that no recourse remains for the Citizen against oppression. It is the same with the States; since the Constitution does not permit them to conclude treaties, to combine among themselves, to emit paper money, to raise troops or taxes without the consent of Congress. In England the right of resistance is part of the Constitution, here it is not even mentioned.—All civil cases will be decided in the supreme Court without benefit of Juries[."]

DHRC, XIII, pp. 423-424.

An American Citizen IV {Tench Coxe} October 21, 1787
Broadside: (excerpts)
Philadelphia

Laws, made after the commission of the fact, have been a dreadful engine in the hands of tyrannical governors. Some of the most virtuous and shining characters in the world have been put to death, by laws *formed to render them punishable*, for parts of their conduct which *innocence permitted*, and to which *patriotism impelled them*. These have been called *ex post facto* laws, and are exploded by the new system. If a time of public contention shall hereafter arrive, *the firm and ardent friends to liberty* may know the length to which they can push their noble opposition, on the foundation of the laws. Should their country's cause impel them further, they will be acquainted with the hazard, and using those arms which Providence has put into their hands, will make a solemn appeal to "*the power above.*" . . .

The old foederal Constitution contained many of *the same things*, which from error or disingenuousness are urged against the new one. *Neither* of them have a bill of rights, *nor does either* notice the liberty of the press, because they are already provided for *by the State Constitutions;* and relating only to *personal* rights, they could not be mentioned *in a contract among sovereign states.* . . .

The apprehensions of the people have been excited, perhaps by persons with good intentions, about the powers of the new government to raise an army. Let us consider this point with moderation and candor. As enemies will sometimes insult us, invade our country, and capture our property, it is clear a power in our government to oppose, restrain or destroy them, is necessary to our honor, safety and existence. The military should, however, be regarded *with a watchful eye;* for it is a profession that is liable to dangerous perversion. But the powers vested in the foederal government *do not go the length* which has been said. *A standing army is not granted or intended,* for there can be no provision for its continuing three years, much less for its *permanent establishment.* Two years are the utmost time for which the money can be given. It will be under all the restrictions which *wisdom and jealousy can suggest,* and the original grant of the supplies must be made by the House of Representatives, *the immediate delegates of the people.* The Senate and President, who also derive their power from *the people,* appoint the officers; and the heads of the departments, *who must submit their accounts to the whole legislature,* are to pay and provide them, *as shall be directed by the laws that shall contain the conditions of the grant.* The militia, *who are in fact the effective part of the people at large,* will render many troops *quite unnecessary.* They will form a *powerful check* upon the regular troops, and will generally be sufficient *to overawe them*—for our *detached* situation will seldom give occasion to raise an army, though *a few scattered companies* may often be necessary. But whenever, *even on the most obvious reasons,* an army shall be raised, the several states shall be called, *by the nature of things,* to attend to the condition of *the militia.* Republican jealousy, *the guardian Angel of these states,* will watch the motions of our military citizens, even though they will be the soldiers of a free people. There is a wide difference between the troops of such a commonwealth as ours, *founded on equal and unalterable principles,* and those of a regal government, where ambition and oppression are *the profession of the king.* In the first case, a military officer is *the occasional servant of the people, employed for their defence;* in the second, he is *the ever ready instrument* to execute the schemes of conquest or oppression, with which the mind of his royal master may be disturbed. . . .

Besides the securities for the liberties of the people arising out of the foederal government, they are guarded by *their state constitutions, and by the nature of things in the separate states.*

DHRC, XIII, pp. 431-436. Reprinted in *Pamphlets*, p. 145.

Louis Guillaume Otto (New York) October 23, 1787
Letter: To Comte de Montmorin (excerpt)

The dissolution of the General Convention having caused a great number of members of Congress to return to New York, this assembly has resumed its sessions. It has begun by debating the plan of the new government, but discovering that the opposition was very strong, they limited themselves to referring this plan to the different states without either approving or disapproving it. It is surprising to see the Congress itself is not in agreement over the great powers which the new Constitution allots it. Mr. Richard Henry Lee, former President, is at the head of the opposition. Although elected a member of the Philadelphia convention, he continually refused to attend it. He does not find the situation of the United States so hopeless, that one might have need of recourse to violent remedies. He disapproves especially that the government might have been accorded immense powers without preceding the Constitution with a *bill of rights,* which has always been regarded as the palladium of a free people. "If," he said, "in place of a virtuous and patriotic President we are given a William the Conqueror, what will become of liberty? How to prevent usurpation? Where is the contract between the nation and the government? The Constitution makes mention only of those who govern, never of the rights of the governed." This new Gracchus, sir, has all the necessary talents for making an impression. He has against him men equally distinguished by their merit, their learning, their services; but he pleads the cause of the people.

DHRC, I, p. 352.

Essay on Federal Sentiments October 23, 1787

Newspaper Article: Philadelphia *Independent Gazetteer* (excerpt)

The best mode of government is occasionally tinctured by the follies and vices of men; without a degree of national virtue it must even lose all energy, because bad men are incapable of liberty. That the Senate could ever erect itself into a permanent aristocracy by assuming the whole sovereign power, is a chimara, that hardly deserves a serious refutation. However great and general national depravity might be, it is impossible that a few men can become kings, while so many are their equals in fortune, and some no doubt in abilities; and while the great majority of the people have a considerable share of property: which must be the case in America for many ages. Aristocracies whether landed or commercial can only arise from a very great inequality of wealth. If the president and the whole senate should happen to be the boldest wealthiest, most artful men in the union, supported by the most powerful connexions, and unanimous in the design of subduing the nation; and if by the concurrence of the representatives they obtained money and troops for the purpose; yet the whole personal influence of the Congress, and their parricide army could never prevail over an hundred thousand men armed and disciplined, owners of the country, animated not only with a spirit of liberty, but ardent resentment against base treacherous tyrants.

DHRC, II Mfm. Pa., pp. 800-801.

A Citizen October 24, 1787

Newspaper Article: *Carlisle Gazette* (excerpt)

To the People of Pennsylvania. . . .
The consideration of the nature and object of this general government will also shew you how weak it is to talk of a bill of rights in it. It is a government of states; not of individuals. The constitution of each state has a bill of rights for its own citizens; and the proposed plan guaranties to every state a republican form of government for ever. But it would be a novelty indeed to form a bill of rights for states. The same observation will apply to the liberty of the press; which is secured by each state to itself—and also to trial by jury in many civil causes that may come before the courts of congress.

DHRC, II Mfm. Pa., p. 820.

Centinel II October 24, 1787
Newspaper Article: Philadelphia *Independent Gazetteer* (excerpts)

To the PEOPLE *of* PENNSYLVANIA.

FRIENDS, COUNTRYMEN, *and* FELLOW-CITIZENS, As long as the liberty of the press continues unviolated, and the people have the right of expressing and publishing their sentiments upon every public measure, it is next to impossible to enslave a free nation. The state of society must be very corrupt and base indeed, when the people in possession of such a monitor as the press, can be induced to exchange the heavenborn blessings of liberty for the galling chains of despotism.—Men of an aspiring and tyrannical disposition, sensible of this truth, have ever been inimical to the press, and have considered the shackling of it, as the first step towards the accomplishment of their hateful domination, and the entire suppression of all liberty of public discussion, as necessary to its support.—For even a standing army, that grand engine of oppression, if it were as numerous as the abilities of any nation could maintain, would not be equal to the purposes of despotism over an enlightened people.

The abolition of that grand palladium of freedom, the liberty of the press, in the proposed plan of government, and the conduct of its authors, and patrons, is a striking exemplification of these observations. The reason assigned for the omission of a *bill of rights,* securing the *liberty of the press,* and *other invaluable personal rights,* is an insult on the understanding of the people. . . .

Mr. *Wilson* asks, "What controul can proceed from the federal government to shackle or destroy that *sacred palladium* of national freedom, the *liberty of the press?*" What!—Cannot Congress, when possessed of the immense authority proposed to be devolved, restrain the printers, and put them under regulation.—Recollect that the omnipotence of the federal legislature over the State establishments is recognized by a special article, viz.—"that this Constitution, and the laws of the United States which shall be made in pursuance thereof, and all treaties made, or which shall be made, under the authority of the United States, shall be the *supreme law* of the land; and the judges in every State shall be bound thereby, any thing in the *Constitutions* or laws of any State to the contrary notwithstanding."—After such a declaration, what security does the *Constitutions* of the several States afford for the *liberty of the press and other invaluable personal rights,* not provided for by the new plan?—Does not this sweeping clause subject every thing to the controul of Congress?

In the plan of Confederation of 1778, now existing, it was thought proper by Article the 2d, to declare that "each State retains its sovereignty, freedom and independence, and every power, jurisdiction and right, which is not by this Confederation expressly delegated to the United States in Congress assembled." *Positive* grant was not *then* thought sufficiently descriptive and restraining upon Congress, and the omission of such a declaration *now,* when such great devolutions of power are proposed, manifests the design of reducing the several States to shadows. But Mr. Wilson tells you, that every right and power not specially granted to Congress is considered as withheld. How does this appear? Is this principle established by the proper authority? Has the Convention made such a stipulation? By no means. Quite the reverse; the *laws* of Congress are to be "the *supreme law* of the land, any thing in the *Constitutions* or laws of any State to the contrary notwithstanding;" and consequently, would be *paramount* to all *State* authorities. The lust of power is so universal, that a speculative unascertained rule of construction would be a *poor* security for the liberties of the people. . . .

Mr. *Wilson* skips very lightly over the danger apprehended from the standing army allowed by the new plan. This grand machine of power and oppression, may be made a fatal instrument to overturn the public liberties, especially as the funds to support the troops may be granted for *two* years, whereas in Britain, the grants ever since the revolution in 1688, have been *from year to year.* A standing army with regular provision of pay and contingencies, would afford a strong temptation to some ambitious man to step up into the throne, and to seize absolute power. The keeping on foot a hired military force *in time of peace,* ought not to be gone into, unless *two thirds* of the members of the federal legislature agree to the necessity of the measure, and adjust the numbers employed. Surely Mr. *Wilson* is not serious when he adduces the instance of the troops now stationed on the Ohio, as a proof of the propriety of a standing army.—they are a mere occasional armament for the purpose of restraining divers hostile tribes of savages. It is contended that under the present confederation, Congress possess the power of raising armies at pleasure; but the opportunity which the states severally have of withholding the supplies necessary to keep these armies on foot, is a sufficient check on the *present* Congress. . . .

From the foregoing illustration of the powers proposed to be devolved to Congress, it is evident, that the general government would necessarily annihilate the particular governments, and that the security of the personal rights of the people by the state constitutions is superseded and destroyed; hence results the necessity of such security being provided for by a bill of rights to be inserted in the new plan of federal government. What excuse can we then make for the omission of this grand palladium, this barrier between *liberty* and *oppression*. For universal experience demonstrates the necessity of the most express declarations and restrictions, to protect the rights and liberties of mankind, from the silent, powerful and ever active conspiracy of those who govern.

The new plan, it is true, does propose to secure the people of the benefit of personal liberty by the *habeas corpus;* and trial by jury for all crimes, except in case of impeachment: but there is no declaration, that all men have a natural and unalienable right to worship Almighty God, according to the dictates of their own consciences and understanding; and that no man ought, or of right can be compelled to attend any religious worship, or erect or support any place of worship, or maintain any ministry, contrary to, or against his own free will and consent; and that no authority can or ought to be vested in, or assumed by any power whatever, that shall in any case interfere with, or in any manner controul, the rights of conscience in the free exercise of religious worship: that the trial by jury in civil causes as well as criminal, and the modes prescribed by the common law for safety of life in ciminal prosecutions shall be held sacred; that the requiring of excessive bail, imposing of excessive fines and cruel and unusual punishments be forbidden; that monopolies in trade or arts, other than to authors of books or inventors of useful arts, for a reasonable time, ought not to be suffered; that the right of the people to assemble peaceably for the purpose of consulting about public matters, and petitioning or remonstrating to the federal legislature ought not to be prevented; that *the liberty of the press be held sacred;* that the people have a right to hold themselves, their houses, papers and possessions free from search or seizure; and that therefore warrants without oaths or affirmations first made, affording a sufficient foundation for them, and whereby any officer or messenger may be commanded or required to search suspected places, or to seize any person or his property, not particularly described, are contrary to that right and ought not to be granted; and that standing armies in time of peace are dangerous to liberty, and ought not to be permitted but when absolutely necessary; all which is omitted to be done in the proposed government.

DHRC, XIII, p. 457-467.

New Haven *Connecticut Journal* October 24, 1787
Newspaper Article: A letter from a gentleman in a neighbouring state (Massachusetts), to a gentleman in this city. (excerpt)[1]

My next objection is to the 12th paragraph of section 8th, in these words: "To raise and support armies, but no appropriation of money to that use shall be for a longer term than two years." A great deal of mischief may be done in two years, with *guns, swords*, and *bayonets*, and armies when once *raised*, it hath sometimes been found difficult to *disband*. I should therefore not think it prudent for Congress ever to raise an army merely to subdue *Wabash Indians* or any one single tribe. Should there be a general combination of all the tribes, or the states be invaded by a foreign enemy, Congress by our present Articles of Confederation are vested with full powers to draw out the military force of the states, nor have the states failed hitherto of compliance in this regard; but to limit them to two years is an affront offered to the dignity of Congress, and appears as tho we were afraid to trust the military force of the states in their hands, when there is just occasion. I take that to be one principal part of the business of congress, to conduct the military arrangements of all the states, when judged necessary for the general safety. My next objection is to the 15th paragraph, which is in these words: "Congress shall have power to provide for calling forth the militia to execute the laws of the union, suppress insurrections, and repel invasions." This looks too much like Baron Stuben's *militia*, by which a *standing army* was meant and intended;[2] I would only observe, to take the military force of the states out of the hands of their respective governors is a manifest indignity offered to them, as they ever have had the sole and exclusive command of the militia of the respective states. I observe the expression used is: "To *execute the laws of the union.*" In fact it means, to convert the *militia* of the states into a *standing army* under the entire command and control of Congress; and I would only observe further, *that government* and *those laws* which require a standing army to enforce them ought not to be supported in any nation under Heaven.[3]

1 DHRC, III, p. 378. Also reprinted in Storing, IV, pp. 11-12.

2 See "A Countryman," January 22, 1788, p. 224, at note 2, for another reference to Baron von Steuben. The Baron indicated in his proposal that it was, in fact, a standing army. His pamphlet was entitled, *A Letter on the Subject of an Established Militia, and Military Arrangements, Addressed to the Inhabitants of the United States*. (New York, [1784], Evans 44601). He also indicated that the "best possible magazine for a Republic" was to have arms and accoutrements "put into the hands of every member of the community."

3 See New Haven *Connecticut Journal*, October 31, 1787, p. 74, for a reply.

Virginia House of Delegates October 25, 1787
Debates (excerpt)

On Thursday last, the House of Delegates of this state took under consideration the resolution of Congress, by which the appointment of a State-Convention was recommended to the different Legislatures in the Union. The Speaker left his seat, and placed Mr. Matthews in the chair.

Mr. Corbin opened the debate; and after having mentioned the critical situation of public affairs, and the necessity of establishing our union on a firm and unalterable basis, spoke with approbation of the new plan of federal government. He closed an elegant and judicious speech with proposing several resolutions, the principal of which was to this effect:—That a Convention should be called, according to the recommendation of Congress.

Mr. Henry rose to oppose the resolution as it then stood. He did not question the propriety or necessity of calling a Convention. No man, he said, was more truly federal than himself: But he conceived that if this resolution was adopted, the convention would only have it in their power to say, that the new plan should *be adopted, or rejected;* and that, however defective it might appear to them, they would not be authorized to propose amendments. The resolution was, that a Convention should be called according to the recommendation of Congress. Congress had recommended that measure, according to the resolution of the Grand Convention; which was merely that a Convention might be called to give their assent and ratification. He therefore thought, that if the people acted under the resolution proposed by Mr. Corbin, the extent of which was only to be ascertained by referring to the resolution of the Federal Convention, the powers of the State Convention would not be sufficient. It was possible that there might be some errors in the new government: Nay, he would not hesitate to declare, that there were errors and defects in it; and he therefore proposed the addition of some words to Mr. Corbin's resolution, by which the power of proposing amendments might be given.

Mr. Corbin defended the resolution which he had proposed.

Mr. George Nicholas seconded his defence. He warmly reprobated Mr. Henry's amendment; because, he said, it would convey an idea to the people of this state, and to the whole continent, that the Legislature of Virginia thought that amendments might be made to the new government; whereas he believed the truth to be, that there was a decided majority in its favour. At the same time neither he nor Mr. Corbin denied the right of the Convention to propose amendments.

Mr. Mason, who had just taken his seat in the House, rose to second Mr. Henry's motion. He told the Committee that he felt somewhat embarrassed at the situation in which he then stood. He had been honored with a seat in the Federal Convention, and all knew that he had refused to subscribe to their proceedings. This might excite some surprize; but it was not necessary at that hour, he said, to make known his reasons. At a proper season, they should be communicated to his countrymen. He would however declare, that no man was more completely federal in his principles than he was: That from the east of New-Hampshire to the south of Georgia, there was not a man more fully convinced of the necessity of establishing some general government: That he regarded our perfect union as the rock of our political salvation: But, that he had considered the new federal government according to that measure of knowledge which God had given him—that he had endeavoured to make himself master of the important subject—that he had deeply and maturely weighed every article of the constitution; and with every information which he could derive, either from his own reflection, or the observations of others, he could not approve it. He said, I thought it wrong, Mr. Chairman,—I thought it repugnant to our highest interests,—and if with these sentiments I had subscribed to it, I might have been justly regarded as a traitor to my country. I would have lost this hand, before it should have marked my name to the new government.

Mr. Marshall, with his usual perspicuity, stated the matter in controversy. He though Mr. Corbin's resolution improper, for the reasons stated by Mr. Henry. He thought Mr. Henry's amendment improper, for the reasons urged by Mr. Nicholas. He wished, he said, that the future Convention should have the fullest latitude in their deliberations—that they should exercise the privilege which belonged to the free representatives of a free country, of considering fully and in every point of view, the nature of the government under which we are to live: But he thought with Mr. Nicholas, that the people should have no reason to suppose that their Legislature disapproved the new federal government; and therefore proposed that the Committee should come to this resolution;—That a Convention should be called, and that the new Constitution should be laid before them for their free and ample discussion.

The Committee came into Mr. Marshall's opinion, and a resolution passed accordingly, without opposition.

DHRC, VIII, pp. 112-114.

An Old Constitutionalist October 26, 1787
Newspaper Article: Philadelphia *Independent Gazetteer* (excerpt)

I will conclude this letter with observing—that it is the undoubted right of every free citizen in America, to take under their consideration the proposed federal constitution, and examine it candidly and deliberately—and if they find that it secures unto them those privileges, which they are intitled to as *freemen*, then let them unanimously adopt it. But on the contrary, if it deprives us of those rights, which should be secured to us by a *bill of rights*, and if we shall not be granted the privilege of either altering or amending, then let us with manly fortitude reject it.

DHRC, II Mfm. Pa., p. 861.

A Confederationalist October 27, 1787
Newspaper Article: Philadelphia *Pennsylvania Herald* (excerpt)[1]

Had the convention thought proper to have published the minutes of their proceedings, then we should have seen who proposed, and who prevented certain measures. We might then have seen the venerable Franklin advocating the liberty of the press, the trial by jury, and all the natural rights of freemen, which are now either not secured or tacitly taken away. We might then have seen a Washington quitting his chair to advocate the rights of his country and insisting upon proper guards and securities for the liberties of the people. But as the public information now stands, the good and the bad are so mingled together, that except in certain cases and as to certain persons we have nothing to judge from. The best propositions for the liberty of the people may have been overruled: and the worst may have been carried. Let not the advocates for despotism think themselves secure in carrying this high handed plan of power, because the respected names of Washington and Franklin appear as witnesses—perhaps unwilling witnesses, that it was agreed to by "the states present." Let it be remembered that they had, but each a vote, and that the vote of ________ was equal to that of the first patriots. Let it be remembered also that General Washington being in the chair he seldom, perhaps never, had it in his power to give his opinion or enter into debate.

But after all, it is a plan submitted to the consideration of the people: and whether the officers of the present government, or those who are arriving at offices under the new, are for it or against, matters not: Those are not the marks by which it ought to be either received or rejected. The jury to question is, whether it is a plan of government formed upon *revolution principles,* and the liberty and happiness of the people fully and effectually secured? If it be such a plan of government as the people, who are, and ought, and WILL be the judges, believe has the essentials for these grand ends: it will be adopted in the face of all the opposition that the officers of the present government can possibly make to it. If not all those who are waiting to fill the numerous offices which will be created by it, if adopted, cannot possibly impose it on the people. I say the question ought to be whether the plan, if adopted, will secure to the people the blessings of a free and equal government? And surely it will be allowed that disputing about the persons who approve or disapprove, will never enable us to answer this question. Let the plan itself be considered, the objections made against it—and the answers to those objections. Certainly this is the only mode upon which a sensible and enlightened people ought to determine. I must own that I read the objections made to the proposed plan of government with a degree of resentment—yet I wished to see them answered. But when I see them repeatedly made, and no attempt to answer them but by abusing the supposed authors, I begin to think them serious, and that they demand attention. The liberty of the press, for example, is said to be invaded, or not secured. How is the objection answered? Why either by direct abuse, or by direct contradiction, without any argument to shew the complaint ill-founded.

Permit me Mr. Editor to make a few remarks upon a piece in the paper of Messrs. Hall and Sellers of Wednesday last, signed, "Federal Constitution."[2] This writer tells us that the convention, "neglected" to mention, "the liberty of the press from a respect to the state constitutions," in each of which it is secured. But surely sir, the gentleman must be mistaken, for it is plain that the constitutions of the states are absolutely destroyed—not by construction only—for the thing is done in plain words: there is nothing equivocal or ambiguous in the expression. The words are, "This constitution, *and all the laws* of the United States which shall be made in pursuance thereof, and all treaties made or which shall be made, under the authority of the United States, *shall be,* the supreme law of the land, and the judges in every state shall be bound thereby, any thing in the constitutions or laws of any state to the contrary notwithstanding." I ask, is there a man of common understanding that can hesitate as to the full and plain meaning of those words? At least to my sense there can be nothing more clearly expressed or easier understood, "he that runs may read." I beg leave to be understood, that I am not now arguing against the propriety of vesting the supreme power in congress, and of setting the constitution and laws of Congress above those of the separate states: perhaps it is right and best that it should be so. But I do insist, that before the people give up to congress the rights and privileges secured to them by the constitution of the state, they ought to have those rights and privileges fully and unequivocally secured to them by an instrument which *shall compose part of the federal constitution.* The writer above hinted at informs us that the "liberty of the press would have been an inherent and political right as long as nothing was said against it." I say that a declaration of those inherent and political rights ought to be made in a BILL OF RIGHTS, that the people may never lose their liberties by construction. If the liberty of the press be an inherent political right, let it be so declared, that no despot however great shall *dare to gain say it.* If it is not so declared it may be denied. Declare it to be an inherent and political right, and that it ought to be held sacred, and we then shall be certain upon what ground we stand. When this declaration is made, let the *attorney general,* of the United States, *file an information* against me for a *libel;* I will carry that declaration in my hand, as my shield and my constitutional defence.

1 DHRC, II Mfm. Pa., pp. 866-870.
2 See "Foederal Constitution," October 10, 1787, p. 37.

An Old Whig IV October 27, 1787
Newspaper Article: Philadelphia *Independent Gazetteer* (excerpt)

In this country perhaps we are possessed of more than our share of political virtue. If we will exercise a little patience, and bestow our best endeavours on the business, I do not think it impossible, that we may yet form a federal constitution, much superior to any form of government, which has ever existed in the world;—but, whenever this important work shall be accomplished, I venture to pronounce, that it will not be done without a *careful attention to the framing of a bill of rights.*

Much has been said and written, on the subject of a bill of rights;—possibly without sufficient attention to the necessity of conveying distinct and precise ideas of the true meaning of a bill of rights. Your readers, I hope, will excuse me, if I conclude this letter with an attempt to throw some light on this subject.

Men when they enter into society, yield up a part of their natural liberty, for the sake of being protected by government. If they yield up all their natural rights they are absolute slaves to their governors.

If they yield up less than is necessary, the government is so feeble, that it cannot protect them.—To yield up so much, as is necessary for the purposes of government; and to retain all beyond what is necessary, is the great point, which ought, if possible, to be attained in the formation of a constitution. At the same time that by these means, the liberty of the subject is secured, the government is really strengthened; because wherever the subject is convinced that nothing more is required from him, than what is necessary for the good of the community, he yields a chearful obedience, which is more useful than the constrained service of slaves.—To define what portion of his natural liberty, the subject shall at all times be entitled to retain, is one great end of a bill of rights. To these may be added in a bill of rights some particular engagements of protection, on the part of government, without such a bill of rights, firmly securing the privileges of the subject, the government is always in danger of degenerating into tyranny; for it is certainly true, that "in establishing the powers of government, the rulers are invested with every right and authority, which is not in explicit terms reserved."—Hence it is, that we find the rulers so often lording over the people at their will and pleasure. Hence it is that we find the patriots, in all ages of the world, so very solicitous to obtain explicit engagements from their rulers, stipulating, expressly, for the preservation of particular rights and privileges.

In different nations, we find different grants or reservations of privileges appealed to in the struggles between the rulers and the people, many of which in the different nations of Europe, have long since been swallowed up and lost by time, or destroyed by the arbitrary hand of power. In England we find the people, with the Barons at their head, exacting a solemn resignation of their rights from king John, in their celebrated *magna charta*, which was many times renewed in Parliament, during the reigns of his successors. The *petition of rights* was afterwards consented to by Charles the first, and contained a declaration of the liberties of the people. The *habeus corpus act*, after the restoration of Charles the Second, *the bill of rights*, which was obtained from the Prince and Princess of Orange on their accession to the throne and the act of settlement, at the accession of the Hanover family, are other instances to shew the care and watchfulness of that nation, to improve every opportunity, of the reign of a weak prince, or the revolution in their government, to obtain the most explicit declarations in favor of their liberties. In like manner the people of this country, at the revolution, having all power in their own hands, in forming the constitutions of the several states, took care to secure themselves by bills of rights, so as to prevent, as far as possible, the encroachments of their future rulers upon the rights of the people. Some of these rights are said to be *unalienable*, such as the rights of conscience: yet even these have been often invaded, where they have not been carefully secured by express and solemn bills and declarations in their favor.

Before we establish a government, whose acts will be THE SUPREME LAW OF THE LAND, and whose power will extend to almost every case without exception, we ought carefully to guard ourselves by a BILL OF RIGHTS, against the invasion of those liberties which it is essential for us to retain, which it is of no real use to government to strip us of; but which in the course of human events have been too often insulted with all the wantonness of an idle barbarity.

DHRC, XIII, pp. 500-502. The series "An Old Whig" is reprinted in Storing, III, starting on p. 17.

M.C. October 27, 1787
Newspaper Article: Philadelphia *Pennsylvania Herald*

The present is universally acknowledged to be a most momentous era, as likely to decide the fate of a world for future ages. This consideration renders it the duty of every individual to submit to the consideration of his fellow citizens whatever he may deem calculated to elucidate the grand subject in general discussion.

The opposition to the new Constitution is said to be made by interested men. This assertion is true only in part. It is possible, indeed, that the most violent, the most active, and the most voluminous writers against the proposed system are generally influenced by sinister and personal considerations. But there are many persons whose apprehensions have been excited by the Centinels, the Old Whigs, the Democratic Federalists, and the Catos, and whose opposition is patriotic and disinterested, as they are fearful for the liberty of posterity and anxious to prevent future encroachments of Congress. To satisfy the minds of those people, I venture, but with great diffidence, to propose a plan, which may possibly remove [a] great part of the present opposition.

Let a meeting of the citizens be called, and a proper committee appointed to frame a bill of rights, for securing the liberty of the press and all other rights which the states hold sacred. Let this bill of rights be transmitted to the several state conventions to be taken into consideration with the new Constitution. Little doubt need be entertained but that it would be universally agreed to.

This measure, if adopted, would draw a line of distinction between the detestable few who would sacrifice the interest and happiness of not only the present, but distant generations to their own emolument, and those who oppose the new system from a patriotic, but perhaps mistaken, dread of danger. The former would be left destitute of the vain covering under which they shelter their want of virtue and public spirit, and the latter would become zealous Federalists.

To the friends of the proposed Constitution, I beg leave to observe, that this measure cannot possibly retard or affect the success of a plan which has justly met with their admiration. Even admitting that no such precaution is really necessary, would it not be advisable to indulge the honest prejudices of many of their fellow citizens? This much, at least, may be said in favor of my plan, that even if it does no good, it can do no possible injury.

I submit it to the candor of the opposers of the new Constitution whether it would not be better to unite in this or some similar plan, than to attempt to defeat the wishes and desires of the continent for an efficient form of government, which is confessedly all that is necessary to restore America to her lost splendor, consequence, credit, and happiness?

Should this hint be attended to and produce the good effect I hope for, I shall esteem it the most fortunate idea that ever occurred to your humble servant, M.C.

DHRC, II, pp. 203-204. Also reprinted in DHRC, XIII, pp. 502-503.

John De Witt II October 27, 1787
Newpaper Article: Boston *American Herald* (excerpts)

[TO THE FREE CITIZENS OF THE COMMONWEALTH OF MASSACHUSETTS]

That the want of a Bill of Rights to accompany this proposed System, is a solid objection to it, provided there is nothing exceptionable in the System itself, I do not assert.—If, however, there is at any time, a propriety in having one, it would not have been amiss here. A people, entering into society, surrender such a part of their natural rights, as shall be necessary for the existence of that society. They are so precious in themselves, that they would never be parted with, did not the preservation of the remainder require it. They are entrusted in the hands of those, who are very willing to receive them, who are naturally fond of exercising of them, and whose passions are always striving to make a bad use of them.—They are conveyed by a written compact, expressing those which are given up, and the mode in which those reserved shall be secured. Language is so easy of explanation, and so diffucult is it by words to convey exact ideas that the party to be governed cannot be too explicit. The line cannot be drawn with too much precision and accuracy. The necessity of this accuracy and this precision encreases in proportion to the greatness of the sacrifice and the numbers who make it.—That a Constitution for the United States does not require a Bill of Rights, when it is considered, that a Constitution for an individual State would, I cannot conceive.—The difference between them is only in the numbers of the parties concerned: They are both a compact between the Governors and Governed, the letter of which must be adhered to in discussing their powers. That which is not expressly granted, is of course retained.

The Compact itself is a recital upon paper of that proportion of the subject's natural rights, intended to be parted with, for the benefit of adverting to it in case of dispute. Miserable indeed would be the situation of those individual States who have not prefixed to their Constitution a Bill of Rights, if, as a very respectable, learned Gentleman at the Southward observes, "the people, when they established the powers of legislation under Representatives with every right and authority which they did not, in explicit terms, reserve; and therefore upon every question, respecting the justification of the House or Assembly, if the Frame of Government is silent, the jurisdiction is efficient and complete." In other words, those powers which the people by their Constitutions expressly give them, they enjoy by positive grant, and those remaining ones, which they never meant to give them, and which the Constitutions say nothing about, they enjoy by tacit implication, so that by one means and by the other, they become possessed of the whole. This doctrine is but poorly calculated for the meridian of America, where the nature of compact, the mode of construing them, and the principles upon which society is founded, are so accurately known and universally diffused. That insatiable thirst for unconditional controul over our fellow-creatures, and the facility of sounds to convey essentially different ideas, produced the first Bill of Rights ever prefixed to a Frame of Government. The people, altho' fully sensible that they reserved every tittle of power they did not expressly grant away, yet afraid that the words made use of, to express those rights so granted might convey more than they originally intended, they chose at the same moment to express in different language those rights which the agreement did not include, and which they never designed to part with, endeavoring thereby to prevent any cause for future altercation and the intrusion into society of that doctrine of tacit implication which has been the favorite theme of every tyrant from the origin of all governments to the present day. . . .

That the power of organizing, arming and disciplining the militia shall be lodged in them, and this thro' fear they shall not be sufficiently attentive to keeping so respectable a body of men as the yeomanry of this Commonwealth, compleatly armed, organized and disciplined; they shall also have the power of raising, supporting and establishing a standing army in time of peace in your several towns, and I see not why in your several houses[.]

Kenyon, pp. 98-101. The "John De Witt" series is reprinted in Storing, IV, starting at p. 15.

George Lee Turberville (Charleston) October 28, 1787
Letter: To Arthur Lee (excerpt)

Mr. Wilsons sophism has no weight with me when he declares—that at the formation of the state Legislatures we gave up all that we did not reserve—& that in this Constitution we retain all that we do not give up, because I cannot observe upon what foundation he has rested this curious observation—the same reason is applicable in both cases, to my comprehension—& this points out to me the absolute necessity of a bill of rights—and that a very full & explanatory one too—where not only the Liberty of the press, the trial by Jury of the vicinage & all those great points—but even every the most trivial priviledge that Citizens have a right to possess—shou'd be expressly stipulated and reserved—& the violation of them most scrupulously & Jealously guarded against—Of what consequence is the federal guarantee of republican governments to the individual states, when the power of the Militia's even is rested in the president—

DHRC, XIII, p. 506.

Arthur Lee (New York) October 29, 1787
Letter: To Edward Rutledge (excerpt)

The proposed Constitution begins to undergoe a very serious discussion. The first impression was so favorable, that you will not be surprised at its losing ground. This change of sentiment is such as to render it very doubful, whether it will be adopted even in Pensylvania.

In this State it is thought there is already a majority against it, & in Virginia the opposition is formidable. For my own part, I do not like it. The want of a promised declaration of rights, when by some exceptions in the Body of it, things, in which no power is expressly given, implies that every thing not excepted is given; is a very material defect.

DHRC, XIII, p. 510. Also reprinted in DHRC, VIII, p. 131.

Richmond *Virginia Independent Chronicle* October 31, 1787

Mr. W[ilson]'s speech to the meeting at Philadelphia, says a correspondent, is really a laughable performance. *When the people,* said the orator, *established the powers of legislation under their separate governments, they vested their representatives with every right and authority, which they did not in explicit terms reserve; but the congressional authority is to be collected from the positive grant alone, expressed in the instrument.* This, it seems, is so self-evident a principle, as to be never in danger of being questioned in future, and it will no doubt be sufficient security for posterity to know, that a Pennsylvania attorney established it; and from thence thought himself sufficiently authorised to draw the following conclusion. "Hence it is *evident* that in the former case every thing which is not reserved is given, but, in the latter the reverse prevails, and every thing which is not given is reserved." Bravo J——y! this is rare security for the liberty of the press, "that sacred palladium of national freedom."

The futility of this assertion, that, "the trial by jury is abolished in civil cases," is detected by him, "taking the advantage of his professional experience," and from this we learn, that it is not yet abolished, but that it may, if Congress think fit; but he undoubtedly knows, that juries are found inconvenient in excise business. He says, that *the vesting of a power in Congress to keep up a standing army in time of peace is no new prerogative, because it is exercised at present on the banks of the Ohio:* But this subtle reasoner did not consider, that it is now a time of war on the banks of the Ohio.

There never was a charge, said he, *made with less reason than that of the dread of an aristocracy from this Foederal Constitution,* and he proves it by Mr. *Adams*'s doctrine of balances; but neither he, nor the *balancer,* ever considered the futility of that doctrine in a country, where the members composing the different departments of government are necessarily of the same rank, have the same views and interests, and where the only balance, which it was of consequence to attend to, is that between the governors and the governed, has been unfortunately forgotten in this Foederal Constitution.

In the next place he tells us, much to the purpose, that *those who have used the word, corporation, are not aware of its extent, that though in common parlance, it signifies petty associations, it may be applied even to the Foederal Union.* In the same manner, it may be said, that those, who make use of the word, *Chief Magistrate,* applied to our governor, do not know the extent of it; as it may also be applied to the *Grand Sultan.* But the strength of his argument is yet to come, for he plainly *proves* that the Foederal Constitution does not annihilate the state governments, because it calls them *Legislatures.* They would be cross children indeed, who would cry for a whistle when they get something in the shape of one, especially, when the name *whistle* is given to it.

But why shall we be so wayward as to be alarmed at Congress's having the power of internal taxation and of laying on excise duties, do not we hear how he says: "I will venture to predict, that the great revenue of the United States must and always will be raised by impost, for being less obnoxious and more productive, the interests of the government will be best promoted by the accommodation of the people." It would seem then, that dominion not revenue was the motive of inserting it; but no matter, let us give up our liberties, there is no danger, he says we shall be kindly used, and that we shall have a LEGISLATURE, sure never there was as more explicit bill of rights!!! He says, that it is only interested people, who set their faces against the Foederal Constitution, it is really a pity that it should miscarry, for he has given the public so striking a specimen of his abilities, that, no doubt, he would get much practice in the supreme Foederal Court, should it be thought advisable to allow the benefit of council there.

DHRC, VIII, pp. 138-139.

Philadelphia *Freeman's Journal* October 31, 1787

A late letter from Boston to a gentleman in this town, says, "Matters have been carried with a high hand here, in regard to the discussion of the new form of government—*Mum* is the word—I am sorry to say that the sentiment of a Roman poet may be applied with too much justice.

"Stranger to flattery and to fear
With pure unsullied honour bright

VIRTUE disdains to lend an ear
To the mad people's sense of right."

Some of the Newsprinters in this city, to their eternal disgrace, have refused to publish any pieces tending to examine that new code, *unless the name of the author or authors be left with them*, which at present is as much as to say, Give me a stick, and I will break your head.—At the same time they, very impertinently, take upon them to style all *such productions* "wicked, rascally, malicious." &c.—I had hitherto supposed *a printer* ought to be above prejudices of this nature, and not capable of being so easily actuated by the *popular frenzy* of the hour.—One poor gentleman having attempted to discuss the matter in the Massachusetts Gazette, was glad to withdraw in time, assuring the public *that he would not trouble them or himself with any more observations on the subject.*—My own idea is, that popular opinions, as being for the most part suddenly taken up, are not always the criterion of truth. A man of sense expects some other proof of a paper being *impious, heretical, or treasonable,* than merely that of its being burned by the hands of the common hangman.—How happy would it be for the honest part of mankind were the whole race of cowards, sycophants, and blockheads extirpated from this earth—farewell."

New Haven *Connecticut Journal* October 31, 1787
Newspaper Article: A Letter from a Gentleman in a neighbouring State (New York), to a Gentleman in this City. (excerpt)[1]

I would next remark: "the 15th paragraph which is in these words: 'Congress shall have power to provide for calling forth the militia, to execute the laws of the union, suppress insurrections, and repel invasions.'" These states, not to mention other nations, have ever made the military power their last resort for executing their laws; this is seldom ever applied to, but on some occasions it is indispensably necessary. The principle is therefore good and agreeable to the sense of the people ever since the settlement of the country. Placing such a power in the hands of congress is the only matter of objection; but, if congress is invested with power to make laws, the power of executing laws in the most ample and effectual manner ought to be lodged there also. Without this, there would have been an inconceivable absurdity in the Constitution. The construction, [p]ut on this particular part, is too absurd to bear a serious refutation. "In fact it means (it is said) to convert the militia of the states into a standing army, under the entire command and control of Congress." But who are the militia? The militia comprehends all the male inhabitants from sixteen to sixty years of age; it includes the knowledge and strength of the nation. Against whom will they turn their swords? Against themselves!—to execute laws which are unconstitutional, unreasonable, and oppressive upon themselves! Absurdity itself could never have thought of raising an objection on this ground. The Constitution in this respect is certainly liberal. It puts the utmost degree of confidence in the people, and is fully correspondent to our ideas of government. It is a sufficient proof that despotism was not the aim of the Convention; had it have been, the execution of the laws of the Union (as a last resort) might have been placed in the hands of a standing army in the service and pay of Congress. In such a case, much might have been said. That when the Congress resort to the militia, which is the body of the people, for the support and execution of the laws of the Union, it is done in confidence that the laws are just and good, and worthy of the support of the people, otherwise Congess can have no reason to expect support from that quarter.[2]

1 DHRC, III, pp. 389-390.

2 This is a reply to an item in the New Haven *Connecticut Journal*, of October, 24, 1787, p. 61.

Agricola November 1, 1787

Newspaper Article: Philadelphia *Independent Gazetteer* (excerpt)

Much has also been said concerning a bill of rights, as if all those rights, which are inherent in us, as members of a free country, could be rendered more secure by a formal acknowledgement of them, by persons acting under an authority derived immediately from ourselves, or irretrievably lost by the silence of our representatives. The fact is, that such an acknowledgement would have been of very little consequence, and the stir which is made about it is only intended to enflame and exasperate weak minds, and by these means excite an opposition to all federal measures.

DHRC, II Mfm. Pa., p. 929.

An Old Whig V November 1, 1787

Newspaper Article: Philadelphia *Independent Gazetteer* (excerpts)

MR. PRINTER, In order that people may be sufficiently impressed, with the necessity of establishing a BILL OF RIGHTS in the forming of a new constitution, it is very proper to take a short view of some of those liberties, which it is of the greatest importance for Freemen to retain to themselves, when they surrender up a part of their natural rights for the good of society. . . .

The more I reflect upon the history of mankind, the more I am disposed to think that it is our duty to secure the essential rights of the people, by every precaution; for not an avenue has been left unguarded, through which oppression could possibly enter in any government; without some enemy of the public peace and happiness improving the opportunity to break in upon the liberties of the people; and none have been more frequently successful in the attempt, than those who have covered their ambitious designs under the garb of a fiery zeal for religious orthodoxy. What has happened in other countries and in other ages, may very possibly happen again in our own country, and for aught we know, before the present generation quits the stage of life. We ought therefore in a *bill of rights* to secure, in the first place, by the most express stipulations, the sacred rights of conscience. Has this been done in the constitution, which is now proposed for the consideration of the people of this country?—Not a word on this subject has been mentioned in any part of it; but we are left in this important article, as well as many others, entirely to the mercy of our future rulers. . . .

It is needless to repeat the necessity of securing other personal rights in the forming a new government. The same argument which proves the necessity of securing one of them shews also the necessity of securing others. Without a bill of rights we are totally insecure in all of them; and no man can promise himself with any degree of certainty that his posterity will enjoy the inestimable blessings of liberty of conscience, of freedom of speech and of writing and publishing their thoughts on public matters, of trial by jury, of holding themselves, their houses and papers free from seizure and search upon general suspicion or general warrants; or in short that they will be secured in the enjoyment of life, liberty and property without depending on the will and pleasure of their rulers.

DHRC, XIII, p. 538-541. The series "An Old Whig" is reprinted in Storing, III, starting on p. 17.

Cincinnatus I November 1, 1787
Newspaper Article: *New York Journal* (excerpt)

[To James Wilson, Esq.]

Your first attempt is to apologize for so very obvious a defect as—the omission of a declaration of rights. This apology consists in a very ingenious discovery; that in the state constitutions, whatever is not reserved is given; but in the congressional constitution, whatever is not given, is reserved. This has more the quaintness of a conundrum, than the dignity of an argument. The conventions that made the state and the general constitutions, sprang from the same source, were delegated for the same purpose—that is, for framing rules by which we should be governed, and ascertaining those powers which it was necessary to vest in our rulers. Where then is this distinction to be found, but in your assumption? Is it in the powers given to the members of convention? no—Is it in the constitution? not a word of it:—And yet on this play of words, this dictum of yours, this distinction without a difference, you would persuade us to rest our most essential rights. I trust, however, that the good sense of this free people cannot be so easily imposed on by professional figments. The confederation, in its very outset, declares—that what is not expressly given, is reserved. This constitution makes no such reservation. The presumption therefore is, that the framers of the proposed constitution, did not mean to subject it to the same exception.

DHRC, XIII, p. 531. The "Cincinnatus" series is reprinted in Storing, VI, starting on p. 5.

Brutus II November 1, 1787
Newspaper Article: *New York Journal*[1]

To the CITIZENS *of the* STATE *of* NEW-YORK.

I flatter myself that my last address established this position, that to reduce the Thirteen States into one government, would prove the destruction of your liberties.

But lest this truth should be doubted by some, I will now proceed to consider its merits.

Though it should be admitted, that the argument against reducing all the states into one consolidated government, are not sufficient fully to establish this point; yet they will, at least, justify this conclusion, that in forming a constitution for such a country, great care should be taken to limit and define its powers, adjust its parts, and guard against an abuse of authority. How far attention has been paid to these objects, shall be the subject of future enquiry. When a building is to be erected which is intended to stand for ages, the foundation should be firmly laid. The constitution proposed to your acceptance, is designed not for yourselves alone, but for generations yet unborn. The principles, therefore, upon which the social compact is founded, ought to have been clearly and precisely stated, and the most express and full declaration of rights to have been made—But on this subjuct there is almost an entire silence.

If we may collect the sentiments of the people of America, from their own most solemn declarations, they hold this truth as self evident, that all men are by nature free. No one man, therefore, or any class of men, have a right, by the law of nature, or of God, to assume or exercise authority over their fellows. The origin of society then is to be sought, not in any natural right which one man has to exercise authority over another, but in the united consent of those who associate. The mutual wants of men, at first dictated the propriety of forming societies; and when they were established, protection and defence pointed out the necessity of instituting government. In a state of nature every individual pursues his own interest; in this pursuit it frequently happened, that the possessions or enjoyments of one were sacrificed to the views and designs of another; thus the weak were a prey to the strong, the simple and unwary were subject to impositions from those who were more crafty and designing. In this state of things, every individual was insecure; common interest therefore directed, that government should be established, in which the force of the whole community should be collected, and under such directions, as to protect and defend every one who composed it. The common good, therefore, is the end of civil government, and common consent, the foundation on which it is established. To effect this end, it was necessary that a certain portion of natural liberty should be surrendered, in order, that what remained should be preserved: how great a proportion of natural freedom is necessary to be yielded by individuals, when they submit to government, I shall not now enquire. So much, however, must be given up, as will be sufficient to enable those, to whom the administration of the government is committed, to establish laws for the promoting the happiness of the community, and to carry those laws into effect. But it is not necessary, for this purpose, that individuals should relinquish all their natural rights. Some are of such a nature that they cannot be surrendered. Of this kind are the rights of conscience, the right of enjoying and defending life, &c. Others are not necessary to be resigned, in order to attain the end for which government is instituted, these therefore ought not to be given up. To surrender them, would counteract the very end of government, to wit, the common good. From these observations it appears, that in forming a government on its true principles, the foundation should be laid in the manner I before stated, by expressly reserving to the people such of their essential natural rights, as are not necessary to be parted with. The same reasons which at first induced mankind to associate and institute government, will operate to influence them to observe this precaution. If they had been disposed to conform themselves to the rule of immutable righteousness, government would not have been requisite. It was because one part exercised fraud, oppression, and violence on the other, that men came together, and agreed that certain rules should be formed, to regulate the conduct of all, and the power of the whole community lodged in the hands of rulers to enforce an obedience to them. But rulers have the same propensities as other men; they are as likely to use the power with which they are vested for private purposes, and to the injury and oppression of those over whom they are placed, as individuals in a state of nature are to injure and oppress one another. It is therefore as proper that bounds should be set to their authority, as that government should have at first been instituted to restrain private injuries.

This principle, which seems so evidently founded in the reason and nature of things, is confirmed by universal experience. Those who have governed, have been found in all ages ever active to enlarge their powers and abridge the public liberty. This has induced the people in all countries, where any sense of freedom remained, to fix barriers against the encroachments of their rulers. The country from which we have derived our origin, is an eminent example of this. Their magna charta and bill of rights have long been the boast, as well as the security, of that nation. I need say no more, I presume, to an American, than, that this principle is a fundamental one, in all the constitutions of our own states; there is not one of them but what is either founded on a declaration or bill of rights, or has certain express reservations of rights interwoven in the body of them.[2] From this it appears, that at a time when the pulse of liberty beat high and when an appeal was made to the people to form constitutions for the government of themselves, it was their universal sense, that such declarations should make a part of their frames of government. It is therefore the more astonishing, that this grand security, to the rights of the people, is not to be found in this constitution.

It has been said, in answer to this objection, that such declaration of rights, however requisite they might be in the constitutions of the states, are not necessary in the general constitution, because, "in the former case, every thing which is not reserved is given, but in the latter the reverse of the proposition prevails, and every thing which is not given is reserved." It requires but little attention to discover, that this mode of reasoning is rather specious than solid. The powers, rights, and authority, granted to the general government by this constitution, are as complete, with respect to every object to which they extend, as that of any state government—It reaches to every thing which concerns human happiness—Life, liberty, and property, are under its controul. There is the same reason, therefore, that the exercise of power, in this case, should be restrained within proper limits, as in that of the state governments. To set this matter in a clear light, permit me to instance some of the articles of the bills of rights of the individual states, and apply them to the case in question.

For the security of life, in criminal prosecutions, the bills of rights of most of the states have declared, that no man shall be held to answer for a crime until he is made fully acquainted with the charge brought against him; he shall not be compelled to accuse, or furnish evidence against himself—The witnesses against him shall be brought face to face, and he shall be fully heard by himself or counsel. That it is essential to the security of life and liberty, that trial of facts be in the vicinity where thay happen. Are not provisions of this kind as necessary in the general government, as in that of a particular state? The powers vested in the new Congress extend in many cases to life; they are authorised to provide for the punishment of a variety of capital crimes, and no restraint is laid upon them in its exercise, save only, that "the trial of all crimes, except in cases of impeachment, shall be by jury; and such trial shall be in the state where the said crimes shall have been committed." No man is secure of a trial in the county where he is charged to have committed a crime; he may be brought from Niagara to New-York, or carried from Kentucky to Richmond for trial for an offence, supposed to be committed. What security is there, that a man shall be furnished with a full and plain description of the charges against him? That he shall see the witnesses against him face to face, or that he shall be fully heard in his own defence by himself or counsel?

For the security of liberty it has been declared, "that excessive bail should not be required, nor excessive fines imposed, nor cruel or unusual punishments inflicted—That all warrants, without oath or affirmation, to search suspected places, or seize any person, his papers or property, are grievous and oppressive."

These provisions are as necessary under the general government as under that of the individual states; for the power of the former is as complete to the purpose of requiring bail, imposing fines, inflicting punishments, granting search warrants, and seizing persons, papers, or property, in certain cases, as the other.

For the purpose of securing the property of the citizens, it is declared by all the states, "that in all controversies at law, respecting property, the ancient mode of trial by jury is one of the best securities of the rights of the people, and ought to remain sacred and inviolable."

Does not the same necessity exist of reserving this right, under this national compact, as in that of this state? Yet nothing is said respecting it. In the bills of rights of the states it is declared, that a well regulated militia is the proper and natural defence of a free government—That as standing armies in time of peace are dangerous, they are not to be kept up, and that the military should be kept under strict subordination to, and controuled by the civil power.

The same security is as necessary in this constitution, and much more so; for the general government will have the sole power to raise and to pay armies, and are under no controul in the exercise of it; yet nothing of this is to be found in this new system.

I might proceed to instance a number of other rights, which were as necessary to be reserved, such as, that elections should be free, that the liberty of the press should be held sacred; but the instances adduced, are sufficient to prove, that this argument is without foundation.—Besides, it is evident, that the reason here assigned was not the true one, why the framers of this constitution omitted a bill of rights; if it had been, they would not have made certain reservations, while they totally omitted others of more importance. We find they have, in the 9th section of the 1st article, declared, that the writ of habeas corpus shall not be suspended, unless in cases of rebellion—that no bill of attainder, or expost facto law, shall be passed—that no title of nobility shall be granted by the United States, &c. If every thing which is not given is reserved, what propriety is there in these exceptions? Does this constitution any where grant the power of suspending the habeas corpus, to make expost facto laws, pass bills of attainder, or grant titles of nobility? It certainly does not in express terms. The only answer that can be given is, that these are implied in the general powers granted. With equal truth it may be said, that all the powers, which the bills of right, guard against the abuse of, are contained or implied in the general ones granted by this constitution.

So far it is from being true, that a bill of rights is less necessary in the general constitution than in those of the states, the contrary is evidently the fact.—This system, if it is possible for the people of America to accede to it, will be an original compact; and being the last, will, in the nature of things, vacate every former agreement inconsistent with it. For it being a plan of government received and ratified by the whole people, all other forms, which are in existence at the time of its adoption, must yield to it. This is expressed in positive and unequivocal terms, in the 6th article, "That this constitution and the laws of the United States, which shall be made in pursuance thereof, and all treaties made, or which shall be made, under the authority of the United States, shall be the supreme law of the land; and the judges in every state shall be bound thereby, any thing in the *constitution*, or laws of any state, *to the contrary* notwithstanding.

"The senators and representatives before-mentioned, and the members of the several state legislatures, and all executive and judicial officers, both of the United States, and of the several states, shall be bound, by oath or affirmation, to support this constitution."

It is therefore not only necessarily implied thereby, but positively expressed, that the different state constitutions are repealed and entirely done away, so far as they are inconsistent with this, with the laws which shall be made in pursuance thereof, or with treaties made, or which shall be made, under the authority of the United States; of what avail will the constitutions of the respective states be to preserve the rights of its citizens? should they be plead, the answer would be, the constitution of the United States, and the laws made in pursuance thereof, is the supreme law, and all legislatures and judicial officers, whether of the general or state governments, are bound by oath to support it. No priviledge, reserved by the bill of rights, or secured by the state government, can limit the power granted by this, or restrain any laws made in pursuance of it. It stands therefore on its own bottom, and must receive a construction by itself without any reference to any other—And hence it was of the highest importance, that the most precise and express declarations and reservations of rights should have been made.

This will appear the more necessary, when it is considered, that not only the constitution and laws made in pursuance thereof, but all treaties made, or which shall be made, under the authority of the United States, are the supreme law of the land, and supersede the constitutions of all the states. The power to make treaties, is vested in the president, by and with the advice and consent of two thirds of the senate. I do not find any limitation, or restriction, to the exercise of this power. The most important article in any constitution may therefore be repealed, even without a legislative act. Ought not a government, vested with such extensive and indefinite authority, to have been restricted by a declaration of rights? It cerainly ought.

So clear a point is this, that I cannot help suspecting, that persons who attempt to persuade people, that such reservations were less necessary under this constitution than under those of the states, are wilfully endeavouring to deceive, and to lead you into an absolute state of vassalage.

1 DHRC, XIII, pp. 524-529.
2 See Appendix A, p. 747, for the state declarations or bills of rights and other provisions relating to individual rights.

Timoleon November 1, 1787

Newspaper Article: *New York Journal* (excerpts)

After some judicious reflections on this subject, which tended to shew the necessity of the most plain and unequivocal language in the all important business of constituting government, which necessarily conveying great powers, is always liable (from the natural tendency of power to corrupt the human heart and deprave the head) to great abuse; by perverse and subtle arguments calculated to extend dominion over all things and all men. . . .
"I now plainly see the necessity of express declarations and reservations in favor of the great, unalienable rights of mankind, to prevent the oppressive and wicked extention of power to the ruin of human liberty. . . . But we may hope that our fellow citizens will not approve of this new plan of government, before they have well considered it and that they will insist on such amendments to it, as will secure from violation the just rights and liberty of the people."

DHRC, XIII, p. 535-538.

George Turner (Philadelphia) November 6, 1787

Letter: To Winthrop Sargent (excerpt)

There are two parties here upon the momentous Business now agitating independent America. One party sees nothing but Danger and Mischief in the proposed Constitution; while the other extols it as a *Chef d'oeuvre* in Politics. In this Case, as in almost every other, there is a middle walk to be trodden, as the directest Road to Truth. For my part, I like the Outlines of the Plan, and, being a Friend to Energy of Government, I approve of most of the Powers proposed to be given. But, as a Friend to the natural Rights of Man, I must hold up my Hand against others. There are certain great and unalienable Rights (which I need not enumerate to you) that should have been secured by a Declaration or Bill of Rights. For that sweeping Clause [Article 6] (as it has been termed) in the proposed Constitution, which places the Authority of Congress over the Laws and Constitutions of the several States renders, in my Opinion, such a Declaration an indispensable Condition. Mr. Wilson has said That 'what is not given is reserved'—but I consider this an unfortunate Declaration on his part; for the Clause alluded to embraces *every thing*.

DHRC, XIII, p. 565. Also reprinted in DHRC, II, p. 209.

Argus November 8, 1787
Newspaper Article: Providence *United States Chronicle*

MR. WHEELER, The Liberty of the Press, or the Liberty which *every Person* in the United States *at present* enjoys, of exhibiting his Sentiments on all public Measures to his Fellow-Citizens, through the Medium of the News-Papers, is a Privilege of infinite Importance—a Privilege, for which (among others) we have fought and bled, and for which I would again shoulder my Musket. I confess the Attempt lately made in Boston, by some of our aristocratical Gentry, to have every Person's Name published who should write against the proposed Federal Constitution, has given many of us a just Alarm. Why, if the proposed Constitution is a good one are its Supporters afraid to have any Thing said against it? Why are they hurrying it down our Throats, before we have opened our Mouths? For what Purpose is it that the Names of its Opposers should be published? Why all this extraordinary Exertion? If it is *very good, very just*, and *wisely calculated* to make us respectable and happy, no Doubt it will be adopted—But pray, my good Friends, give us a Chance to read it once or twice over before we say whether we like it or not. I had written thus far, and intended to have gone on to state my Opinon on this important Subject, when my Son brought me in Mr. Powars' last Boston Paper—I laid down my Pen to read it, and I found a Piece, signed JOHN DE WITT, on the Subject I had proposed to write; who the Author is I know not, but his Sentiments so exactly coincide with mine, that I concluded to write no more, at present, but to request you, Mr. Printer, to publish that Piece in your next Chronicle: By so doing you'll oblige at least one of your Readers.

DHRC, XIII, pp. 320-321.

A Citizen of Philadelphia {Pelatiah Webster} November 8, 1787
Pamphlet: The Weakness of Brutus Exposed (excerpt)
Philadelphia

6. Brutus thinks we can never be too much afraid of the *encroaching avidity of rulers;* but 'tis pretty plain, that however great the natural *lust of power in rulers* may be, the *jealousy of the people in giving it,* is about equal; these two opposite passions, will always operate in opposite directions to each other, and like *action and reaction* in natural bodies, will ever tend to a good ballance.

At any rate, the Congress can never *get* more power than the people will *give,* nor *hold* it any longer than they will *permit;* for should they assume tyrannical powers, and make incroachments on liberty without the consent of the people, they would soon attone for their temerity, with shame and disgrace, and probably with their heads.

DHRC, XIV, p. 70.

Centinel III November 8, 1787
Newspaper Article: Philadelphia *Independent Gazetteer* (excerpt)

Section 8th of article 1st, vests Congress with power "to provide for calling forth the militia to execute the laws of the union, suppress insurrections and repel invasions; to provide for organizing, arming, and disciplining the militia, and for governing such part of them as may be employed in the service of the United States, reserving to the states respectively, the appointment of the officers, and the authority of training the militia according to the discipline prescribed by Congress."—This section will subject the citizens of these states to the most arbitrary military discipline, even death may be inflicted on the disobedient; in the character of militia, you may be dragged from your families and homes to any part of the continent and for any length of time, at the discretion of the future Congress; and as militia you may be made the unwilling instruments of oppression, under the direction of government; there is no exemption upon account of conscientious scruples of bearing arms; no equivalent to be received in lieu of personal services. The militia of Pennsylvania may be marched to Georgia or NewHampshire however incompatible with their interests or consciences;—in short they may be made as meer machines as Prussian soldiers.

DHRC, XIV, p. 60. Centinel addressed this to the People of Pennsylvania.

Hugh Williamson November 8, 1787
Speech at Edenton, North Carolina (excerpt)
Published: New York *Daily Advertiser* February 25, 1788.

It seems to be generally admitted, that the system of Government which has been proposed by the late Convention, is well calculated to relieve us from many of the grievances under which we have been laboring. If I might express my particular sentiments on this subject, I should describe it as more free and more perfect than any form of government that ever has been adopted by any nation; but I would not say it has no faults. Imperfection is inseparable from every human device. Several objections were made to this system by two or three very respectable characters in the Convention, which have been the subject of much conversation; and other objections, by citizens of this State, have lately reached our ears. It is proper that you should consider of these objections. They are of two kinds; they respect the things that are in the system, and the things that are not in it. We are told that there should have been a section for securing the Trial by Jury in Civil cases, and the Liberty of the Press: that there should also have been a Declaration of Rights. In the new system it is provided, that "*The Trial of all crimes*, except in cases of Impeachment," *shall be by Jury*, but this provision could not possibly be extended to all *Civil* cases. For it is well known that the Trial by Jury is not general and uniform throughout the United States, either in cases of Admiralty or of Chancery; hence it became necessary to submit the question to the General Legislature, who might accommodate their laws on this occasion to the desires and habits of the nation. Surely there is no prohibition in a case that is untouched.

We have been told that the Liberty of the Press is not secured by the New Constitution. Be pleased to examine the plan, and you will find that the liberty of the Press and the laws of Mohomet are equally affected by it. The New Government is to have the power of protecting literary property; the very power which you have by a special act delegated to the present Congress. There was a time in England, when neither book, pamphlet, nor paper could be published without a licence from Government. That restraint was finally removed in the year 1694 and by such removal, their press became perfectly free, for it is not under the restraint of any licence. Certainly the new Government can have no power to impose restraints. The citizens of the United States have no more occasion for a second Declaration of Rights, than they have for a section in favor of the press. Their rights, in the several States, have long since been explained and secured by particular declarations, which make a part of their several

Constitutions. It is granted, and perfectly understood, that under the Government of the Assemblies of the States, and under the Government of the Congress, every right is reserved to the individual, which he has not expressly delegated to this, or that Legislature.

DHRC, XVI, p. 202.

Cincinnatus II November 8, 1787
Newspaper Article: *New York Journal* (excerpts)

To James Wilson, Esquire

Sir, I have proved, sir, that not only some power is given in the constitution to restrain, and even to subject the press, but that it is a power totally unlimited; and may certainly annihilate the freedom of the press, and convert it from being the palladium of liberty to become an engine of imposition and tyranny. It is an easy step from restraining the press to making it place the worst actions of government in so favorable a light, that we may groan under tyranny and oppression without knowing from whence it comes.

But you comfort us by saying,—"there is no reason to suspect so popular a privilege will be neglected." The wolf, in the fable, said as much to the sheep, when he was persuading them to trust him as their protector, and to dismiss their guardian dogs. Do you indeed suppose, Mr. Wilson, that if the people give up their privileges to these new rulers they will render them back again to the people? Indeed, sir, you should not trifle upon a question so serious—You would not have us to suspect any ill. If we throw away suspicion—to be sure, the thing will go smoothly enough, and we shall deserve to continue a free, respectable, and happy people. Suspicion shackles rulers and prevents good government. All great and honest politicians, *like yourself,* have reprobated it. Lord Mansfield is a great authority against it, and has often treated it as the worst of libels. But such men as Milton, Sidney, Locke, Montesquieu, and Trenchard, have thought it essential to the preservation of liberty against the artful and persevering encroachments of those with whom power is trusted. You will pardon me, sir, if I pay some respect to these opinions, and wish that the freedom of the press may be *previously* secured as a *constitutional* and *unalienable right,* and not left to the precarious care of popular privileges which may or may not influence our new rulers. You are fond of, and happy at, quaint expressions of this kind in your observation—that a formal declaration would have done harm, by implying, that some degree of power was given when we undertook to define its extent. This thought has really a brilliancy in it of the first water. But permit me, sir, to ask, why any saving clause was admitted into this constitution, when you tell us, every thing is reserved that is not expressly given? Why is it said in sec. 9th, "The migration or importation of such persons as any of the states now existing shall think proper to admit, shall not be prohibited by Congress, prior to the year, 1808." There is no power expressly given to the Congress to prohibit migrations and importations. By your doctrine then they could have none, and it was, according to your own position, nugatory to declare they should not do it. Which are we to believe, sir,—you or the constitution? The text, or the comment. If the former, we must be persuaded, that in the contemplation of the framers of the constitution implied powers were given, otherwise the exception would have been an absurdity. If we listen to you we must affirm it to be a distinctive characteristic of the constitution, that—"what is not expressly given is reserved." Such are the inconsistencies into which men over ingenuous, like yourself, are betrayed in advocating a bad cause. Perhaps four months more consideration of the subject, would have rendered you more guarded.

I come now to the consideration of the trial by jury in civil cases. . . .

I own then, it alarms me, when I see these Doctors of our constitutions cutting in twain this sacred shield of public liberty and justice. Surely my countrymen will think a little before they resign this strong hold of freedom. Our state constitutions have held it sacred in all its parts. They have anxiously secured it. But that these may not shield it from the intended destruction in the new constitution, it is therein as anxiously provided, that "this constitution, and the laws of the United States, which shall be made in pursuance thereof; or which shall be made under the authority of the United States, shall be the supreme laws of the land; and the judges in every state, shall be bound thereby; any thing in the constitution and laws of any state, to the contrary notwithstanding."

Thus this new system, with one sweeping clause, bears down every constitution in the union, and establishes its arbitrary doctrines, supreme and paramount to all the bills and declarations of rights, in which we vainly put our trust, and on which we rested the security of our often declared, unalienable liberties. But I trust the whole people of this country, will unite, in crying out, as did our sturdy ancestors of old—*Nolumus leges anglicae mutari.*—We will not part with our birthright.

DHRC, XIV, pp. 11-14. The "Cincinnatus" series is reprinted in Storing, VI, starting at p. 5.

Federal Farmer November [8], 1787
Pamphlet: Observations Leading to a Fair Examination of the System of Government Proposed by the Late Convention; and to Several Essential and Necessary Alterations in It. In a Number of Letters from the Federal Farmer to the Republican. (excerpts)
New York.

LETTER II.[1] . . .

There are certain unalienable and fundamental rights, which in forming the social compact, ought to be explicitly ascertained and fixed—a free and enlightened people, in forming this compact, will not resign all their rights to those who govern, and they will fix limits to their legislators and rulers, which will soon be plainly seen by those who are governed, as well as by those who govern: and the latter will know they cannot be passed unperceived by the former, and without giving a general alarm—These rights should be made the basis of every constitution; and if a people be so situated, or have such different opinions that they cannot agree in ascertaining and fixing them, it is a very strong argument against their attempting to form one entire society, to live under one system of laws only.—I confess, I never thought the people of these states differed essentially in these respects; they having derived all these rights, from one common source, the British systems; and having in the formation of their state constitutions, discovered that their ideas relative to these rights are very similar. However, it is now said that the states differ so essentially in these respects, and even in the important article of the trial by jury, that when assembled in convention, they can agree to no words by which to establish that trial, or by which to ascertain and establish many other of these rights, as fundamental articles in the social compact. If so, we proceed to consolidate the states on no solid basis whatever.

But I do not pay much regard to the reasons given for not bottoming the new constitution on a better bill of rights. I still believe a complete federal bill of rights to be very practicable.

LETTER III.[2] . . .

The great object of a free people must be so to form their government and laws and so to administer them as to create a confidence in, and respect for the laws; and thereby induce the sensible and virtuous part of the community to declare in favor of the laws, and to support them without an expensive military force. I wish, though I confess I have not much hope, that this may be the case with the laws of Congress under the new Constitution. I am fully convinced that we must organize the national government on different principles, and make the parts of it more efficient, and secure in it more effectually the different interests in the community; or else leave in the state governments some powers proposed to be lodged in it—at least till such an organization shall be found to be practicable. Not sanguine in my expectations of a good federal administration, and satisfied, as I am, of the impracticability of consolidating the states, and at the same time of preserving the rights of the people at large, I believe we ought still to leave some of those powers in the state governments, in which the people, in fact, will still be represented—to define some other powers proposed to be vested in the general government, more carefully, and to establish a few principles to secure a proper exercise of the powers given it. It is not my object to multiply objections, or to contend about inconsiderable powers or amendments. I wish the system adopted with a few alterations; but those, in my mind, are essential ones; if adopted without, every good citizen will acquiesce, though I shall consider the duration of our governments, and the liberties of this people, very much dependant on the administration of the general government. A wise and honest administration, may make the people happy under any government; but necessity only can justify even our leaving open avenues to the abuse of power, by wicked, unthinking, or ambitious men. . . .

By the constitution it is proposed that congress shall have power "to raise and support armies, but no appropriation of money to that use shall be for a longer term than two years; to provide and maintain a navy; to provide for calling forth the militia to execute the laws of the union; suppress insurrections, and repel invasions: to provide for organizing, arming and disciplining the militia: reserving to the states the right to appoint the officers, and to train the militia according to the discipline prescribed by congress;" congress will have unlimited power to raise armies, and to engage officers and men for any number of years; but a legislative act applying money for their support can have operation for no longer term than two years, and if a subsequent congress do not within the two years renew the appropriation, or further appropriate monies for the use of the army, the army, will be left to take care of itself. When an army shall once be raised for a number of years, it is not probable that it will find much difficulty in getting congress to pass laws for applying monies to its support. I see so many men in America fond of a standing army, and especially among those who probably will have a large share in administering the federal system; it is very evident to me, that we shall have a large standing army as soon as the monies to support them can be possibly found. An army is a very agreeable place of employment for the young gentlemen of many families. A power to raise armies must be lodged some where; still this will not justify the lodging this power in a bare majority of so few men without any checks; or in the government in which the great body of the people, in the nature of things, will be only nominally represented. In the state governments the great body of the people, the yeomanry, &c. of the country, are represented: It is true they will chuse the members of congress, and may now and then chuse a man of their own way of thinking; but it is impossible for forty, or thirty thousand people in this country, one time in ten to find a man who can possess similar feeling, views, and interests with themselves: powers to lay and collect taxes and to raise armies are of the greatest moment; for carrying them into effect, laws need not be frequently made, and the yeomanry, &c. of the country ought substantially to have a check upon the passing of these laws; this check ought to be placed in the legislatures, or at least, in the few men the common people of the country, will, probably, have in congress, in the true sense of the word, "from among themselves." It is true, the yeomanry of the country possess the lands, the weight of property, possess arms, and are too strong a body of men to be openly offended—and, therefore, it is urged, they will take care of themselves, that men who shall govern will not dare pay any disrespect to their opinions. It is easily perceived, that if they have not their proper negative upon passing laws in congress, or on the passage of laws relative to taxes and armies, they may in twenty or thirty years be by means imperceptible to them, totally deprived of that boasted weight and strength: This may be done in a great measure by congress, if disposed to do it, by modelling the militia. Should one fifth, or one eighth part of the men capable of bearing arms, be made a select militia, as has been proposed, and those the young and ardent part of the community, possessed of but little or no property, and all the others put upon a plan that will render them of no importance, the former will answer all the purposes of an army, while the latter will be defenceless. The state must train the militia in such form and according to such systems and rules as Congress shall prescribe: and the only actual influence the respective states will have respecting the militia will be in appointing the officers. I see no provision made for calling out the *posse commitatus* for executing the laws of the union, but provision is made for Congress to call forth the militia for the execution of them—and the militia in general, or any select part of it, may be called out under military officers, instead of the sheriff to enforce an execution of federal laws, in the first instance and thereby introduce an entire military execution of the laws.

LETTER IV.[3] . . .

4th. There are certain rights which we have always held sacred in the United States, and recognized in all our constitutions, and which, by the adoption of the new constitution, in its present form will be left unsecured. By article 6, the proposed constitution, and the laws of the United States, which shall be made under the authority of the United States, shall be the supreme law of the land; and the judges in every state shall be bound thereby; any thing in the constitution or laws of any state to the contrary notwithstanding.

It is to be observed that when the people shall adopt the proposed constitution it will be their last and supreme act; it will be adopted not by the people of New-Hampshire, Massachusetts, &c. but by the people of the United States; and whenever this constitution, or any part of it, shall be incompatible with the antient customs, rights, the laws or the constitutions heretofore established in the United States, it will entirely abolish them and do them away: And not only this, but the laws of the United States which shall be made in pursuance of the federal constitution will be also supreme laws, and whenever they shall be incompatible with those customs, rights, laws or constitutions heretofore established, they will also entirely abolish them and do them away.

By the article before recited, treaties also made under the authority of the United States, shall be the supreme law: It is not said that these treaties shall be made in pursuance of the constitution—nor are there any constitutional bounds set to those who shall make them: The president and two thirds of the senate will be empowered to make treaties indefinitely, and when these treaties shall be made, they will also abolish all laws and state constitutions imcompatible with them. This power in the president and senate is absolute, and the judges will be bound to allow full force to whatever rule, article or thing the president and senate shall establish by treaty, whether it be practicable to set any bounds to those who make treaties, I am not able to say: If not, it proves that this power ought to be more safely lodged.

The federal constitution, the laws of congress made in pursuance of the constitution, and all treaties must have full force and effect in all parts of the United States; and all other laws, rights and constitutions which stand in their way must yield: It is proper the national laws should be supreme, and superior to state or district laws; but then the national laws ought to yield to unalienable or fundamental rights—and national laws, made by a few men, should extend only to a few national objects. This will not be the case with the laws of congress: To have any proper idea of their extent, we must carefully examine the legislative, executive and judicial powers proposed to be lodged in the general government, and consider them in connection with a general clause in art. 1. sect. 8. in these words (after enumerating a number of powers) "To make all laws which shall be necessary and proper for carrying into execution the foregoing powers, and all other powers vested by this constitution in the government of the United States, or in any department or officer thereof."—The powers of this government as has been observed, extend to internal as well as external objects, and to those objects to which all others are subordinate; it is almost impossible to have a just conception of these powers, or of the extent and number of the laws which may be deemed necessary and proper to carry them into effect, till we shall come to exercise those powers and make the laws. In making laws to carry those powers into effect, it will be expected, that a wise and prudent congress will pay respect to the opinions of a free people, and bottom their laws on those principles which have been considered as essential and fundamental in the British, and in our government: But a congress of a different character will not be bound by the constitution to pay respect to those principles.

It is said, that when the people make a constitution, and delegate powers, that all powers not delegated by them to those who govern, is reserved in the people; and that the people, in the present case, have reserved in themselves, and in their state governments, every right and power not expressly given by the federal constitution to those who shall administer the national government. It is said, on the other hand, that the people, when they make a constitution, yield all power not expressly reserved to themselves. The truth is, in either case, it is mere matter of opinion, and men usually take either side of the argument, as will best answer their purposes: But the general presumption being, that men who govern, will, in doubtful cases, construe laws and constitutions most favourably for encreasing their own powers; all wise and prudent people, in forming constitutions, have drawn the line, and carefully described the powers parted with and the powers reserved. By the state constitutions, certain rights have been reserved in the people; or rather, they have been recognized and established in such a manner, that state legislatures are bound to respect them, and to make no laws infringing upon them. The state legislatures are obliged to take notice of the bills of rights of their respective states. The bill of rights, and the state constitutions, are fundamental compacts only between those who govern, and the people of the same state.

In the year 1788 the people of the United States make a federal constitution, which is a fundamental compact between them and their federal rulers; these rulers, in the nature of things, cannot be bound to take notice of any other compact. It would be absurd for them, in making laws, to look over thirteen, fifteen, or twenty state constitutions, to see what rights are established as fundamental, and must not be infringed upon, in making laws in the society. It is true, they would be bound to do it if the people, in their federal compact, should refer to the state constitutions, recognize all parts not inconsistent with the federal constitution, and direct their federal rulers to take notice of them accordingly; but this is not the case, as the plan stands proposed at present; and it is absurd, to suppose so unnatural an idea is intended or implied. I think my opinion is not only founded in reason, but I think it is supported by the report of the convention itself. If there are a number of rights established by the state constitutions, and which will remain sacred, and the general government is bound to take notice of them—it must take notice of one as well as another; and if unnecessary to recognize or establish one by the federal constitution, it would be unnecessary to recognize or establish another by it. If the federal constitution is to be construed so far in connection with the state constitutions, as to leave the trial by jury in civil causes, for instance, secured; on the same principles it would have left the trial by jury in criminal causes, the benefits of the writ of habeas corpus, &c. secured; they all stand on the same footing; they are the common rights of Americans, and have been recognized by the state constitutions: But the convention found it necessary to recognize or re-establish the benefits of that writ, and the jury trial in criminal cases. As to EXPOST FACTO laws, the convention has done the same in one case, and gone further in another. It is a part of the compact between the people of each state and the rulers, that no EXPOST FACTO laws shall be made. But the convention, by Art. 1. Sect. 10. have put a sanction upon this part even of the state compacts. In fact, the 9th and 10th Sections in Art. 1. in the proposed constitution, are no more nor less, than a partial bill of rights; they establish certain principles as part of the compact upon which the federal legislators and officers can never infringe. It is here wisely stipulated, that the federal legislature shall never pass a bill of attainder, or EXPOST FACTO law; that no tax shall be laid on articles exported, &c. The establishing of one right implies the necessity of establishing another and similar one.

On the whole, the position appears to me to be undeniable, that this bill of rights ought to be carried farther, and some other principles established, as a part of this fundamental compact between the people of the United States and their federal rulers.

It is true, we are not disposed to differ much, at present, about religion; but when we are making a constitution, it is to be hoped, for ages and millions yet unborn, why not establish the free exercise of religion, as a part of the national compact. There are other essential rights, which we have justly understood to be the rights of freemen; as freedom from hasty and unreasonable search warrants, warrants not founded on oath, and not issued with due caution, for searching and seizing men's papers, property, and persons. The trials by jury in civil causes, it is said, varies so much in the several states, that no words could be found for the uniform establishment of it. If so the federal legislation will not be able to establish it by any general laws. . . .

I confess I do not see in what cases the Congress can, with any pretence of right, make a law to suppress the freedom of the press; though I am not clear, that Congress is restrained from laying any duties whatever on printing and from laying duties particularly heavy on certain pieces printed, and perhaps Congress may require large bonds for the payment of these duties. Should the printer say, the freedom of the press was secured by the constitution of the state in which he lived, Congress might, and perhaps, with great propriety, answer, that the federal constitution is the only compact existing between them and the people; in this compact the people have named no others, and therefore Congress, in exercising the powers assinged them, and in making laws to carry them into execution, are restrained by nothing beside the federal constitution, any more than a state legislature is restrained by a compact between the magistrates and people of a county, city, or town of which the people, in forming the state constitution, have taken no notice.

It is not my object to emumerate rights of inconsiderable importance; but there are others, no doubt, which ought to be established as a fundamental part of the national system. . . .

I am sensible, thousands of men in the United States, are disposed to adopt the proposed constitution, though they percieve it to be essentially defective, under an idea that amendment of it, may be obtained when necessary. This is a pernicious idea, it argues a servility of character totally unfit for the support of free government; it is very repugnant to that perpetual jealousy respecting liberty, so absolutely necessary in all free states[.]

LETTER V.[4] . . .

Thus I have examined the federal constitution as far as a few days leisure would permit. It opens to my mind a new scene; instead of seeing powers cautiously lodged in the hands of numerous legislators, and many magistrates, we see all important powers collecting in one centre, where a few men will possess them almost at discretion. And instead of checks in the formation of the government, to secure the rights of the people against the usurpation of those they appoint to govern, we are to understand the equal division of lands among our people, and the strong arm furnished them by nature and situation, are to secure them against those usurpations. If there are advantages in the equal division of our lands, and the strong and manly habits of our people, we ought to establish governments calculated to give duration to them, and not governments which never can work naturally, till that equality of property, and those free and manly habits shall be destroyed; these evidently are not the natural basis of the proposed constitution. . . . I consider the field of enquiry just opened, and that we are to look to the state conventions for ultimate decisions on the subject before us; it is not to be presumed, that they will differ about small amendments, and lose a system when they shall have made it substantially good; but touching the essential amendments, it is to be presumed the several conventions will pursue the most rational measures to agree in and obtain them; and such defects as they shall discover and not remove, they will probably notice, keep them in view as the ground work of future amendments, and in the firm and manly language which every free people ought to use, will suggest to those who may hereafter administer the government, that it is their expectation, that the system will be so organized by legislative acts, and the government so administered, as to render those defects as little injurious as possible.—Our countrymen are entitled to an honest and faithful government; to a government of laws and not of men; and also to one of their chusing—as a citizen of the country, I wish to see these objects secured, and licentious, assuming, and overbearing men restrained; if the constitution or social compact be vague and unguarded, then we depend wholly upon the prudence, wisdom and moderation of those who manage the affairs of government; or on what, probably, is equally uncertain and precarious, the success of the people oppressed by the abuse of government, in receiving it from the hands of those who abuse it, and placing it in the hands of those who will use it well. . . .

Under these impressions, and keeping in view the improper and unadvisable lodgment of powers in the general government, organized as it at present is, touching internal taxes, armies and militia, the elections of its own members, causes between citizens of different states, &c. and the want of a more perfect bill of rights, &c.—I drop the subject for the present, and when I shall have leisure to revise and correct my ideas respecting it, and to collect into points the opinions of those who wish to make the system more secure and safe, perhaps I may proceed to point out particularly for your consideration, the amendment[s] which ought to be ingrafted into this system,[5] and [not] only in conformity to my own, but the deliberate opinions of others—

1 DHRC, XIV, pp. 27-28.
2 *Ibid.*, pp. 30-39.
3 *Ibid.*, pp. 43-48.
4 *Ibid.*, pp. 48-53.
5 See "Federal Farmer," May, 1788, p. 342, for the "amendments which ought to be engrafted into this system," which are contained in *An Additional Number of Letters from the Federal Farmer to the Republican*.

The Monitor November 9, 1787
Newspaper Article: Philadelphia *Pennsylvania Mercury* (excerpt)

The grand palladium of the freedom of this country, the *Declaration of Rights*, ought to be read and well understood by every citizen; for on them alone rests the political salvation of this country. We there find sufficient energy is given, to compel obedience to legislative authority—a perfect equality is preserved in the several branches of civil power, by a frequent recurrence to fundamental principles,—and the whole is cemented by a firm adherence to moderation and justice. In them, we find the rulers and the ruled equally participating of the blessings of liberty and property, and are equally secured in their rights and privileges as freemen. Of how much importance is it, then, to every citizen, to preserve these inestimable blessings, and duly to consider every subject which might tend to the preservation of them! It *ought* to be the *duty* of *parents* particularly to *inculcate* into the minds of the *rising generation*, the NOBLE PRINCIPLES of VIRTUE and PATRIOTISM—by *example* and *advice* to impress on their minds, the domestic as well as public advantages resulting from industry and oeconomy—for the concomitant blessings of liberty and peace have ever been found, where they have been the prevailing principles.

DHRC, II Mfm. Pa., pp. 1048-1049.

Uncus November 9, 1787
Newspaper Article: Baltimore *Maryland Journal* (excerpts)

The *Centinel* seems almost *expiring with fear*, for "*the liberty of the press*"—By his idea of the subject, one would think he had just made his escape from a *Turkish Haram*, or had been buoyed from the gloomy regions of a *Spanish mine*. It is almost impossible that a man, who was educated in any of the Christian nations of Europe, and really so, that any one, who is an inhabitant of any of the United States of America, should be ignorant that "the liberty of the press" is what the people, for whom the late Convention were acting, look upon as a privilege, with which every inhabitant is born;—a right which Nature, and Nature's God, has given, and too sacred to require being mentioned in the national transactions of these states. . . .

When the Americans shall have lost their virtue—when those sentiments of liberty which pervade the breasts of freemen, shall cease to glow in their bosoms, *bills of right* will not secure their liberties. But whilst they practice *virtue*, and retain *those sentiments*,—from whence can a *Congress* be collected, who will *dare* infringe their liberties; or be ignorantly hardy enough to attempt "*the liberty of the press.*"

DHRC, XIV, p. 78-81.

Vox Populi November 9, 1787
Newspaper Article: Boston *Massachusetts Gazette* (excerpt)

I must renew my address to the publick's indulgence for liberty to make another address to my fellow-citizens, which is for them to consider, how it comports with policy for them to establish a system of government entirely disconnected with a *bill of rights?*

I long sought for the reason why a bill of rights was omitted; at last I had the two following reasons assigned *viz.* first, *as the powers proposed to be vested in Congress were definite, no bill of rights was necessary, for they could exercise no power but what is expressly given them by the constitution. The* other reason is, *because each state has a bill of rights of its own, a federal bill of rights must be wholly useless.*

With regard to the first, it will apply with equal force to any constitution of government extant; we will take our own state's for instance, where we shall find the powers vested in the General Court are as *definite* as those proposed to be vested in Congress; yet, when the constitution was formed, it was deemed absolutely necessary that the people should be protected by an *explicit unequivocal bill of rights*, and the publick are desired to consider whether *that* was a piece of ill-judged policy or not; and if it was not, whether the *nature of things* has so changed since as to render it needless.

The second reason given why it was omitted, I think cannot have much greater force than the former; we may as well say, that because each state has a *constitution* of its own, that a continental constitution was unnecessary, as to say that because we have a *state* bill of rights a *continental* one is unnecessary. But let us consider what is our bill of rights, and what was its original design. If we consider its nature, we shall find it was constucted as a barricado to prevent our own General Court from infringing on certain rights which the people did not mean should be at the disposal of the legislature, and is simply a rule of conduct for our legislature. But what will Congress have to do with *our* bill of rights, any more than they will with the *rest* of our constitution? Will any person suppose that the *other parts* of our constitution will be any rule of *their* conduct? I should imagine if they do, it will curtail some part of the powers which it is meant, by the proposed constitution, they should exercise.

The virtuous and enlightened citizens are requested to pay that attention to this matter which the importance of its nature demands, and act thereon the part which to them shall appear becoming free men, who have hazarded their lives and fortunes to establish a government founded on the principles of genuine civil liberty and *undefiled republicanism.*

Storing, IV, pp. 47-48.

Plain Truth November 10, 1787

Newspaper Article: Philadelphia *Independent Gazetteer* (excerpts)
[This article consists of specific Federalist replies to a list of numbered complaints which originated in a previous Antifederalist article by "An Officer of the Late Continental Army." Ed.]

"2. The powers of Congress extend to the *lives*, the *liberties* and the *property* of every citizen."

2. Is there a government on earth where the life, liberty and property of a citizen may not be forfeited by a violation of the laws of God and man? It is only when justified by such crimes, that the new government has such power; and all crimes (except in cases of impeachment) are expressly to be TRIED BY JURY, *in the state where they may be committed*. (Article 3, section 2.) . . .

"6. Congress being possessed of these immense powers, the liberties of the states and of the people are not secured by a bill or DECLARATION of RIGHTS."

6. Notwithstanding all that has been written against it, I must recur to friend W[ilson]'s definition on this subject. A state government is designed for ALL CASES WHATSOEVER, consequently what is not reserved is tacitly given. A federal government is expressly only for FEDERAL PURPOSES, and its power is consequently bounded by the terms of the compact. In the first case a bill of rights is indispensable, in the second it would be at best useless, and if one right were to be omitted, it might injuriously grant, by implication, what was intended to be reserved. . . .

"9. THE LIBERTY OF THE PRESS is not secured, and the powers of Congress are fully adequate to its destruction, as they are to have the trial of *libels*, or *pretended libels* against the United States, and may by a cursed abominable STAMP ACT (as the *Bowdoin administration* has done in Massachusetts) preclude you effectually from all means of information. *Mr. W*[ilson] *has given you no answer to these arguments*."

The liberty of the press in each state can only be in danger from the laws of that state, and it is everywhere well secured. Besides, as the new Congress can only have the defined powers given, it was needless to say anything about liberty of the press, liberty of conscience, or any other liberty that a freeman ought never to be deprived of. It is remarkable in this instance, that among all the cases to which the federal jurisdiction is to extend (Article 3) not a word is said of *"libels or pretended libels."* Indeed in this extensive continent, and among this enlightened people, no government whatever *could* control the press. For after all that is said about "balance of power," there is one power which no tyranny on earth could subdue if once roused by this great and general grievances, that is THE PEOPLE. This respectable power has preserved the press in Great Britain in spite of government; and none but a madman could ever think of controlling it in America.

"10. Congress have the power of keeping up a STANDING ARMY in time of peace, and Mr. W[ilson] has told you THAT IT IS NECESSARY."

10. The power here referred to is this, "to raise and support armies, *but no appropriation of money to that use shall be for a longer term than two years*." (Article I, section 8.) Thus the representatives of the people have it in their power to disband this army every two years, by refusing supplies. Does not every American feel that no standing army in the power of Congress to raise, could support despotism over this immense continent, where almost every citizen is a soldier? If such an apprehension came, in my opinion, within the bounds of possibility, it would not indeed become my principles to oppose this objection.

DHRC, II, pp. 217-220.

R.S. November 10, 1787
Newspaper Article: Philadelphia *Pennsylvania Herald* (excerpt)

Sir, The most repeated, and certainly the most substantial, charge against the proposed constitution, is the want of a bill of rights. But as our ideas upon the subject are borrowed from Britain, it would not be amiss to recollect the manner in which the celebrated bill of rights of that nation was introduced and adopted. The constitution of England had certainly been established before the interference of the Prince of Orange, before the reign of Charles the first, and even before the reigns of Henry and his father John, for the bill of rights, the petition of rights, and the great charter itself are admitted by the best writers to be only formal acknowledgements of the pre-existing liberties of the people.

DHRC, II Mfm. Pa., p. 1055.

William Grayson (New York) November 10, 1787
Letter: To William Short (excerpt)

With respect to my own sentiments I own I have important objections:—In the first place I think liberty a thing of too much importance to be trusted on the ground of *implication:* it should rest on principles expressed in the clearest & most unequivocal manner. A bill of rights ought then to have preceded. tryals by jury should have been expressly reserved in Civil as well as Criminal cases.

The press ought to have been declared free—

DHRC, XIV, p. 82. Also reprinted in DHRC, VIII, pp. 150-151.

John Adams (London) November 10, 1787
Letter: To Thomas Jefferson (excerpt)

But still I hope the Constitution will be adopted, and amendments be made at a more convenient opportunity.

What think you of a Declaration of Rights? should not such a Thing have preceeded the Model?

DHRC, XIV, p. 463.

James White (New York) November 13, 1787
Letter: To Governor Richard Caswell of North Carolina (excerpt)

I must in candor confess, that I have regretted that the proposed constitution was not more explicit with respect to several essentials: but the great clamor is, that no express provision is made for the TRIAL BY JURY, and LIBERTY OF THE PRESS; things so interwoven with our political, or legal ideas, that I conceive the sacred immutability of these rights to be such, as never to have occurred as questionable objects to the convention. And can it indeed be supposed, that three distinct branches, originating from, & returning to the people, will combine to invade these inviolable first principles? Or would they expect to do it with impunity? The apprehension wears too pusilanimous a complexion.

DHRC, XIV, p. 96.

Thomas Jefferson (Paris) November 13, 1787
Letter: To William Stephens Smith (excerpt)[1]

We have had 13. states independant 11. years. There has been one rebellion. That comes to one rebellion in a century & a half for each state. What country before ever existed a century & a half without a rebellion? & what country can preserve it's liberties if their rulers are not warned from time to time that their people preserve the spirit of resistance? Let them take arms, the remedy is to set them right as to facts, pardon & pacify them. What signify a few lives lost in a century or two? The tree of liberty must be refreshed from time to time with the blood of patriots & tyrants. It is it's natural manure. Our Convention has been too much impressed by the insurrection of Massachusets:[2] and in the spur of the moment they are setting up a kite to keep the hen yard in order. I hope in god this article will be rectified before the new constitution is accepted.

1 DHRC, XIV, p. 465.
2 A reference to Shays' Rebellion.

One of the Late Army November 14, 1787
Newspaper Article: Philadelphia *Freeman's Journal* (excerpt)[1]

As if the deed was already done he[2] tells us "the *old constitution contained* many of the same things, which from error, or disingenuousness, are urged against the *new one.*" But, gentle reader, hear the proof!—"*Neither of them have a bill of rights, nor does either notice the liberty of the press, because they are already provided for by the State constitutions.*"—What effrontery!—Will this writer please to point out the similarity between the two systems upon which he founds this extraordinary observation? Has he reflected that they are wholly different—that the one did not require a *Bill of Rights,* while the other, if adopted, renders this palladium of our unalienable privileges indispensibly essential? Or is the mere omission of it, under one government, an argument for forgetting it in another? O! the depravity of some minds! Has this sophistical writer so soon forgotten that *sweeping* clause (as it has been judiciously termed) which places the authority of Congress *paramount* in all respects to the constitution and laws of every state? Will he dare to say that under this unlimited supreme authority of Congress any *Bill of Rights* is sacred, or that the LIBERTY OF THE PRESS is secure?

1 DHRC, II Mfm. Pa., p. 1096.
2 A reference to the writer of four letters under the pseudonym "A Citizen of America."

A Georgian November 15, 1787
Newspaper Article: *Gazette of the State of Georgia* (excerpt)

Though this new Federal Constitution, I believe, was framed and intended for the good of the United States and, as we are well aware, was assented to by the political saviors of our country, to whom all deference and respect is due, yet the sacredness of these illustrious characters has not been sufficient nor able to prevent several articles from creeping into the said Constitution which, by their different constructions and great latitude given them, an American Sulla or Augustus Octavianus might one day or other make serviceable to his ambition, interest, and to the utter subversion of our SACRED FREEDOM. And as mankind, upon the whole is so depraved as, with pleasure, to trample upon the sacred rights and privileges of their fellow creatures, it is certainly one of our greatest cares, both for ourselves and our offspring, to frame such constitutional laws thereby to prevent such designing tyrants (if ever they be) from grasping at a power, to our destruction, in the said Federal Constitution within their reach; as also to guard with the safest care against all encroachments, and to bar them forever from paving the way to what is worse yet, an ARISTOCRATICAL government, whereby about 70 nabobs would lord over three millions of people as slaves; as also to establish power, harmony, equality and justice, for and among the whole of the United States.

DHRC, III, p. 236.

Brutus III November 15, 1787
Newspaper Article: *New York Journal* (excerpt)

To the CITIZENS *of the* STATE *of* NEW-YORK. . . .

I have attempted to shew, that a consolidation of this extensive continent, under one government, for internal, as well as external purposes, which is evidently the tendency of this constitution, cannot succeed, without a sacrifice of your liberties; and therefore that the attempt is not only preposterous, but extremely dangerous; and I have shewn, independent of this, that the plan is radically defective in a fundamental principle, which ought to be found in every free government; to wit, a declaration of rights.

DHRC, XIV, pp. 119-120.

Cincinnatus III November 15, 1787
Newspaper Article: *New York Journal* (excerpt)

[To James Wilson, Esquire.]

Upon standing armies, sir, your professional dexterity has not abandoned you. The Constitution proposes to give the power of raising and supporting armies—and this without any limitation as to number; and to appropriate money to that object for two years at a time. This you justify by saying, that you "do not know a nation in the world which has not found it necessary and useful to maintain the appearance of strength, in a season of profound tranquility:" your knowledge then, sir, has not extended to free nations. Your phraseology, it is true, is somewhat equivocal; but unless by the term, appearance of strength, we understand, a standing army, we must suppose you to have meant a disingenuous evasion. Your reading might have informed you, sir,—that the Grecian republics, while free, never kept up a standing army—that the Roman republic, while free, never kept up a standing army, but that with them, a standing army and tyranny were co-eval, and concomitant—that in the free Swiss Cantons, no standing army, was ever, or is now permitted; no, sir, in all these great and glorious republics, though surrounded with enemies, their military array was occasional, or at the utmost, annual; nor was there formerly, nor is there now, in the Swiss Cantons, any more appearance of strength kept up in time of peace, than their militia gives: and yet they are free and formidable.

You say a standing army has always been, "a topic of popular declamation." Is it indeed nothing more, sir? Is that which all free nations have studiously avoided, as the rock on which their liberties would suffer shipwreck; that which in fact, is the source and security of tyranny; that which all great political writers concur in condemning; that which has animated the ardor, and inflamed the eloquence of the first orators in the two houses of parliament, in Great-Britain—that which all the art and influence of the crown could never obtain from the people for more than a year—is all that, sir, nothing more than a topic of popular declamation? Is it surprising, that such knowledge, and such sentiments, as this declaration holds out, should have given us such a constitution?

DHRC, XIV, pp. 127-128. The "Cincinnatus" series is reprinted in Storing, VI, starting at p. 5.

Publius {Alexander Hamilton} November 20, 1787
Newspaper Article: *New York Packet* (excerpt)[1]

The FOEDERALIST, No. 8

To the People of the State of New-York. . . .

There is a wide difference also, between military establishments in a country, seldom exposed by its situation to internal invasions, and in one which is often subject to them, and always apprehensive of them. The rulers of the former can have no good pretext, if they are even so inclined, to keep on foot armies so numerous as must of necessity be maintained in the latter. These armies being, in the first case, rarely, if at all, called into activity for interior defence, the people are in no danger of being broken to military subordination. The laws are not accustomed to relaxations, in favor of military exigencies—the civil state remains in full vigor, neither corrupted nor confounded with the principles or propensities of the other state. The smallness of the army renders the natural strength of the community an overmatch for it; and the citizens, not habituated to look up to the military power for [protection][2], or to submit to its oppressions, neither love nor fear the soldiery: They view them with a spirit of jealous acquiescence in a necessary evil, and stand ready to resist a power which they suppose may be exerted to the prejudice of their rights. The army under such circumstances, may usefully aid the magistrate to suppress a small faction, or an occasional mob, or insurrection; but it will be unable to enforce encroachments against the united efforts of the great body of the people.

In a country, in the predicament last described, the contrary of all this happens. The perpetual menacings of danger oblige the government to be always prepared to repel it—its armies must be numerous enough for instant defence. The continual necessity for their services enhances the importance of the soldier, and proportionably degrades the condition of the citizen. The military state becomes elevated above the civil. The inhabitants of territories, often the theatre of war, are unavoidably subjected to frequent infringement on their rights, which serve to weaken their sense of those rights; and by degrees, the people are brought to consider the soldiery not only as their protectors, but as their superiors. The transition from this disposition to that of considering them as masters, is neither remote, nor difficult: But it is very difficult to prevail upon a people under such impressions, to make a bold, or effectual resistance, to usurpations, supported by the military power.

The kindgom of Great Britain falls within the first description. An insular situation, and a powerful marine, guarding it in a great measure aginst the possibility of foreign invasion, supercede the necessity of a numerous standing army within the kingdom. A sufficient force to make head against a sudden descent, till the militia could have time to rally and embody, is all that has been deemed requisite. No motive of national policy have demanded, nor would public opinion have tolerated a larger number of troops upon its domestic establishment. There has been, for a long time past, little room for the operation of the other causes, which have been enumerated as the consequences of internal war. This peculiar felicity of situation has, in a great degree, contributed to preserve the liberty, which that country to this day enjoys, in spite of the prevalent venality and corruption.

1 DHRC, XIV, pp. 142-145.

2 "Perfection" is here given in the source. Undoubtedly a misprint as "protection" is clearly intended. See the next paragraph in the text.

Philadelphia *Freeman's Journal* November 21, 1787
(excerpt)

Extract of a letter from Queen Anne's county, (Maryland) *November* 12.

"You tell me of the beauties of the new constitution, and that great part of your state are for adopting it,—but this is quite different with our people; nobody now supposes that it will go down in this state, without a bill of rights, and very material alterations. You say, that General Wahington's name will force it down in all the states—but you are as much mistaken in that, as I was: I find that our southern states are clearer on this head than any other, that the greatest names ought not to prejudice any man in such an important business; but you will say to this, that the greatest prophet has no honor in his own country. I am often told, when I am arguing with them, that the general would not wish people to adopt it because his name is prefixed to it, and some have told me that the General, Mr. Franklin, and some others, did only sign as witnesses, and that they had no hand in forming it; I have shewn these people Mr. Wilson's speech which you sent me, but I find it does not answer here—pray send me some good, sound, plain, argumentative pieces, for I am looked very slyly at frequently, and I am afraid that there must be some cause for it. Please inform me how I shall get over this sweeping clause, as they call it, *viz.*—'That the constitution and laws of Congress are to have the power of regulating every thing in the state, and to be the supreme law of the land, any thing in the constitutions or laws of any of the states to the contrary notwithstanding;' for in their arguing for a bill of rights they always throw up this in the way, among other objections. Every body I see from Virginia, informs me, that all is going against us all over that state.

DHRC, XIV, p. 163.

Cincinnatus IV November 22, 1787
Newspaper Article: *New York Journal* (excerpt)

To James Wilson, Esquire.

Sir, The public appear to me, sir, to be much indebted to you, for informing them; for what purpose a power was given by the proposed Constitution, of raising and supporting armies.—Some, indeed, might have suspected, that such power, uncontrouled by any declaration, that the military should always be subject to the civil power, might be intended for the purposes of ambition. Your declaration has removed all doubt. Every principle of policy, you say, would be subverted unless we kept up armies—for what—for our defence?—no,—to support declarations of war—to strike home, with despatch and secrecy, before the enemy can be apprized of your intention. Upon the same principle a small army would be rediculous. Nothing less than the Prussian number, about 200,000 men would embrace this salutary object. And as you now say—"no man that regards the dignity and safety of his country can deny the necessity of a military force."—You will next affirm, that no one, for the same reason, can deny the necessity of a large army. The safety of the country, we have already experienced to depend, upon the militia. Switzerland has often experienced the same. Why then, sir, should you be so very positive, that for this purpose a military force is necessary?—But for the dignity of the country, that is for the ambition of its rulers, armies I confess are necessary; and not less in number than other ambitious rulers maintain, by grinding the face of the people. For every thousand in these armies a million of dollars must be levied upon the public, and such armies—raised and supported, would at once maintain the dignity of government, and ensure the submission of the people. We shall be as dignified as the Turks, and equally free.

DHRC, XIV, pp. 186-187. The "Cincinnatus" series is reprinted in Storing, VI, starting at p. 5.

A Citizen November 24, 1787
Newspaper Article: *New York Journal* (excerpt)

Mr. Greenleaf,

On reading your Daily Patriotic Register of the 21st inst. a political piece, under the signature of MEDIUM, engaged my attention—From the name which the author has taken, I flattered myself, that his writings would have been influenced by candor and impartiality; his declarations in the first paragraph, of his having perused the publications for and against the new constitution, "without bias or prejudice," and that his researches had been solely directed to discover on which side the greatest reason prevailed—and, his indiscriminate censures of writers (without my stopping to enquire into the justice of them) confirmed my opinion in favor of his performance: you may judge then of my disappointment when I came to the two last paragraphs; these plainly discover that little dependence can be placed on appearances, and that the people ought to guard against the cunning and insidious arts, employed by desinging men to mislead and betray them; for, it is evidently discernible, that the name which the writer assumes, and the candor that he effects, were purposely designed the better to carry on the business of deception, and to effect the great end which a certain lordly party have in view—the adoption of the new constitution with all its defects; and, of course, risking the dearest rights of mankind to the precarious chance of being secured by future amendments.

In the first place, Medium asserts, that "It may be true, that the constitution is defective, but none have yet been able to prove that it is materially so;" he, however, admits, that it is not accompanied with a bill of rights, which he allows "to be the best security we can have against the encroachments of despotism"—Here it is granted, that the omission of a bill of rights is (whether proved so by other writers or not) "a material defect";—With what degree of consistency then can he urge "the embracing the constitution as it now stands"; certainly, he cannot be ignorant, that if it is agreed to without "that best security against the encroachments of despotism," that our liberties must, hereafter, entirely depend upon acts of an imperfect and unequal congressional legislature, which may be repealed at their pleasure, and, whenever it suits their arbitrary designs.

Storing, VI, pp. 45-46.

Preston, Connecticut November 26, 1787
Instructions of Town Meeting (excerpt)

Voted to give the delegates chosen by this town to attend the state Convention to be holden at Hartford on the first Thursday of January next the following instructions, viz.:

Colonel Jeremiah Halsey and Mr. Wheeler Coit.

Gentlemen: We the inhabitants of the town of Preston legally convened in town meeting having made choice of you, delegates to represent us in the Convention of this state to meet at Hartford in January next to consider of the Constitution proposed to be established in the United States by the late Federal Convention held in Philadelphia, and as we consider ourselves deeply interested and also our posterity in the matter of the proposed Constitution to which for us you are to assent or dissent, we esteem it our right and our duty to instruct you in our opinion and desire on this important subject. It is our ardent wish that an efficient government may be established over these states so constructed that the people may retain all liberties, privileges, and immunities usual and necessary for citizens of a free country and yet sufficient provision made for carrying into execution all the powers vested in government. We are willing to give up such share of our rights as to enable government to support, defend, and preserve the rest. It is difficult to draw the line. All will agree that the people should retain so much power that if ever venality and corruption should prevail in our public councils and government should be perverted and not answer the end of its institution, viz., the well being of society and the good of the whole, in that case the people may resume their rights and put an end to the wantonness of power. In whatever government the people neglect to retain so much power in their hands as to be a check to their rulers, depravity and the love of power is so prevalent in the humane mind, even of the best of men, that tyranny and cruelty will inevitably take place, and the people will be undeceived too late. We agree that the people of these states have no energetic common compact or national existence strictly speaking, and in that respect they are as a number of individuals nearly in a state of natural liberty, and we believe it would be for the benefit of the people that a system of government should take place that we may enjoy national advantages and assume some national importance; but individuals should move with caution in giving up their individual and natural rights to society. Tis much easier to give more power into the hands of government when more is necessary than to recover back where too much is already given. The want of attention to these maxims has enslaved almost all the nations of the world.

DHRC, III, pp. 439-440.

Pennsylvania Convention November 26, 1787
Debates (excerpt)

[Mr. WILSON.]

There necessarily exists, in every government, a power from which there is no appeal, and which, for that reason, may be termed supreme, absolute, and uncontrollable. Where does this power reside? To this question writers on different governments will give different answers. Sir William Blackstone will tell you, that in Britain the power is lodged in the British Parliament; that the Parliament may alter the form of the government; and that its power is absolute, without control. The idea of a constitution, limiting and superintending the operations of legislative authority, seems not to have been accurately understood in Britain. There are, at least, no traces of practice conformable to such a principle. The British constitution is just what the British Parliament pleases. When the Parliament transferred legislative authority to Henry VIII., the act transferring could not, in the strict acceptation of the term, be called unconstitutional.

To control the power and conduct of the legislature, by an overruling constitution, was an improvement in the science and practice of government reserved to the American states.

Perhaps some politician, who has not considered with sufficient accuracy our political systems, would answer that, in our governments, the supreme power was vested in the constitutions. This opinion approaches a step nearer to the truth, but does not reach it. The truth is, that, in our governments, the supreme, absolute, and uncontrollable power *remains* in the people. As our constitutions are superior to our legislatures, so the people are superior to our constitutions. Indeed, the superiority, in this last instance, is much greater; for the people possess over our constitutions control in *act,* as well as right.

The consequence is, that the people may change the constitutions whenever and however they please. This is a right of which no positive institution can ever deprive them.

These important truths, sir, are far from being merely speculative. We, at this moment, speak and deliberate under their immediate and benign influence. To the operation of these truths we are to ascribe the scene, hitherto unparalleled, which America now exhibits to the world—a gentle, a peaceful, a voluntary, and a deliberate transition from one constitution of government to another. In other parts of the world, the idea of revolutions in government is, by a mournful and an indissoluble association, connected with the idea of wars, and all the calamities attendant on wars. But happy experience teaches us to view such revolutions in a very different light—to consider them only as progressive steps in improving the knowledge of government, and increasing the happiness of society and mankind.

Oft have I marked, with silent pleasure and admiration, the force and prevalence, through the United States, of the principle that the supreme power resides in the people, and that they never part with it. It may be called the *panacea* in politics. There can be no disorder in the community but may here receive a radical cure. If the error be in the legislature, it may be corrected by the constitution; if in the constitution, it may be corrected by the people. There is a remedy, therefore, for every distemper in government, if the people are not wanting to themselves; if they are wanting to themselves, there is no remedy. From their power, as we have seen, there is no appeal; of their error there is no superior principle of correction.

Debates, II, pp. 432-433.

Pennsylvania Convention November 28, 1787
Debates (excerpts)

JAMES WILSON: This will be a proper time for making an observation or two, on what may be called the Preamble to this Constitution. I had occasion, on a former day, to mention that the leading principle in the politics, and that which pervades the American constitutions, is, that the supreme power resides in the people; this Constitution, Mr. President, opens with a solemn and practical recognition of that principle: "WE, THE PEOPLE OF THE UNITED STATES, in order to form a more perfect union, establish justice, &c. DO ORDAIN AND ESTABLISH this constitution for the United States of America." It is announced in their name—it receives its political existence from their authority—they ordain and establish. What is the necessary consequence? Those who ordain and establish have the power, if they think proper, to repeal and annul. A proper attention to this principle may, perhaps, give ease to the minds of some, who have heard much concerning the necessity of a bill of rights.

Its establishment, I apprehend, has more force, than a volume written on the subject—it renders this truth evident, that the people have a right to do what they please, with regard to the government. I confess, I feel a kind of pride, in considering the striking difference between the foundation, on which the liberties of this country are declared to stand in this Constitution, and the footing on which the liberties of England are said to be placed. The Magna Charta of England is an instrument of high value to the people of that country. But, Mr. President, from what source does that instrument derive the liberties of the inhabitants of that kingdom? Let it speak for itself. The king says, "*we* have *given* and *granted* to all archbishops, bishops, abbots, priors, earls, barons, and to all the freemen of this our realm, these liberties following, to be kept in our kingdom of England forever." When this was assumed as the leading principle of that government, it was no wonder that the people were anxious to obtain bills of rights, and to take every opportunity of enlarging and securing their liberties. But, here, sir, the fee-simple remains in the people at large, and by this Constitution they do not part with it.[1]

[JOHN SMILIE.]

But the gentleman takes pride in the superiority of this short Preamble when compared with Magna Charta. Why, sir, I hope the rights of men are better understood at this day than at the framing of that deed, and we must be convinced that civil liberty is capable of still greater improvement and extension than is known even in its present cultivated state. True, sir, the supreme authority naturally rests in the people, but does it follow that therefore a declaration of rights would be superfluous? Because the people have a right to alter and abolish government, can it therefore be inferred that every step taken to secure that right would be superfluous and nugatory? The truth is that unless some criterion is established by which it could be easily and constitutionally ascertained how far our governors may proceed, and by which it might appear when they transgress their jurisdiction, this idea of altering and abolishing government is a mere sound without substance. Let us recur to the memorable Declaration of the 4th of July 1776. Here it is said: . . .

"We hold these truths to be self evident; that all men are created equal; that thay are endowed by their Creator with certain unalienable rights; that among these are life, liberty, and the pursuit of happiness. That to secure these rights, governments are instituted among men, deriving their just powers from the consent of the governed; that whenever any form of government becomes destructive of these ends, it is the right of the people to alter or abolish it, and to institute a new government, laying its foundation on such principles, and organizing its powers in such form, as to them shall seem most likely to effect their safety and happiness."

Now, sir, if in the proposed plan, the gentleman can show any similar security for the civil rights of the people I shall certainly be relieved from a weight of objection to its adoption, and I sincerely hope, that as he has gone so far, he will proceed to communicate some of the reasons (and undoubtedly they must have been powerful ones) which induced the late Federal Convention to omit a bill of rights, so essential in the opinion of many citizens to a perfect form of government.[2]

JAMES WILSON: I am called upon to give a reason, why the Convention omitted to add a bill of rights to the work before you. I confess, sir, I did think that in point of propriety, the honorable gentleman [John Smilie] ought first to have furnished some reasons, to show such an addition to be necessary; it is natural to prove the affirmative of a proposition; and if he had established the propriety of this addition, he might then have asked, why it was not made.

I cannot say, Mr. President, what were the reasons, of every member of that Convention, for not adding a bill of rights; I believe the truth is, that such an idea never entered the mind of many of them. I don't recollect to have heard the subject mentioned, till within about three days of the time of our rising, and even then there was no direct motion offered for any thing of the kind. I may be mistaken in this; but as far as my memory serves me, I believe it was the case. A proposition to adopt a measure, that would have supposed that we were throwing into the general government every power not expressly reserved by the people would have been spurned at, in that house, with the greatest indignation; even in a single government, if the powers of the people rest on the same establishment, as is expressed in this Constitution, a bill of rights is by no means a necessary measure. In a government possessed of enumerated powers, such a measure would be not only unnecessary, but preposterous and dangerous.[3]

[JAMES WILSON.]
In civil government it is certain that bills of rights are unnecessary and useless, nor can I conceive whence the contrary notion has arisen. Virginia has no bill of rights, and will it be said that her constitution was the less free?[4]

JOHN SMILIE: The arguments which have been urged, Mr. President, have not, in my opinion, satisfactorily shown that a bill of rights would have been an improper, nay, that it is not a necessary appendage to the proposed system. As it has been denied that Virginia possesses a bill of rights, I shall on that subject only observe, that Mr. Mason, a gentleman certainly of great information and integrity, has assured me that such a thing does exist, and I am persuaded, I shall be able at a future period to lay it before the Convention. But, sir, the State of Delaware has a bill of rights, and I believe one of the honorable members (Thomas M'Kean) who now contests the necessity and propriety of that instrument, took a very conspicuous part in the formation of the Delaware government. It seems however that the members of the Federal Convention were themselves convinced, in some degree, of the expediency and propriety of a bill of rights, for we find them expressly declaring that the writ of *habeas corpus* and the trial by jury in criminal cases shall not be suspended or infringed. How does this indeed agree with the maxim that whatever is not given is reserved? Does it not rather appear from the reservation of these two articles that everything else, which is not specified, is included in the powers delegated to the government? This, sir, must prove the necessity of a full and explicit declaration of rights; and when we further consider the extensive, the undefined powers vested in the administrators of this system, when we consider the system itself as a great political compact between the governors and the governed, a plain, strong, and accurate criterion by which the people might at once determine when, and in what instance, their rights were violated is a preliminary without which this plan ought not to be adopted. So loosely, so inaccurately are the powers which are enumerated in this Constitution defined, that it will be impossible, without a test of that kind, to ascertain the limits of authority and to declare when government has degenerated into oppression. In that event the contest will arise between the people and the rulers. "You have exceeded the powers of your office, you have oppressed us" will be the language of the suffering citizens. The answser of the government will be short: "We have not exceeded our power; you have no test by which you can prove it." Hence, sir, it will be impracticable to stop the progress of tyranny, for there will be no check but the people, and their exertions must be futile and uncertain; since it will be difficult indeed, to communicate to them the violation that has been committed, and their proceedings will be neither systematical nor unanimous. It is said, however, that the difficulty of framing a bill of rights was insurmountable; but, Mr. President, I cannot agree in this opinion. Our experience, and the numerous precedents before us, would have furnished a very sufficient guide. At present there is no security, even for the rights of conscience, and under the sweeping force of the sixth Article every principle of a bill of rights, every stipulation for the most sacred and invaluable privileges of man, are left at the mercy of government.[5]

JAMES WILSON: I do not rely upon the information of Mr. Mason or of any other gentleman on a question of this kind, but I refer to the authenticity of the volume which contains the state constitutions, and in that Virginia has no bill of rights.[6]

[JAMES WILSON.]

Whence comes this notion, that in the United States there is no security without a bill of rights? Have the citizens of South Carolina no security for their liberties? They have no bill of rights. Are the citizens on the eastern side of the Delaware less free, or less secured in their liberties, than those on the western side? The state of New Jersey has no bill of rights. The state of New York has no bill of rights. The states of Connecticut and Rhode Island have no bill of rights. I know not whether I have exactly enumerated the states who have thought it unnecessary to add a bill of rights to their constitution; but this enumeration, sir, will serve to show by experience, as well as principle, that even in single governments, a bill of rights is not an essential or necessary measure. But in a government consisting of enumerated powers, such as is proposed for the United States, a bill of rights would not only be unnecessary, but, in my humble judgment, highly imprudent. In all societies, there are many powers and rights, which cannot be particularly enumerated. A bill of rights annexed to a constitution is an enumeration of the powers reserved. If we attempt an enumeration, every thing that is not enumerated is presumed to be given. The consequence is, that an imperfect enumeration would throw all implied power into the scale of the government; and the rights of the people would be rendered incomplete. On the other hand, an imperfect enumeration of the powers of government reserves all implied power to the people; and, by that means the constitution becomes incomplete; but of the two it is much safer to run the risk on the side of the constitution; for an omission in the enumeration of the powers of government is neither so dangerous, nor important, as an omission in the enumeration of the rights of the people.

Mr. President, as we are drawn into this subject, I beg leave to pursue its history a little farther. The doctrine and practice of declarations of rights have been borrowed from the conduct of the people of England, on some remarkable occasion; but the principles and maxims, on which their government is constituted, are widely different from those of ours. I have already stated the language of Magna Charta. After repeated confirmations of that instrument, and after violations of it, repeated equally often, the next step taken in this business was when the petition of rights was presented to Charles I.

It concludes in this manner, "all of which they most humbly *pray* to be allowed, as their rights and liberties, according to the laws and statutes of this realm." (*8th Par. Hist. 150.*) One of the most material statutes of the realm was Magna Charta; so that we find they continue upon the old ground, as to the foundation on which they rest their liberties. It was not till the era of the revolution that the two houses assume a higher tone, and "*demand* and insist upon all the premises as their undoubted rights and liberties." (*Par. Deb. 261.*) But when the whole transaction is considered, we shall find that those rights, and liberties, are claimed only on the foundation of an original contract, supposed to have been made at some former period, between the king and the people. (*1 Blackstone, 233.*)

But, in this Constitution, the citizens of the United States appear dispensing a part of their original power in what manner and what proportion they think fit. They never part with the whole; and they retain the right of recalling what they part with. When, therefore, they possess, as I have already mentioned, the fee simple of authority, why should they have recourse to the minute and subordinate remedies, which can be necessary only to those, who pass the fee, and reserve only a rent-charge?

To every suggestion concerning a bill of rights, the citizens of the United States may always say, WE reserve the right to do what we please.[7]

ROBERT WHITEHILL: I differ, sir, from the honorable member from the city [James Wilson] as to the impropriety or necessity of a bill of rights. If indeed the Constitution itself so well defined the powers of the government that no mistake could arise, and we were well assured that our governors would always act right, then we might be satisfied without an explicit reservation of those rights with which the people ought not, and mean not to part. But, sir, we know that it is the nature of power to seek its own augmentation, and thus the loss of liberty is the necessary consequence of a loose or extravagant delegation of authority. National freedom has been, and will be the sacrifice of ambition and power, and it is our duty to employ the present opportunity in stipulating such restrictions as are best calculated to protect us from oppression and slavery. Let us then, Mr. President, if other countries cannot supply an adequate example, let us proceed upon our own principles, and with the great end of government in view, the happiness of the people, it will be strange if we err. Government we have been told, sir, is yet in its infancy; we ought not therefore to submit to the shackles of foreign schools and opinions. In entering into the social compact, men ought not to leave their rulers at large, but erect a permanent landmark by which they may learn the extent of their authority, and the people be able to discover the first encroachments on their liberties.[8] . . .

Upon the whole, therefore, I wish it to be seriously considered, whether we have a right to leave the liberties of the people to such future constructions and expositions as may possibly be made upon this system; particularly when its advocates, even at this day, confess that it would be dangerous to omit anything in the enumeration of a bill of rights, and according to their principle, the reservation of the *habeas corpus* and trial by jury in criminal cases may hereafter be construed to be the only privileges reserved by the people. I am not anxious, Mr. President, about forms; it is the substance which I wish to obtain; and therefore I acknowledge, if our liberties are secured by the frame of government itself, the supplementary instrument of a declaration of rights may well be dispensed with. But, sir, we find no security there, except in the two instances referred to, and it will not,

I hope, any longer be alleged that no security is requisite, since those exceptions prove a contrary sentiment to have been entertained by the very framers of the proposed Constitution.[9]

JAMES WILSON: I concur most sincerely, with the honorable gentleman [Robert Whitehill] who was last up in one sentiment, that if our liberties will be insecure under this system of government, it will become our duty not to adopt, but to reject it. On the contrary, if it will secure the liberties of the citizens of America, if it will not only secure their liberties, but procure them happiness, it becomes our duty, on the other hand, to assent to and ratify it. With a view to conduct us safely and gradually to the determination of that important question, I shall beg leave to notice some of the objections that have fallen from the honorable gentleman from Cumberland, (Whitehill.) But, before I proceed, permit me to make one general remark. Liberty has a formidable enemy on each hand; on one there is tyranny, on the other licentiousness. In order to guard against the latter, proper powers ought to be given to government; in order to guard against the former, those powers ought to be properly distributed.[10]

1 DHRC, II, pp. 382-383.
2 *Ibid.*, pp. 385-386.
3 *Ibid.*, pp. 387-388.
4 *Ibid.*, p. 390.
5 *Ibid.*, pp. 391-392.
6 *Ibid.*, p. 390.
7 *Ibid.*, pp. 388-389.
8 *Ibid.*, p. 393.
9 *Ibid.*, p. 398.
10 *Ibid.*, p. 400.

An Old Whig VII November 28, 1787

Newspaper Article: Philadelphia *Independent Gazetter* (excerpt)

1st. Let the Conventions of each state, as they meet, after considering the proposed Constitution, state their objections and propose their amendments.

So far from these objections and amendments clashing with each other in irreconcileable discord, as it has been too often suggested they would do, it appears that from what has been hitherto published in the different states in opposition to the proposed Constitution, we have a right to expect that they will harmonize in a very great degree. The reason I say so is, that about the same time, in very different parts of the continent, the very same objections have been made, and the very same alterations proposed by different writers, who I verily believe, know nothing at all of each other, and were very far from acting a premeditated concert, and that others who have not appeared as writers in the newspapers, in the different states, have appeared to act and speak in perfect unison with those objections and amendments, particularly in the article of a bill of rights. That in short, the very same sentiments seem to have been echoed from the different parts of the continent by the opposers of the proposed Constitution, and these sentiments have been very little contradicted by its friends, otherwise than by suggesting their fears, that by opposing the Constitution at the present proposed, we might be disappointed of any federal government or receive a worse one than the present. It would be a most delightful surprise to find ourselves all of one opinion at last; and I cannot forbear hoping that when we come fairly to compare our sentiments, we shall find ourselves much more nearly agreed than in the hurry and surpise in which we have been involved on this subject, than we ever suffered ourselves to imagine.

DHRC, II, p. 302. The series "An Old Whig" is reprinted in Storing, III, starting at p. 17.

A Federal Republican November 28, 1787
Pamphlet: A Review of the Constitution (excerpt)[1]
Philadelphia

Hitherto we have been considering the blemishes of the Constitution as they statedly exist—other objects are derived from omission. Among these the grand one, upon which is indeed suspended every other, is the omission of a bill of rights.

The remarker upon the address of the sixteen members has answered their objection with much force. "I answer (says he) *this is not true,* it contains a declaration of many rights, and very important ones, i.e., that people shall be obliged to fulfill their contracts, and not avoid them by *tenders* of anything less than the value stipulated—that no *ex post facto* laws shall be made, etc."[2]

The gentleman has here very wittily mistaken the sense of the two terms right and obligation.

They are correlative terms and between two parties. Whenever the former applies to the one, the latter of necessity applies to the other. Whatever anyone has a *right* to expect from me, I am *obliged* to render him. He might as well have said that the Constitution gave the people a *right* to submit to Congress in everything, and that we have a *right* to pay the last farthing of compliance to their despotic whims.

What he mentions is the enforcing of *obligation* and not the declaring of *right*.

One of the learned members of the late Convention, the Honorable Mr. [James] Wilson, observes in his speech that all powers which are not by the Constitution given up to Congress are reserved for the disposition of the several states. This observation is wise and true, because properly speaking it should be so. In entering into the social compact, all rights which are not expressly given up to the governors are reserved to the people. That it is so from a just construction it is easy to discover.

But notwithstanding, if the people are jealous of their rights, where will be the harm in declaring them? If they be meant, as they certainly are, to be reserved to the people, what injury can arise from a positive declaration of it? Although in reasoning it would appear to be unnecessary, yet if the people prefer having their rights stately defined, it is certainly reasonable that it should be done. I am well acquainted with the logical reason that is general[ly] given for it.

It is said that the insertion of a bill of rights would be an argument against the present liberty of the people.

To have the rights of the people declared to them would imply that they had previously given them up or were not in possession of them.

This indeed is a distinction of which the votaries of scholastic philosophy might be proud—but in the political world, where reason is not cultivated independently of action and experience, such futile distinctions ought not to be agitated.

In fact, it does not exist, for I should think it is as rational to declare the right of the people to what they already possess, as to decree to them any new rights. If the people do really possess them, there can be no harm in expressing what is meant to be understood.

A bill of rights should either be inserted, or a declaration made that whatever is not decreed to Congress is reserved to the several states for their own disposal.

In this particular, the Articles of the present Confederation have an evident advantage. The second Article says, that "each state retains its *sovereignty, freedom and independence,* and every *power, jurisdiction, and right, which is not* by this confederation *expressly declared* to [the] United States in Congress assembled."

This will appear the more proper, if we consider that these *are rights* in which all the states are concerned. It is thought proper to delegate to Congress supreme power on all occasions where the *natural* interests of the states are concerned, and why not for the same reason grant and declare to the states a bill of *those rights* which are also *mutual?*

At any rate it is certain that no injury can arise from it, and to do it would be satisfactory and wise.

On the whole, my fellow citizens, this Constitution was *conceived* in wisdom; the thanks of the United States are justly due to the members of the late Convention. But let their productions pass again through the furnace.

Because this once granted they will be fully enabled in the present age to lay the gentle foundation of despotic power, and after a temporary interval of seeming humanity between you and succeeding generations, to rivet upon *them* the chains of slavery beyond the possibility of a rupture.

To guard against this, I could wish to see the proposed Constitution revised and corrected.

If the states are not to be *confederated,* let them be reduced to one compact body.

And if a perfect consolidation of the states is to take place, if the people are to become the source of power, and if Congress is to represent them as the head of this grand body politic, in the name of all that is dear to freemen, permit not the veins through which the life of government itself is to flow from the *heart* to the *head* be any way obstructed—let the passages be free and open that *vital* heat may *animate* every *limb.*

That if all the states were to offer their objections, the Constitution would be reduced to nothing, is an ill-founded idea.

The good-natured simularity which the citizen of America discovered between this Constitution and a piece of painting is perfectly erroneous.

All painting is addressed to the *sense* and relished by *taste* which is various and fluctuating—but this Constitution is addressed to the *understanding* and judged of by *reason* which is fixed and true.

The Constitution is for the most part good, and perhaps many of the objections which have been made to it arise from our not being able to discern *clearly* the collective interest of the states.

Some of them, however, in all probability, exist beyond contradiction.

Let the convention of each state make its exceptions, then let a future and general one receive them all and reconcile them with as much wisdom as possible.

This would certainly be some refinement.

It *could* do no *harm,* but *might* do much *good.*

To conclude, my friends and fellow citizens, have [the] proposed Constitution revised, corrected and amended—have every dubious expression be made plain and clear—have every power accurately defined and well understood, and your own rights and privileges clearly stated or a declaration made that all powers that are not by this Constitution delegated to Congress are reserved for your own disposal.

Then, and not till then, will impartial justice rule over our land, and America become the theater of equity and wisdom, as she has already been the field of patriotism and bravery.

This once obtained, we shall be happy and free, and having enjoyed the blessings of peace and plenty under the ample shade of the tree of *liberty*, we shall deliver them down unimpaired by the corrosive influence of time to the latest posterity.

1 DHRC, II, pp. 303-306. Also reprinted in DHRC, XIV, pp. 274-276. "A Federal Republican" is reprinted in Storing, III, starting at p. 65.

2 See "Seceding Pennsylvania Assemblymen," October 2, 1787, p. 30, for an excerpt from the "address of the sixteen members."

Brutus IV November 29, 1787
Newspaper Article: *New York Journal* (excerpts)

A farther objection against the feebleness of the representation is, that it will not possess the confidence of the people. The execution of the laws in a free government must rest on this confidence, and this must be founded on the good opinion they entertain of the framers of the laws. Every government must be supported, either by the people having such an attachment to it, as to be ready, when called upon, to support it, or by a force at the command of the government, to compel obedience. The latter mode destroys every idea of a free government; for the same force that may be employed to compel obedience to good laws, might, and probably would be used to wrest from the people their constitutional liberties. . . .

If then this government should not derive support from the good will of the people, it must be executed by force, or not executed at all; either case would lead to the total destruction of liberty.—The convention seemed aware of this, and have therefore provided for calling out the militia to execute the laws of the union. If this system was so framed as to command that respect from the people, which every good free government will obtain, this provision was unnecessary—the people would support the civil magistrate. This power is a novel one, in free governments—these have depended for the execution of the laws on the Posse Comitatus, and never raised an idea, that the people would refuse to aid the civil magistrate in executing those laws they themselves had made.

DHRC, XIV, p. 299-301.

Agrippa III November 30, 1787
Newpaper Article: Boston *Massachusetts Gazette* (excerpt)

[TO THE PEOPLE.]

At present this state is one of the most respectable and one of the most influential in the union. If we alone should object to receiving the system without amendments, there is no doubt but it would be amended. But the case is not quite so bad. New-York appears to have no disposition even to call a convention. If they should neglect, are we to lend our assistance to compel them by arms, and thus to kindle a civil war without any provocation on their part? Virginia has put off their convention till May, and appears to have no disposition to receive the new plan without amendments. Pennsylvania does not seem to be disposed to receive it as it is. The same objections are made in all the states, that the civil government which they have adopted and which secures their rights will be subverted. All the defenders of this system undertake to prove that the rights of the states and of the citizens are kept safe. The opposers of it agree that they will receive the least burdensome system which shall defend those rights.

Both parties therefore found their arguments on the idea that these rights ought to be held sacred. With this disposition is it not in every man's mind better to recommit it to a new convention, or to Congress, which is a regular convention for the purpose, and to instruct our delegates to confine the system to the general purposes of the union, than the endeavour to force it through in its present form, and with so many opposers as it must have in every state on the continent?

Essays, pp. 61-62. The "Agrippa" series is reprinted in Storing, IV, starting at p. 68.

Pennsylvania Convention November 30, 1787
Debates (excerpts)

[ROBERT WHITEHILL.]
But in considering, sir, what was necessary to the safety and energy of the government, some attention ought surely to have been paid to the safety and freedom of the people. No satisfactory reason has yet been offered for the omission of a bill of rights; but, on the contrary, the honorable members are defeated in the only pretext which they have been able to assign, that every thing which is not given is excepted,

for we have shown that there are two articles expressly reserved, the writ of *habeas corpus* and the trial by jury in criminal cases; and we have called upon them, in vain, to reconcile this reservation with the tenor of their favorite proposition. For, if there was danger in the attempt to enumerate the liberties of the people, lest it should prove imperfect and defective, how happens it that in the instances I have mentioned, that danger has been incurred? Have the people no other rights worth their attention, or is it to be inferred, agreeably to the maxim of our opponents, that every other right is abandoned? Surely, sir, our language was competent to declare the sentiments of the people and to establish a bar against the intrusions of the general government in other respects as well as these; and when we find some privileges stipulated, the argument of danger is effectually destroyed; and the argument of difficulty, which has been drawn from the attempt to enumerate every right, cannot now be urged against the enumeration of more rights than this instrument contains. In short, Mr. President, it is our duty to take care that the foundation of this system is so laid that the superstructure, which is to be reared by other hands, may not cast a gloom upon the temple of freedom, the recent purchase of our toil and treasure. When, therefore, I consider it as the means of annihilating the constitutions of the several states, and consequently, the liberties of the people, I should be wanting to my constituents, to myself, and to posterity did I not exert every talent with which Heaven has endowed me to counteract the measures that have been taken for its adoption. That it was the design of the late Federal Convention to absorb and abolish the individual sovereignty of the states, I seek no other evidence but this system; for as the honorable delegate [James Wilson] to that body has recommended, I am also satisfied to judge of the tree by its fruit. When, therefore, I behold it thus systematically constructed for the accomplishment of that object, when I recollect the talents of those who framed it, I cannot hesitate to impute to them an intention corresponding with the principles and operation of their own work. Finally, sir, that the dissolution of our state constitutions will produce the ruin of civil liberty is a proposition easy to be maintained, and which, I am persuaded, in the course of these debates, will be incontrovertibly established in the mind of every member, whose judgment is open to conviction and whose vote has not been conclusively pledged for the ratification of this Constitution before its merits were discussed.[1]

[BENJAMIN RUSH.]
Civilians having taught us, Mr. President, that occupancy was the origin of property, I think, it may likewise be considered as the origin

of liberty; and as we enjoy all our natural rights from a preoccupancy, antecedent to the social state, in entering into that state, whence shall they be said to be derived? Would it not be absurd to frame a formal declaration that our natural rights are acquired from ourselves, and would it not be a more ridiculous solecism to say, that they are the gift of those rulers whom we have created, and who are invested by us with every power they possess? Sir, I consider it as an honor to the late Convention that this system has not been disgraced with a bill of rights; though I mean not to blame or reflect upon those states which have encumbered their constitutions with that idle and superfluous instrument. One would imagine however, from the arguments of the opposition that this government was immediately to be administered by foreigners, strangers to our habits and opinions, and unconnected with our interests and prosperity. These apprehensions, sir, might have been excused while we were contending with Great Britain; but, at this time, they are applicable to all governments, as well as that under consideration; and the arguments of the honorable members are, indeed, better calculated for an Indian council fire than the meridian of this refined and enlightened Convention.[2]

[JASPER] YEATES: The objections hitherto offered to this system, Mr. President, may, I think, be reduced to these general heads: first, that there is no bill of rights, and secondly, that the effect of the proposed government will be a consolidation, and not a confederation of the states. Upon the first head, it appears to me, that great misapprehension has arisen, from considering the situation of Great Britain to be parallel to the situation of this country, whereas the difference is so essential that a bill of rights, which was there both useful and necessary, becomes here at once useless and unnecessary. In England a power (by what means it signifies little) was established paramount to that of the people, and the only way which they had to secure the remnant of their liberties was, on every opportunity, to stipulate with that power for the uninterrupted enjoyment of certain enumerated privileges. But our case is widely different, and we find that, upon the opinion of this difference, seven of the thirteen United States have not added a bill of rights to their respective constitutions. Nothing, indeed, seems more clear to my judgment than this, that in our circumstances, every power which is not expressly given is, in fact, reserved. But it is asked, as some rights are here expressly provided for, why should not more? In truth, however, the writ of *habeas corpus* and the trial by jury in criminal cases cannot be considered as a bill of rights, but merely as a reservation on the part of the people and a restriction on the part of their rulers; and I agree with those gentlemen who conceive that a bill of rights, according to the ideas of the opposition, would be accompanied with considerable difficulty and danger; for, it might be argued at a future day by the persons then in power—you undertook to enumerate the rights which you meant to reserve, the pretension which you now make is not comprised in that enumeration, and, consequently, our jurisdiction is not circumscribed.[3]

Mr. M'Kean said yesterday [November 30] in the Convention, that he wished the opponents of the proposed Constitution would not merely find out its defects, but state the remedies. Since they consider a bill of rights so essential, why do they not show us one that we may judge of its necessity? To this Mr. Smilie answered, he was happy to hear the idea suggested, for he had understood that the Convention did not mean to admit either additions or amendments, but let them agree to do this, and he pledged himself to produce such a declaration of rights and such other amendments as would conciliate the opponents of the plan in its present state, who wished not to reject it altogether, but to make it as secure as possible, in favor of the civil liberties of the people.[4]

JOHN SMILIE: We will exhibit a bill of rights, if the Convention will receive it. (1) Great point—Is a bill of rights necessary? (2) Does this system abolish the state governments? Direct taxation, poll tax, standing army are objections.

Freedom almost unknown in the Old World. Are we to go there for precedents of liberty? Bill of rights necessary as the instrument of *original compact* and to mention the rights reserved. The sovereignty and independence of the states should be reserved. There must be a people before there is a king; and the people, in the first instance, have inherent and inalienable rights. We ought to know what rights we *surrender*, and what we *retain*.

Suppose Congress to pass an act for the punishment of libels and restrain the liberty of the press, for they are warranted to do this. What security would a printer have, tried in one of their courts? An aristocratical government cannot bear the liberty of the press.

The Senate will swallow up any thing. What harm from a bill of rights?[5]

1 DHRC, II, pp. 427-428.
2 *Ibid.*, p. 434.
3 *Ibid.*, pp. 436-437.
4 *Ibid.*, p. 444.
5 *Ibid.*, p. 441.

One of the Common People December 3, 1787
Newspaper Article: *Boston Gazette*

Messieurs Edes,

A Writer in the Centinel who calls himself "*One of the middle-interest,*" has gone into a long inquiry to find out "*where we learned the idea of a Bill of Rights.*" It is of little moment where it was learned, since we are possessed of so important and so invaluable a discovery, to guard the *people* against the increasing powers of artificial aristocracy, whose seeds are every where disseminated in free states. This writer thinks it would be superfluous to preface or combine with the federal constitution, a *bill of rights,* because the state constitution is already guarded by one.—If the new plan is adopted, every one knows the state constitution will be very materially and essentially altered; and so far will the security of our rights be precarious and dependent on meer acts of congress, which, without this barrier, may, and by the present tenor of the new constitution, will render our priviledges as undefined as this writer says are those of the subjects of England; which are only to be "*collected from meer opinions of the learned and contradictory authors.*" If we alienate a great part of the powers, at present contained in our state constitution, and vest them in congress, why is it not as necessary that those alienated powers should be secured and limited by a declaration of rights, as that the remaining powers which are left in the hands of the state government should be thus guarded, especially if the greater half are alienated? This writer says, a bill of rights is not necessary, because the first section declares "*that all legislative powers herein* GIVEN (viz. given in the new constitution) *shall be vested in congress;*" and then says, "*the legislative powers* NOT GIVEN *are not surely in congress.*"—But will he say that the powers *therein given* are *clearly* and *explicitly* defined? that the *boundary line* of the legislative jurisdiction *given* to congress is so plain as not to be mistaken or abused? that it will never *clash* with the jurisdiction claimed by the legislature of this state? Is the following clause of such a nature as to have any fixed or definite limits? "*This Constitution, and the laws of the United States which shall be made in pursuance thereof, and all treaties made, or which shall be made under the authority of the United States, shall be the* SUPREME LAW OF THE LAND; *and the judges in every state shall be bound thereby, any thing in the* CONSTITUTION *or laws of any state to the contrary not withstanding.*"—Unless some additional guard is added to define the above clause, here will be a fine field for ambitious or designing men to extend the federal jurisdiction.—In the course of a few years our state legislature will be annihilated, together with our bill of rights, which this writer says is a sufficient security: our *rights* will then depend on the *virtue* of the federal legislature; our *privileges* will then be sought after in a mass of mutilated laws, in *volumes of contradictory reports of the learned*. When this federal government is established, we shall have *two* bodies to legislate for us, and unless the powers which *each* body will have a right to exercise, be clearly defined, we must expect nothing but rival discord and contention, until the federal authority gains the ascendancy, as above predicted; or what may be worse, a revolt from their domination. This writer asks—"*Where is the liberty of the press taken away?*" If congress have a right to controul it, they may be said to have a right to take it away.—Will not the United States Attorney have the power to prosecute any printer for a pretended libel against the United States? Will not a printer be triable for a pretended libel against any foreign minister or consul, or for a libel against any of the individual states, by a federal tribunal? Are not such prosecutions warranted by the following clause in the new constitution? "*all controversies wherein the United States shall be a party, all cases affecting foreign ministers and consuls, and all controversies between a citizen and a state,*" shall be cognizable before a federal tribunal.—Cannot congress by virtue of this clause, restrain all publick information of mal-administration? And will not congress have *absolute* uncontrouled power over printers, and every other person within the United States territory, where there will undoubtedly be a great city?

Never was the trial by jury in civil cases thought so lightly of in America as at this day: we have bled for it, and are now almost ready to trifle it away—because in cases of default (which implies a consent of parties) there is no trial by jury, we must give up that inestimable privilege in all civil cases whatever.—This is fine reasoning sure; because we will not have a jury when we do not want them, we shall not when we do—This gentleman cannot be serious when he asserts, that "*if it were to be expressed* WHAT *civil causes should be tried by jury, it might take a volume of laws, instead of an article of rights;*" If it did I would have the volume, rather than hazard the priviledge.—But I will ask whether it requires this volume of laws to express that privilege in our state constitution? and whether there would be any difficulty in having it declared, that the citizens of each state shall enjoy it conformably to the usage in the state where the tribunal shall be established? he says, "*doubtless congress will make some general regulations in this matter,*" but it will be well to recollect that they may *unmake* them, or *not* make them too, if they please, and *when* they please; but if it is a part of the constitution, the *people alone* will have the power to change or annul it.—It is too great a privilege to be left at loose. I sincerely believe if the federal constitution which shall be *given*, be *clearly defined*, and a *boundary line* be marked out, declaratory of the extent of their jurisdiction, of the rights which the state hold unalienable, and the privilege which the citizens thereof can never part with, the republick of America will last for ages, and be free.

Storing, IV, pp. 120-122.

John De Witt V December 3, 1787
Newspaper Article: Boston *American Herald*[1]

TO THE FREE CITIZENS OF THE COMMONWEALTH OF MASSACHUSETTS.

The chief blessings of society, like individuals, are fond of association, and have a mutual dependence upon each other. They form links of one chain, and are all actuated by the same cause. Where freedom prevails, industry and science there also prevail. Industry produces wealth, and science preserves freedom in purity. The majority of the people in all such countries become so active in their different pursuits, that they are deprived both of their time and opportunity to inform themselves of the principles of the government by which those great blessings are secured to them, and almost implicitly rely both for the explaining and for the enforcing of those principles upon the patriotism of those, their fellow-citizens, who labour but in the field of enquiry, and who spend their whole time in researches after knowledge. Thanks be to Heaven, that in America, that majority always retaining the power, the others have never dared to enforce their principles, without previous explanation, and it has become natural to mankind, wherever they have a system of any kind, a favorite, if it is as genuine and honest in principle, as in appearance, they leave no active powers of the mind unessayed, in elucidating, explaining and enlarging upon its benefits to those whom they wish should adopt it—all its good qualitites are delineated, and every exertion is made to refute all objections offered against it, which exertions will be crowned with success, if the objections in themselves are futile, and will not bear the force of light and argument.

The malevolent passions of the heart are not called in, private faults of individuals are not raked from oblivion and magnified, invidious representations are not made, neither are the slanderous, envenomed darts of malice and envy hurled against those characters, who yesterday were deemed praiseworthy and held sacred for a series of obligations conferred by them upon their country, but to day are execrated with passion, because they do not in all points see as other men see. On the contrary, cool reasoning and dispassionate argument, are of themselves sufficient to build up such a system, to unravel all its mysteries, and to present to the people in expressive, legible colours, the blessings that will result from its adoption. Where this mode of conduct is not pursued by its advocates, where instead of cool reasoning upon the subject in question, artful evasions are presented, the system itself is winked out of sight, instead of dispassionate endeavours to remove difficulties arising in honest minds, which are offered with decency to the public in order to be refuted, those who make them are loaded with the opprobrious terms of *Insurgents, destroyers of all government, bankrupts, defaulters,* and *anti-federalists,* which is worse than *jacobitism:* Where, instead of promoting free discussions upon the most important subject ever before a community, attempts are made to fetter and suppress such discussions, by THREATENING the Printer and DROPPING the papers that contain them: Where, instead of coming forward like men, in the full exercise of reason, like fellow-citizens warmed with a patriotick ardour for their country, emulous to secure and preserve its sacred principles, and with proper weapons disarming their fellow-citizens of those objections, they blast and asperse their characters (the dernier resort of all supporters of a bad cause) I say the people have a fair, undoubted right to presume those objections unanswerable, the system itself essentially defective, and that its advocates are, by their conduct, endeavouring not to reason, but to surprize the people into a hasty approbation of it.—

That this is the case with the supporters of the proceedings of the Foederal Convention, far be it from me to declare.—Judge, my fellow-citizens, for yourselves—examine the public prints from the promulgation of this Constitution. Objections there you will find in score—are they offered with decency? Do they attack men or measures? Are they answered in the same manner? And do you discover a desire in those who wish you to embrace this Government, to inform you of its principles, and the consequences which will probably ensue from such principles—why they have taken from you the sinews of your present government, and instead of revising and amending your confederation; have handed you a new one, contrasted in the plenitude of its powers.—As you answer these questions, so you must make up your opinion upon that which is before you.

They have the power of "organizing, arming and disciplining the militia, and of governing them when in service of the United States, giving to the separate States the appointment of the officers, and the authority of training the militia according to the discipline prescribed by Congress." Let us enquire, why they have assumed this power, for if it is for the purpose of forming you into one uniform, solid body throughout the United States, making you respectable both at home and abroad—of arming you more compleatly and exercising you oftener—of strengthening the power which is now lodged in your hands, and relying upon you and you solely for aid and support to the civil power in the execution of all the laws of the New Congress, it certainly can be no where better placed under the restrictions therein mentioned, than in that body. But is this probable. Does the complection of the proceedings countenance such a supposition? When they unprecedently claim the power of raising and supporting standing armies, do they tell you for what purposes they are to be raised?—How they are to be employed?—How many they are to consist of, and where to be stationed?—Is this power fettered with any one of these necessary restrictions which will shew they depend upon the militia, and not upon this infernal engine of oppression to execute their civil laws. The nature of the demand in itself contradicts such a supposition, and forces you to believe that it is for none of these causes—but rather for the purpose of consolidating and finally destoying your strength, as your respective Governments are to be destroyed.

They well know the impolicy of putting or keeping arms in the hands of a nervous people, at a distance from the Seat of Government, upon whom they mean to exercise the powers granted in that Government.—They have no idea of calling upon the party aggrieved to support and enforce their own grievances. They are aware of the necessity of catching Samson asleep to trim him of his locks. It is asserted by the most respectable writers upon Government, that a well regulated militia, composed of the yeomanry of the country have ever been considered as the bulwark of a free people; and says the celebrated Mr. HUME, "without it, it is folly to think any free government will have stability or security—When the sword is introduced, as in our constitution (speaking of the British) the person entrusted will always neglect to discipline the militia, in order to have a pretext for keeping up a standing army; and it is evident this is a mortal distemper in the British parliament, of which it must finally inevitably perish."—If they have not the same design, why do they wish a standing army unrestrained? It is universally agreed, that a militia and a standing body of troops never yet flourished in the same soil. Tyrants have uniformly depended upon the latter, at the expence of the former. Experience has taught them, that a standing body of regular forces, where ever they can be compleatly introduced, are always efficacious in enforcing their edicts, however arbitrary, and slaves by profession themselves, are "nothing loath" to break down the barriers of freedom with a *gout.*—No, my fellow-citizens, this plainly shews they do not mean to depend upon the citizens of the States alone to enforce their powers, wherefore it is their policy to neglect them, and lean upon something more substantial and summary. It is true, they have left the appointment of officers in the breast of the several States; but this to me, appears an insult, rather than a priveledge, for what avails this right, if they in their pleasure should choose to neglect to arm, organize and discipline the men over whom such Officers are to be appointed. It is a bait, that you might be led to suppose they did intend to apply to them in all cases, and to pay particular attention to making them the bulwark of this Continent.—And would they not be equal to such an undertaking? —Are they not abundantly able to give security and stability to your government as long as it is free? Are they not the only proper persons to do it? Are they not the most respectable body of yeomanry in that character upon earth? Have they not been deeply engaged in some of the most brilliant actions in America, and more than once decided the fate of armies? In short, do they not preclude the necessity of any standing army whatsoever, unless in case of invasion; and in that case it would be time enough to raise them, for no free government under Heaven, with a well disciplined militia was ever yet subdued by mercenary troups.

The advocates at the present day, for a standing army in the New Congress pretend it is necessary for the respectability of government. I defy them to produce an instance in any country, in the Old or New World, where they have not finally done away the liberties of the people:—Every writer upon government,—Lock, Sidney, Hamden, and a list of others have uniformly asserted, that standing armies are a solecism in any government; that no nation ever supported them, that did not resort to, rely on, and finally become a prey to them.—No Western Historians have yet been hardy enough to advance principles that look a different way. What historians have asserted, all the Grecian Republicks have verified.—They are brought up to obedience and unconditional submission.—With arms in their hands, they are taught to feel the weight of rigid discipline:—They are excluded from the enjoyments which liberty gives to its votaries, they, in consequence, hate and envy the rest of the community in which they are placed, and indulge a malignant pleasure in destroying those privileges to which they never can be admitted.—"Without them, says the Marquis of Beccaria, in every society there is an effort constantly tending to confer on one part the height of power, and to reduce the other to the extreme of weakness and misery, and this is of itself sufficient to employ the people's attention." There is no instance of any government being reduced to a confirmed tyranny without military oppression; and the first policy of tyrants has been to annihilate all other means of national activity and defence, and to rely solely upon standing troops.—Repeated were the trials before the Sovereigns of Europe dared to introduce them upon any pretext what-ever; and the whole record of the transactions of mankind cannot furnish an instance (unless the proceedings of the Convention may now be called a part of that record) where the motives which caused their establishment, were not completely disguised.—Pisistratus in Greece, and Dyonysius in Syracuse, Charles in France, and Henry in England, all cloaked their villainous intentions under an idea of raising a small body for a guard to their persons; and Spain, could not succeed in the same nefarious plan, until through the influence of the ambitious Priest, they were called upon to resist the progress of the Infidels. "Ceasar, who first attacked the commonwealth with *mines*, very soon opened his *batteries*."—Notwithstanding all these objections to this engine of oppression, which are made by the most experienced men, and confirmed by every country, where the rays of freedom ever extended.—Yet in America, which has hitherto been her favorite abode—in this civilized territory, where property is valuable, and men are found with feelings that will not patiently submit to arbitrary controul—in this Western region, where, my fellow-countrymen, it is confessedly proper that you should associate and dwell in society from choice and reflection, and not be kept together by force and fear, you are modestly requested to engraft into the component parts of your Constitution, a STANDING ARMY, without any qualifying restraints whatever,—certainly to exist somewhere within the bowels of your country in time of peace. It is very true, that the celebrated Mr. Wilson, a member of the Convention, and who we may suppose breathes, in some measure, the spirit of that body, tells you, it is for the purpose of forming cantonments upon your frontiers, and for the dignity and safety of your country, as it respects foreign nations. No man that loves his country, could object to their being raised for the first of these causes, but for the last it cannot be necessary. GOD has so separated us by an extensive ocean from the rest of mankind, he hath so liberally endowed us with privileges, and so abundantly taught us to esteem them precious, it would be impossible, while we retain our integrity and advert to first principles, for any nation whatever to subdue us. We have succeeded in an opposition to the most powerful people upon the globe; and the wound that America received in the struggle, where is it? As speedily healed as the track in the ocean is buried by the succeeding wave. It has scarcely stopped her progress, and our private dissentions only at this moment, tarnish the lustre of the most illustrious infant nation under Heaven.

You cannot help suspecting this gentleman, when he goes on to tell you, "that standing armies in time of peace, have always been a topic of *popular declamation*, but Europe hath found them necessary to maintain the appearance of strength in a season of the most profound tranquility."—This shews you his opinion, and that he as one of the Convention, was for unequivocally establishing them in time of peace; and to object to them is mere popular declamation. But I will not, my countrymen, I cannot believe you to be of the same sentiment. Where is the standing army in the world, that, like the musquet they make use of, hath been, in time of peace, brightned and burnished for the sake only of maintaining an appearance of strength, without being put to a different use, without having had a pernicious influence upon the morals, the habits, and the sentiments of society, and finally, taking a chief part in executing its laws. But some say, that there is a controul over them, and that consists in the appropriation of monies for their support. Turn your attention to England, and see the popular part of this constitution by the influence of money, by the influence of military and revenue officers, brought gravely to give their annual assent to the existence of a standing army, and for monies to support it. It has long since been an insult on the good sense of that nation.

It may not be amiss to remind you of that swarm of revenue, excise, impost and stamp officers, Continental assessors and collectors, that your new Constitution will introduce among you. They will, of themseves, be a STANDING ARMY to you, and you will see them at your elections, active and industrious to secure the seats of those men who put them into office:—They will be very adequate to give you a surfeit of their company, to make you tired in meddling with government, and disposed to become indifferent about the exercise of it, without the blessed assistance of any military corps.—

Upon the whole, my countymen, it appears to me, that this power as it now stands, is decidedly improper and dangerous. That Congress ought to have the power of raising armies when invaded by our enemies, is certain; that they ought not to have it for any other cause, is equally so. If they did not or do not mean to employ them in any other way, they ought in express terms to say so, in a Bill of Rights. They never ought to exist at all, but in subordination to civil authority. If the people are not in general disposed to execute the powers of government, it is time to suspect there is something wrong in that government, and rather than employ a standing army, they had better have another; for, in my humble opinion, it is yet much too early to set it down for a fact, that mankind cannot be governed, but by force.[2]

1 Storing, IV, pp. 34-40.

2 See Philadelphia *Freeman's Journal*, January 16, 1788, p. 211, for a shortened and altered reprint of this article.

Pennsylvania Convention December 4, 1787
Debates (excerpt)

Mr. WILSON. . . .

A good deal has already been said concerning *a bill of rights.* I have stated, according to the best of my recollection, all that passed in Convention relating to that business. Since that time, I have spoken with a gentleman, who has not only his memory, but full notes that he had taken in that body, and he assures me that, upon this subject, no direct motion was ever made at all; and certainly, before we heard this so violently supported out of doors, some pains ought to have been taken to have tried its fate within; but the truth is, a bill of rights would, as I have mentioned already, have been not only unnecessary, but improper. In some governments, it may come within the gentleman's idea, when he says it can do no harm; but even in these governments, you find bills of rights do not uniformly obtain; and do those states complain who have them not? Is it a maxim in forming governments, that not only all the powers which are given, but also that all those which are reserved, should be enumerated? I apprehend that the powers given and reserved form the whole rights of the people, as men and as citizens. I consider that there are very few who understand the whole of these rights. All the political writers, from *Grotius* and *Puffendorf* down to *Vattel,* have treated on this subject; but in no one of those books, nor in the aggregate of them all, can you find a complete enumeration of rights appertaining to the people as men and as citizens.

There are two kinds of government—that where general power is intended to be given to the legislature, and that where the powers are particularly enumerated. In the last case, the implied result is, that nothing more is intended to be given than what is so enumerated, unless it results from the nature of the government itself. On the other hand, when general legislative powers are given, then the people part with their authority, and, on the gentleman's principle of government, retain nothing. But in a government like the proposed one, there can be no necessity for a bill of rights, for, on my principle, the people never part with their power. Enumerate all the rights of men! I am sure, sir, that no gentleman in the late Convention would have attempted such a thing. I believe the honorable speakers in opposition on this floor were members of the assembly which appointed delegates to that Convention; if it had been thought proper to have sent them into that body, how luminous would the dark conclave have been!—so the gentleman has been pleased to denominate that body. Aristocrats as they were, they pretended not to define the rights of those who sent them there. We ask, repeatedly, What harm could the addition of a bill of rights do? If it can do no good, I think that a sufficient reason to refuse having any thing to do with it. But to whom are we to report this bill of rights, if we should adopt it? Have we authority from those who sent us here to make one?

It is true, we may propose as well as any other private persons; but how shall we know the sentiments of the citizens of this state and of the other states? Are we certain that any one of them will agree with our definitions and enumerations?

In the second place, we are told that there is no check upon the government but the people. It is unfortunate, sir, if their superintending authority is allowed as a check; but I apprehend that, in the very construction of this government, there are numerous checks. Besides those expressly enumerated, the two branches of the legislature are mutual checks upon each other. But this subject will be more properly discussed when we come to consider the form of the government itself; and then I mean to show the reason why the right of *habeas corpus* was secured by a particular declaration in its favor.

In the third place, we are told that there is no security for the rights of conscience. I ask the honorable gentleman, what part of this system puts it in the power of Congress to attack those rights? When there is no power to attack, it is idle to prepare the means of defence.

Debates, II, pp. 453-455.

Publius {Alexander Hamilton} December 4, 1787
Newspaper Article: *New York Packet* (excerpt)

The FOEDERALIST, NO. 16.

To the People of the State of New-York. . . .

But if the execution of the laws of the national government, should not require the intervention of the State Legislatures; if they were to pass into immediate operation upon the citizens themselves, the particular governments could not interrupt their progress without an open and violent exertion of an unconstitutional power. No omissions, nor evasions would answer the end. They would be obliged to act, and in such a manner, as would leave no doubt that they had encroached on the national rights. An experiment of this nature would always be hazardous—in the face of a constitution in any degree competent to its own defence, and of a people enlightened enough to distinguish between a legal exercise and an illegal usurpation of authority. The success of it would require not merely a factious majority in the Legislature, but the concurrence of the courts of justice, and of the body of the people. If the Judges were not embarked in a conspiracy with the Legislature they would pronounce the resolutions of such a majority to be contrary to the supreme law of the land, unconstitutional and void. If the people were not tainted with the spirit of their State representatives, they, as the natural guardians of the constitution, would throw their weight into the national scale, and give it a decided preponderancy in the contest. Attempts of this kind would not often be made with liberty or rashness; because they could seldom be made without danger to the authors; unless in cases of a tyrannical exercise of the Foederal authority.

DHRC, XIV, pp. 339, 342.

Cumberland County Petition December 5, 1787
Petition: *Carlisle Gazette* (excerpts)

To the Honorable Convention of the State of Pennsylvania. The Petition of the Subscribers Inhabitants of the County of Cumberland.

Most humbly showeth: that they consider the present political circumstances of the United States, as very interesting to every citizen who sincerely desires to support our Union, and at the same time to secure to the people the future enjoyment of their unalienable rights and liberties; and as the good of the people is the great end of all good government, and that must be best which affords the best security to their rights and freedom; a solicitude for their own permanent political happiness, and that of their fellow citizens, has induced your petitioners to lay before your honorable house some objections to the adoption of the Constitution, as proposed by the late Continental Convention.

And first: There is no declaration of rights, to secure to the people the liberty of worshiping God according to their consciences; and the sixth Article of the said Constitution declares "that this Constitution and the Laws of the United States which shall be made in pursuance thereof, etc." Therefore the bill of rights contained in the constitutions of the several states are no security, nor are the people secured in the privileges of the common law.

Secondly: The eighth section of the first Article of this Constitution declares, that the Congress shall have power to make all laws necessary and proper for carrying into execution the foregoing powers, and all other powers vested by this Constitution in the government of the United States, or in any department or officer thereof. This, as we conceive, unlimited powers given to Congress, in which they are to be the judges of what laws shall be necessary and proper, uncontrolled by a bill of rights, submits every right of the people of these states, both civil and sacred to the disposal of Congress, who may exercise their power to the expulsion of the jury-trial in civil causes—to the total suppression of the liberty of the press; and to the setting up and establishing of a cruel tyranny, if they should be so disposed, over all the dearest and most sacred rights of the citizens. . . .

These objections, with many others which might be made, induce your petitioners to pray this honorable Convention not to adopt the said proposed plan, until a bill of rights shall be framed and annexed, so as to secure to the citizens of each state, such rights as have been mentioned (we mean to say) those relating to conscience, trial by jury, in civil causes, as well as in criminal cases; the liberty of the press, and such other liberties as to you may seem necessary to be secured and preserved. And your petitioners as in duty bound shall ever pray, etc., etc.

DHRC, II, pp. 310-311.

Philadelphiensis III December 5, 1787

Newspaper Article: Philadelphia *Freeman's Journal* (excerpts)

[I]f we adopt this plan of government in its present form; I say that we shall have reason to curse the day that America became independent. Horrid thought! that the greatest blessing God ever bestowed on a nation, should terminate in its misery and disgrace. Strange reverse this! that the freemen of America, *the favored of heaven,* should submit to a government so arbitrary in its embrio, that even *a bill of rights* cannot be obtained, to secure to the people their unalienable privileges. . . .

But we want an efficient federal government; we want an efficient federal government: this is the constant theme of the day. Well, my friends, I grant this. But what is the ultimate end of an efficient government: in what should it be efficient? I hope you anticipate my answer. The only thing in which a government should be efficient, is to protect the *liberties, lives,* and *property* of the people governed, from foreign and domestic violence. This, and this only is what every government should do effectually. For any government to do more than this is impossible, and every one that falls short of it is defective. Let us now compare the new constitution with this legitimate definition of an efficient government, and we shall find that it has scarce a particle of an efficient government in its whole composition.

In the first place then it does not protect the people in those liberties and privileges that all freemen should hold sacred—The *liberty of conscience,* the *liberty of the press,* the *liberty of trial by jury, &c.* are all unprotected by this constitution. . . . And in respect to the *standing army,* it will only be made up of profligate idle ruffians, whose prowess will chiefly consist in feats of cruelty exercised on their innocent fellow citizens; but in facing a foreign foe, they will prove themselves a body of mean cowards; like the Turkish janizaries, better acquainted with plundering their country than fighting for its protection. In regard to a militia defending the country, the thing is still more absurd if possible. Who in his senses could suppose that people with their spirits broken by oppression, should voluntarily fight for that government, to which they are necessarily disaffected? No truly, common sense would point out to government that its safety could not be the object of the people arming: and hence it is plain, that even were the militia willing to act, such a government would not trust them.

DHRC, XIV, p. 350-352. The "Philadelphiensis" series is reprinted in Storing, III, starting at p. 99.

A True Friend December 6, 1787

Broadside: Richmond

To the ADVOCATES *for the* NEW FEDERAL CONSTITUTION; *and to their* ANTAGONISTS.

GENTLEMEN, You have already pretty nearly agreed, if you be, as I believe you are, well intentioned; at least it is easy to compromise matters between you, unless under the veil of the public good, or of a jealous care for the liberties of your country you are actuated by private or interested motives.

If you are swayed by the pure and chaste love alone of your country, I, this day, offer myself to become arbitrator between you; to reconcile your differences, and if possible, put an end to these ingenious dissertations, which hold the public opinion in suspense.

Let us then, in the first place, agree on a few preliminary positions. You, gentlemen, the preachers up of the new Constitution, will not surely contest a fact proved by the records of all ages and of all nations, that is, *that the liberties and the rights of the people have been always encroached on, and finally destroyed by those, whom they had entrusted with the powers of government;* these have continually abused the confidence reposed in them; and whether this confidence was placed in a single magistrate, or in a body of magistrates, the authority ceded to them by the people has been constantly turned against themselves; has subjected; and in fine enslaved them. The precaution, which they have sometimes taken, to divide this solemn trust amongst the other, has not been hitherto capable of affording a sufficient mound against these dreadful encroachments; for it is unhappily in the nature of men, when collected for any purpose whatsoever into a body, to take a selfish and interested bias, tending invariably towards the encreasing of their prerogatives and the prolonging of the term of their function; but what is yet more unfortunate, those corps have been always victorious over the unconnected, the divided opposition, that men acting individually could make against them: Since then this fact is as certain and incontrovertible a principle in politics, as universal attraction is in physics, the people of this country, blessed with the heavenly boon of liberty, ought to be, to day, not only circumspect, but cautious and suspicious too in the extent of the powers they should delegate, in the choice of the persons they should delegate them to, and in the term of time it may be prudent to continue them in office; thus to guard against incurring the same fate with all the different governments, with which we have been hitherto made acquainted. It would even seem as if the examples, which Poland, Sweden, Geneva, and Holland exhibit, had been reserved by providence for this age, to give this rising empire more striking and experimental lessons.

Neither can you, gentlemen, who oppose the new constitution, disown the pressing necessity there is for a foederal constitution, which may reunite into one whole, and on an uniform regular plan, the different interests and separate advantages of the thirteen states, united at present, 'tis true, in name; though in fact divided and opposed one to the other. You wish, or most undoubtedly you ought to wish, to see good order and mutual confidence established at home, and your credit and reputation flourishing among the nations abroad;

these, these are the means, which must give a rapid progression to our agriculture, to our commerce, and to our navigation. Without these main springs of public felicity, our finances must necessarily remain in their present state of penury and contempt, we shall continue overwhelmed with our debts and difficulties, and be daily forced on ruinous and dishonorable expedients: We shall thus be stunted in our growth, nor can we surely flatter ourselves with being esteemed a free, happy, and recommendable people.

These two cardinal points being thus invariably fixed, and, too true to say, incontestible by either party; the obvious consequences are—1st. A pressing necessity for a new plan of general government; and 2d.—The indispensible obligation we are under to ourselves, to posterity, to the whole world in short, to guard with jealous care and watchful anxiety, in its utmost purity, that glorious and darling deposit, with which Providence has blessed us, perhaps, for the common good of mankind: These should be the aims of every true patriot, and they are doubtless those of both contending parties. To ensure success in the attaining of them, the different states culled out the men of the most enlightened understandings and of the most conspicuous merit: They brought them together in order to discuss, balance and arrange their separate and individual interests, on a uniform comprehensive plan, and into a system founded on justice and reciprocal advantages: It was out of this assembly alone, that we could flatter ourselves that this grand and generous system should arise; there, opinions were contrasted and wisdom united—partial views were banished—salutary and indispensible concessions mutually made;—there, objections were discussed, and satisfactory solutions given to them: It is therefore now both useless and impossible for us to reply to all these, which each state may make, and how much more would the difficulty encrease, should it be attempted to give answers to each individual in those states? None of those are now placed in the proper situation, to take a large and comprehensive view of this extensive prospect; they see but their immediate, partial, and, perhaps, delusive interests: The people in their private capacities are not more likely to discover the solidity or the futility of the reasons, or of the objections of each party. The encomiums and the censures, the attacks and the defences, are set forth with equal acrimony and address; they terrify but do not instruct us: These essays and reasonings give, indeed, proofs of the ingenuity and talents of the champions, and sometimes, alas, of the abuse which they make of them! They likewise prove a melacholy truth; of which every man of reflection had been previously convinced. It is, *the impossibility of framing a good constitution on any one invariable foundation so firmly as never to be shaken*. The best that can be devised will at last be vitiated by the corroding hand of time, and can only be kept pure by continually modifying it according to circumstances, and by bringing it now and then to the test of its general principles: The citizens of America will then, with the utmost reason, repose no confidence in these writers and reasoners, who are ready to level without being able to edify: who raise doubts and fears in order to hinder or to retard the execution of a plan, which is the result of the reflection, the debates and the wisdom of patriots, whom they themselves made choice of: But, as notwithstanding their extensive knowledge and their pure intentions, they are not exempted from the common lot of human frailty, and as it is possible, that they may have erred in some parts of that great art, so difficult to be attained, of *governing without enslaving;* as the extent of our country, our situation, our manners and national character cannot be pertinently compared to any thing, which has hitherto existed on earth, we should not, consequently, model ourselves servilely on any system of government, which has yet appeared, or pin our faith on any political writer whatsoever, be his reputation what it may. Sound reason and urgent necessity lay their positive commands on us to accept the new foederal constitution; but, on the other hand prudence seems to require from us, that we should adopt it on trial only for a certain limited time, for eight, ten, or twelve years: at the expiration of which ever of these periods may be agreed on, we will again call a general convention, in order to rectify the defects or lapses, which the unerring guides, time and experience may discover; this will then reform what our circumstances may point out for reformation. It is a general principle in legislation, which, if well understood, would abridge very much the study of that science for the body of the people, *that the greater the power is with which it invests its governors, the shorter should be the limits of its duration; and on the contrary, that the smaller the power is, the longer it may be permitted to continue.* This may be held as certain an axiom in politics as this is in mechanics; that we cannot increase force but at the expence of velocity, nor increase velocity but at the expence of force. The constitution fixed on at the time of the declaration of our independence was universally admired; it was then, perhaps, the best we could aspire to, we now find it inadequate, and we reform it. The new constitution has its enthusiastic admirers, it is nevertheless imprudent that we should accept it on any other condition, but that of its laying itself open at a stated period for correction, if necessary, or for being confirmed for another stated period, if expedient: Under these two grand guides, time and experience, we shall become expert in the intricate and complicated science of legislation; we shall be looked up to as models by other nations, instead of our servilely copying their institutions; we shall enjoy the singular advantage, hitherto unexampled, to reform our government insensibly and by degrees, without experiencing those violent concussions and catastrophes, which have desolated nations when they attempted a reform. Another precaution seems indispensibly necessary. Notwithstanding Mr. Wilson's assertion, that *every thing which is not given up by this foederal constitution, is reserved to the body of the people;* that security *is not sufficient* to *calm the inquietude* of a *whole nation.* Let us then insert in the first page of this constitution, as a preamble to it, a declaration of our rights, or an enumeration of our prerogatives, as a sovereign people; that they may never hereafter be unknown, forgotten or contradicted by our representatives, our delegates, our servants in Congress: Let the recognition, and solemn ratification by Congress, of this declaration of rights, be made the *sine qua non* of the adoption of this new foederal constitution, by each state. This precious, this comfortable page, will be the ensign, to which on any future contestation, time may induce between the governed and those intrusted with the powers of government, the asserters of liberty may rally, and constitutionally defend it.

The rights of the people should never be left subject to problematical discussion: They should be clear, precise and authenticated: They should never stand in need of the comments or explanations of lawyers or political writers, too apt, we know, to entangle the plainest rights in their net of sophistry: What man of upright intentions will dare to say, that free men giving up such extensive prerogatives to their rulers, as the new foederal constitution requires, should not at the same time put them in mind of the rights, which constitute them such? If there be any person who says, that implication, that forced construction should satisfy their doubts, ye imps of hell whip me such fiend!

I now most earnestly pray, that both the fautors and the opponents of the new foederal constitution, may deign to accept this compromise. If either party refuse to subscribe to it, let them be judged by their country, and if I mistake not, they will be found guilty of the treacherous views, and dark designs with which they are so ready to asperse their antagonists.

DHRC, VIII, pp. 217-220. Also reprinted in DHRC, XIV, pp. 373-377.

Brutus December 6, 1787
Newspaper Article: Alexandria *Virginia Journal* (excerpt)

I now feel myself fully at liberty to answer them [George Mason's objections] in any manner I please consistent with decency and candor.

"There is no bill of rights." As the principles contained in a bill of rights have ever been considered as the foundation of civil liberty, this, at the head of a long string of objections to a government, certainly makes a very formidable appearance, and would of itself be sufficient to condemn the whole system, if it could not be clearly shewn that it was not only unnecessary, but would even have been absurd to have introduced it in the proposed constitution.

In the formation of a political constitution it is necessary that every right and privilege which the people reserve to themselves should be particularly and individually specified; or, that the portion of their natural liberty, which they give up for the enjoyment of civil government, should be expressly mentioned, in the constitution. In the former case, if in the enumeration of the rights and privileges of the people any should be omitted or forgotten, the people cannot assume them. They are lost.—In the latter, that part of natural liberty which is given up at the behest of society is fully and completely denied, and whatever is not there expressly granted remains to the people.—Upon this last mentioned principle the proposed constitution was formed; it would therefore have been not only absurd but even dangerous to have inserted a bill of rights; because, if, in the enumeration of rights and privileges to be reserved, any had been omitted or forgotten, and the people, at a future period, should assume those so omitted, the rulers might with propriety dispute their right to exercise them, as they were not specified in the bill of rights;—and, on the other hand, the people would deny the authority of the rulers to deprive them of the exercise of those rights because they were not expressly given up by them. Thus a bill of rights, in the proposed constitution, instead of securing to the people those rights and privileges which God and nature has rendered unalienable, might have been productive of disputes, contentions, and, perhaps, ultimately of ruin to them. This is the light in which the matter was viewed in the convention, and it was there fully discussed. The powers which the people delegate to their rulers are completely defined, and if they should assume more than is there warranted they would soon find that there is a power in the United States of America paramount to their own, which would bring upon them the just resentment of an injured people.

DHRC, VIII, pp. 212-213.

Philanthropos December 6, 1787
Newspaper Aricle: Alexandria *Virginia Journal* (excerpt)

The new Constitution in its present form, is calculated to produce despotism, thraldom and confusion, and if the United States do swallow it, they will find it a bolus, that will create convulsions to their utmost extremities.—Were they mine enemies, the worst imprecation I could devise would be, may they adopt it: For tyranny, which has been chained (as for a few years past) is always more cursed, and sticks its teeth in deeper than [before?].—Were Col. Mason's objections obviated, the improvement would be very considerable, though even then, not so complete as might be.—The Congress's having power without controul, to borrow money on the credit of the United States: Their having power to appoint their own salaries, and their being paid out of the treasury of the United States, thereby, in some measure, rendering them independent of the individual States, also their being judges of the qualification and election of their own members, by which means they can get men to suit any purpose, together with Col. Mason's wise and judicious objections, are grievances, the very idea of which, is enough to make every honest citizen exclaim in the language of Cato, O liberty, O my country!—Our present constitution, with a few additional powers to Congress, seems better calculated to preserve the rights, and defend the liberties of our citizens, than the one proposed, without proper amendments.

DHRC, VIII, p. 210.

Pennsylvania Convention December 6, 1787
Debates (excerpts)

JOHN SMILIE: (113) I object to the power of Congress over the militia and to keep a standing army. . . .
(123) In a free government there never will be need of standing armies; for it depends on the confidence of the people. If it does not so depend, it is not free.
(124) The Convention, in framing this government, knew it was not a free one; otherwise they would not have asked the power of the purse and the sword.
(125) The last resource of a free people is taken away; for Congress are to have the command of the militia.

(126) The laws of Pennsylvania have hitherto been executed without the aid of the militia.
(127) The governor of each state will be only the drill sergeant of Congress.
(128) The militia officers will be obliged by oath to support the general government against that of their own state.
(129) Congress may give us a select militia which will, in fact, be a standing army—or Congress, afraid of a general militia, may say there shall be no militia at all.
(130) When a select militia is formed; the people in general may be disarmed.
(131) Will the states give up to Congress their last resource—the command of the militia?
(132) Will the milita laws be as mild under the general government as under the state governments? Militia men may be punished with whipping or death. They may [be] dragged from one state to any other.
(133) "Congress guarantees to each State a *Republican* Form of Government." Is this a security for a *free* government?

DHRC, II, pp. 508-509. These excerpts are from James Wilson's notes.

"Z" December 6, 1787
Newspaper Article: Boston *Independent Chronicle* (excerpt)

Again, says the Doctor [Benjamin Franklin], "In these sentiments I agree to this Constitution, with all its faults, if they are such; because I think a general government necessary for us, and there is no FORM of government but what may be a blessing to the people, if well administered." But are we to accept a form of government which we do not entirely approve of, merely in hopes that it *will* be administered well? Does not every man know, that nothing is more liable to be abused than power. Power, without a check, in *any* hands, is tyranny; and such powers, in the hands of even *good men*, so infatuating is the nature of it, will probably be wantonly, if not tyrannically exercised. The world has had experience enough of this, in every stage of it. Those among us who cannot entirely approve the *new* Constitution as it is called, are of opinion, in order that any form may be well administered, and thus be made a blessing to the people, that there ought to be at least, an express reservation of certain inherent unalienable rights, which it would be equally sacrilegious for the people to *give away*, as for the government to *invade*. If the rights of conscience, for instance, are not sacredly reserved to the people, what security will there be, in case the government should have in their heads a predilection for any *one* sect in religion? what will hinder the civil power from erecting a national system of religion, and committing the law to a set of lordly priests, reaching, as the great Dr. *Mayhew* expressed it, from the desk to the skies? An *Hierarchy* which has ever been the grand engine in the hand of civil tyranny; and tyrants in return will afford them opportunity enough to vent their rage on *stubborn hereticks*, by *wholesome severities*, as they were called by national religionists, in a country [England] which has long boasted its freedom. It was doubtless for the peace of *that* nation, that there should be an *uniformity* in religion, and for the same *wise* and *good* reason, the act of uniformity remains *in force* to these enlightened times.

DHRC, XIV, pp. 358-359.

James Madison (New York) December 9, 1787
Letter: To Thomas Jefferson (excerpts)

The Constitution proposed by the late Convention engrosses almost the whole political attention of America. All the Legislatures, except that of R. Island, which have been assembled, have agreed in submitting it to State Conventions. Virginia has set the example of opening a door for amendments, if the Convention there should chuse to propose them. Maryland has copied it. The States which preceded, referred the constitution as recommended by the Genl. Convention, to be ratified or rejected as it stands. . . .
At the head of the 2d. party [in Virginia] which urges amendments are the Govr. [Edmund Randolph] & Mr. Mason. These do not object to the substance of the Governt. but contend for a few additional Guards in favor of the Rights of the States and of the people.

DHRC, XIV, pp. 395-396.

A Landholder VI {Oliver Ellsworth} December 10, 1787
Newspaper Article: Hartford *Connecticut Courant* (excerpts)

[Answers to George Mason's Objections]
There is no Declaration of Rights. Bills of Rights were introduced in England when its kings claimed all power and jurisdiction, and were

considered by them as grants *to the people.* They are insignificant since government is considered as originating from the people, and all the power government now has is a grant *from the people:* the constitution they establish with powers limitted and defined, becomes now to the legislator and magistrate, what originally a bill of rights was to the people. To have inserted in this constitution a bill of rights for the states, would suppose them to derive and hold their rights from the foederal government, when the reverse is the case. . . .

There is no declaration of any kind to preserve the liberty of the press, &c. Nor is liberty of conscience, or of matrimony, or of burial of the dead; it is enough that congress have no power to prohibit either, and can have no temptation. This objection is answered in that the states have all the power originally, and congress have only what the states grant them.

DHRC, XIV, pp. 400-401. "Landholder VI" is reprinted in DHRC, III, starting on p. 487, and in *Essays,* starting on p. 161.

George Lee Turberville (Richmond)   December 11, 1787
Letter: To James Madison (excerpts)

The principal objection that the opponents bring forward against this Constitution, is the total want of a Bill of Rights—this they build upon as an essential—and altho' I am satisfied that an enumeration of those priviledges which we retained—wou'd have left floating in uncertainty a number of non enumerated contingent powers and priviledges—either in the powers granted or in those retained —thereby indisputably trenching upon the powers of the states—& of the Citizens—insomuch as those not specially retained might by just implication have been consider'd as surrender'd—still it wou'd very much assist me in my determination upon this subject if the sense of the Convention and their opinion upon it cou'd be open'd to me—

If the Laws of the United states are to be superior to the Laws & Constitutions of the several states, why was not a Bill of Rights affixed to this Constitution by which the Liberties of individuals might have been secured against the abuse of Foederal Power?

DHRC, XIV, pp. 406-407. Also reprinted in DHRC, VIII, pp. 232-234, and in *Papers,* X, pp. 316-317.

Thomas Johnson (Annapolis) December 11, 1787
Letter: To George Washington (excerpt)

[A]ny necessary Guards for personal Liberty is the common Interest of all the Citizens of America and if it is imagined that a defined power which does not comprehend the Interference with personal Rights needs negative Declarations I presume such may be added by the foederal Legislature with equal Efficacy & more propriety than might have been done by the Convention—

DHRC, XIV, p. 404.

One of the People December 11, 1787
Newspaper Article: Philadelphia *Independent Gazetteer* (excerpt)

Now, Mr. Oswald, I thought it was a bill of rights ascertaining the bounds of the legislative power that gave the judges a right to say when the laws were unconstitutional, and therefore void.

DHRC, II Mfm. Pa., p. 1304.

Uriah Forrest (London) December 11, 1787
Letter: To Thomas Jefferson (excerpt)

I am obliged to own myself one of those, who do not wish to see the people more obedient to their rulers in the next twelve, or any other twelve years, than they have been in the last.—A proper spirit of resistance is the best security for their liberties, and they shou'd now & then warn their rulers of it. As I am in the legislature and shall be in the convention for the consideration of this proposed Constitution, and it is surely a question of the utmost consequence, I wish to acquire every possible information—. If your Excellency will indulge me with such observations on it as hath occur'd to you, it will indeed oblige me—rest assured that no other use shall be made of them, than the correcting of my judgment and opinion on the subject.

DHRC, XIV, pp. 474-475.

Pennsylvania Convention December 12, 1787
Debates (excerpts)

Mr. Whitehill now rose, and having animadverted upon Doctor Rush's metaphysical arguments, and regretted that so imperfect a work should have been ascribed to God, he presented several petitions from 750 inhabitants of Cumberland County, praying, for the reasons therein specified, that the proposed Constitution should not be adopted without amendments, and, particularly, without a bill of rights.[1] The petitions being read from the chair, Mr. M'Kean said, he was sorry that at this stage of the business so improper an attempt should be made. He repeated that the duty of the Convention was circumscribed to the adoption or rejection of the proposed plan, and such had certainly been the sense of the members when it was agreed that only one question could be taken on the important subject before us. He hoped, therefore, that the petitions would not be attended to.[2]

Mr. Whitehill then read, and offered as the ground of a motion for adjourning to some remote day, the consideration of the following articles, which he said might either be taken collectively as a bill of rights, or separately as amendments to the general form of government proposed.

1. The rights of conscience shall be held inviolable, and neither the legislative, executive, nor judicial powers of the United States shall have authority to alter, abrogate, or infringe any part of the constitutions of the several states, which provide for the preservation of liberty in matters of religion.

2. That in controversies respecting property, and in suits between man and man, trial by jury shall remain as heretofore, as well in the federal courts, as in those of the several states.

3. That in all capital and criminal prosecutions, a man has a right to demand the cause and nature of his accusation, as well in the federal courts, as in those of the several states; to be heard by himself or his counsel; to be confronted with the accusers and witnesses, to call for evidence in his favor, and a speedy trial, by an impartial jury of the vicinage, without whose unanimous consent, he cannot be found guilty, nor can he be compelled to give evidence against himself; that no man be deprived of his liberty, except by the law of the land or the judgment of his peers.

4. That excessive bail ought not to be required nor excessive fines imposed, nor cruel or unusual punishments inflicted.

5. That warrants unsupported by evidence, whereby any officer or messenger may be commanded or required to search suspected places,

or to seize any person or persons, his or their property, not particularly described, are grievous and oppressive, and shall not be granted either by the magistrates of the federal government or others.

6. That the people have a right to the freedom of speech, of writing, and of publishing their sentiments, therefore, the freedom of the press shall not be restrained by any law of the United States.

7. That the people have a right to bear arms for the defense of themselves and their own state, or the United States, or for the purpose of killing game; and no law shall be passed for disarming the people or any of them, unless for crimes committed, or real danger of public injury from individuals; and as standing armies in the time of peace are dangerous to liberty, they ought not to be kept up; and that the military shall be kept under strict subordination to and be governed by the civil power.

8. The inhabitants of the several states shall have liberty to fowl and hunt in seasonable times, on the lands they hold, and on all other lands in the United States not enclosed, and in like manner to fish in all navigable waters, and others not private property, without being restrained therein by any laws to be passed by the legislature of the United States.

9. That no law shall be passed to restrain the legislatures of the several states, from enacting laws for imposing taxes, except imposts and duties on goods exported and imported, and that no taxes, except imposts and duties upon goods imported and exported, and postage on letters shall be levied by the authority of Congress.

10. That elections shall remain free, that the House of Representatives be properly increased in number and that the several states shall have power to regulate the elections for Senators and Representatives, without being controlled either directly or indirectly by any interference on the part of Congress, and that elections of Representatives be annual.

11. That the power of organizing, arming, and disciplining the militia (the manner of disciplining the militia to be prescribed by Congress) remain with the individual states, and that Congress shall not have authority to call or march any of the militia out of their own state, without the consent of such state and for such length of time only as such state shall agree.

12. That the legislative, executive, and judicial powers be kept separate, and to this end, that a constitutional council be appointed to advise and assist the President, who shall be responsible for the advice they give (hereby, the Senators would be relieved from almost constant attendance); and also that the judges be made completely independent.

13. That no treaties which shall be directly opposed to the existing laws of the United States in Congress assembled shall be valid until such laws shall be repealed or made conformable to such treaty, neither shall any treaties be valid which are contradictory to the Constitution of the United States, or the constitutions of the individual states.

14. That the judiciary power of the United States shall be confined to cases affecting ambassadors, other public ministers and consuls, to cases of admiralty and maritime jurisdiction, to controversies to which the United States shall be a party, to controversies between two or more states–between citizens claiming lands under grants of different states, and between a state or the citizens thereof and foreign states, and in criminal cases, to such only as are expressly enumerated in the Constitution, and that the United States in Congress assembled shall not have power to enact laws, which shall alter the laws of descents and distributions of the effects of deceased persons, the title of lands or goods, or the regulation of contracts in the individual states.

15. That the sovereignty, freedom, and independency of the several states shall be retained, and every power, jurisdiction and right which is not by this Constitution expressly delegated to the United States in Congress assembled.

Some confusion arose on these articles being presented to the chair, objections were made by the majority to their being officially read, and, at last, Mr. Wilson desired that the intended motion might be reduced to writing, in order to ascertain its nature and extent. Accordingly, Mr. Whitehill drew it up, and it was read from the chair in the following manner.

"That this Convention do adjourn to the ______ day of ______ next, then to meet in the city of Philadelphia, in order that the propositions for amending the proposed Constitution may be considered by the people of this state; that we may have an opportunity of knowing what amendments or alterations may be proposed by other states, and that these propositions, together with such other amendments as may be proposed by other states, may be offered to Congress, and taken into consideration by the United States, before the proposed Constitution shall be finally ratified."

The question being taken on the motion [for adjournment], there appeared for it 23, against it 46. The great and conclusive question was then taken, that "this Convention do assent to and ratify the plan of federal government, agreed to and recommended by the late Federal Convention?" when the same division took place[.][3]

1 See "Cumberland County Petition," December 5, 1787, p. 137.
2 DHRC, II Mfm. Pa., p. 1318.
3 DHRC, II, pp. 597-600. Whitehill's "bill of rights" is contained verbatim in the Dissent of the Minority of the Pennsylvania Convention. See "Pennsylvania Minority," December 18, 1787, pp. 159-161.

A Countryman December 15, 1787

Newspaper Article: *New York Journal* (excerpts)

If all the laws and treaties which may be made, in pursuance of this constitution (provided it be adopted) are to be of *as high authority*, as the constitution, I should be glad to know what security we can have for any one right, however sacred or essential, when there is no explicit proviso, that the laws and treaties which may be made, shall not be repugnant to the constitution?

It is true, that they are to be made in *pursuance* of the constitution; but, *pursuance* is a vague term, and, I presume, generally implies little more than "in consequence, etc."—I have always understood, that the laws derived all their just authority from the constitution, or social compact, as it is sometimes called; and that the latter receives its whole authority, in free governments, from the common consent of the people, and recognizes or acknowledges all their essential rights and liberties, as well as ascertains the reciprocal duties or relations between the governed and their governors, or, perhaps, more properly, their principal public servants, who undertake to manage or conduct the affairs of the community agreeable to certain fixed stipulations, which are mentioned in the original compact or constitution, and not otherwise, but at the risk of being disobeyed, or opposed, as the case may require.

If these ideas of a free government are just, ought there not to have been a positive distinction between the authority of the constitution and that of the laws, treaties, etc. . . .

Does it not appear to you, as if the framers of this clause had profited by the embarrassments which the British ministry frequently met with in their attempts to render acts of parliament, paramount to magna charta, or the great charter of the peoples essential rights, which is acknowleged, by the 43d. of Edward the 3d. not to be in the power of parliament to alter, change, or destroy; as all statutes made or to be made, against, or contrary to that constitution, or bill of rights, are, immediately, to be considered as null and void?

Storing, VI, p. 59-60.

Thomas Jefferson (Paris) December 15, 1787
Letter: To William Carmichael (excerpt)

Our new constitution is powerfully attacked in the American newspapers. The objections are that it's effect would be to form the 13. states into one: that proposing to melt all down into one general government they have fenced the people by no declaration of rights, they have not renounced the power of keeping a standing army, they have not secured the liberty of the press, they have reserved a power of abolishing trials by jury in civil cases, they have proposed that the laws of the federal legislature shall be paramount [to] the laws & constitutions of the states, they have abandoned rotation in office: & particularly their president may be re-elected from 4. years to 4 years for life, so as to render him a king for life, like a king of Poland, & have not given him either the check or aid of a council. To these they add calculations of expence &c. &c. to frighten the people. You will perceive that these objections are serious, and some of them not without foundation.

DHRC, XIV, p. 480.

Pennsylvania Minority December 18, 1787
Newspaper Article: Philadelphia *Pennsylvania Packet*[1]

The Address and Reasons of Dissent of the Minority
of the Convention of the State of Pennsylvania
to their Constituents.

It was not until after the termination of the late glorious contest, which made the people of the United States an independent nation, that any defect was discovered in the present confederation. It was formed by some of the ablest patriots in America. It carried us succesfully through the war; and the virtue and patriotism of the people, with their disposition to promote the common cause, supplied the want of power in Congress.

The requisition of Congress for the five percent impost was made before the peace, so early as the first of February 1781, but was prevented taking effect by the refusal of one state; yet it is probable every state in the union would have agreed to this measure at that period had it not been for the extravagant terms in which it was demanded. The requisition was new molded in the year 1783, and accompanied with an additional demand of certain supplementary funds for 25 years. Peace had now taken place, and the United States found themselves laboring under a considerable foreign and domestic debt, incurred during the war. The requisition of 1783 was commensurate with the interest of the debt, as it was then calculated; but it has been more accurately ascertained since that time. The domestic debt has been found to fall several millions of dollars short of the calculation, and it has lately been considerably diminished by large sales of the western lands. The states have been called on by Congress annually for supplies until the general system of finance proposed in 1783 should take place.

It was at this time that the want of an efficient federal government was first complained of, and that the powers vested in Congress were found to be inadequate to the procuring of the benefits that should result from the union. The impost was granted by most of the states, but many refused the supplementary funds; the annual requisitions were set at naught by some of the states, while others complied with them by legislative acts, but were tardy in their payments, and Congress found themselves incapable of complying with their engagements, and supporting the federal government. It was found that our national character was sinking in the opinion of foreign nations. The Congress could make treaties of commerce, but could not enforce the observance of them. We were suffering from the restrictions of foreign nations, who had shackled our commerce, while we were unable to retaliate; and all now agreed that it would be advantageous to the union to enlarge the powers of Congress; that they should be enabled in the amplest manner to regulate commerce, and to lay and collect duties on the imports throughout the United States. With this view a convention was first proposed by Virginia, and finally recommended by Congress for the different states to appoint deputies to meet in convention, "for the purposes of revising and amending the present articles of confederation, so as to make them adequate to the exigencies of the union." This recommendation the legislatures of twelve states complied with so hastily as not to consult their constituents on the subject; and though the different legislatures had no authority from their constituents for the purpose, they probably apprehended the necessity would justify the measure; and none of them extended their ideas at that time further than "revising and amending the present articles of confederation." Pennsylvania by the act appointing deputies expressly confined their powers to this object; and though it is probable that some of the members of the assembly of this state had at that time in contemplation to annihilate the present confederation, as well as the constitution of Pennsylvania, yet the plan was not sufficiently matured to communicate it to the public.

The majority of the legislature of this commonwealth were at that time under the influence of the members from the city of Philadelphia. They agreed that the deputies sent by them to convention should have no compensation for their services, which determination was calculated to prevent the election of any member who resided at a distance from the city. It was in vain for the minority to attempt electing delegates to the convention, who understood the circumstances, and the feelings of the people, and had a common interest with them. They found a disposition in the leaders of the majority of the house to choose themselves and some of their dependents. The minority attempted to prevent this by agreeing to vote for some of the leading members, who they knew had influence enough to be appointed at any rate, in hopes of carrying with them some respectable citizens of Philadelphia, in whose principles and integrity they could have more confidence; but even in this they were disappointed, except in one member: the eighth member was added at a subsequent session of the assembly.

The continental convention met in the city of Philadelphia at the time appointed. It was composed of some men of excellent characters; of others who were more remarkable for their ambition and cunning, than their patriotism; and of some who had been opponents to the independence of the United States. The delegates from Pennsylvania were, six of them, uniform and decided opponents to the constitution of this commonwealth. The convention sat upwards of four months. The doors were kept shut, and the members brought under the most solemn engagements of secrecy.[(a)] Some of those who opposed their going so far beyond their powers retired, hopeless, from the convention, others had the firmness to refuse signing the plan altogether; and many who did sign it, did it not as a system they wholly approved, but as the best that could be then obtained, and notwithstanding the time spent on this subject, it is agreed on all hands to be a work of haste and accommodation.

Whilst the gilded chains were forging in the secret conclave, the meaner instruments of despotism without were busily employed in alarming the fears of the people with dangers which did not exist, and exciting their hopes of greater advantages from the expected plan than even the best governments on earth could produce.

The proposed plan had not many hours issued forth from the womb of suspicious secrecy, until such as were prepared for the purpose were carrying about petitions for people to sign, signifying their approbation of the system, and requesting the legislature to call a convention. While every measure was taken to intimidate the people against opposing it, the public papers teemed with the most violent threats against those who should dare to think for themselves, and *tar and feathers* were liberally promised to all those who would not immediately join in supporting the proposed government be it what it would. Under such circumstances petitions in favor of calling a convention were signed by great numbers in and about the city, before they had leisure to read and examine the system, many of whom, now they are better acquainted with it, and have had time to investigate its principles, are heartily opposed to it. The petitions were speedily handed into the legislature.

Affairs were in this situation when on the 28th of September last, a resolution was proposed to the assembly by a member [George Clymer] of the house who had been also a member of the federal convention, for calling a state convention, to be elected within *ten* days for the purpose of examining and adopting the proposed constitution of the United States, though at this time the house had not received it from Congress. This attempt was opposed by a minority, who after offering every argument in their power to prevent the precipitate measure, without effect, absented themselves from the house as the only alternative left them, to prevent the measure taking place previous to their constituents being acquainted with the business. That violence and outrage which had been so often threatened was now practiced; some of the members were seized the next day by a mob collected for the purpose, and forcibly dragged to the house, and there detained by force whilst the quorum of the legislature, *so formed*, completed their resolution. We shall dwell no longer on this subject, the people of Pennsylvania have been already acquainted therewith. We would only further observe that every member of the legislature, previously to taking his seat, by solemn oath or affirmation, declares, "that he will not do or consent to any act or thing whatever that shall have a tendency to lessen or abridge their rights and privileges, as declared in the constitution of this state." And that constitution which they are so solemnly sworn to support cannot legally be altered but by a recommendation of the council of censors, who alone are authorized to propose alterations and amendments, and even these must be published at least *six months*, for the consideration of the people. The proposed system of government for the United States, if adopted, will alter and may annihilate the constitution of Pennsylvania; and therefore the legislature had no authority whatever to recommend the calling a convention for that purpose. This proceeding could not be considered as binding on the people of this commonwealth. The house was formed by violence, some of the members composing it were detained there by force, which alone would have vitiated any proceedings, to which they were otherwise competent; but had the legislature been legally formed, this business was absolutely without their power.

In this situation of affairs were the subscribers elected members of the convention of Pennsylvania. A convention called by a legislature in direct violation of their duty, and composed in part of members, who were compelled to attend for that purpose, to consider of a constitution proposed by a convention of the United States, who were not appointed for the purpose of framing a new form of government, but whose powers were expressly confined to altering and amending the present articles of confederation. Therefore the members of the continental convention in proposing the plan acted as individuals, and not as deputies from Pennsylvania.[(b)] The assembly who called the state convention acted as individuals, and not as the legislature of Pennsylvania; nor could they or the convention chosen on their recommendation have authority to do any act or thing, that can alter or annihilate the constitution of Pennsylvania (both of which will be done by the new constitution) nor are their proceedings in our opinion, at all binding on the people.

The election for members of the convention was held at so early a period and the want of information was so great, that some of us did not know of it until after it was over, and we have reason to believe that great numbers of the people of Pennsylvania have not yet had an opportunity of sufficiently examining the proposed constitution. We apprehend that no change can take place that will affect the internal government or constitution of this commonwealth, unless a majority of the people should evidence a wish for such a change; but on examining the number of votes given for members of the present state convention, we find that of upwards of *seventy thousand* freemen who are entitled to vote in Pennsylvania, the whole convention has been elected by about *thirteen thousand* voters, and though *two-thirds* of the members of the convention have thought proper to ratify the proposed constitution, yet those *two-thirds* were elected by the votes of only *six thousand and eight hundred* freemen.

In the city of Philadelphia and some of the eastern counties, the junto that took the lead in the business agreed to vote for none but such as would solemnly promise to adopt the system *in toto*, without exercising their judgment. In many of the counties the people did not attend the elections as they had not an opportunity of judging of the plan. Others did not consider themselves bound by the call of a set of men who assembled at the state house in Philadelphia, and assumed the name of the legislature of Pennsylvania; and some were prevented from voting by the violence of the party who were determined at all events to force down the measure. To such lengths did the tools of despotism carry their outrage, that in the night of the election for members of convention, in the city of Philadelphia, several of the subscribers (being then in the city to transact your business) were grossly abused, ill-treated and insulted while they were quiet in their lodgings, though they did not interfere, nor had anything to do with the said election, but, as they apprehend, because they were supposed to be adverse to the proposed constitution, and would not tamely surrender those sacred rights, which you had committed to their charge.

The convention met, and the same disposition was soon manifested in considering the proposed constitution, that had been exhibited in every other stage of the business. We were prohibited by an express vote of the convention, from taking any question on the separate articles of the plan, and reduced to the necessity of adopting or rejecting *in toto.* Tis true the majority permitted us to debate on each article, but restrained us from proposing amendments. They also determined not to permit us to enter on the minutes our reasons of dissent against any of the articles, nor even on the final question our reasons of dissent against the whole. Thus situated we entered on the examination of the proposed system of government, and found it to be such as we could not adopt, without, as we conceived, surrendering up your dearest rights. We offered our objections to the convention, and opposed those parts of the plan which, in our opinion, would be injurious to you, in the best manner we were able; and closed our arguments by offering the following propositions to the convention.

1. The rights of conscience shall be held inviolable, and neither the legislative, executive, nor judicial powers of the United States shall have authority to alter, abrogate, or infringe any part of the constitutions of the several states, which provide for the preservation of liberty in matters of religion.

2. That in controversies respecting property, and in suits between man and man, trial by jury shall remain as heretofore, as well in the federal courts, as in those of the several states.

3. That in all capital and criminal prosecutions, a man has a right to demand the cause and nature of his accusation, as well in the federal courts, as in those of the several states; to be heard by himself or his counsel; to be confronted with the accusers and witnesses, to call for evidence in his favor, and a speedy trial, by an impartial jury of the vicinage, without whose unanimous consent, he cannot be found guilty, nor can he be compelled to give evidence against himself; that no man be deprived of his liberty, except by the law of the land or the judgment of his peers.

4. That excessive bail ought not to be required nor excessive fines imposed, nor cruel or unusual punishments inflicted.

5. That warrants unsupported by evidence, whereby any officer or messenger may be commanded or required to search suspected places, or to seize any person or persons, his or their property, not particularly described, are grievous and oppressive, and shall not be granted either by the magistrates of the federal government or others.

6. That the people have a right to the freedom of speech, of writing, and of publishing their sentiments, therefore, the freedom of the press shall not be restrained by any law of the United States.

7. That the people have a right to bear arms for the defense of themselves and their own state, or the United States, or for the purpose of killing game; and no law shall be passed for disarming the people or any of them, unless for crimes committed, or real danger of public injury from individuals; and as standing armies in the time of peace are dangerous to liberty, they ought not to be kept up; and that the military shall be kept under strict subordination to and be governed by the civil power.

8. The inhabitants of the several states shall have liberty to fowl and hunt in seasonable times, on the lands they hold, and on all other lands in the United States not enclosed, and in like manner to fish in all navigable waters, and others not private property, without being restrained therein by any laws to be passed by the legislature of the United States.

9. That no law shall be passed to restrain the legislatures of the several states from enacting laws for imposing taxes, except imposts and duties on goods imported or exported, and that no taxes, except imposts and duties upon goods imported and exported, and postage on letters shall be levied by the authority of Congress.

10. That the house of representatives be properly increased in number; that elections shall remain free; that the several states shall have power to regulate the elections for senators and representatives, without being controlled either directly or indirectly by an interference on the part of the Congress; and that elections of representatives be annual.

11. That the power of organizing, arming, and disciplining the militia (the manner of disciplining the militia to be prescribed by Congress) remain with the individual states, and that Congress shall not have authority to call or march any of the militia out ot their own state, without the consent of such state and for such length of time only as such state shall agree.

That the sovereignty, freedom, and independency of the several states shall be retained, and every power, jurisdiction, and right which is not by this constitution expressly delegated to the United States in Congress assembled.

12. That the legislative, executive, and judicial powers be kept separate; and to this end that a constitutional council be appointed, to advise and assist the president, who shall be responsible for the advice they give, hereby the senators would be relieved from almost constant attendance; and also that the judges be made completely independent.

13. That no treaty which shall be directly opposed to the existing laws of the United States in Congress assembled shall be valid until such laws shall be repealed, or made conformable to such treaty; neither shall any treaties be valid which are in contradiction to the constitution of the United States, or the constitutions of the several states.

14. That the judiciary power of the United States shall be confined to cases affecting ambassadors, other public ministers and consuls; to cases of admiralty and maritime jurisdiction; to controversies to which the United States shall be a party; to controversies between two or more states—between a state and citizens of different states—between citizens claiming lands under grants of different states; and between a state or the citizens thereof and foreign states, and in criminal cases, to such only as are expressly enumerated in the constitution, and that the United States in Congress assembled shall not have power to enact laws, which shall alter the laws of descents and distribution of the effects of deceased persons, the titles of lands or goods, or the regulation of contracts in the individual states.

After reading these propositions, we declared our willingness to agree to the plan, provided it was so amended as to meet those propositions, or something similar to them; and finally moved the convention to adjourn, to give the people of Pennsylvania time to consider the subject, and determine for themselves; but these were all rejected, and the final vote was taken, when our duty to you induced us to vote against the proposed plan, and to decline signing the ratification of the same.

During the discussion we met with many insults, and some personal abuse; we were not even treated with decency, during the sitting of the convention, by the persons in the gallery of the house; however, we flatter ourselves that in contending for the preservation of those invaluable rights you have thought proper to commit to our charge, we acted with a spirit becoming freemen, and being desirous that you might know the principles which actuated our conduct, and being prohibited from inserting our reasons of dissent on the minutes of the convention, we have subjoined them for your consideration, as to you alone we are accountable. It remains with you whether you will think those inestimable privileges, which you have so ably contended for, should be sacrificed at the shrine of despotism, or whether you mean to contend for them with the same spirit that has so often baffled the attempts of an aristocratic faction, to rivet the shackles of slavery on you and your unborn posterity.

Our objections are comprised under three general heads of dissent, viz.:

We dissent, first, because it is the opinion of the most celebrated writers on government, and confirmed by uniform experience, that a very extensive territory cannot be governed on the principles of freedom, otherwise than by a confederation of republics, possessing all the powers of internal government; but united in the management of their general, and foreign concerns.

If any doubt could have been entertained of the truth of the foregoing principle, it has been fully removed by the concession of Mr. [James] Wilson, one of majority on this question; and who was one of the deputies in the late general convention. In justice to him, we will give his own words; they are as follows, viz.: "The extent of country for which the new constitution was required produced another difficulty in the business of the federal convention. It is the opinion of celebrated writers that to a small territory, the democratical; to a middling territory (as Montesquieu has termed it) the monarchical; and to an extensive territory, the despotic form of government is best adapted. Regarding then the wide and almost unbounded jurisdiction of the United States, at first view, the hand of despotism seemed necessary to control, connect, and protect it; and hence the chief embarrassment rose. For, we know that, altho our constituents would cheerfully submit to the legislative restraints of a free government, they would spurn at every attempt to shackle them with despotic power." And again in another part of his speech he continues. "Is it probable that the dissolution of the state government and the establishment of one *consolidated empire* would be eligible in its nature and satisfactory to the people in its administration? I think not, as I have given reasons to show that so extensive a territory could not be governed, connected, and preserved, but by the *supremacy of despotic power*. All the exertions of the most potent emperors of Rome were not capable to keeping that empire together, which in extent was far inferior to the dominion of America."

We dissent, secondly, because the powers vested in Congress by this constitution must necessarily annihilate and absorb the legislative, executive, and judicial powers of the several states, and produce from their ruins one consolidated government, which from the nature of things will be *an iron-handed despotism*, as nothing short of the supremacy of despotic sway could connect and govern these United States under one government.

As the truth of this position is of such decisive importance, it ought to be fully investigated, and if it is founded to be clearly ascertained; for, should it be demonstrated, that the powers vested by this constitution in Congress will have such an effect as necessarily to produce one consolidated government, the question then will be reduced to this short issue, viz.: whether satiated with the blessings of liberty; whether repenting of the folly of so recently asserting their unalienable rights, against foreign despots at the expense of so much blood and treasure, and such painful and arduous struggles, the people of America are now willing to resign every privilege of freemen, and submit to the dominion of an absolute government, that will embrace all America in one chain of despotism; or whether they will with virtuous indignation spurn at the shackles prepared for them, and confirm their liberties by a conduct becoming freemen.

That the new government will not be a confederacy of states, as it ought, but one consolidated government founded upon the destruction of the several governments of the states, we shall now show.

The powers of Congress under the new constitution are complete and unlimited over the *purse* and the *sword,*[2] and are perfectly independent of, and supreme over, the state governments; whose intervention in these great points is entirely destroyed. By virtue of their power of taxation, Congress may command the whole, or any part of the property of the people. They may impose what imposts upon commerce; they may impose what land taxes, poll taxes, excises, duties on all written instruments, and duties on every other article that they may judge proper; in short, every species of taxation, whether of an external or internal nature is comprised in section the 8th, of Article the 1st, viz.: "The Congress shall have power to lay and collect taxes, duties, imposts, and excises, to pay the debts, and provide for the common defence and general welfare of the United States."

As there is no one article of taxation reserved to the state governments, the Congress may monopolize every source of revenue, and thus indirectly demolish the state governments, for without funds they could not exist. The taxes, duties, and excises imposed by Congress may be so high as to render it impracticable to levy further sums on the same articles; but whether this should be the case or not, if the state governments should presume to impose taxes, duties, or excises, on the same articles with Congress, the latter may abrogate and repeal the laws whereby they are imposed, upon the allegation that they interfere with the due collection of their taxes, duties, or excises, by virtue of the following clause, part of section 8th, Article 1st, viz.: "To make all laws which shall be necessary and proper for carrying into execution the foregoing powers, and all other powers vested by this constitution in the government of the United States, or in any department or officer thereof."

The Congress might gloss over this conduct by construing every purpose for which the state legislatures now lay taxes, to be for the *"general welfare,"* and therefore as of their jurisdiction.

And the supremacy of the laws of the United States is established by Article 6th, viz.: "That this constitution and the laws of the United States, which shall be made in pursuance thereof, and *all treaties* made, or which shall be made, under the authority of the United States, shall be the *supreme law* of the *land;* and *the judges in every state shall be bound thereby; any thing in the constitution or laws of any state to the contrary notwithstanding."* It has been alleged that the words "pursuant to the constitution" are a restriction upon the authority of Congress; but when it is considered that by other sections they are invested with every efficient power of government, and which may be exercised to the absolute destruction of the state governments, without any violation of even the forms of the constitution, this seeming restriction, as well as every other restriction in it, appears to us to be nugatory and delusive; and only introduced as a blind upon the real nature of the government. In our opinion, "pursuant to the constitution" will be coextensive with the *will* and *pleasure* of Congress, which, indeed, will be the only limitation of their powers.

We apprehend that two coordinate sovereignties would be a solecism in politics. That therefore as there is no line of distinction drawn between the general and state government; as the sphere of their jurisdiction is undefined, it would be contrary to the nature of things, that both should exist together, one or the other would necessarily triumph in the fullness of dominion. However the contest could not be of long continuance, as the state governments are divested of every means of defense, and will be obliged by "the supreme law of the land" *to yield at discretion.*

It has been objected to this total destruction of the state governments, that the existence of their legislatures is made essential to the organization of Congress; that they must assemble for the appointment of the senators and president general of the United States. True, the state legislatures may be continued for some years, as boards of appointment, merely, after they are divested of every other function, but the framers of the constitution foreseeing that the people will soon be disgusted with this solemn mockery of a government without power and usefulness have made a provision for relieving them from the imposition, in section 4th, of Article 1st, viz.: "The times, places, and manner of holding elections for senators and representatives shall be prescribed in each state by the legislature thereof; *but the Congress may at any time, by law make or alter such regulations; except as to the place of chusing senators.*"

As Congress have the control over the time of the appointment of the president general, of the senators and of the representatives of the United States, they may prolong their existence in office, for life, by postponing the time of their election and appointment, from period to period, under various pretenses, such as an apprehension of invasion, the factious disposition of the people, or any other plausible pretense that the occasion may suggest; and having thus obtained life estates in the government, they may fill up the vacancies themselves, by their control over the mode of appointment; with this exception in regard to the senators, that as the place of appoinment for them must, by the constitution, be in the particular state, they may depute somebody in the respective states, to fill up the vacancies in the senate occasioned by death, until they can venture to assume it themselves. In this manner may the only restriction in this clause be evaded. By virtue of the foregoing section, when the spirit of the people shall be gradually broken; when the general government shall be firmly established, and when a numerous standing army shall render opposition vain, the Congress may complete the system of despotism, in renouncing all dependence on the people, by continuing themselves, and [their] children in the government.

The celebrated Montesquieu, in his *Spirit of Laws,* vol. 1, page 12th, says, "That in a democracy there can be no exercise of sovereignty, but by the suffrages of the people, which are their will; now the sovereign's will is the sovereign himself; the laws therefore, which establish the right of suffrage, are fundamental to this government. In fact, it is as important to regulate in a republic in what manner, by whom, and concerning what suffrages are to be given, as it is in a monarchy to know who is the prince, and after what manner he ought to govern." The *time, mode,* and *place* of the election of representatives, senators and president general of the United States ought not to be under the control of Congress, but fundamentally ascertained and established.

The new constitution, consistently with the plan of consolidation, contains no reservation of the rights and privileges of the state governments, which was made in the confederation of the year 1778, by Article the 2d, viz.: "That each state retains its sovereignty, freedom and independence, and every power, jurisdiction and right, which is not by this confederation expressly delegated to the United States in Congress assembled."

The legislative power vested in Congress by the foregoing recited sections is so unlimited in its nature; may be so comprehensive, and boundless [in] its exercise, that this alone would be amply sufficient to annihilate the state governments, and swallow them up in the grand vortex of general empire.

The judicial powers vested in Congress are also so various and extensive, that by legal ingenuity they may be extended to every case, and thus absorb the state judiciaries, and when we consider the decisive influence that a general judiciary would have over the civil polity of the several states, we do not hesitate to pronounce that this power, unaided by the legislative, would effect a consolidation of the states under one government.

The powers of a court of equity, vested by this constitution in the tribunals of Congress; powers which do not exist in Pennsylvania unless so far as they can be incorporated with jury trial, would, in this state, greatly contribute to this event. The rich and wealthy suitors would eagerly lay hold of the infinite mazes, perplexities, and delays, which a court of chancery, with the appellate powers of the supreme court in fact as well as law would furnish him with, and thus the poor man being plunged in the bottomless pit of legal discussion would drop his demand in despair.

In short, consolidation pervades the whole constitution. It begins with an annunciation that such was the intention. The main pillars of the fabric correspond with it, and the concluding paragraph is a confirmation of it. The preamble begins with the words, "We the people of the United States," which is the style of a compact between individuals entering into a state of society, and not that of a confederation of states. The other features of consolidation, we have before noticed.

Thus we have fully established the position, that the powers vested by this constitution in Congress will effect a consolidation of the states under one government, which even the advocates of this constitution admit could not be done without the sacrifice of all liberty.

3. We dissent, thirdly, because if it were practicable to govern so extensive a territory as these United States includes, on the plan of a consolidated government, consistent with the principles of liberty and the happiness of the people, yet the construction of this constitution is not calculated to attain the object, for independent of the nature of the case, it would of itself, necessarily produce a despotism, and that not by the usual gradations, but with the celerity that has hitherto only attended revolutions effected by the sword.

To establish the truth of this position, a cursory investigation of the principles and form of this constitution will suffice.

The first consideration that this review suggests is the omission of a BILL OF RIGHTS ascertaining and fundamentally establishing those unalienable and personal rights of men, without the full, free, and secure enjoyment of which there can be no liberty, and over which it is not necessary for a good government to have the control. The principal of which are the rights of conscience, personal liberty by the clear and unequivocal establishment of the writ of *habeas corpus*, jury trial in criminal and civil cases, by an impartial jury of the vicinage or county; with the common law proceedings, for the safety of the accused in criminal prosecutions; and the liberty of the press, that scourge of tyrants, and the grand bulwark of every other liberty and privilege; the stipulation heretofore made in favor of them in the state constitutions are entirely superseded by this constitution.

The legislature of a free country should be so formed as to have a competent knowledge of its constituents, and enjoy their confidence. To produce these essential requisites, the representation ought to be fair, equal, and sufficiently numerous, to possess the same interests, feelings, opinions, and views, which the people themselves would possess were they all assembled; and so numerous as to prevent bribery and undue influence, and so reponsible to the people, by frequent and fair elections, as to prevent their neglecting or sacrificing the views and interests of their constituents, to their own pursuits.

We will now bring the legislature under this constitution to the test of the foregoing principles, which will demonstrate, that it is deficient in every essential quality of a just and safe representation.

The house of representatives is to consist of 65 members; that is one for about every 50,000 inhabitants, to be chosen every two years. Thirty-three members will form a quorum for doing business, and 17 of these, being the majority, determine the sense of the house.

The senate, the other constituent branch of the legislature, consists of 26 members, being *two* from each state, appointed by their legislatures every six years—fourteen senators make a quorum; the majority of whom, eight, determines the sense of that body; except in judging on impeachments, or in making treaties, or in expelling a member, when two-thirds of the senators present must concur.

The president is to have the control over the enacting of laws, so far as to make the concurrence of *two*-thirds of the representatives and senators present necessary, if he should object to the laws.

Thus it appears that the liberties, happiness, interests, and great concerns of the whole United States may be dependent upon the integrity, virtue, wisdom, and knowledge of 25 or 26 men. How inadequate and unsafe a representation! Inadequate, because the sense and views of 3 or 4 millions of people diffused over so extensive a territory comprising such various climates, products, habits, interests, and opinions cannot be collected in so small a body; and besides, it is not fair and equal representation of the people even in proportion to its number, for the smallest state has as much weight in the senate as the largest, and from the smallness of the number to be chosen for both branches of the legislature; and from the mode of election and appointment, which is under the control of Congress; and from the nature of the thing, men of the most elevated rank in life will alone be chosen. The other orders in the society, such as farmers, traders, and mechanics, who all ought to have a competent number of their best-informed men in the legislature, will be totally unrepresented.

The representation is unsafe because in the exercise of such great powers and trusts, it is so exposed to corruption and undue influence, by the gift of the numerous places of honor and emolument, at the disposal of the executive; by the arts and address of the great and designing; and by direct bribery.

The representation is moreover inadequate and unsafe, because of the long terms for which it is appointed, and the mode of its appointment, by which Congress may not only control the choice of the people, but may so manage as to divest the people of this fundamental right, and become self-elected.

The number of members in the house of representatives *may* be increased to one for every 30,000 inhabitants. But when we consider, that this cannot be done without the consent of the senate, who from their share in the legislative, in the executive, and judicial departments, and permanency of appointment, will be the great efficient body in this government, and whose weight and predominancy would be abridged by an increase of the representatives, we are persuaded that this is a circumstance that cannot be expected. On the contrary, the number of representatives will probably be continued at 65, although the population of the country may swell to treble what it now is; unless a revolution should effect a change.

We have before noticed the judicial power as it would effect a consolidation of the states into one government; we will now examine it, as it would affect the liberties and welfare of the people, supposing such a government were practicable and proper.

The judicial power, under the proposed constitution, is founded on the well-known principles of the *civil law*, by which the judge determines both on law and fact, and appeals are allowed from the inferior tribunals to the superior, upon the whole question; so that *facts* as well as *law*, would be reexamined, and even new facts brought forward in the court of appeals; and to use the words of a very eminent civilian, "The cause is many times another thing before the court of appeals, than what it was at the time of the first sentence."

That this mode of proceeding is the one which must be adopted under this constitution is evident from the following circumstances: 1st. That the trial by jury, which is the grand characteristic of the common law, is secured by the constitution, only in criminal cases. 2d. That the appeal from both *law* and *fact* is expressly established, which is utterly inconsistent with the principles of the common law, and trials by jury. The only mode in which an appeal from law and fact can be established is by adopting the principles and practice of the civil law; unless the United States should be drawn into the absurdity of calling and swearing juries, merely for the purpose of contradicting their verdicts, which would render juries contemptible and worse than useless. 3d. That the courts to be established would decide on all cases *of law and equity,* which is a well-known characteristic of the civil law, and these courts would have conusance [cognizance] not only of the laws of the United States and of treaties, and of cases affecting ambassadors, but of all cases of *admiralty and maritime jurisdiction,* which last are matters belonging exclusively to civil law, in every nation in Christendom.

Not to enlarge upon the loss of the invaluable right of trial by an unbiased jury, so dear to every friend of liberty, the monstrous expense and inconveniences of the mode of proceeding to be adopted are such as will prove intolerable to the people of this country. The lengthy proceedings of the civil law court in the chancery of England, and in the courts of Scotland and France, are such that few men of moderate fortune can endure the expense of; the poor man must therefore submit to the wealthy. Length of purse will too often prevail against right and justice. For instance, we are told by the learned Judge Blackstone, that a question only on the property of an ox, of the value of three guineas, originating under the civil law proceedings in Scotland, after many interlocutory orders and sentences below, was carried at length from the court of sessions, the highest court in that part of Great Britain, by way of *appeal* to the House of Lords, where the question of law and fact was finally determined. He adds, that no pique of spirit could in the court of king's bench or common pleas at Westminster have given continuance to such a cause for a tenth-part of the time, nor have cost a twentieth-part of the expense. Yet the costs in the court of king's bench and common pleas in England are infinitely greater than those which the people of this county have ever experienced. We abhor the idea of losing the transcendent privilege of trial by jury, with the loss of which, it is remarked by the same learned author, that in Sweden, the liberties of the commons were extinguished by an aristocratic senate; and *trial by jury* and the liberty of the people went out together. At the same time we regret the intolerable delay, the enormous expenses and infinite vexation to which the people of this country will be exposed from the voluminous proceedings of the courts of civil law, and especially from the appellate jurisdiction, by means of which a man may be drawn from the utmost boundaries of this extensive country to the seat of the supreme court of the nation to contend, perhaps with a wealthy and powerful adversary. The consequence of this establishment will be an absolute confirmation of the power of aristocratical influence in the courts of justice; for the common people will not be able to contend or struggle against it.

Trial by jury in criminal cases may also be excluded by declaring that the libeler, for instance, shall be liable to an action of debt for a specified sum, thus evading the common law prosecution by indictment and trial by jury. And the common course of proceeding against a ship for breach of revenue laws by information (which will be classed among civil causes) will at the civil law be within the resort of a court, where no jury intervenes. Besides, the benefit of jury trial, in cases of a criminal nature, which cannot be evaded, will be rendered of little value, by calling the accused to answer far from home; there being no provision that the trial be by a jury of the neighborhood or country. Thus an inhabitant of Pittsburgh, on a charge of crime committed on the banks of the Ohio, may be obliged to defend himself at the side of the Delaware, and so *vice versa.* To conclude this head, we observe that the judges of the courts of Congress would not be independent, as they are not debarred from holding other offices during the pleasure of the president and senate, and as they may derive their support in part from fees alterable by the legislature.

The next consideration that the constitution presents is the undue and dangerous mixture of the powers of government: the same body possessing legislative, executive, and judicial powers. The senate is a constituent branch of the legislature, it has judicial power in judging on impeachments, and in this case unites in some measure the characters of judge and party, as all of the principal officers are appointed by the president general, with the concurrence of the senate and therefore they derive their offices in part from the senate. This may bias the judgments of the senators, and tend to screen great delinquents from punishment. And the senate has, moreover, various and great executive powers, viz.: in concurrence with the president general, they form treaties with foreign nations, that may control and abrogate the constitutions and laws of the several states. Indeed, there is no power, privilege, or liberty of the state governments, or of the people, but what may be affected by virtue of this power. For all treaties, made by them, are to be the "supreme law of the land; any thing in the constitution or laws of any state, to the contrary notwithstanding."

And this great power may be exercised by the president and 10 senators (being two-thirds of 14 which is a quorum of that body). What an inducement would this offer to the ministers of foreign powers to compass by bribery *such concessions* as could not otherwise be obtained. It is the unvaried usage of all free states, whenever treaties interfere with the positive laws of the land, to make the intervention of the legislature necessary to give them operation. This became necessary, and was afforded by the parliament of Great Britain in consequence of the late commercial treaty between that kingdom and France. As the senate judges on impeachments, who is to try the members of the senate for the abuse of this power! And none of the great appointments of office can be made without the consent of the senate.

Such various, extensive, and important powers combined in one body of men are inconsistent with all freedom; the celebrated Montesquieu tells us, that "when the legislative and executive powers are united in the same person, or in the same body of magistrates, there can be no liberty, because apprehensions may arise, lest the same monarch or *senate* should enact tyrannical laws, to execute them in a tryannical manner."

"Again, there is no liberty, if the power of judging be not separated from the legislative and executive powers. Were it joined with the legislative, the life and liberty of the subject would be exposed to arbitrary control: for the judge would then be legislator. Were it joined to the executive power, the judge might behave with all the violence of an oppressor. There would be an end of everything, were the same man, or the same body of the nobles, or of the people, to exercise those three powers; that of enacting laws; that of executing the public resolutions; and that of judging the crimes or differences of individuals."

The president general is dangerously connected with the senate; his coincidence with the views of the ruling junto in that body is made essential to his weight and importance in the government, which will destroy all independency and purity in the executive department, and having the power of pardoning without the concurrence of a council, he may screen from punishment the most treasonable attempts that may be made on the liberties of the people, when instigated by his coadjutors in the senate. Instead of this dangerous and improper mixture of the executive with the legislative and judicial, the supreme executive powers ought to have been placed in the president, with a small independent council made personally responsible for every appointment to office or other act, by having their opinions recorded; and that without the concurrence of the majority of the quorum of this council, the president should not be capable of taking any step.

We have before considered internal taxation, as it would effect the destruction of the state governments, and produce one consolidated government. We will now consider that subject as it affects the personal concerns of the people.

The power of direct taxation applies to every individual, as Congress, under this government, is expressly vested with the authority of laying a capitation or poll tax upon every person to any amount. This is a tax that, however oppressive in its nature, and unequal in its operation, is certain as to its produce and simple in its collection; it cannot be evaded like the objects of imposts or excise, and will be paid, because all that a man hath will he give for his head. This tax is so congenial to the nature of despotism, that it has ever been a favorite under such governments. Some of those who were in the late general convention from this state have long labored to introduce a poll tax among us.

The power of direct taxation will further apply to every individual, as Congress may tax land, cattle, trades, occupations, etc. to any amount, and every object of internal taxation is of that nature, that however oppressive, the people will have but this alternative, either to pay the tax, or let their property be taken, for all resistance will be vain. The standing army and select militia would enforce the collection.

For the moderate exercise of this power, there is no control left in the state governments, whose intervention is destroyed. No relief, or redress of grievances can be extended, as heretofore, by them. There in not even a declaration of RIGHTS to which the people may appeal for the vindication of their wrongs in the court of justice. They must therefore, implicitly, obey the most arbitrary laws, as the worst of them will be pursuant to the principles and form of the constitution, and that the strongest of all checks upon the conduct of administration, *responsibility to the people,* will not exist in this government. The permanency of the appointments of senators and representatives, and the control the Congress have over their election, will place them independent of the sentiments and resentment of the people, and the administration having a greater interest in the government than in the community, there will be no consideration to restrain them from oppression and tyranny. In the government of this state, under the old confederation, the members of the legislature are taken from among the people, and their interests and welfare are so inseparably connected with those of their constituents, that they can derive no advantage from oppressive laws and taxes, for they would suffer in common with their fellow citizens; would participate in the burthens they impose on the community, as they must return to the common level, after a short period; and notwithstanding every exertion of influence, every means of corruption, a necessary rotation excludes them from permanency in the legislature.

This large state is to have but ten members in that congress which is to have the liberty, property, and dearest concerns of every individual in this vast country at absolute command, and even these ten persons, who are to be our only guardians, who are to supersede the legislature of Pennsylvania, will not be of the choice of the people, nor amenable to them. From the mode of their election and appointment they will consist of the lordly and high-minded; of men who will have no congenial feelings with the people, but a perfect indifference for, and contempt of them; they will consist of those harpies of power, that prey upon the very vitals; that riot on the miseries of the community. But we will suppose, although in all probability it may never be realized in fact, that our deputies in Congress have the welfare of their constituents at heart, and will exert themselves in their behalf. What security could even this afford; what relief could they extend to their oppressed constituents? To attain this, the majority of the deputies of the twelve other states in Congress must be alike well disposed; must alike forego the sweets of power, and relinquish the pursuits of ambition, which from the nature of things is not to be expected. If the people part with a responsible representation in the legislature, founded upon fair, certain, and frequent elections, they have nothing left they can call their own. Miserable is the lot of that people whose every concern depends on the WILL and PLEASURE of their rulers. Our soldiers will become Janissaries, and our officers of government bashaws; in short, the system of despotism will soon be completed.

From the foregoing investigation, it appears that the Congress under this constitution will not possess the confidence of the people, which is an essential requisite in a good government; for unless the laws command the confidence and respect of the great body of the people, so as to induce them to support them, when called on by the civil magistrate, they must be executed by the aid of a numerous standing army, which would be inconsistent with every idea of liberty; for the same force that may be employed to compel obedience to good laws, might and probably would be used to wrest from the people their constitutional liberties. The framers of this constitution appear to have been aware of this great deficiency; to have been sensible that no dependence could be placed on the people for their support; but on the contrary, that the government must be executed by force. They have therefore made a provision for this purpose in a permanent STANDING ARMY, and a MILITIA that may be subjected to as strict discipline and government.

A standing army in the hands of a government placed so independent of the people may be made a fatal instrument to overturn the public liberties; it may be employed to enforce the collection of the most oppressive taxes, and to carry into execution the most arbitrary measures. An ambitious man who may have the army at his devotion may step up into the throne, and seize upon absolute power.

The absolute unqualified command that Congress have over the militia may be made instrumental to the destruction of all liberty, both public and private; whether of a personal, civil, or religious nature.

First, the personal liberty of every man probably from sixteen to sixty years of age may be destroyed by the power Congress have in organizing and governing of the militia. As militia they may be subjected to corporal punishments of the most disgraceful and humiliating kind, and to death itself, by the sentence of a court martial. To this our young men will be more immediately subjected, as a select militia, composed of them, will best answer the purposes of government.

Secondly, the rights of conscience may be violated, as there is no exemption of those persons who are conscientiously scrupulous of bearing arms. These compose a respectable proportion of the community in the state. This is the more remarkable, because even when the distresses of the late war, and the evident disaffection of many citizens of that description, inflamed our passions, and when every person, who was obliged to risk his own life, must have been exasperated against such as on any account kept back from the common danger, yet even then, when outrage and violence might have been expected, the rights of conscience were held sacred.

At this momentous crisis, the framers of our state constitution made the most express and decided declaration and stipulations in favor of the rights of conscience; but now when no necessity exists, those dearest rights of men are left insecure.

Thirdly, the absolute command of Congress over the militia may be destructive of public liberty; for under the guidance of an arbitrary government, they may be made the unwilling instruments of tyranny. The militia of Pennsylvania may be marched to New England or Virginia to quell an insurrection occasioned by the most galling oppression, and aided by the standing army, they will no doubt be successful in subduing their liberty and independency; but in so doing, although the magnanimity of their minds will be extinguished, yet the meaner passions of resentment and revenge will be increased, and these in turn will be the ready and obedient instruments of despotism to enslave the others; and that with an irritated vengeance. Thus may the militia be made the instruments of crushing the last efforts of expiring liberty, of riveting the chains of despotism on their fellow citizens, and on one another. This power can be exercised not only without violating the constitution, but in strict conformity with it; it is calculated for this express purpose, and will doubtless be executed accordingly.

As this government will not enjoy the confidence of the people, but be executed by force, it will be a very expensive and burthensome government. The standing army must be numerous, and as a further support, it will be the policy of this government to multiply officers in every department: judges, collectors, tax gatherers, excisemen, and the whole host of revenue officers will swarm over the land, devouring the hard earnings of the industrious, like the locusts of old, impoverishing and desolating all before them.

We have not noticed the smaller, nor many of the considerable blemishes, but have confined our objections to the great and essential defects; the main pillars of the constitution, which we have shown to be inconsistent with the liberty and happiness of the people, as its establishment will annihilate the state government, and produce one consolidated government, that will eventually and speedily issue in the supremacy of despotism.

In this investigation, we have not confined our views to the interests or welfare of this state, in preference to the others. We have overlooked all local circumstances; we have considered this subject on the broad scale of the general good; we have asserted the cause of the present and future ages, the cause of liberty and mankind.

a. *The Journals of the conclave are still concealed.*

b. The continental convention in direct violation of the 13th Article of the confederation have declared, "that the ratification of nine states shall be sufficient for the establishment of this constitution, between the states so ratifying the same." Thus has the plighted faith of the states been sported with! They had solemnly engaged that the confederation now subsisting should be inviolably preserved by each of them, and the union thereby formed, should be perpetual, unless the same should be altered by mutual consent.

1 DHRC, II, pp. 618-639. Also reprinted in DHRC, XV, pp. 13-34, and in Storing, III, pp. 145-166.

2 See answer to this charge in "A Pennsylvanian III," February 20, 1788, p. 275.

Philadelphiensis V December 19, 1787

Newspaper Article: Philadelphia *Independent Gazetteer* (excerpt)

Is it improper for freemen to petition for their rights? If it be; then I say that the impropriety consisted only in their not *demanding* them. Propriety requires that the people should approach their representatives with a becoming humility; but the governors of a free people must ever be considered as their servants, and are therefore bound to observe decency towards them, and to act according to their instructions and agreeably to conscience. If the petitions of the freemen of America, couched in decent and respectful terms, will not be attended to; then be it known, that their *demands* must and will be granted: If no better will do, the ultima ratio regum must secure to the people their rights. God in his providence has crowned them with success once already on this head; and there is little doubt, with the same assistance, but a second attempt will terminate just as much in favor of liberty.

DHRC, XV, p. 45. Reprinted in Storing, III, pp. 116-117.

Jacob Trusty December 19, 1787

Newspaper Article: Philadelphia *Freeman's Journal*[1]

Philadelphia County, *Decem.* 12, 1787.

Mr. Bailey,

I wish you would inform me, through the channel of your paper, of the true meaning of disarming the Militia in this State at this solemn period:[2] The county officer shews us an order of Council for to deliver them for cleaning; but we in our county have, upon second thought, resolved to clean them ourselves. Is this a trick for to push upon us the new plan of government whether we will or will not have it; no, Mr. Bailey, those gentlemen in your city who have planned it, are poor politicians, if they depend on our agreeing to give up our mush sticks.—I am, &c.

JACOB TRUSTY

1 DHRC, II Mfm. Pa., p. 1361.

2 For other documents related to the controversy over the collection of publicly owned arms in Pennsylvania, and the complaint that this was intended to disarm the militia, see: "Centinel IX," January 8, 1788, p. 191; Pennsylvania *Carlisle Gazette*, January 9, 1788, p. 194; "Trusty," January 10, 1788, p. 200; "Supreme Executive Council," January 10, 1788, p. 201; "An Old Militia Officer of 1776," January 18, 1788, p. 221; Philadelphia *Freeman's Journal*, January 23, 1788, p. 226; Philadelphia *Pennsylvania Herald*, February 5, 1788, p. 251; Philadelphia *Independent Gazetteer*,

February 27, 1788, p. 286; "James de Caledonia IV," March 12, 1788, p. 298; "Aristocrotis," April [15], 1788, p. 334 at note 2; Philadelphia *Independent Gazetteer*, April 30, 1788, p. 340 at note 3.

Thomas Jefferson (Paris) December 20, 1787
Letter: To James Madison (excerpt)

I will now add what I do not like [about the constitution]. First the omission of a bill of rights providing clearly & without the aid of sophisms for freedom of religion, freedom of the press, protection against standing armies, restriction against monopolies, the eternal & unremitting force of the habeas corpus laws, and trials by jury in all matters of fact triable by the laws of the land & not by the law of Nations. To say, as mr Wilson does that a bill of rights was not necessary because all is reserved in the case of the general government which is not given, while in the particular ones all is given which is not reserved, might do for the Audience to whom it was addressed, but is surely a gratis dictum, opposed by strong inferences from the body of the instrument, as well as from the omission of the clause of our present confederation which had declared that in express terms. It was a hard conclusion to say because there has been no uniformity among the states as to the cases triable by jury, because some have been so incautious as to abandon this mode of trial, therefore the more prudent states shall be reduced to the same level of calamity. It would have been much more just & wise to have concluded the other way that as most of the states had judiciously preserved this palladium, those who had wandered should be brought back to it, and to have established general right instead of general wrong. Let me add that a bill of rights is what the people are entitled to against every government on earth, general or particular, & what no just government should refuse, or rest on inference.

DHRC, XIV, pp. 482-483. Reprinted in *Papers*, X, pp. 336-337.

Robert Yates and John Lansing, Jr. December 21, 1787
Letter: To Governor Clinton of New York.
Published: New York *Daily Advertiser*, January 14, 1788 (excerpts)

[W]e entertained an opinion that a general Government, however guarded by declarations of rights or cautionary provisions, must unavoidably, in a short time, be productive of the destruction of the civil liberty of such citizens who could be effectually coerced by it[.] . . .

[W]e have the strongest apprehensions that a Government so organized as that recommended by the Convention, cannot afford that security to equal and permanent liberty, which we wished to make an invariable object of our pursuit.

DHRC, XV, p. 369-370. Yates and Lansing were delegates from New York to the Federal Convention in Philadelphia. They left the Convention before its work was completed.

Charles Nisbet (Carlisle) December 25, 1787
Letter: To the Earl of Buchan (excerpt)

Mobbish Meetings were held here last Night, to draw up Letters of Thanks to the Minority of the [Pennsylvania] convention, & in these Meetings the Speakers exhorted the People to take up Arms in Defence of their Rights. I hope however that this will be only a Threat. What is worst is, that Congress have Arms for many thousands of Men and a Considerable Quantity of Gun-powder in their Stores here, which they, like wise Men, have ordered to be sold in a few Weeks hence, as if on purpose to Supply the Enemies of their Country. As this Town is the nearest to the Center of the United States, & most commodious for Security, Intelligence & Communication, the Old Congress made Choice of it for their general Magazine[.]

DHRC, XV, pp. 88-89.

Cassius XI December 25, 1787
Newspaper Article: Boston *Massachusetts Gazette* (excerpt)

The 6th section provides, that this constitution, and the laws which shall be made in pursuance thereof, and all treaties made, or which shall be made, in pursuance thereof, under the authority of the United States, shall be the supreme law of the land, and the judges in every state shall be bound thereby, anything in the constitution or laws of any state to the contrary notwithstanding.

This is the article, my countrymen, which knaves and blockheads have so often dressed up in false colours, and requested your attention to the construction of it. Adopt not a constitution, say they, which stipulates that the laws of Congress shall be the supreme law of the land—or, in other words, they request of you not to obey laws of your own making. This is the article which they say is so arbitrary and tyrannical, that unless you have a bill of rights to secure you, you are ruined forever.

But in the name of common sense I would ask, of what use would be a bill of rights, in the present case? . . It can only be to resort to when it is supposed that Congress have infringed the unalienble rights of the people: but would it not be much easier to resort to the federal constitution, to see if therein power is given to Congress to make the law in question? If such power is not given, the law is in fact a nullity, and the people will not be bound thereby. For let it be remembered, that such laws, and such only, as are founded on this constitution, are to be the supreme laws of the land[.]

Essays, pp. 45-46.

Philadelphiensis VI December 26, 1787
Newspaper Article: Philadelphia *Freeman's Journal* (excerpts)

My Fellow-Citizens, If America is to become a respectable nation, the people must retain their freedom in the fullest extent possible; this is the *sine qua non* of our respectability; on this alone must the strength, honor, and national character of this country depend. Indeed any other system defeats the intention of the revolution; freedom was the ultimate object of the war with Britain, and must, from the nature of things, be the object as long as America remains an independent country. The Turkish empire was established by cruelty and dominion, by the swords of bigotted infidels, whose religion taught them to murder without remorse: probably then, that empire should have been extinct long ago, if the same system of despotism and cruelty had not been preserved; (although there are some authors who affirm that even in Turkey great and valuable privileges have always been enjoyed) but be that as it may, the case is widely different with us; nothing short of pure liberty is consistent with revolution principles; the *temple of freedom* that was raised in America, was intended by providence to be the asylum of the poor and the oppressed of every nation and every clime. If then we prostitute this hallowed edifice, to purposes for which providence never designed it, our ruin is inevitable. Our national independence will probably not survive the loss of our liberties a single day. As darkness brings night, so despotism will obliterate the very name of the American empire.

It is a principle almost universally confirmed by the joint evidences of reason and experience, that that nation which is most free, is always most victorious; people who enjoy their civil and religious liberty, according to the true sense and meaning of the phrase, are laborious and brave. As the nature of free government is to protect the lives, liberty, and property of the people, that each may enjoy what he hath by honest industry aquired; so it will be the temper and nature of that people, voluntarily to fight in defence of that government; for its interests and preservation is the same as their own. Hence under a free constitution which secures the rights and privileges of the people, we will find courage, fortitude, and an unshaken loyalty to government: but on the contrary, where despotism and tyranny prevail, the people are indolent and pusillanimous, backward to toil and fight in support of a government which their interest must lead them rather to see annihilated than preserved. If we take a veiw of ancient or modern history, we shall find that freedom and superiority have ever gone hand in hand. The history of England affords us many striking instances to illustrate this truth; the party that fought for their country, in civil broils, has always been victorious over the faction that endeavored to enslave it. But why need I advance examples to prove a point, that the bare mentioning of the American revolution seems to put beyond controversy. If the history of the Turkish empire does not afford an exception to this principle, *that freedom and victory are inseperable,* there can be none found that I know of, without the conquest of the island of Corsica, by the French, be admitted as one; which certainly ought not, for it rather shows that freemen contending for their liberties are invincible.

Since it is obvious from what has been said, that the energy and national strength of America are concomitant with her freedom; it follows then that the adoption of the new constitution which necessarily destroys the latter, must of consequence destroy the former: This constitution, in the first instance, will lop off one half of our sacred rights and privileges, for which we bled and conquered; and the remainder are generally left insecure, and therefore must eventually be lost too; for the cursed lust of dominion can never be satisfied until it is in possession of all power, yea, it even then will be discontent, for it is insatiable. If America is to be *great* she must be *free;* freedom is her heart, her very life-blood; and the liberty of the press, like the great aorta, the prime artery, must convey it to the remotest parts of the extremities. That the adoption of this new constitution, in toto, will destroy the freedom of the press, and every other right and liberty that should adorn the freemen of America, has been proved in a clear and masterly manner be many patriotic writers, even before the dissent of the virtuous minority of the convention of Pennsylvania appeared; but this gives the matter a finishing stroke: he who denies the evidence of their positions is either a designing villain, or one who insults his own reason, and declares himself incapable of judging right from wrong, or freedom from slavery, and consequently unworthy of enjoying American liberty. . . .

There are several who have imagined that this government will for some time be a moderate aristocracy but end in a despotic monarchy; but this is a mistake; for it must commence in despotism, if ever it has a beginning. A large *standing army* will be absolutely necessary to set it in motion; I say a large standing army, for a small military force would only excite opposition in its enemies, and encourage them to attempt its destruction, by an appeal to arms. The impolitic conduct of Britain at the commencement of the American war, is a lesson for despotic governments in future; a decisive blow must be struck at once, otherwise liberty may triumph.

The advocates of the new constitution must be pretty well convinced by this time, that there are in every state a considerable number of people, perhaps one half of the whole, disaffected to it; now if nine states should really come into the measure, would it be prudent to compel the rest. I think not; although it is already whispered about, that if Virginia, or any of the southern states should not adopt it, that force will certainly be applied; but this is Utopian altogether, nor can I conceive even if every state in the union should adopt it, how this *faction* can be crushed, and crushed it must be effectually, before this government is firmly established: I even doubt, whether all the military that the *well born* and their parasites can raise, will complete this piece of business to their satisfaction. Has not America already shown to the world that no power on earth can overcome a *phalanx of freemen* defending their sacred liberties?

Many patriotic writers wishing to compromise matters betweeen the friends and enemies of the proposed government, have imagined that the difference might be amicably settled, if a declaration of rights were prefixed to the constitution, so as to become a part of it; and therefore have recommended this to the parties as a necessary measure to reconcile them again to each other: but these good men did not consider that a declaration of rights would effectually and completely annihilate the constitution; of this however, its advocates were well aware, and consequently could not consent to the amendment. No, no, the haughty lordlings and their sycophants must have no *limits* set to their power; they alone should rule; yes, and rule as they *list* too: why should any poor poltroon speak of rights; what are his rights? Why, to work as a slave for his *well born master*. Ah, my fellow-citizens, this is a trying moment! an awful time indeed! Is it possible that the freemen of America should lose their liberties so soon? I hope not;

and I trust, that the Lord, who is the friend of the poor and oppressed, will defeat the purposes, and confound the counsels of their haughty enemies; so that "They shall take them captives, whose captives they were, and they shall rule over their oppressors." *Amen.*

DHRC, XV, p. 106-109. Reprinted in Storing, III, pp. 119-122.

Publius {Alexander Hamilton} December 26, 1787
Newspaper Article: New York *Independent Journal*

The FOEDERALIST. No. XXVIII.
To the People of the State of New-York.

That there may happen cases, in which the national government may be necessitated to resort to force, cannot be denied. Our own experience has corroborated the lessons taught by the examples of other nations; that emergencies of this sort will sometimes arise in all societies, however constituted; that seditions and insurrections are unhappily maladies as inseparable from the body politic, as tumours and eruptions from the natural body; that the idea of governing at all times by the simple force of law (which we have been told is the only admissible principle of republican government) has no place but in the reveries of those political doctors, whose sagacity disdains the admonitions of experimental instruction.

Should such emergencies at any time happen under the national government, there could be no remedy but force. The means to be employed must be proportioned to the extent of the mischief. If it should be a slight commotion in a small part of a State, the militia of the residue would be adequate to its suppression; and the natural presumption is, that they would be ready to do their duty. An insurrection, whatever may be its immediate cause, eventually endangers all government: Regard to the public peace, if not to the rights of the Union, would engage the citizens, to whom the contagion had not communicated itself, to oppose the insurgents: And if the general government should be found in practice conducive to the prosperity and felicity of the people, it were irrational to believe that they would be disinclined to its support.

If on the contrary the insurrection should pervade a whole State, or a principal part of it, the employment of a different kind of force might become unavoidable. It appears that Massachusetts found it necessary to raise troops for repressing the disorders within that State; that Pennsylvania, from the mere apprehension of commotions among a part of her citizens, has thought proper to have recourse to the same measure. Suppose the State of New-York had been inclined to reestablish her lost jurisdiction over the inhabitants of Vermont; could she have hoped for success in such an enterprise from the efforts of the militia alone? Would she not have been compelled to raise and to maintain a more regular force for the execution of her design? If it must then be admitted that the necessity of recurring to a force different from the militia in cases of this extraordinary nature, is applicable to the State governments themselves, why should the possibility that the national government might be under a like necessity in similar extremities, be made an objection to its existence? Is it not surprising that men, who declare an attachment to the union in the abstract, should urge, as an objection to the proposed constitution, what applies with tenfold weight to the plan for which they contend; and what as far as it has any foundation in truth is an inevitable consequence of civil society upon an enlarged scale? who would not prefer that possibility to the unceasing agitations and frequent revolutions which are the continual scourges of petty republics?

Let us pursue this examination in another light. Suppose, in lieu of one general system, two or three or even four confederacies were to be formed, would not the same difficulty oppose itself to the operations of either of these confederacies? Would not each of them be exposed to the same casualties; and, when these happened, be obliged to have recourse to the same expedients for upholding its authority, which are objected to a government for all the States? Would the militia in this supposition be more ready or more able to support the federal authority than in the case of a general union? All candid and intelligent men must upon due consideration acknowledge that the principle of the objection is equally applicable to either of the two cases; and that whether we have one government for all the States, or different governments for different parcels of them, or even if there should be an intire separation of the States, there might sometimes be a necessity to make use of a force constituted differently from the militia to preserve the peace of the community, and to maintain the just authority of the laws against those violent invasions of them which amount to insurrections and rebellions.

Independent of all other reasonings upon the subject, it is a full answer to those who require a more peremtory provision against military establishments in time of peace, that the whole power of the proposed government is to be in the hands of the representatives of the people. This is the essential, and after all the only efficacious security for the rights and privileges of the people which is attainable in civil society.

If the representatives of the people betray their constituents, there is then no source left but in the exertion of that original right of self-defence, which is paramount to all positive forms of government; and which, against the usurpations of the national rulers, may be exerted with infinitely better prospect of success, than against those of the rulers of an individual State. In a single State, if the persons entrusted with supreme power become usurpers, the different parcels, subdivisions or districts, of which it consists, having no distinct government in each, can take no regular measures for defence. The citizens must rush tumultuously to arms, without concert, without system, without resource; except in their courage and despair. The usurpers, cloathed with the forms of legal authority, can too often crush the opposition in embryo. The smaller the extent of territory, the more difficult will it be for the people to form a regular or systematic plan of opposition; and the more easy will it be to defeat their early efforts. Intelligence can be more speedily obtained of their preparations and movements; and the military force in the possession of the usurpers, can be more rapidly directed against the part where the opposition has begun. In this situation, there must be a peculiar coincidence of circumstances to ensure success to the popular resistance.

The obstacles to usurpation and the facilities of resistance increase with the increased extent of the state; provided the citizens understand their rights and are disposed to defend them. The natural strength of the people in a large community, in proportion to the artificial strength of the government, is greater than in a small; and of course more competent to a struggle with the attempts of the government to establish a tyranny. But in a confederacy the people, without exageration, may be said to be entirely the masters of their own fate. Power being almost always the rival of power; the General Government will at all times stand ready to check the usurpations of the state governments; and these will have the same disposition towards the General Government. The people, by throwing themselves into either scale, will infallibly make it preponderate. If their rights are invaded by either, they can make use of the other, as the instrument of redress. How wise will it be in them by cherishing the Union to preserve to themselves an advantage which can never be too highly prised!

It may safely be received as an axiom in our political system, that the state governments will in all possible contingencies afford complete security against invasions of the public liberty by the national authority. Projects of usurpation cannot be masked under pretences so likely to escape the penetration of select bodies of men as of the people at large. The legislatures will have better means of information. They can discover the danger at a distance; and possessing all the organs of civil power and the confidence of the people, they can at once adopt a regular plan of opposition, in which they can combine all the resources of the community. They can readily communicate with each other in the different states; and unite their common forces for the protection of their common liberty.

The great extent of the country is a further security. We have already experienced its utility against the attacks of a foreign power. And it would have precisely the same effect against the enterprises of ambitious rulers in the national councils. If the foederal army should be able to quell the resistance of one state, the distant states would be able to make head with fresh forces. The advantages obtained in one place must be abandoned to subdue the opposition in others; and the moment the part which had been reduced to submission was left to itself its efforts would be renewed and its resistance revive.

We should recollect that the extent of the military force must at all events be regulated by the resources of the country. For a long time to come, it will not be possible to maintain a large army; and as the means of doing this increase, the population and natural strength of the community will proportionably increase. When will the time arrive, that the foederal Government can raise and maintain an army capable of erecting a despotism over the great body of the people of an immense empire; who are in a situation, through the mediums of their state governments, to take measures for their own defence with all the celerity, regularity, and system of independent nations? The apprehension may be considered as a disease, for which there can be found no cure in the resources of argument and reasoning.

DHRC, XV, pp. 102-105.

An American {Tench Coxe} December 28, 1787
Newspaper Article: Philadelphia *Independent Gazetteer* (excerpt)

[T]he number of people employed in agriculture, is at least *nine parts in ten* of the inhabitants of America, that therefore the planters and farmers form the body of the militia, the bulwark of the nation—that the value of property occupied by agriculure, is manifold greater than that of the property employed in every other way—

DHRC, XV, p. 168.

America {Noah Webster} December 31, 1787
Newspaper Article: New York *Daily Advertiser* (excerpts)[1]

To the DISSENTING MEMBERS of the
late CONVENTION of PENNSYLVANIA.

Gentlemen, . . .

You would likewise restrain Congress from requiring *excessive bail,* or imposing *excessive fines* and *unusual punishment.* But unless you can, in every possible instance, previously define the words *excessive* and *unusual*—if you leave the discretion of Congress to define them on occasion, any restriction of their power by a general indefinite expression, is a nullity—mere *formal nonsense.* What consummate arrogance must you possess, to presume you can *now* make *better* provision for the Government of these States, during the course of ages and centuries, than the future Legislatures can, on the spur of the occasion! Yet your whole reasoning on the subject implies this arrogance, and a presumption that you have a right to legislate for posterity!

But to complete the list of unalienable rights, you would insert a clause in your declaration, *that every body shall, in good weather, hunt on his own land, and catch fish in rivers that are public property.* Here, Gentlemen, you must have exerted the whole force of your genius! Not even the *all-important* subject of *legislating for a world* can restrain my laughter at this clause! As a supplement to that article of your bill of rights, I would suggest the following restriction:—"That Congress shall never restrain any inhabitant of America from eating and drinking, *at seasonable times,* or prevent his lying on his *left side,* in a long winter's night, or even on his back, when he is fatigued by lying on his *right.*"—This article is of just as much consequence as the 8th clause of your proposed bill of rights.[2]

1 DHRC, XV, p. 199.
2 See "Pennsylvania Minority," December 18, 1787, pp. 159-161, for their proposed bill of rights provisions.

Thomas Jefferson (Paris) December 31, 1787
Letter: To Uriah Forrest (excerpt)

I do not pretend to decide what would be the best method of procuring the establishment of the manifold good things in this constitution, & of getting rid of the bad. Whether by adopting it in hopes of future amendment; or, after it shall have been duly weighed

& canvassed by the people, after seeing the parts they generally dislike, & those they generally approve, to say to them, 'We see now what you wish. You are willing to give to your federal govenment such & such powers: but you wish at the same time to have such & such fundamental rights secured to you, & certain sources of convulsion taken away. Be it so. Send together your deputies again. Let them establish your fundamental rights by a sacrosanct declaration, and let them pass the parts of the constitution you have approved. These will give powers to your federal government sufficient for your happiness.' This is what might be said, and would probably produce a speedy, more perfect & more permanent form of government.

DHRC, XIV, p. 490.

George Washington January 1, 1788
Extract of a Letter to a Friend in Fredericksburg (excerpt)
Published: Baltimore *Maryland Journal*

I am not a blind Admirer (for I saw the Imperfections) of the Constitution I aided in the Birth of, before it was handed to the Public; but I am fully persuaded it is the *best that can be obtained at this Time,* that it is free from many of the Imperfections with which it is charged, and that *it* or *Disunion* is before us to choose from. If the first is our Election, when the Defects of it are experienced, a constitutional Door is opened for Amendments, and may be adopted in a peaceable Manner, without Tumult or Disorder.

DHRC, VIII, p. 278.

Marquis de Lafayette (Paris) January 1, 1788
Letter: To George Washington (excerpt)

It is Needless for me to tell You that I Read the New Proposed Constitution With An Unspeackable Eagerness and Attention—I Have Admired it, and find it is a Bold, large, and Solid frame for the Confederation—the Electionneering Principles With Respect to the Two Houses of Congress are Most Happily Calculated—I am only Affraid of two things—1er the Want of a declaration of Rights 2ly the Great Powers and Possible Continuance of the President, Who May one day or other Become a State Holder—Should My observations be well founded, I Still am Easy on two Accounts—The first that a Bill of Rights May Be Made if Wished for by the People Before they Accept the Constitution—My other Comfort is that You Cannot Refuse Being Elected President—

DHRC, XIV, p. 492.

An Old Soldier January 4, 1788
Newspaper Article: New London *Connecticut Gazette* (excerpt)

A bill of rights, or a magna charta, similar to that obtained by the barons of England, would be very pleasing to the people, never to be infringed or altered.

DHRC, XV, p. 258.

Samuel Osgood (New York) January 5, 1788
Letter: To Samuel Adams (excerpt)

I am, Sir, for a fair, explicit & efficient general Government—But I cannot consent, in this Way, to be conclaved out of a Bill of Rights.—This Government is expressly, by its admiring Advocates, to reach the Life Liberty & Property of the Individual Person of every one in the united States, capable of feeling the Government—

DHRC, XV, p. 266.

The Republican January 7, 1788
Newspaper Article: Hartford *Connecticut Courant* (excerpts)[1]

TO THE PEOPLE.

It is generally agreed that the old Articles of Confederation are inadequate to answer the great national purposes for which they were designed. It is likewise generally agreed that the new Constitution is better adapted to answer these great purposes. All the objections which are made against it are reducible to this single one: that it is dangerous to liberty. Say the opposers of it, if we adopt it, our liberties have no security. If this objection be well founded, if the new Constitution does destroy the safeguards of that liberty for which American blood and treasure has been lavished, let us exert every nerve to oppose it. God forbid that we, my countrymen, who have maintained our liberties in spite of the seducing artifices, the hostile arms, and the horrid cruelties which Britain has called into action for the purpose of enslaving us, should now through our folly surrender those precious rights which God and nature have given to men. But on the other hand, if those patriotic citizens, whom we have chosen from among us for their knowledge of government, love of liberty, and love of their country, have formed a plan of government which, without endangering our liberties, is calculated to render us a great, respectable, and happy nation; let us not, through folly and ill-directed jealousy, reject this which is probably the only system for promoting our national felicity which we shall ever have an opportunity of adopting. If we reject this system, which comes recommended to us by the unanimous assent of the ablest and best men that the American continent could appoint, what reason or encouragement can there be for the states ever to appoint another convention? I use the expression *unanimous assent* because those three gentlemen[2] who refused to subscribe to the Constitution did so, not from substantial objections to it, but from partial considerations which can have no weight with a free and enlightened people.

In answer to the objection before stated, I say that adopting the new Constitution will not expose us to the loss of liberty; but the great barriers of liberty will still remain and, in all human probability, will continue to be its security for ages and generations to come. The principal circumstances which render liberty secure are a spirit of liberty among the people—a general diffusion of knowledge—a general distribution of property—a militia of freemen—and a fair representation in the supreme legislature.

The people of the United States possess in a high degree a spirit of liberty. This is a principle which is natural to the human mind. We love to have the command of our own actions and the direction of our own interests. Our minds rise with indignation against oppression and tyranny. These natural feelings have never been eradicated from our minds by subjection to the will of a tyrant. But that freedom with which the principles of liberty have been discussed, that ardor with which they have been inculcated upon the public minds, that long struggle for liberty which has called these principles into action, have so fixed and confirmed the spirit of liberty that it must and will long continue to be a ruling principle of our actions and guard us against the encroachments of tyranny.

Another circumstance highly conducive to the security of liberty is the general diffusion of knowledge among the great body of the people. The American citizens in general are by far better educated and more knowing than the people at large in other countries. And in those states where the people have heretofore had the fewest advantages for learning, they are setting up schools and gaining fast in point of useful knowledge. This is a circumstance of the highest importance to a free people. For where the great body of the citizens are ignorant and incapable of discerning their true interests, they may be duped by artful and factious men and led to do things destructive to their own rights and liberties. But a sensible, intelligent people, who have access to the sources of information and are capable of discerning what measures are conducive to the public welfare, will not be easily induced to act contrary to their own interests and destroy those rights and liberties which are the foundations of public happiness.

Another circumstance highly favorable to liberty is the general distribution of property among the people at large. In most of the American states, property is more equally divided among the great body of the people than it is in any other country. Our laws and customs, which divide great estates among all the children of the deceased owner; the way being open for industrious men, who are born to no inheritance, to acquire property; and the plenty and cheapness of land will long cause property to be diffused among the people at large. The people do and will possess freeholds of their own; they can live comfortably and independently on their farms. Men in such a situation feel the dignity of human nature and scorn to be dependent on the will of a tyrant. When they exercise the important right of choosing men to act for them in a public capacity, they will act independently; we may reasonably presume they will choose those who will be faithful to their country.

It is a capital circumstance in favor of our liberty that the people themselves are the military power of our country. In countries under arbitrary government, the people oppressed and dispirited neither possess arms nor know how to use them. Tyrants never feel secure until they have disarmed the people. They can rely upon nothing but standing armies of mercenary troops for the support of their power. But the people of this country have arms in their hands; they are not destitute of military knowledge; every citizen is required by law to be a soldier; we are all marshaled into companies, regiments, and brigades for the defense of our country. This is a circumstance which increases the power and consequence of the people; and enables them to defend their rights and privileges against every invader.

If in addition to the advantages, which I have before mentioned, for maintaining liberty, a people have a free constitution of government, their liberties are secured by the strongest barriers. The great distinction between a free and an arbitrary government is this: in the former the people give their assent to the laws by which they are governed; in the latter, the laws are made by a power which they cannot control. And the plain reason why the former kind of government secures the rights and liberties of the people is that the people will not consent to laws which are oppressive to themselves. . . .

Now as the people of the United States profess a spirit of liberty to induce them to maintain their rights; as there is such a diffusion of knowledge among them as enables them to judge by what methods liberty is to be supported; as the people at large possess such a share of property as gives them the rank of independent freemen; as the people themselves are the military power of our country; these important supports of liberty, together with our choice of Representatives in the lower branch of the legislature, would secure our rights even supposing the power of the President and Senate were vested in a king and body of nobles independent of the people. I am justified in making this assertion by the circumstances which the people of the United States are in and by the experience of other nations. With all the advantages for maintaining the rights of a free people, which I have mentioned, and when no oppressive measures of government could be taken without the consent of our Representatives, unless by an open violation of our constitutional rights, our liberties would stand firm. The people, we may safely presume, would choose men of abilities and integrity who would withstand every attempt to undermine their liberties. The spirit of the people would oppose every open and direct attempt to enslave them.

1 DHRC, III, pp. 527-531.

2 George Mason and Edmund Randolph from Virginia, and Elbridge Gerry from Massachusetts refused to sign the proposed Constitution.

Centinel IX January 8, 1788

Newspaper Article: Philadelphia *Independent Gazetteer* (excerpt)[1]

The more I consider the manoevres that are practising, the more am I alarmed—foreseeing that the juggle cannot long be concealed, and that the spirit of the people will not brook the imposition, they have guarded as they suppose against any danger arising from the opposition of the people, and rendered their struggles for liberty impotent and ridiculous. What otherwise is the meaning of disarming the milita, for the purpose as it is said, of repairing their musquets at such a particular period?[2] Does not the timing of the measure determine the intention? I was ever jealous of the select militia, consisting of infantry and troops of horse, instituted in this city and in some of the counties, without the sanction of law, and officered principally by the devoted instruments of the *well born,* although the illustrious patriotism of one of them, has not corresponded with the intention of appointing him. Are not these corps provided to suppress the first efforts of freedom, and to check the spirit of the people until a regular and sufficiently powerful military force shall be embodied to rivet the chains of slavery on a deluded nation. What confirms these apprehensions is the declaration of a certain Major, an active instrument in this business, and the echo of the principal conspirators, who has said, he should deem the cutting off of five thousand men, as a small sacrifice, a cheap purchase for the establishment of the new constitution.

1 DHRC, XV, p. 311.

2 For other documents related to the controversy over the collection of publicly owned arms in Pennsylvania, and the complaint that this was intended to disarm the militia, see: "Jacob Trusty," December 19, 1787, p. 176; Pennsylvania *Carlisle Gazette,* January 9, 1788, p. 194; "Trusty," January 10, 1788, p. 200; "Supreme Executive Council," January 10, 1788, p. 201; "An Old Militia Officer of 1776," January 18, 1788, p. 221; Philadelphia *Freeman's Journal,* January 23, 1788, p. 226; Philadelphia *Pennsylvania Herald,* February 5, 1788, p. 251; Philadelphia *Independent Gazetteer,* February 27, 1788, p. 286; "James de Caledonia IV," March 12, 1788, p. 298; "Aristocrotis," April [15], 1788, p. 334 at note 2; Philadelphia *Independent Gazetteer,* April 30, 1788, p. 340 at note 3.

Indignatus January 8, 1788

Newspaper Article: Philadelphia *Independent Gazetteer*

To the PRINTER *of the* INDEPENDENT GAZETTEER.

Sir,

I read with astonishment and indignation, in your paper of this day, these remarkable words, in a speech of Dr. RUSH, in the State Convention on the 30th of November last—"*Sir, I consider it as an* honour *to the late Convention, that this system* (the new constitution) *has not been* DISGRACED *with a* BILL OF RIGHTS."—The only observation I will allow myself upon it is, that it will be an *eternal disgrace* to Pennsylvania that such words were ever uttered in a popular assembly by one of her citizens—Any further remarks on such disgraceful language, would be an insult offered to the understanding of the people—As freemen, and men worthy of freedom, they must *feel* more than I can possibly *express.*

7th January, 1788. INDIGNATUS

DHRC, II Mfm. Pa., p. 1443.

Thomas B. Wait (Portland, Maine) January 8, 1788
Letter: To George Thatcher (excerpt)

My dear friend—

Your kind letter of the 23d ultimo receiv'd.—

My opposition to the proposed plan of Continental Govt. does not, as you suppose, arise from "*violence of passion.*"—

On reception of the Report of the Convention, I perused, and admired it:—Or rather, like many who still *think* they admire it, I loved Geo. Washington—I venerated Benj. Franklin—and therefore concluded that I must love and venerate all the works of their hands:—This, if you please my friend, was "*violence of passion*"—*and to this very violence of passion* will the proposed Constitution owe its adoption—i.e.—should the people ever adopt it. The honest and uninformed *freemen* of America entertain the same opinion of those two gentlemen as do European *slaves* of their Princes,—"*that they can do no wrong*"—

On the unprecendented Conduct of the Pennsylvania Legislature, I found myself disposed to lend an ear to the arguments of the opposition—not with an expectation of being convinced that the new Constitution was defective; but because I thought the minority had been ill used; and I felt a little curious to hear the particulars.

The address of the Seceders was like Thunder of Sinai—it's lightnings were irresistable; and I was obliged to acknowledge, not only that the conduct of the majority was highly reprehensible, but that the Constitution itself might possibly be defective.—My mind has since been open to conviction—I have read & heard every argument, on either side, with a degree of candour, of which I never, on any other occasion, felt myself possessed—And, afer this cool and impartial examination I am constrained—I repeat it, my dear friend—I am constrained to say, that I am dissatisfied with the proposed Constitution.—

Your arguments against the necessity of a Bill of Rights are ingenious; but, pardon me my friend, they are not convincing.—You have traced the origin of a Bill of Rights accurately.—The People of England, as you say, undoubtedly made use of a Bill of Rights to obtain their ~~rights and~~ liberties of their soverigns; but is this an argument to prove that they ought not now to make use of Bills in defence of those liberties?—shall a man throw away his sword, and refuse to defend a piece of property, for no other reason than that his property was obtained by that very sword?—Bills of Rights have been the happy instruments of wresting the privileges and rights of the people from the hand of Despotism; and I trust God that Bills of Rights will still be made use of by the people of America to defend them against future encroachments of despotism—Bills of Rights, in my opinion, are the grand bulwarks of freedom.

But, say you, some however necessary in state Constitutions, there can be no necessity for a Bill of Rights in the Continental plan of Govt.—because every Right is reserved that is not *expressly* given up—Or, in other words, Congress have no powers but those *expressly* given by that Constitution.—This is the *doctrine* of the *celebrated* Mr. Wilson; and as you, my friend, have declared it *orthodox,* be so good as to explain the meaning of the following Extracts from the Constitution—Art. I Sect. 9.—"The privilege of the writ of Habeas Corpus shall *not* be suspended &c."—"*No* bill of attainder or ex post facto law shall be passed."—"*No* money shall be drawn from the treasury" &c.—"*No* title of nobility shall be granted by the United states."—Now, how absurd—how grosly absurd is all this, if Congress, in reality, have no powers but those particularly specified in the Constitution!—

It will not do, my friend—for God's sake let us not deny self-evident propositions—let us not sacrifice the truth, that we may establish a favourite hypothesis;—in the present case, the liberties and happiness of a world may also be sacrificed.—

There is a certain darkness, duplicity and studied ambiguity of expression runing thro' the whole Constitution which renders a Bill of Rights peculiarly necessary.—As it now stands but very few individuals do, or ever will understand it.—Consequently, Congress will be its own *interpreter*—

DHRC, XV, pp. 284-285.

Pennsylvania *Carlisle Gazette* January 9, 1788[1]

State of Pennsylvania, ss.

Cumberland County, 1st. Jan. 1788.

By a resolution of the Honourable the Supreme Executive Council of this State of the fourth of December, 1787, I am directed to collect all the public arms within this county,[2] have them repaired and make return thereof to Council, &c.—I have therefore to require all such as may have public arms in their possession, to inform me thereof, that I may be enabled to conform to the directions of the Honourable the Supreme Executive Council—Those who attempt to conceal public arms, may expect to be proceeded against agreeably to law.

George Gibson, Lieut.

1 DHRC, II Mfm. Pa., p. 1364.

2 For other documents related to the controversy over the collection of publicly owned arms in Pennsylvania, and the Antifederalist complaint that this was intended to disarm the militia, see: "Jacob Trusty," December 19, 1787, p. 176; "Centinel IX," January 8, 1788, p. 191; "Trusty," January 10, 1788, p. 200; "Supreme Executive Council," January 10, 1788, p. 201; "An Old Militia Officer of 1776," January 18, 1788, p. 221; Philadelphia *Freeman's Journal*, January 23, 1788, p. 226; Philadelphia *Pennsylvania Herald*, February 5, 1788, p. 251; Philadelphia *Independent Gazetteer*, February 27, 1788, p. 286; "James de Caledonia IV," March 12, 1788, p. 298; "Aristocrotis," April [15], 1788, p. 334 at note 2; Philadelphia *Independent Gazetteer*, April 30, 1788, p. 340 at note 3.

Philadelphia *Freeman's Journal* January 9, 1788
(excerpt)

[T]here will be a numerous standing army to maintain, as it is allowed by its advocates we are to have them all around us, on every point of the compass: indeed the nature of the government is such, (not possessing the confidence of the people) that it will require to be backed with military aid in every State to make it any how efficient: and this military must not be small, while the militia have arms!

DHRC, II Mfm. Pa., p. 1446.

Publius {Alexander Hamilton} January 9, 1788
Newspaper Article: New York *Independent Journal*

The FOEDERALIST. No. XXXV.

To the People of the State of New-York

The power of regulating the militia and of commanding its services in times of insurrection and invasion are natural incidents to the duties of superintending the common defence, and of watching over the internal peace of the confederacy.

It requires no skill in the science of war to discern that uniformity in the organization and discipline of the militia would be attended with the most beneficial effects, whenever they were called into service for the public defence. It would enable them to discharge the duties of the camp and of the field with mutual intelligence and concert; an advantage of peculiar moment in the operations of an army: And it would fit them much sooner to acquire the degree of proficiency in military functions, which would be essential to their usefulness. This desirable uniformity can only be accomplished by confiding the regulation of the militia to the direction of the national authority. It is therefore with the most evident propriety that the plan of the Convention proposes to empower the union "to provide for organizing, arming, and disciplining the militia, and for governing such part of them as may be employed in the service of the United States, *reserving to the states respectively the appointment of the officers and the authority of training the militia according to the discipline prescribed by Congress.*"

Of the different grounds which have been taken in opposition to the plan of the Convention, there is none that was so little to have been expected, or is so untenable in itself, as the one which from this particular provision has been attacked. If a well-regualted militia be the most natural defence of a free country, it ought certainly to be under the regulation and at the disposal of that body which is constituted the guardian of the national security. If standing armies are dangerous to liberty, an efficacious power over the militia, in the body to whose care the protection of the State is committed, ought as far as possible to take away the inducement and the pretext to such unfriendly institutions. If the foederal government can command the aid of the militia in those emergencies which call for the military arm in support of the civil magistrate, it can the better dispense with the employment of a different kind of force. If it cannot avail itself of the former, it will be obliged to recur to the latter. To render an army unnecessary will be a more certain method of preventing its existence than a thousand prohibitions upon paper.

In order to cast an odium upon the power of calling forth the militia to execute the laws of the Union, it has been remarked that there is no where any provision in the proposed Constitution for calling out the POSSE COMITATUS to assist the magistrate in the execution of his duty; whence it has been inferred that military force was intended to be his only auxiliary. There is a striking incoherence in the objections which have appeared, and sometimes even from the same quarter, not much calculated to inspire a very favourable opinion of the sincerity or fair dealing of their authors. The same persons who tell us in one breath that the powers of the federal government will be despotic and unlimited, inform us in the next that it has not authority sufficient even to call out the POSSE COMITATUS. The latter fortunately is as much short of the truth as the former exceeds it. It would be as absurd to doubt that a right to pass all laws *necessary* and *proper* to execute its declared powers would include that of requiring the assistance of the citizens to the officers who may be entrusted with the execution of those laws; as it would be to believe that a right to enact laws necessary and proper for the imposition and collection of taxes would involve that of varying the rules of descent and alienation of landed property or of abolishing the trial by jury in cases relating to it. It being therefore evident that the supposition of a want of power to require the aid of the POSSE COMITATUS is entirely destitute of colour, it will follow that the conclusion which has been drawn from it, in its application to the authority of the federal government over the militia is as uncandid as it is illogical. What reason could there be to infer that force was intended to be the sole instrument of authority merely because there is a power to make use of it when necessary? What shall we think of the motives which could induce men of sense to reason in this manner? How shall we prevent a conflict between charity and conviction?

By a curious refinement upon the spirit of republican jealousy, we are even taught to apprehend danger from the militia itself in the hands of the federal government. It is observed that select corps may be formed, composed of the young and ardent, who may be rendered subservient to the views of arbitrary power. What plan for the regulation of the militia may be pursued by the national government is impossible to be foreseen. But so far from viewing the matter in the same light with those who object to select corps as dangerous, were the Constitution ratified, and were I to deliver my sentiments to a member of the federal legislature from this State on the subject of a militia establishment, I should hold to him in substance the following discourse:—

"The project of disciplining all the militia of the United States is as futile as it would be injurious, if it were capable of being carried into execution. A tolerable expertness in military movements is a business that requires time and practice. It is not a day or even a week that will suffice for the attainment of it. To oblige the great body of the yeomanry and of the other classes of the citizens to be under arms for the purpose of going through military exercises and evolutions as often as might be necessary, to acquire the degree of perfection which would intitle them to the character of a well-regulated militia, would be a real grievance to the people, and a serious public inconvenience and loss. It would form an annual deduction from the productive labour of the country to an amount which, calculating upon the present numbers of the people, would not fall far short of a million pounds. To attempt a thing which would abridge the mass of labour and industry to so considerable an extent would be unwise; and the experiment, if made, could not succeed, because it would not long be endured. Little more can reasonably be aimed at with respect to the people at large than to have them properly armed and equipped; and in order to see that this be not neglected, it will be necessary to assemble them once or twice in the course of a year.

"But though the scheme of disciplining the whole nation must be abandoned as mischievous or impracticable; yet it is a matter of the utmost importance that a well digested plan should as soon as possible be adopted for the proper establishment of the militia. The attention of the government ought particularly to be directed to the formation of a select corps of moderate extent upon such principles as will really fit them for service in case of need. By thus circumscribing the plan it will be possible to have an excellent body of well trained militia ready to take the field whenever the defence of the State shall require it. This will not only lessen the call for military establishments; but if circumstances should at any time oblige the government to form an army of any magnitude, that army can never be formidable to the liberties of the people, while there is a large body of citizens little if at all inferior to them in discipline and the use of arms, who stand ready to defend their own rights and those of their fellow citizens—This appears to me the only substitute that can be devised for a standing army; the best possible security against it, if it should exist."

Thus differently from the adversaries of the proposed constitution should I reason on the same subject; deducing arguments of safety from the very sources which they represent as fraught with danger and perdition. But how the national Legislature may reason on the point is a thing which neither they nor I can foresee.

There is something so far fetched and so extravagant in the idea of danger to liberty from the militia, that one is at a loss whether to treat it with gravity or with raillery; whether to consider it as a mere trial of skill, like the paradoxes of rhetoricians, as a disingenuous artifice to instill prejudices at any price or as the serious offspring of political fanatism. Where in the name of common sense are our fears to end if we may not trust our sons, our brothers, our neighbours, our fellow-citizens? What shadow of danger can there be from men who are daily mingling with the rest of their countrymen; and who participate with them in the same feelings, sentiments, habits and interests? What reasonable cause of apprehension can be inferred from a power in the Union to prescribe regulations for the militia and to command its services when necessary; while the particular States are to have the *sole and exclusive appointment of the officers?* If it were possible seriously to indulge a jealousy of the militia upon any conceivable establishment under the Foederal Government, the circumstance of the officers being in the appointment of the States ought at once to extinguish it. There can be no doubt that this circumstance will always secure to them a preponderating influence over the militia.

In reading many of the publications against the Constitution, a man is apt to imagine that he is perusing some ill written tale or romance; which instead of natural and agreeable images exhibits to the mind nothing but frightful and distorted shapes—Gorgons, Hydras and Chimeras dire—discoloring and disfiguring whatever it represents and transforming every thing it touches into a monster.

A sample of this is to be observed in the exaggerated and improbable suggestions which have taken place respecting the power of calling for the services of the militia. That of New Hampshire is to be marched to Georgia, of Georgia to New Hampshire, of New York to Kentuke and of Kentuke to Lake Champlain. Nay the debts due to the French and Dutch are to be paid in militiamen instead of Louis d'ors and ducats. At one moment there is to be a large army to lay prostrate the liberties of the people; at another moment the militia of Virginia are to be dragged from their homes five or six hundred miles to tame the republican contumacy of Massachusetts; and that of Massachusetts is to be transported an equal distance to subdue the refractory haughtiness of the aristocratic Virginians. Do the persons, who rave at this rate, imagine, that their art or their eloquence can impose any conceits or absurdities upon the people of America for infallible truths?

If there should be an army to be made use of as the engine of despotism what need of the militia? If there should be no army, whither would the militia, irritated by being called upon to undertake a distant and distressing expedition for the purpose of riveting the chains of slavery upon a part of their countrymen direct their course, but to the seat of the tyrants, who had meditated so foolish as well as so wicked a project; to crush them in their imagined intrenchments of power and to make them an example of the just vengeance of an abused and incensed people? Is this the way in which usurpers stride to dominion over a numerous and enlightened nation? Do they begin by exciting the detestation of the very instruments of their intended usurpations? Do they usually commence their career by wanton and disgustful acts of power calculated to answer no end, but to draw upon themselves universal hatred and execration? Are suppositions of this sort the sober admonitions of discerning patriots to a discerning people? Or are they the inflammatory ravings of chagrined incendiaries or distempered enthusiasts? If we were even to suppose the national rulers actuated by the most ungovernable ambition, it is impossible to believe that they would employ such preposterous means to accomplish their designs.

In times of insurrection, or invasion, it would be natural and proper that the militia of a neighbouring state should be marched into another, to resist a common enemy, or to guard the republic against the violences of faction or sedition. This was frequently the case in respect to the first object in the course of the late war; and this mutual succour is, indeed, a principal end of our political association. If the power of affording it be placed under the direction of the Union, there will be no danger of a supine and listless inattention to the dangers of a neighbour till its near approach had superadded the incitements of self preservation to the too feeble inpulses of duty and sympathy.

DHRC, XV, pp. 318-322.

Trusty January 10, 1788
Newspaper Article: Philadelphia *Independent Gazetteer*[1]

Mr. Oswald,

The captains of the militia not having complied with the order of the Colonel, as inserted in your paper of the 3d instant, their reluctance has induced the Colonel to transmit them a second order—a copy of which I herewith send you for publication; at the same time informing you, that the militia of the country rather choose to repair and clean their own *arms* at this critical juncture, than to deliver them up to any one whatever.[2]

TRUSTY.

REGIMENTAL ORDERS.
December 31, 1787.

"When the public arms are collected, and intimation of it given to the Colonel, he will prevent any further trouble to the Captains, by causing the Regimental Quarter-master to attend the delivery of them to Mr. Perkins, and taking his receipt.

"The reputation of punctuality in complying with orders which Colonel Shee is happy the regiment has acquired, will, he hopes, be maintained in the present instance, as the absolute necessity of repairing the arms belonging to the state must be obvious to every officer."

R. HEYSHAM, Adjutant 3d P.R.

To Captain _____

1 DHRC, II Mfm. Pa., p. 1365.

2 For other documents related to the controversy over the collection of publicly owned arms in Pennsylvania, and the complaint that this was intended to disarm the militia, see: "Jacob Trusty," December 19, 1787, p. 176; "Centinel IX," January 8, 1788, p. 191; Pennsylvania *Carlisle Gazette*, January 9, 1788, p. 194; "Supreme Executive Council," January 10, 1788, p. 201; "An Old Militia Officer of 1776," January 18, 1788, p. 221; Philadelphia *Freeman's Journal*, January 23, 1788, p. 226; Philadelphia *Pennsylvania Herald*, February 5, 1788, p. 251; Philadelphia *Independent Gazetteer*, February 27, 1788, p. 286; "James de Caledonia IV," March 12, 1788, p. 298; "Aristocrotis," April [15], 1788, p. 334 at note 2; Philadelphia *Independent Gazetteer*, April 30, 1788, p. 340 at note 3.

Supreme Executive Council January 10, 1788
Proceedings concerning Militia Arms
Printed: Philadelphia *Pennsylvania Packet*[1]

IN COUNCIL.

Philadelphia, January 10, 1788.

WHEREAS the intention of Council respecting the Public Arms has been misrepresented:

Ordered,

That the Secretary publish the Resolves of this Board respecting them.

IN COUNCIL.

Philadelphia, Monday, November 12, 1787.

It appearing from intelligence received from Washington county, that the Indians have murdered some of the inhabitants of the said county, and that the people there are in want of arms and ammunition.

Resolved, That one hundred stand of arms, four hundred weight of gunpowder, eight hundred weight of lead, and one thousand flints, be purchased by the Comptroller-General, and sent to the Lieutenant of the county of Washington.

Thurday, November 15, 1787.

WHEREAS it is represented to this Board, that the Indians have recently committed divers depredations on the frontier inhabitants of this state: therefore,

Resolved, That the Lieutenants of the several frontier counties may, from time to time, order into actual service, for the protection of the inhabitants, such part of the militia of their respective counties as may appear to them, or any of them, necessary: not exceeding, at any one time, the proportion allowed by law.

Tuesday, November 27, 1787

Ordered, THAT the Comptroller-General be required to furnish Council with an account of all the public arms delivered to the Lieutenants of the city of Philadelphia, and the Lieutenants of all the counties in the state.

Tuesday, December 4, 1787.

On Motion, *Resolved*, THAT the Lieutenants of the city and several counties within this state, be directed to collect all the public arms within their respective counties,[2] have them repaired, and make return to Council, with the accounts and vouchers necessary for payment.

Extract from the Minutes,
CHARLES BIDDLE, *Sec'ry*.

1 DHRC, II Mfm. Pa., pp. 1366-1367.

2 For other documents related to the controversy over the collection of publicly owned arms in Pennsylvania, and the complaint that this was intended to disarm the militia, see: Jacob Trusty, December 19, 1787, p. 176; "Centinel IX," January 8, 1788, p. 191; Pennsylvania *Carlisle Gazette*, January 9, 1788, p. 194; "Trusty," January 10, 1788, p. 200; "An Old Militia Officer of 1776," January 18, 1788, p. 221; Philadelphia *Freeman's Journal*, January 23, 1788, p. 226; Philadelphia *Pennsylvania Herald*, February 5, 1788, p. 251; Philadelphia *Independent Gazetteer*, February 27, 1788, p. 286; "James de Caledonia IV," March 12, 1788, p. 298; "Aristocrotis," April [15], 1788, p. 334 at note 2; Philadelphia *Independent Gazetteer*, April 30, 1788, p. 340 at note 3.

Samuel January 10, 1788

Newspaper Article: Boston *Independent Chronicle* (excerpt)

The most complaints, that I have heard made about the proposed Constitution, are that there is no declaration of rights. In the confederation, there is a declaration of rights, of the contracting parties, viz. The several States. But here is none, either of States or of people. And we by this time see the reason of that omission, viz. because there are no rights left, either to the States or people; and it would have been inconsistent to have attempted any thing of that kind; or declared any rights remaining, after all was given up claimed by this Constitution.

Storing, IV, p. 195.

An Impartial Citizen January 10, 1788
Newspaper Article: Petersburg *Virginia Gazette* (excerpt)

As to amendments, which are so strenuously insisted on by some, the Constitution itself has pointed out a most judicious and most unexceptionable mode of amending, to wit,—that when two-thirds of both Houses think proper, amendments shall be proposed; or, on the application of two thirds of the State Legislatures, a Convention shall be called for that purpose, and the amendments so proposed to become a part of this Constitution, when afterwards ratified by three-fourths of the State Legislatures, or Conventions from three-fourths of the States, as the one or the other mode of ratification shall be proposed by Congress. Now as this mode is so obviously rational and undeniably judicious, to adopt another mode of amending, besides its seeming impracticability, is unnecessary and inexpedient. It is unnecessary, because every inconvenience or possible defect in this system may and can be radically and entirely removed by the amendatory mode included in itself. It is seemingly impracticable to adopt another mode of amending, as the very circumstance of this frame of government's being objected to, strongly proves the difficulty of a general concurrence by all the States, with any proposition. A certain Honorable Gentleman [Richard Henry Lee] in a letter to the Executive, and which has been published, has insisted on the facility and expediency of deputing another Convention to amend the Constitution devised by the last. With deference to so eminent a character, I humbly conceive, that the plan he proposes is by no means so eligible as that pointed out by the Constitution itself, which extends its remedy to every possible defect that experience may prove real; whereas his plan excludes every amendment which the Convention he proposes may not recollect or point out; or then, the omissions will be the ground of another Convention, and so on as often as experience will prove an actual omission or omissions. Moreover, if, as he proposes, another Convention should be deputed to amend, it is very probable, if not certain, that any amendments they may recommend, will be equally as exceptionable and as much objected to, as the Constitution devised by the last Convention: They could not possibly think of amendments that would meet with general approbation, nay, perhaps they might be considered as no melioration of the present system, and then, by this gentleman's way of reasoning, another Convention should be delegated to amend the amendments, &c. which would be endless. Some other eminent persons have asserted that it was impolitic to adopt a form of government which included amendatory provisions; that the idea of entering into a government confessedly defective, and in need of amendments, was enough to disgust any people, and a sufficient reason for its rejection. To which I answer, that all the world has allowed, that it was a good government which had in itself a capacity of amending; that a government which undeniably possesses many excellent regulations, and still provides for such amendments, and secures such remedies, as experience will evince to be necessary, is one of the best systems that human sagacity and ingenuity can devise, must be respected by all the sensible part of mankind, and be the idol, admiration, and envy, of all nations. I add, that as human nature is frail, and no people ever did, or ever can suppose, that the plan of government they first adopt, can at once be perfect, that the bare idea of entering into a form of government confessedly admirable, which provides for the fallibility of human nature, and secures a constitutional mode of amending every possible defect, is sufficient to inspire the good people of this country with respect, confidence, admiration and zeal, for this constitution. I therefore contend that though we have indisputably a right to propose amendments, yet it is unnecessary and inexpedient to exercise that right on the present occasion, and that rejection or adoption of this Constitution is the alternative.

DHRC, VIII, pp. 296-297.

A Farmer January 11, 1788
Newspaper Article: Exeter, New Hampshire *Freeman's Oracle* (excerpts)

My Friends, and Fellow-Farmers,

Much has been said respecting the new Constitution offered you, by the Convention, under the direction of Congress; and much ought to be said, in favour of it, not only from the characters of those gentlemen who composed the Convention (whose characters I revere) but from the many excellencies it contains—Yet, neither the characters of the gentlemen, the excellencies it contains, nor the deranged state of our public affairs, ought to have so much influence upon your minds, as to adopt this Constitution, if it is incompleat. Examine it, my friends, with discernment and candor, and judge for yourselves—I think you will find the foundation is laid, and materials are wanting to render it compleat.

In order to adopt it, as it now stands, with any degree of safety, in my humble opinion, a Bill of Rights is absolutely necessary, to secure the liberties of the people. Although the celebrated Mr. Wilson, in his address to the citizens of Philadelphia, respecting a Bill of Rights, urged, that in a state constitution, every thing that was not reserved, was given; but, in a Federal Constitution, the reverse of the proposition prevailed, and what was not given was reserved. I must confess it was ingeniously got over, but not to my satisfaction, (in many instances people may be silenced, but not convinced) for upon the very principle that Mr. Wilson urged, that there is no need of a bill of rights, for what is not given is reserved, would be the foundation I should go upon to urge the great necessity of one,—for if we look into the Constitution, we shall find the different articles therein contained, are expressed in very general and extensive terms; ONE, in particular, which is sufficient to show the necessity of a Bill of Rights, viz.—"This Constitution and the laws of the United States, which shall be hereafter made in pursuance thereof, shall be the supreme law of the land, and the judges, in every state, shall be bound thereby, any thing in the Constitution or law of any state to the contrary not withstanding;"—Therefore, I say, take this clause, together with the extensive latitude given in several other articles, is too much power to lodge in the hands of any set of men, however virtuous they may be without being properly guarded; nor can I think it in the least derogatory to the honour of the supreme authority of the United States, to have a Bill of Rights stated in the Constitution, wherein it shall be declared thus far you may go and no further. We have found by experience, the great advantage of a Bill of Rights in our State constitution; when the legislature passed sundry laws infringing on the Bill of Rights, we had it in black and white to show them they were wrong; and to their honour be it spoken, they have repealed one; and so far as the necessities of the people would admit the other.

Much has been said respecting Congress exercising exclusive legislation in all cases whatsoever over a jurisdiction, not exceeding ten miles square, in such a place as Congess agree to reside in. If that is a Hobby Horse that Congress wishes to mount, and the state they conclude to reside in will give them the jurisdiction, and the individuals consent to it;—Let them mount, for if we prevent them they may get worse mounted. But on our part,—Let us secure the liberties of individuals of the United States, and guard and fetter the hobby horse, in such a manner, as not to let him kick our heads off, if we should have occasion to pass thro' or remain in that district a certain time— . . .

Standing armies are dangerous *in time of peace to the liberties of a free people,* provided they are kept and voted their continuance yearly, they soon get ingrafted into and become a part of the Constitution, therefore they ought not to be kept up, on any pretext whatsoever, any longer than till the enemy are driven from our doors. War is justifiable on no other principle than self-defence, it is at best a curse to any people; it is comprehensive of most, if not all the mischiefs that do or can afflict mankind; it depopulates nations; lays waste the finest countries; destroys arts and sciences, it many times ruins the best men, and advances the worst, it effaces every trace of virtue, piety and compassion, and introduces all kind of corruption in public affairs; and in short, is pregnant with so many evils, that it ought ever to be avoided if possible; nothing but self-defence can justify it. An army, either in peace or war, is like the locust and caterpillers of Egypt; they bear down all before them—and many times, by designing men, have been used as an engine to destroy the liberties of a people, and reduce them to the most abject slavery. I have both summered and wintered with an army: You, my friends, in general, know nothing of the evils that attend it; guard and secure it well in your Bill of Rights, that it may not be in the power of any set of men to trample your liberties under their feet with it. Organize your militia, arm them well, and under Providence they will be a sufficient security. I have once born arms in defence of my country;—I am now willing to risque myself and property, together with my liberties and privileges, (with a well regulated militia) and when they are invaded, I will gird on my sword and appear in their defence. And, if my children after me will not do it, let them loose theirs with their heads into the bargain. . . .

Rouse up, my friends, a matter of infinite importance is before you on the carpet, soon to be decided in your convention, viz, The New Constitution—Seize the happy moment—Secure to your selves and your posterity the jewel Liberty, which has cost you so much blood and treasure, by a well regulated Bill of Rights, from the encroachments of men in power. . . .

I [do not] wish to see it adopted, without being guarded on all sides with a Magna Chartha, or Bill of Rights, as a bulwark to our liberties. . . .

You are called upon by the legislature to appoint men to meet in Convention, to consider and decide upon the proposed Constitution. Seek, and make choice of such men as served you faithfully through the war, and know the difficulties and dangers of a revolution. No man is debared by our state constitution from sitting in this convention. And let each town, or district, qualified by law to send a member, give him instructions to insist upon the additions of a Bill of Rights to the Constitution, and to have such amendments made in it, as shall effectually secure it on all sides; it had better be done now, in the first setting out, than to have to do it seven years hence—it may be at the purchase of blood.

Storing, IV, pp. 205-209.

Charles Johnson (Strawberry Hill, North Carolina) January 14, 1788
Letter: To James Iredell (excerpt)

For my part I will candidly, and in confidence, declare to you that it is a doubtful point with me, and which I cannot yet bring to a decision, whether it will be better to receive the new Constitution, with all its seeming imperfections on its head, or run the risk of obtaining another Convention, which may revise and amend, expunge those articles that seem repugnant to the liberties of the people—secure our political liberty by separating the executive, legislative, and judicial powers—affix responsibility to every office—and explicitly secure the trial by jury, according to former usage—the liberty of the press, with all the other rights of the individual which are not necessary to be given up to government, and which ought not and cannot be required for any good purpose. Surely, if there is no immediate, impending danger to prevent the adoption of the measure, it is most devoutly to be wished.

DHRC, XV, p. 364.

Agrippa XIII January 14, 1788
Newpaper Article: Boston *Massachusetts Gazette* (excerpt)

TO THE MASSACHUSETTS CONVENTION.
Gentlemen, . . .
Let us now consider the probable effects of a consolidation of the separate states into one mass; for the new system extends so far. Many ingenious explanations have been given of it; but there is this defect, that they are drawn from maxims of the common law, while the system itself cannot be bound by any such maxims. A legislative assembly has an inherent right to alter the common law, and to abolish any of its principles, which are not particularly guarded in the constitution. Any system therefore which appoints a legislature, without any reservation of the rights of individuals, surrenders all power in every branch of legislation to the government. The universal practice of every government proves the justness of this remark; for in every doubtful case it is an established rule to decide in favour of authority. The new system is, therefore, in one respect at least,

essentially inferior to our state constitutions. There is no bill of rights, and consequently a continental law may controul any of those principles, which we consider at present as sacred; while not one of those points, in which it is said that the separate governments misapply their power, is guarded. Tender acts and the coinage of money stand on the same footing of a consolidation of power. It is a mere fallacy, invented by the deceptive powers of Mr. Wilson, that what rights are not given are reserved. The contrary has already been shewn.

Essays, pp. 95-96. The "Agrippa" series is reprinted in Storing, IV, starting on p. 68.

Nathaniel Barrell (Boston) January 15, 1788
Letter: To George Thatcher (excerpts)

[A]fter all the Willsonian orotary—after all the learned arguments I have seen written—after all the labord speeches I have heard in its defence—and after the best investigation I have been able to give it—I see it pregnant with the fate of our libertys and if I should not live to feel its baneful effects, I see it intails wretchedness on my posterity—slavery on my children—for as it now stands congress will be vested with much more extensive powers than ever great Brittain exercisd over us—too great to intrust with any set of men, let their talents & vertues be ever so conspicuous—even tho composd of such exalted amiable characters as the great Washington—for while we consider them as men of like passion the same spontaneous inherent thirst for power with ourselvs—great & good as they may be when they enter upon this important charge, what dependance can we have on their continuing so?—but were we sure they would continue the faithful guardians of our libertys, & prevent any infringments on the priviledges of the people—what assurance can we have that such men will always hold the reins of Government? . . . I think such a Government impracticable among men with such high notions of liberty as we americans. these are the general objections as they occur to my mind, the perticulars I cant bring within the bounds of a letter, all which convince me the federal constitution as it now stands, needs much amendment before 'twill be safe for us to adopt it—therefore as wise men—as the faithful guardians of the peoples libertys—and as we wish well to posterity it becomes to reject it unless such amendments take place as will secure to us & ours that liberty without which life is a burthen.

DHRC, XV, pp. 372-373.

The State Soldier I January 16, 1788
Newspaper Article: Richmond *Virginia Independent Chronicle* (excerpts)

An ADDRESS *to the* GOOD PEOPLE *of* VIRGINIA, *on the* NEW FOEDERAL CONSTITUTION, *by an old State Soldier, in answer to an Officer of the late American army. . . .*

The want of a bill of rights, a charter for the press, and a thousand other things which are now discovered, have been heretofore unnoticed although they existed then in as great a degree as they now do. Whenever any alterations have been made in any of these lesser faults, they have universally been for the better. For instance the appropriation of monies under pretence of providing for our national defence, which then was without hesitation, is now restricted to two years: For although Congress could not absolutely keep a large standing force in time of profound peace, yet they had it in their power to provide for an army when there was not an absolute war: For the declaration being at their sole will, and they not accountable for the necessity, left the appropriation which was given them for supporting the one, entirely at their discretion in time of the other. That when this article shall be viewed independent of the grand object, and considered as one of the smaller faults, separate and distinct from the right of taxation, it must be confessed that part of our SYSTEM has been altered for the better. And thus too respecting a bill of rights, and the liberty of the press, it may also be said, the objection has been diminished by the new plan: For what security had we on this head before but that which was in our state constitutions? And of what is the republican form of government which Congress is now to guarantee to each state to consist? Certainly of any thing each state shall think proper that does not take from Congress what this constitution absolutely claims. Even the very one we now have, or such parts of it as do not extend that far, may be that form of government which this new plan obliges congress to guarantee. That so far from these objections being increased, they are diminished by the new plan; as there will not only be the same state security of these rights then, but also a continental conformation of them—there being nothing in the new system that excludes that part of the old. That it is not, because those smaller faults have not been before seen, they necessarily originate in, or are magnified by the new constitution; but the truth is, they have always been overlooked in beholding that grand blemish which marked the features of the old plan. . . .

In short, as there is nothing in this constitution itself that particularly bargains for a surrender of your liberties, it must be your own faults if you become enslaved. Men in power may usurp authorities under any constitution—and those they govern may oppose their tyranny[.]

DHRC, VIII, pp. 303, 305-306, 308.

Philanthropos {Tench Coxe} January 16, 1788
Newspaper Article: Philadelphia *Pennsylvania Gazette* (excerpts)

When we observe how much the several gentlemen of the late Convention, who declined to sign the foederal constitution, *differ* in *their ground of opposition,* we must see how improbable it is, that another convention would unite in the same degree in any plan. Col. Mason and Mr. Gerry complain of the want of a bill of rights; Governor Randolph does not even mention it as desirable, much less as necessary. . . .
The Minority [of Pennsylvania] say, religious liberty is not duly secured; which is omitted as an objection by all of the three gentlemen above named. The right of the people to fish, fowl and hunt, the freedom of speech, provision against disarming the people, a declaration of the subordination of the military to the civil power, annual elections of the representatives, and the organization and call of the militia, are considered by the Minority of our convention, as on an exceptionable footing; but none of these are even mentioned by Governor Randolph, Mr. Mason or Mr. Gerry. The Minority desire a declaration, that such powers as are not expresly given shall be considered as retained; Mr. Randolph thinks this unnecessary, for that the states retain every thing they do not grant. Mr. Gerry is silent on this head. . . . The minority desire a bill of rights, and object to the smallness of the representation[.]

DHRC, XV, p. 391-393.

Philadelphia *Freeman's Journal* January 16, 1788

The conduct of Congress or the post master-general, in stopping the free circulation of the Newspapers at this critical juncture, is very alarming. From what this extraordinary measure has originated we do not pretend to say; but certainly the freemen of America will never suffer such a bare faced violation of their liberties to pass with impunity. This is a stretch of arbitrary power, that even *Britain* never attempted before the Revolution. By this manoeuvre all communication is cut off between the States, so that the despots may assemble an *army* and subjugate the freemen of one state, before their friends in another hear of it.

Philadelphia *Freeman's Journal* January 16, 1788

Mr. Bailey,
Inclosed you have some extracts from a New-England publication, on the subject of the military powers granted to Congress by the proposed Constitution, which is well worth the attention of your readers—I am, &c.

A LANDHOLDER.

Montgomery County, *Jan.* 3, 1788.

To the PEOPLE OF AMERICA.

Fellow-Citizens,

The Congress under the new Constitution have the power "of organizing, arming and disciplining the militia, and of governing them when in the service of the United States, giving to the separate States the appointment of the officers and the authority of training the militia *according to* the discipline *prescribed by Congress.*" Let us inquire why they have assumed this *great power:* Was it to strengthen the power which is now lodged in your hands, and relying upon you and *you solely* for aid and support to the civil power in the execution of all the laws of the new Congress? Is this probable? Does the complexion of this new plan countenance such a supposition? When they unprecedently claim the power of raising and supporting *armies,* do they tell you for what purposes they are to be raised? How they are to be employed? How many they are to consist of, and where to be stationed? Is this power fettered with any one of those restrictions, which will show they depend upon the militia, and not upon this infernal engine of oppression to execute their civil laws? The nature of the demand in itself contradicts such a supposition, and forces you to believe that it is for none of these causes—but rather for the purpose of consolidating and finally destroying your strength, as your respective governments are to be destroyed. They well know the impolicy of putting or keeping arms in the hands of a nervous people, at a distance from the seat of a government, upon whom they mean to exercise the powers granted in that government.—They have no idea of calling upon or trusting to the party aggrieved to support and enforce their own grievances, (notwithstanding they may select and subject them to as strict subordination as regular troops) unless they have a standing army to back and compel the execution of their orders. It is asserted by the most respectable writers upon government, that a well regulated militia, composed of the yeomanry of the country, have ever been considered as the bulwark of a free people. Tyrants have never placed any confidence on a militia composed of freemen. Experience has taught them that a standing body of regular forces, whenever they can be completely introduced, are always efficacious in enforcing their edicts, however arbitrary; and slaves by profession themselves, are "nothing loth" to break down the barriers of freedom with a *gout.*—No, my fellow citizens, this plainly shows they do not mean to depend upon the citizens of the States alone to enforce their powers; they mean to lean upon something more substantial and summary. They have left the appointment of officers in the breasts of the several States; but this appears to me an insult rather than a privilege, for what avails this right, if they at their pleasure may arm or disarm all or any part of the freemen of the United States, so that when their army is sufficiently numerous, they may put it out of the power of the freemen militia of America to assert and defend their liberties, however they might be encroached upon by Congress. Does any, after reading this provision for a regular standing army, suppose that they intended to apply to the militia in all cases, and to pay particular attention to making them the bulwark of this continent.—And would they not be equal to such an undertaking? —Are they not abundantly able to give security and stability to your government as long as it is free? Are they not the only proper persons to do it? Are they not the most respectable body of yeomanry in that character upon earth? Have they not been engaged in some of the most brilliant actions in America, and more than once decided the fate of princes? In short, do they not preclude the necessity of any standing army whatsoever, unless in case of invasion; and in that case it would be time enough to raise them, for no free government under heaven with a well disciplined militia was ever yet subdued by mercenary troops.

The advocates at the present day, for a standing army in the new Congress, pretend it is necessary for the respectability of government. I defy them to produce an instance in any country, in the Old or New World, where they have not finally done away the liberties of the people.—Every writer upon government—Locke, Sidney, Hambden, and a list of others have uniformly asserted, that standing armies are a solecism in any government; that no nation ever supported them, that did not resort to, rely upon, and finally become a prey to them:—No western historians have yet been hardy enough to advance principles that look a different way. What historians have asserted, all the Grecian republics have verified.—They are brought up to obedience and unconditional submission—With arms in their hands, they are taught to feel the weight of rigid discipline;—they are excluded from the enjoyments which liberty gives to its votaries, they, in consequence, hate and envy the rest of the community in which they are placed, and indulge a malignant pleasure in destroying those privileges to which they never can be admitted.—"Without a standing army, (says the Marquis of Beccaria) in every society there is an effort constantly tending to confer on one part the height and to reduce the other to the extreme of weakness, and this is of itself sufficient to employ the people's attention."

There is no instance of any government being reduced to a confirmed tyranny without military oppression; and the first policy of tyrants has been to annihilate all other means of national activity and defence, when they feared opposition, and to rely solely upon standing troops.—Repeated were the trials before the sovereigns of Europe dared to introduce them upon any pretext whatever; and the whole record of the transactions of mankind cannot furnish an instance (unless the proposed constitution may be called part of that record) where the motives which caused that establishment were not completely disguised. Pisistratus in Greece, and Dionysius in Syracuse, Charles in France, and Henry in England, all cloaked their villainous intentions under an idea of raising a small body as a guard for their persons; and Spain could not succeed in the same nefarious plan, until thro' the influence of an ambitious priest (who have in all countries and in all ages, even at this day, encouraged and preached up arbitrary power) they obtained it. "Ceasar, who first attacked the commonwealth with *mines*, very soon opened his *batteries*." Notwithstanding all these objections to this engine of oppression, which are made by the most experienced men, and confirmed by every country where the rays of freedom ever extended;—yet in America, which has hitherto been her favorite abode—in this civilized territory, where property is so valuable, and men are found with feelings that will not patiently submit to arbitrary controul—in this Western region, where, my fellow-countrymen, it is confessedly proper that you should associate and dwell in society from choice and reflection, and not be kept together by force and fear, you are modestly requested to engraft into the component parts of your constitution a *Standing Army*, without any qalifying restraints whatever—certainly to exist somewhere in the bowels of your country in time of peace. It is very true that Lawyer *Wilson*, member of the Federal Convention, and who we may suppose breathes in some measure the spirit of that body, tells you it is for the purpose of forming cantonments upon your frontiers, and for the dignity and safety of your country, as it respects foreign nations. No man that loves his country could object to their being raised for the first of these causes, but for the last it cannot be necessary. God has so separated us by an extensive ocean from the rest of mankind; he hath so liberally endowed us with privileges, and so abundantly taught us to esteem them precious, it would be impossible while we retain our integrity, and advert to first principles, for any nation whatever to subdue us. We have succeeded in an opposition to the most powerful people upon the globe; and the wound that America received in the struggle, where is it? As speedily healed as the track in the ocean is buried by the succeeding wave. It has scarcely stopped her progress, and our private dissentions only, at this moment, tarnish the lustre of the most illustrious infant nation under Heaven.

You cannot help suspecting this gentleman, when he goes on to tell you, "that standing armies in time of peace, have always been a topic of *popular declamation*, but Europe hath found them necessary to maintain the appearance of strength in a season of the most profound tranquility." This shews you his opinion, and that he, as one of the Convention, was for unequivocally establishing them in time of peace; and to object to them, is a mere popular declamation! But I will not, my countrymen—I cannot believe you to be of the same sentiment. Where is the standing army in the world, that, like the musquet they make use of, hath been in time of peace brightened and burnished for the sake only of maintaining an appearance of strength, without being put to a different use—without having had a pernicious influence upon the morals, the habits, and the sentiments of society, and finally, taking a chief part in executing its laws?—But some say, that there is a controul over them every two years, and that consists in the appropriation of monies for their support. Turn your attention to England, and see the popular part of this constitution, by the influence of money, by the influence of military and revenue officers, brought gravely to give their *annual* assent to the existence of a standing army, and for monies to support it. It has long since been an insult on the good sense of that nation.

It may not be amiss to remind you of that swarm of revenue, excise, impost and stamp officers, continental assessors and collectors, that your new constitution will introduce among you. They will, of themseves, be a *standing army* to you, and you will see them at your elections, active and industrious to secure the seats of those men who put them into office:—They will be very adequate to give you a surfeit of their company, to make you tired in meddling with government, and disposed to become indifferent about the exercising of it, without the blessed assistance of any military corps.

Upon the whole, my countrymen, it appears to me, that this power as it now stands is decidedly improper and dangerous.—That Congress ought to have the power of raising armies when invaded by our enemies, is certain; that they ought not to have it for any other cause, is equally so. If they did not, or do not mean to employ them in any other way, they ought in express terms to say so, in a *Bill of Rights;* especially in such an ill constructed government as the proposed constitution, in which the Legislative, Executive and Judicial powers are blended in one small Senate, without whose consent nothing can be done; the members of which are not appointed by the people; and who have also the power given them to re-elect themselves, or put off the election to any period.

If tyranny is at all feared, the tyranny of *many* is to be guarded against more than that of a *single person.* The Athenians found by sad experience, that 30 tyrants were thirty times worse than one. A bad aristocracy is thirty times worse than a bad monarchy, allowing each to have a standing army as unrestricted as in the proposed constitution.

If the people are not in general disposed to execute the powers of government, it is time to suspect there is something wrong in that government, and rather than employ a standing army, they had better have another; for in my humble opinion, it is yet much too early to set it down for a fact, that mankind cannot be governed, but by *force.*

Reprinted in Borden, pp. 74-77. This article is a shortened reprint, with alterations, of "John De Witt," December 3, 1787, p. 129 (originally printed in the Boston *American Herald.*)

South Carolina Legislature January 18, 1788
Debates (excerpt)

Hon. JAMES LINCOLN, of *Ninety-six,* . . . He had listened with eager attention to all the arguments in favor of the Constitution; but he solemnly declared that the more he heard, the more he was persuaded of its evil tendency. What does this proposed Constitution do? It changes, totally changes, the form of your present government. From a well-digested, well-formed democratic, you are at once rushing into an aristocratic government. What have you been contending for these ten years past? Liberty! What is liberty? The power of governing yourselves. If you adopt this Constitution, have you this power? No: you give it into the hands of a set of men who live one thousand miles distant from you. Let the people but once trust their liberties out of their own hands, and what will be the consequence? First, a haughty, imperious aristocracy; and ultimately, a tyrannical monarchy. No people on earth are, at this day, so free as the people of America. All other nations are, more or less, in a state of slavery. They owe their constitutions partly to chance, and partly to the sword;

but that of America is the offspring of their choice—the darling of their bosom: and was there ever an instance in the world that a people in this situation, possessing all that Heaven could give on earth, all that human wisdom and valor could procure—was there ever a people so situated, as calmly and deliberately to convene themselves together for the express purpose of considering whether they should give away or retain those inestimable blessings? In the name of God, were we a parcel of children, who would cry and quarrel for a hobby-horse, which, when we were once in possession of, we quarrel with and throw it away? It is said this Constitution is an experiment; but all regular-bred physicians are cautious of experiments. If the constitution be crazed a little, or somewhat feeble, is it therefore necessary to kill it in order to cure it? Surely not. There are many parts of this Constitution he objected to: some few of them had not been mentioned; he would therefore request some information thereon. . . .

He would be glad to know why, in this Constitution, there is a total silence with regard to the liberty of the press. Was it forgotten? Impossible! Then it must have been purposely omitted; and with what design, good or bad, he left the world to judge. The liberty of the press was the tyrant's scourge—it was the true friend and firmest supporter of civil liberty; therefore why pass it by in silence? He perceived that not till almost the very end of the Constitution was there any provision made for the nature or form of government we were to live under: he contended it should have been the very first article; it should have been, as it were, the groundwork or foundation on which it should have been built. But how is it? At the very end of the Constitution, there is a clause which says,—"The Congress of the United States shall guaranty to each state a republican form of government." But pray, who are the United States?—A President and four or five senators? Pray, sir, what security have we for a republican form of government, when it depends on the mere will and pleasure of a few men, who, with an army, navy, and rich treasury at their back, may change and alter it as they please? It may be said they will be sworn. Sir, the king of Great Britain, at his coronation, swore to govern his subjects with justice and mercy. We were then his subjects, and continued so for a long time after. He would be glad to know how he observed his oath. If, then, the king of great Britain forswore himself, what security have we that a future President and four or five senators—men like himself—will think more solemnly of so sacred an obligation than he did?

Why was not this Constitution ushered in with the bill of rights? Are the people to have no rights? Perhaps this same President and Senate would, by and by, declare them. He much feared they would.

He concluded by returning his hearty thanks to the gentleman who had so nobly opposed this Constitution: it was supporting the cause of the people; and if ever any one deserved the title of man of the people, he, on this occasion, most certainly did.

Gen. CHARLES COTESWORTH PINCKNEY answered Mr. Lincoln on his objections. . . . With regard to the liberty of the press, the discussion of that matter was not forgotten by the members of the Convention. It was fully debated, and the impropriety of saying any thing about it in the Constitution clearly evinced. The general government has no powers but what are expressly granted to it; it therefore has no power to take away the liberty of the press. That invaluable blessing, which deserves all the encomiums the gentleman has justly bestowed upon it, is secured by all our state constitutions; and to have mentioned it in our general Constitution would perhaps furnish an argument, hereafter, that the general government had a right to exercise powers not expressly delegated to it. For the same reason, we had no bill of rights inserted in our Constitution; for, as we might perhaps have omitted the enumeration of some of our rights, it might hereafter be said we had delegated to the general goverment a power to take away such of our rights as we had not enumerated; but by delegating express powers, we certainly reserve to ourselves every power and right not mentioned in the Constitution.

Debates, IV, pp. 313-316.

An Independent Freeholder January 18, 1788
Newspaper Article: Winchester *Virginia Gazette* (excerpt)

To the CITIZENS of VIRGINIA.

Friends and Countrymen, I shall make no apology for intruding my thoughts on a subject which ought to engage the attention of every American, I mean the Constitution proposed by the late Federal Convention. To this plan many objections have been made. I shall take more particular notice of those published in the Winchester Gazette of sixteenth and twenty-third November last, said to be Observations by R. H. L[ee]. Esquire, and Objections by Colonel M[aso]n; and here I shall not attempt to prove that the Constitution would be inadmissible with their amendments, or absolutely to pronounce that it might not have been improved by the adoption of some of them, to determine this point it would be necessary to see the whole scheme when new modelled so as to receive the amendments, for however pleasing to the people an amendment might be, as a detached sentiment, we cannot otherwise know how it would accord with a plan of Continental Government—having built a convenient dwelling house in a plain style, I would not thank the ablest architect to introduce an highly ornamented Corinthian pillar as one of the supporters of my piazza. *A Bill of Rights* has a pleasing sound, and in some instances has been deemed necessary, but on occasions very different from the present. When by the abdication of James IId. there was a suspension of Regal Government in England, the two houses of Parliament, accompanied the solemn tender of the Crown, which they made to William and Mary, with a Bill of Rights, stating certain acts, which the King, who has the executive powers of government, and is one branch of the legislature, should not do, without the consent of the other two branches the Lords and Commons; but it never entered into the minds of the people of England to declare a Bill of Rights restrictive of the powers of the whole legislative body, tho' they have the choice of one branch only, the other two holding their seats by hereditary right, and one of them claiming by divine. At the American Revolution there was not only an end to the power of the crown, but a total dissolution of government; the people were reduced to a state of nature, under these circumstances several of the states conceived it necessary, previous to granting legislative powers, to declare that certain rights were inherent in the people, and to reserve those rights out of the grant. But is America in the situation Great Britain was in at the time of the revolution in that country, or in which she herself was at the time of the revolution in this? Nothing can be more remote; here is neither a total nor partial dissolution of Government; our social compacts and all our ancient rights remain entire, except such as are expressly granted to Congress. And this affords an answer to many objections, such as that religious liberty, the Freedom of the Press, the right of Petitioning the Legislature, &c. &c. &c. are not secured; no power over these matters being granted to Congress, she never can interpose to destroy them. Much more safely may we rest the Constitution on this ground than on a bill of rights, in that case all powers would be considered as granted which were not expressly reserved, it would not only be incongruous but dangerous, and might tend to sap the foundation of the whole structure. We have not been able to divest ourselves of our early ideas. We have been taught from our infancy to regard those men who opposed the arbitrary exertions of royal power in England as patriots and heroes, and without adverting to the difference of circumstances, conceive, that it is equally meritorious to clog the wheels of government in this country, to circumscribe the legislature, though constituted and chosen by ourselves as narrowly as the people of England have circumscribed the power of their kings.

Yet it appears to me incompatible with the nature of government, that the supreme power in a nation should be restrained from raising an army, or doing any other act which may be necessary for the defence or security of the state, by any other means than the wisdom of the rulers and their regard to the public good, and we have no reason to doubt, from the mode of choosing the members of Congress, but that both these principles will act with full force under the proposed government, I believe such restraint has never been attempted. In England the keeping up standing armies in time of peace was opposed only when it was done by the sole authority of the crown. In this country we complained when troops were stationed among us *without the consent of our Assemblies.*

DHRC, VIII, pp. 310-311.

Luther Martin January 18, 1788
Newspaper Article: Genuine Information IV, Baltimore *Maryland Gazette* (excerpt)

Mr. MARTIN'S *Information to the House of Assembly, continued.*
By the eighth section, . . .
This section proceeds further to give a power to the Congress to provide for calling forth the militia, to execute the laws of the union, suppress insurrections, and repel invasions.—As to *giving such a power* there was no objection; but it was thought by some, that this power *ought* to be given with certain *restrictions*—It was thought that not more than a certain *part* of the militia, of any one State, ought to be obliged to *march out* of the same, or be *employed out* of the same, at any *one time,* without the consent of the legislature of such State—This *amendment* I endeavoured to obtain; but it met with the same fate, which attended almost every attempt to *limit* the powers given to the general government, and *constitutionally* to guard against *their abuse,* it was not adopted.—As it now stands, the Congress will have the power, if they please, to march the *whole* militia of Maryland to the *remotest* part of the union, and keep them in service as long as they think proper, without being in any respect *dependant* upon the *Government of Maryland* for this *unlimited exercise of power over its citizens.—All of whom,* from the *lowest* to the *greatest,* may, during such service, be *subjected* to *military* law, and *tied up* and *whipped* at the *halbert* like the *meanest* of *slaves.*

By the *next* paragraph, Congress is to have the power to provide for *organizing, arming,* and *disciplining* the *militia,* and for *governing* such part of them as may be *employed in the service* of the United States.—

For this *extraordinary* provision, by which the *militia*, the *only defence* and *protection* which the *States* can have for the security of *their rights* agaist *arbitrary encroachments* of the *general government*, is taken entirely *out of the power* of their *respective States*, and placed under the *power of Congress*, it was speciously assigned as a reason, that the general government would cause the militia to be better regulated and better disciplined than the State governments, and that it would be proper for the whole militia of the union, to have a uniformity in their arms and exercise.—To this it was answered, that the reason, however *specious*, was *not just*;—that it would be absurd the militia of the western settlements, who were exposed to an Indian enemy, should either be confined to the *same arms* or *exercise*, as the militia of the eastern or middle States—that the same penalties which would be sufficient to enforce an obedience to militia laws in some States, would be totally disregarded in others—That leaving the power to the several States, they would respectively best know the situation and circumstances of their citizens, and the regulations that would be necessary and sufficient to effect a well regulated militia in each—That we were satisfied the militia had heretofore been as well disciplined, as if they had been under the regulations of Congress; and that the States would now have an *additional* motive to keep their militia well disciplined, and fit for service, as it would be their *only chance* to preserve their *existence* against a general government, armed with powers *sufficient* to destroy them.—These observations, Sir, procured from some of the members an open avowal of those reasons, by which we believed before that they were actuated—They said, that as the States would be opposed to the general government, and at enmity with it, which as I before observed, they *assumed* as a *principle*, if the militia was under the controul and the authority of the respective States, it would *enable them* to *thwart* and *oppose* the general government:—They said the States ought to be at the mercy of the general government, and, therefore, that the militia ought to be put under its power, and not suffered to remain under the power of the respective States.—In answer to these declarations, it was urged, that if after having obtained to the general government the great powers already granted, and among those, that of *raising* and *keeping up regular troops without limitation*, the *power* over the *militia* should be *taken away* from *the States*, and also given to the general government, it ought to be considered as the *last coup de grace* to the *State governments*; that it must be the most convincing proof, the advocates of this system design the *destruction* of the State governments, and that no *professions*, to the contrary, ought to be *trusted;* and that every State in the union, ought to reject such a system with indignation, since, if the general government should attempt to oppress and enslave them, they could not have any possible means of self defence; because the proposed system, taking away from the States the right of organizing, arming and disciplining the militia, the *first attempt* made by a *State* to put the militia in a situation to counteract the arbitrary measures of the general government, would be construed into an *act of rebellion*, or *treason;* and Congress would *instantly march* their *troops* into the State.—It was further observed, that when a government *wishes* to deprive their citizens of freedom, and reduce them to slavery, it *generally makes use of a standing army* for that purpose, and *leaves the militia in a situation as contemptible as possible, least they might oppose its arbitrary designs*—That in *this* system, we give the general government every provision it could wish for, and even *invite* it to *subvert* the *liberties* of the *States* and *their citizens*, since we give them the right to encrease and keep up a standing army as numerous as *it* would wish, and by placing the militia under *its* power, enable it to leave the militia *totally unorganized, undisciplined*, and *even to disarm them;* while the *citizens*, so far from complaining of this *neglect*, might even esteem it a favour in the general government, as thereby they would be freed from the burthen of militia duties, and left to their own private occupations or pleasures.—However, *all* arguments, and every reason that could be urged on *this* subject, as well as on many others, were obliged to yield to *one* that was *unanswerable*, a *majority* upon the division.

DHRC, XV, pp. 410-412.

An Old Militia Officer of 1776 January 18, 1788

Newspaper Article: Philadelphia *Independent Gazetteer*[1]

Mr. Oswald,

The orders, issued by Council, enjoining the delivery of the public arms at this juncture, when a standing army is openly avowed to be necessary, has occasioned no small degree of apprehension amongst some of the officers, who are not in the secret, and in almost every private of the city militia. These orders, the first of the nature issued since the peace, amount, in the most liberal construction, to a temporary disarming of the people.[2] When the arms will be re-delivered, must depend upon the *discretion* of our rulers. In the mean time a militia-man begs leave to advise his fellow citizens to comply with this official mandate; since, if no treachery is intended, their obedience to the government will be praiseworthy and exemplary. But if their good sense should lead them to suspect (and suspicion in a free people is the best of centinels) that these orders originate in that spirit of domination, which has not been illiberally imputed to the new plan of government, will it not be their indispensable duty, as men, as citizens, and as guardians of their own rights, immediately to arm themselves at their own expence? This expedient will convince the enemies of liberty, that the people (their own defenders in the last resort) are prepared for the worst, and that the boasted operations of their intended *standing army* will be found to be as weak and futile, as they are justly apprehended to be insidious and base.[2]

1 DHRC, II Mfm. Pa., pp. 1369-1370.

2 For other documents related to the controversy over the collection of publicly owned arms in Pennsylvania, and the complaint that this was intended to disarm the militia, see: "Jacob Trusty," December 19, 1787, p. 176; "Centinel IX," January 8, 1788, p. 191; Pennsylvania *Carlisle Gazette*, January 9, 1788, p. 194; "Trusty," January 10, 1788, p. 200; "Supreme Executive Council," January 10, 1788, p. 201; Philadelphia *Freeman's Journal*, January 23, 1788, p. 226; Philadelphia *Pennsylvania Herald*, February 5, 1788, p. 251; Philadelphia *Independent Gazetteer*, February 27, 1788, p. 286; "James de Caledonia IV," March 12, 1788, p. 298; "Aristocrotis," April [15], 1788, p. 334 at note 2; Philadelphia *Independent Gazetteer*, April 30, 1788, p. 340 at note 3.

Agrippa XVII January 20, 1788

Newspaper Article: *Massachusetts Gazette* (excerpt)

TO THE MASSACHUSETTS CONVENTION.

Gentlemen, . . .

From this general view of the state of mankind it appears that all the powers of government originally reside in the body of the people; and that when they appoint certain persons to administer the government, they delegate all the powers of government not expressly reserved. Hence it appears that a constitution does not in itself imply any more than a declaration of the relation which the different parts of the government bear to each other, but does not in any degree imply security to the rights of individuals. This has been the uniform practice. In all doubtful cases the decision is in favour of the government. It is therefore impertinent to ask by what right government exercises powers not expressly delegated. Mr. Wilson, the great oracle of federalism, acknowledges, in his speech to the Philadelphians, the truth of these remarks, as they respect the state governments, but attempts to set up a distinction between them and the continental government.

It has been shown in the course of this paper, that when people institute government, they of course delegate all rights not expressly reserved. In our state constitution the bill of rights consists of thirty articles. It is evident therefore that the new constitution proposes to delegate greater powers than are granted to our own government, sanguine as the person was who denied it. The complaints against the separate governments, even by the friends of the new plan, are not that they have not power enough, but that they are disposed to make a bad use of what power they have. Surely then they reason badly, when they purpose to set up a government possess'd of much more extensive powers than the present, and subject to much smaller checks.

Bills of rights, reserved by authority of the people, are, I believe, peculiar to America. A careful observance of the abuse practised in other countries has had its just effect by inducing our people to guard against them. We find the happiest consequences to flow from it. The separate govenments know their powers, their objects, and operations. We are therefore not perpetually tormented with new experiments. For a single instance of abuse among us there are thousands in other countries. On the other hand, the people know their rights, and feel happy in the possession of their freedom, both civil and political. Active industry is the consequence of their security, and within one year the circumstances of the state and of individuals have improved to a degree never before known in this commonwealth. Though our bill of rights does not, perhaps, contain all the cases in which power might be safely reserved, yet it affords a protection to the persons and possessions of individuals not known in any foreign country. In some respects the power of government is a little too confined. In many other countries we find the people resisting their governours for exercising their power in an unaccustomed mode. But for want of a bill of rights the resistance is always, by the principles of their government, a rebellion which nothing but success can justify. In our constitution we have aimed at delegating the necessary powers of government and confining their operation to beneficial purposes. At present we appear to have come very near the truth. Let us therefore have wisdom and virtue enough to reserve it inviolate. It is a stale contrivance, to get the people into a passion, in order to make them sacrifice their liberty. Repentance always comes, but it comes too late. Let us not flatter ourselves that we shall always have good men to govern us. If we endeavour to be like other nations we shall have more bad men than good ones to exercise extensive powers.

Essays, pp. 112-114.

Massachusetts Convention January 21, 1788
Debates (excerpt)

Mr. SINGLETARY. The power [of taxation] is unlimited in Congress—he objects against it—a new case—as much power as was ever given to a despotic prince—will destroy all power in this [state] of raising taxes, and we have nothing left—the only security is, we may have an honest man, but we may not have—we may have an atheist, pagan, Mahommedan—must take care of posterity—few nations enjoy the liberty of Englishmen. Is for giving up some power, but not every thing—no bill of rights—civil and sacred privileges will all go.

Massachusetts, p. 311.

A Countryman January 22, 1788
Newspaper Article: *New York Journal* (excerpts)[1]

Should the new constitution be sufficiently corrected *by a substantial* bill of rights, an equitable representation, chosen annually, or not eligible under two years, the senate chosen triennally, and not eligible in less than three years afterwards, which, apart from it, becoming a more general object to men of learning and genius, might also be a means of preventing monopolies by a few men or families—separating the legislative, judicial and executive departments entirely, and confining the national government to its proper objects; but, by no means admitting a standing army in time of peace, nor a select militia, which last, is a scheme that a certain head has, for some time, been teeming with,[2] and is nothing else but an artful introduction to the other—Nor ought the militia, or any part of it, I think, to be marched out of the state, without the consent of the legislature, and then, not for more than a certain reasonable time, etc.—leaving the states sovereign and independent with respect to their internal police, and relinquishing every idea of drenching the bowels of Africa in gore, for the sake of enslaving its free-born innocent inhabitants, I imagine we might become a happy and respectable people. And, the conduct of the late general convention, by the violent effort which it has made to prostrate our invaluable liberties at the feet of power, fully evinces the absolute necessity of the most express stipulation, for all our essential rights.

But, should the constitution be adopted in its present form, without any amendment, I candidly think, that we should have been much happier, at least for a number of years, in our old connexion with Great-Britain, than with such an absurd heterogeneal kind of government as the convention have proposed for our implicit adoption. Indeed, at present, there are so many dissentients, and others daily becoming so, in all the states, and with arms in their hands, that I cannot see how it could well be organized, without a force superior to every opposition, and that must, of course, absorb all the resources of ways and means immediately, and would defeat many of its own purposes and promises.

Besides, where is the difference between the people's cutting one another's throats, for their own diversion, or cutting them for the pleasure and aggrandizement of one or a few?—If any, I should prefer the former; that is, for my own diversion, etc. I have no idea of being gladiator to any man or body of men whatever; nor marching 500 or 1000 miles to quell an insurrection of such emigrants as are proposed by the new constitution, to be introduced for one and twenty years. No, nor of butchering the natives, that a few great speculators and landholders may engross all the best soil for a song, and revive the old feudal system, which I know to be the wish of some of the advocates for the new government.

1 Storing, VI, pp. 62-63.

2 Baron von Steuben. See DHRC, XV, note pp. 483-484. Von Steuben's 'select militia' proposal was contained in a pamphlet entitled *A Letter on the Subject of an Established Militia, and Military Arrangements, Addressed to the Inhabitants of the United States.* (New York, [1784], Evans 44601). The following is an excerpt from his pamphlet: "The best method of engaging men in service is a bounty; the expence will not be great, and the inconveniency and ill humour which attends draughting be avoided.–The bounty need not exceed ten dollars per man; to this must be added for the whole term of service, a hat, coat, vest, pair of overalls, pair of shoes, and a stock; and at the expiration of his service, provided he has not been capitally censured, his arms and accoutrements should be given to him. In the operation of this system, at the expiration of every third year 7000 well disciplined men, with their arms and accoutrements, will be added to the effective force of the United States, and the best possible magazine for a Republic firmly established, (viz.) arms and accoutrements in the course of a few years be put into the hands of every member of the community, and a perfect knowledge of the duties of a soldier engraved on the mind of every citizen." For another reference to the Baron, see New Haven *Connecticut Journal*, October 24, 1787, p. 61 at note 2.

Helvidius Priscus January 22, 1788

Newspaper Article: Boston *Massachusetts Gazette* (excerpt)

We wish to view every thing on the broad scale of independence to America—the *sovereignty of the United States*, and *the freedom of the people*, who have a just claim thereto, by the birth-right of nature, and the grant of heaven—sealed with the rich blood of martyrs in her cause.—Every member of the community ought diligently to read and to study the constitution of his country, and teach the rising generation to be free. By knowing their rights, they will soon perceive when they are violated, and be the better prepared to resist and defend them.

Storing, IV, p. 158.

Philadelphia *Freeman's Journal* January 23, 1788
Paragraphs from Correspondents.[1]

Whether the motives were good or bad that influnced the Council of Pennsylvania to call in the arms of the state to be cleaned, it matters not; we doubt not, but the measure will terminate in the public good.[2] For, that the attention of the Militia will be roused, both to have their arms in good order, and themselves perfected in Military discipline, is a necessary consequence. Perhaps our Militia, who are the true bulwark of a free country, may soon be called upon to defend our sacred rights and privileges, against the despots and monarchy-men; and to be prepared for the worst, their *arms* and *discipline* ought to undergo a previous examination.

A person of information, in the commercial way, acquaints us, that within these few weeks *large orders* are sent off to Europe for *powder* and *lead*. As these orders have been generally from the northern States, a correspondent wishes to know, what is the object of these extra orders for ammunition. He hopes the high-flying monarchy-men, and the rest of the aristocratics, have no thoughts of letting loose the dogs of war among such of their fellow citizens as intend to oppose the new constitution.

1 DHRC, II Mfm. Pa., p. 1371.

2 For other documents related to the controversy over the collection of publicly owned arms in Pennsylvania, and the complaint that this was intended to disarm the militia, see: "Jacob Trusty," December 19, 1787, p. 176; "Centinel IX," January 8, 1788, p. 191; Pennsylvania *Carlisle Gazette*, January 9, 1788, p. 194; "Trusty," January 10, 1788, p. 200; "Supreme Executive Council," January 10, 1788, p. 201; "An Old Militia Officer of 1776," January 18, 1788, p. 221; Philadelphia *Pennsylvania Herald*, February 5, 1788, p. 251; Philadelphia *Independent Gazetteer*, February 27, 1788, p. 286; "James de Caledonia IV," March 12, 1788, p. 298; "Aristocrotis," April [15], 1788, p. 334 at note 2; Philadelphia *Independent Gazetteer*, April 30, 1788, p. 340 at note 3.

Philadelphiensis VIII January 23, 1788
Newspaper Article: Philadelphia *Freeman's Journal* (excerpts)

In America the freedom of the press is peculiarly interesting: to a people scattered over such a vast continent, what means of information or redress have they, when a conspiracy has been formed against their sacred rights and privileges? None but the press. This is the herald that sounds the alarm, and rouses freemen to guard their liberty. From this scourge, the parricide, the knave of power and his cringing sycophants have every thing to fear; it hurls fury on the guilty heads of such base characters, and drags them to the public altar—And through the medium of the press, the *good and the patriotic* citizen receives the thanks of his grateful countrymen.

The sons of freedom who framed the constitution of Pennsylvania, expresly declared this to be one of the unalienable rights of the people, and therefore it ought not to be restrained. That some evils attend an unrestrained press, is obvious; but these are infinitely overbalanced by its advantages. The very salvation of America, I trust, will be wrought out by it; and the *conspirators* be taken by their own snares, which they so artfully set to seize the liberties of their fellow citizens, to their extreme mortification and disgrace. . . .

The advocates of this government say, that if nine states come into it, they will proceed to organize and put it in operation. They hug themselves up in the idea, that its enemies will cease their opposition and submit peaceably. How they came to make such a silly conclusion, is to me matter of surprise, as I never have observed the smallest change of sentiment among the patriotic gentlemen with whom I have conversed. From some of the writings of its friends, it seems probable, that this idea sprang from the circumstance of the Declaration of Independence. That measure was carried by a bare majority in some of the states, yet the minority gave way and joined cordially in it.—If there were any similarity between the circumstances of the Declaration of Independence and the adoption of the proposed Constitution, this argument would have some weight; but the premises are widely different, and consequently the inference inconclusive. The whole body of the people were determined to defend their liberties, at the hazard of their lives and fortunes, against the tyranny of the British government; so that there was a union of sentiment in respect of the great object, the only difference was in the means of obtaining it; in this case, then, common sense must have pointed out the expediency of the minority accommodating their private sentiments to those of the majority.

But the matter now in debate has no relation to that: the men opposed to the new constitution have the same cause to defend, that the people of America had during the period of a seven years war. Who is he so base, that will peaceably submit to a government that will eventually destroy his sacred *rights and privileges?* The liberty of conscience, the liberty of the press, the liberty of trial by jury, *&c.* must lie at the mercy of a few despots—an infernal junto, that are for changing our *free republican government* into a tyrannical and absolute monarchy. These are what roused the sons of America to oppose Britain, and from the nature of things, they must have a similar effect now.

DHRC, XV, p. 459-461. The "Philadelphiensis" series is reprinted in Storing, III, starting on p. 99.

Massachusetts Convention January 23, 1788
Debates (excerpts)

[Gen. THOMPSON.]
Gentlemen say this section [8th section, Article I] is as clear as the sun, and that all power is retained which is not given. But where is the bill of rights which shall check the power of this Congress; which shall say, *Thus far shall ye come, and no farther.* The safety of the people depends on a bill of rights. If we build on a sandy foundation, is it likely we shall stand? I apply to the feelings of the Convention. There are some parts of this Constitution which I cannot digest: and, sir, shall we swallow a large bone for the sake of a little meat? Some say, Swallow the whole now, and pick out the bone afterwards. But I say, Let us pick off the meat, and throw the bone away. . . .

[Hon. Mr. BOWDOIN.]
With regard to rights, the whole Constitution is a declaration of rights, which primarily and principally respect the general government intended to be formed by it. The rights of particular states, or private citizens, not being the object or subject of the Constitution, they are only incidentally mentioned. In regard to the former, it would require a volume to describe them, as they extend to every subject of legislation, not included in the powers vested in Congress; and, in regard to the latter, as all governments are founded on the relinquishment of personal rights in a certain degree, there was a clear imporpriety in being very particular about them. By such a particularity the government might be embarrassed, and prevented

from doing what the private, as well as the public and general, good of the citizens and states might require.

The public good, in which private is necessarily involved, might be hurt by too particular an enumeration; and the private good could suffer no injury from a deficient enumeration, because Congress could not injure the rights of private citizens without injuring their own, as they must, in their public as well as private character, participate equally with others in the consequences of their own acts. . . .

[Mr. PARSONS.]

It has been objected that we have no bill of rights. If gentlemen who make this objection would consider what are the supposed inconveniences resulting from the want of a declaration of rights, I think they would soon satisfy themselves that the objection has no weight. Is there a single natural right we enjoy, uncontrolled by our own legislature, that Congress can infringe? Not one. Is there a single political right secured to us by our constitution, against the attempts of our own legislature, which we are deprived of by this Constitution? Not one, that I recollect. All the rights Congress can control we have surrendered to our own legislature; and the only question is, whether the people shall take from their own legislatures a certain portion of the several sovereignties, and unite them in one head, for the more effectual securing of the national prosperity and happiness.

The honorable gentleman from Boston [Mr. Bowdoin] has stated at large most of the checks the people have against usurpation, and the abuse of power, under the proposed Constitution; but from the abundance of his matter, he has, in my opinion, omitted two or three, which I shall mention. The oath the several legislative, executive, and judicial officers of the several states take to support the federal constitution, is as effectual a security against the usurpation of the general government as it is against the encroachment of the state governments. For an increase of the powers by usurpation is as clearly a violation of the federal Constitution as a diminution of these powers by private encroachment; and that the oath obliges the officers of the several states as vigorously to oppose the one as the other. But there is another check, founded in the nature of the Union, superior to all the parchment checks that can be invented. If there should be a usurpation, it will not be on the farmer and merchant, employed and attentive only to their several occupations; it will be upon thirteen legislatures, completely organized, possessed of the confidence of the people, and having the means, as well as inclination, successfully to oppose it. Under these circumstances, none but madmen would attempt a usurpation. But, sir, the people themselves have it in their power effectually to resist usurpation, without being driven to an appeal to arms. An act of usurpation is not obligatory; it is not law; and any man may be justified in his resistance. Let him be considered as a criminal by the general government, yet only his own fellow-citizens can convict him; they are his jury, and if they pronounce him innocent, not all the powers of Congress can hurt him; and innocent they certainly will pronounce him, if the supposed law he resisted was an act of usurpation.

Debates, II, pp. 80-81, 87-88, 93-94.

Massachusetts Convention January 24, 1788
Debates (excerpt)

The eighth section was again read.

The Hon. Mr. SEDGWICK went into a general answer to the objections which had been started against the powers to be granted to Congress by this section. He showed the absolute necessity there was that the body which had the security of the whole for their object, should have the necessary means allowed them to effect it; and in order to secure the people against the abuse of this power, the representatives and people, he said, are equally subject to the laws, and can, therefore, have but one and the same interest; that they would never lay unnecessary burdens, when they themselves must bear a part of them; and from the extent of their objects, their power ought necessarily to be illimitable. Men, said he, rarely do mischief for the sake of being mischievous. With respect to the power, in this section, to raise armies, the honorable gentleman said, although gentlemen had thought it a dangerous power, and would be used for the purpose of tyranny, yet they did not object to the Confederation in this particular; and by this, Congress could have kept the whole of the late army in the field, had they seen fit. He asked, if gentlemen could think it possible that the legislature of the United States should raise an army unnecessarily, which, in a short time, would be under the control of other persons; for, if it was not to be under their control, what object could they have in raising it? It was, he said, a chimerical idea to suppose that a country like this could ever be enslaved. How is an army for that purpose to be obtained from the freemen of the United States? They certainly, said he, will know to what object it is to be applied. Is it possible, he asked, that an army could be raised for the purpose of enslaving themselves and their brethren? or, if raised, whether they could subdue a nation of freemen, who know how to prize liberty, and who have arms in their hands? He said, it was a deception in gentlemen to say that this power could be thus used. The honorable gentleman said, that in the Constitution every possible provision against an abuse of power was made; and if gentlemen would candidly investigate for themselves, they would find that the evils they lament cannot ensue therefrom.

Debates, II, pp. 96-97.

William Russell (Aspenville) January 25, 1788
Letter: To William Fleming (excerpt)

Time at present, wont allow me, or my mind might be enlarged on, my fears of the Constitution without amendments; but, am encouriaged from the judicious remarks so many able pens have pointed out, that the people will behold the danger eer it be too late, & make choice of men for, the Conventions of the different States; whom, the hand of Providence, may direct, to wholesome amendments, upon the most permanent basis. I shall now rest my sentiments, hoping shortly for your better judgement, to aid your friend, & the good people of this country, in so important an object.

DHRC, XV, p. 468.

Publius {James Madison] January 25, 1788
Newspaper Article: *New York Packet* (excerpt)

The FOEDERALIST, No. 43.
To the People of the State of New-York. . . .

Bills of attainder, ex post facto laws, and laws impairing the obligation of contracts, are contrary to the first principles of the social compact, and to every principle of sound legislation. The two former are expressly prohibited by the declarations prefixed to some of the State Constitutions, and all of them are prohibited by the spirit and scope of these fundamental charters. Our own experience has taught us, nevertheless, that additional fences against these dangers ought not to be omitted. Very properly therefore have the Convention added this constitutional bulwark in favor of personal security and private rights; and I am much deceived if they have not in so doing as faithfully consulted the genuine sentiments, as the undoubted interests of their constitutents. The sober people of America are weary of the fluctuating policy which has directed the public councils. They have seen with regret and with indignation, that sudden changes and legislative interferences in cases affecting personal rights, become jobs in the hands of enterprizing and influential speculators; and snares to the more industrious and less informed part of the community. They have seen too, that legislative interference, is but the first link of a long chain of repetitions; every subsequent interference being naturally produced by the effects of the preceding.

DHRC, XV, p. 470.

The Yeomanry of Massachusetts January 25, 1788
Newspaper Article: Boston *Massachusetts Gazette* (excerpt)[1]

We do not wish to tire the publick, but would hint to those gentlemen, who would rob the people of their liberties, that their sophistry is not like to produce the effect. We are willing to have a federal constitution. We are willing another trial should be made; this may be done without derogating from the gentlemen, who composed the late convention. In framing a constitution for this commonwealth, two trials were made before one would stick.[2] We are willing to relinquish so much, as to have a firm, energetick government, and this we are sensible may be done, without becoming slaves, to the capricious fancies of any sett of men whatever. It is argued, that there is no danger that the proposed rulers will be disposed to exercise any powers that this constitution puts into their hands, which may enable them to deprive the people of their liberties. But in case, say they, they should make such attempts, the people may, and will rise to arms and prevent it; in answer to which, we have only to say, we have had enough of fighting in the late war, and think it more eligible, to keep our liberties in our own hands, whilst it is in our power thus to do, than to place them in the hands of fallible men, like ourselves, who may if they please, entirely deprive us of them, and so we be at last reduced to the sad alternative of losing them forever, or recovering them back by the point of the sword.

1 Storing, IV, pp. 224-225.

2 A proposed Massachusetts Constitution of 1778 was rejected in part due to the lack of a bill of rights. The Massachusetts Constitution of 1780 included a bill of rights and was adopted. See Appendix A, p. 770, for the Massachusetts Declaration of Rights. For further information on the adoption of the Massachusetts Constitution consult Oscar and Mary Handlin, eds., *The Popular Sources of Political Authority*, (Cambridge: Harvard University Press, 1966.)

John Wilkes I January 26, 1788
Newspaper Article: Philadelphia *Independent Gazetteer* (excerpt)

If the people of England are so jealous of their liberties, of those rights which GOD has trusted them with; and to guard and protect which, they consider as a religious as well as moral duty; will not the Americans, almost the only nation (except them) who continue as yet to enjoy the blessings of such privileges, stand forth in their defence?—Will they sit down and suffer the yoke to be clapped on their necks?—Will they allow the establishment of a government which is only calculated for the meridian of Turkey, the only *seeming* popular part of which is so small, (only 65 for this extensive continent) and so uncertain, so independent of the people, and so very dependent on the will of the well born and powerful branches of the government, that it will be no security to those privileges of freemen, which ought to have been established in a bill of rights, affixed to the constitution.

DHRC, II Mfm. Pa., p. 1588.

Observator January 26, 1788
Newspaper Article: Philadelphia *Independent Gazetteer*

"By their works you will know them."

The public must acknowledge the obligation they are under to the grand writing committee (appointed Friday fortnight) for sundry most excellent, and very elegant and sound argumentative performances, published in the different newspapers; they have taken up all the objections which have been made by the antifederalists, and have fairly and clearly proved them all to be without foundation; the essays signed Conciliator, Watchman, Candidus, Whig of 1776, Old Woman and Deb. Woodcock, prove, that all the clamor which has been raised about the loss of jury tryal, liberty of conscience and the press, dangers of a standing army, &c. &c. has proceeded entirely from interested and factious men: as for Centinel he must be a deceiver—as Candidus says all that has been said against the constitution is mere possibilities, and very justly says the objections would apply to any other constitution. Mr. Conciliator, he has never been equalled by any political writer since the days of *Junius*, to be sure what he says ought to quiet all grumbling in the people, for if our rulers will but establish all our privileges (which have been said are in danger) by a law, and do not repeal that law afterwards, it will be all that can be wanted.

DHRC, II Mfm. Pa., p. 1592.

Publius {James Madison} January 29, 1788
Newspaper Article: *New York Packet* (excerpt)[1]

The FOEDERALIST, No. 45.[2]

To the People of the State of New-York. . . .

The only refuge left for those who prophesy the downfall of the State Governments, is the visionary supposition that the Foederal Government may proviously accumulate a military force for the projects of ambition. The reasonings contained in these papers must have been employed to little purpose indeed, if it could be necessary now to disprove the reality of this danger. That the people and the States should for a sufficient period of time elect an uninterrupted succession of men ready to betray both; that the traitors should throughout this period, uniformly and systematically pursue some fixed plan for the extension of the military establishment; that the governments and the people of the States should silently and patiently behold the gathering storm, and continue to supply the materials, until it should be prepared to burst on their own heads, must appear to everyone more like the incoherent dreams of a delirious jealousy, or the misjudged exaggerations of a counterfeit zeal, than like the sober apprehensions of genuine patriotism. Extravagant as the supposition is, let it however be made. Let a regular army, fully equal to the resources of the country be formed; and let it be entirely at the devotion of the Foederal Government; still it would not be going too far to say, that the State Governments with the people on their side would be able to repel the danger. The highest number to which, according to the best computation, a standing army can be carried in any country, does not exceed one hundredth part of the whole number of souls; or one twenty-fifth part of the number able to bear arms. This proportion would not yield in the United States an army of more than twenty-five or thirty thousand men. To these would be opposed a militia amounting to near half a million of citizens with arms in their hands, officered by men chosen from among themselves, fighting for their common liberties, and united and conducted by governments possessing their affections and confidence. It may well be doubted whether a militia thus circumstanced could ever be conquered by such a proportion of regular troops. Those who are best acquainted with the late successful resistance of this country against the British arms will be most inclined to deny the possibility of it. Besides the advantage of being armed, which the Americans possess over the people of almost every other nation, the existence of subordinate governments to which the people are attached, and by which the militia officers are appointed, forms a barrier against the enterprises of ambition, more insurmountable than any which a simple government of any form can admit of. Notwithstanding the military establishments in the several kingdoms of Europe, which are carried as far as the public resources will bear, the governments are afraid to trust the people with arms. And it is not certain that with this aid alone they would not be able to shake off their yokes. But were the people to possess the additional advantages of local governments chosen by themselves, who could collect the national will, and direct the national force; and of officers appointed out of the militia, by these governments and attached both to them and to the militia, it may be affirmed with the greatest assurance, that the throne of every tyranny in Europe would be speedily overturned, in spite of the legions which surround it. Let us not insult the free and gallant citizens of America with the suspicion that they would be less able to defend the rights of which they would be in actual possession, than the debased subjects of arbitrary power would be to rescue theirs from the hands of their oppressors. Let us rather no longer insult them with the supposition, that they can ever reduce themselves to the necessity of making the experiment, by a blind and tame submission to the long train of insidious measures, which must precede and produce it.[3]

1 DHRC, XV, pp. 488, 492-493. Reprinted in *Papers*, X, pp. 442-443.

2 *The Federalist* Number 45 in the newspapers was Number 46 in the M'Lean edition of the collected essays. See DHRC, XIII, p. 490, for an explanation of their numbering.

3 See "A Pennsylvanian III," February 20, 1788, p. 275, for another Federalist's (Tench Coxe) comments inspired by this essay.

Civis Rusticus January 30, 1788
Newspaper Article: *Virginia Independent Chronicle* (excerpts)[1]

To Mr. DAVIS.

The following "objections to the Constitution of Government formed by the Convention," are stated to be Col. Mason's.

I shall remark on them with that freedom which every person has a right to exercise on publications, but, with that deference, which is due to this respectable and worthy gentleman; to whose great and eminent talents, profound judgment, and strength of mind, no man gives a larger credit, than he, who presumes to criticise his objections—these, falling from so great a height, from one of such authority, may be supposed, if not taken notice of, to contain arguments unanswerable—not obtruding themselves on my mind in that forcible manner, I submit to the decision of the public, whether, what is now offered, contain declamation or reason; cavil, or refutation.

1st. "There is no declaration of rights; and the laws of the general government being paramount to the laws and constitutions of the several states, the declarations of rights in the separate states are no security. Nor are the people secured even in the enjoyment of the benefits of the common law, which stands here upon no other foundation than its having been adopted by the respective acts forming the constitutions of the several states. . . .

Ob. 1st. This objection proves too much, it goes against all sovereignty, "it being paramount to all laws of the several states, the declaration of rights in the separate states are no security," if the declaration of rights in the separate states be no security, which it is confessed are not repealed, neither would a general declaration of rights be any security, for the sovereign who made it could repeal it; "the very title of sovereignty shews the absurdity of an irrevocable law." The people have every security of enjoying the benefits of the common law, and all acts of parliament previous to the fourth of James the first, they ever had—they remain unrepealed, and are the palladium of the rights of the people: as long as *they* retain the spirit of freedom, these rights will exist, amidst the mighty shock of revolutions, the crush of power, the fall of colonies, and the rise of empires.

There are only five states in the union that have declarations of rights[2]—the proposed government is thoroughly popular—the house of representatives are immediately chosen by the people, the senate mediately by their representatives *in Assembly*, and the president by electors, in such manner as the legislature of the state may direct—at the end of four years, he may, and will be removed from his situation, unless he discharge the duties of it, to the approbation of the people, and to the glory and advantage of America. A government thus constituted stands in need of no bill of rights; the liberties of the people never can be lost, until they are lost to themselves, in a vicious disregard of their dearest interests, a sottish indolence, a wild licentiousness, a dissoluteness of morals, and a contempt of all virtue. . . .

10th. There is no declaration of any kind for preserving the liberty of the press, the trial by jury in civil causes; nor against the danger of standing armies in time of peace. . . .

10th. "No declaration of the liberty of the press." Our Bill of Rights declares, and it is not repealed, that the freedom of the press is one of the great bulwarks of the liberty of the people, and never can be restrained, but by despotic power. The people of England have no other security for the liberty of the press, than we have—Their own spirit, and an act of parliament—their act of parliament *may* be repealed—our Bill of Rights *may* be repealed. Of that no man has any fear, of this no man need have, while this spirit is in the people—"This peculiar privilege must last (says a learned writer) as long as our government remains, in any degree, free and independent—it is seldom that liberty of any kind is lost at once—slavery has so frightful an aspect to men accustomed to freedom, that it must steal upon them by degrees, and disguise itself in a thousand shapes in order to be received—But, if the liberty of the press ever be lost, it will be lost at once.—The general laws against sedition and libelling are at present as strong as they can possibly be made, nothing can impose a further restraint, but, either clapping an imprimatur on the press, or giving to the court very large discretionary powers, to punish whatever displeases them—but these concessions would be such a bare faced violation of liberty, that they will probably be the last efforts of a despotic government—Hume's essay vol. 1. p. 17."

The last efforts of a despotic government! Can we then a popular government, a guaranteed republic, fear this more under the proposed, than the present constitution?

A standing army without the consent of the representatives of the people in Congress there never can be: to their wisdom and their discretion we submit—Necessity may oblige America to raise an army—and who can judge of this necessity so well as Congress? Where can this power be more safely reposed? Dr. Smith (in his "Wealth of Nations," book 5. ch. 1.) is of opinion in some cases, that a standing army is not dangerous to liberty—of this the people of America will judge, and a people jealous of their liberty, vigilant over executory magistracy, will oppose with their united voice this institution, when they discover its end to be usurpation and tyranny.

1 DHRC, VIII, pp. 332-338.

2 See Appendix A, p. 747, for the state bills of rights and related provisions. There were actually seven states with formal bills or declarations of rights. Several other state constitutions contained similar individual rights protections within the body of the constitution.

Philadelphia *Pennsylvania Gazette* January 30, 1788

It is curious, says a Correspondent, to observe *the extreme ignorance* or *the disregard to truth*, discovered by certain violent opponents to the proposed constitution. They assert that the Foederalists are sending orders to Europe for large quantities of powder and arms, when it is a well known fact that powder is at a price below what it can be imported for, owing to the perfection of that manufacture,—and arms are to be bought in every seaport in the union for less than their first cost in Europe.

DHRC, II Mfm. Pa., p. 1372.

Franklin County Petition January 30, 1788
Newspaper Article: Pennsylvania *Carlisle Gazette* (excerpt)[1]

Messieurs KLINE & REYNOLDS.

You will oblige a number of your customers by inserting the following address in your useful paper, and through it they ask the opportunity of soliciting the concurrence of their fellow citizens.

To the Honourable the Representatives of the Freemen of the Commonwealth of Pennsylvania, in General Assembly met.

The PETITION of the Subscribers freemen of the County of Franklin.

Most Respectfully Sheweth.

THAT your petitioners are desirous that order and good government should prevail, and that the constitution of this state should not be subverted nor altered in any other way than is therein provided.

That as the members of your honourable house are all sworn or affirmed to do no act or thing prejudicial or injurious to the constitution or government [of Pennsylvania] as established by the convention, by whom the same was framed, they look up to you as the guardians of the rights and liberties therein secured to your petitioners, and pray that they may be protected therein.[2]

That your petitioners are much alarmed at an instrument called a constitution for the United States of America, framed by a convention that had been appointed by several of the states, solely for the purpose of revising the articles of confederation, and to report such alterations and provisions therein, as should when agreed to in congress, and confirmed by the several states, render the federal constitution adequate to the exigencies of government and the preservation of the union, in as much as the liberties, lives and property of your petitioners are not secured thereby.

That the powers therein proposed to be granted to the government of the united states are too great, and that the proposed distribution of these powers are dangerous and inimical to liberty and equality amongst the people.

That they esteem frequent elections and rotation in offices as the great bulwark of freedom.

That they conceive standing armies in time of peace are dangerous to liberty, and that a well organized militia will be the proper security for our defence.

That the rights of conscience should be secured to all men, that none should be molested for his religion, and that none should be compelled contrary to his principles or inclination to hear or support the clergy of any one established religion.

That the liberty of the PRESS should not be insecure or in danger.

That the right of trial by jury should be secured in civil as well as in criminal cases.

That the government as proposed would be burthensome, expensive and oppressive, and that your petitioners are averse from paying taxes to support a numerous train of officers erected thereby, which would be not only unnecessary but dangerous to our liberties.

1 DHRC, II Mfm. Pa., pp. 1612-1614.

2 See Appendix A, "Pennsylvania Constitution," p. 752, for the rights secured to the citizens of Pennsylvania in the state constitution and bill of rights.

Aristides {Alexander Contee Hanson} January 31, 1788
Pamphlet: Remarks on the Proposed Plan of a Federal Government, Addressed to the Citizens of the United States of America, and Particularly to the People of Maryland. (excerpts)
Annapolis

For want of some plain and obvious distinctions, there has been vented so much senseless clamour against standing armies, that they are become a political bugbear. A limited monarch, with the means of maintaining, at all times, an army devoted to his will, might soon trample on the natural and civil rights of his subjects. Could the present congress find means of augmenting the force, which it now maintains, which of you, on that account, would experience the slightest anxiety? Which of all the European powers is destitute of an army? Which of them, if they were free, could be secure of remaining so, without a standing force? I might go further, and demand, whether any of them have lost their liberties, by means of a *standing* army. The troops, continually kept up in Great-Britain, are formidable to its neighbours, and yet no rational Englishman apprehends the destruction of his rights. It is true, that he knows, these troops cannot be maintained, without the consent of his representatives, annually obtained. But the necessity of an army he readily conceives; and the number he leaves to the discretion of parliament. Ought then an American to have greater fears of a president, than an Englishman has of his king? Or may he not trust his representatives and the senate, with as much confidence, as the Englishman reposes in the commons and lords?

Let the federal head be constituted as it may, there can be no perfect security, without both a land force, and naval armament. It is impossible to say how much will, at all times of peace, be sufficient. We have the same security against the abuse of this, as of any other authority. The expences of an army might indeed raise fears of a different kind,—that we shall not be able to maintain force enough for the most proper occasion.

Suppose a limitation in time of peace. What then is to be done on the prospect of a war? Should you make the distinction between profound peace, and a *threatened* war, who is there, but congress, to determine on the exigency? If you make no distinction, then will it be expedient to declare war, at the instant in which the danger shall be conceived, in order that it may be lawful to prepare for only a just defence. In fine, I consider this grand objection, as a mere pretext for terrifying you, like children, with spectres and hobgobblins. It may be material here to remark, that although a well regulated militia has ever been considered as the true defence of a free republic, there are always honest purposes, which are not to be answered by a militia. If they were, the burthen on the militia would be so great, that a free people would, by no means, be willing to sustain it. If indeed it be possible in the nature of things, that congress shall, at any future period, alarm us by an improper augmentation of troops, could we not, in that case, depend on the militia, which is ourselves. In such a case it would be ridiculous to urge, that the federal government is invested with a power over the whole militia of the union. Even when congress shall exercise this power, on the most proper occasions, it is provided in the constitution, that each state shall officer, and train its own militia. . . .

I proceed to attack the whole body of anti-federalists in their strong hold. The proposed constitution contains no *bill of rights*.

Consider again the nature and intent of a federal republic. It consists of an assemblage of distinct states, each completely organized for the protection of its own citizens, and the whole consolidated, by express compact, under one head, for their general welfare and common defence.

Should the compact authorise the sovereign, or head, to do all things it may think necessary and proper, then is there no limitation to its authority; and the liberty of each citizen in the union has no other security, than the sound policy, good faith, virtue, and perhaps proper interests, of the head.

When the compact confers the aforesaid general power, making nevertheless some special reservations and exceptions, then is the citizen protected further, so far as these reservations and exceptions shall extend.

But, when the compact ascertains and defines the power delegated to the federal head, then cannot this government, without manifest usurpation, exert any power not expressly, or by *necessary* implication, conferred by the compact.

This doctrine is so obvious and plain, that I am amazed any good man should deplore the omission of a bill of rights. When we were told, that the celebrated Mr. Wilson had advanced this doctrine in effect, it was said, Mr. Wilson would not dare to speak thus to a CONSTITUTIONALIST. With talents inferior to that gentleman's, I will maintain the doctrine against any CONSTITUTIONALIST who will condescend to enter the lists, and behave like a gentleman.—

It is, however, the idea of another most respectable character, that, as a bill of rights could do no harm, and might quiet the minds of many good people, the convention would have done well to indulge them.—With all due deference, I apprehend, that a bill of rights might not be this innocent quieting instrument. Had the convention entered on the work, they must have comprehended within it every thing, which the citizens of the United States claim as a natural or a civil right. An omission of a single article would have caused more discontent, than is either felt, or pretended, on the present occasion. A multitude of articles might be the source of infinite controversy, by clashing with the powers intended to be given. To be full and certain, a bill of rights might have cost the convention more time, than was expended on their other work. The very appearance of it might raise more clamour than its omission,—I mean from those, who study pretexts for condemning the whole fabric of the constitution.—"What! (might they say) did these exalted spirits imagine, that the natural rights of mankind depend on their gracious concessions. If indeed they possessed that tyrannic sway, which the kings of England had once usurped, we might humbly thank them for their *magna charta,* defective as it is. As that is not the case, we will not suffer it to be understood, that their *new-fangled* federal head shall domineer with the powers not excepted by their precious bill of rights. What! If the owner of 1000 acres of land thinks proper to sell one half, is it necessary for him to take a release from the vendee of the other half? Just as necessary is it for the people to have a grant of their natural rights from a government, which derives every thing it has, from the grant of the people."—

The restraints laid on the state legislatures will tend to secure domestic tranquillity, more than all the bills, or declarations, of rights, which human policy could devise. It is very justly asserted, that the plan contains an avowal of many rights. It provides, that no man shall suffer by ex post facto laws, or bills of attainder.

DHRC, XV, pp. 532-538. Reprinted in *Essays*, pp. 234-243.

A Watchman February, 1788

Newspaper Article: *Worcester Magazine* (excerpts)

To the Citizens of the United States.
Men, Brethren, Sisters,

Hearken! it is now a critical time with us, and a time in which we ought to be upon our watch, and upon our guard. Now is the time for us to look out; now is the time for us to take care; now is the time for us to see that nothing is done to deprive us of our religious, or our civil liberties.

Our government at present is democratical, that is, the power is in the people; we are allowed to choose our rulers, make our own laws, and perform religious worship according to the dictates of our own consciences; and by our constitution a freedom of speech, and the liberty of the press, are allowed to every one of us. But although we are under such an excellent constitution, behold a new one is presented to us for our reception, which appears much like an aristocratical form; and will, if it is established, demolish a part of our democratical government, and deprive us of a part of our liberties.

Before we suffer this new constitution to be established, we ought to consider seriously what it contains, and whether it is calculated to promote our felicity? or whether, like a wolf in sheep's clothing, it is calculated to vest certain men with more power, deprive us of our liberties, and bring our land into lordships, and lead us into vassalage and slavery, . . .

Permit me then, my beloved brethren and sisters, to point out wherein this new constitution is deficient.

1st. There is no bill of rights in it.

Storing, IV, pp. 231-232.

Columbian Patriot {Mercy Warren} February, 1788
Pamphlet: Observations on the New Constitution, and on the Federal and State Conventions. (excerpts)
Boston

Self defence is a primary law of nature, which no subsequent law of society can abolish; this primoeval principle, the immediate gift of the Creator, obliges every one to remonstrate against the strides of ambition, and a wanton lust of domination, and to resist the first approaches of tyranny, which at this day threaten to sweep away the rights for which the brave sons of America have fought with an heroism scarcely paralleled even in ancient republicks. . . .

All writers on government agree, and the feelings of the human mind witness the truth of these political axioms, that man is born free and possessed of certain unalienble rights—that government is instituted for the protection, safety, and happiness of the people, and not for the profit, honour, or private interest of any man, family, or class of men—that the origin of all power is in the people, and that they have an incontestible right to check the creatures of their own creation, vested with certain powers to guard the life, liberty and property of the community: And if certain selected bodies of men, deputed on these principles, determine contrary to the wishes and expectations of their constituents, the people have an undoubted right to reject their decisions, to call for a revision of their conduct, to depute others in their room, or if they think proper, to demand further time for deliberation on matters of the greatest moment: it therefore is an unwarrantable stretch of authority or influence, if any methods are taken to preclude this reasonable, and peaceful mode of enquiry and decision. . . .

6. Though it has been said by Mr. *Wilson* and many others, that a Standing-Army is necessary for the dignity and safety of America, yet freedom revolts at the idea, when the Divan, or the Despot, may draw out his dragoons to suppress the murmurs of a few, who may yet cherish those sublime principles which call forth the exertions, and lead to the best improvement of the human mind. It is hoped this country may yet be governed by milder methods than are usually displayed beneath the bannerets of military law.—Standing armies have been the nursery of vice and the bane of liberty from the Roman legions, to the establishment of the artful Ximenes, and from the ruin of the Cortes of Spain, to the planting the British cohorts in the capitals of America:—By the edicts of authority vested in the sovereign power by the proposed constitution, the militia of the country, the bulwark of defence, and the security of national liberty is

no longer under the controul of civil authority; but at the rescript of the Monarch, or the aristocracy, they may either be employed to extort the enormous sums that will be necessary to support the civil list—to maintain the regalia of power—and the splendour of the most useless part of the community, or they may be sent into foreign countries for the fulfilment of treaties, stipulated by the President and two thirds of the Senate. . . .

14. There is no provision by a bill of rights to guard against the dangerous encroachments of power in too many instances to be named: but I cannot pass over in silence the insecurity in which we are left with regard to warrants unsupported by evidence—the daring experiment of granting *writs of assistance* in a former arbitrary administration is not yet forgotten in the Massachusetts; nor can we be so ungrateful to the memory of the patriots who counteracted their operation, as so soon after their manly exertions to save us from such a detestable instrument of arbitrary power, to subject ourselves to the insolence of any petty revenue officer to enter our houses, search, insult, and seize at pleasure. We are told by a gentleman of too much virtue and real probity to suspect he has a design to deceive—"that the whole constitution is a declaration of rights"—but mankind must think for themselves, and to many very judicious and discerning characters, the whole constitution with very few exceptions appears a perversion of the rights of particular states, and of private citizens.—But the gentleman goes on to tell us, "that the primary object is the general government, and that the rights of individuals are only incidentally mentioned, and that there was a clear impropriety in being very particular about them." But, asking pardon for dissenting from such respectable authority, who has been led into several mistakes, more from his prediliction in favour of certain modes of government, than from a want of understanding or veracity. The rights of individuals ought to be the primary object of all government, and cannot be too securely guarded by the most explicit declarations in their favor. This has been the opinion of the Hampdens, the Pyms, and many other illustrious names, that have stood forth in defence of English liberties; and even the Italian master in politicks, the subtle and renouned Machiavel acknowledges, that no republic ever yet stood on a stable foundation without satisfying the common people. . . .

But when we contemplate the nature of men and consider them originally on an equal footing, subject to the same feelings, stimulated by the same passions, and recollecting the struggles they have recently made, for the security of their civil rights; it cannot be expected that the inhabitants of the Massachusetts, can be easily lulled into a fatal security, by the declamatory effusions of gentlemen, who, contrary to the experience of all ages would perswade them there is no danger to be apprehended, from vesting discretionary powers in the hands of man, which he may, or may not abuse. The very suggestion, that we ought to trust to the precarious hope of amendments and redress, after we have voluntarily fixed the shackles on our own necks should have awakened to a double degree of caution.—This people have not forgotten the artful insinuations of a former Governor, when pleading the unlimited authority of parliament before the legislature of the Massachusetts; not that his arguments were very similar to some lately urged by gentlemen who boast of opposing his measure, *"with halters about their necks."*

We were then told by him, in all the soft language of insinuation, that no form of government of human construction can be perfect—that we had nothing to fear—that we had no reason to complain—that we had only to acquiesce in their illegal claims, and to submit to the requisitions of parliament, and doubtless the lenient hand of government would redress all grievances, and remove the oppressions of the people:—Yet we soon saw armies of mercenaries encamped on our plains—our commerce ruined—our harbours blockaded—and our cities burnt. It may be replied, that this was in consequence of an obstinate defence of our privileges; this may be true; and when the *"ultima ratio"* is called to aid, the weakest must fall. But let the best informed historian produce an instance when bodies of men were intrusted with power, and the proper checks relinquished, if they were ever found destitute of ingenuity sufficient to furnish pretences to abuse it. And the people at large are already sensible, that the liberties which America has claimed, which reason has justified, and which have been so gloriously defended by the sword of the brave; are not about to fall before the tyranny of foreign conquest: it is native usurpation that is shaking the foundations of peace, and spreading the sable curtain of despotism over the United States. . . .

I know not what part the Carolinas will take; but I hope their determinations will comport with the dignity and freedom of this country—their decisions will have great weight in the scale.—But equally important are the small States of New-Hampshire and Rhode-Island:—New-York, the Carolinas, Virginia, Maryland, and these two lesser States may yet support the liberties of the Continent; if they refuse a ratification, or postpone their proceedings till the spirits of the community have time to cool, there is little doubt but the wise measure of another federal convention will be adopted, when the members would have the advantage of viewing, at large, through the medium of truth, the objections that have been made from various quarters; such a measure might be attended with the most salutary effects, and prevent the dread consequences of civil feuds.—But even if some of those large states should hastily accede, yet we have frequently seen in the story of revolution, relief spring from a quarter least expected.

DHRC, XVI, p. 275-288. This pamphlet is reprinted in Storing, IV, starting at p. 270, and in *Pamphlets*, starting at p. 1.

Luther Martin February 1, 1788
Newspaper Article: Genuine Information X, Baltimore *Maryland Gazette* (excerpt)

By the *principles* of the American revolution, *arbitrary power may* and *ought* to be resisted even by *arms* if necessary—

DHRC, XVI, p. 10.

Massachusetts Convention February 1, 1788
Debates (excerpts)[1]

Hon Mr. ADAMS. As your excellency [Jonn Hancock] was pleased yesterday to offer, for the consideration of this Convention, certain propositions intended to accompany the ratification of the Constitution before us, I did myself the honor to bring them forward by a regular motion, not only from the respect due to your excellency, but from a clear conviction, in my own mind, that they would tend to effect the salutary and important purposes which you had in view—"the removing the fears and quieting the apprehensions of many of the good people of this commonwealth, and the more effectually guarding against an undue administration of the federal government."

I beg leave, sir, more particularly to consider those propositions, and, in a very few words, to express my own opinion, that they must have a stong tendency to ease the minds of gentlemen, who wish for the immediate operation of some essential parts of the proposed Constitution, as well as the most speedy and effectual means of obtaining alterations in some other parts of it, which they are solicitous should be made. I will not repeat the reasons I offered when the motion was made, which convinced me that the measure now under consideration will have a more speedy as well as a more certain influence, in effecting the purpose last mentioned, than the measure proposed in the Constitution before us.

Your excellency's first proposition is, "that it be explicitly declared, that all powers not expressly delegated to Congress are reserved to the several states, to be by them exercised." This appears, to my mind, to be a summary of a bill of rights, which gentlemen are anxious to obtain.[2] It removes a doubt which many have entertained respecting the matter, and gives assurance that, if any law made by the federal government shall be extended beyond the power granted by the proposed Constitution, and inconsistent with the constitution of this state, it will be an error, and adjudged by the courts of law to be void. It is consonant with the second article in the present Confederation, that each state retains its sovereignty, freedom, and independence, and every power, jurisdiction, and right, which is not, by this Confederation, expressly delegated to the United States in Congress assembled. I have long considered the watchfulness of the people over the conduct of their rulers the strongest guard against the encroachments of power; and I hope the people of this country will always be thus watchful.

Mr. NASON. . . . Mr. President, let us consider the Constitution without a bill of rights. When I give up any of my natural rights, it is for the security of the rest; but here is not one right secured, although many are neglected. . . . Suffer me, sir, to say a few words on the fatal effects of standing armies, that bane of republican governments. A standing army! Was it not with this that Ceasar passed the *Rubicon,* and laid prostrate the liberties of his country? By this have seven eights of the once free nations of the globe been brought into bondage! Time would fail me, were I to attempt to recapitulate the havoc made in the world by standing armies. Britain attempted to enforce her arbitrary measures by a standing army. But, sir, we had patriots then who alarmed us of our danger; who showed us the serpent, and bade us beware of it. Shall I name them? I fear I shall offend your excellency, but I cannot avoid it. I must. We had a Hancock, an Adams, and a Warren. Our sister states, too, produced a Randolph, a Washington, a Greene, and a Montgomery, who led us in our way. Some of these have given up their lives in defence of the liberties of their country; and my prayer to God is, that, when this race of illustrious patriots shall have bid adieu to the world, from their dust, as from the sacred ashes of the phoenix, another race may arise, who shall take our posterity by the hand, and lead them on to trample on the necks of those who shall dare to infringe on their liberties. Sir, had I a voice like Jove, I would proclaim it throughout the world; and had I am arm like Jove, I would hurl from the globe those villains that would dare attempt to establish in our country a standing army. I wish, sir, that the gentlemen of Boston would bring to their minds the fatal evening of the 5th of March, 1770, when by standing troops they lost five of their fellow-townsmen. I will ask them, What price can atone for their lives? What money can make satisfaction for the loss? The same causes produce the same effects. An army may be raised on pretence of helping a friend; or many pretences might be used. That night, sir, ought to be a sufficient warning against standing armies, except in cases of great emergency. They are too frequently used for no other purpose than dragooning the people into slavery. But I beseech you, my countrymen, for the sake of your posterity, to act like those worthy men who have stood forth in defence of the rights of mankind, and show to the world that you will not submit to tyranny. What occasion have we for standing armies? We fear no foe. If one should come upon us, we have a militia, which is our bulwark. Let Lexington witness that we have the means of defence among ourselves. If, during the last winter there was not much alacrity shown by the militia in turning out, we must consider that they were going to fight their countrymen.[3] Do you, sir, suppose that, had a British army invaded us at that time, such supineness would have been discovered? No, sir; to our enemies' dismay and discomfort, they would have felt the contrary; but against deluded, infatuated men they did not wish to exert their valor or their strength. Therefore, sir, I am utterly opposed to a standing army in time of peace.

1 *Debates*, II, pp. 130-131, 134-137.

2 See "Massachusetts Convention," February 4, 1788, p. 249, for further comments on the intent of this proposed amendment. Also see "Massachusetts Convention," February 6, 1788, p. 260, for Samuel Adams' motion to add protection for several specific individual rights (including the right to keep arms) to this proposed article.

3 A reference to Shays' Rebellion.

The Almanac-Maker February 2, 1788

Newspaper Article: Philadelphia *Pennsylvania Mercury* (excerpt)

[H]e conceives the number of representatives ought to be encreased at least to 400, and that of the senators to 200, and elected annually: And that a *declaration of rights* ought to form a part of the constitution, before the liberties of the people can be properly secured.

DHRC, II Mfm. Pa., p. 1649.

Thomas Jefferson (Paris) February 2, 1788
Letter: To William Stephens Smith (excerpt)

I am glad to learn by letters which come down to the 20th. of December that the new Constitution will undoubtedly be received by a sufficiency of the States to set it a going. Were I in America, I would advocate it warmly till nine should have adopted & then as warmly take, the other side to convince the remaining four that they ought not to come into it till the declaration of rights is annexed to it. By this means we should secure all the good of it, & procure so respectable an opposition as would induce the accepting states to offer a bill of rights. This would be the happiest turn the thing could take. I fear much the effects of the perpetual re-eligibility of the President. But it is not thought of in America, & have therefore no prospect of a change of that article. But I own it astonishes me to find such a change wrought in the opinions of our countrymen since I left them, as that three fourths of them should be contented to live under a system which leaves to their governors the power of taking from them the trial by jury in civil cases, freedom of religion, freedom of the press, freedom of commerce, the habeas corpus laws, & of yoking them with a standing army. This is a degeneracy in the principles of liberty to which I had given four centuries instead of four years. But I hope it will all come about. We are now vibrating between too much & too little government, & the pendulum will rest finally in the middle.

Ford, V, pp. 2-3. Also reprinted in DHRC, XIV, p. 500.

Massachusetts Convention February 4, 1788
Debates (excerpt)[1]

[Dr. JARVIS.]
When we talk of our wanting a bill of rights to the new Constitution, the first article proposed[2] must remove every doubt on this head; as, by positively securing what is not expressly delegated, it leaves nothing to the uncertainty of conjecture, or to the refinements of implication, but is an explicit reservation of every right and privilege which is nearest and most agreeable to the people. There has been scarcely an instance where the influence of Massachusetts has not been felt and acknowledged in the Union. In such a case, her voice will be heard, sir, and I am fully in sentiment, if these amendments are not ingrafted on the Constitution, it will be our own fault. The remaining seven states will have our example before them; and there

is a high probability that they, or at least some of them, will take our conduct as a precedent, and will perhaps assume the same mode of procedure. Should this be the fact, their influence will be united to ours. But your delegates will, besides, be subjected to a perpetual instruction, until its object is completed[.]

1 *Debates*, II, p. 153.

2 A reference to the first article of amendment to the Constitution proposed by John Hancock in the Massachusetts Convention, which stated: "That it be explicitly declared that all powers not expressly delegated by the aforesaid Constitution are reserved to the several states, to be by them exercised." See "Massachusetts Convention," February 1, 1788, p. 247 at note 2, for Samuel Adams' similar viewpoint on this article, and see "Massachusetts Convention," February 6, 1788, p. 260, for Adams' proposal to add a more explicit bill of rights (including the right to keep arms) to this article.

Marquis de Lafayette (Paris) February 4, 1788
Letter: To George Washington (excerpt)

We are Anxiously Waiting for the Result of the State Conventions—the New Constitution Has Been Much Examined and Admired By European Philosophers—It Seems the Want of a declaration of Rights, of An Insurance for the trial By juries, of a Necessary Rotation of the President, are, With the Extensive Powers of the Executive, the Principal Points objected to.—Mr Jefferson and Myself Have Agreed that those objections Appear'd to Us Both Well Grounded, But that None Should Be Started Untill Nine States Had Accepted the Confederation—then Amendments, if thought Convenient, Might Be Made to take in the dissidents—

DHRC, XIV, p. 501.

William Russell February 5, 1788
Letter: To Robert S. Russell

"I find Virginia and all the continent much puzzled about the new Constitution, as is the case here with us. I think there will be a great majority of my own opinion, which after due reflection is decidedly against it, as it is in its nature most dangerous to the liberties of man. I wish it to be amended at all events. The state of your mamma's health prevents me from offering my abilites in opposing it, or rather, advocating its amendment. I wish consequences may not produce much confusion, and it is to be hoped that all who have the good of posterity at heart, will mature all difference of opinion with the utmost calmness"

DHRC, VIII, note 3, pp. 324-325.

Philadelphia *Pennsylvania Herald* February 5, 1788[1]

The enemies of the new constitution, says a correspondent, rely as much on lies for the promotion of their cause, as on any other means. In Boston, a design to bribe the members of the convention, opposed to the proposed plan of government, with "large sums of money, brought from a neighbouring state," is announced in one of the papers. On enquiry it appears the writer dares not discover himself—but shelters his falsehood behind the liberty of the press—the printer will not give up his name. In this state the people are at one time alarmed with a report of disarming the militia, by order of council[2]—at another time, with "large orders for ammunition being sent to Europe"—again, a subscription is set on foot, for the purpose of bribing writers and printers! In fine, to enumerate the various rumours circulated to serve the basest purposes, viz. to generate a spirit of discord and disturbance, would be equally tedious and disgusting.

1 DHRC, II Mfm. Pa., p. 1373.

2 For other documents related to the controversy over the collection of publicly owned arms in Pennsylvania, and the complaint that this was intended to disarm the militia, see: "Jacob Trusty," December 19, 1787, p. 176; "Centinel IX," January 8, 1788, p. 191; Pennsylvania *Carlisle Gazette*, January 9, 1788, p. 194; "Trusty," January 10, 1788, p, 200; "Supreme Executive Council," January 10, 1788, p. 201; "An Old Militia Officer of 1776," January 18, 1788, p. 221; Philadelphia *Freeman's Journal*, January 23, 1788, p. 226; Philadelphia *Independent Gazetteer*, February 27, 1788, p. 286; "James de Caledonia IV," March 12, 1788, p. 298; "Aristocrotis," April [15], 1788, p. 334 at note 2; Philadelphia *Independent Gazetteer*, April 30, 1788, p. 340 at note 3.

Massachusetts Convention February 5, 1788

Debate (excerpt)

Dr. TAYLOR examined the observations of several gentlemen, who had said, that, had the Constitution been so predicated as to require a bill of rights to be annexed to it, it would have been the work of a year, and could not be contained but in volumes. This, if true, he said, was an argument in favor of one being annexed; but so far from its being the case, he believed any gentleman in that Convention could form one in a few hours, as he might take the bill of rights of Massachusetts for a guide. He concluded by objecting to the amendments, because no assurance was given that they ever would become a part of the system.

Mr. PARSONS demonstrated the impracticability of forming a bill, in a national constitution, for securing individual rights, and showed the inutility of the measure, from the ideas, that no power was given to Congress to infringe on any one of the natural rights of the people by this Constitution; and, should they attempt it without constitutional authority, the act would be a nullity, and could not be enforced.

Several other gentlemen spoke in a desultory conversation on the amendments. It was urged again and again, on one side, that it was uncertain whether they ever would be interwoven in the Constitution, and that, therefore, they could not vote for it, on that precarious condition. On the other side, the importance of the opinion of Massachusetts, in other states, in determining on great political questions, the general nature of the amendments proposed, &c., were repeatedly urged in favor of their being a part of the ratification.

Debates, II, pp. 161-162.

Agrippa XVIII February 5, 1788
Newspaper Article: Boston *Massachusetts Gazette* (excerpts)

TO THE MASSACHUSETTS CONVENTION.

Gentlemen,

In my last address I ascertained, from historical records, the following principles: that, in the original state of government, the whole power resides in the whole body of the nation, that when a people appoint certain persons to govern them, they delegate their whole power; that a constitution is not in itself a bill of rights; and that, whatever is the form of government, a bill of rights is essential to the security of the persons and property of the people. It is an idea favourable to the interest of mankind at large, that government is founded in compact. . . .

I know it is often asked against whom in a government by representation is a bill of rights to secure us? I answer, that such a government is indeed a government by ourselves; but as a just government protects all alike, it is necessary that the sober and industrious part of the community should be defended from the rapacity and violence of the vicious and idle. A bill of rights, therefore, ought to set forth the purposes for which the compact is made, and serves to secure the minority against the usurpation and tyranny of the majority. It is a just observation of his excellency, doctor Adams, in his learned defence of the American constitutions that unbridled passions produce the same effect, whether in a king, nobility, or a mob. The experience of all mankind has proved the prevalence of a disposition to use power wantonly. It is therefore as necessary to defend an individual against the majority in a republick as against the king in a monarchy. Our state constitution has wisely guarded this point. The present confederation has also done it. . . . If the new constitution means no more than the friends of it acknowledge, they certainly can have no objection to affixing a declaration in favor of the rights of states and of citizens, especially as a majority of the states have not yet voted upon it.

"Resolved, that the constitution lately proposed for the United States be received only upon the following conditions: . . .

"13. Nothing in this constitution shall deprive a citizen of any state of the benefit of the bill of rights established by the constitution of the state in which he shall reside, and such bill of rights shall be considered as valid in any court of the United States where they shall be pleaded."

Essays, p. 115-119. The "Agrippa" series is reprinted in Storing, IV, starting on p. 68.

The State Soldier II February 6, 1788
Newspaper Article: *Virginia Independent Chronicle* (excerpts)

It is well known that several of the states on the continent have never made any formal declaration of their rights. Well aware of the impossibility of enumerating all those blessings to which by nature they were entitled, and highly sensible of the danger there was intrusting to their recollection of them (knowing that when once they attempted to set to them legal bounds, what ever should by chance be left out, was of course given up) some of the states more prudently thought fit to enumerate on the other hand what should be the powers of their government, when of course what ever was omited on that side, remained as their natural and inviolable rights on the other. And but few states in the world have deemed it safe to do otherwise. . . .

And to forge indiscriminately now those states into a declaration of their rights, who may think it still unsafe to rely on a bare recital of them, particularly in a general government which at its commencement must involve its authors in too great a variety of difficulties and cares, to be sufficiently mindful of every natural right necessary to be secured to each particular state, would be as unjust and inconsistent with our former pretentions, as its natural consequence—the separation of the states—would be contrary to that policy which gave us success.

But why need I labour thus to prove what is in itself so definitely clear?—The constitution itself admits of no amendments till put in force. To adopt it or reject it is all we have to do—

DHRC, VIII, pp. 352-353.

An Old Whig VIII February 6, 1788

Newspaper Article: Philadelphia *Independent Gazetteer*

Mr. PRINTER, It is the fate of political controversies to begin with argument and end with abuse: And hence we find, in many instances, that a subject which for a time, has engaged the most earnest attention of the people, is at length quitted with horror and disgust. The question, however, concerning the total adoption of the plan of government, proposed by the late federal convention, is too important for good men to suffer themselves to be diverted from giving it a full consideration by the bouncing of squibs or the whizzing of political firebrands. I therefore persuade myself that a few candid observations on this subject will yet be heard with attention.

The real question is this;—Whether the people of this country ought to adopt the proposed constitution in its present form, without limitation or alteration, or whether we ought to insist upon amendments being made previous to its adoption.

Most men seem to agree that amendments ought to be made in the proposed plan in some stage of the business; and all seem agreed that an efficient form of continental government ought to be established. Shall we then first adopt the constitution and afterwards amend it; or shall we first amend it and afterwards adopt it? Let us for a moment consider the propriety of adopting it first, and trusting to its being afterwards amended. These necessary amendments, after the constitution is adopted, can only be made in one or two ways;—either by our future rulers in the continental legislature by their own act—or in the way provided for in the fifth article, by a convention to be called for proposing amendments, whenever two-thirds of both houses shall deem it necessary, or whenever the legislatures of two-thirds of the states shall make application for that purpose, such amendments afterwards to be valid if ratified by the legislatures of three-fourths of the states, or by conventions in three-fourths thereof, if Congress should think proper to call them. This latter mode is so intricate, that an attempt to investigate it is like endeavouring to trace the windings of a labyrinth, and I have therefore observed that people willingly turn aside from the subject, as confused and disgusting. Some former observations on this article I found were very little attended to: However I will attempt once more to find a clue to its mazes, after I shall first have considered that more inviting ground of expectation to which most of those who assume the name of federalists turn their eyes with so much confidence.

First then, the general expectation seems to be that our future rulers will rectify all that is amiss. If a bill of rights is wanting, they will frame a bill of rights. If too much power is vested in them, they will not abuse it; nay, they will divest themselves of it. The very first thing they will do, will be to establish the liberties of the people by good and wholesome ordinances, on so solid a foundation as to baffle all future encroachments from themselves or their sucessors. Much good no doubt might be done in this way; if Congress should possess the most virtuous inclinations, yet there are some things which it will not be in their power to rectify. For instance; *the appellate jurisdiction both as to law and fact,* which is given to the supreme court of the continent, and which annihilates the trial by jury in all civil causes, the Congress can only modify:—They cannot extinguish this power, so destructive to the principles of real liberty. It would not by any means be extravagant to say, that a new continental convention ought to be called, if it were only for the sake of preserving that sacred palladium—THE INESTIMABLE RIGHT OF TRIAL BY JURY.—But even if we were to delude ourselves so far as to believe that it would be entirely in the power of the future legislature to set every thing right, to build up our liberties against all invasions, and to protect us from every political calamity, still we ought not to repose all our liberty and all our happiness in the virtue of our future rulers. I speak not with reference to any particular set of men. I pretend not to know who will be our rulers one year hence. In the state of Pennsylvania I have seen the administration of our constitution in the hands of its bitterest enemies, during near one half of its existence; and I shall not be at all surprized to find that if the new continental government shall be set a-going, that the jockies who at present have vaulted into the saddle; should be the first to be thrown into the dirt and trampled upon; nor, on the other hand, that some of those who are foremost in contending for a permanent security to the rights of the people, should be in the first rank of oppressors. These things have frequently happened; and the only safe way of reasoning on political subjects is, to consider men, abstractly as men, with like passions and infirmities throughout the world, in every age, and every country; and to believe that the same guards and checks against arbitrary power, which were necessary two thousand years ago, are equally necessary at present, and will be so two thousand years hence. Idolatry is the parent of errors in politics as well as religion;—and an implicit confidence in our rulers now, will be abused as much as implicit confidence in priests ever was in the days of superstition. I know well that instances of political moderation may be found, and a tyrant has before now descended from the plenitude of power, satiated with dominion, or worn out with care; but there in not one instance on record in all history of a number of men voluntarily abandoning the powers of an aristocracy. Look at the Decemviri, look at the thirty tyrants of Athens, look at all the lordly aristocracies that ever existed, and shew me one instance—such an instance cannot be shewn. Nay farther, a single monarch has many times used his power with moderation; but a number of men combined in an aristocracy, never knew what moderation meant. They are all struggling to be most powerful, all aiming to enrich themselves and provide for their friends, and all of them plundering the people. And shall we foolishly, after so many thousand examples, trust to the virtue and moderation of our future rulers, to divest themselves of those powers which may be abused to our prejudice, and are no way useful to our protection? Not to insist upon Swift's ludicrous tale of Jack's hanging himself at the instigation of Humphry Hocus, on the promise of being cut down before he should be dead, and when he had hanged himself, of being left to kick his heels in the air, the moral of which, by the bye, is strictly founded in human nature;—let us attend to a more serious fable.—"A man, says Aesop, coming into a wood, begged the trees to grant him the favor of a handle to his axe. The whole forest consented; upon which he provided himself with a strong handle; which he had no sooner done, than he began to fell the trees without number, then the trees, though too late, repented of their weakness, and an universal groan was heard throughout the forest. At length, when the man came to cut down the tree which had furnished him with the handle, the trunk fell to the ground uttering these words: Fool that I was! I have been the cause of my own destruction." If we perish in America, we shall have no better comfort than the same mortifying reflection, that we have been the cause of our own destruction.

I have said that many of the liberties which, by the proposed constitution, are to be surrendered up into the hands of our rulers, will be of no use towards the protection of the people; and a little reflection will convice us, that it is certainly the case. If, indeed, government were really strengthened by such surrender, if the body of the people were made more secure, or more happy by the means, we ought to make the sacrifice. An individual ought to submit to be tossed about, imprisoned and treated injuriously, if the good of his country should require it; and every individual in the community ought to strip himself of some convenience for the sake of the public good.

I know it is an error not uncommon to believe, that a government is the more powerful in proportion as it is more tyrannical; but this is not the case: so far from it, that it has always been found, that free countries have been able to exert powers far superior to those in which a more absolute government prevailed. For instance, a senate which is master of its own elections, without any or with very little dependence on the people, would not be able to exert as much force as a senate which is freely elected by the people; because the chearful support which would be yielded in the latter case, would far exceed that which could be exacted by the mere force of authority. Again; how could the stripping people of the right of trial by jury conduce to the strength of the state? Do we find the government in England at all weakened by the people retaining the right of trial by jury? Far from it. Yet these things which merely tend to oppress the people, without conducing at all to the strength of the state, are the last which aristocratic rulers would consent to restore to the people; because they encrease the personal power and importance of the rulers. Judges, unincumbered by juries, have been ever found much better friends to government than to the people. Such judges will always be more desireable than juries to a self-created senate, upon the same principle that a large standing army, and the entire command of the militia and of the purse, is ever desireable to those who wish to enslave the people, and upon the same principle that a bill of rights is their aversion.

In like manner, if we should trace the several branches of the proposed constitution, which are obnoxious to the liberties of the people, we shall find them to consist of such articles as are rather fitted to encrease the powers of the rulers, than the strength of the nation. Union is the great source of strength to a nation, not vassalage. To an aristocratic government vassalage is the great object even at the expence of union among the people. We ought not, therefore, by any means to rely upon the virtue of our future rulers for a reformation of those things which at present are amiss in the proposed constitution. The president and senate will ever be grasping at more and more power until they are completely masters of the people, and the president at last master of all.

Let us then turn to the article in the proposed constitution, which provides for the making alterations at some future period; and let us figure to ourselves the time when two-thirds of both houses of Congress shall think it necessary to call a convention, or two-thirds of the legislatures of the individual states shall apply for the calling of a convention, and when a continental convention shall agree upon amendments, and when the legislatures of three-fourths of the states, or three-fourths of the conventions to be called in the several states, if Congress shall prefer that mode of proceeding, shall ratify such amendments; and again, after all these strainings, and filtrings, and refinings, of the hopes and expectations of the people through the channels of power, when the amendments so asked for, proposed, digested, twistificated, altered, and at last ratified, will be of any essential importance. For my part I would full as soon sit down and take my chance of winning an important privilege to the people, by the casting the dice 'till I could throw sixes an hundred times in succession.—There is no doubt but the thing has been purposely contrived to make alterations extremely difficult; and so it certainly ought to be if the proposed constitution were a good one. I do not therefore so much blame the late federal convention for making their constitution very difficult of alteration, as I insist upon it as an argument in favor of making our amendments beforehand. A machine which cannot be taken to pieces after it is once set a-going, ought to be very well finished at first.

Yet this is not all the difficulty. Inveterate power is at all times very hard to be controuled. Habits, connexions, dependence, and a thousand circumstances in course of time, rivet the chains of slavery 'till we grow either callous to their galling, or too feeble to shake them off, or too listless to resist. Ask the beaten Turk to resume his liberty, or the tired horse to resume his pristine freedom.—As well might you ask the galled sons of America, a few years hence, to assert the native rights of men, if the proposed constitution be once fixed upon us. It will be extremely difficult to change it for the better even in the beginning; but in a little time it will become utterly impossible.

A little prudence, a little patience, and a little serious reflection, would lead us to concur in calling a new convention, to revise the constitution proposed to us. That convention, I have no doubt, if fully, freely, and deliberately chosen, would concur in some essential amendments; and we might yet be a united and a happy people.

DHRC, XVI, pp. 52-56.

Philadelphiensis IX February 6, 1788

Newspaper Article: Philadelphia *Freeman's Journal* (excerpts)

My Fellow-Citizens, Before *martial law* is declared to be the supreme law of the land, and your character of free citizens be changed to that of the subjects of a *military king,* which are necessary consequences of the adoption of the proposed constitution, let me admonish you in the name of *sacred liberty*, to make a solemn pause. Permit a freeman to address you, and to solicit your attention to a cause wherein yourselves and your posterity are concerned. The sun never shone upon a more important one: It is the cause of freedom—of a whole continent—of yourselves and of your fellow men.

Men who have so gloriously asserted the rights of human nature, and overcome tyranny, one ought reasonably to suppose could not have their spirits so much broken as peaceably to submit to it a few years afterwards. By the declaration of peace, wherein Britain acknowledged the independence and sovereignty of the United States, the people of America became citizens of the freest country under heaven. But under the proposed plan of government the least fragment of liberty cannot exist.

The writers against the proposed constitution are denominated, by the *aristocratics*, [as] *incendiaries*, and enemies to America, men whose writings tend to involve this devoted country in anarchy, and in all the horrors of a civil war. Now, in reply to this charge; let me ask the friends of this government, Is that man an *incendiary* who advocates the unalienable rights of the people? Is he an enemy to America who endeavors to protect the *oppressed* from the *oppressor;* who opposes a conspiracy against the liberties of his country, concerted by a few *tyrants*, whose views are to lord it over the rest of their fellow citizens, to trample the poorer part of the people under their feet, that they may be rendered their servants and slaves? If such a writer is an incendiary, and an enemy to America, then I glory in the character. . . .

The thoughts of a military officer possessing such powers, as the proposed constitution vests in the president general, are sufficient to excite in the mind of a freeman the most alarming apprehensions; and ought to rouse him to oppose it at *all events*. Every freeman of America ought to hold up this idea to himself, *that he has no superior but God and the laws*. But this tyrant will be so much his superior, that he can at any time he thinks proper, order him out in the militia to exercise, and to march when and where he pleases. His officers can wantonly inflict the most disgraceful punishment on a peaceable citizen, under pretence of disobedience, or the smallest neglect of militia duty. . . .

To such lengths have these bold conspirators carried their scheme of despotism, that your most sacred rights and privileges are surrendered at discretion. When government thinks proper, under the pretence of writing a libel, &c. it may imprison, inflict the most cruel and unusual punishment, seize property, carry on prosecution, &c. and the unfortunate citizen has no *magna charta*, no *bill of rights*, to protect him; nay, the prosecution may be carried on in such a manner that even a *jury* will not be allowed him. Where is that *base slave* who would not appeal to the *ultima ratio*, before he submits to this government?

If the despots persist in pushing it on, let them answer the consequences; they may fall a sacrifice to their own obstinacy; for liberty will triumph over every obstacle, even were a *standing army* opposed to it.

To preserve the peace of the country, every patriot should exert himself at this awful crisis, and use his influence to have another federal convention called as soon as possible; either to amend the old articles of confederation, or to frame a constitution on revolution principles, that may secure the freedom of America to the remotest time.

DHRC, XVI, p. 57-59. The "Philadelphiensis" series is reprinted in Storing, III, starting on p. 99.

Massachusetts Convention February 6, 1788
Debates (excerpts)

The Hon. Mr. ADAMS introduced some amendments, to be added to those reported by the committee; but, they not meeting the approbation of those gentlemen whose minds they were intended to ease, after they were debated a considerable time, the honorable gentleman withdrew them.[1]

A motion was made and seconded, that the report of the Committee made on Monday last, be amended, so far as to add the following to the first article[2] therein mentioned, viz.: "And that the said Constitution be never construed to authorize Congress to infringe the just liberty of the press, or the rights of conscience; or to prevent the people of the United States, who are peaceable citizens, from keeping their own arms; or to raise standing armies, unless when necessary for the defence of the United States, or of some one or more of them; or to prevent the people from petitioning, in a peaceable and orderly manner, the federal legislature, for a redress of grievances; or to subject the people to unreasonable searches and seizures of their persons, papers or possessions." And the question being put, was determined in the negative.[3,4]

[Rev. Mr. STILLMAN.]

After all, if this Constitution was as perfect as the sacred volume is, it would not secure the liberties of the people, unless they watch their own liberties. Nothing written on paper will do this. It is therefore necessary that the people should keep a watchful, not an over-jealous, eye on their rulers; and that they should give all due encouragement to our colleges, schools of learning, &c., so that knowledge may be diffused through every part of our country. Ignorance and slavery, knowledge and freedom, are inseparably connected. While Americans remain in their present enlightened condition, and warmly attached to the cause of liberty, they cannot be enslaved. Should the general government become so lost to all sense of honor and the freedom of the people, as to attempt to enslave them, they who are the descendants of a race of men who have dethroned kings, would make an American Congress tremble, strip them of their public honors, and reduce them to the lowest state of degradation.[5]

[Ratification: Vote 187 for, 168 against]

The Convention having impartially discussed, and fully considered, the Constitution for the United States of America, reported to Congress by the Convention of Delegates from the United States of America, and submitted to us by a resolution of the General Court of the said Commonwealth, passed the 25th day of October last past,—and acknowledging, with grateful hearts, the goodness of the Supreme Ruler of the universe in affording the people of the United States, in the course of his providence, an opportunity, deliberately and peaceably, without fraud or surprise, of entering into an explicit and solemn compact with each other, by assenting to and ratifying a new Constitution, in order to form a more perfect union, establish justice, insure domestic tranquillity, provide for the common defence, promote the general welfare, and secure the blessings of liberty to themselves and their posterity,—do, in the name and in behalf of the people of the commonwealth of Massachusetts, assent to and ratify the said Constitution for the United States of America.

And as it is the opinion of this Convention, that certain amendments and alterations in the said Constitution would remove the fears, and quiet the apprehensions, of many of the good people of this commonwealth, and more effectually guard against an undue administration of the federal government,—the Convention do therefore recommend that the following alterations and provisions be introduced into the said Constitution:—

I. That it be explicitly declared that all powers not expressly delegated by the aforesaid Constitution are reserved to the several states, to be by them exercised.

II. That there shall be one representative to every thirty thousand persons, according to the census mentioned in the Constitution, until the whole number of the representatives amounts to two hundred.

III. That Congress do not exercise the powers vested in them by the 4th section of the 1st article, but in cases where a state shall neglect or refuse to make the regulations therein mentioned, or shall make regulations subversive of the rights of the people to a free and equal representation in Congress, agreeably to the Constitution.

IV. That Congress do not lay direct taxes but when the moneys arising from the impost and excise are insufficient for the public exigencies, nor then until Congress shall have first made a requisition upon the states to assess, levy, and pay, their respective proportions of such requisition, agreeably to the census fixed in the said Constitution, in such way and manner as the legislatures of the states shall think best; and in such case, if any state shall neglect or refuse to pay its proportion, pursuant to such requisition, then Congress may assess and levy such state's proportion, together with interest thereon at the rate of six per cent. per annum, from the time of payment prescribed in such requisition.

V. That Congress erect no company of merchants with exclusive advantages of commerce.

VI. That no person shall be tried for any crime by which he may incur an infamous punishment, or loss of life, until he be first indicted by a grand jury, except in such cases as may arise in the government and regulation of the land and naval forces.

VII. The Supreme Judicial Federal Court shall have no jurisdiction of causes between citizens of different states, unless the matter in dispute, whether it concerns the realty or personalty, be of the value of three thousand dollars at the least; nor shall the federal judicial powers extend to any actions between citizens of different states, where the matter in dispute, whether it concerns the realty or personalty, is not of the value of fifteen hundred dollars at least.

VIII. In civil actions between citizens of different states, every issue of fact, arising in actions at common law, shall be tried by a jury, if the parties, or either of them, request it.

IX. Congress shall at no time consent that any person, holding an office of trust or profit under the United States, shall accept of a title of nobility, or any other title or office, from any king, prince, or foreign state.

And the Convention do, in the name and in behalf of the people of this commonwealth, enjoin it upon their representatives in Congress, at all times, until the alterations and provisions aforesaid have been considered, agreeably to the 5th article of the said Constitution, to exert all their influence, and use all reasonable and legal methods, to obtain a ratification of the said alterations and provisions, in such manner as is provided in the said article.

And that the United States in Congress assembled may have due notice of the assent and ratification of the said Constitution by this Convention, it is *Resolved,* That the assent and ratification aforesaid be engrossed on parchment, together with the recommendation and injunction aforesaid, and with this resolution; and that his excellency, John Hancock, Esq., president, and the Hon. William Cushing, Esq., vice-president of this Convention, transmit the same, countersigned by the secretary of the Convention, under their hands and seals, to the United States in Congress assembled.

JOHN HANCOCK, *President*
WILLIAM CUSHING, *Vice-President*
GEORGE RICHARDS MINOT, *Secretary.*[6]

1 *Debates,* II, p. 162.

2 A reference to the first article of amendment to the Constitution proposed by John Hancock and adopted by the Massachusetts Convention, which stated: "That it be explicitly declared that all powers not expressly delegated by the aforesaid Constitution are reserved to the several states, to be by them exercised." Samuel Adams attempted to add specific bill of rights provisions to this article. See "Massachusetts Convention," February 1, 1788, p. 247 at note 2 for Samuel Adams' understanding that this article was "a summary of a bill of rights." See "Massachusetts Convention," February 4, 1788, p. 249, for a similar statement by Mr. Jarvis.

3 *Massachusetts,* pp. 86-87.

4 The following contemporary observations of Jeremy Belknap relate to these amendments proposed by Samuel Adams:

> "S. Adams offered some additional amendments to secure the rights of conscience, liberty of the press, right to keep arms, protection of persons and property from seizure, &c.; which *gave an alarm to both parties.* The Antifederalists supposed that so great a politician would not offer these amendments, unless he thought there was danger on these points. The Federalists were afraid the new converts would desert. Adams perceived the mishief, and withdrew his proposal. Another renewed it; but it was voted out, and Adams himself was obliged to vote against it: . . .
>
> "It was matter of speculation how Mr. Adams came to propose *such* amendments. Many suspicions were formed; and some thought he *meant* to overthrow the Constitution. Certainly it was the worst blow which had been given to it. In a week or two afterward came along a *protest* of the Pennsylvania minority, in which these very things are objected to the Constitution which he proposed to guard against by his motion. It is said the copies of these protests were purposely detained on the road; but it is supposed Adams had a copy in a letter before the Convention was dissolved. . . .
>
> "Adams, in the course of debate in Convention, said but little: what he said was *rather in favor* of the Constitution. When it came to the last pinch, his introduced amendments had well-nigh overset it. When he perceived the uneasiness in the minds of both parties, he withdrew his motion. One of the Antifederalists revived it. Adams then opposed it; said he should vote against it, and actually did so. But it is thought his manoeuvre lost several votes for the Constitution.["]

The above excerpts from Belknap's *Minutes* are contained in *Proceedings of the Massachusetts Historical Society,* III, pp. 302-304.

5 *Debates,* II, pp. 160-170.

6 *Debates*, I, pp. 322-323.

Thomas Jefferson (Paris) February 6, 1788
Letter: To James Madison (excerpt)

I am glad to hear that the New Constitution is received with favor. I sincerely wish that the 9 first conventions may receive, & the 4 last reject it. The former will secure it finally, while the latter will oblige them to offer a declaration of rights in order to complete the union. We shall thus have all it's good, and cure it's principal defect. You will of course be so good as to continue to mark to me it's progress.

Ford, V, p. 5. Reprinted in *Papers*, X, p. 474.

Thomas Jefferson (Paris) February 7, 1788
Letter: To Alexander Donald (excerpt)

I wish with all my soul that the nine first Conventions may accept the new Constitution, because this will secure to us the good it contains, which I think great & important. But I equally wish that the four latest conventions, whichever they be, may refuse to accede to it till a declaration of rights be annexed. This would probably command the offer of such a declaration, & thus give to the whole fabric, perhaps as much perfection as any one of that kind ever had. By a declaration of rights I mean one which shall stipulate freedom of religion, freedom of the press, freedom of commerce against monopolies, trial by juries in all cases, no suspensions of the habeas corpus, no standing armies. These are fetters against doing evil which no honest government should decline.

DHRC, VIII, pp. 353-354. Reprinted in Bergh, VI, pp. 425-426.

Anti-Foederalist Nos. I & II February 8, 1788
Newspaper Articles: Exeter *Freeman's Oracle* (excerpts)

Anti-Foederalist, No. I.

To the Inhabitants of New-Hampshire.
The grand topick of the day is the New-Constitution, much has been said for, much has been said against it by able writers—On one side, it is warmly asserted, that the liberties of the people, are sufficiently

secure, as it now stands—On the other it is urged with equal vehemence, they are not, amendments must be made—a Bill of Rights prefixed, or we are undone; so that it is very difficult, for common people to know what is right, any thing that may serve to throw light upon the subject, may be very useful at this juncture. . . .

A Friend to the Rights of the People[1]

Anti-Foederalist, No. II. . . .

It has been said by Mr. Wilson, in support of this Constitution, and against a Bill of Rights, who dare be bold enough to enumerate all the Rights of a people: Such sophistical assertions may do for his phlegmatick Germans, but will not answer for the bold, free and enterprizing people of New-Hampshire—Every honest man ought to be bold enough to declare his rights—at least, such great and essential ones, as never ought to be trusted to the caprice of any set of men—And you, gentlemen, I hope will be bold enough to spurn at a Constitution, offered you without a Bill of Rights; and receive none unless the most essential ones are enumerated—But I shall say no more on this particular, as abler pens have gone before me.— . . .

A Friend to the Republick.[2]

1 Storing, IV, p. 235.
2 *Ibid.*, p. 243.

Candour February 12, 1788
Newspaper Article: Philadelphia *Independent Gazetteer* (excerpt)

I am not now surprised that so much exertion was made to prevent discussion [of the constitution]. I am not surprised that a convention was to be called at ten days notice, in this state—My eyes are now opened—and I am determined hence forward to oppose what is confessedly a system of despotism, and endeavor to procure amendments, and have a bill of rights affixed to it.

DHRC, II Mfm. Pa., p. 1700.

Thomas Jefferson (Paris) February 12, 1788
Letter: To C.W.F. Dumas (excerpt)

With respect to the new government, 9. or 10. states will probably have accepted it by the end of this month. The others may oppose it.

Virginia I think will be of this number. Besides other objections of less moment, she will insist on annexing a bill of rights to the new constitution, i.e. a bill wherein the government shall declare that 1. Religion shall be free. 2. Printing presses free. 3. Trials by jury preserved in all cases. 4. No monopolies in commerce. 5. No standing army. Upon receiving this bill of rights, she will probably depart from her other objections; and this bill is so much of the interest of all the states that I presume they will offer it, and thus our constitution be amended and our union closed by the end of the present year. In this way there will have been opposition enough to do good, and not enough to do harm. I have such reliance on the good sense of the body of the people and the honesty of their leaders, that I am not afraid of their letting things go wrong to any length in any case.

BRDH, I, pp. 613-614.

A Farmer I February 15, 1788
Newspaper Article: Baltimore *Maryland Gazette* (excerpts)[1]

When men, to whom the guardianship of public liberty has been committed, discover a neglect if not contempt for a bill of rights—when they answer reasons by alledging a fact,—which fact too, is no fact at all—it beomes a duty to bear testimony against such conduct, for silence and acquiescence in political language are synonimous terms. . . .

That men who profess an attachment to the liberty of the press, should also require names, is one of those instances of human weakness and inconsistency, that deserves rather pity than resentment. Political as well as religious freedom has ever been and forever will be destroyed by that invariable tendency of enthusiasts and bigots to mark out as objects of public resentment and persecution, those who presume to dispute their opinions or question their infallibility—and whilst there are men, enthusiasm and bigotry will prevail—it is the natural predominance of the passions over reason—The citizens of America are not yet so agitated by the phrenzy of innovation as to forget—that the object of public inquiry is, or ought to be, *truth*—that to convert *truth* into *falsehood, right* into *wrong,* is equally beyond the reach of the *good,* the *bad,* the *great* and the *humble*—A great name may indeed *impose falsehood* for *truth*—*wrong* for *right*—and whenever such voluntarily offer themselves, there may be ground for suspicion—But the people may listen with safety to those, who assert no other claim to their attention, than the *reason* and *merit* of their remarks. . . .

I will confine my inquiry to the English constitution—Example *there,* is in a great measure law *here*—and the authority of an American judge on a point of English law, should be digested with coolness and promulgated with caution, because it is frequently conclusory.

The celebrated and only bill of rights of Great-Britain, which is considered as the supreme law of the land, and not to be questioned or impeached in their courts, was the work of that convention of lords and commons in 1688, which declared that *King James 2d, had abdicated the crown, and that the throne had thereby become vacant,* and who after they had compleated and asserted this glorious declaration of the unalienable rights of their fellow citizens, pursuing the peculiar duty of a convention, conferred the crown of the three kingdoms on an alien and foreigner, William the 3d.

Can any man imagine that this convention could at that time, have considered these rights as the grant of a King, whom they previously declared to have abdicated the throne, or the gracious concessions of a Prince whom they were about to deprive forever of the crown? Or could they have considered this bill of rights as the concession of Prince William, at that time a foreigner and alien, not entitled to hold a foot of land, or any of the common rights of citizenship, and who could afterwards only derive his title to the crown from the same source, which gave authority and sanction to this fundamental and most inestimable law? or, could the British nation at that time, or ever since, have viewed this declaration, as the grant and concession of a King or Prince, when no King or Prince was at that time in existence?—but should there remain any minds yet unsatisfied, I refer such to the debates of that convention, which are preserved in Grey's debates in parliament, and there will be found in them, the principles of equal liberty, the inherent and unalienable rights of men, as amply and ably discussed, and as fully recognized by the authors of that blessing, the artists of that British palladium, as ever they have since been by the animated patriots of America, or the present age.—I also refer them to an inestimable little treatise composed on this occasion by that accomplished lawyer and patriot, afterwards the Lord Somers—High Chancellor of Great-Britain—then a member of the convention, and chiefly instrumental in their great work—a pamphlet that should find a place in the library of every American judge at least—Whoever peruses these, will discover undeniable evidence, that the British convention, considered this their declaration, as the concession of no Prince, but the Prince of Heaven—whom alone they acknowledged as the author of their liberties—they will there find that a bill of rights, is an enumeration of those conditions on which the individuals of the empire agreed to confirm the social compact; and consequently that no power, which they thus conditionally delegated to the majority (in whatever form organized) should be so exercised as to infringe and impair these their natural rights—not vested in SOCIETY, but reserved to each member thereof.

This was not the doctrine of that period alone—It was the common law and constitution of England, so asserted and maintained by the ablest lawyers of every age of the empire. . . .

If I understand Aristides, he says that it would have been considered as an arrogant usurpation of sovereign rights in the members of convention, to have affixed a bill of rights—Can he reconcile this position with another opinion in his remarks, where he maintains that in offering this constitution, they could only act as private individuals, any of whom have a right to propose a constitution to the Americans to adopt at their discretion—In this view they could only have proposed—it is certain they could not have enacted a bill of rights—Nor would there have been any usurpation in WE *the people, of the States of New Hampshire, Massachusetts, &c. securing to ourselves and our posterity the following unalienable rights, &c.* which is the stile of the new constitution—The convention have actually engrafted some of these natural rights, yet no one calls it an usurpation—nor can I believe that any of my fellow-citizens of the United States, would have discovered the least indignation, had they engrafted them all—The universal complaint has been that they have enumerated so few—But says Aristides, it would have been a work of great difficulty, if not impossible to have ascertained them—Are the fundamental rights of mankind at this day unknown? Are they so soon forgot? If they are not imprinted on our hearts, they are in several of the constitutions[2]—Although various in form, they are certainly not contradictory in substance—It did not require the wisdom of a national convention to have reduced them into order, and such as would not have gained the suffrage of a majority, would never have been regretted by America—or, I will venture to assert, what I shall never believe, that the majority were very unworthy of the trust reposed in them—Nor yet can I believe, that the late convention were incompetent to a task that has never been undertaken in the separate States without success.

This constitution is to be the act of the individual members of the American empire—the highest source of terrestrial power with us—As it is a subsequent act, it not only repeals all prior acts of the same authority where it interferes with them—But being a government of the people of all the States, I do not know what right the citizens of Maryland for instance, have to expect that the citizens of Connecticut or New-Jersey, will be governed by the laws or constitution of Maryland—or what benefit a citizen of Maryland could derive from his bill of rights in a court of the United States, which can only be governed by the constitution and laws of the United States—Nor will it help the question to say, what will certainly be denied, that the future Congress may provide by law for this,—that an ordinary law of the United States can make, is an admission that it can unmake, and to submit the bills of rights of the separate States to the power of every annual national parliament, is a very uncertain tenure indeed.

If a citizen of Maryland can have no benefit of his own bill of rights in the confederal courts, and there is no bill of rights of the United States—how could he take advantage of a natural right founded in reason, could he plead it and produce Locke, Sydney, or Montesquieu as authority? How could he take advantage of any of the common law rights, which have heretofore been considered as the birthright of Englishmen and their descendants, could he plead them and produce the authority of the English judges in his support? Unquestionably not, for the authority of the common law arises from the express adoption by the several States in their respective constitutions, and that in various degrees and under different modifications—If admitted at all, I do not see to what extent, and if admitted, it must be admitted as unalterable by ordinary acts of legislation, which would be impossible—and it could never be of use to an individual, but in combating some national law infringing natural right.—To render this more intelligible—suppose for instance, that an officer of the United States should force the house, the asylum of a citizen, by virtue of a general warrant, I would ask, are general warrants illegal by the constitution of the United States? Would a court, or even a jury, but juries are no longer to exist, punish a man who acted by express authority, upon the bare recollection of what once was law and right? I fear not, especially in those cases which may strongly interest the passions of government, and in such only have general warrants been used— . . .

The truth is, that the rights of individuals are frequently opposed to the apparent interests of the majority—For this reason the greater the portion of political freedom in a form of government the greater the necessity of a bill of rights—often the natural rights of an individual are opposed to the presumed interests or heated passions of a large majority of [ ] democratic government; if these rights are not clearly and expressly ascertained, the individual must be lost; and for the truth of this I appeal to every man who has borne a part in the legislative councils of America. In such government the tyranny of the legislative is most to be dreaded.

1 Storing, V, p. 9-15.
2 See Appendix A, p. 747, for the state declarations or bills of rights and related constitutional provisions.

George Nicholas (Charlottesville) February 16, 1788

The last objection that we shall take notice of (for the bounds of a letter will prevent me from going as far as I could wish) is that so much power is given to Congress by this new government that our liberties will be endangered.

If we supposed this true we should be amongst the last persons in America who would advocate this measure; but we can truly say that we are well convinced there is no such [danger?]. We also assert to you as a fact that if the new government shall take place the people of Virginia will part with no more power than they have done already, and that Congress and the legislature of the state will together have no greater power or authority than the present Congress and the legislature of the state now possess: and the only difference will be that of the powers already parted with by the people, under the new government Congress will have a greater share and the legislature of the state less than they now respectively enjoy. Thus the bulk of the people will be greatly benefited because without their parting with any greater share of their natural rights and privileges they will live under a government which will be much better calculated to secure their welfare and prosperity than the one under which they now live. And you may find that it is only a dispute about who shall have the power already given away by the people[.]

DHRC, VIII, pp. 373-374. See source for information on this excerpt.

William Fleming (Botetourt Co., Virginia) February 19, 1788

Letter: To Thomas Madison (excerpt)

I am for the Constitution with such amendments as will secure the liberty of the Subject, for of all Governments an Oligarchy is the worst, and power once parted with can never be reclaimed without bloodshed—

DHRC, XVI, p. 141.

The Impartial Examiner February 20, 1788
Newspaper Article: *Virginia Independent Chronicle* (excerpts)[1]

To the free people of VIRGINIA.

Countrymen and Fellow-Citizens, . . .

In pursuing this address I beg leave to premise that the only true point of distinction between arbitrary and free governments seems to be, that in the former the governors are invested with powers of acting according to their own wills, without any other limits than what they themselves may understand to be necessary for the general good; whereas in the latter they are intrusted with no such unlimited authority, but are restrained in their operations to conform to certain fundamental principles, the preservation whereof is expressly stipulated for in the *civil compact:* and whatever is not so stipulated for is virually and impliedly given up. Societies so constituted invest their supreme governors with ample powers of exerting themselves according to their own judgment in every thing not inconsistent with or derogatory to those principles; and so long as they adhere to such restrictions, their deeds ought not to be rescinded or controuled by any other power whatsoever. Those principles are certain inherent rights pertaining to all mankind in a state of natural liberty, which through the weakness, imperfection, and depravity of human nature cannot be secured in that state. Men, therefore, agree to enter into society, that by the united force of *many* the rights of *each* individual may be protected and secured. These are in all just governments laid down as a foundation to the *civil compact,* which contains a *covenant* between *each* with *all,* that they shall enter into one society to be governed by the same powers; establishes for that purpose the *frame* of government; and consequently creates a *Convention* between *every* member, binding those, who shall at any time be intrusted with power, to a faithful administration of their trust according to the form of the *civil policy,* which they have so constituted, and obliging all to a due obedience therein. There can be no other just origin of civil power, but some such mutual contract of all the people: and although their great object in forming society is an intention to secure their natural rights; yet the relations arising from this *political union* create certain duties and obligations to the state, which require a sacrifice of some portion of those rights and of that exuberance of liberty, which obtains in a state of nature.—This, however, being compensated by certain other adventitious rights and privileges, which are acquired by the social connection; it follows that the advantages derived from a government are to be estimated by the *strength* of the *security,* which is attended at once with the *least sacrifice* and the *greatest acquired benefits.* That government, therefore, which is best adapted for promoting these three *great ends,* must certainly be the best constituted scheme of *civil policy.* Here, then, it may not be improper to remark that persons forming a social community cannot take too much precaution when they are about to establish the plan of their government. They ought to construct it in such a manner as to procure the best possible security for their rights;—in doing this they ought to give up no greater share than what is understood to be absolutely necessary:—and they should endeavor so to organise, arrange and connect it's several branches, that when duly exercised it may tend to promote the *common good* of all, and contribute as many advantages, as the civil institution is capable of. It has been before observed that the only just origin of civil power is a contract entered into by all the people for that purpose.—If this position be true (and, I dare presume, it is not controverted, at least in this country) right reason will always suggest the expediency of adhering to the essential requisites in forming that contract upon true principles. A cautious people will consider all the inducements to enter into the *social state,* from the most important object down to the minutest prospect of advantage. Every motive with them will have its due weight. They will not pay a curious attention to trifles and overlook matters of great consequence:—and in pursuing these steps they will provide for the attainment of *each* point in view with a care—with an earnestness proportionate to its dignity, and according as it involves a *greater* or a *lesser* interest. It is evident, therefore that they should attend most diligently to those sacred rights, which they have received with their birth, and which can neither be retained to themselves, nor transmitted to their posterity, unless they are *expressly reserved:* for it is a maxim, I dare say, universally acknowledged, that when men establish a system of government, in granting the powers therein they are always understood to surrender whatever they do not so expressly reserve. This is obvious from the very design of the civil institution, which is adopted in lieu of the state of natural liberty, wherein each individual, being equally intitled to the enjoyment of all natural rights, and having equally a just authority to exercise full powers of acting, with relation to other individuals, in any manner not injurious to their rights, must, when he enters into society, be presumed to give up all those powers into the hands of the state by submitting his whole conduct to the direction thereof. This being done by every member, it follows, as a regular conclusion, that all such powers, whereof the whole were possessed, so far as they related to each other individually, are of course given up by the mere act of union. If this surrender be made without any reservation, the conclusion is equally plain and regular, that *each* and *all* have given up not only those powers, which relate to others, but likewise every claim, which pertained to themselves, as individuals. For the universality of the grant in this case must necessarily include every *power* of acting, and every *claim* of possessing or obtaining any thing—except according to the regulations of the state. Now a right being properly defined, "a power or claim established by law, to act, or to possess, or to obtain something from others," every natural right is such *power* or *claim* established by the law of nature. Thus, it is manifest, that in a society constituted after this manner, every right whatsoever will be under the power and controul of the civil jurisdiction. This is the leading characteristic of an arbitrary government, and whenever any people establish a system like this, they subject themselves to one, which has not a single property of a free constitution. Hence results the necessity of an *express stipulation* for all such rights as are intended to be exempted from the civil authority. . . .

Suffer me, then, in the first place to advert to a part of the sixth article in this constitution. It may, perhaps, appear somewhat irregular, to begin with this article, since it is almost the last proposed: yet, if it be considered that this at once defines the extent of Congressional authority, and indisputably fixes its supremacy, every idea of impropriety on this head will probably vanish. The clause alluded to contains the following words, "This constitution, and the laws of the United States, which shall be made in pursuance thereof, and all treaties made, or which shall be made, under the authority of the United States, shall be the supreme law of the land; and the judges in every state shall be bound thereby; any thing in the constitution or laws of any state to the contrary, notwithstanding." If this constitution should be adopted, here the sovereignty of America is ascertained and fixed in the foederal body at the same time that it abolishes the present independent sovereignty of each state. Because this government being general, and not confined to any particular part of the continent; but pervading every state and establishing its authority equally in all, its superiority will consequently be recognized in each; and all other powers can operate only in a secondary subordinate degree. For the idea of two sovereignties existing within the same community is a perfect solecism. If they be supposed equal, their operation must be commensurate, and like two mechanical powers of equal *momenta* counteracting each other;—here the force of the one will be destroyed by the force of the other: and so there will be no efficiency in either. If one be greater than the other, they will be similar to two unequal bodies in motion with a given degree of velocity, and impinging each other from opposite points;—the motion of the lesser in this case will necessarily be destroyed by that of the greater: and so there will be efficiency only in the greater. But what need is there for a mathematical deduction to shew the impropriety of two such distinct co-existing sovereignties? The natural undestanding of all mankind perceives the apparent absurdity arising from such a supposition: since, if the word means any thing at all, it must mean that *supreme power*, which must reside somewhere instate; or, in other terms, it is the united powers of each individual member of the state collected and consolidated into *one body*. This collection, this union, this supremacy of power can, therefore, exist only in one body. This is obvious to every man: and it has been very properly suggested that under the proposed constitution each state will dwindle into "the insignificance of a town corporate." This certainly will be their utmost consequence; and, as such, they will have no authority to make laws, even for their own private government any farther than the permissive indulgence of Congress may grant them leave. This, Virginians, will be your mighty, your enviable situation after all your struggles for independence! and, if you will take the trouble to examine, you will find that the great, the supereminent authority, with which this instrument of union proposes to invest the foederal body, is to be created without a single check—without a single article of covenant for the preservation of those inestimable rights, which have in all ages been the glory of freemen. It is true, "the United States shall guarantee to every state in this union a republican form of government": yet they do not guarantee to the different states their present forms of government, or the bill of rights thereto annexed, or any of them; and the expressions are too vague, too indefinite to create such a compact by implication. It is possible that a "republican form" of government may be built upon as absolute principles of despotism as any oriental monarchy ever yet possessed. I presume that the liberty of a nation depends, not on planning the frame of government, which consists merely in fixing and delineating the powers thereof; but on prescribing due limits to those powers, and establishing them upon just principles.

It has been held in a northern state by a zealous advocate for this constitution that there is no necessity for "a bill of rights" in the foederal government; although at the same time he acknowledges such necessity to have existed when the constitutions of the separate governments were established. He confesses that in these instances the people "invested their representatives with every power and authority, which they did not in explicit terms reserve": but "in delegating foederal powers," says he, "every thing, which is not given, is reserved."[2] Here is a distinction, I humbly conceive, without a difference, at least in the present enquiry. How far such a discrimination might prevail with respect to the present system of union, it is immaterial to examine: and had the observation been restrained to that alone, perhaps it might be acknowledged to contain some degree of propriety. For under the confederation it is well known that the authority of Congress cannot extend so far as to interfere with, or exercise any kind of coercion on, the powers of legislation in the different states; but the internal police of each is left free, sovereign and independent: so that the liberties of the people being secured as well as the nature of their constitution will admit; and the declaration of rights, which they have laid down as the *basis* of government, having their full force and energy, any farther stipulation on that head might be unnecessary. But, surely, when this doctrine comes to be applied to the *proposed* foederal constitution, which is framed with such large and extensive powers, as to transfer the individual sovereignty from each state to the *aggregate body*,—a constitution, which delegates to Congress an authority to interfere with, and restrain the legislatures of every state—invests them with supreme powers of legislation throughout all the states—annihilates the separate independency of each; and, in short—swallows up and involves in the plenitude of its jurisdiction all other powers whatsoever:—I shall not be taxed with arrogance in declaring such an argument to be fallacious; and insisting on the necessity of a positive unequivocal declaration in favor of the rights of freemen in this case even more strongly than in the case of their separate governments. For it seems to me that when any civil establishment is formed, the more general its influence, the more extensive the powers, with which it is invested, the greater reason there is to take the necessary precaution for securing a due administration, and guarding against unwarrantable abuses.

1 DHRC, VIII, pp. 387-394. Also reprinted in Storing, V, pp. 173-179.

2 The quoted remarks are from a speech of James Wilson given at the State House Yard in Philadelphia on October 6, 1787.

A Pennsylvanian III {Tench Coxe}   February 20, 1788

Newspaper Article: Philadelphia *Pennsylvania Gazette* (excerpts)

The power of the sword, say the minority of Pennsylvania is in the hands of Congress. My friends and countrymen, it is not so, for THE POWERS OF THE SWORD ARE IN THE HANDS OF THE YEOMANRY OF AMERICA FROM SIXTEEN TO SIXTY. The militia of these free commonwealths, entitled and accustomed to their arms, when compared with any possible army must be *tremendous and irresistable.* Who are these militia? *are they not our selves.* Is it feared, then, that we shall turn our arms *each man against his own bosom.* Congress have no power to disarm the militia. Their swords, and every other terrible implement of the soldier, are *the birthright of an American.* What clause in the state or foederal constitution hath *given away* that important right. It is said, Congress can order the militia of Georgia to New Hampshire! The gentlemen might have gone further, and said, they might order the militia of Maryland TO MARCH OVER THE SURFACE OF THE CHESAPEAK. The latter would be obeyed as soon as the former. These extravagancies operate against all power. The legislature of Pennsylvania may constitutionally order their citizens to pay in taxes one half, or even the whole value of their estates, by the very clause which vests them with the power of providing for the real and evident exigencies of the state government. Further, the power of the sword, even so far as it is placed in the hands of Congress, is subject to the controul of the state legislatures, for they name one branch of the federal government (the Senate) without whom no military officers can be appointed, no monies granted, no armies raised, no navies provided. The state governments also have "*the authority* of training the militia, and *appointing all the officers.* The constitution, instead of providing a standing (or permanent) army, takes care that *it shall not be standing,* shall not *continue,* for it declares it shall find itself *absolutely unprovided* at the end of every two years. If the people see the least reason to apprehend a breach in the constitution by the grant of money for more than two years, they can elect new representatives, and they can by virtue of those military powers, *which are inseparable from their own persons,* suspend every operation of a Congress, which shall have thus ceased to be a lawful and constitutional power. From this circumstance, and from the citizens of the United States possessing the right of creating directly or indirectly every military officer and of granting every military resource, I do not hesitate to affirm, that the unlimited power of the sword is not in the hands of either the *foederal or state governments,* but, where I trust in God it will ever remain, *in the hands of the people. . . .*

Though we readily admitted, that if the proposed constitution for the United States was a *social,* and not a *foederal* one, it would be justly exceptionable, yet as it appears on examination strongly *foederal,* and that it cannot possibly absorb the state governments, so all fear of that *Despotism,* which a *social* government would produce in so extensive a territory, is entirely removed. It may be satisfactory to many of my countrymen to see this point more copiously treated. I remember to have read two very valuable papers, No. 44 and 45, by *the Foederalist* of New-York, who signs himself PUBLIUS, which must give great satisfaction to every discerning and candid mind.

DHRC, II Mfm. Pa., pp. 1778-1780. The author of the pseudonymous series of newspaper pieces by "A Pennsylvanian" has been identified as Tench Coxe of Philadelphia (see DHRC, XVI, p. 241, note 2). Coxe received copies of numbers 44 and 45 of *The Foederlist* from James Madison in early February. *The Foederalist* number 45, written by Madison, discusses the militia, "the advantage of being armed, which the Americans possess over the people of almost every other nation," and the ability of the people of America to protect their rights against the federal government by force if necessary. It influenced Coxe to examine the same subjects in the above article. See "Publius {James Madison}," January 29, 1788, p. 234.

Deliberator February 20, 1788
Newspaper Article: Philadelphia *Freeman's Journal* (excerpt)[1]

They [Congress] shall have power to declare what description of persons shall compose the militia; to appoint the stated times and places for exercising them; to compel personal attendance, whether when called for into actual service, or on other occasions, under what penalties they shall think proper, without regard to scruples of conscience or any other consideration. Their executive officer may march and countermarch them from one extremity of the state to the other—and all this without so much as consulting the legislature of the particular states to which they belong! Where then is that boasted security against the annihilation of the state governments, arising from "the powerful military support"[2] they will have from their militia?

1 DHRC, II Mfm. Pa., p. 1758. Reprinted in Borden, p. 123, and in Storing, III, p. 177.
2 The quote is from "A Freeman II," by Tench Coxe published January 30, 1788. See DHRC, XV, p. 508.

Philadelphiensis X February 20, 1788
Newspaper Article: Philadelphia *Freeman's Journal*[1]

My Fellow-Citizens,

If stupid irony, falsehood, scurrility, and abusive language, be sufficient to silence a writer in the cause of freedom, my sentiments must have been suppressed long ago; but that old saying, that *nothing cuts like the truth,* has encouraged me to address you once more. Probably this essay may be more obnoxious to the friends of the proposed plan of government than any of my former publications; and if so, the above saying is farther confirmed. A freeman must have a *little soul* indeed, whose attention can be diverted from its proper object, by the schemes practised by the friends of unlimited dominion. His own happiness, as being connected with the happiness of his fellow-men, ought to be his chiefest good. The *divine founder* of our religion and his beatified followers had no aim but this, and they pursued it with a zeal consistent with its excellence.

If the proposed plan be a good one upon the whole, why should its friends endeavour to prevent investigating its merits or defects? Why should they hurry it on us before we have even read it? Does not this look suspicious like? Is it not a proof that it is the works of darkness, and cannot bear the light? Why should they summon a Convention in Pennsylvania, before the tenth part of the people had time to judge for themselves, or to know whether it was a free or a tyrannical system of government? Why employ bullies to drag some members of the Assembly per force to the House to make a quorum, in order to call a Convention? The answers of these interrogatives are obvious, and the conclusions deduced from them will in time have their proper effect.

The principles of its framers are now clearly understood; the proceedings of the *dark conclave* have undergone an *ordeal* in Maryland, that exhibits the monarchy-men in convention as a set of the basest conspirators that ever disgraced a free country. At the time that these men were plotting the ruin of their country, and forming a system of national cruelty unequalled in the annals of time, the unsuspecting freemen of America were blessing them, were praying for them in their private families, and in their public churches, and looking up to them for relief; they even called the federal convention an *august body, the most excellent assembly of men that ever appeared in the world.*

The *President-general,* who is to be our *king* after this government is established, is vested with powers exceeding those of the most *despotic monarch* we know of in modern times. What a handsome return have these men made to the people of America for their confidence! Through the misconduct of these bold conspirators we have lost the most glorious opportunity that any country ever had to establish a free system of government. America under one purely democratical, would be rendered the happiest and most powerful nation in the universe; but under the proposed one, composed of an *elective king* and a standing army, officered by his sycophants, the starvelings of the Cincinnati, and an aristocratical Congress of the *well-born,* an iota of happiness, freedom or national strength cannot exist. What a pitiful figure will these ungrateful men make in history;

who, for the hopes of obtaining some lucrative employment, or of receiving a little more homage from the rest of their fellow creatures, framed a system of oppression that must involve in its consequences the misery of their own offspring? There is but one rational way remaining to prevent themselves from being eye witnesses of a dreadful scene, and that is for them to cease immediately every operation that respects the establishing of this plan of government; and then all parties will join heartily in calling another federal convention, and the peace of the country will be preserved.

One of the members of the virtuous minority of the convention of Massachusetts openly declared in that assembly, that pushing on this accursed system would produce a *civil war:* the freemen of New-England, the best soldiers on the continent, have had their eyes opened, and begin to see through the conspiracy; that sacred palladium of liberty, *the freedom of the press,* has dispelled the cloud, and cleared their understandings. In that state, through the influence of the tyrants of Boston, very little information has reached the people; the *press,* generally speaking, was devoted to the *well-born* and their tools; yet out of near 400 members, of which that convention consisted, only a majority of 19 could be procured, notwithstanding every possible method of overawing, threatening and *bribing* was practised.

I conceive that carrying it by so small a majority, is little better than a rejection; in fact it may prove worse, for the breach is only widened so much the more by it, and truly it was wide enough before. The freemen of Massachusetts will never cowardly surrender their sacred rights and liberties into the hands of one man, or any body of men whatever. They know what freedom is, and they will support it at the risque of their lives and fortunes. Their courage, fortitude, and atchievments in the late war have rendered their character, as friends to liberty, immortal.

The amendments proposed by the president[2] will be another source of mischief; the people cannot be so ignorant as to be deceived by so pitiful a manoeuvre. Here is a positive acknowledgement made by one of its advocates, who hopes to be appointed the *little king* if not the *big one,* that it is objectionable; and his amendments are introduced as a blind; the weighty ones are untouched: not a whimper of the extraordinary powers of the *President-general,* the *standing army,* the *liberty of the press, &c.* No, no! if these *glorious parts* be lopped off, what would become of the monarchy-men? And respecting *internal taxation,* is not his amendment a disgrace to himself, and an insult to the understanding of the people? Mr. Hancock knows, or ought to know at least, that the liberties of the citizens of America are not to be trifled with: his schemes are too flimsey not to be seen through.

The allegiance of freeman to government will ever be a consequence of protection; the Congress of America withdrew their allegiance from the king of Great-Britain when he changed his protection into acts of cruelty; and on the same account the citizens of these United States will not chearfully bear allegiance to the new government; which, instead of protecting them in their sacred rights and privileges, will be a system of tyranny and oppression. The unlimited powers of the new Congress in respect to taxation, are abundantly sufficient to alarm the people. While the state assemblies retained the right of *internal taxation*, the country farmers could not be burdened beyond their abilites; these men being the true representatives of the people, would never attempt to levy an oppressive tax; their own feelings and interests being congenial with those of their constituents, their consent must be withheld when a measure was proposed subversive of public good.

That the new Congress will not be the immediate representatives of the people, that their number is too small, their powers too great, their accountability to the people not properly secured, and above all the *executive* dangerously placed in the hands of one man, who is really a *king*, have been fully illustrated by many able writers, and ably proved in the convention of this state and Massachusetts by worthy patriots whose names will be revered as long as time shall remain. Upon the whole, my fellow citizens, if the great characters, who are said to advocate this system of government wish to act consistently, the greatest proof they can give of their love for their country, is to join the rest of their fellow citizens in endeavouring to call another federal convention.

1 DHFFE, IV, pp. 27-29. The "Philadelphiensis" series is reprinted in Storing, III, starting on p. 99.

2 See "Massachusetts Convention," February 6, 1788, pp. 261-262, for the amendments adopted by the Convention, which had been proposed by John Hancock, President of the Convention.

Alexander White February 22, 1788

Newspaper Article: Winchester *Virginia Gazette* (excerpts)[1]

To the CITIZENS of VIRGINIA.

Friends and Countrymen, I some time since addressed you, and in conformity with the general custom, under an assumed name; I then animadverted on objections to the proposed plan of federal government, said to be made by two citizens of this commonwealth.[2] —I shall now take notice of 'the Address and Reasons of Dissent of

the Minority of the Convention of the State of Pennsylvania to their Constituents,' and sign my real name, that those gentlemen may not complain of being attacked by an anonymous writer.— . . .
There are notwithstanding some things in the address which may deserve consideration; these I shall endeavour to answer in the manner best calculated to cast light on the whole subject, without regard to the order in which they occur. There are other things so clearly out of the power of Congress, that the bare recital of them is sufficient, I mean the "rights of conscience, or religious liberty—the rights of bearing arms for defence, or for killing game—the liberty of fowling, hunting and fishing—the right of altering the laws of descents and distribution of the effects of deceased persons and titles of lands and goods, and the regulation of contracts in the individual States." These things seem to have been inserted among their objections, merely to induce the ignorant to believe that Congress would have a power over such objects and to infer from their being refused a place in the Constitution, their intention to exercise that power to the oppression of the people. But if they had been admitted as reservations out of the powers granted to Congress, it would have opened a large field indeed for legal construction: I know not an object of legislation which by a parity of reason, might not be fairly determined within the jurisdiction of Congress.

The freedom of speech and of the press, are likewise out of the jurisdiction of Congress.—But, if by an abuse of that freedom I attempt to excite sedition in the Commonwealth, I may be punished—should I be unjustly accused of such an offence, the trial by a jury of my countrymen is my security—if what I have said or wrote corresponds with their general sense of the subject, I shall be acquitted.

1 DHRC, VIII, pp. 402-405. See "Alexander White," February 29, 1788, p. 288, for excerpts from the continuation of this article.

2 Possibly a reference to "An Independent Freeholder" which had appeared in the same paper on January 18th and 25th; an excerpt from the January 18th item appears above at p. 217.

Publius {Alexander Hamilton} February 23, 1788
Newspaper Article: New York *Independent Journal* (excerpts)[1]

The FOEDERALIST. No. LIX.

To the People of the State of New-York.

We have seen that an incontroulable power over the elections for the federal government could not without hazard be committed to the state legislatures. Let us now see what would be the dangers on the other side; that is, from confiding the ultimate right of regulating its own elections to the union itself. It is not pretended, that this right would ever be used for the exclusion of any state from its share in the representation. The interest of all would in this respect at least be the security of all. But it is alledged that it might be employed in such a manner as to promote the election of some favourite class of men in exclusion of others; by confining the places of election to particular districts, and rendering it impracticable to the citizens at large to partake in the choice. Of all chimerical suppositions, this seems to be the most chimerical. On the one hand no rational calculation of probabilities would lead us to imagine, that the disposition, which a conduct so violent and extraordinary would imply, could ever find its way into the national councils; and on the other, it may be concluded with certainty, that if so improper a spirit should ever gain admittance into them, it would display itself in a form altogether different and far more decisive.

The improbability of the attempt may be satisfactorily inferred from this single reflection, that it could never be made without causing an immediate revolt of the great body of the people,—headed and directed by the state governments. It is not difficult to conceive that this characteristic right of freedom may, in certain turbulent and factious seasons, be violated in respect to a particular class of citizens by a victorioius and overbearing majority; but that so fundamental a privilege, in a country so situated and enlightened, should be invaded to the prejudice of the great mass of the people, by the deliberate policy of the government; without occasioning a popular revolution, is altogether inconceivable and incredible. . . .

Let it however be admitted, for argument sake, that the expedient suggested might be successful; and let it at the same time be equally taken for granted that all the scruples which a sense of duty or an apprehension of the danger of the experiment might inspire, were overcome in the breasts of the national rulers; still, I imagine, it will hardly be pretended, that they could ever hope to carry such an enterprise into exectution, without the aid of a military force sufficient to subdue, the resistance of the great body of the people. The improbability of the existence of a force equal to that object, has been discussed and demonstrated in different parts of these papers[.][2]

1 DHRC, XVI, p. 196-199.

2 See "Publius {James Madison}," January 29, 1788, p. 234, for an excerpt from *The Foederalist* number 45 (number 46 in the M'Lean edition of collected essays.)

Richard Henry Lee (Chantilly) February 26, 1788
Letter: To James Gordon, Jr. (excerpt)

Captain Merry delivered me the letter that you were pleased to write me, on the 11th instant, in which I find you propose the following questions, relative to the new constitution, proposed by the late general convention, and request my answer to them:

First. Whether the United States had not better receive than reject the said constitution?

Secondly. Whether it would not injure our credit in the European world, if we were to dissent therefrom; and whether our country would not thereby be endangered, as there are large demands in Europe against us?

Thirdly. Whether every objection to the plan may not, by instructions from the different states, be made as soon as the said Congress may be assembled?

Fourthly. Whether ruin would await us, unless we are consolidated in one general plan of government?

To the first question, namely, "Whether the United States," &c. I answer, that this question implies a *necessity* of either adopting or rejecting. But I know of no power on earth that has, or ever had, a right to propose such a question of extremity to the people, or any part of the people, of the United States. The happiness or misery of mankind depends so essentially upon government, that, when this is to be established by the people for themselves and their posterity, the right of the people cannot be questioned, of so acting with plans proposed, as to adopt them, reject them, or propose amendments to them.

To the second query, "Whether it would not injure," &c. I reply, that this second question is much founded on the first; and, so far as it is, may receive the same answer. It is divisible into two parts; the first, shall our credit be injured in Europe by *dissenting* from the proposed plan? It is presumable, that credit abroad depends much upon union and happiness at home, as it must always greatly do upon that industry and real strength which grows out of the possession of civil liberty. Those, therefore, who contend for the new plan, by propounding such a question, should prove, in the first place, that the adoption of this constitution will secure union and happiness at home, and those valuable consequences that flow from the possession of civil liberty; and this is the more necessary, as there are such numbers who think that the proffered plan, if admitted without amendments, will empower the administrators of the new government to destroy civil liberty. The second part of this question is, "whether our country will not be endangered by a *dissent,* as there are large demands against us in Europe." I presume that foreigners have no business with the nature of our government. Payment of their debts they are entitled to, but no possible reason can be assigned, why these debts may not as well be paid if the proposed constitution was to be so amended, as to secure the just rights and liberties of the people from violation, by a proper bill of rights; to retain the trial by jury in all cases, civil as well as criminal, as directed by the common law; to secure the rights of conscience, and freedom of the press. Will France, Holland, or Spain, be disturbed at our retaining these valuable privileges? or, will they quarrel with us for so amending this new plan, as to put it out of the power of the new rulers to carry every citizen of the state, by way of appeal, to be tried for every suit for debt, brought by all others than our own state citizens, in the supreme federal court, where distance and expense may ruin multitudes? Have foreigners any thing to do with our amending the proposed constitution, so as to put it out of the power of the rulers under it, to garble elections, by ordering all the elections of any state to be held at any place they shall choose—at Cape Henry, for instance, if they so please at any time. See section fourth, article first, where they have power over time, place, and manner of holding elections for choosing representatives, without restraint or limitation.

To the third query, "Whether every objection," &c. I answer, that the constitution containing these objections, is made by the people of the United States; "and the removal of them by the Congress, would only be a common act of legislation, which may be revoked and repealed by every subsequent meeting of the Congress." So that the power of oppressing will be founded on the strong and lasting ground of a constitution made by the people of the United States, and the remedies (if the new rulers should ever please to declare any,) will rest on feeble and changeable acts of a common legislature. Can it be safe or prudent to suffer this? As for instructions, it is to be remarked, that the senators are chosen by the legislature of the states, and the representatives by all the freeholders—to instruct one, and not both branches of the new legislature, would be doing nothing; and to render instructions of use, the general assembly, and the freeholders of the community, must unite. The almost impossibility of procuring such a union from the majority of the United States, is too obvious, not to show the very little dependence that should be put on such instructions. And, after all, the result could only be a legislative and mutable act against a fixed constitution. But how absurd would it be for the people to agree to a constitutional evil to-day and to-morrow call for a legislative redress of that evil!

The fourth and last question, "Whether ruin would await us," &c. I am clearly of opinion, that our greater strength, safety, and happiness, depends on our union; but I am as clear that this union had infinitely better be on principles that give security to the just rights and liberties of mankind, than on such principles as permit rulers to destroy them. Thus, sir, I hope that I have fully, and to your satisfaction, answered your several questions: so that you may think yourself warranted, if not bound to be a friend to amendments that should be constitutional. To trust to future events for remedy of evils that we have ourselves once created, is like choosing to be sick, because a doctor may possibly cure us!

DHRC, VIII, pp. 417-420.

The Impartial Examiner February 27, 1788

Newspaper Article: *Virginia Independent Chronicle* (excerpt)

It has ever been held that standing armies in times of peace are dangerous to a free country; and no observation seems to contain more reason in it. Besides being useless, as having no object of employment, they are inconvenient and expensive. The soldiery, who are generally composed of the dregs of the people, when disbanded, or unfit for military service, being equally infit for any other employment, become extremely burthensome. As they are a body of men exempt from the common occupations of social life, having an interest different from the rest of the community, they [are] wanton in the lap of ease and indolence, without feeling the duties, which arise from the political connection, though drawing their subsistence from the bosom of the state. The severity of discipline necessary to be observed reduces them to a degree of slavery; the unconditional submission to the commands of their superiors, to which they are bound, renders them the fit instruments of tyranny and oppression.—Hence they have in all ages afforded striking examples of contributing, more or less, to enslave mankind;—and whoever will take the trouble to examine, will find that by far the greater part of the different nations, who have fallen from the glorious state of liberty, owe their ruin to standing armies. It has been urged that they are necessary to provide against sudden attacks. Would not a well regulated militia, duly trained to discipline, afford ample security? Such, I conceive, to be the best, the surest means of protection, which a free people can have when not actually engaged in war. This kind of defence is attended with two advantages superior to any others; first, when it is necessary to embody an army, they at once form a band of soldiers, whose interests are uniformly the same with those of the whole community, and in whose safety they see involved every thing that is dear to themselves: secondly, if one army is cut off, another may be immediately raised already trained for military service. By a policy, somewhat similar to this, the Roman empire rose to the highest pitch of grandeur and magnificence.

DHRC, VIII, pp. 422-423. Reprinted in Storing, V, pp. 181-182.

Philadelphia *Independent Gazetteer* February 27, 1788
(excerpt)[1]

You see we have the town of Boston under our discipline; I wish I could say so of the rest of the state, indeed it is far otherwise, four fifths of the people are against us: But as you say, what need we care for the sentiments of the people, if we can only get the army a-foot.

I was happy to hear you was disarming your militia both for your own safety, and because you will want the arms for the troops; but at the same time I thought it a bold push, and might cause alarm.[2]

1 DHRC, XVI, p. 239. This is antifederalist satire in the form of a fictitious letter from James Bowdoin, former Governor of Massachusetts at the time of Shays' Rebellion, to James Wilson (James de Caledonia), who were both Federalists.

2 For other documents related to the controversy over the collection of publicly owned arms in Pennsylvania, and the complaint that this was intended to disarm the militia, see: "Jacob Trusty," December 19, 1787, p. 176; "Centinel IX," January 8, 1788, p. 191; Pennsylvania *Carlisle Gazette*, January 9, 1788, p. 194; "Trusty," January 10, 1788, p. 200; "Supreme Executive Council," January 10, 1788, p. 201; "An Old Militia Officer of 1776," January 18, 1788, p. 221; Philadelphia *Freeman's Journal*, January 23, 1788, p. 226; Philadelphia *Pennsylvania Herald*, February 5, 1788, p. 251; "James de Caledonia IV," March 12, 1788, p. 298; "Aristocrotis," April [15], 1788, p. 334 at note 2; Philadelphia *Independent Gazetteer*, April 30, 1788, p. 340 at note 3.

Reverend John Leeland February 28, 1788
Letter Enclosure: Objections to the Constitution (excerpts)

According, to your request, I have send you my objections to the *Federal Constitution*, which are as follows,

1st. There is no Bill Rights, whenever Number of men enter into a State of Socity, a Number of individual Rights must be given up to Socity, but there should always be a memorial of those not surrendred, otherwise every natural & domestic right becomes alianable, which raises Tyranny at once, & this is as necessary in one Form of Government as in another— . . .

8ly. We have no assurance that the liberty of the press will be allowed under this Constitution— . . .

10ly. What is dearest of all—*Religious Liberty*, is not Sufficiently Secured, No religious test is required as a Qualification to fill any office under the United States, but if a Majority of Congress with the presedent favour one System more then another, they may oblige all others to pay to the Support of their System as Much as they please, & if Oppression dose not ensue, it will be owing to the Mildness of Administration & not to any Constitutional defense, & if the Manners of People are so far Corrupted, that they cannot live by republican principles, it is Very Dangerous leaving religious Liberty at their Marcy—[2]

1 DHRC, XVI, p. 253-254.

2 Leeland's objections were sent to James Madison in a letter from Joseph Spencer. See DHRC, XVI, p. 254, note 7.

Philadelphia *Independent Gazetteer* February 28, 1788

Newspaper Article: Extract of a letter from a countryman to his friend in New-York. (excerpt)

If all the laws and treaties which may be made, in pursuance of this constitution (provided it be adopted) are to be of *as high authority*, as the constitution, I should be glad to know what security we can have for any one right, however sacred or essential, when there is no explicit proviso, that the laws and treaties which may be made, shall not be repugnant to the constitution?

It is true, that they are to be made in *pursuance* of the constitution; but, *pursuance* is a vague term, and, I presume, generally implies little more than 'in consequence, &c.'—I have always understood, that the laws derived all their just authority from the constitution, or social compact, as it is sometimes called; and that the latter receives its whole authority, in free governments, from the common consent of the people, and recognizes or acknowledges all their essential rights and liberties, as well as ascertains the reciprocal duties or relations between the governed and their governors, or, perhaps, more properly, their principal public servants, who undertake to manage or conduct the affairs of the community agreeable to certain fixed stipulations, which are mentioned in the original compact or constitution, and not otherwise, but at the risk of being disobeyed, or opposed, as the case may require.

DHRC, II Mfm. Pa., pp. 1855-1856.

Alexander White February 29, 1788
Newspaper Article: Winchester *Virginia Gazette* (excerpts)

To the CITIZENS of VIRGINIA.
(Continued from our last.)

Friends and Countrymen, it is objected that there is no Bill of Rights—a clear understanding of that matter will obviate many objections. A Bill of Rights is only necessary, where the rights of different men or orders of men are uncertain, and is rather calculated to inform than to restrain. Paper chains are too feeble to bind the hands of tyranny or ambition. In England the king claimed supreme power, as inseperably annexed to the kingly office, the people claimed privileges, these different claims occasioned many contest[s], until they were defined by a Bill of Rights presented to William and Mary at their accession [in 1689]. But no doubt can arise in the American governments, the fundamental maxim of which is, that sovereignty is vested in the people, a position so plain and simple that the meanest capacity can comprehend it, and so well established both in theory and practice, that no man will deny it. Consequently should Congress attempt to exercise any powers which are not expressly delegated to them, their acts would be considered as void, and disregarded. In America it is the governors not the governed that must produce their Bills of Right: unless they can shew the charters under which they act, the people will not yield obedience. . . .

I have called upon the opposers of the federal system to produce an instance of rulers chosen by the people, who had enslaved them; and rest satisfied it cannot be done; the impracticability of Congress effecting such a measure has likewise been made apparent. I would only beg you to attend to the superior advantages which Great Britain possessed when the contest with her commenced. To all the influence of a civil government to which an unlimited obedience had been paid from time immemorial, she added her military and naval power; the latter surpassing all the nations of the earth; yet, America resisted and success attended her efforts. With how much more ease may you oppose the oppressions of a government which owes its existence to your breath, and which possesses no power independent of you.

DHRC, VIII, p. 438-444. See "Alexander White," February 22, 1788, p. 280, for excerpts from the first part of this article.

The Landholder X February 29, 1788
Newspaper Article: Baltimore *Maryland Journal* (excerpt)

To the Honourable LUTHER MARTIN, Esq; . . .
One hour you sported the opinion, that Congress, afraid of the militia resisting their measures, would neither arm nor organize them: and the next, as if men required no time to breathe between such contradictions, that they would harrass them by long and unnecessary marches, till they wore down their spirit and rendered them fit subjects for despotism.

DHRC, XVI, p. 267. The Landholder is here referring to debates which occurred in the Federal Convention.

A Farmer II February 29, 1788
Newspaper Article: Baltimore *Maryland Gazette* (excerpts)

However, a standing army has from that time destroyed all hopes of a revolution in favour of the rights of mankind [in Spain].

It will be asked how has *England* preserved her liberties, with at least an apparent standing army?—I answer, she did loose them; but as there was no standing army until lately, she regained them again:—She lost them under the Tudors, who broke the then oppressive power of the aristocracy, but the unparalleled avarice of Henry VIIth, the boundless extravagance of Henry VIIIth, the short reign of Edward VIth, (which was but the sickly blaze of a dying candle) the bigotry of that weak woman Mary, who had no other object than religious persecution, and lastly the parsimony of Elizabeth, who had no children of her own to provide for, and who hated her legal successor and his family—all conspired to prevent their establishing a military standing force, sufficient to secure their usurpations; and the nation recovered from their paroxism under the Stuarts, who were too weak and too wicked to command even respect, notwithstanding their dignity.—On the revolution in 1688, the patriots of that day formed some glorious bulwarks, which seem as yet to have secured them from the evils and danger of their present standing army, though still in my opinion, they hold their remaining liberties by a very precarious tenure indeed, as the first enterprizing and popular Prince will most probably convince them.

Let us now examine these defences and compare them with those of the proposed constitution.

In *England,* by their bill of rights, a standing army is declared to be contrary to their constitution, and a militia the only natural and safe defence of a free people—This keeps the jealousy of the nation constantly awake, and has proved the foundation of all the other checks.

In the American constitution, there is no such declaration, or check at all.

In *England,* the military are declared by their constitution to be in *all* cases subordinate to the civil power; and consequently the civil officers have always been active in supporting this pre-eminence.

In the American constitution, there is no such declaration.

In *England,* the mutiny bill can only be passed form year to year, or on its expiration every soldier is as free, and the equal by law of the first general officer of the land.

In *America,* the articles of war (which is the same thing) has been already considered as *perpetual* (as I am well informed) under even the present Congress, although the constitutions of all the States positively forbid any standing troops at all, much less laws for them.

In *England,* the appropriation of money for the support of their army must be from year to year; in America it may be for double the period.

How favorable is this contrast to Britain—that Britain which we lavished our blood and treasure to separate ourselves from, as a country of slavery—But we then held different sentiments from those now become so fashionable; for this I appeal to the constitutions of the several States.

In the declaration of rights of *Massachusetts,* sect. 17.—The people have a right to keep and to bear arms for the common defence. And as in time of peace, armies are dangerous to liberty, they ought not to be maintained without the consent of the legislature, and the military power shall always be held in exact subordination to the civil authority, and be governed by it.

Sect. 27. In time of peace, no soldier ought to be quartered in any house without the consent of the owner; and in time of war, such quarters ought not to be made but by the civil magistrate, in a manner ordained by the legislature.

Declaration of rights of *Pennsylvania,* sect. 13.—That the people have a right to bear arms for the defence of themselves and the State; and as standing armies in the time of peace, are dangerous to liberty, they ought not to be kept up: And that the military should be kept under strict subordination to, and governed by the civil power.

Declaration of rights of *Maryland,* sect. 25.—That a well regulated militia is the proper and natural defence of a free government.

Sect. 26. That standing armies are dangerous to liberty, and ought not to be raised or kept without consent of the legislature.

Sect. 27. That in all cases and at all times the military ought to be under strict subordination to, and controul of the civil power.

Sect. 28. That no soldier ought to be quartered in any house in time of peace, without the consent of the owner; and in time of war, in such manner only as the legislature shall direct.

Declaration of rights of *Delaware,* in the same words as *Maryland.*

Declaration of rights of *North-Carolina,* sect. 17.—That the people have a right to bear arms for the defence of the State; and as standing armies in time of peace are dangerous to liberty, they ought not to be kept up; and that the military should be kept under strict subordination to, and governed by the civil power.

Constitution of *South-Carolina,* sect. 42.—That the military be subordinate to the civil power of the State. . . .

Let the body of the people be interested in the defence of a *good* government, and my countrymen need not fear being surprized by all the slaves and brutes that the despots of the old and new world can arm against them. . . .

I am free to declare, that I never wish to see any measure of government enforced by arms, which the yeomanry of the United States will not turn out to support.

Storing, V, pp. 25-28.

Hugh Henry Brackenridge March 1, 1788

Newspaper Article: *Pittsburgh Gazette* (excerpt)

The want of a *bill of rights* is the great evil. There was no occasion for a bill of *wrongs;* for there will be wrongs enough. But oh! a *bill of rights!* What is the nature of a *bill of rights? It is a schedule or inventory of those powers which Congress do not possess.* But if it is clearly ascertained what powers they have, what need of a catalogue of those powers they have not? Ah! there is the mistake. A minister preaching, undertook, first, to show what was in his text; second, what was not in it. When it is specified what powers are given, why not also what powers are not given? A bill of rights is wanting, and all those things which are usually secured under it.

1. The *rights of conscience* are swept away. The Confession of Faith; the Shorter Catechism, and Pilgrims Progress are to go. The Psalms of Wats I am told, is the only thing of this kind that is to have any quarter at all.

2. The *liberty of the press;* that is gone at the first stroke. Not so much as an advertisement for a stray horse, or a run away negro, can be put in any of the Gazettes.

3. The *trial by jury*, that is knocked in the head, and all that worthy class of men, the lawyers, who live by haranguing and bending the juries, are demolished.

I would submit it to any candid man, if in this constitution there is the least provision for the privilege of shaving the beard? or is there any mode laid down to take the measure of a pair of breeches? Whence then is it that men of learning seem so much to approve, while the ignorant are against it? The cause is perfectly apparent, viz. that reason is an erring guide, while instinct, which is the governing principle of the untaught is certain. Put a pig in a poke, carry it half a day's journey through woods and by ways; let it out and it will run home without deviation. Could Dr. Franklin do this?

DHRC, II Mfm. Pa., pp. 1888-1890. Also reprinted in *Essays*, p. 320. A Federalist satire on Antifederalist views concerning the need for a bill of rights.

The Impartial Examiner March 5, 1788
Newspaper Article: *Virginia Independent Chronicle* (excerpts)

If herein I conceive that you are alarmed at the exceedingly high and extensive authority, which it [the Constitution] is intended to establish, I cannot but see the strongest reasons for such apprehensions. For a system, which is to supercede the present different governments of the states, by ordaining that "laws made in pursuance thereof shall be supreme, and shall bind the judges in every state, any thing in the constitution or laws of any state to the contrary notwithstanding," must be alarming indeed! What cannot this omnipotence of power effect? How will your bill of rights avail you any thing? By this authority the Congress can make laws, which shall bind all, repugnant to your present constitution—repugnant to every article of your rights; for they are a part of your constitution,—they are the basis of it. So that if you pass this new constitution, you will have a naked plan of government unlimited in its jurisdiction, which not only expunges your bill of rights by rendering ineffectual, all the state governments; but is proposed without any kind of stipulation for any of those natural rights, the security whereof ought to be the end of all governments. Such a stipulation is so necessary, that it is an absurdity to suppose any civil liberty can exist without it. Because it cannot be alledged in any case whatsoever, that a breach has been committed—that a right

has been violated; as there will be no standard to resort to—no criterion to ascertain the breach, or even to find whether there has been any violation at all. Hence it is evident that the most flagrant acts of oppression may be inflicted; yet, still there will be no apparent object injured: there will be no unconstitutional infringement. For instance, if Congress should pass a law that persons charged with capital crimes shall not have a *right to demand the cause or nature of the accusation,* shall not be *confronted with the accusers or witnesses, or call for evidence in their own favor;* and a question should arise respecting their authority therein,—can it be said that they have exceeded the limits of their jurisdiction, when *that* has no limits; when no provision has been made for such a right?—When no responsibility on the part of Congress has been required by the constitution? The same observation may be made on any arbitrary or capricious imprisonments *contrary to the law of the land.* The same may be made, if *excessive bail should be required;* if *excessive fines should be imposed;* if *cruel and unusual punishments should be inflicted;* if *the liberty of the press should be restrained:* in a word—if laws should be made totally derogatory to the whole catalogue of rights, which are now secured under your present form of government. . . .
Hence, should it not be a *maxim,* never to be forgotten—that a free people ought to intrust no set of men with powers, that may be abused without controul, or afford opportunities to designing men to carry dangerous measures into execution, without being responsible for their conduct? And as no human foresight can penetrate so far into future events, as to guard always against the effects of vice,—as the securest governments are seldom secure enough;—is it not the greatest imprudence to adopt a system, which has an apparent tendency to furnish ambitious men with the means of exerting themselves—perhaps to the destruction of American liberty?

It is next to impossible to enslave a people immediately after a firm struggle against oppression, while the sense of past injury is recent and strong. But after some time this impression naturally wears off;—the ardent glow of freedom gradually evaporates;—the charms of popular equality, which arose from the *republican plan,* insensibly decline;—the pleasures, the advantages derived from the new kind of government grow stale through use. Such declension in all these vigorous springs of action necessarily produces a supineness. The altar of liberty is no longer watched with such attentive assiduity;—a new train of passions succeeds to the empire of the mind;—different objects of desire take place;—and, if the nation happens to enjoy a series of prosperity, voluptuousness, excessive fondness for riches, and luxury gain admission and establish themselves—these produce venality and corruption of every kind, which open a fatal avenue to bribery. Hence it follows, that in the midst of this general contageon a few men—or one—more powerful than all others, industriously endeavor to obtain all authority; and by means of great wealth—or embezzling the public money,—perhaps totally subvert the government, and erect a system of aristocratical or monarchic tyranny in its room. What ready means for this *work of evil* are numerous standing armies, and the disposition of the great revenue of the United States! Money can purchase soldiers;—soldiers can produce money; and both together can do any thing. It is this depravation of manners, this wicked propensity, my dear countrymen, against which you ought to provide with the utmost degree of prudence and circumspection. All nations pass this *paroxism* of vice at some period or other;—and if at that dangerous juncture your government is not secured upon a solid foundation, and well guarded against the machinations of evil men, the liberties of this country will be lost—perhaps forever!

DHRC, VIII, pp. 461-465. Reprinted in Storing, V, pp. 185-188.

Philadelphia *Freeman's Journal* March 5, 1788

One of the principal arguments which the advocates for a *change* in the government hold out, is, that if after a trial of the new constitution it will not answer, we can mend it; but such fairy tales cannot deceive people of any understanding, they must only be invented to amuse the weak and foolish among themselves. The fable of the ax-man treacherously supplicating the trees in the forest for a handle to his ax, with which he afterwards destroyed them all, is a sufficient explanation of such a fallacious argument. The freemen of America will remember, that it is very easy to change a *free* government into an arbitrary, despotic, or *military* one: but it is very difficult, almost impossible to reverse the matter—very difficult to regain *freedom* once lost. The struggles now existing between the *people* of France and their government is a striking proof of this; for, that government has lately laid (in addition to the other enormous existing taxes) a very heavy *land tax* of 30 per cent. The people complain of it loudly, but what does this avail? their complaints are treated with contempt, as that government has a large *standing army* at their command, and we find those who dare to complain are banished, or sent to the *Bastile!*—So much for the government of the *well-born few,* and standing armies.

Winchester *Virginia Gazette* March 7, 1788
(excerpts)

Messieurs BARTGIS and Co. The Freedom of the PRESS is the unalienable Right of a free Government particularly when matters of the greatest moment demand the serious attention, and free discussion of the citizens.

Your giving a place to the following lines in your entertaining paper, will oblige Your most obedient, humble servant, A VIRGINIA PLANTER.

My dear Countrymen, I beg my intrusion upon your time and patience may be taken in good part, while you read a few sentiments, proceeding from the greatest anxiety of mind, respecting the Federal Constitution, which I have perused impartially, and from the examples of the introduction of the most arbitrary Forms of Government, we may venture to declare this plan to be replete with shackles for the free born sons of America.—Every intelligent person must know, that all the world is now groaning in a Hell of Slavery (America and Switzerland excepted) whereby it becomes absolutely necessary to consider the way and means by which they were brought into that infernal state. Can we produce an instance of one nation that ever recovered from a cursed state of vassalage, to the enjoyment of the just and indubitable rights of mankind?

Are there none in trust that will postpone the adoption of this plan, while the people may reflect cooly upon a system of Government, lest they should subject themselves and millions yet unborn, to a state of political d———n? . . .

What cannot Congress do with an army at their heels, the revenue in their pockets and with the full and absolute disposal of the militia? How do other nations fare in that predicament? History is replete with answers to the question, that they are groveling in the dark regions of slavery, and there they must remain until their own virtue work out their own deliverance, which is impossible, because, slaves and those who submit to slavery, and tyrants, have no idea of virtue, honor, or common justice. . . .

The advanced age of the world has taught us, that the best of men are under the necessity of restraint, in every situation and circumstance respecting power. Power has altered the mildest and most affable character, into the most abandoned cruelty and savage temper. History abounds with innumerable instances of those who, previous to their being cursed with power, appeared as ornaments to human nature. Power is dangerous in the hands of men. Power alters all things, but God. The purpose of delegating power to men, is for the happiness and safety of the community, but with the want of proper limitations, it always proves to be a curse. I have often thought it a paradox in politics, how a few hundred of rulers can ruin the state of millions of subjects into a perfect Hell; the reason is, the few rulers are a junto, acting in close concert.

DHRC, VIII, pp. 469-472.

Philadelphiensis XI March 8, 1788
Newspaper Article: Philadelphia *Independent Gazetteer* (excerpt)

Who is so dimsighted as to suppose that a constitution so essentially differing from the principles of the revolution, and from freedom, and opposed by so respectable a body of freemen, could be established in America; or if it were possible by force or surprise to put it in motion, could it exist any space of time? Nay, the idea is futile, and common sense spurns at it. While it would exist, it must be by the power of a standing army alone; but its warmest advocates know, that all their credit, and influence could not support a standing army, equal to the business, six months.

DHRC, XVI, p. 365. The "Philadelphiensis" series is reprinted in Storing, III, starting at p. 99.

Philodemos March 8, 1788
Newspaper Article: Philadelphia *Federal Gazette* (excerpt)

Every freeman has *a right to the use of the press*, so he has to *the use of his arms*. But if his publications give an unmerited and deadly stroke to *private reputation*, or sap the foundations of *just government*, he abuses his privilege, as unquestionably as if he were to plunge his sword into the bosom of a fellow citizen, and *the good of society* requires that *each offence* should be punished.

DHRC, II Mfm. Pa., p. 1969.

One of the People March 10, 1788
Newspaper Article: Charleston *State Gazette of South Carolina* (excerpt)

It is also said by Mr. Richard Henry Lee, that the people of this country have thought a bill of rights necessary to regulate the exercise of the great power given to their rulers, as appears by the various bills or declarations of rights, whereon the government of the greater number, of the states are founded.

Answer.

Only four states appear, by the book of constitutions, to have a bill of rights which are the lesser number of States.[1]

These, Mr. Goddard, are the arguments used to prejudice the minds of the people against the constitution, some of which it seems, "several gentleman" requested you to publish. For this time, we will suppose these gentleman to have been ignorant of the deceptions they have thus publicly countenanced, because no gentleman would knowingly propagate or countenance untruths.

1 See Appendix A, p. 747, for the bills and declarations of rights of the states. There were actually seven states with formal bills of rights in 1788.

Marcus March 12, 1788
Newspaper Article: *Norfolk and Portsmouth Journal* (excerpt)
[Answer to Objection of George Mason]

There is no danger of the trial by Jury being rejected, when so justly a favorite of the whole people. The Representatives of the people surely can have no interest in making themselves odious for the mere pleasure of being hated; and when a Member of the House of Representatives is only sure of being so for two years, but must continue a citizen all his life, his interest as a citizen, if he is a man of common sense, to say nothing of his being a man of common honesty, must ever be uppermost in his mind. We know the great influence of the monarchy in the British government, and upon what a different tenure the Commons there have their seats in Parliament, from that prescribed to our Representatives. We know also, they have a large standing army. It is in the power of the Parliament if they dare to exercise it, to abolish the trial by jury altogether—but woe be to the man who should dare to attempt it—it would undoubtedly produce an insurrection that would hurl every tyrant to the ground who attempted to destroy that great and just favorite of the English nation. We certainly shall be always sure of this guard at least, upon any such act of folly or insanity in our Representatives: They soon would be taught the consequence of sporting with the feelings of a free people. But when it is evident that such an attempt cannot be rationally apprehended, we have no reason to anticipate unpleasing emotions of that nature. There is indeed little probability, that any degree of tyranny which can be figured to the most discoloured imagination, as likely to arise out of our government, could find an interest in attacking the trial by Jury in civil cases; and in criminal ones, where no such difficulties intervened as in the other, and where there might be supposed temptations to violate the personal security of a citizen, it is sacredly preserved.

DHRC, XVI, p. 383.

James de Caledonia IV March 12, 1788
Newspaper Article: Philadelphia *Freeman's Journal* (excerpt)[1]

On Saturday week ABOVE ONE THOUSAND ARMED MEN assembled in the space of a few hours, at the borough of Carlisle, and after discharging from jail those scoundrels which I wrote you I had imprisoned for abusing me in effigy, they burned the Mittimus, and dismissed the sheriff: they then declared they would oppose our plan at the hazard of their lives, and soon after retired, without making any farther disturbance, to their respective homes.

Such determined and at the same time deliberate conduct, prevails in opposition to us all over the State, that I really begin to be uneasy. I wish all the arms were collected.[2]

I am, my Lord,
Your Lordship's most obedient
and devoted servant,
JAMES DE CALEDONIA.

1 DHRC, II Mfm. Pa., p. 2023. This is an Antifederalist satire on James Wilson. The Pennsylvania Antifederalists used James de Caledonia as a pseudonym for Wilson. For more information on the events described in this excerpt, see DHRC, II, p. 670.

2 For other documents related to the collection of publicly owned arms in Pennsylvania, and the complaint that this was intended to disarm the militia, see: "Jacob Trusty," December 19, 1787, p. 176; "Centinel IX," January 8, 1788, p. 191; Pennsylvania *Carlisle Gazette,* January 9, 1788, p. 194; "Trusty," January 10, 1788, p. 200; "Supreme Executive Council," January 10, 1788, p. 201; "An Old Militia Officer of 1776," January 18, 1788, p. 221; Philadelphia *Freeman's Journal,* January 23, 1788, p. 226; Philadelphia *Pennsylvania Herald,* February 5, 1788, p. 251; Philadelphia *Independent Gazetteer,* February 27, 1788, p. 286; "Aristocrotis," April [15], 1788, p. 334 at note 2; Philadelphia *Independent Gazetteer,* April 30, 1788, p. 340 at note 3.

An Impartial Citizen March 13, 1788
Newspaper Article: Petersburg *Virginia Gazette* (excerpts)

But here the enemies of the new system frighten us with the idea of a standing army. I am a mortal enemy to standing armies, in time of peace particularly; but the necessity of armies in some cases is very obvious. If there be a probability of an attack by foreign nations, or of an overthrow of the government by civil discord, we ought not to wait the enemies attack in either case. It is sophistry in the extreme to suppose, that standing armies will be kept in time of profound peace, when there is no necessity for it. As a regular statement and account of the public receipts and expenditures of money, are to be published from time to time, for the inspection and examination of the public; and as this cannot, on any pretext, be kept secret from the people should armies be unnecessarily maintained the sums which their maintenance would cost would be universally known, and as universally would the measure be reprobated. Every Legislature, and the people in every State, would certainly direct their Representative members and Senators, to vote the dismission of the army. This would be as certainly done; or a neglect of such directions would be severely censured and punished. When a standing army will be unnecessarily maintained in the United States, there will not be a particle of virtue in the people; they will be ripe for the most corrupt government. But the power of raising and collecting taxes, and of providing for arming and disciplining the militia, and governing such part of them as may be employed in the service of the United States, are represented as the means whereby the State Legislatures will be destroyed, and the members of Congress rendered an hereditary aristocracy. . . . The congress cannot make an instrument of tyranny of the militia: The Congress can only provide for arming and disciplining them. The propriety of this results from that of an uniformity of discipline and armour throughout the States, which must be self-evident. The Congress can provide for calling forth the militia only in three cases, viz. to execute the laws of the Union, suppress insurrections, and repel invasions: Ought not these three things to be done? Still the respective States have the authority of training the militia according to the congressional discipline: still they have the appointment of the officers: this renders the States perfectly secure. If the Congress does not prescribe any mode of discipline, the States are not abridged of disciplining them: If the Congress does, still without being trained, and without officers, militia will be useless. Officers appointed by the States would never concur in the destruction of the liberties of their country.

If the congress were to call forth the militia of this State to quel an insurrection in Connecticut, when with infinitely more ease and convenience the Militia of Massachusetts, or some adjacent State, could effect it, the consequence would be an universal, just and irresistable alarm and struggle throughout the Continent: Every State would be deeply interested in opposing so very oppressive an act. It cannot be supposed that the Congress will ever hazard so dangerous a measure. Its members must be idiots or madmen to attempt so wanton a depression of liberty. The members of a Congress who would enact such a measure, would be amenable to their constituents, and every degree of punishment that constituents can any way inflict, would most surely be inflicted on them. They would at all events be never confided in again, nor ever chosen to any office whatever. The people will moreover in every State give positive and pointed directions to their Representatives, and the Legislatures to the Senators, to oppose in Congress, every measure of an oppressive nature. The members from this State will ever compose one fifth at least, of the members present, or will certainly be joined by as many others as would amount to that number. At the request of that number, the yeas and nays on any question, shall be entered on the journals. This will discover the favorers of tyranny. This will prevent corrupt and dangerous proceedings most effectually. But say the antifederalists, the thirst of power will be so great, that the members of Congress will be all but too ready to oppress the people, and too reluctant to relinquish authority. I have already shewn the impracticability of their continuing in Congress, longer than the time pointed out by the Constitution. The only way then whereby Congress can oppress us in any considerable degree, will be by raising money and an army, unnecessarily, and by ordering the militia to be embodied and marched to destroy their fellow citizens. The publication of the applications of the public revenue, and the notoriety of the situation of public affairs, most clearly will prevent the former. The latter cannot be effected without the consent of the militia officers, who being appointed by the States, will be attached to the people, and will never join in the demolition of the freedom of themselves, of their friends and posterity. Besides, the States would, and I conceive *constitutionally* could, oppose this last measure: The Constitution does not say expressly, that the militia shall be marched out of their respective States. And this power by implication will never be suffered to be strained to a most unnecessary and dangerous purpose.

DHRC, VIII, p. 498-500.

Philadelphia *Independent Gazetteer* March 14, 1788

Extract of a letter from a gentleman in Maryland, to his friend in this city, dated March 4.

"The convention of Boston I find have agreed to the new constitution, but in such a manner, as will, in my opinion, considerably affect the system. New-York, Maryland, Virginia, North and South-Carolina, will, I am persuaded, in imitation, propose amendments, and this new government will not be established without paying a deference to the desire of so large a part of the confederation.

"If some amendments should be adopted, it will be all right, and the efforts of the minority have no other object than to secure, in *explicit terms,* some of the essential rights and privileges of freemen. It may be of dangerous consequence to refuse desires so reasonable. If the constitution should pass at all, I hope it will be in such a way as may encrease the unity of the states and the harmony of our citizens, and that we be not a house divided against itself."

DHRC, XVI, p. 536.

Sommers March 15, 1788
Newspaper Article: *Pittsburgh Gazette* (excerpt)

I hope the independent yeomanry of Pennsylvania are not unacquainted with their rights and privileges. You have fought for and are entitled to a government of *laws,* not of *names;* and your happiness depends upon a *full and unequivocal declaration of those rights and privileges in the most full, explicit, and direct terms.* Does this artful, abstruse, and ambiguous plan of government offered to you by our modern patriots, secure these inestimable blessings? No. You are sacrificing your best birth rights at the shrine of ambition and despotism, and courting popularity *for the day,* to become execrable and miserable *for ever.*

DHRC, II Mfm. Pa., p. 2087.

Luther Martin March 18, 1788
Newspaper Article: Baltimore *Maryland Journal* (excerpt)

[*To the* CITIZENS *of* MARYLAND.]

That a system may enable government wantonly to exercise power over the militia, to call out an unreasonable number from any particular state without its permission, and to march them upon, and continue them in, remote and improper services—that the same system should enable the government totally to discard, render useless, and even disarm the militia, when it would remove them out of the way of opposing its ambitious views, is by no means inconsistent, and is really the case in the proposed constitution:—In both these respects it is, in my opinion, highly faulty, and ought to be amended. In the proposed system, the general government has a power not only *without* the *consent,* but *contrary* to the *will* of the *state government,* to call out the *whole* of its militia, without regard to *religious scruples,* or any other consideration, and to continue them in service as long as it pleases, thereby subjecting the *freemen* of a whole state to *martial* law, and reducing them to the situation of *slaves.*—It has also, by another clause, the powers, by *which only* the militia can be organized and armed, and by the neglect of which they may be rendered utterly useless and insignificant, when it suits the ambitious purposes of government:—Nor is the suggestion unreasonable, even if it had been made, that the government might improperly oppress and harass the militia, the better to reconcile them to the idea of regular troops, who might relieve them from the burthen, and to render them less opposed to the measures it might be disposed to adopt for the purpose of reducing them to that state of insignificancy and uselessness.

When the Landholder declared that "I contended the powers and authorities of the new constitution must destroy the liberties of the people," he, for once, stumbled on the truth; but even this he could not avoid coupling with an assertion utterly false. I never suggested that "the same powers could be safely entrusted to the old Congress;"—on the contrary, I opposed many of the powers as being of that nature that, in my opinion, they could not be entrusted to any government whatever, consistent with the freedom of the states and their citizens; and earnestly recommended, what I wish, my fellow citizens, deeply to impress on your minds, that in altering or amending our federal government, no *greater powers* ought to be given than *experience has shown to be necessary,* since it will be *easy to delegate further power* when *time* shall dictate the *expediency* or *necessity;* but powers *once bestowed* upon a government, should they be found ever so *dangerous* or *destructive* to freedom, *cannot be resumed or wrested from government,* but by *another revolution.*

Baltimore, March 14, 1788.

DHRC, XVI, pp. 419-420.

A Ploughman March 19, 1788
Newspaper Article: Winchester *Virginia Gazette*

Messieurs BARTGIS & Co. Your giving a place to the following, in your impartial Gazette will oblige A CUSTOMER.

Dear Countrymen, When we address the People at large, we approach the source of majesty, power and dominion, for all authority and constitutional right of government originates with, and proceeds from, the People; but, when the People become so degenerated as to have no jealousy for their dignity, rights and privileges, they never fail to find usurpers in power and dominion; and various have been the schemes for that purpose, sometimes by artful insinuations, sometimes by sheer deception, and often by open violence. Not long since, the ambitious sons of Britain made wide stretches in their encroachments upon our liberties, but by our virtue and bravery, we shook off the insupportable yoke, and thereby became the most free, happy and renowned people in the universe. But, *Liberty!* That Heaven-born darling of every virtuous soul, must undergo her long-accustomed treatment. When banished from Asia, Africa and Europe, she appeared in all her beauty and excellence, in the dreary regions of America; you see how ambition and avarice beset her, with all their sordid concomitants, and are indefatigably exerting every nerve to force her flight from our world, to those blissful regions from whence she descended.

The happy state of America, in the enjoyment of liberty, roused up the envy of the sons of pride, who never could bear with the happiness of the people in any part of this world, have formed a plan of government, incompatible with, and subversive of, those virtuous plans established by our brave and worthy patriots of the late revolution.

And in order to rivet the chains of perpetual slavery upon us, they have made a standing army an essential of the Federal Constitution, which the world cannot produce an instance of a more permanent foundation to erect the fabrick of tyranny upon; here we are to support and pay our own tormentors, with a bayonet at our breast; to be domineered over by the instruments of tyranny and oppression, and to keep a standing army, gives cause to suspect that the rulers are afraid of the people, or that they have a design upon them. If their designs are oppressive, the army is necessary to compleat the tyranny; if the army is the strongest force in a State, it must be a military government, and it is eternally true, that a free government and a standing army are absolutely incompatible.

An army is so forcible, and at the same time so terrible an instrument, that any hand that wields it may, without much dexterity, perform any operation, and gain any ascendency in human society, and is a mortal distemper in a free government, of which it must inevitably perish.

It was a custom with Lord Walpole when he was minister of state in England, that if any borough did not elect whom he directed, he would send a messenger of satan to buffet them, viz. a company of soldiers to live upon them.

I wish the majesty of the people, together with Congress, would consider, that notwithstanding the throne of tyranny is upheld by an army, it is in continual danger of being overthrown by the same army. Armies have dethroned many a tyrant of their own setting up, and are sure to set up another tyrant in his place. Witness many of the Roman Emperors (of scarlet memory); the Turkish Emperors with their bloody bashaws. Witness the tyrant Charles the first of England; the same army set up the tyrant Cromwell, whom they would murder, had he not concealed himself; but the same army hanged him at Tyburn after he was dead, and that same army set up the tyrant Charles the second; so that an army, with all its inherent malignancy, force and terror, is not to be depended upon; if they do not butcher the people, they will sacrifice their masters; the nature and disposition of an army will not admit of their being inoffensive.

Permit me, my dear fellow citizens, to add one truth more as true as the gospel; that by the Federal Constitution, every soul in America will be an absolute slave; the common people, who are the best and greatest supporters of government, will be slaves to a numberless herd of creeping sycophants; those will be slaves to their employers; their employers will be slaves to Congress, and Congress will be slaves to the army, and the army will be slaves to the &c. &c. &c.

These sentiments are stubborn truths which none upon earth but an American dare hold up to the publick; but if the Federal Constitution be ratified, *the Liberty of the PRESS, that palladium of Freedom, will be lost also.*

Finally, my fellow citizens, you ought to consider this period to be the most interesting you ever saw, or ever will see; now is the time to secure, or to bid an eternal farewell to liberty.

Your interest is inseperably connected with that of Your humble servant, A PLOUGHMAN.

Cherry-lane, March 3, 1788.

DHRC, VIII, pp. 507-509.

Connecticut *Norwich Packet* March 20, 1788

Amidst the rage for forming Constitutions, it is ardently to be wished, says a Correspondent, that Connecticut, would at least *think* of establishing one for herself.—Since the Charter (improved as a substitute) was formed, the circumstances of the State as to population, manners, customs, &c. are so materially varied that it has become indispensably necessary that a Constitution be agreed on, whereby the rights, privileges and immunities, of its citizens be *invariably fixed.*—It may be further urged, with propriety, from the expected operation of the federal government.

DHRC, III, Mfm. Con., p. 346.

A Farmer IV March 21, 1788

Newspaper Article: Baltimore *Maryland Gazette* (excerpt)

The trial by jury is—the democratic branch of the judiciary power—more necessary than representatives in the legislature; for those usurpations, which silently undermine the spirit of liberty, under the sanction of law, are more dangerous than direct and open legislative attacks; in the one case the treason is never discovered until liberty, and with it the power of defence is lost; the other is an open summons to arms, and then if the people will not defend their rights, they do not deserve to enjoy them.

Storing, V, p. 38.

Luther Martin March 21, 1788

Newspaper Article: Baltimore *Maryland Journal* (excerpts)

[This address is an answer to Landholder No.X which charged antifederalist Martin originated the clause in the Federal Convention making the laws of Congress paramount to state laws and constitutions.]

To the CITIZENS *of* Maryland. . . .

When this clause was introduced, it was not established that *inferior* continental courts should be appointed for trial of all questions arising on treaties and on the laws of the general government, and it was my wish and hope that every question of that kind would have been determined, in the first instance, in the courts of the respective states;

had this been the case, the propriety and the necessity that treaties duly made and ratified, and the laws of the general government should be *binding* on the state judiciaries, which were to decide upon them, must be evident to every capacity, while, at the same time, if such treaties or laws were inconsistent with our constitution and bill of rights, the judiciaries of this state would be bound to *reject* the *first* and *abide* by the *last;* since in the form *I* introduced the clause, notwithstanding treaties and the laws of the general government were intended to be superior to the laws of our state government, where they should be opposed to each other, yet that they were not proposed, nor meant to be superior to our *constitution* and bill of rights. It was afterwards altered and amended (if it can be called an amendment) to the form in which it stands in the system now published, and, as inferior continental, and not state, courts are originally to decide on those questions, it is *now worse* than *useless;* for being so altered as to render the treaties and laws made under the general government superior to our constitution, if the system is adopted, it will amount to a total and unconditional surrender to that government, by the citizens of this state, of every right and privilege secured to them by our constitution, and an express compact and stipulation with the general government, that it may, at its discretion, make laws in direct violation of those rights: But on this subject I shall enlarge in a future number. . . .

With respect to a bill of rights—Had the government been formed upon prinicples truly federal, as I wished it, legislating over and acting upon the states only in their collective or political capacity, and not on individuals, there would have been no need of a bill of rights, as far as related to the rights of individuals, but only as to the rights of states:—But the proposed constitution being intended and empowered to act not only on states, but also immediately on individuals, it renders a recognition and a stipulation in favour of the rights both of states and of men, not only proper, but in my opinion, *absolutely* necessary.—I endeavoured to obtain a restraint on the powers of the general government, as to standing armies, but it was rejected. It was my wish that the general government should not have the power of suspending the privilege of the writ of *Habeas Corpus,* as it appears to me altogether unnecessary, and that the power given to it, may and will be used as a dangerous engine of oppression; but I could not succeed.

An honourable member from South-Carolina, most anxiously sought to have a clause inserted, securing the Liberty of the Press, and *repeatedly* brought this subject before the Convention, but could not obtain it.—I am almost positive he made the same attempt to have a stipulation in favour of Liberty of Conscience, but in vain.—The more the system advanced, the more was I impressed with the necessity of not merely attempting to secure a few rights, but of digesting and forming a complete bill of rights, including those of states and of individuals, which should be assented to, and prefixed to the constitution, to serve as a barrier between the general government and the respective states and their citizens; because the more the system advanced, the more clearly it appeared to me that the framers of it did not consider that either states or men had any rights at all, or that they meant to secure the enjoyment of any to either the one or the other; accordingly, I devoted a part of my time to the actually preparing and draughting such a bill of rights, and had it in readiness before I left the Convention, to have laid it before a committee.—I conversed with several members on the subject; they agreed with me on the propriety of the measure, but, at the same time, expressed their sentiments that it would be impossible to procure its adoption if attempted.—A very few days before I left the Convention, I shewed to an honourable member sitting by me, a proposition, which I then had in my hand, couched in the following words, "Resolved, that a committee be appointed to prepare and report a bill of rights, to be prefixed to the proposed constitution," and I then would instantly have moved for the appointment of a committee for that purpose, if he would have agreed to second the motion, to do which he hesitated, not as I understood from any objection to the measure, but from a conviction in his own mind, that the motion would be in vain.

Thus, my fellow-citizens, you see that so far from having no objections to the system on this account, while I was at Convention, I not only then thought a bill of rights necessary, but I took some pains to have the subject brought forward, which would have been done, had it not been for the difficulties I have stated:—At the same time I declare, that when I drew up the motion, and was about to have proposed it to the Convention, I had not the most distant hope it would meet with success.—The rejection of the clauses attempted in favour of particular rights, and to check and restrain the dangerous and exorbitant powers of the general government from being abused, had sufficiently taught me what to expect.

DHRC, XVI, pp. 452-456.

The Political Club (Danville, Kentucky) March 22, 1788

16. Mr Innes The Militia of Kentucky to suppress insurrections in Massachusetts

Mr Muter That Militia may be called to enforce the execution of a Writ &c. and therefore wanted the sentence "executed the Laws &c.["] to be struck out

Seconded by Mr Speed

On Question Over ruled—

Mr Innes Moved an Amendmt. by inserting to enforce &c. instead of Execute

Seconded by Mr McDowell first Division equal—Secy P.T. gave casting Vote in favour of the amendment

In Debate Mr. Muter opposed the amendmt. observing his fears in calling in a Military force that the Civil power by Posse Com[itatus] is sufficient that Militia when embodied are under Military Govt: and therefore dangerous to Freedom, that the case is unprecendented etc seconded by Mr Speed

Mr Innes etc contended that the P. Com. is to all intents a Military Force & such force necessary to enforce the Collection of Taxes instanced Massachusetts Governmt.

DHRC, VIII, p. 414. See source for information on this excerpt.

A Farmer V March 25, 1788
Newspaper Article: Baltimore *Maryland Gazette* (excerpt)

I cannot think that any *able and virtuous citizen,* would in his cool and dispationate moments, wish to blend or risque the fundamental rights of men, with any organization of society that the Americans can or will make for fifty years to come.—Let us keep these rights of individuals—these unalienable blessings—reserved and separated from every constitution and form—If they are unmingled, the attentive eyes of every citizen will be kept fixed upon them. We shall watch them as a sacred deposit, and we may carry them uninjured and unimpaired through every vicissitude and change, from the government we have left, into some other that may be established on the fixed and solid principles of reason.—Nor can there be, I imagine, any *prudent man,* who would trust the whimsical inventions of the day, with that dangerous weapon *a standing army,* in our present unsettled circumstances—striving to substantiate inefficient and unnatural forms—it would wield us into despotism in a moment, and we have surely had throat-cutting enough in our day.

Storing, V, pp. 41-42.

Tullius March 26, 1788
Newspaper Article: Philadelphia *Freeman's Journal*

Great stress has been laid on the knowledge, the jealousy, and that ardent love of liberty which characterise Americans—as qualities that must *ever* watch over their rights, and shield them from encroachment and oppression. The idea would be just, if taken in a less unlimitted sense. It would be comprehensively just, if the senses were always awake—if knowledge were hereditary—and if the divine flame of liberty should never twinkle or be subject to extinction: But the experience of all ages has shewn that there is no stability in man. He may be virtuous to day and corrupt to-morrow. Alive to his rights at one period, and slumbering over them at another.

It is not enough to confine the measure of human rights to the virtuous: We should endeavour to mete out the blessing to ages of depravity (and these will sooner or later take place) as a restorative to virtue. The miseries consequent on depravity are of themselves sufficiently dreadful, without the addition of slavery,—an addition, which once made, *will* rivet shackles on posterity too who may deserve a better fate. The surest way to avoid the evil, and preserve the dignity and happiness of man, is to *begin right*—by clearly defining the powers intended to be delegated by the people to their rulers for the sake of protection—and expresly enumerating the rights to be reserved. Here would appear the *quid pro quo*—and *by appearing*, these rights would be universally understood, and *remembered*. The transition from freedom to slavery would be less easy—for the rights of the people being constantly impressed upon the mind, and the principles of the government fully understood—nothing would be left to the sport of implication, or the construction of arbitrary controul.

Permit me to conclude with the opinion of an honest man—that able statesman and philosopher, Mr. Jefferson: which, tho' it respects religious tyranny founded on certain laws of Virginia, is nevertheless applicable to any subject, and the present important period.*—He says—"Get rid, *while we may*, of those tyrannical laws. It is true we are *yet* secured against them by the spirit of the times. I doubt whether the people of this country would suffer an execution for heresy, or a three years imprisonment for not comprehending the mysteries of the Trinity. But is the spirit of the people an *infallible, a permanent* reliance? *Is it government?* Is this the kind of protection we receive in return for the rights we give up? Besides the spirit of the times may alter—*will alter*. Our rulers will become corrupt, our people careless. A single zealot may commence persecutor, and better men be his victims. *It can never be too often repeated*, THAT THE TIME FOR

FIXING EVERY ESSENTIAL RIGHT ON A LEGAL BASIS, IS WHILE OUR RULERS ARE HONEST, AND OURSELVES UNITED. From the conclusion** of this war we shall be going down hill. It will not then be necessary to resort every moment to the people for support. They will be *forgotten,* therefore, and their rights disregarded. They will forget themselves—but in the sole faculty of making money; and will never think of uniting *to effect a due respect for their rights.* The shackles, therefore, which shall not be knocked off at the conclusion of this war [say, the present system of government] will remain on us long, will be made heavier and heavier, till our rights shall revive, or expire in a convulsion."

TULLIUS.

* *Notes on Virginia, P. 171.*

** Mr. *Jefferson wrote this before the peace.*

Luther Martin March 28, 1788

Newspaper Article: Baltimore *Maryland Journal* (excerpts)

But although almost every one agrees the constitution, as it is, to be both defective and dangerous, we are not wanting in characters who earnestly advise us to adopt it, in its present form, with all its faults, and assure us we may safely rely on obtaining, hereafter, the amendments that are necessary:—but why, I pray you, my fellow-citizens, should we not insist upon the necessary amendments being made now, while we have the liberty of acting for ourselves, before the constitution becomes binding upon us by our assent, as every principle of reason, common sense and safety would dictate?—Because, say they, the sentiments of men are so different, and the interests of the different states are so jarring and dissonant, that there is no probability they would agree if alterations and amendments were attempted.—Thus, with one breath, they tell us that the obstacles to any alterations and amendments being agreed to by the states, are so insuperable, that it is vain to make the experiment, while in the next, they would persuade us it is so certain that states will accede to *those* which shall be necessary; and that *they may* be procured even after the system shall be ratified, that we need not hesitate swallowing the poison, from the ease and security of instantly obtaining the antidote; and they seem to think it astonishing that any person should find a difficulty in reconciling the absurdity and contradiction!

If it is easy to obtain proper amendments, do not let us sacrifice every thing that ought to be dear to freemen, for want of insisting upon its being done, while we have the power.

If the obtaining them will be difficult and improbable, for God's sake do not accept of such a form of government, as without amendments cannot fail of rendering you mere beasts of burthen, and reducing you to a level with your own slaves, with this aggravating distinction, that you *once* tasted the blessings of freedom. . . . what state is there that would have been averse to a bill of rights, or that would have wished for the destruction of jury trial in a great variety of cases, and in a particular manner in *every case,* without exception, where the *government itself is interested?*—These parts of the system, so far from promoting the interest of any state, or states, have an immediate tendency to annihilate *all* the state governments indiscriminately, and to subvert their rights, and the rights of their citizens.—To oppose these, and to procure their alteration, is equally the interest of every state in the union. . . .

Reflect also, I entreat you, my fellow-citizens, that the alterations and amendments which are wanted in the present system, are of such a nature as to *diminish* and *lessen,* to *check* and *restrain* the powers of the general government, not to *increase* and *enlarge* those powers;—If they were of the *last* kind, we might safely adopt it, and trust to giving greater powers hereafter, like a Physician who administers an emetick, *ex re nata,* giving a moderate dose at first, and increasing it afterwards as the constitution of the patient may require.—But I appeal to the history of mankind for this truth, *that when once power and authority are delegated to a government, it knows how to keep it, and is sufficiently and successfully fertile in expedients for that purpose:*—Nay more, the whole history of mankind proves, that so far from parting with the powers actually delegated to it, *government is constantly encroaching on the small pittance of rights reserved by the people to themselves, and gradually wresting them out of their hands, until it either terminates in their slavery, or forces them to arms, and brings about a revolution.*

From these observations it appears to me, my fellow-citizens, that nothing can be more weak and absurd, than to accept of a system that is admitted to stand in need of immediate amendments to render your rights secure; for remember, *if you fail in obtaining them, you cannot free yourselves from the yoke you will have placed on your necks, and servitude must, therefore, be your portion!*

DHRC, XVI, p. 500-502.

J. T. Chase & J. F. Mercer April, 1788
Candidates' Handbill for Maryland Convention Elections.

BILL of RIGHTS.
LIBERTY of CONSCIENCE.
TRIAL by JURY.
NO EXCISE.
NO POLL TAX.
NO STANDING ARMY IN PEACE,
WITHOUT LIMITATION.
NO WHIPPING MILITIA,
NOR MARCHING THEM OUT OF
THE STATE, WITHOUT CONSENT
OF THE GENERAL ASSEMBLY.
NO DIRECT TAXATION,
WITHOUT PREVIOUS
REQUISITION.

J. T. CHASE.
J. F. MERCER.

DHC, IV, pp. 641-642.

A Plebian April, 1788
Pamphlet: An Address to the People of the State of New-York. (excerpts)
New York

Friends and Fellow Citizens,

The advocates for the proposed new constitution, having been beaten off the field of argument, on its merits, have now taken new ground. They admit it is liable to well-founded objections—that a number of its articles ought to be amended; that if alterations do not take place, a door will be left open for an undue administration, and encroachments on the liberties of the people; and many of them go so far as to say, if it should continue for any considerable period, in its present form, it will lead to a subversion of our equal republican forms of government.—But still, although they admit this, they urge that it ought to be adopted, and that we should confide in procuring the necessary alterations after we have received it. Most of the leading characters, who advocate its reception, now profess their readiness to concur with those who oppose it, in bringing about the most material amendments contended for, provided they will first agree to accept the proffered system as it is. These concessions afford strong evidence, that the opposers of the constitution have reason on their side, and that they have not been influenced, in the part they have taken, by the mean and unworthy motives of selfish and private interests with which they have been illiberally charged.—As the favourers of the constitution, seem, if their professions are sincere, to be in a situation similar to that of Agrippa, when he cried out upon Paul's preaching—"almost thou persuadest me to be a christian," I cannot help indulging myself in expressing the same wish which St. Paul uttered on that occasion, "Would to God you were not only almost, but altogether such an one as I am." But alas, as we hear no more of Agrippa's christianity after this interview with Paul, so it is much to be feared, that we shall hear nothing of amendments from most of the warm advocates for adopting the new government, after it gets into operation. When the government is once organized, and all the offices under it filled, the inducements which our great men will have to support it, will be much stronger than they are now to urge its reception. Many of them will then hold places of great honour and emolument, and others will be candidates for such places. It is much harder to relinquish honours and emoluments, which we have in possession, than to abandon the pursuit of them, while the attainment is held in a state of uncertainty.—The amendments contended for as necessary to be made, are of such a nature, as will tend to limit and abridge a number of the powers of the government. And is it probable, that those who enjoy these powers will be so likely to surrender them after they have them in possession, as to consent to have them restricted in the act of granting them? Common sense says—they will not.

When we consider the nature and operation of government, the idea of receiving a form radically defective, under the notion of making the necessary amendments, is evidently absurd.

Government is a compact entered into by mankind, in a state of society, for the promotion of their happiness. In forming this compact, common sense dictates, that no articles should be admitted that tend to defeat the end of its institution. If any such are proposed, they should be rejected. When the compact is once formed and put into operation, it is too late for individuals to object. The deed is executed—the conveyance is made—and the power of reassuming the right is gone, without the consent of the parties.—Besides, when a government is once in operation, it acquires strength by habit, and stability by exercise. If it is tolerably mild in its administration, the people sit down easy under it, be its principles and forms ever so repugnant to the maxims of liberty.—It steals, by insensible degrees, one right from the people after another, until it rivets its powers so as to put it beyond the ability of the community to restrict or limit it. The history of the world furnishes many instances of a people's increasing the powers of their rulers by persuasion, but I believe it would be difficult to produce one in which the rulers have been persuaded to relinquish their powers to the people. Wherever this has taken place, it has always been the effect of compulsion. These observations are so well-founded, that they are become a kind of axioms in politics; and the inference to be drawn from them is equally evident, which is this,—that, in forming a government, care should be taken not to confer powers which it will be necessary to take back; but if you err at all, let it be on the contrary side, because it is much easier, as well as safer, to enlarge the powers of your rulers, if they should prove not sufficiently extensive, than it is to abridge them if they should be too great.

It is agreed, the plan is defective—that some of the powers granted, are dangerous—others not well defined—and amendments are necessary. Why then not amend it? Why not remove the cause of danger, and, if possible, even the apprehension of it? The instrument is yet in the hands of the people; it is not signed, sealed, and delivered, and they have power to give it any form they please.

But it is contended, adopt it first, and then amend it. I ask, why not amend, and then adopt it? Most certainly the latter mode of proceeding is more consistent with our ideas of prudence in the ordinary concerns of life. If men were about entering into a contract respecting their private concerns, it would be highly absurd in them to sign and seal an instrument containing stipulations which are contrary to their interest and wishes, under the expectation, that the parties, after its execution, would agree to make alterations agreeable to their desires.—They would insist upon the exceptionable clauses being altered before they would ratify the contract. And is a compact for the government of ourselves and our posterity of less moment than contracts between individuals? Certainly not. But to this reasoning, which at first view would appear to admit of no reply, a variety of objections are made, and a number of reasons urged for adopting the system, and afterwards proposing amendments.—Such as have come under my observation, I shall state, and remark upon.

It is insisted, that the present situation of our country is such, as not to admit of a delay in forming a new government, or of time sufficient to deliberate and agree upon the amendments which are proper, without involving ourselves in a state of anarchy and confusion.

On this head, all the powers of rhetoric, and arts of description, are employed to paint the condition of this country, in the most hideous and frightful colours. We are told, that agriculture is without encouragement; trade is languishing; private faith and credit are disregarded, and public credit is prostrate; that the laws and magistrates are contemned and set at nought; that a spirit of licentiousness is rampant, and ready to break over every bound set to it by the government; that private embarrassments and distresses invade the house of every man of middling property, and insecurity threatens every man in affluent circumstances: in short, that we are in a state of the most grievous calamity at home, and that we are contemptible abroad, the scorn of foreign nations, and the ridicule of the world. From this high-wrought picture, one would suppose, that we were in a condition the most deplorable of any people upon earth. But suffer me, my countrymen, to call your attention to a serious and sober estimate of the situation in which you are placed, while I trace the embarrassments under which you labour, to their true sources. What is your condition? Does not every man sit under his own vine and under his own fig-tree, having none to make him afraid? Does not every one follow his calling without impediments and receive the reward of his well-earned industry? The farmer cultivates his land, and reaps the fruit which the bounty of heaven bestows on his honest toil. The mechanic is exercised in his art, and receives the reward of his labour. The merchant drives his commerce, and none can deprive him of the gain he honestly acquires; all classes and callings of men amongst us are protected in their various pursuits, and secured by the laws in the possession and enjoyment of the property obtained in those pursuits. The laws are as well executed as they ever were, in this or any other country. Neither the hand of private violence, nor the more to be dreaded hand of legal oppression, are reached out to distress us.

It is true, many individuals labour under embarrassments, but these are to be imputed to the unavoidable circumstances of things, rather than to any defect in our governments. We have just emerged from a long and expensive war. During its existence few people were in a situation to encrease their fortunes, but many to diminish them. Debts contracted before the war were left unpaid while it existed, and these were left a burden too heavy to be borne at the commencement of peace. Add to these, that when the war was over, too many of us, instead of reassuming our old habits of frugality and industry, by which alone every country must be placed in a prosperous condition, took up the profuse use of foreign commodities. The country was deluged with articles imported from abroad, and the cash of the country has been sent out to pay for them, and still left us labouring under the weight of a huge debt to persons abroad. These are the true sources to which we are to trace all the private difficulties of individuals: But will a new government relieve you from these? The advocates for it have not yet told you how it will do it—And I will venture to pronounce, that there is but one way in which it can be effected, and that is by industry and economy; limit your expences within your earnings; sell more than you buy, and every thing will be well on this score. Your present condition is such as is common to take place after the conclusion of a war. Those who can remember our situation after the termination of the war preceding the last, will recollect that our condition was similar to the present, but time and industry soon recovered us from it. Money was scarce, the produce of the country much lower than it has been since the peace, and many individuals were extremely embarrassed with debts; and this happened, although we did not experience the ravages, desolations, and loss of property, that were suffered during the late war.

With regard to our public and national concerns, what is there in our condition that threatens us with any immediate danger? We are at peace with all the world; no nation menaces us with war; Nor are we called upon by any cause of sufficient importance to attack any nation. The state governments answer the purposes of preserving the peace, and providing for present exigencies. Our condition as a nation is in no respect worse than it has been for several years past. Our public debt has been lessened in various ways, and the western territory, which has always been relied upon as a productive fund to discharge the national debt, has at length been brought to market, and a considerable part actually applied to its reduction. I mention these things to shew, that there is nothing special, in our present situation, as it respects our national affairs, that should induce us to accept the proffered system, without taking sufficient time to consider and amend it. I do not mean by this, to insinuate, that our government does not stand in need of a reform. It is admitted by all parties, that alterations are necessary in our federal constitution, but the circumstances of our case do by no means oblige us to precipitate this business, or require that we should adopt a system materially defective. We may safely take time to deliberate and amend, without in the mean time hazarding a condition, in any considerable degree, worse than the present.

But it is said, that if we postpone the ratification of this system until the necessary amendments are first incorporated, the consequence will be a civil war among the states. On this head weak minds are alarmed with being told, that the militia of Connecticut and Massachusetts on the one side, and of New-Jersey and Pennsylvania on the other, will attack us with hostile fury; and either destroy us from off the face of the earth, or at best divide us between the two states adjoining us on either side. The apprehension of danger is one of the most powerful incentives to human action, and is therefore generally excited on political questions: But still, a prudent man, though he foreseeth the evil and avoideth it, yet he will not be terrified by imaginary dangers. We ought therefore to enquire what ground there is to fear such an event?—There can be no reason to apprehend, that the other states will make war with us for not receiving the constitution proposed, until it is amended, but from one of the following causes: either that they will have just cause to do it, or that they have a disposition to do it. We will examine each of these:—That they will have no just cause to quarrel with us for not acceding, is evident, because we are under no obligation to do it, arising from any existing compact or previous stipulation. The confederation is the only compact now existing between the states: By the terms of it, it cannot be changed without the consent of every one of the parties to it. Nothing therefore can be more unreasonable than for part of the states to claim of the others, as matter of right, an accession to a system to which they have material objections. No war can therefore arise from this principle, but on the contrary, it is to be presumed, it will operate strongly the opposite way.—The states will reason on the subject in the following manner: On this momentous question, every state has an indubitable right to judge for itself: This is secured to it by solem compact, and if any of our sister states disagree with us upon the question, we ought to attend to their objections, and accommodate ourselves as far as possible to the amendments they propose.

As to the inclination of the states to make war with us, for declining to accede, until it is amended, this is highly improbable, not only because such a procedure would be most unjust and unreasonable in itself, but for various other reasons.

The idea of a civil war amongst the states is abhorrent to the principles and feelings of almost every man of every rank in the union. It is so obvious to every one of the least reflection, that in such an event we should hazard the loss of all things, without the hope of gaining any thing, that the man who should entertain a thought of this kind, would be justly deemed more fit to be shut up in Bedlam, than to be reasoned with. But the idea of one or more states attacking another, for insisting upon alterations in this system, before it is adopted, is more extravagant still; it is contradicting every principle of liberty which has been entertained by the states, violating the most solemn compact, and taking from the state the right of deliberation. Indeed to suppose, that a people, entertaining such refined ideas of the rights of human nature as to be induced to wage war with the most powerful nation on earth, upon a speculative point, and from the mere apprehension of danger only, should so far be lost to their own feelings and principles, as to deny to their brethren, who were associated with them in the arduous conflict, the right of free deliberation on a question of the first importance to their political happiness and safety, is equally an insult to the character of the people of America, and to common sense, and could only be suggested by a vicious heart and a corrupt mind.

The idea of being attacked by the other states, will appear visionary and chimerical, if we consider that tho' several of them have adopted the new constitution, yet the opposition to it has been numerous and formidable. The eastern states from whom we are told we have most to fear, should a civil war be blown up, would have full employ to keep in awe those who are opposed to it in their own governments. Massachusetts, after a long and dubious contest in their convention, has adopted it by an inconsiderable majority, and in the very act has marked it with a stigma in its present form. No man of candour, judging from their public proceedings, will undertake to say, on which side the majority of the people are. Connecticut, it is true, have acceded to it, by a large majority of their convention; but it is a fact well known, that a large proportion of the yeomanry of the country are against it:—And it is equally true, that a considerable part of those who voted for it in the convention, wish to see it altered. In both these states the body of the common people, who always do the fighting of a country, would be more likely to fight against than for it: Can it then be presumed, that a country, divided among themselves, upon a question where even the advocates for it, admit the system they contend for needs amendments, would make war upon a sister state, who only insist that that should be done before they receive it, which it is granted ought to be done after, and where it is confessed no obligation lies upon them by compact to do it. Can it, I say, be imagined, that in such a case they would make war on a sister state? The idea is preposterous and chimerical.

It is further urged, we must adopt this plan because we have no chance of getting a better. This idea is inconsistent with the principles of those who advance it. They say, it must be altered, but it should be left until after it is put in operation. But if this objection is valid, the proposal of altering, after it is received, is mere delusion.

It is granted, that amendments ought to be made; that the exceptions taken to the constitution, are grounded on just principles, but it is still insisted, that alterations are not to be attempted until after it is received: But why not? Because it is said, there is no probability of agreeing in amendments previous to the adoption, but they may be easily made after it. I wish to be informed what there is in our situation or circumstances that renders it more probable that we shall agree in amendments better after, than before submitting to it? No good reason has as yet been given; it is evident none can be given: On the contrary, there are several considerations which induce a belief, that alterations may be obtained with more ease before, than after its reception, and if so, every one must agree, it is much the safest. The importance of preserving an union, and of establishing a government equal to the purpose of maintaining that union, is a sentiment deeply impressed on the mind of every citizen of America. It is now no longer doubted, that the confederation, in its present form, is inadequate to that end: Some reform in our government must take place. In this, all parties agree: It is therefore to be presumed, that this object will be pursued with ardour and perseverance, until it is attained by all parties. But when a government is adopted that promised to effect this, we are to expect the ardour of many, yea, of most people, will be abated;—their exertions will cease, or be languid, and they will sit down easy, although they may see, that the constitution which provides for this, does not sufficiently guard the rights of the people, or secure them against the encroachments of their rulers. The great end they had in view, the security of the union, they will consider effected, and this will divert their attention from that which is equally interesting, safety to their liberties. Besides, the human mind cannot continue intensely engaged for any great length of time upon one object. As after a storm, a calm generally succeeds, so after the minds of a people have been ardently employed upon a subject, especially upon that of government, we commonly find that they become cool and inattentive: Add to this, that those in the community who urge the adoption of this system, because they hope by it to be raised above the common level of their fellow citizens: because they expect to be among the number of the few who will be benefitted by it, will more easily be induced to consent to the amendments before it is received than afterwards. Before its reception, they will be inclined to be pliant and condescending; if they cannot obtain all they wish, they will consent to take less. They will yield part to obtain the rest. But when the plan is once agreed to, they will be tenacious of every power, they will strenuously contend to retain all they have got; this is natural to human nature, and it is consonant to the experience of mankind. For history affords us no examples of persons once possessed of power, resigning it willingly.

The reasoning made use of to persuade us, that no alterations can be agreed upon previous to the adoption of the system, are as curious as they are futile. It is alledged, that there was great diversity of sentiments in forming the proposed constitution; that it was the effect of mutual concessions and a spirit of accommodation, and from hence it is inferred, that farther changes cannot be hoped for. I should suppose that the contrary inference was the fair one. If the convention, who framed this plan, were possessed of such a spirit of moderation and condescension, as to be induced to yield to each other certain points, and to accommodate themselves to each other's opinions, and even prejudices, there is reason to expect, that this same spirit will continue and prevail in a future convention, and produce an union of sentiments on the points objected to. There is the more reason to hope for this, because the subject has received a full discussion, and the minds of the people much better known than they were when the convention sat. Previous to the meeting of the convention, the subject of a new form of government had been little thought of, and scarcely written upon at all. It is true, it was the general opinion, that some alterations were requisite in the federal system. This subject had been contemplated by almost every thinking man in the union. It had been the subject of many well-written essays, and was the anxious wish of every true friend to America. But it never was in the contemplation of one in a thousand of those who had reflected on the matter, to have an entire change in the nature of our federal government—to alter it from a confederation of states, to that of one entire government, which will swallow up that of the individual states. I will venture to say, that the idea of a government similar to the one proposed, never entered the mind of the legislatures who appointed the convention, and of but very few of the members who composed it, until they had assembled and heard it proposed in that body: much less had the people any conception of such a plan until after it was promulgated. While it was agitated, the debates of the convention were kept an impenetrable secret, and no opportunity was given for well informed men to offer their sentiments upon the subject. The system was therefore never publicly discussed, nor indeed could be, because it was not known to the people until after it was proposed. Since that, it has been the object of universal attention—it has been thought of by every reflecting man—been discussed in a public and private manner, in conversation and in print; its defects have been pointed out, and every objection to it stated; able advocates have written in its favour, and able opponents have written against it. And what is the result? It cannot be denied but that the general opinion is, that it contains material errors, and requires important amendments. This then being the general sentiment, both of the friends and foes of the system, can it be doubted, that another convention would concur in such amendments as would quiet the fears of the opposers, and effect a great degree of union on the subject?—An event most devoutly to be wished. But it is farther said, that there can be no prospect of procuring alterations before it is acceded to, because those who oppose it do not agree among themselves with respect to the amendments that are necessary. To this I reply, that this may be urged against attempting alterations after it is received, with as much force as before; and therefore, if it concludes any thing, it is, that we must receive any system of government proposed to us, because those who object to it do not entirely concur in their objections. But the assertion is not true to any considerable extent. There is a remarkable uniformity in the objections made to the constitution, on the most important points. It is also worthy of notice, that very few of the matters found fault with in it, are of a local nature, or such as affect any particular state; on the contrary, they are such as concern the principles of general liberty, in which the people of New-Hampshire, New-York, and Georgia are equally interested.

It would be easy to shew, that in the leading and most important objections that have been made to the plan, there has been, and is an entire concurrence of opinion among writers, and in public bodies throughout the United States.

I have not time fully to illustrate this by a minute narration of particulars; but to prove that this is the case, I shall adduce a number of important instances.

It has been objected to the new system, that it is calculated to, and will effect such a consolidation of the States, as to supplant and overturn the state governments. In this the minority of Pennsylvania, the opposition in Massachusetts, and all the writers of any ability or note in Philadelphia, New-York, and Boston concur. It may be added, that this appears to have been the opinion of the Massachusetts convention, and gave rise to that article in the amendments proposed, which confines the general government to the exercise only of powers expressly given.

It has been said, that the representation in the general legislature is too small to secure liberty, or to answer the intention of representation. In this there is an union of sentiments in the opposers.

The constitution has been opposed, because it gives to the legislature an unlimited power of taxation, both with respect to direct and indirect taxes, a right to lay and collect taxes, duties, imposts, and excises of every kind and description, and to any amount. In this, there has been as general a concurrence of opinion as in the former.

The opposers to the constitution have said that it is dangerous, because the judicial power may extend to many cases which ought to be reserved to the decision of the State courts, and because the right of trial by jury is not secured in the judicial courts of the general government, in civil cases. All the opposers are agreed in this objection.

The power of the general legislature to alter and regulate the time, place, and manner of holding elections, has been stated as an argument against the adoption of the system. It has been urged, that this power will place in the hands of the general government, the authority, whenever they shall be disposed, and a favorable opportunity offers, to deprive the body of the people, in effect, of all share in the government. The opposers to the constitution universally agree in this objection, and of such force is it, that most of its ardent advocates admit its validity, and those who have made attempts to vindicate it, have been reduced to the necessity of using the most trifling arguments to justify it.

The mixture of legislative, judicial, and executive powers in the senate; the little degree of responsibility under which the great officers of government will be held; and the liberty granted by the system to establish and maintain a standing army, without any limitation or restriction, are also objected to the constitution; and in these, there is a great degree of unanimity of sentiment in the opposers.

From these remarks it appears, that the opponents to the system accord in the great and material points on which they wish amendments. For the truth of the assertion, I appeal to the protest of the minority of the convention of Pennsylvania, to all the publications against the constitution, and to the debates of the convention of Massachusetts. As a higher authority than these, I appeal to the amendments proposed by the Massachusetts; these are to be considered as the sense of that body upon the defects of the system. And it is a fact, which I will venture to assert, that a large majority of that convention were of opinion, that a number of additional alterations ought to be made. Upon reading the articles which they propose as amendments, it will appear, that they object to indefinite powers in the legislature—to the power of laying direct taxes—to the authority of regulating elections—to the extent of the judicial powers, both as it respects the inferior courts and the appellate jurisdiction—to the smallness of the representation, &c.—It is admitted, that some writers have advanced objections that others have not noticed—that exceptions have been taken by some, that have not been insisted upon by others, and it is probable, that some of the opponents may approve what others will reject. But still these differences are on matters of small importance, and of such a nature as the persons who hold different opinions will not be tenacious of. Perfect uniformity of sentiment on so great a political subject is not to be expected. Every sensible man is impressed with this idea, and is therefore prepared to make concessions and accommodate on matters of small importance. It is sufficient that we agree in the great leading principles, which relate to the preservation of public liberty and private security. And on these I will venture to affirm we are as well agreed, as any people ever were on a question of this nature. I dare pronounce, that were the principal advocates for the proposed plan to write comments upon it, they would differ more in the sense they would give the constitution, than those who oppose it do, in the amendments they would wish. I am justified in this opinion, by the sentiments advanced by the different writers in favour of the constitution. . . .

But notwithstanding the local prejudices which operate upon the people of these states, a considerable part of them wish for amendments. It is not to be doubted, that a considerable majority of the people of Connecticut wish for them, and many in Jersey have the same desires, and their numbers are increasing: It cannot be disputed, that amendments would accord with the sentiments of a great majority in Massachusetts, or that they would be agreeable to the greater part of the people of Pennsylvania: There is no reason to doubt but that they would be agreeable to Delaware and Georgia—If then, the states who have already ratified the constitution, are desirous to have alterations made in it, what reason can be assigned why they should not cordially meet with overtures for that purpose from any state, and concur in appointing a convention to effect it? Mankind are easily induced to fall upon measures to obtain an object agreeable to them. In this case, the states would not only be moved by this universal principle of human nature, but by the strong and powerful motive of uniting all the states under a form of government agreeable to them.

I shall now dismiss the consideration of objections made to attempting alterations previous to the adoption of the plan, but before I close, I beg your indulgence, while I make some remarks on the splendid advantages, which the advocates for this system say are to be derived from it.—Hope and fear are two of the most active principles of our nature: We have considered how the latter is addressed on this occasion, and with how little reason: It will appear that the promises it makes, are as little to be relied upon, as its threatenings. We are amused with the fair prospects that are to open, when this government is put into operation—Agriculture is to flourish, and our fields to yield an hundred fold—Commerce is to expand her wings, and bear our productions to all the ports in the world—Money is to pour into our country through every channel—Arts and manufactures are to rear their heads, and every mechanic find full employ—those who are in debt, are to find easy means to procure money to pay them—Public burdens and taxes are to be lightened, and yet all our public debts are soon to be discharged.—With such vain and delusive hopes are the minds of many honest and well meaning people fed, and by these means are they led inconsiderately to contend for a government, which is made to promise what it cannot perform; while their minds are diverted from contemplating its true nature, or considering whether it will not endanger their liberties, and work oppression. . . .

Having remarked upon the arguments which have been advanced, to induce you to accede to this government, without amendments, and I trust refuted them, suffer me to close with an address dedicated by the affection of a brother, and the honest zeal of a lover of his country.

Friends, countrymen, and fellow citizens,

The present is the most important crisis at which you ever have arrived. You have before you a question big with consequences, unutterably important to yourselves, to your childeren, to generations yet unborn, to the cause of liberty and of mankind; every motive of religion and virtue, of private happiness and public good, of honour and dignity, should urge you to consider cooly and determine wisely.

Almost all the governments that have arisen among mankind, have sprung from force and violence. The records of history inform us of none that have been the result of cool and dispassionate reason and reflection: It is reserved for this favoured country to exhibit to mankind the first example.—This opportunity is now given us, and we are to exercise our rights in the choice of persons to represent us in convention, to deliberate and determine upon the constitution proposed: It will be to our everlasting disgrace to be indifferent on such a subject, for it is impossible, we can contemplate any thing that relates to the affairs of this life of half the importance.

You have heard that both sides on this great question, agree, that there are in it great defects; yet the one side tell you, choose such men as will adopt it, and then amend it—while the other say, amend previous to its adoption.—I have stated to you my reasons for the latter, and I think they are unanswerable.—Consider you the common people, the yeomanry of the country, for to such I principally address myself, you are to be the principal losers, if the constitution should prove oppressive. When a tyranny is established, there are always masters as well as slaves; the great and the well-born are generally the former, and the middling class the latter—Attempts have been made, and will be repeated, to alarm you with the fear of consequences; but reflect, there are consequences on both sides, and none can be apprehended more dreadful, than entailing on ourselves and posterity a government which will raise a few to the height of human greatness and wealth, while it will depress the many to the extreme of poverty and wretchedness. Consequences are under the controul of that all-wise and all-powerful being, whose providence directs the affairs of men: Our part is to act right, and we may then have confidence that the consequences will be favourable. The path in which you should walk is plain and open before you; be united as one man, and direct your choice to such men as have been uniform in their opposition to the proposed system in its present form, or without proper alterations: In men of this description you have reason to place confidence, while on the other hand, you have just cause to distrust those who urge the adoption of a bad constitution, under the delusive expectation of making amendments after it is acceded to. Your jealousy of such characters should be the more excited, when you consider that the advocates for the constitution have shifted their ground. When men are uniform in their opinions, it affords evidence that they are sincere: When they are shifting, it gives reason to believe, they do not change from conviction. It must be recollected, that when this plan was first announced to the public, its supporters cried it up as the most perfect production of human wisdom: It was represented either as having no defects, or if it had, they were so trifling and inconsiderable, that they served only, as the shades in a fine picture, to set off the piece to the greater advantage. One gentleman in Philadelphia went so far, in the ardour of his enthusiasm in its favour, as to pronounce, that the men who formed it were as really under the guidance of Divine Revelation, as was Moses, the Jewish lawgiver. Their language is now changed; the question has been discussed; the objections to the plan ably stated, and they are admitted to be unanswerable. The same men who held it almost perfect, now admit it is very imperfect; that it is necessary it should be amended. The only question between us, is simply this: Shall we accede to a bad constitution, under the uncertain prospect of getting it amended, after we have received it, or shall we amend it before we adopt it? Common sense will point out which is the most rational, which is the most secure line of conduct. May heaven inspire you with wisdom, union, moderation and firmness, and give you hearts to make a proper estimate of your invaluable privileges, and preserve them to you, to be transmitted to your posterity unimpaired, and may they be maintained in this our country, while Sun and Moon endure.

A Plebian.

POSTSCRIPT.

Since the foregoing pages have been put to the press, a pamphlet has appeared, entitled, "An address to the people of the state of New-York, on the subject of the new constitution, &c." Upon a cursory examination of this performance (for I have not had leisure to give it more than a cursory examination) it appears to contain little more than declamation and observations that have been often repeated by the advocates of the new constitution.

An attentive reader will readily perceive, that almost every thing deserving the name of an argument in this publication, has received consideration, and, I trust, a satisfactory answer in the preceding remarks, so far as they apply to prove the necessity of an immediate adoption of the plan, without amendments.

I shall therefore only beg the patience of my readers, while I make a few very brief remarks on this piece. . . .

This author tells us, "it is not his design to investigate the merits of the plan, nor of the objections made to it." It is well he did not undertake it, for if he had, from the specimen he has given, the cause he assumes would not have probably gained much strength by it.

He however takes notice of two or three of the many objections brought against the plan.

"We are told, (says he) among other strange things, that the liberty of the press is left insecure by the proposed constitution, and yet that constitution says neither more nor less about it, than the constitution of the state of New-York does. We are told it deprives us of trial by jury, whereas the fact is, that it expressly secures it in certain cases, and takes it away in none, &c. It is absurd to construe the silence of this, or of our own constitution relative to a great number of our rights into a total extinction of them; silence and a blank paper neither grant nor take away anything."

It may be a stange thing to this author [A Citizen of New York] to hear the people of America anxious for the preservation of their rights, but those who understand the true principles of liberty, are no strangers to their importance. The man who supposes the constitution, in any part of it, is like a blank piece of paper, has very erroneous ideas of it. He may be assured every clause has a meaning, and many of them such extensive meaning, as would take a volume to unfold. The suggestion, that the liberty of the press is secure, because it is not in express words spoken of in the constitution, and that the trial by jury is not taken away, because it is not said in so many words and letters it is so, is puerile and unworthy of a man who pretends to reason. We contend, that by the indefinite powers granted to the general govenment, the liberty of the press may be restricted by duties, &c. and therefore the constitution ought to have stipulated for its freedom. The trial by jury, in all civil cases is left at the discretion of the general government, except in the supreme court on the appellate jurisdiction, and in this I affirm it is taken away, not by express words, but by fair and legitimate construction and inference; for the supreme court have expressly given them an appellate jurisdiction, in every case to which their powers extend (with two or three exceptions) both as to *law and fact.* The court are the judges; every man in the country, who has served as a juror, knows, that there is a distinction between the court and the jury, and that the lawyers in their pleading, make the distinction. If the court, upon appeals, are to determine both the law and the fact, there is no room for a jury, and the right of trial in this mode is taken away.

The author manifests equal levity in referring to the constitution of this state, to shew that it was useless to stipulate for the liberty of the press, or to insert a bill of rights in the constitution. With regard to the first, it is perhaps an imperfection in our constitution that the liberty of the press is not expressly reserved; but still there was not equal necessity of making this reservation in our State as in the general Constitution, for the common and statue law of England, and the laws of the colony are established, in which this privilege is fully defined and secured. It is true, a bill of rights is not prefixed to our constitution, as it is in that of some of the states; but still this author knows, that many essential rights are reserved in the body of it; and I will promise, that every opposer of this system will be satisfied, if the stipulations that they contend for are agreed to, whether they are prefixed, affixed, or inserted in the body of the constitution, and that they will not contend which way this is done, if it be but done. I shall add but one remark, and that is upon the hackneyed argument introduced by the author, drawn from the character and ability of the framers of the new constitution. The favourers of this system are not very prudent in bringing this forward. It provokes to an investigation of characters, which is an invidious task. I do not wish to detract from their merits, but I will venture to affirm, that twenty assemblies of equal number might be collected, equally repectable both in point of ability, integrity, and patriotism.

Storing, VI, pp. 129-146. Also reprinted in *Pamphlets*, pp. 89-115.

A Farmer VI April 1, 1788
Newspaper Article: Baltimore *Maryland Gazette* (excerpt)

Retired in the country the publication by *Aristides* did not reach the *Farmer* until this moment. The object of the remarks by the *Farmer* was to draw the attention of the public to a question of the greatest magnitude to them and their posterity; and the *cause* in which he has ventured to publish his sentiments is a *cause* of the United States.—The great and manifest defects in the *national* government proposed for America.—the omission of a declaration to ascertain the *rights* of the several *States*, and the *rights* of *individuals*, the primary object of every good and free government, particularly the trial by jury on suit against a *federal* officer for abuse of authority;—the want of proper checks to prevent the abuse, or annihilation of those rights;—the manifest danger to public liberty from a standing army, without limitation of number, in time of peace;—and the pernicious doctrines of *Aristides;* alone induced the *Farmer* to lay his reflections before the tribunal of public opinion. . . .

Is not the *supreme federal* court superior to the *State* courts? Is it not superior to the bills of rights, and the constitutions, of the several States?

Storing, V, p. 51-53.

Massachusetts Delegates April 9, 1788
Newspaper Article: Reasons for Dissent, Northampton *Hampshire Gazette* (excerpts)

We the subscribers being of the number, who did not assent to the ratification of the federal constitution, under consideration in the late state convention, held at Boston, to which we were called by the suffrages of the corporations to which we respectively belong—beg leave, through the channel of your paper to lay before the public in general, and our constituents in particular, the reasons of our dissent, and the principles which governed us in our decision of this important question.

Fully convinced, ever since the late revolution, of the necessity of a firm, energetic government, we should have rejoiced in an opportunity to have given our assent to such a one; and should in the present case, most cordially have done it, should we at the same time been happy to have seen the liberties of the people and the rights of mankind properly guarded and secured. We conceive that the very notion of government carries along with it the idea of justice and equity, and that the whole design of instituting government in the world, was to preserve men's properties from rapine, and their bodies from violence and bloodshed. . . .

But it was pled by some of the ablest advocates of the constitution, that if congress should exercise such powers to the prejudice of the people (and they did not deny but they could if they should be disposed) they (the people) would not suffer it. They would have recourse to the *ultima ratio,* the *dernier resort* of the oppressed—*the sword.*

But it appeared to us a piece of *superlative incongruity* indeed, that the people, whilst in the full and indefeasible possession of their liberties and privileges, should be so very profuse, so very liberal in the disposal of them, as consequently to place themseves in a predicament miserable to an extreme. . . .

Consider Arms
Malichi Maynard
Samuel Field

Storing, IV, pp. 255-258.

Aristocrotis April [15], 1788

Pamphlet: The Government of Nature Delineated or An Exact Picture of the New Federal Constitution. (excerpts)[1]

Carlisle, Pennsylvania

[This is an Antifederalist satire upon Federalist views. Ed.]

The present is an active period; Europe is in a ferment breaking their constitutions, America is in a similar state, making a constitution—For this valuable purpose a convention was appointed, consisting of such as excelled in wisdom and knowledge, who met in Philadelphia last May. For my own part, I was so smitten with the character of the members, that I had assented to their production, while it was yet in embrio; and I make no doubt but every good republican did so too; but how great was my surprize, when it appeared with such a venerable train of names annexed to its tail, to find some of the people under different signatures; such as *Centinel, Old Whig, Brutus, etc.,* daring to oppose it, and that too with barefaced arguments, obstinate reason and stubborn truth. This is certainly a piece of the most extravagant impudence to presume to contradict the collected wisdom of the United States; or to suppose a body, who engrossed the whole wisdom of the continent, was capable of erring. I expected the superior character of the convention would have secured it from profane sallies of a plebeian's pen; and its inherent infaliability, debarred the interference of impertinent reason or truth. It was too great an act of condescension to permit the people, by their state conventions, "to assent and ratify," what the grand convention prescribed to them; but to enquire into its priciples, or investigate its properties, was a presumption too daring to escape resentment. Such licentious conduct practised by the people, is a striking proof of our feeble governments, and calls aloud for the pruning knife, viz. the establishment of some proper plan of discipline. This the convention, in the depth of their united wisdom hath prescribed, which when established, will certainly put a stop to the growing evil. A consciousness of this, is, no doubt, the cause which stimulates the people to oppose it with so much vehemence; they deprecate the idea of being confined within their proper sphere; they cannot endure the thoughts of being obliged to mind their own business, and leave the affairs of government to those whom nature hath destined to rule. I say nature, for it is a fundamental principle, as clear as an axiom, that nature hath placed proper degrees and subordinations amongst mankind, and ordained a few to rule, and many to obey. . . .

A government founded agreeable to nature must be intirely independant; that is, it must be beyond the reach of annoyance or controul from every power on earth. Now in order to render it thus, several things are necessary.

1st. The means of their own support must be within the immediate reach of rulers: for this purpose they must possess the sole power of taxation. . . .

2ndly. It will create and diffuse a spirit of industry among the people; they will then be obliged to labour for money to pay their taxes: . . .

3dly. This will make the people attend to their own business; and not be dabbling in politics—things they are entirely ignorant of; nor is it proper they should understand. But it is very probable that the exercise of this power may be opposed by the refractory plebians, who (such is the perverseness of their natures) often refuse to comply with what is manifestly for their advantage; but to prevent all inconveniency from this quarter the congress have power to raise and support armies. This is the second thing necessary to render government independent. . . .

4thly. To render government entirely independent, they must have the sole and absolute command of the militia without restriction or reserve, either as to time or place, principle or conscience; and with this power the constitution hath amply furnished them—see article 1st sect. 8. "the congress shall have power to provide for calling forth the militia to execute the laws of the union, suppress insurrections, and repel invasions, to provide for organising, arming, and disciplining the militia, and for governing such part of them as may be employed in the service of the united states." By this clause the militia is divided into two classes, viz. active and inactive; the active militia will be those employed "in the service of the united states," or in other words in the service of congress; they will consist of young men chiefly, who will not be attached to any particular place, on account of their families: or such eccentric genius's as by their superior address or daring spirit may gain an ascendency over the minds of the vulgar, and so become the heads of liberty factions.

Such persons as these will best suit the purpose of government; and if they are judiciously culled and picked, will compose a very respectable army; from which many great advantages may result to government. 1st. They will assist, in conjunction with the standing army, to quell insurrections that may arise in any part of the empire on account of pretensions to support liberty, redress grievances, and the like. 2dly. This power will enable congress to fulfill their engagements with foreign nations, their allies; should they stipulate in the treaty of alliance, to furnish a number of troops (in consideration of a certain sum of money) to be employed in the service of these allies, when they are engaged in war, the active militia will always be ready. . . .

The second class or inactive militia, comprehends all the rest of the peasants; viz. the farmers, mechanics, labourers, etc. which good policy will prompt government to disarm. It would be dangerous to trust such a rable as this with arms in their hands. They might employ them in opposing the supreme laws of the land instead of employing them to execute them. 4thly To render government independent, the people must be divested of all the privileges they have wrested from their rulers in times of anarchy and confusion. In modern times the people for the most part have these privileges arranged together in one instrument, which commonly serves as a preliminary to their constitution—this instrument, they call their bill of rights.* These rights are claims which the people have extorted from weak, timid, irresolute rulers—However the grand convention in framing the new constitution, hath omitted the dangerous ceremony, and left it in the power of congress, to irradicate every vestage of so daring an encroachment. One particular article provided for in these bills of rights, is the liberty of the press, which the people pretend ought never to be restrained, altho' it is undeniable that it has ever been the vehicle of slander, and the source of innumerable evils; it hath filled the world with seditions, insurrections, rebellions, conspiracies, murders, heresies, and the most dangerous innovations of every sort; wherever it is tolerated it is impossible to divest the people of those dangerous privileges, which they have usurped in time of turbulence and disorder; through this channel they will receive early intelligence of the schemes of government, and be ready on the slightest offence, to unite in support of what they deem their natural and unalienable rights; so that it might prove difficult for the best appointed army, that congress could possibly raise or support, to repel their fury, or reduce them to obedience; but as there is no provision made for its security in the new frame of government, congress may abolish it at pleasure, which they will soon find it their interest to do, and its own native licentiousness will furnish them with reasons plausible enough to form a preamble for the act; as none but friends of government will then have an opportunity of communicating their sentiments to the public, or displaying their genius: so none but they will care to acquire sentiments, or cultivate genius. Learning will then flourish in its native soil, and science run in its proper channel; for a knowledge of letters among the vulgar is the bane of good government. Another privilege which the people possesses at present, and which the new congress will find it their interest to deprive them of, is trial by jury—for of all the powers which the people have wrested from government, this is the most absurd; it is even a gross violation of common sense, and most destructive to energy. In the first place it is absurd, that twelve ignorant plebians, should be constituted judges of a law, which passed through so many learned hands;—first a learned legislature after many learned animadversions and criticisms have enacted it—Second, learned writers have explained and commented on it.—Third, learned lawyers twisted, turned and new modeled it—and lastly, a learned judge opened up and explained it. Yet after all these learned discussions, an illiterate jury (who have scarce a right to think for themselves instead of judging for others) must determine whether it applies to the fact or not; and by their verdict the learned judge must be governed in passing sentence; and perhaps a learned gentleman be cast in an action with an insignificant cottager. . . .

There are many other rights claimed by the people besides these mentioned; but as they are of little consequence, I shall leave the discussion of them to the new congress themselves, who no doubt will be quick sighted enough to discern them, and prudent enough to provide for their removal. But before I conclude, I must take notice of an incumbrance upon government, which have been more general in its operation than any yet mentioned; viz. religion. There has been but few nations in the world, where the people possessed the privilege of electing their rulers; of prefixing a bill of rights to their constitutions, enjoyed a free press, or trial by jury; but there was never a nation in the world whose government was not circumscribed by religion. . . .

I shall now suggest a few directions to my worthy friends, the inventors and advocates of this admirable constitution—1st. that the people may be brought speedily to "assent and ratify" this constitution, they must have very short time given them for consideration;** it may take well enough with them while they know it only by report, but if time and leasure is allowed them to examine it, they will surely reject it. 2dly. everything like argument in its defence must be carefully avoided, and instead thereof, the profound wisdom of the convention, the great men of which it was composed, particularly the names of a Washington and a Franklin, must be rung in the people's ears: it must be declared a crime bordering on blasphemy, to say any thing against the production of such men as these, and if any thing is wrote concerning it, it must be panegyrick, eulogium, or rhapsody; but by all means avoid reasoning, or you will betray the good cause in which you are engaged. 3rdly. All who presume to speak or write against this constitution, must be branded as enemies to their country and to the union of the states; to impress this upon the minds of the vulgar, they must be termed antifederalists,*** all their personal faults must be searched out and exposed; and the people must be warned not to listen to their reasoning on the subject, as they are interested persons, being either officers of government, or expectants of offices, and that their opposition arises from sinister views, and selfish motives, and not from a conviction of its evil: but beware of encountering their arguments, or you will certainly expose this darling constitution to popular execration. 4thly. The people must be told, that the revenue of the nation will be chiefly raised by impost under the new constitution, and that internal taxation will seldom if ever be recurred to; this will amuse them in the mean time while they possess the power, but we hope congress will have more wisdom than to verify this prophecy, as it would be very injurious to the interest of our well beloved brother Robert Morris, and all our brethren in high life throughout the nation: a land, but in particular a high poll-tax, will be the most effectual method of collecting the finances; some other articles, such as stamp duties; a tax on candles, leather, soap, etc. may turn to a very good account; and the money raised from the sale of the active militia to foreigners, will be no contemptable source of revenue. 5thly. All communication between the people of the different states must as much as possible be prevented—therefore our own friends must be posts and postmasters, and they must have full power to break open all packets, letters, and papers of every sort, and if they contain any thing against the new constitution they must be suppressed, if not closed up again and sent to the persons to whom they are directed; and it is requested of all our trusty friends throughout the country, that they intercept all papers, which come in their way; examine their contents, and if possible destroy them, if they contain any thing against this glorious plan. 6thly. The militia must be disarmed; for this purpose all the public arms must be called in, upon pretence of having them cleaned;[2] this will not only deprive our enemies of using them against us, but they will be ready to put in the hands of our friends, or men raised by them for the establishment of the constitution if coercion is necessary. 7thly. The distress of the people must be magnified as much as possible; they must be told that they are ruined and miserable, that they are all bankrupts; and that all these calamities is occasioned by their feeble governments (although in fact it is by their own extravagance); and that the new plan will effectually relieve all their wants, and redress all their grievances; although in reality it must be their own industry and economy; but this they must not know for the present. 8thly. They must be told that the new congress will immediately pay off all the debts of the union; but if they ask you how? you must evade the question the best way you can; for if you tell them the truth, that it will be by levying high taxes on themselves, they will be sure to spurn your argument and constitution too. 9thly. The highly and elevated station, to which this will raise America amongst the nations, must be held forth with great vehemence. The people are mighty fond of pomp and splendor, and will almost grant anything to raise their country to grandeur and magnificence. 10thly. They must be told that anarchy will inevitably be the consequence, if they reject the proposed plan; for there are no more wise men on the continent capable to frame another system; and the same men which composed the late grand convention will not meet a second time. Finally, these directions, if strictly observed, may be of great utility; but they are not to be implicitly confided in. Standing armies are the most proper instruments, both for maintaining and establishing a good government; therefore to secure all beyond a doubt, a standing army must be speedily provided[.]

* Dr. Rush, in the state convention, amongst many other wise and learned sayings, hath the following remarkable observation, "I am happy sir, to find that the convention hath not disgraced this constitution with a bill of rights."

** Our friends in Pennsylvania and some other states, have wisely anticipated this advice, and thereby carried their favourite scheme. But I am sorry to find that Virginia and several other states have given too much time for the plebeians to scrutinize and cavil; which may perhaps disconcert the whole plot, so artfully contrived.

*** I hope none of my friends will imagine that I wish for a federal union, because I have called the new plan of government the FEDERAL CONSTITUTION. I assure my friends (by whose interest I expect to receive my share of the loaves and fishes when they are dividing after the constitution is established) I abhor every idea of a federal union; I am decidedly for an incorporate or consolidated union; and I am sensible that this sort of union is effectually secured by the new constitution, the only system capable to exalt the rulers and reduce [the] people; but I have applyed the word federal to the constitution, to chagrin the vulgar, who are enthusiastically fond of it; and as few of them are capable to distinguish betwixt the name and the thing, they may be brought to adopt it under this plausible sanction; also by calling the constitution federal, we can apply the odious term antifederalists to our opponents with more propriety.

1 Storing, III, p. 198-211. Reprinted in DHRC, II Mfm. Pa., pp. 2511-2540.

2 For other documents related to the controversy over the collection of publicly owned arms in Pennsylvania, and the complaint that this was intended to disarm the militia, see: "Jacob Trusty," December 19, 1787, p. 176; "Centinel IX," January 8, 1788, p. 191; Pennsylvania *Carlisle Gazette,* January 9, 1788, p. 194; "Trusty," January 10, 1788, p. 200; "Supreme Executive Council," January 10, 1788, p. 201; "An Old Militia Officer of 1776," January 18, 1788, p. 221; Philadelphia *Freeman's Journal,* January 23, 1788, p. 226; Philadelphia *Pennsylvania Herald,* February 5, 1788, p. 251; Philadelphia *Independent Gazetteer,* February 27, 1788, p. 286; "James de Caledonia IV," March 12, 1788, p. 298; Philadelphia *Independent Gazetteer,* April 30, 1788, p. 340 at note 3.

George Lee Turberville (Epping, Richmond County) April 16, 1788

Letter: To James Madison (excerpt)

The result of a very cool enquiry into the probable effects of the new Constitution in my mind—in a few Words, is that it is adequate to every beneficial consequence for which Governments are or ought to be instituted—whilst at the same time the Checks are so ingeniously interposed between the Rulers and Citizens as to leave all power—in the hands of the people—and therefore it is impossible that it shou'd ever continue perverted to bad purposes untill it is dangerous—unless the great mass of the people shou'd become *Corrupt!* ignorant of their Birthright—and regardless of their posterity. Shou'd such at any period be the unhappy Characteristick of My fellow Citizens—they will then deserve—& must inevitably wear the Yoke of slavery—it will not be in the power of Folios of Bills of rights to maintain their Liberties. The rights of Freemen are only to be maintain'd by Freemen—and when the Spirit of Freedom (that has ever elevated those who felt its influence amongst Mankind) becomes extinct in the bosoms of men Liberty itself will be a curse to them.

Experience the parent of Wisdom has already taught us that unanimity amongst us can be successfull—& that an attempt to Tyrannize hath already given unanimity to America. Each state will still have a Legislature possessing its confidence as effectually as the old Assemblies did—as adequate to the purposes of calling forth the forces and resources of the States, and as free to commune with the assemblies of the sister states. Have we any reason then to suppose that an Act of Oppression wou'd pass unnoticed when issued by the New Congress? that the states wou'd not be unanimous in their opposition? or that the general government which depends for support upon the individual states wou'd be enabled to triumph over the Liberties of America—when the Fleets and Armies of the British King supported by the Wealth of Britain were inadequate?

Papers, XI, pp. 23-24.

A Farmer April 23, 1788
Newspaper Article: Philadelphia *Freeman's Journal* (excerpt)

It is only free republics that can completely and safely form a federal republic; I say free republics, for there are republics who are not free, such as Venice, where a citizen carrying arms is punished with instant death, and where even the nobles dare not converse with strangers, and scarcely with their friends, and are liable by law to be put to death secretly without trial—

DHRC, II Mfm. Pa., pp. 2449-2450. Also reprinted in Storing, III, p. 185.

Philadelphia *Pennsylvania Gazette* April 23, 1788
(excerpt)

The men who object to the new government, says another correspondent, because the mode of altering the old confoederation was not strictly *constitutional*, remind us of the conduct of the loyalists in the beginning of the late war, who objected to *associating*, *arming* and *fighting*, in defence of our liberties, because these measures were not *constitutional*. A free people should always be left in a condition competent to all their wants, and with every possible power to promote their own happiness. The people, as the sovereigns of a country, are above all constitutions, and a *majority* of them have a right to alter, or abolish, their constitutions at *any* time, and in *any* way they may think proper. The contrary opinion is the doctrine of Hobbes, and other advocates for passive obedience, accommodated to the present state of government in the United States.

DHRC, II Mfm. Pa., p. 2483.

Albany Antifederal Committee April 26, 1788

Newspaper Article: *New York Journal* (excerpts)

Albany, April 10, 1788

On the last Tuesday of April inst. delegates are to be chosen, by the people, to determine the important question, whether the proposed new constitution shall be adopted or rejected—A determination of the utmost consequence to the citizens of the state and to posterity. From an apprehension that the constitution, if adopted in its present form, would deprive the people of their dearest rights and liberties, a number of gentlemen, from different parts of this county, met for the purpose of nominating and recommending delegates for convention, and unanimously resolved on the following gentlemen:

Robert Yates, John Lansing, jun., Henry Oothoudt, Peter Vrooman, Dirck Swart, Israel Thompson, Anthony Ten Eyck.

As we have been informed, that the advocates for the new constitution, have lately travelled through the several districts in the county, and propogated an opinion, that it is a good system of government; we beg leave to state, in as few words as possible, some of the many objections against it. . . .

The great and extensive powers granted to the new government over the lives, liberties, and property of every citizen.

These powers in many instances not defined or sufficiently explained, and capable of being interpreted to answer the most ambitious and arbitrary purposes. . . .

The power to raise, support, and maintain a standing army *in time of peace*. The bane of a republican government; by a standing army most of the once free nations of the globe have been reduced to bondage; and by this Britain attempted to inforce her arbitrary measures.

The power to call forth the militia to any part of the continent, without any limitation of time or place, under the command of the president, or such continental officers as shall be appointed over them.

Men conscienciously scrupulous of bearing arms, made liable to perform military duty. . . .

The not securing the rights of conscience in matters of religion, of granting the liberty of worshipping God agreeable to the mode thereby dictated; whereas the experience of all ages proves that the benevolence and humility inculcated in the gospel, are no restraint on the love of domination. . . .

No provision being made to prevent placemen and pensioners.

Nor for the liberty of the press, that grand palladium of liberty and scourge of tyrants.

The tryal by jury, that sacred bulwark of liberty, is not provided for in civil cases. . . .

By the articles of confederation each state retains what is not expressly granted to Congress; but in the new constitution, there is no provision or bill of rights, to secure any of the fundamental rights and liberties of the people. . . .

With regard to amendments, some of the strongest and most zealous advocates for the new constitution, at first, and for a long time, affect to hold it up as a good system of government; but after various and repeated journies into the country (having discovered that the people were generally opposed to the constitution, and that they can and will judge on a matter of such consequence to themselves and their posterity) these same zealous advocates have since changed their ground, and altered their plan of operations: They now acknowledge it to be defective but endeavour to prevail on the people, first to adopt it, and afterwards (like Massachusetts) trust to a recommendation for future amendments. Would it be prudent or safe for the people to surrender their dearest rights and liberties, to the discretionary disposal of their future rulers? First to make a surrender and afterwards ask for terms of capitulation.

The free men of America have fought and bled to oppose the oppression and usurpation of Great-Britain; and shall they now resign these rights and privileges, to a government which, if possible, may be still more arbitrary and despotic? Sacred as well as profane history afford abundant examples to prove that the most strenuous assertors of liberty, in all ages, after having successfully triumphed over tyranny, have themselves become tyrants, when intrusted by the people with unlimited and uncontroulable powers. . . .

These, among many others, are the reasons that have induced us to oppose the new constitution in its present form. A constitution destructive of the fundamental principles of the general as well as all the state governments; dangerous to the rights and liberties of the people, and which, if adopted without previous amendments, will, in our opinion, terminate in slavery.

Storing, VI, p. 122-126.

Philadelphia *Independent Gazetteer* April 30, 1788
Extract of a letter from Franklin County[1]

"The necessary arrangements," as they are termed here, have taken place in these counties; committees of observation and correspondence are appointed in every township, who correspond with the militia officers and leading men in every county in the state; the counties of Cumberland, Dauphine, and Franklin, appear to take the lead, and have been long since repairing and cleaning their arms, and every young fellow who is able to do it, is providing himself with a *rifle* or musket, and amunition: They have also nominated a commanding officer, it is said to be General ______, and say that they can turn out, at ten days warning, TWENTY THOUSAND expert woodsmen, completely armed; this is I believe very true, as all the counties, this side the Susquehanna, are nearly unanimous, and near three fourths of the other counties. They say the strength of their opponents are in the city, and give out that it will be in vain for them to make any resistance; they mean to make * and are promised assistance from a neighbouring state, who, I find, are as warmly opposed as this state to the system. The *lawyers*, &c. when they precipitated with such fraud and deception the new system upon us, it seems to me, did not recollect, that the militia had arms; however, it will be an awful lesson to tyrants, if they should feel the resentment of an enraged people; I can assure Mr. Wilson, that the people are now as *determined* to secure their liberties as he is *anxious* for power and offices; and let the worst come to the worst, the opposition have the constitution of the state, the established law of the land, on their side; this yet remains good and firm, any doings, *or acts of a faction, or illegal mob convention, to the contrary notwithstanding*. *A civil war* is dreadful, but a little blood spilt now, will perhaps prevent much more hereafter. However, another general convention being called, will prevent any thing like it happening; the people appear anxious for farther powers being granted to Congress; and are generally agreed, that those offered by the minority of the convention of this state would be quite sufficient, and all their rights and privileges would be then secured by the proposed bill of rights,[2] consequently unity and harmony would follow: on the other hand, if the votaries of power and offices do not agree to peaceable measures, by having another general convention called, I dread the consequences to themselves.

N.B. I hear no more of the attempt to execute the order of Council to disarm the militia.[3] I believe the *sub-liutenants* in most of the counties refused to deliver up the arms, it was well enough, for the people were detemined not to part with them. It is hinted that since the western members went down, they cancelled the order.

1 DHRC, II Mfm. Pa., pp. 2548-2550.

2 See "Pennsylvania Minority," December 18, 1787, pp. 159-161, for their proposed bill of rights.

3 For other documents related to the controversy over the collection of publicly owned arms in Pennsylvania, and the complaint that this was intended to disarm the militia, see: "Jacob Trusty," December 19, 1787, p. 176; "Centinel IX," January 8, 1788, p. 191; Pennsylvania *Carlisle Gazette,* January 9, 1788, p. 194; "Trusty," January 10, 1788, p. 200; "Supreme Executive Council," January 10, 1788, p. 201; "An Old Militia Officer of 1776," January 18, 1788, p. 221; Philadelphia *Freeman's Journal,* January 23, 1788, p. 226; Philadelphia *Pennsylvania Herald,* February 5, 1788, p. 251; Philadelphia *Independent Gazetteer,* February 27, 1788, p. 286; "James de Caledonia IV, March 12, 1788, p. 298; "Aristocrotis," April [15], 1788, p. 334 at note 2.

John Francis Mercer [May], 1788
Letter (excerpts)[1]

To the Members of the Conventions of New York and Virginia— . . . this *Constitution* and the Laws made under it are declared paramount even to the unalienable rights, which have heretofore been assured to the Citizens of these States by their Constitutional compacts.—

Altho' this new Constitution can boast indeed of a Bill of Rights of seven Articles—yet of what nature is that Bill of Rights? to hold out such a security to the rights of property as might lead very wealthy and influential Men and Families into a blind compliance and adoption—whilst the Rights that are essential to the great body of Yeomanry of America are entirely disregarded.—

Moreover those very powers, which are to be expressly vested in the new Congress, are of a nature most liable to abuse—They are those which tempt the avarice and ambition of Men to a violation of the rights of their fellow Citizens, and they will be screend under the sanction of an undefined and unlimited authority—Against the *abuse* and *improper* exercise of these special powers, the People have a right to be secured by a sacred Declaration, defining the rights of the Individual and limiting by them, the extent of the exercise—The People were secured against the abuse of those Powers by fundamental Laws and a Bill of Rights, under the Government of Britain and under their own Constitutions—That Government which permits the abuse of Power, recommends it; and will deservedly experience the tyranny which it authorizes; for the history of Mankind establishes the truth of this political adage—*that in Government what may be done will be done.*

The most blind admirer of this Constitution must in his heart confess that it is as far inferior to the British Constitution, of which it is an imperfect imitation, as darkness is to light—In the British Constitution, the rights of Men, the primary objects of the social Compact—are fixed on an immoveable foundation and clearly defined and ascertained by their Magna Charta, their Petition of Rights and Bill of Rights; and their Effective administration by ostensible Ministers, secures Responsibility—In this new Constitution—a complicated System sets responsibility at defiance and the Rights of Men, neglected and undefined, are left at the mercy of events; . . .

When We turn our Eyes back to the scenes of blood and desolation which we have waded through to separate from Great Britain—we behold with manly indignation that our blood and treasure have been wasted to establish a Government in which the Interest of the *few* is preferred to the Rights *of the Many*—When We see a Government so every way inferior to that we were born under, proposed as the reward of our sufferings in an eight years calamitous war—our astonishment is only equalled by our resentment—On the conduct of Virginia and New York, two important States, the preservation of Liberty in a great measure depends—the chief security of a Confoederacy of Republics was boldly disregarded and the old Confoederation violated by requiring Nine instead of 13 voices to alter the Constitution.—But still the resistance of either of these States, in the present temper of America (for the late conduct of the Party here[2] must open the eyes of the People in Massachusetts with respect to the fate of their amendments) will secure all that we mean to contend for—*The natural and unalienable Rights of Men* in a constitutional manner—At the distant appearance of danger to these, We took up arms in the late Revolution—and may we never have cause to look back with regret on that period when connected with the Empire of Great Britain, We were *happy, secure,* and *free.*

1 Storing, V, pp. 104-106.
2 Mercer was referring to the Federalists in Maryland.

Federal Farmer May, 1788
Pamphlet: An Additional Number of Letters from the Federal Farmer to the Republican. (excerpts)
New York

LETTER VI.[1] . . .

Three states have now adopted the constitution without amendments; these, and other circumstances, ought to have their weight in deciding the question, whether we will put the system into operation, adopt it, enumerate and recommend the necessary amendments, which afterwards, by three-fourths of the states, may be ingrafted into the system, or whether we will make the amendments prior to the adoption—I only undertake to shew amendments are essential and necessary—how far it is practicable to ingraft them into the plan, prior to the adoption, the state conventions must determine. Our situation is critical, and we have but our choice of evils—We may hazard much by adopting the constitution in its present form—we may hazard more by rejecting it wholly—we may hazard much by long contending about amendments prior to the adoption. The greatest political evils that can befal us, are discords and civil wars—the greatest blessings we can wish for, are peace, union, and industry, under a mild, free, and steady government. Amendments recommended will tend to guard and direct the administration—but there will be danger that the people, after the system shall be adopted, will become inattentive to amendments—Their attention is now awake—the discussion of the subject, which has already taken place, has had a happy effect—it has called forth the able advocates of liberty, and tends to renew, in the minds of the people, their true republican jealousy and vigilance, the strongest guard against the abuses of power; but the vigilance of the people is not sufficiently constant to be depended on—Fortunate it is for the body of a people, if they can continue attentive to their liberties, long enough to erect for them a temple, and constitutional barriers for their permanent security: when they are well fixed between the powers of the rulers and the rights of the people, they become visible boundaries, constantly seen by all, and any transgression of them is immediately discovered: they serve as centinels for the people at all times, and especially in those unavoidable intervals of inattention. . . .

We might as well call the advocates and opposers [of the Constitution] tories and whigs, or any thing else, as federalists and anti-federalists. To be for or against the constitution, as it stands, is not much evidence of a federal disposition; if any names are applicable to the parties, on account of their general politics, they are those of republicans and anti-republicans. The opposers are generally men who support the rights of the body of the people, and are properly republicans. The advocates are generally men not very friendly to those rights, and properly anti-republicans. . . .

The supreme power is in the people, and rulers possess only that portion which is expressly given them; yet the wisest people have often declared this is the case on proper occasions, and have carefully formed stipulation to fix the extent, and limit the exercise of the power given.

The people by Magna Charta, &c. did not acquire powers, or receive privileges from the king, they only ascertained and fixed those they were entitled to as Englishmen; the title used by the king "we grant," was mere form. Representation, and the jury trial, are the best features of a free government ever as yet discovered, and the only means by which the body of the people can have their proper influence in the affairs of government. . . .

A free and mild government is that in which no laws can be made without the formal and free consent of the people, or of their constitutional representatives; that is, of a substantial representative branch. Liberty, in its genuine sense, is security to enjoy the effects of our honest industry and labours, in a free and mild government, and personal security from all illegal restraints.

Of rights, some are natural and unalienble, of which even the people cannot deprive individuals: Some are constitutional or fundamental; these cannot be altered or abolished by the ordinary laws; but the people, by express acts, may alter or abolish them—These, such as the trial by jury, the benefits of the writ of habeas corpus, &c. individuals claim under the solemn compacts of the people, as constitutions, or at least under laws so strengthened by long usuage as not to be repealable by the ordinary legislature—and some are common or mere legal rights, that is, such as individuals claim under laws which the ordinary legislature may alter or abolish at pleasure. . . .

The following, I think, will be allowed to be unalienable or fundamental rights in the United States:—

No man, demeaning himself peaceably, shall be molested on account of his religion or mode of worship—The people have a right to hold and enjoy their property according to known standing laws, and which cannot be taken from them without their consent, or the consent of their representatives; and whenever taken in the pressing urgencies of government, they are to receive a reasonble compensation for it—Individual security consists in having free recourse to the laws—The people are subject to no laws or taxes not assented to by their representatives constitutionally assembled—They are at all times intitled to the benefits of the writ of habeas corpus, the trial by jury in criminal and civil causes—They have a right, when charged, to a speedy trial in the vicinage; to be heard by themselves or counsel, not to be compelled to furnish evidence against themselves, to have witnesses face to face, and to confront their adversaries before the judge—No man is held to answer a crime charged upon him till it be substantially described to him; and he is subject to no unreasonable searches or seizures of his person, papers or effects—The people have a right to assemble in an orderly manner, and petition the government for a redress of wrongs—The freedom of the press ought not to be restrained—No emoluments, except for actual service—No hereditary honors, or orders of nobility, ought to be allowed—The military ought to be subordinate to the civil authority, and no soldier be quartered on the citizens without their consent—The militia ought always to be armed and disciplined, and the usual defence of the country—The supreme power is in the people, and power delegated ought to return to them at stated periods, and frequently—The legislative, executive, and judicial powers, ought always to be kept distinct—others perhaps might be added.

LETTER VII.[2]

In viewing the various governments instituted by mankind, we see their whole force reducible to two principles—the important springs which alone move the machines, and give them their intended influence and controul, are force and persuasion: by the former men are compelled, by the latter they are drawn. We denominate a government despotic or free, as the one or other principle prevails in it. Perhaps it is not possible for a government to be so despotic, as not to operate persuasively on some of its subjects; nor is it, in the nature of things, I conceive, for a government to be so free, or so supported by voluntary consent, as never to want force to compel obedience to the laws. In despotic governments one man, or a few men, independant of the people, generally make the laws, command obedience, and inforce it by the sword: one-fourth part of the people are armed, and obliged to endure the fatigues of soldiers, to oppress the others and keep them subject to the laws. In free governments the people, or their representatives, make the laws; their execution is principally the effect of voluntary consent and aid; the people respect the magistrate, follow their private pursuits, and enjoy the fruits of their labour with very small deductions for the public use. . . .

To obviate difficulties on this head, as well as objections to the representative branch, generally, several observations have been made— . . .

That the people possess the strong arm to overawe their rulers, and the best checks in their national character against the abuses of power, that the supreme power will remain in them.

LETTER IX.[3] . . .

I shall only observe, at present, that in the state legislatures the body of the people will be genuinely represented, and in congress not; that the right of resisting oppressive measures is inherent in the people, and that a constitutional barrier should be so formed, that their genuine representatives may stop an oppressive ruinous measure in its early progress, before it shall come to maturity, and the evils of it become in a degree fixed.

LETTER X.[4]

It is said that our people have a high sense of freedom, possess power, property, and the strong arm; meaning, I presume, that the body of the people can take care of themselves, and awe their rulers; and, therefore, particular provision in the constitution for their security may not be essential. When I come to examine these observations, they appear to me too triffling and loose to deserve a serious answer.

LETTER XVI.[5]

Having gone through with the organization of the government, I shall now proceed to examine more particularly those clauses which respect its powers. I shall begin with those articles and stipulations which are necessary for accurately ascertaining the extent of powers, and what is given, and for guarding, limiting, and restraining them in their exercise. We often find, these articles and stipulations placed in bills of rights; but they may as well be incorporated in the body of the constitution, as selected and placed by themselves. The constitution, or whole social compact, is but one instrument, no more or less, than a certain number of articles or stipulations agreed to by the people, whether it consists of articles, sections, chapters, bills of rights, or parts of any other denomination, cannot be material. Many needless observations, and idle distinctions, in my opinion, have been made respecting a bill of rights. On the one hand, it seems to be considered as a necessary distinct limb of the constitution, and as containing a certain number of very valuable articles, which are applicable to all societies; and, on the other, as useless, especially in a federal government, possessing only enumerated power—nay, dangerous, as individual rights are numerous, and not easy to be enumerated in a bill of rights, and from articles, or stipulations, securing some of them, it may be inferred, that others not mentioned are surrendered. There appears to me to be general indefinite propositions without much meaning—and the man who first advanced those of the latter description, in the present case, signed the federal constitution, which directly contradicts him. The supreme power is undoubtedly in the people, and it is a principle well established in my mind, that they reserve all powers not expressly delegated by them to those who govern; this is as true in forming a state as in forming a federal government. There is no possible distinction but this founded merely in the different modes of proceeding which take place in some cases. In forming a state constitution, under which to manage not only the great but the little concerns of a community: the powers to be possessed by the government are often too numerous to be enumerated; the people to adopt the shortest way often give general powers, indeed all powers, to the government, in some general words, and then, by a particular enumeration, take back, or rather say they however reserve certain rights as sacred, and which no laws shall be made to violate: hence the idea that all powers are given which are not reserved; but in forming a federal constitution, which *ex vi termine,* supposes state governments existing, and which is only to manage a few great national concerns, we often find it easier to enumerate paricularly the powers to be delegated to the federal head, than to unumerate paricularly the individual rights to be reserved; and the principle will operate in its full force, when we carefully adhere to it. When we particularly enumerate the powers given, we ought either carefully to enumerate the rights reserved, or be totally silent about them; we must either particularly enumerate both, or else suppose the particular enumeration of the powers given adequately draws the line between them and the rights reserved, particularly to enumerate the former and not the latter, I think most advisable: however, as men appear generally to have their doubts about these silent reservations, we might advantageously enumerate the powers given, and then in general words, according to the mode adopted in the 2d art. of the confederation, declare all powers, rights and privileges, are reserved, which are not explicitly and expressly given up. People, and very wisely too, like to be express and explicit about their essential rights, and not to be forced to claim them on the precarious and unascertained tenure of inferences and general principles, knowing that in any controversy between them and their rulers, concerning those rights, disputes may be endless, and nothing certain:—But admitting, on the general principle, that all rights are reserved of course, which are not expressly surrendered, the people could with sufficient certainty assert their rights on all occasions, and establish them with ease, still there are infinite advantages in paricularly enumerating many of the most essential rights reserved in all cases; and as to the less important ones, we may declare in general terms, that all not expressly surrendered are reserved. We do not by declarations change the nature of things, or create new truths, but we give existence, or at least establish in the minds of the people truths and principles which they might never otherwise have thought of, or soon forgot. If a nation means its systems, religious or political, shall have duration, it ought to recognize the leading principles of them in the front page of every family book. What is the usefulness of a truth in theory, unless it exists constantly in the minds of the people, and has their assent:—we discern certain rights, as the freedom of the press, and the trial by jury, &c. which the people of England and of America of course believe to be sacred, and essential to their political happiness, and this belief in them is the result of ideas at first suggested to them by a few able men, and of subsequent experience; while the people of some other countries hear these rights mentioned with the utmost indifference; they think the privilege of existing at the will of a despot much preferable to them. Why this difference amongst beings every way formed alike. The reason of the difference is obvious—it is the effect of education, a series of notions impressed upon the minds of the people by examples, precepts and declarations. When the people of England got together, at the time they formed Magna Charta, they did not consider it sufficient, that they were indisputably entitled to certain natural and unalienable rights, not depending on silent titles, they, by a declaratory act, expressly recognized them, and explicitly declared to all the world, that they were entitled to enjoy those rights; they made an instrument in writing, and enumerated those they then thought essential, or in danger, and this wise men saw was not sufficient; and therefore, that the people might not forget these rights, and gradually become prepared for arbitrary government, their discerning and honest leaders caused this instrument to be confirmed near forty times, and to be read twice a year in public places, not that it would lose its validity without such confirmations, but to fix the contents of it in the minds of the people, as they successively come upon the stage.—Men, in some countries do not remain free, merely because they are entitled to natural and unalienable rights; men in all countries are entitled to them, not because their ancestors once got together and enumerated them on paper, but because, by repeated negociations and declarations, all parties are brought to realize them, and of course to believe them to be sacred. Were it necessary, I might shew the wisdom of our past conduct, as a people, in not merely comforting ourselves that we were entitled to freedom, but in constantly keeping in view, in addresses, bills of rights, in news-papers, &c. the particular principles on which our freedom must always depend.

It is not merely in this point of view, that I urge the engrafting in the constitution additional declaratory articles. The distinction, in itself just, that all powers not given are reserved, is in effect destroyed by this very constitution, as I shall paricularly demonstrate—and even independent of this, the people, by adopting the constitution, give many general undefined powers to congress, in the constitutional exercise of which, the rights in question may be effected. Gentlemen who oppose a federal bill of rights, or further declaratory articles, seem to view the subject in a very narrow imperfect manner. These have for their objects, not only the enumeration of the rights reserved, but principally to explain the general powers delegated in certain material points, and to restrain those who exercise them by fixed known boundaries. Many explanations and restrictions necessary and useful, would be much less so, were the people at large all well and fully acquainted with the principles and affairs of government. There appears to be in the constitution, a studied brevity, and it may also be probable, that several explanatory articles were omitted from a circumstance very common. What we have long and early understood ourselves in the common concerns of the community, we are apt to suppose is understood by others, and need not be expressed; and it is not unnatural or uncommon for the ablest men most frequently to make this mistake. To make declaratory articles unnecessary in an instrument of government, two circumstances must exist; the rigths reserved must be indisputably so, and in their nature defined; the powers delegated to the government, must be precisely defined by the words that convey them, and clearly be of such extent and nature as that, by no reasonable construction, they can be made to invade the rights and prerogatives intended to be left in the people.

The first point urged, is, that all power is reserved not expressly given, that particular enumerated powers only are given, that all others are not given, but reserved, and that it is needless to attempt to restrain congress in the exercise of powers they possess not. This reasoning is logical, but of very little importance in the common affairs of men; but the constitution does not appear to respect it even in any view. To prove this, I might cite several clauses in it. I shall only remark on two or three. By article I, section 9, "No title of nobility shall be granted by congress." Was this clause omitted, what power would congress have to make titles of nobility? In what part of the constitution would they find it? The answer must be, that congress would have no such power—that the people, by adopting the constitution, will not part with it. Why then by a negative clause, restrain congress from doing what it would have no power to do? This clause, then, must have no meaning, or imply, that were it omitted, congress would have the power in question, either upon the principle that some general words in the constitution may be so construed as to give it, or on the principle that congress possess the powers not expressly reserved. But this clause was in the confederation, and is said to be introduced into the constitution from very great caution. Even a cautionary provision implies a doubt, at least, that it is necessary; and if so in this case, clearly it is also alike necessary in all similar ones. The fact appears to be, that the people in forming the confederation, and the convention, in this instance, acted, naturally, they did not leave the point to be settled by general principles and logical inferences; but they settle the point in a few words, and all who read them at once understand them.

The trial by jury in criminal as well as in civil causes, has long been considered as one of our fundamental rights, and has been repeatedly recognized and confirmed by most of the state conventions. But the constitution expressly establishes this trial in criminal, and wholly omits it in civil causes. The jury trial in criminal causes, and the benefit of the writ of habeas corpus, are already as effectually established as any of the fundamental or essential rights of the people in the United States. This being the case, why in adopting a federal constitution do we now establish these, and omit all others, or all others, at least with a few exceptions, such as again agreeing there shall be no ex post facto laws, no titles of nobility, &c. We must consider this constitution, when adopted, as the supreme act of the people, and in construing it hereafter, we and our posterity must strictly adhere to the letter and spirit of it, and in no instance depart from them: in construing the federal constitution, it will be not only impracticable, but improper to refer to the state constitutions. They are entirely distinct instruments and inferior acts: besides, by the people's now establishing certain fundamental rights, it is strongly implied, that they are of opinion that they would not otherwise be secured as a part of the federal system, or be regarded in the federal administration as fundamental. Further, these same rights, being established by the state constitutions, and secured to the people, our recognizing them now, implies, that the people thought them insecure by the state establishments, and extinguished or put afloat by the new arrangement of the social system, unless re-established.—Further, the people, thus establishing some few rights, and remaining totally silent about others similarly circumstanced, the implication indubitably is, that they mean to relinquish the latter, or at least feel indifferent about them. Rights, therefore, inferred from general principles of reason, being precarious and hardly ascertainable in the common affairs of society, and the people, in forming a federal constitution, explicitly shewing they conceive these rights to be thus circumstanced, and accordingly proceed to enumerate and establish some of them, the conclussion will be, that they have established all which they esteem valuable and sacred. On every principle, then, the people especially having began, ought to go through enumerating, and establish particularly all the rights of individuals, which can by any possibility come in question in making and executing federal laws. I have already observed upon the excellency and importance of the jury trial in civil as well as in criminal causes, instead of establishing it in criminal causes only; we ought to establish it generally;—instead of the clause of forty or fifty words relative to this subject, why not use the language that has always been used in this country, and say, "the people of the United States shall always be entitled to the trial by jury." This would shew the people still hold the right sacred, and enjoin it upon congress substantially to preserve the jury trial in all cases, according to the usage and custom of the country. I have observed before, that it is *the jury trial* we want; the little different appendages and modifications tacked to it in the different states, are no more than a drop in the ocean: the jury trial is a solid uniform feature in a free government; it is the substance we would save, not the little articles of form.

Security against expost facto laws, the trial by jury, and the benefits of the writ of habeas corpus, are but a part of those inestimable rights the people of the United States are entitled to, even in judicial proceedings, by the course of the common law. These may be secured in general words, as in New-York, the Western Territory, &c. by declaring the people of the United States shall always be entitled to judicial proceedings according to the course of the common law, as used and established in the said states. Perhaps it would be better to enumerate the particular essential rights the people are entitled to in these proceedings, as has been done in many of the states, and as has been done in England. In this case, the people may proceed to declare, that no man shall be held to answer to any offence, till the same be fully described to him; nor to furnish evidence against himself: that, except in the government of the army and navy, no person shall be tried for any offence, whereby he may incur loss of life, or an infamous punishment, until he be first indicted by a grand jury: that every person shall have a right to produce all proofs that may be favourable to him, and to meet the witnesses against him face to face: that every person shall be entitled to obtain right and justice freely and without delay: that all persons shall have a right to be secure from all unreasonable searches and seizures of their persons, houses, papers, or possessions; and that all warrants shall be deemed contrary to this right, if the foundation of them be not previously supported by oath, and there be not in them a special designation of persons or objects of search, arrest, or seizure: and that no person shall be exiled or molested in his person or effects, otherwise than by the judgment of his peers, or according to the law of the land. A celebrated writer observes upon this last article, that in itself it may be said to comprehend the whole end of political society. These rights are not necessarily reserved, they are established, or enjoyed but in few countries: they are stipulated rights, almost peculiar to British and American laws. In the execution of those laws, individuals, by long custom, by magna charta, bills of rights &c. have become entitled to them. A man, at first, by act of parliament, became entitled to the benefits of the writ of habeas corpus—men are entitled to these rights and benefits in the judicial proceedings of our state courts generally: but it will by no means follow, that they will be entitled to them in the federal courts, and have a right to assert them, unless secured and established by the constitution or federal laws. We certainly, in federal processes, might as well claim the benefits of the writ of habeas corpus, as to claim trial by a jury—the right to have council—to have witnesses face to face—to be secure against unreasonable search warrants, &c. was the constitution silent as to the whole of them:—but the establishment of the former, will evince that we could not claim them without it; and the omission of the latter, implies they are relinquished, or deemed of no importance. These are rights and benefits individuals acquire by compact; they must claim them under compacts, or immemorial usage—it is doubtful, at least, whether they can be claimed under immemorial usage in this country; and it is, therefore, we generally claim them under compacts, as charters and constitutions.

The people by adopting the federal constitution, give congress general powers to institute a distinct and new judiciary, new courts, and to regulate all proceedings in them, under the eight limitations mentioned in a former letter; and the further one, that the benefits of the habeas corpus act shall be enjoyed by individuals. Thus general powers being given to institute courts, and regulate their proceedings, with no provision for securing the rights principally in question, may not congress so exercise those powers, and constitutionally too, as to destroy those rights? Clearly, in my opinion, they are not in any degree secured. But, admitting the case is only doubtful, would it not be prudent and wise to secure them and remove all doubts, since all agree the people ought to enjoy these valuable rights, a very few men excepted, who seem to be rather of opinion that there is little or nothing in them? Were it necessary I might add many observations to shew their value and political importance.

The constitution will give congress general powers to raise and support armies. General powers carry with them incidental ones, and the means necessary to the end. In the exercise of these powers, is there any provision in the constitution to prevent the quartering of soldiers on the inhabitants? you will answer, there is not. This may sometimes be deemed a necessary measure in the support of armies; on what principle can the people claim the right to be exempt from this burden? they will urge, perhaps, the practice of the country, and the provisions made in some of the state constitutions—they will be answered, that their claim thus to be exempt is not founded in nature, but only in custom and opinion, or at best, in stipulations in some of the state constitutions, which are local, and inferior in their operation, and can have no controul over the general government—that they had adopted a federal constitution had noticed several rights, but had been totally silent about this exemption—that they had given general powers relative to the subject, which, in their operation, regularly destroyed the claim. Though it is not to be presumed, that we are in any immediate danger from this quarter, yet it is fit and proper to establish, beyond dispute, those rights which are particularly valuable to individuals, and essential to the permanency and duration of free government. An excellent writer observes, that the English, always in possession of their freedom, are frequently unmindful of the value of it: we, at this period, do not seem to be so well off, having, in some instances abused ours; many of us are quite disposed to barter it away for what we call energy, coercion, and some other terms we use as vaguely as that of liberty—There is often as great a rage for change and novelty in politics, as in amusements and fashions.

All parties apparently agree, that the freedom of the press is a fundamental right, and ought not to be restrained by any taxes, duties, or in any manner whatever. Why should not the people, in adopting a federal constitution, declare this, even if there are only doubts about it. But, say the advocates, all powers not given are reserved:—true; but the great question is, are not powers given, in the excercise of which this right may be destroyed? The people's or the printers claim to a free press, is founded on the fundamental laws, that is, compacts, and state constitutions, made by the people. The people, who can annihilate or alter those constitutions, can annihilate or limit this right. This may be done by giving general powers, as well as by using particular words. No right claimed under a state constitution, will avail against a law of the union, made in pursuance of the federal constitution: therefore the question is, what laws will congress have a right to make by the constitution of the union, and paricularly touching the press? By art. 1. sect. 8. congress will have power to lay and collect taxes, duties, imposts and excise. By this congress will clearly have power to lay and collect all kind of taxes whatever—taxes on houses, lands, polls, industry, merchandize, &c.—taxes on deeds, bonds, and all written instruments—on writs, pleas, and all judicial proceedings, on licences, naval officers papers, &c. on newspapers, advertisements, &c. and to require bonds of the naval officers, clerks, printers, &c. to account for the taxes that may become due on papers that go through their hands. Printing, like all other business, must cease when taxed beyond its profits; and it appears to me, that a power to tax the press at discretion, is a power to destroy or restrain the freedom of it. There may be other powers given, in the exercise of which this freedom may be effected; and certainly it is of too much importance to be left thus liable to be taxed, and constantly to constructions and inferences. A free press is the channel of communication as to mercantile and public affairs; by means of it the people in large countries ascertain each others sentiments; are enabled to unite, and become formidable to those rulers who adopt improper measures. Newspapers may sometimes be the vehicles of abuse, and of many things not true; but these are but small inconveniencies, in my mind, among many advantages. A celebrated writer, I have several times quoted, speaking in high terms of the English liberties, says, "lastly the key stone was put to the arch, by the final establishment of the freedom of the press." I shall not dwell longer upon the fundamental rights, to some of which I have attended in this letter, for the same reasons that these I have mentioned, ought to be expressly secured, lest in the exercise of general powers given they may be invaded: it is pretty clear, that some other of less importance, or less in danger, might with propriety also be secured.

LETTER XVII.[6] . . .

By the proposed system, the federal head will possess, without limitation, almost every species of power that can, in its exercise, tend to change the government, or to endanger liberty; while in it, I think it has been fully shewn, the people will have but the shadow of representation, and but the shadow of security for their rights and liberties.

LETTER XVIII.[7] . . .

The power to controul the military forces of the country, as well as the revenues of it, requires serious attention. Here again I must premise, that a federal republic is a compound system, made up of constituent parts, each essential to the whole: we must then expect the real friends of such a system will always be very anxious for the security and preservation of each part, and to this end, that each constitutionally possess its natural portion of power and influence—and that it will constantly be an object of concern to them, to see one part armed at all points by the constitution, and in a manner destructive in the end, even of its own existence, and the others left constitutionally defenceless.

The military forces of a free country may be considered under three general descriptions—1. The militia. 2. the navy—and 3. the regular troops—and the whole ought ever to be, and understood to be, in strict subordination to the civil authority—and that regular troops, and select corps, ought not to be kept up without evident necessity. Stipulations in the constitution to this effect, are perhaps, too general to be of much service, except merely to impress on the minds of the people and soldiery, that the military ought ever to be subject to the civil authority, &c. But particular attention, and many more definite stipulations, are highly necessary to render the military safe, and yet useful in a free government; and in a federal republic, where the people meet in distinct assemblies, many stipulations are necessary to keep a part from transgressing, which would be unnecessary checks against the whole met in one legislature, in one entire government.—A militia, when properly formed, are in fact the people themselves, and render regular troops in a great measure unnecessary. The powers to form and arm the militia, to appoint their officers, and to command their services, are very important; nor ought they in a confederated republic to be lodged, solely, in any one member of the government. First, the constitution ought to secure a genuine and guard against a select militia, by providing that the militia shall always be kept well organized, armed, and disciplined, and include, according to the past and general usuage of the states, all men capable of bearing arms; and that all regulations tending to render this general militia useless and defenceless, by establishing select corps of militia, or distinct bodies of military men, not having permanent interests and attachments in the community[8] to be avoided. I am persuaded, I need not multiply words to convince you of the value and solidity of this principle, as it respects general liberty, and the duration of a free and mild government: having this principle well fixed by the constitution, then the federal head may prescribe a general uniform plan, on which the respective states shall form and train the militia, appoint their officers and solely manage them, except when called into the service of the union, and when called into that service, they may be commanded and governed by the union. This arrangement combines energy and safety in it; it places the sword in the hands of the solid interest of the community, and not in the hands of men destitute of property, of principle, or of attachment to the society and government, who often form the select corps of peace or ordinary establishments: by it, the militia are the people, immediately under the management of the state governments, but on a uniform federal plan, and called into the service, command, and government of the union, when necessary for the common defence and general tranquility. But, say gentlemen, the general militia are for the most part employed at home in their private concerns, cannot well be called out, or be depended upon; that we must have a select militia; that is, as I understand it, particular corps or bodies of young men, and of men who have but little to do at home, particularly armed and disciplined in some measure, at the public expence, and always ready to take the field. These corps, not much unlike regular troops, will ever produce an inattention to the general militia; and the consequence has ever been, and always must be, that the substantial men, having families and property, will generally be without arms, without knowing the use of them, and defenceless; whereas, to preserve liberty, it is essential that the whole body of the people always possess arms, and be taught alike, especially when young, how to use them; nor does it follow from this, that all promiscuously must go into actual service on every occasion. The mind that aims at a select militia, must be influenced by a truly anti-republican principle; and when we see many men disposed to practice upon it, whenever they can prevail, no wonder true republicans are for carefully guarding against it. As a farther check, it may be proper to add, that the militia of any state shall not remain in the service of the union, beyond a given period, without the express consent of the state legislature.

1 *An Additional Number of Letters from the Federal Farmer to the Republican . . .*, (Chicago: Quadrangle, 1962) pp. 48-53. Note that this second pamphlet of the Federal Farmer containing letters VI-XVIII is paged consecutively with his first pamphlet, *Letters of the Federal Farmer to the Republican*, which contains letters I-V. See "Federal Farmer," November [8], 1787, p. 89 for excerpts from the first pamphlet.

2 *Ibid.*, pp. 56-64.

3 *Ibid.*, p. 80.

4 *Ibid.*, p. 82.

5 *Ibid.*, pp. 142-153.

6 *Ibid.*, p. 161.

7 *Ibid.*, pp. 168-170.

8 This sentence was later utilized as part of a proposed bill or declaration of rights introduced into the New York convention by John Lansing. See "New York Convention," July 7, 1788, p. 474 at note 2.

Thomas Jefferson (Paris) May 2, 1788
Letter: To George Washington (excerpt)

I had intended to have written a word to your Excellency on the subject of the new Constitution, but I have already spun out my letter to an immoderate length. I will just observe, therefore, that according to my ideas, there is a great deal of good in it. There are two things, however, which I dislike strongly. 1. The want of a declaration of rights. I am in hopes the opposition of Virginia will remedy this, and produce such a declaration. 2. The perpetual re-eligibility of the President.

Bergh, VI, p. 454.

Maryland Minority May 6, 1788
Address to the People of Maryland (excerpts)
Published: Baltimore *Maryland Gazette*

The following facts, disclosing the conduct of the late Convention of Maryland, are submitted to the serious consideration of the citizens of the state. . . .

On Thursday [April 24], the members who were opposed to the ratification of the constitution, without such *previous* amendments could be obtained as they thought essentially necessary to secure the liberty and happiness of the people (being confined by the last resolution to consider in one view the whole of the plan of government) stated some of their objections to the constitution.—The convention met in the evening, when Mr. Paca, member from Hartford, having just taken his seat, rose and informed the president, that he had great objection to the constitution proposed, in its present form, and meant to propose a variety of amendments, not to prevent, but to accompany, the ratification, . . .

[April 26, in Convention after ratification by a vote of 63 to 11] . . . Mr. Paca again rose and laid before the convention his propositions for amending the Constitution thus adopted; which he had prepared by leave of the house, declaring that he had only given his assent to the government under the firm persuasion, and in full confidence, that such amendments would be peaceably obtained, as to enable the people to live happy under the government;—that the people of the county he represented, and that he himself, would support the government with such amendments, but without them, not a man in the State, and no people, would be more firmly opposed to it than himself and those he represented. Sentiments highly favorable to amendments were expressed, and a general murmur of approbation seemed to arise from all parts of the house, expressive of a desire to consider amendments, either in their characters as members of convention, or in their individual capacities as citizens; . . .

And then it was resolved, "That the amendments proposed to the Constitution by the delegate from Hartford-county, should be referred to the above committee." . . .

The following amendments to the proposed Constitution were separately agreed to by the committee, most of them by a *unanimous* vote, and all of them by a *great majority.*

1. That Congress shall exercise no power but what is expressly delegated by this Constitution.

By this amendment, the general powers given to Congress by the first and last paragraphs of the 8th sect. of art. 1, and the second paragraph of the 6th article, would be in a great measure restrained: those dangerous expressions by which the bills of rights and constitutions of the several states may be repealed by the laws of Congress, in some degree moderated, and the exercise of *constructive* powers wholly prevented.

2. That there shall be trial by jury in all criminal cases, according to the course of proceeding in the state where the offence is committed; and that there be no appeal from matter of fact, or second trial after acquittal; but this provision shall not extend to such cases as may arise in the government of the land or naval forces.

3. That, in all actions on debts or contracts, and in all other controversies respecting property, of which the inferior federal courts have jurisdiction, the trial of facts shall be by jury, if required by either party; and that it be expressly declared, that the State courts, in such cases, have a concurrent jurisdiction with the federal courts, with an appeal from either, only as to matter of law, to the supreme federal court, if the matter in dispute be of the value of   dollars.

4. That the inferior federal courts shall not have jurisdiction of less than   dollars; and there may be an appeal in all cases of revenue, as well to matter of fact as law and Congress may give the State courts jurisdiction of revenue cases, for such sums, and in such manner, as they may think proper.

5. That, in all cases of trespasses done within the body of a county, and within the inferior federal jurisdiction, the party injured shall be entitled to trial by jury in the State where the injury shall be committed; and that it be expressly declared, that the State courts, in such cases, shall have concurrent jurisdiction with the federal courts; and there shall be no appeal from either, except on matter of law; and

that no person be exempt from such jurisdiction and trial but ambassadors and ministers privileged by the law of nations.

6. That the federal courts shall not be entitled to jurisdiction by fictions or collusion.

7. That the federal judges do not hold any other office of profit, or receive the profits of any other office under Congress, during the time they hold their commission.

The great objects of these amendments were, 1st. To secure the trial by jury in all cases, the boasted birth-right of Englishmen, and their descendants, and the palladium of civil liberty; and to prevent the *appeal from fact,* which not only destroys that trial in civil cases, but by *construction,* may also exlude it in criminal cases; a mode of proceeding both expensive and burthensome; and also by blending law with fact, will destroy all check on the judiciary authority, render it almost impossible to convict judges of corruption, and may lay the foundation of that gradual and silent attack on individuals, by which the approaches of tyranny become irresistible. 2d. To give a concurrent jurisdiction to the State courts, in order that Congress may not be compelled, as they will be under the present form, to establish inferior federal courts, which if not numerous will be inconvenient, and if numerous very expensive; the circumstances of the people being unequal to the increased expense of double courts, and double officers; an arrangement that will render the law so complicated and confused, that few men can know how to conduct themselves with safety to their persons or property, the great and only security of freemen. 3dly. To give such jurisdiction to the State courts, that transient foreigners, and persons from other States, committing injuries in this state, may be amenable to the State, whose laws they violate, and whose citizens they injure. 4thly, To prevent an extension of the federal jurisdiction, which may, and in all probability will, swallow up the State jurisdictions, and consequently sap those rules of descent and regulations of personal property, by which men now hold their estates; and lastly, To secure the independence of the federal judges, to whom the happiness of the people of this great continent will be so greatly committed by the extensive powers assigned them.

8. That all warrants without oath, or affirmation of a person conscientiously scrupulous of taking an oath, to search suspected places, or seize any person or his property, are grievous and oppressive; and all general warrants to search suspected places, or to apprehend any person suspected, without naming or describing the place or person in special, are dangerous, and ought not to be granted.

This amendment was considered indispensable by many of the committee, for Congress having the power of laying excises, the horror of a free people, by which our dwelling-houses, those castles considered so sacred by the English law, will be laid open to the insolence and oppression of office, there could be no constitutional check provided, that would prove so effectual a safeguard to our citizens. General warrants too, the great engine by which power may destroy those individuals who resist usurpation, are also hereby forbid to those magistrates who are to administer the general government.

9. That no soldier be enlisted for a longer time than four years except in time of war, and then only during the war.

10. That soldiers be not quartered, in time of peace upon *private* houses, without the consent of the owners.

11. That no mutiny bill continue in force longer than two years.

These were the only checks that could be obtained against the unlimited power of raising and regulating standing armies, *the natural enemies to freedom,* and even with these restrictions, the new Congress will not be under such constitutional restraints as the Parliament of Great-Britain; restraints which our ancestors have bled to establish, and which have hitherto preserved the liberty of their posterity.

12. That the freedom of the press be inviolably preserved.

In prosecutions in the federal courts for libels, the constitutional preservation of this great and fundamental right, may prove invaluable.

13. That the militia shall not be subject to martial law, except in time of war, invasion or rebellion.

This provision to restrain the powers of Congress over the militia, although by no means so ample as that provided by magna charta, and the other fundamental constitutional laws of Great-Britain, (it being contrary to magna charta to punish a freeman by martial law in time of peace, and murder to execute him,) yet it may prove an inestimable check; for all other provisions in favour of the rights of men, would be vain and nugatory, if the power of subjecting all men able to bear arms to martial law at any moment, should remain vested in Congress.

Thus far the amendments were agreed to.

The following amendments were laid before the committee, and negatived by a majority.

1. That the militia, unless selected by lot, or volutarily enlisted, shall not be marched beyond the limits of an adjoining State, without the consent of their legislature or executive.

2. That the Congress shall have no power to alter or change the time, place, or manner, of holding elections for senators or representatives, unless a State shall neglect to make regulations, or to execute its regulations, or shall be prevented by invasion or rebellion; in which cases only Congress may interfere, until the cause be removed.

3. That, in every law of Congress imposing *direct* taxes, the *collection* thereof shall be *suspended* for a certain reasonable time therein limited, and on payment of the sum by any State, by the time appointed, such taxes shall not be collected.

4. That no standing army shall be kept up *in time of peace,* unless with the consent of two thirds of the members present of each branch of Congress.

5. That the president shall not command the army in person, without the consent of Congress.

6. That no treaty shall be effectual to repeal or abrogate the *constitutions* or *bills of rights* of the States, or any part of them.

7. That no regulation of commerce, or navigation act, shall be made, unless with the consent of two thirds of the members of each branch of Congress.

8. That no member of Congress shall be eligible to any office of profit under Congress during the time for which he shall be appointed.

9. That Congess shall have no power to lay a *poll-tax*.

10. That no person, conscientiously scrupulous of bearing arms in any case, shall be compelled *personally* to serve as a soldier.

11. That there be a responsible council to the president.

12. That there be no national religion established by law, but that all persons be equally entitled to protection in their religious liberty.

13. That all imposts and duties laid by Congress shall be placed to the credit of the State in which the same shall be collected, and be deducted out of such State's quota of the common or general expenses of government.

14. That every man hath a right to petition the legislature for the redress of grievances in a peaceable and orderly manner.

15. That it be declared, that all persons intrusted with the legislative or executive powers of government are the *trustees and servants* of the public, and as such accountable for their conduct. Wherefore, whenever the ends of government are perverted, and public liberty manifestly endangered, and all other means of redress are ineffectual, the people may, and of right ought, to reform the old, or establish a new government; the doctrine of non-resistance against arbitrary power and oppression is absurd, slavish, and destructive of the good and happiness of mankind. . . .

We consider the proposed form of national government as very defective, and that the liberty and happiness of the people will be endangered if the system be not greatly changed and altered. The amendments agreed to by the committee, and those proposed by the minority, are now laid before you for your consideration, that you may express your sense as to such alterations as you may think proper to be made in the new Constitution.

We remain persuaded that the importance of the alterations proposed, calculated to preserve public liberty, by those checks on power which the experience of ages has rendered venerable, and to promote the happiness of the people by a due attention to their ease and convenience, will justify the steps we have taken to obtain them, to our constituents, and the world.

Having no interest that can distinguish us from the rest of the community, we neither fear censure, nor wish applause. Having thus discharged the duty of citizens and trustees of the public, we shall now submit to the people those precautions and securities which, after mature reflection on this momentous subject, we deem necessary for their safety and happiness.

May the all-wise and omnipotent Being, who made us masters of a fair and fruitful empire, inspire us with wisdom and fortitude to perpetuate to posterity that freedom which we received from our fathers!

Members of the Committee.—William Paca, Samuel Chase, John F. Mercer, Jeremiah T. Chase.
Members of the Convention.—John Love, Charles Ridgely, Edward Cockey, Nathan Cromwell, Charles Ridgely, of Wm., Luther Martin, Benjamin Harrison, Wm. Pinckney.

Storing, V, pp. 92-100. Reprinted in *Debates*, II, pp. 547-556.

Richard Henry Lee (Westmoreland County) May 7, 1788
Letter: To George Mason (excerpt)[1]

Give me leave now, dear sir, to make a few observations on the important business that will call you to Richmond next month.[2] It seems pretty clear at present, that four other States, viz., North Carolina, New York, Rhode Island, and New Hampshire, will depend much upon Virginia for their determination on the Convention project of a new constitution; therefore it becomes us to be very circumspect and careful about the conduct we pursue, as, on the one hand, every possible exertion of wisdom and firmness should be employed to prevent danger to civil liberty, so, on the other hand, the most watchful precaution should take place to prevent the foes of union, order, and good government, from succeeding so far as to prevent our acceptance of the good part of the plan proposed. I submit to you, sir, whether, to form a consistent union of conduct, it would not be well for six or eight leading friends to amendments to meet privately, and, having formed the best possible judgment of the members' sentiments from knowledge of the men, to see how far it may be safe to press either for modes of amendment or the extent of amendments, and to govern accordingly. But, certainly, the firmest stand should be made against the very arbitrary mode that has been pursued in some States, that is, to propose a question of absolute rejection or implicit admission. For though it is true that the Convention plan looks something like this, yet I think every temperate man must agree that neither the Convention, nor any set of men upon earth, have or had a right to insist upon such a question of extremity. To receive the good and reject the bad is too necessary and inherent a right to be parted with. As some subtle managers will be upon the Convention, I believe you will find entrapping questions proposed at first as a ground-work of proceeding, which will hamper, confine, and narrow all attempts to proper investigation or necessary amendment, and this will be done under the plausible pretext of losing all by attempting *any* change. I judge that it will be so here, because I observe a similar conduct has been pursued in other places, as in Maryland and Pennsylvania. I trust that such uncandid and dangerous stratagems will be opposed and prevented in the Convention of Virginia, and a thorough, particular, and careful examination be first made into all its parts as a previous requisite to the formation of any question upon it. During this process a tolerable judgment may be formed of the sentiments of the generality, and a clue furnished for forming successful propositions for amendment, as the candid friends to this system admit that amendments may be made to improve the plan, but say that these amendments ought to be made, and may be obtained from the new Congress without endangering a total loss of the proposed Constitution. I say that those who talk thus, if they are sincere, will not object to this plan which, as I propose it, is something like the proceeding of the Convention Parliament of 1688; in the form of ratification, insert plainly and strongly such amendments as can be agreed upon, and say, that the people of Virginia do claim, demand and insist upon these as their undoubted rights and liberties which they mean not to part with,[3] and if these are not obtained and secured by the mode pointed out in the fifth article of the Convention plan, in two years after the meeting of the new Congress, that Virginia shall, in that case, be considered as disengaged from this ratification. Under this proposition a development will be made of the sincerity of those who advocate the new plan, the beneficial parts of it retained, and a just security given to civil liberty. In the fifth article it is stated that two-thirds of Congress may propose amendments, which, being approved by three-fourths of the legislatures, become parts of the

Constitution. By this mode, the new Congress may obtain our amendments without risking the convulsion of conventions, and the friends of the plan will be gratified in what they say is necessary, the putting the government in motion, when, as they again say, amendments may and ought to be obtained. By this mode, too, in all probability, the undetermined States, may be brought to harmonize, and the formidable minorities, in the assenting States, may be quieted. By this friendly and reasonable accommodation, the perpetual distrust and opposition, that will inevitably follow the total adoption of the plan, from the State legislatures, may be happily prevented, and friendly united exertions take place. Much reflection has convinced me that this mode is the best that I have had an opportunity of cultivating. I have, therefore, taken the liberty of recommending it to your serious and patriotic attention; in the formation of these amendments *localities* ought to be avoided as much as possible.

1 Rowland, II, pp. 215-217.

2 Mason had been elected to the Virginia convention called to ratify the United States Constitution.

3 This idea is quite similar to New York's ratification of the Constitution which contains a long list of rights that the New York Convention declared "cannot be abridged or violated." See "New York Convention," July 26, 1788, p. 480. Rhode Island followed New York's example in this. See "Rhode Island Convention," May 29, 1790, p. 733.

South Carolina Convention May 20, 1788
Debates (excerpt)

Speech of Mr. PATRICK DOLLARD, *of Prince Frederick's.*

Mr. President, I rise, with the greatest diffidence, to speak on this occasion, not only knowing myself unequal to the task, but believing this to be the most important question that ever the good people of this state were called together to deliberate upon. This Constitution has been ably supported, and ingeniously glossed over by many able and respectable gentlemen in this house, whose reasoning, aided by the most accurate eloquence, might strike conviction even in the predetermined breast, had they a good cause to support. Conscious that they have not, and also conscious of my inability to point out the consequences of its defects, which have in some measure been defined by able gentlemen in this house, I shall therefore confine myself within narrow bounds: that is, concisely to make known the sense and language of my constituents. The people of Prince Frederick's Parish, whom I have the honor to represent, are a brave, honest, and industrious people. In the late bloody contest, they bore a conspicuous part, when they fought, bled, and conquered, in defence of their civil rights and privileges, which they expected to transmit untainted to their posterity. They are nearly all, to a man, opposed to this new Constitution, because, they say, they have omitted to insert a bill of rights therein, ascertaining and fundamentally establishing, the unalienable rights of men, without a full, free, and secure enjoyment of which there can be no liberty, and over which it is not necessary that a good government should have the control. They say that they are by no means against vesting Congress with ample and sufficient powers; but to make over to them, or any set of men, their birthright, comprised in Magna Charta, which this new Constitution absolutely does, they can never agree to. Notwithstanding this, they have the highest opinion of the virtues and abilities of the honorable gentlemen from this state, who represented us in the General Convention; and also a few other distinguished characters, whose names will be transmitted with honor to future ages; but I believe, at the same time, they are but mortal, and, therefore, liable to err; and as the virtue and abilities of those gentlemen will consequently recommend their being first employed in jointly conducting the reins of this government, they are led to believe it will commence in a moderate aristocracy: but, that it will, in its future operations, produce a monarchy, or a corrupt and oppressive aristocracy, they have no manner of doubt. Lust of dominion is natural in every soil, and the love of power and superiority is as prevailing in the United States, at present, as in any part of the earth; yet in this country, depraved as it is, there still remains a strong regard for liberty: an American bosom is apt to glow at the sound of it, and the splendid merit of preserving that best gift of God, which is mostly expelled from every country in Europe, might stimulate Indolence, and animate even Luxury to consecrate herself at the alter of freedom.

My constituents are highly alarmed at the large and rapid strides which this new government has taken towards despotism. They say it is big with political mischiefs, and pregnant with a greater variety of impending woes to the good people of the Southern States, especially South Carolina, than all the plagues supposed to issue from the poisonous box of Pandora. They say it is particularly calculated for the meridian of despotic aristocracy; that it evidently tends to promote the ambitious views of a few able and designing men, and enslave the rest; that it carries with it the appearance of an old phrase, formerly made use of in despotic reigns, and especially by Archbishop Laud, in the reign of Charles I., that is, "non-resistance." They say they will resist against it; that they will not accept of it unless compelled by force of arms, which this new Constitution plainly threatens; and then, they say, your standing army, like Turkish janizaries enforcing despotic laws, must ram it down their throats with the points of bayonets. They warn the gentlemen of this Convention, as the guardians of their liberty, to beware how they will be accessory to the disposal of, or rather sacrificing, their dear-bought rights and privileges. This is the sense and language, Mr. President, of the people; and it is an old saying, and I believe a very true one, that the general voice of the people is the voice of God. The general voice of the people, to whom I am responsible, is against it. I shall never betray the trust reposed in me by them; therefore, shall give my hearty dissent.

Debates, IV, pp. 336-338. The South Carolina Convention ratified the Constitution on May 23, 1788, by a vote of 149 to 73. The Convention also made the following declaration: "This Convention doth also declare, that no section or paragraph of the said Constitution warrants a construction that the states do not retain every power not expressly relinquished by them, and vested in the general government of the Union." See *Debates*, I, p. 325.

George Mason May 26, 1788
Letter: To Thomas Jefferson (excerpt)

I make no Doubt that you have long ago received Copys of the new Constitution of Government, framed last Summer by the Delegates of the several States, in general Convention, at Philadelphia. Upon the most mature Consideration I was capable of, and from Motives of sincere Patriotism, I was under the Necessity of refusing my Signature, as one of the Virginia Delegates; and drew up some general Objections; which I intended to offer, by Way of Protest; but was discouraged from doing so, by the precipitate, & intemperate, not to say indecent Manner, in which the Business was conducted, during the last Week of the Convention, after the Patrons of this new plan found they had a decided Majority in their Favour, which was obtained by a Compromise between the Eastern, and the two Southern States, to permit the latter to continue the Importation of Slaves for twenty odd Years; a more favourite Object with them than the Liberty and Happiness of the People.

These Objections of mine were first printed very incorrectly, without my Approbation, or Privity; which laid me under some kind of Necessity of publishing them afterwards, myself. I take the Liberty of enclosing you a Copy of them. You will find them conceived in general Terms; as I wished to confine them to a narrow Compass. There are many other things very objectionable in the proposed new

Constitution; particularly the almost unlimited Authority over the Militia of the several States; whereby, under Colour of regulating, them may disarm, or render useless the Militia, the more easily to govern by a standing Army; or they may harrass the Militia, by such rigid Regulations, and intollerable Burdens, as to make the People themselves desire it's Abolition. By their Power over the Elections, they may so order them, as to deprive the People at large of any Share in the Choice of their Representatives. By the Consent of Congress, Men in the highest Offices of Trust in the United States may receive any Emolument, Place, or Pinsion from a forreign Prince, or Potentate, which is setting themselves up to the highest Bidder. But it wou'd be tedious to enumerate all the Objections; and I am sure they cannot escape Mr. Jefferson's Observation. Delaware—Pensylvania—Jersey—Connecticut—Georgia, and Maryland have ratifyed the new Government (for surely it is not a Confederation) without Amendments. Massachusets has accompanyed the Ratification with proposed Amendments. Rhode Island has rejected it. New Hampshire, after some deliberation, adjourned their Convention to June. The Convention of South Carolina is now sitting. The Convention of new York meets in June—that of North Carolina in July—and the convention of Virginia meets on the first Monday in June. I shall set out for Richmond this week, in order to attend it. From the best Information I have had, the Members of the Virginia Convention are so equally divided upon the Subject, that no Man can, at present, form any certain Judgement of the Issue. There seems to be a great Majority for Amendments; but many are for ratifying first, and amending afterwards. This Idea appears to me so utterly absurd, that I can not think any Man of Sense candid, in Proposing it.

Rutland, III, pp. 1044-1046.

Thomas Jefferson (Paris) May 27, 1788
Letter: To Edward Carrington (excerpt)

I learn with great pleasure the progress of the new Constitution. Indeed I have presumed it would gain on the public mind, as I confess it has on my own. At first, tho' I saw that the great mass & ground work was good, I disliked many appendages. Reflection and discussion have cleared off most of these. You have satisfied me as to the query I had put to you about the right of direct taxation. My first wish was that 9 States would adopt it in order to ensure what was good in it, & that the others might, by holding off, produce the necessary amendments. But the plan of Massachusetts is far preferable, and will I hope be followed by those who are yet to decide. There are two amendments only which I am anxious for. 1. A bill of rights, which it is so much the interest of all to have, that I conceive it must be yielded. The 1st amendment proposed by Massachusetts will in some degree answer this end, but not so well. It will do too much in some instances & too little in others. It will cripple the federal government in some cases where it ought to be free, and not restrain it in some others where restraint would be right.

Ford, V, pp. 19-20.

Thomas Jefferson (Paris) June 3, 1788
Letter: To William Carmichael (excerpt)

I was much pleased with many & essential parts of this instrument from the beginning. But I thought I saw in it many faults, great & small. What I have read & reflected has brought me over from several of my objections of the first moment, and to acquiesce under some others. Two only remain, of essential consideration, to wit, the want of a bill of rights, & the expunging the principle of necessary rotation in the offices of President & Senate. At first I wished that when 9. states should have accepted the constitution, so as to ensure us what is good in it, the other 4. might hold off till the want of the bill of rights at least might be supplied. But I am now convinced that the plan of Massachusetts is the best. That is, to accept, and to amend afterwards. If the states which were to decide after her should all do the same, it is impossible but they must obtain the essential amendments. It will be more difficult if we lose this instrument, to recover what is good in it, than to correct what is bad after we shall have adopted it. It has therefore my hearty prayers, and I wait with anxiety for news of the votes of Maryland, S. Carolina, & Virginia.

Ford, V, p. 25.

Virginia Convention June 5, 1788
Debates (excerpts)

[Mr. HENRY.]
I wish I was possessed with talents, or possessed of any thing that might enable me to elucidate this great subject. I am not free from

suspicion: I am apt to entertain doubts. I rose yesterday to ask a question which arose in my own mind. When I asked that question, I thought the meaning of my interrogation was obvious. The fate of this question and of America may depend on this. Have they said, We, the states? Have they made a proposal of a compact between states? If they had, this would be a confederation. It is otherwise most clearly a consolidated government. The question turns, sir, on that poor little thing—the expression, We, the *people*, instead of the *states*, of America. I need not take much pains to show that the principles of this system are extremely pernicious, impolitic, and dangerous. Is this a monarchy, like England—a compact between prince and people, with checks on the former to secure the liberty of the latter? Is this a confederacy, like Holland—an association of a number of independent states, each of which retains its individual sovereignty? It is not a democracy, wherein the people retain all their rights securely. Had these principles been adhered to, we should not have been brought to this alarming transition, from a confederacy to a consolidated government. We have no detail of these great considerations, which, in my opinion, ought to have abounded before we should recur to a government of this kind. Here is a resolution as radical as that which separated us from Great Britain. It is radical in this transition; our rights and privileges are endangered, and the sovereignty of the states will be relinquished: and cannot we plainly see that this is actually the case? The rights of conscience, trial by jury, liberty of the press, all your immunities and franchises, all pretensions to human rights and privileges, are rendered insecure, if not lost, by this change, so loudly talked of by some, and inconsiderately by others. Is this tame relinquishment of rights worthy of freemen? Is it worthy of that manly fortitude that ought to characterize republicans? It is said eight states have adopted this plan. I declare that if twelve states and a half had adopted it, I would, with manly firmness, and in spite of an erring world, reject it. You are not to inquire how your trade may be increased, nor how you are to become a great and powerful people, but how your liberties can be secured; for liberty ought to be the direct end of your government.

Having premised these things, I shall, with the aid of my judgment and information, which, I confess, are not extensive, go into the discussion of this system more minutely. Is it necessary for your liberty that you should abandon those great rights by the adoption of this system? Is the relinquishment of the trial by jury and the liberty of the press necessary for your liberty? Will the abandonment of your most sacred rights tend to the security of your liberty? Liberty, the greatest of all earthly blessings—give us that precious jewel, and you may take every thing else! But I am fearful I have lived long enough to become an old-fashioned fellow. Perhaps an invincible attachment to the dearest rights of man may, in these refined, enlightened days, be deemed old-fashioned; if so, I am contented to be so. I say, the time has been when every pulse of my heart beat for American liberty, and which, I believe, had a counterpart in the breast of every true American; but suspicions have gone forth—suspicions of my integrity—publicly reported that my professions are not real. Twenty-three years ago was I supposed a traitor to my country? I was then said to be the bane of sedition, because I supported the rights of my country. I may be thought suspicious when I say our privileges and rights are in danger. But, sir, a number of the people of this country are weak enough to think these things are too true. I am happy to find that the gentleman on the other side declares they are groundless. But, sir, suspicion is a virtue as long as its object is the preservation of the public good, and as long as it stays within proper bounds: should it fall on me, I am contented: conscious rectitude is a powerful consolation. I trust there are many who think my professions for the public good to be real. Let your suspicion look to both sides. There are many on the other side, who possibly may have been persuaded to the necessity of these measures, which I conceive to be dangerous to your liberty. Guard with jealous attention the public liberty. Suspect every one who approaches that jewel. Unfortunately, nothing will preserve it but downright force. Whenever you give up that force, you are inevitably ruined. I am answered by gentlemen, that, though I might speak of terrors, yet the fact was, that we were surrounded by none of the dangers I apprehended. I conceive this new government to be one of those dangers: it has produced those horrors which distress many of our best citizens. We are come hither to preserve the poor commonwealth of Virginia, if it can be possibly done: something must be done to preserve your liberty and mine. The Confederation, this same despised government, merits, in my opinion, the highest encomium: it carried us through a long and dangerous war; it rendered us victorious in that bloody conflict with a powerful nation; it has secured us a territory greater than any European monarch possesses: and shall a government which has been thus strong and vigorous, be accused of imbecility, and abandoned for want of energy? Consider what you are about to do before you part with the government. Take longer time in reckoning things; revolutions like this have happened in almost every country in Europe; similar examples are to be found in ancient Greece and ancient Rome—instances of the people losing their liberty by their own carelessness and the ambition of a few. We are cautioned by the honorable gentleman, who presides, against faction and turbulence. I acknowledge that licentiousness is dangerous, and that it ought to be provided against: I acknowledge, also, the new form of government may effectually prevent it: yet there is another thing it will as effectually do—it will oppress and ruin the people. . . .

I shall be told I am continually afraid: but, sir, I have strong cause of apprehension. In some parts of the plan before you, the great rights of freemen are endangered; in other parts, absolutely taken away. How does your trial by jury stand? In civil cases gone—not sufficiently secured in criminal—this best privilege is gone. But we are told that we need not fear; because those in power, being our representatives, will not abuse the powers we put in their hands. I am not well versed in history, but I will submit to your recollection, whether liberty has been destroyed most often by the licentiousness of the people, or by the tyranny of rulers. I imagine, sir, you will find the balance on the side of tyranny. Happy will you be if you miss the fate of those nations, who, omitting to resist their oppressors, or negligently suffering their liberty to be wrested from them, have groaned under intolerable despotism! Most of the human race are now in this deplorable condition; and those nations who have gone in search of grandeur, power, and splendor, have also fallen a sacrifice, and been the victims of their own folly. While they acquired those visionary blessings, they lost their freedom. My great objection to this government is, that it does not leave us the means of defending our rights, or of waging war against tyrants. It is urged by some gentlemen, that this new plan will bring us an acquisition of strength—an army, and the militia of the states. This is an idea extremely ridicuous; gentlemen cannot be earnest. This acquisition will trample on our fallen liberty. Let my beloved Americans guard against that fatal lethargy that has pervaded the universe. Have we the means of resisting disciplined armies, when our only defence, the militia, is put into the hands of Congress? The honorable gentleman said that great danger would ensue if the Convention rose without adopting this system. I ask, Where is that danger? I see none. Other gentlemen have told us, within these walls, that the union is gone, or that the union will be gone. Is not this trifling with the judgment of their fellow-citizens? Till they tell us the grounds of their fears, I will consider them as imaginary. I rose to make inquiry where those dangers were; they could make no answer: I believe I never shall have that answer. Is there a disposition in the people of this country to revolt against the dominion of laws? Has there been a single tumult in Virginia? Have not the people of Virginia, when laboring under the severest pressure of accumulated distresses, manifested the most cordial acquiescence in the execution of the laws? What could be more awful than their unanimous acquiescence under general distresses? Is there any revolution in Virginia? Whither is the spirit of America gone? Whither is the genius of America fled? It was but yesterday, when our enemies marched in triumph through our country. Yet the people of this country could not be appalled by their pompous armaments: they stopped their career, and victoriously captured them. Where is the peril, now, campared to that? Some minds are agitated by foreign alarms. Happily for us, there is no real danger from Europe; that country is engaged in more arduous business: from that quarter there is no cause of fear: you may sleep in safety forever for them.

Where is the danger? If, sir, there was any, I would recur to the American spirit to defend us; that spirit which has enabled us to surmount the greatest difficulties: to that illustrious spirit I address my most fervent prayer to prevent our adopting a system destructive to liberty. Let not gentlemen be told that it is not safe to reject this government. Wherefore is it not safe? We are told there are dangers, but those dangers are ideal; they cannot be demonstrated. To encourage us to adopt it, they tell us that there is a plain, easy way of getting amendments. When I come to comtemplate this part, I suppose that I am mad, or that my countrymen are so. The way to amendment is, in my conception, shut. Let us consider this plain, easy way. "The Congress, whenever two thirds of both houses shall deem it necessary, shall propose amendments to this Constitution, or on the application of the legislatures of two thirds of the several states, shall call a Convention for proposing amendments, which, in either case, shall be valid to all intents and purposes, as part of this Constitution, when ratified by the legislatures of three fourths of the several states, or by the Conventions in three fourths thereof, as the one or the other mode of ratification may be proposed by the Congress. Provided, that no amendment which may be made prior to the year 1808, shall in any manner affect the 1st and 4th clauses in the 9th section of the 1st article; and that no state, without its consent, shall be deprived of its equal suffrage in the Senate."

Hence it appears that three fourths of the states must ultimately agree to any amendments that may be necessary. Let us consider the consequence of this. However uncharitable it may appear, yet I must tell my opinion—that the most unworthy characters may get into power, and prevent the introduction of amendments. Let us suppose—for the case is supposable, possible, and probable—that you happen to deal those powers to unworthy hands; will they relinquish powers already in their possession, or agree to amendments? Two thirds of the Congress, or of the state legislatures, are necessary even to propose amendments. If one third of these be unworthy men, they may prevent the application for amendments; but what is destructive and mischievous, is, that three fourths of the state legislatures, or of the state conventions, must concur in the amendments when proposed! In such numerous bodies, there must necessarily be some designing, bad men. To suppose that so large a number as three fourths of the states will concur, is to suppose that they will possess genius, intelligence, and integrity, approaching to miraculous. It would indeed be miraculous that they should concur in the same amendments, or even in such as would bear some likeness to one another; for four of the smallest states, that do not collectively contain one tenth part of the population of the United States, may obstruct the most salutary and necessary amendments. Nay, in these four states, six tenths of the people may reject these amendments; and suppose that amendments shall be opposed to amendments, which is highly probable,—is it possible that three fourths can ever agree to the same amendments? A bare majority in these four small states may hinder the adoption of amendments; so that we may fairly and justly conclude that one twentieth part of the American people may prevent the removal of the most grievous inconveniences and oppression, by refusing to accede to amendments. A trifling minority may reject the most salutary amendments. Is this an easy mode of securing the public liberty? It is, sir, a most fearful situation, when the most contemptible minority can prevent the alteration of the most oppressive government; for it may, in many respects, prove to be such. Is this the spirit of republicanism?

What, sir, is the genius of democracy? Let me read that clause of the bill of rights of Virginia which relates to this: 3d clause:—that government is, or ought to be, instituted for the common benefit, protection, and security of the people, nation, or community. Of all the various modes and forms of government, that is best, which is capable of producing the greatest degree of happiness and safety, and is most effectually secured against the danger of mal-administration; and that whenever any government shall be found inadequate, or contrary to those purposes, a majority of the community hath an indubitable, and indefeasible right to reform, alter, or abolish it, in such manner as shall be judged most conducive to the public weal.

This, sir, is the language of democracy—that a majority of the community have a right to alter government when found to be oppressive. But how different is the genius of your new Constitution from this! How different from the sentiments of freemen, that a contemptible minority can prevent the good of the majority! If, then, gentlemen, standing on this ground, are come to that point, that they are willing to bind themselves and their posterity to be oppressed, I am amazed and inexpressibly astonished. If this be the opinion of the majority, I must submit; but to me, sir, it appears perilous and destructive. I cannot help thinking so. Perhaps it may be the result of my age. These may be feelings natural to a man of my years, when the American spirit has left him, and his mental powers, like the members of the body, are decayed. If, sir, amendments are left to the twentieth, or tenth part of the people of America, your liberty is gone forever. We have heard that there is a great deal of bribery practised in the House of Commons, in England, and that many of the members raise themselves to preferments by selling the rights of the whole of the people. But, sir, the tenth part of that body cannot continue oppressions on the rest of the people. English liberty is, in this case, on a firmer foundation than American liberty. It will be easily contrived to procure the opposition of one tenth of the people to any alteration, however judicious. The honorable gentleman who presides told us that, to prevent abuses in our government, we will assemble in Convention, recall our delegated powers, and punish our servants for abusing the trust reposed in them. O sir, we should have fine times, indeed, if, to punish tyrants, it were only sufficient to assemble the people! Your arms, wherewith you could defend yourselves, are gone; and you have no longer an aristocratical, no longer a democratical spirit. Did you ever read of any revolution in a nation, brought about by the punishment of those in power, inflicted by those who had no power at all? You read of a riot act in a country which is called one of the freest in the world, where a few neighbors cannot assemble without the risk of being shot by a hired soldiery, the engines of despotism. We may see such an act in America.

A standing army we shall have, also, to execute the execrable commands of tyranny; and how are you to punish them? Will you order them to be punished? Who shall obey these orders? Will your mace-bearer be a match for a disciplined regiment? In what situation are we to be? The clause before you gives a power of direct taxation, unbounded and unlimited, exclusive power of legislation, in all cases whatsoever, for ten miles square, and over all places purchased for the erection of forts, magazines, arsenals, dockyards, &c. What resistance could be made? The attempt would be madness. You will find all the strength of this country in the hands of your enemies; their garrisons will naturally be the strongest places in the country. Your militia is given up to Congress, also, in another part of this plan: they will therefore act as they think proper: all power will be in their own possession. You cannot force them to receive their punishment: of what service would militia be to you, when, most probably, you will not have a single musket in the state? for, as arms are to be provided by Congress, they may or may not furnish them.

Let me here call your attention to that part which gives the Congress power "to provide for organizing, arming, and disciplining the militia, and for governing such part of them as may be employed in the service of the United States—reserving to the states, respectively, the appointment of the officers, and the authority of training the militia according to the discipline prescribed by Congress." By this, sir, you see that their control over our last and best defence is unlimited. If they neglect or refuse to discipline or arm our militia, they will be useless: the states can do neither—this power being exclusively given to Congress. The power of appointing officers over men not disciplined or armed is ridiculous; so that this pretended little remains of power left to the states may, at the pleasure of Congress, be rendered nugatory. Our situation will be deplorable indeed: nor can we ever expect to get this government amended, since I have already shown that a very small minority may prevent it, and that small minority interested in the continuance of the oppression. Will the oppressor let go the oppressed? Was there ever an instance? Can the annals of mankind exhibit one single example where rulers overcharged with power willingly let go the oppressed, though solicited and requested most earnestly? The application for amendments will therefore be fruitless. Sometimes, the oppressed have got loose by one of those bloody struggles that desolate a country; but a willing relinquishment of power is one of those things which human nature never was, nor ever will be, capable of.

Debates, III, pp. 44-56.

Virginia Convention June 6, 1788
Debates (excerpts)

[Gov. RANDOLPH.]
The honorable gentleman [Patrick Henry] attacks the Constitution, as he thinks it is contrary to our bill of rights. Do we not appeal to the people, by whose authority all government is made? That bill of rights is of no validity, because, I conceive, it is not formed on due authority. It is not a part of our Constitution; it has never secured us against any danger; it has been repeatedly disregarded and violated. . . .

I beg leave to remind you of the strength of Massachusetts and other states to the north; and what would their conduct be to us, if disunited from them? In case of a conflict between us and Maryland, or Pennsylvania, they would be aided by the whole strength of the more northern states; in short, by that of the adopting states. For these reasons, I conceive that, if Virginia supposes she has no cause of apprehension, she will find herself in a fatal error.

Suppose the American spirit in the fullest vigor in Virginia; what military preparations and exertions is she capable of making? The other states have upwards of 330,000 men capable of bearing arms: this will be a good army, or they can very easily raise a good army out of so great a number. Our militia amounts to 50,000: even stretching it to the improbable amount (urged by some) of 60,000,—in case of an attack, what defence can we make? Who are militia? Can we depend solely upon these? I will pay the last tribute of gratitiude to the militia of my country: they performed some of the most gallant feats during the last war, and acted as nobly as men inured to other avocations could be expected to do: but, sir, it is dangerous to look to them as our sole protectors. Did ever militia defend a country? Those of Pennsylvania were said to differ very little from regulars; yet these, sir, were insufficient for the defence of that state. The militia of our country will be wanted for agriculture. On this noblest of arts depend the virtue and the very existence of a country; if it be neglected, every thing else must be in a state of ruin and decay. It must be neglected if those hands which ought to attend to it are occasionally called forth on military expeditions. Some also will be necessary for manufactures, and those mechanic arts which are necessary for the aid of the farmer and planter. If we had men sufficient in number to defend ourselves, it could not avail without other requisites.

Debates, III, pp. 70, 76-77.

Virginia Convention June 7, 1788

Debates (excerpts)

[Mr. CORBIN.]

The honorable gentleman then urges an objection respecting the militia, who, he tells us, will be made the instruments of tyranny to deprive us of our liberty. Your militia, says he, will fight against you. Who are the militia? Are we not militia? Shall we fight against ourselves? No, sir; the idea is absurd. We are also terrified by the dread of a standing army. It cannot be denied that we ought to have the means of defence, and be able to repel an attack.

If some of the community are exclusively inured to its defence, and the rest attend to agriculture, the consequence will be, that the arts of war and defence, and of cultivating the soil, will be undersood.

Agriculture will flourish, and military discipline will be perfect. If, on the contrary, our defence be solely intrusted to militia, ignorance of arms and negligence of farming will ensue: the former plan is, in every respect, more to the interest of the state. By it we shall have good farmers and soldiers; by the latter we shall have neither. If the inhabitants be called out on sudden emergencies of war, their crops, the means of their subsistence, may be destroyed by it. If we are called in the time of sowing seed, or of harvest, the means of subsistence might be lost; and the loss of one years's crop might have been prevented by a trivial expense, if appropriated to the purpose of supporting a part of the community, exclusively occupied in the defence of the whole. I conceive that this idea, if it be a new one, is yet founded on solid and very substantial reasons. But, sir, we are told of the expediency and propriety of previous amendments. What end would it answer to attempt it? Will the states which have adopted the Constitution rescind their adopting resolutions? Had we adopted it, would we recede from it to please the caprice of any other state? Pride, sir, revolts at the idea. Admitting this state proposes amendments previous to her adoption, must there not be another federal convention? Must there not be also a convention in each state? Suppose some of our proposed conditions to be rejected; will not our exclusion out of the Union be the consequence? Or would other conventions again be called, and would be eternally revolving and devising expedients, without coming to a final decision? The loss of the union, sir, must be the result of a pertinacious demand of precedent conditions. My idea is, that we should go hand in hand with Massachusetts: adopt it first, and then propose amendments of a general nature; for local ones cannot be expected. Consider the situation of Massachusetts, commanding the north, and the importance and respectability of Virginia to the south. These, sir, are the two most populous, wealthy, and powerful states in the Union. Is it not very probable that their influence would have very great weight in carrying any amendments? Would any gentleman turn a deaf ear to their solicitations? By union alone can we exist: by no other means can we be happy. Union must be the object of every gentleman here. I never yet have heard any gentleman so wild and frantic in his opposition as to avow an attachment to partial confederacies. By previous adoption, the union will be preserved; by insisting on alterations previous to our adoption, the union may be lost, and our political happiness destroyed by internal dissensions.[1]

Mr. HENRY. I have thought, and still think, that a full investigation of the actual situation of America ought to precede any decision on this great and important question. That government is no more than a choice among evils, is acknowledged by the most intelligent among mankind, and has been a standing maxim for ages. If it be demonstrated that the adoption of the new plan is a little or a trifling evil, then, sir, I acknowledge that adoption ought to follow; but, sir, if this be a truth, that its adoption may entail misery on the free people of this country, I then insist that rejection ought to follow. Gentlemen strongly urge, its adoption will be a mighty benefit to us; but, sir, I am made of so incredulous materials, that assertions and declarations do not satisfy me. I must be convinced, sir. I shall retain my infidelity on that subject till I see our liberties secured in a manner perfectly satisfactory to my understanding.

There are certain maxims by which every wise and enlightened people will regulate their conduct. There are certain political maxims which no free people ought ever to abandon—maxims of which the observance is essential to the security of happiness. It is impiously irritating the avenging hand of Heaven, when a people, who are in the full enjoyment of freedom, launch out into the wide ocean of human affairs, and desert those maxims which alone can preserve liberty. Such maxims, humble as they are, are those only which can render a nation safe or formidable. Poor little humble republican maxims have attracted the admiration, and engaged the attention, of the virtuous and wise in all nations, and have stood the shock of ages. We do not now admit the validity of maxims which we once delighted in. We have since adopted maxims of a different, but more refined nature—new maxims, which tend to the prostration of republicanism.

We have one, sir, *that all men are by nature free and independent, and have certain inherent rights, of which, when they enter into society, they cannot by any compact deprive or divest their posterity.* We have a set of maxims of the same spirit, which must be beloved by every friend to liberty, to virtue, to mankind: our bill of rights contains those admirable maxims.[2]

Now, sir, I say, let us consider whether the picture given of American affairs ought to drive us from those beloved maxims.

The honorable gentleman, Governor Randolph, has said that it is too late in the day for us to reject this new plan. That system which was once execrated by the honorable member must now be adopted, let its defects be ever so glaring. That honorable member will not accuse me of want of candor, when I cast in my mind what he has given the public, [alluding to his excellency's letter on that subject to the speaker of the House of Delegates] and compare it to what has happened since. It seems to me very strange and unaccountable that that which was the object of his execration should now receive his encomiums. Something extraordinary must have operated so great a change in his opinion. It is too late in the day! Gentlemen must excuse me if they should declare, again and again, that it was too late, and I should think differently. I never can believe, sir, that it is too late to save all that is precious: if it be proper, and, independently of every external consideration, wisely constructed, let us receive it: but, sir, shall its adoption by eight states induce us to receive it, if it be replete with the most dangerous defects? They urge that subsequent amendments are safer than previous amendments, and that they will answer the same ends.

At present we have our liberties and privileges in our own hands. Let us not relinquish them. Let us not adopt this system till we see them secure. There is some small possibility that, should we follow the conduct of Massachusetts, amendments might be obtained. There is a small possibility of amending any government; but, sir, shall we abandon our most inestimable rights, and rest their security on a mere possibility? The gentleman fears the loss of the Union. If eight states have ratified it unamended, and we should rashly imitate their precipitate example, do we not thereby disunite from several other states? Shall those who have risked their lives for the sake of the Union be at once thrown out of it? If it be amended, every state will accede to it; but by an imprudent adoption in its defective and dangerous state, a schism must inevitably be the consequence. I can never, therefore, consent to hazard our most unalienable rights on an absolute uncertainty. . . .

The honorable member advises us to adopt a measure which will destroy our bill of rights[.] . . .

If we are to have one representative for every thirty thousand souls, it must be by implication. The Constitution does not positively secure it. Even say it is a natural implication,—why not give us a right to that proportion in express terms, in language that could not admit of evasions or subterfuges? If they can use implication for us, they can also use implication against us. We are giving power; they are getting power; judge, then, on which side the implication will be used! When we once put it in their option to assume constructive power, danger will follow. Trial by jury, and liberty of the press, are also on this foundation of implication. If they encroach on these rights, and you give your implication for a plea, you are cast; for they will be justified by the last part of it, which gives them full power "to make all laws which shall be necessary and proper to carry their power into execution." Implication is dangerous, because it is unbounded: if it be admitted at all, and no limits be prescribed, it admits of the utmost extension. They say that every thing that is not given is retained. The reverse of the proposition is true by implication. They do not carry their implication so far when they speak of the general welfare no implication when the sweeping clause comes. Implication is only necessary when the existence of privileges is in dispute. The existence of powers is sufficiently established. If we trust our dearest rights to implication, we shall be in a very unhappy situation.

Implication, in England, has been a source of dissension. There has been a war of implication between the king and people. For a hundred years did the mother country struggle under the uncertainty of implication. The people insisted that their rights were implied; the monarch denied the doctrine. The Bill of Rights, in some degree, terminated the dispute. By a bold implication, they said they had a right to bind us in all cases whatsoever. This constructive power we opposed, and successfully. Thirteen or fourteen years ago, the most important thing that could be thought of was to exclude the possibility of construction and implication. These, sir, were then deemed perilous. The first thing that was thought of was a bill of rights. We were not satisfied with your constructive, argumentative rights.

Mr. Henry then declared a bill of rights indispensably necessary; that a general positive provision should be inserted in the new system, securing to the states and the people every right which was not conceded to the general government; and that every implication should be done away. It being now late, he concluded by observing, that he would resume the subject another time.[3]

1 *Debates,* III, pp. 112-113.
2 See Appendix A, p. 747 for the Virginia Declaration of Rights.
3 *Debates,* pp. 137-139, 143, 149-150.

A Militiaman June 7, 1788

Newspaper Article: Philadelphia *Independent Gazetteer* (excerpt)

From the *Maryland Gazette,* printed by Mr. *Hayes.*
WHIPPING MILITIA! . . .

But the great body of the yeomanry of England cannot by their constitution—by their Magna Charta—be subjected to martial law, or deprived of the trial by their Peers, unless it be *flagrante bello*—Whereas the great body of the yeomanry of America may, at any time, and at all times, *by the new Constitution,* be subject to MARTIAL LAW, which Sir Matthew Hale observes is really *no law at all,* but arbitrary proceedings of men acting by no settled rules.—Thus the militia of this country, which includes almost the whole yeomanry of America, may by deprived *at will* of every right, and continue so subjected to arbitrary and despotic rule during their whole lives.—What may be done in government will certainly at some period be actually done;—this has become, from the constant observation of mankind, a political apothegm, and as such is never controverted by those whose sense or candour entitle them to controvert—

George Mason (Richmond) June 9, 1788
Letter: To John Lamb (excerpt)[1]

I have had the Honor to receive your Letter, dated the 18th of May, in behalf of the foederal republican Committee of New York, upon the Subject of the government proposed by the late convention to the respective States for their Adoption, and have communicated it to several respectable Gentlemen of the Convention now met in this City, who are opposed to the Adoption without previous Amendments. They receive, with pleasure, the proposition of your Committee for a free Correspondence on the Subject of Amendments, and have requested me to transmit to your Committee such as we have agreed on as necessary for previous Adoption.[2]

Although there is a general Concurrence in the Convention of this State that Amendments are necessary, yet, the Members are so equally divided with respect to the Time and Manner of obtaining them, that it cannot now be ascertained whether the Majority will be on our Side or not; if it should be so, I have no doubt but that an Official Communication will immediately take place between the convention of this State and yours.

1 Rutland, III, pp. 1057-1058.

2 See "George Mason," [June 11, 1788], p. 388, for the bill of rights portion of the proposals of the Richmond Antifederal Committee. See Rutland, III, p. 1071 for details concerning how and when the proposed amendments were actually sent to the New York Committee.

Virginia Convention June 9, 1788
Debates (excerpts)

[Mr. HENRY.]
They [Congress] are also to have magazines in each state. These depositories for arms, though within the state, will be free from the control of its legislature. Are we at last brought to such an humiliating and debasing degradation, that we cannot be trusted with arms for our

own defence? Where is the difference between having our arms in our own possession and under our own direction, and having them under the management of Congress? If our defence be the *real* object of having those arms, in whose hands can they be trusted with more propriety, or equal safety to us, as in our own hands? If our legislature be unworthy of legislating for every foot in this state, they are unworthy of saying another word.

The clause which says that Congress shall "provide for arming, organizing, and disciplining the militia, and for governing such part of them as may be employed in the service of the United States, reserving to the states respectively the appointment of the officers," seemed to put the states in the power of Congress. I wished to be informed, if Congress neglected to discipline them, whether the states were not precluded from doing it. Not being favored with a particular answer, I am confirmed in my opinion, that the states have not the power of disciplining them, without recurring to the doctrine of constructive implied powers. If, by implication, the states may discipline them, by implication, also, Congress may officer them; because, in a partition of power, each has a right to come in for part; and because implication is to operate in favor of Congress on all occasions, where their object is the extension of power, as well as in favor of the states. We have not one fourth of the arms that would be sufficient to defend ourselves. The power of arming the militia, and the means of purchasing arms, are taken from the states by the paramount powers of Congress. If Congress will not arm them, they will not be armed at all.

There have been no instances shown of a voluntary cession of power, sufficient to induce me to grant the most dangerous power; a possibility of their future relinquishment will not persuade me to yield such powers.

Congress, by the power of taxation, by that of raising an army, and by their control over the militia, have the sword in one hand, and the purse in the other. Shall we be safe without either? Congress have an unlimited power over both: they are entirely given up by us. Let him candidly tell me, where and when did freedom exist, when the sword and purse were given up from the people? Unless a miracle in human affairs interposed, no nation ever retained its liberty after the loss of the sword and purse. Can you prove, by any argumentative deduction, that it is possible to be safe without retaining one of these? If you give them up, you are gone.[1]

[Mr. LEE, (of Westmoreland).]

This plan provides for the public defence as it ought to do. Regulars are to be employed when necessary, and the service of the militia will always be made use of. This, sir, will promote agricultural industry and skill, and military discipline and science.

I cannot understand the implication of the honorable gentleman, that, because Congress may arm the militia, the states cannot do it: nor do I understand the reverse of the proposition. The states are, by no part of the plan before you, precluded from arming and disciplining the militia, should Congress neglect it. . . .

But says he, "The President will enslave you; Congress will trample on your liberties; a few regiments will appear, Mr. Chief Justice must give way; our mace-bearer is no match for a regiment." It was inhuman to place an individual against a whole regiment. A *few* regiments will not avail; I trust the supporters of the government would get the better of *many* regiments. Were so mad an attempt made, the people would assemble in thousands, and drive thirty times the number of their few regiments. We would then do as we have already done with the regiments of that king whom he so often tells us of. . . .

It was necessary to provide against licentiousness, which is so natural to our climate. I dread more from the licentiousness of the people than from the bad government of rulers. Our privileges are not, however, in danger: they are better secured than any bill of rights could have secured them.

I say that this new system shows, in stronger terms than words could declare, that the liberties of the people are secure. It goes on the principle that all power is in the people, and that rulers have no powers but what are enumerated in that paper. When a question arises with respect to the legality of any power, exercised or assumed by Congress, it is plain on the side of the governed: *Is it enumerated in the Constitution?* If it be, it is legal and just. It is otherwise arbitrary and unconstitutional. Candor must confess that it is infinitley more attentive to the liberties of the people than any state government.

[Mr. Lee then said, that, under the state governments, the people reserved to themselves certain enumerated rights, and that the rest were vested in their rulers; that, consequently, the powers reserved to the people were but an inconsiderable exception from what were given to their rulers; but that, in the federal government, the rulers of the people were vested with certain defined powers, and that what were not delegated to those rulers were retained by the people. The consequence of this, he said, was, that the limited powers were only an exception to those which rested in the people, and that they knew what they had given up, and could be in no danger. He exemplified the proposition in a familiar manner. He observed, that, if a man delegated certain powers to an agent, it would be an insult upon common sense to suppose that the agent could legally transact any business for his principal which was not contained in the commission whereby the powers were delegated; but that, if a man empowered his representative or agent to transact all his business except certain enumerated parts, the clear result was, that the agent could lawfully transact every possible part of his principal's business except the enumerated parts; and added, that these plain propositions were sufficient to demonstrate the inutility and *folly* (were he permitted to use the expression) of bills of rights.][2]

[Gov. RANDOLPH.]

He said that Magna Charta destroyed all implication. This was not the object of Magna Charta, but to destroy the power of the king, and secure the liberty of the people. The bill of rights was intended to restore the government to its primitive principles. . . .

I am surprised at his proposition of previous amendments, and his assertion that subsequent ones will cause disunion. Shall we not lose our influence and weight in the government to bring about amendments, if we propose them previously? Will not the senators be chosen, and the electors of the President be appointed, and the government brought instantly into action, after the ratification of nine states? In this disunion, when will the effect proposed be produced? But no man here is willing to believe what the honorable gentleman says on this point. . . .

Why have we been told that maxims can alone save nations; that our maxims are our bill of rights; and that the liberty of the press, trial by jury, and religion, are destroyed? Give me leave to say, that the maxims of Virginia are union and justice. . . .

I should not say so much on this occasion, were it not that I perceive that the flowers of rhetoric are perverted, in order to make impressions unfavorable and inimical to an impartial and candid decision. What security can arise from a bill of rights? The predilection for it has arisen from a misconception of its principles. It cannot secure the liberties of this country. A bill of rights was used in England to limit the king's prerogative; he could trample on the liberties of the people in every case which was not within the restraint of the bill of rights.

Our situation is radically different from that of the people of England. What have we to do with bills of rights? Six or seven states have none. Massachusetts has declared her bill of rights as no part of her Constitution. Virginia has a bill of rights, but it is no part of her

Constitution. By not saying whether it is paramount to the Constitution or not, it has left us in confusion. Is the bill of rights consistent with the Constitution? Why, then, is it not inserted in the Constitution? Does it add any thing to the Constitution? Why is it not in the Constitution? Does it except any thing from the Constitution? Why not put the exceptions in the Constitution? Does it oppose the Constitution? This will produce mischief. The judges will dispute which is paramount. Some will say, the bill of rights is paramount: others will say, that the Constitution, being subsequent in point of time, must be paramount. A bill of rights, therefore, accurately speaking, is quite useless, if not dangerous to a republic.

I had objections to this Constitution. I still have objections to it. [Here he read the objections which appeared in his public letter.] The gentleman asks, How comes it to pass that you are now willing to take it? I answer, that I see Virginia in such danger, that, were its defects greater, I would adopt it. These dangers, though not immediately present to our view, yet may not be far distant, if we disunite from the other states. I will join any man in endeavoring to get amendments, after the danger of disunion is removed by a previous adoption.[3]

1 *Debates*, III, pp. 168-169.
2 *Ibid.*, pp. 178-179, 181, 185-186.
3 *Ibid.*, pp. 190-192.

Virginia Convention June 10, 1788
Debates (excerpts)

[Mr. MONROE.]

As it will operate on all states and individuals, powers given it generally should be qualified. It may be attributed to the prejudice of my education, but I am a decided and warm friend to a bill of rights—the polar star and great support of American liberty; and I am clearly of opinion that the general powers conceded by that plan, such as the impost, &c, should be guarded and checked by a bill of rights.

Permit me to examine the reasoning that admits that all powers not given up are reserved. Apply this. If you give to the United States the power of direct taxation, in making all laws necessary to give it operation, (which is a power given by the last clause in the 8th section of the 1st article,) suppose they should be of opinion that the right of the trial by jury was not one of the requisites to carry it into effect; there is no check in this Constitution to prevent the formal abolition of it. There is a general power given to them to make all laws that will enable them to carry their powers into effect. There are no limits pointed out. They are not restrained or controlled from making any law, however oppressive in its operation, which they may think necessary to carry their powers into effect. By this general, unqualified power, they may infringe not only on the trial by jury, but the liberty of the press, and every right that is not expressly secured or excepted from that general power. I conceive that such general powers are very dangerous. Our great unalienable rights ought to be secured from being destroyed by such unlimited powers, either by a bill of rights, or by an express provision in the body of the Constitution. It is immaterial in which of these two modes rights are secured. . . .

Mr. HARRISON. . . He added some observations on the plan of government; that it certainly would operate an infringement of the rights and liberties of the people; that he was amazed that gentlemen should attempt to misrepresent facts to persuade the Convention to adopt such a system; and that he trusted they would not ratify it as it then stood.

Debates, III, pp. 217-218, 236.

Virginia Convention June 11, 1788
Debates (excerpts)

[Mr. MASON.]
It is urged that no new power is given up to the general government, and that the Confederation had those powers before. That system derived its power from the state governments. When the people of Virginia formed their government, they reserved certain great powers in the bill of rights. They would not trust their own citizens, who had a similarity of interest with themselves, and who had frequent and intimate communication with them. They would not trust their own fellow-citizens, I say, with the exercise of those great powers reserved in the bill of rights. Do we not, by this system, give up a great part of the rights, reserved by the bill of rights, to those who have no fellow-feeling for the people—to a government where the representatives will have no communication with the people? I say, then, there are great and important powers, which were not transferred to the state government, given up to the general government by this Constitution.

Let us advert to the 6th article. It expressly declares, that "this Constitution, and the laws of the United States which shall be made in pursuance thereof, and all treaties made, or which shall be made, under the authority of the United States, shall be the supreme law of the land, and the judges in every state shall be bound thereby; any thing in the Constitution or laws of any state to the contrary notwithstanding." Now, sir, if the laws and Constitution of the general government, as expressly said, be paramount to those of any state, are not those rights with which we were afraid to trust our own citizens annulled and given up to the general government? The bill of rights is a part of our own Constitution. The judges are obliged to take notice of the laws of the general government; consequently, the rights secured by our bill of rights are given up. If they are not given up, where are they secured? By implication! Let gentlemen show that they are secured in a plain, direct, unequivocal manner. It is not in their power. Then where is the security? Where is the barrier drawn between the government and the rights of the citizens, as secured in our own state government? These rights are given up in that paper; but I trust that this Convention will never give them up, but will take pains to secure them to the latest posterity. If a check be necessary in our own state government, it is much more so in a government where our representatives are to be at the distance of a thousand miles from us, without any responsibility. . . .

We wish only our rights to be secured. We must have such amendments as will secure the liberties and happiness of the people on a plain, simple construction, not on a doubtful ground. We wish to give the government sufficient energy, on real republican principles; but we wish to withhold such powers as are not absolutely necessary in themselves, but are extremely dangerous. We wish to shut the door against corruption in that place where it is most dangerous—to secure against the corruption of our own representatives. We ask such amendments as will point out what powers are reserved to the state governments, and clearly discriminate between them and those which are given to the general government, so as to prevent future disputes and clashing of interest. Grant us amendments like these, and we will cheerfully, with our hands and hearts, unite with those who advocate it, and we will do every thing we can to support and carry it into execution. But in its present form we never can accede to it. Our duty to God and to our posterity forbids it. We acknowledge the defects of the Confederation, and the necessity of a reform. We ardently wish for a union with our sister states, on terms of security. This I am bold to declare is the desire of most of the people. On these terms we will most cheerfully join with the warmest friends of this Constitution. On another occasion I shall point out the great dangers of this Constitution, and the amendments which are necessary. I will likewise endeavor to show that amendments after ratification are delusive and fallacious—perhaps utterly impracticable.

Debates, III, pp. 265-266, 271-272.

Denatus June 11, 1788
Newspaper Article: Richmond *Virginia Independent Chronicle* (excerpt)

To the Members of the Virginia Federal Convention, collectively, and individually. . . .

I object to it also, because, it appears to be a huddled piece of work: and (that in the general bustle) they forgot to put a bill of rights to it. A bill of rights! say Mr. Wilson and others, to confederated powers, is unnecessary—very truly, to powers properly confederated, but this is no confederation. It is a national government, i.e. through a little time, the incroachment will so prevail, that the foederal constitution will expunge entirely the state constitutions—It appears to be a confederation now, but the monarch who is asleep in its bosom, at a convenient time, will awaken with a vengeance! —There would be no need of a bill of rights, were the states properly confederated. The land-mark clearly drawn between the powers that give, and the power given:—And where the remaining parts of the powers that give, are ever to be held sacred by the power given. The remaining parts of the powers that give, or the residue, of our state constitutions, would be a bill of rights, to the power given, or the foederal constitution. Had this distinction been clearly fixed, so as to prevent any future controversy, the constitution in question, would have been a glorious, and an immortal example of human wisdom. But alas! this is not the case—There is no barrier to the power of the foederal constitution. It will easily overleap our state constitutions with impunity. When this comes to be the case, and the foederal constitution sovereign in all things, we ought to have a bill of rights; to save us from oppression. The want of this, is of an alarming nature, and I hope will be one of your amendments.

Storing, V, p. 263.

George Mason [June 11, 1788]
Richmond Antifederal Committee Proposed Bill of Rights

That there be a Declaration or Bill of Rights, asserting and securing from Encroachment the essential and unalienable Rights of the People, in some such Manner as the following.

1. That all Freemen have certain essential inherent Rights, of which they can not by any Compact, deprive or divest their Posterity; among which are the Enjoyment of Life and Liberty, with the Means of acquiring, possessing, and protecting Property, and pursueing and obtaining Happiness and Safety.
2. That all Power is naturally vested in, and consequently derived from the People; that Magistrates therefore are their Trustees and Agents; and at all times amenable to them.
3. That Government ought to be instituted for the common Benefit, Protection, and Security of the People; and that whenever any government shall be found inadequate or contrary to these Purposes, a Majority of the community hath an indubitable, unalienable, and indefeasible Right to reform, alter, or to abolish it, and Establish another, in such Manner as shall be judged most conducive to the Public Weal; and that the Doctrine of non resist[ance] against arbitrary Power & oppression is absurd, slavish, & destructive of the Good & Happiness of Mankind.
4. That no Man, or set of Men, are entitled to exclusive or separate public Emoluments or privileges from the Community, but in Consideration of public Services; which not being descendible, neither ought the Offices of Magistrate Legislator, or Judge, or any other public Office, to be hereditary.
5. That the legislative executive and judiciary powers of Government shou'd be separate & distinct; and that the Members of the two first may be restrained from Oppression, by feeling and participating in the public Burthens, they shou'd at fixed Periods, be reduced to a private Station, return into the Mass of the People, and the Vacancys be supplied by certain & regular Elections; in which all, or any Part of the former Members to be eligible, or ineligible, as the Rules of the constitution of Government, & the Laws shall direct.
6. That the Right of the People to participate in the Legislature is the best Se[c]urity of Liberty, and the Foundation of all free government; for this Purpose Elections ought to be free, & frequent; and all men having sufficient Evidence of permanent common Interest with, and Attachment to the Community, ought to have the Right of Suffrage and that no aid charge Tax, or fee can be set rated or levyed upon the People, without their own Consent or that of their Representatives, so

elected, nor can they be bound by any Law to which they have not, in like Manner, assented, for the public Good.

7. That all Power of suspending Laws, or the Execution of Laws, by any Authority, without the consent of the Representatives of the People in the Legislature, is injurious to their Rights, and ought not to be exercised.

8. That in all capital or Criminal Prosecutions, a Man hath a Right to demand the Cause and nature of his Accusation, to be confronted with the Accusers and Witnesses, to call for Evidence, & be admitted Councel in his Favour, and to a fair & speedy Trial by an impartial Jury of his Vicinage; without whose unanimous Consent he can not be found guilty, (except in the Government of the Land and Naval Forces in time of actual War, Invasion, or Rebellion) nor can he be compelled to give Evidence against himself.

9. That no freeman ought to be taken, imprisoned, or disseized of his Freehold, Liberties, privileges, or Franchises, or outlawed, or exiled, or in any manner destroyed, or deprived of his Life, Liberty, or Property but by the Law of the Land.

10. That every freeman restrained of his Liberty, is entitled to a Remedy, to enquire into the Lawfulness thereof, and to remove the same if unlawful, and that such Remedy ought not to be denyed, or delayed.

11. That in Controversies respecting Property, and in Suits between Man and Man, the ancient Trial by Jury of Facts, where they arise, is one of the greatest Securities to the Rights of a free People, and ought to remain sacred and inviolable.

12. That every Freeman ought to find a certain Remedy, by Recourse to the Laws, for all Injurys or Wrongs he may receive in his Person property or Character. He ought [to] obtain Right and Justice freely, without Sale, compleatly & without Denial, promptly and without Delay; and that all Establishments or Regulations contravening these Rights are oppressive and unjust.

13. That excessive Bail ought not to be required, nor excessive Fines imposed, nor cruel and unusual Punishments inflicted.

14. That every free man has a Right to be secure from all unreasonable Searches and Seizures of his Person, his papers, and his property. All Warrants therefore to search suspected places, or to seize any freeman, his papers, or Property, without Information upon Oath (or Affirmation of a Person religiously scrupulous of taking an Oath) of legal and sufficient Cause, are grievous and oppressive; and all general Warrants to search suspected places, or to apprehend any suspected Person, without specially naming or describing the place or Person, are dangerous, and ought not to be granted.

15. That the People have a Right peaceably to assemble together to consult for their common good or to instruct their Representatives, and that every freeman has a right to petition, or apply to the Legislature for Redress of Grievances.
16. That the People have a Right to Freedom of Speech, and of Writing and publishing their Sentiments; that the Freedom of the Press is one of the great Bulwarks of Liberty, and ought not to be violated.
17. That the People have a Right to keep & to bear Arms; that a well regulated Militia, composed of the Body of the People, trained to Arms, is the proper natural and safe Defence of a free State; that standing Armys in time of Peace are dangerous to Liberty, and therefore ought to be avoided, as far as the Circumstances and Protection of the Community will admit; and that in all Cases, the Military shou'd be under strict Subordination to and govern'd by the Civil Power.
18. That no Soldier in time of Peace ought to be quartered in any House without the Consent of the Owner; and in time of War, only by the Civil Magistrate in such manner as the Laws direct.
19. That any Person religiously scrupulous of bearing Arms ought to be exempted, upon payment of an Equivalent, to employ another to bear Arms in his Stead.
20. That Religion, or the duty which we owe to our Creator, and the Manner of discharging it, can be directed only by Reason and Conviction, not by Force or Violence, and therefore all Men have an equal natural and unalienable Right to the free Exercise of Religion, according to the Dictates of Conscience, And that no particular religious Sect or Society of Christians ought to be favoured or established by Law, in Preference to others.

Rutland, III, pp. 1068-1071. This bill of rights was sent to Antifederalist leaders in New York. See *Ibid.*, note on p. 1071, and "Robert Yates," p. 444, below.

Virginia Convention June 12, 1788
Debates (excerpts)

[Mr. PENDLETON.]
Permit me to deliver a few sentiments on the great and important subject of previous and subsequent amendments. When I sat down to read that paper, I did not read it with an expectation that it was perfect, and that no man would object to it. I had learned, sir, that an expectation of such perfection in any institute devised by *man*, was as vain as the search for the philosopher's stone. I discovered objections—I thought I saw there some sown seeds of disunion—not

in the immediate operation of the government, but which *might* happen in some future time. I wish amendments to remove these. But these remote possible errors may be eradicated by the amendatory clause in the Constitution. I see no danger in making the experiment, since the system itself points out an easy mode of removing any errors which shall have been experienced. In this view, then, I think we may safely trust in the government. With respect to the eight states who have already acceded to it, do gentlemen believe that, should we propose amendments as the *sine qua non* of our adoption, they would listen to our proposals? I conceive, sir, that they would not retract. They would tell us—*No, gentlemen, we cannot accept of your conditions. You put yourselves upon the ground of opposition. Your amendments are dictated by local considerations. We, in our adoption, have been influenced by considerations of general utility to the Union. We cannot abandon principles, like these, to gratify you.* Thus, sir, by previous amendments, we present a hostile countenance. If, on the contrary, we imitate the conduct of those states, our language will be conciliatory and friendly. Gentlemen, we put ourseves on the same ground that you are on. We are not actuated by local considerations, but by such as affect the people of America in general. This conduct will give our amendments full weight.

I was surprised when I heard introduced the opinion of a gentleman (Mr. Jefferson) whom I highly respect. I know the great abilites of that gentleman. Providence has, for the good of mankind, accompanied those extensive abilites with a disposition to make use of them for the good of his fellow-beings; and I wish, with all my heart, that he was here to assist us on this interesting occasion. As to his letter, impressed as I am with the force of his authority, I think it was improper to introduce it on this occasion. The opinion of a private individual, however enlightened, ought not to influence our decision. But, admitting that this opinion ought to be conclusive with us, it strikes me in a different manner from the honorable gentleman. I have seen the letter in which this gentleman has written his opinion upon this subject. It appears that he is possessed of that Constitution, and has in his mind the idea of amending it—he has in his mind the very question, of subsequent or previous amendments, which is now under consideration. His sentiments on this subject are as follows: "I wish, with all my soul, that the nine first conventions may accept the new Constitution, because it will secure to us the good it contains, which I think great and important. I wish the four latest, whichever they be, may refuse to accede to it till amendments are secured." He then enumerates the amendments which he wishes to be secured, and adds, "We must take care, however, that neither this nor any other objection to the form, produce a schism in our Union. That would be an incurable evil; because friends falling out never cordially reunite." Are these sentiments in favor of those who wish to prevent its adoption by previous amendments? He wishes the first nine states to adopt it. What are his reasons? Because he thinks it will secure to us the good it contains, which he thinks *great* and *important;* and he wishes the other four may refuse it, because he thinks it may tend to obtain necessary amendments.[1]

[Mr. HENRY.]

The honorable gentleman has endeavored to explain the opinion of Mr. Jefferson, our common friend, into an advice to adopt this new government. What are his sentiments? He wishes nine states to adopt, and that four states may be found somewhere to reject it. Now, sir, I say, if we pursue his advice, what are we to do? To prefer form to substance? For, give me leave to ask, what is the substantial part of his counsel? It is, sir, that four states should *reject*. They tell us that, from the most authentic accounts, New Hampshire will adopt it. When I denied this, gentlemen said they were absolutely certain of it. Where, then, will four states be found to reject, if we adopt it? If we do, the counsel of this enlightened and worthy countryman of ours will be thrown away; and for what? He wishes to secure amendments and a bill of rights, if I am not mistaken. I speak from the best information, and if wrong, I beg to be put right. His amendments go to that despised thing, called *a bill of rights,* and all the rights which are dear to human nature—trial by jury, the liberty of religion and the press, &c. Do not gentlemen see that, if we adopt, under the idea of following Mr. Jefferson's opinion, we amuse ourselves with the shadow, while the substance is given away? If Virginia be for adoption, what states will be left, of sufficient respectability and importance to secure amendments by their rejection? As to North Carolina, it is *a poor, despised place.* Its dissent will not have influence to introduce any amendments. Where is the American spirit of liberty? Where will you find attachment to the rights of mankind, when Massachusetts, the great northern state, Pennsylvania, the great middle state, and Virginia, the great southern state, shall have adopted this government? Where will you find magnanimity enough to reject it? Should the remaining states have this magnanimity, they will not have sufficient weight to have the government altered. This state has weight and importance. Her example will have powerful influence—her rejection will procure amendments. Shall we, by our adoption, hazard the loss of amendments? Shall we forsake that importance and respectability which our station in America commands, in hopes that relief will come from an obscure part of the Union? I hope my countrymen will spurn at the idea.

The necessity of amendments is universally admitted. It is a word which is reechoed from every part of the continent. A majority of those who hear me think amendments are necessary. Policy tells us they are necessary. Reason, self-preservation, and every idea of propriety, powerfully urge us to secure the dearest rights of human nature. Shall we, in direct violation of these prinicples, rest this security upon the uncertainty of its being obtained by a few states, more weak and less respectable than ourselves, and whose virtue and magnanimity may be overborne by the example of so many adopting states? *Poor* Rhode Island, and North Carolina, and even New York, surrounded with federal walls on every side, may not be magnanimous enough to reject; and if they do reject it, they will have but little influence to obtain amendments. I ask, if amendments be necessary, from whence can they be so properly proposed as from this state? The example of Virgnina is a powerful thing, particularly with respect to North Carolina, whose supplies must come *through* Virginia. Every possible opportunity of procuring amendments is gone, our power and political salvation are gone, if we ratify unconditionally. . . .

We are told that all powers not given are reserved. I am sorry to bring forth hackneyed observations. But, sir, important truths lose nothing of their validity or weight, by frequency of repetition. The English history is frequently recurred to by gentlemen. Let us advert to the conduct of the people of that country. The people of England lived without a declaration of rights till the war in the time of Charles I. That king made usurpations upon the rights of the people. Those rights were, in a great measure, before that time undefined. Power and privilege then depended on implication and logical discussion. Though the declaration of rights was obtained from that king, his usurpations cost him his life. The limits between the liberty of the people, and the prerogative of the king, were still not clearly defined.

The rights of the people continued to be violated till the Stuart family was banished, in the year 1688. The people of England magnanimously defended their rights, banished the tyrant, and prescribed to William, Prince of Orange, by the bill of rights, on what terms he should reign; and this bill of rights put an end to all construction and implication. Before this, sir, the situation of the public liberty of England was dreadful. For upwards of a century, the nation was involved in every kind of calamity, till the bill of rights put an end to all, by defining the rights of the people, and limiting the king's prerogative. Give me leave to add (if I can add any thing to so splendid an example) the conduct of the American people. They, sir, thought a bill of rights necessary. It is alleged that several states, in the formation of their government, omitted a bill of rights. To this I answer, that they had the substance of a bill of rights contained in their constitutions, which is the same thing. I believe that Connecticut has preserved it, by her Constitution, her royal charter, which clearly defines and secures the great rights of mankind—secures to us the great, important rights of humanity; and I care not in what form it is done.

Of what advantage is it to the American Congress to take away this great and general security? I ask, Of what advantage is it to the public, or to Congress, to drag an unhappy debtor, not for the sake of justice, but to gratify the malice of the plaintiff, with his witnesses, to the federal court, from a great distance? What was the principle that actuated the Convention in proposing to put such dangerous powers in the hands of any one? Why is the trial by jury taken away? All the learned arguments that have been used on this occasion do not prove that it is secured. Even the advocates for the plan do not all concur in the certainty of its security. Wherefore is religious liberty not secured? One honorable gentleman, who favors adoption, said that he had had his fears on the subject. If I can well recollect, he informed us that he was perfectly satisfied, by the powers of reasoning, (with which he is so happily endowed,) that those fears were not well grounded. There is many a religious man who knows nothing of argumentative reasoning, there are many of our most worthy citizens who cannot go through all the labyrinths of syllogistic, argumentative deductions, when they think that the rights of conscience are invaded. This sacred right ought not to depend on constructive, logical reasoning.

When we see men of such talents and learning compelled to use their utmost abilities to convince themselves that there is no danger, is it not sufficient to make us tremble? Is it not sufficient to fill the minds of the ignorant part of men with fear? If gentlemen believe that the apprehensions of men will be quieted, they are mistaken, since our best-informed men are in doubt with respect to the security of our rights. Those who are not so well informed will spurn at the government. When our common citizens, who are not possessed with such extensive knowledge and abilities, are called upon to change their bill of rights (which, in plain, unequivocal terms, secures their most valuable rights and privileges) for construction and implication, will they implicitly acquiesce? Our declaration of rights tells us that "all men are by nature free and independent," &c. [Here Mr. Henry read the declaration of rights.][2] Will they exchange these rights for logical reasons? If you had a thousand acres of land dependent on this, would you be satisfied with logical construction? Would you depend upon a title of so disputable a nature? The present opinions of individuals will be buried in entire oblivion when those rights will be thought of. That sacred and lovely thing religion, ought not to rest on the ingenuity of logical deduction. Holy religion, sir, will be prostitued to the lowest purposes of human policy. What has been more productive of mischief among mankind than religious disputes? Then here, sir, is a foundation for such disputes, when it requires learning and logical deduction to perceive that religious liberty is secure.[3]

Rulers are the servants and agents of the people; the people are their masters. Does the new Constitution acknowledge this principle? Trial by jury is the best appendage of freedom. Does it secure this? Does it secure the other great rights of mankind? Our own Constitution preserves these principles. The honorable gentleman contributed to form that Constitution. The applauses so justly due to it should, in my opinion, go to the condemnation of that paper. . . .

The honorable gentleman did our judiciary honor in saying that they had firmness to counteract the legislature in some cases. Yes, sir, our judges opposed the acts of the legislature. We have this landmark to guide us. They had fortitude to declare that they were the judiciary, and would oppose unconstitutional acts. Are you sure that your federal judiciary will act thus? Is that judiciary as well constructed, and as independent of the other branches, as our state judiciary? Where are your landmarks in this government? I will be bold to say you cannot find any in it. I take it as the highest encomium on this country, that the acts of the legislature, if unconstitutional, are liable to be opposed by the judiciary.[4]

[Mr. MADISON.]

The honorable member has introduced the subject of religion. Religion is not guarded; there is no bill of rights declaring that religion should be secure. Is a bill of rights a security for religion? Would the bill of rights, in this state, exempt the people from paying for the support of one particular sect, if such sect were exclusively established by law? If there were a majority of one sect, a bill of rights would be a poor protection for liberty. Happily for the states, they enjoy the utmost freedom of religion. This freedom arises from that multiplicity of sects which pervades America, and which is the best and only security for religious liberty in any society; for where there is such a variety of sects, there cannot be a majority of any one sect to oppress and persecute the rest. Fortunately for this commonwealth, a majority of the people are decidedly against any exclusive establishment. I believe it to be so in the other states. There is not a shadow of right in the general government to intermeddle with religion. Its least interference with it would be a most flagrant usurpation. I can appeal to my uniform conduct on this subject, that I have warmly supported religious freedom. It is better that this security should be depended upon from the general legislature, than from one particular state. A particular state might concur in one religious project. But the United States abound in such a variety of sects, that it is a strong security against religious persecution; and it is sufficient to authorize a conclusion, that no one sect will ever be able to outnumber or depress the rest.[5]

1 *Debates*, III, pp. 303-304.
2 See Appendix A, p. 747 for the Virginia Declaration of Rights.
3 *Debates*, III, pp. 314-318.
4 *Ibid.*, p. 324-325.
5 *Ibid.*, p. 330.

Sydney June 13, 1788
Newspaper Article: *New York Journal* (excerpt)

TO THE CITIZENS OF THE STATE OF NEW YORK. . . .

The omission of a bill of rights in this State has given occasion to an inference that the omission was equally warrantable in the constitution for the United States. On this it may be necessary to observe that while the constitution of this State was in agitation, there appeared doubts upon the propriety of the measure, from the peculiar situation in which the country then was; our connection with Britain dissolved, and her government formally renounced—no substitute devised—all the powers of government avowedly temporary, and solely calculated for defence; it was urged by those in favor of a bill of rights that the power of the rulers ought to be circumscribed, the better to protect the people at large from the oppression and usurpation of their rulers. The English petition of rights, in the reign of Charles the First, and the bill of rights in the reign of king William, were mentioned as examples to support their opinions. Those in opposition admitted that in established governments, which had an implied constitution, a declaration of rights might be necessary to prevent the usurpation of ambitious men, but that was not our situation, for upon the declaration of independence it had become necessary that the exercise of every kind of authority "under the former government should be totally suppressed, and all the power of government exerted under the authority of the people of the colonies;" that we could not suppose that we had an existing constitution or form of government, express or implied, and therefore our situation resembled a people in a state of nature, who are preparing "to institute a government, laying its foundation on such principles, and organizing its powers in such form as to them shall seem most likely to effect their safety and happiness," and as such, the constitution to be formed would operate as a bill of rights.

These and the like considerations operated to induce the convention of New York to dismiss the idea of a bill of rights, and the more especially as the legislative state officers being elected by the people at short periods, and thereby rendered from time to time liable to be displaced in case of mal-conduct. But these reasons will not apply to the general government, because it will appear in the sequel that the state governments are considered in it as mere dependencies, existing solely by its toleration, and possessing powers of which they may be deprived whenever the general government is disposed so to do. If then the powers of the state governments are to be totally absorbed, in which all agree, and only differ as to the mode, whether it will be effected by a rapid progression, or by as certain, but slower, operations: what is to limit the oppression of the general government? Where are the rights, which are declared to be incapable of violation? And what security have people against the wanton oppression of unprincipled governors? No constitutional redress is pointed out, and no express declaration is contained in it, to limit the boundaries of their rulers; beside which the mode and period of their being elected tends to take away their responsibility to the people over whom they may, by the power of the purse and the sword, domineer at discretion; nor is there a power on earth to tell them, What dost thou? or, Why dost thou so?

Essays, pp. 299-300. "Sydney" is reprinted in Storing, VI, starting at p. 108.

Cassandra June 14, 1788
Newspaper Article: Philadelphia *Independent Gazetteer* (excerpts)[1]

Mr. Printer,

The cry of adopting the constitution proposed by the late federal convention IN TOTO, seems to have subsided. Even those who of late so very devoutly held it up as the work of divine legation, to which whosoever should add, or from which whosoever should take away, his part should be taken out of the book of life;—even these blind persecuting zealots relent. It seems now to be admitted that amendments are absolutely necessary; and amendments too of the most essential consequence to the liberty of the subject and the security of the individual states. To this principle the states of Massachusetts and South-Carolina have formally borne testimony by the acts of their state conventions; and though the conventions of some of the other states have ratified the plan of government without exception or reserve, yet the sense of the people seems to be sufficiently manifest, that the proposed system of government is calculated more for the benefit of the future rulers than for the good of the people; and that some alterations, either in the form of a bill of rights or otherwise, are indispensably necessary. Few men are found hardy enough to contradict this opinion. . . .

Every part of the continent seems agreed that the powers of Congress should be increased; that the regulation of foreign trade should be in their hands, and that they should be clothed with every power that is not destructive of those liberties which are secured by the constitutions of the separate states.[2] Is there any man who wishes to go farther? If there be, he must have interested motives and sinister views; such as he will hardly venture to explain.

The only question that seems to make any difference amongst us appears to be, Whether we shall adopt those amendments, in which we seem all to be agreed, before we raise up a body of governors and rulers with a separate interest, whose wish and inclination it will be, to leave the people as small a share of liberty as possible; or whether we shall trust to our future rulers to do it hereafter? At present it is in our own power; hereafter it will be at the will and pleasure of our rulers to secure the liberties of the people.

The continent most certainly ought to be united; but we ought as certainly to secure our liberties before the new government is set in motion.

WE SHALL NEVER DO IT AFTERWARDS.

1 DHRC, II Mfm. Pa., p. 2638-2640.
2 For the state bills of rights, see Appendix A, p. 747.

A Freeman June 14, 1788
Newspaper Article: *Providence Gazette*

From the INDEPENDENT GAZETTEER.

The conduct of the majority in the Maryland Convention is a striking display of the nature of power, and a sample of what the freemen of America would experience from the great Congress, if established:—Inebriated with a temporary superiority, they arrogantly refused to discuss the merits of a system of government that was to determine the fate of a great people, that would prove either the instrument of their freedom and prosperity, or of their slavery and misery, for ages to come; but observed a contemptuous silence, notwithstanding some of the greatest and most able men in Maryland, with all the ardour of patriotism, represented the dangers with which the new Constitution was replete, and repeatedly urged the majority to invalidate their objections, if in their power. A greater insult than this was never offered to freemen, and the infatuation of the people must indeed be astonishing, if they are not aroused by it to a sense of the imposition practising upon them. The conduct of the Maryland Convention also shews the folly of trusting to future amendments; for they have already thrown aside the masque, and avowed the intention of establishing the new Constitution in all its plenitude of powers, without any reservation in favour of the liberty of the people. After amusing the minority with hopes that suitable amendments would be recommended by them, they at length, in a despotic manner, dissolved the Convention.

What must be the feelings of the great body of the people in Massachusetts, who were deluded into the adoption of this system of government, by specious assurances that the amendments would be acceded to by all the States, and certainly incorporated in the government—that it argued ignorance of the weight of Massachusetts in the union, to entertain the smallest doubt that her example would not be followed by all the others? I rejoice that the rash confidence of the advocates of the new Constitution, has led them to discover so soon this dangerous, deceptive game of the amendments, by which they had imposed upon so many. The question now is simply, Whether the people will submit to the absolute establishment of a form of government, which all, even the most designing, are obliged to allow is defective? I recommend the perusal of the narrative of facts and propositions of amendments, subscribed by the minority of the Maryland Convention, to every person who wishes to continue free.[1]

1 See "Maryland Minority," May 6, 1788, p. 356, for excerpts from the narrative referred to.

Virginia Convention June 14, 1788
Debates (excerpts)

[The 8th section read.]

Mr. CLAY wished to be informed why the Congress were to have power to provide for calling forth the militia, to put the laws of the Union into execution.

Mr. MADISON supposed the reasons of this power to be so obvious that they would occur to most gentlemen. If resistance should be made to the execution of the laws, he said, it ought to be overcome. This could be done only in two ways—either by regular forces or by the people. By one or the other it must unquestionably be done. If insurrections should arise, or invasions should take place, the people ought unquestionably to be employed, to suppress and repel them, rather than a standing army. The best way to do these things was to put the militia on a good and sure footing, and enable the govenment to make use of their services when necessary.

Mr. GEORGE MASON. Mr. Chairman, unless there be some restrictions on the power of calling forth the militia, to execute the laws of the Union, suppress insurrections, and repel invasions, we may very easily see that it will produce dreadful oppressions. It is extremely unsafe, without some alterations. It would be to use the militia to a very bad purpose, if any disturbance happened in New Hampshire, to call them from Georgia. This would harass the people so much that they would agree to abolish the use of the militia, and establish a standing army. I conceive the general government ought to have power over the militia, but it ought to have some bounds. If gentlemen say that the militia of a neighboring state is not sufficient, the government ought to have power to call forth those of other states, the most convenient and contiguous. But in this case, the consent of the state legislatures ought to be had. On *real* emergencies, this consent will never be denied, each state being concerned in the safety of the rest. This power may be restricted without any danger. I wish such an amendment as this—that the militia of any state should not be marched beyond the limits of the adjoining state; and if it be necessary to draw them from one end of the continent to the other, I wish such a check, as the consent of the state legislature, to be provided. Gentlemen may say that this would impede the government, and that the state legislatures would counteract it by refusing their consent. This argument may be applied to all objections whatsoever. How is this compared to the British constitution? Though the king may declare war, the Parliament has the means of carrying it on. It is not so here. Congress can do both. Were it not for that check in the British government, the monarch would be a despot. When a war is necessary for the benefit of the nation, the means of carrying it on are never denied. If an unjust requisition be made on Parliament, it will be as it ought to be, refused. The same principle ought to be observed in our government. In times of real danger, the states will have the same enthusiasm in aiding the general government, and granting its demands, which is seen in England, when the king is engaged in a war apparently for the interest of the nation. This power is necessary; but we ought to guard against danger. If ever they attempt to harass and abuse the militia, they may abolish them, and raise a standing army in their stead. There are various ways of destroying the militia. A standing army may be perpetually established in their stead. I abominate and detest the idea of a government, where there is a standing army. The militia may be here destroyed by that method which has been practised in other parts of the world before; that is, by rendering them useless—by disarming them. Under various pretences, Congress may neglect to provide for arming and disciplining the militia; and the state governments cannot do it, for Congress has an exclusive right to arm them, &c. Here is a line of division drawn between them—the state and general governments. The power over the militia is divided between them. The national government has an exclusive right to provide for arming, organizing, and disciplining the militia, and for governing such part of them as may be employed in the service of the United States. The state governments have the power of appointing the officers, and of training the militia, according to the discipline prescribed by Congress, if they should think proper to prescribe any. Should the national government wish to render the militia useless, they may neglect them, and let them perish, in order to have a pretence of establishing a standing army.

No man has a greater regard for the military gentlemen than I have. I admire their intrepidity, perseverance, and valor. But when once a standing army is established in any country, the people lose their liberty. When, against a regular and disciplined army, yeomanry are the only defence,—yeomanry, unskilful and unarmed,—what chance is there for preserving freedom? Give me leave to recur to the page of history, to warn you of your present danger. Recollect the history of most nations of the world. What havoc, desolation, and destruction, have been perpetrated by standing armies! An instance within the memory of some of this house will show us how our militia may be destroyed. Forty years ago, when the resolution of enslaving America was formed in Great Britain, the British Parliament was advised by an artful man [Sir William Keith], who was governor of Pennsylvania, to disarm the people; that it was the best and most effectual way to enslave them; but that they should not do it openly, but weaken them, and let them sink gradually, by totally disusing and neglecting the militia. [Here Mr. Mason quoted sundry passages to this effect.] This was a most iniquitous project. Why should we not provide against the danger of having our militia, our real and natural strength, destroyed? The general government ought, at the same time, to have some such power. But we need not give them power to abolish our militia. If they neglect to arm them, and prescribe proper discipline, they will be of no use. I am not acquainted with the military profession. I beg to be excused for any errors I may commit with respect to it. But I stand on the general principles of freedom, whereon I dare to meet any one. I wish that, in case the general government should neglect to arm and discipline the militia, there should be an express declaration that the state governments might arm and discipline them. With this single exception, I would agree to this part, as I am conscious the government ought to have the power.

They may effect the destruction of the militia, by rendering the sevice odious to the people themselves, by harassing them from one end of the continent to the other, and by keeping them under martial law.

The English Parliament never pass a mutiny bill but for one year. This is necessary; for otherwise the soldiers would be on the same footing with the officers, and the army would be dissolved. One mutiny bill has been here in force since the revolution. I humbly conceive there is extreme danger of establishing cruel martial regulations. If, at any time, our rulers should have unjust and iniquitous designs against our liberties, and should wish to establish a standing army, the first attempt would be to render the service and use of militia odious to the people themselves—subjecting them to unnecessary severity of discipline in time of peace, confining them under marial law, and disgusting them so much as to make them cry out, "Give us a standing army!" I would wish to have some check to exclude this danger; as, that the militia should never be subject to martial law but in time of war. I consider and fear the natural propensity of rulers to oppress the people, I wish only to prevent them from doing evil. By these amendments I would give necessary powers, but no unnecessary power. If the clause stands as it is now, it will take from the state legislatures what divine Providence has given to every individual—the means of self-defence. Unless it be moderated in some degree, it will ruin us, and introduce a standing army.

Mr. MADISON. Mr. Chairman, I most cordially agree, with the honorable member last up, that a standing army is one of the greatest mischiefs that can possibly happen. It is a great recommendation for this system, that it provides against this evil more than any other system known to us, and, particularly, more than the old system of confederation. The most effectual way to guard against a standing army, is to render it unnecessary. The most effectual way to render it unnecessary, is to give the general government full power to call forth the militia, and exert the whole natural strength of the Union, when necessary. Thus you will furnish the people with sure and certain protection, without recurring to this evil; and the certainty of this protection from the whole will be a strong inducement to individual exertion. Does the organization of the government warrant a belief that this power will be abused? Can we believe that a government of a federal nature, consisting of many coequal sovereignties, and particularly having one branch chosen from the people, would drag the militia unnecessarily to an immense distance? This, sir, would be unworthy the most arbitrary despot. They have no temptation whatever to abuse this power; such abuse could only answer the purpose of exciting the universal indignation of the people, and drawing on themselves the general hatred and detestation of their country.

I cannot help thinking that the honorable gentleman has not considered, in all its consequences, the amendment he has proposed. Would this be an equal protection, sir, or would it not be a most partial provision? Some states have three or four states in contact. Were this state invaded, as it is bounded by several states, the militia of three or four states would, by this proposition, be obliged to come to our aid; and those from some of the states would come a far greater distance than those of others. There are other states, which, if invaded, could be assisted by the militia of one state only, there being several states which border but on one state. Georgia and New Hampshire would be infinitely less safe than the other states. Were we to adopt this amendment, we should set up those states as butts for invasions, invite foreign enemies to attack them, and expose them to peculiar hardships and dangers. Were the militia confined to any limited distance from their respective places of abode, it would produce equal, nay, more inconveniences. The principles of equality and reciprocal aid would be destroyed in either case.

I cannot conceive that this Constitution, by giving the general government the power of arming the militia, takes it away from the state governments. The power is concurrent, and not exclusive. Have we not found, from experience, that, while the power of arming and governing the militia has been solely vested in the state legislatures, they were neglected and rendered unfit for immediate sevice? Every state neglected too much this most essential object. But the general government can do it more effectually. Have we not also found that the militia of one state were almost always insufficient to succor its harassed neighbor? Did all the states furnish their quotas of militia with sufficient promptitude? The assistance of one state will be of little avail to repel invasion. But the general head of the whole Union can do it with effect, if it be vested with power to use the aggregate strength of the Union. If the regulation of the militia were to be committed to the executive authority alone, there might be reason for providing restrictions. But, sir, it is the legislative authority that has this power. They must make a law for the purpose.

The honorable member is under another mistake. He wishes martial law to be exercised only in time of war, under an idea that Congress can establish it in time of peace. The states are to have the authority of training the militia according to the congressional discipline; and of governing them at all times when not in the service of the Union. Congress is to govern such part of them as may be employed in the actual sevice of the United States; and such part only can be subject to martial law. The gentlemen in opposition have drawn a most tremendous picture of the Constitution in this respect. Without considering that the power was absolutely indispensable, they have alarmed us with the possible abuse of it, but have shown no inducement or motive to tempt them to such abuse. Would the legislature of the state drag the militia of the eastern shore to the western frontiers, or those of the western frontiers to the eastern shore, if the local militia were sufficient to effect the intended purpose? There is something so preposterous, and so full of mischief, in the idea of dragging the militia unnecessarily from one end of the continent to the other, that I think there can be no ground of apprehension. If you limit their power over the militia, you give them a pretext for substituting a standing army. If you put it in the power of the state governments to refuse the militia, by requiring their consent, you destroy the general government, and sacrifice the particular states. The same principles and motives which produce disobedience to requisitions, will produce refusal in this case.

The restrictions which the honorable gentleman mentioned to be in the British constitution are all provisions against the power of the executive magistrate; but the House of Commons may, if they be so disposed, sacrifice the interest of their constituents in all those cases. They may prolong the duration of mutiny bills, and grant supplies to the king to carry on an impolitic war. But they have no motives to do so; for they have strong motives to do their duty. We have more ample security than the people of Great Britain. The powers of the government are more limited and guarded, and our representatives are more responsible than the members of the British House of Commons.

Mr. CLAY apprehended that, by this power, our militia might be sent to the Mississippi. He observed that the sheriff might raise the *posse comitatus* to execute the laws. He feared it would lead to the establishment of a military government, as the militia were to be called forth to put the laws into execution. He asked why this mode was preferred to the old, established custom of executing the laws.

Mr. MADISON answered, that the power existed in all countries; that the militia might be called forth, for that purpose, under the laws of this state and every other state in the Union; that public force must be used when resistance to the laws required it, otherwise society itself must be destroyed; that the mode referred to by the gentleman might not be sufficient on every occasion, as the sheriff must be necessarily restricted to the *posse* of his own county. If the *posse* of one county were insufficient to overcome the resistance to the execution of the laws, this power must be resorted to. He did not, by any means, admit that the old mode was superseded by the introduction of the new one. And it was obvious to him, that, when the civil power was sufficient, this mode would never be put in practice.

Mr. HENRY. Mr. Chairman, in my judgment the friends of the opposition have to act cautiously, We must make a firm stand before we decide. I was heard to say, a few days ago, that the sword and purse were the two great instruments of government; and I professed great repugnance at parting with the purse, without any control, to the proposed system of government. And now, when we proceed in this formidable compact, and come to the national defence, the sword, I am persuaded we ought to be still more cautious and circumspect; for I feel still more reluctance to surrender this most valuable of rights.

The honorable member [Madison] who has risen to explain several parts of the system was pleased to say, that the best way of avoiding the danger of a standing army, was, to have the militia in such a way as to render it unnecessary; and that, as the new government would have power over the militia, we should have no standing army—it being unnecessary. This argument destroys itself. It demands a power, and denies the probability of its exercise. There are suspicions of power on one hand, and absolute and unlimited confidence on the other. I hope to be one of those who have a large share of suspicion. I leave it to this house, if there be not too small a portion on the other side, by giving up too much to that government. You can easily see which is the worst of two extremes. Too much suspicion may be corrected. If you give too little power to-day, you may give more to-morrow. But the reverse of the proposition will not hold. If you give too much power to-day, you cannot retake it to-morrow: for to-morrow will never come for that purpose. If you have the fate of other nations, you will never see it. It is easier to supply deficiencies of power than to take back excess of power. This no man can deny.

But, says the honorable member, Congress will keep the militia armed; or, in other words, they will do their duty. Pardon me if I am too jealous and suspicious to confide in this remote possibility. My honorable friend went on a supposition that the American rulers, like all others, will depart from their duty without bars and checks. No government can be safe without checks. Then he told us they had no temptation to violate their duty, and that it would be their interest to perform it. Does he think you are to trust men who cannot have separate interests from the people? It is a novelty in the political world (as great a novelty as the system itself) to find rulers without private interests, and views of personal emoluments, and ambition. His supposition, that they will not depart from their duty, as having no interest to do so, is no satisfactory answer to my mind. This is no check. The government may be most intolerable and destructive, if this be our only security.

My honorable friend attacked the honorable gentleman with universal principles—that, in all nations and ages, rulers have been actuated by motives of individual interest and private emoluments, and that in America it would be so also. I hope, before we part with this great bulwark, this noble palladium of safety, we shall have such checks interposed as will render us secure. The militia, sir, is our ultimate safety. We can have no security without it. But then, he says that the power of arming and organizing the militia is concurrent, and to be equally exercised by the general and state governments. I am sure, and I trust in the candor of that gentleman, that he will recede from that opinion, when his recollection will be called to the particular clause which relates to it.

As my worthy friend said, there is a positive partition of power between the two governments. To Congress is given the power of "arming, organizing, and disciplining the militia, and governing such part of them as may be employed in the service of the United States." To the state legislatures is given the power of "appointing the officers, and training the militia according to the discipline prescribed by Congress." I observed before, that, if the power be concurrent as to arming them, it is concurrent in other respects. If the states have the right of arming them, &c., concurrently, Congress has a concurrent power of appointing the officers, and training the militia. If Congress have that power, it is absurd. To admit this mutual concurrence of powers will carry you into endless absurdity—that Congress has nothing exclusive on the one hand, nor the states on the other. The rational explanation is, that Congress shall have exclusive power of arming them, &c., and that the state governments shall have exclusive power of appointing the officers, &c. Let me put it in another light.

May we not discipline and arm them, as well as Congress, if the power be concurrent? so that our militia shall have two sets of arms, double sets of regimentals, &c.; and thus, at a very great cost, we shall be doubly armed. The great object is, that every man be armed. But can the people afford to pay for double sets of arms, &c.? Every one who is able may have a gun. But we have learned, by experience, that, necessary as it is to have arms, and though our Assembly has, by a succession of laws for many years, endeavored to have the militia completely armed, it is still far from being the case. When this power is given up to Congress without limitation or bounds, how will your militia be armed? You trust to chance; for sure I am that that nation which shall trust its liberties in other hands cannot long exist. If gentlemen are serious when they suppose a concurrent power, where can be the impolicy to amend it? Or, in other words, to say that Congress shall not arm or discipline them, till the states shall have refused or neglected to do it? This is my object. I only wish to bring it to what they themselves say is implied. Implication is to be the foundation of our civil liberties; and when you speak of arming the militia by a concurrence of power, you use implication. But implication will not save you, when a strong army of veterans comes upon you. You would be laughed at by the whole world for trusting your safety implicitly to implication.

The argument of my honorable friend was, that rulers might tyrannize. The answer he received was, that they will not. In saying that they would not, he admitted they might. In this great, this essential part of the Constitution, if you are safe, it is not from the Constitution, but from the virtues of the men in government. If gentlemen are willing to trust themselves and posterity to so slender and improbable a chance, they have greater strength of nerves than I have.

The honorable gentleman, in endeavoring to answer the question why the militia were to be called forth to execute the laws, said that the civil power would probably do it. He is driven to say, that the civil power may do it instead of the militia. Sir, the military power ought not to interpose till the civil power refuse. If this be the spirit of your new Constitution, that the laws are to be enforced by military coercion, we may easily divine the happy consequences which will result from it. The civil power is not to be employed at all. If it be, show me it. I read it attentively, and could see nothing to warrant a belief that the civil power can be called for. I should be glad to see the power that authorizes Congress to do so. The sheriff will be aided by military force. The most wanton excesses may be committed under color of this; for every man in office, in the states, is to take an oath to support it in all its operations. The honorable gentleman said, in answer to the objection that the militia might be marched from New Hampshire to Georgia, that the members of the government would not attempt to excite the indignation of the people. Here, again, we have the general unsatisfactory answer, that they will be virtuous, and that there is no danger.

Will gentlemen be satisfied with an answer which admits of dangers and abuses if they be wicked? Let us put it out of their power to do mischief. I am convinced there is no safety in the paper on the table as it stands now. . . .

But it is said that our Congress are more responsible than the British Parliament. It appears to me that there is no real, but there may be some specious responsibility. If Congress, in the execution of their unbounded powers, shall have done wrong, how will you come at them to punish them, if they are at the distance of five hundred miles? At such a great distance, they will evade responsibility altogether. If you have given up your militia, and Congress shall refuse to arm them, you have lost every thing. Your existence will be precarious, because you depend on others, whose interests are not affected by your infelicity. If Congress are to arm us exclusively, the man of New Hampshire may vote for or against it, as well as the Virginian. The great distance and difference between the two places render it impossible that the people of that country can know or pursue what will promote our convenience. I therefore contend that, if Congress do not arm the militia, we ought to provide for it ourselves.

Mr. NICHOLAS. Mr. Chairman, the great object of government, in every country, is security and public defence. I suppose, therefore, that what we ought to attend to here, is, what is the best mode of enabling the general government to protect us. One of three ways must be pursued for this purpose. We must either empower them to employ, and rely altogether on, a standing army; or depend altogether on militia; or else we must enable them to use the one or the other of these two ways, as may be found most expedient. The least reflection will satisfy us that the Convention has adopted the only proper method. If a standing army were alone to be employed, such an army must be kept up in time of peace as would be sufficient in war. The dangers of such an army are so striking that every man would oppose the adoption of this government, had it been proposed by it as the only mode of defence. Would it be safe to depend on militia alone, without the agency of regular forces, even in time of war? Were we to be invaded by a powerful, disciplined army, would we be safe with militia? Could men unacquainted with the hardships, and unskilled in the discipline of war,—men only inured to the peaceable occupations of domestic life,—encounter with success the most skilful veterans, inured to the fatigues and toils of campaigns? Although some people are pleased with the theory of reliance on militia, as the sole defence of a nation, yet I think it will be found, in practice, to be by no means adequate. Its inadequacy is proved by the experience of other nations. But were it fully adequate, it would be unequal. If war be supported by militia, it is by personal service. The poor man does as much as the rich. Is this just? What is the consequence when war is carried on by regular troops? They are paid by taxes raised from the people, according to their property; and then the rich man pays an adequate share.

But, if you confine yourselves to militia alone, the poor man is oppressed. The rich man exempts himself by furnishing a substitute. And, although it be oppressive to the poor, it is not advantageous to the rich? For what he gives would pay regular troops. It is therefore neither safe nor just to depend entirely on militia. As these two ways are ineligible, let us consider the third method. Does this Constitution put this on a proper footing? It enables Congress to raise an army when necessary, or to call forth the militia when necessary. What will be the consequence of their having these two powers? Till there be a necessity for an army to be raised, militia will do. And when an army will be raised, the militia will still be employed, which will render a less numerous army sufficient. By these means, there will be a sufficient defence for the country, without having a standing army altogether, or oppressing the people. The worthy member has said, that it ought to be a part of the Constitution that the militia ought not to go out of the state without the consent of the state legislature. What would be the consequence of this? The general defence is trusted to the general government. How is it to protect the Union? It must apply to the state governments before it can do it. Is this right? Is it not subjecting the general will to the particular will, and exposing the general defence to the particular caprice of the members of the state governments? This would entirely defeat the power given to Congress to provide for the general defence; and unless the militia were to aid in the execution of the laws when resisted, the other powers of Congress would be nugatory. But he has said that this idea is justified by the English history; for that the king has the power of the sword, but must apply to the commons for the means of using it—for the purse. This is not a similar case. The king and commons are parts of the same government. But the general government is separate and perfectly distinct from the individual governments of the states. Should Congress be obliged to apply to the particular states for the militia, they may be refused, and the government overturned. To make the case similar, he ought to show us that the king and Parliament were obliged to call on some other power to raise forces, and provide for the means of carrying on war; for, otherwise, there is no similitude.

If the general government be obliged to apply to the states, a part will be thereby rendered superior to the whole. What are to be the effects of the amendments proposed? To destroy one of the most beneficial parts of the Constitution, put an obstacle in the way of the general government, and put it in the power of the state governments to take away the aid of the militia. Who will be most likely to want the aid of the militia? The Southern States, from their situation. Who are the most likely to be called for? The Eastern States, from their strength, &c. Should we put it in the power of particular states to refuse the militia, it ought to operate against ourselves. It is the height of bad policy to alter this part of the system. But it is said, the militia are to be disarmed. Will they be worse armed than they are now? Still, as my honorable friend said, the states would have power to arm them. The power of arming them is concurrent between the general and state governments; for the power of arming them rested in the state governments before; and although the power be given to the general government, yet it is not given exclusively; for, in every instance where the Constitution intends that the general government shall exercise any power exclusively of the state governments, words of exclusion are particularly inserted. Consequently, in every case where such words of exclusion are not inserted, the power is concurrent to the state governments and Congress, unless where it is impossible that the power should be exercised by both. It is, therefore, not an absurdity to say, that Virginia may arm the militia, should Congress neglect to arm them. But it would be absurd to say that we should arm them after Congress had armed them, when it would be unnecessary; or that Congress could appoint the officers, and train the militia, when it is expressly excepted from their powers.

But his great uneasiness is, that the militia may be under martial law when not on duty. A little attention will be sufficient to remove this apprehension. The Congress is to have power "to provide for the arming, organizing, and disciplining the militia, and for governing such part of them as may be employed in the service of the United States." Another part tells you that they are to provide for calling them forth, to execute the laws of the Union, suppress insurrections, and repel invasions. These powers only amount to this—that they can only call them forth in these three cases, and that they can only govern such part of them as may be in the actual service of the United States. This causes a sufficient security that they will not be under martial law but when in actual service. If, sir, a mutiny bill has continued since the revolution, recollect that this is done under the present happy government. Under the new government, no appropriation of money, to the use of raising or supporting an army, shall be for a longer term than two years. The President is to command. But the regulation of the army and navy is given to Congress. Our representatives will be a powerful check here. The influence of the commons, in England, in this case, is very predominant. But the worthy member on the other side of the house has said that the militia are the great bulwark of the nation, and wishes to take no step to bring them into disuse. What is the inference? He wishes to see the militia employed. The Constitution provides what he wants. This is, to bring them frequently into use. If he expects that, by depriving the general government of the power of calling them into more frequent use, they will be rendered more useful and expert, he is greatly deceived. We ought to part with the power to use the militia to somebody. To whom? Ought we not to part with it for the general defence? If you give it not to Congress, it may be denied by the states. If you withhold it, you render a standing army absolutely necessary; for if they have not the militia, they must have such a body of troops as will be necessary for the general defence of the Union.

It was said, by the gentleman, that there was something singular in this government, in saying that the militia shall be called forth to execute the laws of the Union. There is a great difference between having the power in three cases, and in all cases. They cannot call them forth for any other purpose than to execute the laws, suppress insurrections, and repel invasions. And can any thing be more demonstrably obvious, than that the laws ought to be enforced if resisted, and insurrections quelled, and foreign invasions repelled? But it is asked, Why has not the Constitution declared that the civil power shall be employed to execute the laws? Has it said that the civil power shall not be employed? The civil officer is to execute the laws on all occasions; and, if he be resisted, this auxiliary power is given to Congress of calling forth the militia to execute them, when it shall be found absolutely necessary.

From his argument on this occasion, and his eulogium on the executive magistrate of Britain, it might be inferred that the executive magistrate here was to have the power of calling forth the militia. What is the idea of those gentlemen who heard his argument on this occasion? Is it not that the President is to have this power—that President, who, he tells us, is not to have those high feelings, and that fine sensibility, which the British monarch possesses? No, sir, the President is not to have this power. God forbid we should ever see a public man in this country who should have this power. Congress only are to have the power of calling forth the militia. And will the worthy member say that he would trust this power to a prince, governed by the dictates of ambition, or mere motives of personal interest, sooner than he would trust it in the hands of Congress? I will trust Congress, because they will be actuated by motives of fellow-feeling. They can make no regulations but what will affect themselves, their friends, and relations. But I would not trust a prince, whose ambition and private views would be the guide of his actions. When the government is carried on by representatives, and persons of my own choice, whom I can follow when far removed, who can be displaced at stated and short periods,—I can safely confide the power to them. It appears to me that this power is essentially necessary; for, as the general defence is trusted to Congress, we ought to intrust fully the means. This cannot be fully done without giving the power of calling forth the militia; and this power is sufficiently guarded.

Mr. MADISON. Mr. Chairman, the honorable gentleman has laid much stress on the maxim, that the purse and sword ought not to be put in the same hands, with a view of pointing out the impropriety of vesting this power in the general government. But it is totally inapplicable to this question. What is the meaning of this maxim? Does it mean that the sword and purse ought not to be trusted in the hands of the same government? This cannot be the meaning; for there never was, and I can say there never will be, an efficient government, in which both are not vested. The only rational meaning is, that the sword and purse are not to be given to the same member. Apply it to the British government, which has been mentioned. The sword is in the hands of the British king; the purse in the hands of the Parliament. It is so in America, as far as any analogy can exist. Would the honorable member say that the sword ought to be put in the hands of the representatives of the people, or in other hands independent of the government altogether? If he says so, it will violate the meaning of that maxim. This would be a novelty hitherto unprecedented. The purse is in the hands of the representatives of the people. They have the appropriation of all moneys. They have the direction and regulation of land and naval forces. They are to provide for calling forth the militia; and the President is to have the command, and, in conjunction with the Senate, to appoint the officers. The means ought to be commensurate to the end. The end is general protection. This cannot be effected without a general power to use the strength of the Union.

We are told that both sides are distinguished by these great traits, confidence and distrust. Perhaps there may be a less or greater tincture of suspicion on one side than the other. But give me leave to say that, where power can be safely lodged, if it be necessary, reason commands its cession. In such case, it is imprudent and unsafe to withhold it. It is universally admitted that it must be lodged in some hands or other. The question, then, is, in what part of the government it ought to be placed; and not whether any other political body, independent of the government, should have it or not. I profess myself to have had a uniform zeal for a republican government. If the honorable member, or any other person, conceives that my attachment to this system arises from a different source, he is greatly mistaken. From the first moment that my mind was capable of contemplating political subjects, I never, till this moment, ceased wishing success to a well-regulated republican government. The establishment of such in America was my most ardent desire.[1]

[Mr. HENRY.]

The means, says the gentleman, must be commensurate to the end. How does this apply? All things in common are left with this government. There being an infinitude in the government, there must be an infinitude of means to carry it on. This is a sort of mathematical government that may appear well on paper, but cannot sustain examination, or be safely reduced to practice. The delegation of power to an adequate number of representatives, and an unimpeded reversion of it back to the people, at short periods, form the principal traits of a republican government. The idea of a republican government, in that paper, is something superior to the poor people. The governing persons are the servants of the people. There, the servants are greater than their masters; because it includes infinitude, and infinitude excludes every idea of subordination. In this the creature has destroyed and soared above the creator. For if its powers be infinite, what rights have the people remaining? By that very argument, despotism has made way in all countries where the people unfortunately have been enslaved by it. We are told, the sword and purse are necessary for the national defence. The junction of these, without limitation, in the same hands, is, by logical and mathematical conclusions, the description of despotism.

The reasons adduced here to-day have long ago been advanced in favor of passive obedience and non-resistance. In 1688, the British nation expelled their monarch for attempting to trample on their liberties. The doctrine of divine right and passive obedience was said to be commanded by Heaven—it was inculcated by his minions and adherents. He wanted to possess, without control, the sword and purse. The attempt cost him his crown. This government demands the same powers. I see reason to be more and more alarmed. I fear it will terminate in despotism. As to his objection of the abuse of liberty, it is denied. The political inquiries and promotions of the peasants are a happy circumstance. A foundation of knowledge is a great mark of happiness. When the spirit of inquiry after political discernment goes forth among the lowest of the people, it rejoices my heart. Why such fearful apprehensions? I defy him to show that liberty has been abused. There has been no rebellion here, though there was in Massachusetts. Tell me of any country which has been so long without a rebellion. Distresses have been patiently borne, in this country, which would have produced revolutions in other countries. We strained every nerve to make provisions to pay off our soldiers and officers. They, though not paid, and greatly distressed at the conclusion of the war, magnanimously acquiesced. The depreciation of the circulating currency very much involved many of them, and thousands of other citizens, in absolute ruin; but the same patient fortitude and forbearance marked their conduct. What would the people of England have done in such a situation? They would have resisted the government, and murdered the tryant. But in this country, no abuse of power has taken place. It is only a general assertion, unsupported, which suggests the contrary. Individual licentiousness will show its baneful consequences in every country, let its government be what it may.

Gov. RANDOLPH. Mr. Chairman, our attention is summoned to this clause respecting the militia, and alarms are thrown out to persuade us that it involves a multiplicity of danger. It is supposed by the honorable gentleman lately up, and another gentleman, that the clause for calling forth the militia to suppress insurrections, repel invasions, and execute the laws of the Union, implies that, instead of using civil force in the first instance, the militia are to be called forth to arrest petty offenders against the laws. Ought not common sense to be the rule of interpreting this Constitution? Is there an exclusion of the civil power? Does it provide that the laws are to be enforced by military coercion in all cases? No, sir. All that we are to infer is, that when the civil power is not sufficient, the militia must be drawn out. Who are they? He says (and I cheerfully acquiesce in the rectitude of the assertion) that they are the bulwarks of our liberties. Shall we be afraid that the people, this bulwark of freedom, will turn instruments of slavery? The officers are to be appointed by the states. Will you admit that they will act so criminally as to turn against their country? The officers of the general government are attached to it, because they derive their appointment from it. Admitting the militia officers to be corrupt, what is to make them be in favor of the general government? Will not the same reason attach them to the state governments? But it is feared that the militia are to be subjected to martial law when not in service. They are only to be called out in three cases, and only to be governed by the authority of Congress when in the actual service of the United States; so that their articles of war can no longer operate upon them than when in the actual service of the Union.

Can it be presumed that you can vest the supreme power of the United States with the power of defence, and yet take away this natural defence from them? You risk the general defence by withholding this power. . . .

With respect to a standing army, I believe there was not a member in the federal Convention, who did not feel indignation at such an institution. What remedy, then, could be provided? Leave the country defenceless? In order to provide for our defence, and exclude the dangers of a standing army, the general defence is left to those who are the objects of defence. It is left to the militia, who will suffer if they become the instruments of tyranny. The general government must have power to call them forth when the general defence requires it. In order to produce greater security, the state governments are to appoint the officers. The President, who commands them when in actual service of the Union, is appointed secondarily by the people. This is a further security. Is it not incredible that men who are interested in the happiness of their country—whose friends, relations, and connections, must be involved in the fate of their country—should turn against their country? I appeal to every man whether, if any of our own officers were called upon to destroy the liberty of their country, he believes they would assent to such an act of suicide. The state governments, having the power of appointing them, may elect men who are the most remarkable for their virtue of attachment to their country.

Mr. GEORGE MASON, after having read the clause which gives Congress power to provide for arming, organizing, and disciplining the militia, and governing those in actual service of the Union, declared it as his firm belief, that it included the power of annexing punishments, and establishing necessary discipline, more especially as the construction of this, and every other part of the Constitution was left to those who were to govern. If so, he asked if Congress would not inflict ignominious punishments on the most worthy citizens of the community. Would freemen submit to such indignant treatment? It might be thought a strained contruction, but it was no more than congress might put upon it. He thought such severities might be exercised on the militia as would make them wish the use of the militia to be utterly abolished, and assent to the establishment of a standing army. . . .

Mr. LEE, (of Westmoreland.) . . . We say that it will secure our liberty and happiness, and that it is so contructed and organized, that we need apprehend no danger. . . .

But gentlemen say that we must apply to the militia to execute the constitutional laws, without the interposition of the civil power, and that a military officer is to be substituted for the sheriff in all cases. This unwarrantable objection is urged, like many others, to produce the rejection of this government, though contrary to reason. What is the meaning of the clause under debate? Does not their explanation violate the natural meaning of language? Is it to be inferred that, when the laws are not opposed, judgments must be executed by the militia? Is this the right and liberal way of discussing the general national objects? I am astonished that gentlemen should attempt to impose so absurd a construction upon us. . . .

Mr. CLAY. . . . He was not, however, convinced that the civil power would be employed. If it was meant that the militia should not be called out to execute the laws in all cases, why were they not satisfied with the words, "repel invasions, suppress insurrections"? He thought the word *insurrection* included every opposition to the laws; and if so, it would be sufficient to call them forth to suppress insurrections, without mentioning that they were to execute the laws of the Union. He added that, although the militia officers were appointed by the state governments, yet, as they were sworn to obey the superior power of Congress, no check or security would result from their nomination of them.

Mr. MADISON. Mr. Chairman, I cannot think that the explanation of the gentleman last up is founded in reason. It does not say that the militia shall be called out in all cases, but in certain cases. There are cases in which the execution of the laws may require the operation of militia, which cannot be said to be an invasion or insurrection. There may be a resistance to the laws which cannot be termed an insurrection. . . .

Mr. CLAY wished to know the instances where an opposition to the laws did not come within the idea of an insurrection.

Mr. MADISON replied, that a riot did not come within the legal definition of an insurrection. There might be riots, to oppose the execution of the laws, which the civil power might not be sufficient to quell. This was one case, and there might probably be other cases. He referred to the candor of the committee, whether the militia could ever be used to destroy themselves.[2]

1 *Debates*, III, pp. 378-394.
2 *Ibid.*, pp. 396-397, 400-402, 406-408, 410.

Virginia Convention June 16, 1788
Debates (excerpts)

[The 8th section still under consideration.]

Mr. HENRY thought it necessary and proper that they should take a collective view of this whole section, and revert again to the first clause. He adverted to the clause which gives Congress the power of raising armies, and proceeded as follows: To me this appears a very alarming power, when unlimited. They are not only to raise, but to support, armies; and this support is to go to the utmost abilities of the United States. If Congress shall say that the general welfare requires it, they may keep armies continually on foot. There is no control on Congress in raising or stationing them. They may billet them on the people at pleasure. This unlimited authority is a most dangerous power: its principles are despotic. If it be unbounded, it must lead to despotism; for the power of a people in a free government is supposed to be paramount to the existing power.

We shall be told that, in England, the king, lords, and commons, have this power; that armies can be raised by the prince alone, without the consent of the people. How does this apply here? Is this government to place us in the situation of the English? Should we suppose this government to resemble king, lords, and commons, we of this state should be like an English county. An English county cannot control the government. Virginia cannot control the government of Congress any more than the county of Kent can control that of England. Advert to the power thoroughly. One of our first complaints, under the former government, was the quartering of troops upon us. This was one of the principal reasons for dissolving the connection with Great Britain. Here we may have troops in time of peace. They may be billeted in any manner—to tyrannize, oppress, and crush us.

We are told, we are afraid to trust ourselves; that our own representatives—Congress—will not exercise their powers oppressively; that we shall not enslave ourselves; that the militia cannot enslave themselves, &c. Who has enslaved France, Spain, Germany, Turkey, and other countries which groan under tyranny? They have been enslaved by the hands of their own people. If it will be so in America, it will be only as it has been every where else. I am still persuaded that the power of calling forth the militia, to execute the laws of the Union, &c., is dangerous. We requested the gentleman to show the cases where the militia would be wanting to execute the laws. Have we received a satisfactory answer? When we consider this part, and compare it to other parts, which declare that Congress may declare war, and that the President shall command the regular troops, militia, and navy, we shall find great danger. Under the order of Congress, they shall suppress insurrections. Under the order of Congress, they shall be called to execute the laws. It will result, of course, that this is to be a government of force. Look at the part which speaks of excises, and you will recollect that those who are to collect excises and duties are to be aided by military force. They have power to call them out, and to provide for arming, organizing, disciplining, them. Consequently, they are to make militia laws for this state.

The honorable gentleman said that the militia should be called forth to quell riots. Have we not seen this business go on very well to-day without military force? It is a long-established principle of the common law of England, that civil force is sufficient to quell riots. To what length may it not be carried? A law may be made that, if twelve men assemble, if they do not disperse, they may be fired upon. I think it is so in England. Does not this part of the paper bear a strong aspect? The honorable gentleman, from his knowledge, was called upon to show the instances, and he told us the militia may be called out to quell riots. They may make the militia travel, and act under a colonel, or perhaps under a constable. Who are to determine whether it be a riot or not? Those who are to execute the laws of the Union? If they have power to execute their laws in this manner, in what situation are we placed! Your men who go to Congress are not restrained by a bill of rights. They are not restrained from inflicting unusual and severe punishments, though the bill of rights of Virginia forbids it. What will be the consequence? They may inflict the most cruel and ingnominious punishments on the militia, and they will tell you that it is necessary for their discipline.

Give me leave to ask another thing. Suppose an exciseman will demand leave to enter your cellar, or house, by virtue of his office; perhaps he may call on the militia to enable him to go. If Congress be informed of it, will they give you redress? They will tell you that he is executing the laws under the authority of the continent at large, which must be obeyed, for that the government cannot be carried on without exercising severity. If, without any reservation of rights or control, you are contented to give up your rights, I am not. There is no principle to guide the legislature to restrain them from inflicting the utmost severity of punishment. Will gentlemen voluntarily give up their liberty? With respect to calling the militia to enforce every execution indiscriminately, it is unprecendented. Have we ever seen it done in any free country? Was it ever so in the mother country? It never was so in any well-regulated country. It is a government of force, and the genius of despotism expressly. It is not proved that this power is necessary, and if it be unnecessary, shall we give it up?

Mr. MADISON. Mr. Chairman, I will endeavor to follow the rule of the house, but must pay due attention to the observations which fell from the gentleman. I should conclude, from abstracted reasoning, that they were ill founded. I should think that, if there were any object which the general government ought to command, it would be the direction of the national forces. And as the force which lies in militia is most safe, the direction of that part ought to be submitted to, in order to render another force unnecessary. The power objected to is necessary, because it is to be employed for national purposes. It is necessary to be given to every government. This is not opinion, but fact. The highest authority may be given, that the want of such authority in the government protracted the late war, and prolonged its calamities.

He says that one ground of complaint, at the beginning of the revolution, was, that a standing army was quartered upon us. This was not the whole complaint. We complained because it was done without the local authority of this country—without the consent of the people of America. As to the exclusion of standing armies in the bill of rights of the states, we shall find that though, in one or two of them, there is something like a prohibition, yet, in most of them, it is only provided that no armies shall be kept without the legislative authority; that is, without the consent of the community itself. Where is the impropriety of saying that we shall have an army, if necessary? Does not the notoriety of this constitute security? If inimical nations were to fall upon us when defenceless, what would be the consequence? Would it be wise to say, that we should have no defence? Give me leave to say, that the only possible way to provide against standing armies is to make them unnecessary.

The way to do this is to organize and discipline our militia, so as to render them capable of defending the country against external invasions and internal insurrections. But it is urged that abuses may happen. How is it possible to answer objections against the possibility of abuses? It must strike every logical reasoner, that these cannot be entirely provided against. I really thought that the objection in the militia was at an end. Was there ever a constitution, in which if authority was vested, it must not have been executed by force, if resisted? Was it not in the contemplation of this state, when contemptuous proceedings were expected, to recur to something of this kind? How is it possible to have a more proper resource than this? That the laws of every country ought to be executed, cannot be denied. That force must be used if necessary, cannot be denied. Can any government be established, that will answer any purpose whatever, unless force be provided for executing its laws? The Constitution does not say that a standing army shall be called out to execute the laws. Is not this a more proper way? The militia ought to be called forth to suppress smugglers. Will this be denied? The case actually happened at Alexandria. There were a number of smugglers, who were too formidable for the civil power to overcome. The military quelled the sailors, who otherwise would have perpetrated their intentions. Should a number of smugglers have a number of ships, the militia ought to be called forth to quell them. We do not know but what there may be a combination of smugglers in Virginia hereafter. We all know the use made of the Isle of Man. It was a general depository of contraband goods. The Parliament found the evil so great, as to render it necessary to wrest it out of the hands of its possessor.

The honorable gentleman says that it is a government of force. If he means military force, the clause under consideration proves the contrary. There never was a government without force. What is the meaning of government? An institution to make people do their duty. A government leaving it to a man to do his duty or not, as he pleases, would be a new species of government, or rather no government at all. The ingenuity of the gentleman is remarkable in introducing the riot act of Great Britain. That act has no connection, or analogy, to any regulation of the militia; nor is there any thing in the Constitution to warrant the general government to make such an act. It never was a complaint, in Great Britain, that the militia could be called forth. If riots should happen, the militia are proper to quell it, to prevent a resort to another mode. As to the infliction of ignominious punishments, we have no ground of alarm, if we consider the circumstances of the people at large. There will be no punishments so ignominious as have been inflicted already. The militia law of every state to the north of Maryland is less rigorous than the particular law of this state. If a change be necessary to be made by the general government, it will be in our favor. I think that the people of those states would not agree to be subjected to a more harsh punishment than their own militia laws inflict. An observation fell from a gentleman, on the same side with myself, which deserves to be attended to. If we be dissatisfied with the national government, if we should choose to renounce it, this is an additional safeguard to our defence. I conceive that we are peculiarly interested in giving the general government as extensive means as possible to protect us. If there be a particular discrimination between places in America, the Southern States are, from their situation and circumstances, most interested in giving the national government the power of protecting its members.

[Here Mr. Madison made some other observations, but spoke so very low, that his meaning could not be comprehended.]

An act passed, a few years ago, in this state, to enable the government to call forth the militia to enforce the laws when a powerful combination should take place to oppose them. This is the same power which the Constitution is to have. There is a great deal of difference between calling forth the militia, when a combination is formed to prevent the execution of the laws, and the sheriff or constable carrying with him a body of militia to execute them in the first instance; which is a construction not warranted by the clause. There is an act, also, in this state, empowering the officers of the customs to summon any persons to assist them when they meet with obstruction in executing their duty. This shows the necessity of giving the government power to call forth the militia when the laws are resisted. It is a power vested in every legislature in the Union, and which is necessary to every government. He then moved that the clerk should read those acts—which were accordingly read.

Mr. GEORGE MASON asked to what purpose the laws were read. The objection was, that too much power was given to Congress—power that would finally destroy the state governments more effectually by insidious, underhanded means, than such as could be openly practised. This, said he, is the opinion of many worthy men, not only in this Convention, but in all parts of America. These laws could only show that the legislature of this state could pass such acts. He thought they militated against the cession of this power to Congress, because the state governments could call forth the militia when necessary, so as to compel a submission to the laws; and as they were competent to it, Congress ought not to have the power. The meeting of three or four persons might be called an insurrection, and the militia might be called out to disperse them. He was not satisfied with the explanation of the word *organization* by the gentleman in the military line, (Mr. Lee.)

He thought they were not confined to the technical explanation, but that Congress could inflict severe and ignominious punishments on the militia, as a necessary incident to the power of organizing and disciplining them. The gentleman had said there was no danger, because the laws respecting the militia were less rigid in the other states than this. This was no conclusive argument. His fears, as he had before expressed, were, that grievous punishments would be inflicted, in order to render the service disagreeable to the militia themselves, and induce them to wish its abolition, which would afford a pretence for establishing a standing army. He was convinced the state governments ought to have the control of the militia, except when they were absolutely necessary for general purposes. The gentleman had said that they would be only subject to martial law when in actual service. He demanded what was to hinder Congress from inflicting it always, and making a general law for the purpose. If so, said he, it must finally produce, most infallibly, the annihilation of the state governments. These were his apprehensions; but he prayed God they might be groundless.

Mr. MADISON replied, that the obvious explanation was, that the states were to appoint the officers, and *govern all* the militia except that part which was called into the actual service of the United States. He asked, if power were given to the general government, if we must not give it executive power to use it. The vice of the old system was, that Congress could not execute the powers nominally vested in them. If the contested clause were expunged, this system would have nearly the same defect.

Mr. HENRY wished to know what authority the state governments had over the militia.

Mr. MADISON answered, that the state governments might do what they thought proper with the militia, when they were not in the actual service of the United States. They might make use of them to suppress insurrections, quell riots, &c., and call on the general government for the militia of any other state, to aid them, if necessary.

Mr. HENRY replied that, as the clause expressly vested the general government with power to call them out to suppress insurrections, &c., it appeared to him, most decidedly, that the power of suppressing insurrections was *exclusively* given to congress. If it remained in the states, it was by implication.

Mr. CORBIN, after a short address to the chair, in which he expressed extreme reluctance to get up, said, that all contentions on this subject might be ended, by adverting to the 4th section of the 4th article, which provides, "that the United States shall guaranty to every state in the Union a republican form of government, and shall protect each of them against invasion, and, on application of the legislature, or of the executive, (when the legislature cannot be convened,) against domestic violence." He thought this section gave the states power to use their own *militia*, and call on Congress for the militia of other states. He observed that our representatives were to return every second year to mingle with their fellow-citizens. He asked, then, how, in the name of God, they would make laws to destroy themselves. The gentleman had told us that nothing could be more humiliating than that the *state governments* could not control the general government. He thought the gentleman might as well have complained that one county could not control the state at large. Mr. Corbin then said that all confederate goverments had the care of the national defence, and that Congress ought to have it. Animadverting on Mr. Henry's observations, that the French had been the instruments of their own slavery, that the Germans had enslaved the Germans, and the Spaniards the Spaniards, &c., he asked if those nations knew any thing of representation. The want of this knowledge was the principal cause of their bondage. He concluded by observing that the general government had no power but such as the state government had, and that arguments against the one held against the other.

Mr. GRAYSON, in reply to Mr. Corbin, said he was mistaken when he produced the 4th section of the 4th article, to prove that the state governments had a right to intermeddle with the militia. He was of opinion that a previous application must be made to the federal head, by the legislature when in session, or otherwise by the executive of any state, before they could interfere with the militia. In his opinion, no instance could be adduced where the states could employ the militia; for, in all the cases wherein they could be employed, Congress had the exclusive direction and control of them. Disputes, he observed, had happened in many countries, where this power should be lodged. In England, there was a dispute between the Parliament and King Charles who should have power over the militia. Were this government well organized, he would not object to giving it power over the militia. But as it appeared to him to be without checks, and to tend to the formation of an aristocratic body, he could not agree to it. Thus organized, his imagination did not reach so far as to know where this power should be lodged. He conceived the state governments to be at the mercy of the generality. He wished to be open to conviction, but he could see no case where the states could command the militia. He did not believe that it corresponded with the intentions of those who formed it, and it was altogether without an equilibrium. He humbly apprehended that the power of providing for organizing and disciplining the militia, enabled the government to make laws for regulating them, and inflicting punishments for disobedience, neglect, &c. Whether it would be the spirit of the generality to lay unusual punishments, he knew not; but he thought they had the power, if they thought proper to exercise it. He thought that, if there was a constructive implied power left in the states, yet, as the line was not clearly marked between the two governments, it would create differences. He complained of the uncertainty of the expression, and wished it to be so clearly expressed that the people might see where the states could interfere.

As the exclusive power of arming, organizing, &c., was given to Congress, they might entirely neglect them; or they might be armed in one part of the Union, and totally neglected in another. This he apprehended to be a probable circumstance. In this he might be thought suspicious; but he was justified by what had happened in other countries. He wished to know what attention had been paid to the militia of Scotland and Ireland since the union, and what laws had been made to regulate them. There is, says Mr. Grayson, an excellent militia law in England, and such as I wish to be established by the general government. They have thirty thousand select militia in England. But the militia of Scotland and Ireland are neglected. I see the necessity of the concentration of the forces of the Union. I acknowledge that militia are the best means of quelling insurrections, and that we have an advantage over the English government, for their regular forces answer the purpose. But I object to the want of checks, and a line of discriminaton between the state governments and the generality.

Mr. JOHN MARSHALL asked if gentlemen were serious when they asserted that, if the state governments had power to interfere with the militia, it was by implication. If they were, he asked the committee whether the least attention would not show that they were mistaken. The state governments did not derive their powers from the general government; but each government derived its powers from the people, and each was to act according to the powers given it. Would any gentleman deny this? He demanded if powers not given were retained by implication. Could any man say so? Could any man say that this power was not retained by the states, as they had not given it away? For, says he, does not a power remain till it is given away? The state legislatures had power to command and govern their militia before, and have it still, undeniably, unless there be something in this Constitution that takes it away.

For Continental purposes Congress may call forth the militia,—as to suppress insurrections and repel invasions. But the power given to the states by the people is not taken away; for the Constitution does not say so. In the Confederation Congress had this power; but the state legislatures had it also. The power of legislating given them within the ten miles square is exclusive of the states, becuase it is expressed to be exclusive. The truth is, that when power is given to the general legislature, if it was in the state legislature before, both shall exercise it; unless there be an incompatibility in the exercise by one to that by the other, or negative words precluding the state government from it. But there are no negative words here. It rests, therefore, with the states. To me it appears, then, unquestionable that the state governments can call forth the militia, in case the Constitution should be adopted, in the same manner as they could have done before its adoption. Gentlemen have said that the states cannot defend themselves without an application to congress, because Congress can interpose! Does not every man feel a refutation of the argument in his own breast? I will show that there could not be a combination, between those who formed the Constitution, to take away this power. All the restraints intended to be laid on the state governments (besides where an exclusive power is expressly given to Congress) are contained in the 10th section of the 1st article. This power is not included in the restrictions in that section. But what excludes every possibility of doubt, is the last part of it—that "no state shall engage in war, unless actually invaded, or in such imminent danger as will not admit of delay." When invaded, they can engage in war, as also when in imminent danger. This clearly proves that the states can use the militia when they find it necessary. The worthy member last up objects to the Continental government's possessing the power of disciplining the militia, because, though all its branches be derived from the people, he says they will form an aristocratic government, unsafe and unfit to be trusted.

Mr. GRAYSON answered, that he only said it was so constructed as to form a great aristocratic body.

Mr. MARSHALL replied, that he was not certain whether he understood him; but he thought he had said so. He conceived that, as the government was drawn from the people, the feelings and interests of the people would be attended to, and that we should be safe in granting them power to regulate the militia. When the government is drawn from the people, continued Mr. Marshall, and depending on the people for its continuance, oppressive measures will not be attempted, as they will certainly draw on their authors the resentment of those on whom they depend. On this government, thus depending on ourselves for its existence, I will rest my safety, notwithstanding the danger depicted by the honorable gentleman. I cannot help being surprised that the worthy member thought this power so dangerous. What government is able to protect you in time of war? Will any state depend on its own exertions? The consequence of such dependence, and withholding this power from Congress, will be, that state will fall after state, and be a sacrifice to the want of power in the general government. *United we are strong, divided we fall.* Will you prevent the general government from drawing the militia of one state to another, when the consequence would be, that every state must depend on itself? The enemy, possessing the water, can quickly go from one state to another. No state will spare to another its militia, which it conceives necessary for itself. It requires a superintending power, in order to call forth the resources of all to protect all. If this be not done, each state will fall a sacrifice. This system merits the highest applause in this respect. The honorable gentleman said that a general regulation may be made to inflict punishments. Does he imagine that a militia law is to be ingrafted on the scheme of government, so as to render it incapable of being changed? The idea of the worthy member supposes that men renounce their own interests. This would produce general inconveniences throughout the Union, and would be equally opposed by all the states. But the worthy member fears, that in one part of the Union they will be regulated and disciplined, and in another neglected. This danger is enhanced by leaving this power to each state; for some states may attend to their militia, and others may neglect them. If Congress neglect our militia, we can arm them ourselves. Cannot Virginia import arms? Cannot she put them into the hands of her militia-men?

He then concluded by observing, that the power of governing the militia was not vested in the states by implication, because, being possessed of it antecedent to the adoption of the government, and not being divested of it by any grant or restriction in the Constitution, they must necessarily be as fully possessed of it as ever they had been. And it could not be said that the states derived any powers from that system, but retained them, though not acknowleged in any part of it.

Mr. GRAYSON acknowledged that all power was drawn from the people. But he could see none of those checks which ought to characterize a free government. It had not such checks as even the British government had. He thought it so organized as to form an aristocratic body. If we looked at the democratic branch, and the great extent of country, he said, it must be considered, in a great degree, to be an aristocratic representation. As they were elected with craving appetites, and wishing for emoluments, they might unite with the other two branches. They might give reciprocally good offices to one another, and mutually protect each other; for he considered them all as united in interest, and as but one branch. There was no check to prevent such a combination; nor, in cases of concurrent powers, was there a line drawn to prevent interference between the state governments and the generality.

Mr. HENRY still retained his opinion, that the states had no right to call forth the militia to suppress insurrections, &c. But the right interpretation (and such as the nations of the earth had put upon the concession of power) was that, when power was given, it was given exclusively. He appealed to the committee, if power was not confined in the hands of a *few* in almost all countries of the world. He referred to their candor, if the construction of conceded power was not an exclusive concession, in nineteen twentieth parts of the world. The nations which retained their liberty were comparatively few. America would add to the number of the oppressed nations, if she depended on constructive rights and argumentative implication. That the powers given to Congress were exclusively given, was very obvious to him. The rights which the states had must be founded on the restrictions on Congress. He asked, if the doctrine which had been so often circulated, that rights not given were retained, was true, why there were negative clauses to restrain Congress. He told gentlemen that these clauses were sufficient to shake all their implication; for, says he, if Congress had no power but that given to them, why restrict them by negative words? Is not the clear implication this—that, if these restrictions were not inserted, they could have performed what they prohibit?

The worthy member had said that Congress ought to have power to protect all, and had given this system the highest encomium. But he insisted that the power over the militia was concurrent. To obviate the futility of this doctrine, Mr. Henry alleged that it was not reducible to practice. Examine it, says he; reduce it to practice. Suppose an insurrection in Virginia, and suppose there be danger apprehended of an insurrection in another state, from the exercise of the government; or suppose a national war, and there be discontents among the people of this state, that produce, or threaten, an insurrection; suppose Congress, in either case, demands a number of militia,—will they not be obliged to go? Where are your reserved rights, when your militia go to a neighboring state? Which call is to be obeyed, the congressional call, or the call of the state legislature? The call of Congress must be obeyed. I need not remind this committee that the sweeping clause will cause their demands to be submitted to. This clause enables them "to make all laws which shall be necessary and proper to carry into execution all the powers vested by this Constitution in the government of the United States, or in any department or officer thereof." Mr. Chairman, I will turn to another clause which relates to the same subject, and tends to show the fallacy of their argument.

The 10th section of the 1st article, to which reference was made by the worthy member, militates against himself. It says, that "no state shall engage in war, unless actually invaded." If you give this clause a fair construction, what is the true meaning of it? What does this relate to? Not domestic insurrections, but war. If the country be invaded, a state may go to war, but cannot suppress insurrections. If there should happen an insurrection of slaves, the country cannot be said to be invaded. They cannot, therefore, suppress it without the interposition of Congress. The 4th section of the 4th article gives Congress power to call forth the militia to quell insurrections: there cannot, therefore, be a concurrent power. The state legislatures ought to have power to call forth the efforts of the militia, when necessary. Occasions for calling them out may be urgent, pressing, and instantaneous. The states cannot now call them, let an insurrection be ever so perilous, without an application to Congress. So long a delay may be fatal.

There are three clauses which prove, beyond the possibility of doubt, that Congress, and *Congress only*, can call forth the militia. The clause giving Congress power to call them out to suppress insurrections, &c.; that which restrains a state from engaging in war except when actually invaded, and that which requires Congress to protect the states against domestic violence,—render it impossible that a state can have power to intermeddle with them. Will not Congress find refuge for their actions in these clauses? With respect to the concurrent jurisdiction, it is a political monster of absurdity. We have passed that clause which gives Congress an unlimited authority over the national wealth; and here is an unbounded control over the national strength. Notwithstanding this clear, unequivocal relinquishment of the power of controlling the militia, you say the states retain it, for the very purposes given to Congress. Is it fair to say that you give the power of arming the militia, and at the same time to say you reserve it? This great national government ought not to be left in this condition. If it be, it will terminate in the destruction of our liberties.

Mr. MADISON. Mr. Chairman, let me ask this committee, and the honorable member last up, what we are to understand from this reasoning. The power must be vested in Congress, or in the state governments; or there must be a division or concurrence. He is against division. It is a political monster. He will not give it to Congress for fear of oppression. Is it to be vested in the state governments? If so, where is the provision for general defence? If ever America should be attacked, the states would fall successively. It will prevent them from giving aid to their sister states; for, as each state will expect to be attacked, and wish to guard against it, each will retain its own militia for its own defence. Where is this power to be deposited, then, unless in the general government, if it be dangerous to the public safety to give it exclusively to the states? If it must be divided, let him show a better manner of doing it than that which is in the Constitution. I cannot agree with the other honorable gentleman, that there is no check. There is a powerful check in that paper. The state governments are to govern the militia when not called forth for general national purposes; and Congress is to govern such part only as may be in the actual service of the Union. Nothing can be more certain and positive than this. It expressly empowers Congress to govern them when in the service of the United States. It is, then, clear that the states govern them when they are not. With respect to suppressing insurrections, I say that those clauses which were mentioned by the honorable gentleman are compatible with a concurrence of the power. By the first, Congress is to call them forth to suppress insurrections, and repel invasions of foreign powers. A concurrence in the former case is necessary, because a whole state may be in insurrection against the Union. What has passed may perhaps justify this apprehension. The safety of the Union and particular states requires that the general government should have power to repel foreign invasions. The 4th section of the 4th article is perfectly consistent with the exercise of the power by the states. The words are, "The United States shall guaranty to every state in this Union a republican form of government, and shall protect each of them against invasion, and, on application of the legislature, or of the executive, (when the legislature cannot be convened,) against domestic violence." The word *invasion* here, after power had been given in the former clause to repel invasions, may be thought tautologous, but it has a different meaning from the other. This clause speaks of a particular state. It means that it shall be protected from invasion by other states. A republican government is to be guarantied to each state, and they are to be protected from invasion from other states, as well as from foreign powers; and, on application by the legislature or executive, as the case may be, the militia of the other states are to be called to suppress domestic insurrections. Does this bar the states from calling forth their own militia? No; but it gives them a supplementary security to suppress insurrections and domestic violence.

The other clause runs in these words: "No state shall, without the consent of Congress, lay any duty on tonnage, keep troops or ships of war in time of peace, enter into any agreement or compact with another state, or with a foreign power, or engage in war, unless actually invaded, or in such imminent danger as will not admit of delay." They are restrained from making war, unless invaded, or *in imminent danger*. When in such danger, they are not restrained. I can perceive no competition in these clauses. They cannot be said to be repugnant to a concurrence of the power. If we object to the Constitution in this manner, and consume our time in verbal criticism, we shall never put an end to the business.

Mr. GEORGE MASON. Mr. Chairman, a worthy member has asked who are the militia, if they be not the *people* of this country, and if we are not to be protected from the fate of the Germans, Prussians, &c., by our representation? I ask, Who are the militia? They consist now of the whole people, except a few public officers. But I cannot say who will be the militia of the future day. If that paper on the table gets no alteration, the militia of the future day may not consist of all classes, high and low, and rich and poor; but they may be confined to the lower and middle classes of the people, granting exclusion to the higher classes of the people. If we should ever see that day, the most ignominious punishments and heavy fines may be expected. Under the present government, all ranks of people are subject to militia duty. Under such a full and equal representation as ours, there can be no ignominious punishment inflicted. But under this national, or rather consolidated government, the case will be different. The representation being so small and inadequate, they will have no fellow-feeling for the people. They may discriminate people in their own predicament, and exempt from duty all the officers and lowest creatures of the national government. If there were a more particular definition of their powers, and a clause exempting the militia from martial law except when in actual service, and from fines and punishments of an unusual nature, then we might expect that the militia would be what they are. But, if this be not the case, we cannot say how long all classes of people will be included in the militia. There will not be the same reason to expect it, because the government will be administered by different people. We know what they are now, but know not how soon they may be altered.

Mr. GEORGE NICHOLAS. Mr. Chairman, I feel apprehensions lest the subject of our debates should be misunderstood. Every one wishes to know the true meaning of the system; but I fear those who hear us will think we are captiously quibbling on words. We have been told, in the course of this business, that the government will operate like a *screw*. Give me leave to say that the exertions of the opposition are like that instrument. They catch at every thing, and take it into their vortex. The worthy member says that this government is defective, because it comes from the people. Its greatest recommendation, with me, is putting the power in the hands of the people. He disapproves of it because it does not say in what particular instances the militia shall be called out to execute the laws. This is a power of the Constitution, and particular instances must be defined by the legislature. But, says the worthy member, those laws which have been read are arguments against the Constitution, because they show that the states are now in possession of the power, and competent to its execution. Would you leave this power in the states and by that means deprive the general government of a power which will be necessary for its existence? If the state governments find this power necessary, ought not the general government to have a similar power? But, sir, there is no state check in this business. The gentleman near me has shown that there is a very important check.

Another worthy member says there is no power in the states to quell an insurrection of slaves. Have they it now? If they have, does the Constitution take it away? If it does, it must be in one of the three clauses which have been mentioned by the worthy member. The first clause gives the general government power to call them out when necessary. Does this take it away from the states? No. But it gives an additional security; for, besides the power in the state governments to use their own militia, it will be the duty of the general government to aid them with the strength of the Union when called for. No part of this Constitution can show that this power is taken away.

But an argument is drawn from that clause which says "that no state shall engage in war unless actually invaded, or in such imminent danger as will not admit of delay." What does this prohibition amount to? It must be a war with a foreign enemy that the states are prohibited from making; for the exception to the restriction proves it. The restriction includes only offensive hostility, as they are at liberty to engage in war when invaded, or in imminent danger. They are, therefore, not restrained from quelling domestic insurrections, which are totally different from making war with a foreign power. But the great thing to be dreaded is that, during an insurrection, the militia will be called out from the state. This is his kind of argument. Is it possible that, at such a time, the general government would order the militia to be called? It is a groundless objection, to work on gentlemen's apprehensions within these walls. As to the 4th article, it was introduced wholly for the particular aid of the states. A republican form of government is gaurantied, and protection is secured against invasion and domestic violence on application. Is not this a guard as strong as possible? Does it not exclude the unnecessary interference of Congress in business of this sort?

The gentleman over the way cannot tell who will be the militia at a future day, and enumerates dangers of select militia. Let me attend to the nature of gentlemen's objections. One objects because there will be select militia; another objects because there will be no select militia; and yet both oppose it on these contradictory principles. If you deny the general government the power of calling out the militia, there must be a recurrence to a standing army. If you are really jealous of your liberties, confide in Congress.

Mr. MASON rose, and said that he was totally misunderstood. The contrast between his friend's objection and his was improper. His friend had mentioned the propriety of having select militia, like those of Great Britain, who should be more thoroughly exercised than the militia at large could possibly be. But *he*, himself, had not spoken of a selection of militia, but of the exemption of the highest classes of the people from militia service; which would justify apprehensions of severe and ignominious punishments.

Mr. NICHOLAS wished to know whether the representatives of the people would consent to such exemptions, as every man who had twenty-five acres of land could vote for a federal representative. . . .

Mr. GRAYSON. . . . A well-regulated militia ought to be the defence of this country. In some of our constitutions it is said so. This Constitution should have inculcated the principle. Congress ought to be under some restraint in this respect.[1]

[Mr. PENDLETON.]

They say that the state governments have no power at all over the militia. The power of the general government to provide for arming and organizing the militia is to introduce a uniform system of discipline to pervade the United States of America. But the power of *governing* the militia, so far as it is in Congress, extends only to such parts of them as may be employed in the service of the United States. When not in their service, Congress has no power to govern them. The states then have the sole government of them; and though Congress *may* provide for arming them, and prescribe the mode of discipline, yet the states have the authority of training them, according to the uniform discipline prescribed by Congress. But there is nothing to preclude them from arming and disciplining them, should Congress neglect to do it. As to calling the militia to execute the laws of the Union, I think the fair construction is directly opposite to what the honorable member says. The 4th section of the 4th article contains nothing to warrant the supposition that the states cannot call them forth to suppress domestic insurrections. [*Here he read the section.*] All the restraint here contained is, that Congress may, at their pleasure, on application of the state legislature, or (in vacation) of the executive, protect each of the states against domestic violence. This is a restraint on the general government not to interpose. The state is in full possession of the power of using its own militia to protect itself against domestic violence; and the power in the general government cannot be exercised, or interposed, without the application of the state itself. This appears to me to be the obvious and fair construction.

With respect to the necessity of the ten miles square being superseded by the subsequent clause, which gives them power to make all laws which shall be necessary and proper for carrying into execution the forgoing powers, and all other powers vested by this Constitution in the government of the United States, or in any department or officer thereof, I understand that clause as not going a single step beyond the delegated powers. What can it act upon? Some power given by this Constitution. If they should be about to pass a law in consequence of this clause, they must pursue some of the delegated powers, but can by no means depart from them, or arrogate any new powers; for the plain language of the clause is, to give them power to pass laws in order to give effect to the delegated powers.

Mr. GEORGE MASON. Mr. Chairman, gentlemen say there is no new power given by this clause. Is there any thing in this Constitution which secures to the states the powers which are said to be retained? Will powers remain to the states which are not expressly guarded and reserved? I will suppose a case. Gentlemen may call it an impossible case, and suppose that Congress will act with wisdom and integrity. Among the enumerated powers, Congress are to lay and collect taxes, duties, imposts, and excises, and to pay the debts, and to provide for the general welfare and common defence; and by that clause (so often called the *sweeping clause*) they are to make all laws necessary to execute those laws. Now, suppose oppressions should arise under this government, and any writer should dare to stand forth, and expose to the community at large the abuses of those powers; could not Congress, under the idea of providing for the general welfare, and under their own construction, say that this was destroying the general peace, encouraging sedition, and poisoning the minds of the people? And could they not, in order to provide against this, lay a dangerous restriction on the press? Might they not even bring the trial of this restriction within the ten miles square, when there is no prohibition against it? Might they not thus destroy the trial by jury? Would they not extend their implication? It appears to me that they may and will. And shall the support of our rights depend on the bounty of men whose interest it may be to oppress us? That Congress should have power to provide for the general welfare of the Union, I grant. But I wish a clause in the Constitution, with respect to all powers which are not granted, that they are retained by the states. Otherwise, the power of providing for the general welfare may be perverted to its destruction.

Many gentlemen, whom I respect, take different sides of this question. We wish this amendment to be introduced, to remove our apprehensions. There was a clause in the Confederation reserving to the states respectively every power, jurisdiction, and right, not expressly delegated to the United States. This clause has never been complained of, but approved by all. Why not, then, have a similar clause in this Constitution, in which it is the more indispensably necessary than in the Confederation, because of the great augmentation of power vested in the former? In my humble apprehension, this clause now under consideration will go to any thing our rulers may think proper. Unless there be some express declaration that every thing not given is retained, it will be carried to any power Congress may please.

Mr. HENRY moved to read from the 8th to the 13th article of the declaration of rights; which was done.[2]

[The sections read are as follows: Ed.]

8. That in all capital or criminal prosecutions a man hath a right to demand the cause and nature of his accusation, to be confronted with the accusers and witnesses, to call for evidence in his favour, and to a speedy trial by an impartial jury of his vicinage, without whose unanimous consent he cannot be found guilty, nor can he be compelled to give evidence against himself; that no man be deprived of his liberty except by the law of the land, or the judgment of his peers.

9. That excessive bail ought not to be required, nor excessive fines imposed, nor cruel and unusual punishments inflicted.

10. That general warrants, wherby any officer or messenger may be commanded to search suspected places without evidence of a fact committed, or to seize any person or persons not named, or whose offence is not particularly described and supported by evidence, are grievous and oppressive, and ought not to be granted.

11. That in controversies respecting property, and in suits between man and man, the ancient trial by jury is preferable to any other, and ought to be held sacred.

12. That the freedom of the press is one of the great bulwarks of liberty, and can never be restrained but by despotick governments.

13. That a well regulated militia, composed of the body of the people, trained to arms, is the proper, natural, and safe defence of a free state; that standing armies, in time of peace, should be avoided, as dangerous to liberty: and that, in all cases, the military should be under strict subordination to, and governed by, the civil power.[3]

Mr. GEORGE NICHOLAS, in reply to the gentlemen opposed to the clause under debate, went over the same grounds, and developed the same principles, which Mr. Pendleton and Mr. Madison had done. The opposers of the clause, which gave the power of providing for the general welfare, supposed its dangers to result from its connection with, and extension of, the powers granted in the other clauses. He endeavored to show the committee that it only empowered Congress to make such laws as would be necessary to enable them to pay the public debts and provide for the common defence; that this general welfare was united, not to the general power of legislation, but to the particular power of laying and collecting taxes, imposts, and excises, for the purpose of paying the debts and providing for the common defence,—that is, that they could raise as much money as would pay the debts and provide for the common defence, in consequence of this power. The clause which was affectedly called the *sweeping clause* contained no new grant of power. To illustrate this position, he observed that, if it had been added at the end of every one of the enumerated powers, instead of being inserted at the end of all, it would be obvious to any one that it was no augmentation of power. If, for instance, at the end of the clause granting power to lay and collect taxes, it had been added that they should have power to make necessary and proper laws to lay and collect taxes, who could suspect it to be an addition of power? As it would grant no new power if inserted at the end of each clause, it could not when subjoined to the whole.

He then proceeded thus: But, says he, who is to determine the extent of such powers? I say, the same power which, in all well-regulated communities, determines the extent of legislative powers. If they exceed these powers, the judiciary will declare it void, or else the people will have a right to declare it void. Is this depending on any man? But, says the gentleman, it may go to any thing. It may destroy the trial by jury; and they may say it is necessary for providing for the general defence. The power of providing for the general defence only extends to raise any sum of money they may think necessary, by taxes, imposts, &c. But, says he, our only defence against oppressive laws consists in the virtue of our representatives. This was misrepresented. If I understand it right, no new power can be exercised. As to those which are actually granted, we trust to the fellow-feelings of our representatives; and if we are deceived, we then trust to altering our government. It appears to me, however, that we can confide in their discharging their powers rightly, from the peculiarity of their situation, and connection with us. If, sir, the powers of the former Congress were very inconsiderable, that body did not deserve to have great powers.

It was so constructed that it would be dangerous to invest it with such. But why were the articles of the bill of rights read? Let him show us that those rights are given up by the Constitution. Let him prove them to be violated. He tells us that the most worthy characters of the country differ as to the necessity of a bill of rights. It is a simple and plain proposition. It is agreed upon by all that the people have all power. If they part with any of it, is it necessary to declare that they retain the rest? Liken it to any similar case. If I have one thousand acres of land, and I grant five hundred acres of it, must I declare that I retain the other five hundred? Do I grant the whole thousand acres, when I grant five hundred, unless I declare that the five hundred I do not give belong to me still? It is so in this case. After granting some powers, the rest must remain with the people.

Gov. RANDOLPH observed that he had some objections to the clause. He was persuaded that the construction put upon it by the gentlemen, on both sides, was erroneous; but he thought any construction better than going into anarchy.

Mr. GEORGE MASON still thought that there ought to be some express declaration in the Constitution, asserting that rights not given to the general government were retained by the states. He apprehended that, unless this was done, many valuable and important rights would be concluded to be given up by implication. All governments were drawn from the people, though many were perverted to their oppression. The government of Virginia, he remarked, was drawn from the people; yet there were certain great and important rights, which the people, by their bill of rights, declared to be paramount to the power of the legislature. He asked, Why should it not be so in this Constitution? Was it because we were more substantially represented in it than in the state government? If, in the state government, where the people were substantially and fully represented, it was necessary that the great rights of human nature should be secure from the encroachments of the legislature, he asked if it was not more necessary in this government, where they were but inadequately represented? He declared that artful sophistry and evasions could not satisfy him. He could see no clear distinction between rights relinquished by a positive grant, and lost by implication. Unless there were a bill of rights, implication might swallow up all our rights.

Mr. HENRY. Mr. Chairman, the necessity of a bill of rights appears to me to be greater in this government than ever it was in any government before. I have observed already, that the sense of the European nations, and particularly Great Britain, is against the construction of rights being retained which are not expressly relinquished. I repeat, that all nations have adopted this construction—that all rights not expressly and unequivocally reserved to the people are impliedly and incidentally relinquished to rulers, as necessarily inseparable from the delegated powers. It is so in Great

Britain; for every possible right, which is not reserved to the people by some express provision or compact, is within the king's prerogative. It is so in that country which is said to be in such full possession of freedom. It is so in Spain, Germany, and other parts of the world. Let us consider the sentiments which have been entertained by the people of America on this subject. At the revolution, it must be admitted that it was their sense to set down those great rights which ought, in all countries, to be held inviolable and sacred. Virginia did so, we all remember. She made a compact to reserve, expressly, certain rights.

When fortified with full, adequate, and abundant representation, was she satisfied with that representation? No. She most cautiously and guardedly reserved and secured those invaluable, inestimable rights and privileges, which no people, inspired with the least glow of patriotic liberty, ever did, or ever can, abandon. She is called upon now to abandon them, and dissolve that compact which secured them to her. She is called upon to accede to another compact, which most infallibly supersedes and annihilates her present one. Will she do it? This is the question. If you intend to reserve your unalienable rights, you must have the most express stipulation; for, if implication be allowed, you are ousted of those rights. If the people do not think it necessary to reserve them, they will be supposed to be given up. How were the congressional rights defined when the people of America united by a confederacy to defend their liberties and rights against the tyrannical attempts of Great Britain? The states were not then contented with implied reservation. No, Mr. Chairman. It was expressly declared in our Confederation that every right was retained by the states, respectively, which was not given up to the government of the United States. But there is no such thing here. You, therefore, by a natural and unavoidable implication, give up your rights to the general government.

Your own example furnishes an argument against it. If you give up these powers, without a bill of rights, you will exhibit the most absurd thing to mankind that ever the world saw—a government that has abandoned all its powers—the powers of direct taxation, the sword, and the purse. You have disposed of them to Congress, without a bill of rights—without check, limitation, or control. And still you have checks and guards; still you keep barriers—pointed where? Pointed against your weakened, prostrated, enervated state government! You have a bill of rights to defend you against the state government, which is bereaved of all power, and yet you have none against Congress, though in full and exclusive possession of all power! You arm yourselves against the weak and defenceless, and expose yourselves naked to the armed and powerful. Is not this a conduct of unexampled absurdity? What barriers have you to oppose to this most strong, energetic government? To that government you have nothing to oppose. All your defence is given up. This is a real, actual defect. It must strike the mind of every gentleman. When our government was first instituted in Virginia, we declared the common law of England to be in force.

That system of law which has been admired, and has protected us and our ancestors, is excluded by that system. Added to this, we adopted a bill of rights. By this Constitution, some of the best barriers of human rights are thrown away. Is there not an additional reason to have a bill of rights? By the ancient common law, the trial of all facts is decided by a jury of impartial men from the immediate vicinage. This paper speaks of different juries from the common law in criminal cases; and in civil controversies excludes trial by jury altogether. There is, therefore, more occasion for the supplementary check of a bill of rights now than then. Congress, from their general powers, may fully go into business of human legislation. They may legislate, in criminal cases, from treason to the lowest offence—petty larceny. They may define crimes and prescribe punishments. In the definition of crimes, I trust they will be directed by what wise representatives ought to be governed by. But when we come to punishments, no latitude ought to be left, nor dependence put on the virtue of representatives. What says our bill of rights?—"that excessive bail ought not to be required, nor excessive fines imposed, nor cruel and unusual punishments inflicted." Are you not, therefore, now calling on those gentlemen who are to compose Congress, to prescribe trials and define punishments without this control? Will they find sentiments there similar to this bill of rights? You let them loose; you do more—you depart from the genius of your country. That paper tells you that the trial of crimes shall be by jury, and held in the state where the crime shall have been committed. Under this extensive provision, they may proceed in a manner extremely dangerous to liberty: a person accused may be carried from one extremity of the state to another, and be tried, not by an impartial jury of the vicinage, acquainted with his character and the circumstances of the fact, but by a jury unacquainted with both, and who may be biased against him. Is not this sufficient to alarm men? How different is this from the immemorial practice of your British ancestors, and your own! I need not tell you that, by the common law, a number of hundredors were required on a jury, and that afterwards it was sufficient if the jurors came from the same county. With less than this the people of England have never been satisfied. That paper ought to have declared the common law in force.

In this business of legislation, your members of Congress will loose the restriction of not imposing excessive fines, demanding excessive bail, and inflicting cruel and unusual punishments. These are prohibited by your declaration of rights. What has distinguished our ancestors?—That they would not admit of tortures, or cruel and barbarous punishment. But Congress may introduce the practice of the civil law, in preference to that of the common law. They may introduce the practice of France, Spain, and Germany—of torturing to extort a confession of the crime. They will say that they might as well draw examples from those countries as from Great Britain, and they will tell you that there is such a necessity of strengthening the arm of government, that they must have a criminal equity, and extort confession by torture, in order to punish with still more relentless severity. We are then lost and undone. And can any man think it troublesome, when we can, by a small interference, prevent our rights from being lost? If you will, like the Virginian government, give them knowledge of the extent of the rights retained by the people, and the powers of themselves, they will, if they be honest men, thank you for it. Will they not wish to go on sure grounds? But if you leave them otherwise, they will not know how to proceed; and, being in a state of uncertainty, they will assume rather than give up powers by implication.

A bill of rights may be summed up in a few words. What do they tell us?—That our rights are reserved. Why not say so? Is it because it will consume too much paper? Gentlemen's reasoning against a bill of rights does not satisfy me. Without saying which has the right side, it remains doubtful. A bill of rights is a favorite thing with the Virginians and the people of the other states likewise. It may be their prejudice, but the government ought to suit their geniuses; otherwise, its operation will be unhappy. A bill of rights, even if its necessity be doubtful, will exclude the possibility of dispute; and, with great submission, I think the best way is to have no dispute. In the present Constitution, they are restrained from issuing general warrants to search suspected places, or seize persons not named, without evidence of the commission of a fact, &c. There was certainly some celestial influence governing those who deliberated on that Constitution; for they have, with the most cautious and enlightened circumspection, guarded those indefeasible rights which ought ever to be held sacred! The officers of Congress may come upon you now, fortified with all the terrors of paramount federal authority. Excisemen may come in multitudes; for the limitation of their numbers no man knows. They may, unless the general government be restrained by a bill of rights, or some similar restriction, go into your cellars and rooms, and search, ransack, and measure, every thing you eat, drink, and wear. They ought to be restrained within proper bounds. With respect to the freedom of the press, I need say nothing; for it is hoped that the gentlemen who shall compose Congress will take care to infringe as little as possible the rights of human nature. This will result from their integrity. They should, from prudence, abstain from violating the rights of their constituents. They are not, however, expressly restrained. But whether they will intermeddle with that palladium of our liberties or not, I leave you to determine.

Mr. GRAYSON thought it questionable whether rights not given up were reserved. A majority of the states, he observed, had expressly reserved certain important rights by bills of rights, and that in the Confederation there was a clause declaring expressly that every power and right not given up was retained by the states. It was the general sense of America that such a clause was necessary; otherwise, why did they introduce a clause which was totally unnecessary? It had been insisted, he said, in many parts of America, that a bill of rights was only necessary between a prince and people, and not in such a government as this, which was a compact between the people themselves. This did not satisfy his mind; for so extensive was the power of legislation, in his estimation, that he doubted whether, when it was once given up, *any thing* was retained. He further remarked, that there were some negative clauses in the Constitution, which refuted the doctrine contended for by the other side. For instance; the 2d clause of the 9th section of the 1st article provided that "the privilege of the writ of *habeas corpus* shall not be suspended, unless when, in cases of rebellion or invasion, the public safety may require it." And, by the last clause of the same section, "no title of nobility shall be granted by the United States." Now, if these restrictions had not been here inserted, he asked whether Congress would not most clearly have had a right to suspend that great and valuable right, and to grant titles of nobility. When, in addition to these considerations, he saw they had an indefinite power to provide for the general welfare, he thought there were great reasons to apprehend great dangers. He thought, therefore, that there ought to be a bill of rights.[4]

1 *Debates*, III, pp. 410-430.
2 *Ibid.*, pp. 440-442.
3 DHRC, VIII, p.531.
4 *Debates*, III, pp. 442-449.

Virginia Convention June 17, 1788
Debates (excerpts)

Mr. TYLER . . . This seemed to him to demonstrate most clearly the necessity of restraining them, by a bill of rights, from infringing our unalienable rights. It was immaterial whether the bill of rights was by itself, or included in the Constitution. But he contended for it one way or the other. It would be justified by our own example and that of England. . . .

Mr. HENRY. Mr. Chairman, we have now come to the 9th section, and I consider myself at liberty to take a short view of the whole. I wish to do it very briefly. Give me leave to remark that there is a bill of rights in that government.

There are express restrictions, which are in the shape of a bill of rights; but they bear the name of the 9th section. The design of the negative expressions in this section is to prescribe limits beyond which the powers of Congress shall not go. These are the sole bounds intended by the American government. Whereabouts do we stand with respect to a bill of rights? Examine it, and compare it to the idea manifested by the Virginian bill of rights, or that of the other states. The restraints in this congressional bill of rights are so feeble and few, that it would have been infinitely better to have said nothing about it. The fair implication is, that they can do every thing they are not forbidden to do. What will be the result if Congress, in the course of their legislation, should do a thing not restrained by this 9th section? It will fall as an incidental power to Congress, not being prohibited expressly in the Constitution. The first prohibition is, that the privilege of the writ of *habeas corpus* shall not be suspended but when, in case of rebellion or invasion, the public safety may require it. It results clearly that, if it had not said so, they could suspend it in all cases whatsoever. It reverses the position of the friends of this Constitution, that every thing is retained which is not given up; for, instead of this, every thing is given up which is not expressly reserved. It does not speak affirmatively, and say that it shall be suspended in those cases; but that it shall not be suspended but in certain cases; going on a supposition that every thing which is not negatived shall remain with Congress. If the power remains with the people, how can Congress supply the want of an affirmative grant? They cannot do it but by implication, which destroys their doctrine. The Virginia bill of rights interdicts the relinquishment of the sword and purse without control. That bill of rights secures the great and principal rights of mankind. But this bill of rights extends to but very

few cases, and is destructive of the doctrine advanced by the friends of that paper. . . .
Our own government triumphs, with infinite superiority, when put in contrast with that paper. The want of a bill of rights will render all their laws, however oppressive, constitutional.

If the government of Virginia passes a law in contradiction to our bill of rights, it is nugatory. . . . You are told that your rights are secured in this new government. They are guarded in no other part but this 9th section. The few restrictions in that section are your only safeguards. They may control your actions, and your very words, without being repugnant to that paper. The existence of your dearest privileges will depend on the consent of Congress, for they are not within the restrictions of the 9th section.

If gentlemen think that securing the slave trade is a capital object; that the privilege of the *habeas corpus* is sufficiently secured; that the exclusion of *ex post facto* laws will produce no inconvenience; that the publication from time to time will secure their property; in one word, that this section alone will sufficiently secure their liberties,—I have spoken in vain. Every word of mine, and of my worthy coadjutor, is lost. I trust that gentlemen, on this occasion, will see the great objects of religion, liberty of the press, trial by jury, interdiction of cruel punishments, and every other sacred right, secured, before they agree to that paper. These most important human rights are not protected by that section, which is the only safeguard in the Constitution. My mind will not be quieted till I see something substantial come forth in the shape of a bill of rights. . . .

[Gov. RANDOLPH.]

On the subject of a bill of rights, the want of which has been complained of, I will observe that it has been sanctified by such reverend authority, that I feel some difficulty in going against it. I shall not, however, be deterred from giving my opinion on this occasion, let the consequence be what it may. At the beginning of the war, we had no certain bill of rights; for our charter cannot be considered as a bill of rights; it is nothing more than an investiture, in the hands of the Virginia citizens, of those rights which belonged to British subjects. When the British thought proper to infringe our rights, was it not necessary to mention, in our Constitution, those rights which ought to be paramount to the power of the legislature? Why is the bill of rights distinct from the Constitution? I consider bills of rights in this view—that the government should use them, when there is a departure from its fundamental principles, in order to restore them.

Debates, III, pp. 454, 460-462, 466.

Many June 18, 1788
Newspaper Article: Richmond *Virginia Independent Chronicle* (excerpt)

We see our way now more clearly than at first outset; several of our objections have been ably answered. But so attached are we to old forms, or from some other cause, we are not yet satisfied, with the want of what is called a BILL OF RIGHTS.—What, if the expression was varied, and it should be termed *incontrovertable truths, or fundamental laws*—Why might not the new constitution be prefaced by such an instrument of writing? The use we would wish to see made of it, is a resort, or recurrence, a test, to try all the acts of the national legislature by.—It is known that the bulk of the people do not understand abstruse, or lengthy political disquisitions. The fundamental laws of a nation, might be expressed in a few articles, and those in a few words, yet plain, and pithy, to which the people would pay a similar deference, as to the decalogue. . . .

Such are the sentiments of
Many.

Storing, V, p. 275.

Virginia Convention June 19, 1788
Debates (excerpts)

Mr. HENRY. . . .

We are told that the state rights are preserved. Suppose the state right to territory be preserved; I ask and demand, How do the rights of persons stand, when they have power to make any treaty, and that treaty is paramount to constitutions, laws, and every thing? When a person shall be treated in the most horrid manner, and most cruelly and inhumanly tortured, will the security of territorial rights grant him redress? . . .

I might go on in this discrimination; but it is too obvious that the security of territory is no security of individual safety. I ask, How are the state rights, individual rights and national rights, secured? Not as in England; for the authority quoted from Blackstone would, if stated right prove, in a thousand instances, that, if the king of England attempted to take away the rights of individuals, the law would stand against him. The acts of Parliament would stand in his way. The bill and declaration of rights would be against him. The common law is fortified by the bill of rights. The rights of the people cannot be destroyed, even by the paramount operation of the law of nations, as the case of the Russian ambassador evinces. If you look for a similar security in the paper on your table, you look in vain. That paper is defective without such a declaration of rights. It is unbounded without such restrictions. If the Constitution be paramount, how are the constitutions and laws of the states to stand? Their operation will be totally controlled by it; for it is paramount to every thing, unless you can show some guard against it. The rights of persons are exposed as it stands now. . . .

[Mr. MADISON.]
I conceive that, as far as the bills of rights in the states do not express any thing foreign to the nature of such things, and express fundamental principles essential to liberty, and those privileges which are declared necessary to all free people, these rights are not encroached on by this government.

Debates, III, pp. 512-513, 516.

Robert Yates (Poughkeepsie) June 21, 1788
Letter: To George Mason (excerpt)[1]

Your Letter of the 9th Inst. directed to John Lamb Esquire at Newyork Chairman of the federal Republican Committee in that City enclosing your proposed Amendments to the new Constitution, has been by him transmitted to such of the Members of our Convention, who are in Sentiment with him. In consequence of this Communication a Committee has been appointed by the Members in Opposition to the New System (of which they have appointed me their Chairman) with a special View to continue our Correspondence on this necessary and important Subject.

We are happy to find that your Sentiments with respect to the Amendments correspond so nearly with ours, and that they stand on the Broad Basis of securing the Rights, and equally promoting the Happiness of every Citizen in the Union.[2]

1 Rutland, III, p. 1111.
2 See George Mason, [June 11, 1789], p. 388, for the bill of rights proposals referred to by Yates.

New Hampshire Convention June 21, 1788
Ratification of the United States Constitution

IN CONVENTION OF THE DELEGATES OF THE PEOPLE OF THE STATE OF NEW HAMPSHIRE, *June the 21st,* 1788.

The Convention having impartially discussed and fully considered the Constitution for the United States of America, reported to Congress by the Convention of Delegates from the United States of America, and submitted to us by a resolution of the General Court of said state, passed the 14th day of December last past, and achnowledging with grateful hearts the goodness of the Supreme Ruler of the universe in affording the people of the United States, in the course of his providence, an opportunity, deliberately and peaceably, without fraud or surprise, of entering into an explicit and solemn compact with each other, by assenting to and ratifying a new Constitution, in order to form a more perfect union, establish justice, insure domestic tranquility, provide for the common defence, promote the general welfare, and secure the blessings of liberty to themselves and their posterity,—Do, in the name and behalf of the people of the state of New Hampshire, assent to and ratify the said Constitution for the United States of America. And as it is the opinion of this Convention, that certain amendments and alterations in the said Constitution would remove the fears and quiet the apprehensions of many of the good people of this state, and more effectually guard against an undue administration of the federal government,—The Convention do therefore recommend that the following alterations and provisions be introduced in the said Constitution:—

I. That it be explicitly declared that all powers not expressly and particularly delegated by the aforesaid Constitution are reserved to the several states, to be by them exercised.

II. That there shall be one representative to every thirty thousand persons, according to the census mentioned in the Constitution, until the whole number of representatives amount to two hundred.

III. That Congress do not exercise the powers vested in them by the fourth section of the first article but in cases when a state shall neglect or refuse to make the regulations therein mentioned, or shall make regulations subversive of the rights of the people to a free and equal representation in Congress; nor shall Congress in any case make regulations contrary to a free and equal representation.

IV. That Congress do not lay direct taxes but when the moneys arising from impost, excise, and their other resources, are insufficient for the public exigencies, nor then, until Congress shall have first made a requisition upon the states to assess, levy, and pay, their respective proportions of such requisition, agreeably to the census fixed in the said Constitution, in such way and manner as the legislature of the state shall think best; and in such case, if any state shall neglect, then Congress may assess and levy such state's proportion, together with the interest thereon, at the rate of six per cent. per annum, from the time of payment prescribed in such requisition.

V. That Congress shall erect no company of merchants with exclusive advantages of commerce.

VI. That no person shall be tried for any crime by which he may incur an infamous punishment, or loss of life, until he first be indicted by a grand jury, except in such cases as may arise in the government and regulation of the land and naval forces.

VII. All common-law cases between citizens of different states shall be commenced in the common-law courts of the respective states; and no appeal shall be allowed to the federal court, in such cases, unless the sum or value of the thing in controversy amount to three thousand dollars.

VIII. In civil actions between citizens of different states, every issue of fact, arising in actions at common law, shall be tried by jury, if the parties, or either of them, request it.

IX. Congress shall at no time consent that any person, holding an office of trust or profit under the United States, shall accept any title of nobility, or any other title or office, from any king, prince, or foreign state.

X. That no standing army shall be kept up in time of peace, unless with the consent of three fourths of the members of each branch of Congress; nor shall soldiers, in time of peace, be quartered upon private houses, without the consent of the owners.

XI. Congress shall make no laws touching religion, or to infringe the rights of conscience.

XII. Congress shall never disarm any citizen, unless such as are or have been in actual rebellion.

And the Convention do, in the name and in behalf of the people of this state enjoin it upon their representatives in Congress, at all times until the alterations and provisions aforesaid have been considered agreeably to the fifth article of the said Constitution, to exert all their influence, and use all reasonable and legal methods, to abtain a ratification of the said alterations and provisions, in such manner as is provided in the article.

And that the United States in Congress assembled may have due notice of the assent and ratification of the said Constitution by this Convention, it is *Resolved,* That the assent and ratification aforesaid be engrossed on parchment, together with the recommendation and injunction aforesaid, and with this resolution; and that John Sullivan, Esq., president of the Convention, and John Langdon, esq., president of the state, transmit the same, countersigned by the secretary of Convention, and the secretary of state, under their hands and seals, to the United States in Congress assembled.

Debates, I, pp. 325-327.

James Madison (Richmond) June 22, 1788
Letter: To Rufus King (excerpt)

We are at length approaching the close of our deliberations on the several parts of the Constitution. The Judiciary Department has been gone over; though perhaps it may receive some additional disquisitions. The attack has apparently been less formidable than I had apprehended. Independently of some particular interests, the objections against it have not been calculated in my opinion to make any deep impressions. In the eyes of many this part of the plan stands in a less vulnerable point of view than had been conceived prior to the examination of it. As soon as the remaining articles shall be despatched, some general propositions will be agitated. The opponents will bring forward a bill of rights with sundry other amendments as conditions of ratification; & in case of disappointment will probably aim at an adjournment. Some apprehend a secession; but there are too many moderate and respectable characters on that side to admit such a supposition. It has been judged prudent nevertheless to maintain so exemplary a fairness on our part, (and even in some points to give way to unreasonable pretensions) as will withold every pretext for so rash a step. On the side of the Constitution it is in contemplation to preface the ratification with a declaration of a few obvious truths which can not affect the validity of the act, and to follow it with a recommendation of a few amendments to be pursued in the constitutional mode. This expedient is necessary to conciliate some individuals who are in general well affected, but have certain scruples drawn from their own reflexions, or from the temper of their Constituents.

Papers, XI, p. 167. Madison, a leader of the Federalists in the Virginia Convention, is here describing each party's strategy within the Convention.

Virginia Convention June 24, 1788
Debates (excerpts)

[Mr. WYTHE.]

He then proceeded to the consideration of the question of previous or subsequent *amendments*. The critical situation of America, the extreme danger of dissolving the Union, rendered it necessary to adopt the latter alternative. He saw no danger from this. It appeared to him, most clearly, that any amendments which might be thought necessary would be easily obtained *after ratification*, in the manner proposed by the Constitution, as amendments were desired by all the states, and had already been proposed by the several states. He then *proposed* that the committee *should ratify the Constitution*, and that whatsoever amendments might be deemed necessary should be recommended to the consideration of the Congress which should first assemble under the Constitution, to be acted upon according to the mode prescribed therein.

[The resolution of ratification proposed by Mr. Wythe was then read by the clerk; which see hereafter in the report of the committee to the Convention.][1]

Mr. HENRY, after observing that the proposal of ratification was premature, and that the importance of the subject required the most mature deliberation, proceeded thus:—

The honorable member must forgive me for declaring my dissent from it; because, if I understand it rightly, it admits that the new system is defective, and most capitally; for, immediately after the proposed ratification, there comes a declaration that the paper before you is not intended to violate any of these three great rights—the liberty of religion, liberty of the press, and the trial by jury. What is the inference when you enumerate the rights which you are to enjoy? That those not enumerated are relinquished. There are only three things to be retained—religion, freedom of the press, and jury trial. Will not the ratification carry every thing, without excepting these three things? Will not all the world pronounce that we intended to give up all the rest? Every thing it speaks of, by way of rights, is comprised in these things. Your subsequent amendments only go to these three amendments.

I feel myself distressed, because the necessity of securing our *personal rights* seems not to have pervaded the minds of men; for many other valuable things are omitted:—for instance, general warrants, by which an officer may search suspected places, without evidence of his crime, ought to be prohibited. As these are admitted, any man may be seized, any property may be taken, in the most arbitrary manner, without any evidence or reason. Every thing the most sacred may be searched and ransacked by the strong hand of power. We have infinitely more reason to dread general warrants here than they have in England, because there, if a person be confined, liberty may be quickly obtained by the writ of *habeas corpus*. But here a man living many hundred miles from the judges may get in prison before he can get that writ.

Another most fatal omission is with respect to standing armies. In our bill of rights of Virginia, they are said be to dangerous to liberty, and it tells you that the proper defence of a free state consists in militia; and so I might go on to ten or eleven things of immense consequence secured in your bill of rights, concerning which that proposal is silent. Is that the language of the bill of rights in England? Is it the language of the American bill of rights, that these three rights, and these only, are valuable? Is it the language of men going into a new government? Is it not necessary to speak of those things before you go into a compact? . . .

With respect to subsequent amendments, proposed by the worthy member, I am distressed when I hear the expression. It is a new one altogether, and such a one as stands against every idea of fortitude and manliness in the states, or any one else. Evils admitted in order to be removed subsequently, and tyranny submitted to in order to be excluded by a subsequent alteration, are things totally new to me. But I am sure the gentleman meant nothing but to amuse the committee. I know his candor. His proposal is an idea dreadful to me. I ask, does experience warrant such a thing from the beginning of the world to this day? Do you enter into a compact first, and afterwards settle the terms of the government? It is admitted by every one that this is a compact.

Although the Confederation be lost, it is a compact, constitution, or something of that nature. I confess I never heard of such an idea before. It is most abhorrent to my mind. You endanger the tranquillity of your country, you stab its repose, if you accept this government unaltered. How are you to allay animosities?—for such there are, great and fatal.

He flatters me, and tells me that I could influence the people, and reconcile them to it. Sir, their sentiments are as firm and steady as they are patriotic. Were I to ask them to apostatize from their native religion, they would despise me. They are not to be shaken in their opinions with respect to the propriety of preserving their rights. You never can persuade them that it is necessary to relinquish them. Were

I to attempt to persuade them to abandon their patriotic sentiments, I should look on myself as the most infamous of men.

I believe it to be a fact that the great body of yeomanry are in decided opposition to it. I may say with confidence that, for nineteen counties adjacent to each other, nine tenths of the people are conscientiously opposed to it. I may be mistaken, but I give you it as my opinion; and my opinion is founded on personal knowledge, in some measure, and other good authority. I have not hunted *popularity* by declaiming to injure this government. Though public fame might say so, it was not owing to me that this flame of opposition has been kindled and spread. These men never will part with their political opinions. If they should see their political happiness secured to the latest posterity, then, indeed, they may agree to it. Subsequent amendments will not do for men of this cast. Do you consult the Union in proposing them? You may ammuse them as long as you please, but they will never like it. You have not solid reality—the hearts and hands of the men who are to be governed. . . .

If you will, in the language of freemen, stipulate that there are rights which no man under heaven can take from you, you shall have me going along with you; not otherwise.

[Here Mr. Henry informed the committee that he had a resolution prepared, to refer a declaration of rights, with certain amendments to the most exceptionable parts of the Constitution, to the other states in the confederacy, for their consideration, previous to its ratification. The clerk then read the resolution, the declaration of rights, and amendments which were nearly the same as those ultimately proposed by the Convention; which see at the conclusion.][2]

Mr. HENRY then resumed the subject. I have thus candidly submitted to you, Mr. Chairman, and this committee, what occurred to me as proper amendments to the Constitution, and a declaration of rights containing those fundamental, unalienable privileges, which I conceive to be essential to liberty and happiness. I believe that, on a review of these amendments, it will still be found that the arm of power will be sufficiently strong for national purposes, when these restrictions shall be a part of the government. I believe no gentleman who opposes me in sentiments will be able to discover that any one feature of a strong government is altered; and at the same time your unalienable rights are secured by them. The government unaltered may be terrible to America, but can never be loved till it be amended. You find all the resources of the continent may be drawn to a point. In danger, *the President* may concentre to a point every effort of the continent. If the government be constructed to satisfy the people, and remove their apprehensions, the wealth and the strength of the continent will go where public utility shall direct. This government, with these restrictions, will be a strong government, united with the privileges of the people. In my weak judgment, a government is strong when it applies to the most important end of all government—the rights and privileges of the people. In the honorable member's proposal, jury trial, the press and religion, and other essential rights, are not to be given up. Other essential rights—what are they? The world will say that you intended to give them up. When you go into an enumeration of your rights, and stop that enumeration, the inevitable conclusion is, that what is omitted is intended to be surrendered.[3]

[Mr. DAWSON.]

That sacred palladium of liberty, the freedom of the press, (the influence of which is so great that it is the opinion of the ablest writers that no country can remain long in slavery where it is unrestrained,) has not been expressed; nor are the liberties of the people ascertained and protected by any declaration of rights; that inestimable privilege, (the most important which freemen can enjoy,) the trial by jury in all civil cases, has not been guarded by the system;—and while they have been inattentive to these all-important considerations, they have made provision for the introduction of standing armies in time of peace. These, sir, ever have been used as the grand machines to suppress the liberties of the people, and will ever awaken the jealousy of republicans, so long as liberty is dear, and tyranny odious, to mankind.[4]

1 See "Virginia Convention," June 25, 1788, p. 454, for the form of ratification.

2 See "Virginia Convention," June 27, 1788, p. 456, for the Declaration of Rights and other Amendments.

3 *Debates*, III, pp. 587-594.

4 *Ibid.*, pp. 610-611.

Virginia Convention June 25, 1788

Debates (excerpts)

[Mr. ZACHARIAH JOHNSON.]

I shall consider several other parts which are much objected to. As to the regulation of the militia, I feel myself doubly interested. Having a numerous offspring, I am careful to prevent the establishment of any regulation that might entail oppression on them. When gentlemen of high abilities in this house, and whom I respect, tell us that the militia may be subjected to martial law in time of peace, and whensoever Congress may please, I am much astonished. My judgment is astray, and exceedingly undiscerning, if it can bear such a construction. Congress has only the power of arming and disciplining them. The states have the appointment of the officers, and the authority of training the militia, according to the discipline prescribed by Congress. When called into the actual service of the United States, they shall be subject to the marching orders of the United States. Then, and then only, it ought to be so. When we advert to the plain and obvious meaning of the words, without twisting and torturing their natural signification, we must be satisfied that this objection is groundless. Had we adverted to the true meaning, and not gone farther, we should not be here to-day, but should have come to a decision long ago. We are also told that religion is not secured; that religious tests are not required. You will find that the exclusion of tests will strongly tend to establish religious freedom. If tests were required, and if the Church of England, or any other, were established, I might be excluded from any office under the government, because my conscience might not permit me to take the test required. The diversity of opinions and variety of sects in the United States have justly been reckoned a great security with respect to religious liberty. The difficulty of establishing a uniformity of religion in this country is immense. The extent of the country is very great. The multiplicity of sects is very great likewise. The people are not to be disarmed of their weapons. They are left in full possession of them. The government is administered by the representatives of the people voluntarily and freely chosen.

Under these circumstances, should any one attempt to establish their own system, in prejudice of the rest, they would be universally detested and opposed, and easily frustrated. This is a principle which secures religious liberty most firmly. The government will depend on the assistance of the people in the day of distress. This is the case in all governments. It never was otherwise. . . .

I shall make a comparison, to illustrate my observations, between the state and the general government. In our state government, so much admired by the worthy gentleman over the way, though there are 1700 militia in some counties, and but 150 in others, yet every county sends two members, to assist in legislating for the whole community. There is disproportion between the respectable county of Augusta, which I have the honor to represent, and the circumscribed, narrow county of Warwick. Will any gentleman tell us that this is a more equal representation than is fixed in the Constitution, whereby 30,000 are to send one representative, in whatever place they may reside? . . .

Mr. President now resumed the chair, and Mr. Matthews reported, that the committee had, according to order, again had the proposed Constitution under their consideration, and had gone through the same, and come to several resolutions thereupon, which he read in his place, and afterwards delivered in at the clerk's table, where the same were again read, and are as followeth:—

"Whereas the powers granted under the proposed Constitution are the gift of the people, and every power not granted thereby remains with them, and at their will,—no right, therefore, of any denomination, can be cancelled, abridged, restrained, or modified, by the Congress, by the Senate or House of Representatives, acting in any capacity, by the President, or any department or officer of the United States, except in those instances in which power is given by the Constitution for those purposes; and, among other essential rights, liberty of conscience and of the press cannot be cancelled, abridged, restrained, or modified, by any authority of the United States.

"And whereas any imperfections, which may exist in the said Constitution, ought rather to be examined in the mode prescribed therein for obtaining amendments, than by a delay, with a hope of obtaining previous amendments, to bring the Union into danger,—

"*Resolved,* That it is the opinion of this committee, that the said Constitution be ratified. But in order to relieve the apprehensions of those who may be solicitous for amendments,—

"*Resolved,* That it is the opinion of this committee, that whatsoever amendments may be deemed necessary, be recommended to the consideration of the Congress which shall first assemble under the said Constitution, to be acted upon according to the mode prescribed in the 5th article thereof."

The 1st resolution being read a second time, a motion was made, and the question being put, to amend the same by substituting, in lieu of the said resolution and its *preamble,* the following resolution,—

"*Resolved,* That, previous to the ratification of the new Constitution of government recommended by the late federal Convention, a declaration of rights, asserting, and securing from encroachment, the great principles of civil and religious liberty, and the unalienable rights of the people, together with amendments to the most exceptionable parts of the said Constitution of government, ought to be referred by this Convention to the other states in the American confederacy for their consideration,"—

It passed in the negative—ayes, 80; noes, 88. . . .

And then, the *main question* being put that the Convention do *agree* with the committee in the said 1st resolution, it was resolved in the *affirmative*—ayes, 89; noes, 79. . . .

The 2d resolution being then read a second time, a motion was made, and, the qestion being put to amend the same by striking out the preamble thereto, it was resolved in the affirmative.

And then, the main question being put, that the Convention do agree with the committee in the 2d resolution so amended, it was resolved in the affirmative.

On motion, *Ordered,* That a committee be appointed to prepare and report a form of ratification pursuant to the first resolution; and that Governor Randolph, Mr. Nicholas, Mr. Madison, Mr. Marshall, and Mr. Corbin, compose the said committee.

On motion, *Ordered,* that a committee be appointed to prepare and report such amendments as by them shall be deemed necessary, to be recommended, pursuant to the second resolution; and that the Hon. George Wythe, Mr. Harrison, Mr. Matthews, Mr. Henry, Governor Randolph, Mr. George Mason, Mr. Nicholas, Mr. Grayson, Mr. Madison, Mr. Tyler, Mr. John Marshall, Mr. Monroe, Mr. Ronald, Mr. Bland, Mr. John Blair, and Mr. Simms, compose the said committee.

His excellency, Governor RANDOLPH, reported, from the committee appointed, according to order, *a form of ratification,* which was read and agreed to by the Convention, in the words following:
VIRGINIA, TO WIT:

"We, the delegates of the people of Virginia, duly elected in pursuance of a recommendation from the General Assembly, and now met in Convention, having fully and freely investigated and discussed the proceedings of the federal Convention, and being prepared, as well as the most mature deliberation hath enabled us, to decide thereon, Do, in the name and in behalf of the people of Virginia, declare and make known, that the powers granted under the Constitution, being derived from the people of the United States, be resumed by them whensoever the same shall be perverted to their unjury or oppression, and that every power, *not granted thereby, remains with them, and at their will;* that, therefore, no right, of any denomination, can be cancelled, abridged, restrained, or modified, by the Congress, by the Senate or House of Representatives, acting in any capacity, by the President, or any department or officer of the United States, except in those instances in which power is given by the Constitution for those purposes; and that, among other essential rights, the liberty of conscience and of the press cannot be cancelled, abridged, restrained, or modified, by any authority of the United States.

"With these impressions, with a solemn appeal to the Searcher of hearts for the purity of our intentions, and under the conviction that whatsoever imperfections may exist in the Constitution ought rather to be examined in the mode prescribed therein, than to bring the Union into danger by delay, with a hope, of obtaining amendments previous to the ratification,—

"We, the said delegates, in the name and behalf of the people of Virginia, do, by these presents, *assent to* and *ratify the Constitution,* recommended on the seventeenth day of September, one thousand seven hundred and eighty-seven, by the federal Convention, for the government of the United States; hereby announcing to all those whom it may concern, that the said Constitution is binding upon the said people, according to an authentic copy hereunto annexed[."]

Debates, III, pp. 645-646, 652-656.

A Delegate Who Has Catched Cold June 25, 1788
Newspaper Article: Richmond *Virginia Independent Chronicle* (excerpt)

As we may propose and recommend amendments to Congress, and to avoid the reproach of making them either partial, or numerous and contradictory, let us be satisfied with presenting a bill of rights of the people of America, in such general terms; so expressive, so clear, and at the same time so short, as never to require either comment or interpretations. Nothing that has been yet laid before the public is satisfactory; may it be written by men conscious of its necessity and of the dignity of their subject, that it may be an honorable introduction to the constitution of the United States of America.

Our rights as a free people, were fixed and fully expressed at the head of our different constitutions. Why then should they not be placed also at the head of this general foederation, which may supercede these? Some states, it is true, have no bill of rights, but it is an additional reason for inserting one in the foederal; since as Americans their rights are the same, and making a greater concession of those rights to the foederal body, that precaution is at present indispensible: it is not possible now to be ignorant of our rights, and to contest them, being so near of the glorious epoch of their acquisition; but it will be attempted in the future time and the history of all ages announce that they will no more be spared, than those of all the people who have preceded us, if we have no more care for their preservation.

In considering all peoples existing on the earth and the nations who have preceded them, it is not possible to sustain, that they have been reduced in that state of servitude with their full consent and by the free concession of their rights! but in contrary it is certain, that they have lost them imperceptibly and have been subjugated by gradation, or by a violent revolution occasioned by anarchy; if they had well known, established and maintained their prerogatives and their government, they should have prevented those two extremes, who have constrained them to creep under a chief, and becoming conqueror, or conquered people.

Those rights characterise the man, essentially the true republican, the citizen of this continent; their enumeration, in head of the new constitution, can inspire and conserve the affection for the native country, they will be the first lesson of the young citizens becoming men, to sustain the dignity of their being; in fine the publication of those prerogatives has drawn us the envy and the admiration of all Europe, and being the preamble of our foederal constitution, they may be the means of a considerable emigration to this continent.

Storing, V, pp. 272-273.

New York Journal June 26, 1788

Extract of a Letter from Boston.

There seems to be a general infatuation here among the *magi;* the vulgar have caught it, so that there is no reasoning with them on the subject, though of the greatest importance. Ask any of them, *high* or *low,* whether they have any ill apprehensions from the adoption of the new system, they answer, without hesitation, *yes;* but they say, Congress will *certainly* make the proposed alterations. Ministers, lawyers, and merchants made a large proportion of our Convention, so that it is no great wonder that the people *at large* are so many of them *deluded;* yet, I believe, could the voice of the people in general be taken, a very large majority would be found in opposition to the proposed plan. Of this I am convinced from the frequent conversations I have had with farmers, etc.

DHFFE, I, pp. 443-444.

Virginia Convention June 27, 1788

Proposed Declaration of Rights and other Amendments

Mr. WYTHE reported, from the committee appointed, such *amendments* to the proposed Constitution of government for the United States as were by them deemed necessary to be recommended to the consideration of the Congress which shall first assemble under the said

Constitution, to be acted upon according to the mode prescribed in the 5th article thereof; and he read the same in his place, and afterwards delivered them in at the clerk's table, where the same were again read, and are as follows;—

"That there be a declaration or bill of rights asserting, and securing from encroachment, the essential and unalienable rights of the people, in some such manner as the following:—

"1st. That there are certain natural rights, of which men, when they form a social compact, cannot deprive or divest their posterity; among which are the enjoyment of life and liberty, with the means of acquiring, possessing, and protecting property, and pursuing and obtaining happiness and safety.

"2d. That all power is naturally invested in, and consequently derived from, the people; that magistrates therefore are their *trustees* and *agents*, at all times amenable to them.

"3d. That government ought to be instituted for the common benefit, protection, and security of the people; and that the doctrine of non-resistance against arbitrary power and oppression is absurd, slavish, and destructive to the good and happiness of mankind.

"4th. That no man or set of men are entitled to separate or exclusive public emoluments or privileges from the community, but in consideration of public services, which not being descendible, neither ought the offices of magistrate, legislator, or judge, or any other public office, to be hereditary.

"5th. That the legislative, executive, and judicial powers of government should be separate and distinct; and, that the members of the two first may be restrained from oppression by feeling and participating the public burdens, they should, at fixed periods, be reduced to a private station, return into the mass of the people, and the vacancies be supplied by certain and regular elections, in which all or any part of the former members to be eligible or ineligible, as the rules of the Constitution of government, and the laws, shall direct.

"6th. That the elections of representatives in the legislature ought to be free and frequent, and all men having sufficient evidence of permanent common interest with, and attachment to, the community, ought to have the right of suffrage; and no aid, charge, tax, or fee, can be set, rated, or levied, upon the people without their own consent, or that of their representatives, so elected; nor can they be bound by any law to which they have not, in like manner, assented, for the public good.

"7th. That all power of suspending laws, or the execution of laws, by any authority, without the consent of the representatives of the people in the legislature, is injurious to their rights, and ought not to be exercised.

"8th. That, in all criminal and capital prosecutions, a man hath a right to demand the cause and nature of his accusation, to be confronted with the accusers and witnesses, to call for evidence, and be allowed counsel in his favor, and to a fair and speedy trial by an impartial jury of his vicinage, without whose unanimous consent he cannot be found guilty, (except in the government of the land and naval forces;) nor can he be compelled to give evidence against himself.

"9th. That no freeman ought to be taken, imprisoned, or disseized of his freehold, liberties, privileges, or franchises, or outlawed, or exiled, or in any manner destroyed, or deprived of his life, liberty, or property, but by the law of the land.

"10th. That every freeman restrained of his liberty is entitled to a remedy, to inquire into the lawfulness thereof, and to remove the same, if unlawful, and that such remedy ought not to be denied nor delayed.

"11th. That, in controversies respecting property, and in suits between man and man, the ancient trial by jury is one of the greatest securities to the rights of the people, and to remain sacred and inviolable.

"12th. That every freeman ought to find a certain remedy, by recourse to the laws, for all injuries and wrongs he may receive in his person, property, or character. He ought to obtain right and justice freely, without sale, completely and without denial, promptly and without delay, and that all establishments or regulations contravening these rights are oppressive and unjust.

"13th. That excessive bail ought not to be required, nor excessive fines imposed, nor cruel and unusual punishments inflicted.

"14th. That every freeman has a right to be secure from all unreasonable searches and seizures of his person, his papers, and property; all warrants, therefore, to search suspected places, or seize any freeman, his papers, or property, without information on oath (or affirmation of a person religiously scrupulous of taking an oath) of legal and sufficient cause, are grievous and oppressive; and all general warrants to search suspected places, or to apprehend any suspected person, without specially naming or describing the place or person, are dangerous, and ought not to be granted.

"15th. That the people have a right peaceably to assemble together to consult for the common good, or to instruct their representatives; and that every freeman has a right to petition or apply to the legislature for redress of grievances.

"16th. That the people have a right to freedom of speech, and of writing and publishing their sentiments; that freedom of the press is one of the greatest bulwarks of liberty, and ought not to be violated.

"17th. That the people have a right to keep and bear arms; that a well-regulated militia, composed of the body of the people trained to arms, is the proper, natural, and safe defence of a free state; that standing armies, in time of peace, are dangerous to liberty, and therefore ought to be avoided, as far as the circumstances and protection of the community will admit; and that, in all cases, the military should be under strict subordination to, and governed by, the civil power.

"18th. That no soldier in time of peace ought to be quartered in any house without the consent of the owner, and in time of war in such manner only as the laws direct.

"19th. That any person religiously scrupulous of bearing arms ought to be exempted, upon payment of an equivalent to employ another to bear arms in his stead.

"20th. That religion, or the duty which we owe to our Creator, and the manner of discharging it, can be directed only by reason and conviction, not by force or violence; and therefore all men have an equal, natural, and unalienable right to the free exercise of religion, according to the dictates of conscience, and that no particular religious sect or society ought to be favored or established, by law, in preference to others.

AMENDMENTS TO THE CONSTITUTION

"1st. That each state in the Union shall respectively retain every power, jurisdiction, and right, which is not by this Constitution delegated to the Congress of the United States, or to the departments of the federal government.

"2d. That there shall be one representative for every thirty thousand according to the enumeration or census mentioned in the Constitution until the whole number of representatives amounts to two hundred; after which, that number shall be continued or increased, as Congress shall direct, upon the principles fixed in the Constitution, by apportioning the representatives of each state to some greater number of the people, from time to time, as population increases.

"3d. When the Congress shall lay direct taxes or excises, they shall immediately inform the executive power of each state, of the quota of such state, according to the census herein directed, which is proposed to be thereby raised; and if the legislature of any state shall pass a law which shall be effectual for raising such quota at the time required by Congress, the taxes and excises laid by Congress shall not be collected in such state.

"4th. That the members of the Senate and House of Representatives shall be ineligible to, and incapable of holding, any civil office under the authority of the United States, during the time for which they shall respectively be elected.

"5th. That the journals of the proceedings of the Senate and House of Representatives shall be published at least once in every year, except such parts thereof, relating to treaties, alliances, or military operations, as, in their judgment require secrecy.

"6th. That a regular statement and account of receipts and expenditures of public money shall be published at least once a year.

"7th. That no commercial treaty shall be ratified without the concurrence of two thirds of the whole number of the members of the Senate; And no treaty ceding, contracting, restraining, or suspending, the territorial rights or claims of the United States, or any of them, or their, or any of their, rights or claims of fishing in the American seas, or navigating the American rivers, shall be made, but in cases of the most urgent and extreme necessity; nor shall any such treaty be ratified without the concurrence of three fourths of the whole number of the members of both houses respectively.

"8th. That no navigation law, or law regulating commerce, shall be passed without the consent of two thirds of the members present, in both houses.

"9th. That no standing army, or regular troops, shall be raised, or kept up, in time of peace, without the consent of two thirds of the members present, in both houses.

"10th. That no soldier shall be enlisted for any longer term than four years, except in time of war, and then for no longer term than the continuance of the war.

"11th. That each state respectively shall have the power to provide for organizing, arming, and disciplining its own militia, whensoever Congress shall omit or neglect to provide for the same. That the militia shall not be subject to martial law, except when in actual service, in time of war, invasion, or rebellion; and when not in the actual service of the United States, shall be subject only to such fines, penalties, and punishments, as shall be directed or inflicted by the laws of its own state.

"12th. That the exclusive power of legislation given to Congress over the federal town and its adjacent district, and other places, purchased or to be purchased by Congress of any of the states, shall extend only to such regulations as respect the police and good government thereof.

"13th. That no person shall be capable of being President of the United States for more than eight years in any term of sixteen years.

"14th. That the judicial power of the United States shall be vested in one Supreme Court, and in such courts of admiralty as Congress may from time to time ordain and establish in any of the different states. The judicial power shall extend to all cases in law and equity arising under treaties made, or which shall be made, under the authority of the United States; to all cases affecting ambassadors, other foreign ministers, and consuls; to all cases of admiralty and maritime jurisdiction; to controversies to which the United States shall be a party; to controversies between two or more states, and between parties claiming lands under the grants of different states. In all cases affecting ambassadors, other foreign ministers, and consuls, and those in which a state shall be a party, the Supreme Court shall have original jurisdiction; in all other cases before mentioned, the Supreme Court shall have appellate jurisdiction, as to matters of law only, except in cases of equity, and of admiralty, and maritime jurisdiction, in which the Supreme Court shall have appellate jurisdiction both as to law and fact, with such exceptions and under such regulations as the Congress shall make: but the judicial power of the United States shall extend to no case where the cause of action shall have originated before the ratification of this Constitution, except in disputes between states about their territory, disputes between persons claiming lands under the grants of different states, and suits for debts due to the United States.

"15th. That, in criminal prosecutions, no man shall be restrained in the exercise of the usual and accustomed right of challenging or excepting to the jury.

"16th. That Congress shall not alter, modify, or interfere in the times, places, or manner of holding elections for senators and representatives, or either of them, except when the legislature of any state shall neglect, refuse, or be disabled, by invasion or rebellion, to prescribe the same.

"17th. That those clauses which declare that Congress shall not exercise certain powers, be not interpreted, in any manner whatsoever, to extend the power of Congress; but that they be construed either as making exceptions to the specified powers where this shall be the case, or otherwise, as inserted merely for greater caution.

"18th. That the laws ascertaining the compensation of senators and representatives for their services, be postponed, in their operation, until after the election of representatives immediately succeeding the passing thereof; that excepted which shall first be passed on the subject.

"19th. That some tribunal other than the Senate be provided for trying impeachments of senators.

"20th. That the salary of a judge shall not be increased or diminished during his continuance in office, otherwise than by general regulations of salary, which may take place on a revision of the subject at stated periods of not less than seven years, to commence from the time such salaries shall be first ascertained by Congress.

And the convention do, in the name and behalf of the people of this commonwealth, enjoin it upon their representatives in Congress to exert all their influence, and use all reasonable and legal methods, to obtain a ratification of the foregoing alterations and provisions, in the manner provided by the 5th article of the said Constitution; and, in all congressional laws to be passed in the mean time, to conform to the spirit of these amendments, as far as the said Constitution will admit.

And so much of the said amendments as is contained in the first twenty articles, constituting the bill of rights, being read again, *Resolved,* That this Convention doth concur therein.

The other amendments to the said proposed Constitution, contained in twenty-one articles, being then again read, a motion was made, and the question being put,—to amend the same by striking out the third article, containing these words,—

"When Congress shall lay direct taxes . . ."

It passed in the negative—ayes, 65; noes, 85. . . .

On motion, *Ordered,* That the foregoing amendments be fairly engrossed upon parchment, signed by the president of this Convention, and by him transmitted, together with the ratification of the federal Constitution, to the United States in Congress assembled.

On motion, *Ordered,* That a fair, engrossed copy of the ratifiction of the federal Constitution, with the subsequent amendments this day agreed to, signed by the president, and attested by the secretary of this Convention, be transmitted by the president, in the name of the Convention, to the executive or legislature of each state in the Union.

Ordered, That the secretary do cause the journal of the proceedings of this Convention to be fairly entered into a well-bound book, and, after being signed by the president, and attested by the secretary, that he deposit the same in the archives of the privy council, or council of state.

On motion, *Ordered,* That the printer to this Convention do strike, forthwith, fifty copies of the ratification and subsequent amendments of the federal Constitution, for the use of each county in the commonwealth. . . .

And then the Convention adjourned, "*sine die.*"

Debates, III, pp. 657-661.

Philadelphia *Independent Gazetteer* June 27, 1788
A Correspondent (excerpt)

And why should the *many* resign their birthrights into the hands of the *few*, the *well born*, as Mr. Adams calls them? Perhaps some of them, like *Ceasar*, are panting for an *Imperial Crown*.

But let those violent men [Federalists] now be told that Americans are entitled to an honest and faithful government; to a government of *laws* not *men;* to the freedom of the Press and Trial by Jury of the vicinage, which the new constitution has totally annihilated; and, therefore, it cannot, must not, be established:—nothing, concludes our correspondent, but a DECLARATION OF RIGHTS in favor of the people at large, founded on the principles of equal liberty, can possibly save this devoted country from internal commotion—For

"The birthright we hold
Shall never be sold.
But sacred maintain to our graves;
Nay, 'ere we comply,
We'll gallantly die,
For we must not, nor will not be slaves."

DHRC, II Mfm. Pa., p. 2844.

New York Convention June 27, 1788
Debates (excerpt)

[Mr. WILLIAMS.]

Sir, I yesterday expressed my fears that this clause [Article 1, section 8] would tend to annihilate the state governments. I also observed, that the powers granted by it were indefinite, since the Congress are authorized to provide for the common defence and general welfare, and to pass all laws necessary for the attainment of those important objects. The legislature is the highest power in a government. Whatever they judge necessary for the proper administration of the powers lodged in them, they may execute without any check or impediment. Now, if the Congress should judge it a proper provision, for the common defence and general welfare, that the state governments should be essentially destroyed, what, in the name of common sense, will prevent them? Are they not constitutionally authorized to pass such laws? Are not the terms, *common defence and general welfare,* indefinite, undefinable terms? What checks have the state governments against such encroachments?

Why, they appoint the senators once in six years. So do the electors of Germany appoint their emperor. And what restraint have they against tyranny in their head? Do they rely on any thing but arms, the *ultima ratio?* And to this most undesirable point must the states recur, in order to secure their rights. But have they the means necessary for the purpose? Are they not deprived of the command of the purse and the sword of their citizens? Is not the power, both over taxation and the militia, wrested from their hands by this Constitution, and bestowed upon the general government? Yes, sir, it is. But it may be said (I expect to be answered) that the states have concurrent jurisdiction with Congress, as to taxation. I answer, that the Constitution does not say so: it is a mere opinion, a mere construction, a thing of too much uncertainty to risk the rights of the states upon, which I have heard, with peculiar pleasure, an honorable gentleman from New York acknowledge to be of great utility to the people. The constitution grants the power of taxation to Congress, but is silent with regard to the power in the states. If it is inferred from this that it is not taken away from the states, we may, sir, with equal justice, deduce, from the positive establishment of the trial by jury in criminal cases, that it is annihilated in civil. Ingenious men may assign ingenious reasons for opposite constructions of the same clause. They may heap refinement upon refinement, and subtilty upon subtilty, until they construe away every republican principle, every right sacred and dear to man. I am, sir, for certainty in the establishment of a constitution which is not only to operate upon us, but upon millions yet unborn. I would wish that little or no latitude might be left to the sophistical constructions of men who may be interested in betraying the rights of the people, and elevating themselves upon the ruins of liberty. Sir, it is an object of infinitely too much importance to be committed to the sport of caprice, and the construction of interested men. If we adopt this Constitution, it is impossible, absolutely impossible, to know what we give up, and what we retain. I wish that this may, as far forth as possible, be ascertained; and, for this purpose, it is absolutely necessary that this clause should be amended.

Debates, II, pp. 338-339.

New York Convention July 2, 1788
Debates (excerpts)

[Mr. TREDWELL.]

Sir, I introduce these observations to combat certain principles which have been daily and confidently advanced by the favorers of the present Constitution, and which appear to me totally indefensible. The first and grand leading, or rather misleading, principle in this debate, and on which the advocates for this system of unrestricted powers must chiefly depend for its support, is that, in forming a constitution, whatever powers are not expressly granted or given the government, are reserved to the people, or that rulers cannot exercise any powers but those expressly given to them by the Constitution. Let me ask the gentlemen who advanced this principle, whether the commission of a Roman dictator, which was in these few words—to take care that the state received no harm—does not come up fully to their ideas of an energetic government; or whether an invitation from the people to one or more to come and rule over them, would not clothe the rulers with sufficient powers. If so, the principle they advance is a false one. Besides, the absurdity of this principle will evidently appear, when we consider the great variety of objects to which the powers of the government must necessarily extend, and that an express enumeration of them all would probably fill as many volumes as Pool's Synopsis of the Critics. But we may reason with sufficient certainty on the subject, from the sense of all the public bodies in the United States, who had occasion to form new constitutions. They have uniformly acted upon a direct and contrary principle, not only in forming the state constitutions and the old Confederation, but also in forming this very Constitution, for we do not find in every state constitution express resolutions made in favor of the people; and it is clear that the late Convention at Philadelphia, whatever might have been the sentiments of some of its members, did not adopt the principle, for they have made certain reservations and restrictions, which, upon that principle, would have been totally useless and unnecessary; and can it be supposed that that wise body, whose only apology for the great ambiguity of many parts of that perfomance, and the total omission of some things which many esteem essential to the security of liberty, was a great desire of brevity, should so far sacrifice that great and important object, as to insert a number of provisions which they esteemed totally useless? Why is it said that the privilege of the writ of *habeas corpus* shall not be suspended, unless, in cases of rebellion or invasion, the public safety may require it? What clause in the constitution, except this very clause itself, gives the general government a power to deprive us of that great privilege, so sacredly secured to us by our state constitutions? Why is it provided that no bill of attainder shall be passed, or that no title of nobility shall be granted? Are there any clauses in the Constitution extending the powers of the general government to these objects? Some gentlemen say that these, though not necessary, were inserted for greater caution. I could have wished, sir, that a greater caution had been used to secure to us the freedom of election, a sufficient and responsible representation, the freedom of the press, and the trial by jury both in civil and criminal cases.

These, sir, are the rocks on which the Constitution should have rested; no other foundation can any man lay, which will secure the sacred temple of freedom against the power of the great, the undermining arts of ambition, and the blasts of profane scoffers—for such there will be in every age—who will tell us that all religion is in vain; that is, that our political creeds, which have been handed down to us by our forefathers as sacredly as our Bibles, and for which more of them have suffered martyrdom than for the creed of the apostles, are all nonsense; who will tell us that paper constitutions are mere paper, and that parchment is but parchment, that jealousy of our rulers is a sin, &c. I could have wished also that sufficient caution had been used to secure to us our religious liberties, and to have prevented the general government from tyrannizing over our consciences by a religious establishment—a tyranny of all others most dreadful, and which will assuredly be exercised whenever it shall be thought necessary for the promotion and support of their political measures. It is ardently to be wished, sir, that these and other invaluable rights of freemen had been as cautiously secured as some of the paltry local interests of some of the individual states. But it appears to me, that, in forming this Constitution, we have run into the same error which the lawyers and Pharisees of old were charged with; that is, while we have secured the tithes of mint, anise, and cumin, we have neglected the weightier matters of the law, judgment, mercy, and faith. Have we not neglected to secure to ourselves the weighty matters of judgment or justice, by empowering the general government to establish one supreme, and as many inferior, courts as they please, whose proceedings they have a right to fix and regulate as they shall think fit, so that we are ingnorant whether they shall be according to the common, civil, the Jewish, or Turkish law? What better provisions have we made for mercy, when a man, for ignorantly passing a counterfeit continental note, or bill of credit, is liable to be dragged to a distant county, two or three hundred miles from home, deprived of the support and assistance of friends, to be tried by a strange jury, ignorant of his character, ignorant of the character of the witnesses, unable to contradict any false testimony brought against him by their own knowledge of facts, and with whom the prisoner being unaquainted, he must be deprived totally of the benefit of his challenge? and besides all that, he may be exposed to lose his life, merely for want of property to carry his witnesses to such a distance;

and after all this solemn farce and mockery of a trial by jury, if they should acquit him, it will require more ingenuity than I am master of, to show that he does not hold his life at the will and pleasure of the Supreme Court, to which an appeal lies, and consequently depend on the tender mercies, perhaps, of the wicked, (for judges may be wicked;) and what those tender mercies are, I need not tell you. You may read them in the history of the Star Chamber Court in England, and in the court of Philip, and in your Bible.

This brings me to the third and last weighty matter mentioned in the text—to wit, faith. The word *faith* may, with great propriety, be applied to the articles of our political creed, which, it is absolutely necessary, should be kept pure and uncorrupted, if we mean to preserve the liberties of our country and the inestimable blessings of a free government. And, sir, I cannot but be seriously alarmed on this head, as has frequently been the case during the present discussion,—gentlemen of the first rank and abilities openly opposing some of the most essential principles of freedom, and endeavoring, by the most ingenious sophistry, and the still more powerful weapons of ridicule, to shake or corrupt our faith therein. Have we not been told that, if government is but properly organized, and the powers were suitably distributed among the several members, it is unnecessary to provide any other security against the abuse of its power? that power thus distributed needs no restriction? Is this a whig principle? Does not every constitution on the continent contradict this position? Why are we told that all restrictions of power are found to be inconvenient? that we ought to put unlimited confidence in our rulers? that it is not our duty to be jealous of men in power? Have we not had an idea thrown out of establishing an aristrocracy in our own country,—a government than which none is more dreadful and oppressive?

What the design of the preacher on this occasion is, I will not attempt to determine; far be it from me to judge men's hearts: but thus much I can say, from the best authority, they are deceitful above all things, and desperately wicked. But whatever be the design of the preachers, the tendency of their doctrines is clear; they tend to corrupt our political faith, to take us off our guard, and lull to sleep that jealousy which, we are told by all writers,—and it is proved by all experience,—is essentially necessary for the preservation of freedom. But notwithstanding the strongest assertions that there are no wolves in our country, if we see their footsteps in every public path, we should be very credulous and unwise to trust our flocks abroad, and to believe that those who advised us to do it were very anxious for their preservation.

In this Constitution, sir, we have departed widely from the principles and political faith of '76, when the spirit of liberty ran high, and danger put a curb on ambition. Here we find no security for the rights of individuals, no security for the existence of our state governments; here is no bill of rights, no proper restriction of power; our lives, our property, and our consciences, are left wholly at the mercy of the legislature, and the powers of the judiciary may be extended to any degree short of almighty. Sir, in this Constitution we have not only neglected,—we have done worse,—we have openly violated, our faith,—that is, our public faith. . . .

There are other objections to this Constitution, which are weighty and unanswerable; but they have been so clearly stated, and so fully debated, in the course of this discussion, that it would be an unjustifiable intrusion on the patience of the house to repeat them. I shall therefore content myself with a few observations on the general plan and tendency. We are told that this is a federal government. I think, sir, there is as much propriety in the name, as in that which its advocates assume, and no more; it is, in my idea as complete a consolidation as the government of this state, in which legislative powers, to a certain extent, are exercised by the several towns and corporations. The sole difference between a state government under this Constitution, and a corporation under a state government, is, that a state being more extensive than a town, its powers are likewise proportionably extended, but neither of them enjoys the least share of sovereignty; for, let me ask, what is a state government? What sovereignty, what power is left to it, when the control of every source of revenue, and the total command of the militia, are given to the general government? That power which can command both the property and the persons of the community, is the sovereign, and the sole sovereign. The idea of two distinct sovereigns in the same country, separately *possessed* of sovereign and supreme power, in the same matters at the same time, is as supreme an absurdity, as that two distinct separate circles can be bounded exactly by the same circumference. This, sir, is demonstration; and from it I draw one corollary, which, I think, clearly follows, although it is in favor of the Constitution, to wit—that at least that clause in which Congress guaranties to the several states a republican *form* of government, speaks honestly; that is, that no more is intended by it than is expressed; and I think it is clear that, whilst the mere form is secured, the substance—to wit, the whole power and sovereignty of our state governments, and with them the liberties of the country—is swallowed up by the general government; for it is well worth observing, that, while our state governments are held up to us as the great and sufficient security of our rights and privileges, it is carefully provided that they shall be disarmed of all power, and made totally dependent on the bounty of Congress for their support, and conseqeuntly for their exsitence,—so that we have scarce a single right secured under either.

Is this, sir, a government for freemen? Are we thus to be duped out of our liberties? I hope, sir, our affairs have not yet arrived to that long-wished-for pitch of confusion, that we are under the necessity of accepting such a system of government as this.

I cannot, sir, express my feelings on a late occasion, when I consider with what unspeakable indignation the spirit of a Montgomery, a Herkimer, a Paris, &c., must have fired at insults offered to their memories on this floor, and that not by a stanger, but by a brother, when their names, which will ever be dear to freemen, were profanely called upon as an inducement for us to surrender up those rights and privileges, in the defence of which they so gallantly fought, and so gloriously died. We are called upon at this time (I think it is an early day) to make an unconditional surrender of those rights which ought to be dearer to us than our lives.

But I hope, sir, that the memory of these patriot heroes will teach us a duty on this occasion. If we follow their example, we are sure not to err. We ought, sir to consider—and it is a most solemn consideration—that we may now give away, by a vote, what it may cost the dying groans of thousands to recover; that we may now surrender, with a little ink, what it may cost seas of blood to regain; the dagger of Ambition is now pointed at the fair bosom of Liberty, and, to deepen and complete the tragedy, we, her sons, are called upon to give the fatal thrust. Shall we not recoil at such a deed, and all cry out with one voice, "Hands off!" What distraction has seized us? Is she not our mother, and if the frenzy of any should persist in the parricidal attempt, shall we not instantly interpose, and receive the fatal point into our own bosom? A moment's hesitation would ever prove us to be bastards, not sons. The liberties of the country are a deposit, a trust, in the hands of individuals; they are an entailed estate, which the possessors have no right to dispose of; they belong to our children, and to them we are bound to transmit them as a representative body. The trust becomes tenfold more sacred in our hands, especially as it was committed to us with the fullest confidence in our sentiments, integrity, and firmness. If we should betray that trust on this occasion, I fear (think there is reason to fear) that it will teach a lesson dangerous to liberty—to wit, that no confidence is to be placed in men.

But why, sir, must we be guilty of this breach of trust? Why surrender up the dear-bought liberties of our country? Because we are told, in very positive terms, that nothing short of this will satisfy, or can be accepted by, our future rulers? Is it possible that we can be at a loss for an answer to such declarations as these? Can we not, ought we not to speak like freemen on this occasion, (this perhaps may be the last time when we shall dare to do it,) and declare, in as positive terms, that we cannot, we will not, give up our liberties; that, if we cannot be admitted into the Union as freemen, we will not come in as slaves? This I fully believe to be the language of my constituents; this is the language of my conscience; and, though I may not dare longer to make it the language of my tongue, yet I trust it will ever be the language of my heart. If we act with coolness, firmness, and decision, on this occasion, I have the fullest confidence that the God who has so lately delivered us out of the paw of the lion and the bear, will also deliver us from this Goliath, this uncircumcised Philistine. This government is founded in sin, and reared up in iniquity; the foundations are laid in a most sinful breach of public trust, and the top-stone is a most iniquitous breach of public faith; and I fear, if it goes into operation, we shall be justly punished with the total extinction of our civil liberties. We are invited, in this instance, to become partakers in other men's sins; if we do, we must likewise be content to take our share in the punishment.

Debates, II, pp. 398-405.

Philadelphia *Pennsylvania Gazette* July 2, 1788
(excerpt)

The citizens of America, says a correspondent, have in the course of thirteen years acquired more immortal honour, more unfading laurels, and more well-won fame, than all the heroes of antiquity, and conquerors of modern times. They are the only people who ever assumed a military character, and without discipline or experience, and surrounded by a thousand difficulties, ventured to oppose the well-trained bands, the hardy veterans of a powerful tyrant. Nor did they oppose them in vain—Engaged in one common cause, inspired with the same generous flame, they were successful in asserting their own rights, the rights of their country, of their posterity, and of mankind—They burst the bands of tyranny, and taught others how to become free. They provided a last retreat for liberty, and "an asylum for the oppressed of all nations." But they have shewn themselves no less wise in council, than brave in the field: They have calmly and deliberately formed and adopted a plan of government, which (when we consider the heterogeneous materials afforded for its construction by thirteen distinct states, almost all of them different in their interests, manners and customs) may justly be called a masterpiece of human wisdom. While the revolutions of government, in other countries, have given rise to most horrid scenes of carnage and bloodshed, America alone can boast of a constitution framed by her chosen sages, and, after the most mature deliberation, approved of by the people at large, without tumultuous disorders or intestine broils, notwithstanding the industrious efforts of a few desperate incendiaries.

DHFFE, IV, pp. 40-41.

Cumberland County (Pennsylvania) Meeting July 3, 1788
Proceedings and Circular Letter

PROCEEDINGS[1]

At Mr. James Bell's, in a meeting of delegates from the several townships of the beforesaid county, Benjn. Blyth in the chair, called for the purpose of advising the most eligible mode of obtaining such amendments in the Constitution, proposed by the General Convention for the government of these United States, as may remove the causes of jealousy and fears of a tyrannical aristocracy the foundation of which appears to be in many parts of the said Constitution, and secure and hand down to posterity the blessings of dear bought freedom; and thereby most cordially engage each state and every citizen, not only for wrath but conscience sake, to aid and support the officers of the government in the due execution thereof; after seriously considering the importance of the subject and the duty of citizens, have come to the following resolution, viz.,

Resolved, that it is the opinion of this meeting that the Constitution proposed by the General convention of the United States is in several parts destructive of that liberty for which so much blood and treasure has been spent, and subversive of the several state governments by which the rights and liberties of the people have been guarded and secured; that it is the indispensable duty of every citizen to use all lawful means to obtain such amendments in the said Constitution or take such measures as shall be necessary for the security of religion and liberty.

Resolved, that it is the opinion of the members of this meeting that it will be expedient to collect as soon and as accurately as possible the sentiments of the citizens of this state touching such amendments and such mode of obtaining them as shall be to said citizens most agreeable.

Resolved, that in order to effectuate the foregoing resolution, that a circular letter be written, signed by the chairman and addressed to such societies in each county as have already been formed for political purposes, and to such as shall be formed in any county where none is yet formed or to such persons as shall be judged fit, requesting that measures be taken to call a meeting of delegates from each township within the respective counties to meet as soon as conveniently may be and take into consideration the necessity and propriety of amending the Constitution of the United States. And for that purpose to appoint delegates to meet in a general conference of the state at Harrisburg on the third day of September 1788, then and there to consider and devise a plan the most likely to succeed in obtaining the desired amendments. Resolved by the meeting, that five members be chosen by the county Cumberland or three out of the five to represent said county in the conference to be held at Harrisburg the 3d day of September 1788; the place and time aforesaid.

CIRCULAR LETTER[2]

That ten states have already, unexpectedly, without amending, ratified the Constitution proposed for the government of these United States, cannot have escaped the notice of the friends of liberty. That the way is prepared for the full organization of the government, with all its foreseen and consequent dangers, is too evident, and unless prudent steps be taken to combine the friends to amendments in some place in which they may confidently draw together and exert their power in unison, the liberty of the American citizens must lie at the discretion of congress, and most probably, posterity become slaves to the officers of government.

The means adopted and proposed by a meeting of delegates from the townships of this county for preventing the alleged evils and also the calamities of a civil war, are, as may be observed in perusing the proceedings of the said meeting herewith transmitted to request such persons as shall be judged fit within the counties respectively, to use their influence to obtain a meeting of delegates from each township to take into consideration, the necessity of amending the Constitution of these United States, and for that purpose to nominate and appoint a number of delegates to represent the county, in a general conference of the counties of this commonwealth, to be held at Harrisburg on the third day of September next, then and there, to devise such amendments, and such mode of obtaining them, as in the wisdom of the delegates shall be judged most satisfactory and expedient.

A law will no doubt be soon enacted by the General Assembly for electing eight members to represent this state in the new Congress. It will therefore be expedient to have proper persons put in nomination by the delegates in conference, being the most likely method of directing the views of the electors to the same object and of obtaining the desired end.

The society of which you are chairman is requested to call a meeting agreeably to the foregoing designs, and lay before the delegates the proceeding of this county, to the intent that the state may unite in casting off the yoke of slavery and once more establish union and liberty.

1 DHFFE, I, p. 239. Reprinted in DHRC, II Mfm. Pa., pp. 2658-2660.
2 DHFFE, I, p.240.

New York Convention July 7, 1788
Proceedings (excerpts)

Mr. LANSING then read, and presented to the committee, a *bill of rights* to be prefixed to the Constitution.[1]

DECLARATION of RIGHTS

THAT all freemen have essential rights, of which they cannot by any contract deprive or divest their posterity, among which are the enjoyment of life and liberty.

That all power is origninally vested in, and consequently derived from the people; and that government is instituted for their common benefit, protection and security.

That in all cases in which a man may be subjected to a capital or infamous punishment, no one ought to be put to his trial unless on an indictment by a grand jury; and that in all capital or criminal prosecutions, the accused hath a right to demand the cause and nature of his accusation; to be confronted with his accusers and witnesses; to produce testimony and have council in his defence: and to a fair, public and speedy trial by an impartial jury of the county in which the crime was committed, without whose unanimous consent he ought not to be found guilty (except in the government of the land and naval forces, in time of actual war, invasion or rebellion;) nor ought he to be compelled to give evidence against himself.

That no freeman ought to be taken, imprisoned or disseized of his freehold, or be exiled or deprived of his privileges, franchises, life, liberty or property, but by the law of the land.

That no person ought to be put in jeopardy of life or limb, or otherwise punished twice for one and the same offence, unless upon impeachment.

That every freeman restrained in his liberty is entilted to an enquiry into the lawfulness of such restraint, without denial or delay, and to a removal thereof, if unlawful.

That in all controversies respecting property, and in all suits between man and man, the ancient trial of facts by jury is one of the greatest securities of the rights of a free people, and ought to remain sacred and inviolated for ever.

That excessive bail ought not to be required nor excessive fines imposed, nor cruel nor unusual punishments inflicted.

That every freeman has a right to be secure from all unreasonable searches and seizures of his person, his papers and his property; and that therefore all warrants to search suspected places, or to seize any freeman, his papers or property, without information upon oath (or affirmation of a person religiously scrupulous of taking oaths) of sufficient cause, are grievous and oppressive; and all general warrants to search suspected places, or to apprehend any suspected person, without specially naming or describing the place or person, are dangerous and oppresive, and ought not to be granted.

That people have a right peaceably to assemble together, to consult for their common good, or to instruct their representatives; and that every freeman has a right to petition or apply to the legislature for redress of grievances.

That the freedom of the press ought not to be violated or restrained.

That the militia should always be kept well organized, armed and disciplined, and include, according to past usages of the states, all the men capable of bearing arms, and that no regulations tending to render the general militia useless and defenceless, by establishing select corps of militia, or distinct bodies of military men, not having permanent interests and attachments to the community, ought to be made;[2] and that the militia ought not to be subject to martial law, except in time of war, invasion or rebellion; and that in all cases the military should be under strict subordination to and governed by the civil power.

That no soldier in time of peace ought to be quartered in any house without the consent of the owner, and in time of war only by the civil magistrate, in such manner as the laws may direct.

That any person religiously scrupulous of bearing arms, ought to be exempted therefrom upon payment of an equivalent.

That the free and peaceable exercise and enjoyment of religious profession and worship, is a natural and unalienable right, and ought never to be abridged or violated.[3]

1 *Debates*, II, p. 410.

2 Up to this point, this article of the proposed Declaration of Rights is adapted almost verbatim from *An Additional Number of Letters from the Federal Farmer to the Republican*, Letter XVIII. The "Federal Farmer" intended this to "secure a genuine" militia of the people and "guard against a select militia." He considered this as essential to "general liberty and the duration of a free and mild government." See "Federal Farmer," May, 1788, p. 354 at note 8.

3 Philadelphia *Independent Gazetteer*, July 16, 1788, p. 3.

Pennsylvania *Carlisle Gazette* July 9, 1788
Description of Antifederalist 4th of July Celebration.

On Friday the 4th July instant, being the anniversary of the 13th year of American independence, a number of the respectable inhabitants of the borough of Carlisle, and adjacent townships, together with the volunteer company of militia, and detachments from other militia companies, convened in the public square of this borough. After attending a discourse suitable on the occasion, delivered by the Reverend Dr. Robert Davidson, they marched from thence to the Meetinghouse Springs, to celebrate the day, when a genteel repast was prepared; after partaking of which, the following toasts were drank, each accompanied with a discharge of musketry.

1. May the thirteen American states forever remain united, on real federal principles.
2. May such amendments be speedily framed, and unanimously adopted, as may render the proposed Constitution for the United States truly democratical.
3. May agriculture, manufactures and commerce forever flourish in America.
4. May America continue the asylum of civil and religous liberty to the latest ages.
5. May the example of America, in the late Revolution, be copied by every enslaved people throughout the world.
6. May the fate of Great Britain in the late contest be the fate of all tyrants.
7. The memory of the heroes who fell in support of American independence.
8. The virtuous minority of the late Convention of Pennsylvania.
9. The minorities of our sister state conventions.
10. The constitution of Pennsylvania.

11. Our friends in Europe.

12. May the designs of such as endeavor to enslave the citizens of America prove abortive.

13. May America remain forever free from tyranny, anarchy, and consolidation.

After which they marched in order to the public square, from thence to the commons south of town, where after firing three volleys they repaired again to the public square, and dispersed. We are happy to announce to the public, that joy, peace, and good order pervaded the whole scene.

DHFFE, I, pp. 242-243.

New York Convention July 10, 1788
Proceedings (excerpts)

Mr. LANSING submitted a plan of amendments, on a new arrangement, and with material alterations. They are divided into three—1st, explanatory; 2d, conditional; 3d, recommendatory.[1]

When the Convention met on thursday Mr Lansing came forward with the amendments, arranged in three classes—explanatory, conditional and recommendatory. The bill of rights is among those that are explanatory.[2] The following are conditional. 1. That there shall be no standing army in time of peace, without the consent of two thirds of Congress: 2. That there shall be no direct taxes, nor excises on american manufactures. 3. That the militia shall not be ordered out of the state, except by the previous consent of the executive thereof; nor then for a longer time than six weeks, without the consent of the state Legislature; & 4thly. That there shall be no interference in the elections, unless when a state shall neglect or refuse to provide for the same.[3]

1 *Debates*, II, p. 410.
2 See "New York Convention," July 7, 1788, p. 473, for the bill of rights provisions.
3 BRDH, II, pp. 921-922.

New York Convention July 19, 1788
Debates (excerpts)

SATURDAY, *July* 19, 1788; when Mr. LANSING moved to postpone the several propositions before the house, in order to take into consideration a draft of a conditional ratification, with a *bill of rights* prefixed, and amendments subjoined. Debates arose on the motion, and it was carried. The committee then proceeded to consider separately the amendments proposed in this plan of ratification.[1]

1—Articles of the Bill of rights read.[2]

Jay, why not insert all the unallianible rights & these three selected.

Harper—if the Gent. wants any added—wishes he would suggest them.

Jay—if there was any necessity to mention them or have a Bill o[f] rights at all—he would do it.

Lansing—if the line was to be drawn between the Jurisdictions of the state & Genl. Govt. so that the power of the Genl. Govt. shall not extend to individuals this may be proper.

Jay—Govt. must have power to restrain—as the clause stands it is so inaccurate, he cannot vote for it—if the committee will agree to amend it he will agree.

the question put on the sentiment, or principle of the first article—Unanimous.

Jones—wishes the whole of the bill of rights should be committed to select com[mitt]ee.

2 Article read—agreed.

3 Do.

Jay—you cannot make a right—you can only declare what a right is.

Govr. [Clinton]—it is a political right.

Smith—the source is—this is a right which we all enjoy before this New Govt. should be adopted.

Tredwell—we insert it before here because, we cannot find it in the new constn.

Ham[ilton]—the spirit of the 2d. clause he agrees with—& will agree in—the Jury of the vicinage in some cases cannot be good—however will not insist on it—a Jury—is security sufficient—without saying of the Country—Moves to strike out "of the country."

Govr. [Clinton]—wishes it should stand.

Jones—Do.—who shall designate whence the Jury should be called—the prosecutor may lay his venue where he pleases.

Ham[ilton]—this could be done by the Legislature—in Engd. this has been done—as in the rebellion in Scotland.

questn. on the 3d. article—agreed.

4th—article—Do.

5—Do.—

6—Do.—

7—Do.—

Ham[ilton]—this article he thinks includes more than Gent. intend—in the Admiralty—& Chancery there is no Jury—"to remain" may be intended to qu[a]llify this—in some states—the trial by Jury in both the Courts above mentd. are in use.

On treaties & Laws of Nations—the supreme Judicial ought to be the last resort.

difficultied to remedy this—so as to agree to it—& not clash with other states.

Yates—the object, to secure the trial by Jury in all cases where they heretofore were of use—this ought to be held inviolate—and was intended to provide agt. the Genl. Govt. taking this right away.

Jay—the word "accustomed" will not take the objectn. away—because in admiralty cases an appeal should lay—where the whole matter should go up.

Ham[ilton]—Comn. Law—will not do in Connecticut—neither accustomed.

Govr. [Clinton]—we wish to get the Idea.

Jones—we can get over the difficulty & yet retain an Idea—if we say—according to the com. Law will do—The Court of Exchequer in Engd.—proceed in both with, in some cases—in other without a Jury—In Jersey & Connecticut—since the revolution, have directed the Court of Admiralty must be by Jury.

Lansing—we only want the sentiment.

Smith—the committee will word it.

7th article as amended—agreed to.

8—Bail—or unusual excessive punisht.—agreed.

9—every freeman secure agt. Genl. Warrants—agreed.

10—rights of the people to consult and petition—agreed.

11—the freedom of the press—agreed.

12—Militia—according to ancient Usage.

Ham[ilton]—opposed to the leading idea of this clause—it tends to render the Militia of no service—in swisd. & england—there must be select corps—the whole people can never be fully trained if we agree to this, you oblidge the govt. to have a standing army.

does not depend on regulations on paper for safety—but on the Genius of our country—was mistaken as to the clause.

objects only to the words "past usages."

Govr [Clinton]—the object is to keep the Militia well armed, the Comee will word it.

Jones—will mention one difficulty "past usages" are indeffinate—as there have been in our state many alterations.

12—Art—agreed.

13—standing armies—agreed.

14—quartering soldiers-agreed.

15—exemption of Quakers.

Jay—if it means Quakers—is content—but if it will comprehend every person who in time of War will declare they are con[sc]ientious about it—he will not.

Smith—this must be defined by the law—as there are more sects than one which are scrupulous.

Jones—it may opperate ill—those who are scrupulous to bear arms—object to pay the fine.

Ham[ilton]—is willing those who are now scrupulous may be exempted—but does not wish to encourage this idea.

the sence of the committee on this clause taken—to be transposed—agreed.

16—liberty of conscience—agreed.[3]

1 *Debates*, II, pp. 411-412.

2 See "New York Convention," July 7, 1788, p. 473 for the bill of rights articles referred to.

3 BRDH, II, pp. 896-898. This excerpt of notes taken in the New York Convention is from the Gilbert Livingston Papers (New York Public Library.)

Abraham Clark (New York) July 23, 1788

Letter: To Thomas Sinnickson (excerpt)

As to my sentiments respecting the New System of Government, altho' you do not ask, yet, as I find by your Letter it will be Acceptable, I think it not amiss to give them.—They have at no time been concealed.—I never liked the System in all its parts. I considered it from the first, more a Consolidated government than a federal, a government too expensive, and unnecessarily Oppressive in its Opperation; Creating a Judiciary undefined and unbounded.—with all these imperfections about it, I nevertheless wished it to go to the States from Congress just as it did, without any Censure or Commendation, hoping that in Case of a general Adoption, the Wisdom of the States would soon amend it in the exceptionable parts; Strong fears however remained upon my mind untill I found the Custom of Recommending amendments with the Adoptions began to prevail.—This set my mind at ease. It became clear in my opinion from the Oppositions, and the general concurrence in proposing amendmts that the present plan must undergo some alterations to make it more agreable to the minds of the great Numbers who dislike it in its present form. The Amendments I wish are not numerous;—Many proposed by the different Conventions appear of but little Consequence, yet some are important and must be Acceded to if ever the Government sits easy. From this State of the matter, wishing amendmts, as I do, you will readily conclude I anxiously wish every State may come into the adoption in order to effect a measure with me so desireable; in which case, from the general current of amendments proposed, we shall retain all the important parts in which New Jersey is interested.

DHFFE, III, p. 117.

New York Convention July 26, 1788
Ratification of the United States Constitution

We, the delegates of the people of the state of New York, duly elected and met in Convention, having maturely considered the Constitution for the United States of America, agreed to on the 17th day of September, in the year 1787, by the convention then assembled at Philadelphia, in the common wealth of Pennsylvania, (a copy whereof precedes these presents,) and having also seriously and deliberately considered the present situation of the United States,—Do declare and make known,—

That all power is originally vested in, and consequently derived from, the people, and that government is instituted by them for their common interest, protection, and security.

That the enjoyment of life, liberty, and the pursuit of happiness, are essential rights, which every government ought to respect and preserve.

That the powers of government may be reassumed by the people whensoever it shall become necessary to their happiness; that every power, jurisdiction, and right, which is not by the said Constitution clearly delegated to the Congress of the United States, or the departments of the government thereof, remains to the people of the several states, or to their respective state governments, to whom they may have granted the same; and that those clauses in the said Constitution, which declare that Congress shall not have or exercise certain powers, do not imply that Congress is entitled to any powers not given by the said Constitution; but such clauses are to be construed either as exceptions to certain specified powers, or as inserted merely for greater caution.

That the people have an equal, natural, and unalienable right freely and peaceably to exercise their religion, according to the dictates of conscience; and that no religious sect or society ought to be favored or established by law in preference to others.

That the people have a right to keep and bear arms; that a well-regulated militia, including the body of the people *capable of bearing arms,* is the proper, natural, and safe defence of a free state.

That standing armies, in time of peace, are dangerous to liberty, and ought not to be kept up, except in cases of necessity; and that at all times the military should be under strict subordination to the civil power.

That, in time of peace, no soldier ought to be quartered in any house without the consent of the owner, and in time of war only by the civil magistrate, in such manner as the laws may direct.

That no person ought to be taken, imprisoned, or disseized of his free hold, or be exiled, or deprived of his privileges, franchises, life, liberty, or property, but by due process of law.

That no person ought to be put twice in jeopardy of life or limb, for one and the same offence; nor, unless in case of impeachment, be punished more than once for the same offence.

That every person restrained of his liberty is entitled to an inquiry into the lawfulness of such restraint, and to a removal thereof if unlawful; and that such inquiry or removal ought not to be denied or delayed, except when, on account of public danger, the Congress shall suspend the privilege of the writ of *habeas corpus.*

That excessive bail ought not to be required, nor excessive fines imposed, nor cruel or unusual punishments inflicted.

That (except in the government of the land and naval forces, and of the militia when in actual service, and in cases of impeachment) a presentment or indictment by a grand jury ought to be observed as a necessary preliminary to the trial of all crimes cognizable by the judiciary of the United States; and such trial should be speedy, public, and by an impartial jury of the county where the crime was committed; and that no person can be found guilty without the unanimous consent of such jury. But in cases of crimes not committed within any county of any of the United States, and in cases of crimes committed within any county in which a general insurrection may prevail, or which may be in the possession of a foreign enemy, the inquiry and trial may be in such county as the Congress shall by law direct; which county, in the two cases last mentioned, should be as near as conveniently may be to that county in which the crime may have been committed;—and that, in all criminal prosecutions, the accused ought to be informed of the cause and nature of his accusation, to be confronted with his accusers and the witnesses against him, to have the means of producing his witnesses, and the assistance of counsel for his defence; and should not be compelled to give evidence against himself.

That the trial by jury, in the extent that it obtains by the common law of England, is one of the greatest securities to the rights of a free people, and ought to remain inviolate.

That every freeman has a right to be secure from all unreasonable searches and seizures of his person, his papers, or his property; and therefore, that all warrants to search suspected places, or seize any freeman, his papers, or property, without information, upon oath or affirmation, of sufficient cause, are grievous and oppressive, and that all general warrants (or such in which the place or person suspected are not particularly designated) are dangerous, and ought not to be granted.

That the people have a right peaceably to assemble together to consult for their common good, or to instruct their representatives, and that every person has a right to petition or apply to the legislature for redress of grievances.

That the freedom of the press ought not to be violated or restrained.

That there should be, once in four years, an election of the President and Vice-President, so that no officer, who may be appointed by the Congress to act as President, in case of the removal, death, resignation, or inability, of the President and Vice-President, can in any case continue to set beyond the termination of the period for which the last President and Vice-President were elected.

That nothing contained in the said Constitution is to be construed to prevent the legislature of any state from passing laws at its discretion, from time to time, to divide such state into convenient districts, and to apportion its representatives to and amongst such districts.

That the prohibition contained in the said Constitution, against *ex post facto* laws extends only to laws concerning crimes.

That all appeals in causes determinable according to the course of the common law, ought to be by writ of error, and not otherwise.

That the judicial power of the United States, in cases in which a state may be a party, does not extend to criminal prosecutions, or to authorize any suit by any person against a state.

That the judicial power of the United States, as to contoversies between citizens of the same state, claiming lands under grants from different states, is not to be construed to extend to any other controversies between them, except those which relate to such lands, so claimed, under grants of different states.

That the jurisdiction of the Supreme Court of the United States, or of any other court to be instituted by the Congress, is not in any case to be increased, enlarged, or extended, by any faction, collusion, or mere suggestion; and that no treaty is to be construed so to operate as to alter the Constitution of any state.

Under these impressions, and declaring that the rights aforesaid cannot be abridged or violated, and that the explanations aforesaid are consistent with the said Constitution, and in confidence that the amendments which shall have been proposed to the said Constitution will recieve an early and mature consideration,—We, the said delegates, in the name and in the behalf of the people of the state of New York, do, by these presents, assent to and ratify the said Constitution. In full confidence, nevertheless, that, until a convention shall be called and convened for proposing amendments to the said Constitution, the militia of this state will not be continued in service out of this state for a longer term than six weeks, without the consent of the legislature thereof; that the Congress will not make or alter any regulation in this state, respecting the times, places, and manner, of holding elections for senators or representatives, unless the legislature of this state shall neglect or refuse to make laws or regulations for the purpose, or from any circumstance be incapable of making the same; and that, in those cases, such power will only be exercised until the legislature of this state shall make provision in the premises; that no excise will be imposed on any article of the growth, production, or manufacture of the United States, or any of them, within this state, ardent spirits excepted; and the Congress will not lay direct taxes within this state, but when the moneys arising from the impost and excise shall be insufficient for the public exigencies, nor then, until Congress shall first have made a requisition upon this state to assess, levy, and pay, the amount of such requisition, made agreeably to the census fixed in the said Constitution, in such way and manner, as the legislature of this state shall judge best; but that in such case, if the state shall neglect or refuse to pay its proportion, pursuant to such requisition, then the Congress may assess and levy this state's proportion, together with interest, at the rate of six per centum per annum, from the time at which the same was required to be paid.

Done in Convention, at Poughkeepsie, in the county of Duchess, in the state of New York, the 26th day of July, in the year of our Lord 1788.

By order of the Convention. GOE. CLINTON, *President.*
Attested. John M'Kesson, A.B. Banker, *Secretaries.*

And the Convention do, in the name and behalf of the people of the state of New York, enjoin it upon their representatives in Congress to exert all their influence, and use all reasonable means, to obtain a ratification of the following amendments to the said Constitution, in the manner prescribed therein; and in all laws to be passed by the Congress, in the mean time, to conform to the spirit of the said amendments, as far as the Constitution will admit.

That there shall be one representative for every thirty thousand inhabitants, according to the enumeration or census mentioned in the Constitution, until the whole number of representatives amounts to two hundred, after which that number shall be continued or increased, but not diminished, as the Congress shall direct, and according to such ratio as the Congress shall fix, in conformity to the rule prescribed for the apportionment of representatives and direct taxes.

That the Congress do not impose any excise on any article (ardent spirits excepted) of the growth, production, or manufacture of the United States, or any of them.

That Congress do not lay direct taxes but when the moneys arising from the impost and excise shall be insufficient for the public exigencies, nor then, until Congress shall first have made a requisition upon the states to assess, levy, and pay, their respective proportions of such requisition, agreeably to the census fixed in the said Constitution, in such way and manner as the legislatures of the respective states shall judge best; and in such case, if any state shall neglect or refuse to pay its proportion, pursuant to such requisition, then Congress may assess and levy such state's proportion, together with interest at the rate of six per centum per annum, from the time of payment prescribed in such requisition.

That the Congress shall not make or alter any regulation, in any state, respecting the times, places, and manner, of holding elections for senators and representatives, unless the legislature of such state shall neglect or refuse to make laws or regulations for the purpose or from any circumstance be incapable of making the same, and then only until the legislature of such state shall make provision in the premises; provided, that Congress may prescribe the time for the election of representatives.

That no persons, except natural-born citizens, or such as were citizens on or before the 4th of July, 1776, or such as held commissions under the United States during the war, and have at any time since the 4th day of July, 1776, become citizens of one or other of the United States, and who shall be freeholders, shall be eligible to the places of President, Vice-President, or members of either house of the Congress of the United States.

That the Congress do not grant monopolies, or erect any company with exclusive advantages of commerce.

That no standing army or regular troops shall be raised, or kept up, in time of peace, without the consent of two thirds of the senators and representatives present in each house.

That no money be borrowed on the credit of the United States without the assent of two thirds of the senators and representatives present in each house.

That the Congress shall not declare war without the concurrence of two thirds of the senators and representatives present in each house.

That the privilege of the *habeas corpus* shall not, by any law, be suspended for a longer term than six months, or until twenty days after the meeting of the Congress next following the passing the act for such suspension.

That the right of Congress to exercise exclusive legislation over such district, not exceeding ten miles square, as may, by cession of a particular state, and the acceptance of Congress, become the seat of government of the United States, shall not be so exercised as to exempt the inhabitants of such district from paying the like taxes, imposts, duties, and excises, as shall be imposed on the other inhabitants of the state in which such district may be; and that no person shall be privileged within the said district from arrest for crimes committed, or debts contracted, out of the said district.

That the right of exclusive legislation, with respect to such places as may be purchased for the erection of forts, magazines, arsenals, dock-yards, and other needful buildings, shall not authorize the Congress to make any law to prevent the laws of the states, respectively, in which they may be, from extending to such places in all civil and criminal matters, except as to such persons as shall be in the service of the United States; nor to them with respect to crimes committed without such places.

That the compensation for the senators and representatives be ascertained by standing laws; and that no alteration of the existing rate of compensation shall operate for the benefit of the representatives until after a subsequent election shall have been had.

That the Journals of the Congress shall be published at least once a year, with the exception of such parts, relating to treaties or military operations, as, in the judgment of either house, shall require secrecy; and that both houses of Congress shall always keep their doors open during their sessions, unless the business may, in their opinion, require secrecy. That the yeas and nays shall be entered on the Journals whenever two members in either house may require it.

That no capitation tax shall ever be laid by Congress.

That no person be eligible as a senator for more than six years in any term of twelve years; and that the legislatures of the respective states may recall their senators, or either of them, and elect others in their stead, to serve the remainder of the time for which the senators so recalled were appointed.

That no senator or representative shall, during the time for which he was elected, be appointed to any office under the authority of the United States.

That the authority given to the executives of the states to fill up the vacancies of senators be abolished, and that such vacancies be filled by the respective legislatures.

That the power of Congress to pass uniform laws concerning bankruptcy shall only extend to merchants and other traders; and the states, respectively, may pass laws for the relief of other insolvent debtors.

That no person shall be eligible to the office of President of the United States a third time.

That the executive shall not grant pardons for treason, unless with the consent of the Congress; but may, at his discretion, grant reprieves to persons convicted of treason, until their cases can be laid before the Congress.

That the President, or person exercising his powers for the time being, shall not command an army in the field in person, without the previous desire of the Congress.

That all letters patent, commissions, pardons, writs, and processes of the United States, shall run in the name of *the people of the United States,* and be tested in the name of the President of the United States, or the person exercising his powers for the time being, or the first judge of the court out of which the same shall issue, as the case may be.

That the Congress shall not constitute, ordain, or establish, any tribunals of inferior courts, with any other than appellate jurisdiction, except such as may be necessary for the trial of cases of admiralty and maritime jurisdiction, and for the trial of piracies and felonies committed on the high seas; and in all other cases to which the judicial power of the United States extends, and in which the Supreme Court of the United States has not original jurisdiction, the causes shall be heard, tried, and determined, in some one of the state courts, with the right of appeal to the Supreme Court of the United States, or other proper tribunal, to be established for that purpose by the Congress, with such exceptions, and under such regulations, as the Congress shall make.

That the court for the trial of impeachments shall consist of the Senate, the judges of the Supreme Court of the United States, and the first or senior judge, for the time being, of the highest court of general and ordinary common-law jurisdiction in each state; that the Congress shall, by standing laws, designate the courts in the respective states, answering this description, and, in states having no courts exactly answering this description, shall designate some other court, preferring such, if any there be, whose judge or judges may hold their places during good behavior; provided, that no more than one judge, other than judges of the Supreme Court of the United States, shall come from one state.

That the Congress be authorized to pass laws for compensating the judges for such services, and for compelling their attendance; and that a majority, at least, of the said judges shall be requisite to constitute the said court. That no person impeached shall sit as a member thereof; that each member shall, previous to the entering upon any trial, take an oath or affirmation honestly and impartially to hear and determine the cause; and that a majority of the members present shall be necessary to a conviction.

That persons aggrieved by any judgment, sentence, or decree, of the Supreme Court of the United States, in any cause in which that court has original jurisdiction, with such exceptions, and under such regulations, as the Congress shall make concerning the same, shall, upon application, have a commission, to be issued by the President of the United States to such men learned in the law as he shall nominate, and by and with the advice and consent of the Senate appoint, not less than seven, authorizing such commissioners, or any seven or more of them, to correct the errors in such judgment, or to review such sentence and decree, as the case may be, and to do justice to the parties in the premises.

That no judge of the Supreme Court of the United States shall hold any other office under the United States, or any of them.

That the judicial power of the United States shall extend to no controversies respecting land, unless it relate to claims of territory or jurisdiction between states, and individuals under the grants of different states.

That the militia of any state shall not be compelled to serve without the limits of the state, for a longer term than six weeks, without the consent of the legislature thereof.

That the words *without the consent of the Congress,* in the seventh clause of the ninth section of the first article of the Constitution, be expunged.

That the senators and representatives, and all executive and judicial officers of the United States, shall be bound by oath or affirmation not to infringe or violate the constitutions or rights of the respective states.

That the legislatures of the respective states may make provision, by law, that the electors of the election districts, to be by them appointed, shall choose a citizen of the United States, who shall have been an inhabitant of such district for the term of one year immediately preceding the time of his election, for one of the representatives of such state.

Done in Convention, at Poughkeepsie, in the county of Duchess, in the state of New York, the 26th day of July, in the year of our Lord 1788.

By order of the Convention. GEO. CLINTON, *President.*

Attested. John M'Kesson, Ab. B. Banker, *Secretaries.*

Debates, I, pp. 327-331.

New York Convention July 28, 1788

Circular Letter of the Convention

THE CIRCULAR LETTER,

from the Convention of the State of New York to the governors of the several states in the Union.

Poughkeepsie, July 28, 1788

Sir:

We, the members of the Convention of this state, have deliberately and maturely considered the Constitution proposed for the United States. Several articles in it appear so exceptionable to a majority of us that nothing but the fullest confidence of obtaining a revision of them by a general convention, and an invincible reluctance to separating from our sister states, could have prevailed upon a sufficient number to ratify it, without stipulating for previous amendments. We all unite in opinion, that such a revision will be necessary to recommend it to the approbation and support of a numerous body of our constituents.

We observe that amendments have been proposed, and are anxiously desired, by several of the states, as well as by this; and we think it of great importance that effectual measures be immediately taken for calling a convention, to meet at a period not far remote; for we are convinced that the apprehensions and discontents, which those articles occasion, cannot be removed or allayed, unless an act to provide for it be among the first that shall be passed by the new Congress.

As it is essential that an application for the purpose should be made to them by two thirds of the states, we earnestly exhort and request the legislature of your state to take the earliest opportunity of making it. We are persuaded that a similar one will be made by our legislature, at their next session; and we ardently wish and desire that the other states may concur in adopting and promoting the measure.

It cannot be necessary to observe, that no government, however constructed, can operate well, unless it possesses the confidence and good-will of the great body of the people; and as we desire nothing more than that the amendments proposed by this or other states be submitted to the consideration and decision of a general convention, we flatter ourselves that motives of mutual affection and conciliation will conspire with the obvious dictates of sound policy to induce even such of the states as may be content with every article in the Constitution to gratify the reasonable desires of that numerous class of American citizens who are anxious to obtain amendments of some of them.

Our amendments will manifest that none of them originated in local views, as they are such, as if acceded to, must equally affect every state in the Union. Our attachment to our sister states, and the confidence we repose in them, cannot be more forcibly demonstrated than by acceding to a government which many of us think very imperfect, and devolving the power of determining whether that government shall be rendered perpetual in its present form, or altered agreeably to our wishes, and a minority of the states with whom we unite.

We request the favor of your excellency to lay this letter before the legislature of your state; and we are persuaded that your regard for our national harmony and good government will induce you to promote a measure which we are unanimous in thinking very conducive to those interesting objects.

We have the honor to be, with the highest respect, your excellency's most obedient servants.

By the unanimous order of the Convention,

GEORGE CLINTON,
President

Debates, II, pp. 413-414. Reprinted in DHFFE, I, pp. 44-45.

North Carolina Convention July 28, 1788
Debates (excerpts)

[Mr. SPENCER.]
Our rights are not guarded. There is no declaration of rights, to secure to every member of the society those unalienable rights which ought not to be given up to any government. Such a bill of rights would be a check upon men in power. Instead of such a bill of rights, this Constitution has a clause which may warrant encroachments on the power of the respective state legislatures. I know it is said that what is not given up to the United States will be retained by the individual states. I know it ought to be so, and should be so understood; but, sir, it is not *declared* to be so. In the Confederation it is expressly declared that all rights and powers, of any kind whatever, of the several states, which are not given up to the United States, are expressly and absolutely retained, to be enjoyed by the states. There ought to be a bill of rights, in order that those in power may not step over the boundary between the powers of government and the rights of the people, which they may do when there is nothing to prevent them. They may do so without a bill of rights; notice will not be readily taken of the encroachments of rulers, and they may go a great length before the people are alarmed. Oppression may therefore take place by degrees; but if there were express terms and bounds laid down, when these were passed by, the people would take notice of them, and oppressions would not be carried on to such a length. I look upon it, therefore, that there ought to be something to confine the power of this government within its proper boundaries. I know that several writers have said that a bill of rights is not necessary in this country; that some states had them not, and that others had. To these I answer, that those states that have them not as bills of rights, strictly so called, have them in the frame of their constitution, which is nearly the same.

There has been a comparison made of our situation with Great Britain. We have no crown, or prerogative of a king, like the British constitution. I take it, that the subject has been misunderstood. In Great Britain, when the king attempts to usurp the rights of the people, the declaration and bill of rights are a guard against him. A bill of rights would be necessary here to guard against our rulers. I wish to have a bill of rights, to secure those unalienable rights, which are called by some respectable writers the *residuum* of human rights, which are never to be given up. At the same time that it would give security to individuals, it would add to the general strength. It might not be so necessity to have a bill of rights in the government of the United States, if such means had not been made use of as endanger a consolidation of all the states; but at any event, it would be proper to have one, because, though it might not be of any other service, it would at least satisfy the minds of the people. . . .

[Mr. MACLAINE.]

The gentleman has wandered out of his way to tell us—what has so often been said out of doors—that there is no declaration of rights; that consequently all our rights are taken away. It would be very extraordinary to have a bill of rights, because the powers of Congress are expressly defined; and the very definition of them is as valid and efficacious a check as a bill of rights could be, without the dangerous implication of a bill of rights. The powers of Congress are limited and enumerated. We say we have given them those powers, but we do not say we have given them more. We retain all those rights which we have not given away to the general government. The gentleman is a professional man. If a gentleman had made his last will and testament, and devised or bequeathed to a particular person the sixth part of his property, or any particular specific legacy, could it be said that that person should have the whole estate? If they can assume powers not enumerated, there was no occasion for enumerating any powers. The gentleman is learned. Without recurring to his learning, he may only appeal to his common sense; it will inform him that, if we had all power before, and give away but a part, we still retain the rest. It is as plain a thing as possibly can be, that Congress can have no power but what we expressly give them. There is an express clause which, however disingenuously it has been perverted from its true meaning, clearly demonstrates that they are confined to those powers which are given them. This clause enables them to "make all laws which shall be necessary and proper for carrying into execution the foregoing powers, and all other powers vested by this Constitution in the government of the United States, or any department or officers thereof." This clause specifies that they shall make laws to carry into execution *all the powers vested* by this Constitution; consequently, they can make no laws to execute any other power. This clause gives no new power, but declares that those already given are to be executed by proper laws. I hope this will satisfy gentlemen. . . .

[Mr. IREDELL.]

With regard to a bill of rights, this is a notion originating in England, where no written constitution is to be found, and the authority of their government is derived from the most remote antiquity. Magna Charta itself is no constitution, but a solemn instrument ascertaining certain rights of individuals, by the legislature for the time being; and every article of which the legislature may at any time alter. This and a bill of rights also, the invention of later times, were occasioned by great usurpations of the crown, contrary, as was conceived, to the principles of their government, about which there was a variety of opinions. But neither that instrument, nor any other instrument, ever attempted to abridge the authority of Parliament, which is supposed to be without any limitations whatever. Had their constitution been fixed and certain, a bill of rights would have been useless, for the constitution would have shown plainly the extent of that authority which they were disputing about. Of what use, therefore, can a bill of rights be in this Constitution, where the people expressly declare how much power they do give, and consequently retain all they do not? It is a declaration of particular powers by the people to their representatives, for particular purposes. It may be considered as a great power of attorney, under which no power can be exercised but what is expressly given. Did any man ever hear, before, that at the end of a power of attorney it was said that the attorney should not exercise more power than was there given him? Suppose, for instance, a man had lands in the counties of Anson and Caswell, and he should give another a power of attorney to sell his lands in Anson, would the other have any authority to sell the lands in Caswell?—or could he, without absurdity, say, "'Tis true you have not expressly authorized me to sell the lands in Caswell; but as you had lands there, and did not say I should not, I thought I might as well sell those lands as the other." A bill of rights, as I conceive, would not only be incongruous, but dangerous. No man, let his ingenuity be what it will, could enumerate all the individual rights not relinquished by this Constitution. Suppose, therefore, an enumeration of a great many, but an omission of some, and that, long after all traces of our present disputes were at an end, any of the omitted rights should be invaded, and the invasion be complained of; what would be the plausible answer of the government to such a complaint? Would they not naturally say, "We live at a great distance from the time when this Constitution was established. We can judge of it much better by the ideas of it entertained at the time, than by any ideas of our own. The bill of rights, passed at that time, showed that the people did not think every power retained which was not given, else this bill of rights was not only useless, but absurd. But we are not at liberty to charge an absurdity upon our ancestors, who have given such strong proofs of their good sense, as well as their attachment to liberty. So long as the rights enumerated in the bill of rights remain unviolated, you have no reason to complain. This is not one of them." Thus a bill of rights might operate as a snare rather than a protection. If we had formed a general legislature, with undefined powers, a bill of rights would not only have been proper, but necessary; and it would have then operated as an exception to the legislative authority in such particulars. It has this effect in respect to some of the American constitutions, where the powers of legislation are general. But where they are powers of a particular nature, and expressly defined, as in the case of the Constitution before us, I think, for the reasons I have given, a bill of rights is not only unnecessary, but would be absurd and dangerous.

Debates, IV, pp. 137-138, 140-141, 148-149.

North Carolina Convention July 29, 1788
Debates (excerpts)

[Mr. SPENCER.]
The gentleman said, all matters not given up by this form of government were retained by the respective states. I know that it ought to be so; it is the general doctrine, but it is necessary that it should be expressly declared in the Constitution, and not left to mere construction and opinion. I am authorized to say it was heretofore thought necessary. The Confederation says, expressly, that all that was not given up by the United States was retained by the respective states. If such a clause had been inserted in this Constitution, it would have superseded the necessity of a bill of rights. But that not being the case, it was necessary that a bill of rights, or something of that kind, should be a part of the Constitution. It was observed that, as the Constitution is to be a delegation of power from the several states to the United States, a bill of rights was unnecessary. But it will be noticed that this is a different case.

The states do not act in their political capacities, but the government is proposed for individuals. The very caption of the Constitution shows that this is the case. The expression, "We, the people of the United States," shows that this government is intended for individuals; there ought, therefore, to be a bill of rights. I am ready to acknowledge that the Congress ought to have the power of executing its laws. Heretofore, because all the laws of the Confederation were binding on the states in their political capacities, courts had nothing to do with them; but now the thing is entirely different. The laws of Congress will be binding on individuals, and those things which concern individuals will be brought properly before the courts. In the next place, all the officers are to take an oath to carry into execution this general government, and are bound to support every act of the government, of whatever nature it may be. This is a forth reason for securing the rights of individuals. It was also observed that the federal judiciary and the courts of the states, under the federal authority, would have concurrent jurisdiction with respect to any subject that might arise under the Constitution. I am ready to say that I most heartily wish that, whenever this government takes place, the two jurisdictions and the two governments—that is, the general and the several state governments—may go hand in hand, and that there may be no interference, but that every thing may be rightly conducted. But I will never concede that it is proper to divide the business between the two different courts. I have no doubt that there is wisdom enough in this state to decide the business, without the necessity of federal assistance to do our business. The worthy gentleman from Edenton dwelt a considerable time on the observations on a bill of rights, contending that they were proper only in monarchies, which were founded on different principles from those of our government; and, therefore, though they might be necessary for others, yet they were not necessary for us. I still think that a bill of rights is necessary. This necessity arises from the nature of human societies. When individuals enter into society, they give up some rights to secure the rest. There are certain human rights that ought not to be given up, and which ought in some manner to be secured. With respect to these great essential rights, no latitude ought to be left. They are the most inestimable gifts of the great Creator, and therefore ought not to be destroyed, but ought to be secured. They ought to be secured to individuals in consideration of the other rights which they give up to support society. . . .

Mr. MACLAINE. Mr. Chairman, I beg leave to make a few observations. One of the gentleman's objections to the Constitution now under consideration is, that it is not the act of the states, but of the people; but that it ought to be the act of the states; and he instances the delegation of power by the states to the Confederation, at the commencement of the war, as a proof of this position. I hope, sir, that all power is in the people, and not in the state governments. If he will not deny the authority of the people to delegate power to agents, and to devise such a government as a majority of them thinks will promote their happiness, he will withdraw his objection. The people, sir, are the only proper authority to form a government. They, sir, have formed their state governments, and can alter them at pleasure. Their transcendent power is competent to form this or any other government which they think promotive of their happiness. But the gentleman contends that there ought to be a bill of rights, or something of that kind—something declaring expressly, that all power not expressly given to the Constitution ought to be retained by the states, and he produces the Confederation as an authority for its necessity. When the confederation was made, we were by no means so well acquainted with the principles of government as we are now. We were then jealous of the power of our rulers, and had an idea of the British government when we entertained that jealousy. There is no people on earth so well acquainted with the nature of government as the people of America generally are. We know now that it is agreed upon by most writers, and men of judgment and reflection, that all power is in the people, and immediately derived from them. The gentleman surely must know that, if there be certian rights which never can, nor ought to, be given up, these rights cannot be said to be given away, merely because we have omitted to say that we have not given them up. Can any security arise from declaring that we have a right to what belongs to us? Where is the necessity of such a declaration? If we have this inherent, this unalienable, this indefeasible title to those rights, if they are not given up, are they not retained? If Congress should make a law beyond the powers and the spirit of the Constitution, should we not say to Congres, "You have no authority to make this law. There are limits beyond which you cannot go. You cannot exceed the power prescribed by the Constitution. You are amenable to us for your conduct. This act is unconstitutional. We will disregard it, and punish you for the attempt." . . .

Mr. SPENCER answered, that the gentleman last up [Mr. Maclaine] had misunderstood him. He did not object to the caption of the Constituion, but he instanced it to show that the United States were not, merely as states, the objects of the Constitution; but that the laws of Congress were to operate upon individuals, and not upon states. He then continued: I do not mean to contend that the laws of the general government should not operate upon individauls. I before observed that this was necessary, as laws could not be put in execution against states without the agency of the sword, which, instead of answering the ends of government, would destroy it. I endeavored to show that, as the government was not to operate against states, but against individuals, the rights of individuals ought to be properly secured. In order to constitute this security, it appears to me there ought to be such a clause in the Constitution as there was in the Confederation, expressly declaring, that every power, jurisdiction, and right, which are not given up by it, remain in the states. Such a clause would render a bill of rights unnecessary. But as there is no such clause, I contend that there should be a bill of rights, ascertaining and securing the great rights of the states and people. . . .

[Mr. Iredell.]
In like manner, I say, the future Congress can have no right to exercise any power but what is contained in that paper. Negative

words, in my opinion, could make the matter no plainer than it was before. The gentleman says that unalienable rights ought not to be given up. Those rights which are unalienable are not alienated. They still remain with the great body of the people. If any right be given up that ought not to be, let it be shown. Say it is a thing which affects your country, and that it ought not to be surrendered: this would be reasonable. But when it is evident that the exercise of any power not given up would be a usurpation, it would be not only useless, but dangerous, to enumerate a number of rights which are not intended to be given up; because it would be implying, in the strongest manner, that every right not included in the exception might be impaired by the government without usurpation; and it would be impossible to enumerate every one. Let any one make what collection or enumeration of rights he pleases, I will immediately mention twenty or thirty more rights not contained in it. . . .

Mr. SPENCER. Mr. Chairman, the gentleman expresses admiration as to what we object with respect to a bill of rights, and insists that what is not given up in the Constitution is retained. He must recollect I said, yesterday, that we could not guard with too much care those essential rights and liberties which ought never to be given up. There is no express negative—no fence against their being trampled upon. They might exceed the proper boundary without being taken notice of. When there is no rule but a vague doctrine, they might make great strides, and get possession of so much power that a general insurrection of the people would be necessary to bring an alteration about. But if a boundary were set up, when the boundary is passed, the people would take notice of it immediately. These are the observations which I made; and I have no doubt that, when he reflects, he will acknowledge the necessity of it. I acknowledge, however, that the doctrine is right; but if that Constitution is not satisfactory to the people, I would have a bill of rights, or something of that kind, to satisfy them.

Debates, IV, pp. 153-154, 160-163, 166-167, 168.

North Carolina Convention July 30, 1788
Debates (excerpts)

Mr. LENOIR. Mr. Chariman, I conceive that I shall not be out of order to make some observations on this last part of the system, and take some retrospective view of some other parts of it. I think it not proper for our adoption, as I consider that it endangers our liberties. When we consider this system collectively, we must be surprised to think that any set of men, who were delegated to amend the Confederation, should propose to annihilate it; for that and this system are utterly different, and cannot exist together. It has been said that the fullest confidence should be put in those characters who framed this Constitution. We will admit them, in private and public transactions, to be good characters. But, sir, it appears to me, and every other member of this committee, that they exceeded their powers. Those gentlemen had no sort of power to form a new constitution altogether; neither had the citizens of this country such an idea in their view. I cannot undertake to say what principles actuated them. I must conceive they were mistaken in their politics, and that this system does not secure the unalienable rights of freemen. It has some aristocratical and some monarchical features, and perhaps some of them intended the establishment of one of these governments. Whatever might be their intent, according to my views, it will lead to the most dangerous aristocracy that ever was thought of—an aristocracy established on a constitutional bottom! I conceive (and I believe most of this committee will likewise) that this is so dangerous, that I should like as well to have no constitution at all. Their powers are almost unlimited.

A constitution ought to be understood by every one. The most humble and trifling characters in the country have a right to know what foundation they stand upon. I confess I do not see the end of the powers here proposed, nor the reasons for granting them. The principal end of a constitution is to set forth what must be given up for the community at large, and to secure those rights which ought never to be infringed. The proposed plan secures no right; or if it does, it is in so vague and undeterminate a manner, that we do not understand it. My constituents instructed me to oppose the adoption of this Constitution. The principal reasons are as follow: The right of representation is not fairly and explicitly preserved to the people, it being easy to evade that privilege as provided in this system, and the terms of election being too long. If our General Assembly be corrupt, at the end of the year we can make new men of them by sending others in their stead. It is not so here. If there by any reason to think that human nature is corrupt, and that there is a disposition in men to aspire to power, they may embrace an opportunity, during their long continuance in office, by means of their powers, to take away the rights of the people. The senators are chosen for six years, and two thirds of them, with the President, have most extensive powers. They may enter into a dangerous combination. And they may be continually reelected. The President may be as good a man as any in existence, but he is but a man. He may be corrupt. He has an opportunity of forming plans dangerous to the community at large. I shall not enter into the *minutiae* of this system, but I conceive, whatever may have been the intention of its framers, that it leads to a most dangerous aristocracy. It appears to me that, instead of securing the sovereignty of the states, it is calculated to melt them down into one solid empire. If the citizens of this state like a consolidated government, I hope they will have virtue enough to secure their rights. I am sorry to make use of the expression, but it appears to me to be a scheme to reduce this government to an aristocracy. It guaranties a republican form of government to the states; when all these powers are in Congress, it will only be a form. It will be past recovery, when Congress has the power of the purse and the sword. The power of the sword is in explicit terms given to it. The power of direct taxation gives the purse. They may prohibit the trial by jury, which is a most sacred and valuable right. There is nothing contained in this Constitution to bar them from it. The federal courts have also appellate cognizance of law and fact, the sole cause of which is to deprive the people of that trial, which it is optional in them to grant or not. We find no provision against infringement on the rights of conscience. Ecclesiastical courts may be established, which will be destructive to our citizens. They may make any establishment they think proper. They have also an exclusive legislation in their ten miles square, to which may be added their power over the militia, who may be carried thither and kept there for life. Should any one grumble at their acts, he would be deemed a traitor, and perhaps taken up and carried to the exclusive legislation, and there tried without a jury. We are told there is no cause to fear. When we consider the great powers of Congress, there is great cause of alarm. They can disarm the militia. If they were armed, they would be a resource against great oppressions. The laws of a great empire are difficult to be executed. If the laws of the Union were oppressive, they could not carry them into effect, if the people were possessed of proper means of defence.

It was cried out that we were in a most desperate situation, and that Congress could not discharge any of their most sacred contracts. I believe it to be the case. But why give more power than is necessary? The men who went to the Federal convention went for the express purpose of amending the government, by giving it such additional powers as were necessary. If we should accede to this system it may be thought proper, by a few designing persons, to destroy it, in a future age, in the same manner that the old system is laid aside. The Confederation was binding on all the states. It could not be destroyed but with the consent of all the states. There was an express article to that purpose. The men who were deputed to the Convention, instead of amending the old, as they were solely empowered and directed to do, proposed a new system. If the best characters departed so far from their authority, what may not be apprehended from others, who may be agents in the new govenment?

It is natural for men to aspire to power—it is the nature of mankind to be tyrannical; therefore it is necessary for us to secure our rights and liberties as far as we can. But it is asked why we should suspect men who are to be chosen by ourselves, while it is their interest to act justly, and while men have self-interest at heart. I think the reasons which I have given are sufficient to answer that question. We ought to consider the depravity of human nature, the predominant thirst of power which is in the breast of every one, the temptations our rulers may have, and the unlimited confidence placed in them by this system. These are the foundation of my fears. They would be so long in the general government that they would forget the grievances of the people of the states.

But it is said we shall be ruined if separated from the other states, which will be the case if we do not adopt. If so, I put less confidence in those states. The states are all bound together by the Confederation, and the rest cannot break from us without violating the most solemn compact. If they break that, they will this.

But it is urged that we ought to adopt, because so many other states have. In those states which have patronized and ratified it, many great men have opposed it. The motives of those states I know not. It is the goodness of the Constitution we are to examine. We are to exercise our own judgments, and act independently. And as I conceive we are not out of the Union, I hope this Constituion will not be adopted till amendments are made. Amendments are wished for by the other states. . . .

I wish not to be so understood as to be so averse to this system, as that I should object to all parts of it, or attempt to reflect on the reputation of those gentlemen who formed it; though it appears to me that I would not have agreed to any proposal but the amendment of the Confederation. If there were any security for the liberty of the people, I would, for my own part, agree to it. But in this case, as millions yet unborn are concerned, and deeply interested in our decision, I would have the most positive and pointed security. I shall therefore hope that, before this house will proceed to adopt this Constitution, they will propose such amendments to it as will make it complete; and when amendments are adopted, perhaps I will be as ready to accede to it as any man. One thing will make it aristocratical.

Its powers are very indefinite. There was a very necessary clause in the Confederation, which is omitted in this system. That was a clause declaring that every power, &c., not given to Congress, was reserved to the states. The omission of this clause makes the power so much greater. Men will naturally put the fullest construction on the power given them. Therefore lay all restraint on them, and form a plan to be understood by every gentleman of this committee, and every individual of the community. . . .

Mr. J. M'DOWALL. Mr. Chairman, I was in hopes that amendments would have been brought foreward to the Constitution before the idea of adopting it had been thought of or proposed. From the best information, there is a great proportion of the people in the adopting states averse to it as it stands. I collect my information from respectable authority. I know the necessity of a federal goverment. I therefore wish this was one in which our liberties and privileges were secured; for I consider the Union as the rock of our political salvation. I am for the strongest federal govenment. A bill of rights ought to have been inserted, to ascertain our most valuable and unalienable rights. . . .
A large majority of the people of this country are against this Constitution, because they think it replete with dangerous defects. They ought to be satisfied with it before it is adopted; otherwise it cannot operate happily. Without the affections of the people, it will not have sufficient energy. To enforce its execution, recourse must be had to arms and bloodshed. How much better would it be if the people were satisfied with it! From all these considerations, I now rise to oppose its adoption; for I never will agree to a government that tends to the destruction of the liberty of the people. . . .

[Mr. LANCASTER.]
Treaties are to be the supreme law of the land. This has been sufficiently discussed: it must be amended some way or other. If the Constitution be adopted, it ought to be the supreme law of the land, and a perpetual rule for the governors and governed. But if treaties are to be the supreme law of the land, it may repeal the laws of different states, and render nugatory our bill of rights.

Debates, IV, pp. 201-206, 210-212, 215.

North Carolina Convention July 31, 1788
Debates (excerpts)

Mr. WILLIE JONES. Mr. Chairman, the gentleman last up has mentioned the resolution of Congress now laying before us, and the act of Assembly under which we meet here, which says that we should deliberate and determine on the Constitution. What is to be inferred from that? Are we to ratify it at all events? Have we not an equal right to reject? We do not determine by neither rejecting nor adopting. It is objected we shall be out of the Union. So I wish to be. We are left at liberty to come in at any time. It is said we shall suffer a great loss for want of a share of the impost. I have no doubt we shall have it when we come in, as much as if we adopted now. I have a resolution in my pocket, which I intend to introduce if this resolution is carried, recommending it to the legislature to lay an impost, for the use of Congress, on goods imported into this state, similar to that which may be laid by Congress on goods imported into the adopting states. This shows the committee what is my intention, and on what footing we are to be. This being the case, I will forfeit my life that we shall come in for a share. It is said that all the offices of Congress will be filled, and we shall have no share in appointing the officers. This is an objection of very little importance. Gentlemen need not be in such haste. If left eighteen months or two years without offices, it is no great cause of alarm. The gentleman further said that we could send no representatives, but must send ambassadors to Congress, as a foreign power. I assert the contrary; and that, whenever a convention of the states is called, North Carolina will be called upon like the rest. I do not know what these gentlemen would desire.

I am very sensible that there is a great majority against the Constitution. If we take the question as they propose, they know it would be rejected, and bring on us all the dreadful consequences which they feelingly foretell, but which can never in the least alarm me. I have endeavored to fall in with their opinion, but could not. We have a right, in plain terms, to refuse it if we think proper. I have, in my proposition, adopted, word for word, the Virginia amendments, with one or two additional ones. We run no risk of being excluded from the Union when we think proper to come in. Virginia, our next neighbor, will not oppose our admission. We have a common cause with her. She wishes the same alterations. We are of the greatest importance to her. She will have great weight in Congress; and there is no doubt but she will do every thing she can to bring us into the Union. South Carolina and Georgia are deeply interested in our being admitted. The Creek nation would overturn these two states without our aid. They cannot exist without North Carolina. There is no doubt we shall obtain our amendments, and come into the Union when we please. Massachusetts, New Hampshire, and other states, have proposed amendments. New York will do also, if she ratifies. There will be a majority of the states, and the most respectable, important, and extensive states also, desirous of amendments, and favorable to our admission.

As great names have been mentioned, I beg leave to mention the authority of Mr. Jefferson, whose great abilities and respectability are well known. When the Convention sat in Richmond, in Virginia, Mr. Madison received a letter from him. In that letter he said he wished nine states would adopt it, not because it deserved ratification, but to preserve the Union. But he wished that the other four states would reject it, that there might be a certainty of obtaining amendments. Congress may go on, and take no notice of our amendments; but I am confident they will do nothing of importance till a convention be called. If I recollect rightly, amendments may be ratified either by conventions or the legislatures of the states. In either case, it may take up about eighteen months. For my part, I would rather be eighteen years out of the Union than adopt it in its present defective form.

Debates, IV, pp. 225-226. Reprinted in BRDH, II, pp. 958-959.

Thomas Jefferson (Paris) July 31, 1788
Letter: To James Madison (excerpts)

I sincerely rejoice at the acceptance of our new constitution by nine states. It is a good canvass, on which some strokes only want retouching. What these are, I think are sufficiently manifested by the general voice from North to South, which calls for a bill of rights. It seems pretty generally understood that this should go to Juries, Habeas corpus, Standing armies, Printing, Religion & Monopolies. I conceive there may be difficulty in finding general modifications of these, suited to the habits of all the states. But if such cannot be found then it is better to establish trials by Jury, the right of Habeas corpus, freedom of press & freedom of religion, in all cases, and to abolish standing armies in time of peace, and Monopolies in all cases, than not do it in any. The few cases wherein these things may do evil, cannot be weighed against the multitude wherein the want of them will do evil. . . . A declaration that the federal government will never restrain the presses from printing anything they please, will not take away the liability of the printers for false facts printed. The declaration that religious faith shall be unpunished, does not give impunity to criminal acts dictated by religious error. The saying there shall be no monopolies lessens the incitements to ingenuity, which spurred on by the hope of a monopoly for a limited time, as of 14 years; but the benefit even of limited monopolies is too doubtful to be opposed to that of their general suppression. If no check can be found to keep the number of standing troops within safe bounds, while they are tolerated as far as necessary, abandon them altogether, discipline well the militia, & guard the magazines with them. More than magazine guards will be useless if few, & dangerous if many. No European nation can ever send against us such a regular army as we need fear, & it is hard if our militia are not equal to those of Canada or Florida. My idea then is, that tho' proper exceptions to these general rules are desirable, & probably practicable, yet if the exceptions cannot be agreed on, the establishment of the rules in all cases will do ill in very few. I hope therefore a bill of rights will be formed to guard the people against the federal government, as they are already guarded against their state governments in most instances.

Ford, V, pp. 45-46. Reprinted in *Papers*, XI, pp. 212- 213.

North Carolina Convention August 1, 1788
Refusal to Ratify the United States Constitution

"*Resolved*, That a declaration of rights, asserting and securing from encroachment the great principles of civil and religious liberty, and the unalienable rights of the people, together with amendments to the most ambiguous and exceptionable parts of the said Constitution of government, ought to be laid before Congress, and the convention of the states that shall or may be called for the purpose of amending the said Constitution, for their consideration, previous to the ratification of the Constitution aforesaid on the part of the state of North Carolina."

DECLARATION OF RIGHTS.

"1. That there are certain natural rights, of which men, when they form a social compact, cannot deprive or divest their posterity, among which are the enjoyment of life and liberty, with the means of acquiring, possessing, and protecting property, and pursuing and obtaining happiness and safety.

"2. That all power is naturally vested in, and consequently derived from, the people; that magistrates, therefore, are their trustees and agents, and at all times amenable to them.

"3. That government ought to be instituted for the common benefit, protection, and security, of the people; and that the doctrine of nonresistance against arbitrary power and oppression is absurd, slavish, and destructive to the good and happiness of mankind.

"4. That no man or set of men are entitled to exclusive or separate public emoluments or privileges from the community, but in consideration of public services, which not being descendible, neither ought the offices of magistrate, legislator, or judge, or any other public office, to be hereditary.

"5. That the legislative, executive, and judiciary powers of government should be separate and distinct, and that the members of the two first may be restrained from oppression by feeling and participating the public burdens: they should, at fixed periods, be reduced to a private station, return into the mass of the people, and the vacancies be supplied by certain and regular elections, in which all or any part of the former members to be eligible or ineligible, as the rules of the constitution of government and the laws shall direct.

"6. That elections of representatives in the legislature ought to be free and frequent, and all men having sufficient evidence of permanent common interest with, and attachment to, the community, ought to have the right of suffrage; and no aid, charge, tax, or fee, can be set, rated, or levied, upon the people without their own consent, or that of their representatives so elected; nor can they be bound by any law to which they have not in like manner assented for the public good.

"7. That all power of suspending laws, or the execution of laws, by any authority, without the consent of the representatives of the people in the legislature, is injurious to their rights, and ought not to be exercised.

"8. That, in all capital and criminal prosecutions, a man hath a right to demand the cause and nature of his accusation, to be confronted with the accusers and witnesses, to call for evidence, and be allowed counsel in his favor, and a fair and speedy trial by an impartial jury of his vicinage, without whose unanimous consent he cannot be found guilty, (except in the government of the land and naval forces;) nor can he be compelled to give evidence against himself.

"9. That no freeman ought to be taken, imprisoned, or disseized of his freehold, liberties, privileges, or franchises, or outlawed or exiled, or in any manner destroyed, or deprived of his life, liberty, or property, but by the law of the land.

"10. That every freeman, restrained of his liberty, is entitled to a remedy to inquire into the lawfulness thereof, and to remove the same if unlawful; and that such remedy ought not to be denied nor delayed.

"11. That, in controversies respecting property, and in suits between man and man, the ancient trial by jury is one of the greatest securities to the rights of the people, and ought to remain sacred and inviolable.

"12. That every freeman ought to find a certain remedy, by recourse to the laws, for all injuries and wrongs he may receive in his person, property, or character; he ought to obtain right and justice freely without sale, completely and without denial, promptly and without delay; and that all establishments or regulations contravening these rights are oppressive and unjust.

"13. That excessive bail ought not to be required, nor excessive fines imposed, nor cruel and unusual punishments inflicted.

"14. That every freeman has a right to be secure from all unreasonable searches and seizures of his person, his papers and property; all warrants, therefore, to search suspected places, or to apprehend any suspected person, without specially naming or describing the place or person, are dangerous, and ought not to be granted.

"15. That the people have a right peaceably to assemble together, to consult for the common good, or to instruct their representatives; and that every freeman has a right to petition or apply to the legislature for redress of grievances.

"16. That the people have a right to freedom of speech, and of writing and publishing their sentiments; that freedom of the press is one of the greatest bulwarks of liberty, and ought not to be violated.

"17. That the people have a right to keep and bear arms; that a well regulated militia, composed of the body of the people, trained to arms, is the proper, natural, and safe defence of a free state; that standing armies, in time of peace, are dangerous to liberty, and therefore ought to be avoided, as far as the circumstances and protection of the community will admit; and that, in all cases, the military should be under strict subordination to, and governed by, the civil power.

"18. That no soldier, in time of peace, ought to be quartered in any house without the consent of the owner, and in time of war, in such manner only as the laws direct.

"19. That any person religiously scrupulous of bearing arms ought to be exempted, upon payment of an equivalent to employ another to bear arms in his stead.

"20. That religion, or the duty which we owe to our Creator, and the manner of discharging it, can be directed only by reason and conviction, not by force or violence; and therefore all men have an equal, natural, and unalienable right to the free exercise of religion, according to the dictates of conscience; and that no particular religious sect or society ought to be favored or established by law in preference to others."

AMENDMENTS TO THE CONSTITUTION

"1. That each state in the Union shall respectively retain every power, jurisdiction, and right, which is not by this Constitution delegated to the Congress of the United States, or to the departments of the federal government.

"2. That there shall be one representative for every thirty thousand according to the enumeration or census mentioned in the Constitution, until the whole number of representatives amounts to two hundred; after which that number shall be continued or increased as Congress shall direct, upon the principles fixed in the Constitution, by apportioning the representatives of each state to some greater number of the people, from time to time, as the population increases.

"3. When Congress shall lay direct taxes or excises, they shall immediately inform the executive power of each state of the quota of such state, according to the census herein directed, which is proposed to be thereby raised; and if the legislature of any state shall pass any law which shall be effectual for raising such quota at the time required by Congress, the taxes and excises laid by Congress shall not be collected in such state.

"4. That the members of the Senate and House of Representatives shall be ineligible to, and incapable of holding, any civil office under the authority of the United States, during the time for which they shall respectively be elected.

"5. That the Journals of the proceedings of the Senate and House of Representatives shall be published at least once in every year, except such parts thereof relating to treaties, alliances, or military operations, as in their judgment require secrecy.

"6. That a regular statement and account of receipts and expenditures of all public moneys shall be published at least once in every year.

"7. That no commercial treaty shall be ratified without the concurrence of two thirds of the whole number of the members of the Senate. And no treaty, ceding, contracting, restraining, or suspending, the territorial rights or claims of the United States, or any of them, or their, or any of their, rights or claims of fishing in the American seas, or navigating the American rivers, shall be made, but in cases of the most urgent and extreme necessity; nor shall any such treaty be ratified without the concurrence of three fourths of the whole number of the members of both houses respectively.

"8. That no navigation law, or law regulating commerce, shall be passed without the consent of two thirds of the members present in both houses.

"9. That no standing army or regular troops shall be raised or kept up in time of peace, without the consent of two thirds of the members present in both houses.

"10. That no soldier shall be enlisted for any longer term than four years, except in time of war, and then for no longer term than the continuance of the war.

"11. That each state respectively shall have the power to provide for organizing, arming, and disciplining its own militia, whensoever Congress shall omit or neglect to provide for the same; that the militia shall not be subject to martial law, except when in actual service in time of war, invasion, or rebellion; and when not in the actual service of the United States, shall be subject only to such fines, penalties, and punishments, as shall be directed or inflicted by the laws of its own state.

"12. That Congress shall not declare any state to be in rebellion, without the consent of at least two thirds of all the members present in both houses.

"13. That the exclusive power of legislation given to Congress over the federal town and its adjacent district, and other places purchased or to be purchased by Congress of any of the states, shall extend only to such regulations as respect the police and good government thereof.

"14. That no person shall be capable of being President of the United States for more than eight years in any term of fifteen years.

"15. That the judicial power of the United States shall be vested in one Supreme Court, and in such courts of admiralty as Congress may from time to time ordain and establish in any of the different states. The judicial power shall extend to all cases in law and equity arising under treaties made, or which shall be made, under the authority of the United States; to all cases affecting ambassadors, other foreign ministers, and consuls; to all cases of admiralty and maritime jurisdiction; to controversies to which the United States shall be a party; to controversies between two or more states, and between parties claiming lands under the grants of different states. In all cases affecting ambassadors, other foreign ministers, and consuls, and those in which a state shall be a party, the Supreme Court shall have original jurisdiction. In all other cases before mentioned, the Supreme Court shall have appellate jurisdiction as to matters of law only, except in cases of equity, and of admiralty and maritime jurisdiction, in which the Supreme Court shall have appellate jurisdiction both as to law and fact, with such exceptions, and under such regulations, as the

Congress shall make: but the judicial power of the United States shall extend to no case where the cause of action shall have originated before the ratification of this Constitution, except in disputes between states about their territory, disputes between persons claiming lands under the grants of different states, and suits for debts due to the United States.

"16. That, in criminal prosecutions, no man shall be restrained in the exercise of the usual and accustomed right of challenging or excepting to the jury.

"17. That Congress shall not alter, modify, or interfere in, the times, places, or manner, of holding elections for senators and representatives, or either of them, except when the legislature of any state shall neglect, refuse, or be disabled, by invasion or rebellion, to prescribe the same.

"18. That those clauses which declare that Congress shall not exercise certain powers be not interpreted in any manner whatsoever to extend the power of Congress; but that they be construed either as making exceptions to the specified powers, where this shall be the case, or otherwise as inserted merely for greater caution.

"19. That the laws ascertaining the compensation of senators and representatives for their services, be postponed in their operation until after the election of representatives immediately succeeding the passing thereof, that excepted which shall first be passed on the subject.

"20. That some tribunal other than the Senate be provided for trying impeachments of senators.

"21. That the salary of a judge shall not be increased or diminished during his continuance in office, otherwise than by general regulations of salary, which may take place on a revision of the subject at stated periods of not less than seven years, to commence from the time such salaries shall be first ascertained by Congress.

"22. That Congress erect no company of merchants with exclusive advantages of commerce.

"23. That no treaties which shall be directly opposed to the existing laws of the United States in Congress assembled shall be valid until such laws shall be repealed, or made conformable to such treaty; nor shall any treaty be valid which is contradictory to the Constitution of the United States.

"24. That the latter part of the 5th paragraph of the 9th section of the 1st article be altered to read thus: 'Nor shall vessels bound to a particular state be obliged to enter or pay duties in any other; nor, when bound from any one of the states, be obliged to clear in another.'

"25. That Congress shall not, directly or indirectly, either by themselves or through the judiciary, interfere with any one of the states in the redemption of paper money already emitted and now in circulation, or in liquidating and discharging the public securities of any one of the states: but each and every state shall have the exclusive right of making such laws and regulations, for the above purposes, as they shall think proper.

"26. That Congress shall not introduce foreign troops into the United States without the consent of two thirds of the members present of both houses."

Debates, IV, pp. 242-247.

Abraham G. Lansing (Albany) August 3, 1788
Letter: To Abraham Yates, Jr. (excerpt)

I received your Letter of the 30 Ulto. by last evening's Stage—the News of the adoption had been in Town some days past, and our Friends are much better pleased with it then we had reason to expect—the Bill of Rights which is interwoven with the adoption is considered by the Majority of those to whom I have shewn it as a security against the Encroachments of the Genl. Government—I do not suppose the Idea altogether futile but the adoption is notwithstanding unconditional in every acceptation of the words—upon the whole I believe or *endeavour* to believe that it is best to both in a political and private light—for had the Constitution been so adopted as that Congress would not accept it—yourself and our Friends would have incurred blame & Cesure if any serious commotions had ensued—as we stand our Friends in this quarter are firmly united—and I trust we shall be able to send such Members as will assist in bringing about the reformation we wish—Hints have been given that you will be proposed for a Senator—I wish you to favor me with your Confidential Sentiments & wishes on this Subject that I may Conduct myself accordingly.

DHFFE, III, p. 202.

Tench Coxe (Philadelphia) August 5, 1788
Letter: To Robert Smith (excerpt)

A combination was taken up in the back parts and center of Pennsylvania for the purpose of obtaining amendments in concert with the opposition in New York, who were then supposed to have an absolute command in that state. They proposed to meet at Harrisburg and meant to term themselves a convention. The unexpected adoption by the convention of New York has staggered them a good deal, but I do not think they will drop their measures, tho they may be less extravagant and assuming for that check.

A fact of a very curious nature occurred to me about the time Virginia was determining. Some little question arose in conversation between a strong and sensible opponent and myself on the probable nature of the Virginia amendments, as they would be proposed to Congress. We thought differently on them when he made this remark. "It is not worth making a question about the amendments for I have *a copy of them in my pocket.*" It is but a single fact, but it comes in confirmation of the many symptoms of *concert* in this plan, which are daily presenting themselves.

DHFFE, I, p. 248.

Thomas Jefferson (Paris) August 12, 1788
Letter: To William Carmichael (excerpts)

Since my last to you, I have been honoured with your's of the 18th & 29th of May & 5th of June. My latest american intelligence is of the 24th of June when 9 certainly & probably 10 states had accepted the new constitution, and there was no doubt of the 11th (North-Carolina) because there was no opposition there. . . . Tho' I am much pleased with this succesful issue of the new constitution, yet I am more so to find that one of it's principal defects (the want of a Declaration of rights) will pretty certainly be remedied. I suppose this, because I see that both people & Conventions in almost every state have concurred in demanding it. Another defect, the perpetual re-eligibility of the same president, will probably not be cured during the life of General Washington. His merit has blinded our countrymen to the dangers of making so important an officer re-eligible.

DHFFE, IV, p. 50.

James Hanna (Newtown) August 15, 1788
Letter: To John Vandegrift, Nathan Vansant, and Jacob Vandegrift[1]
Published: Philadelphia *Pennsylvania Gazette,* September 10, 1788.

The important crisis now approaching (confident I am you will think with me) demands the most serious attention of every friend of American liberty. The constitution of the United States is now adopted by eleven states in the Union, and no doubt the other two will follow their example; for, however just the sentiments of the opposition may be, I do conceive it would be the height of madness and folly, and in fact a crime of very detrimental consequence to our country, to refuse to acquiesce in a measure received in form by so great a majority of our country; not only to ourselves individually, but to the community at large. For the worst that we can expect from a bad form of government is anarchy and confusion, with all its common train of grievances, and by an opposition in the present situation of affairs, we are sure of it. On the other hand, by a sullen and inactive conduct, it will give the promoters and warm advocates of the plan an opportunity (if any such design they have) to shackle us with those manacles that we fear may be formed under color of law, and we be led to know it is constitutional, when it is too late to extricate ourselves and posterity from a lasting bondage.

To you it is not worth while to animadvert on the plain and pointed tendency the Constitution has to this effect, and how easily it may be accomplished in power under its influence. That virtue is not the standard which has principally animated the adoption of the Constitution in this state I believe is too true. Let us, therefore, as we wish to serve our country, and show the world that those only who wished amendments were truly Federal, adopt the conduct of our fellow citizens in the back counties. Let us, as freemen, call a meeting of those citizens who wish for amendments, in a committee of the county, delegated from each township, for the purpose expressed in a copy of the (circular) enclosed.[2] In promoting a scheme of this kind, I hope we shall not only have the satisfaction of seeing the minds and exertions of all who wish for amendments center in this object, which will swallow others more injurious, but that we will enjoy the supreme felicity of having assisted in snatching from slavery a once happy and worthy people.

I therefore hope you will undertake to call together your township, have delegates chosen to represent them in a committee to be held at the house of George Piper, on Monday the 21st inst. at nine o'clock in the forenoon, for the purpose of appointing delegates to represent them in the state conference, and for giving them instructions, etc.

If you should apprehend the people will not call a town meeting for the purpose, that you will, as we intend here, write or call on a few of the most respectable people of your township, to attend at the general meeting, as they intend to do at Philadelphia, if they cannot accomplish their purpose in the other way.

Your usual public spirit on occasions of this kind, I am sure, needs no spur. We shall, therefore, rest assured that we will meet a representation of the township *committed to your charge* on the day appointed.

1 DHFFE, I, pp. 250-251.
2 For the circular letter, see "Cumberland County Meeting," July 3, 1788, p. 472.

Fayette County (Pennsylvania) Delegates August 18, 1788
Certificate of Election

We whose names are hereunto subscribed, at a conference held at Union Town for the County of Fayette, being appointed a committee, do certify that the Honorable John Smilie and Mr. Albert Galatin were chosen by the people then convened, to represent them in a general conference of the state to be held at Harrisburg the third day of September, in order to conclude upon such amendments and such mode of obtaining them as the conference in their wisdom may judge proper: Given under our hands at Union Town August the eighteenth Anno Domini 1788.

[Signed:] Nathanial Breading, James Finley, Daniel Cannon, Zadok Springer, Joseph Torrence

DHFFE, I, pp. 252-253.

Solon, jun. August 23, 1788
Newspaper Article: *Providence Gazette* (excerpt)

Time has at length discovered to us, that a great many of the people, and some respectable States in the Union, are of opinion, that the New Constitution needs amendments.—The ratification of it by the State of New York bears a singular complexion; and North-Carolina has refused to ratify it.

The most eligible mode of obtaining these amendments is therefore now on the tapis.—Two only strike me at present.—It must be done by the States under the old confederation—or as an operation of the New Constitution.

Eleven States having ratified the Constitution unconditionally, it is not likely that they will so far recede from that measure, as to humour the remaining two States in holding a Convention under the old confederation—this indeed would be an indecent request from the two non-complying States, were they more respectable than they are. It therefore follows, that the necessary amendments are to be sought for by the operations of the New Constitution.—Let us therefore attend to the fifth article thereof, which points out the process.

In case two-thirds of the New Congress are of opinion that amendments are necessary—they have authority to draught such as they please, and transmit them to the States they represent for ratification.—It is at the option of the New Congress to direct that these amendments shall be submitted to the Legislatures of the States, or to Conventions in the several states, for ratification; and in case such amendments shall be ratified by three-fourths either of the Legislatures or Conventions of such States, they become valid and binding. In this method amendments are obtainable under the New Constitution, without another General Convention.

But, secondly, although two-thirds of the New Congress should not be in favour of any amendments; yet if two-thirds of the Legislatures of the States they represent are for amendments, on the application of such two-thirds, the New Congress will call a General Convention for the purpose of considering and proposing amendments, to be ratified in the same manner as in case they had been proposed by the Congress themselves.

From this brief application of the process in obtaining amendments under the operation of the New Constitution, it is clear that the non-complying States can have no agency whatever in the business. They will not be represented on the floor of the New Congress, and so cannot act in amendments originating with that body; nor can they have a seat in any future Conventions directed by that body, in which amendments may originate, and so can have neither part nor lot in the matter.

It is scarcely to be expected, that eight of the eleven States, assembled under the powers of the New Constitution, will agree [?] of any amendments at all; and the voices of seven States, being less than two-thirds of that body, cannot originate any amendments—they will be unavailing—the voices of the Legislatures of seven of those States for a General Convention will also be unavailing for the same reason: But let us suppose that the two outstanding States should come in, after the manner of New-York, their two voices, added to the seven in the New Congress, or the voices of their two-Legislatures added to the other seven, would make more than two-thirds of the whole—for a moderate skill in arithmetic will discover, that although *seven* is less than two-thirds of *eleven, nine* is more than two-thirds of *thirteen.*

The line of policy appears therefore clearly chalked out to the non-complying States, if they wish to facilitate and secure amendments, and more especially if they wish to have a voice in making those amendments. Under this impression, no doubt, the Convention of New-York ratified the Constitution—and what wiser views influenced the North-Carolinians we are yet to learn.

James Tilghman (Chestertown) August 24, 1788
Letter: To Tench Coxe (excerpt)

There is a great deal to do before the present form of Government can get into operation. It must first be revised and amended whether by the Congress themselves or by a New Convention is somewhat incertain. I am apprehensive the New York circular letter will take with many People. I thought I saw many defects and Errors in the Constitution which I imagined the New Congress wd. rectify and supply otherwise I would not have promoted it. I still think they will do it if they have any degree of Sense and prudence. This makes a good choice of delegates and Senators a matter of vast importance. We shall see how the mode of chusing delegates will succeed. I never did like it. The choice of Senators is upon a better plan—I have said much more upon the Subject than I intended and find it time to say Yr affte hble sevt.

DHFFE, II, p. 144.

Bucks County (Pennsylvania) Meeting August 25, 1788
Proceedings (excerpts)
Published: Philadelphia *Pennsylvania Packet* September 2, 1788

The ratification of the federal Constitution and its expected operation forming a new era in the American world, and giving cause of hope to some and fear to others; it has been thought proper that the freemen of the state, or delegates chosen by them, should meet together and deliberate on the subject. Accordingly it has been proposed that a meeting of deputies from the different counties be held at Harrisburg the third day of September next. A Circular Letter, bearing the above proposition was sent to this county, and in pursuance thereof there met this day at Piper's Tavern, in Bedminster Township, the following gentlemen. . . .

[Forty persons are listed along with their townships. Ed.]

Samuel Smith, Esquire, chosen chairman, and James Hanna, Esquire, secretary. After some time spent in duscussing the business of the meeting, Resolved, that the Reverend Nathaniel Erwin, Richard Backhouse, Samuel Smith, John Crawford, and James Hanna, esquires, be a committee to draw up resolves expressive of the sense of this meeting on the subject before them.

In a short time thereafter the following were presented by the gentlemen appointed, and unanimously approved.

Resoved 1. That it is the opinion of this meeting that the plan of government for the United States, formed by the General Convention, having been adopted by eleven of the states, ought, in conformity to the resolves of said convention, to come into operation, and have force until altered in a constitutional way.

2. That as we mean to act the part of peaceable citizens ourselves, so we will support the said plan of government and those who act under it against all illegal violence.

3. That the said plan of government will admit of very considerable amendment, which ought to be made in the mode pointed out in the Constitution itself.

4. That as few governments once established have ever been altered in favor of liberty without confusion and bloodshed, the requisite amendments in said Constitution ought to be attempted as soon as possible.

5. That we will use our utmost endeavors in a pacific way to procure such alterations in the Federal Constitution as may be necessary to secure the rights and liberties of ourselves and posterity.

6. That we approve of a state meeting being held at Harrisburg the third day of September next, on the subject of the above resolves.

7. That four persons ought to be delegated from this county to attend said meeting, and join with the deputies from other counties who may meet with them (in a recommendation to the citizens of this state) of a suitable set of men to represent them in the new Congress, and generally to acquiesce and assist in the promotion of such plan or plans as may be designed by the said state conferees for the purpose of obtaining the necessary amendments of said Constitution, as far as is consistent with our views, expressed in the foregoing resolves.

Agreeably to the resolve last past the Reverend Nathaniel Erwin, Richard Backhouse, John Crawford, and James Hanna, esquires, or any two of them, were appointed to represent us in said conference to be held at Harrisburg.

Resolved, that James Hanna, Esquire be requested to hand the foregoing proceedings to the press for publication.

DHFFE, I, pp. 255-257.

Solon August 28, 1788
Newspaper Article: Boston *Independent Chronicle*

Fellow Countrymen and Citizens: Animated by those noble principles of *virtuous freedom,* which are the dignity of human nature, you spurned the idea of dependence and vassalage, asserted your rights, and, under the smiles of Heaven to the wonder of an admiring world, established your *independence* and sovereignty.

Actuated by sentiments of wisdom and foresight, you have generally adopted a Federal Constitution, which is ere long to be put in practice, and to an eye of reason promises, if well administered, to *confirm* your independence and sovereignty, to render you prosperous and happy at home, and respected abroad. But it has been, and still is the opinion of many, that *certain amendments* are absolutely necessary to render the Constitution still more perfect, and to secure to you, and your posterity, under every administration, the blessings of that liberty you have so dearly purchased, and which it is the duty of enlightened freemen ever to provide. These considerations have induced me to address you at this time, and with all deference to interest, that you do not lose sight of the important object so highly interesting to yourselves and posterity. The amendments which have been proposed by the different state conventions are not local, they equally concern all the states; but whether all that have been mentioned are absolutely necessary is not for me to determine. But in some of them, there is such a general concurrence, that but little, if any doubt can remain of their eligibility. It is not improbable that there will be found some who do not wish for *any* amendments; or that any further *checks* should be provided, than are at present in the Constitution. But I assure myself, that a large majority of you think otherwise, and that you will not be diverted from proper and necessary endeavors to obtain the object by any animadversion, cant, or ridicule that may be thrown out on the subject. It is to be observed, that this is already beginning to discover itself. The Circular Letter from the Convention of New York has had the epithets of *impertinent* and *impudent* bestowed upon it, and probably more will be advanced, as the time draws near. If amendments are necessary, they *claim* an *early consideration,* and measures for the purpose merit your *first* attention. Will it be improper to hint, that in the choice of *Senators* and *Representatives,* this object among others naturally presents itself to your consideration, and that such *instructions* as may be necessary, be *seasonably prepared;* you have hitherto been the peculiar care of a kind Povidence, may you, and your posterity after you, be a name and a praise among the nations of the earth, is the ardent wish of SOLON.

DHFFE, I, pp. 454-455.

A Friend to Amendments August 28, 1788

Newspaper Article: Boston *Independent Chronicle* (excerpt)

It is not doubted the sentiments of the people will be united in such men as are *known to be* the friends to our country, independent of sinister motives, and who are advocates for amendments in our Federal Constitution, as a large and respectable majority of the states have earnestly recommended them.

A friend to amendments has now become the criterion of a Federalist, and none but a set of headstrong aristocratics, who will ever disregard the voice of the people, will endeavor to introduce those men into our new government, who are not strenuous advocates for amendments.

DHFFE, I, p. 452.

A Republican September 1, 1788

Newspaper Article: *Boston Gazette*

The political scene is opened, the canvass is begun, in order to prepare the minds of an enlightened people for the choice of their federal legislators. Much depends upon the wisdom of the first choice. While the citizens of Massachusetts carefully guard against giving their suffrages for such as wish for an inefficient and feeble government, it is to be hoped, that equal caution will be observed towards those persons who are so ardently desirous of erecting a government of an arbitrary, oppressive, and tyrannical complexion. We have many of this last description of men among us; they are violently opposed to any alterations of the new Constitution in favor of the freedom of the people, while they secretly wish for alterations on the side of arbitrary power. But as three-fourths of the people are desirous of amendments not favorable to their views, they dare not hazard their principles in public, and content themselves at present in endeavoring to prevent the amendments already recommended, from being adopted. To effect this, they insist upon our trying the

Constitution first, in order, they say, by that means to discover its defects, well knowing, if once put in motion under their administration, no amendments favorable to liberty will ever be obtained thereafter. These aristocratical tyrants are ever insulting and abusing the old patriots and true friends of our country, because they are not as despotically inclined as themselves, and also with the view of raising themselves upon their ruin. They compare the Honorable Mr. Adams with Governor Hutchinson and other traitors to our country. A republican is called a Shayite and a destroyer of all government, if he only wishes the adoption of one alteration recommended; although if it had not been for the expectation of amendments, the Constitution would have been rejected in this state, by a majority of more than two to one of our Convention. Thus notwithstanding it is the wish of the people that the alterations recommended should take place, these arbitrary aristocratics are perpetually scribbling in the little papers to induce the people to neglect the true patriots of our country, that themselves may be chosen into the federal legislature. How absurd and inconsistent will it appear, Messieurs Printers, after having recommended amendments, to elect such men to administer the federal government, as have publicly declared themselves opposed to all amendments which have been recommended? "But as we have hitherto been the care of Divine Providence, we have reason to hope, that our federal councils will be preserved from the direction" of *Recanting Tories, British Agents,* and *Aristocratical* and *Monarchical Tyrants.*

DHFFE, I, pp. 453-454.

William Shippen, Jr. (Philadelphia) September 2, 1788
Letter: To Thomas Lee Shippen (excerpt)

There is a great convention now sitting at Harrisburg on the Susquehanna, composed of Antifederalists from every county. Blair McClenachan is gone from Philadelphia County and George Bryan and Charles Pettit from the city. Their business is to agree upon and recommend such alterations as they may think necessary and there is so respectable a minority in every state that I think one of the first acts of the new government will be to propose a general convention of the people to make these necessary alterations, till when the minds of a great part of the United States will not be easy. To effect this measure I am apt to think at our next election the Constitutionalists will prevail.

DHFFE, I, p. 258.

Harrisburg Convention September 6, 1788
Proceedings

Agreeably to a Circular Letter which originated in the county of Cumberland, inviting to a conference such of the citizens of this state, who conceive that a revision of the federal system, lately proposed for the general government of the United States, is necessary, a number of gentlemen from the city of Philadelphia and counties of Philadelphia, Bucks, Chester, Lancaster, Cumberland, Berks, Northumberland, Bedford, Fayette, Washington, Franklin, Dauphin, and Huntingdon, assembled at this place for the said purpose, viz. Hon. George Bryan, Charles Pettit, Blair M'Clenachan, Richard Backhouse, James Hanna, Joseph Sterrit, William Rodgers, William Petriken, Jonathan Hoge, John Bishop, Daniel Montgomery, John Lytle, John Dickey, Hon. John Smiley, Albert Gallatin, James Marshall, Benjamin Elliot, Richard Baird, James Crooks, Adam Orth, John Rodgers, Thomas Murray, Robert M'Kee, John Kean, John A. Hanna, Daniel Bradly, Robert Smith, James Anderson.

Blair M'Clenachan, Esquire, was unanimously elected chairman, and John A. Hanna, Esquire, secretary.

After free discussion and mature deliberation had upon the subject before them, the following resolutions and propositions were adopted.

The ratification of the Federal Constitution having formed a new era in the American world highly interesting to all the citizens of the United States, it is no less the duty than the privilege of every citizen to examine with attention the principles and probable effects of a system, on which the happiness or misery of the present as well as future generations so much depend. In the course of such examination many of the good citizens of the state of Pennsylvania have found their apprehensions excited, that the Constitution, in its present form, contains in it some principles which may be perverted to purposes injurious to the rights of free citizens, and some ambiguities which may probably lead to contentions incompatible with order and good government. In order to remedy these inconveniencies and to avert the apprehended dangers, it has been thought expedient that delegates, chosen by those who wish for early amendments in the said Constitution should meet together for the purpose of deliberating on the subject, and uniting in some constitutional plan for obtaining the amendments which they may deem necessary.

We the conferees, assembled for the purpose aforesaid, agree in opinion,

That a federal government only can preserve the liberties and secure the happiness of the inhabitants of a country so extensive as these United States; and experience having taught us that the ties of our Union, under the Articles of Confederation, were so weak as to deprive us of some of the greatest advantages we had a right to expect from it. We are fully convinced that a more efficient government is indispensably necessary; but although the Constitution proposed for the United States is likely to obviate most of the inconveniencies we labored under, yet several parts of it appear so exceptionable to us that we are clearly of opinion considerable amendments are essentially necessary. In full confidence, however, of obtaining a revision of such exceptionable parts, by a general convention, and from a desire to harmonize with our fellow citizens, we are induced to aquiesce in the organization of the said Constitution.

We are sensible that a large number of the citizens, both in this and the other states, who gave their assent to its being carried into execution, previous to any amendments, were actuated more by the fear of the dangers that might arise from delays than by a conviction of its being perfect; we therefore hope they will concur with us in pursuing every peaceable method of obtaining a speedy revision of the Constitution in the mode therein provided; and when we reflect on the present circumstances of the Union, we can entertain no doubt that motives of conciliation and the dictates of policy and prudence will conspire to induce every man of true federal principles to give his support to a measure, which is not only calculated to recommend the new Constitution to the approbation and support of every class of citizens, but even necessary to prevent the total defection of some of the members of the Union.

Strongly impressed with these sentiments, we have agreed to the following resolutions:

I. Resolved, that it be recommended to the people of this state to acquiesce in the organization of the said government; but although we thus accord in its organization, we by no means lose sight of the grand object of obtaining very considerable amendments and alterations, which we consider essential to preserve the peace and harmony of the Union and those invaluable privileges for which so much blood and treasure have been recently expended.

II. Resolved, that it is necessary to obtain a speedy revision of said Constitution by a general convention.

III. Resolved, that in order to effect this desirable end, a petition be presented to the legislature of this state, requesting that honorable body to take the earliest opportunity to make application for that purpose to the new Congress.

The petition proposed is as follows:

To the Honorable Representatives of the Freemen of the Commonwealth of Pennsylvania, in General Assembly met.

The petition and representation of the subscribers humbly show,

That your petitioners possess sentiments completely federal, being convinced that a confederacy of republican states, and no other, can secure political liberty, happiness, and safety throughout a territory so extended as the United States of America. They are well apprised of the necessity of devolving extensive powers to Congress, and of vesting the supreme legislature with every power and resource of a general nature; and consequently they acquiesce in the general system of government framed by the late Federal Convention; in full confidence, however, that the same will be revised without delay: for however worthy of approbation the general principles and outlines of the said system may be, your petitioners conceive that amendments in some parts of the plan are essential, not only to the preservation of such rights and privileges as ought to be reserved in the respective states, and in the citizens thereof, but to the fair and unembarrassed operation of the government in its various departments. And as provision is made in the Constitution itself for the making of such amendments as may be deemed necessary; and your petitioners are desirous of obtaining the amendments which occur to them as more immediately desirable and necessary, in the mode admitted by such provision,

They pray that your honorable House, as the representatives of the people in this commonwealth, will, in the course of your present session, take such measures as you in your wisdom shall deem most effectual and proper to obtain a revision and amendment of the Constitution of the United States, in such parts and in such manner as have been or shall be pointed out by the conventions or assemblies of the respective states; and that such revision be by a general convention of representatives from the several states in the Union.

Your petitioners consider the amendments pointed out in the propositions hereto subjoined as essentially necessary, and as such they suggest them to your notice, submitting to your wisdom the order in which they shall be presented to the consideration of the United States.

The amendments proposed are as follow, viz.,

I. That Congress shall not exercise any powers whatsoever, but such as are expressly given to that body by the Constitution of the United States: nor shall any authority, power or jurisdiction be assumed or exercised by the executive or judiciary departments of the Union under color or pretense of construction or fiction: But all the rights of sovereignty which are not by the said Constitution expressly and plainly vested in the Congress shall be deemed to remain with, and shall be exercised by the several states in the Union according to their respective constitutions: And that every reserve of the rights of individuals made by the several constitutions of the states in Union to the citizens and inhabitants of each state respectively, shall remain inviolate, except so far as they are expressly and manifestly yielded or narrowed by the national Constitution.

II. That the number of Representatives be for the present, one for every twenty thousand inhabitants according to the present estimated numbers in the several states, and continue in that proportion till the whole number of Representatives shall amount to two hundred; and then to be so proportioned and modified as not to exceed that number till the proportion of one Representative for every thirty thousand inhabitants shall amount to the said number of two hundered. (Article I, Section 2, Paragraph 3.)

III. That Senators, tho chosen for six years, shall be liable to be recalled, or superseded by other appointments, by the respective legislatures of the states at any time. (Section 3.)

IV. That Congress shall not have power, to make or alter regulations concerning the time, place and manner of electing Senators and Representatives except in case of neglect or refusal by the state, to make regulations for the purpose: and then only for such time as such neglect or refusal shall continue. (Section 4.)

V. That when Congress shall require supplies which are to be raised by direct taxes, they shall demand from the several states their respective quotas thereof, giving a reasonable time to each state to procure and pay the same; and if any state shall refuse, neglect or omit to raise and pay the same within such limited time, then Congress shall have power to assess, levy and collect the quota of such state, together with interest for the same from the time of such delinquency, upon the inhabitants and estates therein, in such manner as they shall by law direct, provided that no poll tax be imposed. (Section 8).

VI. That no standing army of regular troops shall be raised or kept up in time of peace, without the consent of two-thirds of both houses in Congress. (Section 8.)

VII. That the clause respecting the exclusive legislation over a district not exceeding ten miles square, be qualified by a proviso that such right of legislation extend only to such regulations as respect the police and good order thereof. (Section 8.)

VIII. That each state respectively shall have power to provide for organizing, arming and disciplining the militia thereof, whensoever Congress shall omit or neglect to provide for the same. That the militia shall not be subject to marial law, but when in actual service in time of war, invasion or rebellion: and when not in the actual service of the United States, shall be subject to such fines, penalties, and punishments only, as shall be directed or inflicted by the laws of its own state: nor shall the militia of any state be continued in actual service longer than two months under any call of Congress, without the consent of the legislature of such state, or, in their recess, the executive thereof. (Aricle I, Section 8.)

IX. That the clause respecting vessels bound to or from any one of the states be explained. (Section 9.)

X. That Congress establish no courts other than the Supreme Court except such as shall be necessary, for determining causes of admiralty jurisdiction. (Article 3, Section 1.)

XI. That a proviso be added at the end of the second clause of the second section of the third article to the following effect, viz. Provided that such appelate jurisdiction, in all cases of common law cognizance, be by writ of error, and confined to matters of law only, and that no such writ of error shall be admitted except in revenue cases, unless the matter in controversy exceed the value of three thousand dollars. (Section 2, Paragraph 2.)

XII. That to article 6, clause 2, be added the following proviso, viz. Provided always, that no treaty which shall hereafter be made, shall be deemed or construed to alter or effect any law of the United States, or of any particular state, until such treaty shall have been laid before, and assented to by the House of Representatives in Congress. (Article 6, Paragraph 2.)

Resolved, that the foregoing proceedings be committed to the chairman for publication.

Blair M'Clenachan, Chairman

Attest: John A. Hanna, Secretary

DHFFE, I, pp. 260-264. Reprinted in *Debates*, II, pp. 542-546.

Boston *Massachusetts Centinel* September 6, 1788
A Correspondent.

The legislature (thank God *they* choose the Senators) and the freemen of the county of Suffolk, in particular, will undoubtedly fix their eyes upon men of *real* federalism, *consistent, independent* characters, who have judgment to *discern,* and spirit to *pursue,* the best interests of their country. You will not find such men pledging themselves to *alter* the Constitution. The proposition is treason against the majesty of the people. It is their *own Constitution,* by a fairer and better title than any nation under Heaven can boast, having been conceded to in its *present form* by a greater proportion of the free citizens, than we can naturally suppose any alterations ever will, and therefore we may safely repeat, that unconditional promises to support and bring about alterations, previous to a *full trial* and experience of its competency to the great purposes of the Union, is TREASON AGAINST THE MAJESTY OF THE PEOPLE.

DHFFE, I, p. 458. For a response to this item, see "A Federal Correspondent," September 11, 1788, directly below.

A Federal Correspondent September 11, 1788
Newspaper Article: Boston *Independent Chronicle*[1]

A federal correspondent observes, that howsoever a correspondent of the Centinel[2] of Saturday last may amuse himself with air, "thin air," the enlightened freemen of the United States of America are not so destitute of common sense, as not to see and laugh at any suggestions, direct or implied, that convey an idea, that it is treason against themselves, to propose, and endeavor to obtain, in the constitutional way, necessary amendments, to their own Constitution; "treason against the majesty of the people" lies on the other hand. The people of this commonwealth, in particular, by their very respectable Convention, in February last, at the ratification of the Federal Constitution, after stating sundry amendments, then enumerated, did, "In the name and in the behalf of the people of this Commonwealth, enjoin it upon their Representatives in Congress, at all times, until the alterations and provisions aforesaid, have been considered, agreeably to the fifth article of the said Constitution, to exert all their influence, and use all reasonable and legal methods to obtain a ratification of the said alterations and provisions, in such manner, as is provided in the said article."

Is it then, this correspondent asks, the holding up the propriety and importance, of obtaining, if possible, this enjoined object of the people; or sentiments, advanced in opposition to it, that exhibits most, the complexion of TREASON AGAINST THE MAJESTY OF THE PEOPLE. Of this the enlightened people are fully competent to determine for themselves. But not only the Convention of this commonwealth, but those of several other states (the whole included, being entitled, as fixed by the Constitution, to a majority of Representatives, of those states which have adopted the system) have likewise proposed amendments. And it is highly probable, that if the mode of first adopting the Constitution, and then proposing amendments, had been at first thought of, all the ratifying states, would have pursued nearly the same line of conduct. The freemen of these states, have a foresight to discern, that their liberties may be in danger, although not attacked, if an avenue is left open, through which they may, at some future time, be attacked; they will, therefore, naturally be anxious, that any aperture in the barrier between powers delegated and retained, be closed, explicitly defined, and well understood. To leave matters to a full trial of experience, as some are urging, may perhaps be compared to the loaning a man's money, untold and without proper security for the payment thereof, in order to ascertain his honor and honesty; or to neglect to repair a breach in the walls of a city liable to be besieged, in order to discover whether the assailants would avail themselves of the advantage offered them. The loss of property, however, in the one case, and a lodgment gained behind the breach, in the other, would render after precaution unavailable.

1 DHFFE, I, pp. 460-461.
2 See "Boston *Massachusetts Centinel*," September 6, 1788, directly above.

A Marylander September 12, 1788
Newspaper Article: Baltimore *Maryland Gazette* (excerpt)

To the *Inhabitants* of *Baltimore-Town*

It is industriously held out, that the federal constitution is now so firmly fixed, as to render it immaterial, what are the political sentiments of our representatives in the ensuing assembly—For my part I think a federalist ought to vote against his own brother, who will not unequivocally pledge himself to put the government in motion, vote for no man as a senator, but what has been uniformly an advocate for the adoption of the government, previous to the proposal of amendments, so as to secure the union from dissolution, and support no alterations, which shall subvert or enervate the constitution—No man, who is for depriving the general government of the exclusive direction of foreign affairs, and confirmation or rejection of treaties; of the command of the militia (thereby laying a foundation for civil wars among the different States;) of the direction and appropriation of all excises and duties upon imports and exports to the uses of the union, and the power of laying direct taxes, in cases of emergency, can with propriety be termed a federalist, those being the cardinal points of the new constitution—It is customary here to call out amendments, amendments, and upbraiding the two Doctors [McHenry and Coulter] for being opposed to any whatever—Almost every person agrees, that explanatory amendments, more accurately defining the great rights of the people, are necessary, but we should take care, that no *alterations*, sapping the most energetic parts of the government, should be carried, under the popular cry of *amendments*—The two Doctors ought to explain at the Town Meeting, HOW FAR THEY WILL GO, and the two Lawyers [Chase and McMechan], WHERE THEY WILL STOP.

DHFFE, II, p. 145.

Providence Gazette **September 13, 1788**
Datelined Petersburg, August 14 (excerpt)

We learn from North-Carolina, that the Convention of that State have not absolutely rejected the new Constitution—but have proposed a bill of rights, and amendments to the most exceptionable parts of the same—which they conceive ought to be laid before Congress and the States, previous to the ratification of the Constitution on the part of the State of North-Carolina—The bill of rights and amendments are nearly the same as those proposed by this State [Virginia], except in two instances; but this locality does not militate against the interest of any other States. The new Constitution was discussed clause by clause, in a Committee of the whole Convention, and the report of the Committee was a bill of rights and amendments previous to the ratification, which was agreed to by the Convention by a majority of 102—Yeas, 184—Nays, 82. It was the opinion of that Convention, that the Congress will call a general Convention to consider the proposed amendments; that the deliberations of that Convention be submitted to Conventions in the several States; and that their State not having rejected the Constitution absolutely, will not be precluded from calling a Convention to adopt it, should they think proper so to do.

A Republican September 17, 1788
Newspaper Article: New York *Daily Advertiser* (excerpts)

But North-Carolina has not adopted the new Constitution, and therefore it is alleged that she is antifederal, and an enemy to good government. This is the last charge, and like the rest, it is worse founded than people are apt to believe. It is now generally agreed that the new Constitution will admit of some amendments—they have been pointed out. It will also admit of several explanations or alterations, by which it may be rendered, not a better system, but a safer one against the machinations of wicked men. Some of these explanations will doubtless be made by the general concurrence of the states, because they obviate powers, which no man can advocate:— . . . The state wishes to see the alterations made which she has pointed out, and for this very reason, she wishes to see the new government commence. If eight states only had confederated, when the Convention of North-Carolina sat, perhaps they ought to have made the ninth, but ten states had confederated, consequently the general system was secure.

The pause that North-Carolina has made can occasion no delay in the necessary measures, and no state, except herself, can be injured by it. We are told, indeed, that she ought to have adopted the new system, that so she might have assisted in making the proposed amendments; but she replies that, if other states are seriously disposed to make reasonable and profitable alterations, they can do it in a short time without her assistance; but if they are dissembling—if they are about to drop the spirit of accommodation, and to hold by majorities what they have gained by accident, she is safest where she stands. A cautious politician has little faith.

DHFFE, IV, p. 316.

Civis September 19, 1788
Newspaper Article: *Pennsylvania Packet*[1]

The publication of the proceedings of a late meeting at Harrisburg[2] has afforded to me, and probably to many others, an agreeable disappointment. From what we had heard of the disposition of the people who promoted the meeting, there was reason to expect a result widely different from that which their proceedings exhibit. The moderation they have shown on this occasion does honor to those who were assembled, and entitles the measures they have recommended to attention and respect. However widely some of them may have heretofore strayed from the line of sound policy and good citizenship in their conduct concerning the Federal Constitution, they had, or imagined they had, sufficient cause for the opposition they gave. If in the manner of doing it passion should be supposed to have unduly interposed its influence, candid reflection on the occurrences shortly after the promulgation of the plan of government, may extenuate though it may not excuse the fault. But however this may be, they have now made a conciliatory advance, which ought to be met and cherished by those from whom they have differed in opinion, as well for the sake of promoting harmony in the state, as to give fair operation to the plan of confederation. For although in a free government, the *will* of the majority may, and ought to predominate, a wise and prudent majority will nevertheless calculate and conduct their measures in as conciliating a manner as is consistent with the dignity and energy of government, and cautiously avoid giving unnecessary cause of irritation or disgust to the minority. Success naturally produces moderation, complacency and dignity in cultivated minds. These effects are therefore expected to be found in the conduct of a majority; and when it is otherwise they generally diminish their own strength, by adding to that of the minority, and not unfrequently change places with them. I wish, therefore, as one of the majority, to see our public measures so conducted as to leave no ground for prejudice itself to generate alarms upon, and in such manner as may be most likely to improve the *acquiescence* of the minority into *approbation*.

A large proportion, probably a majority of those who have assented to the ratification of the new Constitution in its present form, are desirous that it should be amended in some parts as early as such amendments can be made without impeding its operation, or hazarding its being destroyed, by being wholly submitted to the arbitration of another general convention. The amendments proposed are but few, and pointed to particular parts, which may be subjected to revision by a general convention, without danger to the general principles or vital parts of the Constitution, and without impeding its organization and operation in the meantime. Several of the most considerable of the states have accompanied their adoption with an instruction to procure amendments as early as possible. As the Convention of Pennsylvania omitted this accompaniment to their ratification on a supposition, it is imagined, that their power was limited to the mere adoption or rejection of the instrument laid before them. The Assembly, who are expressly authorized by the Constitution itself to propose amendments, are now requested to do it. Whether they will comply with this request or not, is with them to determine.

May wisdom govern their choice!

1 DHFFE, I, pp. 276-277.
2 See "Harrisburg Convention," September 6, 1788, p. 519 for the proceedings referred to.

DeWitt Clinton (New York) September 19, 1788
Letter: To Dr. Charles Clinton (excerpt)[1]

I suppose you have heard that North Carolina has rejected the Constitution by a majority of 102. This step is imputed to letters from this state giving reason to suppose that our Convention would set the example. I imagine P[atrick] Henry's mighty influence in that state has assisted in bringing about the measure. A meeting of delegates from every county in Pennsylvania was held the 3d instant at Harrisburg. The ostensible design is this: that the opponents to the new Constitution may concenter their endeavors in the election of Antifeds to the new Congress. Some suppose it was intended to prevent the operation of the government in that state, but the result of their proceedings evinces the contrary.

After a great struggle between the Northern and Southern members in Congress as to the place of the meeting of the first Congress under the new Constitution, it is finally determined by an ordinance that this city shall be the place, the first Wednesday of January next the time of appointing Electors throughout the several states, the first Wednesday of February next the day of electing the President, and the first Wednesday of March the day of putting the government in operation. I always supposed that subsequent amendments were never the serious design of the great friends of the new government and that the idea was only a political maneuver to lead the people to its adoption. In some of the Philadephia and Boston newspapers, emendations to the government are evidently reprobated, the Circular Letter and proposed amendments of our convention styled impertinent and destructive, and an attempt to procure alterations, until the government is tried, called high treason against the majesty of the people. Messieurs Samuel Adams and [Elbridge] Gerry are nominated in the Massachusetts newspapers as Senators for that state. The first is earnest for amendments[2] and the second was a member of the General Convention and refused to subscribe to the Constitution. By a cooperation of influence, it is supposed they may get in.

1 DHFFE, I, pp. 140-141.

2 See "Massachusetts Convention," February 6, 1788, p. 260 at note 3, for Samuel Adams' proposed amendments in the Convention, which included the right of the people to keep their own arms.

Pittsburgh Gazette September 20, 1788

County Committee Report (excerpts)

Report of the Committee: A committee having been chosen, at a meeting held in Greensburg, for the County of Westmoreland on the 5th day of August, and authorized to correspond with other counties of this state, respecting the propriety of joining with other states in endeavoring to procure amendments to the Constitution for the general government of the United States; and the respective citizens present at the said meeting, having unanimously voted that amendments were necessary, and the committee having received letters on the subject, think it their duty to express their own sentiments, and what they believe to be the prevailing sentiments of the people of the County of Westmoreland on this important subject.

They profess to possess sentiments completely federal, and do believe that no other than a federal republican form of government can secure political liberty in an empire so extensive as the United States. They are also fully convinced of the necessity of vesting more extensive powers in Congress, than it could exercise under the Confederation, consequently they heartily approve of vesting the general government with every power and resource which is of a general nature, and which is generally relating to all the states; such as imposts or duties arising from importation, regulation of commerce, treaties of all sorts, armies, navies, coin, post office, etc. etc. But they regret that the general government goes much farther than these federal principles will admit, and vests Congress with such extensive local powers, in addition to the necessary general powers, as must eventually destroy the state governments, and absorb the whole sovereignty [and] consequently prove to be one entire consolidated government, which in our extensive situation must be a despotic one. They therefore wish that it may be expressly stipulated, that Congress shall not assume or exercise any further or other powers than what is expressly defined and clearly vested therein by the express words of the Constitution. . . .

Fifthly, they apprehend that the unlimited power of keeping standing armies in time of peace, especially as combined with the power over every source of revenue is inconsistent with the principles of a federal republican government, and the freedom of the citizens.

They therefore earnestly recommend, that if keeping standing armies in time of peace should be thought necessary, the power should be put under such checks, as to secure the liberty of the community at large, and the personal safety of individuals; and this they conceive may be accomplished by rendering a majority of three-fourths of the Senate and House of Representatives agreeing to the necessity and propriety of raising a standing army in time of peace necessary, and by keeping the military in due subordination to the civil law.

Sixthly, they conceive that by so imperfect a bill or declaration of rights as the new plan of general government contains, whereby the trial by jury in criminal cases, the habeas corpus act, etc., only is secured; trial by jury in civil cases, and every other essential right of freemen is impliedly given up to the arbitrary will of future men. They therefore wish that such a declaration of rights may be added to the general frame of government as may secure to posterity those privileges which are essential to the proper limiting the extent of sovereign power, and securing those rights which are essential to freemen; and that Congress may not have power to pass any laws which in their effects may infringe on or tend to subvert the constitution of any particular state, except in such cases as are mentioned in the first clause to be of a general nature, and properly belonging to Congress.

Seventhly, they further observe, that the undue mixture of legislative and executive powers in the Senate is highly corrupting in its nature, and dangerous to liberty in its influence; and that the power of putting the militia under the terrors of martial law in time of peace, or of marching them, perhaps, to destroy the freedom of an oppressed sister state, without any check or control from the state governments, stand also in absolute need of revision and amendments.

The foregoing particulars the committee have tho't proper to point out as amongst the most obvious exceptionable powers vested by the new system of general government in the future Congress: at the same time they believe that the people of the County of Westmoreland are willing to concur with such further, or other amendments, as shall render the proposed plan a government of freedom, confidence and energy.

DHFFE, I, p. 277-279.

Thomas Jefferson (Paris) September 20, 1788
Letter: To William Short (excerpt)

The convention of Virginia annexed to their ratification of the new Constitution a copy of the state Declaration of rights, not by way of Condition, but to announce their attachment to them. They added also propositions for specific alterations of the constitution. Among these was one for rendering the President incapable of serving more than 8. years in any term of 16. New York has followed the example of Virginia, expressing the substance of her bill of rights, (i.e. Virginia's) & proposing amendments.

Ford, V, pp. 48-49.

James Madison (New York) September 21, 1788
Letter: To Thomas Jefferson (excerpt)

The Circular letter fom the New York Convention has rekindled an ardor among the opponents of the federal Constitution for an immediate revision of it by another General Convention. You will find in one of the papers inclosed the result of the consultations in Pennsylvania on that subject. Mr. Henry and his friends in Virginia enter with great zeal into the scheme. Governor Randolph also espouses it; but with a wish to prevent if possible danger to the article which extends the power of the Government to internal as well as external taxation. It is observable that the views of the Pennsylva[nia] meeting do not rhyme very well with those of the Southern advocates for a Convention; the objects most eagerly pursued by the latter being unnoticed in the Harrisburg proceedings. The effect of the circular letter on other States is less known. I conclude that it will be the same everywhere among those who opposed the Constitution, or contended for a conditional ratification of it. Whether an early Convention will be the result of this united effort, is more than can at this moment be foretold. The measure will certainly be industriously opposed in some parts of the Union, not only by those who wish for no alterations, but by others who would prefer the other mode provided in the Constitution, as most expedient at present, for introducing those supplemental safeguards to liberty agst. which no objections can be raised; and who would moreover approve of a Convention for amending the frame of the Government itself, as soon as time shall have somewhat corrected the feverush state of the public mind, and trial have pointed its attention to the true defects of the system.

BRDH, II, pp. 929-930. Reprinted in *Papers*, XI, pp. 257-258.

Abraham Yates, Jr. (New York) September 22, 1788
Letter: To William Smith

I have your favour of the 19th before me—In Respect to the New government we exactly Agree in Opinion—The case now is simple All agree that Amendmt are Indispensibly necessary—And where we had it in our own power before the Convention have transferred it to the union at Large and we now cant get the amendments unless 2/3 of the states first agree to a Convention and as many to agree to the Amendments—And then 3/4 of the several Legislatures to Confirm them: That this will be an uphill Affair—You may see when you call to mind that Congress lately had ten weeks before they could agree where the New government was to meet—But so it is And we must make the best of it. our only safety now is in geting the Amendments Confirmed—I mean to try for it and I believe the first thing Necessary will be to pass a Law to Inhibit the state officers (the Legislature Executive And Judicial) from takeing the Oath to support the New government untill our amendments have been Confirmed in due form—my Next will contain more upon this subject I have no time (Your son goes off to manor) than to add that I Remain Your sincere friend And Humble sert

DHFFE, III, p. 203.

Governor Samuel Huntington (Connecticut) September 23, 1788
Letter: To Governor Samuel Johnston of North Carolina[1]

I have been honoured with your several letters of the 12th.[2]& 24th. ulto., the former covering an Extract from the Journals of the late Convention of your State & the latter accompanied with two Resolves passed by your Convention.

These papers will be communicated to the General Assembly of this State at their approaching Session.

The Convention in this State, at the time they ratified the new federal Constitution, would have preferred some Alterations & Amendments rather than the present form, if I may judge from the sentiments that were thrown out in discussing the subject; but deemed it too dangerous to hazard Delays under a tottering Constitution, until every diffuculty should be removed, so as to obtain a Constitution which would meet the entire approbation of all the States in the Union, which it is not probable would ever be the Case.

Perhaps from the nature of the case, it must be left to the wisdom & virtue of the States to make Amendments in future, in the mode provided by the Constitution, as experience shall dictate: No Constitution of Government can make a people happy without Virtue and Wisdom.

A Bill of Rights in former times hath been judged necessary, but in this enlightened age, when it seems a self evident truth, acknowledged almost as indisputably as any Axiom, that all right & authority in Government is derived from the People, & may be resumed whenever the safety or happiness of the people renders it necessary; is it necessary, or expedient, for them to form a Bill of Rights which seems at least to call in question a truth of such importance & which ought ever to be held indisputable?

1 DHFFE, II, pp. 12-13.

2 The letter of the 12th had included the Declaration of Rights and Amendments to the Constitution which were proposed by the North Carolina Convention. See *Ibid.*, p. 13, note 2. See "North Carolina Convention," August 1, 1788, pp. 503-509, for these items.

Federalism September 26, 1788

Newspaper Article: Baltimore *Maryland Journal* (excerpt)[1]

It is said, with great confidence, by all the enemies of the federal constitution, that the government is constitutionally confirmed, and that nothing can prevent its being put in motion as the constitution of *America.* Sir, this is but half the truth—this is an idea which they have carefully circulated, through every part of this continent. It is manifestly intended to make the people at rest—to lull their minds asleep to a further prosecution of the business—and at our present situation, when in reality the constitution is but half established —when recovered from an imperfect, an enfeebled state of infancy, and just obtained a healthful tone, at this imperfect crisis, we hear and see plans forming in several states to give the constitution a secret stab through the medium of *particular amendments,* which will destroy every federal feature, and crush all its efficient powers.—This may be considered a harsh accusation—This kind of conduct in men, may be considered as beneath the utmost depravity of mankind—But I am sorry to see this truth upon record—I am sorry to think and know we have men so base amongst us.

The *inclination* and *power* in men to do *certain acts,* is sufficient ground for the rational mind to conclude that these *acts* will be executed, if not prevented by circumstances opposite, or men of contrary sentiments.—That it is the *will* or *inclination* of certain men, in the different states, to throw our public affairs into confusion and prevent the federal government taking effect, I appeal to facts—I appeal to the proceedings of the minority of the state of *Pennsylvania.*—What was the conduct of these men while in their state convention? When they met in that body, by the voice of their country, and by the consent of themselves, when they found a majority in the house for adopting the constitution, did they not, with violence, attempt to break up the house, and in the fury of their malice bursted the doors; and those who absconded from the house, were they not dragged to their duty, to the business of their country, by force?[2]—And what was their conduct afterwards?—Did they not publish an address to the people in the most inflammatory language that could be penned, and in this address advised the people "to oppose the constitution then offered to them," and adopted by their state, "*in the same manner, and with the same spirit, that they resisted the tyranny of* Great-Britain *in the late revolution.*" Sir, this was the language of these men, it is upon record, and in the hands of almost every person—and this is their language still. The leaders of these very men, and some of the men themselves, were in the late convention that sat at *Harrisburg*—The names of these men are annexed to and accompany the *amendments,* that are now published by that convention and offered for our acceptance.—Are these men to be trusted?—Can credulity itself place confidence in men who, but a few months since, advised their constituents to take *up arms against each other*—to introduce all the *horrors of civil war* in this country, and *draw the sword* against that *constitution which they now say they mean to put in motion.*

Now permit me to call your attention to the enemies of the constitution, collected in the minority in the late convention of this state: Although, in fact, their conduct was not as openly expressive of their malicious designs against the constitution; but in proportion to their numbers, compared with those in *Pennsylvania,* they were equally as much so; yet, I say, the final issue of their deliberations were the same, and the amendments of each may be considered this issue.—Every person who can read, may compare the amendments of each minority, and acknowledge their similitude.—In those points that are not materially necessary either way—and those also that are expressed by the one and not mentioned by the other, still of little or no consequence, they differ; but in the great leading points, that are necessary to the execution of their plan, the distruction of the federal constitution, *they exactly agree.*—Does not this shew a premeditated plan?—Does not this discover an inclination to destroy, *by particular amendments,* our federal governments?—This inclination being thus proved, as far as actions are declarative of intentions or wishes, it only remains to shew that these men have it in their power, if their numbers in state-legislatures are sufficient, to defeat the government in a *constitutional manner.*—This will appear evident from the following considerations.

The means by which amendments, agreeably to the constitution, are to be made to the federal government, are two—First, by Congress—Secondly, by the legislatures of the several states —Congress will be composed of a President, of a Senate, and a House of Representatives—Congress is a body *yet to be formed*—the people appoint immediately the House of Representatives as one part; but the Senate and President, the other parts, are created by other powers—The President will be appointed by electors, and these electors are to be chosen, out of the body of the people, in such manner as the legislatures of the several states shall order.—Here is great discretionary power.—So that in truth the President of Congress will be the mediate creature of the state-legislatures.—This constitutional truth being duly considered and established, let us suppose, for a moment, that which is much to be feared we will be obliged to admit, an antifederal representation present in the state-legislatures: under these circumstances, I beg leave to ask every friend and foe to the constitution, if it is not probable, if it is not reasonable, if it is not consistent with human nature to expect, that states so represented will choose antifederal electors, and those electors will make choice of an antifederal President.

The Senate is the next object. The same reasons urged above, with respect to the President, apply in the present case, and in a much more forcible manner; because the Senate is appointed by the state-legislatures immediately, and their voice will determine the complexion of the Senate for six years, when it will be in vain to counteract what they have done.

But, Sir, this is not all—These great chances are not the only ones that the enemies to the constitution have to defeat the government—they have another power, if you will permit their numbers to be sufficient, in the state-legislatures, to do what they please—and to have such amendments as they *choose,* without the intervention of Congress or any other power to control them.—All these powers appear evident to every candid and reasonable person, and all clearly expressed on the face of the constitution, as will appear from the following statement of part of the fifth article thereof, *viz.* "The Congress, whenever two-thirds of both houses shall deem it necessary, shall propose amendments to this constitution; *or on the application of the legislatures of two-thirds of the several states, shall call a convention for proposing amendments, which will in either case be valid to all intents and purposes as a part of this constitution, when ratified by the legislatures of three fourths of the several states,* or by conventions in three-fourths thereof, as the one or the other mode of ratification may be proposed by Congress," &c.

The second means by which amendments are to be made to the constitution, that is by the legislature, I conceive will be the way by which the enemies to the constitution mean to make their first attack upon the government; this will be the unfortunate avenue through which these political serpents mean to insinuate their baneful poison into our public measures—and our next assemblies, I fear, will bear testimony to the sad catastrophe—It will, perhaps, be then in their power to bring forward those amendments which have been already offered to us, and rejected by the real friends to our country; and if their present plan succeeds, that of obtaining a sufficient number of antifederals in the state-assemblies, they will do the business at once.—They will not wait the issue of another election; and before the people will have another voice in the business, our beloved and once befriended federal government will be done away, or rendered useless, by the *addition of particular amendments*—and amendments too proposed and incorporated in the government in the above constitutional manner.—This is the reason why we hear the constant cry of antifederalism in every corner—"*We want amendments, and we will pledge ourselves to the people that we will make them in a constitutional manner.*"

Sir, I flatter myself it is now plain to the most domestic capacity, the danger we are yet in and the great probability of our federal government being defeated.—After all our trouble—after the united exertions of the collected wisdom and virtue of the tried friends of *America,* assembled in General Convention—after the Constitution has passed triumphant thro' the strictest constitutional investigation that freemen can give it, and at length has been adopted by our country by a great majority of states, more than was sufficient, as prescribed by the constitution, to give efficacy to it—I say, after all this labour, there is a great probability that this constitution will yet be defeated.

1 DHFFE, II, pp. 118-121.

2 The author apparently here confused the Minority of the Pennsylvania Convention with the Seceding Pennsylvania Assemblymen. See "Seceding Pennsylvania Assemblymen," October 2, 1787, p. 30 and "Pennsylvania Minority," December 18, 1787, p. 154.

Richard Henry Lee (Chantilly) October 15, 1788
Letter: To Theodorick Bland

Long acqaintance and friendship, with very similar political opinions, will apologize for my troubling you with my wishes that amendments may be procured to the new constitution, by means of the new Congress; and that I am willing to exert my faculties for the obtaining such amendments in the senate of the new legislature, if it shall please the Assembly to send me there; and this information to my friends is the more necessary, because I know it is a common art, in these times, to prevent elections by asserting that persons proposed will not serve, if elected. That amendments are necessary to this system, cannot, I think, be doubted by any sensible and dispassionate man. The thing itself, the judgment of many respectable states, and great numbers of individuals, all proclaim it. Nor will amendments, probably, fail to be made, unless the legislatures should choose men so zealously and blindly devoted as to prevent them from seeing defects that all other men do see. As the subject has been very fully considered, and a majority have received it, professedly under the idea of expected amendments, I should think that, as good citizens, it now becomes us to exert our faculties so to conduct the business as that a wise, energetic, and free government, may result from properly amending the present form. Should this fortunately be your opinion, the community will have the aid of your knowledge and experience in the new legislature.

DHFFE, II, pp. 259-260. See "Theodorick Bland," October 28, 1788, p. 545 for an excerpt from Bland's reply.

James Madison (New York) October 17, 1788
Letter: To Thomas Jefferson (excerpt)[1]

The little pamphlet herewith inclosed will give you a collective view of the alterations which have been proposed for the new Constitution.[2] Various and numerous as they appear they certainly omit many of the true grounds of opposition. The articles relating to Treaties—to paper money, and to contracts, created more enemies than all the errors in the System positive & negative put together. It is true nevertheless that not a few, particularly in Virginia have contended for the proposed alterations from the most honorable & patriotic motive; and that among the advocates for the Constitution, there are some who wish for further guards to public liberty & individual rights. As far as these may consist of a constitutional declaration of the most essential rights, it is probable they will be added; though there are many who think such addition unnecessary, and not a few who think it misplaced in such a Constitution. There is scarce any point on which the party in opposition is so much divided as to its importance and its propriety. My own opinion has always been in favor of a bill of rights; provided it be so framed as not to imply powers not meant to be included in the enumeration. At the same time I have never thought the omission a material defect, nor been anxious to supply it even by *subsequent* amendment, for any other reason than that it is anxiously desired by others. I have favored it because I supposed it might be of use, and if properly executed could not be of disservice. I have not viewed it in an important light 1. because I conceive that in a certain degree, though not in the extent argued by Mr. Wilson, the rights in question are reserved by the manner in which the federal powers are granted. 2 because there is great reason to fear that a positive declaration of some of the most essential rights could not be obtained in the requisite latitude. I am sure that the rights of Conscience in particular, if submitted to public definition would be narrowed much more than they are likely ever to be by an assumed power. One of the objections in New England was that the Constitution by prohibiting religious tests opened a door for Jews Turks & infidels. 3. because the limited powers of the federal Government and the jealousy of the subordinate Governments, afford a security which has not existed in the case of the State Governments, and exists in no other. 4 because experience proves the inefficacy of a bill of rights on those occasions when its controul is most needed. Repeated violations of these parchment barriers have been committed by overbearing majorities in every State. In Virginia I have seen the bill of rights violated in every instance where it has been opposed to a popular current. Notwithstanding the explicit provision contained in that instrument for the rights of Conscience it is well known that a religious establishment wd. have taken place in that State, if the legislative majority had found as they expected, a majority of the people in favor of the measure; and I am persuaded that if a majority of the people were now of one sect, the measure would still take place and on narrower ground than was then proposed, notwithstanding the additional obstacle which the law has since created. Wherever the real power in a Government lies, there is the danger of oppression. In our Governments the real power lies in the majority of the Community, and the invasion of private rights is *cheifly* to be apprehended, not from acts of Government contrary to the sense of its constituents, but from acts in which the Government is the mere instrument of the major number of the constituents. This is a truth of great importance, but not yet sufficiently attended to: and is probably more strongly impressed on my mind by facts, and reflections suggested by them, than on yours which has contemplated abuses of power issuing from a very different quarter. Wherever there is an interest and power to do wrong, wrong will generally be done, and not less readily by a powerful & interested party than by a powerful and interested prince. The difference, so far as it relates to the superiority of republics over monarchies, lies in the less degree of probability that interest may promote abuses of power in the former than in the latter; and in the security in the former agst. oppression of more than the smaller part of the society, whereas in the former[3] it may be extended in a manner to the whole. The difference so far as it relates to the point in question—the efficacy of a bill of rights in controuling abuses of power—lies in this, that in a monarchy the latent force of the nation is superior to that of the sovereign, and a solemn charter of popular rights must have a great effect, as a standard for trying the validity of public acts, and a signal for rousing & uniting the superior force of the community; whereas in a popular Government, the political and physical power may be considered as vested in the same hands, that is in a majority of the people, and consequently the tyrannical will of the sovereign is not [to] be controuled by the dread of an appeal to any other force within the community. What use then it may be asked can a bill of rights serve in popular Governments? I answer the two following which though less essential than in other Governments, sufficiently recommend the precaution. 1. The political truths declared in that solemn manner acquire by degrees the character of fundamental maxims of free Government, and as they become incorporated with the national sentiment, counteract the impulses of interest and passion. 2. Altho' it be generally true as above stated that the danger of oppression lies in the interested majorities of the people rather than in usurped acts of the Government, yet there may be occasions on which the evil may spring from the latter sources; and on such, a bill of rights will be a good ground for an appeal to the sense of the community. Perhaps too there may be a certain degree of danger, that a succession of artful and ambitious rulers, may by gradual & well-timed advances, finally erect an independent Government on the subversion of liberty. Should this danger exist at all, it is prudent to guard agst. it, especially when the precaution can do no injury. At the same time I must own that I see no tendency in our governments to danger on that side. It has been remarked that there is a tendency in all Governments to an augmentation of power at the expence of liberty. But the remark as usually undersood does not appear to me well founded. Power when it has attained a certain degree of energy and independence goes on generally to further degrees. But when below that degree, the direct tendency is to further degrees of relaxation, until the abuses of liberty beget a sudden transition to an undue degree of power. With this explanation the remark may be true; and in the latter sense only is it in my opinion applicable to the Governments in America. It is a melancholy reflection that liberty should be equally exposed to danger whether the Government have too much or too little power, and that the line which divides these extremes should be so inaccurately defined by experience.

Supposing a bill of rights to be proper the articles which ought to compose it, admit of much discussion. I am inclined to think that *absolute* restictions in cases that are doubtful, or where emergencies may overrule them, ought to be avoided. The restrictions however strongly marked on paper will never be regarded when opposed to the decided sense of the public; and after repeated violations in extraordinary cases, they will lose even their ordinary efficacy. Should a Rebellion or insurrection alarm the people as well as the Government, and a suspension of the Hab. Corp. be dictated by the alarm, no written prohibitions on earth would prevent the measure. Should an army in time of peace be gradually established in our neighbourhood by Britn: or Spain, declarations on paper would have as little effect in preventing a standing force for the public safety. The best security agst. these evils is to remove the pretext for them. With regard to monopolies they are justly classed among the greatest nusances in Government. But is it clear that as encouragements to literary works and ingenious discoveries, they are not too valuable to be wholly renounced? Would it not suffice to reserve in all cases a right to the Public to abolish the privilege at a price to be specified in the grant of it? Is there not also infinitely less danger of this abuse in our Governments, than in most others? Monopolies are sacrifices of the many to the few. Where the power is in the few it is natural for them to sacrifice the many to their own partialities and corruptions. Where the power, as with us, is in the many not in the few, the danger can not be very great that the few will be thus favored. It is much more to be dreaded that the few will be unnecessarily sacrificed to the many.

1 *Papers,* XI, pp. 297-300. Also reprinted in BRDH, I, pp. 615-618.

2 The pamphlet was *The Ratifications of the New Foederal Constitution, Together with the Amendments, Proposed by the Several States.* It was printed in Richmond, and contained the ratifications of those states which had proposed amendments. See *Papers,* XI, p. 300, note 2.

3 Madison clearly intended "latter" here, not "former."

4 See "Thomas Jefferson," March 15, 1789, p. 635 for Jefferson's reply to this letter concerning a bill of rights.

Charles Smith (Sunbury) October 18, 1788
Letter: To Tench Coxe (excerpt)[1]

Enclosed you have a copy of the instructions of a number of the inhabitants of Northumberland County to their deputies appointed to attend at the state conference at Lancaster;[2] which I beg you will commit to the press, for the sole purpose of acquainting our friends and fellow citizens with the decisive measures we have pursued in consequence of the circular letter from Philadelphia. To investigate and fix upon proper characters to form a Federal ticket is surely a matter of considerable moment, and which requires coolness and deliberation. To purge the minds of thousands of our fellow citizens of the poison with which they have been infected will and ought to be an important object with the Representatives of this great commonwealth. Perhaps, indeed, all their fears are vain—but when popular passions are roused, and those passions kept alive by designing and ambitious men, an attempt to reason them down is frequently construed into insult. It seems, therefore, to be the wish of the moderate and reasonable men of all parties that some necessary explanations should take place, in order to quiet the minds of our dissenting fellow citizens, and to introduce union and harmony throughout the state. Attention to this subject ought to be considered as a duty incumbent upon our first federal Representatives.

1 DHFFE, I, p. 315.
2 The conference at Lancaster (which met on November 3, 1788) was the Pennsylvania Federalists' counterpart of the Antifederalist conference which had been held at Harrisburg on September 3. For the Proceedings of the latter, see "Harrisburg Convention," September 6, 1788, p. 519.

James Madison (New York) October 20, 1788
Letter: To Edmund Pendleton (excerpt)

I am glad to find you concurring in the requisite expedients for preventing antifederal elections, and a premature Convention. The circular letter from this State [New York] has united and animated the efforts on the adverse side with respect to both these points. An early Convention threatens discord and mischeif. It will be composed of the most heterogenious characters—will be actuated by the party spirit reigning among their constituents—will comprehend men having insidious designs agst. the Union—and can scarcely therefore terminate in harmony or the public good. Let the enemies to the System wait untill some experience shall have taken place, and the business will be conducted with more light as well as with less heat. In the mean time the other mode of amendments may be employed to quiet the fears of many by supplying those further guards for private rights which can do no harm to the system in the judgments even of its most partial friends, and will even be approved by others who have steadily supported it.

Papers, XI, p. 307.

Real Farmer October 22, 1788
Newspaper Article: Springfield *Hampshire Chronicle* (excerpt)

The time is now approaching when the new government is to be organized and put into operation in the United States of America. The Constitution has been adopted by the conventions of more than nine states. In several of those conventions, the members have been nearly equally divided. In most of them, a number of amendments have been resolved upon as highly expedient for securing the liberties and welfare of the people, on the one hand, and for preventing the baneful effects of the abuse of power, on the other. In a situation thus critical, it is ardently to be wished, if not confidently expected, that the legislatures in the several states, and the people at large, may proceed in the organization of this government with the highest degree of candor, prudence, and sagacity. In transacting this all-important business, violent parties and venal measures would, probably, produce a corrupt and violent administration of government.

DHFFE, I, p. 468.

Christian Farmer October 23, 1788
Newspaper Article: Connecticut *Norwich Packet* (excerpt)

Mr. Trumbull,

Please to insert the following in your impartial Paper, and you will oblige a number of your Readers.

CHRISTIAN FARMER.

It is of the utmost importance to found our principles on the solid basis of truth; and before we declare ourselves on this or the other side of any question we ought thoroughly to understand the matter in debate, & seriously consider the consequence of adopting this or the other opinion: when we have done this, we are fitted for a manly and uniform prosecution of what we take in hand. Reason points out to us the method; and a consciousness of our being right, supplieth us with resolution and fortitude to pursue it.

It is of the greatest moment to every society, that a just estimate be formed of the powers of government, and the liberties of the people; for on this depends every thing which is held dear; whether of a civil or religious nature; and what makes it still more interesting is, that every one in this case is like Adam the representative of a future race, who are to be rewarded for the virtues or suffer for the guilt of their progenitors.

Never was there a people whom it more immediately concerned to search into the nature and extent of their rights and privileges, than it doth the people of America at this day; what is once dedicated to legislative authority is seldom if ever recovered without bloodshed, although it is improved to the oppression of the people who meant it to be exercised for their benefit.

My Christian Brethren and Fellow Citizens, we cannot easily be too critical in examining a Constitution which has been compiled and thus far approved by the aristocratic or court part of this infant nation, pray dont let us be discouraged and think the trial is over and decided. Remember it is the right of Americans to have a fair trial by jury. I think their virdict on the trial has been forgotten or not taken in by the court. Except only in the State of Rhode Island, and there we are informed the democratic or jury part were about four fifths against the Constitution, in North Carolina a large majority of their Convention were against it, and have wisely and judiciously drawn up a bill of rights, and proposed material amendments, which ought to take place previous to the new government; of those Conventions that have adopted the Constitution, it has, in most of them, been by a small majority, and several of them have proposed amendments. New-York Convention have in a judicious, pertinent and respectful circular letter to the supreme executives of the respective States; proposed, that a national Convention be appointed to make the amendments. Whom else can make the alterations that are proposed? Surely Congress cannot. For the design and subject of a Constitution and Bill of Rights is to be a law to Congress, to teach them what they are impowered to do for the general good of the people; and what they shall not do that might hurt or oppress the community, methinks it could not be rationally expected that the first Convention should do any more than lay a foundation, and prepare the way to bring up the sense and feelings of the nation on so weighty a subject. Especially when we reflect thay originated only from a creature or creatures of the people, made by the people at large for another purpose, viz. to legislate under their respective State Constitutions, which gave them no power to make such a great political creature bigger than themselves and their Constituents united.

DHFFE, II, pp. 13-14.

Theodorick Bland (Richmond) October 28, 1788
Letter: To Richard Henry Lee (excerpt)[1]

Not lightly unadvisedly or wantonly did I take up my opinion with regard to the new Constitution, and however matured I considered those opinions in my own mind—I confess they have received great additional strength from their concurrence with those of so many of my Friends, who have long been numbered among the first and most active Patriots—when I mention this Class of our fellow Citizens I presume Sr. that I need not particularize one who has borne the highest honors as well as the most heavy Burthens, incident to and consequent on our virtuous and well *meant* Struggle. A uniform consentaniety of political opinions grounded on and growing out of a Basis which is the surest foundation of Political happiness (viz a government in which the Essential rights of a free People are well secured,) has knit us together and calls loudly on us to strengthen those Bonds which may enable us *together* to stem the Torrent, which bids fair to bear down every thing before it. The Virtuous Principles which have dictated our political opinions, I trust do still remain in full vigor in the breasts of some of us, and will I hope lead us to exertions which will in the end render that government secure and harmless, which in its outset threatens Tyranny and oppression. This Sr. in my humble apprehension can only be done by men wedded to freedom and the rights of *men,* and by measures carried on in concert and steadily opposed to whatever shall tend to trample on those rights; Convinced as I am sr. that you hold these principles you may be well assured that my exertions will not be wanting to place you in those councils, where your Experience, abilities, and Inclination will I hope cooperate to introduce such *amendments* as can alone render the new government *tolerable,* and which I beleive the far greater part of the People of the United States wish to see adopted—

1 DHFFE, II, p. 267.
2 See "Richard Henry Lee," October 15, 1788, p. 538, for Lee's letter which prompted this reply.

John Harris (Harrisburg) October 28, 1788
Letter: To Tench Coxe

I received your kind letter with the pamphlet and almanac, for which I thank you. We must set up manufactories, be frugal and industrious, and then we shall make the times better. It's all in our own power. If any British vessels are arrived, please to send Mr. Maclay's two boxes of window glass by the bearer, Christian Flakingar, a wag[one]r, who will be very careful of them. I carried my point with respect of Mr. Carson. The meeting at Lancaster will be by one side of the question. I hope they'll name good men. There will be a party election. If good men are elected as our Representatives, it will answer the public utility. A few amendments will please every honest man to the Constitution, and none called for, but what's reasonable (and necessary) and not a string of them that would destroy the whole Constitution, which might be attended with bad consequences. I hope for the best, and means to be a good subject as I ever has been. A few lines from you with a late paper will be very acceptable to, sir, your most humble servant.

P.S. I write from home with a very bad pen, in haste.

DHFFE, I, p. 321. Harris (founder of Harrisburg) was Pennsylvania Senator elect Maclay's father-in-law. See *Ibid.*, note 1.

Virginia House of Delegates October 29, 1788
Resolution: As contained in a letter from George Lee Turberville to James Madison (excerpt)[1]

"Whereas . . . the Convention of Delegates of the People of Virginia did ratify a constitution for the people of the United states also declare that sundry Amendments agreed to by the said Convention involves *all* the *great unalienable* & essential rights of Freemen—many of which if not cancelled are render'd insecure—under the said Constitution untill the same shall be alter'd and amended— . . .

"Resolved as the opinion of this Committee that for quieting the minds of the good Citizens of the Commonwealth & for securing their dearest rights & priviledges & preventing those disorders which must arise under a government not founded in the confidence of the

People—Application be made to the Congress of the United states —so soon as they shall Assemble under the new Constitution to call a Convention for proposing Amendments to the same according to the mode therein described.["][2]

1 *Papers*, XI, pp. 323-324. This resolution was approved by the House the following day.
2 In a subsequent letter, Turberville reported to Madison that the above resolution and preamble "passed by a majority of 85. to 39." *Papers*, XI, p. 340.

Charles Lee (Richmond) October 29, 1788
Letter: To George Washington (excerpt)[1]

For a few days past the Assembly has been engaged upon the subject of the federal constitution: the house of delegates in committee has come to several resolutions with respect to putting it into operation. One of them distributes the commonwealth into ten districts each of which is to choose a representative in Congress, and another appoints that there shall be twelve districts each of which is to choose an Elector of the President, and every freeman is at this election to have a vote. These matters were introduced by Mr. Corbin who seems to me not to have the confidence even of those who are friends to the fair trial of the new government and as they have made but small progress, I cannot tell what will become of them. For Mr. Henry to day took occasion to declare that he should oppose every measure tending to the organization of the government unless accompanied with measures for the amendment of the Constitution for which purpose he proposes that another General Convention of deputies from the different states shall be held as soon as practicable. He offered to the Committee of the whole house several resolutions to be agreed to upon this point, one of them that the Legislature of Virginia should apply to the new Congress expressive of the desire of this state that another General Convention be immediately held to amend the constitution—The language of this resolution contains a direct and indecent censure on all those who have befriended the new constitution holding them forth as the betrayers of the dearest rights of the people—Applying to the constitution these words are used "whereby the most precious rights of the people if not cancelled are rendered insecure." With some difficulty and after much entreaty Mr. Henry *conceded* (I use his expression) to suffer the resolution to lie on the table for consideration till tomorrow. Mr. Corbin who spoke several times but never against the resolution concluded with saying that the resolution as proposed was unobjectionable and Zach. Johnson was the only member who declared his disapprobation in positive terms. If Mr. Henry pleases he will carry the resolution in its present terms, than which none in my opinion can be more exceptionable or inflamatory though as he is sometimes kind and condescending, he may perhaps be induced to alter it. The other resolution proposed that a committee should be appointed, to answer the circular letter of New york and in conformity with the object of that letter, to address the assemblies of the other states.

I am told Mr. Henry has publickly said that no person who wishes the constitution to be amended should vote for Mr. Madison to be in the senate, and there is much reason to fear he will not be elected. Col R. H. Lee is considered as certain—and Col Grayson is expected to be the choice for the Senate.[2]

1 DHFFE, II, pp. 268-269.

2 Lee and Grayson, both of whom favored amending the Constitution, were later selected as Senators for Virginia.

Honestus October 30, 1788

Newspaper Article: Boston *Independent Chronicle* (excerpt)

I have observed in some late publications a disposition to inculcate among the people, an idea, *that those persons who are in favor of the proposed amendments, are not to be trusted in our federal government;* and some have gone even so far as to brand all such persons with the opprobrious epithet of *Antifederalists.* This being the case, I conceive it has now become a serious question to be determined: *Whether the amendments were proposed with an intention of having them adopted, or whether they were artfully introduced to deceive the members of the Convention?* We cannot in candor suppose, that any members of that respectable body (particularly the gentleman who introduced them) meant to betray their constituents, by pretending to adopt a Constitution under the mask of amendments, and then desert them after its ratification. We cannot, in justice to those respectable characters who composed that august assembly, conceive that so much cunning and subtlety should prevail among any individuals; neither ought we to presume, that men possessing so much political wisdom, would have been so *impolitic,* as to introduce the new government, by deceiving the people in its first establishment. Such a mode of conduct, they must be sensible, would have a tendency to raise a jealousy in the minds of the public, which would ever operate as a clog on all the future operations of government. No policy can be more destructive, than to raise a distrust of the *integrity* of those with whom we have intrusted our political concerns. What must be the sentiments of the people with respect to the Convention, if we are now told, *that the amendments are not to be regarded;* and that they were only introduced as a measure to pass the Constitution; and that our members for the federal government would be of that class of men who are *openly opposed* to any amendments whatever. Provided this is the case (but which I conceive was far from the intention of the Convention) would not a distrust naturally prevail among the body of the people? What must be their conjectures? Will they think more favorably of that government, which needs such deception for its adoption? What decisions can they trust to in future, if this solemn form of ratification, signed by a man in whom they have ever confided, is to be treated as words of no signification? If the determinations of a body of men, consisting of characters as respectable for their wisdom and patriotism as any in the commonwealth, are to be considered only as the mere trick of state policy, how will the people be ever able to ascertain the reality of any doings hereafter, however solemnly and deliberately resolved? Surely then if we mean to act consistent with the principles of *common prudence,* or wish to effect a lasting and beneficial government, founded on the CONFIDENCE of the PEOPLE, we ought at least to avoid those persons whom we have reason to believe are opposed to the proposed amendments. As the Convention have pledged to the people, that exertions shall be made to effect the adoption of the propositions, we should be careful to have such members as are disposed to comply with these resolutions; that if the amendments are of any importance, they may be adopted; if not, that they may be set aside, after that decent investigation which is due to the propositions of this commonwealth.

If we attend to the words of the recommendation, we cannot but consider them of some importance, "And the Convention do in the name, and in behalf of the people of this Commonwealth, enjoin it upon their Representatives in Congress, at all times, until the alterations and provisions aforesaid, have been considered, agreeably to the 5th article of the said Constitution, to exert all their influence, and use every reasonable and legal method to obtain a ratification of the said alterations and provisions, in such manner as is provided in the said article".

After reading the form of the ratification, it is the highest reflection on their probity, to doubt of the sentiments of the Convention, with respect to the *importance* of the amendments. How abusive and uncandid then to stigmatize those who are for adhering to them, as

Antifederalists? Certainly those who are opposed to them, may with greater propriety be styled such, as they are opposed to the decided voice of the Convention. If we are to *enjoin* upon our Representatives the alterations and provisions mentioned—and they are *bound to exert* all their influence for these purposes—how absurd to think of choosing men, whom we have reason to suppose will rather use their influence to backward any attempts for their adoption? Real Federal men are those who are for the propositions submitted; for REAL FEDERALISM *consists in promoting the harmony and union of all the states.* These happy consequences are most likely to be effected by complying with the decisions of the several states, as far as their proposals can be adopted. But to disregard the several propositions, and pretend to choose men professedly with a view to backward any attempt to gratify the people, must have a direct tendency to destroy that UNION, which must ever be our national support.

Besides, what dependence can we place in men, who arrogantly presume to disregard the almost unanimous voice of the conventions of the several states!

DHFFE, I, pp. 473-474.

Virginia House of Delegates October 31, 1788
Proceedings on an Act for Federal Elections (excerpt)

Resolved, that it is the opinion of this Committee that the returns of the Militia or any other official mode of ascertaining the number of White Inhabitants in each County within this Commonwealth ought to be their guide in the distribution of Districts both for the Choice of Representatives to serve in Congress and for the Choice of Electors to choose a President.

DHFFE, II, p. 284.

A Friend to the People November 1, 1788
Newspaper Article: Exeter, N. H. *Freeman's Oracle* (excerpt)

I beg leave further to differ from your correspondent to say, I do not think His Honor the Chief Justice is a suitable person to represent us in Congress at this time as a Senator. I do not wish to hurt his feelings, for I love and respect his abilities, but the call of my country is more extensive than my feelings for a bosom friend. The amendments to the new Constitution is the most important object we are looking for, at the settling of the new Congress. *Vox populi, est vox Dei*—the voice of the people cry aloud for it. Every gentleman has a right to give his own sentiments, and His Honor the Chief Justice delivered his in the Convention with a great degree of firmness, "*that the Constitution was now complete without any amendments.*" If so, why should we send him to Congress and at the same time deprive us of a gentleman on the superior bench that time will scarce ever replace? Were I to recommend any person for the office of Senator, I should be careful to avoid any character who had a hand in framing the Constitution, as it is, in some measure, a child of their own making. Consequently, they would wish to support it at any rate. Witness the expression of a respectable character in the late convention, viz., "*that the Constitution was now complete; the amendments would not take place in five hundred years.*" On the other hand, I should avoid those who wish to destroy the whole. But take the middle path and choose some gentleman who wishes well to the whole community, and whose acquaintance and extensive knowledge will be serviceable in bringing about the amendments.

DHFFE, I, pp. 776-777.

James Madison (New York) November 2, 1788
Letter: To George Turberville

Your favor of the 20th. Ult: not having got into my hands in time to be acknowledged by the last mail, I have now the additional pleasure of acknowledging along with it your favor of the 24. which I recd. yesterday.

You wish to know my sentiments on the project of another general Convention as suggested by New York. I shall give them to you with great frankness, though I am aware they may not coincide with those in fashion at Richmond or even with your own. I am not of the number if there be any such, who think the Constitution, lately adopted a faultless work. On the contrary there are amendments wch. I wished it to have received before it issued from the place in which it was formed. These amendments I still think ought to be made according to the apparent sense of America and some of them at least I presume will be made. There are others concerning which doubts are entertained by many, and which have both advocates and opponents on each side of the main question. These I think ought to receive the light of actual experiment, before it would be prudent to admit them into the Constitution. With respect to the first class, the only question is which of the two modes provided be most eligible for the discussion and adoption of them. The objections agst. a Convention which give a preference to the other mode in my judgment are the following 1. It will add to the difference among the States on the merits, another and an unnecessary difference concerning the mode. There are amendments which in themselves will probably be agreed to by all the States, and pretty certainly by the requisite proportion of them. If they be contended for in the mode of a Convention, there are unquestionably a number of States who will be so averse and apprehensive as to the mode, that they will reject the merits rather than agree to the mode. A convention therefore does not appear to be the most convenient or probable channel for getting to the object. 2. A convention cannot be called without the unanimous consent of the parties who are to be bound by it, if first principles are to be recurred to; or without the previous applications of 2/3 of the State legislatures, if the forms of the Constitution are to be pursued. The difficulties in either of these cases must evidently be much greater than will attend the origination of amendments in Congress, which may be done at the instance of a single State Legislature, or even without a single instruction on the subject. 3. If a General Convention were to take place for the avowed and sole purpose of revising the Constitution, it would naturally consider itself as having a greater latitude than the Congress appointed to administer and support as well as to amend the system; it would consequently give greater agitation to the public mind; an election into it would be courted by the most violent partizans on both sides; it wd. probably consist of the most heterogeneous characters; would be the very focus of that flame which has already too much heated men of all parties; would no doubt contain individuals of insidious views who under the mask of seeking alterations popular in some parts but inadmissible in other parts of the Union might have a dangerous opportunity of sapping the very foundations of the fabric. Under all these circumstances it seems scarcely to be presumeable that the deliberations of the body could be conducted in harmony, or terminate in the general good. Having witnessed the difficulties and dangers experienced by the first Convention which assembled under every propitious circumstance, I should tremble for the result of a Second, meeting in the present temper of America, and under all the disadvantages I have mentioned. 4. It is not unworthy of consideration that the prospect of a second Convention would be viewed by all Europe as a dark and threatening Cloud hanging over the Constitution just established, and perhaps over the Union itself; and wd. therefore suspend at least the advantages this great event has promised us on that side. It is a well known fact that this event has filled that quarter of the Globe with equal wonder and veneration, that its influence is already secretly but powerfully working in favor of liberty in France, and it is fairly to be inferred that the final event there may be materially affected by the prospect of things here. We are not sufficiently sensible of the importance of the example which this Country may give to the world: nor sufficiently attentive to the advantages we may reap from the late reform if we avoid bringg. it into danger. The last loan in Holland and that alone, saved the U.S. from Bankruptcy in Europe; and that loan was obtained from a belief that the Constitution then depending wd. be certainly speedily, quietly, and finally established, & by that means put America into a permanent capacity to discharge with honor & punctuality all her engagements.

DHFFE, II, pp. 271-272.

Father Abraham November 3, 1788
Newspaper Article: Litchfield, Connecticut *Weekly Monitor* (excerpt)

The constitution recently adopted is, indeed, the foundation on which they [Congress] must build; but is it therefore no matter of what materials the superstructure is made. This constitution, like all others, has its defects; yet we may set down satisfied, provided a wise, judicious and munificent administration take place. It exhibits some general and fundamental maxims; but many of them capable of variant construction, and may by some fortuitous circumstance, be rendered either salutary or destructive.—Several states have proposed amendments, and made such animadversions on the more unguarded expressions as they thought necessary, the more effectually to secure the rights of the people.—All those, and an infinite variety of other matters of the utmost importance, will demand the attention of Congress; 'tis therefore indispensably necessary that they be men of the first and best characters; men of the clearest heads and purest hearts;—men of wisdom, sagacity and penetration; capable of discerning, projecting and executing;—men of stability and firmness; that will neither be led nor drove to counteract their own judgment;—men of religion and piety, who will glorify the Almighty by promoting the felicity of his people;—men of virtue and honour, who will resist tyranny sword in hand, and spurn at meanness in whatever garb it appear;—men possessing a good fund of common sense, and political knowledge, and, if possible, *men* of *experience*, whose past services have, in times of difficulty and danger, afforded ample testimony of ability and integrity.

DHFFE, II, pp. 35-36.

Federal Republican Committee (New York) November 4, 1788
Letter: To County Committees of New York

Gentlemen,

The circumstances and Situation of Things both before, and some time after, our Convention had met, warranted an universal Opinion among all Federal Republicans, that it was proper to adopt the new Constitution, only on Condition that those important Alterations, which were considered Necessary to the Protection of political and civil Liberty, should be made; and this was founded not only on the defects of the Constitution, but on the Anticipation that there would have been a Majority in several of the State Conventions of the same Sentiment with our own, from whom we should have derived Support; but in pursuing our Opposition in this Form, the Sentiments and Opinions of many in our convention were changed, not, as we have reason to believe, as to the Principles of Opposition, but as to the expediency of adopting it under an Alteration of Circumstances, so that this State should continue in the Union; at the same time giving such Constructions to some of its Articles, and relying on the Sentiments of a Majority in the United States with Respect to an Opinion of its Defects, that the Government would be restrained in the exercise of its most offensive and dangerous Powers until a new Convention should have an Opportunity of reconsidering and revising it before it should have its full operation—This Alteration of Sentiment with respect to a conditional Adoption, and the Mode of adopting it in its present Manner, it is to be presumed was caused by the Reception of it by nine States successively, by which the Government was capable to be put in Operation, and likewise the immediate and subsequent Adoption of it by Virginia, perhaps one of the most influential and important States in the Union—The Confidence of those who were of these Sentiments, was excited because many of the most important States had acknowledged it by small Majorities, and almost all in such a Way as was expressive of its Defects, and hence they considered Amendments as certain, subsequent as precedent—Thus, unsupported by any of the States in the Prospect of a conditional Adoption, and for these Reasons, it became a political Calculation with them, whether it was not most for the Interest of this State, under all Circumstances, to continue in the Union, and trust, for the Reasons aforesaid, for amendments: Unhappily this occasioned a Diversity of Opinion among our Friends in the Convention, who were for a conditional Adoption only—however, the Question, as you well know, was at last carried in the way it now Stands. Altho' a Division took place, both within, and without the Convention, on this Point, and for these Reasons, yet we hope that a Confidence remains on the Minds of all, that each was governed by the Principles of Rectitude, and that the Efforts and Exertions of each other collectively, as well as individually, will be considered as a Duty in future, and made use of to obtain the great Objects we have all had, and still have in View, to wit, the requisite amendments, by having a general Convention called immediately, or as soon as possible after the Organization of the New Government.

With this design we conceive it will be very necessary to advert to the ensuing Election of Members to represent this State in the Assembly of the General Government, and to endeavour to elect such Characters who are in Sentiment with us on the Subject of Amendments; nor is the Mode of Election a Matter of small Importance, when it is considered that one Mode may throw the Balance in the Hands of the Advocates of an arbitrary Government, while another may be favourable to equal Liberty.

The Activity and Duplicity of the principal of those who have contended for unequivocal Adoption, and an uncontrouled Exercise of the New Constitution, notwithstanding their Promises to assist in procuring a Convention for the Purposes already mentioned, have given us just Causes of Suspicion, that those Promises were made with a View to deceive.

To facilitate a Communication of Sentiment and free Discussion on this Subject with you and our Friends in the other Counties, and thereby further the great Objects of our Pursuit, and oppose with successs the subtle Practices of the Adversaries of consitutional Liberty, have induced us to form ourselves into a Society for the purpose of procuring a general Convention agreable to the circular Letter of the late Convention of this State, and we beg leave to recommend to your Considerations the propriety of you joining together, without Delay, for the like Design.

We have only to add, that whatever diversity of sentiment may have taken place among the friends of equal Liberty in our late Convention, we are fully persuaded, that they will unite their utmost Exertions in the only mode that is now left, and should the present Opportunity which is now offered at the organization of the Government not be properly improved, it is highly probable such a favourable one will not be again presented, and the liberties of the People will then depend on the arbitrary Decrees of their Rulers.

DHFFE, III, pp. 207-208.

Foreign Spectator November 7, 1788
Newspaper Article: Philadelphia *Federal Gazette* (excerpts)

REMARKS *on the Amendments to the federal Constitution, proposed by the Conventions of Massachusetts, New-Hampshire, New-York, Virginia, South and North-Carolina, with the minorities of Pennsylvania and Maryland, by a* FOREIGN SPECTATOR.

NUMBER VI.

We proceed to consider the amendments that regard the military power of the federal government. It is pleasing to find that the states of Massachusetts, and South-Carolina are entirely silent on this important subject:—They having wisely reflected, that although a friend may possibly point that weapon to my breast, which I give him to defend me against an assassin, yet it would be absurd either to tye his right arm, or to give him only half a sword; especially when I am well armed myself. . . . If the country is not in a proper state of defence, it will the sooner invite an enemy, opens its bosom to him, and may receive a dangerous wound before the arms can ward off the stroke; but all the disadvantage of collecting an army of perhaps 10 or 15,000 men without eminent necessity, is to impose some new taxes, which can never be oppressive, as the greatest part of the money is directly laid out in the country. As to any danger to liberty from such an army, it is altogether visionary; and it is needless to repeat what has been so often said on that subject. While the people have property, arms in their hands, and only a spark of a noble spirit, the most corrupt congress must be mad to form any project of tyranny.

A Friend to Liberty and Union November 7, 1788
Newspaper Article: Philadelphia *Federal Gazette* (excerpt)

Liberty was the avowed object of the late glorious Revolution, in search of which we waded with patience and resolution, through all the horrors of a civil war; and the constitutions of the several states were framed with admirable wisdom, according to the best models, and upon the noblest principles of civil liberty. One only defect remained. The general government of the continent, under the late Articles of Confederation, was too feeble to secure the safety of the people. Its defects were evident; and yet, as if by a studied contrivance, they were suffered to remain, with hardly an attempt to remedy them, until the public affairs of the continent had sunk into utter imbecility and ruin. The cry, at length, for a new form of continental government, became loud and universal.

A continental Convention was called; the hopes of the people were raised to the highest pitch of expectation, and the sun never beheld a more glorious opportunity of establishing a happy form of government. Nothing short of the most glaring defects could have excited any shadow of opposition. But it is to be feared, some selfish and artful men amongst us were but too willing to avail themselves of so favorable an opportunity of consulting the profit and power of the future governors of the continent, at the expense of the liberties of the people. Whether, however, it was the effect of accident or design, most glaring defects appear in the Constitution which they have proposed to the people. These defects have been freely stated by writers in the public papers, throughout the continent, as well as in the debates of the several state conventions. Indeed many of these defects seem now to be generally acknowledged, even by those men who, there is too much reason to fear, would still wish to evade their amendment and to retain them in the system. Some of these defects are very glaring and important: others perhaps, in the heat of contention have been exagerated. One or two of the most considerable, I shall attempt briefly to lay before you.

The future Congress, if the new Constitution be not amended, will be vested with unlimited powers: the state governments, which have been founded on the most excellent constitutions in the world, will crumble into ruin or dwindle into shadows, and, in their stead, an enormous unwieldy government will be erected, which must speedily fall to pieces by its own weight, and leave us to the wretched alternative of anarchy or tyranny: whereas by a due temperature, the continental government may be clothed with all necessary powers, for the management of foreign affairs, and leave the state governments in possession of such powers, as will enable them to regulate our internal concerns, which a continental government can never effectually reach. It is just as absurd to suppose, that the general government of the whole empire can regulate the internal police of the several states, as to believe that the several states could regulate our foreign trade, and protect us in our intercourse with foreign nations. The latter we have already tried without success: the former will be found equally impracticable.

Another defect in the Federal Constitution is equally alarming. No security is provided for the rights of individuals; no bill of rights is framed, nor is any privilege of freemen secured from the invasion of the governors. Trust me, my fellow citizens! We shall not be more powerful or more respected abroad, for being liable to oppression at home; but on the contrary, the freest states have been ever the most powerful. Yet with us no barriers will remain against slavery, under the new continental government, if it be not amended: the state governments, by the express terms of the Constitution, can afford no protection to their citizens, and not even a single right is defined or stipulated, which the subject may appeal to against the will and pleasure of the moment.

These circumstances and others of a like tendency, have excited great opposition; but the absolute necessity of a continental government of some sort, has silenced the opposition of those, who were dissatisfied with the present constitution, first in the Continental Convention, and afterwards in most of the conventions of the states. The wiser, if not the major, part of the Continental Convention, would have produced to us a much better form of continental Union, had it been in their power; but they preferred this to none, and, in the different states, the wisest and best of the people have acquiesced in the scheme of adopting it in its present form, from the hope of obtaining those amendments, which the Constitution itself has provided for the attaining: provided two-thirds of Congress, or two-thirds of the state legislatures, shall concur in requiring them. Without such a clause of obtaining amendment, there is little doubt but a majority of the freemen of America, would have spurned at the idea of subjecting themselves to the other terms of the new Constitution: with this clause of obtaining amendments, it has become the duty of good citizens to make a beginning with the Constitution as it is, confiding in the hope of obtaining all essential amendments in a constitutional mode. In this mode which is provided, it is certainly more eligible to reform the Constitution, than by any violent or irregular opposition to attempt to overthrow it. We must have a continental government, or we are an undone people: at the same time, we ought to preserve our liberties, if possible, so far as they may consist with our essential protection. If these two points can be attained, and this extensive continent held together, in the course of a few years, we may, at once, be the greatest and happiest people on earth.

Impressed with these sentiments, and in the hope of reconciling the wishes of all parties, which, on the present question, we trust, when fairly explained, are more nearly the same, than possibly were those of any people, who, by the arts of intriguing men, were ever set at variance; a large number of the freemen of Pennsylvania have, without noise or disturbance, resolved to invite their fellow citizens to accord with their inclinations, which they trust are the inclinations of a great majority of the freemen of this state. They wish most ardently for a Continental Union and a continental government, upon free principles. They wish to set the proposed government in motion: but they wish for amendments. They think that the strength of this great continent

may be exerted, without impairing the private and essential rights of the meanest individual.
[The remainder of this article goes on to propose candidates who are in favor of amendments. Ed.]

DHFFE, I, pp. 332-334.

Annapolis *Maryland Gazette* November 13, 1788

Extract of a letter from a gentleman in Fredericksburg to his friend in this city, dated November 4, 1788.

On the other side is a resolution, carried ayes 85, noes 39, which will shew that we repent of our folly in adopting a constitution without previous amendment—But, since it is done, the assembly are proceeding to organize it agreeably to the constitution, at least as they understand it, that is, to have the electors, and the delegates chosen by the people, by districts, the elected to be residentees; this was nearly the unanimous vote; but, by what rule the districts are to be measured, is yet in doubt—The delegates have at present adopted the rule by that of the militia—But, as they had but a majority of 6, and the senate are opposed to it, I expect the rule of tythes will be their guide—that is, to take in three fifths of the blacks, the which, I conceive to be right, as our delegation is increased by that rule, and we are also to be taxed accordingly.

Whereas the convention of this state did, &c. ratify a constitution for the United States, and did also declare that sundry amendments to exceptionable parts of the same ought to be adopted: And whereas the subject matter of the amendments agreed to by the said convention *involves all the great unalienable and essential rights, liberties and privileges, of freemen,* many of which, if *not cancelled,* are rendered *insecure* under the *said constitution* until they shall be altered and amended: RESOLVED, *as the opinion of this committe,* That, for quieting the minds of the good citizens of this commonwealth, and securing their dearest rights and privileges, and preventing those disorders which must arise under a government not founded in the confidence of the people, application be made to the congress of the United States, so soon as they shall assemble under the said constitution, to call a convention for proposing amendments to the same according to the mode therein directed,

RESOLVED, *also,* That a circular letter be written to the different legislatures, &c. on the foregoing subject.

Ayes	85
Noes	39
	46 Majority

These resolutions were introduced by Mr. Henry—opposed by F. Corbin—an amendment offered to *recommend* it to the *delegates in Congress* to have the amendments offered by the states considered by congress, and, when amended, to be submitted to the consideration of the legislatures, as in the alternative mentioned in the 5th article.

You are not to suppose that thirty-nine members approved of this—but that number divided for the amendment—because many thought Henry's resolution contained reflections on the late Virginia and continental conventions—but I do not think six members would have voted for amendments by congress instead of a convention.—I was in the house and heard the great ground of objection applied to the language.

DHFFE, II, p. 373.

Federal Republican Committee (New York) November 13, 1788
Letter: To Antifederalists in Other States.

Sir,

The federal Republicans in this State are of opinion, that it is of great importance in the election of vice president, that the choice fall on a person who will be zealously engaged in promoting such amendments to the new Constitution as will render the Liberties of the Country secure under it—

For this purpose they have consulted some Gentlemen in Virginia, who are united in sentiment with us, and are informed that they have it in view in that State, to vote for Governer Clinton of this State for that office—We have reason to believe that the Electors of this State will generally give their votes in his favor—

It is highly probable, if your State would unite with Virginia and ours, that Governer Clinton will be elected—We need not make any observations to shew, the influence that the Vice President will have in the administration of the new Government—Nor is it necessary to say any thing respecting the talents or sentiments of this Gentleman —Both are well known throughout the union—If you should concur with us in opinion, you will take such measures to communicate the matter to the Electers of your State as your prudence may direct.

DHFFE, IV, p. 91.

Virginia House of Delegates November 14, 1788
Proceedings relative to amending the Constitution[1]

The House according to the Order of the day, resolved itself into a Committee of the whole House on an application to Congress to call a Convention of the States, to take into consideration the defects of the Constitution, and report the necessary amendments; also on the draft of a Letter to Governor Clinton, and to the several States on the same subject; and after some time spent therein Mr. Speaker resumed the Chair, and Mr. Bullitt reported, that the Committee had, according to Order, had the said application and draft of Letters under their consideration, and amended the same, and, he read the said application and draft of Letters, as amended, in his place and afterwards delivered them in at the Clerk's table, where the same were again read, and are as followeth:

Resolved, that it is the opinion of this Committee, that an application ought to be made, in the name and on behalf of the Legislature of this Commonwealth, to the Congress of the United States, in the words following, to wit:

The Good People of this Commonwealth,

"In Convention assembled, having ratified the Constitution submitted to their consideration, this Legislature has, in conformity to that Act, and the Resolutions of the United States in Congress assembled, to them transmitted, thought proper to make the arrangments that were necessary, for carrying it into effect.—Having thus shewn themselves obedient to the voice of their Constituents, all America will find, that so far as it depends on them, that plan of Government will be carried into immediate operation.

"But the sense of the people of Virginia would be but in part complied with, and but little regarded, if we went no further. In the very moment of adoption, and coeval with the Ratification of the new plan of government, the General voice of the Convention of this State, pointed to objects, no less interesting to the People we represent, and equally intituled to your attention. At the same time that from motives of affection for our Sister States, the Convention yeilded their assent to the Ratification, they gave the most unequivocal proofs, that they dreaded its operation under the present form."

"In acceding to a government under this impression, painful must have been the prospect, had they not derived consolation from a full expectation, of its imperfections being speedily amended. In this resource therefore, they placed their confidence—A confidence, that will continue to support them, whilst they have reason to believe, they have not calculated upon it in vain.

"In making known to you, the objections of the People of this Commonwealth, to the new plan of Government, we deem it unnecessary to enter into a particular detail of its defects, which they consider as involving all the great and unalienable rights of Freemen: For their sense on this subject, we refer you to the proceedings of their late Convention, and the sense of this General Assembly, as expressed in their Resolutions of the thirtieth day of October, 1788.[2]

"We think proper however to delcare that in our opinion, as those objections were not founded in speculative theory, but deduced from principles, which have been established, by the melancholy example of other Nations in different Ages—So they never will be removed, untill the cause itself shall cease to exist. The sooner therefore the public apprehensions are quieted, and the Government is possessed of the confidence of the people, the more salutary will be its operations, and the longer its duration.

"The cause of amendments, we consider as a common cause, and since concessions have been made from political motives, which we conceive may endanger the Republic; we trust that a commendable Zeal will be shewn for obtaining those provisions, which experience has taught us, are necessary to secure from danger, the unalienable rights of human nature.

"The anxiety with which our Countrymen press for the accomplishment of this important end, will ill admit of delay. The slow forms of Congressional discussion and recommendation, if indeed they should ever agree to any change, would we fear be less certain of success. Happily for their wishes, the Constitution hath presented an alternative, by admitting the submission to a convention of the States. To this therefore we resort, as the source from whence they are to derive relief from their present apprehensions.—We do therefore, in behalf of our Constituents, in the most earnest and solemn manner, make this application to Congress, that a Convention be immediately called, of deputies from the several States with full power, to take into their consideration the defects of this Constitution that have been suggested by the State Conventions, and report such amendments thereto, as they shall find best suited to promote our common interests, and secure to ourselves, and our latest posterity, the great and unalienable rights of Mankind."

Draft of a letter to Governor Clinton on the same subject.

Sir,

"The Letter from the Convention of the State of New York, hath been laid before us, since our present Session. The subject which it contemplated, was taken up, and we have the pleasure to inform you, of the entire concurrence in sentiment between that Honorable Body, and the Representatives, in Senate and Assembly, of the freemen of this Commonwealth. The propriety of immediately calling a Convention of the States, to take into consideration the defects of the Constitution was admitted, and in consequence thereof, an application agreed to, to be presented to the Congress so soon as it shall be conven'd, for the accomplishment of that important end. We herewith transmit to your Excellency, a Copy of this application, which we request may be laid before your Assembly at their next meeting. We take occasion to express our most earnest wishes that it may obtain the approbation of New York, and of all other sister States."

Draft of a Letter to the several States on the same subject.

"The freemen of this Commonwealth in Convention Assembled, having, at the same time that they ratified the Foederal Constitution, expressed a desire that many parts which they considered as exceptionable parts, should be amended, the General Assembly, as well from a sense of duty as a conviction of its defects, have thought proper to take the earliest measures in their power, for the accomplishment of this important object. They have accordingly agreed upon an application, to be presented to the Congress, so soon as it shall be assembled, requesting that Honorable Body, to call a Convention of deputies from the several States, to take the same into their consideration, and report such amendments, as they shall find best calculated to answer the purpose. As we conceive that all the good people of the United States, are equally interested in obtaining those amendments, that have been proposed, we trust that there will be an harmony in their sentiments, and measures, upon this very interesting subject. We herewith transmit to you a Copy of this application and take the liberty to subjoin our earnest wishes that it may have your concurrence."

And the said application and Draft of Letters, being again severally read at the Clerk's table, a motion was made, and the question being put, to amend the same, by substituting in lieu thereof, the following form of an application and draft of Letters, to wit:

[Proposed Federalist substitutes which were rejected.]

The Legislature of Virginia, to the Congress of the United States, send Greeting.

"The Convention of the Representatives of the good people of this Commonwealth, having on the twenty fifth day of June last, ratified the Constitution or form of Government, proposed by the Foederal

Convention on the seventeenth of September 1787, and having declared in their act of Ratification, that any imperfections which might exist in the said Constitution, ought rather to be examined in the mode prescribed therein for obtaining amendments, than by a delay, with a hope of obtaining previous amendments, to bring the Union into danger, and in order to relieve the apprehentions of those who might be solicitous for amendments, having resolved that whatever amendments might be deemed necessary, ought to be recommended to the consideration of Congress, which should first assemble under the said Constitution, to be acted upon according to the mode prescribed in the fifth article thereof. And on the twenty seventh day of the same Month of June agreed to certain amendments to the said Constitution, which were transmitted, together with the Ratification of the Foederal Constitution, to the United States in Congress Assembled; which amendments the said Convention did, in the name and behalf of the People of this Commonwealth, enjoin it upon their Representatives in Congress, to exert all their influence, and use all legal and reasonble methods to obtain a Ratification of in the manner provided by the said Constitution. And in all Congresional laws to be passed in the mean time, to conform to the spirit of the said amendments as far as the said Constitution would admit.

"This Legislature fully concurring in sentiment with the said Convention, and solicitous to promote the salutary measures by them recommended. Do, in consideration of the unanimity with which the said amendments were agreed to, and a just sense of their utility, earnestly call upon the Congress of the United States, to take the said amendments under their immediate consideration, and also those which may have been submitted by the Conventions of other States, and to act thereupon in the manner prescribed by the fifth article of the Foederal Constitution; either by proposing the necessary alterations, to the consideration of the States; or by calling a Convention to deliberate on the subject, as to them shall seem most likely to promote the peace and general good of the Union. We pray that Almighty God in his goodness and wisdom, will direct your counsels to such measures, as will establish our lasting peace and welfare, and secure to our latest posterity the blessings of freedom; and that he will always have you in his holy keeping."

Draft of a Latter to GOVERNOR CLINTON on the same subject.

Sir,

"Early in our present session, the Circular Letter from the Honorable the Convention of the state of *New-York,* transmitted by your Excellency, was laid before us for our consideration. While we are sensible of the obligations which we in common with all America, owe to the patriotism, and exertions of so noble and generous a people; while we feel all the respect due to their virtue, and every inclination to comply with their wishes, especially when pointed to an object so dear to us all, the preservation of our common Liberties; and while at the same time, we ardently desire such amendments to our new system of Government, as will guard our rights from every possible danger, and quiet the present apprehensions of many of the good Citizens, as well of this Commonwealth, as of our sister states, we feel great pain in finding that we cannot entirely accord with so wise and august a body, in the mode of obtaining these alterations and additional provisions. We acknowledge with them the propriety of introducing the necessary amendments as soon as possible into our system, so as to induce a general confidence under the operations of a government, which we flatter ourselves will relieve us from our present embarrassments, and again raise us to that respect and importance, which we once held among the nations of the world. It is therefore with the greatest respect and deference to the opinions of a people we so highly value, and whom we love with all the affection of brethren, who have bled in the same common cause of Liberty and Mankind, that we submit to their attention the propriety of an application to the first Congress, which shall assemble under the new plan, expressive of a desire, that they will immediately take into their consideration the amendments, which have been recommended by the Conventions of the several states which have ratified the same, and either make the necessary provisions consonant to the general sense of America, and submit them to the Legislatures of the respective states at their next sessions, for their adoption; or call a general convention to deliberate on that subject; as to their wisdom, viewing all circumstances, may appear to be most proper.

We consider Conventions as Assemblies, which ought never to be resorted to, except in cases where the ordinary administration is inadequate to the object. Here the ordinary administration is fully adequate to the object, being vested with powers expressly comprehending the present case. The Senate being chosen by the Legislatures of the respective states, and the other branch by the people themselves, must feel every obligation, and every inclination to pursue such measures, as will accord with the sentiments of the constituents, and establish that confidence in government which alone can render it prosperous and happy. If therefore the Foederal Legislature as soon as they shall assemble, shall recommend to the states the necessary amendments, the fears of our Fellow Citizens throughout America, concerning the public Liberty, will be sooner allayed, and the public confidence sooner restored, than by the delays which must necessarily occur in the summoning and the assembling of another Convention the result of whose deliberations must finally undergo the same discussion in every state, as a recommendation from the Congress. Viewing the subject as we do, and anxious to pursue the most safe and speedy way of obtaining amendments, we most ardently hope, that our endeavours will be aided by similar efforts on the part of *New-York* and the rest of our sister states, and they will unite with us in making an immediate application to congress, similar to the one we take the liberty of enclosing for the consideration of the Legislature of *New-York*. We cannot but flatter ourselves with the happiest success from so united an effort; and that Congress will take the most speedy and effectual measures, to remove every uneasy sensation from the hearts of our fellow citizens, and to fence our unalienable rights from every possible encroachment, and this without the delay and danger of a Convention. Approving in the highest degree the jealous watchfulness of our brethren of *New-York*, and promising to guard with equal care, our common Liberties—We pray that Almighty God may direct their counsels, and ours, to the lasting good of our common Country, and that he will always have *them* in his Holy keeping."

Draft of a Letter to the several States on the same subject.

"We beg leave to submit to your consideration, a Copy of our answer to the Circular Letter from the Convention of our Sister State of New York, and also the Copy of an address, which we think it our duty to make to the Congress at their first meeting. We flatter ourselves that you will not hesitate in making a similar application, the object being to establish our rights and Liberties on the most immutable basis. May God have you in his holy keeping."

1 DHFFE, II, pp. 274-278. The Federalist substitute letters were rejected by a vote of 72 to 50.

2 See "Virginia House of Delegates," October 29, 1788, p. 546, for Patrick Henry's resolution calling for a convention to amend the Constitution.

Centinel XXII November 14, 1788

Newspaper Article: Philadelphia *Independent Gazetteer* (excerpt)

We are now hastening to a crisis that will determine the fate of this great country, that will decide whether the United States is to be ruled by a free government, or subjected to the supremacy of *a lordly and profligate few*. Hitherto the gratification of party spirit and prejudice was attended with the ruin of the honest whigs and the emolument and aggrandizement of the Republicans at the common expense; but now it would be attended with the loss of all liberty and the establishment of a general thralldom—men of all descriptions, except our rulers, would equally wear the fetters, and experience the evils of despotism; it therefore behooves every man who has any regard for the welfare and happiness of his country, of himself, or his posterity, to endeavor to divest himself of all prejudices that may bias or blind his judgment on this great occasion. In confidence of a dispassionate perusal and consideration, I will now take up the address [of Lucullus] and expose its fallacy. It begins "you will be called upon, on the last Wednesday of the present month, to give your votes for eight persons to represent you in the legislature of the United States. You never were called upon to exercise the privilege of electing rulers upon a more important occasion. Two tickets will be offered you. The one will contain men who will support the new Constitution *in its present form;* the other ticket will contain men, who will overset the government under the specious pretext of amending it." Here is a plain, explicit avowal that the new Constitution is to be supported in its *present form;* I hope this declaration will open the eyes of those people who have been deluded by the deceitful promises of amendments, and, that being thereby convinced of the fallacy of the reiterated assurances of amendments, they will now embrace the only method left of obtaining them, by giving their suffrages and influence to the other ticket. The bugbear raised to intimidate the people from voting for this ticket, viz., "that the design is to destroy the government under the specious pretext of amending it," I trust will be treated with the deserved contempt, and that this low device will only confirm the people the more in their determination to support men favorable to amendments.

DHFFE, I, pp. 341-342.

Foreign Spectator November 14, 1788
Newspaper Article: Philadelphia *Federal Gazette*

REMARKS *on the Amendments to the Federal Constitution, proposed by the Conventions of Massachusetts, New-Hampshire, New-York, Virginia, South and North-Carolina, with the minorities of Pennsylvania and Maryland, by a* FOREIGN SPECTATOR.

NUMBER VIII.

A Good militia is the natural, easy, powerful and honorable defence of a country. Even those nations which are surrounded with formidable neighbours, need not altogether depend on great standing armies, which are not favourable to liberty, and create an enormous expence. Indeed regular troops are more excellent, as they resemble a militia; which is evidently seen in the Swedish army, and acknowledged by the best military writers of different nations. America will be well defended against any attack by the united strength of a small but well appointed army, and a numerous well ordered militia. The federal government is empowered to provide for the organizing and calling forth this principal branch of national defence, by the 15th and 16 par. in 8th sect. of 1st art. on which the following amendments are proposed. *That each state respectively shall have the power to provide for organizing, arming and disciplining its own militia, whensoever congress shall omit or neglect to provide for the same. That the militia shall not be subject to martial law, except when in actual service, in time of war, invasion, or rebellion: and when not in the actual service of the United States, shall be subject only to such fines, penalties, and punishments as shall be directed or inflicted by the laws of its own state.* Convent. of Virginia and N. Carol. 11 am[endment]. *That the power of organizing, arming, and disciplining the militia (the manner of disciplining the militia to be prescribed by Congress) remain with the individual states; and that Congress shall not have authority to call or march any of the militia out of their own state, without the consent of such state, and for such length of time only as such state shall agree.* Minor. of Pennsylvania, 11 am. *That the militia shall not be subject to martial law, except in time of war, invasion, or rebellion; and that it shall not, unless selected by lot, or voluntarily enlisted, be marched beyond the limits of an adjoining state, without the consent of their legislature or executive.* Min. of Maryl. 11 and 1 am.* *That the militia of any state shall not be compelled to serve without the limits of the state for a longer term than six weeks, without the consent of the legislature thereof.* Conv. of New-York, 20 am. Before I enter on the discussion of these amendments, I beg leave to observe the want of agreement, and the silence of the New-Hampshire convention with those of South-Carolina and Massachusetts, who, as was remarked above, are satisfied with the military powers of the new constitution. The request, that each state respectively may provide for organizing, &c. its own militia, whensoever Congress shall omit or neglect to provide for the same, I humbly presume to be a mere suggestion of jealousy. Congress never can omit such an important and general duty without a treasonable design, which supposes many preceding degrees of corruption; but this corruption cannot continue and accumulate in a body formed and freqently changed by the people, except the people themselves are thoroughly corrupted.

The proposition, that a state-government may controul the power of Congress to call the militia out of the state, must be regarded as hastily formed in the fermentation of party, and now disavowed by every American, who regards the safety and honor of the union and of his own state. If a powerful enemy invades any part of the United States, he must be opposed with all possible expedition, before he gets possession of any important passes, lays the country under contributions, defeats the weak forces that fall in his way, and creates the usual calamities of war. Sympathy with a sister state, and the assurance that she will in time of need repay the obligation, are sufficient motives to lend what aid the common guardian requires. The federal power watches for the whole union, views the magnitude of the danger, knows the resources of every state, and feels impartially for all; it is therefore the best judge of what they should in every emergency do and suffer for each other. That the militia should not be called to a further distance, and in greater numbers, or kept in the field for a longer time than is necessary, every person of sense will readily grant; that a select body is in real danger, much preferable to a multitude of ordinary militia, every military man well knows; but every regulation on this important matter should be left to the general government. It will certainly not be so liable to an abuse of such power as a state-government, which, with all its generosity, cannot in the same manner think and feel for the United States. What may be the consequence of recalling the militia on the eve of a decisive battle? Perhaps the conquest of two or three states, and the miseries of war for several years!

The constitution *reserves to the states respectively the appointment of the officers, and the authority of training the militia according to the discipline prescribed by Congress.* This surely is a perfect security to any state against an encroachment of the federal power. The safety of the union requires that the militia of every state should be well armed, and in every respect qualified for the defence of the country, consequently general and effectual regulations must be made by Congress. Fines, penalties, and punishments of a proper kind are a necessary part of discipline; if these are to be exercised by the several states, it is needless to compliment the Congress with the ridiculous power of organizing the militia.

A citizen, as a militia man is to perform duties which are different from the usual transactions of civil society; and which consequently must be enforced by congenial laws and regulations. These military duties have in time of peace no other object than a compleat preparation for war, and therefore do not require that rigour of martial law, which is indespensible in actual service;—yet when we consider the extreme importance of every military duty in time of war, and the necessity of acquiring an habitual exercise of them in time of peace, it would be childish to enervate by a scrupulous delicacy that manly discipline, which is the bulwark of the country—Give us then, for heaven's sake, martial law enough to be truly martial when we are to face the veterans of a powerful enemy.

Fines alone are very insufficient to prevent the various kinds of neglect and misdemeanor in the militia service, because they will not affect the rich, and at the best only produce a mechanical compliance without life and spirit. Disgrace in different and just degrees is the most effectual penalty; and it will keep alive that high sense of military honor, without which a militia is only a disorderly populace, or a mass of animal machines. With an equitable allowance for age, bodily infirmities, religious opinions, and pressing avocations, absence and the hiring of substitutes should be held dishonorable. Not to join your company, because you can earn more than the fine in your shop or your field; or because you had rather loll in an easy chair; or because you like the gambling table better than the drum; oh, for shame! not to learn that noble art, by which you can defend your life, liberty and property; your parents, wife and children! in a day of danger to be defended by others like a weak woman and a helpless child! A man of spirit will be delighted with the play of arms in all the manoeuvres that present the image of real war. Though worth 10,000*l.* a year he chearfully takes his place in the rank with a day-laborer, who is his brother-citizen, and defender of the common country—His fortune only inspires the noble pride of a greater application to the theory and practice of the military art, that by superior abilities he may deserve the honor to command a band of patriots.

As the constitution makes no mention of martial law, it is not my business to enter further into this subject; only observing that the only means to render a standing army useless, is to form a truly warlike militia.

* *This minority has two sets of amendments; the latter negatived by a majority of the committee.*

Patrick Henry (Richmond) November 15, 1788
Letter: To Richard Henry Lee

I postponed answering your Favor until I could have the pleasure of congratulating you on your Election to the Office of Senator for Virga. in the new Congress, which I now do. The Friends of the System are much displeased that [Mr.?] Madison was left out of the Choice. They urged his Election most warmly—claiming as a sort of Right the admission of one federal Member; but in vain—For to no purpose must the Efforts of Virga. have been expected to procure Amendments, if one of her Senators had been found adverse to that Scheme—the universal Cry is for Amendments, & the federals are obliged to join in it; but whether to amuse, or conceal other Views seems dubious—You have been too long used to political Measures not to see the Ground of this Doubt, & how little Dependance can be placed on such occasional conformity—And you know too well the Value of the Matters in Contest to trust their Safety to those whose late Proceedings, if they do not manifest Enmity to public Liberty, yet shew too little Sollicitude or Zeal for its Preservation—

Your Age & mine seems to exempt us from the Task of stepping forth again into the busy Scenes which now present themselves—I am glad to know that you have Health & Spirits enough to decline [no exertion?]—I shall not claim it further than it will extend to distant Operations—I mean not to take any Part in Deliberations held out of this State—unless in Carolina from which I am not very distant & to whose Politics I wish to be attentive—If Congress do not give us substantial Amendmts. I will turn my Eyes to that Country a Connection with which may become necessary for me as an Individual. I am indeed happy where I now live in the Unanimity which prevails on this Subject; for in near 20 adjoining Countys I think at least 19/20ths. are antifederal—& this great Extent of Country in Virga. lays adjoining to No. Carolina & with her forms a great Mass of Opposition not easy to surmount. This Opposition it is the Wish of my Soul to see wise, firm, temperate. It will scarcely Preserve the latter Epithet longer than Congress shall hold out the Hope of forwarding Amendmts—I really dread the Consequences following from a Conduct manifesting in that Body, an Aversion to that System—I firmly belieive the *American Union depends on the Success* of Amendments —God [grant?] I may never see the Day when it shall be the Duty of whigg[ish?] Americans to seek for Shelter under any other Government than that of the united States—The old Charges of Turbulence & Ambition have been plentifully bestowed on me. You have not escaped; but as to us who have so long been accustomed to despise these Attempts, they will have little Effect further than to excite Pity—

I have no Correspondancys at present on the Subject of Politics—For that Reason I beg you will now & then dr[op?] me a Line when you may find Leisure—The Progress of Things under the new Govermt. in its Commencement, will be highly interesting & important to be known. Letters addressed to the Care of George Fleming Esqr. in this City, will reach me.

After expressing my ardent Wishes for your Welfare & Success in your late appointment & every other Circumstance, I beg Leave to [tell you?] of the high Esteem & regard with which I am, Dear Sir affectionatly yours

DHFFE, II, pp. 374-375.

Thomas Jefferson (Paris) November 18, 1788
Letter: To James Madison (excerpt)

As to the bill of rights however I still think it should be added and I am glad to see that three states have at length considered the perpetual re-eligibility of the president as an article which should be amended. I should deprecate with you indeed the meeting of a new convention. I hope they will adopt the mode of amendment by Congress & the Assemblies, in which case I should not fear any dangerous innovation in the plan. But the minorities are too respectable not to be entitled to some sacrifice of opinion in the majority especially when a great proportion of them would be contented with a bill of rights.

Ford, V, p. 53.

Alfred November 19, 1788
Newspaper Article: Philadelphia *Independent Gazetteer*
Reprint from the *Massachusetts Spy* (excerpt)

Finding ourselves thus one nation, united by one government, having only one sovereignty, the question will be, whether the constitution needs amendments in order to secure the rights and liberties of the people?

It is frequently said, that the people cannot be enslaved or deprived of their liberties—and that therefore it is not material what constitution they have, but the same reasoning will prove, that none at all is necessary, if it proves any thing. He is now called by some an enemy in his country, who would attempt amendments, and we are told that the propositions for that purpose in the convention, were only conciliatory, and the constitution being adopted, there can be no need of them. And did a *Hancock* introduce the propositions, did *Adams* support them, did the leaders in convention advocate and agree to them, in order to obtain a vote—in order to beguile the majority into what they would not have done unless they had been thus deceived?

America has not yet made such strides in political vice and deception, as to be contented with such chicanery and cunning, and the people can have no reason to conclude, from the base insinuations of a few individuals, that after his excellency our governor, and many other patriots, have sacredly pledged themselves to attemp amendments, that they will now basely desert the people, and avow an unexampled piece of chicanery that would disgrace the character of a Nero or a Caligula. Indeed the man who has consented to the adoption of the new constitution upon the propositions introduced in the several conventions, and will now oppose a revision of those propositions in congress, or vote for a member who would oppose an investigation into the necessity of them, ought to be branded with the epithet of a betrayer of the country's freedom—and never can be trusted by the people.

Philadelphia *Independent Gazetteer* November 22, 1788

Extract of a letter from a gentleman of information in New York to his friend in this city. (excerpt)

All good Feds as well as Antis in this state call for amendments, and are astonished at some paragraphs against amendments published from your papers; certainly there must be some among you, who would go to any length to carry the new government in its present form, would involve America in all the horrors of a civil war and dissolve the Union, if the people would be led by them into such measures. You know the office hunters would be much sorrowed in their prospects when amendments take place.

None go into Congress from this state except they promise to secure the rights of the people by amendments—and we will admit no lawyers into the House of Representatives or popular part of Congress. How careful should the people be to appoint good men to hold their purse strings, when the great men are always watching to peculate!

Our legislature will take up the business of the Union the first in order, and will, I have no doubt, adopt amendments.

DHFFE, I, p. 355.

James Wilson November 23, 1788
Newspaper Article: Philadelphia *Federal Gazette* (excerpts)

Last evening, agreeably to advertisement, a large and respectable number of the citizens of Philadelphia met at the Statehouse, for the purpose of receiving the report of their conferees who had attended at Lancaster, to settle a general Federal ticket for Representatives in the Congress of the United States. . . .

Mr. Wilson addressed the meeting. . . .

We know that unfortunately for this state, the sentiments of all its inhabitants have not been unanimous with regard to the Federal Constitution itself. We know, for the period is too recent to be forgot, that a number of citizens, but far from a majority have expressed themselves unfavorable with regard to it; we know that some have attacked it with the bitterest malignity; and if I am not mistaken, an attempt is now made to bring forward some of those characters in order to administer this very Constitution; this I think appears, from a ticket that has been published and has been named "the amendment ticket." I make no observations that are personal, but I submit it whether some of those, whose names are to be found in that ticket are not the same whom many of you now present heard about twelve months ago, most warm, most earnest, and most anxious to obtain the rejection of that system of government. You will recollect this gentlemen, for you heard the debates within these walls. Now say, is it natural that those who were for the rejection of this system, should be its supporters? Or ought such to be appointed to carry it into execution? I think it is not natural on their part to expect it: but it would certainly be more unnatural for its friends to throw it into their hands.

No doubt, gentlemen the pretense of amendment is a specious one. It is well known, that everything *human* is *capable* of being amended; it may therefore be said, and said truly, that this system, like every other production of the human mind, is capable of improvement. But let me ask, who is most likely to improve it, its friends or its opposers? This question is easily answered, and upon that answer your votes will be formed. I have no doubt but they will be formed in the same manner throughout the state.

DHFFE, I, p. 324-327.

William R. Davie November 25, 1788
Letter: To James Iredell (excerpt)

The House of Delegates in Virginia have passed resolutions to the following effect, one, "that application be made to the Congress of the United States, so soon as they shall assemble under the new Constitution to call a Convention for proposing amendments according to the mode therein described"—another, "that a writing whall be drawn up expressing the reasons which induce them to urge their application so early." A third—"that a letter be sent in answer to Govr. Clinton circular letter—and a circular letter on the same subject to the other States in the *Union.*"

R. H. Lee and Grayson are chosen for their Senators, both *Anties.* This shews that this denomination of politicians prevails at present at least in the Assembly—Madison lost the election by 5. votes only.—

It appears to me that the States should immediately concur in calling another Convention, it would satisfy the Honest part of the opposition—and stop the mouths of the rest.

DHFFE, IV, p. 317.

David Humphreys (Mount Vernon) November 29, 1788
Letter: To Thomas Jefferson (excerpt)

The general opinion of the Advocates for the Government is, that some explanations & amendments are highly necessary. They conceive, however, that it might be dangerous to put every thing afloat, in seeking that object, before some degree of stability shall have been given to the System, by its being carried into effect. But it is thought that some who push for premature amendments, wish to sap its very existance. That is to say, its opponents in the State of New York. Be that as it may, the probability amounts almost to a certainty, that it will be quietly carried into effect in March next.

DHFFE, IV, p. 100.

Jonathan Jackson (Newburyport) December, 1788
Letter: To William Eustice (excerpts)[1]

[N]othing is more true in a country so free as this than that public measures must be conformed to public opinions and sentiments, for if the public mind is not previously prepared for the measures you would propose, the success of them will be very uncertain. The late Governor Cushing has at different times remarked to me, when we were about reforming our constitution of government in this state, which you know was several times attempted before it was effected,[2] that the wisest way to do this was by degrees, as necessity and the public conviction called for alterations, and that reforms thus introduced would be more thoroughly kept up to, as well as the public tranquility be better preserved. The remark, whether originally his own or another's, has struck me as that of a politician of some experience; and could we rationally expect always to have *honest and skillful pilots* at *helm,* we might be as well be done troubling our heads about these matters and leave all to them. For though upon paper we might not appear to have so perfect a constitution and so systematical, yet as far as we had one, if it was always kept up to and upon new exigencies or alterations of circumstances easy judicious reforms were made and the government well administered according to its professed principles, our political happiness might at least be equal to what it now is. The universal experience of mankind testifies that those at helm are neither always the most knowing nor the best disposed of any in the community. We therefore very justly choose to prescribe them rules of action. But are we not too tenacious of power, and like the dog in the manger growlingly forbid others to use that we cannot use ourselves—though perhaps others might use it for our benefit? We learned from our British ancestors to be jealous of all rulers, and perhaps have not yet distinguished the difference between those who rule by prescription and inheritance, and those whom we create; and whom we can destroy when we please. The difference it must be acknowledged is immense. . . .

Are not the two leading principles laid down in the early part of your letter stated, my good sir, rather too much in the spirit of republican jealousy? Can the people by themselves exercise the functions of government? If not, must they not deputize somebody to do it for them? Which is most rational: to depute so many that no hope can be formed of their doing it well, or only such a number as may be sufficient to know all the people can wish, or require with reason? Which is most rational: to devolve the trust upon any who present without any tolerable means of judging of their qualifications, or by creating responsibility in all who are concerned in devolving the trust, to endeavor to obtain the favorite few of Bolingbroke at least in the higher departments of the government, presuming on the favorable side of human nature that among them will be some of the well disposed who can always go far in keeping the rest to their duty when they are small in number and men of thorough information? If it be granted that the people must depute others to act for them, it appears to me absurd not to give them all the powers which it is probable will be wanted in the exercise of a thorough administration. To be parsimonious in such a case is expecting the end to be obtained without the necessary means, and by not allowing them enough we shall tempt our governors to encroachment and usurpation; and this with a plausible pretense for the public good, and at first perhaps honestly meant so it would not be difficult to point out some stretching of this kind in the present existing Congress beyond the limits prescribed them by the Confederation. I cannot subscribe to the first part of your second position that the happiness of the many is secured in proportion as power is retained in their hands, for I believe it absolutely necessary that full powers should be imparted to a few that the happiness of the many may be secured. I am decidedly in favor of "this delegated power's reverting often enough into the hands of the many" to secure their control over the few, and to learn these a thorough dependence upon their fellow citizens for creation and support, but I profess myself as real a republican as any of you, though charged with aristocratical principles, and am willing to try the system in any shape that will promise us good government. There is a latitude for such a variety of opinion that scarcely two speculatists will take up the subject with the same view, or reason upon it from like notices imbibed. It must be granted that it is strongly in the disposition of man to abuse power when placed in his hands, as also to avail himself of superior advantages when possessed of them, to the prejudice of his fellow men. To provide against this evil, a well-constructed government must be organized with different bodies for different departments and with reciprocal checks upon as well as mutual assistances to each other. In this machinery some modern schemes of government appear to have the advantage of any ancient ones. It must be granted when reasoning *a priori* (I believe the logicians call it) to establish such checks we may sometimes err, or if not that, the wit and ingenuity of man are probably at different periods so nearly equal that those who follow may be ingenious enough to break through or leap over the barriers prescribed by the constitution mongers of the former age and plead necessity for so doing. But distinct from all checks marked out by constitutions on paper, we have one that I believe has by some kind or other among the people of every country—that is public opinion, or what is called [their?] [---] or mode of thinking—to which the administrators of every government must in a great degree conform. The check last mentioned must in this country for many years to come have a peculiar force from the spirit with which it has been exercised for many years past. The right, everywhere tacitly acknowledged and in some states expressly reserved, freely to declare and publish our opinions upon public measures and the conductors of them, if exercised with half the freedom which our presses permit and give a great facility in doing, will serve to keep public men very generally to their duty, after our institutions have pointed out expressly "whose *watch and ward it is,*" or where the responsibility lies, for without this there is no knowing the point of attack. Are not the present people of this country inclinable enough to political enquiries, and public investigations to deter those at helm from practicing any undue arts to impose upon the people or infringe their rights? But after recognizing the genius of the people of this country from its early settlement, and recurring to the spirit with which the late Revolution was begun and in some respects carried out, when at the same time we view them in the singular instance of a whole people with arms in their hands and for such well instructed in the use of them, what idea can be more chimerical than that the despotism of the few, while we in the gross keep clear of confusion, shall advance upon us without our notice and without the power to restrain it in its early approaches—and this with the simple apparatus by which a paper war is carried on, and not by that more hazardous as well as more inhuman one the sword. The late dissents concerning the new Constitution are sufficient to evince no want of political combatants, some of whom can sound even false alarms where real ones are wanting. The word liberty, it is true, has been much abused and little understood in this country as well as all others. There is not, I believe, such a mighty difference between different countries in the actual enjoyment of it as some men are apt to imagine. "A rational man however, whether American or any other, would in making up his mind upon this subject wish to have his property and such personal rights as he can exercise in social life secured to him by known established laws," and in this country I conceive he need be abridged of few or no such rights which are conducive to his political happiness.

1 DHFFE, I, pp. 591-594.

2 The Massachusetts Constitution of 1780 was the second one proposed to the people of that state. One major reason for the rejection of the proposed Constitution of 1778 was the lack of a bill of rights. See Oscar and Mary Handlin, eds., *The Popular Sources of Political Authority*, (Cambridge, Mass., 1966).

Thomas Jefferson (Paris) December 4, 1788
Letter: To George Washington (excerpt)

I have seen, with infinite pleasure, our new Constitution accepted by eleven States, not rejected by the twelfth; and that the thirteenth happens to be a State of the least importance. It is true, that the minorities in most of the accepting States have been very respectable; so much so as to render it prudent, were it not otherwise reasonable, to make some sacrifice to them. I am in hopes, that the annexation of a bill of rights to the Constitution will alone draw over so great a proportion of the minorities as to leave little danger in the opposition of the residue; and that this annexation may be made by Congress and the Assemblies, without calling a convention, which might endanger the most valuable parts of the system.

Bergh, VII, p. 223.

James Madison (Philadelphia) December 8, 1788
Letter: To Thomas Jefferson (excerpts)

Notwithstanding the formidable opposition made to the New federal Government, first in order to prevent its adoption, and since in order to place its administration in the hands of disaffected men, there is now both a certainty of its peaceable commencement in March next, and a flattering prospect that it will be administered by men who will give it a fair trial. . . .

The questions which divide the public at present relate 1. to the extent of the amendments that ought to be made to the Constitution. 2. to the mode in which they ought to be made. The friends of the Constitution; some from an approbation of particular amendments, others from a spirit of conciliation, are generally agreed that the system should be revised. But they wish the revisal to be carried no farther than to supply additional guards for liberty, without abridging the sum of power transferred from the States to the general Government or altering previous to trial, the particular structure of the latter and are fixed in opposition to the risk of another Convention whilst the purpose can be as well answered by the other mode provided for introducing amendments. Those who have opposed the Constitution, are on the other hand, zealous for a second Convention, and for a revisal which may either not be restrained at all, or extend at least as far as alterations have been proposed by any State. Some of this class, are no doubt, friends to an effective Government and even to the substance of the particular Government in question. It is equally certain that there are others who urge a Second Convention with the insidious hope of throwing all things into Confusion, and of subverting the fabric just established if not the Union itself. If the first Congress embraces the policy which circumstances mark out, they will not fail to propose of themselves every desireable safeguard for popular rights; and by thus separating the well meaning from the designing opponents fix on the latter their true character and give to the Government its due popularity and stability.

DHFFE, IV, p. 109. Reprinted in *Papers*, XI, pp. 381-383.

Governor George Clinton December 11, 1788

Speech to the Assembly and Senate of New York (excerpt)

Gentlemen of the Senate and Assembly,

I WAS induced to convene you at this time, that I might have a seasonable opportunity of laying before you the proceedings of the Convention of this State, lately held at Poughkeepsie, and the ordinance of Congress for putting into operation the Constitution for the United States, which was adopted by that Convention.

While I submit this important subject to the Legislature, it is my duty to call your particular attention to the amendments proposed by our Convention, to this new system of general Government. It will appear from the instrument of ratification, that a declaration of rights with certain explanations are inserted, in order to remove doubtful constructions, and to guard against an undue and improper administration; and that it was assented to on the express confidence, that the exercise of different powers would be suspended, until it should undergo a revision by a General Convention of the States. You will also perceive by the Circular Letter addressed to our Sister States, that several articles of it appeared so exceptionable to a majority of the Convention, that nothing short of the fullest confidence of obtaining such a revision, could have prevailed upon a sufficient number to have ratified it, without stipulating for previous amendments; and that all united in opinion, that a speedy revisal of the system would be necessary to recommend it to the approbation and support of a numerous body of our Constituents, and to allay the apprehensions and discontents which the exceptionable articles of it had occasioned. These considerations, and a conviction of the truth of the observation, "that no Government, however constructed, can operate well, unless it possesses the confidence and good will of the great body of the people," will, I am persuaded, be sufficient to engage your best endeavors for effecting a measure so earnestly recommended by the Convention, and anxiously desired by your Constituents.

DHFFE, III, pp. 217-218.

A Federal Republican December 11, 1788
Newspaper Article: *New York Journal* (excerpt)

The FEDERAL REPUBLICAN, *No.* 2. . . .
No revolution ever took place, that could more truly be said to be for the people, than the one which we have seen in this country—Power was in great measure opposed to it through the whole union.—It originated in the purest whig principles—was supported on the broad basis of the equal rights of mankind—and the form of government which were agreed to, recognized these principles, and the administration has moved upon them. In the progress of the general government, it has appeared to the conviction of almost every man, that the powers under the confederation were not adequate to the management of the general concerns of the union. A very general concurrence of sentiment therefore took place to revise the system—For this purpose a convention of the states by their delegates assembled, and the result of their deliberations was not merely an extension of the powers, but a change of the form of government, this has been submitted to all the states, and acceded to by eleven of them. The officers are now choosing, and the system will soon be in operation. An entire revolution is about taking place without war or bloodshed. In the discussion of this great question there has been a great division of sentiments with regard to the merits of the plan proposed—It has been urged by those who were opposed to it, that the great principles of the revolution has been too little attended to in its formation—that it embraces objects not necessary to be committed to the care of a general government—that sufficient checks are not placed in it to restrain the rulers from an abuse of power—that it will annihilate the state governments on whom we must depend for the preservation of our liberties; and, that it will operate to deprive the people of those rights, which they have so dearly earned—On the other side, it has been said, that these apprehensions are imaginary—that although there are imperfections in the plan, yet, on the whole, it is a well ballanced government, and that sufficient security is afforded against every abuse by committing the power of

electing their rulers to the people. To this it is replied, that very little safety will be derived from the right of the people to elect—For that this power will be rather nominal than real—that the number of representatives will be so small, and so great a number concerned in chusing them, that the influence of a few will always predominate.—It is not my design to investigate this subject, as to repeat all that has been said upon it—It is not necessary for my purpose—It has been the general opinion in this state, of both parties, if we may judge from their professions that there are defects in the plan—the same sentiment has prevailed throughout the union. And hence it is, that the most prevailing arguments that the advocates for the system have used, have been drawn, not from its merits, but from the expediency of adopting it, considering the [critical] situation in which the country was. The language has been, if we must have a government adopt this, and we will cordially unite in making amendment. No inducement whatever would have prevailed upon the convention of this state to have ratified the constitution, had they not had confidence that a general union would have prevailed to submit it to the revision of another general convention. It is manifest from the proceedings of the conventions of the other states, that the same motives influenced them. In our own state, almost every sober thinking man declared, without reserve, their wishes to have the system revised—But what is the present language of many of the leading men who advocated the adoption of the constitution. Do they now urge the necessity and propriety of another convention? Nothing is further from their present persuit. They now say, it is wise and proper to give the government a trial. The goodness or badness of the scheme will be proved from experiment—If it should prove defective on a trial of ten or twenty years, then we shall be better able to amend it—But if it be true that the liberties of the people are not well secured under it, in twenty years it may, and probably will be too late to secure them. What are we to think of men who hold this language after they have pledged themselves to unite in procuring another convention? Can we refrain from suspecting that they are unfriendly to equal liberty,—that they have in view a system of government which they dare not avow, and which they mean to fix over the people of this country by insensible degrees, and without their perceiving it until it is accomplished? It is time for every disinterested man and real friend to his country to open his eyes, and act with decision.

All who were sincere in declaring that they wished for a reconsideration and amendments to the system will do so, and will give their voices decidedly in favor of such men to represent them as will firmly pursue the plan recommended by the convention of this state. A variety of unanswerable arguments, beside the defects in the constitution itself, point this out as the wise, prudent, and patriotic line of conduct which ought to be pursued.

DHFFE, III, pp. 214-215.

Belasarius December 15, 1788
Newspaper Article: *Boston Gazette* (excerpt)

The great objects of the new government are as clear as our necessities and sufferings can make them. Agriculture, manufactures, and commerce, the restoration of public faith and private credit, economy in our public expenditures, together with the greatest caution and frugality in the creation of offices and the annexment of salaries, are among the great and leading points, which will no doubt first attract the attention and engage the wisdom of the federal legislature. In the order of things, relief in our difficulties will precede every attempt to meliorate the new system, so as to prevent the probability of abuse in its administration, by adding such amendments as the concurring opinions of a whole continent have in a manner agreed to be necessary to confirm the wavering, and to conciliate its opponents. Our public faith, the honor of the state, and our reputation for consistency depend upon something being done, agreeably to the form of our own ratification.

DHFFE, I, p. 560.

George Mason (Gunston Hall) December 18, 1788
Letter: To John Mason (excerpt)

North Carolina has rejected the new Government, unless previous Amendments, almost the same with the subsequent Amendments proposed by Virginia, can be obtained; Rhode Island has yet done nothing decisive on the Subject. New York, discouraged by the Adoption in Virginia, with a Majority in their Convention of two to one against the new Form of Government, received it; upon the Minority's agreeing to recommend unanimously, Amendments similar to those of Virginia, & voting a circular Letter, from their President, Governor Clinton, to invite the Concurrence of the other States, in an immediate Application to the new Congress for calling another federal Convention, to consider them—the other States have all adopted. Connecticut, Jersey, Pensylvania, Delaware, & Maryland without recommending any Amendments—New Hampshire, Massachusetts, South Carolina, and (I think) Georgia, with a Recommendation of Amendments. The Virginia Legislature, now sitting, have taken up the Subject, upon the Ground of the New York circular Letter, & by a large Majority, have voted an Application to Congress for immediately calling a federal Convention, to consider the Amendments proposed by this & the other States; their Address to Congress for this purpose is a very firm & in my opinion, proper one; they have also wrote a Circular to the other States, desiring their concurrence. Your Brother George will send you a Collection of American Papers, in which you will see the Particulars.

Colo. Richd. Henry Lee, & Colo. Grayson, are appointed Senators for this State. Mr. Madison was proposed but lost his Election by a considerable Majority. Virginia is divided into ten districts, as nearly equal as Circumstances will admit; the Rule of Computation being the Number of Militia in each County; each District to chuse one Representative (who has been a Resident in the district for 12 Months last past) in the new Government; and it is thought the Elections will go, very generally, in favour of Men, who are for calling a federal Convention, to make Amendments. Our District consists of the Countys of Loudoun, Fairfax, Prince William, Fauquier, Stafford & King George; several Candidates are talked of by the other Party, vizt. Ludwell Lee—Dr. Stuart—Mr. Fitzhugh of Chatham—Levin Powell, & Martin Picket; but they will hardly, I suppose, be foolish enough to start more than one. The Gentlemen for Amendments have not yet fixed upon a Candidate, & I doubt we shall be at a Loss for one; several who have been applyed to having refused; if we can prevail upon a proper Person to offer, I think there will be little Doubt of his Succeeding. Mr. Jas. Monroe of Fredericksburg (late Member of Congress) opposes Mr. Maddison in the Spotsylvania & Orange District, & it's thought will carry his Election.

Rutland, III, pp. 1135-1136.

John Francis Mercer December 20, 1788
Broadside: Declaration of Candidacy for Congress (excerpt)
Annapolis

The organization of the new federal government has presented a very awful crisis to these States—Individual happiness and national prosperity are deeply involved in its first movements—The contrariety of opinion discovered throughout the continent with respect to its leading features—splended expectations on one part—fears and disquietude on the other—the existing separation of two states heretofore united by the ties of blood, common interest, sufferings and success—the terms and instructions which five others have annexed to their ratifications, must satisfy every dispassionate mind, that mutual concession can alone produce that harmony and concord, without which the government will be neither happy in its operations, or of lasting duration—they must also prove, that to elect men to administer this government, who are altogether the enthusiastic admirers of this constitution without any amendments, will not produce a real representation of the interests and wishes of the people, but tend to establish that violent adherence to party spirit and views, which destroys the mild influence of reason, the only true principle of republican government.

With these sentiments, I offer myself to represent the third district of this state in the new congress.

DHFFE, II, p. 160.

Thomas Jefferson (Paris) December 25, 1788
Letter: To William Carmichael (excerpt)

You have long ago known that 11. states ratified our new constitution, and that N. Carolina, contrary to all expectation, has declined either accepting or refusing, but has proposed amendments copied verbatim from those of Virginia. Virginia and Massachussetts had preferred this method of amendment, that is to say, desiring Congress to propose specific amendments to the several legislatures, which is one of the modes of amendment provided in the new constitution. In this way nothing can be touched but the parts specifically pointed out. New York has written circular letters to the legislatures to adopt the other mode of amendment, provided also by the constitution that is to say to assemble another federal convention. In this way the whole fabric could be submitted to alteration. It's friends therefore unite in endeavoring to have the first method adopted, and they seem agreed to concur in adding a bill of rights to the Constitution. This measure will bring over so great a part of the Opposition that what will remain after that will have no other than the good effects of watching, as centinels, the conduct of government, and laying it before the public.

BRDH, II, p. 994.

Election Appeal for James Monroe January, 1789

Gent.

My Solicitude for the liberty of my Country constrains me to Call your attention to the Subject of Electing a Representative for this District to Congress under the General Government. You are Sensible that the Constitution in its present form has not the hearts and affections of the people: Their fears and apprehensions are greatly alarmed and in my opinion Very justly: the Convention in June last at the Same time they Ratified it, agreed it was so far defective as to Require a Bill of Rights and a number of Amendments which you Cannot be Strangers to: also enjoined it on their Representatives in Congress to exart all their influence and use all reasonable and legal methods to obtain the same and Even went so far as to Recommend that all Congressional laws which Should be passed in the mean time Should Conform to the Spirit of the amendments as far as the Said Constitution would admit, the late Assembly has taken Great pains to Clear the way for this Great and desirable object, by making application to Congress, at their first Meeting to Call a General Convention of the States to Consider of the amendments and have at the Same time written a Circular letter to the Differant States to join them in Similar application, which is agreeable to the fifth article of the Constitution and thare Remains little doubt, if proper men are elected but the Amendments will take place and thareby the minds of the people quieted and I hope peace Safety and happiness Secured, when you Consider thare are at least nine tenth's of the Habitable Globe are immersed in & Groaning under the most, Dreadful oppressions of Tyrany: and that it neaver was the Design of Providance in forming Such an order of Beings that they Should be thus Circumstanced and that it is only by a strange and unacountable perversion of his Benevolent intensions to mankind that they were Ever Deprived of liberty. I hope you will Consider the Necessity of uniting in favor of a Gent. who has been uniformly in favour of Amendments I mean James Munroe Esq. a man who possesses great abilites integrity and a most amiable Character who has been many years a member of Congress of the House of Delegates and of the Privy Council and whome I have Prevaled on to offer in our District, Considering him as being able to Render his Country great Servises on this important occasion. It is now Submitted to your Consideration whether you wish for amendments or not, and if you do who is the most likely to obtain them, the man who has been uniformly in favor of them, or one who has been uniformly against them. This is so clear that I am persuaded you will all join with me in opinion, that the object of amendments Can alone be premoted by one who feels a desire for their introduction, if the people at large had always united against Tyranny and oppression, thare would have been no Such Monsters in the world, but from some fatality or other, we generally get Devided by men who are fond of power and thus the liberty of the people has always been Endangred if not Snatched away. When we Consider that the human mind is not to be Satisfied with power, and that Powers once parted with, are Seldom if Ever Recovered, it shews how necessary it is to Elect the Gent. I have taken the liberty to mention, whose heart and mind is bent on obtaining the amendments[.] it is not my wish or Design to influence the Suffrage of any person, but have stated the above Observations for the free Exercise of your best judgments. I have thus Spoke to you the language of my heart, which if you approve I shall be happy, if not, Shall be Content, haveing done what I conceive to be my Duty, and hope if by a Contrary Conduct you Should Entale Misery on your Selves and posterity that I shall stand acquitted from haveing had any hand in it.

DHFFE, II, pp. 329-330.

Arthur Lee January, 1789
Broadside: Announcement of Candidacy for Congress.
Fredericksburg

To the FREEHOLDERS of the Counties of GLOUCESTER, MIDDLESEX, ESSEX, KING and QUEEN, KING WILLIAM, CAROLINE, WESTMORELAND, RICHMOND, NORTHUMBERLAND, and LANCASTER:

WOODBERRY, in Richmond County.

GENTLEMEN,

When I offer myself, as a Candidate to represent you in the General Congress of the United States, I think it proper to declare the Principles, which shall govern my Conduct, if I have the Honour of being elected.

In my Mind, it is the Duty of every good Man to submit to the Determination of the Majority of his Fellow-Citizens; and therefore, although in my Judgement, the Constitution required Amendments, previous to its Adoption, yet I shall always think it incumbent on me to support what the Convention—after a full and fair Discussion—has adopted, until it shall be altered in the Mode which the Constitution itself points out.

For the same Reason, I shall deem it my duty to use every Effort for obtaining those Amendments, which have been sanctioned by so great a Majority of the Convention, and by almost the unanimous Sense of the General Assembly. There is every Reason to hope, that the new Constitution—so amended as to remove the Apprehensions and secure the Confidence of the People—will promote our Interests at home, and our Respectibility abroad. But this will very much depend upon the Laws and Regulations of the first congress, and the Train of Administration in which they place the new Government.

After twelve Years public Employment in the high and confidential Offices of Government, both at home and abroad, it may be permitted me to hope, that I, in some Measure, merit the Confidence of my Country, both as to Discernment of what is useful to the Public, and Integrity to pursue it.—Upon this Hope, and upon the Principles I have declared, I must rest the Success of my Election:—But whatever may be your Determination, Gentlemen, I shall always wish the Prosperity of the People, under the new Government, and endeavour to promote, as far as may be in my Power the particular Interests of this District.

I have the Honour to be, with the greatest Respect,
GENTLEMEN,
Your most obedient Servant,
ARTHUR LEE

DHFFE, II, p. 352.

Aristides January 1, 1789
Newspaper Article: Annapolis *Maryland Gazette* (excerpt)

To the PEOPLE of MARYLAND

You are at length called upon to perform the last thing on your part, for giving life, motion and vigour, to the new system of government. It has hitherto triumphed over all opposition—It's enemies are now "*in the last ditch.*" But despair will perhaps redouble their efforts, and the strength of the whole will be directed to a point. Let their conduct in this one particular be imitated. Unite, and the work is complete.—

For the sake of yourselves and posterity, for the honour of human nature, and the general good of mankind, let not your behaviour on this critical occasion defeat all you have done. Dash not those elevated hopes, from the beginning, conceived by almost every good and wise man, that the fairest experiment, the world ever saw, would ultimately be crowned with success.

It has been asserted, and with a confidence which generally marks the assertors, that a majority of the people of Maryland are disposed for amendments. The position is so far true, that the people wish ardently for the best possible form of government. They suppose the new constitution, as it is the work of man, must *somewhere* be defective. But it is not true, that they perceive the necessity, or expedience, of any one amendment, or alteration, which hath yet been proposed.—

That you are attached to the trial by jury; that you value, as you ought, the freedom of the press; that you are averse from those fetters, with which superstition and bigotry would enslave the mind,—all this I stedfastly believe.—That the most inestimable mode of trial is done away; and that the privilege of declaring and publishing your opinions, and the right of worshiping God in your own way, depend on a speedy revision of the system, is what no true federalist, that I know of, has ever yet admitted.

The particulars alluded to, constitute, as I am told, the "capital" objections of men, who would embrace the system with only its less material faults. They must permit me to make some few remarks on a subject which, although trite and hackneyed, appears not yet fully understood—

If congress can claim no authority, independent of the constitution, and yet enjoys absolute unlimited power; for what purpose, in the name of common speech, and common sense were particular powers enumerated and defined?

The constitution, I conceive, is a compact, according to which a number of states have consented to be governed, for the purpose of common defence and general welfare.

If the true construction of this compact allow congress the right of legislating in all cases whatever, he that would now restrain that absolute power no further, than by preventing it from abolishing the trial by jury, shackling the press, and establishing a national church, would allow them far greater authority, than any sound federal expositor, I have yet heard, or perused.

Allow not declamation and sophistry to bewilder your minds. Read carefully the constitution, and rely upon this,—that it requires no depth of science to discover the meaning of a contract.—A form of government, being no more than a general agreement, entered into by each member of society, must be construed, like other agreements, according to the plain common acceptation of the words—.

Suppose then an agreement between two men for the sale of property from one to the other.—The vendor would be thought ridiculous in the last degree, should he suppose it necessary to except and reserve in the deed that part of his property, about which there was no bargain at all.—Suppose him to be feifed of four tracts of land, and intending to convey only the first.—It would be a stange mode of effecting his intent, should the deed convey generally the whole of his real estate, *except* the three tracts therein described. The deed ought certainly to pursue the common mode of conveyancing, that is, it should do no more than convey the first tract by express words, describing it, according to course and distance, or metes and bounds. I demand whether such a deed would give the slightest pretext for the vendee to claim the other three tracts?

In like manner, my fellow-citizens, the constitution, or agreement of the whole people of America, is the only thing, which creates the powers of congress; when it enumerates and defines those powers; when it contains no general clause, which, [by] the most strained constuction, can confer unlimited authority; is it possible, a man of common sense will believe, that congress may *rightfully* exercise power, not mentioned, or even alluded to, by the enumeration?

I say *rightfully;* because if you will suppose congress wicked enough to contravene the plain meaning of the contract, and to usurp authority, under an arbitrary construction, you ought not to suffer congress, or any other body of men, to legislate for America. But, if you will have a legislative body for these United States, it can make only one difference, whether you say to them in effect—"Thus far may you legislate." Or whether you say thus—"Do as you shall think best, provided you deprive us not of the trial by jury, abridge the freedom of religion, restrain the press, levy more than a reasonable proportion on the poll, &c. &c. &c.—" The convention adopted the former mode of conferring the powers of government; and they did right. When men are conferring particular definite powers, they consider cautiously every thing, which may be done under those powers; but when men confer general power, limited only by express reservations and exceptions, they may probably omit such exceptions, as may afterwards be found material.

I have spoken thus far with respect to the necessity of amendments.

To men of extreme caution, who say, that amendments are expedient to quiet apprehension, (and such indeed is the language of more than one state convention,) I propose these simple questions.

May not the first congress remove every plausible or rational objection; and cure every uneasy scruple of the most timid mind, by a solemn declaration, to be entered on its jounal, and deposited in all the archives of America?

Is it not probable, that a wise federal congress will immediately adopt this method of at once blasting opposition?

Would a declaration like this be held less sacred than a bill of rights, ingrafted on the constitution?

I mean not, that the declaration, in any manner, should be repugnant to the constitution.—I mean only, that it should explain, according to the ideas of the best and wisest federal men, those parts (if any) which are dubious, or "broad" enough to afford pretext for arbitrary power.

Will it not be early enough to appoint a general convention, and thereby set all things afloat on a wild tempestuous sea, when the first congress shall have failed of performing that, which every rational federalist expects and requires?

I shall not waste time, in urging a consideration, which hath often been suggested, and never once been answered.

The best body of men, America ever produced, an assembly of its heroes, patriots and sages, devoted many months, to the most laborious and painful investigation of truth; seeking light from the precious remains of antiquity; adverting to the experience of more modern times; contemplating our own hasty institutions, and the evils resulting from their defects; above all attending to documents of the various interests of the states, with the manners, customs, habits and opinions, of a people, spread over this great and extended continent. Is it then conceivable, that an illiterate demagogue, or even the most sagacious theorist, shall be able to point out with certainty, and correct, the errors of their system? And if that body of men be capable of betraying their country, is it likely, that another general convention, chosen under the most unfavourable auspices, will be more zealous to preserve your rights, and promote your welfare?—Away then with the baneful project of a revisal! Or wait, till time and experience shall demonstrate the defects and mistakes!

DHFFE, II, pp. 175-177.

Adolphus January 1, 1789

Newspaper Article: Boston *Independent Chronicle* (excerpt)

In the county of Middlesex, there were seventeen members in the Convention in favor of ratifying the Constitution, and twenty-five against it; of the county of Worcester there were seven members for it, and forty-three against it; in the whole Convention, there were one hundred and eighty-seven for, and one hundred and sixty-eight against it, although it was proposed with such amendments as essentially altered it for the better. We might suppose that on such a division as this, one might decently utter an opinion in favor of amendments, without being liable to such torrents of abuse, as have been retailed in the paper called the [*Massachusetts*] *Centinel*, and of which Governor Clinton, Governor Randolph, Governor Hancock, and others of the first patriots in the country have in some measure been the objects.

When Governor Hancock proposed the amendments in Convention, the Honorable S[amuel] Adams said "a proposal of this sort coming from Massachusetts, from her importance, will have its weight. It appears to me that such a measure will have the most salutary effect throughout the Union. I apprehend, sir, that these states will be influenced by the proposition." But who will mind him? He is a son of liberty! Young Mr. Bowdoin said that "he could not but express his approbation of the propositions made by His Excellency." He added, "Your Excellency's propositions, are calculated to quiet the apprehensions of gentlemen, lest Congress should exercise an unreasonable control over the state legislatives, with regard to the times, places and manner of holding elections, which by the 4th section of the first article, are prescribed, etc. I have had my fears lest this control should infringe the freedom of elections, which ought ever to be held sacred." The Honorable Judge Sumner said "that the probability was very great, that if the amendments proposed were recommended by this Convention, that they would, on the first meeting of Congress, be adopted by the general government." The Honorable Judge Dana proposed and carried a very important article in the proposal for amendments, respecting a requisition on the states, before Congress assessed a tax upon them, and said that "if they were recommended to be adopted by the Convention it was very probable that two-thirds of Congress would concur in proposing them." The Hon. Mr. Strong went into a particular discussion of the several amendments recommended in the proposition submitted by His Excellency, each of which he considered with much attention. He anticipated the good effects it must have in conciliating the various sentiments of gentlemen upon the subject, and expressed his firm belief that if it was recommended by the Convention, IT WOULD BE INSERTED IN THE CONSTITUTION; Mr. Parsons, Colonel Orne, Hon. Mr. Phillips, and others spoke in favor of the proposition as a conciliatory measure, *and the probability of the amendments being adopted*." Doctor Jarvis said, "there has scarce been an instance where the influence of Massachusetts has not been felt, and acknowledged in the Union. In such a case her voice will be heard, sir, and I am fully in sentiment if the *amendments* are not engrafted on the Constitution, it will be our own fault." Mr. Ames observed, "that the mode of obtaining amendments is pointed out in the Constitution itself; if, however, there was an irregularity in the proceeding, the General Court would not delay to confirm it." Mr. Turner said "in my judgment there is a rational probability, a moral certainty, that the proposed amendments will meet the approbation of the several states in the Union."

It would be too much to detail all that was said in favor of amendments; what I have mentioned is taken from the printed proceedings of the Convention, where much more remains of the same tenor.

Finally, the Convention adopted the form of government, by a small majority, with the most solemn injunctions upon the Representatives of the commonwealth in Congress, to exert their influence to obtain the proposed alterations, and amendments.

Were these men sincere, or were they jesting with the people? If they were honest, and sincere, why should there be an objection to Mr. Gerry because he is in favor of these amendments and alterations? These men, or some of them, at least, spoke their sentiments, but there are others who having obtained a vote for a ratification, now laugh at amendments, and revile eveyone who is in favor of them; but you my fellow citizens know your friends. Your eyes are now opened by the perfidy and duplicity of men, who are too lazy to dig, and are ashamed to beg. But Mr. Gerry loves the people too well to participate in wealth arising from their misery, and so you are not to vote for him.

There is neither policy or propriety in this violent opposition to amendments. Three-quarters of the people in this commonwealth expect them to be attempted. The general assemblies of Virginia, and the Convention of New York, two very important states, have written circular letters in favor of them. The two Northern States, and one of the Southern, have ratified the Constitution by a small majority, and on the express stipulation of exertions for alterations. Six other states have adopted it, generally by small majorities, but all in consideration, that there could be amendments made. North Carolina and Rhode Island have rejected it. In this situation, is it wise to make such a violent opposition to the sense and understanding of so large a majority?

DHFFE, I, pp. 637-638.

James Madison (Orange) January 2, 1789
Letter: To George Eve

Being informed that reports prevail not only that I am opposed to any amendments whatever to the new federal Constitution, but that I have ceased to be a friend to the rights of Conscience; and inferring from a conversation with my brother William, that you are disposed to contradict such reports as far as your knowledge of my sentiments may justify, I am led to trouble you with this communication of them. As a private Citizen it could not be my wish, that erroneous opinions should be entertained, with respect to either of those points, particularly, with respect to religious liberty. But having been induced to offer my services to this district as its representative in the federal Legislature, considerations of a public nature make it proper that, with respect to both, my principles and views should be rightly understood.

I freely own that I have never seen in the Constitution as it now stands those serious dangers which have alarmed many respectable Citizens. Accordingly whilst it remained unratified, and it was necessary to unite the States in some one plan, I opposed all previous alterations as calculated to throw the States into dangerous contentions, and to furnish the Secret enemies of the Union with an opportunity of promoting its dissolution. Circumstances are now changed: The Constitution is established on the ratifications of eleven States and a very great majority of the people of America; and amendments, if pursued with a proper moderation and in a proper mode, will be not only safe, but may serve the double purpose of satisfying the minds of well meaning opponents, and of providing additional guards in favor of liberty. Under this change of circumstances, it is my sincere opinion that the Constitution ought to be revised, and that the first Congress meeting under it, ought to prepare and recommend to the States for ratification, the most satisfactory provisions for all essential rights, particularly the rights of Conscience in the fullest latitude, the freedom of the press, trials by jury, security against general warrants &c. I think it will be proper also to provide expressly in the Constitution, for the periodical increase of the number of Representatives until the amount shall be entirely satisfactory; and to put the judiciary department into such a form as will render vexatious appeals impossible. There are sundry other alterations which are either eligible in themselves, or being at least safe, are recommended by the respect due to such as wish for them.

I have intimated that the amendments ought to be proposed by the first Congress. I prefer this mode to that of a General Convention, 1st.

because it is the most expeditious mode. A Convention must be delayed, until 2/3 of the State Legislatures shall have applied for one; and afterwards the amendments must be submitted to the States; whereas if the business be undertaken by Congress the amendments may be prepared and submitted in March next.—2dly. because it is the most certain mode. There are not a few States who will absolutely reject the proposal of a Convention, and yet not be averse to amendments in the other mode.—lastly, it is the safest mode. The Congress, who will be appointed to execute as well as to amend the Government, will probably be careful not to destroy or endanger it. A convention, on the other hand, meeting in the present ferment of parties, and containing perhaps insidious characters from different parts of America, would at least spread a general alarm, and, be but too likely to turn every thing into confusion and uncertainty. It is to be observed however that the question concerning a General Convention, will not belong to the federal Legislature. If 2/3 of the States apply for one, Congress can not refuse to call it: if not, the other mode of amendments must be pursued.

DHFFE, II, pp. 330-331. Reprinted in *Papers*, XI, pp. 404-405.

Samuel Sterett January 2, 1789
Newspaper Article: Circular Letter and Address to the Public
Baltimore *Maryland Journal*

Sir,

Encouraged by the Patronage and promised Support of a Number of very respectable Characters, I take the Liberty of offering myself a Candidate to represent this State in Congress, and soliciting your Vote and Interest to place me on the Return, at the ensuing Election for the Fourth District.

To see immediate energetic Operation given to the New-Government, is the great Object of my Wishes. I should then be happy to promote such Amendments as will produce Union and Harmony among the States, and guard the great and fundamental Rights of the People, without impairing or injuring, in the smallest Degree, the real Vigour or true Beauty of the System. The Trial by Jury ought to be unequivocally secured, and a Bill of Rights would quiet the Apprehensions of many Citizens, and ought to be granted.

Under this Impression, and with these Sentiments, I offer my humble Services to my Country, and shall consider myself very happy in having your Approbation, and the Honour of your Suffrage and Interest.

With Sentiments of Respect, I am, Sir, Your obedient Servant,

SAMUEL STERETT

DHFFE, II, p. 183.

A Native of Baltimore January 6, 1789
Newspaper Article: Baltimore *Maryland Gazette* (excerpts)

My Fellow-Citizens!

You are told the new government wants amendments, and, perhaps, that trial by jury, liberty of the press, and other great rights are not secured by it; many of you admit the facts, to such I respectfully offer the following hints.

In an address published here the 6th of May, 1788, it appears that Messrs. Gale, Hanson and Tilghman, agreed in a committee of the [Maryland] convention to certain amendments, in which those rights above particularized, would be effectually secured—it is needless to inform you why they were not agreed to by the convention—It was only my design to shew you that these gentlemen, who are now candidates for congressmen and electors, are friends to those rights, and that others in oppostition to them are not alone solicitous for them.—Give me leave to remind you of certain alterations (which I suppose must be the rights not specified) advocated in the afore mentioned committee, and which is also published in that address by Messrs. Mercer, J.T. Chase and C. Ridgely, of William, opponents to the former gentlemen: "That in every law of congress imposing direct taxes, the collection thereof shall be suspended for a certain reasonable time therein limitted, and on payment of the sum by any state, by the time appointed, such taxes shall not be collected—That all imposts and duties laid by congress, shall be placed to the credit of the state in which the same be collected, and shall be deducted out of such state's quota of the common or general expences of government—That no treaty shall be effectual to repeal or abrogate the constitutions or bills of rights of the states or any part of them." . . .

These amendments, the framers of them and their supporters, may justly be deemed antifederal, and men who oppose them are, of course, the only real federalists.

Many have submitted to the dishonorable appellation of an anti from mistaken patriotism and an honest zeal to have the best rights of freemen secured to them and their posterity—whereas it is the opinion of many of our wisest men as well as my own, that they are in no danger, and if we consider that congress can claim no powers not vested in them by the constitution, we may rest assured of our safety, especially whilst we may have a *Washington, Adams, or Hancock,* at the helm of affairs.

DHFFE, II, pp. 188-189.

Civis January 6, 1789
Newspaper Article: Baltimore *Maryland Journal* (excerpt)

Two Tickets for Representatives in the Congress, are now offered to you, the one *Federal,* and the other is called the *Antifederal* Ticket. Various have been the means by which the latter characters have endeavoured to unfetter themselves from the disgraceful *name* of *Antifederal.* But their *struggles* only tend to bind them faster. The hatred they have to their just name, is a conclusive evidence of the reproaches of conscience, and the corruption of their principles. If they dislike the name, in reality, why do they not abandon their principles which gave them the *title!* I hope that federal condour will still prevail, and that jutice will perpetuate the distinction as long as the cause exists which gave rise to it; and permit not their hatred to their self-acquired name to diminish our dislike and opposition to their degenerate principles.

The *State electioneering* argument of "amendments and security of the important rights of the people," is again revived and brought forward at the present Election; but it merits no attention. The policy of such language is easily understood—There are animals who cry *piteously* at one moment, in order to devour at the next. Who are these merciful men who plead the cause of the people with so much seeming sympathy on the present subject?—Upon inquiry we shall find some of them are at the head of an antifederal party in one County, and others the *pliant tools* of enemies to the Constitution in another. The *Black-List* brings up the rear in all the majesty of iniquity! Such men are not to be trusted. They urge these arguments in order to impress an idea, that the men in the opposition are against amendments, and wish not to have the rights of the people secure. But there is not a man in the Federal Ticket, who possesses such a thought.—It is to their interest to secure the rights of the people, as well as their duty, and it is an absurdity to suppose they will act at variance with these great rules of human conduct.

DHFFE, II, p. 187.

A True Federalist January 7, 1789
Newspaper Article: New York *Daily Advertiser* (excerpt)[1]

The following statement of FACTS *is submitted to the candid and dispassionate* CONSIDERATION *of the* INDEPENDENT FREEHOLDERS *of VIRGINIA, by a Friend to* Truth *and* Liberty.

From the foregoing extracts from the Journal of the [Virginia] house of delegates, it will appear that the majority and minority have differed only in the mode of pursuing of amendments—it becomes the public to determine whose conduct has been the most temperate, consistent and dignified, and best adapted to the attainment of the great end—the amendments which we all think necessary. To take a full view of the subject, it will be proper to recur to the resolutions introduced into the house of delegates by Mr. *Henry*, and which were sanctioned by their approbation.[2] To a dispassionate enquirer, it must appear strange, that a man of such great endowments should suffer himself to be led so far from the bounds of moderation, into the violent expressions therein contained; and under the pretext of using the bold language of republicanism; so far forget the proper demeanor of a good citizen, as to criminate in the stongest terms the conduct of the people themselves in full and free convention assembled, by accusing them of having assented to a government which, "if it does not cancel, renders insecure all the great, essential, and unalienable rights of freemen." How hasty and ungrounded such aspersions are, a candid attention to the conduct of that august body must bring to the view of every friend to truth, to decorum, and to the peace and happiness of his country. But however strange his conduct may appear, it may be accounted for from human frailty; accustomed to govern the counsels of his country, unused to any control, and habituated to see his political opinions triumph over all opposition—the check which he experienced in the convention, composed of our best and most illustrious citizens, may have wounded his ambition and soured his temper. But that a majority of the legislature, chosen about the same time at which the convention was elected, and for very different purposes, should concur in such measures, is wholly inexplicable on any rational or justifiable principle; and furnishes a melancholy proof of the unbounded influence of an individual, who, to use the mildest terms, may be as liable to error as other men. To accuse the legislature of an intention wantonly to insult the people, is what I am unwilling to do; but I must say that they have been fatally misled from the line of their duty, and the dignified manner which ought to have characterised their proceedings, into measures which teem with the virulence of *party spirit,* instead of being animated with the noble and generous zeal of an enlightened people, knowing their rights, and conscious of their freedom.

It is true, that the legislature had a right to exercise the power vested in them by the constitution, to apply to Congress to call another general convention. But they ought to have exercised this right with decency and respect; and not to have endeavored to stain the character of a convention, chosen by the people with unusual solemnity and circumspection, and composed of the best and wisest patriots of our country. They ought to have reflected, that this convention was elected in the month of *March,* for a special and solemn purpose, and they, in the *April* following, for the ordinary objects of legislation. The convention having determined on the subject which was specially and exclusively committed to their decision;—the legislature ought with modest propriety to have confined their attention to the legitimate objects of their appointment. But how do they act? They no sooner assemble, than they undertake to arraign the conduct of this august assembly—an assembly which embraced the collected wisdom, experience, and patriotism of our country. These men of the most unblemished characters,—of long tried virtue—and acknowledged abilities, are accused of treason against their country,—of having sacrificed "all the great, essential, and unalienable rights of freemen"; and an *ordinary* legislature, "cloathed with a little brief authority," dare say this.—My countrymen, what an insult to your understandings!

I have said that the legislature possesses a power to apply to Congress, whenever they may think it necessary, to call a convention. But they ought to exercise this right with propriety and dignity; and not to convert it into a dagger to stab the peace of their country; or use it as the vehicle of private resentment or party virulence. This power seems to have been wisely vested by the constitution in the legislatures, to provide for the occasional admission of such amendments, as experience, the great guide in human affairs, should point out to be necessary. It never therefore could have been the expectation of its framers, or of our convention which ratified it, that any attempt would be made to exercise this power before we had actually experienced the defects of the government from its operation. If our state convention had thought another general convention necessary to introduce the amendments, which they had suggested, it would have been as easy for them, to have recommended to our legislature, and to the legislatures of the other states, to apply to Congress as soon as it should assemble, for another convention, as to have expressed themselves in the terms they have used. But they recollected that there was another way of amending the constitution, viz. "The Congress, whenever two-thirds of both houses shall deem it necessary, shall propose amendments to this constitution, which shall be valid to all intents and purposes as part of this constitution, when ratified by the legislatures of three fourths of the several states." They therefore were of opinion, that they did enough in solemnity, enjoining it on our representative in Congress, "To pursue all reasonable and legal methods to obtain a ratification of the alterations and provisions, which they deemed proper." They saw the impropriety of perpetual conventions. They saw the danger in the present ferment of mens' minds of collecting the violent and discordant opinions of America to a point; whence the most fatal dissensions might spread over our country, and not only cut off our present hopes, but obliterate all future prospects of happiness and safety. Under these impressions, they very prudently determined that a resort to an extraordinary assembly would be as unwise as it was unnecessary. They reflected that Congress was vested with powers fully adequate to the object of their wishes, and being chosen by the people themselves, would feel the strongest obligations of duty and interest to pursue every measure, which tended to the greater security of our liberties, and the restoration of general confidence. They asked themselves these simple questions:—Cannot the people send as virtuous and wise men to the Congress as to a convention? And if Congress be composed of virtuous and wise men, will they not be as fit to be trusted as a convention? And if deserving of equal confidence, will it not prevent delay, save expence, and avoid the danger of civil feuds to submit the consideration of our amendments to Congress? Congress can transmit to the legislatures of the several states at their next sessions, such amendments as the collected wisdom of America shall determine to be proper. The legislatures will ratify, and the public confidence be re-established. If this reasoning be natural, just and conclusive—was there any necessity for the assembly in November to vary from the measures of the convention in June? It is true indeed, that since June the convention of New-York has solicited another general convention.

But shall the opinion of the convention of another state be regarded more than that of our own? Our people in convention assembled thought another general convention unnecessary, if not dangerous. The people in the other states of the union thro' their conventions, expressed similar sentiments. And such of their legislatures as have assembled, have spoke the same language. Because one state requested a convention, was it prudent in us to indulge them in a measure, which might prove so fatal to our concord, if not to our safety? As much as I respect the state of New York, I think on this occasion, we have carried our politeness to an unjustifiable extent. The minority, however, were willing to go as far as the convention had gone;—they were willing to go further—to desire Congress to call a convention, if on a view of all circumstances they should deem it necessary. But, to repeat it, if nothing could satisfy the majority, but an application for a convention: What necessity was there to insult our own convention, and our sister states, by declaring that they had adopted a government, which cancelled all the great, essential and unalienable rights of freemen—It was wantonness in the extreme:—It derogated from the character of our country; it scandalized the cause of amendments; and might eventually injure it, if the magnanimity of our sister states did not supercede resentment for so ungenerous a wound—It looked more like the impotent revenge of a disappointed party—than the noble and manly effort of freemen.

1 DHFFE, II, pp. 387-389.

2 See "Virginia House of Delegates," October 29, 1788, p. 546 and November 14, 1788, p. 561 for Henry's resolution and the action taken by the Virginia legislature to request that a convention be called by Congress to consider amending the Constitution.

Thomas Rodney (Poplar Grove, Delaware) January 10, 1789
Letter: To Ceasar Augustus Rodney (excerpt)

The Objects of a True Patriot are To Protect and defend his Country against all foreign Attacks; To protect the Citizens in their just rights and liberties, and guard them against the Tyrany & Injustice of Government; To Comfort the unfortunate, and persue Such Measures as Will Make the people happy and render the State great & prosperous.

DHFFE, II, pp. 78-79.

Elbridge Gerry (Cambridge) January 12, 1789
Letter: To Samuel Dexter

I was absent when your letter of the 8th was left at my house, in answer to which I can only inform you, that I am now as I ever have been since the commencement of our independence anxious for an efficient federal government, with every power for promoting the welfare and sufficient *checks* for securing the liberties of the people. The *latter* is what I have contended for, and those who wish to prey on the people by means of a corrupt government are loading me and everyone else who opposes them with anathemas for urging amendments. I consider myself bound by the voice of a majority whether in favor of the Cosntitution as it now stands or of amendments, but wish not for a seat in the federal legislature and make this communication for your own satisfaction and not to answer any purpose of electioneering. I am no ways concerned at the invectives against myself, for the authors know themselves incapable of supporting it, and the people will in due time be able to determine who are the *real* friends of their liberty.

DHFFE, I, p. 644.

James Madison (Louisa) January 13, 1789
Letter: To Thomas Mann Randolph, Sr.
Published: Richmond *Virginia Independent Chronicle,* January 28, 1789

Being informed, that report has ascribed to me many opinions relating to the public trust, for which I am a Candidate in this District, and being unable to rectify the mistakes by personal explanations, I have thought it proper to give written communications of my real opinions, to several of my acquaintances in your, and the other Counties. It has been with reluctance in every instance, that I have taken such a liberty; and in none have I felt more, than in troubling you with the grounds, on which my services are offered. Whatever hopes I may indulge, that my opinions are not materially inconsonant to yours, and that my pretensions, may not in other respects, be disapproved by you, I have no particular warrant for either, that renders an apology unnecessary. The best, perhaps, I can make, is the one which departs least from the truth; that as far as my opinions, and pretentsions, may not receive your approbation, I rely on your candor, for a proper interpretation of the motives, with which they are communicated; and that, as far as I may be favored in both respects, with your approbation, you will not only excuse the liberty I take, but feel sufficient inducements, as opportunities may fall in your way, to set the misinformed part of your county right.

The report, which, I have reason to believe is most injurious, charges me, with being a strenuous advocate for the perfection of the

Constitution as it stands, and an inflexible opponent to the change of a single letter. The truth, on the contrary is, that I have ever thought it might be improved in several points, although I never could see the dangers which alarmed many; and what is more, was an unsuccessful advocate in the General convention, which framed the instrument, for several of the very amendments, since recommended by this, and other States. But, if my own judgment, did not entirely concur in the scheme of revising the work of that Assembly, I should hold myself bound by the strongest motives, to wish for such an alteration of it as may banish the party heats, which have so long, and so injuriously prevailed.

Whilst the Constitution was unratified, those who viewed the difficulty of uniting the various interests, and prejudices of the States, and the various opinions, and speculations of their political leaders, in any one plan whatever, were naturally led to withstand all previous amendments, as a dangerous road to public confusion. That this policy was warranted by the general state of things in America, is, perhaps, the belief of a greater majority of the people of the United States at this time, than then concurred in it. Whatever opinion may be entertained as to this point, however, it is evident, that the change of situation produced by the establishment of the Constitution, leaves me in common with other friends of the Constitution, free, and consistent in espousing such a revisal of it, as will either make it better in itself; or without making it worse, will make it appear better to those, who now dislike it. It is accordingly, my sincere opinion, and wish, that in order to effect these purposes, the Congress, which is to meet in March, should undertake the salutary work. It is particularly, my opinion, that the clearest, and strongest provision ought to be made, for all those essential rights, which have been thought in danger, such as the rights of conscience, the freedom of the press, trials by jury, exemption from general warrants, &c. I think also, that the periodical increase of the House of Representatives, until it attains a certain number, ought to be expressly provided for, instead of being left to the discretion of the government. There is room likewise in the Judiciary department for amendment. It ought to be so regulated, as to render vexatious, and superfluous appeals, impossible. In a number of other particulars, alterations are eligible either on their own account, or on account of those, who wish for them.

I have said, that I think the amendments ought to be undertaken by the Congress. I prefer that mode, to a General Convention, as most expeditious, most certain (since there are States who will object to the mode of a Convention, without being averse to amendments in themselves) as most safe, and as most oeconomical. It will not have escaped you, however, that the question concerning a General Convention, does not depend on the discretion of Congress. If two-thirds of the States make application, Congress cannot refuse to call one; if not, Congress have no right to take the step.

DHFFE, II, pp. 338-340. Reprinted in *Papers*, XI, pp. 415-417.

New York Assembly January 20, 1789
Debates (excerpts)
Printed: New York *Daily Advertiser* (January 30 & 31, 1789)
[During debate on the issue of district elections, the subject of the ratification of the Constitution by the New York Convention was discussed. Ed.]

Mr. *B. Livingston.* The sentiments of the honorable gentleman, who was last on the floor, and my own, differ very widely on the present occasion. I did not, however, expect that he would have had recourse to the explanatory amendments of our convention to support the doctrine he contends for, but that he would have drawn his arguments from the constitution itself. For my own part I consider those explanations in a very different light. I consider that our convention have *unconditionally* adopted the new constitution, and that they have only expressed a *confidence* that certain powers will only be exercised in a certain way. . . .

Mr. *Lansing*—If the gentleman has given such sentiments as can be supported, the consequence is that the people of this state have been cajoled; if this sentiment is to prevail, the language is, that the people have ratified one constitution, and are bound by another; but I am induced to believe that on reflection the gentleman will correct that sentiment.

To convince the committee, if they place a confidence in the ratification, I need only refer to it for our authority to divide the state into districts; but if the explanations and reservations therein contained are to be of no effect, then it is clear that the people of this state have been cajoled, and are bound by a contract they did not intend to agree to. But the national government has no power over the people of this state, except what is derived from the ratification by our convention; which, if it is binding on us, is also binding on the general government; if they accept it, it must be with our explanations. I must confess, Sir, that the sentiments I have heard advanced are peculiarly distressing, when we consider our present situation. It is well known that there was a great diversity of sentiment in the state on this subject, and that a great majority of the people were opposed to it; the members of the convention, therefore, were fully impressed with the necessity of a revision of the constitution, and making a proper explanation in the ratification, of these rights which their constituents wished secured to them; at present it is said that these reservations in favor of the people are not binding: Sir, I wish we may hear no more assertions of this kind in this house. I hold that the whole of the compact must be taken together, and that if any part of it is binding, the whole is. Sir, I should not animadvert on this subject, if I did not suppose the sentiment was such as could not be maintained. This is not, however, the matter under consideration; the question is, whether we have a right to annex qualifications unknown to the constitution? If the constitution is to be the line of our conduct, we must amend the bill in the manner I propose.

Mr. *B. Livingston*—The honorable gentleman who has just favored us with his sentiments, has treated the subject in a much more serious light than any thing that dropped from me would justify. Had the gentleman attended to my arguments, he would have spared several observations he has been pleased to make. I did not assert that all our explanatory amendments were to be totally disregarded. This is a sentiment I have heard from no one but the gentleman himself, who has been pleased to put it into my mouth to shew with how much ingenuity he could refute it. I said, Sir, that these explanations were not binding on the national government—that our convention had power only to adopt or reject the constitution, not to explain it; or to make any previous stipulations on the subject. If our convention had this right, that of Delaware had the same, and so had every state in the union—Suppose then these explanations should differ, as they certainly would, who should determine which state had fallen upon the true construction?—I therefore consider nothing as obligatory either upon this state or the national government, but the ratification; at the same time I have so much confidence in the characters who will probably compose the new Congress, as not to doubt that a due regard will be paid to all the explanations of the different states, so far as they can consistently be attended to.

I can hardly think, Sir, that there is any room for the honorable gentleman's suspecting that he has been *cajoled* in this business. Methinks the members who composed that convention were incapable of cajoling each other.

Mr. *Lansing*—Sir, when we ratified that constitution we were freemen, and had a right to make our own stipulations. We declared that we adopted the constitution under certain explanations, and that ratification having been accepted, those explanations are part of the compact.

Mr. *Harrison*—Sir, government is and ought to be considered as a contract between the persons governed, and the governors. When therefore the new constitution was offered to the people, it was as the subject of that compact, of which they might approve or disapprove; they might declare that they would take it in the whole, or in part—it was in the power of the United State, as the governors, to agree to the stipulations made by the people, or to reject them. Sir, if we attend to this idea, I believe gentlemen will be fully convinced that the explanations that are annexed to the ratification must be considered as binding upon the United States; they offered to the consideration of the people of this state, a certain constitution; the people of the state assembled in convention took up that constitution, and say that we understand certain parts of it may admit of doubt, but we are willing to accept, provided that such a sense is affixed to paricular articles of it.—If then the United States accept of a ratification containing such an explanation; the explanation is as binding as any part of it. This is the case with all contracts. Sir, when the most common instrument of writing is brought to a man, will it not be in his power to say, I understand a particular article in such a way, and if he signs it under such an explanation, does not his explanation become a part of the contract. This is plain reasoning on the subject. These are my sentiments, and such as I shall always think it my duty to support. I think, however, that we are drawn from the subject.

DHFFE, III, p. 333-335. See "New York Convention," July 10, 1788, p. 476 for reference to the explanatory amendments, and July 26, 1788, pp. 480-483 for the ratification with the explanatory bill of rights.

An Observer January 22, 1789
Newspaper Article: Boston *Independent Chronicle* (excerpt)

The great body of the community is certainly in favor of amendments, and will not knowingly vote for anybody who is against them. They have been much alarmed at the bold claims of those who openly assert, that the amendments were proposed only as an expedient to procure a majority, and that the rights of mankind are not originally equal. These things, being published here so frequently as they have been, have much lessened the influence of this town [Boston] upon the country, where an high value is set upon constitutional liberty, by a people who cannot bear to be contradicted upon principles which they hold sacred.

DHFFE, I, p. 669.

Elbridge Gerry January 22, 1789
Letter: To the Electors of Middlesex
Published: Boston *Independent Chronicle*

Friends and Fellow Citizens,

It appearing by your suffrages that I am one of your candidates for a federal Representative, give me leave for this evidence of your confidence, to express my warmest acknowledgments, but at the same time to request, that such of you as may again be disposed to honor me with your votes will turn your attention to some other candidate, for although I have been long honored with the confidence of my countrymen, and am conscious that a real regard to their political happiness has been the sole motive of my conduct, yet circumstanced as I am, to me an election would by no means be agreeable. Since however, my name is again, without any effort or inclination of my own, brought into public view, I embrace this opportunity to explain that conduct for which I have been treated with so much invective and abuse.

When the question on the Constitution was put in the Federal Convention, conceiving myself to be in a land of liberty, where the privilege of deliberating and voting with freedom would in the fullest extent be firmly supported, I voted against the Constitution, it being in my mind, in many instances, *defective.* Had my opinion been founded in error, it would have been but an error in judgment, for the fabricated falsehoods against me have been frequently and fully exposed. But five states having ratified the Constitution in the fullest expectation of amendments, and two having rejected it, no one can I think deny, that my opinion on this subject has been confirmed by the proceedings of a majority of the Union. An attempt has been made by means of *invective,* which must be condemned by this, and by every respectable community, to impair or destroy the privilege mentioned; a privilege, which no good citizen will ever permit to die in his hands, and which the good sense of the community will undoubtedly protect as one of the great pillars of a free state.

Some have endeavored to hold me up as an enemy to the Constitution, than which, nothing is more remote from the truth. Since the commencement of the Revolution, I have been ever solicitous for an efficient federal government, conceiving that without it, we must be a divided, an unhappy people. A government too democratical have I ever deprecated, but wished for one that should possess every power requisite for the welfare of the Union, and at the same time be so balanced, as to secure the *governed* from the rapacity and domination of lawless and insolent ambition. To an unconditional ratification of the Constitution was I therefore opposed, because thereby every necessary amendment would be rendered precarious. But as the system is adopted, I am clearly of opinion, that every citizen of the ratifying states is in duty bound to support it, and that an opposition to a due administration of it would not only be unjustifiable, but highly criminal.

Amendments, every citizen has still a right to urge, without exciting a spirit of persecution, which is unnecessary in a good, and never gains proselytes in a bad cause. Every friend to a vigorous government must, as I conceive, be desirous of such amendments, as will remove the just apprehensions of the people, and secure their confidence in, and affection for, the new government. For to defeat amendments of this description, must be in effect, to defeat the Constitution itself. But when the question on amendments shall have received a constitutional decision, I shall cheerfully acquiesce in it, and, in any event, shall be happy to promote the true interest of the respectable county of Middlesex, of this commonwealth, and of the United States.

The part which I have had to act, and the uncandid treatment which I have received in this matter, will I trust justify me in being thus explicit; for I am conscious, that every part of my political conduct has had for its object, the public welfare.

DHFFE, I, pp. 647-648. Gerry won the election.

Philadelphia *Independent Gazetteer* January 23, 1789

A gentleman from Virginia, whose information may be relied on, asserts that the controversy between *federalists* and *anti-federalists*, which have for some time past distracted and divided the Councils of the several states, has entirely subsided in that quarter, relative to the proposed amendments to the new constitution for the United States; it being agreed, on all hands, that a *bill of rights*, declaratory of the *freedom of the press, trial by jury*, &c. ought to be annexed, and other *essential* points explained and defined, so as to fix the liberties of the people on the most safe and permanent foundation; and that the only question amongst them now, is, Whether the *poll*—or *capitation* tax, should be levied on the people, both parties being convinced the *impost* will be inadequate to the expences of the general government? The *federalists* are for the measure; the *anti-federalists* oppose it; and this, at present, seems to be the *bone of contention*, among the people of the *ancient dominion*.

DHFFE, II, p. 397.

James Madison January 27, 1789
Published: Fredericksburg *Virginia Herald,* January 29, 1788

Extract of a letter from the Hon. JAMES MADISON, *jun. to his friend in this county.*

The offer of my services to the district, rests on the following grounds:—That although *I* always conceived the constitution might be improved, yet *I* never could see in it, as it stands, the dangers which have alarmed many respectable citizens; that I held it my duty therefore, whilst the constitution remained unratified, and it was necessary to unite the various opinions, interests and prejudices of the different states, in some one plan, to oppose every previous amendment, as opening a door for endless and dangerous contentions among the states, and giving an opportunity to the secret enemies of the union to promote its dissolution:—That the change of circumstances produced by the secure establishment of the plan proposed, leaves me free to espouse such amendments as will, in the most satisfactory manner, guard essential rights, and will render certain vexatious abuses of power impossible:—That it is my wish, particularly, to see specific provision made on the subject of *the Rights of Conscience, the Freedom of the Press, Trials by Jury, Exemption from General Warrants, &c,* to see, effectual provision made also for the periodical increase of the representatives, until the number shall amount to the fullest security on that head, and for prohibiting appeals to the federal court in cases that might be vexatious or superfluous:—That there are a variety of other alterations which ought to be inserted, as either eligible in themselves, or as due to those who think them so.

With regard to the mode of obtaining amendments, I have not withheld my opinion that they ought to be recommended by the first Congress, rather than be pursued by way of a General Convention: 1st, Because the former is the most expeditious mode. If congress undertake the business, the amendments may be prepared in March next, and immediately submitted to the states; whereas a convention must be delayed until two-thirds of the states shall have assembled their legislatures, and these shall have applied for one; and after a convention itself shall have been formed, and agreed on amendments, the same formalities will remain, as if the amendments should be proposed by Congress in March next.—2dly, Because it is the most certain mode. There are not a few states who will in no case agree to a convention, and yet have no objection to amendments in themselves—3dly, Because it is the safest mode. No danger can be apprehended from the deliberations of Congress on the subject. What might result from a Convention, meeting in the present foment of parties, and consisting, as would probably be in part the case, of insidious characters from different quarters of the union, is more than can be foreseen. It is a sufficient objection against the experiment, if the same avowed end can be otherwise answered, that a great part of America is filled with the most serious apprehensions from it. One thing, however, ought not to be disregarded, to wit, that the question relating to a Convention will in no respect depend on the discretion of Congress, and consequently the sentiments of the candidates for that body, on that point, cannot affect their pretensions. If two-thirds of the states apply for a Convention, Congress cannot refuse to call one. If not, Congress have no right to take such a step, but must proceed in the other mode pointed out by the Constitution.

DHFFE, II, pp. 340-341. Reprinted in *Papers*, XI, pp.428-429.

New York Election Law January 27, 1789
(excerpt)

And be it further enacted by the Authority aforesaid, That no Officer or other Person shall call or order any of the Militia of this State to appear or Exercise, on any day or at any time during any such Election, or at any time within twenty days before the Ordinary and Established days of Election, (except in cases of Invasion or Insurrection) on pain of Forfeiting the sum of Two hundred pounds for every such Offence, to be recovered by any Person who will Sue for the same, with Costs, the one Moiety of such Penalty to his own use, and the other Moiety thereof to the People of this State.

DHFFE, III, p. 364.

Spectator January 27, 1789
Newspaper Article: Boston *Herald of Freedom*

I was much surprised last evening to hear Mr. Bowdoin of Dorchester, son to our late worthy governour, assert, in the House of Representatives, that the Legislature of New-York wished to destroy the new federal Constitution. Unfortunately for that state, as well as the rest of the union, the two branches of their Legislature could not agree as to the mode of choosing their electors and Senators; and after a Committee of conference between the two Houses, on this subject, on which much ingenuity was displayed, the time passed, and the injury was of course irretrievable. This being the true state of the case, it appears the more astonishing that any gentleman should make such a round assertion on such very slender information. The Senate of that state is unquestionably federal, and their answer to the message of the governour of that Commonwealth, is at once a proof of their patriotism and discretion. Nor does it ever appear, by any authentick documents—that their House of Representatives is opposed to the Constitution, unless wishing for amendments is to be considered as evidence, and, in that case, more than two thirds of the whole people of America are in the same way of thinking. This sort of official abuse had best be restrained, for it can have no other tendency than to irritate and mislead, without answering a single valuable purpose.

DHFFE, III, p. 366.

Abraham Clark February 4, 1789
Newspaper Article: Elizabethtown *New Jersey Journal* (excerpt)

One of their insinuations is that I am antifoederal, and an enemy to the new government. The charge of antifoederalism is of so general and undefined a nature, that had it not been followed by that of an enemy to the government, I should not have thought it worthy of notice, as that epithet is frequently given to all those who dare venture to suspect the least defect in the Constitution, in which is included by far the greatest part of the inhabitants of the United States: How far this charge is applicable to me, I leave the impartial public to judge. That I used every means in my power in the different stations I filled, to obtain an efficient government, is well known and cannot be denied. When the plan of the new government appeared, I found it not such as I had wished and expected; I perceived, as I supposed, some parts of it bearing too hard upon the liberties of the people, and giving some unnecessary powers to those who were to administer it: This I never scrupled to mention when my opinion was desired. Notwithstanding my dislike to some parts, considering the situation the United States was in, and the provision made in the Constitution for amendments, I cheerfully gave my assistance to send it to the states for their consideration, judging that New-Jersey, from its local situation and circumstances, could not with propriety reject it, notwithstanding its imperfections; presuming at the same time, that the new Congress would endeavor to amend it as soon as other important business for putting the government into operation would admit. This I yet hope and expect will, in a proper time, be effected in Congress, but not by a future general convention, which would be inexpedient and dangerous to the union by leaving us without government for years to come. The story so industriously propogated, that I made offers to, and used endeavors with the Convention of Jersey to prevent their ratifying the Constitution, is so far from being true, that I never exchanged one word to my remembrance or belief, with any one member of our Convention on the subject of the Constitution, until long after its ratification, or ever wrote to one of them upon that subject; nor did I use any means whatever tending to a rejection of it, which I had a right to do if I thought proper, when the Constitution was under consideration; a right which I trust I shall at all times, if necessary, exercise without fear or scruple, when our liberties are the subject of deliberation. This in brief, as near as I can state it, is the sum total of my antifoederalism and enmity to the new government, if any are pleased to call it such.

DHFFE, III, pp. 119-120.

New York Assembly February 4, 1789
Debates (excerpt)

The house then went again into committee on the draft of an application to Congress to call a convention to revise and propose amendments to the new constitution.

Mr. Webster in the chair.

The following draft of an application to Congress was read.

Resolved (if the honorable the senate concur herein) that an application be made to the Congress of the United States of America in the name and behalf of the legislature of this state, in the words following, to wit

The people of the state of New-York having ratified the constitution agreed on the 17th September, 1787, by the convention then assembled at Philadelphia, as explained by the said ratification, in the fullest confidence of obtaining a revision of the several articles of the said constitution by a general convention. In compliance, therefore, with the unanimous sense of the convention of this state, who all united in opinion, that such a revision was necessary to recommend the said constitution to the approbation and support of a numerous body of their constituents, and a majority of whom conceived the constitution so exceptionable that nothing but such confidence, and an invincible reluctance to separate from our sister states could have prevailed upon a sufficient number to assent to it without stipulating for previous amendments, and from a conviction that the apprehensions or discontents which those articles occasion, cannot be removed or allayed, unless an act to revise the said constitution be among the first that shall be passed by the new Congress; WE, the legislature of the state of New-York, DO, in behalf of our constituents, in the most earnest and solemn manner, make this application to the Congress, that a convention of deputies from the several states be immediately called, with full power to take the said constitution into their consideration, and to report such amendments thereto as they shall find best suited to promote our common interests, and secure to ourselves and our latest posterity the great and unalienable rights of mankind.

Mr. *B. Livingston*—I do not rise, Mr. Chariman, to oppose an application to Congress for a revision of the new Constitution, but to state my objections to its being made in the form of the resolution now under consideration. I must, however, be indulged in declaring that when I give my assent to making any application to Congress upon this subject, it is not from a conviction that any amendments whatever are necessary. I consider the constitution as perfect as we could reasonably have expected it from the hands of men. But as a revision of the system will have a tendency to render it more universally acceptable, it may not be improper to take some measures on our part to obtain it in a constitutional way. It is with us to determine in what mode this revision should be had, so as to promote the salutary ends we all have in view.

Sir, the constitution of the United States provides that amendments may be obtained either by Congress proposing them to the legislatures of the different states, or by calling a new convention for the purpose. Will it not then be prudent to leave it to the discretion of Congress to determine which of these two modes will be best calculated to answer the end the resolution has in view, and not to insist on their calling a convention immediately?

Conventions are assemblies which should as seldom as possible be resorted to, where the ordinary administration is adequate to the object. Here the government are vested with powers expressly comprehending the present case. Is there any danger that these powers will not be called into exercise if the public good requires it? Of whom will Congress be composed? Are not the senators chosen by the different state legislatures, and the other branch by the people themselves? Will they not be acquainted with the sentiments and wishes of their constituents? Will they not feel every obligation, as well as inclination, to pursue such measures as will best accord with those sentiments and wishes? From an assembly thus constituted, may we not expect that the proper amendments will be proposed as soon as possible after their first meeting? To whom are those amendments to be submitted? To the legislatures of the several states, who will doubtless ratify such of them as in their estimation will be acceptable to their constituents. This mode of proceeding is attended with fewer embarrassments, and will take up much less time, than what must necessarily elapse before a convention can be assembled; the result of whose deliberations (should they ever agree) must undergo the same discussion as those which may be proposed by Congress. Should Congress believe a majority of the people wish for amendments, it is probable that the legislature of this state, at their very next meeting, may be employed in deliberating on some of their proposing—while, from the time that must unavoidably transpire in the summoning and meeting of a convention, the advocates for amendments can scarcely flatter themselves with a speedy revision of the system in that way.

But delay is not the only inconvenience attendant on a new convention. Dangers of a more serious nature are to be apprehended. It is well known that this state, as well as some others, are divided into two parties, federal and antifederal. These terms are not used with a view of casting an odium on the one or the other; but because I do not recollect an other term that is so generally applied, or is better understood. Gentlemen have been blamed for mentioning that parties exist in the state; but when the notoriety of the fact renders concealment impossible, and when pertinent arguments may be drawn from the present situation of the country, where can be the impropriety in taking notice of it. If then parties exist, what will be their conduct in the case of a convention? Will not federalists choose federalists; and those of an opposite character, send members possessing the same sentiments with themselves? Will members thus chosen feel all that independence of sentiment so essential to a cool and dispassionate consideration of the constitution they are to revise? Will a body composed of such heterogeneous materials, be likely to accord in any one amendment? Will not the same spirit of party which influenced their election, continue to actuate the different members of the convention, until they are compelled to return home, without effecting any alteration in the new system of government? Should this be the case, will all those who desire amendments feel disposed to acquiesce in that disappointment? We might indeed have expected that this would have been the case, had not an honorable gentleman, who was one of the managers in a late conference between the two houses, declared in the presence of both, that he hoped his constituents would never rest satisfied until they had obtained the amendments they desired. This, sir, is going much farther than our convention have gone, and it is to be sincerely hoped that the gentleman may be mistaken in the sentiments he entertains of his constituents. Should these, however, be the real intentions of so respectable a part of the community, and should pains be taken to disseminate them still farther, what are we to expect in case of the conventions's rising without proposing amendments, but a civil war? The gentleman who made this declaration may have familiarised himself to such an event. His nerves may be sufficient to meet it, and to carry him through without emotion; but, for my own part, I cannot, while the devastations of the late war are fresh in my memory, but tremble at the idea of a repetition of them.

Having stated some objections to the immediate calling of a convention, I shall offer a resolution by way of amendment to the one which has just been read, by which Congress are left at liberty to call a convention, or to propose amendments in the other way, as they shall think best. The resolution is as follows:

Resolved, (if the honourable the senate concur herein) that an application be made to the Congress of the United States of America, in the name and behalf of the legislature of the state, in the words following, to wit,

Whereas the convention of the good people of the state of New-York, on the 26th day of July last past, assented to and ratified the Constitution proposed on the 17th day of September, in the year of our Lord 1787, by the Convention then assembled at Philadelphia, in confidence nevertheless, "*that the amendments which might be proposed to the said constitution, would receive an early and mature consideration*"

And whereas the said convention at the same time agreed to sundry amendments, and in the name and behalf of their constituents, "*enjoined it upon their representatives in Congress to exert all their influence to obtain a ratification of the same in the manner prescribed in the said constitution.*" Therefore, we the representatives of the people of the state of New-York, in senate and assembly convened, in compliance with the sense of our convention, and anxious that the *necessary amendments* may be introduced as soon as possible, do earnestly and in the most solemn manner call upon the Congress of the United States, to take the amendments recommended by our convention, and by those of our sister states, into their "*early and mature consideration,*" and to take effectual measures to obtain a ratification of such of them as may be deemed necessary to induce a general confidence in the government, either by proposing the same to the legislatures of the different states, or by calling a convention to meet at a period not far remote, agreeable to the manner prescribed by the fifth article of the constitution aforesaid, as the one or the other mode of ratification may to them appear best calculated to promote the peace and welfare of the union.

After reading the resolution Mr. Livingston proceeded.

Sir, In framing this resolution I have followed as nearly as possible the sentiments of our convention as expressed in their instrument of ratification. In one place they express a confidence that the amendments which might be proposed, would receive an early and mature consideration, but are silent as to the mode in which that consideration was to be had; in another part, they enjoin it upon their representatives in Congress, to exert all their influence to obtain a ratification of certain amendments in the manner prescribed in the constitution. Here again, nothing is said of a convention.

I am aware it will be mentioned, that by their circular letter, they have recommended the calling of a convention to all the other states. But, Sir, notwithstanding the respect we entertain for the honorable gentlemen who composed that convention; notwithstanding the gratitude we must all feel for their having ratified a form of government which cannot fail of producing the most solid advantages to our country, yet I trust we shall not think ourselves precluded by the advice contained in this letter, further than as it corresponds with our own ideas of propriety. Far be it from me to censure those who signed that letter, yet to prevent its having an undue influence, I shall stand excused from reminding the committee that our convention were chosen for the sole purpose of taking into consideration the new constitution. If we recur to the resolution under which they acted, we shall find no other authority delegated to them; whatever, therefore, they have done beyond ratifying the constitution, and particularly this letter, must be considered in the light of advice, which we are at liberty to follow or not, as the same may appear expedient or otherwise.

Upon the whole, the amendment which is brought forward is so unexceptionable, that I cannot but hope it will meet with the approbation of the committee.

Mr. *Jones.*—I am not a little surprized at what I have heard. The arguments appear to me to be extraordinary. We are told, in the first place, that it would be improper to call a convention immediately, because there are parties in the states, and that the persons chosen to go to the convention will be the representatives of those parties. But, the representatives to be chosen in the several states, to represent them in Congress, are not to be men of party; they are to be divested of all those prejudices which have been created since the new constitution has been the subject of political speculation and party rage. Sir, is there not a contradiction in this reasoning? Will not these parties have as much influence in the choice of members of Congress, as in the choice of members of convention? Can this be doubted? Why then are we to look to Congress, as a body in whom party heats and prejudices will be unknown? It is said too, that it is too soon to call a convention—that bad consequences will follow from it, in case they do not come to a happy result; and yet, if we leave it to the new government to propose amendments, notwithstanding every thing will be new to them, and it will be a long time before they get organized, and can take up the subject; yet it is said we shall probably be deliberating on amendments that they shall propose, before even a convention can be called. Really, sir, these arguments have no weight in them—they are fallacious. Again, it is said that the convention of the state did not request that a convention should be called immediately. But, sir, this sentiment is expressed in the ratification; if the gentleman will recur to it, he will find the proposed application conformable thereto. Sir, we need not apprehend that a convention will be called too soon—it will take a long period of time for the new government to get organized; and tho' I have not the smallest doubt of two thirds of the states in the union making an application, yet two years at least will elapse before an act can be passed, and a convention called. Sir, the arguments of the gentleman, as it respects the ratification of the convention, is not fair; the inference he draws from it is not just. The convention could not, in the instrument of ratification, insist upon the calling of a convention; but if they could, it would not have been prudent in them to have attempted it. But they could express their sentiments in a circular letter, and it is well known that they did this, and unanimously recommended the calling a convention; how far they had a right to do this I submit to the committee, and to the world. And I have not a doubt but their conduct is approved of. Sir, the convention of this state never would have ratified the constitution, if they had not been persuaded that their sister states in the union would have consented to call a convention, and if the circular letter had not been agreed to by both parties. Indeed this may be considered as a condition on which the constitution was ratified. Can it then be expected of us that we will submit to the general government to make the amendments? Was it ever known that the rulers themselves would say, you have trusted us with too much power, we therefore beg of you to take back a part of it? That they may want more power is highly probable; but it is not in the nature of man to suppose that too much confidence is reposed in them; they are never disposed to contemplate an abuse of power which they hold in their own hands. Shall we, therefore, trust to our own rulers to make amendments for us? The reason why there are two modes of obtaining amendments prescribed by the constitution I suppose to be this—it could not be known to the framers of the constitution, whether there was too much power given by it or too little; they therefore prescribed a mode by which Congress might procure more, if in the operation of the government it was found necessary; and they prescribed for the states a mode of restraining the powers of the government, if upon trial it should be found they had given too much. In my opinion, therefore, we ought to call for a convention as the proper line chalked out by the constitution for the people to obtain such amendments as to them appear essential to their happiness.

I am sorry that the sentiments of an individual, who he is I do not know, should be taken up as the sentiments of the people. The sentiments of the convention ought to have the preference; and we ought to pay deference to that sentiment only. The convention have declared a convention of the states to be necessary—even if no amendments are made; it will certainly quiet the apprehensions of a great number of people, and thereby give additional spirit to the new government itself. And, sir, I believe that peace will never be perfectly restored to the United States, until a convention is called, and they either declare that no amendments are necessary, or propose some.

But, sir, with respect to the existence of parties, it is natural, and is to be expected as a consequence resulting from freedom. There are parties in all free governments—at least, I have no knowledge of any in which party did not exist. One will sometimes be strongest —sometimes the other: In our country, which ever may prevail, I hope they will always pursue the great rights of mankind.

Mr. *Lansing*. In discussing this business, I shall pay some attention to the remarks of the gentleman who has brought forward the amendment; and I believe I can convince the committee that it would be improper to adopt it, unless they hold the same ideas as the gentleman himself. If agreed to, it would appear, instead of urging to Congress the necessity of calling a convention, that we did it barely in compliance with the recommendation of the late convention, and that it is repugnant to our own sentiments. The resolution as reported by the committee who were appointed to essay it, declares that the people of the state of New-York wish a convention called to revise the new system of general government. Sir, we are to believe that the resolution reported by them is the sense of the people, in as much as it is conformable to the unanimous sentiment of the late convention, who were elected by the people, for the special purpose of giving their sentiments on that subject—and further, sir, I believe it speaks the sense of the state. As the convention I say were called to express the sense of the people on the new constitution, we ought to respect their opinion. That convention adopted the constitution, not because they approved of it, but because the pressure of circumstances, and the ratification of it by a number of our sister states, had an influence on a majority of the members of that body. Sir, when the subject was under their consideration, men of all parties—of all descriptions—and all views, united in the opinion that a convention of the states, and the immediate revision of the system was necessary; indeed the unanimity which prevailed in the convention on the subject of the circular letter, is the strongest proof of the sentiments of the people. I am not apprehensive therefore that the sense of our constituents can be conveyed in too strong terms. This being my sentiment, it can not be supposed that I shall advocate the amendment proposed by the gentleman—for it will not in my opinion convey the sentiments of the people of the state. Is it probable that a revision will take place in the mode prescribed by the gentleman? the national government will be a long time making the necessary arrangements—for it is yet to be organized—and they will have a variety of important objects to pay immediate attention to; indeed much more than they can accomplish in two or three years. We are not to suppose that they will abandon all the national objects that will be before them to decide on the different amendments that have been proposed—After all this time expires, and Congress do propose amendments, then they are to go to the states, where another considerable period of time must elapse before three-fourths of the states agree to them. In the one instance we submit the propriety of making amendments to men who are sent, some of them for six years, from home, and who lose that knowledge of the wishes of the people by absence, which men more recently from them, in case of a convention, would naturally possess. Besides, the Congress, if they propose amendments, can only communicate their reasons to their constituents by letter, while if the amendments are made by men sent for the express purpose, when they return from the convention, they can detail more satisfactorily, and explicitly the reasons that operated in favour of such and such amendments—and the people will be able to enter into the views of the convention, and better understand the propriety of acceding to their proposition.

The hon. gentleman who has brought forward the amendment is fearful that the convention will be called at too early a day; for my part, I wish it was possible to anticipate the business; for the sooner amendments are made, the better. I should have preferred calling a convention before the meeting of Congress, was it practicable.

Sir, we have heard the word party too often mentioned. I suppose there is a material difference in what is now termed party, than that which originates in particular attachments to particular men—the present division of the people, arising from constitutional causes. One part of them supposing the new constitution a good one and the other supposing it dangerous to their happiness; this is the opinion of the majority of our constituents, as is evidenced by the complexion of this house. The reason why a different sentiment prevails in the senate may be accounted for from this cause; that that branch of the legislature is composed of men not so recently elected by the people; they were most of them chosen at a time when the present political dispute was unthought of; but, sir, this house speaks the sentiments of the people; for the majority of the members have been elected under that influence which is opposed to the new government. I am pained when I make these observations; but I do it to explain the distinctions that prevail at present, and they are such as are founded on fact. But, sir, it is insinuated, that if we do not leave this power with Congress, it will be supposing them not trustworthy. Sir, this is not a fair supposition, for it is impossible for any member to entertain such opinions without knowing of what characters Congress may be composed. But, sir, it is reasonable to expect that Congress will be unwilling to relinquish any of the powers that are given. Mankind are not disposed to give up advantages that they possess; it is easier to give power than to reclaim it. The contest between the two houses clearly proves this principle.

Mr. *B. Livingston.*—I shall be very short in my reply to the remarks of the two gentlemen who were last on the floor. In opposition to the proposed resolution, it is said that Congress will be too much embarrassed by a variety of important business, during their first session to attend to the subject of amendments. In answering this objection it may be asked, whether any more important object can claim their attention than the revision of the very system by which they are constituted, nor will this subject require as much time or avocation from their other concerns, as is apprehended. All the amendments which have been proposed by the different states, will lay before them. From these may be selected and recommended to the different legislatures such as may be deemed the most salutary: But should Congress be of opinion that a majority of their constituents are satisfied with the constitution in its present form, they will certainly act wisely not to recommend any innovations until experience shall have evinced the necessity of them.

Again, it is said, that a majority of the good people of the United States, and of this state in particular, are solicitous for the immediate assembling of a new convention. Was I satisfied of this being the fact, averse as I feel to this mode of obtaining amendments, I should think it my duty to give it every support. But I am yet to be convinced that this is the case: Several states, have unanimously ratified the new constitution, others have done it by very large majorities, without saying a syllable upon the subject of amendments, or a new convention; whence then is it to be inferred, that a major part of the people are anxious for this measure. It is by no means certain that a majority of our immediate constituents think it expedient.

One other remark which escaped those gentlemen ought not to pass unnoticed. They both observed that the new constitution would probably not have been adopted by our convention, unless the gentlemen who had from the first advocated this measure, had consented to sign the circular letter. If this information be true, (and it certainly is, for it comes from two gentlemen who had the honor of being members of that convention) it militates much against the attention which ought otherwise to be paid to a proceeding which had the appearance of being adopted with so much unanimity. If I say this letter was the result of compromise or compassion, surely as much credit is not due to it, as if every member had signed it voluntarily and without any other consideration than a conviction of its being an eligible step. This was so far from being the case, that several gentlemen, whose names appear to that letter, from the information which has been given the committee, seem to have been placed in such a situation as to have no alternative but that of signing the letter or losing the constitution. They preferred the former as the least of the two evils. The respect we were all ready to pay to the unanimous recommendation of our convention, must be much weakened now we are informed by what means this unanimity was effected.

I shall make but one observation more. The proposed resolution goes much farther than the circular letter of our convention. By the latter it is recommended that a convention meet at *a period not far remote.* By the application before us, we desire a convention may be assembled *immediately*. There is a very great and manifest difference between these terms. From this guarded expression of our convention we may conclude, that while they wished measures might be immediately taken to *call* a convention to satisfy a part of their constituents, they did not judge it expedient that this convention should assemble until experience had pointed out the defects of the new system, and therefore fixed the time of their meeting to *a period not far remote.*

Mr. *Jones.*—With respect to the circular letter, I have no recollection if I said they were compelled to sign it. I think that I did not say so. The fact is, thay were not compelled to sign it. The friends of the constitution dictated it themselves. There are some of the members in both houses who were of that convention—let them declare the fact.

Mr. *Lansing.*—If I conveyed an idea that there was compulsion in the framing of the circular letter, it was what I did not intend—nor do I beleive I did express a sentiment of the kind. Sir, I said that the change that took place between the time of election and the time of ratification, had an influence on a majority of the convention to ratify the constitution—tho' it did not alter their sentiments in respect to the merits of it. The question then was, how were they to shew the disapprobation of the state on the subject?—and all parties agreed in the measure of writing a circular letter, inviting our sister states to join with us to effect a revision of the system;—the better to secure the liberties of the people.

Mr. *Gilbert.*—I think a great deal of what has been said, is foreign to the subject; the only question before the committee is, whether we shall apply to Congress to call a convention, or whether we shall leave it to them to exercise their discretion in either calling a convention, or proposing amendments. We are to answer this question, in my opinion, by asking another—Are the proceedings of the convention binding?—if they are binding, are they so in the whole, or in part? For my part I think them binding in the whole; if so, we are bound to respect them, and we have no discretion on the present question—we must vote for calling a convention.

Mr. *Harrison.*—I feel myself peculiarly circumstanced upon the present occasion. I could wish to have remained silent—but it may be necessary that I give the committee my ideas. I am in sentiment opposed to the amendment offered by the gentleman from New York;—and yet I differ with the gentlemen who oppose it. I shall not however, enter into any argument on the subject, as my sense of amendments to the new constitution will appear on the journals of the convention—and I have hitherto seen no reason to alter my opinion. I think that if the amendments which were proposed in that body were adopted, that it would defeat the constitution by rendering it useless. But as a member of that convention, when I consider the situation of the state, and the sentiments that prevailed among a great number of the people, and the heats that had taken place, I was induced to think that every measure which could allay the apprehensions of the people, and prevent mischiefs which were then contemplated, ought to be adopted. Under these impressions I signed the circular letter. I was willing that the constitution should be submitted to a convention; not doubting but the good sense of the citizens of America would not rashly make such alterations as would impair its beauty—or enervate any of its essential parts; and that they would weigh well all that could be said for and against it. I am not unwilling, sir, to trust my countrymen; if I am mistaken in my opinion, I will submit to their's. And tho' the constitution is in my opinion as good as can be expected, yet I do not consider it so perfect as not to want improvement; if therefore a convention can point out any alterations tending to promote the happiness of the people, I shall think it my duty to acquiesce. And I must confess that I think the calling of a convention, the only means to restore peace and harmony to our country, and to destroy those parties that exist amongst us;—under this impression I shall vote against the amendment.

Sir, I can not think it right that any invidious comparisons should be drawn between the two houses. I consider both of them as the representatives of the people, with whose sentiments I suppose them equally acquainted. We do not, sir, know what may be the sense of the people, in respect to the proceedings of this legislature; but to the bar of the public the two houses will have to appeal; where, if the conduct of the one or the other is approved of, they will again be sent foreward as their representatives. Sir, gentlemen in either house may maintain opposite principles; but it is cruel to suppose they do not originate in pure motives. We are to suppose that both houses act conscientiously.

Mr. *Lansing*—I believe, sir, that the gentlemen of the committee will recollect the expressions I made; and what I said cannot be construed into an invidious distinction. I stated facts, and they can not be contradicted. I say, that the last year, when an election was had, that throughout the state, it took a complexion from the sentiments of the people, as they respect the new constitution; and the consequence is, that in this house we have a majority for amendments. I say, too, that the senate, having been elected at an earlier period, do not entertain the same sentiments, and that this difference in the two houses, arises from the senate not having come so recently from the people. When I state these facts, I disclaim any intention of injuring the feelings of the senate.

On the question to agree to the amendment proposed by Mr. B. Livingston . . . [it was defeated by a vote of 43 to 9]

DHFFE, III, pp. 395-403.

New York Assembly February 5, 1789
Proceedings (excerpt)

Mr. Webster, from the committee of the whole House, on the draft of an application by the Legislature of this State to the Congress of the United States of America, to call a Convention for revising the Constitution for the said United States, adopted by the Convention of this State, on the 26th day of July last, reported, that after the said draft had been this day read in the committee, a paragraph thereof was again read, in the words following, viz.

"We, the Legislature of the State of New-York, do, in behalf of our Constituents, in the most earnest and solemn manner, make this application to the Congress, that a Convention of Deputies from the several States be immediately called, with full powers to take the said Constitution into their consideration, and to propose such amendments thereto, as they shall find best calculated to promote our common interests, and secure to ourselves and our latest posterity, the great and unalienable rights of mankind."

That the said paragraph having been read, Mr. Livingston made a motion, that the word *immediately* be obliterated, and the words *at a period not far remote,* inserted after the word *called.*

That the question having been put, whether the committee did agree to the amendment proposed by the motion of Mr. Livingston, it passed in the negative in the manner following, viz. . . .[by a vote of 33 to 18]

That Mr. Macomb then made a motion, that the word *immediately* be obliterated, and the words *as early as possible,* inserted after the word *called.*

That the question having been put, whether the committee did agree to the amendment proposed by the motion of Mr. Macomb, it was carried in the affirmative, in the manner following, viz. . . . [by a vote of 28 to 21]

That Mr. Livingston then made a motion for an amendment, to obliterate the words, *the said Constitution,* and instead thereof to insert the words, *amendments proposed by this or the other States,* whereby that part of the said paragraph, would be in the words following, viz.

"We, the Legislature of the State of New-York, do, in behalf of our Constituents, in the most earnest and solemn manner, make this application to the Congress, that a Convention of Deputies from the several States be called as early as possible, with full powers to take *the amendments proposed by this or other States,* into their consideration."

That the question having been put, whether the committee did agree to the amendment proposed by the motion of Mr. Livingston, it passed in the negative, in the manner following, viz. . . . [by a vote of 37 to 10]

That it was thereupon *Resolved*, that the committee did agree to the said resolution and application, which he was directed to report to the House; and he read the report in his place, and delivered the said draft of a resolution and application in at the table; where the same were again read, and agreed to by the House. Thereupon,

Resolved, (if the Honorable the Senate concur therein) That an application be made to the Congress of the United States of America, in the name and behalf of the Legislature of this State, in the words following, to wit:

THE PEOPLE OF THE STATE OF NEW-YORK, having ratified the constitution agreed to on the seventeenth day of September, in the year of our Lord one thousand seven hundred and eighty seven, by the convention then assembled at Philadelphia, in the State of Pennsylvania, as explained by the said ratification, in the fullest confidence of obtaining a revision of the said Constitution by a General Convention; and in confidence that certain powers in and by said Constitution granted, would not be exercised, until a Convention should have been called and convened, for proposing amendments to the said Constitution. In compliance, therefore, with the *unanimous* sense of the Convention of this State, who all united in opinion, that such a revision was necessary to recommend the said Constitution to the approbation and support of a numerous body of their Constituents, and a majority of the members of which, conceived several articles of the Constitution so exceptionable, that nothing but such confidence, and an invincible reluctance to separate from our sister States, could have prevailed upon a sufficient number to assent to it, without stipulating for previous amendments: And from a conviction, that the apprehensions and discontents which those articles occasion, cannot be removed or allayed, unless an act to revise the said Constitution, be among the first that shall be passed by the new Congress; WE, *the legislature of the state of New-York,* DO, in behalf of our constituents, in the *most earnest and solemn manner,* make this application to the Congress, that a Convention of Deputies from the several states be called, as early as possible, with full powers to take the said Constitution into their consideration, and to propose such amendments thereto as they shall find best calculated to promote our common interests, *and secure to ourselves and our latest posterity the great and unalienable rights of mankind.*

Ordered, that Mr. Jones and Mr. Carman deliver a copy of the preceding resolution, to the Honorable the Senate.

DHFFE, III, pp. 404-408.

Thomas Jefferson (Paris) February 9, 1789
Letter: To William Short (excerpt)

[A] majority of federalists are secured in the Senate and expected in the H of representatives. Genl Washington will be president and probably Mr. Adams vice president. So that the constitution will be put under way by those who will give it a fair trial. It does not seem probable that the attempt of N York to have another convention to make amendments will succeed, tho' Virginia concurs in it. It is tolerably certain that Congress will propose amendments to the assemblies, as even the friends of the constitution are willing to make amendments, some from a conviction they are necessary, others from a spirit of conciliation. The addition of a bill of rights will probably be the most essential change.

Ford, V, p. 70.

A. B. February 13, 1789
Newspaper Article: Baltimore *Maryland Journal* (excerpt)

The rule laid down by Dr. Price, and other political writers (if true) of taking one *fifth* of all the inhabitants of a country, to ascertain the number of *sencible* men, or men capable of bearing arms, is not applicable, and can by no means ascertain the number of *voters* in this State. No man can vote before 21, and unless he has 30L. property: a man can bear arms between 15 and 21, and without any property.

DHFFE, II, p. 217. The excerpt relates to a discussion of the number of voters in Washington County, Maryland. On March 3, 1789 the *Maryland Journal* printed another article by "A.B." on this same subject which contained the following: "In Dr. Price's consideration on the measures carrying on with respect to the British Colonies in North-America, p. 22, after mentioning the number of *free* people in the Colonies, he adds, "the common calculation is of one *sencible,* or fighting man, in *five* persons, and this is supposed to be rather under than over the truth." (DHFFE, II, p. 226 at note 4.)

Baltimore *Maryland Gazette* February 17, 1789
(excerpt)

A Correspondent observes, that it gave him great satisfaction to find the anties, in this town and county, at the late election, equally eager for placing the American Fabius in the presidential chair, with the warm federals, which ought to silence all clamour against them, as *their* sincerity cannot reasonably be doubted, especially when it contradicts the erroneous opinion, too generally entertained, of their acting systematically in close concert with those of the same way of thinking in other states, particularly the violent anties in the back counties of Pennsylvania, who generally and openly, when chusing electors, avowed their wish for Mr. R. H. Lee to be president, and Governor Clinton vice-president, as men most likely to promote the calling a new general convention, for the purpose of obtaining such *amendments* as would unequivocally "ascertain, secure and protect the great rights of the people."

DHFFE, IV, p. 178.

A Republican February 23, 1789
Newspaper Article: *Boston Gazette*[1]

Messrs. Edes,

The correspondent in Wednesday's Centinel, has an extraordinary faculty in discovering the views, designs, and *feelings* of those he is pleased to call Antifederalists; he represents them as *mortified* and *chagrined* at the probable election of *Washington* and *Adams* as President and Vice-President of the United States.—This vile suggestion, I believe to be groundless in general, and as it respects this Commonwealth in particular, every man's own observation will give him complete evidence of its untruth. *Washington* when in the Field, and cloathed in Martial Power, ever respected the Rights of the Citizens; and as a true Republican never trampled upon their privileges.—Had his Republican principles been fully awake, when he left the Field, he never would have concurred in erecting an *Order* of *Nobility* in America, nor have accepted the *Presidency* of that *Order*, which his brother Officers more ambitious than himself, in a manner forced upon him; but even *this* the people are willing to overlook in *him*, like a spot in the Sun, it is swallowed up by his many resplendant virtues—All parties and descriptions of men revere him—there is hardly one but ardently wishes his election, whether

Federalist or Antifederalist, Aristocratic or Republican.—The vile suggestion of the Centinel Correspondent, is equally untrue as it [refers?] to our Countryman and distinguished Patriot, the Hon. John Adams, Esq. His virtues and abilities are equalled but by few, and his genuine Republican principles are undoubted. Never were contrary parties more perfectly united than in these two friends to liberty and mankind. From these men the Antifederalists (so called) have every thing to hope, and little to fear: they have full confidence in their integrity and patriotism, nor doubt but they will favour, and concur in, every safe and equitable measure to meliorate, and improve the Constitution; in securing to the people their just rights and privileges, and placing them beyond the reach of *Aristocratic Fraud* and *Usurpation.* The correspondent of the Centinel takes occasion by a contrast with these eminent characters, obliquely to stigmatize two others, highly meritorious for their Patriotism—I mean the Hon. Patrick Henry of Virginia, and Governour Clinton of New-York; men who have been great, and uniform friends, to their Country, and to the Revolution; and who stand high in the estimation of their Countrymen. This Correspondent of the Centinel advances as another cause of *chagrin* to the Antifederalists, "That the Senators of Nine States are *consistent* Federalists." He does not define the kind of *consistency* with which their sentiments comport—If he means that they are honest men, who wish well to the Community, I believe he will not find the Antifederalists opposed to them; but if he means, as I think he does, that they are *consistent* with the political principles of *Robert the Cofferer,*[2] and such like over-grown *Monsters* of *Aristocracy,* who keep up a chain of communication and influence from New-Hampshire to Georgia, and whose wishes are to subject the People to *Vassallage,* I will venture to say that he is mistaken, at least in part; and whatever may be the wicked *design* of a *few* in that august Body, I presume they will not dare to counteract the well founded expectations of the Majority of their Constituents, in *defining, checking,* and *guarding* the Constitution, so as to secure a good and faithful Administration of the Federal Government, and preserve to the People that high bequest of Heaven—their Freedom.

This correspondent of the Centinel brings as another instance of *mortification* to the Antifederalists that "of the six Representatives already chosen in this State, neither of them will second their designs to *destroy the Union*"—God grant that they may never destroy the Union: nor did the idea ever enter the brain of any one except the correspondent of the Centinel, and a few others like him, and it is promulgated by them for the purposes only of promoting divisions and jealousy. Every one knows that the gentlemen elected were not the favorite of the Aristocratics (one only excepted).—Therefore we may fairly conclude that they were elected by the Antifederalists, (so called,) or in other words by the Republicans: for the true distinction of the parties which divide the Commonwealth at this time, is that of the *Republicans* and of the *Aristocratics*, and in these are all others swallowed up—the former wish the Federal Constitution *defined* and *amended* that it may be a Government of *Laws* and not of *Men*:—and the latter wish it *indefinite* and *ambiguous*, that it may be a Government of *Men* and not of *Laws*:—And lastly, this pitiful correspondent of the Centinel pretends as another cause of *chagrin* to the Antis, that the Hon. Mr. GERRY has changed his sentiments of the Federal Constitution, and from a D —— l, as he was before represented by the violent Aristocratics, he has now become an Angel. It was but the other day the Centinel teemed with torrents of abuse from that party, against this respectable Patriot: but since his election as a Federal Representative, they make a virtue of necessity, & their policy now is to court him to their interest—Such are the machinations of this artful, cunning and over-bearing junto.—In *Mr. G*, they are mistaken in their man; he has too keen a sense of feelings speedily to forget their many injuries, and too much integrity not to act for the general good—He has too independent a principle to become the dupe of their measures, and too much knowledge to fall into their serpentine embraces.

1 DHFFE, IV, pp. 183-184.
2 Robert Morris, Senator-elect from Pennsylvania.

Joshua Atherton (Amherst) February 23, 1789
Letter: To John Lamb (excerpt)

It would be unentertaining to you to be informed by what means the Federalists (if I after them may use so improper a term) have eventually brought about their own measures, notwithstanding they seemed throughout the course of the whole transactions, to have been on the brink of failure. In our General Assembly, [where for a] long time there was a decided majority against the new system, opposition has ceased—and the language is "It is adopted, let us try it." No slaves could speak a language more agreeable to their masters. And the unavailing measure of choosing a committee to consider the address of New York relative to a new convention for the purpose of amendments was all the Assembly of New Hampshire found leisure to do.

Not to descend too far into particulars, it is very obvious, that a kind of aristocratical influence throughout the states buoys up and carries forward a system of government wherein all the solid foundations of liberty are (strange to relate) totally forgotten. To carry on the farce the Federalists have taken the liberty to step onto the ground of their opponents, and, clothing themselves with their armor, talk high of amendments—and by a kind of duplicity, often successful if not discovered, are taking possession of the political citadel under the style of friends.

You, sir, live in the very focus of the maze of collected wisdom from the body of our political system, and will discover how the planets move. Happy should I be, to owe to your goodness (so far as is compatible with propriety and your convenience) the earliest information of the real characteristics of this new collection of satellites. Will they prove by their ordinances that they have the general liberty firmly at heart? Will they establish the common law for the rule of the judicial department? Or will they canonize the civil law, that imperceptible, but sure engine of political slavery? Will they unequivocally guard us against the oppression of standing armies? Will they separate with inviolable boundaries the legislative, the executive, and the judicial departments? Will they make us a free and happy people? Or in other words, that I may sum up the whole in one sentence, will they make the real liberty of the citizens, the immediate object of all legislation? If they should be so happy as to speedily determine upon amendments, will they take it upon themselves to do it? Their authority seems much better suited to the calling a convention for the purpose.

Before I conclude, it may not be improper to add by way of apology, that New York, Virginia, and other states having gone so fully into the detail of amendments, the strokes of abler hands ha[ve] rendered the lines of my feeble pen unnecessary.

DHFFE, I, pp. 839-840.

Cassius March 3, 1789

Newspaper Article: Poughkeepsie *Country Journal*

To the PEOPLE of the STATE of
NEW YORK.

The next Election will perhaps be as important to the general interests of America, as any that ever have been or will be held in this country; for it may greatly depend upon them, whether the new constitution is to continue in its present form, or to receive such amendments as have been proposed by many of the State Conventions, and are anxiously desired by so great a proportion of the citizens of these United States. That the leaders of the federal party, throughout these States, are opposed to those amendments, which we consider as the most essential, I believe is now beyond a doubt. Their conduct in all the legislatures whose proceedings we have had any account of, the sentiments held out by their writers in the public papers, and the indefatigable pains taken to get in those who call themselves federalists at the ensuing election for State and Continental Representatives, establish this truth in my opinion beyond all contradiction—for if they are not opposed to the amendments, why are they opposed to our having such persons to represent us, as we may be assured will use their endeavours to obtain them? I defy any one to give a satisfactory answer to this question, (for it is clear that the highest or farthest object which the warmest opponent to the new constitution can now have in view, is to have the amendments take place which are so generally esteemed to be necessary for the security of our State governments, and of the inestimable rights of freemen.) We may easily see from this, if we wish for the amendments, the absolute necessity of exerting ourselves to get into the elective offices, both of our own, and of the general government, persons possessed of the same wishes. We cannot suppose any one to be a sincere friend to amendments who shall advise us to trust those of a contrary character to obtain them; the absurdity of such a supposition would be too glaring not to strike the most common observer. It is a favorite sentiment with the federal writers, to postpone amending, till we experience the defects in the system by its operations; which is as much as to say, bow your unwilling necks to the yoke, till the experiment can be fairly tried, whether the people cannot be goaded into a tame submission to this system without alterations. Is this the language of those who wish for amendments? Surely not. For the sake of every thing which is dear to freemen, let us not suffer ourselves to be deceived upon this occasion by *artful* and insidious professions; but let us be fully impressed with this important truth, established by the invariable experience of ages, that if we wait till the fetters are fairly and completely rivetted on, nothing but steel will be able to file them off. The people of these States have it yet in their power, by proper and judicious elections, to retrieve and establish their liberties on a sure and permanent foundation.

Every scheme and artifice which can be devised are now using, and will be used to oust our present Governor [Clinton] at the next election, for no other reason but because he is a whig, a republican, a friend of the liberties of the common people, and a professed enemy to aristocracy; which he and all writers and thinkers upon the subject, justly esteem to be the most oppressive kind of government on earth. They can justly find no fault with his character, none with his public administration; and I believe that no one who is acquainted with the history of his life, will dare to accuse me of partiality, when I say I believe him to be one of the best public characters on the continent. From his (legal) infancy he has been in our assembly an able and steady asserter of the rights of the people, until the commencement of the late war, through which, amidst innumerable difficulties, he has defended them with equal activity, abilities and firmness in the field. Nor was his merit less conspicuous, in the peace and good order which immediately took place upon our taking possession of the southern district of this State, between the jarring elements which came together upon that occasion. When resentments ran so high as to threaten the destruction of part of the community, the peace was preserved, the dignity of government kept up, and the authority of the laws prevailed.—And what is now peculiar to his character, and distinguishes it from most of the shining ones of the time, is, that he does not ask, he does not wish, as a reward for his services, a surrender of those rights into his own hands, but still remains the same steady and sincere friend to the liberties of his country, and the same determined opposer of tyranny, whether it comes in the shape of a royal Prerogative, an act of Parliament, or in one less alarming, and consequently more dangerous.

Some time ago, at a meeting of near forty of the members of the Legislature, friends to amendments, it was by a unanimous ballot, determined to hold up at the ensuing election his excellency George Clinton, Esquire, for Governor, and the honorable Pierre Van Cortlandt, Esquire, for Lieutenant-Governor. It would be highly imprudent if not dangerous to make any great changes in the officers of government at this time, when the cold water which is thrown upon the amendments to the new constitution, will probably prove as oil to the fire of discontent already kindled throughout this continent, by that system of government, which, in its present form, is justly looked upon to be so very defective and dangerous. It would be unwise to dismiss from the helm of government, a pilot of experienced skill, courage and integrity, at a time when the political horizon lowers so heavily.

The friends of freedom in our sister states, at present overpowered by the arts, deceptions, and influence of their great men, turn their eyes to us from every part of the continent with the most anxious solicitude and concern, depending chiefly upon the active exertions of this state and Virginia, and the still, but powerful influence arising from the determination of North-Carolina and Rhode-Island, not to adopt the system in its present form, to support the cause of amendments, on which depends the liberties of America.

The Conventions of Massachusetts, New-Hampshire, New-York, Virginia and South-Carolina, and a respectable and virtuous minority in the convention of Pennsylvania, have declared to the world in the most unequivocal manner, by the amendments they have proposed to this system, that they look upon it as dangerous to liberty: And the states of North Carolina and Rhode-Island, have still more forcibly, though not more clearly, expressed the same sentiment, by their refusing to adopt it. What then, my fellow citizens, must we think of those, who are endeavouring to persuade us, that the amendments are matters of no consequence, that the government will not abuse its powers; that we ought to sit still, and not seek for any alterations, until, like the rest of the nations of the world, we *feel* ourselves enslaved and oppressed (should they not add) and like them unable to resist or shake off the tyranny? What must we think of those who are endeavouring, by insidious and malicious insinuations, and the most low and despicable falsehoods, to destroy our confidence in those whose fidelity we have sufficiently proved, by their having long enjoyed that confidence, and having never abused or betrayed it, who have steadily opposed foreign and open attempts upon the liberties of their country, and as steadily refuted the more artful, sly and concealed encroachments of domestic tyranny? What can we think of those who vilify that excellent mode of trial by jury, and thereby shew an inclination to persuade us to give up that invaluable privilege? Is it possible we can suppose that they are friends to our liberties? May Heaven forbid so fatal an infatuation!—It is high time to open our eyes to our true situation. Is not the declared sense of so many respectable public bodies of the defects and dangers in that constitution sufficient to awaken our attention? Is it not a ground that will justify at least some small degree of jealousy concerning the design of those who are opposed to the amendments; especially when we look round and observe who they are? are they not generally the rich, the powerful, the great, the well born and the upstart, the governors (except our own) the senators and the high officers of government? Is it not sufficient to evince the necessity at least of our being cautious whom we trust with power, until the necessary amendments to the new constitution shall be obtained, whereby the powers of the government may be clearly defined and limited, the rights of the state governments (most of them sufficiently extensive for free ones) properly ascertained & established, every idea of their consolidation erased (an idea I will be bold to say, never contemplated by Congress, or one of the state legislatures, or by the people of any of the states) and the rights and privileges of freemen permanently secured to us and our late posterity?—Let us upon this occasion convince the world that we have the good sense to guard those rights, which we have so lately had the courage to defend.

DHFFE, III, pp. 438-441.

Thomas Jefferson (Paris) March 4, 1789
Letter: To William Carmichael (excerpt)

N. Carolina has fixed a day for another convention, but a very distant one. It is the anti-federalism of Virginia which levens the mass. Rhode island has again refused to call a convention. Genl. Washington, tho' with vast reluctance, will undertake the presidency if called to it, & there was no doubt he would be so called. The only candidates for the vice presidency, with their own consent, are Mr. Hancock and Mr. J. Adams. The latter, it was thought, would be chosen. The friends of the new constitution agree pretty generally to add a declaration of rights to it, and the opposition becomes daily weaker, so that the government, confided generally to friendly hands, and gaining on the esteem of the nation, begins, *this very day*, under the most auspicious appearances.

Ford, V, p. 73. Reprinted in DHFFE, IV, p. 190.

Thomas Jefferson (Paris) March 13, 1789
Letter: To Francis Hopkinson (excerpt)

You say that I have been dished up to you as an antifederalist, and ask me if it be just. My opinion was never worthy enough of notice to merit citing: but since you ask it I will tell it you. I am not a Federalist, because I never submitted the whole system of my opinions to the creed of any party of men whatever in religion, in philosophy, in politics, or in any thing else where I was capable of thinking for myself. Such an addiction is the last degradation of a free and moral agent. If I could not go to heaven but with a party, I would not go there at all. Therefore I protest to you I am not of the party of federalists. But I am much farther from that of the Antifederalists. I approved from the first moment, of the great mass of what is in the new constitution, the consolidation of the government, the organisation into Executive, legislative and judiciary, the subdivision of the legislative, the happy compromise of interests between the great and little states by the different manner of voting in the different houses, the voting by persons instead of by states, the qualified negative on laws with the judiciary also as in New York, and the power of taxation. I thought at first that the latter might have been limited. A little reflection soon convinced me it ought not to be. What I disapproved from the first moment also was the want of a bill of rights to guard liberty against the legislative as well as executive branches of the government, that is to say to secure freedom in religion, freedom of the press, freedom from monopolies, freedom from unlawful imprisonment, freedom from a permanent military, and a trial by jury in all cases determinable by the laws of the land. I disapproved also the perpetual reeligibility of the President. To these points of disapprobation I adhere. My first wish was that the 9. first conventions might accept the constitution, as the means of securing to us the great mass of good it contained, and that the 4. last might reject it, as the means of obtaining amendments. But I was corrected in this wish the moment I saw the much better plan of Massachusetts and which had never occurred to me. With respect to the declaration of rights I suppose the majority of the United states are of my opinion: for I apprehend all the antifederalists, and a very respectable proportion of the federalists think that such a declaration should now be annexed. The enlightened part of Europe have given us the greatest credit for inventing this instrument of security for the rights of the people, and have been not a little surprised to see us so soon give it up.

Ford, V, pp. 76-77. Reprinted in Boyd, XIV, p. 649, and in BRDH, I, p. 618.

Thomas Jefferson (Paris) March 15, 1789
Letter: To James Madison (excerpt)[1]

Your thoughts on the subject of the Declaration of rights in the letter of Oct 17. I have weighed with great satisfaction.[2] Some of them had not occurred to me before, but were acknoleged just in the moment they were presented to my mind. In the arguments in favor of a declaration of rights, you omit one which has great weight with me, the legal check which it puts into the hands of the judiciary. This is a body, which if rendered independent & kept strictly to their own department merits great confidence for their learning & integrity. In fact what degree of confidence would be too much for a body composed of such men as Wythe, Blair & Pendleton? On characters like these the "*civium ardor prava jubilentium*" would make no impression. I am happy to find that on the whole you are a friend to this amendment. The Declaration of rights is like all other human blessings alloyed with some inconveniences, and not accomplishing fully it's object. But the good in this instance vastly overweighs the evil. I cannot refrain from making short answers to the objections which your letter states to have been raised. 1. That the rights in question are reserved by the manner in which the federal powers are granted. Answer. A constitutive act may certainly be so formed as to need no declaration of rights. The act itself has the force of a declaration as far as it goes; and if it goes to all material points nothing more is wanting. In the draught of a constitution which I had once a thought of proposing in Virginia, & printed afterwards, I endeavored to reach all the great objects of public liberty, and did not mean to add a declaration of rights. Probably the object was imperfectly executed; but the deficiencies would have been supplied by others, in the course of discussion. But in a constitutive act which leaves some precious articles unnoticed, and raises implications against others, a declaration of rights becomes necessary by way of supplement. This is the case of our new federal consitution. This instrument forms us into one state as to certain objects, and gives us a legislative & executive body for these objects. It should therefore guard us against their abuses of power within the field submitted to them. 2. A positive declaration of some essential rights could not be obtained in the requisite latitude. Answer. Half a loaf is better than no bread. If we cannot secure all our rights, let us secure what we can. 3. The limited powers of the federal government & jealousy of the subordinate governments afford a security which exists in no other instance. Answer. The first member of this seems resolvable into the first ojection before stated. The jealousy of the subordinate governments is a precious reliance. But observe that those governments are only agents. They must have principles furnished them whereon to found their opposition. The declaration of rights will be the text whereby they will try all the acts of the federal government, In this view it is necessary to the federal government also; as by the same text they may try the opposition of the subordinate governments. 4. Experience proves the inefficacy of a bill of rights. True. But tho it is not absolutely efficacious under all circumstances, it is of great potency always, and rarely inefficacious. A brace the more will often keep up the building which would have fallen with that brace the less. There is a remarkable difference between the characters of the Inconveniences which attend a Declaration of rights, & those which attend the want of it. The inconveniences of the Declaration are that it may cramp government in it's useful exertions. But the evil of this is short-lived, trivial & reparable. The inconveniences of the want of a Declaration are permanent, afflicting & irreparable. They are in constant progression from bad to worse. The executive in our governments is not the sole, it is scarcely the principal object of my jealousy. The tyranny of the legislatures is the most formidable dread at present, and will be for long years. That of the executive will come in it's turn, but it will be at a remote period. I know there are some among us who would now establish a monarchy. But they are inconsiderable in number and weight of character. The rising race are all republicans. We were educated in royalism; no wonder if some of us retain that idolatry still. Our young people are educated in republicanism, an apostasy from that to royalism is unprecedented & impossible. I am much pleased with the prospect that a declaration of rights will be added; and hope it will be done in that way which will not endanger the whole frame of the government, or any essential part of it.

1 Ford, V, pp. 80-83. Also reprinted in *Papers*, XII, pp. 13-16.
2 See "James Madison," October 17, 1788, p. 538 for the letter referred to.

Thomas Jefferson (Paris) March 18, 1788
Letter: To David Humphreys (excerpt)

The operations which have taken place in America lately, fill me with pleasure. In the first place they realize the confidence I had that whenever our affairs go obviously wrong the good sense of the people will interpose and set them to rights. The example of changing a constitution by assembling the wise men of the State, instead of assembling armies, will be worth as much to the world as the former examples we had given them. The constitution too which was the result of our deliberations, is unquestionably the wisest ever yet presented to men, and some of the accommodations of interest which it has adopted are greatly pleasing to me who have before had occasions of seeing how difficult those interests were to accommodate. A general concurrence of opinion seems to authorize us to say it has some defects. I am one of those who think it a defect that the important rights, not placed in security by the frame of the constitution itself were not explicitly secured by a supplementary declaration. There are rights which it is useless to surrender to the government, and which governments have yet always been fond to invade. These are the rights of thinking, and publishing our thoughts by speaking or writing; the rights of free commerce; the right of personal freedom. There are instruments for administering the government, so peculiarly trust-worthy, that we should never leave the legislature at liberty to change them. The new constitution has secured these in the executive & legislative departments; but not in the judiciary. It should have established trials by the people themselves, that is to say by jury. There are instruments so dangerous to the rights of the nation, and which place them so totally at the mercy of their governors, that those governors, whether legislative or executive, should be restrained from keeping such instruments on foot, but in well-defined cases. Such an instrument is a standing army. We are now allowed to say such a declaration of rights, as a supplement to the constitution where that is silent, is wanting to secure us in these points. The general voice has legitimated this objection.

Ford, V, pp. 89-90.

Thomas Jefferson (Paris) March 23, 1789
Letter: To John Paul Jones (excerpts)

Our new Constitution was acceded to in the course of the last summer by all the states except North Carolina and Rhode Island. Massachusetts, Virginia and New York though they accepted unconditionally yet gave it as a perpetual instruction to their future delegates never to cease urging certain amendments. North Carolina insisted that the amendments should be made before she would accede. The more important of these amendments will be effected by adding a bill of rights; and even the friends of the Constitution are become sensible of the expediency of such an addition were it only to conciliate the opposition. In fact this security for liberty seems to be demanded by the general voice of America and we may conclude it will unquestionably be added. . . .

Though the new Constitution was adopted in eleven states, yet in those of Massachusetts, Virginia and New York it was by very small majorities; and the minorities in the two last are far from the laudable acquiescence of that of Massachusetts. Governor Clinton of New York and Mr. Henry in Virginia are moving heaven and earth to have a new convention to make capital changes. Buy they will not succeed. There has been just opposition enough to produce probably further guards to liberty without touching the energy of the government and this will bring over the bulk of the opposition to the side of the new government.

Bergh, XIX, p. 57-58.

Paine Wingate (New York) March 25, 1789
Letter: To Timothy Pickering (excerpt)

I think the members of both houses [of Congress] will almost unanimously be firm friends to the government. Those who have heretofore had their objections will be so few, that they will probably not think it expedient to raise difficulties. I am told that your old friend Mr. Gerry speaks very moderately upon the subject. Nobody thinks that a general convention will be called. Possibly in a convenient time Congress may take up the consideration of amendments or alterations, and may recommend some that may quiet the fears & jealousies of the well designing & not affect the essentials of the present system. I am rather inclined to suppose that this cannot be attended to immediately, but must be postponed for other more important matters.—

DHFFE, IV, p. 207.

H.G. April 7, 1789
Newspaper Article: New York *Daily Advertiser* (excerpt)

The friends of the Governor [Clinton] tell us that after the adoption of the constitution, he declared in convention that he should conceive himself bound to maintan the public peace, and to concur in putting the system *into operation*. This was saying as little as possible. Luckily, the public peace was in no danger, and his Excellency with all his hardihood would not dare to refuse an official co-operation in putting the government established by the people, *in motion*. I attended the debates of the convention, and I could not forbear remarking, that the Governor, in the speech alluded to, seemed carefully to confine his assurances to a mere *official compliance*. The impression made upon my mind by the *two* last speeches he delivered was this, that he would as Governor of the state, in mere official transactions *conform* to the constitution, but that he should think it expedient to keep alive the spirit of opposition in the people, until the *amendments proposed*, or another convention (I am not certain which) could be obtained. In this impression I am not singular; there were others who understood him in the same sense.

No reasonable man can doubt that such a sentiment was an unjustifiable one. The United States are to determine on the propriety of amendments, and on the expediency of a convention. Both must be referred to their judgment. If they think both improper, or unnecessary, it is the duty of a particular member to acquiesce. This is the fundamental principle of the social compact. To threaten the continuance of an opposition therefore till either of those purposes was accomplished, was in every view intemperate and unwarrantable. That there will be a reconsideration of parts of the system, and that certain amendments will be made, I devoutly wish and confidently expect. I have no doubt that the system is susceptible of improvement, and I anxiously desire that every prudent means may be used to conciliate the honest opponents of it. But I reprobate the idea of keeping up an opposition to the government upon principles, which derogate from those, on which the union is, and must necessarily be supported. I reprobate the idea of one state giving law to the rest.

DHFFE, III, p. 432.

James Madison (New York) April 8, 1789
Letter: To Edmund Pendleton (excerpt)

The subject of amendments has not yet been touched—From appearances there will be no great difficulty in obtaining reasonable ones. It will depend however entirely on the temper of the federalists, who predominate as much in both branches, as could be wished. Even in this State, notwithstanding the violence of its antifederal symtoms, three of its six representatives at least will be zealous friends to the Constitution, and it is not improbable that a fourth will be of the same description.

DHFFE, IV, p. 229. Reprinted in *Papers*, XII, p. 51.

James Madison (New York) April 12, 1789
Letter: To Edmund Randolph (excerpt)[1]

On the subject of amendments nothing has been publickly and very little privately said. Such as I am known to have espoused, will as far as I can gather, be attainable from the federalists, who sufficiently predominate in both branches; though with some, the concurrence will proceed from a spirit of conciliation rather than conviction. Connecticut is least inclined though I presume not inflexibly opposed, to a moderate revision. A paper wch. will probably be republished in the Virga. Gazettes, under the signature of a Citizen of New Haven, unfolds *Mr. Shermans* opinions. Whatever the amendments may be it is clear that they will be attempted in no other way than thro' Congress. Many of the warmest of the opponents of the Govt. disavow the Mode contended for by Virginia.[2]

1 *Papers*, XII, p. 76.

2 Virginia had voted to request that Congress call a convention to amend the Constitution. See "Virginia House of Delegates," November 14, 1788, p. 561.

Republican Committee April 21, 1789

Newspaper Article: *Hudson Weekly Gazette* (excerpts)

Copy of a letter circulating through the western district of the state of New-York; particularly handed to the freeholders of said district.

Albany, 7th April, 1789.

From a persuasion that the same principles actuate you, which formerly induced you to contend for amendments to the new constitution, previous to its adoption, we take the liberty again to address you on the subject of the next election.

We are aware that it has been said, that the election of governor, senators and representatives of assembly cannot influence the measures to be pursued for obtaining amendments to the new constitution; but, as two senators for the new government will probably be chosen by the legislature, it is of great importance that such state officers be elected, as will be decidedly in favor of amendments, and will be disposed to favor the calling of a general convention for the purpose, and against which convention many of those who call themselves federal are opposed. It is an undoubted truth, that several declared, that the next election will decidedly discover the opinion of the people on that occasion; and hence, if you join in giving your votes in favor of those candidates who are opposed to amendments, you will either appear to confess that you have been mistaken in the measures you have formerly taken in favor of amendments, or that you are not anxious to obtain them. . . .

We are, Your most obedient, humble servants,
By order of the Republican Committee, lately called the Anti-Federal Committee,

Jer. Van Rensselear, Chairman.
Mat. Visscher, Secretary.

1 DHFFE, III, pp. 513-514.

President George Washington April 30, 1789
Innaugural Address (excerpts)[1]

FELLOW-CITIZENS of the SENATE and of the HOUSE of REPRESENTATIVES: . . .

Besides the ordinary objects submitted to your care, it will remain with your judgment to decide, how far an exercise of the occasional power delegated by the fifth article of the constitution is rendered expedient at the present juncture by the nature of objections which have been urged against the system, or by the degree of inquietude which has given birth to them.—Instead of undertaking particular recommendations on this subject, in which I could be guided by no lights derived from official opportunities, I shall again give way to my entire confidence in your discernment and pursuit of the public good:—for I assure myself that whilst you carefully avoid every alteration which might endanger the benefits of an united and effective government, or which ought to await the future lessons of experience; a reverence for the characteristic rights of freemen, and a regard for the public harmony, will sufficiently influence your deliberations on the question how far the former can be more impregnably fortified, or the latter be safely and advantageously promoted.[2]

1 DHFFE, IV, pp. 263, 265. Reprinted in *Papers*, XII, pp. 121, 123.
2 Washington's Innaugural speech was written by James Madison. See *Papers*, XII, p. 120.

House of Representatives May 4, 1789
Proceedings (excerpt)

Before the House adjourned, Mr. Madison gave notice, that he intended to bring on the subject of amendments to the constitution, on the 4th Monday of this month.

BRDH, II, p. 1012.

House of Representatives May 5, 1789
Proceedings (excerpts)[1]

Mr. Madison, from the committee appointed to prepare an address on the part of this House to the President of the United States, in answer to his speech to both Houses of Congress,[2] reported as followeth: *The Address of the House of Representatives to George Washington, President of the United States. . . .*

The question arising out of the fifth article of the Constitution, will receive all the attention demanded by its importance; and will, we trust be decided, under the influence of all the considerations to which you allude. . . .

Mr. Bland presented to the House the following application from the Legislature of Virginia, to wit:[3]

1 BRDH, II, pp. 1012-1013.
2 See "President George Washington," April 30, 1789, p. 642.
3 See "Virginia House of Delegates," November 14, 1788, p. 561, for the application to Congress for calling a convention to amend the Constitution.

House of Representatives May 6, 1789
Proceedings (excerpt)[1]

Mr. Lawrence, from New York, presented to the House an application, in the name and behalf of the Legislature of that State, addressed to the Congress of the United States; which being read, was ordered to be filed.[2]

1 BRDH, II, p. 1016.
2 See "New York Assembly," February 5, 1789, p. 624, for the application to Congress for calling a convention to amend the Constitution.

James Madison (New York) May 27, 1789
Letter: To Thomas Jefferson (excerpt)

The subject of amendments was to have been introduced on monday last; but is postponed in order that more urgent business may not be delayed. On Monday sevennight it will certainly come forward. A Bill of rights, incorporated perhaps into the Constitution will be proposed, with a few other alterations most called for by the opponents of the Government and least objectionable to its friends.

Papers, XII, p. 186. Also reprinted in BRDH, II, p. 1045.

Richard Henry Lee (New York) **May 28, 1789**
Letter: To Patrick Henry (excerpt)

It must never be forgotton, however, that the liberties of the people are not so safe under the gracious manner of government, as by the limitation of power. Mr. Madison has given notice, that, on Monday s'n-night he will call for the attention of the house to the subject of amendments. I apprehend that his ideas, and those of our convention, on this subject, are not similar. We shall carefully attend to this, and when the plan comes to the senate, we shall prepare to abridge, or enlarge, so as to effect, if possible, the wishes of our legislature. I think, from what I hear and see, that many of our amendments will not succeed, but my hopes are strong that such as may effectually secure civil liberty will not be refused. As two-thirds of the legislatures have refused to apply for a general convention, the Congress, it seems, can constitutionally only submit their propositions of amendments to the legislatures, or to state conventions; but, I suppose, neither of these modes will fail, where the design is more effectually to secure civil liberty; the wish to do which, was, I assure you, the sole reason that could have influenced me to come here, for I agree perfectly with you that your time of life and mine, after the turbulence we have passed through, renders repose necessary to our declining years.

Henry, III, p. 388. Lee was a United States Senator from Virginia.

President George Washington **[May 31, 1789]**
Letter: To James Madison (excerpt)

As far as a momentary consideration has enabled me to judge, I see nothing exceptionable in the proposed amendments. Some of them, in my opinion, are importantly necessary, others, though in themselves (in my conception) not very essential, are necessary to quiet the fears of some respectable characters and well meaning Men. Upon the whole, therefore, not foreseeing any evil consequences that can result from their adoption, they have my wishes for a favorable reception in both houses.

Papers, XII, p. 191. The source indicates that this letter was endorsed by James Madison as follows: "Amendments to the Constitution proposed by J. M. at the first Session of Congress in 1789." See "House of Representatives," June 8, 1789, pp. 654-656, for the amendments.

James Madison June 8, 1789
Notes for speech in Congress supporting Amendments.

Reasons urging amendts.
1. to prove fedts. friends to liberty
2. remove remaining inquietudes
3. bring in N.C. & R. Island.
4. to improve the Constitution

Reasons for moderating the plan
1. No stop if door opend to theoretic amendts.
2. as likely to make worse as better till trial
3. insure passage by 2/3 of Congs. & 3/4 of Sts.

Objectns. of 3 kinds vs the Constn:
1. vs. the theory of its structure
2. vs. substance of its powers—elections & direct taxes
3. vs omission of guards in favr. of rights & libertys

The last most urged & easiest obviated.
Read the amendments—

They relate 1st. to private rights—

Bill of Rights—useful—not essential—

---

fallacy on both sides—especy as to English Decln. of Rts—
1. mere act of parlt.
2. no freedom of press—Conscience
Gl. Warrants—Habs. corpus
jury in Civil Causes —criml.
attainders—arms to Protestts.

---

frequent parlts cheif trust—

---

freedom of press & of Conscience unknown to Magna Cha. & Pet: Rts

---

Contents of Bills of Rhts—
1. assertion of primitive equality &c.
2. do. of rights exerted in formg. Govts.
3. *natural rights*, retained—as Speech, Con:
4. positive rights resultg—as trial by jury
5. Doctrinl. artics. as Depts. distinct—Electns free
6. moral precepts for the administrn. & natil. character—as justice—OEconomy —&c—

Object of Bill of Rhts
To limit & qualify powr. by exceptg. from grant cases in wch. it shall not be exercised or exd. in a particular manner.
to guard 1. vs. Executive & in Engd. &c—
2. Legislative as in Sts—
3. the majority of people

---

ought to point vs greatest danger which in Rep: is Prerogative of majority—

Here proper, tho' less nessary., than in small Repubs—

Objectns. vs. Bill of Rhts.
1. in Elective Govt. all power in people
hence unnec[e]ssary & improper—this vs Sts—
2. In fedl. Govt. all not given retained—
Bill of powers—needs no bill of Rhts—

Sweeping clause—Genl Warrants &c
3. St: Bills not repeald.—

---

too uncertain

Some Sts have not bills—others defect:—others—injurious—as Protestts.
4. dispar[a]ge other rights—or constructively enlarge—

---

the first goes vs St: Bills—

---

both guarded vs. by amendt.
5. Not effectl. vs Sts also—but some check

Courts will aid—also Ex: also.

Sts Legisls: watch

Time sanctify—incorporate public Sentiment

Bill fo Rts ergo. *proper*—

II increase of Reps. 2 for each H.

III pay of Congs.

IV Interdict to States as to Conscience—press—& Jury—

---

this more necsy. to Sts. than Congs.

V Check on appeals—& Common law—

VI. partn. as to 3 Depts. & do. as to Genl. & St: Govts.

Papers, XII, pp. 193-195.

House of Representatives June 8, 1789
Debates (excerpts)

Amendments to the Constitution

Mr. Madison rose, and reminded the House that this was the day that he had heretofore named for bringing forward amendments to the constitution, as contemplated in the fifth article of the constitution, addressing the Speaker as follows: This day, Mr. Speaker, is the day assigned for taking into consideration the subject of amendments to the constitution. As I considered myself bound in honor and in duty to do what I have done on this subject, I shall proceed to bring the amendments before you as soon as possible, and advocate them until they shall be finally adopted or rejected by a constitutional majority of this House. With a view of drawing your attention to this important object, I shall move that this House do now resolve itself into a Committee of the whole on the state of the Union; by which an opportunity will be given, to bring forward some propositions, which I have strong hopes will meet with the unanimous approbation of this House, after the fullest discussion and most serious regard. I therefore move you, that the House now go into a committee on this business.

Mr. Smith . . . [Against motion.]

Mr. Jackson: I am of opinion we ought not to be in a hurry with respect to altering the constitution. For my part, I have no idea of speculating in this serious manner on theory. . . . [Against motion—proposed postponement until 1790.]

Mr. Goodhue: I believe it would be perfectly right in the gentleman who spoke last, to move a postponement to the time he has mentioned; because he is opposed to the consideration of amendments altogether. But I believe it will be proper to attend to the subject earlier; because it is the wish of many of our constituents, that something should be added to the constitution, to secure in a stronger manner their liberties from the inroads of power. Yet I think the present time premature; inasmuch as we have other business before us, which is incomplete, but essential to the public interest. When that is finished, I shall concur in taking up the subject of amendments.

Mr. Burke thought amendments to the constitution necessary, but this was not the proper time to bring them foreward. . . . [Against motion.]

Mr. Madison: The gentleman from Georgia (Mr. Jackson) is certainly right in his opposition to my motion for going into a Committee of the whole, because he is unfriendly to the object I have in contemplation; but I cannot see that the gentlemen who wish for amendments to be proposed at the present session, stand on good ground when they object to the House going into committee on this business.

When I first hinted to the House my intentions of begging their deliberations to this object, I found the pressure of other important matters had submitted the propriety of postponing this till the more urgent business was despatched; but finding that business not despatched, when the order of the day for considering amendments arrived, I thought it a good reason for a farther delay; I moved the postponement accordingly. I am sorry the same reason still exists in some degree, but operates with less force, when it is considered that it is not now proposed to enter into a full and minute discussion of every part of the subject, but merely to bring it before the House, that our constituents may see we pay a proper attention to a subject they have much at heart; and if it does not give that full gratification which is to be wished, they will discover that it proceeds from the urgency of business of a very important nature. But if we continue to postpone from time to time, and refuse to let the subject come into view, it may occasion suspicions, which, though not well founded, may tend to inflame or prejudice the public mind against our decisions. They may think we are not sincere in our desire to incorporate such amendments in the constitution as will secure those rights, which they consider as not sufficiently guarded. The applications for amendments come from a very respectable number of our consitutents, and it is certainly proper for Congress to consider the subject, in order to quiet that anxiety which prevails in the public mind. Indeed, I think it would have been of advantage to the Government, if it had been practicable to have made some proposition for amendments the first business we entered upon; it would have stifled the voice of complaint, and made friends of many who doubted the merits of the constitution. Our future measures would then have been more generally agreeably supported; but the justifiable anxiety to put the Government into operation prevented that; it therefore remains for us to take it up as soon as possible. I wish then to commence the consideration at the present moment; I hold it to be my duty to unfold my ideas, and explain myself to the House in some form or other without delay. I only wish to introduce the great work, and, as I said before, I do not expect it will be decided immediately; but if some step is taken in the business, it will give reason to believe that we may come to a final result. This will inspire a reasonable hope in the advocates for amendments, that full justice will be done to the important subject; and I have reason to believe their expectation will not be defeated. I hope the House will not decline my motion for going into a committee.

Mr. Sherman: I am willing that this matter should be brought before the House at a proper time. . . . For my part, I question if any alteration which can be now proposed would be an amendment, in the true sense of the word; but nevertheless, I am willing to let the subject be introduced. If the gentleman only desires to go into committee for the purpose of receiving his propositions, I shall consent; but I have strong objections to being interrupted in completing the more important business; because I am well satisfied it will alarm the fears of twenty of our constituents where it will please one.

Mr. White: I hope the House will not spend much time on this subject, till the more pressing business is despatched; but, at the same time, I hope we shall not dismiss it altogether, because I think a majority of the people who have ratified the constitution, did it under the expectation that Congress would, at some convenient time, examine its texture and point out where it was defective, in order that it might be judiciously amended. Whether, while we are without experience, amendments can be digested in such a manner as to give satisfaction to a constitutional majority of this House, I will not pretend to say; but I hope the subject may be considered with all convenient speed. I think it would tend to tranquillize the public mind; therefore, I shall vote in favor of going into a Committee of the whole, and, after receiving the subject, shall be content to refer it to a special committee to arrange and report. I fear, if we refuse to take up the subject, it will irritate many of our constituents, which I do not wish to do. If we cannot, after mature consideration, gratify their wishes, the cause of complaint will be lessened, if not removed. But a doubt on this head will not be a good reason why we should refuse to inquire. I do not say this as it affects my immediate constituents, because I believe a majority of the district which elected me do not require alterations; but I know there are people in other parts who will not be satisfied unless some amendments are proposed.

Mr. Smith, of South Carolina, thought the gentleman who brought forward the subject had done his duty: he had supported his motion with ability and candor, and if he did not succeed, he was not to blame. On considering what had been urged for going into a committee, he was induced to join the gentleman; but it would be merely to receive his propositions, after which he would move something to this effect: That, however desirous this House may be to go into the consideration of amendments to the constitution, in order to establish the liberties of the people of America on the securest foundation, yet the important and pressing business of the Government prevents their entering upon that subject at present.

Mr. Page: My colleague tells you he is ready to submit to the Committee of the whole his ideas on this subject. If no objection had been made to his motion, the whole business might have been finished before this. He has done me the honor of showing me certain propositions which he has drawn up; they are very important, and I sincerely wish the House may receive them. After they are published, I think the people will wait with patience till we are at leisure to resume them. But it must be very disagreeable to them to have it postponed from time to time, in the manner it has been for six weeks past; they will be tired out by a fruitless expectation. Putting myself into the place of those who favor amendments, I should suspect Congress did not mean seriously to enter upon the subject; that it was vain to expect redress from them. I should begin to turn my attention to the alternative contained in the fifth article, and think of joining the Legislatures of those States which have applied for calling a new convention. How dangerous such an expedient would be I need not mention; but I venture to affirm, that unless you take early notice of this subject, you will not have power to deliberate. The people will clamor for a new convention; they will not trust the House any longer. Those, therefore, who dread the assembling of a convention, will do well to acquiesce in the present motion, and lay the foundation of a most important work. I do not think we need consume more than half an hour in the Committee of the whole; this is not so much time but we may conveniently spare it, considering the nature of the business. I do not wish to divert the attention of Congress from the organization of the Government, nor do I think it need be done, if we comply with the present motion.

Mr. Vining: . . . [Against motion for committee of the whole on amendments.]

Mr. Madison: I am sorry to be accessary to the loss of a single moment of time by the House. If I had been indulged in my motion, and we had gone into a Committee of the whole, I think we migh have rose and resumed the consideration of other business before this time; that is, so far as it depended upon what I proposed to bring forward. As that mode seems not to give satisfaction, I will withdraw the motion, and move you, sir, that a select committee be appointed to consider and report such amendments as are proper for Congress to propose to the Legislatures of the several States, conformably to the fifth article of the constitution.

I will state my reasons why I think it proper to propose amendments, and state the amendments themselves, so far as I think they ought to be proposed. If I thought I could fulfil the duty which I owe to myself and my constituents, to let the subject pass over in silence, I most certainly should not trespass upon the indulgence of this House. But I cannot do this, and am therefore compelled to beg a patient hearing to what I have to lay before you. And I do most sincerely believe, that if Congress will devote but one day to this subject, so far as to satisfy the public that we do not disregard their wishes, it will have a salutary influence on the public councils, and prepare the way for a favorable reception of our future measures. It appears to me that this House is bound by every motive of prudence, not to let the first session pass over without proposing to the State Legislatures some things to be incorporated into the constitution, that will render it as acceptable to the whole people of the United States, as it has been found acceptable to a majority of them. I wish, among other reasons why something should be done, that those who have been friendly to the adoption of this constitution may have the opportunity of proving to those who were opposed to it that they were as sincerely devoted to liberty and a Republican Government, as those who charged them with wishing the adoption of this constitution in order to lay the foundation of an aristocracy or despotism. It will be a desirable thing to extinguish from the bosom of evey member of the community, any apprehensions that there are those among his countrymen who wish to deprive them of the liberty for which they valiantly fought and honorably bled. And if there are amendments desired of such a nature as will not injure the constitution, and they can be ingrafted so as to give satisfaction to the doubting part of our fellow-citizens, the friends of the Federal Government will evince that spirit of deference and concession for which they have hitherto been distinguished.

It cannot be a secret to the gentlemen of this House, that, notwithstanding the ratification of this system of Government by eleven of the thirteen United States, in some cases unanimously, in others by large majorities; yet still there is a great number of our constituents who are dissatisfied with it; among whom are many respectable for their talents and patriotism, and respectable for the jealousy they have for their liberty, which, though mistaken in its object, is honorable in its motive. There is a great body of the people falling under this description, who at present feel much inclined to join their support to the cause of Federalism, if they were satisfied on this one point. We ought not to disregard their inclination, but, on principles of amity and moderation, conform to their wishes and expressly declare the great rights of mankind secured under this constitution. The acceptance which our fellow-citizens show under the Government, calls upon us for a like return of moderation. But perhaps there is a stronger motive than this for our going into a consideration of the subject. It is to provide those securities for liberty which are required by a part of the community: I allude in a particular manner to those two States that have not thought fit to throw themselves into the bosom of the Confederacy. It is a desirable thing, on our part as well as theirs, that a re-union should take place as soon as possible. I have no doubt, if we proceed to take those steps which would be prudent and requisite at this juncture, that in a short time we should see that disposition prevailing in those States which have not come in, that we have seen prevailing in those States which have embraced the constitution.

But I will candidly acknowledge, that, over and above all these considerations, I do conceive that the constitution may be amended; that is to say, if all power is subject to abuse, that then it is possible the abuse of the powers of the General Government may be guarded against in a more secure manner than is now done, while no one advantage arising from the exercise of that power shall be damaged or endangered by it. We have in this way something to gain, and, if we proceed with caution, nothing to lose. And in this case it is necessary to proceed with caution; for while we feel all these inducements to go into a revisal of the constitution, we must feel for the constitution itself, and make that revisal a moderate one. I should be unwilling to see a door opened for a reconsideration of the whole structure of the Government—for a re-consideration of the principles and the substance of the powers given; because I doubt, if such a door were opened, we should be very likely to stop at that point which would be safe to the Government itself. But I do wish to see a door opened to consider, so far as to incorporate those provisions for the security of rights, against which I believe no serious objection has been made by any class of our constituents: such as would be likely to meet with the concurrence of two-thirds of both Houses, and the approbation of three-fourths of the State Legislatures. I will not propose a single alteration which I do not wish to see take place, as intrinsically proper in itself, or proper because it is wished for by a respectable number of my fellow-citizens; and therefore I shall not propose a single alteration but is likely to meet the concurrence required by the constitution. There have been objections of various kinds made against the constitution. Some were levelled against its structure because the President was without a council; because the Senate, which is a legislative body, had judicial powers in trials on impeachments; and because the powers of that body were compounded in other respects, in a manner that did not correspond with a particular theory; because it grants more power than is supposed to be necessary for every good purpose, and controls the ordinary powers of the State Governments. I know some respectable characters who opposed this Government on these grounds; but I believe that the great mass of the people who opposed it, disliked it because it did not contain effectual provisions against encroachments on particular rights, and those safeguards which they have been long accustomed to have interposed between them and the magistrate who exercises the sovereign power; nor ought we to consider them safe, while a great number of our fellow-citizens think these securities necessary.

It is a fortunate thing that the objection to the Government has been made on the ground I stated, because it will be practicable, on that ground, to obviate the objection, so far as to satisfy the public mind that their liberties will be perpetual, and this without endangering any part of the constitution, which is considered as essential to the existence of the Government by those who promoted its adoption.

The amendments which have occurred to me, proper to be recommended by Congress to the State Legislatures, are these:

First, That there be prefixed to the constitution a declaration, that all power is originally vested in, and consequently derived from, the people.

That Government is instituted and ought to be exercised for the benefit of the people; which consists in the enjoyment of life and liberty, with the right of acquiring and using property, and generally of pursuing and obtaining happiness and safety.

That the people have an indubitable, unalienable, and indefeasible right to reform or change their Government, whenever it be found adverse or inadequate to the purposes of its institution.

Secondly, That in article 1st, section 2, clause 3, these words be struck out, to wit:

"The number of Representatives shall not exceed one for every thirty thousand, but each State shall have at least one Representative, and until such enumeration shall be made;" and that in place thereof be inserted these words, to wit: "After the first actual enumeration, there shall be one Representative for every thirty thousand, until the number amounts to ___, after which the proportion shall be so regulated by Congress, that the number shall never be less than ___, nor more than ___, but each State shall, after the first enumeration, have at least two Representatives; and prior thereto."

Thirdly, That in article 1st, section 6, clause 1, there be added to the end of the first sentence, these words, to wit: "But no law varying the compensation last ascertained shall operate before the next ensuing election of Representatives."

Fourthly, That in article 1st, section 9, between clauses 3 and 4, be inserted these clauses, to wit: The civil rights of none shall be abridged on account of religious belief or worship, nor shall any national religion be established, nor shall the full and equal rights of conscience be in any manner, or on any pretext, infringed.

The people shall not be deprived or abridged of their right to speak, to write, or to publish their sentiments; and the freedom of the press, as one of the great bulwarks of liberty, shall be inviolable.

The people shall not be restrained from peaceably assembling and consulting for their common good; nor from applying to the Legislature by petitions, or remonstrances, for redress of their grievances.

The right of the people to keep and bear arms shall not be infringed; a well armed and well regulated militia being the best security of a free country; but no person religiously scrupulous of bearing arms shall be compelled to render military service in person.

No soldier shall in time of peace be quartered in any house without the consent of the owner; nor at any time, but in a manner warranted by law.

No person shall be subject, except in cases of impeachment, to more than one punishment or one trial for the same offence; nor shall be compelled to be a witness against himself; nor be deprived of life, liberty, or property, without due process of law; nor be obliged to relinquish his property, where it may be necessary for public use, without a just compensation.

Excessive bail shall not be required, nor excessive fines imposed, nor cruel and unusual punishments inflicted.

The rights of the people to be secured in their persons; their houses, their papers, and their other property, from all unreasonable searches and seizures, shall not be violated by warrants issued without probable cause, supported by oath or affirmation, or not particularly describing the places to be searched, or the persons or things to be seized.

In all criminal prosecutions, the accused shall enjoy the right to a speedy and public trial, to be informed of the cause and nature of the accusation, to be confronted with his accusers, and the witnesses against him; to have a compulsory process for obtaining witnesses in his favor; and to have the assistance of counsel for his defence.

The exceptions here or elsewhere in the constitution, made in favor of particular rights, shall not be so construed as to diminish the just importance of other rights retained by the people, or as to enlarge the powers delegated by the constitution; but either as actual limitations of such powers, or as inserted merely for greater caution.

Fifthly, That in article 1st, section 10, between clauses 1 and 2, be inserted this clause, to wit:

No State shall violate the equal rights of conscience, or the freedom of the press, or the trial by jury in criminal cases.

Sixthly, That, in article 3d, section 2, be annexed to the end of clause 2d, these words, to wit:

But no appeal to such court shall be allowed where the value in controversy shall not amount to ____ dollars: nor shall any fact triable by jury, according to the course of common law, be otherwise re-examinable than may consist with the principles of common law.

Seventhly, That in article 3d, section 2, the third clause be struck out, and in its place be inserted the clauses following, to wit:

The trial of all crimes (except in cases of impeachments, and cases arising in the land or naval forces, or the militia when on actual service, in time of war or public danger) shall be by an impartial jury of freeholders of the vicinage, with the requisite of unanimity for conviction, of the right of challenge, and other accustomed requisites; and in all crimes punishable with loss of life or member, presentment or indictment by a grand jury shall be an essential preliminary, provided that in cases of crimes committed within any county which may be in possession of an enemy, or in which a general insurrection may prevail, the trial may by law be authorized in some other county of the same State, as near as may be to the seat of the offence.

In cases of crimes committed not within any county, the trial may by law be in such county as the laws shall have prescribed. In suits at common law, between man and man, the trial by jury, as one of the best securities to the rights of the people, ought to remain inviolate.

Eighthly, That immediately after article 6th, be inserted, as article 7th, the clauses following, to wit:

The powers delegated by this constitution are appropriated to the departments to which they are respectively distributed: so that the legislative department shall never exercise the powers vested in the executive or judicial nor the executive exercise the powes vested in the legislative or judicial, nor the judicial exercise the powers vested in the legislative or executive departments.

The powers not delegated by this constitution, nor prohibited by it to the States, are reserved to the States respectively.

Ninthly, That article 7th be numbered as article 8th.

The first of these amendments relates to what may be called a bill of rights. I will own that I never considered this provision so essential to the federal constitution, as to make it improper to ratify it, until such an amendment was added; at the same time, I always conceived, that in a certain form, and to a certain extent, such a provision was neither improper nor altogether useless. I am aware, that a great number of the most respectable friends to the Government, and champions for republican liberty, have thought such a provision, not only unnecessary, but even improper; nay, I believe some have gone so far as to think it even dangerous. Some policy has been made use of, perhaps, by gentlemen on both sides of the question: I acknowledge the ingenuity of those arguments which were drawn against the constitution, by a comparison with the policy of Great Britain, in establishing a declaration of rights; but there is too great a difference in the case to warrant the comparison: therefore, the arguments drawn from that source were in a great measure inapplicable. In the declaration of rights which that country has established, the truth is, they have gone no farther than to raise a barrier against the power of the Crown; the power of the Legislature is left altogether indefinite.

Although I know whenever the great rights, the trial by jury, freedom of the press, or liberty of conscience, come in question in that body, the invasion of them is resisted by able advocates, yet their Magna Charta does not contain any one provision for the security of those rights, respecting which the people of America are most alarmed. The freedom of the press and rights of conscience, those choicest privileges of the people, are unguarded in the British constitution.

But although the case may be widely different, and it may not be thought necessary to provide limits for the legislative power in that country, yet a different opinion prevails in the United States. The people of many States have thought it necessary to raise barriers against power in all forms and departments of Government, and I am inclined to believe, if once bills of rights are established in all the States as well as the federal constitution, we shall find that although some of them are rather unimportant, yet, upon the whole, they will have a salutary tendency.

It may be said, in some instances, they do no more than state the perfect equality of mankind. This, to be sure, is an absolute truth, yet it is not absolutely necessary to be inserted at the head of a constitution.

In some instances they assert those rights which are exercised by the people in forming and establishing a plan of Government. In other instances, they specify those rights which are retained when particular powers are given up to be exercised by the Legislature. In other instances, they specify positive rights, which may seem to result from the nature of the compact. Trial by jury cannot be considered as a natural right, but a right resulting from a social compact which regulates the action of the community, but is as essential to secure the liberty of the people as any one of the pre-existent rights of nature. In other instances, they lay down dogmatic maxims with respect to the construction of the Government; declaring that the legislative, executive, and judicial branches shall be kept separate and distinct. Perhaps the best way of securing this in practice is, to provide such checks as will prevent the encroachment of the one upon the other.

But whatever may be the form which the several States have adopted in making declarations in favor of particular rights, the great object in view is to limit and qualify the powers of Government, by excepting out of the grant of power those cases in which the Government ought not to act, or to act only in a particular mode. They point these exceptions sometimes against the abuse of the executive power, sometimes against the legislative, and, in some cases, against the community itself; or, in other words, against the majority in favor of the minority.

In our Government it is, perhaps, less necessary to guard against the abuse in the executive department than any other; because it is not the stronger branch of the system, but the weaker. It therefore must be levelled against the legislative, for it is the most powerful, and most likely to be abused, because it is under the least control. Hence, so far as a declaration of rights can tend to prevent the exercise of undue power, it cannot be doubted but such declaration is proper. But I confess that I do conceive, that in a Government modified like this of the United States, the great danger lies rather in the abuse of the community than in the legislative body. The prescriptions in favor of liberty ought to be levelled against that quarter where the greatest danger lies, namely, that which possesses the highest prerogative of power. But it is not found in either the executive or legislative departments of Government, but in the body of the people, operating by the majority against the minority.

It may be thought that all paper barriers against the power of the community are too weak to be worthy of attention. I am sensible they are not so strong as to satisfy gentlemen of every description who have seen and examined thoroughly the texture of such a defence; yet, as they have a tendency to impress some degree of respect for them, to establish the public opinion in their favor, and rouse the attention of the whole community, it may be one means to control the majority from those acts to which they might be otherwise inclined.

It has been said, by way of objection to a bill of rights, by many respectable gentlemen out of doors, and I find opposition on the same principles likely to be made by gentlemen on this floor, that they are unnecessary articles of a Republican Government, upon the presumption that the people have those rights in their own hands, and that is the proper place for them to rest. It would be a sufficient answer to say, that this objection lies against such provisions under the State Governments, as well as under the General Government: and there are, I believe, but few gentlemen who are inclined to push their theory so far as to say that a declaration of rights in those cases is either ineffectual or improper. It has been said, that in the Federal Government they are unnecessary, because the powers are enumerated, and it follows, that all that are not granted by the constitution are retained; that the constitution is a call of powers, the great residuum being the rights of the people; and, therefore, a bill of rights cannot be so necessary as if the residuum was thrown into the hands of the Government. I admit that these arguments are not entirely without foundation; but they are not conclusive to the extent which has been supposed. It is true, the powers of the General Government are circumscribed, they are directed to particular objects; but even if

Government keeps within those limits, it has certain discretionary powers with respect to the means, which may admit of abuse to a certain extent, in the same manner as the powers of the State Governments under their constitutions may to an indefinite extent; because in the constitution of the United States, there is a clause granting to Congress the power to make all laws which shall be necessary and proper for carrying into execution all the powers vested in the Government of the United States, or in any department or officer thereof; this enables them to fulfil every purpose for which the Government was established. Now, may not laws be considered necessary and proper by Congress, for it is for them to judge of the necessity and propriety to accomplish those special purposes which they may have in comtemplation, which laws in themselves are neither necessary nor proper; as well as improper laws could be enacted by the State Legislatures, for fulfilling the more extended objects of those Governments. I will state an instance, which I think in point, and proves that this might be the case. The General Government has a right to pass all laws which shall be necessary to collect its revenue; the means for enforcing the collection are within the direction of the Legislature: may not general warrants be considered necessary for this purpose, as well as for some purposes which it was supposed at the framing of their constitutions the State Governments had in view? If there was reason for restraining the State Governments from exercising this power, there is like reason for restraining the Federal Government.

It may be said, indeed it has been said, that a bill of rights is not necessary, because the establishment of this Government has not repealed those declarations of rights which are added to the several State constitutions; that those rights of the people, which had been established by the most solemn act, could not be annihilated by a subsequent act of that people, who meant, and declared at the head of the instrument, that they ordained and established a new system, for the express purpose of securing to themselves and posterity the liberties they had gained by an arduous conflict.

I admit the force of this observation, but I do not look upon it to be conclusive. In the first place, it is too uncertain ground to leave this provision upon, if a provision is at all necessary to secure rights so important as many of those I have mentioned are conceived to be, by the public in general, as well as those in particular who opposed the adoption of this constitution. Besides, some States have no bills of rights, there are others provided with very defective ones, and there are others whose bills of rights are not only defective, but absolutely improper; instead of securing some in the full extent which republican principles would require, they limit them too much to agree with the common ideas of liberty.

It has been objected also against a bill of rights, that, by enumerating particular exceptions to the grant of power, it would disparage those rights which were not placed in that enumeration; and it might follow, by implication, that those rights which were not singled out, were intended to be assigned into the hands of the General Government, and were consequently insecure. This is one of the most plausible arguments I have ever heard urged against the admission of a bill of rights into this system; but, I conceive, that it may be guarded against. I have attempted it, as gentlemen may see by turning to the last clause of the fourth resolution.

It has been said, that it is unnecessary to load the constitution with this provision, because it was not found effectual in the constitution of the particular States. It is true, there are a few particular States in which some of the most valuable articles have not, at one time or other, been violated; but it does not follow but they may have, to a certain degree, a salutary effect against the abuse of power. If they are incorporated into the constitution, independent tribuals of justice will consider themselves in a peculiar manner the guardians of those rights; they will be an impenetrable bulwark against every assumption of power in the legislative or executive; they will be naturally led to resist every encroachment upon rights expressly stipulated for in the constitution by the declaration of rights. Besides, this security, there is a great probability that such a declaration in the federal system would be enforced; because the State Legislatures will jealously and closely watch the operations of this Government, and be able to resist with more effect every assumption of power, than any other power on earth can do; and the greatest opponents to a Federal Government admit the State Legislatures to be sure guardians of the people's liberty. I conclude, from this view of the subject, that it will be proper in itself, and highly politic, for the tranquillity of the public mind, and the stability of the Government, that we should offer something, in the form I have proposed, to be incorporated in the system of Government, as a declaration of the rights of the people.

In the next place, I wish to see that part of the constitution revised which declares that the number of Representatives shall not exceed the proportion of one for every thirty thousand persons, and allows one Representative to every State which rates below that proportion. If we attend to the discussion of this subject, which has taken place in the State conventions, and even in the opinion of the friends to the constitution, an alteration here is proper. It is the sense of the people of America, that the number of Representatives ought to be increased, but particularly that it should not be left in the discretion of the Government to diminish them, below that proportion which certainly is in the power of the Legislature as the constitution now stands; and they may, as the population of the country increases, increase the House of Representatives to a very unwieldy degree. I confess I always thought this part of the constitution defective, though not dangerous; and that it ought to be particularly attended to whenever Congress should go into the consideration of amendments.

There are several minor cases enumerated in my proposition, in which I wish also to see some alteration take place. That article which leaves it in the power of the Legislature to ascertain its own emolument, is one to which I allude. I do not believe this is a power which, in the ordinary course of Government, is likely to be abused. Perhaps of all the powers granted, it is least likely to abuse; but there is a seeming impropriety in leaving any set of men without control to put their hand into the public coffers, to take out money to put in their pockets; there is a seeming indecorum in such power, which leads me to propose a change. We have a guide to this alteration in several of the amendments which the different conventions have proposed. I have gone, therefore, so far as to fix it, that no law, varying the compensation shall operate until there is a change in the Legislature; in which case it cannot be for the particular benefit of those who are concerned in determining the value of the service.

I wish also, in revising the constitution, we may throw into that section, which interdict the abuse of certain powers in the State Legislatures, some other provisions of equal, if not greater importance than those already made. The words, "No State shall pass any bill of attainder, ex post facto law," &c. were wise and proper restrictions in the constitution. I think there is more danger of those powers being abused by the State Governments than by the Government of the United States. The same may be said of other powers which they possess, if not controlled by the general principle, that laws are unconstitutional which infringe the rights of the community. I should therefore wish to extend this interdiction, and add, as I have stated in the 5th resolution, that no State shall violate the equal right of conscience, freedom of the press, or trial by jury in criminal cases; because it is proper that every Government should be disarmed of powers which trench upon those particular rights. I know, in some of the State constitutions, the power of the Government is controlled by such a declaration; but others are not. I cannot see any reason against obtaining even a double security on those points; and nothing can give a more sincere proof of the attachment of those who opposed this constitution to these great and important rights, than to see them join in obtaining the security I have now proposed; because it must be admitted, on all hands, that the State Governments are as liable to attack the invaluable privileges as the General Government is, and therefore ought to be as cautiously guarded against.

I think it will be proper, with respect to the judiciary powers, to satisfy the public mind of those points which I have mentioned. Great inconvenience has been apprehended to suitors from the distance they would be dragged to obtain justice in the Supreme Court of the United States, upon an appeal on an action for a small debt. To remedy this, declare that no appeal shall be made unless the matter in controversy amounts to a particular sum; this, with the regulations respecting jury trials in criminal cases, and suits at common law, it is to be hoped, will quiet and reconcile the minds of the people to that part of the constitution.

I find, from looking into the amendments proposed by the State conventions, that several are particularly anxious that it should be declared in the constitution, that the powers not therein delegated should be reserved to the several States. Perhaps words which may define this more precisely than the whole of the instrument now does, may be considered as superfluous. I admit they may be deemed unnecessary: but there can be no harm in making such a declaration, if gentlemen will allow that the fact is as stated. I am sure I understand it so, and do therefore propose it.

These are the points on which I wish to see a revision of the constitution take place. How far they will accord with the sense of this body, I cannot take upon me absolutely to determine; but I believe every gentleman will readily admit that nothing is in contemplation, so far as I have mentioned, that can endanger the beauty of the Government in any one important feature, even in the eyes of its most sanguine admirers. I have proposed nothing that does not appear to me as proper in itself, or eligible as patronized by a respectable number of our fellow-citizens; and if we can make the constitution better in the opinion of those who are opposed to it, without weakening its frame, or abridging its usefulness, in the judgment of those who are attached to it, we act the part of wise and liberal men to make such alterations as shall produce that effect.

Having done what I conceived was my duty, in bringing before this House the subject of amendments, and also stated such as I wish for and approve, and offered the reasons which occurred to me in their support, I shall content myself, for the present, with moving "that a committee be appointed to consider of and report such amendments as ought to be proposed by Congress to the Legislatures of the States, to become, if ratified by three-fourths thereof, part of the constitution of the United States." By agreeing to this motion, the subject may be going on in the committee, while other important business is proceeding to a conclusion in the House. I should advocate greater despatch in the business of amendments, if I were not convinced of the absolute necessity there is of pursuing the organization of the Government; because I think we should obtain the confidence of our fellow-citizens, in proportion as we fortify the rights of the people against the encroachments of the Government.

Mr. Jackson: The more I consider the subject of amendments, the more I am convinced it is improper. I revere the rights of my constituents as much an any gentleman in Congress, yet I am against inserting a declaration of rights in the constitution, and that for some of the reasons referred to by the gentleman last up. . . .

If we actually find the constitution bad upon experience, or the rights and privileges of the people in danger, I here pledge myself to step foreward among the first friends of liberty to prevent the evil; and if nothing else will avail, I will draw my sword in the defence of freedom, and cheerfully immolate at that shrine my property and my life. But how are we now proceeding? Why, on nothing more than theoretical speculation, pursuing a mere *ignis fatuus,* which may lead us into serious embarrassments. The imperfections of the Government are now unknown; let it have a fair trial, and I will be bound they show themselves; then we can tell where to apply the remedy, so as to secure the great object we are aiming at. . . .

Mr. Gerry: I do not rise to go into the merits or demerits of the subject of amendments; nor shall I make any other observations on the motion for going into a Committee of the whole on the state of the Union, which is now withdrawn, than merely to say, that, referring the subject to that committee, is treating it with the dignity its importance requires. . . .

I say I wish as early a day as possible may be assigned for taking up this business, in order to prevent the necessity which the States may think themselves under of calling a new convention. For I am not, sir, one of those blind admirers of this system, who think it all perfection; nor am I so blind as not to see its beauties. The truth is, it partakes of humanity; in it is blended virtue and vice, errors and excellence. But I think, if it is referred to a new convention, we run the risk of losing some of its best properties; this is a case I never wish to see. Whatever might have been my sentiments of the ratification of the constitution without amendments, my sense now is, that the salvation of America depends upon the establishment of this Government, whether amended or not. If the constitution which is now ratified should not be supported, I despair of ever having a government of these United States.

I wish the subject to be considered early for another reason. There are two States not in the union; it would be a very desirable circumstance to gain them. I should therefore be in favor of such amendments as might tend to incite them and gain their confidence; good policy will dictate to us to expedite that event. Gentlemen say, that we shall not obtain the consent of two-thirds of both Houses to amendments. Are gentlemen willing then to throw Rhode Island and North Carolina into the situation of foreign nations? They have told you that they cannot accede to the Union, unless certain amendments are made to the constitution; if you deny a compliance with their request in that particular, you refuse an accommodation to bring about that desirable event, and leave them detached from the Union. . . .

Some gentlemen consider it necessary to do this to satisfy our constituents. I think referring the business to a special committee will be attempting to amuse them with trifles. Our fellow-citizens are possessed of too much discernment not to be able to discover the intention of Congress by such procedure. It will be the duty of their representatives to tell them, if they were not able to discover it of themselves, they require the subject to be fairly considered; and if it be found to be improper to comply with their reasonable expectations, to tell them so. I hope there is no analogy between federal and punic faith; but unless Congress shall candidly consider the amendments which have been proposed in confidence by the State conventions, federal faith will not be considered very different from the *punica fides* of Carthage. The ratification of the constitution in several States would never have taken place, had they not been assured that the objections would have been duly attended to by Congress. And I believe many members of these conventions would never have voted for it, if they had not been persuaded that Congress would notice them with that candor and attention which their importance requires. I will say nothing respecting the amendments themselves; they ought to stand or fall on their own merits. If any of them are eligible, they will be adopted; if not, they will be rejected.

Mr. Livermore was against this motion; not that he was against amendments at a proper time. . . .

Mr. Sherman: . . . I would prefer to have it referred to a Committee of the whole, rather than a special committee, and therefore shall not agree to the motion now before the House.

Mr. Gerry moved, that the business lie over until the 1st day of July next, and that it be the order for that day.

Mr. Sumter: I consider the subject of amendments of such great importance to the Union, that I shall be glad to see it undertaken in any manner. I am not, Mr. Speaker, disposed to sacrifice subtance to form; therefore, whether the business shall originate in a Committee of the whole, or in the House, is a matter of indifference to me, so that it be put in train. Although I am seriously inclined to give this subject a full discussion, yet I do not wish it to be fully entered into at present, but am willing it should be postponed to a future day, when we shall have more leisure. With respect to referring to a select committee, I am rather against it; because I consider it as treating the applications of the State conventions rather slightly; and I presume it is the intention of the House to take those applications into consideration as well as any other. If it is not, I think it will give fresh cause for jealously; it will rouse the alarm which is now suspended, and the people will become clamorous for amendments. They will decline any further application to Congress, and resort to the other alternative pointed out in the constitution. I hope, therefore, this House, when they do go into the business, will receive those propositions generally. This I apprehend will tend to tranquillize the public mind, and promote that harmony which ought to be kept up between those in the exercise of the powers of Government, and those who have clothed them with the authority, or, in other words, between Congress and the people. Without a harmony and confidence subsist between them, the measures of Government will prove abortive, and we shall have still to lament that imbecility and weakness which have long marked our public councils.

Mr. Vining . . . a bill of rights was unnecessary in a Government deriving all its powers from the people; and the constitution enforced the principle in the strongest manner by the practical declaration prefixed to that instrument; he alluded to the words, "We the people do ordain and establish."

There were many things mentioned by some of the State conventions which he would never agree to, on any conditions whatever; they changed the principles of the Government, and were therefore obnoxious to its friends. The honorable gentleman from Virginia [Mr. Madison] had not touched upon any of them; he was glad of it, because he could by no means bear the idea of an alteration respecting them; he referred to the mode of obtaining direct taxes, judging of elections, &c.

He found he was not speaking to the question; he would therefore return to it, and declare he was against committing the subject to a select committee; if it was to be committed at all, he preferred a Committee of the whole, but hoped the subject would be postponed.

Mr. Madison found himself unfortunate in not satisfying gentlemen with respect to the mode of introducing the business; he thought, from the dignity and peculiarity of the subject, that it ought to be referred to a Committee of the whole. He accordingly made that motion first, but finding himself not likely to succeed in that way, he had changed his ground. Fearing again to be discomfited, he would change his mode, and move the propositions he had stated before, and the House might do what they thought proper with them. He accordingly moved the propositions by way of resolutions be adopted by the House.

Mr. Livermore objected to these propositions, because they did not take up the amendments of the several States.

Mr. Page was much obliged to his colleague for bringing the subject forward in the manner he had done. He conceived it to be just and fair. What was to be done when the house would not refer it to a committee of any sort, but bring the question at once before them? He hoped it would be the means of bringing about a decision.

Mr. Lawrence moved to refer Mr. Madison's motion to the Committee of the whole on the state of the Union.

Mr. Lee thought it ought to be taken up in that committee; and hoped his colleague would bring the propositions before the committee, when on the state of the Union, as he had originally intended.

Mr. Boudinot wished the appointment of a select committee, but afterwards withdrew his motion.

At length Mr. Lawrence's motion was agreed to, and Mr. Madison's propositions were ordered to be referred to a Committee of the whole. Adjourned.

BRDH, II, pp. 1016-1042.

William R. Davie June 10, 1789
Letter: To James Madison (excerpt)

My private acquaintance with you would by no means warrant a correspondence of this kind, but the interest we have in your public character and exertions will sufficiently apologize for the freedom.

You are well acquainted with the political situation of this State [North Carolina], its unhappy attachment to paper money and that wild scepticism which has prevailed in it since the publication of the Constitution. It has been the uniform cant of the enemies of the Government, that Congress would exert all their influence to prevent the calling of a convention, and would never propose an amendment themselves, or consent to an alteration that would in any manner diminish their powers. The people whose fears had been already alarmed, have received this opinion as fact, and become confirmed in their opposition; your notification however of the 4th of May has dispersed almost universal pleasure, we hold it up as a refutation of the gloomy prophecies of the leaders of the opposition, and the honest part of our antifederalists have publicly expressed great satisfaction on this event. Our Convention meet again in November, with powers to adopt the Constitution and any amendments, that may be proposed; this renders it extremely important that the amendments, if any, should be proposed before that time—and although we may be nominally a foreign State, yet I hope the alterations will come officially addressed to the people of this country, an attention however trifling in itself, that will be of importance in the present state of the public mind here.

That farrago of amendments borrowed from Virginia is by no means to be considered as the sense of this country; they were proposed amidst the violence and confusion of party heat, at a critical moment in our Convention, and adopted by the opposition without one moment's consideration—I have collected with some attention the objections of the honest and serious—they are but few and perhaps necessary—they require some explanation rather than alteration of the power of Congress over elections—an abridgement of the jurisdiction of the federal Court in a few instances, and some fixed regulations respecting appeals—they also insist on the trial by jury being expressly secured to them in all cases—and a constitutional guaruntee for the free exercise of their religious rights and privileges—the rule of representation is thought to be too much in the power of Congress—and the Constitution is silent with respect to the existing paper money an important and interesting property. Instead of a Bill of rights attempting to enumerate the rights of the individuals or the State Governments, they seem to prefer some general negative confining Congress to the exercise of the powers particularly granted, with some express negative restriction in some important cases.—I am extremely anxious to know the progress of this delicate and interesting business; and if you could find leisure from the duties of office and the obligations of Friendship to give me some information on this subject, it might perhaps be of some consequence to this country, and would in any event be gratefully acknowledged.

BRDH, II, pp. 979-980.

Fisher Ames (New York) June 11, 1789
Letter: To Thomas Dwight (excerpt)

Mr. Madison has introduced his long expected amendments. They are the fruit of much labor and research. He has hunted up all the grievances and complaints of newspapers, all the articles of conventions, and the small talk of their debates. It contains a bill of rights, the right of enjoying property, of changing the government at pleasure, freedom of the press, of conscience, of juries, exemption from general warrants, gradual increase of representatives, till the whole number, at the rate of one to every thirty thousand, shall amount to , and allowing two to every State, at least. This is the substance. There is too much of it. Oh! I had forgot, the right of the people to bear arms.

Risum teneatis amici?

Upon the whole, it may do some good towards quieting men, who attend to sounds only, and may get the mover some popularity, which he wishes.

Ames, I, pp. 52-53. Ames was a Massachusetts congressman.

Fisher Ames (New York) June 12, 1789
Letter: To George Richards Minot (excerpt)

Mr. Madison has inserted, in his amendments, the increase of representatives, each State having two at least. The rights of conscience, of bearing arms, of changing the government, are declared to be inherent in the people. Freedom of the press, too. There is a prodigious great dose for a medicine. But it will stimulate the stomach as little as hasty-pudding. It is rather food than physic. Am immense mass of sweet and other herbs and roots for a diet drink.

Ames, I, p. 54. Ames was a Massachusetts congressman.

William Grayson (New York) June 12, 1789
Letter: To Patrick Henry (excerpt)[1]

I am exceedingly sorry it is out of my power to hold out to you any flattering expectations on the score of amendments; it appears to me that both houses are almost wholly composed of federalists; those who call themsleves Antis are so extremely lukewarm as scarcely to deserve the appellation: Some gentlemen here from motives of policy have it in contemplation to effect amendments which shall effect personal liberty alone, leaving the great points of the Judiciary, direct taxation &c, to stand as they are; their object is in my opinion unquestionably to break the spirit of the party by divisions; after this

I presume many of the most sanguine expect to go on coolly in sapping the independence of the state legislatures:—In this system however of *divide &c impera,* they are opposed by a very heavy column, from the little States, who being in possession of rights they had no pretensions to in justice, are afraid of touching a subject which may bring into investigation or controversy their fortunate situation: Last Monday a string of amendments were presented to the lower House; these altogether respected personal liberty; & I would now enclose you a copy, did I not know that Parker had done it already:[2]—Even these amendments were opposed by Georgia, New Hampshire & Connecticut:—they were however submitted to a comm[itt]ee of the whole on the State of the nation, & it is thought will not be taken up again for one while. I understood that the mover was so embarrassed in the course of the business, that he was once or twice on the point of withdrawing the motion, & it was thought by some that the commitment was more owing to personal respect than a love of the subject introduced.

1 Henry, III, pp. 391-392. Grayson was a United States Senator from Virginia.
2 See "House of Representatives," June 8, 1789, pp. 654-656, for the amendments introduced by James Madison.

James Madison (New York) June 13, 1789
Letter: To Thomas Jefferson (excerpt)

The Newspaper inclosed will shew you the form and extent of the amendments which I thought it adviseable to introduce to the H. of Representatives as most likely to pass thro' 2/3 of that Hs. & of the Senate & 3/4 of the States. If I am not mistaken they will if passed, be satisfactory to [a] majority of those who have opposed the Constitution. I am persuaded they will be so to a majority of that Description in Virginia.

Papers, XII, pp. 217-218.

James Madison (New York) June 15, 1789
Letter: To Edmund Randolph (excerpt)[1]

The inclosed paper contains the proposition made on Monday last on the subject of amendments.[2] It is limited to points which are important in the eyes of many and can be objectionable in those of none. The structure & stamina of the Govt. are as little touched as possible. Nothing of a controvertible nature can be expected to make its way thro' the caprice & discord of opinions which would encounter it in Congs. when 2/3 must concur in each House, & in the State Legislatures, 3/4 of which will be requisite to its final success. The article which I fear most for is that which respects the representation. The small States betray already a coolness towards it. And I am not sure that another local policy may not mingle its poison in the healing experiment.

1 *Papers*, XII, p. 219.
2 See "House of Representatives," June 8, 1789, pp. 654-656, for Madison's proposal which consisted of a bill of rights and other amendments.

A Pennsylvanian {Tench Coxe} June 18, 1789
Newspaper Article: Philadelphia *Federal Gazette*[1]

REMARKS *on the first part of the* AMENDMENTS *to the* FEDERAL CONSTITUTION, *moved on the 8th instant in the House of Representatives.*

The manifestation of good faith, which this motion carries, is matter of no dishonorable reflection on the friends of the new Constitution, and the ingenuousness and moderation discovered by the gentlemen of the house, who have desired amendments, excites feelings of the most comfortable nature. The people must rejoice to find, that their rulers, of however diversified opinions, are equally anxious for their country's happiness.

The first article, pursuing the republican spirit with which the convention of 1787 designed to animate every part of the Constitution, declares in the most unequivocal terms, that all power is the exclusive right of the people—That from them alone therefore it can be justly derived—that it is granted by them for the promotion of their own benefit, that it can only be exercised to increase and preserve their happiness—that *whenever* this frame of government shall prove unequal to the attainment or destructive of that essential object, *the public good,* it must be reformed or altered, and that it can be at any time reformed and altered by *an indubitable, unalienable and indefeasible right, which always remains in the people.* This is indeed the creed of liberty, to which every American will give his unqualified assent.

The second article provides for a larger representation of the people, than the present number, that members, still more minutely acquainted with local interests and the feelings of the people, may be returned.—Rhode-Island by this liberal clause will have two members in the house of representatives, which will increase those weighty and prudential considerations, that, we trust, are now inclining that state to join her political family.

The third article wisely provides, that no future house of representatives shall determine the wages of that Congress, of which it shall be a part, but may fix the allowance to its successors for two years. This is a new thought admirably calculated to protect the purses of the people from extravagant wages.

The next article establishes religious liberty, and all those political rights, which by various tricks of state have been wounded through its means, on the firmest ground. The tender, the almost sacred rights of conscience, says this inestimable article, shall by no means, on no account be abridged or interfered with. No self-righteous or powerful church shall set up its impious domination over all the rest. Every pious man may pay to the divine author of his existence the tribute of thanksgiving and adoration, in the manner of his forefathers.

The following paragraph declares the freedom of the press to be a main bulwark of liberty, and reasoning unanswerably from its usefulness and indispensable necessity, declares, that it shall be inviolable.

As civil rulers, not having their duty to the people, duly before them, may attempt to tyrannize, and as the military forces which shall be occasionally raised to defend our country, might pervert their power to the injury of their fellow-citizens, the people are confirmed by the next article in their right to keep and bear their private arms.

The humane and wholesome maxim of the common law, which protects even the guilty from double punishment, is recognized in another clause, and legal oppression, in the shape of excessive bail, is absolutely prohibited.

Oppression and inhumanity have contaminated the fountains of justice in many countries, by the subjection of offenders to exhorbitant fines, or new and barbarous punishments.—The passions of men have co-operating with necessary policy, stained the character of nations, and rendered their legislators infamous and execrable. Free governments are particularly liable to these things, for enemies of the people have no friends, and the popular voice is unceasing and loud against them. To interpose the moderation of cooler moments, seems therefore wise in Congress, and accordingly they have enabled the most odious offenders to remind their country, "that *excessive* fines ought not to be imposed, nor *cruel, and unusual* punishments inflicted."

1 See "A Pennsylvanian," June 30, 1789, p. 764, for remarks on the second part of Madison's proposed amendments.

Tench Coxe (Philadelphia) June 18, 1789
Letter: To James Madison (excerpt)[1]

I observe you have brought forward the amendments you proposed to the federal Constitution.[2] I have given them a very careful perusal, and have attended particularly to their reception by the public. The most decided friends of the constitution admit (generally) that they will meliorate the government by removing some points of litigation and jealousy, and by heightening and strengthening the barriers between necessary power and indispensible liberty. In short the most ardent & irritable among our friends are well pleased with them. On the part of the opposition I do not observe any unfavorable animadversion. Those who are honest are well pleased at the footing on which the press, liberty of conscience, original right & power, trial by jury &ca. are rested. Those who are not honest have hitherto been silent, for in truth they are stript of every rational, and most of the popular arguments they have heretofore used. I will not detain you with further remarks, but feel very great satisfaction in being able to assure you generally, that the proposed amendments will greatly tend to promote harmony among the late contending parties and a general confidence in the patriotism of Congress. It has appeared to me that a few well tempered observations on these propositions might have a good effect. I have therefore taken an hour from my present Engagements, which on account of my absence are greater than usual, and have thrown together a few remarks upon the first part of the Resolutions. I shall endeavour to pursue them in one or two more short papers. It may perhaps be of use in the present turn of the public opinions in New York state that they should be republished there. It is in fed. Gazette of 18th. instant.[3,4]

1 *Papers*, XII, pp. 239-240.

2 See "House of Representatives," June 8, 1789, pp. 654-656, for Madison's proposed amendments.

3 See "A Pennsylvanian," June 18 and June 30, 1789, directly above and p. 674, respectively, for Coxe's remarks on Madison's proposals.

4 See "James Madison (New York)," June 24, 1789, p. 673, for Madison's reply, including a comment upon Coxe's published remarks relating to the amendments proposed by Madison.

James Madison (New York) June 21, 1789
Letter: To Samuel Johnston (excerpt)

In the inclosed paper is a copy of a late proposition in Congress on the subject of amending the Constitution. It aims at the twofold object of removing the fears of the discontented and of avoiding all such alterations as would either displease the adverse side, or endanger the success of the measure. I need not remark to you the hazard of attempting any thing of a controvertible nature which is to depend on the concurrence of 2/3 of both Houses here, and the ratification of 3/4 of the State Legislatures. It will be some time before the proposed amendments will become a subject of discussion in Congress; The bills relating to revenue, and the organization of the Judiciary and Executive Departments, being likely to remain for some time on hand.

Papers, XII, p. 250. Reprinted in BRDH, II, p. 1049.

Joseph Jones (Richmond) June 24, 1789
Letter: To James Madison (excerpt)[1]

I thank you for the copy of the amendments proposed to the constitution which you lately inclosed to me[2]—they are calculated to secure the personal rights of the people so far as declarations on paper can effect the purpose, leaving unimpaired the great Powers of the government—they are of such a nature as to be generally acceptable and of course more likely to obtain the assent of Congress than wod. any proposition tending to separate the powers or lessen them in either branch.

1 *Papers*, XII, pp. 258-259.
2 See "House of Representatives," June 8, 1789, pp. 654-656, for Madison's proposals.

James Madison (New York) June 24, 1789
Letter: To Tench Coxe (excerpt)[1]

Accept my acknowledgments for your favor of the 18th. instant.[2] The printed remarks inclosed in it are already I find in the Gazettes here.[3] It is much to be wished that the discon[ten]ted part of our fellow Citizens could be reconciled to the Government they have opposed, and by means as little as possible unacceptable to those who approve the Constitution in its present form. The amendments proposed in the H. of Reps. had this twofold object in view; besides the third one of avoiding all controvertible points which might endanger the assent of 2/3 of each branch of Congs and 3/4 of the State Legislatures. How far the experiment may succeed in any of these respects is wholly uncertain. It will however be greatly favored by explanatory strictures of a healing tendency, and is therefore already indebted to the co-operation of your pen.

1 *Papers*, XII, p. 257.
2 See "Tench Coxe (Philadelphia)," June 18, 1789, p. 672, for Coxe's letter to Madison.
3 See "A Pennsylvanian {Tench Coxe}," June 18, 1789, p. 670, for Coxe's newspaper article supporting Madison's proposed amendments. Note paragraph number seven relating to the right of the people to "keep and bear their private arms."

A Pennsylvanian {Tench Coxe} June 30, 1789
Newspaper Article: Philadelphia *Federal Gazette*[1]

REMARKS *on the second part of the* AMENDMENTS, *moved on the 8th instant, in the House of Representatives.*

General warrants have been ever peculiarly alarming to the subjects of arbitrary princes, and proportionally odious to the citizens of free governments. It will be therefore highly satisfactory to the people of these states, that an explicit provision against that dangerous process has been proposed in Congress.

An unnecessary or injurious *delay* of justice is in part a *denial* of it, therefore, says the next amendment, trials shall be speedy, and they shall not, like the proceedings of a Star Chamber, or an inquisition, be in private. The cause and nature of the accusation shall be laid open, that the injured may turn the malice of their accusers, however powerful, upon their own heads. Nor shall any one suffer from the great name of his prosecutors, or the want of knowledge and skill to demonstrate his innocence; for even the most timid and unwilling witnesses shall be compelled to attend, and counsellors of learning, virtue and firmness may in all cases be employed in his defence.

A previous accusation by twelve grand jurors at least—the trial by *jury*, and that of the *vicinage*—the necessity of every voice of the traverse jurors to constitute a legal conviction—the right of excepting against the inimical, the severe, the partial or the dishonest on the jury list, and every other just and humane privilege of the common law, are expressly confirmed.

Whenever an invasion, or any public disorder shall prevent an undisturbed and uninfluenced session of court, the trial shall not be at the will of the executive or judiciary, but at such place as the legislature, *the representatives of the states and of the people,* shall fix and determine. So also will affairs be ordered, when offences shall be committed on the waters, or without the limits of any country. These wholesome provisions are well calculated to prevent not only those interruptions of justice, which internal disorders frequently occasion, but those stretches of power, which the executive and judicial authority in every country have sometimes unwarily but always unwarrantably hazarded on such occasions.

It has been argued by many against a bill of rights, that the omission of some in making the detail would one day draw into question those that should not be particularized. It is therefore provided, that no inference of that kind shall be made, so as to diminish much less to alienate an ancient tho' unnoticed right, nor shall either of the branches of the Federal Government argue from such omission any increase or extension of their powers.

The fifth proposition is an admirable thought. The Congress of the United States not only declare that liberty of conscience—the freedom of the press—and trial by jury are due *from them* to the people of this Union, but deeming them as precious as the republican form of our government, they declare, that no State under pretence of a separate jurisdiction, shall violate either of them. How insurmountable are the obstructions to the progress of tyranny, which this inestimable proposition will create?

In the re-examination of the verdicts of a jury, of which a party may complain, the known and settled principles and directions of the common law are ever to be remembered and observed.

The wisdom of every free country has adopted that rule of civil policy, which separates the legislative, executive and judicial powers, and renders them as far as possible, independent of each other. The eighth proposition therefore, wisely declares that to be the intention of the American people, in constructing their frame of general government; and upon all future questions regarding this point, the article proposed, will dictate such mode of proceeding, as shall most perfectly conform with the explained spirit of the original constitution.

To render more distinct and indelible the line which is drawn between the powers of the several States, and those of the general government, it is proposed by Congress to declare, that the States respectively, retain all such powers as are not delegated to Congress, or the exercise of which is not prohibited by the federal constitution. This must remove all apprehensions that the government of the States will be absorbed by that of the Union.

Whatever may be the fate of some of these propositions, either in Congress, or in the State Legislatures, every ingenuous citizen of America will admit, that they manifest an attentive regard to the convenience, and a virtuous solicitude for the safety and happiness of the people, while they leave unimpaired those wholesome and necessary powers which *the freemen* of the United States have wisely granted to their national government.

1 See "A Pennsylvanian," June 18, 1789, p. 670, for remarks on the first part of Madison's proposed amendments.

Hugh Williamson (Baltimore) July 2, 1789
Letter: To James Madison (excerpt)[1]

I verily believe that unless you can persuade Congress seriously to take up & agree to some such Amendm[en]ts as you have proposed[2] North Carolina will not confederate but of this more particulars when I have the Pleasure of seeing you which I hope will be about the End of next Week.

1 *Papers*, XII, pp. 274-275.
2 See "House of Representatives," June 8, 1789, pp. 654-656, for Madison's proposals which included a provision regarding the right of the people to keep and bear arms.

One of the People July 2, 1789
Newspaper Article: Philadelphia *Federal Gazette*

ON A BILL OF RIGHTS; addressed to the friends of amendments in Congress and out of it.

It is a singular property in the human mind, to transfer the habits of one country into another, where they are often both ridiculous and improper.

The natives of Holland, build their houses with projections from the upper story, in order to raise their furniture by means of a rope and pulley from the water, which in many of their cities runs by their doors. This form the first settlers gave to their houses, twenty miles from navigable water, in the state of New-York.

The same attachment to *forms* and *habits* has obtained in America upon the subject of government, that has obtained among the Hollanders upon the subject of footstoves and houses.

A bill of rights has been demanded in England, because in that country the kings *confer* liberty upon the people.

In the United States, the people derive their liberty from nature, and they delegate such parts of it only to their servants, as are necessary for its better preservation.

The very idea of a bill of rights, and of a compact, is a dishonorable one to freemen. It implies that we are insensible of our dignity, as the sovereigns of our country, and as the only source of power. It changes the places of rulers and ruled. It disposes us to look upon our rulers as our masters,—whereas they are nothing but our servants.

What should we think of a gentleman, who, upon hiring a waiting-man, should say to him—"my friend, please to take notice, before we come together, that I shall always claim the liberty of eating when and what I please, of fishing and hunting upon my own ground, of keeping as many horses and hounds as I can maintain, and of speaking and writing my sentiments upon all subjects." A servant must be a fool, who would not suppose such a master to be a madman. If he replied to him at all, he would certainly tell him, that "he had a right to do as he pleased—that his business was only to obey his orders—and that when he refused to do this, he was at liberty to discharge him."

Liberty can never be safe, nor can government ever be reformed in America, 'till we banish European, and in particular British, ideas of the nature of the one and of the origin of the other.

Place the sovereignty in the PEOPLE, and all the mysteries of government which have arisen out of kingcraft and priestcraft tumble to the dust.

We walked so long half-bent under the British government, that we have not, in the twelfth year of our Independence, learned to walk upright. We resemble old soldiers who have been discharged from an army, who, though independent and affluent afterwards, irresistibly and mechanically pull off their hats, at the sight of an officer who has formerly commanded them.

Instead of forming creatures to treat *us* with respect and homage, when we choose our rulers, we immediately become idolaters, and worship the work of *our own* hands. No wonder therefore, rulers are so prone to tyranny. They are encouraged to it by the want of knowledge among the people. The sight of a bill of rights is at any time enough to kindle a fire of persecution against liberty[.] "I gave," says a ruler—and therefore "I have a right to take away."

Let these truths sink deep into our hearts: that the people are the masters of their rulers and that rulers are the servants of the people—that men cannot *give* to themselves what they *own* from nature—that a free government is no more than a few plain directions to a number of servants, how to take care of a part of their masters property—and that a master reserves to himself the exclusive care of all that property, and of *every thing else* which he has not committed to the care of those servants.

When the people of America are as much enlightened upon the affairs of government, as they now are upon other things, they will consider the noise that has been made about a bill of rights, as we now consider the stories that were told a century ago about conjurors and witches.

Governor and Council of North Carolina July 9, 1789
Address: To President George Washington (excerpts)

The following ADDRESS of the governor and Council of this State has lately been presented to General WASHINGTON, President of the United States: . . . To his Excellency *GEORGE WASHINGTON,* Esq: President of the United States.

SIR,

AMIDST the congratulations which surround you from all quarters, WE, the Governor and Council of the State of North-Carolina, beg leave to offer ours, with equal sincerity with any which can be presented to you. Though this State be not yet a member of the Union under the new form of government, we look forward with the pleasing hope of its shortly becoming such; and in the mean time consider ourselves bound in a common interest and affection with the other States, waiting only for the happy event of such alterations being proposed as will remove the apprehensions of many of the good citizens of this State, for those liberties for which they have fought and suffered in common with others. This happy event, we doubt not, will be accelerated by your Excellency's appointment to the first office in the Union, since we are well assured the same greatness of mind, which in all scenes has so eminently characterised your Excellency, will induce you to advise every measure calculated to compose party divisions, and to abate any animosity that may be excited by a mere difference of opinion.

Providence Gazette, August 1, 1789, p. 2.

House of Representatives July 21, 1789
Debates (excerpt)

Mr. Madison then moved, that the house resolve itself into a committee, in order to take into consideration the subject of amendments to the constitution.

Several members suggesting that it would be more proper to refer the subject to a special committee, a motion was made in form, that a committee of one member from each state be appointed to take in consideration the motion of the [8]th of June (Mr. Madison's motion, offering certain amendments), together with the amendments proposed by the conventions of the different states, and to report thereon.

Upon this motion a diffusive debate ensued, which turned altogether upon the point of expediency as to the mode; it being agreed that it would be proper for the house to take the subject into consideration. The principal argument in favour of the motion was drawn from the infinite embarrassments which would take place, if the subject in its present irregular and disordered state should come first before the whole House, and the great delay which it would occasion.

On the other hand it was chiefly contended, that the method proposed would not give satisfaction to the people; and that it would not facilitate the business, since the whole subject would, on the report of the committee, lie open to the House.

The motion was however carried by a large majority, and the House proceeded to ballot for the committee, which, on counting the ballots, was found to consist of Mr. Gilman, Mr. Goodhue, Mr. Sherman, Mr. Benson, Mr. Boudinot, Mr. Clymer, Mr. Vining, Mr. Gale, Mr. Madison, Mr. Burke, and Mr. Baldwin. *Adjourned*

Philadelphia *Freeman's Journal,* July 29, 1789, p. 2. For a more detailed account of these debates, see BRDH, II, pp. 1057-1061.

Fisher Ames (New York) July 23, 1789
Letter: To George Richards Minot (excerpt)

We have had the amendments on the *tapis,* and referred them to a committee of one from a State. I hope much debate will be avoided by this mode, and that the amendments will be more rational, and less *ad populum,* than Madison's. It is necessary to conciliate, and I would have amendments. But they should not be trash, such as would dishonor the Constitution, without pleasing its enemies. Should we propose them, North Carolina would accede. It is doubtful, in case we should not.

Ames, I, p. 65. Ames was a congressman from Massachusetts.

House of Representatives July 28, 1789
Proceedings on Amendments

Mr. Vining from the committee of eleven, to whom it was referred to take the subject of amendments to the constitution of the United States, generally into their consideration, and to report thereupon, made a report, which was read, and is as followeth:

In the introductory paragraph before the words, "We the people," add, "Government being intended for the benefit of the people, and the rightful establishment thereof being derived from their authority alone."

Art. 1, Sec. 2, Par. 3—Strike out all between the words, "direct" and "and until such," and instead thereof insert, "After the first enumeration there shall be one representative for every thirty thousand, until the number shall amount to one hundred; after which the proportion shall be so regulated by Congress, that the number of representatives shall never be less than one hundred, nor more than one hundred and seventy-five, but each state shall always have at least one representative."

Art. 1, Sec. 6—Between the words "United States," and "shall in all cases," strike out "they," and insert, "But no law varying the compensation shall take effect until an election of representatives shall have intervened. The members."

Art. 1, Sec. 9—Between Par. 2 and 3, insert, "No religion shall be established by law, nor shall the equal rights of conscience be infringed."

"The freedom of speech, and of the press, and of the right of the people peaceably to assemble and consult for their common good, and to apply to the government for redress of grievances, shall not be infringed."

"A well regulated militia, composed of the body of the people, being the best security of a free state, the right of the people to keep and bear arms shall not be infringed, but no person religiously scrupulous shall be compelled to bear arms."

"No soldier shall in time of peace be quartered in any house without the consent of the owner, nor in time of war but in a manner to be prescribed by law."

"No person shall be subject, except in case of impeachment, to more than one trial or one punishment for the same offence, nor shall be compelled to be a witness against himself, nor be deprived of life, liberty or property without due process of law, nor shall private property be taken for public use without just compensation."

"Excessive bail shall not be required, nor excessive fines imposed, nor cruel and unusual punishments inflicted."

"The right of the people to be secure in their person, houses, papers and effects, shall not be violated by warrants issuing, without probable cause supported by oath or affimation, and not particularly describing the places to be searched, and the persons or things to be seized."

"The enumeration in this constitution of certain rights shall not be construed to deny or disparage others retained by the people."

Article 1, Sec. 10, between the 1st and 2d par. insert "No state shall infringe the equal rights of conscience, nor the freedom of speech, or of the press, nor of the right of trial by jury in criminal cases."

Art. 3, Sec. 2, add to the 2d Par. "but no appeal to such court shall be allowed, where the value of controversy shall not amount to one thousand dollars; nor shall any fact triable by a jury according to the course of the common law, be otherwise reexaminable than according to the rules of common law."

Art. 3, Sec. 2—Strike out the whole of the 3d paragraph, and insert—"In all criminal prosecutions the accused shall enjoy the right to a speedy and public trial, to be informed of the nature and cause of the accusation, to be confronted with the witnesses against him, to have compulsory process for obtaining witnesses in his favor, and to have the assistance of counsel for his defence."

"The trial of all crimes (except in cases of impeachment, and in cases arising in the land or naval forces, or in the militia, when in actual service in time of war or public danger) shall be by an impartial jury of freeholders of the vicinage, with the requisite of unanimity for conviction, the right of challenge and other accustomed requisites; and no person shall be held to answer for a capital, or otherwise infamous crime, unless on a presentment or indictment by a grand-jury, but if a crime be committed in a place in the possession of an enemy, or in which an insurrection may prevail, the indictment and trial may by law be authorised in some other place within the same state; and if it be committed in a place not within a state, the indictment and trial may be at such place or places as the law may have directed."

"In suits at common law, the right of trial by jury shall be preserved."

Immediately after Art. 6, the following to be inserted as Art. 7.

"The powers delegated by this constitution to the government of the United States, shall be exercised as therein appropriated, so that the legislative shall never exercise the powers vested in the executive or the judicial; nor the executive, the powers vested in the legislative or judicial; nor the judicial, the powers vested in the legislative or executive."

"The powers not delegated by this constitution, nor prohibited by it to the states, are reserved to the states respectively."

Art. 7 to be made Art. 8.

Upon motion of Mr. Gerry, it was voted, that 100 copies be struck off for the accommodation of the members.

Philadelphia *Freeman's Journal*, August 5, 1789, p. 1.

George Mason (Gunston Hall) July 31, 1789
Letter: To John Mason (excerpt)[1]

You were mistaken in your Suggestion, that the Publication you saw of Mr. Madison's, was a certain Indication of proper Amendments to the Government being obtained. It was indeed, natural enough to think so. But the *Fact* was, Mr. Madison [knew that he cou]'d not be elected, without making some such promises. By them he carryed his Election; and in order to appear as good as his Word, he has made some Motions in Congress on the Subject; and to carry on the Farce, is now the ostensible Patron of Amendments. Perhaps some Milk & Water Propositions may be made by Congress to the State Legislatures by Way of th[r]owing out a Tub to the Whale; but of important & substantial Amendments, I have not the least Hope.[2]

1 Rutland, III, p. 1164.

2 See "George Mason," September 8, 1789, p. 710, for Mason's views on the amendments as actually proposed by the House of Representatives. Mason must not have been aware of Madison's proposals in the House of Representatives of June 8, 1789 (see above at pp. 654-656) when he wrote this. The "Publication you saw of Mr. Madison's" might have been a newspaper reference to Madison's notice that he intended to bring foreward amendments.

James Madison (New York) August 2, 1789
Letter: To Wilson Cary Nicholas (excerpt)[1]

The proposed amendments of which I sent you a copy[2] have since been in the hands of a committee composd of a member from each State. Their report is inclosed.[3] [Some] of the changes are perhaps for the better, others for the worse. From the concord of the Come. and the language used in the House on the last discussion, I indulge a confidence that something will be effected. For the Senate I can less answer, but I have no reason for distrust in case the plan be kept within its present limits.

1 *Papers*, XII, p. 321.
2 See "House of Representatives," June 8, 1789, pp. 654-656, for Madison's proposals.
3 See "House of Representatives," July 28, 1789, p. 680, for the amendments proposed by the select committee.

Pierce Butler (New York) August 11, 1789
Letter: To James Iredell (excerpt)

If you wait for substantial amendments, you will wait longer than I wish you to do, speaking *interestedly*. A few *milk-and-water* amendments have been proposed by Mr. M[adison], such as liberty of conscience, a free press, and one or two general things already well secured. I suppose it was done to keep his promise with his constituents, to move for alterations; but, if I am not greatly mistaken, he is not hearty in the cause of amendments.

DHFFE, IV, p. 319. Butler was a United States Senator from South Carolina.

Fisher Ames (New York) August 12, 1789
Letter: To George Richards Minot (excerpt)

We are beginning the amendments in a committee of the whole. We have voted to take up the subject, in preference to the Judiciary, to incorporate them into the Constitution, and not to require, in committee, two thirds to a vote. This cost us the day. To-morrow we shall proceed. Some General, before engaging, said to his soldiers, "Think of your ancestors, and think of your posterity." We shall make a dozen or two of rights and privileges for our posterity. If I am to be guided by your advice, to marry and live in Boston, it behooves me to interest myself in the affair. It will consume a good deal of time, and renew the party struggles of the States. It will set Deacon Smead and many others to constitution-making, a trade which requires little stock, and often thrives without much custom. The workman is often satisfied to be the sole consumer. Our State [Massachusetts] is remarkable for it. We made several frames of government, which did not pass. The timber was so green, the vessels rotted on the stocks. However, I am persuaded it is proper to propose amendments, without delay, and if the *antis* affect to say that they are of no consequence, they may be reproached with their opposition to the government, because they protested that the principles were important.

Ames, I, pp. 66-67. Ames was a Massachusetts congressman.

House of Representatives August 13, 1789
Debates (excerpts)

Amendments to the Constitution

Mr. Lee moved that the House now resolve itself into a Committee of the whole, on the report of the committee of eleven, to whom it had been referred to take the subject of amendments to the constitution of the United States generally into their consideration.

Mr. Page hoped the House would agree to the motion of his colleague without hesitation, because he conceived it essentially necessary to proceed and finish the business as speedily as possible; for whatever might be the fact with respect to the security which the citizens of America had for their rights and liberties under the new constitution, yet unless they saw it in that light, they would be uneasy, not to say dissatisfied.

He thought, likewise, that the business would be expedited by the simplicity and self-evidence which the propositions reported possessed, as it was impossible that much debate could take place.

Mr. Sedgwick was sorry that the motion was made, because he looked upon this as a very improper time to enter upon the consideration of a subject which would undoubtedly consume many days; and when they had so much other and more important business requiring immediate attention, he begged gentlemen to recollect that all they had hitherto done was of little or no effect; their impost and tonnage laws were but a dead letter.

Mr. Madison did not think it was an improper time to proceed in this business; the House had already gone through with subjects of a less interesting nature; now if the Judiciary bill was of such vast importance, its consideration ought not to have been postponed for those purposes.

He would remind gentlemen that there were many who conceived amendments of some kind necessary and proper in themselves; while others who are not so well satisfied of the necessity and propriety, may think they are rendered expedient from some other consideration. Is it desirable to keep up a division among the people of the United States on a point in which they consider their most essential rights are concerned? If this is an object worthy the attention of such a numerous part of our constituents, why should we decline taking it into our consideration, and thereby promote that spirit of urbanity and unanimity which the Government itself stands in need of for its more full support?

Already has the subject been delayed much longer than could have been wished. If after having fixed a day for taking it into consideration, we should put it off again, a spirit of jealously may be excited, and not allayed without great inconvenience. . . .

Mr. Smith. . . .

An honorable gentleman from Virginia observed to us that these propositions were self-evident, that little or no debate could grow out of them. That may be his opinion, but truly, sir, it is not mine; for I think some of them are not self-evident, and some of them will admit of lengthy discussion; and some others, I hope, may be rejected, while their place may be better supplied by others hereafter to be brought foreward. Some members are pledged to support amendments, and will, no doubt, support them with all the arguments their fancy or ingenuity can suggest. Viewing it in this light, it is not to be expected that the discussion will be ended in less than a fortnight or three weeks; and let gentlemen consult their own feelings whether they have so much time now to spare.

Mr. Hartley thought the judicial system ought to be finished before any other business was entered upon, and was willing to consider of amendments to the constitution when the House was more disengaged; because he wished very much that the constitution was so modified as to give satisfaction to honest and candid minds. Such would be satisfied with securing to themselves and their posterity all those blessings of freedom which they are now possessed of. As to the artful and designing, who had clamored against the whole work, he had not the smallest desire to gratify them: he hoped and trusted their numbers were but few.

Mr. Gerry thought the discussion would take up more time than the House could now spare; he was, therefore, in favor of postponing the consideration of the subject, until the Judicial bill, and the bill for registering and clearing vessels, and some other bills relating to the revenue business, were gone through. . . .

Mr. Lawrence had no objections to consider amendments at a proper time, but did not think that the present was a proper time to enter upon them, nor did he suppose that gentlemen would be precluded from a full discussion of the whole subject whenever it was taken up. . . .

Mr. Madison: I beg leave to make one or two remarks more, in consequence of the observations which have fallen from the different sides of the House. Some gentlemen seem to think that additional propositions will be brought forward; whether they will or not, I cannot pretend to say; but if they are, I presume they will be no impediment to our deciding upon those contained in the report. But gentlemen who introduce these propositions will see, that if they are to produce more copious debate than has hitherto taken place, they will consume a great part of the remainder of the session. I wish the subject well considered, but I do not wish to see any unnecessary waste of time; and gentlemen will please to remember that this subject has yet to go before the Senate.

I admit, with the worthy gentleman who preceded me, that a great number of the community are solicitous to see the Government carried into operation; but I believe that there is a considerable part also anxious to secure those rights which they are apprehensive are endangered by the present constitution. Now, considering the full confidence they reposed at the time of its adoption in their future representatives, I think we ought to pursue the subject to effect. I confess it has already appeared to me, in point of candor and good faith, as well as policy, to be incumbent on the first Legislature of the United States, at their first session, to make such alterations in the constitution as will give satisfaction, without injuring or destroying any of its vital principles.

I should not press the subject at this time because I am well aware of the importance of the other business enumerated by the gentlemen who are adverse to the present motion, but from an apprehension that, if it is delayed until the other is gone through, gentlemen's patience and application will be so harassed and fatigued, as to oblige them to leave it in an unfinished state until the next session; besides, were the Judicial bill to pass now, it could not take effect until others were enacted, which probably at this time are not drawn up. . . .

Mr. Fitzsimons wished gentlemen would suffer the question to be put, and not consume the time in arguing about what should be done. If a majority was not in favor of considering amendments, they might proceed to some other business.

Mr. Page was positive the people would never support the Government unless their anxiety was removed. They, in some instances, adopted it, in confidence of its being speedily amended; they will complain of being deceived unless their expectations are fulfilled. So much time has elapsed since the subject was first brought forward, said he, that people will not think us serious, unless we now set about and complete it.

He begged gentlemen to consider the importance of the number of citizens, who were anxious for amendments; if these had been added to those who openly opposed the constitution, it possibly might have met a different fate. Can the Government, under these circumstances, possess energy, as some gentlemen suppose? Is not the confidence of the people absolutely necessary to support it?

The question was now put, and carried in the affirmative.

The House then resolved itself into a Committee of the whole, Mr. Boudinot in the chair, and took the amendments under consideration. . . .[1]

The report of the Committee was then read—the first article of which is in these words, viz.

In the introductory paragraph of the Constitution, before the words, "We the people," add "Government being intended for the benefit of the people, and the rightful establishment thereof being derived from their authority alone."

Mr. Sherman. I am opposed to this mode of making amendments to the Constitution—and am for striking out from the report of the Committee the first article entirely. I concieve that we cannot incorporate these amendments in the body of the Constitution. . . . Mr. Sherman then read a proposition, which he moved should be substituted in place of the article in the report.

This being seconded, brought on an interesting debate—Whether the amendments should be incorporated in the body of the Constitution, or be made a distinct supplementary act.

Several gentlemen spoke repeatedly upon the subject—the question on motion being taken, it passed in the negative.[2]

1 BRDH, II, pp. 1062-1066.
2 *Providence Gazette*, August 29, 1789, p. 3.

House of Representatives August 14, 1789
Debates (excerpt)[1]

Mr. Gerry: The presumption is, that if provision is not made for the increase of the House of Representatives, by the present Congress, the increase never will be made. Gentlemen ought to consider the difference between the Government in its infancy and when well established. The people suppose their liberties somewhat endangered; they have expressed their wishes to have them secured, and instructed their representatives to endeavor to obtain for them certain amendments, which they imagine will be adequate to the object they have in view. Besides this, there are two States not in the Union; but which we hope to annex to it by the amendments now under deliberation. These are inducements for us to proceed and adopt this amendment, independent of the propriety of the amendment itself, and such inducements as no future Congress will have, the principle of self-interest and self-importance will always operate on them to prevent any addition to the number of representatives. Cannot gentlemen contemplate a difference in situation between this and a future Congress on other accounts. We have neither money nor force to administer the constitution; but this will not be the case hereafter. In the progress of this Government its revenues will increase, and an army will be established; a future Legislature will find other means to influence the people than now exist.

This circumstance proves that we ought to leave as little as possible to the discretion of the future Government; but it by no means proves that the present Congress ought not to adopt the amendment moved by my colleague, Mr. Sedgwick.[2]

1 BRDH, II, p. 1085.
2 "The amendment moved" was to increase the upper limit of representatives from 175 to 200.

House of Representatives August 15, 1789
Debates (excerpts)

Amendments to the Constitution

The House again went into a Committee of the whole on the proposed amendments to the constitution, Mr. Boudinot in the chair.

The fourth proposition being under consideration, as follows:

Article 1. Section 9. Between paragraphs two and three insert "no religion shall be established by law, nor shall the equal rights of conscience be infringed."

Mr. Sylvester had some doubts of the propriety of the mode of expression used in this paragraph. He apprehended that it was liable to a construction different from what had been made by the committee. He feared it might be thought to have a tendency to abolish religion altogether.

Mr. Vining suggested the propriety of transposing the two members of the sentence.

Mr. Gerry said it would read better if it was, that no religious doctrine shall be established by law.

Mr. Sherman thought the amendment altogether unnecessary, inasmuch as Congress had no authority whatever delegated to them by the constitution to make religious establishments; he would, therefore, move to have it struck out.

Mr. Carroll: As the rights of conscience are, in their nature, of peculiar delicacy, and will little bear the gentlest touch of governmental hand; and as many sects have concurred in opinion that they are not well secured under the present constitution, he said he was much in favor of adopting the words. He thought it would tend more towards conciliating the minds of the people to the Government than almost any other amendment he had heard proposed. He would not contend with gentlemen about the phraseology, his object was to secure the substance in such a manner as to satisfy the wishes of the honest part of the community.

Mr. Madison said, he apprehended the meaning of the words to be, that Congress should not establish a religion, and enforce the legal observation of it by law, nor compel men to worship God in any manner contrary to their conscience. Whether the words are necessary or not, he did not mean to say, but they had been required by some of the State Conventions, who seemed to entertain an opinion that under the clause of the constitution, which gave power to Congress to make all laws necessary and proper to carry into execution the constitution, and the laws made under it, enabled them to make laws of such a nature as might infringe the rights of conscience, and establish a national religion; to prevent these effects he presumed the amendment was intended, and he thought it as well expressed as the nature of the language would admit.

Mr. Huntington said that he feared, with the gentleman first up on this subject, that the words might be taken in such latitude as to be extremely hurtful to the cause of religion. He understood the amendment to mean what had been expressed by the gentleman from Virginia; but others might find it convenient to put another construction upon it. The ministers of their congregations to the Eastward were maintained by the contributions of those who belonged to their society; the expense of building meeting-houses was contributed in the same manner. These things were regulated by bylaws. If any action was brought before a Federal Court on any of these cases, the person who had neglected to perform his engagements could not be compelled to do it; for a support of ministers, or building of places of worship might be construed into a religious establishment.

By the charter of Rhode Island, no religion could be established by law; he could give a history of the effects of such a regulation; indeed the people were now enjoying the blessed fruits of it. He hoped, therefore, the amendment would be made in such a way as to secure the rights of conscience, and a free exercise of the rights of religion, but not to patronize those who professed no religion at all.

Mr. Madison thought, if the word national was inserted before religion, it would satisfy the minds of honorable gentlemen. He believed that the people feared one sect might obtain a pre-eminence, or two combine together, and establish a religion to which they would compel others to conform. He though if the word national was introduced, it would point the amendment directly to the object it was intended to prevent.

Mr. Livermore was not satisfied with that amendment; but he did not wish them to dwell long on the subject. He thought it would be better if it was altered, and made to read in this manner, that Congress shall make no laws touching religion, or infringing the rights of conscience.

Mr. Gerry did not like the term national, proposed by the gentleman from Virginia, and he hoped it would not be adopted by the House. It brought to his mind some observations that had taken place in the convention at the time they were considering the present constitution. It had been insisted upon by those who were called antifederalists, that this form of Government consolidated the Union; the honorable gentleman's motion shows that he considers it in the same light. Those who were called antifederalist at that time complained that they had injustice done them by the title, because they were in favor of a Federal Government, and the others were in favor of a national one; the federalists were for ratifying the constitution as it stood, and the others not until amendments were made. Their names then ought not to have been distinguished by federalists and antifederalist, but rats and antirats.

Mr. Madison withdrew his motion, but observed that the words "no national religion shall be established by law," did not imply that the Government was a national one; the question was then taken on Mr. Livermore's motion, and passed in the affirmative, thirty-one for, and twenty against it.

The next clause of the fourth proposition was taken into consideration, and was as follows: "The freedom of speech and of the press, and the right of the people peaceably to assemble and consult for their common good, and to apply to the Government for redress of grievances, shall not be infringed."

Mr. Sedgwick submitted to those gentlemen who had contemplated the subject, what effect such an amendment as this would have; he feared it would tend to make them appear triffling in the eyes of their constituents; what, said he, shall we secure the freedom of speech, and think it necessary, at the same time, to allow the right of assembling? If people freely converse together, they must assemble for that purpose; it is a self-evident, unalienable right which the people possess; it is certainly a thing that never would be called in question; it is derogatory to the dignity of the House to descend to such minutiae; he therefore moved to strike out "assemble and."

Mr. Benson: The committee who framed this report proceeded on the principle that these rights belonged to the people; they conceived them to be inherent; and all that they meant to provide against was their being infringed by the Government.

Mr. Sedgwick replied, that if the committee were governed by that general principle, they might have gone into a very lengthy enumeration of rights; they migh have declared that a man should have a right to wear his hat if he pleased; that he might get up when he pleased, and go to bed when he thought proper; but he would ask the gentleman whether he thought it necessary to enter these trifles in a declaration of rights, in a Government where none of them were intended to be infringed.

Mr. Tucker hoped the words would not be struck out, for he considered them of importance; besides, they were recommended by the States of Virginia and North Carolina, though he noticed that the most material part proposed by those States was omitted, which was, a declaration that the people should have a right to instruct their representatives. He would move to have those words inserted as soon as the motion for striking out was decided.

Mr. Gerry was also against the words being struck out, because he conceived it to be an essential right; it was inserted in the constitutions of several States; and though it had been abused in the year 1786 in Massachusetts, yet that abuse ought not to operate as an argument against the use of it. The people ought to be secure in the peaceable enjoyment of this privilege, and that can only be done by making a declaration to that effect in the constitution.

Mr. Page: The gentleman from Massachusetts, (Mr. Sedgwick) who made this motion, objects to the clause, because the right is of so trivial a nature. He supposes it no more essential than whether a man has a right to wear his hat or not; but let me observe to him that such rights have been opposed, and a man has been obliged to pull off his hat when he appeared before the face of authority; people have also been prevented from assembling together on their lawful occasions, therefore it is well to guard against such stretches of authority, by inserting the privilege in the declaration of rights. If the people could be deprived of the power of assembling under any pretext whatsoever, they might be deprived of every other privilege contained in the clause.

Mr. Vining said, if the thing was harmless, and it would tend to gratify the States that had proposed amendments, he should agree to it.

Mr. Hartley observed, that it had been asserted in the convention of Pennsylvania, by the friends of the constitution, that all the rights and powers that were not given to the Government were retained by the States and the people thereof. This was also his own opinion; but as four or five States had required to be secured in those rights by an express declaration in the constitution, he was disposed to gratify them; he thought every thing that was not incompatible with the general good ought to be granted, if it would tend to obtain the confidence of the people in the Government; and, upon the whole, he thought these words were as necessary to be inserted in the declaration of rights as most in the clause.

Mr. Gerry said, that his colleague contended for nothing, if he supposed that the people had a right to consult for the common good, because they could not consult unless they met for the purpose.

Mr. Sedgwick replied that if they were understood or implied in the word consult, they were utterly unnecessary, and upon that ground he moved to have them struck out.

The question was now put upon Mr. Sedgwick's motion, and lost by a considerable majority.

Mr. Tucker then moved to insert these words, "to instruct their Representatives." . . .

Mr. Madison: I think the committee acted prudently in omitting to insert these words in the report they have brought forward; if, unfortunately, the attempt of proposing amendments should prove abortive, it will not arise from the want of a disposition in the friends of the constitution to do what is right with respect to securing the rights and privileges of the people of America, but from the difficulties arising from discussing and proposing abstract propositions, of which the judgment may not be convinced. I venture to say, that if we confine ourselves to an enumeration of simple, acknowledged principles, the ratification will meet with but little difficulty. Amendments of a doubful nature will have a tendency to prejudice the whole system; the proposition now suggested partakes highly of this nature. It is doubted by many gentlemen here; it has been objected to in intelligent publications throughout the Union; it is doubted by many members of the State Legislatures. In one sense this declaration is true, we have asserted the right sufficiently in what we have done; if we mean nothing more than this, that the people have a right to express and communicate their sentiments and wishes, we have provided for it already. The right of freedom of speech is secured; the liberty of the press is expressly declared to be beyond the reach of this Government; the people may therefore publicly address their representatives, may privately advise them, or declare their sentiment by petition to the whole body; in all these ways they may communicate their will. If gentlemen mean to go further, and to say that the people have a right to instruct their representatives in such a sense as that the delegates are obliged to conform to those instructions, the declaration is not true. Suppose they instruct a representative, by his vote, to violate the constitution; is he at liberty to obey such instructions? Suppose he is instructed to patronize certain measures, and from circumstances known to him, but not to his constituents, he is convinced that they will endanger the public good; is he obliged to sacrifice his own judgment to them? Is he absolutely bound to perform what he is instructed to do. Suppose he refuses, will his vote be the less valid, or the community be disengaged from that obedience which is due to the laws of the Union? If his vote must inevitably have the same effect, what sort of a right is this in the constitution, to instruct a representative who has a right to disregard the order, if he pleases? In this sense the right does not exist, in the other sense it does exist, and is provided largely for.

The honorable gentleman from Massachusetts asks if the sovereignty is not with the people at large. Does he infer that the people can, in detached bodies, contravene an act established by the whole people? My idea of the sovereignty of the people is, that the people can change the constitution if they please; but while the constitution exists, they must conform themselves to its dictates. But I do not believe that the inhabitants of any district can speak the voice of the people; so far from it, their ideas may contradict the sense of the whole people; hence the consequence that instructions are binding on the representative is of a doubtful, if not of a dangerous nature. I do not conceive, therefore, that it is necessary to agree to the proposition now made; so far as any real good is to arise from it, so far that real good is provided for; so far as it is of a doubtful nature, so far it obliges us to run the risk of losing the whole system. . . .

Mr. Gerry: . . .

If this amendment is introduced into the constitution, I do not think we shall be much troubled with instructions; a knowledge of the right will operate to check a spirit that would render instruction necessary.

The honorable gentleman from Virginia asked, will not the affirmative of a member who votes repugnant to his instructions bind the community as much as the votes of those who conform? There is no doubt, sir, but it will; but does this tend to show that the constituent has no right to instruct? Surely not. I admit, sir, that instructions contrary to the constitution ought not to bind, though the sovereignty resides in the people. The honorable gentleman acknowledges that the sovereignty vests there; if so, it may exercise its will in any case not inconsistent with a previous contract. The same gentleman asks if we are to give the power to the people in detached bodies to contravene the Government while it exists. Certainly not; nor does the proposed proposition extend to that point; it is only intended to open for them a convenient mode in which they may convey their sense to their agents. The gentleman therefore takes for granted what is inadmissible, that Congress will always be doing illegal things, and make it necessary for the sovereign to declare its pleasure.

He says the people have a right to alter the constitution, but they have no right to oppose the Government. If, while the Government exists, they have no right to control it, it appears they have divested themselves of the sovereignty over the constitution. Therefore, our language, with our principles, must change, and we ought to say that the sovereignty existed in the people previous to the establishment of this Government. This will be ground for alarm indeed, if it is true; but I trust, sir, too much to the good sense of my fellow-citizens ever to believe that the doctrine will generally obtain in this country of freedom. . . .

Mr. Madison was unwilling to take up any more of the time of the committee; but, on the other hand, he was not willing to be silent after the charges that had been brought against the committee, and the gentleman who introduced the amendments, by the honorable members on each side of him, (Messrs. Sumter and Burke.) Those gentlemen say that we are precipitating the business, and insinuate that we are not acting with candor. I appeal to the gentlemen who have heard the voice of their country, to those who have attended the debates of the State conventions, whether the amendments now proposed are not those most strenuously required by the opponents to the constitution? It was wished that some security should be given for those great and essential rights which they had been taught to believe were in danger. I concurred, in the convention of Virginia, with those gentlemen, so far as to agree to a declaration of those rights which corresponded with my own judgment, and the other alterations which I had the honor to bring forward before the present Congress. I appeal to the gentlemen on this floor who are desirous of amending the constitution, whether these proposed are not compatible with what are required by our constituents? Have not the people been told that the rights of conscience, the freedom of speech, the liberty of the press, and trial by jury, were in jeopardy? that they ought not to adopt the constitution until those important rights were secured to them?

But while I approve of these amendments, I should oppose the consideration at this time of such as are likely to change the principles of the Government, or that are of a doubtful nature; because I apprehend there is little prospect of obtaining the consent of two-thirds of both Houses of Congress, and three-fourths of the State Legislatures, to ratify propositions of this kind; therefore, as a friend to what is attainable, I would limit it to the plain, simple, and important security that has been required. If I were inclined to make no alteration in the constitution, I would bring forward such amendments as were of a dubious cast, in order to have the whole rejected. . . .

The question [on the right to instruct representatives] was now called for from several parts of the House; but a desultory conversation took place before the question was put. At length the call becoming general, it was stated from the chair, and determined in the negative, 10 rising in favor of it, and 41 against it.

BRDH, II, pp. 1087-1091, 1096-1097, 1099, 1104-1105.

House of Representatives August 17, 1789
Debates (excerpt)

Amendments to the Constitution

The House again resolved itself into a committee, Mr. Boudinot in the chair, on the proposed amendments to the constitution. The third clause of the fourth proposition in the report was taken into consideration, being as follows: "A well regulated militia, composed of the body of the people, being the best security of a free state, the right of the people to keep and bear arms shall not be infringed; but no person religiously scrupulous shall be compelled to bear arms."

Mr. Gerry: This declaration of rights, I take it, is intended to secure the people against the mal-administration of the Government; if we could suppose that, in all cases, the rights of the people would be attended to, the occasion for guards of this kind would be removed. Now, I am apprehensive, sir, that this clause would give an opportunity to the people in power to destroy the constitution itself. They can declare who are those religiously scrupulous, and prevent them from bearing arms.

What, sir, is the use of a militia? It is to prevent the establishment of a standing army, the bane of liberty. Now, it must be evident, that, under this provision, together with their other powers, Congress could take such measures, with respect to a militia, as to make a standing army necessary. Whenever Governments mean to invade the rights and liberties of the people, they always attempt to destroy the militia, in order to raise an army upon their ruins. This was actually done by Great Britain at the commencement of the late revolution. They used every means in their power to prevent the establishment of an effective militia to the eastward. The Assembly of Massachusetts, seeing the rapid progress that administration were making to divest them of their inherent privileges, endeavored to counteract them by the organization of the militia; but they were always defeated by the influence of the Crown.

Mr. Seney wished to know what question there was before the committee, in order to ascertain the point upon which the gentleman was speaking.

Mr. Gerry replied that he meant to make a motion, as he disapproved of the words as they stood. He then proceeded. No attempts that they made were successful, until they engaged in the struggle which emancipated them at once from their thraldom. Now, if we give a discretionary power to exclude those from militia duty who have religious scruples, we may as well make no provision on this head. For this reason, he wished the words to be altered so as to be confined to persons belonging to a religious sect scrupulous of bearing arms.

Mr. Jackson did not expect that all the people of the United States would turn Quakers or Moravians; consequently, one part would have to defend the other in case of invasion. Now this, in his opinion, was unjust, unless the constitution secured an equivalent: for this reason he moved to amend the clause, by inserting at the end of it, "upon paying an equivalent, to be established by law."

Mr. Smith, of South Carolina, inquired what were the words used by the conventions respecting this amendment. If the gentleman would conform to what was proposed by Virginia and Carolina, he would second him. He thought they were to be excused provided they found a substitute.

Mr. Jackson was willing to accommodate. He thought the expression was, "No one, religiously scrupulous of bearing arms, shall be compelled to render military service, in person, upon paying an equivalent."

Mr. Sherman conceived it difficult to modify the clause and make it better. It is well known that those who are religiously scrupulous of bearing arms, are equally scrupulous of getting substitutes or paying an equivalent. Many of them would rather die than do either one or the other; but he did not see an absolute necessity for a clause of this kind. We do not live under an arbitrary Government, said he, and the

States, respectively, will have the government of the militia, unless when called into actual service; besides, it would not do to alter it so as to exclude the whole of any sect, because there are men amongst the Quakers who will turn out, notwithstanding the religious principles of the society, and defend the cause of their country. Certainly it will be improper to pre[v]ent the exercise of such favorable dispositions, at least whilst it is the practice of nations to determine their contests by the slaughter of their citizens and subjects.

Mr. Vining hoped the clause would be suffered to remain as it stood, because he saw no use in it if it was amended so as to compel a man to find a substitute, which, with respect to the Government, was the same as if the person himself turned out to fight.

Mr. Stone inquired what the words "religiously scrupulous" had reference to: was it of bearing arms? If it was, it ought to be expressed.

Mr. Benson moved to have the words "but no person religiously scrupulous shall be compelled to bear arms," struck out. He would always leave it to the benevolence of the Legislature, for, modify it as you please, it will be impossible to express it in such a manner as to clear it from ambiguity. No man can claim this indulgence of right. It may be a religious persuasion, but it is no natural right, and therefore ought to be left to the discretion of the Government. If this stands part of the constitution, it will be a question before the Judiciary on every regulation you make with respect to the organization of the militia, whether it comports with this declaration or not. It is extremely injudicious to intermix matters of doubt with fundamentals.

I have no reason to believe but the Legislature will always possess humanity enough to indulge this class of citizens in a matter they are so desirous of; but they ought to be left to their discretion.

The motion for striking out the whole clause being seconded, was put, and decided in the negative—22 members voting for it, and 24 against it.

Mr. Gerry objected to the first part of the clause, on account of the uncertainty with which it is expressed. A well regulated milita being the best security of a free State, admitted an idea that a standing army was a secondary one. It ought to read, "a well regulated militia, trained to arms;" in which case it would become the duty of the Government to provide this security, and furnish a greater certainty of its being done.

Mr. Gerry's motion not being seconded, the question was put on the clause as reported; which being adopted,

Mr. Burke proposed to add to the clause just agreed to, an amendment to the following effect: "A standing army of regular troops in time of peace is dangerous to public liberty, and such shall not be raised or kept up in time of peace but from necessity, and for the security of the people, nor then without the consent of two-thirds of the members present of both Houses; and in all cases the military shall be subordinate to the civil authority." This being seconded.

Mr. Vining asked whether this was to be considered as an addition to the last clause, or an amendment by itself. If the former, he would remind the gentleman the clause was decided; if the latter, it was improper to introduce new matter, as the House had referred the report specially to the Committee of the whole.

Mr. Burke feared that, what with being trammelled in rules, and the apparent disposition of the committee, he should not be able to get them to consider any amendment; he submitted to such proceeding because he could not help himself.

Mr. Hartley thought the amendment in order, and was ready to give his opinion on it. He hoped the people of America would always be satisfied with having a majority to govern. He never wished to see two-thirds or three-fourths required, because it might put it in the power of a small minority to govern the whole Union.

The question on Mr. Burke's motion was put, and lost by a majority of thirteen.

The fourth clause of the fourth proposition was taken up as follows: "No soldier shall, in time of peace, be quartered in any house, without the consent of the owner, nor in time of war, but in a manner to be prescribed by law."

Mr. Sumter hoped soldiers would never be quartered on the inhabitants, either in time of peace or war, without the consent of the owner. It was a burthen, and very oppressive, even in cases where the owner gave his consent; but where this was wanting, it would be a hardship indeed! Their property would lie at the mercy of men irritated by a refusal, and well disposed to destroy the peace of the family.

He moved to strike out all the words from the clause but "no soldier shall be quartered in any house without the consent of the owner."

Mr. Sherman observed that it was absolutely necessary that marching troops should have quarters, whether in time of peace or war, and that it ought not to be put in the power of an individual to obstruct the public service; if quarters were not to be obtained in publick barracks, they must be procured elsewhere. In England, where they paid considerable attention to private rights, they billeted the troops upon the keepers of public houses, and upon private houses also, with the consent of the magistracy.

Mr. Sumter's motion being put, was lost by a majority of sixteen.

Mr. Gerry moved to insert between "but" and, "in a manner" the words "by a civil magistrate," observing that there was no part of the Union but where they could have access to such authority.

Mr. Hartley said those things ought to be intrusted to the Legislature; that cases might arise where the public safety would be endangered by putting it in the power of one person to keep a division of troops standing in the inclemency of the weather for many hours; therefore he was against inserting the words.

Mr. Gerry said either his amendment was essential, or the whole clause was unnecessary.

On putting the question, thirteen rose in favor of the motion, thirty-five against it; and then the clause was carried as reported.

BRDH, II, pp. 1107-1110.

House of Representatives August 18, 1789
Debates (excerpt)

The 9th proposition, in the words following, was considered, "The powers not delegated by the constitution, nor prohibited by it to the States, are reserved to the States respectively."

Mr. Tucker proposed to amend the proposition, by prefixing to it "all powers being derived from the people." He thought this a better place to make this assertion than the introductory clause of the constitution, where a similar sentiment was proposed by the committee. He extended his motion also, to add the word "expressly," so as to read "the powers not expressly delegated by this constitution."

Mr. Madison objected to this amendment, because it was impossible to confine a Government to the exercise of express powers; there must necessarily be admitted powers by implication, unless the constitution descended to recount every minutia. He remembered, the word "expressly" had been moved in the convention of Virginia, by the opponents to the ratification, and, after full and fair discussion, was given up by them, and the system allowed to retain its present form.

Mr. Sherman coincided with Mr. Madison in opinion, observing that corporate bodies are supposed to possess all powers incident to a corporate capacity, without being absolutely expressed.

Mr. Tucker did not view the word "expressly" in the same light with the gentleman who opposed him; he thought every power to be expressly given that could be clearly comprehended within any accurate definition of the general power.

Mr. Tucker's motion being negatived,

Mr. Carroll proposed to add to the end of the proposition, "or to the people;" this was agreed to.

The 10th proposition, "Art. 7 to be made Art. 8," agreed to.

The committee then rose, and reported the amendments as amended by the committee.

BRDH, II, p. 1118.

House of Representatives August 19, 1789
Debates (excerpt)

Amendments to the Constitution

The House then took into consideration the amendments to the constitution, as reported by the Committee of the whole.

Mr. Sherman renewed his motion for adding the amendments to the constitution by way of supplement.

Hereupon ensued a debate similar to what took place in the Committee of the whole, but, on the question, Mr. Sherman's motion was carried by two-thirds of the House; by consequence it was agreed to.

BRDH, II, pp. 1125-1126.

James Madison (New York) August 19, 1789
Letter: To Richard Peters (excerpt)

The papers inclosed will shew that the nauseous project of amendments has not yet been either dismissed or despatched. We are so deep in them now, that right or wrong some thing must be done. I say this not by way of apology, for to be sincere I think no apology requisite. 1. because a constitutional provision in favr. of essential rights is a thing not improper in itself and was always viewed in that light by myself. It may be less necessary in a republic, than a Monarchy, & in a fedl. Govt. than the former, but it is in some degree rational in every Govt., since in every Govt. power may oppress, and declarations on paper, tho' not an effectual restraint, are not without some influence. 2. In many States the Constn. was adopted under a tacit compact in favr. of some subsequent provisions on this head. In Virga. It would have been *certainly* rejected, had no assurances been given by its advocates that such provisions would be pursued. As an honest man *I feel* my self bound by this consideration. 3. If the Candidates in Virga. for the House of Reps. had not taken this conciliary ground at the election, that State would have [been] represented almost wholly by disaffected characters, instead of the *federal* reps. now in Congs. 4. If amendts. had not been proposed from the federal side of the House, the proposition would have come *within three days,* from the adverse side. It is certainly best that they should appear to be the free gift of the friends of the Constitution rather than to be extorted by the address & weight of its enemies. 5. It will kill the opposition every where, and by putting an end to the disaffection to the Govt. itself, enable the administration to venture on measures not otherwise safe. Those who hate the Govt. will always join the party disaffected to measures of the admi[ni]s[tra]tion, and such a party will be created by every important measure. 6. If no amendts. be proposed the language of antifedl. leaders to the people, will be, we advised you not to adopt the Constn. witht. previous amendts—You listened to those who told you that subsequent securities for your rights would be most easily obtained—We urged you to insist on a Convention as the only effectual mode of obtaining these—You yielded to the assurances of those who told you that a Convention was unecessary, that Congs. wd. be the proper channel for getting what was wanted. &c &c. Here are fine texts for popular declaimers who wish to revive the antifedl. cause, and at the fall session of the Legislares. to blow the trumpet for a second Convention. In Virga. a majority of the Legislature last elected, is bitterly opposed to the Govt. and will be joined, if no amends. be proposed, by great nos. of the other side who will complain of being deceived. 7. Some amendts. are necssy for N. Carola. I am so informed by the best authorities in that State.

Papers, XII, pp. 346-347.

Philadelphia *Independent Gazetteer*   August 20, 1789
Letter to the Editors

From the (Boston) INDEPENDENT CHRONICLE

Messrs. Adams & Nourse,

It may well be remembered that the following "amendments" to the new constitution for these United States, were introduced to the convention of this commonwealth by its present Lieutenant Governor, that venerable patriot, SAMUEL ADAMS.[1]—It was his misfortune to have been misconceived, and the proposition was accordingly withdrawn—lest the business of the convention (the session of which was then drawing to a period) might be unexpectedly protracted. His enemies triumphed exceedingly, and affected to represent his proposal as not only an artful attempt to prevent the constitution being adopted in this state, but as an unnecessary and improper alteration of a system, which did not admit of improvements. To the honor of this gentleman's penetration, and of his just way of thinking on this important subject, every one of the intended alterations, but one, have been already reported by the committee of the House of Representatives in Congress, and most probably will be adopted by the federal legislature. In justice therefore to that long tried Republican, and his numerous friends, you gentlemen, are requested to re-publish his intended alterations, in the same paper that exhibits to the public, the amendments which the committee have adopted, in order that they may be compared together.

Propositions submitted to the Convention of this State, by the Honorable SAMUEL ADAMS, *Esquire.*

"THAT the report of the committee made on Monday last, be amended so far as to add the following to the first article therein mentioned,[2] viz.—And that the said constitution be never construed to authorize Congress to infringe the just liberty of the Press, or the rights of Conscience; or to prevent the people of the United States who are peaceable citizens, from keeping their own arms; or to raise standing armies, unless when necessary for the defence of the United States, or of some one of them; or to prevent the people from petitioning in a peaceable and orderly manner, the federal Legislature, for a redress of grievances; or to subject the people to unreasonable searches and seizures of their persons, papers, or possessions."

1 See "Massachusetts Convention," February 6, 1788, p. 260, for Samuel Adams' introduction of amendments.

2 The first article of the Massachusetts Convention amendments was, "That it be explicitly declared that all powers not expressly delegated by the aforesaid Constitution are reserved to the several states, to be by them exercised."

House of Representatives August 20, 1789
Debates

Amendments to the Constitution

The House resumed the consideration of the report of the Committee of the whole on the subject of amendments to the constitution.

Mr. Ames's proposition was taken up. Five or six other members introduced propositions on the same point, and the whole were, by mutual consent, laid on the table. After which, the House proceeded to the third amendment, and agreed to the same.

On motion of Mr. Ames, the fourth amendment was altered so as to read "Congress shall make no law establishing religion, or to prevent the free exercise thereof, or to infringe the rights of conscience." This being adopted,

The first proposition was agreed to.

Mr. Scott objected to the clause in the sixth amendment, "No person religiously scrupulous shall be compelled to bear arms." He observed that if this becomes part of the constitution, such persons can neither be called upon for their services, nor can an equivalent be demanded; it is also attended with still further difficulties, for a militia can never be depended upon. This would lead to the violation of another article in the constitution, which secures to the people the right of keeping arms, and in this case recourse must be had to a standing army. I conceive it, said he, to be a legislative right altogether. There are many sects I know, who are religiously scrupulous in this respect; I do not mean to deprive them of any indulgence the law affords; my design is to guard against those who are of no religion. It has been urged that religion is on the decline; if so, the argument is more strong in my favor, for when the time comes that religion shall be discarded, the generality of persons will have recourse to these pretexts to get excused from bearing arms.

Mr. Boudinot thought the provision in the clause, or something similar to it, was necessary. Can any dependence, said he, be placed in men who are conscientious in this respect? or what justice can there be in compelling them to bear arms, when, according to their religious principles, they would rather die than use them? He adverted to several instances of oppression on this point, that occurred during the war. In forming a militia, an effectual defence ought to be calculated, and no characters of this religious description ought to be compelled to take up arms. I hope that in establishing this Government, we may show the world that proper care is taken that the Government may not interfere with the religious sentiments of any person. Now, by striking out the clause, people may be led to believe that there is an intention in the General Government to compel all its citizens to bear arms.

Some further desultory conversation arose, and it was agreed to insert the words "in person" to the end of the clause; after which, it was adopted, as was the fourth, fifth, sixth, seventh, and eighth clauses of the fourth proposition; then the fifth, sixth, and seventh propositions were agreed to, and the House adjourned.

BRDH, II, pp. 1126-1127.

James Madison (New York) August 21, 1789
Letter: To Edmund Randolph (excerpt)

For a week past the subject of amendts. has exclusively occupied the H. of Reps. Its progress has been exceedingly wearisome not only on account of the diversity of opinions that was to be apprehended, but of the apparent views of some to defeat by delaying a plan short of their wishes, but likely to satisfy a great part of their companions in opposition throughout the Union. It has been absolutely necessary in order to effect any thing, to abbreviate debate, and exclude every proposition of a doubtful & unimportant nature. Had it been my wish to have comprehended every amendt. recommended by Virg. I should have acted from prudence the very part to which I have been led by choice. Two or three contentious additions would even now frustrate the whole project.

Papers, XII, pp. 348-349. Reprinted in BRDH, II, pp. 1138-1139.

James Madison (New York) August 21, 1789
Letter: To Edmund Pendleton (excerpt)

The last 8 or 10 days have been spent on the subject of amendts. The work has been extremely difficult and fatiguing, as well on account of the dilatory artifices of which some of the antifederal members are suspected, as of the diversity of opinions & fancies inseparable from such an Assembly as Congress. At present there is a prospect of finishing to day, the plan so far as it lies with the H. of Reps. It does not differ much from the original propositions offered on that subject.

Papers, XII, p. 348.

Samuel Adams August 22, 1789
Letter: To Elbridge Gerry (excerpt)

I hope Congress, before they adjourn, will take into very serious Consideration the necessary Amendments of the Constitution. Those whom I call the best—the most judicious & disinterested Federalists, who wish for the perpetual Union, Liberty & Happiness of the States & their respective Citizens, many of them if not all are anxiously expecting them. They wish to see a Line drawn as clearly as may be, between the federal Powers vested in Congress and the distinct Sovereignty of the several States upon which the private & personal Rights of the Citizens depend. Without such Distinction there will be Danger of the Constitution issuing imperceptibly and gradually into a consolidated Government over all the States; which, altho it may be wished for by some was reprobated in the Idea by the highest Advocates for the Constitution as it stood without Amendm[en]ts. I am fully persuaded that the population of the U S liv[in]g in different Climates, of different Habits & feelings under one consolidated Governm[en]t can not long remain free, or indeed remain under any kind of Govern[men]t but despotism.

Cushing, IV, p. 332.

James Madison (New York) August 24, 1789
Letter: To Alexander White (excerpt)

The week past has been devoted to the subject of amendments. All that remains is a formal vote on a fair transcript which will be taken this morning; and without debate I hope as each of the propositions has been agreed to by two thirds of the House. The substance of the report of the Committee of eleven has not been much varied. It became an unavoidable sacrifice to *a few* who knew their concurrence to be necessary, to the despatch if not the success of the business, to give up the form by which the amendts. when ratified would have fallen into the body of the Constitution, in favor of the project of adding them by way of appendix to it. It is already apparent I think that some ambiguities will be produced by this change, as the question will often arise and sometimes be not easily solved, how far the original text is or is not necessarily superceded, by the supplemental act. A middle way will be taken between the two modes, of proposing all the amendts. as a single act to be adopted or rejected in the gross, and of proposing them as independent amendts. each of which shall take place or not, as it may be individually decided on. The several propositions will be *classed* according to their affinity to each other, which will reduce them to the number of 5 or 6 in the whole, to go forth as so many amendts. unconnected with one another.

Papers, XII, pp. 352-353.

House of Representatives August 24, 1789
Proceedings

Mr. Benson, from the committee appointed [on August 22] for the purpose, reported an arrangement of the articles of amendment to the constitution of the United States, as agreed to by the House on Friday last; also, a resolution prefixed to the same, which resolution was twice read and agreed to by the House, as follows:

> Resolved by the Senate and House of Representatives of the United States of America in Congress assembled, (two-thirds of both Houses deeming it necessary,) That the following articles be proposed to the Legislatures of the several States as amendments to the constitution of the United States, all or any of which articles, when ratified by three-fourths of the said Legislatures, to be valid to all intents and purposes as part of the said constitution.

Ordered, That the clerk of this House do carry to the Senate a fair engrossed copy of the said proposed articles of amendment, and desire their concurrence.[1]

Articles in addition to, and amendment of, the constitution of the United States of America, proposed by Congress, and ratified by the legislatures of the several states, pursuant to the fifth article of the original constitution.

Art. 1. After the first enumeration, required by the first article of the constitution, there shall be one representative for every thirty thousand, until the number shall amount to one hundred, after which the proportion shall be so regulated by Congress, that there shall be not less than one hundred representatives, nor less than one representative for every forty thousand persons, until the number of representatives shall amount to two hundred, after which the proportion shall be so regulated by Congress, that there shall not be less than two hundred representatives, nor less than one representative for every fifty thousand persons.

Art. 2. No law varying the compensation to the members of Congress, shall take effect, until an election of representatives shall have intervened.

Art. 3. Congress shall make no law establishing religion or prohibiting the free exercise thereof, nor shall the rights of conscience be infringed.

Art. 4. The freedom of speech, and of the press, and the right of the people peaceably to assemble, and consult for the common good, and to apply to the government for a redress of grievances, shall not be infringed.

Art. 5. A well regulated militia, composed of the body of the people, being the best security of a free state, the right of the people to keep and bear arms, shall not be infringed, but no one religiously scrupulous of bearing arms, shall be compelled to render military service in person.

Art. 6. No soldier shall, in time of peace, be quartered in any house without the consent of the owner, nor in time of war, but in a manner to be prescribed by law.

Art. 7. The right of the people to be secure in their persons, houses, papers and effects, against unreasonble searches and seizures, shall not be violated, and no warrants shall issue, but upon probable cause, supported by oath or affirmation, and particularly describing the place to be searched, and the persons or things to be seized.

Art. 8. No person shall be subject, except in case of impeachment, to more than one trial, or one punishment for the same offence, nor shall be compelled in any criminal case, to be a witness against himself, nor be deprived of life, liberty or property without due process of law; nor shall private property be taken for public use without just compensation.

Art. 9. In all criminal prosecutions, the accused shall enjoy the right to a speedy and public trial, to be informed of the nature and cause of the accusation, to be confronted with the witnesses against him, to have compulsory process for obtaining witnesses in his favor, and to have the assistance of counsel for his defence.

Art. 10. The trial of all crimes (except in cases of impeachment, and in cases arising in the land or naval forces, or in the militia when in actual service in time of war or public danger) shall be by an impartial jury of the vicinage, with the requisite of unanimity for conviction, the right of challenge, and other accustomed requisites; and no person shall be held to answer for a capital, or otherwise infamous crime, unless on a presentment or indictment by a grand jury; but if a crime be committed in a place in the possession of an enemy, or in which an insurrection may prevail, the indictment and trial may by law be authorised in some other place within the same state.

Art. 11. No appeal to the supreme court of the United States, shall be allowed, where the value in controversy shall not amount to one thousand dollars, nor shall any fact, triable by a jury according to the course of common law, be otherwise re-examinable, than according to the rules of common law.

Art. 12. In suits at common law, the right of trial by jury shall be preserved.

Art. 13. Excessive bail shall not be required, nor excessive fines imposed, nor cruel and unusual punishments inflicted.

Art 14. No state shall infringe the right of trial by jury in criminal cases, nor the rights of conscience, nor the freedom of speech, or of the press.

Art. 15. The enumeration in the constitution of certain rights, shall not be construed to deny or disparage others retained by the people.

Art. 16. The powers delegated by the constitution to the government of the United States, shall be exercised as therein appropriated, so that the legislative shall never exercise the powers vested in the executive or judicial; nor the executive the powers vested in the legislative or judicial; nor the judicial the powers vested in the legislative or executive.

Art. 17. The powers not delegated by the constitution, nor prohibited by it, to the states, are reserved to the states respectively.[2]

1 BRDH, II, p. 1138.
2 Philadelphia *Freeman's Journal,* September 2, 1789, pp. 2-3.

Samuel Adams August 24, 1789
Letter: To Richard Henry Lee (excerpt)

I mean, my friend, to let you know how deeply, I am impressed with a sense of the Importance of Amendments; that the good People may clearly see the distinction, for there is a distinction, between the *federal* Powers vested in Congress, and the *sovereign* Authority belonging to the several States, which is the Palladium of the private, and personal rights of the Citizens. I freely protest to you that I earnestly wish some Amendments may be judiciously, and deliberately made without partial or local considerations—that there may be no uncomfortable Jarrings among the several Powers; that the whole People may in every State contemplate their own safety on solid grounds, and the Union of the States be perpetual.

Cushing, IV, p. 334.

Thomas Jefferson (Paris) August 28, 1789
Letter: To James Madison (excerpt)

I must now say a word on the declaration of rights you have been so good as to send me. I like it as far as it goes; but I should have been for going further. For instance the following alterations & additions would have pleased me. Art 4. "The people shall not be deprived or abridged of their right to speak, to write or *otherwise* to publish anything but false facts affecting injuriously the life, liberty, property, or reputation of others or affecting the peace of the confederacy with foreign nations. Art 7. All facts put in issue before any judicature shall be tried by jury except 1, in cases of admiralty jurisdiction wherein a foreigner shall be interested; 2, in cases cognizable before a court martial concerning only the regular officers & souldiers of the U. S. or members of the militia in actual service in time of war or insurrection, & 3, in impeachments allowed by the constitution. Art 8. No person shall be held in confinement more than ____ days after they shall have demanded & been refused a writ of Hab. corp. by the judge appointed by law nor more than ____ days after such a writ shall have been served on the person holding him in confinement & no order given on due examination for his remandment or discharge, nor more than ____ hours in any place at a greater distance than ____ miles from the usual residence of some judge authorized to issue the writ of Hab. corp., nor shall that writ be suspended for any term exceeding one year nor in any place more than ____ miles distant from the station or encampment of enemies or of insurgents. Art. 9. Monopolies may be allowed to persons for their own productions in literature & their own inventions in the arts, for a term not exceeding ____ years but for no longer term & no other purpose. Art. 10. All troops of the U. S. shall stand *ipso facto* disbanded at the expiration of the term for which their pay & subsistence shall have been last voted by Congress, and all officers & souldiers not natives of the U. S. shall be incapable of serving in their armies by land except during a foreign war." These restrictions I think are so guarded as to hinder evil only. However if we do not have them now, I have so much confidence in my countrymen as to be satisfied that we shall have them as soon as the degeneracy of our government shall render them necessary.

Ford, V, pp. 112-113. Also reprinted in *Papers*, XII, pp. 363-364, and in BRDH, II, p. 1143.

United States Senate September 4, 1789
Proceedings on Amendments Proposed by the House (excerpt)

On motion, Upon the fifth Article, to subjoin the following proposition, to wit:

"That standing armies, in time of peace, being dangerous to Liberty, should be avoided as far as the circumstances and protection of the community will admit; and that in all cases the military should be under strict subordination to, and governed by the civil Power.—That no standing army or regular troops shall be raised in time of peace, without the consent of two thirds of the Members present in both Houses, and that no soldier shall be inlisted for any longer term than the continuance of war."

Nays 9 Yeas 6

Did not pass.

On motion, To adopt the fifth Article of the Amendments proposed by the House of Representatives, amended to read as followeth—

"A well regulated militia, being the best security of a free State, the right of the people to keep and bear arms, shall not be infringed"—

It passed in the Affirmative.

DePauw, I, pp. 153-154.

George Mason (Gunston Hall) September 8, 1789
Letter: To Samuel Griffin (excerpt)

I have received much Satisfaction from the Amendments to the federal Constitution, which have lately passed the House of Representatives; I hope they will also pass the Senate. With two or three further Amendments—Such as confining the federal Judiciary to Admiralty & Maritime Jurisdiction, and to Subjects merely federal—fixing the Mode of Elections either in the Constitution itself (which I think wou'd be preferable) or securing the Regulation of them to the respective States—Requiring more than a bare Majority to make Navigation & Commercial Laws, and appointing a constitutional amenable council to the President, & lodging with them most of the Executive Powers now vested in the Senate—I cou'd chearfully put my Hand & Heart to the new Government.

Rutland, III, p. 1172.

Centinel, Revived, No. XXIX September 9, 1789
Newspaper Article: Philadelphia *Independent Gazetteer* (excerpts)

To the PEOPLE *of* PENNSYLVANIA.
Friends and Fellow-Citizens,

What would be your opinion of the man who, living where thieves were so numerous and vigilant as to improve every opportunity of plunder, should go to sleep at night in thoughtless security, with his doors wide open, trusting for the preservation of his property from depredation, to the care with which he had fastened the window shutters. Would you not laugh at his stupidity and folly?

Similar would be the conduct of the people of the United States, if they rest the security of their invaluable privileges upon the partial amendments making by Congress to the new constitution: for although many of these amendments are very proper and necessary, yet whilst the constitution is suffered to retain powers that may not only defeat their salutary operation, but may, and incontrovertibly will be so decisively injurious as to sweep away every vestige of liberty; it is an insult upon the understanding and discernment of the people to flatter them with the secure enjoyment of privileges, that are held by so precarious and transient a tenure.

Besides, some of even these limited, insecure amendments, which, to a superficial observer, seem to contain useful provisions, when examined with attention, are found to be delusive and inoperative. I will instance two or three of them. . . .

It was a serious objection to the new constitution, that as certain personal rights and privileges were expressly provided for, whilst many others were omitted, that agreeably to the usual and established rule of construction in such case, the latter were abrogated, or at best left at the mere discretion of Congress. To obviate the apprehensions of people on this head, a specious amendment is proposed, as follows, viz. Article the 15th. "The enumeration in the constitution of certain rights, shall not be construed to deny, or disparage others *retained* by the people." This sounds very well; But what is the amount of these shewy words when brought to the test of rational construction? why really nothing. For to give them any meaning or operation, it must be first shewn in what part of the new constitution there is any reservation made of the rights or privileges of the people, other than those expressly enumerated, which I challenge the most ingenious to do. The fact incontrovertibly is, that there are none retained but what are specifically inserted. This proposed amendment, therefore, makes no provision for the defect, and will be absolutely inoperative and nugatory.

Article 5th of the proposed amendments—"A well regulated militia, composed of the body of the people, being the best security of a free state, the right of the people to keep and bear arms, shall not be infinged, &c." It is remarkable that this article only makes the observation, "that a well regulated militia, composed of the *body* of the people, is the best security of a free state;" it does not ordain, or constitutionally provide for, the establishment of such a one. The absolute command vested by other sections in Congress over the militia, are not in the least abridged by this amendment. The militia may still be subjected to martial law and all its concomitant severities, and disgraceful punishments, may still be marched from state to state and made the unwilling instruments of crushing the last efforts of expiring liberty.

United States Senate September 9, 1789
Proceedings on Amendments Proposed by the House (excerpt)

On motion, To amend Article the fifth by inserting these words, "For the common defence," next to the words "Bear arms"—

It passed in the Negative.

On motion, To strike out of this Article, line the second, these words, "The best," and insert in lieu thereof "Necessary to the"

It passed in the Affirmative.

On motion, On Article the fifth, to strike out the word "Fifth," after "Article the," and insert "Fourth"—

And to amend the Article to read as follows,

"A well regulated militia being [necessary to] the security of a free State, the right of the people to keep and bear arms, shall not be infringed"—

It passed in the Affirmative.

DePauw, I, pp. 166-167.

James Madison (New York) September 14, 1789
Letter: To Edmund Pendleton (excerpt)

The Senate have sent back the plan of amendments with some alterations which strike in my opinion at the most salutary articles. In many of the States juries even in criminal cases, are taken from the State at large—in others from districts of conside[rable] extent—in very few from the County alone. Hence a [dis]like to the restraint with respect to *vicinage*, which has produced a negative on that clause. A fear of inconvenience from a constitutional bar to appeals below a certain value, and a confidence that such a limitation is not *necessary*, have had the same effect on another article. Several others have had a similar fate. The difficulty of uniting the minds of men accustomed to think and act differently can only be conceived by those who have witnessed it.

Papers, XII, p. 402.

Richard Henry Lee (New York) September 14, 1789
Letter: To Patrick Henry (excerpt)

I have since waited to see the issue of the proposed amendments to the constitution, that I might give you the most exact accounts of that business. As they came from the house of Representatives, they were far short of the wishes of our convention, but as they are returned by the Senate they are certainly much weakened. You may be assured that nothing on my part was left undone to prevent this, and every possible effort was used to give success to all the amendments proposed by our country. We might as well have attempted to move Mount Atlas upon our shoulders. In fact the idea of subsequent amendments, was little better than putting oneself to death first, in expectation that the doctor, who wished our destruction, would afterwards restore us to life. I am grieved to see too many look at the rights of the people as a miser examines a security, to find a flaw in it. The great points of free election, jury trial in criminal cases, and the unlimited rights of taxation, and standing armies, remain as they were. The most essential danger from the present system arises, in my opinion, from its tendency to a consolidated government, instead of a union of confederated states. The history of the world and reason concur in proving, that so extensive a territory as the United States comprehend, never was, or can be, governed in freedom under the former idea; under the latter it is abundantly more practicable, because extended representation, knowledge of characters, and confidence in consequence, secure that good opinion of rulers, without which fear, the offspring of force, can alone answer; for all free government resting on opinion, if that fails force must succeed; hence standing armies and despotism follow. I take this reasoning to be irrefutable, and therefore it becomes the friends of liberty to guard with perfect vigilance every right that belongs to the states, and to protest against every invasion of them, taking care always to procure as many protesting states as possible; this kind of vigilance will create caution, and establish such a mode of conduct as will create a system of precedent that will prevent a consolidating effect from taking place by slow but sure degrees. A sufficinet number of legislatures cannot be got at present to agree in demanding a convention, but I shall be very much mistaken indeed, if ere long a great sufficiency will not concur in this measure. The preamble to the amendments is really curious. A careless reader would be apt to suppose that the amendments desired by the states had been graciously granted, but when the thing done is compared with that desired, nothing can be more unlike. Some valuable rights are indeed declared, but the power to violate them to all intents and purposes remains unchanged.

Henry, III, pp. 399-400.

Archibald Maclaine (Wilmington, North Carolina) September 17, 1789

Letter: To John Hay (excerpt)

So far as I am informed of Elections, I am pleased with them —There are many good men elected who were left out last year—I am certain there are some, and I believe many, who will vote differently than what they did, when they had the honor to be Willie Jones's puppets—By the way, I do not hear anything of him, nor who are elected for Halifax & Northampton.—If he is a member, he has now a fair opportunity of changing sides, without incurring the charge of inconsistency, as the amendments proposed and carried by such a large majority, can leave no room to doubt of their adoption. In any event, I do not believe that Mr. Jones will a second time lead such a number by the nose.

DHFFE, IV, p. 320. This letter concerns the elections for the second North Carolina Convention called to ratify the United States Constitution.

State Gazette of North Carolina **September 24, 1789**

WILMINGTON, *September 10.*

The amendments to the constitution of the United States, proposed by congress will undoubtedly satisfy the minds of *all* its enemies. —Not a door is left open for complaint, should the amendments be ratified by three fourths of the legislatures of the several states.

Every friend to the Union may now with pleasure anticipate the adoption of the constitution by this state, and of its again becoming one of its members.

The enemies to the federal constitution in this state, says a correspondent, have nothing to boast in the completion of so desirable an object to them, as amendments to the constitution, this state not being represented in congress.

It is an almost unparalled instance, of a public body possessed of power, abridging it, and fully contradicts the grand argument of the opponents to the constitution, that—"*if Congress are once possessed of the power vested in the constitution, they never will relinquish or amend it conformable to our wishes.*"

DHFFE, IV, p. 321.

United States Congress September 26, 1789
Proposed Amendments to the Constitution

CONGRESS OF THE UNITED STATES.

Begun and held at the City of New-York, on Wednesday, the fourth of March, One thousand seven hundred and eighty-nine.

The CONVENTIONS of a number of the states having, at the time of their adopting the Constitution, expressed a desire, in order to prevent misconstruction or abuse of its powers, that further declaratory and restrictive clauses should be added: And as extending the ground of public confidence in the government will best insure the beneficent ends of its institution—

RESOLVED, by the Senate and House of Representatives of the United States of America, in Congress assembled, two thirds of both Houses concurring, that the following Articles be proposed to the Legislatures of the several states, as amendments to the Constitution of the United states, all or any of which articles, when ratified by three-fourths of the said Legislatures, to be valid to all intents and purposes, as part of the said Constitution, viz.

ARTICLES in addition to, and amendment of, the Constitution of the United States of America, proposed by Congress, and ratified by the legislatures of the several States, pursuant to the first [fifth] article of the original Constitution.

ART. I. After the first enumeration required by the first article of the Constitution, there shall be one representative for every thirty thousand, until the number shall amount to one hundred, after which the proportion shall be so regulated by Congress, that there shall be no less than one hundred representatives, nor less than one representative for every forty thousand persons, until the number of representatives shall amount to two hundred, after which the proportion shall be so regulated by Congress, that there shall not be less than two hundred representatives, nor more than one representative for every fifty thousand persons.

ART. II. No law varying the compensation for the services of the Senators and Representatives shall take effect, until an election of representatives shall have intervened.

ART. III. Congress shall make no laws respecting an establishment of religion, or prohibiting the free exercise thereof, or abridging the freedom of speech, or of the press; or the right of the people peaceably to assemble, and to petition the government for a redress of grievances.

ART. IV. A well regulated militia being necessary to the security of a free State, the right of the people to keep and bear arms shall not be infringed.

ART. V. No soldier shall, in time of peace, be quartered in any house, without the consent of the owner, nor in time of war, but in a manner to be prescribed by law.

ART. VI. The right of the people to be secure in their persons, houses, papers, and effects, against unreasonable searches and seizures, shall not be violated, and no warrants shall issue, but upon probable cause, supported by oath or affirmation, and particularly describing the place to be searched, and the persons or things to be seized.

ART. VII. No person shall be held to answer for a capital or otherwise infamous crime, unless on a presentment or indictment of a grand jury, except in cases arising in the land or naval forces, or in the militia, when in actual service in time of war or public danger; nor shall any person be subject for the same offence to be twice put in jeopardy of life or limb; nor shall be compelled in any criminal case to be a witness against himself, nor be deprived of life, liberty or property, without due process of law; nor shall private property be taken for public use without just compensation.

ART. VIII. In all criminal prosecutions, the accused shall enjoy the right to a speedy and public trial, by an impartial jury of the State and district wherein the crime shall have been committed, which district shall have been previously ascertained by law, and to be informed of the nature and cause of the accusation: to be confronted with the witnesses against him; to have compulsory process for obtaining witnesses in his favor, and to have the assistance of counsel for his defence.

ART. IX. In suits at common law, where the value in controversy shall exceed twenty dollars, the right of trial by jury shall be preserved, and no fact, tried by a jury, shall be otherwise re-examined in any court of the United States, than according to the rules of the common law.

ART. X. Excessive bail shall not be required, nor excessive fines imposed, nor cruel and unusual punishments inflicted.

ART. XI. The enumeration in the Constitution, of certain rights, shall not be construed to deny or disparage others retained by the people.

ART. XII. The powers not delegated to the United States by the Constitution, nor prohibited by it to the States, are reserved to the States respectively, or to the people.

Philadelphia *Federal Gazette*, November 28, 1789, p. 3.

Richard Henry Lee (New York) September 27, 1789
Letter: To Patrick Henry (excerpts)

My third letter to you on the 14th inst will satisfy you how little is to be expected from Congress, that shall be any ways satisfactory on the subject of amendments. Your observation is perfectly just, that right without power to protect it, is of little avail. Yet small as it is, how wonderfully scrupulous have they been in stating rights? The english language has been carefully culled to find words feeble in their nature, or doubtful in their meaning. . . . By an address, received two days ago from the Assembly of R. Island (copy of which I will send you by my brother) to the federal government, it appears to me as if they intended to keep out of the Union until effectual amendments were made. We ought in common prudence to have done the same. Does N. C. design to act in the same manner?

Henry, III, p. 402-404. Lee was a United States Senator from Virginia.

William Grayson (New York) September 29, 1789
Letter: To Patrick Henry (excerpt)

With respect to amendments matters have turned out exactly as I apprehended from the extraordinary doctrine of playing the after game. The lower house sent up amendments which held out a safeguard to personal liberty in great many instances, but this disgusted the senate, and though we made every exertion to save them, they are so mutilated and gutted that in fact they are good for nothing, and I believe, as many others do, that they will do more harm than benefit. The Virginia amendments were all brought into view and regularly rejected. Perhaps they may think differently on the subject the next session; as Rhode Island has refused for the present acceding to the constitution; her reasons you will see in the printed papers.

Henry, III, p. 406. Grayson was a United States Senator from Virginia.

President George Washington (New York) October 2, 1789
Letter: To Governor Samuel Huntington of Connecticut[1]

In pursuance of the enclosed resolution I have the honor to transmit to your Excellency a copy of the amendments proposed to be added to the Constitution of the United States.

I have the honor to be with due consideration Your Excellency's most obedient Servant.

Resolution

Congress of the United States, In the House of Representatives,
Thursday, the 24th of September 1789

Resolved by the Senate and House of Representatives of the United States of America in Congress assembled, that the President of the United States be requested to transmit to the Executives of the several States which have ratified the Constitution, Copies of the Amendments proposed by Congress, to be added thereto; and like Copies to the Executives of the States of Rhode Island and North Carolina.

Attest,
John Beckley, Clerk

United States of America
In Senate, September the 26th 1789

Resolved, that the Senate do concur in this Resolution.

Attest,
Sam. A. Otis, Secy.

[Here followed the twelve proposed amendments.][2]

1 BRDH, II, pp. 1172-1173.
2 See "United States Congress," September 26, 1789, p. 715, for the proposed amendments.

New York *Gazette of the United States* October 14, 1789
(excerpts)

Extract of a letter from Fayette-Ville, North-Carolina, dated September 12.

"I think there is not a doubt that the Convention which is to meet here in November will adopt the Constitution—the amendments will do the business.

The right of the people to keep and bear arms has been recognized by the General Government; but the best security of that right after all is, that military spirit, that taste for martial exercises, which has always distinguished the free citizens of these States: From various parts of the Continent the most pleasing accounts are published of reviews and parades in large and small assemblies of the militia.—The people appear determined to avail themselves of the circumstance, which our patriotic and beloved President pointed out in one of his messages to Congress, viz. That fund of military knowledge which is diffused through the States by the officers of the late Continental Army. A spirit of emulation is excited; and not only in cities and towns, where the people being more compact, can with greater ease concert and carry their plans into execution—but in the country towns also, whole Regiments are clothed in Uniform—and bodies of Horse completely equipped have been raised and disciplined.—Such men form the best barrier to the Liberties of America.—And when called to defend their Country—they fight for all that gives worth to existence.

James Madison (Orange) November 20, 1789
Letter: To George Washington (excerpt)

[T]he amendments have been taken up [in the Virginia Assembly], and are likely to be put off to the next Session, the present house having been elected prior to the promulgation of them. This reason would have more force, if the amendments did not so much correspond as far as they go with the propositions of the State Convention, which were before the public long before the last Election. At any rate, the Assembly might pass a vote of *approbation* along with the postponement, and Assign the reason of referring the *ratification* to their successors. It is probably that the scruple has arisen with the disaffected party. If it be construed by the public into a latent hope of some contingent opportunity for prosecuting the war agst. the Genl.

Government; I am of opinion the experiment will recoil on the authors of it. As far as I can gather, the great bulk of the late opponents are entirely at rest, and more likely to censure a further opposition to the Govt. as now Administered than the Government itself. One of the principal leaders of the Baptists lately sent me word that the amendments had entirely satisfied the disaffected of his Sect, and that it would appear in their subsequent conduct.

Papers, XII, p. 453.

New Jersey Council November 20, 1789
Ratification of proposed Amendments to the Constitution. (excerpt)

Article the fourth. A well regulated Militia being necessary to the security of a free State the right of the people to keep and bear Arms shall not be infringed.

DHC, II, p. 327. See "United States Congress," September 26, 1789, p. 715, for the proposed Amendments. New Jersey ratified all of the proposals except number 2 relating to the pay of Senators and Representatives.

Hardin Burnley (Richmond) November 28, 1789
Letter: To James Madison (excerpt)

The fate of the Amendments proposed by Congress to the General Government is still in suspence [in the Virginia Assembly]. In a committee of the whole house the fi[r]st ten were acceeded to with but little opposition for on a question taken, on each seperately, there was scarcely a dissenting voice. On the two last a debate of some length took place, which ended in rejection. Mr. E[dmund] Randolph who advocated all the others stood in this contest in the front of opposition. His principal objection was pointed against the word *retained* in the eleventh proposed amendment, and his argument if I understood it was applied in this manner, that as the rights declared in the first ten of the proposed amendments were not all that a free people would require the exercise of; and that as there was no criterion by which it could be determined whether any other particular right was retained or not, it would be more safe, & more consistant with the spirit of the 1st. & 17th. amendments proposed by Virginia, that this reservation against constructive power, should operate rather as a provision against extending the powers of Congress by their own authority, than as a protection to rights reducable to no definitive certainty. But others among whom I am one see not the force of the distinction, for by preventing an extension of power in that body from which danger is apprehended safety will be ensured if its powers are not too extensive already, & so by protecting the rights of the people & of the States, an improper extension of power will be prevented & safety made equally certain. If the house should agree to the resolution for rejecting the two last I am of opinion that it will bring the whole into hazzard again, as some who have been decided friends to the ten first think it woud be unwise to adopt them without the 11th. & 12th.

Papers, XII, p. 456. Reprinted in BRDH, II, pp. 1188-1189.

Hardin Burnley (Richmond) [December] 5, 1789
Letter: To James Madison (excerpt)

Since the date of my letter to you which I wrote a few days ago the resolutions of the Committee on the amendments proposed by Congress have been reported. Those which respect the ten first were agreed to with even less opposition than they experienced in the Committee, & that wh. passed on the 11th & 12th. was rescinded by a majority of about twelve. The amendments with the resolutions on them are now with the Senate, where from the best information which I have been able to collect there is such a division in opinion as not to furnish a ground for probable conjecture as to their decision. Some of that body I am informed propose rejection in toto, others adoption, & others again wish to postpone a decision on them 'till next Session of assembly. I believe it may be said with certainty that the greater part of those who wish either to postpone or reject, are not dissatisfied with the amendments so far as they have gone, but are apprehensive that the adoption of them at this time will be an obstacle to the chief object of their persuit, the amendment on the subject of direct taxation.

Papers, XII, p. 460. Letter misdated November. Also reprinted in BRDH, II, pp. 1184-1185. Burnley is referring to actions by the Virginia Legislature concerning the amendments proposed by Congress.

James Madison (Orange) December 5, 1789
Letter: To George Washington (excerpt)[1]

The difficulty started agst. the amendments [in the Virginia Assembly] is really unlucky, and the more to be regretted as it springs from a friend to the Constitution. It is still greater cause of regret, if the distinction be, as it appears to me, altogether fanciful. If a line can be drawn between the powers granted and the rights retained, it would seem to be the same thing, whether the latter be secured, by declaring that they shall not be abridged, or that the former shall not be extended. If no line can be drawn, a declaration in either form would amount to nothing. If the distinction were just it does not seem to be of sufficient importance to justify the risk of losing the amendts. of furnishing a handle to the disaffected, and of arming N. C. with a pretext, if she be disposed, to prolong her exile from the Union.

1 *Papers*, XII, p. 459. Reprinted in BRDH, II, p. 1190.
2 Hardin Burnley's letter to Madison (November 28, 1789, p. 720) was repeated verbatim by Madison in this letter to Washington.

Virginia Senate December 12, 1789
Objections to and Reasons for Postponement of Articles 3, 8, 11, and 12 of the Proposed Amendments to the United States Constitution.[1]
Published: Richmond *Virginia Independent Chronicle*, January 13, 1790.

The Senate of Virginia having determined to postpone until the next session of Assembly, the third, eighth, eleventh, and twelfth[2] articles of the amendments to the Constitution of the United States, recommended by Congress, we, the underwritten members of the majority on that question, deem it incumbent on us, not only from the respect we owe to our constituents, and our responsibility to them, but in order to prevent doubt and misrepresentation, to enter on the Journals of the House the considerations which have influenced our decision on this subject, and our principal objections to those articles. We are satisfied that the people of Virginia would never have ratified the Constitution of the United States, but from a confident hope and firm persuasion of speedily seeing it much more materially altered and amended than it would be by ratifying the propositions lately submitted by Congress to the State Legislatures. That although we consider some of the amendments offered as similar, and others nearly equivalent, to a part of the amendments proposed by Virginia and other States, yet that some of them which seem analogous to other amendments so proposed, are not substantially the same and fall short of affording the same security to personal rights, or of so effectually guarding against the apprehended mischiefs of the government; of this description we consider the 3rd, 8th, 11th and 12th articles. We conceive that the 3rd article, which seems given in lieu of the 15th, 16th, 19th and 20th[3] articles of the bill of rights proposed by the Virginia Convention, will not bear a comparison with these articles. The 15th expressly declares the rights of the people to assemble together to consult for the common good, to instruct their representatives, and to petition for redress of grievances. The 16th asserts the right of the people to freedom of speech, and of writing and publishing their sentiments, and secures the liberty of the press. The 19th and 20th hold sacred the rights of conscience, secure to every religious sect or society the most perfect equality, and effectually guard against any religious establishments.

The 3rd amendment, recommended by Congress, does not prohibit the rights of conscience from being violated or infringed; and although it goes to restrain Congress from passing laws establishing any national religion, they might, notwithstanding, levy taxes to any amount, for the support of religion or its preachers; and any particular denomination of Christians might be so favored and supported by the General Government as to give it a decided advantage over others, and in process of time render it as powerful and dangerous as if it was established as the national religion of the country.

This amendment does not declare and assert the right of the people to speak and publish their sentiments, nor does it secure the liberty of the press. Should these valuable rights be infringed or violated by the arbitrary decisions of Judges, or by any other means than a legislative act directly to that effect, the people would have no avowed principle in the Constitution to which they might resort for the security of these rights.

The right of the people to instruct their representatives, and their right to consult with each other for the common good, seem too evident to be questioned in a republican government; yet, these rights are denied by Congress, and they have refused to allow any amendment declaratory of them, as we discover by their Journals; and even the humble privilege of petitioning against oppression is not fully asserted or secured; as this privilege may be abridged or rendered nugatory without any law upon the subject; not to mention other means, it migh be defeated by a rule of either House, without violating the 3rd article of the amendments.

This amendment then, when considered as it relates to any of the rights it is pretended to secure, will be found totally inadequate, and betrays an unreasonable, unjustifiable, but a studied departure from the amendment proposed by Virginia and other States, for the protection of their rights. We conceive that this amendment is dangerous and fallacious, as it tends to lull the apprehensions of the people on these important points, without affording them security; and mischievous, because by setting bounds to Congress, it will be considered as the only restriction on their power over these rights; and thus certain powers in the government, which it has been denied to possess, will be recognized without being properly guarded against abuse.

The 8th article of the proposed amendments, so far from securing the valuable trial by jury of the vicinage in criminal prosecutions, leaves Congress the same power to abridge this right as they possess by the original Constitution. They have already by law fixed the district co-extensive with the respective States; and they will at all times possess the power of regulating the districts at pleasure, so that there appears to us nothing in this amendment to restrain government from carrying a man accused of a crime, out of his own neighborhood to any distance within the limits of a State, to be tried by strangers, perhaps enemies, where the advantages of this excellent mode of trial might be entirely defeated, and where a person obnoxious to Congress, might fall an innocent sacrifice to their resentment.

We do not find that the 11th article is asked for by Virginia or any other state; we therefore conceive that the people of Virginia should be consulted with respect to it, even if we did not doubt the propriety of adopting it; but it appears to us highly exceptionable. If it is meant to guard against the extension of the powers of Congress by implication, it is greatly defective, and does by no means comprehend the idea expressed in the 17th article of amendments proposed by Virginia; and as it respects personal rights might be dangerous, because should the rights of the people be invaded or called in question, they might be required to show by the Constitution what rights they have *retained;* and such as could not from that instrument be proved to be retained, they might be denied to possess. Of this there is ground to be apprehensive, when Congress are already seen denying certain rights of the people heretofore deemed clear and unexceptionable.

We conceive that the 12th article would come up to the 1st article of the Virginia amendments, were it not for the words 'or to the people.' It is not declared to be the people of the respective States; but the expression applies to the people generally as citizens of the United States, and leaves it doubtful what powers are reserved to the State Legislatures. Unrestrained by the Constitution or these amendments, Congress, might, as the supreme ruler of the people, assume those powers which properly belong to the respective States, and thus gradually effect an entire consolidation.

We consider that of the many and important amendments recommended by the Conventions of Virginia and other States, these propositions contain all that Congress are disposed to grant; that all the rest are by them deemed improper, and that these are offered in full satisfaction of the whole: and although the ratification of a part of the amendments that have been prayed for by Virginia would not absolutely preclude us from urging others, yet we conceive that by the acceptance of particular articles, we are concluded as to the points they relate to. Considering therefore that they are far short of what the people of Virginia wish, and have asked, and deeming them by no means sufficient to secure the rights of the people, or to render the government safe and desirable, we think our countrymen ought not to be put off with amendments so inadequate.

That being satisfied of the defects and dangerous tendency of these four articles of the proposed amendments, we are constrained to withhold our assent to them; but unwilling for the present to determine on their rejection, we think it our duty to postpone them until the next session of Assembly, in order that the people of Virginia may have an opportunity to consider of them, and judge for themselves; and that the members of the Legislature may be enabled to consult with, and know the sentiments of their constituents on the subject.

1 Rowland, II, pp. 320-323.

2 For the amendments proposed by Congress, see "United States Congress," September 26, 1789, p. 715.

3 For the bill of rights amendments proposed by Virginia, see "Virginia Convention," June 27, 1788, pp. 456-459.

John Dawson (Richmond) December 17, 1789

Letter: To James Madison (excerpt)

The amendments recommended by Congress were taken up and all of them pass'd our house—the Senate amended the resolution by posponing the consideration of the 3d, 8th, 11th, & 12th, untill the next session of assembly—we adher'd, and so did they. A conference took place, and both houses remain'd obstinate, consequently the whole resolution was lost, and none of the amendments will be adopted by this assembly.

Papers, XII, p. 461. Dawson's comments relate to actions in the Virginia Legislature. See "Virginia Senate," December 12, 1789, directly above, regarding the Senate's reasons for postponing articles 3, 8, 11, and 12 of the proposed amendments.

Maryland Senate December 19, 1789
Ratification of proposed Amendments to the Constitution. (excerpt)

Article the fourth. A well regulated Militia being necessary to the security of a free State, the right of the people to keep and bear Arms, shall not be infringed.

DHC, II, p. 332. See "United States Congress," September 26, 1789, p. 715, for the twelve proposed Amendments. Maryland ratified all twelve proposals.

Edward Carrington (Richmond) December 20, 1789
Letter: To James Madison (excerpt)

Somewhat later in the [Virginia Assembly] session the subject of the amendments was taken up—the ten first were, with the exception of perhaps not more than ten Members, unanimously agreed to—on the eleventh and twelfth some difficulty arose, from Mr. E. Randolphs objecting to them as unsatisfactory—after much debate they were rejected in the Committee of the whole but the report being defered a few days they were accepted in the House by a pretty good Majority thus the whole were adopted in the lower house—they went to the senate in one resolution where they remained long—the resolution at length returned with a proposition to amend by striking out the 3d. 8th. 11th. & 12, these to be refered to the consideration of the people. To this amendment the lower house disagreed and requested a conference—the Senate insisted, and assented to the conference, this was however, productive of conviction on neither side, the Committee on the part of the Senate returned with S. T. Mason at their head, to their House, which upon his Motion, immediately adhered before any thing further passed between the two Houses; the delegates could in no stage have seen cause to recede from their disagreement, but under this intemperate and unprecendented Conduct they were left without a choice of any thing but to adhere also, and thus the whole amendments have fallen. The sense of the house of delegates was fairly & fully passed on the propriety of adopting them, and the intemperance manifested in the conduct of the Senate, will doubtless shew the people whether this fate of the amendments, was produced from a want of merit in them, or in the senate. Through the whole course of the business in that house there was on the several questions equal divisions of the members, so, as to leave the decision to the chair. Notwithstanding the unequivocal decision in the house of delegates for adopting the amendments, yet in the course of the discussion some intemperance was generated—this led to propositions which in the earlier parts of the session none would have thought of, and it was with difficulty that a proposition for demanding a compliance with the amendments proposed by our convention, so far as they have not been agreed to, by Congress was prevented from passing. This proposition was presented to the house as often as three times, at first it was rejected by a great majority, at the next attempt it was rejected by a less majority, and at the third by the vote of the Speaker. Had Mr. Henry conceived that such would have been the temper in the latter stages of the session, he would not have left us. My information from the various parts of the Country is that the people are at ease on the subject of amendments, expecting nothing but that those sent on would be adopted and that others will be supplied as further deliberation and experience shall discover the want of them. This I think I am warranted in supposing to be true, because the heats which have appeared in the latter part of the session would have shewn themselves sooner had they been amongst the people when their representatives came from their Counties, but they have been generated here in the course of the discussions upon the amendments.

Papers, XII, pp. 463-465. Reprinted in BRDH, II, pp. 1192-1193.

Governor Alexander Martin December 22, 1789

Message from the Governor to the General Assembly of North Carolina (excerpt)

Received from his Excellency the Governor the following message:

To the Honourable the General Assembly.

Gentlemen, . . .

Although some of the great establishments [of the Federal Government] have been formed, in which it is to be wished this state had borne her part at an earlier period, yet an ample field is still open to distinguish herself, and give weight to the continental scale. Perhaps it is all for the better that this state hesitated, and was not precipitate in ratifying a form of government intended to last for ages, without maturely deliberating how far the lives, liberties and properties of her citizens were to be protected and secured by it—a jealousy of their rulers ought to subsist in all free governments, as the grand check that freedom hath over tyranny.

DHFFE, IV, p. 350.

North Carolina General Assembly December 22, 1789
Ratification of proposed Amendments to the Constitution. (excerpt)

Article IV A well regulated militia being necessary to the security of a free State, the right of the people to keep and bear arms, shall not be infringed.

DHC, II, p. 337. See "United States Congress," September 26, 1789, p. 715, for the proposed Amendments to the Constitution. North Carolina ratified all twelve proposals.

Philadelphia *Independent Gazetteer* December 28, 1789

AN IDEA OF A CONSTITUTION.

TO secure an equality of right to each, and the greatest quantity of happiness to all is the great end of human society. To effect this every individual brings into the public stock all that quantity of power and of privilege, the exercise of which is not necessary to his own existence, happiness, and rank in nature: and this collective mass of authority is committed to the management of one or of a few. But there are some rights too essential to be delegated—too sacred to be infringed. These each individual reserves to himself; in the free enjoyment of these the whole society engages to protect him; and this engagement is the principle and foundation of government—All these essential and sacred rights, it would be difficult, if not impossible, to recount, but some, in every social compact, it is proper to enumerate, as specimens of many others, as illustrations of the general nature of all, and as useful memorials to the people of the existence, nature, extent, and limitation of those powers which are neither to be transferred nor obstructed. Moreover, in establishing the frame and operation of government, all powers intrusted to any man, or any number of men, ought to be distinctly and accurately defined—Thus the people knowing their privileges, and the Magistates their authority, all incroachments, made by the one body on the other, may be plainly discerned, and speedily restrained.

Philadelphia *Pennsylvania Packet* December 29, 1789

New York, Dec. 23 . . . The amendments to the constitution proposed by Congress to the several states, appear to receive that cordial approbation which does honour to the candour and patriotism of the respective state legislatures, to whom they have been submitted. If they do not in every respect meet the ideas of those who never liked the constitution, it ought to be remembered that they are the result of a concession on the part of the majority, who were satisfied with the system in its original form—but from the best motives were induced to aquiesce in amendments to reconcile, if possible, opposition, and to conciliate the doubting.

1 BRDH, II, p. 1180.

Philadelphia *Federal Gazette* January 5, 1790
(excerpt)

A bill of rights for freemen appears to be a contradiction in terms. From whom are they received? From themselves? Do freemen relinquish those rights that are not specified in a bill? To whom do they relinquish them? To themselves, or their rulers? Who are their rulers but the creatures of their own forming? If freemen retain no rights but those specified in a bill, they divest themselves of *thousands*, where they retain *one*. What avails a bill of rights to those who violate the laws? and in a free country, every right of human natu[r]e which are as numerous as sands upon the sea shore, belong to the quiet, peaceable citizen.

President George Washington January 8, 1790
Speech to both Houses of Congress (excerpts)

Among the many interesting objects which will engage your attention, that of providing for the common defence will merit particular regard.—To be prepared for war, is one of the most effectual means of preserving peace.

A free people ought not only to be armed, but disciplined; to which end a uniform and well digested plan is requisite: And their safety and interest require that they should promote such manufactories as tend to render them independent on others, for essential, particularly for military supplies. . . . Knowledge is in every country the surest basis of public happiness. In one in which the measures of government receive their impression so immediately from the sense of the community, as in ours, it is proportionably essential. To the security of a free Constitution it contributes in various ways: by convincing those who are entrusted with the public administration, that every valuable end of government is best answered by the enlightened confidence of the people: And by teaching the people themselves to know and to value their own rights: to discern and provide against invasions of them; to distinguish between oppression and the necessary exercise of lawful authority; between burthens proceeding from a disregard to their convenience, and those resulting from the inevitable exigencies of society; to discriminate the spirit of liberty from that of licentiousness, cherishing the first, avoiding the last, and uniting a speedy but temperate vigilance against encroachments, with an inviolable respect to the laws.

Providence Gazette, January 16, 1790, p. 2.

South Carolina Senate January 19, 1790
Ratification of proposed Amendments to the Constitution. (excerpt)

"Article 4th A well regulated Militia being necessary to the security of a free State, the right of the people to keep and bear Arms shall not be infringed"—

DHC, II, p. 342. See "United States Congress," September 26, 1789, p. 715, for Congress' proposals to amend the Constitution. South Carolina ratified all twelve proposed Amendments.

New Hampshire Legislature January 25, 1790
[On this date the New Hampshire Legislature voted to ratify all of the proposed Amendments to the Constitution, except the second relating to the compensation of Senators and Representatives.]

DHC, II, p. 346. See "United States Congress," September 26, 1789, p. 715, for the proposed Amendments.

Delaware Legislature January 28, 1790
Ratification of proposed Amendments to the Constitution. (excerpt)

Article the Fourth,......A well regulated Militia, being necessary to the security of a free State, the right of the people to keep and bear arms, shall not be infringed.

DHC, II, p. 349. See "United States Congress," September 26, 1789, p. 715, for the proposed Amendments. Delaware ratified all except number 1 relating to the ratio of Representatives to population.

Governor John Hancock January 28, 1790

Newspaper Article: *New York Journal*

On the 9th inst. his Excellency the Governor of Massachusetts made a speech to both houses of the Legislature. In this speech his Excellency, among many important matters, mentions the amendments to the Constitution of the United States on which he observes:—"In all free governments, a share in the administration of the laws aught to be vested in, or reserved to the people; this prevents a government from verging towards despotism, secures the freedom of debate, and supports that independence of sentiment, which dignifies the citizen, and renders the government permanently respectable. The institutions of grand and petit Juries are admirably calculated to produce these happy effects, and to afford security to the best rights of men in civil society: These articles, therefore, I believe will meet your ready approbation: Some of the others appear to me as very important to that personal security which is so truly characteristic of a free government.["] After speaking of the state of the union, he observes:—"Notwithstanding a general government is well established by the free consent of the people, we are to continue to support our own government, with unabating anxiety for its welfare and prosperity: indeed, the general government of the United States is founded in an assemblage of republican governments; and it depends essentially on these, not only for its dignity and energy, but for its very existence in the form it now possesses; therefore, whatever is done to support the commonwealth, has a tendency to advance the interest and honor of all the states. Hence we are called upon in an especial manner, to maintain an equal and regular system of revenue and taxation, to support the faith, and perform the engagements of our republic; to arm and cause our militia to be disciplined according to the mode which shall be provided by Congress; and to see that they are officered with men, who are capable of making the greatest progress in the art military, and who delight in the freedom and happiness of their country. A well regulated and disciplined militia, is at all times a good objection to the introduction of that bane of all free governments—a standing army."

BRDH, II, pp. 1178-1179.

New York Senate February 24, 1790
Ratification of proposed Amendments to the Constitution. (excerpt)

ARTICLE THE FOURTH..A well regulated Militia being necessary to the Security of a free State, the right of the People to keep and bear arms shall not be infringed.

DHC, II, p. 359. See "United States Congress," September 26, 1789, p. 715, for the proposed Amendments. New York ratified all of the proposals except number 2 relating to the compensation of Senators and Representatives.

Pennsylvania General Assembly March 10, 1790
Ratification of proposed Amendments to the Constitution. (excerpt)

"Article 4th A well regulated Militia being necessary to the security of a free State, the right of the people to keep and bear Arms shall not be infringed.["]

DHC, II, p. 354. See "United States Congress," September 26, 1789, p. 715, for the proposed Amendments. Pennsylvania ratified all except numbers 1 and 2 on this date. It later reconsidered and adopted number 1 on September 21, 1791.

Governor Arthur Fenner (Rhode Island) May 20, 1790
Letter: To President George Washington (excerpt)

And since the Publication of the Constitution and the Adoption of it by the other States the Various and numerous proceedings of the legislature [of Rhode Island] respecting it, from time to time, have been [more?] influenced by party considerations than a determination finally to reject it. And as I can now assure your Excellency that all the other States having joined the New Confederacy and many important Amendments having been proposed, some of which have already been agreed to, many persons of influence who have heretofore opposed the Adoption of the New Constitution here, have withdrawn their opposition, There is therefore reason to suppose that it will be very soon adopted in this State[.]

DHFFE, IV, p. 398.

Rhode Island Convention May 29, 1790
[The Constitution of the United States of America precedes the following ratification.]

Ratification of the Constitution by the Convention of the State of Rhode Island and Providence Plantations.

We, the delegates of the people of the state of Rhode Island and Providence Plantations, duly elected and met in Convention, having maturely considered the Constitution for the United States of America, agreed to on the seventeenth day of September, in the year one thousand seven hundred and eighty-seven, by the Convention then assembled at Philadelphia, in the commonwealth of Pennsylvania, (a copy whereof precedes these presents,) and having also seriously and deliberately considered the present situation of this state, do declare and make known,—

I. That there are certain natural rights of which men, when they form a social compact, cannot deprive or divest their posterity, —among which are the enjoyment of life and liberty, with the means of acquiring, possessing, and protecting property, and pursuing and obtaining happiness and safety.

II. That all power is naturally vested in, and consequently derived from, the people; that magistrates, therefore, are their trustees and agents, and at all times amenable to them.

III. That the powers of government may be reassumed by the people whensoever it shall become necessary to their happiness. That the rights of the states respectively to nominate and appoint all state officers, and every other power, jurisdiction, and right, which is not by the said Constitution clearly delegated to the Congress of the United States, or to the departments of government thereof, remain to the people of the several states, or their respective state governments, to whom they may have granted the same; and that those clauses in the Constitution which declare that Congress shall not have or exercise certain powers, do not imply that Congress is entitled to any powers not given by the said Constitution; but such clauses are to be construed as exceptions to certain specified powers, or as inserted merely for greater caution.

IV. That religion, or the duty which we owe to our Creator, and the manner of discharging it, can be directed only by reason and conviction, and not by force and violence; and therefore all men have a natural, equal, and unalienable right to the exercise of religion according to the dictates of conscience; and that no particular religious sect or society ought to be favored or established, by law, in preference to others.

V. That the legislative, executive, and judiciary powers of government should be separate and distinct; and, that the members of the two first may be restrained from oppression, by feeling and participating the public burdens, they should, at fixed periods, be reduced to a private station, returned into the mass of the people, and the vacancies be supplied by certain and regular elections, in which all or any part of the former members to be eligible or ineligible, as the rules of the constitution of government and the laws shall direct.

VI. That elections of representatives in legislature ought to be free and frequent, and all men having sufficient evidence of permanent common interest with, and attachment to, the community, ought to have the right of suffrage; and no aid, charge, tax, or fee, can be set, rated, or levied, upon the people without their own consent, or that of their representatives so elected, nor can they be bound by any law to which they have not in like manner consented for the public good.

VII. That all power of suspending laws, or the execution of laws, by any authority, without the consent of the representatives of the people in the legislature, is injurious to their rights, and ought not to be exercised.

VIII. That, in all capital and criminal prosecutions, a man hath the right to demand the cause and nature of his accusation, to be confronted with the accusers and witnesses, to call for evidence, and be allowed counsel in his favor, and to a fair and speedy trial by an impartial jury in his vicinage, without whose unanimous consent he cannot be found guilty, (except in the government of the land and naval forces,) nor can he be compelled to give evidence against himself.

IX. That no freeman ought to be taken, imprisoned, or disseized of his freehold, liberties, privileges, or franchises, or outlawed, or exiled, or in any manner destroyed or deprived of his life, liberty, or property, but by the trial by jury, or by the law of the land.

X. That every freeman restrained of his liberty is entitled to a remedy, to inquire into the lawfulness thereof, and to remove the same if unlawful, and that such remedy ought not to be denied or delayed.

XI. That in conroversies respecting property, and in suits between man and man, the ancient trial by jury, as hath been exercised by us and our ancestors, from the time whereof the memory of man is not to the contrary is one of the greatest securities to the rights of the people, and ought to remain sacred and inviolable.

XII. That every freeman ought to obtain right and justice, freely and without sale, completely and without denial, promptly and without delay; and that all establishments or regulations contravening these rights are oppressive and unjust.

XIII. That excessive bail ought not to be required, nor excessive fines imposed, nor cruel or unusual punishments inflicted.

XIV. That every person has a right to be secure from all unreasonable searches and seizures of his person, his papers, or his property; and therefore, that all warrants to search suspected places, to seize any person, his papers, or his property, without information upon oath or affirmation of sufficient cause, are grievous and oppressive; and that all general warrants (or such in which the place or person suspected are not particularly designated) are dangerous, and ought not to be granted.

XV. That the people have a right peaceably to assemble together to consult for their common good, or to instruct their representatives; and that every person has a right to petition or apply to the legislature for redress of grievances.

XVI. That the people have a right to freedom of speech, and of writing and publishing their sentiments. That freedom of the press is one of the greatest bulwarks of liberty, and ought not to be violated.

XVII. That the people have a right to keep and bear arms; that a well-regulated militia, including the body of the people capable of bearing arms, is the proper, natural, and safe defence of a free state; that the militia shall not be subject to martial law, except in time of war, rebellion, or insurrection; that standing armies, in time of peace, are dangerous to liberty, and ought not to be kept up, except in cases of necessity; and that, at all times, the military should be under strict subordination to the civil power; that, in time of peace, no soldier ought to be quartered in any house without the consent of the owner, and in time of war only by the civil magistrates, in such manner as the law directs.

XVIII. That any person religiously scrupulous of bearing arms ought to be exempted upon payment of an equivalent to employ another to bear arms in his stead.

Under these impressions, and declaring that the rights aforesaid cannot be abridged or violated, and that the explanations aforesaid are consistent with the said Constitution, and in confidence that the amendments hereafter mentioned will receive an early and mature consideration, and, conformably to the fifth article of said Constitution, speedily become a part thereof,—We, the said delegates, in the name and in the behalf of the people of the state of Rhode Island and Providence Plantations, do, by these presents, assent to and ratify the said Constitution. In full confidence, nevertheless, that, until the amendments hereafter proposed and undermentioned shall be agreed to and ratified, pursuant to the aforesaid fifth article, the militia of this state will not be continued in service out of this state, for a longer term than six weeks, without the consent of the legislature thereof; that the Congress will not make or alter any regulation in this state respecting the times, places, and manner, of holding elections for senators or representatives, unless the legislature of this state shall neglect or refuse to make laws or regulations for the purpose, or, from any circumstance, be incapable of making the same; and that, in those cases, such power will only be exercised until the legislature of this state shall make provision in the premises; that the Congress will not lay direct taxes within this state, but when the moneys arising from impost, tonnage, and excise, shall be insufficient for the public exigencies, nor until the Congress shall have first made a requisition upon this state to assess, levy, and pay, the amount of such requisition made agreeable to the census fixed in the said Constitution, in such way and manner as the legislature of this state shall judge best; and that congress will not lay any capitation or poll tax.

Done in Convention, at Newport, in the county of Newport, in the state of Rhode Island and Providence Plantations, the twenty-ninth day of May, in the year of our Lord one thousand seven hundred and ninety, and in the fourteenth year of the independence of the United States of America.

By order of the Convention.
(signed) DANIEL OWEN, *President*
Attest. DANIEL UPDIKE, *Secretary*

And the Convention do, in the name and behalf of the people of the state of Rhode Island and Providence Plantations, enjoin it upon their senators and representatives, which may be elected to represent this state in Congress, to exert all their influence, and use all reasonable means, to obtain a ratification of the following amendments to the said Constitution, in the manner prescribed therein; and in all laws to be passed by the Congress in the mean time, to conform to the spirit of the said amendments, as far as the Constitution will admit.

AMENDMENTS

I. The United States shall guaranty to each state its sovereignty, freedom, and independence, and every power, jurisdiction, and right, which is not by this Constitution expressly delegated to the United States.

II. That Congress shall not alter, modify, or interfere in, the times, places, or manner, of holding elections for senators and representatives, or either of them, except when the legislature of any state shall neglect, refuse, or be disabled, by invasion or rebellion, to prescribe the same, or in case when the provision made by the state is so imperfect as that no consequent election is had, and then only until the legislature of such state shall make provision in the premises.

III. It is declared by the Convention, that the judicial power of the United States, in cases in which a state may be a party, does not extend to criminal prosecutions, or to authorize any suit by any person against a state; but, to remove all doubts or controversies respecting the same, that it be especially expressed, as a part of the Constitution of the United States, that Congress shall not, directly or indirectly, either by themselves or through the judiciary, interfere with any one of the states, in the redemption of paper money already emitted, and now in circulation, or in liquidating and discharging the public securities of any one state; that each and every state shall have the exclusive right of making such laws and regulations for the before-mentioned purpose as they shall think proper.

IV. That no amendments to the Constitution of the United States, hereafter to be made, pursuant to the fifth article, shall take effect, or become a part of the Constitution of the United States, after the year one thousand seven hundred and niney-three, without the consent of eleven of the states heretofore united under the Confederation.

V. That the judicial powers of the United States shall extend to no possible case where the cause of action shall have originated before the ratification of this constitution, except in disputes between states about their territory, disputes between persons claiming lands under grants of different states, and debts due to the United States.

VI. That no person shall be compelled to do military duty otherwise than by voluntary enlistment, except in cases of general invasion; any thing in the second paragraph of the sixth article of the Constitution, or any law made under the Constitution, to the contrary notwithstanding.

VII. That no capitation or poll tax shall ever be laid by Congress.

VIII. In cases of direct taxes, Congress shall first make requisitions on the several states to assess, levy, and pay, their respective proportions of such requisitions, in such way and manner as the legislatures of the several states shall judge best; and in case any state shall neglect or refuse to pay its proportion, pursuant to such requisition, then congress may assess and levy such state's proportion, together with interest, at the rate of six per cent, per annum, from the time prescribed in such requisition.

IX. That Congress shall lay no direct taxes without the consent of the legislatures of three fourths of the states in the Union.

X. That the Journal of the proceedings of the Senate and House of Representatives shall be published as soon as conveniently may be, at least once in every year, except such parts thereof relating to treaties, alliances, or military operations, as in their judgment require secrecy.

XI. That regular statements of the receipts and expenditures of all public moneys shall be published at least once a year.

XII. As standing armies, in time of peace, are dangerous to liberty, and ought not to be kept up, except in cases of necessity, and as, at all times, the military should be under strict subordination to the civil power, that, therefore, no standing army or regular troops shall be raised or kept up in time of peace.

XIII. That no moneys be borrowed, on the credit of the United States, without the assent of two thirds of the senators and representatives present in each house.

XIV. That the Congress shall not declare war without the concurrence of two thirds of the senators and representatives present in each house.

XV. That the words "without the consent of Congress," in the seventh clause in the ninth section of the first article of the Constitution, be expunged.

XVI. That no judge of the Supreme Court of the United States shall hold any other office under the United States, or any of them; nor shall any officer appointed by Congress, or by the President and Senate of the United States, be permitted to hold any office under the appointment of any of the states.

XVII. As a traffic tending to establish or continue the slavery of any part of the human species is disgraceful to the cause of liberty and humanity, that Congress shall, as soon as may be, promote and establish such laws and regulations as may effectually prevent the importation of slaves of every description into the United States.

XVIII. That the state legislatures have power to recall, when they think it expedient, their federal senators, and to send others in their stead.

XIX. That Congress have power to establish a uniform rule of inhabitancy or settlement of the poor of the different states throughout the United States.

XX. That Congress erect no company with exclusive advantages of commerce.

XXI. That when two members shall move and call for the ayes and nays on any question, they shall be entered on the Journals of the houses respectively.

Done in Convention, at Newport, in the county of Newport, in the state of Rhode Island and Providence Plantations, the twenty-ninth day of May, in the year of our Lord one thousand seven hundred and ninety, and the 14th year of the independence of the United States of America.

By order of the Convention.
(Signed) DANIEL OWEN, *President*
Attest. DANIEL UPDIKE, *Secretary*

Debates, I, pp. 334-337. This ratification, by a vote of 34 to 32, took place at an adjourned meeting of the Rhode Island Convention. The first meeting in March, 1790, refused to ratify and proposed a bill of rights and other amendments. That bill of rights was the same as the one presented above. The amendments were basically the same, except the first set ended at number 18 which stated: "And that the amendments proposed by Congress, in March, 1789, be adopted by this Convention, except the second article therein contained." See Foster, pp. 93-98.

Richard Henry Lee (New York) June 10, 1790
Letter: To Patrick Henry (excerpt)

There appears to be no prospect of further amendments to the constitution this session, and I own 'tis my wish that the amendments generally, as proposed at the last session, had been adopted by our legislature; for although there is much force in your observation, upon that subject, yet when I consider one great object of declarations beyond which government may not go, to wit: that they inculcate upon the minds of the people, just ideas of their rights, it will always be hazardous for rulers, however possessed of means, to undertake a violation of what is generally known to be right, and to be encroachments on the rights of the community; besides that by getting as much as we can at different times, we may at last come to obtain the greatest part of our wishes. It would probably contribute as much to this end, if at the ensuing election of representatives, instructions were given by the people of those districts that send influential members here, to exert themselves to procure such additional amendments as have not yet been made.

Henry, III, pp. 421-422.

Rhode Island General Assembly June [15], 1790
Ratification of proposed Amendments to the Constitution. (excerpt)

4 A well regulated Militia being necessary to the Security of a free State, the Right of the people to keep & bear Arms shall not be infringed.

DHC, II, p. 364. See "United States Congress," September 26, 1789, p. 715, for the proposed Amendments to the Constitution. Rhode Island ratified all twelve of the proposals.

Thomas Jefferson (Philadelphia) December 4, 1790
Letter: To Noah Webster (excerpt)

In mentioning me in your essays, and canvassing my opinions, you have done what every man has a right to do, and it is for the good of society that that right should be freely exercised. No republic is more real than that of letters, and I am the last in principles, as I am the least in pretensions, to any dictatorship in it. Had I other dispositions, the philosophical & dispassionate spirit with which you have expressed your own opinions in opposition to mine, would still have commanded my approbation. A desire of being set right in your opinion, which I respect too much not to entertain that desire, induces me to hazard to you the following observations. It had become an universal and almost uncontroverted position in the several states, that the purposes of society do not require a surrender of all our rights to our ordinary governors: that there are certain portions of right not necessary to enable them to carry on an effective government, & which experience has nevertheless proved they will be constantly encroaching on, if submitted to them: that there are also certain fences which experience has proved peculiarly efficacious against wrong, and rarely obstructive of right, which yet the governing powers have ever shown a disposition to weaken and remove. Of the first kind, for instance, is freedom of religion: of the second, trial by jury, Habeas corpus laws, free presses. These were the settled opinions of all the states, of that of Virginia, of which I was writing, as well as of the others. The others had in consequence delineated these unceded portions of right, and these fences against wrong, which they meant to exempt from the power of their governors, in instruments called declarations of rights & constitutions: and as they did this by Conventions which they appointed for the express purpose of reserving these rights, and of delegating others to their ordinary legislative, executive and judiciary bodies, none of the reserved rights can be touched without resorting to the people to appoint another convention for the express purpose of permitting it. Where the consitutions then have been so formed by conventions named for this express purpose they are fixed & unalterable but by a convention or other body to be specially authorized.

Ford, V, pp. 254-255.

A Farmer January 29, 1791
Newspaper Article: Philadelphia *Independent Gazetteer*

To the YEOMANRY of PENNSYLVANIA.
(Continued from No. 1323.)
LETTER XIV.

KNOWING what constitutes your rights, you should comply with that duty you owe to yourselves, and to your posterity, and support such rights.

Do not suffer ambitious and designing men to mislead you into an opinion, that whilst you enjoy the freedom of electing your Legislators there is no danger of your rights being violated. This is a dangerous and false doctrine; for laws made by the immediate representatives of the people, are not always just. Britian which is regarded by many of our politicians, as an example worthy of imitation, is continually enacting laws, not only unjust, but oppressive to her most valuable citizens. You can only be regarded as a free people whilst your Legislature adheres strictly to the laws of nature, and calculates every one of its regulations for the protection of PROPERTY, and for promoting the *general happiness* of the community. This principle is too frequently stifled by the voice of avarice and ambition; the wealthy citizens by intrigue, sumptuous entertainments, and bribery, influence the conduct of Legislators; and when by such means a law is obtained in favor of the few, however the general rights of the community may be violated, yet it must never be altered or repealed, from a mock apprehension of a breach of public faith.

Under such circumstances of finesse and imposition, it is necessary that you should support a regular militia; otherwise an army of mercenaries may be thought necessary to procure obedience to laws. This has taken place in England to support the most unjust and oppressive excise laws; and the Ministry of that country depends more on a willing, obedient soldiery, than on the justice of laws, to procure a submission to them.

Under every government the dernier resort of the people, is an appeal to the sword; whether to defend themselves against the open attacks of a foreign enemy, or to check the insidious encroachments of domestic foes. Whenever a people are so enervated by luxury as to intrust the defence of their country to a regular, standing army, composed of mercenaries, the power of that country will remain under the direction and influence of the most wealthy citizens. The history of Holland and other modern republics will manifest, how far a *mere monied interest* is to be intrusted with the liberties of the people. —This subject requires your most serious consideration. Whatever form your government may assume, your liberties will be safe as long as you support a well regulated militia. Those who experience the labor of acquiring property, will ever be the best defenders of it.

Vermont General Assembly November 3, 1791
[Vermont had become a member of the Union on March 4, 1791. With the addition of Vermont to the Union, eleven states were required to adopt the proposed Amendments instead of ten. Vermont was the tenth state to take action when it ratified all twelve proposals on November 3rd.]

DHC, II, p. 375. See "United States Congress," September 26, 1789, p. 715, for the twelve proposed Amendments.

Virginia Senate December 15, 1791
[The Virginia Senate finished ratifying all 12 proposed Amendments to the Constitution on this date. With Virginia's ratification, Articles 3 through 12 of the proposed Amendments had received the necessary number of ratifications to become part of the Constitution.]

DHC, II, pp. 387-390. See "United States Congress," September 26, 1789, p. 715, for the proposed Amendments. See "Virginia Senate," December 12, 1789, p. 722, for the reasons why previous action upon proposed Amendments numbers 3, 8, 11, and 12 was postponed, which resulted in no action on ratification by Virginia in 1789.

Thomas Jefferson March 1, 1792
Letter: From the Secretary of State to the Governor of Maryland

Sir,

I have the honor to send you herein enclosed two copies, duly authenticated, of an Act concerning certain fisheries of the United States, and for the regulation and government of the fishermen employed therein; also of an Act to establish the Post office and Post roads within the United States; also the ratifications, by three-fourths of the legislatures of the several States, of certain articles in addition to & amendment of the Constitution of the United States, proposed by Congress to the said Legislatures; and of being with sentiments of the most perfect respect

Your Excellency's Most obedient & Most humble serv[an]t.

National Archives Publication No. 67-4, p. 21. Jefferson sent the same letter to each of the state Governors, along with a printed copy of all twelve of the proposed amendments and the ratifications of the states indicating that only Articles 3 through 12 had actually been ratified by a sufficient number of states. See source, p. 3. See "United States Congress," September 26, 1789, p. 715, for the amendments.

Philadelphia *Freeman's Journal* March 14, 1792[1]

Articles of AMENDMENT, *to the* Constitution *of the* United States, *proposed by* Congress *to the* Legislatures *of the* several states, *pursuant to the* Fifth Article of the Constitution, and which, when ratified by three fourths of the said Legislatures, to be valid to all intents and purposes, as part of the said Constitution. } *By what States and when Ratified.*

ARTICLE I.

AFTER the first enumeration required by the first article of the constitution, there shall be one Representative for every thirty thousand, until the number shall amount to one hundred, after which the proportion shall be so regulated by Congress, that there shall be not less than one hundred Representatives nor less than one Representative for every forty thousand persons, until the number of Representatives shall amount to two hundred; after which the proportion shall be so regulated by Congress, that there shall not be less than two hundred Representatives, nor more than one Representative for every fifty thousand persons. } N. Hampshire, Jan. 25, 1790[;] Vermont, Novem. 3, 1791[;] Rhode-Island, June 1790[;] N. York, March 27, 1790[;] N. Jersey, August 3, 1790[;] Pennsylvania, Sep. 21, 1791[;] Maryland, Decem. 19, 1789[;] Virginia, November 3, 1791[;] N. Carolina, Dec. 22, 1789[;] S. Carolina, Jan. 19, 1790

ARTICLE II.

No law varying the compensation for the services of the Senators and Representatives, shall take effect, until an election of Representatives shall have intervened. } Vermont, Novem. 3, 1791[;] Delaware, January 28, 1790[;] Maryland, Decem. 19, 1789[;] Virginia, Decem. 15, 1791[;] N. Carolina, Dec. 22, 1789[;] S. Carolina, Jan. 19, 1790

ARTICLE III.

Congress shall make no law respecting an establishment of religion, or prohibiting the free exercise thereof, or abridging the freedom of speech, or of the press; or the right of the people peaceably to assemble, and to petition the government for a redress of grievances. } N. Hampshire, Jan. 25, 1790[;] Vermont, Novem. 3, 1791[;] Rhode-Island, June, 1790[;] N. York, March, 27, 1790[;] N. Jersey, August 3, 1790[;] Pennsylvania, Mar. 10, 1790[;] Delaware, January 28, 1790[;] Maryland, Decem. 19, 1789[;] Virginia, Decem. 15, 1791[;] N. Carolina, Dec. 22. 1789[;] S. Carolina, Jan. 19, 1790

ARTICLE IV.

A well regulated militia being necessary to the security of a free state, the right of the people to keep and bear arms shall not be infringed. } N. Hampshire, Jan. 25, 1790[;] Vermont, Novem. 3, 1791[;] Rhode-Island, June, 1790[;] N. York, March 27, 1790[;] N. Jersey, August 3, 1790[;] Pennsylvania, Mar. 10, 1790[;] Delaware, Jan. 28, 1790[;] Maryland, Decem. 19, 1789[;] Virginia, Decem. 15, 1791[;] N. Carolina, Dec, 22, 1789[;] S. Carolina, Jan. 19, 1790

ARTICLE V.

No soldier shall in time of peace be quartered in any house without the consent of the owner; nor in time of war, but in a manner to be prescribed by law. } N. Hampshire, Jan. 25, 1790[;] Vermont, Nov. 3, 1791[;] Rhode-Island, June, 1790[;] N. York, March 27, 1790[;] N. Jersey, August 3, 1790[;] Pennsylvania, Mar. 10, 1790[;] Delaware, Jan. 28, 1790[;] Maryland, Dec. 19, 1789[;] Virginia, Dec. 15, 1791[;] N. Carolina, Dec. 22, 1789[;] S. Carolina, Jan. 19, 1790

ARTICLE VI.

The right of the people to be secure in their persons, houses, papers, and effects, against unreasonable searches and seizures, shall not be violated; and no warrants shall issue but upon probable cause, supported by oath or affirmation, and particularly describing the place to be searched, and the persons or things to be seized. } N. Hampshire, Jan. 25, 1790[;] Vermont, Novem. 3, 1791[;] Rhode-Island, June, 1790[;] N. York, March 27, 1790[;] N. Jersey, August 3, 1790[;] Pennsylvania, Mar. 10, 1790[;] Delaware, Jan. 28, 1790[;] Maryland, Decem. 19, 1789[;] Virginia, Decem. 15, 1791[;] N. Carolina, Dec, 22, 1789[;] S. Carolina, Jan. 19, 1790

ARTICLE VII.

No person shall be held to answer for a capital, or otherwise infamous crime, unless on a presentment or indictment of a grand jury, except in cases arising in the land or naval forces, or in the militia when in actual service in time of war or public danger; nor shall any person be subject for the same offence to be twice put in jeopardy of life or limb; nor shall be compelled in any criminal case to be a witness against himself, nor be deprived of life, liberty, or property, without due process of law; nor shall private property be taken for public use without just compensation. } N. Hampshire, Jan. 25, 1790[;] Vermont, Novem. 3, 1791[;] Rhode-Island, June, 1790[;] N. York, March 27, 1790[;] N. Jersey, August 3, 1790[;] Pennsylvania, Mar. 10, 1790[;] Delaware, Jan. 28, 1790[;] Maryland, Decem. 19, 1789[;] Virginia, Decem. 15, 1791[;] N. Carolina, Dec, 22, 1789[;] S. Carolina, Jan. 19, 1790

ARTICLE VIII.

In all criminal prosecutions, the accused shall enjoy the right to a speedy and public trial, by an impartial jury of the state and district wherein the crime shall have been committed, which district shall have been previously ascertained by law, and to be informed of the nature and cause of the accusation; to be confronted with the witnesses against him; to have compulsory process for obtaining witnesses in his favour and to have the assistance of counsel for his defence. } N. Hampshire, Jan. 25, 1790[;] Vermont, Novem. 3, 1791[;] Rhode-Island, June, 1790[;] N. York, March 27, 1790[;] N. Jersey, August 3, 1790[;] Pennsylvania, Mar. 10, 1790[;] Delaware, Jan. 28, 1790[;] Maryland, Decem. 19, 1789[;] Virigina, Decem. 15, 1791[;] N. Carolina, Dec, 22, 1789[;] S. Carolina, Jan. 19, 1790

ARTICLE IX.

In suits at common law, where the value in controversy shall exceed twenty dollars, the right of trial by jury shall be preserved; and no fact, tried by a jury shall be otherwise re-examined in any court of the United States, than according to the rules of the common law. } N. Hampshire, Jan. 25, 1790[;] Vermont, Novem. 3, 1791[;] Rhode-Island, June, 1790[;] N. York, March 27, 1790[;] N. Jersey, August 3, 1790[;] Pennsylvania, Mar. 10, 1790[;] Delaware, Jan. 28, 1790[;] Maryland, Decem. 19, 1789[;] Virigina, Decem. 15, 1791[;] N. Carolina, Dec, 22, 1789[;] S. Carolina, Jan. 19, 1790

ARTICLE X.

Excessive bail shall not be required, nor excessive fines imposed, nor cruel and unusual punishments inflicted. } N. Hampshire, Jan. 25, 1790[;] Vermont, Novem. 3, 1791[;] Rhode-Island, June, 1790[;] N. York, March 27, 1790[;] N. Jersey, August 3, 1790[;] Pennsylvania, Mar. 10, 1790[;] Delaware, Jan. 28, 1790[;] Maryland, Decem. 19, 1789[;] Virginia, Decem. 15, 1791[;] N. Carolina, Dec, 22, 1789[;] S. Carolina, Jan. 19, 1790

ARTICLE XI.

The enumeration in the constitution, of certain rights, shall not be construed to deny or disparage others retained by the people. } N. Hampshire, Jan. 25, 1790[;] Vermont, Novem. 3, 1791[;] Rhode-Island, June, 1790[;] N. York, March 27, 1790[;] N. Jersey, August 3, 1790[;] Pennsylvania, Mar. 10, 1790[;] Delaware, Jan. 28, 1790[;] Maryland, Decem. 19, 1789[;] Virginia, Decem. 15, 1791[;] N. Carolina, Dec, 22, 1789[;] S. Carolina, Jan. 19, 1790

ARTICLE XII.

The powers not delegated to the United States by the constitution, nor prohibited by it to the states, are reserved to the states respectively or to the people. } N. Hampshire, Jan. 25, 1790[;] Vermont, Novem. 3, 1791[;] Rhode-Island, June, 1790[;] N. York, March 27, 1790[;] N. Jersey, August 3, 1790[;] Pennsylvania, Mar. 10, 1790[;] Delaware, Jan. 28, 1790[;] Maryland, Decem. 19, 1789[;] Virginia, Decem. 15, 1791[;] N. Carolina, Dec. 22, 1789[;] S. Carolina, Jan. 19, 1790

AMENDMENTS RATIFIED[2]

N. Hampshire	1		3	4	5	6	7	8	9	10	11	12
Massachusetts												
Vermont	1	2	3	4	5	6	7	8	9	10	11	12
Rhode-Island	1		3	4	5	6	7	8	9	10	11	12
Connecticut												
New-York	1		3	4	5	6	7	8	9	10	11	12
New-Jersey	1		3	4	5	6	7	8	9	10	11	12
Pennsylvania	1		3	4	5	6	7	8	9	10	11	12
Delaware		2	3	4	5	6	7	8	9	10	11	12
Maryland	1	2	3	4	5	6	7	8	9	10	11	12
Virginia	1	2	3	4	5	6	7	8	9	10	11	12
N. Carolina	1	2	3	4	5	6	7	8	9	10	11	12
S. Carolina	1	2	3	4	5	6	7	8	9	10	11	12
Georgia												

1 Note that Articles 1 and 2 of the proposed amendments were not ratified by a sufficient number of the State Legislatures to become part of the Constitution. Thus, Articles 3 through 12 became the first 10 amendments to the Constitution.

2 Massachusetts, Connecticut, and Georgia did not take the necessary action to ratify the Bill of Rights until 1939.

APPENDIX A

State Declarations & Bills of Rights
and Related Constitutional Provisions
in effect during the formation of the
Federal Bill of Rights—
1787-1789

Virginia Bill of Rights June 12, 1776

Bill of Rights

A declaration of rights made by the representatives of the good people of Virginia, assembled in full and free Convention; which rights do pertain to them, and their posterity, as the basis and foundation of government.

SECTION 1. That all men are by nature equally free and independent, and have certain inherent rights, of which, when they enter into a state of society, they cannot, by any compact, deprive or divest their posterity; namely, the enjoyment of life and liberty, with the means of acquiring and possessing property, and pursuing and obtaining happiness and safety.

SEC. 2. That all power is vested in, and consequently derived from, the people; that magistrates are their trustees and servants, and at all times amenable to them.

SEC. 3. That government is, or ought to be, instituted for the common benefit, protection, and security, of the people, nation, or community; of all the various modes and forms of government, that is best which is capable of producing the greatest degree of happiness and safety, and is most effectually secured against the danger of maladministration; and that, when any government shall be found inadequate or contrary to these purposes, a majority of the community hath an indubitable, unalienable, and indefeasible right, to reform, alter, or abolish it, in such manner as shall be judged most conducive to the public weal.

SEC. 4. That no man, or set of men, are entitled to exclusive or separate emoluments or privileges from the community, but in consideration of public services; which, not being descendible, neither ought the offices of magistrate, legislator, or judge to be hereditary.

SEC. 5. That the legislative and executive powers of the state should be separate and distinct from the judiciary; and that the members of the two first may be restrained from oppression, by feeling and participating the burthens of the people, they should, at fixed periods, be reduced to a private station, return into that body from which they were originally taken, and the vacancies be supplied by frequent, certain, and regular elections, in which all, or any part of the former members, to be again eligible, or ineligible, as the laws shall direct.

SEC. 6. That elections of members to serve as representatives of the people, in assembly, ought to be free; and that all men, having sufficient evidence of permanent common interest with, and attachment to, the community, have the right of suffrage, and cannot be taxed or deprived of their property for public uses, without their own consent, or that of their representatives so elected, nor bound by any law to which they have not, in like manner, assented, for the publick good.

SEC. 7. That all power of suspending laws, or the execution of laws, by any authority, without consent of the representatives of the people, is injurious to their rights, and ought not to be exercised.

SEC. 8. That in all capital or criminal prosecutions a man hath a right to demand the cause and nature of his accusation, to be confronted with the accusers and witnesses, to call for evidence in his favor, and to a speedy trial by an impartial jury of twelve men of his vicinage, without whose unanimous consent he cannot be found guilty; nor can he be compelled to give evidence against himself; that no man be deprived of his liberty except by the law of the land, or the judgment of his peers.

SEC. 9. That excessive bail ought not to be required, nor excessive fines imposed, nor cruel and unusual punishments inflicted.

SEC. 10. That general warrants, whereby an officer or messenger may be commanded to search suspected places without evidence of a fact committed, or to seize any person or persons not named, or whose offence is not particularly described and supported by evidence, are grievous and oppressive, and ought not to be granted.

SEC. 11. That in controversies respecting property, and in suits between man and man, the ancient trial by jury is preferable to any other, and ought to be held sacred.

SEC. 12. That the freedom of the press is one of the great bulwarks of liberty, and can never be restrained but by despotic governments.

SEC. 13. That a well-regulated militia, composed of the body of the people, trained to arms, is the proper, natural, and safe defence of a free state; that standing armies, in time of peace, should be avoided, as dangerous to liberty; and that in all cases the military should be under strict subordination to, and governed by, the civil power.

SEC. 14. That the people have a right to uniform government; and, therefore, that no government separate from, or independent of, the government of Virginia, ought to be erected or established within the limits thereof.

SEC. 15. That no free government, or the blessings of liberty, can be preserved to any people, but by a firm adherence to justice, moderation, temperance, frugality, and virtue, and by frequent recurrence to fundamental principles.

SEC. 16. That religion, or the duty which we owe to our Creator and the manner of discharging it, can be directed only by reason and conviction, not by force or violence; and therefore all men are equally entitled to the free exercise of religion, according to the dictates of conscience; and that it is the mutual duty of all to practice Christian forbearance, love, and charity towards each other.

Thorpe, VII, pp. 3812-3814.

New Jersey Constitution July 3, 1776

[Provisions of the New Jersey Constitution which relate to individual rights or to provisions contained in other state bills of rights.]

XVI. That all criminals shall be admitted to the same privileges of witnesses and counsel, as their prosecutors are or shall be entitled to.

XVII. That the estates of such persons as shall destroy their own lives, shall not, for that offence, be forfeited; but shall descend in the same manner, as they would have done, had such persons died in the natural way; nor shall any article, which may occasion accidentally the death of any one, be henceforth deemed a deodand, or in anywise forfeited, on account of such misfortune.

XVIII. That no person shall ever, within this Colony, be deprived of the inestimable privilege of worshipping Almighty God in a manner agreeable to the dictates of his own conscience; nor, under any pretence whatever, be compelled to attend any place of worship, contrary to his own faith and judgment; nor shall any person, within this Colony, ever be obliged to pay tithes, taxes, or any other rates, for the purpose of building or repairing any other church or churches, place or places of worship, or for the maintenance of any minister or ministry, contrary to what he believes to be right, or has deliberately or voluntarily engaged himself to perform.

XIX. That there shall be no establishment of any one religious sect in this Province, in preference to another; and that no Protestant inhabitant of this Colony shall be denied the enjoyment of any civil right, merely on account of his religious principles; but that all persons, professing a belief in the faith of any Protestant sect, who shall demean themselves peaceably under the government, as hereby established, shall be capable of being elected into any office of profit or trust, or being a member of either branch of the Legislature, and shall fully and freely enjoy every privilege and immunity, enjoyed by others, their fellow subjects.

XXII. That the common law of England, as well as so much of the statute law, as have been heretofore practised in this Colony, shall still remain in force, until they shall be altered by a future law of the Legislature; such parts only excepted, as are repugnant to the rights and privileges contained in this Charter; and that the inestimable right of trial by jury shall remain confirmed as a part of the law of this Colony, without repeal, forever.

Thorpe, V, pp. 2597-2598.

Delaware Declaration of Rights September 11, 1776

A Declaration of Rights and Fundamental Rules of the Delaware State, formerly stiled, The Government of the counties of New-Castle, Kent and Sussex, upon Delaware.

SECTION 1. That all government of right originates from the people, is founded in compact only, and instituted solely for the good of the whole.

SECT. 2. That all men have a natural and unalienable right to worship Almighty God according to the dictates of their own consciences and understandings; and that no man ought or of right can be compelled to attend any religious worship or maintain any ministry contrary to or against his own free will and consent, and that no authority can or ought to be vested in, or assumed by any power whatever that shall in any case interfere with, or in any manner controul the right of conscience in the free exercise of religious worship.

SECT. 3. That all persons professing the Christian religion ought forever to enjoy equal rights and privileges in this state, unless, under colour of religion, any man disturb the peace, the happiness or safety of society.

SECT. 4. That people of this state have the sole exclusive and inherent right of governing and regulating the internal police of the same.

SECT. 5. That persons intrusted with the Legislative and Executive Powers are the Trustees and servants of the public, and as such accountable for their conduct; wherefore whenever the ends of government are perverted, and public liberty manifestly endangered by the Legislative singly, or a treacherous combination of both, the people may, and of right ought to establish a new, or reform the old government.

SECT. 6. That the right in the people to participate in the Legislature, is the foundation of liberty and of all free government, and for this end all elections ought to be free and frequent, and every freeman, having sufficient evidence of a permanent common interest with, and attachment to the community, hath a right of suffrage.

SECT. 7. That no power of suspending laws, or the execution of laws, ought to be exercised unless by the Legislature.

SECT. 8. That for redress of grievances, and for amending and strengthening of the laws, the Legislature ought to be frequently convened.

SECT. 9. That every man hath a right to petition the Legislature for the redress of grievances in a peaceable and orderly manner.

SECT. 10. That every member of society hath a right to be protected in the enjoyment of life, liberty and property, and therefore is bound to contribute his proportion towards the expense of that protection, and yield his personal service when necessary, or an equivalent thereto; but no part of a man's property can be justly taken from him or applied to public uses without his own consent or that of his legal Representatives: Nor can any man that is conscientiously scrupulous of bearing arms in any case be justly compelled thereto if he will pay such equivalent.

SECT. 11. That retrospective laws, punishing offences committed before the existence of such laws, are oppressive and unjust, and ought not to be made.

SECT. 12. That every freeman for every injury done him in his goods, lands or person, by any other person, ought to have remedy by the course of the law of the land, and ought to have justice and right for the injury done to him freely without sale, fully without any denial, and speedily without delay, according to the law of the land.

SECT. 13. That trial by jury of facts where they arise is one of the greatest securities of the lives, liberties and estates of the people.

SECT. 14. That in all prosecutions for criminal offences, evey man hath a right to be informed of the accusation against him, to be allowed counsel, to be confronted with the accusers or witnesses, to examine evidence on oath in his favour, and to a speedy trial by an impartial jury, without whose unanimous consent he ought not to be found guilty.

SECT. 15. That no man in the Court of Common Law ought to be compelled to give evidence against himself.

SECT. 16. That excessive bail ought not to be required, nor excessive fines imposed, nor cruel or unusual punishments inflicted.

SECT. 17. That all warrants without oath to search suspected places, or to seize any person or his property, are grievous and oppressive; and all general warrants to search suspected places, or to apprehend all persons suspected, without naming or describing the place or any person in special, are illegal and ought not to be granted.

SECT. 18. That a well regulated militia is the proper, natural and safe defence of a free government.

SECT. 19. That standing armies are dangerous to liberty, and ought not to be raised or kept up without the consent of the Legislature.

SECT. 20. That in all cases and at all times the military ought to be under strict subordination to and governed by the civil power.

SECT. 21. That no soldier ought to be quartered in any house in time of peace without the consent of the owner; and in time of war in such manner only as the Legislature shall direct.

SECT. 22. That the independency and uprightness of judges are essential to the impartial administration of justice, and a great security to the rights and liberties of the people.

SECT. 23. That the liberty of the press ought to be inviolably preserved.

Perry, pp. 338-340.

Pennsylvania Constitution September 28, 1776
(excerpts)

A DECLARATION OF THE RIGHTS OF THE INHABITANTS OF THE COMMONWEALTH, OR STATE OF PENNSYLVANIA

I. That all men are born equally free and independent, and have certain natural, inherent and inalienable rights, amongst which are, the enjoying and defending life and liberty, acquiring, possessing and protecting property, and pursuing and obtaining happiness and safety.

II. That all men have a natural and unalienable right to worship Almighty God according to the dictates of their own consciences and understanding: And that no man ought or of right can be compelled to attend any religious worship, or erect or support any place of worship, or maintain any ministry, contrary to, or against, his own free will and consent: Nor can any man, who acknowledges the being of a God, be justly deprived or abridged of any civil right as a citizen, on account of his religious sentiments or peculiar mode of religious worship: And that no authority can or ought to be vested in, or assumed by any power whatever, that shall in any case interfere with, or in any manner controul, the right of conscience in the free exercise of religious worship.

III. That the people of this State have the sole, exclusive and inherent right of governing and regulating the internal police of the same.

IV. That all power being originally inherent in, and consequently derived from, the people; therefore all officers of government, whether legislative or executive, are their trustees and servants, and at all times accountable to them.

V. That government is, or ought to be, instituted for the common benefit, protection and security of the people, nation or community; and not for the particular emolument or advantage of any single man, family, or sett of men, who are a part only of that community; And that the community hath an indubitable, unalienable and indefeasible right to reform, alter, or abolish government in such manner as shall be by that community judged most conducive to the public weal.

VI. That those who are employed in the legislative and executive business of the State, may be restrained from oppression, the people have a right, at such periods as they may think proper, to reduce their public officers to a private station, and supply the vacancies by certain and regular elections.

VII. That all elections ought to be free; and that all free men having a sufficient evident common interest with, and attachment to the community, have a right to elect officers, or to be elected into office.

VIII. That every member of society hath a right to be protected in the enjoyment of life, liberty and property, and therefore is bound to contribute his proportion towards the expence of that protection, and yield his personal service when necessary, or an equivalent thereto: But no part of a man's property can be justly taken from him, or applied to public uses, without his own consent, or that of his legal representatives: Nor can any man who is conscientiously scrupulous of bearing arms, be justly compelled thereto, if he will pay such equivalent, nor are the people bound by any laws, but such as they have in like manner assented to, for their common good.

IX. That in all prosecutions for criminal offences, a man hath a right to be heard by himself and his council, to demand the cause and nature of his accusation, to be confronted with the witnesses, to call for evidence in his favour, and a speedy public trial, by an impartial jury of the country, without the unanimous consent of which jury he cannot be found guilty; nor can he be compelled to give evidence against himself; nor can any man be justly deprived of his liberty except by the laws of the land, or the judgment of his peers.

X. That the people have a right to hold themselves, their houses, papers, and possessions free from search and seizure, and therefore warrants without oaths or affirmations first made, affording a sufficient foundation for them, and whereby any officer or messenger may be commanded or required to search suspected places, or to seize any person or persons, his or their property, not particularly described, are contrary to that right, and ought not to be granted.

XI. That in controversies respecting property, and in suits between man and man, the parties have a right to trial by jury, which ought to be held sacred.

XII. That the people have a right to freedom of speech, and of writing, and publishing their sentiments; therefore the freedom of the press ought not to be restrained.

XIII. That the people have a right to bear arms for the defence of themselves and the state; and as standing armies in the time of peace are dangerous to liberty, they ought not to be kept up; and that the military should be kept under strict subordination to, and governed by, the civil power.

XIV. That a frequent recurrence to fundamental principles, and a firm adherence to justice, moderation, temperance, industry, and frugality are absolutely necessary to preserve the blessings of liberty, and keep a government free: The people ought therefore to pay particular attention to these points in the choice of officers and representatives, and have a right to exact a due and constant regard to them, from their legislatures and magistrates, in the making and executing such laws as are necessary for the good government of the state.

XV. That all men have a natural inherent right to emigrate from one state to another that will recieve them, or to form a new state in vacant countries, or in such countries as they can purchase, whenever they think that thereby they may promote their own happiness.

XVI. That the people have a right to assemble together, to consult for their comnon good, to instruct their representatives, and to apply to the legislature for redress of grievances, by address, petition, or remonstrance.

[Related provisions from the body of the Pennsylvania Constitution.]

Sect. 5. The freemen of this commonwealth and their sons shall be trained and armed for its defence under such regulations, restrictions, and exceptions as the general assembly shall by law direct, preserving always to the people the right of choosing their colonels and all commissioned officers under that rank, in such manner and as often as by the said laws shall be directed.

Sect. 25. Trials shall be by jury as heretofore: And it is recommended to the legislature of this state, to provide by law against every corruption or partiality in the choice, return, or appointment of juries.

Sect. 29. Excessive bail shall not be exacted for bailable offences: And all fines shall be moderate.

Sect. 35. The printing presses shall be free to every person who undertakes to examine the proceedings of the legislature, or any part of government.

Sect. 43. The inhabitants of this state shall have liberty to fowl and hunt in seasonable times on the lands they hold, and on all other lands therein not inclosed; and in like manner to fish in all boatable waters, and others not private property.

Sect. 46. The declaration of rights is hereby declared to be a part of the constitution of this commonwealth, and ought never to be violated on any pretence whatever.

Thorpe, V, pp. 3082-3091.

Maryland Declaration of Rights November 11, 1776

A Declaration of Rights, and the Constitution and Form of Government agreed to by the Delegates of Maryland, in free and full Convention assembled.

A DECLARATION OF RIGHTS, &C.

THE parliament of Great Britain, by a declaratory act, having assumed a right to make laws to bind the Colonies in all cases whatsoever, and, in pursuance of such claim, endeavoured, by force of arms, to subjugate the United Colonies to an unconditional submission to their will and power, and having at length constrained them to declare themselves independent States, and to assume government under the authority of the people;—Therefore we, the Delegates of Maryland, in free and full Convention assembled, taking into our most serious consideration the best means of establishing a good Constitution in this State, for the sure foundation and more permanent security thereof, declare,

I. That all government of right originates from the people, is founded in compact only, and instituted solely for the good of the whole.

II. That the people of this State ought to have the sole and exclusive right of regulating the internal government and police thereof.

III. That the inhabitants of Maryland are entitled to the common law of England, and the trial by jury, according to the course of that law, and to the benefit of such of the English statutes, as existed at the time of their first emigration, and which, by experience, have been found applicable to their local and other circumstances, and of such others as have been since made in England, or Great Britain, and have been introduced, used and practised by the courts of law or equity; and also to acts of Assembly, in force on the first of June seventeen hundred and seventy-four, except such as may have since expired, or have been or may be altered by acts of Convention, or this Declaration of Rights—subject, nevertheless, to the revision of, and amendment or repeal by, the Legislature of this State: and the inhabitants of Maryland are also entitled to all property, derived to them, from or under the Charter granted by his Majesty Charles I. to Caecilius Calvert, Baron of Baltimore.

IV. That all persons invested with the legislative or executive powers of government are the trustees of the public, and, as such, accountable for their conduct; wherefore, whenever the ends of government are perverted, and public liberty manifestly endangered, and all other means of redress are ineffectual, the people may, and of right ought, to reform the old or establish a new government. The doctrine of non-resistance, against arbitrary power and oppression, is absurd, slavish, and destructive of the good and happiness of mankind.

V. That the right in the people to participate in the Legislature is the best security of liberty, and the foundation of all free government; for this purpose, elections ought to be free and frequent, and every man, having property in, a common interest with, and an attachment to the community, ought to have a right of suffrage.

VI. That the legislative, executive and judicial powers of government, ought to be forever separate and distinct from each other.

VII. That no power of suspending laws, or the execution of laws, unless by or derived from the Legislature, ought to be exercised or allowed.

VIII. That freedom of speech and debates, or proceedings in the Legislature, ought not to be impeached in any other court or judicature.

IX. That a place for the meeting of the Legislature ought to be fixed, the most convenient to the members thereof, and to the depository of public records; and the Legislature ought not to be convened or held at any other place, but from evident necessity.

X. That, for redress of grievances, and for amending, strengthening and preserving the laws, the Legislature ought to be frequently convened.

XI. That every man hath a right to petition the Legislature, for the redress of grievances, in a peaceable and orderly manner.

XII. That no aid, charge, tax, fee, or fees, ought to be set, rated, or levied, under any pretence, without consent of the Legislature.

XIII. That the levying taxes by the poll is grievous and oppressive, and ought to be abolished; that paupers ought not to be assessed for the support of government; but every other person in the State ought to contribute his proportion of public taxes, for the support of government, according to his actual worth, in real or personal property, within the State; yet fines, duties, or taxes, may properly and justly be imposed or laid, with a political view, for the good government and benefit of the community.

XIV. That sanguinary laws ought to be avoided, as far as is consistent with the safety of the State: and no law, to inflict cruel and unusual pains and penalties, ought to be made in any case, or at any time hereafter.

XV. That retrospective laws, punishing facts committed before the existence of such laws, and by them only declared criminal, are oppressive, unjust, and incompatible with liberty; wherefore no *ex post facto* law ought to be made.

XVI. That no law, to attaint particular persons of treason or felony, ought to be made in any case, or at any time hereafter.

XVII. That every freeman, for any injury done him in his person or property, ought to have remedy, by the course of the law of the land, and ought to have justice and right freely without sale, fully without any denial, and speedily without delay, according to the law of the land.

XVIII. That the trial of facts where they arise, is one of the greatest securities of the lives, liberties and estates of the people.

XIX. That, in all criminal prosecutions, every man hath a right to be informed of the accusation against him; to have a copy of the indictment or charge in due time (if required) to prepare for his defence; to be allowed counsel; to be confronted with the witnesses against him; to have process for his witnesses; to examine the witnesses, for and against him, on oath; and to a speedy trial by an impartial jury, without whose unanimous consent he ought not to be found guilty.

XX. That no man ought to be compelled to give evidence against himself, in a common court of law, or in any other court, but in such cases as have been usually practised in this State, or may hereafter be directed by the Legislature.

XXI. That no freeman ought to be taken, or imprisoned, or disseized of his freehold, liberties, or privileges, or outlawed, or exiled, or in any manner destroyed, or deprived of his life, liberty, or property, but by the judgment of his peers, or by the law of the land.

XXII. That excessive bail ought not to be required, nor excessive fines imposed, nor cruel or unusual punishments inflicted, by the courts of law.

XXIII. That all warrants, without oath or affirmation, to search suspected places, or to seize any person or property, are grievous and oppressive; and all general warrants—to search suspected places, or to apprehend suspected persons, without naming or describing the place, or the person in special—are illegal, and ought not to be granted.

XXIV. That there ought to be no forfeiture of any part of the estate of any person, for any crime except murder, or treason against the State, and then only on conviction and attainder.

XXV. That a well-regulated militia is the proper and natural defence of a free government.

XXVI. That standing armies are dangerous to liberty, and ought not to be raised or kept up, without consent of the Legislature.

XXVII. That in all cases, and at all times, the military ought to be under strict subordination to and control of the civil power.

XXVIII. That no soldier ought to be quartered in any house, in time of peace, without the consent of the owner; and in time of war, in such manner only, as the Legislature shall direct.

XXIX. That no person, except regular soldiers, mariners, and marines in the service of this State, or militia when in actual service, ought in any case to be subject to or punishable by martial law.

XXX. That the independency and uprightness of Judges are essential to the impartial administration of justice, and a great security to the rights and liberties of the people; wherefore the Chancellor and Judges ought to hold commissions during good behaviour; and the said Chancellor and Judges shall be removed for misbehaviour, on conviction in a court of law, and may be removed by the Governor, upon the address of the General Assembly; *Provided*, That two-thirds of all the members of each House concur in such address. That salaries, liberal, but not profuse, ought to be secured to the Chancellor and the Judges, during the continuance of their commissions, in such manner, and at such times, as the Legislature shall hereafter direct, upon consideration of the circumstances of this State. No Chancellor or Judge ought to hold any other office, civil or military, or receive fees or perquisites of any kind.

XXXI. That a long continuance, in the first executive departments of power or trust, is dangerous to liberty; a rotation, therefore, in those departments, is one of the best securities of permanent freedom.

XXXII. That no person ought to hold, at the same time, more than one office of profit, nor ought any person, in public trust, to receive any present from any foreign prince or state, or from the United States, or any of them, without the approbation of this State.

XXXIII. That, as it is the duty of every man to worship God in such manner as he thinks most acceptable to him; all persons, professing the Christian religion, are equally entitled to protection in their religious liberty; wherefore no person ought by any law to be molested in his person or estate on account of his religious persuasion or profession, or for his religious practice; unless, under colour of religion, any man shall disturb the good order, peace or safety of the State, or shall infringe the laws of morality, or injure others, in their natural, civil, or religious rights; nor ought any person to be compelled to frequent or maintain, or contribute, unless on contract, to maintain any particular place of worship, or any particular ministry; yet the Legislature may, in their discretion, lay a general and equal tax, for the support of the Christian religion; leaving to each individual the power of appointing the payment over of the money, collected from him, to the support of any particular place of worship or minister, or for the benefit of the poor of his own denomination, or the poor in general of any particular county: but the churches, chapels, glebes, and all other property now belonging to the church of England, ought to remain to the church of England forever. And all acts of Assembly, lately passed, for collecting monies for building or repairing particular churches or chapels of ease, shall continue in force, and be executed, unless the Legislature shall, by act, supersede or repeal the same: but no county court shall assess any quantity of tobacco, or sum of money, here after, on the application of any vestrymen or church-wardens; and every encumbent of the church of England, who hath remained in his parish, and performed his duty, shall be entitled to receive the provision and support established by the act, entitled "An act for the support of the clergy of the church of England, in this Province," till the November court of this present year, to be held for the county in which his parish shall lie, or partly lie, or for such time as he hath remained in his parish, and performed his duty.

XXXIV. That every gift, sale, or devise of lands, to any minister, public teacher, or preacher of the gospel, as such, or to any religious sect, order or denomination, or to or for the support, use or benefit of, or in trust for, any minister, public teacher, or preacher of the gospel, as such, or any religious sect, order or denomination—and every gift or sale of goods, or chattels, to go in succession, or to take place after the death of the seller or donor, or to or for such support, use or benefit—and also every devise of goods or chattels to or for the support, use or benefit of any minister, public teacher, or preacher of the gospel, as such, or any religious sect, order, or denomination, without the leave of the Legislature, shall be void; except always any sale, gift, lease or devise of any quantity of land, not exceeding two acres, for a church, meeting, or other house of worhsip, and for a burying-ground, which shall be improved, enjoyed or used only for such purpose—or such sale, gift, lease, or devise, shall be void.

XXXV. That no other test or qualification ought to be required, on admission to any office of trust or profit, than such oath of support and fidelity to this State, and such oath of office, as shall be directed by this Convention, or the Legislature of this State, and a declaration of belief in the Christian religion.

XXXVI. That the manner of administering an oath to any person, ought to be such, as those of the religious persuasion, profession, or denomination, of which such person is one, generally esteem the most effectual confirmation, by the attestation of the Divine Being. And that the people called Quakers, those called Dunkers, and those called Menonists, holding it unlawful to take an oath on any occasion, ought to be allowed to make their solemn affirmation, in the manner that Quakers have been heretofore allowed to affirm; and to be of the same avail as an oath, in all such cases, as the affirmation of Quakers hath been allowed and accepted within this State, instead of an oath. And further, on such affirmation, warrants to search for stolen goods, or for the apprehension or commitment of offenders, ought to be granted, or security for the peace awarded, and Quakers, Dunkers or Menonists ought also, on their solemn affirmation as aforesaid, to be admitted as witnesses, in all criminal cases not capital.

XXXVII. That the city of Annapolis ought to have all its rights, privileges and benefits, agreeable to its Charter, and the acts of Assembly confirming and regulating the same, subject nevertheless to such alteration as may be made by this Convention, or any future Legislature.

XXXVIII. That the liberty of the press ought to be inviolably preserved.

XXXIX. That monopolies are odious, contrary to the spirit of a free government, and the principles of commerce; and ought not to be suffered.

XL. That no title of nobility, or hereditary honours, ought to be granted in this State.

XLI. That the subsisting resolves of this and the several Conventions held for this Colony, ought to be in force as laws, unless altered by this Convention, or the Legislature of this State.

XLII. That this Declaration of Rights, or the Form of Government, to be established by this Convention, or any part or either of them, ought not to be altered, changed or abolished, by the Legislature of this State, but in such manner as this Convention shall prescribe and direct.

This Declaration of Rights was assented to, and passed, in Convention of the Delegates of the freemen of Maryland, begun and held at Annapolis, the 14th day of August, A.D. 1776.

By order of the Convention.

Thorpe, III, pp. 1686-1691.

North Carolina Constitution December 18, 1776

(excerpts)

A DECLARATION OF RIGHTS, &C.

I. That all political power is vested in and derived from the people only.

II. That the people of this State ought to have the sole and exclusive right of regulating the internal government and police thereof.

III. That no man or set of men are entitled to exclusive or separate emoluments or privileges from the community, but in consideration of public services.

IV. That the legislative, executive, and supreme judicial powers of government, ought to be forever separate and distinct from each other.

V. That all powers of suspending laws, or the execution of laws, by any authority, without consent of the Representatives of the people, is injurious to their rights, and ought not to be exercised.

VI. That elections of members, to serve as Representatives in General Assembly, ought to be free.

VII. That, in all criminal prosecutions, every man has a right to be informed of the accusation against him, and to confront the accusers and witnesses with other testimony, and shall not be compelled to give evidence against himself.

VIII. That no freeman shall be put to answer any criminal charge, but by indictment, presentment, or impeachment.

IX. That no freeman shall be convicted of any crime, but by the unanimous verdict of a jury of good and lawful men, in open court, as heretofore used.

X. That excessive bail should not be required, nor excessive fines imposed, nor cruel or unusual punishments inflicted.

XI. That general warrants—whereby an officer or messenger may be commanded to search suspected places, without evidence of the fact committed, or to seize any person or persons, not named, whose offences are not particularly described, and supported by evidence—are dangerous to liberty, and ought not to be granted.

XII. That no freeman ought to be taken, imprisoned, or desseized of his freehold, liberties or privileges, or outlawed, or exiled, or in any manner destroyed, or deprived of his life, liberty, or property, but by the law of the land.

XIII. That every freeman, restrained of his liberty, is entitled to a remedy, to inquire into the lawfulness thereof, and to remove the same, if unlawful; and that such remedy ought not to be denied or delayed.

XIV. That in all controversies at law, respecting property, the ancient mode of trial, by jury, is one of the best securities of the rights of the people, and ought to remain sacred and inviolable.

XV. That the freedom of the press is one of the great bulwarks of liberty, and therefore ought never to be restrained.

XVI. That the people of this State ought not to be taxed, or made subject to the payment of any impost or duty, without the consent of themselves, or their Representatives in General Assembly, freely given.

XVII. That the people have a right to bear arms, for the defence of the State; and, as standing armies, in time of peace, are dangerous to liberty, they ought not to be kept up; and that the military should be kept under strict subordination to, and governed by, the civil power.

XVIII. That the people have a right to assemble together, to consult for their common good, to instruct their Representatives, and to apply to the Legislature, for redress of grievances.

XIX. That all men have a natural and unalienable right to worship Almighty God according to the dictates of their own consciences.

XX. That, for redress of grievances, and for amending and strengthening the laws, elections ought to be often held.

XXI. That a frequent recurrence to fundamental principles is absolutely necessary, to preserve the blessings of liberty.

XXII. That no hereditary emoluments, privileges or honors ought to be granted or conferred in this State.

XXIII. That perpetuities and monopolies are contrary to the genius of a free State, and ought not to be allowed.

XXIV. That retrospective laws, punishing facts committed before the existence of such laws, and by them only declared criminal, are oppressive, unjust, and incompatible with liberty; wherefore no *ex post facto* law ought to be made.

[Related provisions from the body of the North Carolina Constitution.]

XXXIV. That there shall be no establishment of any one religious church or denomination in this State, in preference to any other; neither shall any person, on any pretence whatsoever, be compelled to attend any place of worship contrary to his own faith or judgment, nor be obliged to pay, for the purchase of any glebe, or the building of any house of worship, or for the maintenance of any minister or ministry, contrary to what he believes right, or has voluntarily and personally engaged to perform; but all persons shall be at liberty to exercise their own mode of worship:—*Provided,* That nothing herein contained shall be construed to exempt preachers of treasonable or seditious discourses, from legal trial and punishment.

XLIV. That the Declaration of Rights is hereby declared to be part of the Constitution of this State, and ought never to be violated, on any pretence whatsoever.

Thorpe, V, pp. 2787-2794.

Georgia Constitution February 5, 1777

[Provisions of the Georgia Constitution which relate to individual rights or to provisions contained in other state bills of rights.]

Art. LVI. All persons whatever shall have the free exercise of their religion; provided it be not repugnant to the peace and safety of the State; and shall not, unless by consent, support any teacher or teachers except those of their own profession.

Art. LIX. Excessive fines shall not be levied, nor excessive bail demanded.

Art. LX. The principles of the *habeas-corpus* act shall be a part of this constitution.

Art. LXI. Freedom of the press and trial by jury to remain inviolate forever.

Thorpe, II, pp. 784-785.

New York Constitution April 20, 1777
[Provisions from the New York Constitution which relate to individual rights or are similar to provisions from other state bills of rights.]

XIII. And this convention doth further, in the name and by the authority of the good people of this State, ordain, determine, and declare, that no member of this State shall be disfranchised, or deprived of any the rights or privileges secured to the subjects of this State by this constitution, unless by the law of the land, or the judgment of his peers.

XXXIV. *And it is further ordained,* That in every trial on impeachment, or indictment for crimes or misdemeanors, the party impeached or indicted shall be allowed counsel, as in civil actions.

XXXVIII. And whereas we are required, by the benevolent principles of rational liberty, not only to expel civil tyranny, but also to guard against that spiritual oppression and intolerance wherewith the bigotry and ambition of weak and wicked priests and princes have scourged mankind, this convention doth further, in the name and by the authority of the good people of this State, ordain, determine, and declare, that the free exercise and enjoyment of religious profession and worship, without discrimination or preference, shall forever hereafter be allowed, within this state, to all mankind: *Provided,* That the liberty of conscience, hereby granted, shall not be so construed as to excuse acts of licentiousness, or justify practices inconsistent with the peace or safety of this State.

XL. And whereas it is of the utmost importance to the safety of every State that it should always be in a condition of defence; and it is the duty of every man who enjoys the protection of society to be prepared and willing to defend it; this convention therefore, in the name and by the authority of the good people of this State, doth ordain, determine, and declare that the militia of this State, at all times hereafter, as well in peace as in war, shall be armed and disciplined, and in readiness for service. That all such of the inhabitants of this State being of the people called Quakers as, from scruples of conscience, may be averse to the bearing of arms, be therefrom excused by the legislature; and do pay to the State such sums of money, in lieu of their personal service, as the same may, in the judgment of the legislature, be worth. And that a proper magazine of warlike stores, proportionate to the number of inhabitants, be, forever hereafter, at the expense of this State, and by acts of the legislature, established, maintained, and continued in every county in this State.

XLI. And this convention doth further ordain, determine, and declare, in the name and by the authority of the good people of this State, that trial by jury, in all cases in which it hath heretofore been used in the colony of New York, shall be established and remain inviolate forever. And that no acts of attainder shall be passed by the legislature of this State for crimes, other than those committed before the termination of the present war; and that such acts shall not work a corruption of blood. And further, that the legislature of this State shall, at no time hereafter, institute any new court or courts, but such as shall proceed according to the course of the common law.

Thorpe, V, pp. 2632-2637.

Vermont Constitution July 8, 1777
(excerpts)
[Note that New York claimed Vermont as part of its territory until 1791. For this reason, Vermont was not recognized as one of the original 13 states in the union.]

Chapter I
A Declaration of the Rights of the Inhabitants of the State of Vermont

I. That all men are born equally free and independent, and have certain natural, inherent and unalienable rights, amongst which are the enjoying and defending life and liberty; acquiring, possessing and protecting property, and pursuing and obtaining happiness and safety. Therefore, no male person, born in this country, or brought from over sea, ought to be holden by law, to serve any person, as a servant, slave or apprentice, after he arrives to the age of twenty-one years, nor female, in like manner, after she arrives to the age of eighteen years, unless they are bound by their own consent, after they arrive to such age, or bound by law, for the payment of debts, damages, fines, costs, or the like.

II. That private property ought to be subservient to public uses, when necessity requires it; nevertheless, whenever any particular man's property is taken for the use of the public, the owner ought to receive an equivalent in money.

III. That all men have a natural and unalienable right to worship ALMIGHTY GOD, according to the dictates of their own consciences and understanding, regulated by the word of GOD; and that no man ought, or of right can be compelled to attend any religious worship, or erect, or support any place of worship, or maintain any minister, contrary to the dictates of his conscience; nor can any man who professes the protestant religion, be justly deprived or abridged of any civil right, as a citizen, on account of his religious sentiment; or peculiar mode of religious worship, and that no authority can, or ought to be vested in, or assumed by, any power whatsoever, that shall, in any case, interfere with, or in any manner controul, the rights of conscience, in the free exercise of religious worship: nevertheless, every sect or denomination of people ought to observe the Sabbath, or the Lord's day, and keep up, and support, some sort of religious worship, which to them shall seem most agreeable to the revealed will of GOD.

IV. That the people of this State have the sole, exclusive and inherent right of governing and regulating the internal police of the same.

V. That all power being originally inherent in, and consequently, derived from, the people; therefore, all officers of government, whether legislative or executive, are their trustees and servants, and at all times accountable to them.

VI. That government is, or ought to be, instituted for the common benefit, protection, and security of the people, nation or community; and not for the particular emolument or advantage of any single man, family or set of men, who are a part only of that community; and that the community hath an indubitable, unalienable and indefeasible right to reform, alter, or abolish, government, in such manner as shall be, by that community, judged most conducive to the public weal.

VII. That those who are employed in the legislative and executive business of the State, may be restrained from oppression, the people have a right, at such periods as they may think proper, to reduce their public officers to a private station, and supply the vacancies by certain and regular elections.

VIII. That all elections ought to be free; and that all freemen, having a sufficient, evident, common interest with, and attachment to, the community, have a right to elect officers, or be elected into office.

IX. That every member of society hath a right to be protected in the enjoyment of life, liberty and property, and therefore, is bound to contribute his proportion towards the expense of that protection, and yield his personal service, when necessary, or an equivalent thereto; but no part of a man's property can be justly taken from him, or applied to public uses, without his own consent, or that of his legal representatives; nor can any man who is conscientiously scrupulous of bearing arms, be justly compelled thereto, if he will pay such equivalent; nor are the people bound by any law, but such as they have, in like manner, assented to, for their common good.

X. That, in all prosecutions for criminal offences, a man hath a right to be heard, by himself and his counsel—to demand the cause and nature of his accusation—to be confronted with the witnesses—to call for evidence in his favor, and a speedy public trial, by an impartial jury of the country; without the unanimous consent of which jury, he cannot be found guilty; nor can he be compelled to give evidence against himself; nor can any man be justly deprived of his liberty, except by the laws of the land or the judgment of his peers.

XI. That the people have a right to hold themselves, their houses, papers and possessions free from search or seizure; and therefore warrants, without oaths or affirmations first made, affording a sufficient foundation for them, and whereby any officer or messenger may be commanded or required to search suspected places, or to seize any person or persons, his, her or their property, not particularly described, are contrary to that right, and ought not to be granted.

XII. That no warrant or writ to attach the person or estate, of any freeholder within this State, shall be issued in civil action, without the person or persons, who may request such warrant or attachment, first make oath, or affirm, before the authority who may be requested to issue the same, that he, or they, are in danger or losing his, her or their debts.

XIII. That, in controversies respecting property, and in suits between man and man, the parties have a right to a trial by jury; which ought to be held sacred.

XIV. That the people have a right to freedom of speech, and of writing and publishing their sentiments; therefore, the freedom of the press ought not be restrained.

XV. That the people have a right to bear arms for the defence of themselves and the State; and, as standing armies, in the time of peace, are dangerous to liberty, they ought not to be kept up; and that the military should be kept under strict subordination to, and governed by, the civil power.

XVI. That frequent recurrence to fundamental principles, and a firm adherence to justice, moderation, temperance, industry and frugality, are absolutely necessary to preserve the blessings of liberty, and keep government free. The people ought, therefore, to pay particular attention to these points, in the choice of officers and representatives, and have a right to exact a due and constant regard to them, from their legislators and magistrates, in the making and executing such laws as are necessary for the good government of the State.

XVII. That all people have a natural and inherent right to emigrate from one State to another, that will receive them; or to form a new State in vacant countries, or in such countries as they can purchase, whenever they think thereby they can promote their own happiness.

XVIII. That the people have a right to assemble together, to consult for their common good—to instruct their representatives, and to apply to the legislature for redress of grievances, by address, petition or remonstrance.

XIX. That no person shall be liable to be transported out of this State for trial, for any offence committed within this State.

[Related provisions from the body of the Vermont Constitution.]

Section V. The freemen of this Commonwealth, and their sons, shall be trained and armed for its defence, under such regulations, restrictions and exceptions, as the general assembly shall, by law, direct; preserving always to the people, the right of choosing their colonels of militia, and all commissioned officers under that rank, in such manner, and as often, as by the said laws shall be directed.

Section XXII. Trials shall be by jury; and it is recommended to the legislature of this State to provide by law, against every corruption or partiality in the choice, and return, or appointment, of juries.

Section XXVI. Excessive bail shall not be exacted for bailable offences: and all fines shall be moderate.

Section XXXII. The printing presses shall be free to every person who undertakes to examine the proceedings of the legislature, or any part of government.

Section XXXIX. That the inhabitants of this State, shall have liberty to hunt and fowl, in seasonable times, on the land they hold, and on other lands (not enclosed;) and, in like manner, to fish in all boatable and other waters, not private property, under proper regulations, to be hereafter made and provided by the General Assembly.

Section XLIII. The declaration of rights is hereby declared to be a part of the Constitution of this State, and ought never to be violated, on any pretence whatsoever.

Thorpe, VI, pp. 3739-3748.

South Carolina Constitution March 19, 1778

[Provisions of the South Carolina Constitution which relate to individual rights or to provisions contained in other state bills of rights.]

XXXVIII. That all persons and religious societies who acknowledge that there is one God, and a future state of rewards and punishments, and that God is publicly to be worshipped, shall be freely tolerated. The Christian Protestant religion shall be deemed, and is hereby constituted and declared to be, the established religion of this State. That all denominations of Christian Protestants in this State, demeaning themselves peaceably and faithfully, shall enjoy equal religious and civil privileges. . . .

XLI. That no freeman of this State be taken or imprisoned, or disseized of his freehold, liberties, or privileges, or outlawed, exiled or in any manner destroyed or deprived of his life, liberty, or property, but by the judgment of his peers or by the law of the land.

XLII. That the military be subordinate to the civil power of the State.

XLIII. That the liberty of the press be inviolably preserved.

Thorpe, VI, pp. 3255-3257.

Massachusetts Constitution October 25, 1780
(excerpt)

PREAMBLE

The end of the institution, maintenance, and administration of government, is to secure the existence of the body politic, to protect it, and to furnish the individuals who compose it with the power of enjoying in safety and tranquillity their natural rights, and the blessings of life: and when ever these great objects are not obtained, the people have a right to alter the government, and to take measures necessary for their safety, prosperity, and happiness.

The body politic is formed by a voluntary association of individuals: it is a social compact, by which the whole people covenants with each citizen, and each citizen with the whole people, that all shall be governed by certain laws for the common good. It is the duty of the people, therefore, in framing a constitution of government, to provide for an equitable mode of making laws, as well as for an impartial interpretation and a faithful execution of them; that every man may at all times, find his security in them.

We, therefore, the people of Massachusetts, acknowledging, with grateful hearts, the goodness of the great Legislator of the universe, in affording us, in the course of His providence, an opportunity, deliberately and peaceably, without fraud, violence, or surprise, of entering into an original, explicit, and solemn compact with each other; and of forming a new constitution of civil government, for ourselves, and posterity; and devoutly imploring His direction in so interesting a design, do agree upon, ordain, and establish, the following *Declaration of Rights, and Frame of Government,* as the CONSTITUTION OF THE COMMONWEALTH OF MASSACHUSETTS.

PART THE FIRST

A DECLARATION OF THE RIGHTS OF THE INHABITANTS OF THE COMMONWEALTH OF MASSACHUSETTS

ARTICLE I. All men are born free and equal, and have certain natural, essential, and unalienable rights; among which may be reckoned the right of enjoying and defending their lives and liberties; that of acquiring, possessing, and protecting property; in fine, that of seeking and obtaining their safety and happiness.

II. It is the right as well as the duty of all men in society, publicly, and at stated seasons, to worship the SUPREME BEING, the great Creator and Preserver of the universe. And no subject shall be hurt, molested, or restrained, in his person, liberty, or estate, for worshipping GOD in the manner and season most agreeable to the dictates of his own conscience; or for his religious profession of sentiments; provided he doth not disturb the public peace, or obstruct others in their religious worship.

III. As the happiness of a people, and the good order and preservation of civil government, essentially depend upon piety, religion, and morality; and as these cannot be generally diffused through a community but by the institution of the public worship of GOD, and of public instructions in piety, religion, and morality: Therefore, to promote their happiness, and to secure the good order and preservation of their government, the people of this commonwealth have a right to invest their legislature with power to authorize and require, and the legislature shall, from time to time, authorize and require, the several towns, parishes, precincts, and other bodies politic, or religious societies, to make suitable provision, at their own expense, for the institution of the public worship of GOD, and for the support and maintenance of public Protestant teachers of piety, religion, and morality, in all cases where such provision shall not be made voluntarily.

And the people of this commonwealth have also a right to, and do, invest their legislature with authority to enjoin upon all the subjects an attendance upon the instructions of the public teachers aforesaid, at stated times and seasons, if there be any on whose instructions they can conscientiously and conveniently attend.

Provided, notwithstanding, that the several towns, parishes, precincts, and other bodies politic, or religious societies, shall, at all times, have the exclusive right of electing their public teachers, and of contracting with them for their support and maintenance.

And all moneys paid by the subject to the support of public worship, and of the public teachers aforesaid, shall, if he require it, be uniformly applied to the support of the public teacher or teachers of his own religious sect or denomination, provided there be any on whose instructions he attends; otherwise it may be paid towards the support of the teacher or teachers of the parish or precinct in which the said moneys are raised.

And every denomination of Christians, demeaning themselves peaceably, and as good subjects of the commonwealth, shall be equally under the protection of the law: and no subordination of any one sect or denomination to another shall ever be established by law.

IV. The people of this commonwealth have the sole and exclusive right of governing themselves, as a free, sovereign, and independent state; and do, and forever hereafter shall, exercise and enjoy every power, jurisdiction, and right, which is not, or may not hereafter be, by them expressly delegated to the United States of America, in Congress assembled.

V. All power residing originally in the people, and being derived from them, the several magistrates and officers of government, vested with authority, whether legislative, executive, or judicial, are their substitutes and agents, and are at all times accountable to them.

VI. No man, nor corporation, or association of men, have any other title to obtain advantages, or particular and exclusive privileges, distinct from those of the community, than what arises from the consideration of services rendered to the public; and this title being in nature neither hereditary, nor transmissible to children, or descendants, or relations by blood, the idea of a man born a magistrate, lawgiver, or judge, is absurd and unnatural.

VII. Government is instituted for the common good; for the protection, safety, prosperity, and happiness of the people; and not for the profit, honor, or private interest of any one man, family, or class of men: Therefore the people alone have an incontestible unalienable, and indefeasible right to institute government; and to reform, alter, or totally change the same, when their protection, safety, prosperity, and happiness require it.

VIII. In order to prevent those who are vested with authority from becoming oppressors, the people have a right, at such periods and in such manner as they shall establish by their frame of government, to cause their public officers to return to private life; and to fill up vacant places by certain and regular elections and appoinments.

IX. All elections ought to be free; and all the inhabitants of this commonwealth, having such qualifications as they shall establish by their frame of government, have an equal right to elect officers, and to be elected, for public employments.

X. Each individual of the society has a right to be protected by it in the enjoyment of his life, liberty, and property, according to standing laws. He is obliged, consequently, to contribute his share to the expense of this protection; to give his personal service, or an equivalent, when necessary: but no part of the property of any individual can, with justice, be taken from him, or applied to public uses, without his own consent, or that of the representative body of the people. In fine, the people of this commonwealth are not controllable by any other laws than those to which their constitutional representative body have given their consent. And whenever the public exigencies require that the property of any individual should be appropriated to public uses, he shall receive a reasonable compensation therefor.

XI. Every subject of the commonwealth ought to find a certain remedy, by having recourse to the laws, for all injuries or wrongs which he may receive in his person, property, or character. He ought to obtain right and justice freely, and without being obliged to purchase it; completely, and without any denial; promptly, and without delay; conformably to the laws.

XII. No subject shall be held to answer for any crimes or offence, until the same is fully and plainly, substantially, and formally, described to him; or be compelled to accuse, or furnish evidence against himself. And every subject shall have a right to produce all proofs that may be favorable to him; to meet the witnesses against him face to face, and to be fully heard in his defence by himself, or his counsel, at his election. And no subject shall be arrested, imprisoned, despoiled, or deprived of his property, immunities, or privileges, put out of the protection of the law, exiled, or deprived of his life, liberty, or estate, but by the judgment of his peers, or the law of the land.

And the legislature shall not make any law that shall subject any person to a capital or infamous punishment, excepting for the government of the army and navy, without trial by jury.

XIII. In criminal prosecutions, the verification of facts, in the vicinity where they happen, is one of the greatest securities of the life, liberty, and property of the citizen.

XIV. Every subject has a right to be secure from all unreasonable searches, and seizures, of his person, his houses, his papers, and all his possessions. All warrants, therefore, are contrary to this right, if the cause or foundation of them be not previously supported by oath or affirmation, and if the order in the warrant to a civil officer, to make search in suspected places, or to arrest one or more suspected persons, or to seize their property, be not accompanied with a special designation of the persons or objects of search, arrest, or seizure; and no warrant ought to be issued but in cases, and with the formalities prescribed by the laws.

XV. In all controversies concerning property, and in all suits between two or more persons, except in cases in which it has heretofore been otherways, used and practised, the parties have a right to a trial by jury; and this method of procedure shall be held sacred, unless, in causes arising on the high seas, and such as relate to mariners' wages, the legislature shall hereafter find it necessary to alter it.

XVI. The liberty of the press is essential to the security of freedom in a state it ought not, therefore, to be restricted in this commonwealth.

XVII. The people have a right to keep and to bear arms for the common defence. And as, in time of peace, armies are dangerous to liberty, they ought not to be maintained without the consent of the legislature; and the military power shall always be held in an exact subordination to the civil authority, and be governed by it.

XVIII. A frequent recurrence to the fundamental principles of the constitution, and a constant adherence to those of piety, justice, moderation, temperance, industry, and frugality, are absolutely necessary to preserve the advantages of liberty, and to maintain a free government. The people ought, consequently, to have a particular attention to all those principles, in the choice of their officers and representatives: and they have a right to require of their lawgivers and magistrates an exact and constant observance of them, in the formation and execution of the laws necessary for the good administration of the commonwealth.

XIX. The people have a right, in an orderly and peaceable manner, to assemble to consult upon the common good; give instructions to their representatives, and to request of the legislative body, by the way of addresses, petitions, or remonstrances, redress of the wrongs done them, and of the grievances they suffer.

XX. The power of suspending the laws, or the execution of the laws, ought never to be exercised but by the legislature, or by authority derived from it, to be exercised in such particular cases only as the legislature shall expressly provide for.

XXI. The freedom of deliberation, speech, and debate, in either house of the legislature, is so essential to the rights of the people, that it cannot be the foundation of any accusation or prosecution, action or complaint, in any other court or place whatsoever.

XXII. The legislature ought frequently to assemble for the redress of grievances, for correcting, strengthening, and confirming the laws, and for making new laws, as the common good may require.

XXIII. No subsidy, charge, tax, impost, or duties ought to be established, fixed, laid, or levied, under any pretext whatsoever, without the consent of the people or their representatives in the legislature.

XXIV. Laws made to punish for actions done before the existence of such laws, and which have not been declared crimes by preceding laws, are unjust, oppressive, and inconsistent with the fundamental principles of a free government.

XXV. No subject ought, in any case, or in any time, to be declared guilty of treason or felony by the legislature.

XXVI. No magistrate or court of law shall demand excessive bail or sureties, impose excessive fines, or inflict cruel or unusual punishments.

XXVII. In time of peace, no soldier ought to be quartered in any house without the consent of the owner; and in time of war, such quarters ought not to be made but by the civil magistrate, in a manner ordained by the legislature.

XXVIII. No person can in any case be subject to law-martial, or to any penalties or pains, by virtue of that law, except those employed in the army or navy, and except the militia in actual service, but by authority of the legislature.

XXIX. It is essential to the preservation of the rights of every individual, his life, liberty, property, and character, that there be an impartial interpretation of the laws, and administration of justice. It is the right of every citizen to be tried by judges as free, impartial, and independent as the lot of humanity will admit. It is, therefore, not only the best policy, but for the security of the rights of the people, and of every citizen, that the judges of the supreme judicial court should hold their offices as long as they behave themselves well; and that they should have honorable salaries ascertained and established by standing laws.

XXX. In the government of this commonwealth, the legislative department shall never exercise the executive and judicial powers, or either of them: the executive shall never exercise the legislative and judicial powers, or either of them: the judicial shall never exercise the legislative and executive powers, or either of them: to the end it may be a government of laws and not of men.

Thorpe, III, pp. 1888-1893.

New Hampshire Bill of Rights June 2, 1784

PART I.—THE BILL OF RIGHTS

ARTICLE I. All men are born equally free and independent; therefore, all government of right originates from the people, is founded in consent, and instituted for the general good.

II. All men have certain natural, essential, and inherent rights; among which are—the enjoying and defending life and liberty—acquiring, possessing and protecting property—and in a word, of seeking and obtaining happiness.

III. When men enter into a state of society, they surrender up some of their natural rights to that society, in order to insure the protection of others; and, without such an equivalent, the surrender is void.

IV. Among the natural rights, some are in their very nature unalienable, because no equivalent can be given or received for them. Of this kind are the RIGHTS OF CONSCIENCE.

V. Every individual has a natural and unalienable right to worship GOD according to the dictates of his own conscience, and reason; and no subject shall be hurt, molested, or restrained in his person, liberty or estate for worshipping GOD, in the manner and season most agreeable to the dictates of his own conscience, or for his religious profession, sentiments or persuasion; provided he doth not disturb the public peace, or disturb others, in their religious worship.

VI. As morality and piety, rightly grounded on evangelical principles, will give the best and greatest security to government, and will lay in the hearts of men the strongest obligations to due subjection; and as the knowledge of these, is most likely to be propagated through a society by the institution of the public worship of the DEITY, and of public instruction in morality and religion; therefore, to promote those important purposes, the people of this state have a right to impower, and do hereby fully impower the legislature to authorize from time to time, the several towns, parishes, bodies-corporate, or religious societies within this state, to make adequate provision at their own expence, for the support and maintenance of public protestant teachers of piety, religion and morality:

Provided notwithstanding, That the several towns, parishes, bodies-corporate, or religious societies, shall at all times have the exclusive right of electing their own public teachers, and of contracting with them for their support and maintenance. And no portion of any one particular religious sect or denomination, shall ever be compelled to pay towards the support of the teacher or teachers of another persuasion, sect or denomination.

And every denomination of christians demeaning themselves quietly, and as good subjects of the state, shall be equally under the protection of the law: and no subordination of any one sect or denomination to another, shall ever be established by law.

And nothing herein shall be understood to affect any former contract made for the support of the ministry; but all such contracts shall remain, and be in the same state as if this constitution had not been made.

VII. The people of this state, have the sole and exclusive right of governing themselves as a free, sovereign, and independent state, and do, and forever hereafter shall, exercise and enjoy every power, jurisdiction and right pertaining thereto, which is not, or may not hereafter be by them expressly delegated to the United States of America in Congress assembled.

VIII. All power residing originally in, and being derived from the people, all the magistrates and officers of government, are their substitutes and agents, and at all times accountable to them.

IX. No office or place whatsoever in government, shall be hereditary—the abilities and integrity requisite in all, not being transmissible to posterity or relations.

X. Government being instituted for the common benefit, protection, and security of the whole community, and not for the private interest or emolument of any one man, family or class of men; therefore, whenever the ends of government are perverted, and public liberty manifestly endangered, and all other means of redress are ineffectual, the people may, and of right ought, to reform the old, or establish a new government. The doctrine of non-resistance against arbitrary power, and oppression, is absurd, slavish, and destructive of the good and happiness of mankind.

XI. All elections ought to be free, and every inhabitant of the state having the proper qualifications, has equal right to elect, and be elected into office.

XII. Every member of the community has a right to be protected by it in the enjoyment of his life, liberty and property; he is therefore bound to contribute his share in the expence of such protection, and to yield his personal service when necessary, or an equivalent. But no part of a man's property shall be taken from him, or applied to public uses, without his own consent, or that of the representative body of the people. Nor are the inhabitants of this state controllable by any other laws than those to which they or their representative body have given their consent.

XIII. No person who is conscientiously scrupulous about the lawfulness of bearing arms, shall be compelled thereto, provided he will pay an equivalent.

XIV. Every subject of this state is entitled to a certain remedy, by having recourse to the laws, for all injuries he may receive in his person, property or character, to obtain right and justice freely, without being obliged to purchase it; completely, and without any denial; promptly, and without delay, conformably to the laws.

XV. No subject shall be held to answer for any crime, or offence, until the same is fully and plainly, substantially and formally, described to him; or be compelled to accuse or furnish evidence against himself. And every subject shall have a right to produce all proofs that may be favorable to himself; to meet the witnesses against him face to face, and to be fully heard in his defence by himself, and counsel. And no subject shall be arrested, imprisoned, despoiled, or deprived of his property, immunities, or privileges, put out of the protection of the law, exiled or deprived of his life, liberty, or estate, but by the judgment of his peers or the law of the land.

XVI. No subject shall be liable to be tried, after an acquittal, for the same crime or offence.—Nor shall the legislature make any law that shall subject any person to a capital punishment, excepting for the government of the army and navy, and the militia in actual service, without trial by jury.

XVII. In criminal prosecutions, the trial of facts in the vicinity where they happen, is so essential to the security of the life, liberty and estate of the citizen, that no crime or offence ought to be tried in any other county than that in which it is committed; except in cases of general insurrection in any particular county, when it shall appear to the Judges of the Superior Court, that an impartial trial cannot be had in the county where the offence may be committed, and upon their report, the assembly shall think proper to direct the trial in the nearest county in which an impartial trial can be obtained.

XVIII. All penalties ought to be proportioned to the nature of the offence. No wise legislature will affix the same punishment to the crimes of theft, forgery and the like, which they do to those of murder and treason; where the same undistinguishing severity is exerted against all offences; the people are led to forget the real distinction in the crimes themselves, and to commit the most flagrant with as little compunction as they do those of the lightest dye: For the same reason a multitude of sanguinary laws is both impolitic and unjust. The true design of all punishments being to reform, not to exterminate, mankind.

XIX. Every subject hath a right to be secure from all unreasonable searches and seizures of his person, his houses, his papers, and all his possessions. All warrants, therefore, are contrary to this right, if the cause or foundation of them be not previously supported by oath, or affirmation; and if the order in the warrant to a civil officer, to make search in suspected places, or to arrest one or more suspected persons, or to seize their property, be not accompanied with a special designation of the persons or objects of search, arrest, or seizure; and no warrant ought to be issued but in cases, and with the formalities prescribed by the laws.

XX. In all contoversies concerning property, and in all suits between two or more persons, except in cases in which it has been heretofore otherwise used and practiced, the parties have a right to a trial by jury; and this method of procedure shall be held sacred, unless in causes arising on the high seas, and such as relate to mariners wages, the legislature shall think it necessary hereafter to alter it.

XXI. In order to reap the fullest advantage of the inestimable privilege of the trial by jury, great care ought to be taken that none but qualified persons should be appointed to serve; and such ought to be fully compensated for their travel, time and attendance.

XXII. The Liberty of the Press is essential to the security of freedom in a state; it ought, therefore, to be inviolably preserved.

XXIII. Retrospective laws are highly injurious, oppressive and unjust. No such laws, therefore, should be made, either for the decision of civil causes, or the punishment of offences.

XXIV. A well regulated militia is the proper, natural, and sure defence of a state.

XXV. Standing armies are dangerous to liberty, and ought not to be raised or kept up without the consent of the legislature.

XXVI. In all cases, and at all times, the military ought to be under strict subordination to, and governed by the civil power.

XXVII. No soldier in time of peace, shall be quartered in any house without the consent of the owner; and in time of war, such quarters ought not to be made but by the civil magistrate, in a manner ordained by the legislature.

XXVIII. No subsidy, charge, tax, impost or duty shall be established, fixed, laid, or levied, under any pretext whatsoever, without the consent of the people or their representatives in the legislature, or authority derived from that body.

XXIX. The power of suspending the laws, or the execution of them, ought never to be exercised but by the legislature, or by authority derived therefrom, to be exercised in such particular cases only as the legislature shall expressly provide for.

XXX. The freedom of deliberation, speech, and debate, in either house of the legislature, is so essential to the rights of the people, that it cannot be the foundation of any action, complaint, or prosecution, in any other court or place whatsoever.

XXXI. The legislature ought frequently to assemble for the redress of grievances, for correcting, strengthening and confirming the laws, and for making new ones, as the common good may require.

XXXII. The people have a right in an orderly and peaceable manner, to assemble and consult upon the common good, give instructions to their representatives; and to request of the legislative body, by way of petition or remonstrance, redress of the wrongs done them, and of the grievances they suffer.

XXXIII. No magistrate or court of law shall demand excessive bail or sureties, impose excessive fines, or inflict cruel or unusual punishments.

XXXIV. No person can in any case be subjected to law martial, or to any pains, or penalties, by virtue of that law, except those employed in the army or navy, and except the militia in actual service, but by authority of the legislature.

XXXV. It is essential to the preservation of the rights of every individual, his life, liberty, property and character, that there be an impartial interpretation of the laws, and administration of justice. It is the right of every citizen to be tried by judges as impartial as the lot of humanity will admit. It is therefore not only the best policy, but for the security of the rights of the people, that the judges of the supreme (or superior) judicial court should hold their offices so long as they behave well; and that they should have honorable salaries, ascertained and established by standing laws.

XXXVI. Economy being a most essential virtue in all states, especially in a young one; no pension shall be granted, but in consideration of actual services, and such pensions ought to be granted with great caution, by the legislature, and never for more than one year at a time.

XXXVII. In the government of this state, the three essential powers thereof, to wit, the legislative, executive and judicial, ought to be kept as separate from and independent of each other, as the nature of a free government will admit, or as is consistent with that chain of connection that binds the whole fabric of the constitution in one indissoluble bond of union and amity.

XXXVIII. A frequent recurrence to the fundamental principles of the Constitution, and a constant adherence to justice, moderation, temperance, industry, frugality, and all the social virtues, are indispensably necessary to preserve the blessings of liberty and good government; the people ought, therefore, to have a particular regard to all those principles in the choice of their officers and representatives: and they have a right to require of their law-givers and magistrates, an exact and constant observance of them in the formation and execution of the laws necessary for the good administration of government.

Thorpe, IV, pp. 2453-2457.

APPENDIX B

Bill of Rights Provisions Comparison Chart

The chart on pages 782-783 compares the provisions in the United States Bill of Rights with the provisions contained in its immediate antecedents, the state ratifying convention proposals and the state bills of rights.

The left column lists the source document titles. At the top is the United States Bill of Rights. Below this are listed in reverse chronological order the six state ratifying conventions which proposed amendments to the Constitution, the seven state bills of rights (plus Vermont's), and the English Bill of Rights. To the right on the top line are the first ten amendments to the Constitution with vertical descriptive headings in italics below the amendment number. In the columns below these headings an "X" is placed if the source document in the left column of that line contains a related provision.

Source[1]	An "X" Below				
United States Bill of Rights	Article #		I		
General Subject {	*Religion*	*Speech*	*Press*	*Assembly*	*Petition*
North Carolina Amendments	X	X	X	X	X
New York Amendments[2]	X		X	X	X
Virginia Amendments	X	X	X	X	X
New Hampshire Amendments	X				
South Carolina Amendments[3]					
Massachusetts Amendments					
New Hampshire Bill of Rights	X	X[4]	X	X	X
Massachusetts Declaration of Rights	X	X[4]	X	X	X
Vermont Declaration of Rights	X	X	X	X	X
North Carolina Declaration of Rights	X		X	X	
Maryland Declaration of Rights	X	X[4]	X	X	X
Pennsylvania Declaration of Rights	X	X	X	X	X
Delaware Declaration of Rights	X		X		X
Virginia Bill of Rights	X		X		
English Bill of Rights		X[6]			X

1 The Rhode Island amendments are not included.
2 These were understandings contained in the ratification.
3 This understanding was contained in the ratification.
4 Freedom of speech for legislators in the legislature.

Indicates a Related Provision in Source

II	III	IV	V	VI	VII	VIII	IX	X
Bear Arms	*Quartering*	*Search*	*Due Process*	*Procedure*	*Jury Trial*	*Punishments*	*Enumeration*	*Construction*
X	X	X	X	X	X	X	X	X
X	X	X	X	X	X	X	X	X
X	X	X	X	X	X	X	X	X
X	X		X		X			X
								X
			X		X			X
X	X	X	X	X	X	X		
X	X	X	X	X	X	X		
X		X	X	X	X	X[5]		
X		X	X	X	X	X		
X	X	X	X	X	X	X		
X		X	X	X	X	X[5]		
X	X	X	X	X	X	X		
X		X	X	X	X	X		
X[7]						X		

5 This provision contained in the body of the Constitution.
6 Freedom of speech for members of Parliament in Parliament.
7 "That the subjects which are protestants may have arms for their defence suitable to their conditions and as allowed by law."

APPENDIX C

Estimates of popular support for the Constitution and Bill of Rights.

The following tables and statistics relate to the twelve state conventions which met in 1787 and 1788. The population figures are estimates utilized in the Federal Convention and are taken from *Debates*, vol. I, p. 194. This appendix does not include statistics relating to the second North Carolina convention of 1789, nor the Rhode Island convention of 1790, both of which ratified the Constitution after the amendments to the Constitution were proposed by Congress.

TABLE I.

Table of State conventions; * indicates state constitution contains a bill of rights, numbers of delegates, delegate votes for and against Constitution in each, estimated state population (not including slaves), population per convention vote.

State Convention	Convention Delegates	Vote For	Vote Against	State Population	Populati Per Vote
Delaware*	30	30	0	37,000	1,233
Pennsylvania*	69	46	23	341,000	4,942
New Jersey	38	38	0	138,000	3,632
Georgia	26	26	0	27,000	1,038
Connecticut	168	128	40	202,000	1,202
Massachusetts*	355	187	168	352,000	991
Maryland*	74	63	11	174,000	2,351
South Carolina	162	149	13	93,000	574
New Hampshire*	104	57	47	82,000	788
Virginia*	168	89	79	300,000	1,786
New York	57	30	27	238,000	4,175
North Carolina*	268	84	184	181,000	675

Population in states with a bill of rights—1,467,000
Population in states with no bill of rights— 698,000

TABLE II.

Portions of population for and against ratification extrapolated from the population per vote of delegates in convention for the twelve conventions held in 1787 and 1788. For states marked ** the convention proposed amendments to the Constitution. The states are divided into three equal groups of four based upon their chronological order of ratification. This arrangement more clearly demonstrates trends.

State	Vote For	Vote Against
Delaware	37,000	0
Pennsylvania	227,333	113,667
New Jersey	138,000	0
Georgia	27,000	0
Subtotal	429,333	113,667
Connecticut	153,905	48,095
Massachusetts**	185,420	166,580
Maryland	148,135	25,865
South Carolina**	85,537	7,463
Subtotal	572,997	248,003
New Hampshire**	44,942	37,058
Virginia**	158,929	141,071
New York**	125,263	112,737
North Carolina**	56,731	124,269
Subtotal	385,865	415,135

Examining the subtotals of the votes for each group of four conventions and relating them to some of the occurrences during the ratification period, some general trends are evident.

Note that three of the first four conventions ratified unanimously (Delaware, New Jersey, Georgia). No other states did so. Also note that the unanimous votes were in relatively small states. The representatives of twenty one per cent of the population in the first four conventions voted against ratification.

In the middle four states two of the conventions proposed amendments (Massachusetts, South Carolina). The percentage against ratification increased from twenty one to thirty per cent.

In the last group of four states all of the conventions proposed amendments. One convention did not ratify and insisted that a bill of rights be added first (North Carolina), and one ratified with the understanding that a specified bill of rights was in effect and consistent with the Constitution (New York). The percentage of the population against ratification increased to fifty two per cent.

In every convention which proposed amendments (six of the twelve conventions), the votes for ratification are votes for the proposed amendments. All votes against ratification are votes expressive of a desire for amendments prior to ratification.

Generally, the Constitution had great momentum at first, but as the latter conventions met, there was more opposition, more desire for amendments, and ratification became contingent upon amendments, especially a bill of rights, being added subsequent to ratification.

Examining the totals:

For the Constitution without amendments 34%	731,373
For the Constitution with proposed amendments 30%	656,822
Against Constitution / For previous amendments 36%	776,805

It appears that a significant majority required amendments (66%). The largest single total is against the constitution and in favor of previous amendments (36%). Those who liked the Constitution just as it was (34%) and those who favored with proposed amendments (30%) managed to get the Constitution ratified due to their combined efforts (64%). In general, close to one third of the populace was in each category with two thirds in favor of the ratification of the Constitution, and two thirds in favor of a bill of rights.

These figures which are population related are not necessarily conclusive for at least four reasons. First, the population figures are estimates. Second, the actual population represented by each delegate to a state convention could vary considerably within a state. Third, not all constituents of a delegate would have agreed with the delegates vote. Fourth, there is no certainty that a vote of the citizens themselves would have coincided with the votes of their delegates in convention. However, for purposes of examining some broad general trends, and considering that this data is fairly accurate, the information should be reliable for the purposes used here.

INDEX

"A. B.," 626n; article by, 626
Adams, John, 72, 252, 463, 597, 626, 627, 628, 634
–Letter from, 101
Adams, Samuel, 250n2, 263n2, 518, 573, 592, 701-702, 702n1; comments in the Massachusetts Convention, 246; every one of his amendments proposed in the Massachusetts Convention has been reported by the committee of the House of Representatives, 702; introduction of amendments in the Massachusetts Convention, 260; nominated for U.S. Senator in Massachusetts, 529; proposed a bill of rights in the Massachusetts convention, xlix
–Letters from, 704, 708
–Letters to, 31, 188
"Adolphus," article by, 591
"Agricola," article by, 75
"Agrippa," 253n; articles by, 123, 207, 222, 252
Albany Antifederal Committee, article by, 337
"Alfred," article by, 572
"Almanac-Maker, The," article by, 248
Amendment Ticket, 574
Amendments to the Constitution, xxxiv, xxxvii, 32, 35, 37, 62, 96, 97, 101, 118, 123, 145, 147, 187, 203, 231, 250, 254, 310, 312-327, 338, 361-363, 366, 367, 371-373, 374, 397-398, 455, 471-472, 475, 479-480, 488-489, 501-502, 510, 511, 512-514, 515, 516, 517-518, 519, 524, 525-526, 532, 533, 534-537, 538, 545, 546, 549, 551, 558-559, 560, 561-566, 571, 572-573, 575, 582, 585, 586, 587-588, 590, 591-592, 594-595, 600, 604, 607-608, 612-623, 626, 629, 630, 632, 635, 639-641, 642, 645-647, 666-667, 668, 670, 670n2, 673, 676, 676n1, 679, 683n2, 683n3, 684-700, 702-703, 705, 709, 713, 714, 717, 731; according to the apparent sense of America, 551; action of Maryland Convention respecting, 399; action on those proposed by Congress in Virginia, 721; advocates for, 517; agreement to add at the end of the Constitution, 700; all excluded of a doubtful or unimportant nature, 704; a large proportion, probably a majority of those who assented to the Constitution in its present form are desirous of, 528; all good federalists and antifederalists call for, 573; a majority of the most respectable, important, and extensive states will be in favor of, 502; as have been proposed by many state conventions, 631; as proposed by the House of Representatives, 706; anxiously desired by several of the states, 488; anxiously desired by so great a proportion of the citizens of these states, 631; are essential and necessary, 342; avoid electing those opposed to the proposed amendments, 549; beginning discussion of in a committee of the whole House of Representatives, 683; bill of rights, 119, 387, 656; bill of rights will be proposed in Congress, 643; checks on government for securing the liberties of the people, 602; comparison chart of proposed amendments, state bills of rights, and the Federal Bill of Rights provisions, 782-783; comparison of proposed amendments of Virginia and Congress, 722-725; conduct of North Carolina regarding, 527; Congress had right to insert, 30; Congress may take up the consideration of, 639; Congress would never propose, 666; Constitution needs, 512; custom of recommending with ratifications of the Constitution began to prevail, 479; dangerous and fallacious, 724; deceitful promises of, 567; difficulty started against those proposed by Congress in Virginia, 722; discussion of in the House of Representatives, 647-666; essential, 367; explanatory ones more accurately defining the great rights of the people are necessary, 526; explanatory ones in

the New York ratification, 605; extent of, 579; fallacy of the reiterated assurances of, 567; farrago of borrowed from Virginia, 667; fate of those proposed by Congress in Virginia, 720; favorable comments upon in the Massachusetts Convention, 592-593; favorable to liberty, 518; Federalist and Antifederalist proposed modes of obtaining in the New York Assembly, 612-623; Federalists now talk highly of, 630; five states having ratified in the fullest expectation of, 607; first Massachusetts amendment related to a bill of rights, 367; folly of future ones, 399; for guarding against an undue administration of the federal government, 445; for securing the liberties of the people, 543; for the security of the important rights of the people, 597; friend to, 631; friends of, 471; general arguments concerning, xli-xlv; George Mason received much satisfaction from those proposed by the House of Representatives, 710; good for nothing, 718; governor of Massachusetts and many other patriots sacredly pledged to attempt adoption of, 573; have been proposed by Massachusetts, New Hampshire and other states, 502; if North Carolina, Rhode Island, and New York reject the Constitution, they will have litte influence to obtain, 393; importance of, 708; in Congress are limited and insecure, 711; in Congress are specious, 711; in favor of essential rights, 700; in favor of liberty, 43; in the House of Representatives, xxxix; important and substantial, 682; incorporated into the Constitution or made a supplementary act, 687, 705; indispensably necessary, 533; influence upon Rhode Island to ratify the Constitution, 732; introduced by Samuel Adams in the Massachusetts Convention, 260, 701-702; involves all the great unalienable & essential rights of freemen, 546; making their way through Congress, 711; mode of obtaining, xxxvii, 25, 254, 513, 536-537, 551-553, 572, 579, 585, 598, 603, 641; no prospect of further ones from Congress, 739; necessary, 515, 530, 648; not dissatisfied with, 721; not from a conviction that any whatever are necessary, 613; object of being to establish our rights and liberty on the most immutable basis, 566; objections of the Virginia Senate to those proposed by Congress, 722; objects of Madison's, 673-674; observations on action relating to in Virginia, 726-727; opinion of advocates of Constitution is that some are highly necessary, 575; pamphlet collection of, 538; people of Massachusetts deluded into seeking future, 399; pretence of is a specious one, 574; previous ones insisted upon by North Carolina, 583; previous to ratification of the Constitution, 356, 380, 453, 455, 488, 499, 559, 580, 587; previous versus subsequent, 342, 376, 383, 390-393, 398, 448, 701; probability of adding to Constitution, 257-258; proceedings in New York Assembly for application to Congress to call a convention for, 624-625; proper, 310; proposed by Massachusetts, 279, 322; proposed by Massachusetts, Virginia and New York, 638; proposed by New York, 580, 639; proposed by several states, 553; proposed by the South Carolina Convention, compared, 782; proposed by the state conventions, 564; proposed by Virginia and other states, 584; proposed in order to get Constitution ratified, xxxiii; proposed only as an expedient to procure a majority in favor of the Constitution, 606; proposed relating to control of the militia, 568; ratifications of by the states, 720, 726, 728, 730, 732, 739, 742; reasons for postponement of Congress' by the Virginia Senate, 722-725; recommended to the first Congress, 453; referred to a special committee, 650; remarks on, 556; restrained from proposing in the Pennsylvania Convention, 159; right of the people to propose, 283; rights mentioned in first ten of those proposed by Congress were not all that a free people would require the exercise of, 720; secure the rights of the people by, 573; should follow the example of Massachusetts by adopting the Constitution first and proposing amendments, 376; small possibility of should we follow the example of Massachusetts, 378; South Carolina will propose, 301; subsequent to ratification of the Constitution, 449, 529, 713; support for analyzed, xxxvi; support for and against analyzed, 784-786; table showing ratifications of, 746; texts of and states ratifying, 743-746; the concurring opinions of a whole continent have agreed to be necessary, 583; the great body of the community is certainly in favor of, 606; the liberties of America depend upon the cause of, 633; the whole of have fallen in Virginia, 726; those of Virginia adopted word for word, 501; those proposed by Congress sent to the states, 718; those proposed by Congress taken up in the Virginia Assembly, 719; those proposed by Congress will convince North Carolina to adopt the Constitution, 719; those proposed by James Madison and by the conventions of the different states, 679; those proposed by the Massachusetts Convention are not to be regarded, 549; those sent up from the House of Representatives held out a safeguard to personal liberty in great many instances, 717; those to secure civil liberty will not be refused, 644; those who are opposed to, 633; those who favor, 548; to ascertain, secure and protect the great rights of the people, 627; to guard essential rights, 609; to guard our rights from every possible danger, 565; to guard the great and fundamental rights of the people, 595; to protect personal rights, 723; to secure liberty, 208; to secure the just rights and liberty of the people, 83; to secure the liberty of the people, 386; to secure the liberty of the subject, 270; to secure the liberties of the people of America, 650; to secure the rights and liberties of the people, 572; to secure the rights of the people, 553; those of North Carolina are nearly the same as Virginia's, 526; three fourths of the people are desirous for, 517; two thirds of the whole people of America wish for, 611; universal cry is for, 571; voice of the people cry aloud for, 551; which related to individual rights, xxxix; which shall effect personal liberty alone, 668; which will render the liberties of the country secure, 560; will be attempted in no other way than through Congress, 641; wished for by other states, 499

–Congress, proposed by, 714, 728; text of, 715-717

–Harrisburg Convention, proposed by, text of, 522-523

–House Select Committee, proposed by, text of, 680-682

–James Madison, comments of George Washington on those proposed by, 644; copy of those proposed by sent to Samuel Johnston, 673; gave notice that he intended to bring on the subject of in the House of Representatives, 642; general comments on, 700-701; grouped those relating to rights of individuals together, xxxviii; his announcement of plan to bring up subject in House of Representatives dispersed almost universal pleasure, 667; his proposed amendments altogether respected personal liberty, 669; his proposed amendments relate to things already well secured, 683; in favor of, 603; introduced in the House of Representatives by, xxxviii; is now the ostensible patron of, 682; made some motions on in Congress, 682; milk and water amendments introduced by, 683; newspaper remarks upon those proposed by in Congress, 670; North Carolina will not approve the Constitution unless Congress agrees to amendments similar to those proposed by James Madison, 676; observations on those proposed by, 672; on the mode of obtaining, 609-610; ones proposed by are those most strenuously required by the opponents of the Constitution, 694; report he is opposed to, 594; sent Edmund Randolph a copy of those he introduced into the House of Representatives, 669; sent Thomas Jefferson a copy of those he introduced into the House of Representatives, 669; text of those proposed by, 654-656; thanked for a copy of his proposed amendments

sent to Joseph Jones, 673; those proposed by, 672n4; those proposed by the House of Representatives do not differ much from those originally proposed by, 704
–Maryland Minority, proposed, text of, 357-360
–Massachusetts Convention, also proposed by New Hampshire convention, 445-446; enjoined it upon future representatives in Congress to work for adoption of, 524; proposed, 252, 279, 322, 591-593, 782, text of, 261-262
–New Hampshire Convention, proposed, text of, 445-447
–New York Convention, proposed by, 584; compared, 782; text of, 480-488
–North Carolina Convention, proposed by, compared, 782; text of, 503-509
–Pennsylvania Minority, proposed, text of, 150-152, 159-161
–Rhode Island Convention, proposed, text of, 733-738
–Richmond Antifederal Committee, proposed, 444; text of, 388-390
–Virginia Convention, proposed by, compared, 782; text of, 457-462
–See also: Bill of Rights, Declaration of Rights, Rights
"America," {Noah Webster}, article by, 186
"American, An" {Tench Coxe}, article by, 185
"American Citizen, An" {Tench Coxe}, broadside by, 54
American Herald (Boston), xlviii; articles from, 69, 129
American Revolution, xxiii, xxvi, xxviii, xxxvi, 180, 218, 246, 303, 341, 402, 419, 437, 475, 478, 535, 578, 607; object of, 556; principles of, 286, 581
Ames, Fisher, (Ma.), 592, 668n, 680n; comments in the House of Representatives on amendments, 703
–Letters from, 667, 668, 679, 683
Antifederalists, xxiii, xxxiv, 300, 333, 335, 342, 518, 542n2, 548, 573, 608, 627, 634, 667, 690; defined, 629; considered Constitution defective, xxxi; strategy of for the Virginia Convention, 361-363; tried to introduce all of the ratifying convention amendments in Congress, xxxix; unanimity among for a bill of rights, xlv; views on a bill of rights, xli
Anti-republicans, not friendly to the rights of the people, 343
"Anti-Foederalist," articles by, 264, 265
"Argus," article by, 84
"Aristides," {Alexander Contee Hanson}, 268, 328; article by, 588; pamphlet by, 239
Aristocratics, defined, 629
"Aristocrotis," 177n2, 192n2, 195n2, 201n2, 202n2, 222n2, 226n2, 251n2, 286n2, 298n2, 340n3; pamphlet by, 329
Arm, militia, 731; the freemen of America, 212
Armed, a free people ought to be, 729; a hundred thousand men armed and disciplined, 57; Americans possess the advantage of being armed over the people of almost every other nation, 234-235; freemen of Vermont and their sons shall be armed, 768; I am well armed myself analogy, 556; one fourth of people in despotic governments are armed to oppress the others, 344; people are, xlv; the freemen and their sons shall be, 755; the militia of New York at all times hereafter shall be armed, 764; the whole body of the people are, 40
–See Also: Disarm, Disarmed, Disarming, Militia
Armed Populace, xxiv, xxv, li; constitutional protection for, lii; duscussion of protection for, xlv-lii; protected in every state bill of rights, xxvi
–See also: Militia–Well Regulated
Arms, 500; a whole people with arms in their hands, 578; advised their constitutents to take up, 535; appeal to, 230; appeal to against despotic government, 181; arbitrary power ought to be resisted by, 246; available in every seaport, 238; bear for the common defence, 712; public ones called in for cleaning, 226; a citizen carrying in a republic which is not free such as Venice is punished with instant death, 336; citizens rush tumultuously to, 184; collect all the public, 193; compelling them to bear, 703; Congress may or may not furnish them, 373; conscientiously scrupulous of bearing, 174, 338, 479, 655, 696-697, 751, 764, 777; Constitution shall

never be construed to authorize Congress to prevent the people from keeping their own arms, xlix, 260, 702; controversy over collection of in Pennsylvania, 176, 176n2, 191, 192n2, 194, 195n2, 200, 201n2, 201, 202n2, 221, 222n2, 226, 226n2, 251, 251n2, 286, 286n2, 298, 298n2, 334, 335n2, 340, 340n3; dangerous to trust in hands of all the farmers, mechanics, laborers, 331; desireability of having supplied by the government, xlix; every young fellow is providing himself with a rifle or musket, 339; impolicy of puting or keeping in the hands of a nervous people, 131; in the hands of the people enables them to defend their rights and privileges against every invader, 190; kingdoms of Europe afraid to trust the people with arms, 235; let people take in spirit of resistance, 102; militia choose to repair and clean their own, 200; militia shall have two sets of, 406; nation of freemen with arms in their hands, 231; not possessed by people in countries under arbitrary government, 190; people exhorted to take up in defence of their rights, 178; people forced to by encroachments of the government on their rights, 311; people have in their hands, 556; people left in full possession of, 452; people of the United States keeping their own, 260; proportion of men capable of bearing in population, 626; public ones must be called in upon pretence of having them cleaned, 334; religiously scrupulous of bearing, 360, 390, 459, 474, 505, 695, 703, 707, 735; repairing and cleaning their own, 339; right of bearing declared inherent in the people, 668; right of the people to bear, xxviii, 151, 668, 783; right of people to bear for the defence of the state, 762; right of the people to bear for the defence of themselves and the state, 290, 291, 754, 762, 767; right of the people to bear for the defense of themselves and their own state, or the United States, or for the purpose of killing game, xlviii, 151, 160; right of the people to keep, 248n2, 250n2, 263n4, 703; right of the people to keep and bear, xxviii, li, 290, 390, 459, 481, 505, 676n3, 735; right of the people to keep and bear shall not be infringed, 654, 680, 695, 707, 710, 712, 716, 720, 726, 728, 730, 732, 739, 744; right of the people to keep and bear their private arms, 671, 674n3; right of the people to keep and to bear for the common defence, 290, 712, 773; the militia of these free commonwealths, entitled and accustomed to their arms, 275-276; the right of the people to keep and bear arms has been recognized by the general government, 719; the yeomanry possess, 91; the rights of bearing arms for defence, or killing game, 281; the ultima ratio, 464; those conscientiously scrupulous of bearing arms shall not be compelled to serve as a soldier, 360; to enforce the Constitution recourse must be had to, 500; we took up during the Revolution at the distant appearance of danger to the natural and unalienable rights of men, 341; wherewith you could defend yourselves are gone, 373; which Providence has put into the hands of friends to liberty, 55; while the militia have, 195; wish all of were collected, 298

Arms, Consider, 329

Army, xxiv, 2, 11, 26, 30, 43, 46, 55, 57, 105, 106, 108, 199, 210, 211, 216, 234, 286, 332, 370, 637, 645, 741; active militia will compose a very respectable, 331; capable of erecting a despotism over the great body of the people, 185; Continental, xxv; could they subdue a nation of freemen with arms in their hands, 230; dangerous to liberty, 290, 773; infernal engine of oppression, 211; power of Congress to raise and support, 19, 352; quell resistance, 185; render unnecessary by use of the militia, 196
  –See Also: Standing Army

Articles of Confederation, See: Confederation–Articles of

Assembly, right of, See: Rights–Of Assembly

Atherton, Joshua
  –Letter from, 629

Bail, excessive, 80, 150, 159, 186, 293, 389, 434, 439, 458, 474, 481, 505, 655,

671, 681, 707, 717, 735, 745, 748, 752, 758, 762, 763, 768, 774, 779
Barrell, Nathaniel
–Letter from, 208
Bastile, 294
Bear Arms, See: Arms, People, Rights–Arms, Keeping and/or Bearing
"Belasarius," article by, 583
Belknap, Jeremy, 263n4
Benson, Egbert, (N.Y.), comments in the House of Representatives on amendments, 691, 697
Bill of Rights, xxiii, xxvi, xxxiii, xxxv, 28, 30, 32, 38, 41, 46, 49, 50, 51, 53, 55, 56, 57, 58, 64, 66, 67, 68, 69, 70, 73, 75, 84, 88, 89, 98, 99, 101, 103, 104, 107, 112, 117, 120, 127, 135, 138, 147, 149, 179, 186, 188, 193-194, 204-206, 209, 210, 214, 216, 218, 224, 229, 237n2, 240-242, 244, 247, 249, 250n2, 251, 255, 260, 265, 266-270, 288, 291, 297, 311, 331, 334, 335, 340, 345-353, 355n2, 367, 379, 392, 395, 396-397, 398, 436-440, 441-442, 443-444, 444n2, 455, 476, 479n2, 500, 531, 534, 538-541, 572, 578n2, 579, 585, 586, 595, 608, 626, 635, 645, 657, 667, 668, 670n2, 675, 676, 678, 725n2, 739n; a law to Congress, to teach them what they shall not do that might hurt or oppress the community, 544; absolute necessity of, 71; all of the state constitutions founded upon one or contain express reservations, 79; answer to Mason's objection concerning lack of, 144; appears to be a contradiction in terms, 729; as an amendment, 387, 656; as conditions of ratification, 447; ascertaining and fundamentally establishing the unalienable rights of men, 364; best security against encroachments of despotism, 109; by which the liberties of individuals might have been secured against the abuse of federal power, 148; comparison of provisions in state, federal and proposed, 781-783; complaint about lack of, 242; concept of attacked by Federalists, xliii; Constitution is inferior to state constitutions because it lacks one, 208; Constitution not disgraced with one, 125, 192; Constitution of each state has one for its own citizens, 57; contains the more important of the amendments proposed by the state conventions, 638; controlling abuses of power, 540; dangers of in Constitution, 492; dangerous to a republic, 384; discussion of in the New York Convention, 477-479; essential, 252; federal, 782; fundamental maxims of free government, 540; fundamentally establishing those unalienable and personal rights of men without the secure enjoyment of which there can be no liberty, 167; general arguments concerning, xli-xlv; general voice calls for, 502; governments of greater number of states are founded upon, 27; grand bulwarks of freedom, 193; incontrovertible truths of are a test to try all the acts of the national legislature, 443; incorporated into the Rhode Island ratification, 733-735; indispensably necessary, 379; individual rights, 345; ingrafted on the constitution, 591; kindles a fire of persecution against liberty, 677; lack of, 101, 224, 286; Madison's opinion on, 539; more necessary in the Constitution than in state constitutions, 81; most states had and so should Constitution, 440; necessary for the Constitution of the United States as well as for an individual state, 70; necessary for the personal rights of the people, 59; necessity of, 307; necessity of greater in Constitution than any government before, 436; needed in Constitution, xxxi; no satisfactory reason for the omission of, 123; not found in the Constitution, 79; not needed in Constitution because it is a government of states, not of individuals, 57; none in Constitution, 34; none to secure the privileges of freemen from their governors, 557; objections to, 658-660; omission of, 167, 177, 396-397; ought to have in Constitution to save us from oppression, 387; partial one in Constitution, 94; people are entitled to against every government on earth, 177; people use to defend rights against future encroachments of despotism, 193; polar star and great support of American liberty, 384; privileges of freemen, 233;

provisions, 263; purpose of, 348; purpose is to restrain and regulate rulers, 27; related to Article II of the Confederation, 338; Richard Henry Lee brings up in Congress, 27; secure our great unalienable rights, 385; secures liberty of the press and other invaluable personal rights, 58; summary of, 247; support for analyzed, 784-786; to confine the power of the government within proper boundaries, 490; to guard the people against the federal government, as they are already guarded against their state governments, 503; the safety of the people depends upon, 228; that woven into the New York ratification is a security against the encroachments of the general government, 509; they forgot to put one in the Constitution, 387; to secure the just rights and liberties of the people from violation, 284; to secure the rights of individuals, 494; to secure those unalienable rights which are never to be given up, 490; to secure to every member of the society those unalienable rights which ought not to be given up to any government, 490; Virginia will insist upon annexing one, 266; virtually assured, xxxvi; voted down in the Federal Convention, xxx; well regulated, 206; what benefit would a citizen have from a state bill of rights in a federal court, 269; will be exhibited in the Pennsylvania convention, 126; will unquestionably be added to the Constitution, 638; without one implication might swallow up all our rights, 436; you have one to defend you against the state government, but none to defend you against Congress, 437

–Delaware, 114, 782; text of, 750-752

–English, xliii, 29, 79, 101, 193, 218, 267, 288, 290, 341, 379, 383, 393, 396, 449, 490, 492, 677, 782

–Maryland, 782; text of, 755-761

–Massachusetts, 782; might be taken as a guide to annex one to the U. S. Constitution, 251; text of, 770-775

–New Hampshire, 782; text of, 775-780

–New York, has none, 327; omission of one in state constitution related to omission of one in the U. S. Constitution, 396-397

–New York Convention, has followed the example of Virginia and expressed the substance of the Virginia bill of rights, 532; text of, 480-483

–North Carolina, 782; text of, 761-763

–North Carolina Convention, 526, 544; text of, 503-506

–Pennsylvania, 52, 782; text of, 752-754

–Pennsylvania Minority, xlviii, 339; text of, 159-161

–Rhode Island Convention, text of, 733-736

–Richmond Antifederal Committee, text of, 388-390

–State, xxix, 93, 218, 223, 270n2, 297n1, 306, 393-394, 398n1, 419, 490, 596, 747; are no security under Constitution, 34; do not limit the federal government, 94; fundamental principles essential to liberty, and privileges necessary to all free people, 444; not guaranteed under the Constitution, 274; not repealed, 646; origin of, 41; provisions relating to a well regulated militia added so people could protect liberty from the government, li; proposal that they shall be valid under the U. S. Constitution, 253, 522; sacred principles of not secured in the federal Constitution, 208; some states do not have, 646; that of the state will not limit Congress, 99; to prevent encroachments of future rulers, 67; treaties may render nugatory, 500; treaties shall not repeal or abrogate, 360; will not limit the federal government, 82

–Vermont, 782; text of, 765-768

–Virginia, 372, 383, 385, 436, 449, 782; controversy over existence of in the Pennsylvania convention, 114-115; how will it avail you under Constitution, 292; is of no validity, 374; contains republican political maxims of a free people, 377; secures the great and principal rights of mankind, 441; substance of expressed in the New York Convention bill of rights, 532; text of, 747-749; U. S. Constitution will destroy, 378; why were articles 8

through 13 read from, 435
–Virginia Convention, 723; text of, 457-459
–See Also: Amendments, Declaration of Rights, Rights, specific individual rights
Blackstone, William, 110
Blair, John, 454
Bland, Theodorick, 454
–Letter from, 545
–Letter to, 538
Boston, 73; attempt to stifle freedom of the press in, 84
Boston Gazette, articles from, 127, 517, 583, 627
Boudinot, Elias, (N.J.), comments in the House of Representatives on amendments, 666, 703
Bowdoin, James, 229, 286n1, 592, 610; comments in the Massachusetts Convention, 228
Brackenridge, Hugh Henry, article by, 291
Broadsides
"A True Friend," text of, 139
"An American Citizen," {Tench Coxe}, text of, 54
Announcement of candidacy for Congress by Arthur Lee, text of, 587
Declaration of Candidacy for Congress by John Francis Mercer, text of, 584
"Seceding Pennsylvania Assemblymen," text of, 30
"Brutus," 329; articles by: (N.Y.), II, 77; III, 104; IV, 122; (Va.), 144
Buchan, Earl of
–Letter to, 178
Bucks County Meeting, proceedings, 514
Burgh, James, 47
Burke, Aedanus, (S.C.), comments in the House of Representatives on amendments, 697-698
Burnley, Hardin, 722n2
–Letters from, 720, 721
Butler, Pierce, (S.C.), comments in the Federal Convention, 4
–Letter from, 683

"Caledonia, James de," 177n2, 192n2, 195n2, 201n2, 202n2, 222n2, 226n2, 251n2, 286n2, 335n2, 340n3; article by, 298
"Candidus," 233
"Candour," article by, 265
Carlisle Gazette, (Pa.), 176n2, 192n2, 201n2, 202n2, 222n2, 226n2, 251n2, 286n2, 298n2, 335n2, 340n3; articles from, 57, 137, 193, 238, 475
Carmichael, William
–Letters to, 154, 367, 510, 585, 634
Carrington, Edward
–Letter from, 726
–Letter to, 366
Carroll, Daniel, (Md.), comments in the House of Representatives on amendments, 688, 700
"Cassandra," article by, 397
"Cassius," articles by, 178, 630
Caswell, Richard, (Governor, N.C.)
–Letter to, 102
"Cato," 68
"Centinel," 68, 97, 176n2, 195n2, 201n2, 202n2, 222n2, 226n2, 233, 251n2, 286n2, 298n2, 329, 335n2, 340n3; articles by: I, 33; II, 58; III, 85; IX, 191; XXII, 566; XXIX, 711
Charles the First, 67, 101, 304, 364, 393, 396, 423
Charles the Second, 67, 304
Chase, Jeremiah T., 361; election handbill of, 312
Chase, Samuel, 361
"Christian Farmer," article by, 543
"Cincinattus," 89n, articles by, I, 77; II, 87; III, 104; IV, 107
Circular Letter, 514, 542
–Cumberland County (Pa.), 519; text of, 472
–New York, 516, 529, 532, 542, 544, 555, 562, 564, 566, 580, 583-584, 585, 593, 616, 621-622; text of, 488
–Virginia, 586, 593; text of, 563
"Citizen, A" articles by, 57, 108
"Citizen of America, A" {Noah Webster}, 103n2; pamphlet by, 38
"Citizen of New York, A" 326
"Citizen of Pennsylvania, A" article by, 41
"Citizen of Philadelphia, A" {Peletiah Webster}, pamphlet by, 85
Civil Liberty, 28, 31, 99, 112, 144, 177, 216, 283, 361, 475, 503, 556, 600, 644; amendments to secure will not be refused, 644; implication is to be the foundation of under the Constitution, 407; in imminent danger, 27; ruin of, 124; state constitution framed upon best principles of, 556; the total extinction of, 470
–See Also: Civil Rights, Liberty, Rights

Civil Rights, 112, 244, 364
 –See Also: Civil Liberty, Liberty, Rights
Civil War, 10, 38, 316-318, 339, 342, 472, 526, 535, 556, 573, 615
"Civis," articles by, 527, 597
"Civis Rusticus," article by, 235
Clark, Abraham, address to the public, 611
 –Letter from, 479
Clay, Charles, comments in the Virginia Convention, 399, 404, 416
Clinton, DeWitt
 –Letter from, 529
Clinton, Charles
 –Letter to, 529
Clinton, George, (Governor, N.Y.), 489, 560, 575, 592, 627, 628, 632, 638; speech to the New York Assembly, 580
 –Letters to, 177, 562
"Columbian Patriot," {Mercy Warren}, pamphlet by, 243
Common Defence, 15, 290, 463, 712, 773
"Conciliator," 233
Concord, Massachusetts, xxv
Confederation, 437, 494
 –Articles of, xxviii, 58, 77, 188, 556
 –Article II of, xxix, 46, 49, 120, 165, 247, 346, 440, 490, 494, 495, 500; Article II of related to a bill of rights, 338, 494, 495
 –Congress of the, xxix, 2, 30, 31n, 33n, 41; cannot maintain an army, 3; excerpts from debates in, 27
"Confederationalist," 37n, article by, 64
Congress of the Confederation, See: Confederation–Congress
Congress, United States, 2, 15, 17, 26, 27, 50, 52, 54, 56, 57, 58, 59, 62, 68, 72, 74, 89, 93, 98, 154, 230, 255, 280, 412, 718n2, 720n, 725n2, 726n, 728n, 730n, 732n, 740n, 742n, 743n; acts of become the supreme law of the land, 44; amend the Constitution, 514; amendment to restrict powers of, 260; amendments should be proposed by, 594-595; amendments to be considered by, 560; and amendments, 362-363; application to by Virginia for calling a convention to amend the Constitution, 561; application to call a convention to amend the Constitution, 547; blamed for stopping free circulation of the newspapers, 210; can disarm the militia, 498; cannot employ illegal and unconstitutional methods due to the militia, 45; comparison of under Confederation and Constitution, 46; Constitution shall never be construed to authorize Congress to prevent the people from keeping their own arms, 260, 702; defects of its power under the Articles of Confederation, 155; has no power to disarm the militia, 276; hopes will take into consideration the necessary amendments, 704; must be mad to form any project of tyranny, 556; power over the militia, 174; powers of, 18, 99, 145, 277; propose amendments to the states, 609-610; proposed amendments to the Constitution, text of, 715-717; recommend amendments to, 455; remote possibility that they will keep the militia armed, 405; request for calling a convention to amend the Constitution, 563; shall never disarm any citizen, 446; should be left at liberty to propose amendments or call a convention, 615; should endeavor to amend the Constitution, 612; should propose amendments instead of calling a convention, 613-614; will be its own interpreter, 193; will certainly make the proposed alterations, 456; will not possess the confidence of the people, 173
Connecticut Courant (Hartford), articles from, 147, 188
Connecticut Gazette (New London), article from, 188
Connecticut Jounal (New Haven), 61, 225n2; articles from, 61, 74
Connecticut, failed to ratify the Bill of Rights, xli; ratification vote, xxxiii
Conscience, See: Freedom of Conscience, Freedom of Religion, Liberty of Conscience, Liberty of Religion, Religious Freedom, Religious Liberty, Rights–Of Conscience
Constitution
 –Pennsylvania, 33, 238, 239n2
 –State, absolutely destroyed, 65; of states framed upon the best principles of civil liberty, 556
 –United States, xxx, 15, 31, 32, 34, 36, 46, 54, 56, 71, 78, 83, 154, 238, 529; adopt or reject is all we have to

do, 254; amend previous or subsequent to ratification, 367; amend then adopt, 314; amendment of, 556-558; Article V of, 642, 643; Article VI of, 52, 273; body of the common people who always do the fighting of a country would more likely fight against it, 318; charge that criticism of was being suppressed, xxxiii; construction of powers delegated under, 345-353, 461, 480, 508; dangerous to the liberties of man, 250; dangerous to the rights and liberties of the people, 338; defective, 556-558; defective and dangerous, 632; defects of, 561; defects of involve all the great and unalienable rights of freemen, 562; described, xxix; did not contain effectual provisions against encroachments on particular rights, 653; differing from the principles of the revolution, 296; does not secure the unalienable rights of freemen, 497; does not sufficiently guard the rights of the people, or secure them against the encroachments of their rulers, 319; doubts about, 48; endangers our liberties, 497; further declaratory and restrictive clauses, 715; has been adopted, 543; liable to strong and fundamental objections, 44; no means provided to amend previous to ratification, xxx; shall never be construed to authorize Congress to prevent the people from keeping their own arms, 260, 702; ought to secure a genuine militia, and guard against a select militia, 354; people dreaded the operation of, 561; possibly defective, 193; prospects for ratification of, 366; rejection or adoption is the alternative, 204; replete with dangerous defects, 500; representation under is inadequate and unsafe, 168; support for analyzed, 318, 784-786; text of, 15-26; will resist against it, 364; James Wilson's distinction concerning construction of state and federal, 46; would deprive the people of their dearest rights and liberties, 337; would have been certainly rejected in Virginia, 700; would have been rejected in Massachusetts if it had not been for the expectation of amendments, 518
  –See also: Free Constitution

Constitutionalists, of Pennsylvania, xxxi

Construction, proper construction of the powers of Congress, 46
  –See Also: James Wilson

Convention, another federal, 37, 244, 260, 585; another general, 15, 532, 582, 591; application to Congress for, 612; general called for by the Virginia Assembly, 586; people will clamor for if Congress does not pursue amendments, 650; proceedings in New York Assembly for application to Congress for, 624-625; second, 579; state, 35, 62; to amend the Constitution, 44, 207, 488, 501, 503, 514, 520, 526, 542, 544, 547, 554-555, 562-566, 572, 575, 595, 604, 609, 612, 626, 627, 629, 630, 639, 641, 643, 643n3, 650, 666, 701, 715; Virginia's application to Congress to call, 599
  –See Also: Federal Convention, Harrisburg Convention, Convention listings under each state.

Corbin, Francis, 423, 454, 547, 560; comments in the Virginia House of Delegates, 62; comments in the Virginia Convention, 375-376, 422-423

Country Journal (Poughkeepsie), article from, 630

"Countryman, A" 61n; articles by, 153, 224

Coxe, Tench, 235n3, 277n, 674n3; articles by, 210, 275, 670, 674; broadside by, 54; wrote the article by "A Pennsylvanian," 672
  –Letters from, 510, 672
  –Letters to, 514, 542, 546, 673

Cromwell, Oliver, 304

Cruel, and unusual punishments, See: Punishments

Cumberland County Meeting, (Pa.), 512n2; proceedings, 471

Cushing, William, 263

Daily Advertiser (New York), articles from, 86, 186, 527, 598, 604, 639

Dana, Francis, 592

Davie, William R.
  –Letters from, 575, 666

Dawson, John, comments in the Virginia Convention, 451
  –Letter from, 725

Dayton, Jonathan, (N.J.), comments in the Federal Convention, 3, 9; motion in the Federal Convention on regulation of the militia, 8
Declaration of Independence, xxiv, 227
Declaration of Rights, 30, 54, 84, 86, 88, 97, 99, 104, 143, 147, 154, 172, 181, 187, 202, 229, 235, 244, 248, 250, 253, 264, 297, 297n1, 301, 328, 356, 443-444, 463, 491, 531, 634, 637, 692, 695; ascertain and protect the liberties of the people, 451; asserting and securing from encroachment the great principles of civil and religious liberty, and the unalienable rights of the people, 453, 503; comparison of provisions in state and federal, 781-783; defining the rights of the individual against the abuse and improper exercise of power, 340; entered by Congress on its journal [not part of Constitution], 590; fundamental principle which ought to be found in every free government, 104; fundamental, unalienable privileges, which are essential to liberty, 450; inculcate just ideas of their rights upon the people, 739; Jefferson's remarks on, 635-637; necessity of a full and explicit one, 114; none in the Constitution, 34; not necessary because the state declarations are not repealed, 12, 659; objection to the Constitution, 137; omission of, 77; proposed by Patrick Henry in the Virginia Convention, 450; proposed in the New York Convention by John Lansing Jr., text of, 473-475; purpose of, 348; sacrosanct, 187; support for analyzed, 784-786; there is none in the Constitution, 490; to secure those rights which are essential to freemen, 531; to secure to posterity those privileges which are essential to the proper limiting the extent of sovereign power, 531; want of will pretty certainly be remedied, 510
-Delaware, 291; text of, 750-752
-English, 645, 656; See Also: Bill of Rights, English
-Maryland, 290; is part of the state constitution, 761; text of, 755-761
-Massachusetts, 232n2, 290; text of, 770
-New York Convention, to remove doubtfull constructions, and to guard against an undue and improper administration, 580; text of, 480-483
-North Carolina, 291; is part of the state constitution, 763; text of, 761-763
-North Carolina Convention, 534n2; text of, 503-506
-Pennsylvania, 290; is part of the state constitution, 755; text of, 752-754
-State, 270n, 740; all of the state constitutions founded upon one or contain express reservations, 79; the great object is to limit and qualify the powers of government, 657
-Vermont, is part of the state constitution, 768; text of, 765-768
-Virginia, 379n2, 394, 396n2, 439; annexed to the Virginia Convention ratification of the Constitution, 532; Articles 8 through 13 read in the Virginia Convention, 434; text of, 747-749
-Virginia Convention, text of, 457-462
-See Also: Amendments, Bill of Rights, Rights, specific individual rights
Defence, proper means of for the people, 498
Delaware, bill of rights provisions compared, 782; bill of rights provision on a well regulated militia, xxvii; declaration of rights, text of, 750; unanimous vote for ratification of the Constitution, xxxiii
-Legislature, article the fourth of the amendments of Congress as adopted by, 730
"Delegate Who Has Catched Cold, A" article by, 455
"Deliberator," article by, 277
"Democratic Federalist, A" articles by, 45, 68
"Denatus," 387
Despotic Government, 344
Despotism, 58, 145, 193, 245, 370, 413, 567, 652, 713, 731; a bill of rights is the best security against encroachments of, 109; no standing army of Congress could support despotism over this continent, 100
"De Witt, John," xlviii, 71n, 84, 215n; articles by: II, 69; V, 129
Dexter, Samuel
-Letter to, 601

Dickinson, John, (Del.), comments in the Federal Convention on regulation of the militia, 4
Disarm, Congress has no power to disarm the militia, 276; Congress may arm or disarm all or any part of the freemen of the United States, xlviii, 212; Congress shall never disarm any citizen, 446; people, xlvii; protection against disarming the people, 210
–Militia, xlix, 176, 176n2, 191, 192n2, 195n2, 221, 251, 251n2, 286, 286n2, 289n2, 302, 331, 335, 340, 340n3, 366, 401, 498
Disarmed, 8; militia must be, 334; people, 146; people disarmed by tyrants, 190; people must be before a standing army can rule, 40; people not to be disarmed of their weapons, 452
Disarming, no law shall be passed for disarming the people, xlviii, 151, 160; temporary disarming of the people, 221
Dollard, Patrick, comments in the South Carolina convention, 363
Donald, Alexander
–Letter to, 264
Dumas, C.W.F.
–Letter to, 265
Dwight, Thomas
–Letter to, 667

Earl of Oxford, 47
Elections, 538, 542, 567, 630, 631; address of Samuel Sterett, 595; amendment ticket, 574; announcement of candidacy for Congress by Arthur Lee, 587; appeal for James Monroe, 586; avoid electing those opposed to amendments, 549; declaration of candidacy for Congress by John Francis Mercer, 584; federal, 517-518; for Congress and state legislators, xxxvii; for second North Carolina Convention, 714; of vice president, 560; relation to amendments, xxxvii; federal and antifederal tickets, 597
Ellsworth, Oliver, (Con.), article by, 147; comments in the Federal Convention, against select militia, 5, on regulation of the militia, 7; motion in the Federal Convention on regulation of the militia, 4
Enumeration, of certain rights in the Constitution, 681, 708, 711, 717, 746, 783
"Essay on Federal Sentiments," article, 57
Eustice, William
–Letter to, 575
Eve, George
–Letter to, 594
Ex Post Facto Law, 20

"Farmer, A" articles by, (Md.), 266, 289, 305, 308, 328; (N.H.), 204; (Pa.), 336, 741
"Father Abraham," article by, 553
Fayette County Delegates, certificate of election, 512
Federal Convention, xxiii, xxix, 36, 37, 62, 498, 556, 558; bill of rights voted down in, xxx, 12; excerpts from debates in, 2, 6, 7, 11, 12, 13
"Federal Correspondent, A" article by, 524
"Federal Farmer," li, 97n2, 355n1, 475n2; pamphlets by, 89, 342
Federal Gazette, (Phil.), articles from, 296, 556, 567, 574, 670, 676, 729
"Federal Republican, A" 122n1; article by, 581; pamphlet by, 119
Federal Republican Committee (N.Y), 444
–Letters from, 554, 560
"Federalism," article by, 534
Federalist, The, 235n2, 277, 277n, 282n2; texts of: VIII, 105; XVI, 136, XXVIII, 182; XXXV, 195; XLIII, 231; XLV, 234; LIX, 281
Federalists, xxiii, xxxiv, 69, 238, 342, 526, 542n2, 573, 596, 608, 626, 628, 634, 640, 668, 690, 704; attack the concept of a bill of rights, xliii; Constitution considered perfect by some, xxxi; defined, xxiii, 629; friend to amendments has now become the criterion of, 517; tried to limit amendments in Congress to those relating to individual rights, xxxix; views concerning a bill of rights, xlii; views on amendments, xli
Fenner, Arthur, (Governor, R.I.)
–Letter from, 732
Field, Samuel, 329
Fines, excessive, 80, 150, 159, 186, 293, 389, 434, 439, 458, 474, 481, 505, 655, 671, 681, 707, 717, 735, 745, 748, 752, 758, 762, 763, 774, 779; militia, 570; shall be moderate, 768

Fitzsimons, Thomas, (Pa.), comments in the House of Representatives on amendments, 686

Fleming, William
 –Letter from, 270
 –Letter to, 231

"Foederal Constitution," 65, 66n; article by, 37

"Foreign Spectator," articles by, 11, 26, 556, 567

Forrest, Uriah
 –Letter from, 149
 –Letter to, 186

Franklin, Benjamin, 64, 107, 146, 193, 292, 333

Free Constitution, 180, 190, 729; a declaration of personal rights premised in most, 34
 –See Also: Free Country, Free Government, Free Nation, Free Republic, Free State

Free Country, 167, 196, 347, 418, 575, 675, 729; a well armed and well regulated militia being the best security of, 654-655; liberties, privileges, and immunities usual and necessary for citizens of, 110; militia true bulwark of, 226; standing armies dangerous to, 285
 –See Also: Free Constitution, Free Government, Free Nation, Free Republic, Free State

Free Government, xxviii, 30, 32, 39, 81, 95, 104, 122, 145, 146, 153, 180, 191, 287, 290, 294, 295, 328, 343, 354, 388, 426, 467, 475n2, 528, 538, 566, 618, 671, 674, 678, 713, 731, 749, 751, 756, 774; a jealousy of rulers ought to subsist in all, 727; a standing army is the bane of, 731; a well regulated militia is the proper and natural defence of a free government, xxvii, 290, 758; a well regulated militia is the proper, natural and safe defence of a free government, xxvi, 752; as opposed to a despotic government, 344; as opposed to a government by a lordly and profligate few, 566; distinction between arbitrary and, 271; fundamental maxims of, 540; incompatible with a standing army, 303; power of people in is supposed to be paramount to the existing power, 417; republican, xlv, 228; rests upon power of the people, 2
 –See Also: Free Constitution, Free Country, Free Nation, Free Republic, Free State

Free Nation, 58, 105; reduced to bondage by standing army, 337
 –See Also: Free Constitution, Free Country, Free Government, Free Republic, Free State

Free People, 89, 93, 96, 222, 285, 289, 290, 293, 298, 336, 359, 389, 474, 545, 626n; a well regulated militia composed of the yeomanry have ever been considered as the bulwark of, 211; militia is the last resource of, 145; ought to be armed, 729; political maxims of, 377; rights of, 191; rights of as were fully expressed at the head of our different constitutions, 455; the rights a free people would require the exercise of, 720

Free Press, See: Freedom of the Press

Free Republic, 336; a well regulated militia is the true defence of, 240
 –See Also: Free Constitution, Free Country, Free Government, Free Nation, Free State

Free State, xxvii, 95, 607; a well regulated militia being necessary to the security of, 712, 716, 720, 726, 728, 730, 732, 739, 744; a well regulated militia being the best security of, 697, 710; a well regulated militia composed of the body of the people being the best security of, 680, 695, 707, 712; a well regulated militia composed of the body of the people trained to arms is the proper, natural, and safe defence of, xxvi, li, 390, 435, 459, 505, 748; a well regulated militia including the body of the people capable of bearing arms is the proper, natural and safe defence of, li, 481, 735; proper defence of consists in militia, 449
 –See Also: Free Constitution, Free Country, Free Government, Free Nation, Free Republic

Freedom, from a permanent military, 635; republican constitutions and principles of, 41

Freedom of Conscience, 138
 –See Also: Freedom of Religion, Liberty of Conscience, Liberty of Relgion, Religious Freedom, Religious Liberty, Rights–Of Conscience

Freedom of Religion, 27, 60, 95, 177, 249, 264, 266, 343, 383, 390, 392, 395, 451, 475, 481, 498, 502, 505, 589, 590, 635, 645, 646, 654, 667, 668, 688-690, 703, 733, 740, 743, 749, 750, 752, 759, 762, 763, 764, 765, 768, 770, 775, 782
 –See Also: Freedom of Conscience, Liberty of Conscience, Liberty of Religion, Religious Freedom, Religious Liberty, Rights–Of Conscience
Freedom of Speech, 33, 76, 151, 160, 242, 281, 390, 458, 505, 638, 646, 654, 680, 690, 692, 694, 706, 707, 716, 723, 735, 743, 754, 767, 782
Freedom of the Press, 6, 27, 30, 33, 34, 35, 38, 40, 42, 45, 76, 78, 87, 95, 101, 151, 160, 177, 180, 218, 227, 249, 264, 266, 279, 281, 284, 295, 296, 344, 352, 353, 359, 378, 390, 434, 440, 448, 451, 458, 463, 466, 474, 478, 482, 502, 505, 589, 590, 594, 603, 608, 609, 635, 638, 645, 654, 655, 657, 668, 671, 675, 680, 681, 690, 706, 707, 716, 735, 740, 743, 748, 754, 755, 762, 763, 767, 768, 782; abolished, 34; cannot be abridged by Congress, 38; declared inherent in the people, 668; may be restrained, 43; one of the unalienable rights of the people, 227; sacred, 347; secured in each of the state constitutions, 37; the palladium of liberty, 37
 –See Also: Liberty of the Press
"Freeman, A" {Tench Coxe}, 277n2; article by, 398
Freeman's Journal, (Phil.), 176n2, 195n2, 201n2, 202n2, 222n2, 251n2, 286n2, 298n2, 335n2, 340n3, 679n, 682n, 708n2; articles from, 73, 103, 107, 138, 176, 179, 195, 210, 211, 226, 227, 258, 277, 294, 298, 309, 743
Freeman's Oracle, (Exeter, N.H.), articles from, 204, 264, 550
Freemen, 310, 368, 270, 388, 389, 398, 415, 469, 470, 514, 516, 524, 558, 597, 634, 676, 677, 729; a declaration of rights to secure those rights which are essential to, 531; a nation of freemen know how to prize liberty, 230-231; all the great unalienable and essential rights, liberties and principles of, 559; and their sons shall be armed, 755, 768; Congress at their pleasure may arm or disarm all or any part of the freemen of the United States, so that when their army is sufficiently numerous, they may put it out of the power of the freemen militia of America to assert and defend their liberties, xlviii, 212; every other essential right of is impliedly given up under the Constitution, 531; how far the characteristic rights of may be more impregnably fortified, 642; invaluable rights of, 466; liberties of may be in danger, 525; liberty of is secure due to the existence of a militia of freemen, 189; militia powers of government may be used to subject the freemen of a whole state to martial law, 302; natural rights of, 64; no bill of rights to secure the privileges of from their governors, 557; phalanx of defending their sacred liberties, 181; privileges of, 233, 301, 373; the Constitution does not secure the unalienable rights of, 497; the Constitution renders insecure all the great, essential, and unalienable rights of, 598; the inestimable rights of, 631; the rights of are only to be maintained by freemen, 335; the Virginia Convention amendments involve all the great unalienable and essential rights of, 546
"Friend to Amendments, A" article by, 517
"Friend to Liberty and Union, A" article by, 556
"Friend to the People, A" article by, 550
"Friend to the Republic, A" 265
"Friend to the Rights of the People, A" 264

Gallatin, Albert, 512, 519
Gazette of the State of Georgia, (Savannah), articles from, 28, 103
Gazette of the United States, (New York), article from, 719
General Militia, See: Militia–General
General Warrants, 33, 60, 76, 80, 95, 150, 160, 244, 269, 358, 389, 434, 439, 448, 458, 474, 478, 482, 505, 594, 603, 609, 645, 646, 655, 659, 668, 674, 681, 702, 707, 716, 735, 744, 748, 752, 754, 758, 762, 767, 772, 778, 783
 –See Also: Unreasonable Searches,

Writs of Assistance
General Welfare, 15, 32, 164, 463
"Georgian, A" article by, 103
Georgia, constitutional provisions, text of, 763; failed to ratify the Bill of Rights, xli; unanimous vote for ratification of the Constitution, xxxiii
Gerry, Elbridge, xxx, xxxi, 191n2, 210, 593, 629, 639, 682; candidate for Congress, 607; nominated for a U. S. Senator in Massachusetts, 529; objections to the Constitution, 51; was a member of the Federal Convention who refused to sign the Constitution, 529
−Comments in the Federal Convention, 5; regulation of the militia, 8; against national power over the militia, 10; against standing armies in time of peace, 3; liberty not as safe under national government as under the states, 9; objections to the Constitution, 14; trial by jury, 12; motion for a bill of rights, 12; motion relating to a free press, 13; motion for a limitation on number of troops, 3
−Comments in the House of Representatives on amendments, 663-664, 685, 687-688, 690, 691, 692, 693-694, 695, 696, 699
−Letters from, 51, 601, 607
−Letter to, 704
Gilbert, William W., comments in the New York Assembly, 622
Goodhue, Benjamin, (Ma.), comments in the House of Representatives on amendments, 648
Gordon, James Jr.
−Letter to, 283
Gorham, Nathaniel, (Ma.), comments in the Federal Convention, 3, on trial by jury, 12
Government, arbitrary, 191; despotic, 344; general comments on, 575-578; new federal will commence in March next, 579; supporters of would get the better of many regiments of troops, 382
−See Also: Free Government
Grayson, William, 454, 548n2, 669n1; chosen a U.S. Senator for Virginia, 575, 584; comments in the Virginia Convention, 423-424, 425, 426, 432, 440
−Letters from, 101, 668, 717
Griffin, Samuel
−Letter to, 710

"H.G.," article by, 639
Habeas Corpus, 6, 20
Hale, Matthew, 379
Hampden, John, 132, 212, 244
Hamilton, Alexander, articles by, 105, 136, 182, 195, 281
Hampshire Chronicle, (Springfield, Ma.), article from, 543
Hampshire Gazette, (Northampton, Ma.), article from, 328
Hancock, John, (Governor, Ma.), 247, 250n2, 263, 263n2, 280n2, 573, 592, 597, 634; speech to the Massachusetts legislature, text of, 731
Hanna, James, 515, 519, 523
−Letter from, 511
Hanson, Alexande Contee, article by, 588; pamphlet by, 239
Harris, John
−Letter from, 546
Harrisburg Convention, 510, 512, 514, 515, 518, 527, 529, 529n2, 532, 535, 542n2; call for, 471; called for in Cumberland County (Pa.) Circular letter, 472; proceedings of, 519
Harrison, Benjamin, 454; comments in the Virginia Convention, 385
Harrison, Richard, comments in the New York Assembly, 606, 622-623
Hartley, Thomas, (Pa.), comments in the House of Representatives on amendments, 685, 692, 698, 699
Hay, John
−Letter to, 714
"Helvidius Priscus," article by, 225
Henry, Patrick, 374, 423, 454, 529, 532, 547, 548, 560, 598, 628, 638, 727; comments in the Virginia House of Delegates in favor of the Virginia Convention being authorized to propose amendments to the Constitution, 62; proposes declaration of rights in the Virginia Convention, 450
−Comments in the Virginia Convention, 367-374, 376-379, 380-381, 392-395, 405-408, 413-414, 417-418, 422, 426-428, 434, 436-440, 441-442, 443-444, 448-451
−Letter from, 571
−Letters to, 644, 668, 713, 717, 739
Herald of Freedom, (Boston), article from, 610

Hobbes, Thomas, 337
"Honestus," article by, 548
Hopkinson, Francis
–Letter to, 634
House of Representatives, 15, 55, 297, 669n2, 670, 670n2, 672n2, 673n2, 676n2, 782n2, 683n2, 683n3; amendments to the Constitution proposed by, text of, 706-708; excerpts from debates in concerning amendments to the Constitution, 647-666, 679, 684, 687, 688, 695, 699, 700, 702; proceedings on amendments to the Constitution, 642, 643, 680; resolved into a committee of the whole on amendments, 687; shred or rag of representation, 44
Hudson Weekly Gazette, article from, 641
Hume, David, 47
Humphreys, David
–Letter from, 575
–Letter to, 637
Huntington, Samuel, (Governor, Con.)
–Letter from, 533
–Letter to, 718
Huntington, Benjamin, (Con.), comments in the House of Representatives on amendments, 689-690

"Impartial," article by, 45
"Impartial Citizen, An," articles by, 203, 299
"Impartial Examiner, The," articles by, 271, 285, 292
Impeachment, 17, 23
Implication, 71, 143, 241, 249, 309, 393, 394, 427, 437, 439, 724; arming the militia by a concurrence of power, 407; might swallow up all our rights without a bill of rights, 436; power by, 300, 378, 381, 699; rights secured by, 379; rights secured only by, 386
Independent Chronicle, (Boston), 701; articles from, 146, 202, 209, 516, 517, 547, 591, 606, 607
"Independent Freeholder, An," 281n2; article by, 217
Independent Gazetteer, (Phil.), 176n2, 177n2, 192n2, 195n2, 201n2, 202n2, 222n2, 226n2, 251n2, 286n2, 298n2, 335n2, 340n3, 475n2; articles from, 11, 26, 33, 34, 43, 45, 48, 51, 57, 58, 64, 66, 75, 85, 99, 118, 149, 176, 185, 191, 192, 200, 233, 265, 286, 287, 296, 301, 339, 379, 397, 463, 566, 572, 573, 608, 701, 711, 728, 741
Independent Journal, (N.Y.), articles from, 182, 281
"Indignatus," article by, 192
Iredell, James, comments in the North Carolina Convention, 491-493, 495-496
–Letters to, 207, 575, 683

Jackson, Jonathan
–Letter from, 575
Jackson, James, (Ga.), comments in the House of Representatives on amendments, 648, 663, 696
James the 2nd, 218, 267
Jarvis, Charles, 263n2; comments in the Massachusetts Convention, 249
Jefferson, Thomas, 308-309, 542n4, 743n; opinions of regarding the Constitution discussed in the North Carolina Convention, 502; opinions of regarding the Constitution discussed in the Virginia Convention, 391, 392
–Letters from, 102, 154, 177, 186, 249, 264, 265, 356, 366, 367, 502, 510, 532, 572, 579, 585, 626, 634, 635, 637, 638, 709, 740, 742
–Letters to, 101, 147, 149, 365, 532, 538, 575, 579, 643, 669
Johnson, Charles
–Letter from, 207
Johnson, Thomas
–Letter from, 149
Johnson, Zachariah, 547; comments in the Virginia Convention, 451-452
Johnston, Samuel, (Governor, N.C)
–Letters to, 533, 673
Jones, John Paul
–Letter to, 638
Jones, Joseph
–Letter from, 673
Jones, Samuel, comments in the New York Assembly, 616-618, 622
Jones, Willie, 714; comments in the North Carolina Convention, 501-502
Judicial Power, 23
Jury Trial, in civil cases, See: Trial by Jury

Keep Arms, See: Arms, People, Rights–Arms, Keeping and/or Bearing
King, Rufus (Ma.)
–Comments in the Federal Convention, free government rests upon the power of the people, 2;

object of the Federal Convention is to increase power of the general government at the expense of the state governments, 2; organizing, arming and disciplining the militia, 8; rights or power of the people should not be diminished, 2
–Letter to, 447

Lafayette, Marquis de
–Letters from, 187, 250
Lamb, John, 444
–Letters to, 380, 629
Lancaster Conference, 542, 542n2, 546
Lancaster, William, comments in the North Carolina Convention, 500
"Landholder, A" {Oliver Ellsworth}, article by, 147
"Landholder, The," 302, 305; article by, 289
Langdon, John, (N.H.), comments in the Federal Convention, 3, 5, 9
Lansing, Abraham G.
–Letter from, 509
Lansing, John Jr., 355n8, 337; comments in the New York Assembly, 604-605, 618-620, 623; introduced a bill of rights in the New York Convention, 473, 476
–Letter from, 177
Laud, Archbishop, 364
Lawrence, Mr., (John Laurence, N.Y.) comments in the House of Representatives on amendments, 666, 685
Laws, 610; militia, xxiv; tyrannical, 309
Lee, Arthur, broadside announcing candidacy for Congress, 587
–Letter from, 71
–Letter to, 71
Lee, Charles
–Letter from, 547
Lee, Mr. H. (of Westmoreland), comments in the Virginia Convention, 382, 415-416
Lee, Richard Bland, (Va.), comments in the House of Representatives on amendments, 666, 684
Lee, Richard Henry, 31, 44n2, 56, 203, 217, 297, 546n2, 548n2, 627; comments in the Confederation Congress on the proposed Constitution, 27; considered as certain to be selected a U.S. Senator for Virginia, 548; elected as a U.S. Senator for Virginia, 575, 584; opposed Constitutioin in the Confederation Congress, xxxi; proposed a bill of rights in Congress, 27, 30; wishes amendments proposed by the United States Congress had been adopted by Virginia, 739
–Letters from, 31, 44, 283, 361, 538, 644, 713, 717, 739
–Letters to, 545, 571, 708
Leeland, John, objections to the Constitution, 286
Lenoir, William, comments in the North Carolina Convention, 496-499
Lexington, Massachusetts, xxv, 47, 248
Liberties, 193, 208, 209, 442, 467; a patriot protects the citizens in their just rights and liberties, 601; all the great unalienable and essential rights, liberties and privileges of freemen, 559; amendments for securing, 543; amendments to secure to the people of America, 650; apprehensions of the good citizens of North Carolina for, 678; Constitution would deprive the people of their dearest, 337; constitutional liberties wrested from people by standing army, 173; deprive the people of, 232; destroy the militia to invade the rights and liberties of the people, 696; destroyed by an army, 206; duped out of, 469; encroachments upon the people's, 312; essential liberties which ought never to be given up, 496; general government could not triumph over the liberties of America if Britain was unable to, 336; how far protected and secured by the Constitution, 727; implication is to be the foundation of civil liberties, 407; in our own hands, 378; inquire how they are to be secured, 368; not well secured under the Constitution, 582; of freemen may be in danger, 525; of the people, 198, 385, 644; out of the power of the freemen militia of America to assert and defend their liberties, 212; people have it in their power to retrieve and establish on a sure and permanent foundation, 631; preservation of, 581, 565; sacred, 181, 279; secured by the constitution of Pennsylvania, 33, 238; secured by the constitutions of the states, 398; something should be added to the

Constitution to secure the liberties of our constituents from the inroads of power, 648; the best barrier to, 719; the greater security of our liberties, 600; the total extinction of civil liberties, 470; we will not give up, 470; will be safe so long as people support a well regulated militia, 742

Liberty, xxvi, 15, 26, 27, 29, 31, 39, 43, 46, 53, 54, 56, 57, 58, 65, 68, 79, 85, 87, 88, 97, 98, 101, 126, 167, 169, 173, 176, 178, 206, 215, 227, 255, 279, 303, 305, 317, 321, 336, 338, 342, 343, 365, 377, 382, 413, 415, 451, 465, 473, 492, 511, 515, 520, 571, 645, 654, 658, 705; a bill of rights is the polar star and great support of, 384; a bill of rights kindles a fire of persecution against, 677; a bill of rights securing liberty seems to be demanded by the general voice of America, 638; a nation of freemen know how to prize, 230-231; additional guards in favor of, 594; amendments favorable to, 518; amendments in favor of, 43; amendments to effect personal liberty, 668; amendments to secure civil liberty will not be refused, 644; American, 293; Americans' love of will shield their rights from encroachments and oppression, 309; an high value is set upon consitutional liberty, 606; blessings of, 749; champions of republican, 656; civil, 28, 31, 99, 112, 144, 177, 216, 283, 361, 475, 503; civil and religious, 180, 475; common ideas of, 660; Constitution destructive of liberty, 471; Constitution is dangerous to, 188; creed of, 670; danger to from the militia, 198; dependent upon a real militia, 354; destruction of all due to Congress' unqualified command over the militia, 174; destruction of the people's, 500; endangered by the Constitution, 360; equal, 463; essential guards of, 30; every vestige of will be swept away by the injurious powers of Congress, 711; five state Conventions, and the Pennsylvania Minority, have declared the Constitution dangerous to liberty by their amendments, 633; for which they valiantly fought and bled, 652; friends of, 471, 628; friends of equal, 555; friends to the Constitution wish amendments for additional guards for, 579; further guards to, 638; further guards to public, 538; gone forever, 373; greatest of all earthly blessings, 368; in imminent danger from the proposed Constitution, 27; jealousy of necessary in all free states, 95; last retreat for, 470; liberty is secure due to the existence of a militia of freemen, 189; loss of, 117; Madison's amendments altogether respected personal liberty, 669; Madison's amendments will strengthen barriers for indispensible liberty, 672; nations which retained were compartively few, 427; natural, 271; nothing will preserve it but downright force, 369; of fowling, hunting, fishing, 150, 151, 281, 755, 768; of the people, 356, 499; patriotic, 437; people cannot be deprived of while they retain power in their own hands, 40; people in the United States derive from nature, 677; personal, 149, 174; political and civil, 554; power of defence lost with, 305; preservation of, 341; public, 79; ruins of, 464; safety of, 9; securities for, 652; should follow example of Switzerland to defend with militia alone, 48; solid foundations of totally forgotten, 630; spirit of, 189, 468, 730; standing army dangerous to, xxvii, 10, 81, 239, 291, 328, 459, 556, 710, 735, 748, 752, 754, 758, 762, 767, 773, 778; standing army not dangerous to, 237; state constitution framed upon best principles of civil liberty, 556; subversion of, 540; supplemental safeguards to against which no objections can be raised, 532; there can be none without the full, free, and secure enjoyment of the unalienable rights of men, 364; those who would give up essential liberty to purchase a little temporary safety deserve neither liberty nor safety, 44; to preserve liberty it is essential that the whole body of the people always possess arms, 355; total destruction of, 122; true principles of, 326-327; two states have declared Constitution dangerous to liberty by

their refusal to adopt, 633; was the object of the American Revolution, 556; will gentlemen voluntarily give it up, 418
—See Also: Civil Liberty, Civil Rights, Rights, specific individual rights

Liberty of Conscience, 76, 139, 228, 233, 307, 453, 454, 479, 657, 675
—See Also: Freedom of Conscience, Freedom of Religion, Liberty of Religion, Religious Freedom, Religious Liberty, Rights–Of Conscience

Liberty of Religion, 394, 448
—See Also: Freedom of Conscience, Freedom of Religion, Liberty of Conscience, Religious Freedom, Religious Liberty, Rights–Of Conscience

Liberty of the Press, 52, 55, 57, 58, 60, 64, 65, 68, 71, 84, 86, 97, 100, 102, 103, 126, 128, 138, 139, 148, 154, 167, 180, 207, 209, 216, 217, 228, 233, 235-236, 239, 242, 260, 263n4, 266, 287, 292, 293, 304, 306, 326, 331, 338, 368, 383, 385, 392, 453, 454, 596, 693, 694, 702, 723, 752, 760, 769, 772, 778
—See Also: Freedom of the Press

Lincoln, James, comments in the South Carolina Legislature, 215

Livermore, Samuel, (N.H.), comments in the House of Representatives on amendments, 664, 666, 690

Livingston, Brockholst, comments in the New York Assembly, 604, 605, 613-616, 620-621

Livingston, William, (N.J.), report in the Federal Convention on regulation of the militia, 7

Locke, John, 87, 132, 212, 269

"M.C.," article by, 68

Maclaine, Archibald, comments in the North Carolina Convention, 491, 494-495
—Letter from, 714

Madison, James, (Va.), 277n, 282n2, 287n2, 434, 454, 547n2, 548, 571, 575, 584, 637n2, 642n2, 643, 645n, 669n2, 670n2, 672n2, 682, 722n2; amendments proposed by in House of Representatives, 654-656; articles by, 231, 234; gave notice he will introduce subject of amendments, 644; his amendments, 668; introduced amendments in the House of Representatives, xxxviii; introduced his amendments, 667; moves for a select committee to consider amendments, 651; notes for speech in Congress supporting amendments to the Constitution, 645-647; remarks to Tench Coxe concering Coxe's newpaper article about Madison's amendments, 674; under obligations to support a bill of rights, xxxviii
—Comments in the Federal Convention, against standing armies, 13; on militia and a standing army, 10; on organizing, arming, and disciplining the militia, 8; on regulation of the militia, 5, 9
—Comments in the House of Representatives on amendments, 647, 648-649, 651-663, 665-666, 679, 684, 686, 689, 690, 692-693, 694-695, 699
—Comments in the Virginia Convention, 395-396, 400, 402-404, 405, 412-413, 416, 419-421, 422, 428-429, 444
—Letters from, 29, 147, 447, 532, 538, 542, 551, 579, 594, 602, 609, 640, 643, 669, 673, 682, 700, 704, 705, 712, 719, 722
—Letters to, 148, 177, 264, 335, 502, 546, 572, 635, 644, 666, 672, 673, 676, 709, 720, 721, 725, 726

Madison, Thomas
—Letter to, 270

Magna Charta, 67, 79, 112, 116, 153, 206, 341, 343, 347, 359, 364, 379, 383, 491, 645, 657

Mansfield, Lord, 87

"Many," article by, 443

"Marcus," article by, 297

Marshall, John, 454, comments in the Virginia Convention, 424-425, 425-426; comments in the Virginia House of Delegates, 63

Martial Law, xlvii, 258, 302, 359, 379, 402, 410, 430, 452, 523, 569-570, 712, 758

Martin, Alexander, (Governor, N.C.), message to the general assembly of North Carolina, 727

Martin, Luther, (Md.), 289, 361; articles by, 219, 246, 301, 305, 310; comments in the Federal Convention on regulation of the militia, 9; motion in the Federal Convention on limiting the number of troops, 3

Maryland, convention ratifies the Constitution, xxxiv; letter to governor of, 742
-Bill of Rights, bill of rights provision for a well regulated militia, xxvii; compared, 782; is part of the state constitution, 761; text of, 755-761
-Senate, article the fourth of the amendments proposed by Congress as adopted by, 726
"Marylander, A" article by, 525
Maryland Gazette, (Baltimore), articles from, 219, 266, 289, 305, 308, 328, 356, 525, 596, 627
Maryland Gazette, (Annapolis), articles from, 559, 588
Maryland Journal, (Baltimore), 626n; articles from, 97, 187, 289, 301, 305, 310, 534, 595, 597, 626
Maryland Minority, 399, 399n1, 535; article by, 356
Mason, George, xxx, xxxi, 30, 145, 147, 191n2, 210, 217, 235, 297, 363n2, 380n2, 444n2, 454, 682n2; objections to the Constitution, 34; received much satisfaction from the amendments proposed by the House of Representatives, 710; Richmond Antifederal Committee Bill of Rights, 388
-Comments in the Federal Convention, against the constitution, 14; proposes a bill of rights, 12; on the regulation of the militia and opposing a standing army, 2; on a select militia, 4
-Comments in the Virginia Convention, 385-387, 400-402, 415, 421-422, 430, 432, 433-434, 436
-Comments in the Virginia House of Delegates, 63
-Letters from, 34, 365, 380, 583, 682, 710
-Letters to, 361, 444
-Motions in the Federal Convention, against standing armies, 12; appointment of militia officers by the states, 4; limiting control over the militia, 5; limiting power over the militia to one tenth part, 4; regulation of the militia, 3
Mason, John
-Letters to, 583, 682
Mason, S. T., 726
Massachusetts, bill of rights, 232n2; bill of rights compared, 782; bill of rights provision on the right to keep and bear arms, xxviii; bill of rights, text of, 770-774; failed to ratify the Federal Bill of Rights, xli; letter to the General Court, 51; ratification action, xxxiii
-Convention, 248n2, 263n2, 280n2, 530n2, 633, 702n2; bill of rights defeated in, xlix; excerpts from debates in, 224, 228, 230, 246, 249, 251, 260; proposed amendments compared, 782; ratification and proposed amendments, text of, 261-263; what was said in favor of amendments in, 591-593
Massachusetts Centinel, (Boston), 525n2; articles from, 51, 524
Massachusetts Delegates, article by, 328
Massachusetts Gazette, (Boston), articles from, 98, 123, 178, 207, 222, 225, 232
Maxims, republican political maxims of a free people, 377
Mayhew, Thomas, 147
Maynard, Malichi, 329
M'Dowall, Joseph, comments in the North Carolina Convention, 500
"Medium," 108
Meetings, See: Bucks County, Cumberland County
Mercer, John Francis, 361; broadside declaring candidacy for Congress, 584; election handbill, 312
-Letter from, 340
Military, establishments, 183; force, 40, 184; forces, 354; forces sufficient to subdue the great body of the people, 282; military powers are inseparable from the persons of the people, 276; ought to be under strict subordination to and governed by the civil power, 749, 752, 754, 758, 762, 767, 773, 778; power, 556; powers, 90; subordinate to the civil power, 6, 769
-See Also: Army, Militia, Standing Army
Militia, 47, 55, 61, 74, 90, 105, 106, 108, 139, 145, 174, 182, 195-200, 210, 224, 243-244, 248, 259, 289, 290, 299-300, 301, 308, 316, 354, 359, 375-376, 380-381, 382, 399-416, 417-418, 475, 478, 483, 487, 498, 503, 567-570, 610, 655, 695, 703; able to overawe the regular troops, 55; absolute command of Congress over, 174,

712; absolute disposal of, 295; active and inactive, 331; active, sale of, 333; all men able to bear arms, 359; all the militia of the United States, 197; almost unlimited authority over, 366; an armed militia is a fundamental or unalienable right, 343-344; are the people, 355; are we not militia, 376; arm, 731; arm them well and they will be a suffient security for your liberties, 206; arming, defined, 8; army must be large while militia have arms, 195; at all times hereafter shall be armed, 764; body of formed by farmers, 185; body of the people, 75; bulwark of the nation, 185; bulwarks of our liberties, 414; cannot enslave themselves, 417; cannot say who will be the militia of a future day if the Constitution gets no alteration, 430; command of, 526; complaint concerning powers of Congress over, 85; comprehends all the male inhabitants from sixteen to sixty, 74; Congress at their pleasure may arm or disarm all or any part of the freemen of America, so that when their army is sufficiently numerous, they may put it out of the power of the freemen militia of America to assert and defend their liberties, 212; Congress has no power to disarm, 276; Congress has power to declare what description of persons shall compose, 277; Congress may say there shall be none, 146; control of, 417-432; crush tyrants in their imagined intrenchments of power, 199; destroy to invade the rights and liberties of the people, 696; disciplining, defined, 8; election districts in Virginia determined by the number of militia in each county, 559, 584; every man, 764; every man from 16 to 60, 174; free citizens of Massachusetts, 131; freemen of a whole state, 302; genuine, 354; given up to Congress, 373; government can discard and render useless, 302; government would not trust the people arming, 139; great body of, 5; guard against our real and natural strength being destroyed, 401; have arms, 339; if armed they would be a resource against great oppressions, 498; inactive militia comprehends farmers, mechanics, laborers, 331; includes all men capable of bearing arms, 354, 474; is ourselves, 240; justification of powers of Congress over, 408-412; large and small assemblies of, 719; last and best defence, 374; last defence of the people against unconstitutional acts, xlv; last resource of a free people, 145; law to prevent influence over militiamen at elections in New York, 610; laws, xxiv; make service odius to the people in order to destroy the militia, 402; means of government destroying, xlvii; modelling, xlvii, 91; must be disarmed, 334; need not give them power to abolish our militia, 401; number of in counties used as comparison of unequal representation, 452; numerous well ordered, 568; of no service as you will probably not have a single musket in the state, 373; only a disorderly populace, 570; ordinary, 569; organize, 206; organizing, arming and disciplining, 7, 10, 19, 39, 71, 130, 160, 211, 219, 374, 381, 401, 406-407, 415, 523; organizing, defined, 8; ought always to be armed and disciplined, 344; our only defence is put into the hands of Congress, 370; our ultimate safety, we can have no security without it, 405; part of, 4, 19; people, 414, 498; people took into their own hands, xxv; people would not become tools for enslaving themselves, 26; possible ways the government can abuse, 430; power to arm, 381; powerful chech upon the regular troops, 55; powers of Congress to regulate, xlv, 19, 71, 85, 90, 195, 337, 460, 464, 507; powers over may be used to destroy strength of the yeomanry, 91; prepared for defence, 339; President is commander in chief of, 22; proper security for defence, 239; proposed amendment to powers over, 151, 160, 460, 483, 507, 735-736; Prussian, 34; regular, xxv, 741; regulation of, 2-6, 219-221, 402-404, 451-452; remote possibility that Congress will keep them armed, 405; rendering useless by disarming, 401; returns of, used to ascertain the number of white inhabitants, 550;

safety of the union requires that the militia of every state be well armed, 569; should always be kept well organized, armed and disciplined, and include, according to past usages of the states, all the men capable of bearing arms, 354, 474; size of compared to the largest possible standing army, 234; sole and absolute command of, 330; Swiss, 105, 478; ten times the number of a veteran army, 26; the general defence is left to those who are the objects of defence, 415; the great body of the yeomanry of America, 379; the great object is that every man be armed, 407; the militia comprehends all the male inhabitants from sixteen to sixty, 74; the object is to keep the militia well armed, 478; the people, 414, 498; the persons of the community, 468; the safety of an oppressive government could not be the purpose of the people arming, 139; there are 330,000 men capable of bearing arms not including those of Virginia, 375; they are ourselves, 276; they consist now of the whole people, except a few public officers, 430; useless if Congress neglect or refuse to discipline or arm, 374; Virginia's amounts to 50,000 to 60,000, 375; who are in fact the effective part of the people at large, 55; who are the militia, 430; who are they, 276; when embodied are under military government, 308; when properly formed are the people themselves, 354; whipping, 379; whole, 4; whole natural strength of the union, 402; will always have it in their power to command redress for any illegal and unconstitutional methods employed by Congress, 45; will not be armed at all, 381; yeomanry from sixteen to sixty, 275-276; you can defend your life, liberty and property, your parents, wife and children, 570; you, the free citizens of Massachusetts, 131

–Disarm, xlix, 176, 176n2, 191, 192n2, 195n2, 201n2, 202n2, 221, 222n2, 226n2, 251, 251n2, 286, 286n2, 298n2, 302, 331, 335, 340, 340n3, 401, 498; disarming of was equivalent to disarming the entire population, xlviii; good policy will prompt the government to disarm the inactive militia, 331; will render the militia useless, 366

–General: 474, Congress afraid of, 146, disarmed, xlviii

–Select, xxv, xlvii, 3, 4, 5, 146, 172, 192, 197, 224, 354, 431, 432, 474, 475n2, 478, 569; defined, 355; in England, 424; one fifth or one eighth part of the men capable of bearing arms, 91; people may be disarmed, 146; plan for, 198; supporters of are anti-republican, 355

–Well Regulated, 47, 81, 196, 211, 220, 285-286, 432, 731; being necessary to the security of a free state, 712, 716, 720, 726, 728, 730, 732, 739, 744; being the best security of a free state, 697, 710; best security of a free country, 654; bulwark of a free people, 131; composed of the body of the people being the best security of a free state, 680, 695, 707, 712; composed of the body of the people trained to arms is the proper, natural and safe defence of a free state, xxvi, li, 390, 434, 459, 505, 748; composed of the people themselves, xxv; composed of the yeomanry have ever been considered as the bulwark of a free people, 211; including the body of the people capable of bearing arms is the proper, natural and safe defence of a free state, li, 481, 735; is the proper and natural defence of a free government, xxvii, 290, 758; is the proper, natural and safe defence of a free government, xxvii, 752; is the proper, natural, and sure defence of a state, 778; liberties will be safe as long as people support, 742; people trained themselves as, xxv; same security for necessary in Constitution as in state bills of rights, 81; the Constitution should have inculcated the principle of as some of the state constitutions do, 432; the degree of perfection in military exercises which would entitle the great body of the yeomanry and other classes of citizens to the character of, 197; the true defence of a free republic, 240

"Militiaman, A" article by, 379

Milton, John, 87

Minot, George Richards, 263
 –Letters to, 668, 679, 683
M'Kean, Thomas, 114; comments in the Pennsylvania Convention, 126
"Monitor, The" article by, 97
Monroe, James, 454, 584; comments in the Virginia Convention, 384-385; election appeal for, 586
Montesquieu, 87, 165, 171, 269; *The Spirit of the Laws*, 165
Montmorin, Comte de
 –Letters to, 54, 56
Morris, Gouverneur, (Pa.), comments in the Federal Convention on standing armies, 13
Morris, Robert, 333, 629n2
Musket, every young fellow is providing himself with a rifle or musket, 339; not have a single one in the state, 373; would shoulder again in defence of liberty, 84

Nason, Samuel, comments in the Massachusetts Convention, 247
"Native of Baltimore, A" article by, 596
New Hampshire
 –Bill of Rights, compared, 782; provision on a well regulated militia, xxvii; text of, 775-780
 –Convention, 633; adjourned, xxxiv; proposal to prevent disarming of the citizens, 446; ratification of the United States Constitution and proposed amendments, text of, 445-446; ratifies Constitution and proposes amendments, xxxiv
 –Legislature; ratifies the amendments proposed by Congress, 730
New Jersey, article the fourth of the amendments proposed by Congress as adopted by, 720; constitutional provisions, text of, 749; unanimous vote for ratification of the Constitution, xxxiii
New Jersey Journal, (Elizabeth Town), article from, 611
New York, constitutional provisions, text of, 764; election law, 610; voted to request Congress to call a convention to amend the Constitution, xxxviii
 –Assembly, 643n2; application to Congress for calling a Convention to amend the Constitution, 625; excerpts from debates in, 604, 612; proceedings, 624
 –Convention, 355n2, 363n3, 476n2, 479n2, 606n, 633; bill of rights from ratification compared, 782; bill of rights proposal on right to keep and bear arms, li, 481; bill of rights proposed in Convention, text of, 473-475; circular letter, xxxviii, 514, 516, 529, 532, 542, 544, 555, 562, 564, 566, 580, 583-584, 585, 593, 616, 621-622; circular letter, text of, 488; excerpts from debates in, 463, 464, 476; observations on, 554-555; proceedings, 473, 476; ratified with incorporated bill of rights, and proposed amendments, xxxv; ratification of the United States Constitution with bill of rights and proposed amendments, text of, 480-488; the Rhode Island Convention emulates the New York Convention by incorporating a bill of rights in its ratification, xl
 –Senate, article the fourth of the amendments proposed by Congress as adopted by, 732
New York Journal, articles from, 77, 83, 87, 104, 108, 122, 153, 224, 337, 396, 456, 581, 731
New York Packet, articles from, 105, 136, 231, 234
Nicholas, George, 454; comments in the Virginia Convention, 408-412, 430-431, 432, 434; comments in the Virginia House of Delegates, 62
 –Letter from, 270
Nicholas, Wilson Cary
 –Letter to, 682
Nisbet, Charles
 –Letter from, 178
Non-resistance, 364; same reasons adduced in Virginia Convention discussion of the militia were advanced to support in 1688 England, 413; the doctrine of against arbitrary power and oppression is absurd, slavish, and destructive, 360, 388, 457, 504, 756, 776
Norfolk and Portsmouth Journal, article from, 297
North Carolina, bill of rights compared, 782; bill of rights provision on the right to bear arms, xxviii; bill of rights, text of, 761-763; constitutional provisions, text of, 763; determination not to adopt the Constitution in its present form, 633;

doubtful if will adopt the Constitution without amendments being proposed by Congress, 679; Governor and Council's address to President George Washington, 678; has fixed a distant day for another state convention, 634; legislature ratifies amendments, xl; not in the union unless certain amendments are added, 664; some amendments are necessary for, 701; the state declaration of rights is part of the state constitution, 763
–Convention, xxxix, 534n2; amendments nearly the same as Virginia's, li, 526; copied verbatim the amendments of Virginia, 585; excerpts from debates in, 490, 493, 496, 501; excerpts from the journals of, 533; insisted upon previous amendments, 638; proposed a declaration of rights and amendments, xxxv; proposed amendments compared, 782; proposed declaration of rights and other amendments, text of, 503-509; refusal to ratify the Constitution, xxxv, 503, 512, 529, 583, 593
–General Assembly, article the fourth of the amendments of Congress as adopted by, 728
Norwich Packet, (Con.), articles from, 305, 543
Notes on the State of Virginia, 310

Obedience, people will not yield, 288
"Observator," article by, 233
"Observer, An" article by, 606
"Officer of the Late Continental Army, An" 99
"Old Constitutionalist, An" article by, 64
"Old Militia Officer of 1776, An" 176n2, 192n2, 195n2, 201n2, 202n2, 226n2, 251n2, 286n2, 295n2, 298n2, 335n2, 340n3; article by, 221
"Old Soldier, An" article by, 188
"Old Whig, An" 44n, 51n, 53n, 68, 68n, 76n, 329; articles by: I, 43; II, 48; III, 51; IV, 66; V, 75; VII, 118; VIII, 254
"Old Woman," 233
"One of the Common People," article by, 127
"One of the Late Army," article by, 103
"One of the Middle-Interest," 127
"One of the People," articles by, 45, 149, 297, 676
Opposition, to rulers, 287
Oppression, 54, 55, 59, 79, 172, 189, 245, 280, 281, 285, 288, 293, 303, 306, 309, 336, 338, 359, 372, 374, 387, 397, 400, 428, 436, 451, 490, 498, 539, 540, 544, 545, 557, 586, 633, 671, 703, 723, 730, 734, 756; legal oppression, 315; non-resistance against is absurd, slavish, and destructive, 360, 388, 457, 504, 756, 776
Orne, Colonel, 592
Osgood, Samuel
–Letter from, 188
Otto, Louis Guillaume
–Letters from, 54, 56

Paca, William, 361, 356
Page, John, (Va.), comments in the House of Representatives on amendments, 650, 666, 684, 685-687, 691
Pamphlets, *A Review of the Constitution*, by "A Federal Republican," 119; *An Additional Number of Letters from the Federal Farmer to the Republican*, 342; *An Address to the People of the State of New-York*, by "A Plebian," 312; *An Examination into the leading principles of the Federal Constitution*, by "A Citizen of America," {Noah Webster}, 38; *A LETTER of His Excellency EDMUND RANDOLPH, Esquire, on the Federal Constitution*, 35; *Letters from the Federal Farmer to the Republican*, 89; *Observations on the New Constitution, and on the Federal and State Conventions*, by "A Columbian Patriot," {Mercy Warren}, 243; *Remarks on the Proposed Plan of a Federal Government*, by "Aristides," {Alexander Contee Hanson}, 239; *The Government of Nature Delineated or An Exact Picture of the New Federal Constitution*, by "Aristocrotis," 329; *The Weakness of Brutus Exposed*, by "A Citizen of Philadelphia," {Pelatiah Webster}, 85
Parliament, 50, 110, 218, 297, 400, 402, 423, 492, 632
Parsons, Theophilus, 592; comments in the Massachusetts Convention, 229, 252

Patriot, 67, 102, 141, 280, 289, 301, 601, 701
Pendleton, Edmund, 434; comments in the Virginia Convention, 390-392, 432-433
–Letters to, 542, 640, 704, 712
Pennsylvania, 71; bill of rights comparison, 782; bill of rights provision on right to bear arms, xxviii; bill of rights, text of, 752-755; constitution, 239n2; constitutional provisions, text of, 755; the state declaration of rights is part of the state constitution, 755
–Assembly, xxxii, 30n; article the fourth of the amendments of Congress as adopted by, 732; requested to call a convention for amending the Constitution, 528
–Convention, 692; excerpts from debates in, 110, 112, 123, 135, 145, 150; ratifies constitution, xxxii
Pennsylvania Gazette, (Phil.), articles from, 37, 45, 237, 336, 470, 511
Pennsylvania Herald, (Phil.), 45, 176n2, 192n2, 195n2, 201n2, 202n2, 222n2, 226n2, 286n2, 298n2, 335n2, 340n3; articles from, 45, 64, 68, 101, 251
Pennsylvania Mercury, (Phil.), articles from, 97, 248
Pennsylvania Minority, xxxii, 153n2, 178, 186, 186n2, 210, 263n2, 275, 281, 321, 322, 339, 340n2, 475, 535, 537n2; protest of, text of, 154
Pennsylvania Packet, (Phil.), articles from, 41, 154, 201, 527, 728
"Pennsylvanian, A" {Tench Coxe}, 175n2, 235n3, 277n, 672n3, 674n3, 676n1; articles by, 275, 670, 674
People, a free people ought to be armed, 729; a whole people with arms in their hands, 578; all power is the exclusive right of the people, 670; American people assumed a military character, burst the bands of tyranny, and taught others how to become free, 470; are armed, xlv; are the military power, 190; arms in the hands of enables them to defend their rights and privileges against every invader, 190; arms not possessed by in countries under arbitrary government, 190; besides the advantage of being armed which the Americans possess over the people of almost every other nation, 234-235; body of the common people who always do the fighting of a country would be more likely to fight against the Constitution, 318; confirmed in their right to keep and bear their private arms, 671; constitute a force superior to any band of regular troops, 40; deceiving them in the establishment of the Constitution, 548; dernier resort of is an appeal to the sword, 741; determined to secure their liberties, 339; disarmed, 146; exhorted to take up arms in defence of their rights, 178; forced to arms by encroachments of the government on their rights, 311; freedom of, 517; government founded on confidence of, 549; great mass of those who opposed Constitution did so because it did not contain effectual provisions against encroachments on particular rights, 653; great rights of, 526, 627; have a right to declare acts void which exceed constitutional powers, 435; have arms in their hands, 556; impolicy of puting or keeping arms in the hands of a nervous people, 131; in many states, have thought it necessary to raise barriers against the abuse of power in all forms and departments of government, 657; in the United States derive their liberty from nature, 677; kingdoms of Europe afraid to trust the people with arms, 235; left in full possession of their arms, 452; let people take arms in spirit of resistance, 102; make use of state government as instrument of redress against national, and vice versa, 184; most essential rights of, 684; no law shall be passed for disarming, xlviii; not to be disarmed of their weapons, 452; of this country have arms in their hands, 190; possess the strong arm to overawe their rulers, 345; possessed of proper means of defence, 498; prepared to resist and defend their rights, 226; right of to bear arms, xxviii, 151, 668, 783; right of to bear arms declared inherent in, 668; right of to bear arms for the defence of the state, 762; right of to bear arms for the defence of themselves and the state, 290, 291, 754, 762, 767;

right of to bear arms for the defense of themselves and their own state, or the United States, or for the purpose of killing game, xlviii, 151, 160; right of to keep arms, 248n2, 250n2, 263n4, 703; right of to keep and bear arms, xxxviii, li, 290, 390, 459, 481, 505, 676n3, 735; right of to keep and bear arms has been recognized by the general government, 719; right of to keep and bear arms shall not be infringed, 654, 680, 695, 707,710, 712, 716, 720, 726, 728, 730, 732, 739, 744; right of to keep and bear their private arms, 671, 674n3; right of to keep and to bear arms for the common defence, 290, 773; rise to arms to prevent rulers depriving them of their liberties, 232; should retain so much power that they may resume their rights and put an end to the wantonness of power, 110; supreme power resides in, 111; teaching to know and value their rights, 730; temporary disarming of, 221; the Constitution shall never be construed to authorize Congress to prevent from keeping their own arms, 702; the power of is paramount in a free government, 417; the rights a free people would require the exercise of, 720; the safety of an oppressive government could not be the purpose of the people arming, 139; treason against the majesty of, 524, 525; would assemble in thousands and drive thirty times the number of their few regiments, 382

Peters, Richard
  –Letter to, 700

Petition, Cumberland County, 153n1, text of, 137; Franklin County, text of, 238; Harrisburg Convention, text of, 521

Petition of Rights, (English), 341

"Philadelphiensis," 139n, 228n, 260n, 280n1; articles by: III, 138; V, 176; VI, 179; VIII, 227; IX, 258; X, 277; XI, 296

"Philanthropos," (Pa.), {Tench Coxe}, article by, 210; (Va.), article by, 145

Phillips, William, 592

"Philodemos," article by, 296

Pickering, Timothy
  –Letter to, 639

Pierce, William
  –Letter from, 28

Pinckney, Charles, (S.C.), comment in the Federal Convention on scanty faith in militia, 5; motion in the Federal Convention on freedom of the press, 13; proposals in the Federal Convention relating to individual rights, 6

Pinckney, Charles Cotesworth, (S.C.), comments in the Federal Convention: 3; on regulation of the militia, 9; that states will not properly discipline the militia, 4; comments in the South Carolina Legislature, 217

Pittsburgh Gazette, articles from, 291, 301, 530

"Plain Truth," article by, 99

"Plebian, A" pamphlet by, 312

"Ploughman, A" article by, 303

Political Club, (Danville, Ky.), minutes of meeting, 307

Postmaster, blamed for stopping the free circulation of the newspapers, 210

Posse Comitatus, 91, 122, 196, 308, 404, 405; to all intents is a military force, 308

Power, abuse of, 577; arbitrary power ought to be resisted by arms, 246; by implication, 378, 381; citizens stand ready to resist a power which they suppose may be exerted to the prejudice of their rights, 106; limitation of, 644; of people is paramount in a free government, 417; non-resistance against arbitrary power is absurd, slavish, and destructive, 388, 457, 504, 756, 776; people cannot be deprived of liberty while they retain power in their own hands, 40; people should retain so much that they may resume their rights and put an end to the wontonness of power, 110; security against the abuse of, 467; the people in many states have thought it necessary to raise barriers against power in all forms and departments of government, 657; true republican jealousy and vigilance is the strongest guard against the abuses of, 342

Powers of Congress, do not see the end of under the Constitution, 497
  –Amendment of, all powers are

reserved which are not expressly delegated, 445; to explain proper construction of, (#17) 460, (#18) 508
–Construction of, 345-353; we retain all that we have not given away, 491; those not delegated to the government are reserved to the people under the Constitution, 465; those not delegated to the United States are reserved to the states or to the people, 717, 746; Wilson's doctrine examined, 382-383, 384
–See Also: James Wilson

President, of the United States, 18, 21, 26, 55

Preston, Connecticut, 109

Price, Richard, 626, 626n2

Prince of Orange, 67, 101

Prince William, 393; See Also: Prince of Orange

Privileges, 66, 67; privileges and immunities, 24; secured by the constitution of Pennsylvania, 33

Providence Gazette, 678n, 687n2; articles from, 398, 512, 526, 678

Pseudonyms, "A. B.," 626, 626n; "Adolphus," 591; "Agricola," 75; "Agrippa," 123, 207, 222, 252, 253n; "Alfred," 572; "The Almanac-Maker," 248; "America," {Noah Webster}, 186; "An American," {Tench Coxe}, 185; "An American Citizen," {Tench Coxe}, 54; "Anti-Foederalist," 264, 265; "Argus," 84; "Aristides," {Alexander Contee Hanson}, 239, 268, 328, 588; "Aristocrotis," 177n2, 192n2, 195n2, 201n2, 202n2, 222n2, 226n2, 251n2, 286n2, 298n2, 329, 340n3; "Belasarius," 583; "Brutus," 77, 122, 144, 329; "Candidus," 233; "Candour," 265; "Cassandra," 397; "Cassius," 178, 630; "Cato," 68; "Centinel," 33, 58, 68, 85, 97, 176n2, 191, 195n2, 201n2, 202n2, 222n2, 226n2, 233, 251n2, 286n2, 298n2, 329, 335n2, 340n3, 566, 711; "Christian Farmer," 543; "Cincinnatus," 77, 87, 89n, 104, 107; "A Citizen," 57, 108; "A Citizen of America," {Tench Coxe}, 38, 103n2; "A Citizen of New York," 326; "A Citizen of Pennsylvania," 41; "A Citizen of Philadelphia," {Pelatiah Webster}, 85; "Civis," 527, 597; "Civis Rusticus," 235; "Columbian Patriot," {Mercy Warren}, 243; "Conciliator," 233; "A Confederationalist," 37n, 64; "A Countryman," 61n, 153, 224; "Deb. Woodcock," 233; "A Delegate Who Has Catched Cold," 455; "Deliberator," 277; "A Democratic Federalist," 45, 68; "Denatus," 387; "A Farmer," (Md.) 266, 289, 305, 308, 328, (N.H.) 204, (Pa.) 336, 741; "Father Abraham," 553; "A Federal Correspondent," 524; "Federal Farmer," li, 89, 97n2, 342, 355n1, 475n2; "Federalism," 534; "A Federal Republican," 119, 122n1, 581; "Foederal Constitution," 37, 65, 66n2; "Foreign Spectator," 11, 26, 556, 567; "A Freeman," {Tench Coxe}, 277n2, 398; "A Friend to Amendments," 517; "A Friend to Liberty and Union," 556; "A Friend to the People," 550; "A Friend to the Republick," 265; "A Friend to the Rights of the People," 264; "A Georgian," 103; "H.G.," 639; "Helvidius Priscus," 225; "Honestus," 548; "Impartial," 45; "An Impartial Citizen," 203, 299; "The Impartial Examiner," 271, 285, 292; "An Independent Freeholder," 217, 281n2; "Indignatus," 192; "Jacob Trusty," 176, 192n2, 195n2, 201n2, 202n2, 222n2, 226n2, 251n2, 286n2, 298n2, 335n2, 340n3; "James de Caledonia," 177n2, 192n2, 195n2, 201n2, 202n2, 222n2, 226n2, 251n2, 286n2, 298, 335n2, 340n3; "John De Witt," xlviii, 69, 71n, 84, 129, 215n; "John Wilkes," 233; "A Landholder," {Oliver Ellsworth}, 147; "The Landholder," 289, 302, 305; "M.C.," 68; "Many," 443; "Marcus," 297; "A Marylander," 525; "Medium," 108; "A Militiaman," 379; "The Monitor," 97; "A Native of Baltimore," 596; "Observator," 233; "An Observer," 606; "An Officer of the Late Continental Army," 99; "An Old Constitutionalist," 64; "An Old Militia Officer of 1776," 176n2, 192n2, 195n2, 201n2, 202n2, 221, 226n2, 251n2, 286n2, 298n2, 335n2, 340n3; "An Old Soldier," 188; "An Old Whig," 43, 44n, 48, 51, 51n, 53n, 66, 68, 68n, 75, 76n, 118, 254, 329; "Old Woman," 233; "One of the Common People," 127; "One of the Late Army," 103; "One of the

Middle-Interest," 127; "One of the People," 45, 149, 297, 676; "A Pennsylvanian," {Tench Coxe}, 175n2, 235n3, 275, 277n, 670, 672n3, 674, 674n3, 676n1; "Philadelphiensis," 138, 139n, 176, 179, 227, 228n, 258, 260n, 277, 280n1, 296; "Philanthropos," (Pa.), {Tench Coxe}, 210; "Philanthropos," (Va.), 145; "Philodemos," 296; "Plain Truth," 99; "A Plebian," 312; "A Ploughman," 303; "Publius," 277, 277n, 282n2, {Alexander Hamilton}, 105, 136, 182, 195, 281, {James Madison}, 231, 234; "R.S.," 101; "Real Farmer," 543; "A Republican," 517, 527, 627; "The Republican," 188; "Samuel," 202; "Solon," 516; "Solon, jun.," 512; "Sommers," 301; "Spectator," 610; "The State Soldier," 209, 253; "Sydney," 396; "Timoleon," 83; "A True Federalist," 598; "A True Friend," 139; "Trusty," 176n2, 192n2, 195n2, 200, 202n2, 222n2, 226n2, 251n2, 286n2, 298n2, 335n2, 340n3; "Tullius," 309; "Uncus," 97; "Vox Populi," 98; "A Watchman," 233, 242; "Whig of 1776," 233; "The Yeomanry of Massachusetts," 232

"Publius," 277, 277n, 282n2; articles by, {Alexander Hamilton}, 105, 136, 182, 195, 281, {James Madison}, 231, 234

Punishments, 35; cruel and unusual, 28, 60, 80, 150, 159, 258, 293, 389, 434, 439, 458, 474, 481, 505, 655, 671, 681, 707, 717, 735, 745, 748, 752, 758, 762, 774, 779, 783; unusual, 186

Pym, John, 244

Quartering of Soldiers, 352, 359, 390, 417, 419, 459, 474, 479, 481, 505, 655, 680, 698-699, 707, 716, 735, 744, 752, 758, 774, 778, 783

"R.S.," article by, 101

Randolph, Edmund, (Va.), xxx, xxxi, 35, 44n2, 147, 191n2, 210, 377, 454, 532, 592, 720, 726
- –Comments in the Federal Convention, in favor of amendments by the state conventions, 13; on regulation of the militia, 9
- –Comments in the Virginia Convention, 374-375, 383-384, 414-415, 436, 442
- –Letter from, (pamphlet), 35
- –Letters to, 44, 640, 669, 704

Randolph, Thomas Mann Sr.
- –Letter to, 602

Ratification, North Carolina's refusal of for the new Constitution, 503
- –Of Amendments Proposed by Congress, 746; Del., 730; Md., 726; N.C., 728; N.H., 730; N.J., 720; N.Y., 732; R.I., 739; S.C., 730; Va., 742; Vt., 742
- –Of the Constitution, 25; Ma., 261; N.H., 445; N.Y., 480; R.I., 733; Va., 454

"Real Farmer," article by, 543

Read, George, (Del.), comments in the Federal Convention on regulation of the militia, 6

Rebellion, 54, 102, 414

Regular Militia, xxv
- –See Also: Militia

Religious Freedom, 459
- –See Also: Freedom of Conscience, Freedom of Religion, Liberty of Conscience, Liberty of Religion, Religious Liberty, Rights–Of Conscience

Religious Liberty, 210, 218, 242, 281, 287, 360, 466, 475, 503, 671
- –See Also: Freedom of Conscience, Freedom of Religion, Liberty of Conscience, Liberty of Religion, Religious Freedom, Rights–Of Conscience

Representatives, 15; number of under Constitution, 16; are the only efficacious security for the rights and privileges of the people, 183

Republican, 368, 451, 456, 567, 577, 628, 631, 637, 702; constitutions and principles of freedom, 41; defined, 629; form of government, 24, 312, 429, 468, 675; jealousy, 41; government, 337, 413, 530, 585, 651, 658; jealousy and vigilance, the strongest guard against abuses of power, 342; maxims, 377; plan, 293; political party in Pennsylvania, xxxi; principles, 386, 659-660; spirit, 670; a republican supports the rights of the people, 342-343

"Republican, A" articles by, 517, 527, 627

"Republican, The" article by, 188

Republican Committee
- –Letter from, 641

Republicanism, 99

Resistance, 54, 106, 373; against British, 234; against encroachments,

51; against unjust and oppressive laws, 40; any man justified in against act of usurpation, 230; armed, xxiv; citizens of America capable of, xxxvi; let people take arms in spirit of, 102; of encroachments, 41; of people against national rulers, 184; of the great body of the people, 282; right of, 54; proper spirit of is the best security for the liberties of the people, 149; right of against oppressive measures is inherent in the people, 345

Resist, 288; arbitrary power by arms, 246; citizens stand ready to resist a power which they suppose may be exerted to the prejudice of their rights, 106; people prepared to resist and defend rights, 226; the Constitution, 364

Revolt, immediate revolt of the great body of the people, 282

Revolution, 260, 311, 359, 373, 414, 456, 681, 696; another to resume powers from government, 302; government forces people to arms by encroaching on the rights they have reserved, 311; in favor of the rights of mankind, 289; of 1688, (English), 29, 289; popular, 282; principles, 65
 –See Also: American Revolution

Rhode Island, appears as if they intend to keep out of the union until effectual amendments were made, 717; determination not to adopt the Constitution in its present form, 633
 –Convention, 363n3, 733; ratification of the Constitution with bill of rights and proposed amendments, text of, 733-739; ratifies Constitution and incorporates a bill of rights, xl
 –General Assembly, article the fourth of the amendments of Congress as adopted by, 739; ratifies the amendments proposed by Congress, xl

Richmond Antifederal Committee, 380n2; proposed bill of rights, 388

Rights, 66, 67, 176, 181, 217, 349, 418, 496, 605, 634, 645, 653, 741; a patriot protects the citizens in their just rights and liberties, 601; all power is the exclusive right of the people, 670; all the great unalienable and essential of freemen, 546; amendments to ascertain, secure and protect the great rights of the people, 627; amendments to protect the private and essential rights of the meanest individual, 558-559; amendments which will guard essential, 609; are the people to have none, 216; as a free people were fully expressed at the head of our different constitutions, 455; betrayers of the dearest rights of the people, 547; birth, 301; certain great and important rights which the people declared to be paramount to the power of the legislature, 436; characteristic rights of freemen, how far they can be more impregnably fortified, 642; citizens are the guardians of their own rights, 222; civil, 112, 244, 364; Congress denying rights of the people which were formerly deemed clear and unexceptionable, 724; Congress not restrained from violating except by their integrity and prudence, 440; Constitution contains some principles which may be perverted to purposes injurious to the rights of free citizens, 519; Constitution did not contain effectual provisions against encroachments on particular rights, 653; Constitution paramount to the unalienable rights of the citizens secured in the state constitutions, 340; Constitution renders insecure all the great, essential, and unalienable rights of freemen, 598; Constitution would deprive the people of their dearest, 337; constitutional declaration of the most essential, 539; constitutional or fundamental, 343; constitutional provision in favor of essential, 700; constructive, 427; dearer to us than our lives, 469; deprive the people of their, 581; endangered by transition to new government, 368; enumeration of certain in the Constitution shall not disparage others retained by the people, 681, 708, 711, 717, 746, 783; errect constitutional barriers for the permanent security of the liberties of the people, 342, 708, 746; essential, 346, 453, 454, 473, 594, 700; essential and sacred, 728; essential inherent, 388; essential natural, 79; essential of freemen are impliedly given up under Constitution, 531; essential to freemen, 301, 531; essential which ought never to be given up, 496; every desireable safeguard for popular, 580; explanatory amendments more accurately defining the great rights of the people are necessary, 526; expressly declare the great rights of mankind secure under this Constitution, 652; fought British to prevent oppression, and shall now resign to a government still more arbitrary, 338; free citizens of America able to defend the rights they are in possession of, 235; fundamental, 187; fundamental, unalienable, 308; given up, 386; government steals one after another from the people, 313-314; great, 448; great and unalienable should have been secured in a bill of rights, 84; great essential ought to be secured to individuals, 494; held inviolable and sacred, 437; if people will not defend, they do not deserve to enjoy, 305; inestimable, 378; infringe upon, 578; inherent, 271, 747; invaluable rights of freemen, 466; invaluable, inestimable, 437; just ideas of, 739; means of defending, 370; most essential of the people, 684; nature and extent of, 544; natural, 32, 78, 125, 268, 292, 503, 646, 733; natural and unalienable, 343; natural, essential and inherent, 775; natural, essential, and unalienable, 752, 770, 765; natural rights of freemen, 64; natural, took up arms at distant appearance of danger to, 341; necessity of securing our personal, 448; none left to states or people, 202; not guarded, 490; object of amendments being to establish our rights and liberties on the most immutable basis, 566; of citizens, protected in state constitutional declarations, 86; of Englishmen, 29; of freemen are only to be maintained by freemen, 335; of ourselves and posterity, 515; of persons, 443; of persons exposed as it stands now, 444; of the people, 35, 147, 385, 553; other essential, what are they, 451; other great rights are not secured by the Constitution, 596; other rights retained by the people, 655; our great unalienble rights ought to be secured by a bill of rights, 385; out of the power of Congress, 281; people of Virginia do claim, demand and insist upon as their undoubted, 362; personal, 42, 55, 58, 76, 149, 723; private, 645; protected in state declarations of rights, 740; retained by the people, 439; right without power to protect it is of little avail, 717; sacred, 180, 228, 279; sacred and dear to man, 464; sacred or essential, 287; secure those which are endangered by the Constitution, 686; secured by the Pennsylvania Minority proposed bill of rights, 339; secured by the state constitutions ought to be secured in the federal constitution, 66; secured by the state governments, 471; secured by the constitution of Pennsyvania, 238; secured in the Virginia constitution but not under the proposed U. S. Constitution, 386; securing the just rights and privileges of the people, 628; securing the rights and privileges of the people of America, 692; security for however sacred or essential, 153; security for the rights of individuals, 222, 468; security of in the Constitution, 723; should be held sacred, 123; should be invariably fixed in new Connecticut constitution, 305; some too essential to be delegated to government, to sacred to be infringed, 728; some valuable ones are indeed declared in the new Constitution, 714; supports of, 191; teaching the people to know and value, 730; that a free people would require the exercise of, 720; the great unalienable and essential rights, liberties and privileges of freemen, 559; the inestimable rights of freemen, 631; the people be the better prepared to resist and defend them, 226; the private and personal of the citizens, 705, 708; the reserve of rights in the constitutions of the states shall remain inviolate, 522; the Richmond Antifederal Committee amendments stand on the broad basis of securing the rights of every citizen in the Union, 444; they may infringe every right not expressly

secured, 385; those aforesaid cannot be abridged or violated, (R.I. Ratification) 483, (N.Y. ratification) 735; those which the people consider as not sufficiently guarded, 649; to fish, fowl and hunt, 210; took up arms at the distant appearance of danger to the unalienable rights, 341; tyranny threatens to sweep away, 243; unalienable, 68, 137, 267, 378; unalienable and fundamental, 89; unalienable or fundamental, 92; unalienable right to hunt and fish, 186; which no man under heaven can take from you, 450; which ought never to be infringed, 497; why not place rights as a free people at the head of the general federation, which may supercede the states, 455
–Arms: Keeping and/or Bearing, of citizens to keep their own arms, xlix; of keeping arms, 248n2, 250n2, 263n4, 703; of people to bear arms, xxviii, 151, 668, 783; of people to bear arms for the defence of the state, 762; of people to bear arms for the defence of themselves and the state, 290, 291, 754, 762, 767; of the people to bear arms for the defense of themselves and their own state, or the United States, or for the purpose of killing game, xlviii, 151, 160; of people to keep and bear arms, xxviii, li, 390, 459, 481, 505, 676n3, 735; of people to keep and bear arms has been recognized by the general government, 719; of people to keep and bear arms shall not be infringed, 654, 680, 695, 707, 710, 712, 716, 720, 726, 728, 730, 732, 739, 744; original right of self defence, 184; people confirmed in their right to keep and bear their private arms, 671, 674n3; reasons for constitutional amendment in favor of, li-lii, 671; right of bearing arms declared inherent in the people, 668; right of the people to keep and to bear arms for the common defence, 290, 712, 773; the rights of bearing arms for defence, or killing game, 281; to the use of arms, 296
–Of Assembly, 28, 60, 390, 458, 474, 482, 505, 654, 680, 690, 706, 716, 723, 735, 743-744, 754, 762, 768, 773, 779, 782
–Of Conscience, 147, 150, 159, 167, 174, 239, 260, 263n4, 284, 291, 338, 368, 446, 594, 603, 609, 655, 680, 681, 694, 702, 706, 707, 723; declared inherent in the people, 668; See Also: Freedom of Conscience, Freedom of Religion, Liberty of Conscience, Liberty of Religion, Religious Liberty, Religious Freedom
–Individual, xxiii, 42, 207, 244, 306, 345, 350, 557; all the other rights of the individual, 207; amendments related to, xxxix; further guards to, 538; Madison grouped amendments relating to together, xxxviii; reasons for securing in a bill of rights, 494; sacred deposit, 308; security for the rights of, 222, 468
–See Also: Amendments, Bill of Rights, Declaration of Rights, listings for specific individual rights

Rodney, Ceasar Augustus
–Letter to, 601

Rodney, Thomas
–Letter from, 601

Rush, Benjamin, 192; comments in the Pennsylvania Convention, 124

Russell, Robert S.
–Letter to, 250

Russell, William
–Letters from, 231, 250

Rutledge, Edward
–Letter to, 71

"Samuel," article by, 202

Sargent, Winthrop
–Letter to, 83

Scott, Thomas, (Pa.), comments in the House of Representatives on amendments, 703

Searches, unreasonable, See: General Warrants, Writs of Assistance

Seceding Pennsylvania Assemblymen, xxxii, 33n, 122n2, 193, 537n2; broadside by, 30

Second Amendment, to the Constitution, xxii, xxiii, xxxviii-xxxix, xli

Second General Convention, See: Convention

Sedgwick, Theodore, (Ma.), comments in the House of Representatives on amendments, 684, 690-691, 692; comments in the Massachusetts Convention, 230

Self Defence, 184; is a primary law of nature, 243; the people have a right to bear arms for the defence of themselves, xlviii, 151, 160, 290, 291,

754, 762, 767
Select Militia, See: Militia–Select
Senate, United States, 15, 16, 55; proceedings on amendments to the Constitution, 710, 712
Seney, Joshua, (Md.), comments in the House of Representatives on amendments, 696
Shays' Rebellion, 6n2, 248n3, 286n3
Sherman, Roger (Con.)
–Comments in the Federal Convention, against a bill of rights, 12; against motion for a free press, 13; on regulation of the militia, 5, 10; motion in the Federal Convention on regulation of the miltia, 7
–Comments in the House of Representatives on amendments to the Constitution, 649, 664, 688, 696, 698, 699
Shippen, Thomas Lee
–Letter to, 518
Shippen, William Jr.
–Letter from, 518
–Letter to, 31
Short, William
–Letters to, 101, 532, 626
Sidney, Algernon, 87, 132, 212, 269
Singletary, Amos, comments in the Massachusetts Convention, 224
Sinnickson, Thomas
–Letter to, 479
Smiley, John, 512, 519; comments in the Pennsylvania Convention, 112, 114, 126, 145
Smith, Adam, 237
Smith, Charles
–Letter from, 542
Smith, Melancton, 30
Smith, Robert
–Letter to, 510
Smith, William
–Letter to, 533
Smith, William Loughton, (S.C.), comments in the House of Representatives on amendments, 650, 685, 696
Smith, William Stephens
–Letters to, 102, 249
Soldier, almost every citizen is one, 100
–See Also: Militia
"Solon," article by, 516
"Solon, jun.," article by, 512
Somers, Lord, 267
"Sommers," article by, 301
South Carolina, constitutional provisions, text of, 768
–Convention, 633; amendments compared, 782; excerpts from debates in, 363; ratifies Constitution and proposes amendments, xxxiv
–Legislature, excerpts from debates in, 215
–Senate, article the fourth of the amendments proposed by Congress as adopted by, 730
"Spectator," article by, 610
Speech, freedom of, See: Freedom of Speech
Spencer, Joseph, 287n2
Spencer, Samuel, comments in the North Carolina Convention, 490, 493-494, 496
Spirit of the Laws, The, 165
Standing Army, xxv, xlvii, xlviii, xlix, 2, 11, 27, 30, 34, 35, 38, 40, 43, 46, 47, 55, 58, 59, 60, 61, 71, 72, 74, 90, 100, 104, 106, 131, 133, 139, 145, 151, 154, 160, 172, 173, 174, 177, 181, 195, 198, 205, 212, 213, 221, 222, 224, 233, 234, 237, 239-240, 243, 247, 249, 260, 264, 266, 276, 278, 285, 289, 294, 296, 299, 306, 308, 334, 359, 360, 365, 366, 373, 401, 402, 405, 408, 415, 419, 446, 449, 460, 476, 478, 479, 481, 485, 502, 507, 522, 530, 568, 630, 638, 695, 697-698, 702, 703, 710, 713, 731, 738, 741; advocates of tyranny support, 47; bane of republican government, 337; before a standing army can rule, the people must be disarmed, 40; dangerous to liberty, xxvii, 10, 81, 239, 291, 328, 459, 556, 710, 735, 748, 752, 754, 758, 762, 767, 773, 778; dangerous to public liberty, 328; great support of tyrants, 47; highest number is one twenty-fifth part of the number able to bear arms, 234; in conjunction with the active militia will quell insurrections which support liberty, 331; incompatible with a free government, 303; must be numerous, 175; size of compared to the numbers of militia, 234; tyrants can rely upon nothing but, 190
–See Also: Army, Militia
State Gazette of North Carolina (New Bern), article from, 714
State Gazette of South Carolina (Charleston), article from, 297
"State Soldier, The" articles by, I, 209;

II, 253
Sterett, Samuel, address to the public, 595
Steuben, Baron von, 61, 61n, 225n2
Stillman, Samuel, comments in the Massachusetts Convention, 261
Stone, Michael Jenifer, (Md.), comments in the House of Representatives on amendments, 697
Strong Arm, people possess to overawe their rulers, 345; will secure rights of the people against usurpation, 96
Sumner, Judge, 592
Sumter, Thomas, (S.C.), comments in the House of Representatives on amendments, 664-665, 698
Supreme Court, 23
Supreme Executive Council, (Pennsylvania), xlix, 176n2, 192n2, 195n2, 201n2, 222n2, 226, 226n2, 251n2, 286n2, 298n2, 335n2, 340n3; proceedings concerning militia arms, 201
Supreme Law of the Land, 25, 32, 50, 52, 58, 65, 68, 82, 88, 92, 127, 178, 273, 386, 500
 –See Also: Sweeping Clause
Sweeping Clause, 58, 84, 88, 103, 107, 379, 646; necessary and proper clause, xlv, 19, 59, 378, 427, 433, 435
 –See Also: Supreme Law of the Land
Switzerland, 108; and America only countries not groaning in a hell of slavery, 295; preserved its freedom for ages with the sole help of militia, 48
Sword, The, 4, 11, 14, 40, 215, 381, 405, 464, 495, 498, 578; dernier resort of the oppressed, 329; obedience compelled by the power of the sword in despotic governments, 276; power of is in the hands of the people, 276; synonym for military power, 4, 11; the dernier resort of the people is an appeal to under any government, 741; the power of is in the hands of the yeomanry from sixteen to sixty, 275; the power of is not in hands of either the federal or state governments, 276
 –See Also: Ultima Ratio
"Sydney," article by, 396
Sylvester, Peter, (Peter Silvester), (N.Y.), comments in the House of Representatives on amendments, 688
Tax, power to tax the press is the power to destroy the freedom of it, 353
Taylor, John, comments in the Massachusetts Convention, 251
Thatcher, George
 –Letters to, 193, 208
Thompson, Gen., comments in the Massachusetts Convention, 228
Tilghman, James
 –Letter from, 514
"Timoleon," article by, 83
Title of Nobility, 20
Treaties, powers under the Constitution, 25; See Also: Supreme Law of the Land
Tredwell, Thomas, comments in the New York Convention, 464-470
Trenchard, John, 87
Trial by Jury, in civil cases, xlv, 27, 30, 33, 35, 40, 45, 47, 52, 57, 60, 64, 71, 72, 76, 80, 81, 86, 88, 89, 94, 101, 102, 128, 138, 139, 150, 154, 159, 167, 169-170, 177, 207, 228, 233, 239, 249, 255, 262, 264, 266, 284, 292, 297, 305, 311, 322, 326, 328, 332, 338, 343, 349, 357-358, 368, 370, 378, 384, 389, 392, 394, 433, 434, 438, 446, 448, 451, 458, 463, 464, 466, 474, 478, 482, 502, 505, 531, 589, 590, 594, 595, 596, 603, 608, 609, 618, 633, 635, 638, 645, 646, 655, 656, 657, 667, 668, 675, 694, 707, 717, 733, 740, 745, 748, 750, 754, 755, 756, 762, 763, 765, 767, 772, 778, 782; a most sacred and valuable right, 498; juries are judges, 33; sacred, 347
Troops, 182
"True Federalist, A" article by, 598
"True Friend, A" broadside by, 139
"Trusty," 176n2, 192n2, 195n2, 202n2, 222n2, 226n2, 251n2, 286n2, 298n2, 335n2, 340n3; article by, 200
"Trusty, Jacob," 192n2, 195n2, 202n2, 222n2, 226n2, 251n2, 286n2, 298n2, 335n2, 340n3; article by, 176
Tucker, Thomas Tudor, (S.C.), comments in the House of Representatives on amendments, 691, 692, 699
Tucker, St. George
 –Letter to, 28
"Tullius," article by, 309
Turberville, George Lee, 547n2
 –Letters from, 71, 148, 335, 551, enclosure, 546
 –Letter to, 551

Turner, George
 –Letter from, 83
Tyler, John, 454; comments in the Virginia Convention, 441
Tyranny, 40, 237, 248, 280, 285, 286, 294, 298, 303, 324, 338, 340, 370, 373, 449, 466, 470, 476, 535, 545, 553, 557, 586, 601, 632, 633, 677, 727; advocates of argue for a standing army, 47; attempts of government to establish, 184; Congress must be mad to form any projects of, 556; favorers of, 300; men may oppose, 209; rulers are so prone to, 677
Tyrants, 102, 518; assemble the people to punish, 373; never feel secure until have disarmed the people, 190

Ultima Ratio, 245, 260; arms, 464; the sword, the dernier resort of the oppressed, 329; the ultima ratio regum must secure to the people their rights, 176
 –See Also: Sword
Unalienable, See: Rights, Unalienable
Unconsititutional, 495; laws, 75, 149, 395, 661
"Uncus," article by, 97
United States
 –Congress, See: Congress, United States
 –Constitution, See: Constitution–United States
 –House of Representatives, See: House of Representatives
 –Senate, See: Senate, United States
United States Chronicle (Providence), article from, 84
Unreasonable Searches, 28, 260
 –See Also: General Warrants, Writs of Assistance
Usurpation, 56, 96, 229-230, 237, 245, 289, 628; of national rulers, 184; resistance against, 106, 184, 230

Vandegrift, Jacob
 –Letter to, 511
Vandegrift, John
 –Letter to, 511
Vansant, Nathan
 –Letter to, 511
Vermont, xxvi; bill of rights compared, 782; bill of rights provision on the right to bear arms, xxviii; bill of rights, text of, 765-768; constitutional provisions, text of, 765; General Assembly ratifies the proposed amendments, xl, 742; the state declaration of rights is part of the state constitution, 768
Vining, John, (Del.), comments in the House of Representatives on amendments, 665, 688, 692, 697, 698; reports amendments approved by the House committee of eleven, 680
Virginia, 72; action on the amendments proposed by Congress, 721; bill of rights compared, 782; bill of rights, text of, 747-749; circular letter, 563, 586, 593; Constitution would have been certainly rejected in, 700; fate of amendments proposed by Congress in, 720; first state to form a constitution and bill of rights, xxvi; observations on action relating to amendments in, 726-727; reasons why none of Congress' amendments adopted by, 725; senate opposes articles 3, 8, 11, and 12 of the proposed amendments, xl; voted to request Congress to call a convention to amend the Constitution, xxxviii
 –Convention, 451n1, 633, 699, 723, 725n1; amendments compared, 782; Antifederalist strategy for, 361-363; declaration of rights and other amendments proposed by, text of, 457-462; excerpts from debates in, 367, 374, 375, 380, 384, 385, 390, 399, 417, 441, 443, 448, 451, 456; form of ratification, 454-455; members of equally divided over previous versus subsequent amendments, 380; ratification vote, 453; ratifies and proposes a bill of rights and other amendments, xxxv
 –House of Delegates, 566n2, 575, 601n2, 641n2, 643n2; excerpts from debates in, 62; letter to speaker of, 35; proceedings, 550; proceedings relative to amending the Constitution, 561; resolution for requesting Congress to call a convention to amend the Constitution, 546
 –Senate, 726n, 742n; objections to the amendments of Congress, 722; ratifies the amendments proposed by Congress, 742
Virginia Gazette (Petersburg), articles from, 44, 203, 299
Virginia Gazette (Winchester), articles

from, 217, 280, 288, 295, 303
Virginia Herald (Fredericksburg), article from, 609
Virginia Independent Chronicle (Richmond), articles from, 72, 235, 253, 271, 285, 292, 387, 443, 455, 602, 722
Virginia Journal (Alexandria), articles from, 34, 144, 145
"Vox Populi," article by, 98

Wait, Thomas B.
 –Letter from, 193
Warrants, See: General Warrants
Warren, Mercy, pamphlet by, 243
War, civil, 279, 316, 339, 342, 471, 535, 556, 573; waging war against tyrants, 370
Washington, George, 64, 107, 193, 208, 247, 333, 510, 597, 626, 627, 634, 643, 722n2; address from the Governor and Council of North Carolina, 678; innaugural address, 642; speech to Congress, 729
 –Letters from, 187, 644, 718
 –Letters to, 29, 34, 149, 187, 250, 356, 547, 579, 719, 722, 732
"Watchman, A" 233; article by, 242
Wealth of Nations, The 237
 –See Also: Adam Smith
Weapons, people are not to be disarmed of, they are left in full possession of, 452
Webster, Noah, article by, 186; pamphlet by, 38
 –Letter to, 740
Webster, Pelatiah, pamphlet by, 85
Weekly Monitor, (Litchfield, Con.), article from, 553
Well Regulated Militia, See: Militia–Well Regulated
Westmoreland County Committee, report of, 530
"Whig of 1776," 233
White, Alexander, (Va.), articles by, 280, 281n1, 288, 288n; comments in the House of Representatives on amendments, 649
 –Letter to, 705
White, James
 –Letter from, 102
Whitehill, Robert, 152; comments in the Pennsylvania Convention, 117, 123, 150; introduces amendments (bill of rights) into Pennsylvania Convention, 150
"Wilkes, John" article by, 233
William and Mary, 218
William the 3rd, 267
Williams, John, comments in the New York Convention, 463
Williamson, Hugh, (N.C.), comments in the Federal Convention, 3, on trial by jury, 11; speech by, 86
 –Letter from, 676
Wilson, James, 52, 58, 59, 71, 72, 77, 84, 87, 100, 104, 107, 120, 143, 152, 162, 177, 193, 204, 213, 222, 241, 243, 265, 275n2, 286n2, 298n2, 339, 387, 539; comments in the Pennsylvania Convention, 110, 112, 118, 135, on omission of a bill of rights, 113-114, 115-116; doctrine of concerning distinction between powers under the state and federal constitutions, xliii, 45, 48; report on the Lancaster Conference, 574
Wingate, Paine
 –Letter from, 639
"Woodcock, Deb." 233
Worcester Magazine, article from, 242
Writs of Assistance, 244
 –See Also: General Warrants, Unreasonable Searches
Wythe, George, 454; comments in the Virginia Convention, 448; reports the proposed amendments to the Constitution recommended to the consideration of Congress by the Virginia Convention, 456-457

Yates, Abraham Jr.
 –Letter from, 533
 –Letter to, 509
Yates, Robert, 337, 390n, 444n2
 –Letters from, 177, 444
Yeates, Jasper, comments in the Pennsylvania Convention, 125
Yeomanry, 71, 291, 340, 401; a well regulated militia composed of have ever been considered as the bulwark of a free people, 211; Congress may not keep them completely armed, organized and disciplined, 71; great body of, 197; possess arms, 91; the militia consists of the yeomanry from sixteen to sixty, 275-276; the militia of America consisting of the great body of the yeomanry, 379; too strong a body of men to be openly offended by Congress, 91
"Yeomanry of Massachusetts, The" article by, 232

"Z", article by, 146

Zenger, John Peter, 46